Date Due

MR 18 '59			
JUN 9 '78			

A History of Preaching

VOL. I.

FROM THE APOSTOLIC FATHERS TO
THE GREAT REFORMERS
A. D. 70—1572

BY
EDWIN CHARLES DARGAN, D. D., LL. D.
Professor of Homiletics in the Southern Baptist Theological
Seminary, Louisville, Kentucky
1892 - 1907

Introduction by
J. B. WEATHERSPOON

BAKER BOOK HOUSE
GRAND RAPIDS 6, MICHIGAN
1954

PHOTOLITHOPRINTED BY CUSHING - MALLOY, INC.
ANN ARBOR, MICHIGAN, UNITED STATES OF AMERICA
1954

Introduction to the 1954 Edition

In its republication of Dargan's *History of Preaching,* the Baker Book House is performing a much needed service in making available to ministers, theological students, and libraries the most comprehensive work in that field. Since its first publication early in this century no comparable history of preaching has been produced. There have been numerous biographies, books dealing with particular periods and aspects of preaching, but none so ambitious and encyclopaedic as Dargan's. Its reappearance will, therefore, supply the want of teachers who have been handicapped in giving courses in the history of preaching because no comprehensive basic text was available for library and personal use.

Originally this work was in two volumes, the first dealing with the period from the Apostolic Fathers to the Reformation; the second covering the story of the seventeenth, eighteenth, and nineteenth centuries (exclusive of American preaching which Dr. Dargan planned to include in a third volume). It is a great gain that now the two are combined in one volume.

Several features of Dr. Dargan's method are of particular value. The first is the illuminating presentation in every instance of the political, social, literary, and general cultural conditions of a period in their relation to preaching. The interplay between these factors and preaching is significantly displayed. Another feature is a careful critical analysis of the qualities of preaching that affected its creativity in both the periods of decline and those of spiritual advance in the church. Of great value also are the biographical sketches of many of the greater preachers in Christian history. It is remarkable how the author in the brief space given to the individual character was able to give a clear portrait and turn the spot-light on the central qualities of his personality and preaching. If to achieve greatness one must have a vision of greatness and habitually gaze upon the best achievement in any field, this galaxy of the great in the field of preaching affords for the aspiring preacher of our day an inspiring vision.

On behalf of the ministry at large, I would congratulate the publishers for their service in reissuing this monumental work.

J. B. Weatherspoon

Department of Preaching
Southern Baptist Theological Seminary
Louisville, Kentucky

TABLE OF CONTENTS

VOL. I.

TABLE OF CONTENTS.

PREFACE

The following work is the fruit of studies pursued and judgments formed during eleven years of service as professor of Homiletics in the Southern Baptist Theological Seminary, at Louisville, Kentucky. It was the custom of the distinguished and lamented Dr. John A. Broadus, the first incumbent of that chair, to give every year instructive and delightful lectures on the History of Preaching. Under his inspiring teaching my interest as a student was awakened in the subject, and when years afterwards it fell to me first to share his labors of instruction and then to succeed to them, I became more and more deeply interested in the historical part of the course in Homiletics.

The remarkable lack of treatises on the History of Preaching, especially in English, early impressed me, and aroused a desire to do something, however little, towards supplying the need. The difficulty of the task and the pressure of other and heavy burdens have occasioned many misgivings and delays, and there have been of necessity changes of plan in the execution of the work. As now planned the present volume is the first of three proposed books. It deals with the history up to and including the Reformation, the next will treat of Modern European preaching, and the last will present a History of Preaching in the United States. Some material is in hand for these later works, and should this one be fortunate enough to find a public, and should life and leisure be granted me, I hope in time to produce them.

For the completion of the present volume opportunity was kindly afforded by the Trustees of the Seminary in granting me leave of absence for some months to visit Europe. While abroad from June, 1902, to January, 1903, I had time not only to write up much material already gathered, but to visit some of the places made famous in the history of the pulpit, and to read somewhat in a number of the great libraries, including those at Berlin,

Leipzig, Rome, Zurich, Geneva, and Paris. I am indebted for courtesies to the managers at these and other places.

In the use of the materials which I had to study, both at home and abroad, three methods have found place: (1) Much of the work done and critical judgments reached is based on personal and independent study of the original sources; (2) Much more, however, is of that mingled sort which rests partly and often chiefly on the work of others, and yet has been confirmed, enlarged or modified by contact with the sources; (3) In a few cases, where circumstances warranted or seemed to require it, I have simply adopted information obtained or views expressed by others. I have endeavored, either in the text or footnotes, to give the requisite indications as to which method has been used. But every one who has attempted this kind of writing knows how utterly impossible it is in all cases to distinguish sharply between what may be properly regarded as the author's own work, and that which he owes to others. I can only say that I have tried to make an honest book, and hereby cheerfully acknowledge my great indebtedness to many excellent workers in this field. I trust the book may find, both among my brethren of the Christian ministry and among others, readers who in their turn may find some pleasure and profit in perusing even so imperfect a presentation of the History of Preaching.

E. C. D.

Louisville, Kentucky, December, 1904.

INTRODUCTION

1. The Need of a History of Preaching

The history of preaching has not yet been adequately written. A few works, all of them more or less fragmentary and incomplete, deal with the subject as a whole; a larger number, some of them remarkably good and satisfactory, treat of particular epochs or phases of the history; some attention, incidental and often superficial, has been given to preaching by writers of general, ecclesiastical, and literary histories; and this is all. A thorough, comprehensive, well-proportioned and reasonably complete account of preaching in all periods and countries does not exist, either as the great work of a single author or as a connected series of studies by different authors.

This lack of suitable historic treatment has been variously noticed by different writers. Thus Van Oosterzee,[1] in commenting on the lack of historic knowledge among preachers themselves concerning their work, says, "There is still wanting a good history of the art of preaching from the earliest times to the present day;" and further, "The wish cannot be suppressed that a qualified and vigorous hand might yet be impelled satisfactorily to fill up this gap in the historic-theologic literature." Christlieb,[2] in noticing the failure yet to produce an "all-round, satisfying, comprehensive history," seems to give up the expectation as hopeless, because no one is likely to have the "capacity and leisure" for so vast an undertaking. A recent French Catholic writer, the Abbé Boucher,[3] rather lightly dismisses the matter with the remark that such a work would be unnecessary as it would really be a history of the progress of Christianity. This is too superficial a view; and the suggestion of Christlieb is no more appropriate for the history of

[1] *Practical Theology* (Am. ed.), pp. 67, 68.

[2] *Geschichte der Predigt,* article in the Herzog-Plitt *Real-Encyklopädie,* Bd. 18, S. 466.

[3] *L'Eloquence de la Chaire,* Introduction.

preaching than for other subjects which cover vast fields, long periods, and practically limitless materials.

The materials for writing the history of the Christian pulpit are abundant, for some epochs superabundant. Only for a few and comparatively unimportant periods and departments of the subject is there scarcity. These materials consist, first of all, in the innumerable biographies and sketches of preachers of all ages and lands, and in the practically infinite quantity of published sermons. Then account must be taken of ecclesiastical histories and archæologies, as these are obviously very closely related to preaching. And then the histories of civilization and of literature contain much that bears on preaching, directly and indirectly; and of course some knowledge, and the more the better, of general history is requisite to understanding that of the pulpit. Besides these sources of information at first hand there is a considerable literature which discusses different branches of the general subject, and is indispensable as a help to the historian. There are not a few excellent treatises and monographs which greatly reduce the necessity for research in some quarters of the field. Evidently the historian of preaching has at his disposal ample material for his work.

In fact the great abundance of the material is one of the chief difficulties in the way of writing the history of preaching. Even allowing for all the helps, and pressing the principle of selection as far as is admissible, there still remains a vast bulk of literature to go over, a deal of information to accumulate, study, digest, arrange, and finally set forth in writing. On the other hand, another difficulty arises from the lacks and gaps in the literature. Many periods and branches of the subject are still without adequate treatment, and there are very few general works to serve as basis, guide, or even warning, in the production of a really complete general history. When we add to these intrinsic difficulties of the task the exacting requisites which the modern critical and scientific spirit lays down for the writing of history,[1] we cannot

[1] See, for example, how these are set forth by Langlois and Seignobos, in their valuable *Introduction to the Study of History* (Eng. trans.).

wonder that so little has yet been accomplished in this department. It is as impossible to reach perfection in writing history as in any other human undertaking, and even to attain to excellence requires a rare combination of aptitude, learning, practice, enthusiasm, patience and leisure which might well appall the most competent.

On the other hand, it must be remembered that if difficulties of this sort were allowed their full force nobody worth attending to would have the courage to write history at all; for these obstacles are more or less incident to all historical research and writing. There is no more reason why a history of preaching should be given up as hopeless than histories of literature, of philosophy, of art, and the like.

A very slight glance at what has already been done will justify this conclusion, and at the same time lead to a consideration of what remains to be done in this too much neglected field. Foot-notes in the body of this work will give a fuller account of the literature.[1] Here only some brief statements are proposed. The literature naturally falls into the two groups of general and special works.

Of treatises bearing on the general history of preaching three sorts may be specified. First, there are those somewhat fragmentary works which may be called contributions to the history. Here, for example, belongs the old but still serviceable book of Lentz, *Geschichte der Homiletik,* published in 1839, containing brief biographical and critical notices of some of the more noted preachers of ancient, mediæval and modern times, with selections from their sermons. Somewhat like this, but with full sermons and proportionately less of biographical and critical matter is the valuable collection by H. C. Fish, *Masterpieces of Pulpit Eloquence*, published at New York in 1850, and still reprinted. Besides these are several later works, in various languages, of this general character.

[1] Paniel, *Geschichte der Christlichen Beredsamkeit,* in the introduction ably reviews the earlier literature up to 1831. Christlieb, in his two articles in Herzog-Plitt—*Geschichte der Predigt* and *Homiletik*—also has a good review of the literature to about 1886. Broadus mentions some of the best books in the appendix to his *Lectures on the History of Preaching.*

A second class of writings dealing with the whole subject are certain sketches, or compendious outlines. One of the best of these is that of J. J. Van Oosterzee in his *Practical Theology* (translation published at New York about 1879); and there are several by German authors on Homiletics, as Th. Harnack, Hering, and others; also the sketch by Professor Hoppin in his *Homiletics* is specially noteworthy, as he discusses American preachers neglected by the others. But by far the most comprehensive and thorough sketch, so complete indeed that one hesitates to call it a sketch, is the great article by Christlieb, *Geschichte der Predigt,* in the supplement to the eighteenth volume of the Herzog-Plitt *Real Encyclopädie.*[1] Even in its present form it is the nearest approach yet made to a complete though necessarily compendious history.

The remaining class of general histories of preaching are those few works which in some measure present a connected view of the whole field. In 1839 a German scholar, Paniel, published the first volume of a proposed general history of preaching under the title *Pragmatische Geschichte der Christlichen Beredsamkeit.* It was a well-planned work and showed both research and the scientific spirit, but unhappily it remains only a fragment, having got no further than Augustine in the fifth century. It is still valuable for the early centuries. Next should be mentioned the *Geschichte der Predigt von den Anfangen bis auf Schleiermacher* of Richard Rothe, edited from his manuscript remains by Trümpelmann, and published in 1881. This came nearer being a general history than any other work that had yet appeared, but it is full of gaps, much of it is mere compilation, and it lacks completeness and finish in many ways. In 1876 Dr. John A. Broadus published a small volume of *Lectures on the History of Preaching,* which had been delivered at Newton Theological Institution, near Boston. The book does not profess to cover the ground as a formal or scientific treatise, but contains some excellent work in the way of historical generalization and comment, of discussion of certain periods and men, and of

[1] At the time of this writing the new edition (ed. by Professor Hauck of Leipzig) has not reached this article.

keen and sympathetic criticism. Similar in method are the *Lectures on the History of Preaching* (1888), of Dr. John Ker of Scotland, which give a slight account of ancient and mediæval preaching, but chiefly present in a very pleasing way some of the modern German preachers. There is a spirited and readable course of lectures by the late Fleming James, D.D., *The Message and the Messengers* (1897), which is not a history, but, as the subtitle correctly describes it, a series of "lessons from the history of preaching." The most recent work is that of the late Professor T. Harwood Pattison, of Rochester Theological Seminary, Rochester, New York, *The History of Christian Preaching*. The work is much too brief to present adequate consideration of the great mass of material, and it does not claim to be a complete history; but it gives a series of brilliant short sketches of many of the leading preachers, with some comment on the condition of preaching in all the Christian ages.

When we come to works which treat of special epochs, countries, sects, or other departments of the history of preaching, a very much better showing can be made for the literature. There are numerous treatises of varying authorship, date, and language. Many of them have been of inestimable service in the preparation of this work, and are mentioned in the foot-notes where appropriate, so that detailed notice is not here needed.

From this brief general mention we may see that while something has been done, much remains yet to be done in this inviting field of religious history.

There is, and of course always will be, place for that class of writings called "contributions" to history, that is, accumulations of material in the way of biographical, critical, and other monographs, which will facilitate research and study, and sometimes even render them unnecessary where the historian can depend upon a careful and judicious investigator. Some of the special works spoken of in the previous paragraphs are admirable specimens of this sort of writing, but there is need for many more of the same sort.

But the most pressing present need is a general history. Such a work might take one, or indeed all, of three forms: (1) A compendious manual covering the whole ground, but briefly and clearly; (2) A larger work of several volumes, going more into biographical, critical and general historical detail; (3) A *magnum opus* of many volumes really covering the subject and remaining a complete and enduring authority. It would be very difficult for any one scholar nowadays to produce a work of the third kind, for it would require a lifetime of leisure and plenty of means to accomplish the task, but it might be done in shorter time by the coöperation under competent editorship of a number of scholars who should devote themselves to particular epochs and countries. The books of Broadus, Ker, and especially Pattison, fall under the first head. It is the aim of the author to meet in some modest measure the second of the forementioned needs. But it will require many works of many laborers and through many years before the place of preaching in human history can be adequately set forth. To some consideration of that great sphere we may now appropriately turn.

2. The Place of Preaching in History

Since Christianity became an active force in human affairs there has been upward and onward movement, and one mighty factor in that progress has been preaching. There are a number of ways in which the importance of preaching in history may be shown.

The most remote point of connection should be first noted, that is, the influence of preaching upon the general course of events. The influence has necessarily been reciprocal—preaching has shaped events, and events have affected preaching. More detailed statements will make the point clearer.

The life and progress of nations, the rise and fall of governments have often been closely connected with preaching. This is no extravagant claim, as we shall have some occasion to see in the course of this work. The great names of the Apostle Paul, of John Chrysostom, of Augustine and Ambrose, of Leo and Gregory, of Boniface and Bernard, of Wiclif and Savonarola, of Luther and Calvin and Knox, of Edwards, Whitefield and Wesley, are some of those which suggest how variously and profoundly the larger life of nations has sometimes been influenced by the preacher.

In regard to customs and morals, however, the contact of preaching with history is more visible and fruitful. Preaching has profoundly and for the most part wholesomely influenced the morals and customs of mankind. And in those few cases where the influence of the pulpit may be justly open to criticism, the injurious effects have been comparatively trivial and not permanent. On the other hand preaching has, sometimes for the better and sometimes for the worse, received moulding from contemporary customs and standards of ethics. While this sensitiveness to environment has often kept the pulpit from stagnation and given to it greater power to deal with the needs of the times, we must confess that sometimes public sentiment and entrenched evil, rather than the ostensibly accepted higher authorities, have colored the language of sermons.

Progress in the arts and sciences has contributed in many ways to preaching. Here it has received more than it has given; but its influence has not been void of good and help even in this direction; for the pulpit has many a time given intelligent aid and stimulus to material enterprises which had in view the present and permanent good of mankind. So also preaching has availed itself of the advantages of commerce to herald the gospel to other lands and peoples, and used many an improvement and device in the material sphere to make more effective its work at home.

The connection of preaching with the progress of human culture is real and extensive. Sometimes there has been conflict, sometimes mutual jealousy, but more frequently reciprocal and cordial help. Let us notice some of the particulars.

As to art it is beyond doubt that music, painting, sculpture, architecture, and even the industrial arts, have owed something to preaching, and preaching something to them. But no great amount of reciprocal influence is claimed in this sphere.

In philosophy, however, the mutual influence has been profound and profoundly important. The effect has not always been for the best on either party, but it is safe to say that preaching has oftener been hurt by philosophy than philosophy by preaching. But there has also been wholesome and helpful interaction. Theology and ethics are fundamental in pulpit work, and their relations to philosophy are necessarily close. Names of preachers who have been eminent in philosophical work and influence are numerous; a few of the most important are Justin Martyr, Origen, Gregory of Nyssa, Augustine, among the ancients; Anselm, Aquinas, and others of the great schoolmen of the middle ages; Eckhart among the mystics; Calvin among the theologians of the Reformation; Edwards among American Puritans.

In regard to science there has often been full and cordial mutual recognition. Some eminent scientists have not failed in reverence for Christian institutions, the pulpit included; and some preachers here and there have been skilled scientists in various branches. But on the whole it must be sadly admitted that the relations between science and the pulpit have not been as friendly and mutually profitable as could be wished. If the progress of science has at times suffered from the dogmatism of the pulpit, even so the preaching of a sorely needed gospel has been sometimes hindered or harmed in effect by the dogmatism of science. Preachers have been known to assail science in an unchristian spirit, and scientists have perhaps as often denounced and discredited preaching in an unscientific spirit. Pulpit ignorance of science has been fairly matched by scientific ignorance of the aims and realities of the pulpit. Narrowness and arrogance on both sides have done their full share of mischief. It is time for a better understanding, for mutual respect, for more cordial united service between these two great agencies for human good. Reverent science seeking hidden truth should surely be no foe to earnest preaching proclaiming revealed truth; and the herald of God's saving grace in Christ should not be the enemy of the searcher after God's wondrous thought in creation. There is room in God's world for both the scientist and the preacher; there should be room in their hearts for each other.

In the very nature of the preacher's work lies his relation to the study and use of language. The proclamation of the gospel, the translation of the Bible, and the creation of a literature of Christian instruction in many languages of the earth have been largely the work of preachers. The impetus thus given to linguistic science has been great and fruitful. Nor must the study and employment of language for the high purposes of discourse be forgotten; not a few preachers have been masters and models of eloquence.

In the sphere of literature there has been great and hearty reciprocal service. Preaching has both directly and indirectly contributed much to literature. Yet it must be said that while many a Paul has met with his surprised and admiring Festus, it is also true that too often literature, especially fiction, has done the pulpit injustice by its one-sided presentation of the weaker or extreme types of ministerial character. But on the whole literature and the preacher have through many moons been dear lovers. Illiterate preachers have served to emphasize by contrast the learning of their more cultured brethren. Incidentally to their main work numbers of preachers have won enduring laurels in the republic of letters. Often, too, the pen of the writer and the tongue of the preacher have been allied forces in campaigns against ignorance and error.

As to education no openminded observer can fail to recognize the intimate relations between it and preaching. The debt is reciprocal and large; and it has been so all along the history of the pulpit. There has hardly ever been any really good educational movement which has failed to receive the steadfast and efficient support of the preachers as a class. In turn education has given her choicest treasures and her best discipline to the pulpit. Scientific and literary training have both served the preacher, naturally the latter more; and especially has there been necessarily close affinity between preaching and rhetorical culture. Sometimes this has been unduly neglected, and sometimes unduly magnified. Artistic, not to say artificial, oratory has not seldom been ambitiously substituted for simple and earnest proclamation of divine truth. On the other hand, the faithful presentation of the gospel has often exemplified the noblest uses of rhetoric, and the work of the pulpit has exhibited not a few specimens of the highest oratory. Thus in many ways is the history of preaching interwoven with that of civilization and culture.

It remains to consider the largest surface of contact between preaching and history, and this, of course, is its place in the religious life and progress of mankind. Preaching is an essential part and a distinguishing feature of Christianity, and accordingly the larger history of general religious movements includes that of preaching. Here, as before, a reciprocal influence must be reckoned with: the movement has sometimes produced the preaching, the preaching sometimes the movement, but most commonly they have each helped the other. Illustrations readily occur.

The spread of Christianity, both geographically and numerically, has been largely the work of preaching. The preacher as a missionary has always been the advance herald of the gospel. From apostolic days, through the long Middle Ages, and even down to present times this has been true. Moreover, the leavening of the nations already reached by the gospel, the adding to the church daily those who are being saved, is, on the human side and to a great extent, the result of preaching. We must not underestimate the value and effect of personal example and suasion, but history forbids that we should assign an inferior place to preaching in bringing men to know Christ as Saviour and Lord, and in training them in the Christian life, doctrine and service. For spiritual life, doctrine and service are the very marrow of the gospel, and therefore of the preaching of the gospel. The message of the true preacher in every age has had to do with these fundamental things. On the other hand, Christian life as expressed and exemplified in ecclesiastical institutions, and Christian doctrine as formally stated in creeds, or even when only vaguely underlying accepted beliefs and usages, have in their turn powerfully influenced the character and aims of preaching. Alas! the story is not always a pleasing one; for doctrinal and sectarian polemics have too often been the preacher's chief concern.

Human progress of every kind is usually not steady

and continuous, but rather goes by waves, like the rising tide. Declension and revival, forward and backward, up and down, these are the common Christian phenomena, individual, local, general. Even the most superficial study reveals the connection, at once causal and resultant, between movements of the kind described and preaching. Decline of spiritual life and activity in the churches is commonly accompanied by a lifeless, formal, unfruitful preaching, and this partly as cause, partly as effect. On the other hand, the great revivals of Christian history can most usually be traced to the work of the pulpit, and in their progress they have developed and rendered possible a high order of preaching.

Again and again in the following pages we shall see illustrations of the positions taken in this discussion, and the right of preaching to a fair large room in history's many-chambered mansion may easily be vindicated and assured. So it is appropriate at this point of our introductory studies to say something as to the historic origins of preaching.

3. The Historic Origins of Preaching

History is a study of origins and developments in human affairs. Strictly speaking the actual beginnings of most human institutions are difficult to discover, and our knowledge of them is chiefly conjectural or inferential. What we call beginnings or causes are themselves effects of previous causes and movements, and what we call effects may be the causes of subsequent events; and so the ceaseless current of time and change flows on and on. The history of any people or subject, to be complete, must begin as far back as knowledge reaches and come down to present times. But the narrative may confine itself within more or less arbitrary limits at the discretion of the historian. The scope of the present volume is to trace the history of preaching from the Apostolic Fathers at the end of the first century to and including the great Reformers of the sixteenth century. But it seems desirable to give here at least a summary sketch of the origin and development of preaching before the point at which the more detailed account begins, in order that the reader may have before him to some extent the story from the beginnings of our knowledge.

There are three great converging lines of preparation in the way of materials, tendencies and events, which under providential guidance conspired to start, in the age immediately following the Apostles, that series of causes and effects which we are to study under the name of the history of preaching. These three elements of origination, named in the ascending order of their immediacy and importance, are the ancient oratory, the Hebrew prophecy, and the Christian gospel. From this last, as directly resting upon the second, and after a time considerably influenced by the first, came preaching as history knows it. Oratory and prophecy were preparatory and contributing forces, the gospel was the real originating cause, which took to itself elements of tendency and power from both the others.

How soon did men find and use the gift of persuasive speech? How long came oratory after language itself? There is no answer to these questions. It is likely indeed that oratory grew out of conversation, but its use and development do not tell the story of its origin. Passing by any vague theories, whether serious or humorous, of a possible derivation from the chatterings of supposititious simian ancestors, we may hazard some more plausible conjectures as to the rise and use of oratory before we discover certain traces of it in existing records. It is a natural inference that, connected with the desire and capacity of one person to influence another, language should at once have been employed for this purpose, and that from such use in conversation and dialogue it should have come to be employed by one in address to several others, from two or three to a multitude.

Spencer[1] conjectures that oratory, especially religious oratory, grew out of laudatory harangues at first addressed to heroes on returning from victorious wars, and then made in favor of deified heroes, and so of the gods. He thinks he sees traces of this custom in the acclamations of Israel at the Red Sea, and at the victory of David over Goliath, and outside of the Biblical records in some observances of the Fiji Islanders. In the same way arose

[1] *Principles of Sociology,* Vol. III., pp. 216 ff.

epic poetry, and the drama. The conjecture seems far-fetched, a pound of inference from a pennyweight of observation.

If the ethnological theory be accepted that the North American Indians represent in some respects the stage of development reached by man in the so-called Stone Age previous to recorded history, it may be plausibly claimed that the remarkable eloquence sometimes exhibited by these "untutored children of the forest" was a sample of prehistoric oratory, and gives real trace of a very remote origin of the use of persuasive speech for personal or public ends. But leaving these theories, let us come to actual history.

The three great civilizations of the ancient world—Egyptian, Assyrian, Persian—have not sent down to us any notable contribution to oratory. It is a commonplace among students of the subject that despotic governments are not favorable to eloquence, and it is probable that oratory was not much cultivated among these great peoples. Yet there are traces of its existence. The councils of war and of state, the royal audiences, petitions, pleas for justice, and the like, of which the records tell us, indicate at least some place and need for oratory as an art. In the Biblical account of Egyptian and Assyrian affairs there are a few traces of the use of public persuasive speech. The effort of Moses to be excused from going to Egypt to bring up the Israelites, on the ground of his lack of eloquence,[1] is suggestive of his acquaintance with the need of gifts in that direction in order to secure the end sought. In later times the insolent speeches of Rabshakeh, recorded in the eighteenth chapter of Second Kings, afford evidence that the art was not unknown among the Assyrians. Among the Hebrews, besides the work of the prophets to which more detailed attention will be given later, there are notices here and there of an oratory not especially or at all religious. The speech of Lamech[2] to his wives Adah and Zillah has been adduced as a specimen of antediluvian oratory, but it more properly belongs to poetry. Professor Sears[3] pertinently inquires as to what kind of oratory the author of the Book of Job must have heard in order to produce such

[1] Exod. 4:10 ff. [2] Gen. 4:23. [3] *History of Oratory*, p. 28.

speeches as those uttered by the interlocutors in that drama. The pathetic and simply beautiful speech of Judah[1] before Joseph in Egypt is justly admired as a choice specimen of unpretentious eloquence. In the ninth chapter of the Book of Judges we have an interesting speech from Jotham,[2] who compared the selection of his murderous half-brother, Abimelech, to be ruler or " king " over a part of Israel, to the choice of the bramble as king by the trees of the forest. Besides, there are a few other traces of a secular, or at least not distinctively religious, oratory in the Old Testament. But on the whole the oratory of the ancient peoples before the Grecian and Roman times was not abundant in quantity nor of the highest quality. Its value as literature and its significance in history alike are slight.

A widely different state of affairs greets us when we come to study the oratory of the Greeks. Both the literary value and the historic importance of their orations are of the highest sort. Ancient eloquence, on its secular and artistic side, reached its culmination among this gifted and versatile people. The speeches in the Homeric Poems show that in the earliest, semi-mythical times the Greeks employed and prized the gift of eloquence. The growth of political freedom, the early and vigorous development of dialectic philosophy, the cultivation and excellence of art and literature, along with the imaginative and lively intellect and the flexible and powerful language of the Greeks, all contributed to their marvellous and abiding attainments in the field of oratory.[3] It was cultivated in all the Greek countries, but reached its highest stage of development at Athens, and its personal acme in Demosthenes. Along with the practice of public speaking came the theory, the reduction to principles and rules, the teaching of rhetoric as an art. It is a notable coincidence that Demosthenes, the greatest orator of ancient times, and Aristotle, the great philosopher, and author of the most original and suggestive treatise on rhetoric in ancient literature, should have lived at the same time and died the same year, 322, B.C. With the passing away of

[1] Gen. 44: 18. [2] See Broadus, *History of Preaching*, p. 8.

[3] See Grote's *History of Greece*, chaps. 46 and 67; Jebb's *Attic Orators*, introd.; Sears' *History of Oratory*, chaps. II.-V.

these masters, and the political overthrow of ancient Greece, the oratory of the Greeks rapidly degenerated. But its lasting impress had been left on the history of oratory, and of civilization.

The Latin oratory was not of so excellent quality nor of so long duration as the Greek. Here too theory and practice developed together, but with the difference that the Romans had both the advantage and the disadvantage of possessing the Greek models. In the early days of the Republic, though there was some Greek influence, the Roman oratory was more independent and original, and was giving promise of a development and power of its own. But after the conquest of Greece the influence of the better Greek ideas and achievements in this as in other lines of literature was irresistible, and Latin oratory is, for the comparatively brief period of its development, mostly imitation or adaptation of the Greek.

The chief representative of Roman oratory is Cicero, who died B.C. 43. But there were a number of others too, and these gave a peculiar Roman stamp to their oratory. The Latin mind was much too vigorous not to be something of a Samson even in the chains of its enthrallment to Greek models. The best Latin treatise on rhetoric, that of Quintilian, was published probably in the latter part of the first Christian century, or the early part of the second. It is one of the very best works of all time on that subject, and has been a storehouse for all subsequent writers on rhetoric. In literary finish, in proportionate treatment of subjects, in fulness of material and completeness of range it excels the more original, suggestive and profound work of Aristotle.

Among both Greeks and Romans there was ample provision for instruction in the art of oratory.[1] In fact this was the chief element of ancient education. So we find that at the coming of Christianity rhetorical treatises, teachers and schools abounded, many speeches of the

[1] Information is obtainable from the works of Grote and Jebb, previously named; and from Davidson's *Aristotle and the Ancient Educational Ideals,* Hatch's Hibbert Lectures for 1888 on *The Influence of Greek Ideas and Usages upon the Christian Church,* and from a very entertaining and instructive article by M. Gaston Boissier in the *Revue des Deux Mondes* for March 15, 1884 (Vol. LXII), p. 316 ff. on *Instruction Publique dans l'Empire Romain.*

greatest Greek and Roman orators were preserved and potent in the culture of the age, and these two languages were dominant in all the social life of the peoples, among whom the new religion was to make its principal advances for centuries to come.

The Græco-Roman oratory at its best estate was lacking in one great essential to the highest eloquence. It had no religious content, and but incidentally a moral one. The accepted division of oratory into its kinds was threefold: deliberative, or political; forensic, or judicial; and epideictic, or declamatory. The first two are easily enough understood, the last is not so clear. At first it was meant to embrace funeral or memorial orations, or panegyrical discourses upon living persons, or patriotic speeches, or, as Aristotle defines it, was concerned chiefly with praise and blame. But in this classification of orations there is notable omission of the didactic element. There was nothing in ancient oratory corresponding to our lecture platform or pulpit. Lectures by teachers were hardly considered as belonging to oratory at all, and their declamations given as models to their pupils would probably have been classed under the third division, if anywhere. Of course, moral teaching could, and to some extent actually did, find place in all three kinds of speeches, but it was incidental to their main purpose in each case. A fourth kind of oratory, not that of the deliberative political assembly, not that of the law courts, not that of the memorial or panegyrical occasion, but that which as its main purpose should convey instruction with a view to ethical and religious culture and activity, was wanted before the trained gift of eloquence could find its noblest content and its best use. We are now to see how this lack was supplied. When Roman imperialism had conspired with other causes to ruin deliberative eloquence and depress the other two, Christian preaching gradually arose to devote oratory to a new service and fill it with a grander message. But before we reach the historical confluence of ancient oratory with distinctively Christian eloquence we must trace the separate line of development along which in the order of divine Providence gospel preaching arose.

In the ancient Hebrew prophecy we have exactly the

counterpart, in respect of moral and religious content and aim, to the Græco-Roman oratory. Of distinctively political, judicial, or declamatory speaking the Israelites probably had little or none, but their prophets were an order of orators charged with divine messages and devoted to the moral and spiritual culture of the people. We must beware of thinking exclusively of the predictive element in the work of Israel's prophets.[1] "It was by no means the main business of the prophets to predict the future, as people are now apt to suppose from our modern use of the word prophet, but they spoke of the past and the present, often much more than of the future. The prophets reminded the people of their sins, exhorted them to repent, and instructed them in religious and moral, in social and personal duties; and when they predicted the future it was almost always in the way of warning or encouragement, as a motive to forsake their sins and serve God. . . . . The prophets were preachers." These words of Dr. Broadus state the case clearly and well.

In the earliest ages it is said that "Enoch also, the seventh from Adam, prophesied."[2] And Noah is called "a preacher of righteousness."[3] Thus accepted Hebrew tradition recognized the beginnings of distinctively religious oratory in the most remote patriarchal times. The blessings of Isaac[4] and of Jacob[5] are examples of formal and solemn religious address in the poetical style. The book of Deuteronomy is a series of addresses repeating and expanding and enforcing in this form much of the legislation of Moses. Later as a sort of supplement we have the two farewell discourses of Joshua,[6] filled with earnest and wholesome counsel and appeal.[7]

From the time of Samuel (B.C. 1050) to that of Jeremiah (B.C 629), was the great prophetic period in Israel's history. Within this time appeared Samuel, Nathan, Gad, Azariah, Elijah, Elisha, Joel, Micah,

[1] See Broadus, *History of Preaching,* pp. 10-18.
[2] Jude 14. [3] 2 Peter 2:5. [4] Gen. 27:27-29.
[5] Gen. 49:3-27. [6] Josh. chaps. 23 and 24.
[7] The poetical prophecies of the singularly gifted Oriental seer Balaam, and the lofty discourses in the drama of Job are beside the direct line of Hebrew prophecy in the proper sense.

Micaiah, Isaiah, Jeremiah, and others.[1] These men of God came to people and kings with their certified divine messages, often introducing their great addresses with the formula, "Thus saith the Lord." They pleaded, warned, rebuked, encouraged; they crushed with sovereign threatenings and judgments; they built up with glowing divine promises of unspeakable and enduring glory to come. By no means are all the incidents of their careers related, nor is more than a fraction of their addresses preserved, but judging from what is known of their lives and works we surely gather vivid impressions of the greatness of their characters, the strength of their influence, and the lasting value of their discourses.

The last period of Hebrew prophecy extended from Ezekiel and Daniel to Malachi, from the exile to the restoration and later. In this period of the Jewish national life the character and influence of prophecy did not materially change. It was still the voice of God through chosen men to his chosen people. In form and content it still ministered to the religious life and aims of the people, both by preaching to the present and pointing to the future. But for long years the voice of prophecy was mute, awaiting the coming of the Promised One, the dawn of a new era.

During this period the worship of the Jews had a very important development, and one specially significant in the history of preaching. This was the hortatory exposition of the Sacred Writings in connection with the services of the synagogue. While the actual origin of the synagogue has not been definitely fixed, the growth of the institution into an established feature of Jewish religious life occurs during the time now under review. In the eighth chapter of Nehemiah there is record of the great occasion, soon after the return from the exile, when "Ezra the scribe stood upon a pulpit of wood, which they had made for the purpose," and others assisted him, and

[1] For a good treatment of the homiletical value of the preaching of the prophets see Stalker's *The Preacher and His Models.* The matter finds instructive comment in Ker's *Lectures on the History of Preaching,* and in James' *Message and the Messengers.* For a discussion from the point of view of the modern critical school see George Adam Smith's *Modern Criticism and the Preaching of the Old Testament.*

"they read in the book in the law of God distinctly, and gave the sense, and caused [the people] to understand the reading." Philo[1] gives testimony to the effect that at the time of the introduction of Christianity the services of the synagogue, "consisted chiefly of oral instruction and of free extended speaking." We find both our Lord and the Apostles availing themselves of this custom to proclaim the gospel. Thus we see that there was a clearly defined basis for Christian preaching in the sacred speech of that people from whom in the divine ordering of events Christianity sprang. And so in the widely separated lines of development which the sacred and the secular oratory of the ancient world pursued before the coming of our Lord, God was laying the foundation for the use of public speech as a means in the spread and the establishment of Christianity. Prophecy was preparation only. The proclaiming of the gospel of the kingdom of God was the actual initial step in the historic progress of Christian preaching. In this proclamation there are three distinct but successive, and therefore not wholly separate stages, namely, the preaching of John the Baptist, of our Lord himself, and of the Apostles and their fellow-workers.

John was the connecting link between the Old Testament and the New, the last and greatest of the prophets, the first preacher of the new dispensation. The character of the man was marked by great originality (though he was much like Elijah) and power. He was brusque, bold, candid, ready; but modest, devoted and faithful. The great fact that he announced was the immediate coming of the promised reign of God, "the Kingdom of Heaven is at hand." The promised Messiah was now about to arrive, and he himself was but a voice preparing the way of the Lord. In the greater work and glory of the Coming One he must be lost to view. Along with announcing this fact he had a great duty to enjoin, that of immediate preparation for the kingdom by a sincere

[1] Quoted by Hoppin, *Homiletics*, p. 23. On the relation of synagogue worship to preaching see Maybaum, *Jüdische Homiletik*, Einleitung. This writer, however, makes the mistake of leaving out of his definition of preaching the prophetic element and confining it to the exposition of Scripture. Something also may be found on the subject in Schürer's (Eng. trans.) *Jewish People in the Time of Christ*, Vol. II., p. 54.

and fruitful repentance. This he enforced by many an apt illustration and example, many a strong and brave application. His work was fortified and his message of repentance strikingly symbolized in the rite of baptism from which he gets his name.[1] It had not been uncommon for the older prophets to employ external things as signs, tokens, illustrations of their messages. John does not seem to have used the synagogues, but to have preached altogether to the crowds in the open air. In both character and work he has received the highest possible endorsement in the encomium of his Lord, "Among them that are born of women there hath not arisen a greater than John the Baptist."

In the work of Jesus himself, however, lies the main foundation of Christian preaching for all time.[2] It is not within the plan of this volume to give a thorough study of our Lord as a preacher. The theme demands a book to itself.[3] The purpose here is merely to indicate the salient features of Christ's preaching as the basis of subsequent historic development.

In comparing our Lord's preaching with that of John we notice that its burden was the same, but with a difference. Matthew tells us,[4] "From that time Jesus began to preach, and to say, Repent, for the kingdom of heaven is at hand." But as we go on to study the contents of his teaching from the beginning to the close of his ministry we observe more and more that the burden of his message is himself. He proclaims himself as the fulfillment of prophecy, as the Son, and therefore, the revealer of God, and cautiously at first, but with increasing distinctness, as the king of a spiritual realm, and finally throughout his ministry as the Saviour and Deliverer of men, the Way to God, the Good Shepherd who giveth his life for

[1] Cf. Broadus, *History of Preaching,* pp. 19-21.

[2] For the preaching of our Lord see Broadus, *op. cit.,* pp. 22-36, also his *Lectures on Jesus of Nazareth,* p. 43 ff.; Pattison's *History of Christian Preaching,* p. 14 ff; Stalker's *Imago Christi,* chaps. XII.-XV.; Armitage's *Lectures on Preaching,* Lects. I., II. Of course the subject is touched in most of the numerous works on the Life of Christ.

[3] Such a book has recently appeared in the *Jesus und seine Predigt* of Erich von Schrenck. But his treatment is rather exegetical and theological than homiletical.

[4] Matt. 4: 17.

the sheep, the Redeemer who would give his life as a ransom for many. He is his own gospel.

Accordingly the duty which he enjoins is not distinctively repentance (though this is understood) as preparation for a coming Lord, but rather faith in the Lord who has now come. He offers himself and his work to the acceptance of his hearers. He is the revelation and embodiment of God's gracious ways with men, and as such he is to be received and trusted. His message is, "Come unto me . . . . and I will give you rest."[1] . . . . "Believe in God, and believe in me."[2] . . . . "He that believeth on me hath everlasting life."[3]

The occasions and audiences of his preaching varied greatly. He sometimes conversed with individuals, announcing the great truths and distinctive principles of his gospel. Sometimes he talked with small groups, and sometimes he preached to great multitudes. Now we see him in the synagogue on the Sabbath day using the opportunity of worship for the proclamation of his message, and again we find him by sea or on mountain declaring the principles of his kingdom to those whom his teaching or his miracles had attracted.

The character of his preaching was a wonderful union of power and of charm. Its dominant note was authority, supreme confidence in God, in himself, in his mission and message. He ranged from scathing invective to tender invitation; he employed argument, aphoristic saying, parable, exposition of Scripture, with wonderful skill and effect; he mingled with all a yearning for men's good and God's honor which abides the ideal motive for all worthy preaching.

During his ministry our Lord twice[4] sent out bands of his disciples, two and two, to proclaim his kingdom. He gave them both their message and practical instructions for their guidance. It is not impossible that he did more of this work than these two recorded instances. After the Ascension we find the Apostles and others waiting at Jerusalem for the promised enduement of the Holy Spirit. In the book of Acts and in the Epistles we have traces of the Apostles' preaching after Pentecost had

[1] Matt. 11:28. [2] John 14:1. [3] John 6:47; *et sim.*
[4] Matt. chap. 10; Luke chap. 10.

given them their mission. Adequate treatment of this topic also does not fall within the scope of this treatise, but as the transition from the personal ministry of Jesus to the later history, the preaching of the Apostles and their colaborers claims at least a brief consideration.[1]

The apostolic preaching was accompanied by more immediate and consciously felt manifestation and direction of the Holy Spirit than was the case with later preaching. Along with this there were certain supernatural gifts which seem to have been granted for the attestation of the apostolic ministry, and to have continued with declining frequency and clearness a little way into the post-apostolic age. Such were the gifts of tongues, healings, miracles.

The content of the preaching was fundamentally the same as that of the Lord, with only the important difference made by the great facts of his crucifixion, resurrection and ascension, and the great promise of his second coming. Christ himself was still the central and dominant theme of the gospel message. Both repentance and faith, the union of John's burden with that of his Master, found due emphasis in the apostolic preaching. It proclaims a crucified, risen, reigning and coming Saviour and Lord. It is universal in time, having touch with past, present and future; in extent, reaching out to all men of every race and class in the world; and in character, holding the one remedy for all sin, the one way of reconciliation with God, the one path to eternal life.

In regard to method we see in the reported discourses of the Acts, and inferentially in the style and contents of the Epistles,[2] that the Apostles were greatly influenced by the ancient prophets in their general mode of address.

[1] Cf. the works previously mentioned of Broadus, Pattison, Stalker and Armitage. James does not treat the matter at length. The numerous modern works on the church of the apostolic age pay some attention to the preaching of the times. See, for example, Lightfoot's notes to his commentaries on Galatians and Philippians; Hort's *Ecclesia;* Lindsay's *Church and Ministry in the Early Centuries;* Allen's *Christian Institutions;* articles in Hastings' *Bible Dictionary,* and many others. In most works of this nature some caution is requisite in the reading, because of the tendency toward the over-use of inference and conjecture, from confessedly scanty materials, to establish critical or ecclesiastical theories.

[2] Cf. Broadus, *History of Preaching,* p. 36 ff.

Unless Paul's discourse at Athens[1] be an exception, we can detect little if any trace of influence from the ancient classical oratory. The two permanent elements of Christian preaching appear: evangelism and instruction. There is free speaking to men anywhere and everywhere in announcement of the gospel and in urgency of its claims, and there is orderly and authorized public instruction and edification of believers in their assemblies for worship, based upon the ancient Scriptures and the gospel tradition now becoming Scripture. For these ends there are apostles and prophets, elders, pastors and teachers, and evangelists. Thus in all essential respects we find in the apostolic preaching the regulative basis for Christian preaching in all times. The preaching of John was transitional, that of Jesus was unique, that of the Apostles and their fellow workers is our abiding model.

We are ready now to begin to trace the history of preaching from its origins. In the ancient classical oratory we have the artistic and effective use of language, as an instrument for the proclamation and enforcement of truth, brought to its highest degree of power. In the fervid moral and religious addresses of the Old Testament prophets we see exemplified the best possible employment to which oratory can be put. In the Christian gospel as proclaimed by Jesus and his appointed spokesmen we perceive the greatest and best content with which oratory can be charged for all time. On these historic foundations the fabric of preaching has been reared through the Christian centuries. We must give attention to its outlines.

4. Outline of the History of Preaching

History cannot be forced into arbitrary divisions, for at the borders there is always overlapping. The history of any age is dependent upon the preceding, and contributory to the subsequent ages; the history of any people touches that of other peoples; and the history of any subject is related to that of kindred subjects. Yet there is manifest propriety, not to say necessity, in having divisions of all the sorts indicated. Also the marking of

[1] Acts 17:22-31.

periods in the history of any people or subject is at once a convenience of study and a requirement of the subject-matter; but we must always remember that these boundaries are only approximate, never exact. It is true that in the course of events there are different facts and phases of life to be dealt with, and certain decisive occurrences or strongly marked changes emphasize their dates as turning points. But while some dates are practically accepted by all historians as suitable turning points, it is evident that particular considerations of people, place, subject, and the like, give rise to unavoidable differences in locating the exact time for recording the change or event. Thus while the division of general history into ancient, mediæval and modern is generally accepted, the particular dates of the transitions are by no means unanimously agreed upon; and for particular countries and subjects there must of necessity be different periods. The epochs of English history, for example, do not coincide with those of German or French history, nor the dates of the history of philosophy with those of the history of art, of literature, or of preaching; though at some points there is interesting connection because of some general event or mode of thought influencing all, or because of special relations at various times. Again, the assignment of periods must be largely the prerogative of each historian, according to his conception of his subject-matter, or his practical aim in writing, or other subjective considerations. In surveying the history of preaching as a whole we shall find that its course corresponds, as we should naturally expect, in marked degree with that of both general and ecclesiastical history; we shall note longer and shorter seasons of varying character, prosperity and power; and we shall be able to assign with at least approximate accuracy the dates which may be best assumed as turning points.

After the death of the Apostles and their fellow workers there is a time of decline, until gradually preaching rises in power to its ancient culmination in the fourth and early fifth century. Then it falls into a long night of obscurity and weakness, till with the preaching of the Crusades and the rise of Scholasticism it begins to revive, and reaches the height of its mediæval power in the thirteenth century. Then again there is a general and fearful falling off in purity and power; but the Reformation comes as another high wave gathering force slowly to its crest in the early part of the sixteenth century. After that, the unity of Christendom being forever broken, and other things coöperating, the modern period exhibits so great diversities in the character of preaching in different lands that it is not so easy to describe preaching in general terms. For while it flourishes in one country, it is often depressed in another, and while exhibiting one character in one sect or people, it may have another in others. Thus during the ascendency of Puritan doctrinal preaching in England there was the culmination of Catholic oratorical preaching in France; and the progress of the Wesleyan revival in England was contemporary with the dry-rot of rationalism in Germany. Yet in a general way, allowing for exceptions of all sorts, it is not inaccurate to describe the period next after the Reformation as one of decline, wherein doctrinal controversies too much occupied the pulpit; and while this was especially true of Germany it also found illustration elsewhere. The later modern period, chiefly in the nineteenth century, is undoubtedly the greatest in the history of the Christian pulpit, leaving out, of course, the originating period which is not included in our scheme, and for many reasons is unique and not to be compared with any subsequent one. Both the revival and the missionary impulses which have characterized this last period entitle it preëminently to be called the evangelical age. Its close is placed at the end of the nineteenth century only for convenience, for the obvious reason that even if we contemporaries seem to recognize the beginnings of a new epoch in preaching about this time, we cannot foresee its general character and course with sufficient distinctness to give it limits and a name. But waiving the matter of dates and boundaries as impossible, and looking only at the great tendencies in the religious life of our times, we should not perhaps guess very far amiss if we predict that later historians may have to describe the period of preaching on which we have just entered as the humanitarian or social age.

Bearing in mind the explanations made, we may assume

six fairly well defined periods for the general history of preaching, as follows:

Period I. A.D. 70-430.—The Ancient, or Patristic, Age. From the times of the Apostolic Fathers to the close of the labors of Chrysostom (d. 407) and of Augustine (d. 430).

Period II. 430-1095.—The Early Mediæval, or Dark, Age. After the times of Chrysostom and Augustine up to the preaching of the first Crusade, by Peter the Hermit and Pope Urban II.

Period III. 1095-1361.—The Central Mediæval, or Scholastic, Age. From the times of Peter the Hermit and Urban II. to the close of Tauler's (d. 1361) and the beginning of Wiclif's (ordained 1361) ministry.

Period IV. 1361-1572.—The Transitional, or Reformatory, Age. From the times of Tauler and Wiclif to the death of John Knox, the last of the great Reformers.

Period V. 1572-1738.—The Early Modern, or Dogmatic, Age. After the times of the great Reformers up to the beginning of the English revival under Whitefield and Wesley.

Period VI. 1738-1900.—The later Modern, or Evangelical, Age. From the times of Whitefield and Wesley to the end of the nineteenth century.

In the present volume it is proposed to treat of only the first four of these periods, tracing the general history of preaching down to the close of the work of the great Reformers. Of these Zwingli died in 1531, Luther in 1546, Calvin in 1564, and Knox in 1572. While the work of the Reformation went on in its effects and struggles beyond this time, the preaching of the Reformation reached its culmination in these men and their contemporaries.

PERIOD I

THE ANCIENT, OR PATRISTIC, AGE

A.D. 70–430

From the times of the Apostolic Fathers to the death of Chrysostom (407) and of Augustine (430)

CHAPTER I.

PREACHING DURING THE FIRST THREE CENTURIES.

In the introduction some attention has been paid to the origin of preaching in the work of Christ and his Apostles. We begin here to trace its development and progress from this beginning on through the ages down to the close of the work of the great Reformers in the sixteenth century. The first general period laid out for our study extends from the fall of Jerusalem in A.D. 70 to the death of the great theologian, bishop and preacher, Augustine, in 430. In this chapter only so much of that period as covers the first three centuries will be brought under review.

1. GENERAL VIEW OF THE FIRST THREE CENTURIES.

The fall of Jerusalem in A.D. 70 marks the end of the Jewish commonwealth, and is in many ways a significant and impressive event in general and church history. It also has a particular bearing on the history of preaching, and in time nearly coincides with the death of the apostles Peter and Paul, who probably suffered under Nero in 68.

At the end of the third and early in the fourth century Christianity was strong enough to withstand the last furious persecution (under Diocletian), and induce Constantine to change the attitude of the imperial government from contempt and opposition to tolerance and patronage. Within these centuries there were many events and forces which had great influence in determining the character and shaping the future of Christianity as an institution, and likewise profoundly affected the development of preaching. And so for a proper understanding of the course of preaching it is fitting that we first give at least a hurried glance at the general state of the Empire and of Christianity during these centuries.

Titus, the conqueror of Jerusalem, fell heir to an empire which, extending from Rome and Italy as a centre, reached westward and included Spain and Portugal; northwestward it took in France, the Netherlands and England; northward it held the German debatable territories on both sides of the Rhine; northeastward it claimed sovereignty to the Danube, and sometimes beyond, but could not always make good its claims in this direction; eastward it took in Dalmatia, Thrace, Greece, Asia Minor, and Armenia; southeastward it held the ancient lands of Egypt, Syria, Palestine, and far in to where Parthian and Persian disputed its eager lust of power by the Euphrates and Tigris; southward it embraced the territories of its ancient rival Carthage, and the provinces of Northern Africa stretching westward to the ocean, where at the Straits of Gibraltar the circuit is completed.

The varied character of the population of this mighty empire is, of course, evident at a glance, nor was it possible for even so powerful a government as that of Rome to weld these varied nations into a homogeneous people. Yet, with many minute variations, the Græco-Roman type of civilization was generally prevalent; and the use of both the Greek and Latin languages was widely spread. In the East the extension of Greek ideas and the conquest of Alexander had prepared the way for the predominance and perpetuation of the Hellenic elements of the dual culture; while in the West the Latinizing of North Africa, Spain and Gaul, partly begun under republican and early achieved under imperial rule, emphasized the Roman elements. The Eastern Empire was essentially Greek with infusion of Latin and Oriental ingredients; the Western Empire was essentially Roman with infusion of Hellenic and barbarian ingredients. The failure of Rome to conquer and assimilate the Germanic peoples as it had done the Iberian and Keltic races left an open door for barbarian conquest, and hastened, soon after the permanent division, the downfall of the Western Empire. The surging and mingling of races, with all accompanying forces of discord and corruption, were fairly under way in Vespasian's time, and went on with marked results throughout our period.

Building on the foundations of the older Roman rule, the wonderful political genius of Cæsar and of Augustus had constructed a fabric which stood the shock of the tyrannies and crimes of their degenerate followers till Vespasian retrieved the fallen glories of imperial rule, and his successors—except Domitian, and until Commodus—governed with great ability. Confusion followed, but Diocletian at the end of the third century again made imperial rule strong and respected. But we should go far astray if we regarded the imperial court and headquarters alone in our study of Roman government. The provinces and cities of the empire were also fields for the display of that marvellous administrative faculty which distinguished the Roman people. It was their settled policy not to interfere with local and popular institutions any further than was necessary to the maintenance of their military supremacy and the management of the imperial revenues. But these items necessarily involved the enactment of many laws and the general administration of justice. And thus in various ways, throughout this vast extent of lands and among peoples so diverse, the complicated system of Roman government held for ages its mighty sway over the most active and progressive races of mankind.

The imperial succession, and the characters and doings of the emperors during this period were all forces of importance in shaping events. The confusion after the wicked and tyrannical Nero was ended by the accession of the able general and ruler Vespasian, whose son Titus, the conqueror of Jerusalem, followed in a short though promising reign, to be himself followed for fifteen years by the mad tyrant Domitian. Then followed the "five good emperors"—Nerva, Trajan, Hadrian, Antoninus Pius, Marcus Aurelius—whose mostly beneficent reigns filled out not quite a century (96-180). After the good emperors came, through a little more than a century (180-306), a long succession of short reigns. From Commodus to Constantine were more than thirty emperors. Many of them were bad, some unfortunate, a few were able rulers. Diocletian associated others with himself, divided the empire, and thus paved the way for discord and civil wars. Meantime we are more concerned with the rise and growth of another power destined to play even a greater part than Rome in the history of the world, and that is Christianity.

Already in Paul's lifetime that apostle could write[1] of the gospel as being "in all the world bearing fruit and increasing;" his own extensive labors are familiarly known, and it is reasonable to suppose that even at the commencement of our period the gospel had at least been made known in all parts of the empire. Soon it had reached even beyond those bounds, and by the end of the time we have in view it had adherents in all the world. "From Britain to India the name of Christ was honored."[2] How numerous these adherents were at any given time it is of course impossible to say. They were certainly a minority of the population, but yet a very strong minority, even at the time of Diocletian's persecution.

As Christianity was not a legalized religion till Constantine, the imperial policy before that time wavered between toleration and persecution, and this lack of a settled attitude is illustrated among both the bad and the good emperors. Thus Nero, Domitian and Maximin were persecutors, but so were Marcus Aurelius and Diocletian. Trajan and Hadrian were tolerant, but so was Caracalla. It was largely as popular feeling or the whim of the emperor pleased.

Not only in the outward relations of Christianity, but also in its inner development there were noteworthy events and forces. The simple polity and worship of the

[1] Col. 1: 5, 6.
[2] A. H. Newman, *Manual of Church History,* Vol. I., p. 291.

apostolic churches soon began to develop toward a more complicated organization and a more elaborate ritual. The pastors came to be distinguished as bishops and presbyters, and the deacons were made an order of ministry. A powerful stimulus was given toward the developments of later times. Centering about the observance of the Lord's Supper, and commemorating sacred seasons, worship became at once enriched and corrupted by ceremonial accretions, and grew into an imposing ritual.

Nothing in the history of the first three centuries of Christianity is more notable than the defence and gradual formulation of Christian doctrine. Already in apostolic times the Gnostic heresies were beginning to appear. Others followed, and the teachings of the gospel had to be guarded from corrupt forms of professedly Christian faith. Opposition from without called forth the Apologists with their statements, and the natural tendency of study and speculation developed the theologians of various schools.

2. Particular Relation of Some Events to Preaching.

We shall have frequent occasion to observe that preaching, like all other special institutions, is responsive to general influences; and so it shared, more or less directly, in the whole character and movement of the age as briefly outlined in the preceding section. But besides this general influence of the times there are several matters of great importance which had a more particular influence in shaping the development and character of preaching. These were, the dispersion and final overthrow of the Jews as a nation, the great extension of the Roman empire, and the imperial persecutions of the Christians.

From the time of the Captivity under the Assyrian and Babylonian kings the Israelites had begun to be scattered among the nations of the earth, and this movement was accelerated during the time we are now studying by the great events which then occurred. Already during the labors of the Apostles there were Jewish communities and synagogues in the chief cities which they visited;

and these influenced preaching partly by the opportunity they offered and the mode they suggested for the proclamation of the gospel, and partly also by the stimulus of opposition and rejection which turned the Apostles and early preachers more and more to the Gentiles.

In A. D. 70 the long and dreadful siege of Jerusalem by the Roman armies ended in the capture and destruction of the city. The horrors of that awful event are equaled in impressiveness only by its momentous lessons. Israel had failed to meet the splendid opportunities of the divine election. It now passes as a nation from the historic page, leaving written behind it the warning moral of its checkered story. The overthrow of the Holy City and the destruction of the Temple published in tremendous tones what the rejection and crucifixion of Jesus had already made a settled thing, namely, the end of the Jewish and the inauguration of the Christian dispensation, as the special channel of God's revelation to men. The first Christians were mostly Jews. After the overthrow of Jerusalem they had no more a Jewish commonwealth to live for—they were citizens of the kingdom of heaven. The effect of this change of view in their religious relations had its effect on the preaching of the sub-apostolic age. Prophecy was fulfilled, and a new and impressive message must go with the proclamation of the gospel to all the world. The failure of all attempts to re-establish the Jewish nation only marked finality upon what had been so impressively taught by the fall of Jerusalem.

Let it be noted just here that the widest extent of the Roman Empire was reached in this age, under the Emperor Trajan (A. D. 98-117); but both before and after this time the vast and varied empire under one strong government was a mighty force in the progress of civilization, and thus lent its aid to the development of Christian preaching. The wide extent of Roman influence, the great roads and lines of communication, the prevalence of the Greek and Latin languages, were all factors of no small importance in that development.

We must now say a word as to the imperial persecutions. Up to the beginning of the fourth century Christianity was an unlawful religion in the Roman Empire. As such it was the object of popular hatred, and received much social persecution. Sometimes also the government was aroused to violent action against the Christians. These imperial persecutions were rather spasmodic in character, but some of them were very severe while they lasted. Some were local and some more extensive. The worst of them were those under Marcus Aurelius (165), Decius (250), Valerian (258), and Diocletian (303). They did not suppress Christianity, but made Christians more earnest and determined. This deep earnestness no doubt made itself felt in the preaching of the period. Another way in which the persecutions affected preaching was more external. They hindered, though they could not prevent, the gathering of large assemblies; and they interfered with and retarded the building of churches. Thus the preaching in large measure lacked these aids to oratorical development, and as a matter of fact it remained rather informal and personal in character throughout this early epoch. Other causes contributed to this, but it is not unlikely that the persecutions had something to do with it.

3. The Inner Development of Preaching.

More important, however, for us is the inner development of preaching during the second and third centuries. It is an obscure period, and we therefore cannot trace the development with as much accuracy and clearness as is desirable; but there are not wanting some valuable hints and data whereby a tolerably distinct view of the preaching of the age may be presented. That there was great decline in the power of preaching after the death of the Apostles and on to the times of Hippolytus, Origen and Cyprian in the latter part of the second and early part of the third century seems quite certain. For about a hundred years after the death of Peter and Paul (say from 70-170) the traces of preaching are extremely scanty, and do not exhibit any great degree of power. The very meagreness of our information, while it prevents our forming a safe judgment, is in itself an indication of weakness. For had there been a very powerful preaching in this era it is hardly conceivable that it would not have left more evidence of itself both in tradition and in literature. But toward the end of the second century, with the work of Clement and Origen at Alexandria, and of Irenaeus and Hippolytus in the West there is clear evidence of increased power in the ministry of the word. And this rise of strength prepared the way for the greater oratorical triumphs of the fourth century. But taking in the whole period of about two hundred and thirty years from the close of the apostolic age to the beginning of the fourth century, we may group the characteristics of preaching about the following points: (1) the preacher and his audience, (2) the contents of the preaching, (3) the form of the discourse, and (4) the preservation of sermons.

The essential personal factors in all speaking—the speaker and hearer—are necessarily to be considered in preaching, and their contribution to the character of the discourse must be duly estimated. Was preaching in this early time confined to an official class, or was it regarded as the privilege and duty of every believing man? It is probable that the regular church preaching, the exhortation or teaching addressed to the congregations of believers, was at first quite free, and was done by those who would volunteer for the service. At the same time it appears that even in apostolic times there was, parallel with this freedom and voluntariness, distinct recognition of "teachers"[1] and of "evangelists" also, in addition to the "apostles" and the "prophets," all of whom were in some sense especially charged with the duty of preaching. In regard to heralding, or evangelistic preaching, this would naturally vary from the conversational appeal and teaching, addressed to one or a few, up to the more extended and formal discourse addressed to a crowd or to some orderly assemblage. All this, no doubt, was guided by circumstances—in the nature of things preaching cannot be reduced to one type at any time. But it was natural that along with the developments in church organization, and the tendency toward increasing officialism therein displayed, there should also be a growing tendency to confine the work of preaching to an official class of duly authorized men. It appears[2] that very soon after

[1] 1 Cor. 12:28 and Eph. 4:11, 12.

[2] Paniel's *Geschichte der Christlichen Beredsamkeit,* S. 73 ff.; Rothe's *Geschichte der Predigt,* S. 8.

apostolic times preaching in the Christian assemblies was confined to the presbyters and bishops. Evangelistic preaching (which was more informal), and personal dealing with individuals (or smaller groups than assemblies) were not sharply distinguished and were recognized as the duty of all; but the exigencies of orderly worship and correct teaching required the appointment and qualification of a special class. How far apostolic initiative and sanction were followed in this matter does not clearly appear, but the qualifications required of the bishops in the third chapter of First Timothy, as well as some other indications, show that apostolic authority was not wholly lacking. The *Didache*[1] mentions travelling "apostles" and "prophets," as well as settled "teachers," who must be supported; and also notices that the "teachers" at least were elected by the churches.

In the latter part of our period it is clear that the regular church preaching has now come to be generally recognized as the duty of a special class. Others than presbyters could not formally preach in the churches without especial permission of the bishop, and it seems that the privilege was not granted to the presbyters themselves when a bishop was present without the request or sanction of the higher officer. The case of Origen, though peculiar, illustrates the point; at first he was permitted and encouraged to expound the Scriptures at Alexandria, but on his being ordained a presbyter at Cæsarea in later years his bishop, Demetrius of Alexandria, urgently objected.[2] In the less formal evangelistic preaching there does not seem to have been any rigid custom or rule. For Justin Martyr was never ordained a presbyter, but he doubtless preached much.

In regard to the details of posture and delivery the preacher usually sat, and spoke freely.[3] Eusebius[4] quotes Irenaeus as saying that he remembered "the very place where the blessed Polycarp was accustomed to sit

[1] See chaps. 11, 12, 13, 15. For travelling preachers of a later time see Eusebius, *H. E.*, III., 27. Cf. Lindsay, *The Church and Ministry of the Early Centuries*, chap. III.

[2] Euseb., *H. E.*, VI., 8, 23.

[3] This was in accord with Hebrew custom (Matt. 5:1; Luke 4:20), but the Greek orators stood.

[4] *H. E.*, V., 20.

and discourse." But while the extemporaneous delivery was the rule there is indication in at least one striking relic of the early times—the Ancient Homily—that the preacher sometimes read his discourse to the worshipping assembly. Broadus remarks,[1] "The apostolical Epistles were not in general expected to be read by all or by many of those to whom they were sent, but were written addresses designed to be read [2] out in meeting and listened to." Early Christian teachers, as Clement, Irenæus and others, followed the apostolic custom and wrote letters to be read to the churches. From this there was a possible transition to the reading of the address by the author himself, and this quite certainly was done by the writer of the ancient homily known as the Second Epistle of Clement, though erroneously assigned to him. If this was done in one instance, why not in others? Still all we can say is that such cases of written and read discourses must have been exceptions to the general rule of the freely spoken address.

It is impossible to describe in general terms, with any degree of accuracy, the character of the audiences to which the preaching of the early centuries was addressed. The audiences were of course greatly varied according to times, places and circumstances. The two general classes of believers and unbelievers among the hearers must be recognized; but we have to consider whether any given audience was composed exclusively or predominantly of one class or the other, or whether the two classes were pretty evenly divided. These conditions have always characterized the hearing of Christian preaching, and they are too general to be of any special significance in the age which we are now studying, further than to occasion the remark that this twofold or threefold character of the audiences must already be dealt with, even in the beginnings of the history of preaching. Unbelievers were reached mainly by personal interviews, but there must have been some preaching to groups or crowds. In the apostolic times, as we know from the book of Acts, frequent use was made of the Jewish synagogues for proclaiming the gospel to the unbelieving Jews, and also to the Gentiles

[1] *Hist. Prea.*, p. 36.

[2] Rev. 1:3.

who might be in attendance. After that time, however, there must have been some falling off in this custom, as the antagonism of the Jews was intensified, and as Christianity became more and more Gentile in its personnel. Further, as the number of Christians grew, notwithstanding persecution, there would be increased attendance upon Christian worship by unbelievers, partly as led by curiosity and interest, and partly because of social, domestic, or other relations with Christian families.[1] Thus in various ways opportunity would be given and employed for heralding the gospel to unbelievers.

The regular customary assemblies for Christian worship were, however, the principal audiences for preaching. All through this period teaching and exhortation appear as part of the established order of worship in the churches. The custom came from the synagogue, and has been perpetuated through all the centuries. In the order of services, as was natural, the preaching usually followed the reading of the Scriptures, of which it was commonly a sort of exposition or hortatory application. We must also bear in mind the mixed character of the congregations even when properly called Christian. The old and young were there, men and women, the new convert and the tried and ripe believer, the hesitating and the stanch, the half doubter and the loyal, the far-off inquirer and the scoffing visitor, the nearer inquirers, of two kinds, "energumens" and "catechumens." The audiences were thus sufficiently varied in character to require different modes of address as circumstances might demand.

The material or contents of the early preaching did not in general character present any marked contrast to that which has ever since been the main staple of which sermons are made, but there was, as always, great difference in the details of volume, of grasp, of relative importance, and of presentation. The main elements of Christian discourse were three: the apostolic tradition, Scripture, and the personal contribution of the preacher. The last was then and always has been a greatly variable quantity, and the importance assigned to the first two

[1] Paul clearly intimates the possible presence of unbelievers in the assemblies for worship at Corinth in 1 Cor. 14:23.

has likewise varied much in different ages and in the minds of different preachers.

Just after the Apostles, and while the canon of Scripture was forming, it is easy to see that the apostolic tradition must justly have had a more prominent and authoritative place than it could properly claim in later times. For the Apostles themselves passed on to others what they knew and had received concerning the great facts and doctrines of the Christian faith.[1] Those who learned these things from the Apostles and their fellow laborers were the preachers of the early part of our period, and in the next remove those who learned them from the pupils of the apostolic men were the preachers of at latest the middle part of it, while in the latter part of this time the tradition still was comparatively fresh. But in process of time and in passing from one to another the newness became tarnished, accretions were made, distortions occurred, heresies crept in, and trustworthiness declined. Such deterioration must have soon set in, and later times only too sadly witness to the evil wrought by giving undue authority to untrustworthy legends, and to principles and customs falsely regarded as descending straight from the Apostles.

But in the good providence of God as the value of tradition declined the authority of Scripture, particularly of the New Testament books, came to be more and more recognized. The Old Testament scriptures had from the first been received by our Lord and his first followers as the sacred revelation of God to his chosen people. To early Jewish-Christians these holy writings were part both of their national heritage and of their new faith. By early Gentile-Christians they were readily accepted as God's word. The synagogue was the depository and the interpreter of the Old Testament, and the church easily and gladly received the sacred trust. Soon too the written Christian tradition as embodied in the Gospels and Acts began to correct or confirm the fainter growing oral testimony, while the Letters of the Apostles, carefully preserved, became the precious treasure of doctrine and duty for all the churches. All during the period under review the writings of the New Testament

[1] See Luke 1:1-4; 1 Cor. 11:2 (R. V.); 2 Tim. 2:2.

were coming more and more to be regarded as a part of the inspired revelation of God; and thus the canon of Scripture, substantially as we have it to-day, was practically completed by the end of the third century. Thus as the apostolic tradition became less direct, and what passed for it grew more corrupt, the preachers were furnished with that treasury of divine truth which the true Christian pulpit has ever recognized as the source of its teachings and the authority for its message. We shall see as we go on more in detail how the preaching of the early centuries dealt with the Scriptures in the way of interpretation and application. The treatment was inadequate and often unwise, but in this first age, as in all following ones, the Bible furnished the main basis and the most valuable element of preaching.

There is yet to be mentioned the personal element. Judging from the few remains that have come down to us, we can see that what has always been true of preaching since was true of it in the period we are studying. There was more or less individual freedom in handling both the scriptural and the traditional elements; and the illustration, reasoning, exposition, and application were largely the preacher's own work. His personality—thought, feeling, method—must mingle with his sources and characterize his product.

In form the sermons of the early times were unpretentious addresses, as their name "homilies"—conversations, talks—sufficiently indicates. They were without much logical order, and give little if any indication of a previously prepared outline. The character of the audience would determine whether the talk should be chiefly didactic or evangelistic, and the circumstances and purpose of the preacher would decide whether it should be principally doctrinal, expository, or hortatory; or how far any or all of these elements might be combined in one discourse. There was progress both toward a more orderly structure and a more expository character, and these tendencies were powerfully furthered by the example and teaching of Origen toward the end of the third century. Before his time Scripture was used in the homilies, but rather by way of quotation and application than as furnishing a text for exposition. But in his hands continuous exposition with hortatory application became the rule.

In regard to the preservation and publication of sermons the age, as in many other things, was one of beginnings and tendencies. Sermon literature proper belongs to a later time. There is reason to suppose that in many cases the material used in epistles and other treatises had been first employed in oral address, and the apostolic epistles and others, as we have seen, were much of the nature of addresses. For sermons themselves, then as now, there were two ways of preservation: to be written by the preacher himself before or after delivery; and to be reported by others during or after delivery, with or without the author's revision. The Ancient Homily, which will presently claim fuller notice, is an example of the first method; the numerous homilies of Origen are an example of the second.[1] Shorthand writing (tachygraphy) was in vogue in those times, and oral discourses were often reported in this way. It has been reasonably conjectured[2] that the recognized superiority and value of the expository over the hortatory homilies led to the taking down and preservation of more of the expository kind than of others. It is to this that we owe our possession of comparatively so many more of Origen's expository homilies than of others. We cannot but wish that some of those old reporters had foreseen and benevolently considered the scholarly curiosity of our times.

4. The Principal Preachers of the Age.

It is common to divide the literature of the first three centuries into three groups: the Apostolic Fathers, the Apologists, and the Ante-Nicene Theologians. While this classification is like all similar ones in not being rigidly accurate, it is very far from being arbitrary, for it is founded in the nature of the material and it corresponds fairly well with the course of events. It is also quite as convenient for the history of preaching as for that of general Christian literature, and is therefore

[1] Euseb., *H. E.*, VI., 23; and L., 6.
[2] Rothe, *Gesch. der Pred.*, S. 13.

adopted here. It will be noticed in the discussion following that the time limits of the different groups overlap, though there is succession. Thus the Apologists followed the Apostolic Fathers, but began before their predecessors had finished their work; and the Theologians prior to the Nicene council were many of them contemporary with the later Apologists.

The literary remains embraced under the title Apostolic Fathers consist of the writings of men who were, or may reasonably be supposed to have been, in direct contact with some of the Apostles themselves. Their age may be considered as extending from the death of the Apostles (68 or 100) to a date just past the middle of the second century, say 160. The literature of the period is scanty in amount and of little intrinsic value, but because it is all that we have its relative importance is beyond estimate. Its homiletical worth is almost nothing, as it contains only one homily properly so-called, and its notices of preaching are not very numerous or clear. We need not discuss these writings, but only notice the three foremost preachers of the time, and give some account of its only remaining sermon.

Polycarp (69?-155), bishop or pastor of the church at Smyrna, was a loving disciple of John the Apostle. He suffered martyrdom under the reign of Antoninus Pius in 155. When asked to renounce his faith in view of the stake he said that he had been serving his Lord for eighty-six years and could not renounce him now. This would put back the date of his birth or baptism to the year 69, according as he meant all his life or all his Christian life. He was a noble and beloved man and pastor. One of his writings, an Epistle to the Philippians (date probably before 150), remains, and indicates his pious character and a warm earnestness which must have marked his preaching.

Ignatius was bishop at Antioch. He also suffered martyrdom, and the date of his death lies between the years 107 and 115. There remain a number of epistles attributed to him, but their genuineness is much disputed. Allowing that a few, in substance at least, are really his, they exhibit more intellectual power than Polycarp had and a greater vehemence of nature, but less of poise, moderation, holiness. Yet he must have been a preacher of considerable force.

The most important of the three, however, is perhaps Clement of Rome (d. c. 100), whose Epistle to the Corinthians, of date about 97, is the oldest specimen of post-apostolic literature. He may be the Clement of whom Paul speaks in Philippians 4:3, and was one of the first bishops of the Roman church. His letter shows the Roman dignity and capacity for administration. Of his preaching there is no mention nor certain trace, but his force of character and his position render some testimony to his power as a teacher of the word.

But passing the preachers we notice now the only homiletical relic of this earliest age. This is an ancient document which has been commonly called the Second Epistle of Clement.[1] Only a fragment of it was known to modern scholars till a comparatively recent date. But even in this fragmentary form its Clementine authorship was disputed, and its true nature as a homily rather than an epistle was suspected. The discovery of the complete text has confirmed both these opinions, and makes it now clear that Clement of Rome was not its author. From a passage in the writing itself [2] we learn that it was read by the author to the congregation immediately after the reading of the Scriptures in worship, and from this and other indications its homiletical character is established. The authorship must be left in doubt, but Lightfoot's ingenious conjecture may be provisionally accepted, that it is a homily of a bishop or presbyter of the Corinthian church. Its date is probably about 135-140, but it is not certainly fixed.

The theme of the homily is the duty of living the right sort of Christian life as a recompense to Christ for the gift of salvation. There is no clear-cut division of the matter, but the two leading thoughts are, confession of Christ, and repentance, as necessary to the Christian life. These are repeatedly urged and enforced in a variety of ways and from a variety of motives. The doctrine is not elaborate, the homily being hortatory in character, but the main great teachings of the Christian faith are

[1] Riddle's notes, and the translation of the homily in *Ante-Nicene Fathers,* Vol. VII., p. 372 ff and p. 512 ff. [2] Chap. 19.

implied, and for all that appears to the contrary the treatment is orthodox. The morality urged is sound and elevated. The style is natural, simple and appropriate; but is not marked by special oratorical excellence, is somewhat feeble, and is marred by much repetition. The use of Scripture is reverent. There is no text, but the quotations and allusions are frequent, and derived from both the Old and the New Testament. This is significant for the early recognition of the New Testament writings as authoritative in pulpit use. The interpretation and application are fairly good. There is no wild allegorizing or forcing of Scripture. The tone and spirit are admirable—faith, hope, and love, with humility and sincerity, are apparent throughout. Particularly worthy of note is a passage near the end, where the preacher modestly declares that though conscious of imperfection he tries to do what he urges upon others, and begs his hearers to think on these things after they leave the house of worship and go about their affairs. He earnestly exhorts them in view of the future life, and tenderly consoles them in the midst of present trials, concluding with a doxology.

Next after these Apostolic Fathers we take up the important group of early Christian writers known as the Apologists. The reigns of the so-called, "Five Good Emperors," extending over about eighty years and lying chiefly within the second century, are the golden age of Roman imperial rule. Yet within these reigns Christians were hated and persecuted, though not so severely as in later times. It is a painful fact that Marcus Aurelius, the best of all the Roman emperors, and one of the wisest, most humane and just of all earthly rulers, looked upon Christianity with contempt, and permitted, if he did not encourage, the persecution of its votaries. Before his time the peaceful and energetic administration of Hadrian (117-138) offered a fair occasion for the rise of a notable class of Christian writers, who defended their faith from the attacks of its enemies, and the succeeding reigns were such as to render this kind of work still necessary and not hopeless. Hence we have the Christian Apologists of the second century.[1] There was demand

[1] Cf. A. H. Newman, *Manual of Ch. Hist.*, Vol. I., p. 237 ff., and many other authorities, especially also *The Ante-Nicene Fathers*, Am. ed.

and response. The persecution and misrepresentation of Christianity called for defence. Its remarkable progress among the people and its growing favor with some among the upper classes of society had called forth not only violent social and ostensibly legal opposition, but also many foul calumnies as a pretext for persecution. There were now among the Christians a number of acute and educated men, philosophers, lawyers and others, who were capable of doing this work, and they did it.

Besides those whose writings place them among the Apologists, there were, no doubt, many excellent and worthy preachers in this time. One of these was Dionysius, bishop of Corinth, of whom Eusebius [1] says, "He imparted freely not only to his own people but to others abroad also the blessings of his divine labors." Among the Apologists whose names and works (or notices of them) have come down to us, some were preachers, though not all. Of these the most important for us were Justin Martyr and Tertullian, who, though his *Apologeticus* and other writings place him in this group, is more properly reckoned among the Theologians. Others were: Quadratus, who is probably to be identified with a bishop, and therefore a preacher, at Athens in that time; Melito, bishop of Sardis, who was a strong man, and is called a "prophet;" and Theophilus the sixth bishop of Antioch, whose apology addressed to one Autolycus is vigorous and written in a good style which suggests his power as a speaker.

On the whole, while technically no sermons remain from this group of preachers, their writings and those of their lay fellow-laborers reveal traces of a vigorous and fruitful ministry of the Word. The Apologists had as a rule more culture and more intellectual power than the Apostolic Fathers. There is evidence in their writings of wide reading, considerable acquaintance with literature and philosophy, and no small degree of vigor and grasp of mind.

Their best representative was Justin (c. 100-165), afterwards called the Martyr. He was a very able and interesting man. He was born probably about the beginning of the second century, at Neapolis (the ancient

[1] *H. E.*, IV., 23.

Sychem) in Samaria, of heathen parents. It is uncertain whether they were of Greek or Roman extraction. Justin was well educated, and seems to have had means sufficient to lead a life of travel and study. He sought mental rest in various systems of philosophy, except Epicureanism which he hated, and was about to settle down into Platonism when he was converted to Christianity. He met one day near the seashore a pleasant-faced old man, who engaged him in conversation and made known to him the Christian faith. This led to his conversion, and he found peace of mind. He became an earnest defender of Christianity. He travelled much, retaining his philosopher's cloak, not so much now because it was a badge of distinction, as because it gave him the opportunity to teach, with the authority of culture, the truths of his religion. He was not ordained a presbyter, but found frequent occasion to discourse to the few or many who might be attracted to hear him concerning the faith. He awakened the jealousy and opposition of a philosopher named Crescens, at whose instigation probably he was condemned and martyred under Marcus Aurelius, about 165. His three writings—the First and Second Apology and the Dialogue with Trypho the Jew—are of great value for what they teach as to the doctrines and customs of the Christians of his time. They also give us a fairly good idea of his views, his mental capacity, and his style. He handled the Scriptures quite freely, dealing mainly with the prophecies as fulfilled in Christ. He had some wrong notions, but was deeply in earnest and must have been a preacher of some eloquence and power.

The third group of early Christian writers is that of the Ante-Nicene Theologians, whose work may be regarded as covering the time from Irenæus, say 180, to Arnobius, about 300.[1] This was a time of short reigns and great confusion and turmoil in the empire. It was also the period in which occurred the worst persecutions of the Christians; those under Severus (202), Maximin (235-238), Decius (249-251), Valerian (257-258), and Diocletian (303), being very severe. It was too late to

[1] Various editions of their works. For American readers *The Ante-Nicene Fathers,* as before.

suppress Christianity by governmental force. In spite of opposition it had only grown stronger. Now with this accession of strength there came men of classical and philosophical culture, to whom it was natural to philosophize about the faith and to endeavor to formulate its truths. Parallel with this tendency was the work of the Apologists already noticed, and the development of church unity and organization. And, most influential of all, there had been from earliest times heresies and sects disturbing the clear stream of Christian doctrine. All these things contributed to the rise of the class of theologians who grappled with the great thoughts revealed in Scripture, and sought to develop them into something of a philosophic system. Allowing for individual differences, it is fair to say in general terms of these Christian thinkers that for the most part they were men of fine mental gifts, good education, ample learning, deep knowledge of Scripture, elevated morals, and devoted piety. As scholars and theologians, notwithstanding some faults and vagaries, they must ever hold high rank in religious history, and their writings are a priceless source of knowledge concerning the men, events, customs, and opinions of Christianity in their time.

Many of these theologians were notable and useful preachers of the word, yet very few specimens of their homiletic work remain, except in the single case of Origen. We are dependent upon their writings, and upon such scanty notices of their preaching as may be given by others, for our imperfect estimate of their work and power as preachers. During their time and in their hands the informal and familiar homily of previous times made decided advance toward the more oratorical and elaborate address or sermon of the next period. While others contributed to this development, the greatest single personal force in it was the eminent scholar and teacher Origen, of Alexandria and Cæsarea. He was one of those leaders of thought whose faculty and privilege it is to perceive, exemplify and guide, if they do not originate, some tendency or tendencies of the age in which they live. A more particular account of him will be given later. It is sufficient to quote here the summary statement of Christlieb;[1] "Through Origen the sermon received the

[1] Art. *Gesch. der Predigt,* Herzog, *R. E.,* 18, supplement.

fixed form of an explanation and application of a text."

For convenience of study we may consider the great theologians as falling into an eastern and a western group, in each of which there are again two clearly distinguished schools, namely, in the East the Alexandrian and Antiochian, and in the West the Græco-Roman and the North African. We shall notice them in the order just given.

At Alexandria there was founded in early times, date not known, a school for the instruction of catechumens. It grew into a school for the training of teachers and preachers, and was at various times under the headship of highly distinguished men. Of these the two most important for us are Clement and Origen.

Clement (c. 160-220) was born probably at Athens near the middle of the second century. He was highly educated, and trained in the Greek philosophy. Seeking light he came to Alexandria, and was brought to Christianity by Pantænus at that time head of the catechetical school there. About 190 he succeeded Pantænus as leader in the school, was banished about 202, and probably died not later than 220. Not much can be known of his preaching from his great and valuable theological writings. But among them is an Outline (Hypotyposis) of the Catholic Epistles which is a sort of expository discourse, and in it, as Christlieb says, "the first germs of the homily show themselves." Clement was a many-sided man, theologian, exegete, poet, preacher. His influence on Origen was deep and formative, and through his illustrious pupil he has left a broad mark on preaching and on Christian thought.

As a point of secondary importance in his relation to preaching it may be noted that for polemical purposes he has preserved in his writings[1] two homilies (fragments) of the famous Gnostic, Valentinus. Of these Broadus[2] says that they "are of curious interest but not homiletically instructive." But they, at least, show that the form of the "homily" was already coming into vogue, and that heretics as well as the orthodox preached.

The greatest name among the Alexandrian theologians is that of the learned scholar and eminent Christian,

[1] *Stromat.*, IV., 13. [2] *Hist. Prea.*, p. 45.

Origen (185-254). He was born at Alexandria, probably about 185, of Christian parents. He was trained in Christian lore from his childhood, and like many another clever boy puzzled his father with precocious and hard questions. When his father suffered martyrdom in 202 Origen exhorted him to courage and himself desired the martyr's crown, boy though he was, but was hindered from giving himself up to the inquisitors by the ingenuity of his mother, who hid all his clothes while he was undressed, and thus kept him at home till the danger or the impulse had passed by. He was from his youth a rigorous ascetic.[1] As a student he became so proficient in the Scriptures that on the banishment of his master Clement he was, though a very young man, appointed to succeed that great teacher in the catechetical school. His expository lectures were so highly valued that they were written or dictated after delivery, and published as commentaries. A wealthy man named Ambrosius was his friend and patron, and furnished the means for employing the amanuenses and copyists. To this man's kind liberality and appreciation of genius we owe our possession of so many of Origen's works. Later, according to Eusebius,[2] when he was sixty years of age, he permitted his extemporaneous discourses to be taken down by shorthand writers. This was after his ordination as a presbyter, and these discourses are his homilies on various books of the Bible.

So marked was his success as an expounder of Scripture that on a visit to Palestine he was invited to preach in church. This led to trouble with his bishop, Demetrius of Alexandria. On a later visit the bishop of Jerusalem ordained him a presbyter. This gave great offence to his own bishop at Alexandria, by whom in 232 a council was called and Origen was deposed.[3] On this account he permanently left Alexandria and set up a school at Cæsarea in Palestine. Here he died under persecution in 254.

His services to the development of preaching were

[1] In an excess of youthful zeal, to avoid temptation, and taking Matt. 19:12 literally, he mutilated himself.

[2] *H. E.*, L., 6.

[3] One of the principal grounds urged for this action was his mutilation. He was also accused of heresy.

great.[1] He showed by example the importance of expository preaching. He was a careful scholar, and took great pains to expound the Scriptures and to make the sacred text the real basis of preaching. But with this good service must be reckoned the harm he did by lending the sanction of his great influence to the allegorical method of interpretation. He held and taught a threefold sense of Scripture—grammatical, moral, spiritual (or allegorical)—and regarded the last as the best. While he was not, strictly speaking, the originator of this method, he is perhaps more responsible than any one else for giving it dignity and enabling it to fasten such a tremendous grip on the pulpit of all ages.

In regard to Origen's character and his views as a preacher, we have some interesting statements by Eusebius, and some hints here and there in his own writings. Not only did his extraordinary ability attract many to his lectures, both at Alexandria in his youth and at Cæsarea in his age, but his warmth of nature, his enthusiasm and his sympathy won men to him. All this stirred up enemies and persecutors. But he bravely and faithfully held on his course. Eusebius [2] tells of all this and quotes as a current saying concerning Origen that "as his doctrine, so was his life; and as his life, so also was his doctrine."

Origen left no formal treatise on preaching, but Nebe [3] has gathered and put together from his writings a number of items regarding the spirit and method of his work. He believed both in the divine call and qualification of the preacher, and also in the need of human effort to acquire and improve the divine gift of prophecy. He cared little for heathen rhetoric and art in speech, but much for the simple, clear, forcible exposition of God's word. He insisted that the preacher should himself be pure and reverent that he might properly teach his hearers the truth of God. There is a tradition—certainly true to the spirit of the man if not actually a fact—that once when he was going to preach his eyes chanced to fall on Psalm

[1] See Broadus, *Hist. Prea.*, p. 51 ff. For his qualities as a preacher see Lentz, *Christliche Homiletik,* Bd. I., S. 33 ff., Paniel, S. 178 ff., and Nebe, *Zur Geschichte der Predigt,* Bd. I., S. 1 ff., an especially good discussion.

[2] *H. E.,* VI., 3.

[3] *Zur Gesch. der Pred.,* I., S. 8 ff.

50:16, "But unto the wicked God saith, What hast thou to do to declare my statutes, or that thou shouldest take my covenant in thy mouth?" and that he was so overcome with emotion he could not go on for his tears. As the source of the sermon must be the word of God, so its supreme end must be the spiritual edification of the hearer, and to this end there must be both instruction and exhortation. So he insists that the teacher should know both the word and the hearts of men. It was this earnest desire to make all the word of God alike spiritually profitable, which led him into the mistake of extreme allegorical interpretation. In this he has no consistent principle, and often gives the rein to fancy. His Greek was simple, conversational, chaste. He soared to no oratorical heights, nor did he descend to the colloquial and vulgar.

Nearly two hundred of his homilies on the Bible remain, chiefly in the free and inaccurate Latin translations of Rufinus and Jerome. In the original Greek there are extant only nineteen, all on the book of Jeremiah.[1] Of these, according to Klostermann, there were originally probably forty-three, but only the nineteen have been preserved. The same scholar thinks that they were probably delivered at Cæsarea between the years 242 and 244, and were among those mentioned by Eusebius as having been taken down by shorthand writers as they were delivered. We have the Latin translations of these also, and they show how very free and often inaccurate the translators were.

As a sample of Origen's manner the following literal translation of the opening paragraph of the sixteenth homily on Jeremiah is offered:[2] Jer. 16:16, "Behold I will send for many fishers, saith the Lord, and they shall fish them; and after will I send for many hunters and they shall hunt them from every mountain, and from every hill, and out of the holes of the rocks."

"It is written in the Gospel according to Matthew that our Saviour came by the Sea of Galilee and saw Simon and Andrew his brother casting a net into the sea; for they were fishers. Then says the Word that the

[1] See Migne, *Pat. Gr.*, tom. 13, col. 255 ss., also Klostermann in *Texte und Untersuchungen*, neue Folge, I., 3, *Die Überlieferung der Jeremia-Homilien des Origenes.*

[2] Migne, *Pat. Gr.*, tom. 13, col. 457 ss.

Saviour seeing them said, 'Come after me, and I will make you fishers of men; but they, leaving their nets, followed him.' And Jesus made them still to take up fishing. And he found two other brothers, James the son of Zebedee and John his brother, in the boat with their father mending the nets; and these he called to the same craft [lit. skill]. He has made them also fishers of men. Now, if any one should consider those who have from God a grace of speech filled as a dragnet, and woven from the holy Scriptures as a cast-net, so that the network should encompass the souls of the hearers; and should also cleverly perceive that this came about according to the skill which Jesus taught; he will see how not only then, but also now our Saviour sends fishers of men, training them in order that we may be able to come up from the sea and flee its bitter waves. But those fish, the irrational ones, coming up in the seines and in the cast-nets and in the dragnets or on the hooks, die a real death because life does not follow death. But he who is taken by the fishers of Jesus, and comes up from the sea, he also indeed dies, but he dies to the world, he dies to sin, and after dying to the world and to sin, he is made alive by the word of God and takes on another life; as though you could by supposition see the soul of the fish changing, after it had come out of the fishy body, and becoming something better than a fish. I take this as an example. Let no one make objection concerning things he never heard of—let him imagine such a thing. Thou hast come up from the sea, falling into the nets of the disciples of Jesus; coming forth thou changest thy soul, thou art no longer a fish, passing thy time in the briny waves of the sea; but at once thy soul changes, and is transformed, and becomes something better and diviner than it formerly was. But that it is transformed and changed hear Paul saying, 'But we all with unveiled face gazing as in a mirror upon the glory of the Lord are transformed into the same image from glory to glory, as from the Lord, the Spirit.' And being thus transformed, the fish that is caught by the fishers of Jesus, leaving the haunts of the sea makes his haunts in the mountains, so that he no longer needs the fishers who bring him up from the sea, but those second ones, such as are called hunters, who hunt from every mountain and from every hill. Thou, therefore, having come up from the sea, and having been caught in the nets of the disciples of Jesus, change from the sea, forget it, come up upon the mountains, the prophets, and upon the hills, the righteous, and make there thy haunts, in order that after these things, when the time of thy departure is at hand, the many hunters may be sent forth, other than the fishers. But who could these be but those who have been appointed for the purpose of receiving the souls that are in the hills, that are no longer lying below? And see if the prophet has not mystically called out saying these things, and offering this thought, when he says, 'Behold I send many fishers, saith the Lord, and they shall fish them; and afterwards I will send many hunters and they shall hunt them upon every mountain, and upon every hill.'"

Here we see something of Origen's exuberant fancy in interpretation, but he has much that is more extreme than this. Here too we catch glimpses of his reverent spirit, and observe his engaging, unpretentious, but not lofty or moving style. His lack of orderly method is also apparent. In his work generally there is considerable acuteness of interpretation with much fanciful allegorizing, but there is also earnest appeal and sound practical application. He was not an orator, but a teacher by instinct and experience. But take him all in all, both for what he himself did and for what he influenced others to do, he was the most important preacher of the third century.

A devoted pupil of Origen during his Cæsarean ministry was Gregory, afterward surnamed Thaumaturgus (Wonderworker) in order to distinguish him from others of the name. He was born at Neo-Cæsarea in Pontus, about 210. Coming to Palestine on some business he heard of Origen's lectures at Cæsarea and came to hear him. This led to his conversion to Christianity and to his lifelong devotion to his great teacher and friend. He studied with Origen eight years, and then took leave of him in a fulsome panegyric which has come down to us. It was in the fashion of the time and decidedly overdone; but it exhibits both a high appreciation of his teacher and a certain rhetorical power.

Returning to his home in Pontus, Gregory devoted himself to religious work among his own people. Soon on account of his piety, ability and zeal he was, much against his will, made bishop. It is said that he found on his return from Palestine only seventeen Christians in his neighborhood; but his earnest and fruitful labors for thirty years spread Christianity through all that region, and hundreds were brought to Christ through him. This great success, perhaps, rather than reputation for miracle-working, earned him his surname of Thaumaturgus. His success speaks more of his power as a preacher than his overwrought Panegyric on Origen, or the few and probably not genuine homilies which have been ascribed to him.

These three were the most important of the oriental group of preachers among the Theologians, but a word must be said regarding the other school of eastern theologians which had its seat at Antioch.[1] Its most famous representatives belong to a later time. But Lucian and Dorotheus are named as having been in charge of a school at Antioch as early as 280. This is regarded as the beginning of the line of theologians and preachers of the Antiochian school, whose distinction it was to urge and exemplify the literal, historical and grammatical interpretation of Scripture as opposed to the fanciful allegorical method of the Alexandrian school.

We must now turn our attention to the western group of the Ante-Nicene Theologians, and give brief consideration to those among them who are chiefly important as preachers. And here we observe a very important line of distinction. Some of these men used the Greek tongue in their writings, and presumably also in speech. This was in Italy and Gaul. But in North Africa, chiefly though not exclusively, there arose a great line of thinkers who used the Latin, and became the founders of the Latin theology.

Clement and other early bishops of the Roman church used the Greek language. How long it was before Latin asserted its rightful claim, and became the churchly as it was the vernacular speech of the West, is not known. Most probable is the conjecture[2] that both languages were

[1] See Cruttwell, *Literary History of Christianity*, Vol. II., p. 532.
[2] Cruttwell, *op. cit.*, II., p. 405.

used for a while in worship and documents. But about the time of bishop Victor (187) there is a decided change toward the dominant use of Latin. Among the leaders who are worthy of mention as preachers two only need claim our notice here.

Some time before the middle of the second century there was born somewhere in Asia Minor one who was to receive the name of Irenæus—the peaceful one—was to be a pupil of the venerable Polycarp, who had sat at the feet of the beloved John, and yet was to be in the far West in mature life the laborious bishop and the stout antagonist of "all the heresies." In his youth Irenæus received a good education, and was well taught in the Scriptures and in the earlier Christian writings. He became a man of great piety and simplicity of character. While he was working as a missionary in Gaul, the bishop of Lyons was martyred (177), and the courageous evangelist succeeded to the dangerous post. Schaff says of him, "He combined vast literary and missionary activity." He is lost to view after 190. A somewhat doubtful tradition tells that he suffered martyrdom under Septimius Severus in 202. His greatest work, *Against Heresies,* appeared about 185. No sermons remain. His writings are hard and tedious. He modestly disclaims eloquence, and he probably had no high oratorical gifts, but he was an able, wise, earnest, useful pastor and diligent preacher.

Much more notable as a preacher was the great controversialist, Hippolytus (170-236), of whom Schaff[1] cleverly says that he has lived three lives: the real one in the third century, a fictitious one as a canonized saint in the Middle Ages, and a literary one in the nineteenth century since the recovery of his works. Of his real life little is known. His name and his use of Greek indicate Grecian parentage, though not necessarily eastern birth. He is mentioned by Eusebius[2] as a bishop, but without designation of place, and Jerome in his *Illustrious Men*

[1] *Church Hist.,* Vol. II., p. 758. Cf. also Bunsen, *Hippolytus and Callistus;* and a supplement (on Hippolytus' relations to Origen) by Trümpelmann in Rothe's *Geschichte der Predigt.* Further, Cruttwell, *op. cit.,* II., p. 403, and Achelis, in *Texte und Untersuchungen,* N. F., I., 4. [2] *H. E.,* VI., 20, 22.

speaks of him as bishop of "some church" (*cujusdam ecclesiæ*); but his real place remains unknown. Later tradition says he was bishop of Portus near the mouth of the Tiber, while some have conjectured that he was assistant bishop, or rival bishop, of Rome. At any rate he was called a bishop, had a good deal to do with the Roman church, and got into a quarrel with Callistus, the contemporary Roman bishop, whom he handles very severely in one of his writings. It seems that he was banished by the Emperor Maximin, about 235, to the mines of Sardinia, where he soon died.

In the sixteenth century a sitting statue, supposed to be his, was found. On the back of it a number of writings attributed to him are enumerated. He wrote a large number of controversial works. What of his preaching? Eusebius speaks of him as an "eloquent" man, and Jerome tells how he once delivered a notable sermon on the Praise of the Lord and Saviour, in a church at Rome, in presence of Origen who was visiting there at the time. This sermon has not come down to us, but there is preserved one on the Holy Theophany[1] at the baptism of Jesus, which with some probability may be regarded as genuine.[2] It is a baptismal sermon addressed to a candidate—probably a prominent person—for baptism, and at the same time to the congregation. It followed the reading of the Scripture lesson, on which it is based as a text. There is considerable quotation of Scripture. The doctrine is not elaborate. It is sound on the Trinity, does not discuss atonement or grace, and teaches, but not baldly, the necessity of baptism to salvation. In the conclusion the preacher exhorts his hearers to come and be baptized, but only on the basis of a sound repentance and in the exercise of faith. In structure and style the homily is suggestive and eloquent, and secures for its author a place among the true preachers of his age.

It is a curious fact that the beginnings of Latin theology are found in North Africa rather than in Rome. Of those who were notable among the North African theologians two at least claim notice as preachers.

[1] Translated in *Ante-Nicene Fathers*, Vol. V., p. 234.

[2] Questioned by Achelis, *op. cit.*, S. 199 ff., but accepted by Zahn, Lightfoot and others.

One of the most eminent Christian writers of his own or any age was Tertullian (150-220). He was born about the year 150 at Carthage, where his father was a centurion in the Roman army in the service of the proconsul of the province. Tertullian received a good education in his youth, and became an advocate, it seems at Rome. After a somewhat wild youth he was converted when about forty years old, and became a very earnest Christian. Later he joined the strict sect of the Montanists. He was at one time a presbyter, probably at Carthage, as we learn from Jerome; but he was not promoted, and, probably on account of his Montanism, never attained distinction as a church officer. His chief title to consideration is in his numerous and variously valuable writings. Apologetic, doctrinal and controversial treatises flowed from his hand in rapid succession. Of these Broadus says,[1] "The writings of Tertullian amply show that he was a born orator. His penetrating insight into subjects, his splendid imagination, his overpowering passion, the torrent-like movement of his style, heedless of elegance and of grammatical accuracy, his very exaggerations and his fiery assaults upon his antagonists, all seem to show the man born to be a speaker." His treatises on moral and spiritual subjects, especially the beautiful ones on Patience and on Penitence, have decided oratorical character. They read as if they had been written out after first being spoken as hortatory addresses or sermons.

Like Tertullian, his predecessor and master, Cyprian (c. 200-258) was the son of a Roman officer, and born and bred at Carthage. He was educated for a teacher of rhetoric, but was early converted to Christianity and became one of the most celebrated churchmen and writers of his time. He was greatly indebted to Tertullian, though it does not appear that there was any personal contact. If there was it was when Tertullian was very old and Cyprian very young. On his conversion in 246 Cyprian gave both himself and his means to Christianity. His piety, learning and ability, both in letters and affairs were recognized at home, and he was soon made bishop of his native city. During the Decian persecution he pru-

[1] *Hist. of Prea.*, p. 45 ff.

dently retired, but kept the oversight of his flock, and his letters at this period are an interesting and valuable body of literature. Though not dictated by cowardice, his retirement was misunderstood and criticized. So during the persecution under Valerian he remained at his post and was banished, but on venturing back he was martyred in 258. He met his end with dignity and composure.

He was a theological writer of marked ability and importance, and was especially distinguished for his advocacy of church unity and catholicity. He did not, however, as is frequently supposed, admit the papal supremacy of the Roman bishop, though allowing great weight to that see in ecclesiastical affairs. As in case of Tertullian we must judge of Cyprian's preaching from his writings. Those which bear on Scriptural and moral subjects may probably have first served as sermons. His charming exposition of the Lord's Prayer,[1] for example, has many homiletical excellences, and reads much like a reproduced address. In his letter to Donatus[2] he discusses briefly but intelligently the difference between secular and sacred eloquence, and his speech is highly praised by Lactantius,[3] who says: "He had a ready, copious and pleasant faculty, and that clearness which is the greatest excellence in a discourse, so that it would be difficult to say whether he was more ornate in stating, or ready in illustrating, or powerful in persuading."

5. Summary.

In closing this imperfect survey of preaching during the important, fruitful but disappointingly obscure age that elapsed from the close of the work of the Apostles in the first century to the great council of Nicæa in the early part of the fourth, we may attempt a brief summary of its leading characteristics.

1. There was profound conviction of the truth of the gospel, and of its power to redeem men from sin. Along with this there was true earnestness in presenting it to the minds and hearts of men, both as a scheme of salvation and as a rule of thought and life.

[1] Fish's *Masterpieces of Pulpit Eloquence*, I., p. 36 ff.
[2] Quoted in Ker's *History of Preaching*, p. 99. [3] *Ibid.*

2. For the most part the preaching of the time teaches a pure and lofty morality, in marked contrast to the principles and practices of the age.

3. The preaching is firmly based on the authority of the Scriptures, both of the Old and of the New Testament, as a revelation of the thought and will of God; and is increasingly occupied with the exposition and application of the Word.

4. Of doctrinal preaching, as later and now commonly understood, there was little if any. Yet the main great teachings of the Christian system, while not yet formally stated, are with more or less clearness held or implied. The term *trinity* (in Greek *trias*) has already appeared, to describe the relations of the three Persons of the Godhead; man's sinful nature and need of deliverance by Christ are recognized; repentance and faith are insisted on, as the proper relation of man toward God, and the means of securing the blessing of salvation; and the ideas of the future life of glory or of punishment are firmly held. Along with this there is a growing conception of church unity and universality, and of the efficacy of the ordinances, particularly of baptismal regeneration.

On the whole our actual knowledge of the preaching and preachers of that age is confessedly inadequate and scanty. We are left largely to inference and conjecture. But from such specimens, traditions and traces as we have, we certainly know that there were those who planted and those who watered in that obscure early time, to whose labors God gave the increase, for they like Apollos were "mighty in the Scriptures," and their preaching like that of Paul "was in demonstration of the Spirit and of power."

CHAPTER II

The Culmination of Ancient Preaching in the Fourth Century

The course of events in empire and church from the accession of Constantine (306) to and including the reigns of Arcadius in the East (d. 408) and of Honorius in the West (d. 423) had profound influence upon the history of civilization, of Christianity, of preaching. Schaff[1] eloquently summarizes the main points of the situation as follows: "The reign of Constantine the Great marks the transition of the Christian religion from under persecution by the secular government to union with the same—the beginning of the state-church system. The Græco-Roman heathenism, the most cultivated and powerful form of idolatry which history knows, surrenders, after three hundred years' struggle, to Christianity, and dies of incurable consumption. . . . The successor of Nero, Domitian, and Diocletian appears in the imperial purple at the council of Nice as protector of the church, and takes his golden throne at the nod of bishops who still bear the marks of persecution. The despised sect, which, like its Founder in the days of his humiliation, had not where to lay its head, is raised to sovereign authority in the state, enters into the prerogatives of the pagan priesthood, grows rich and powerful, builds countless churches out of the stones of idol temples to the honor of Christ and his martyrs, employs the wisdom of Greece and Rome to vindicate the foolishness of the cross, exerts a molding power upon civil legislation, rules the national life, and leads off the history of the world." These are no extravagant words, but a sound, if glowing, statement of the facts.

The troubled reigns of the sons of Constantine prepared the way for the brief and ineffectual reaction toward paganism under their cousin the emperor Julian, commonly known as the Apostate, because he hated Christianity and tried to re-establish the old heathen religion in the empire. This he did not try to do by persecution, however, but by ridicule, social contempt, and various other ways. But the effort to revive heathenism came too late. Julian's successor, Jovian, was a Christian, and in his brief reign restored imperial favor to Christianity. This was true of Valentinian also and his successors. Valens, associated with Valentinian, and emperor of the East, favored the Arian party and thus caused much trouble. Theodosius the Great, called to the sovereignty of the East on the death of Valens, favored orthodoxy, or the Athanasian party. He was a great and

[1] *Hist. of the Christian Church,* Vol. III., pp. 4, 5.

capable ruler, with some serious faults of character, but according to his light a sincere Christian. After him the empire was finally divided, his two weak sons being his successors, Arcadius in the East, Honorius in the West. Under these degenerate princes affairs went sadly enough. The western empire was tottering to its fall, while in the East corruption, luxury, effeminacy and decay were rife. And while the Goths without and decay within were hastening the ruin of the old Roman civilization, fierce controversies were tearing Christianity in twain. It was a strange, fearful, corrupt, uneasy age. Yet in such a time as this lived and spoke the greatest preachers of the ancient Christian world; for it is precisely in the fourth and the early years of the fifth century that Christian preaching in its ancient development reached its culmination.

1. Conditions Favorable to the Development of Preaching

We have already observed, and shall have frequent occasion to do so again as we go along, how responsive preaching is to its environment. Like every other great exercise of the spirit of man it is in touch with each successive age through which it works. Hindering and favoring forces meet it in every period, and it will decline or flourish as one set or the other are stronger. When favorable conditions are in the ascendant what would be serious drawbacks often become incitements to higher life and greater activity. Thus a pleasure-loving, corrupt age may be both a hindrance and a stimulus to preaching, and other things must help to decide in each case or time which it shall rather be. Now these conditions lie partly in external affairs and partly in preaching itself.

In the affairs of the empire and the church there came together many things at this time to exercise from without a favorable influence upon the oratorical development of preaching.

During the intervals of persecution, and indeed to some extent stimulated by persecution, there had been great extension of Christian power and influence. The church was also growing in organization and deepening its influence as a great visible power over its own members. At the opening of the fourth century it was distinctly a power in society that had to be reckoned with. Diocletian's last and terrible attempt to suppress Christianity by imperial force had clearly failed. Society and government must accept as an established institution this obstinate and irrepressible body of followers of Jesus Christ. So as the church forced itself more and more into social recognition, all that concerned it, especially its worship, must acquire respect and dignity. As a part of the worship preaching had its own claim to recognition. And as the worship became more elaborate and attractive, more observed and attended, this peculiar feature of it came to be a more formal and stately affair. The development of preaching toward an oratorical form was thus an integral part of the general ecclesiastical movement.

Whatever we may think of the conversion of Constantine, he was at least wise enough to see that as a matter of statecraft it was time to change the policy of many preceding emperors. Christianity was here to stay, it could not be crushed, why not use it? Christians were a numerous and a worthy class of citizens, why not give them a better chance? Was not their friendship and aid better than their hatred and opposition? At any rate, whatever his motives, Constantine reversed the policy of Diocletian and Galerius, even persuading the latter to join him in the first decree of toleration in 311. Two years later a stronger decree was enacted, and thus in 313 Christianity was the recognized religion of the empire. Ten years more passed, and in 323 Constantine became sole emperor with power to make his wishes respected throughout the Roman world. And in two years more, 325, we find him presiding at the first general church council called by him at the instance of Christian dignitaries to decide the great controversy between Arians and Athanasians as to the divinity of Christ.

With the exception of Julian, as already noted, Constantine's successors followed his general policy, but favored now the Arian and now the orthodox party in the church. The emperor was to all intents and purposes as supreme in the church as in the state. This brought a dangerous gift of political and social prestige to the church and inevitably disturbed its spirituality and purity, but at the same time it gave a certain distinction to all the institutions and characteristic actions of the church, including preaching. Attending church and hearing preachers became a social function. As Broadus aptly says,[1] " Fashionable people in Constantinople, Alexandria, Antioch, and hundreds of smaller towns, began to speak (so Chrysostom intimates) almost as enthusiastically about the favorite preacher of the hour as they spoke of the favorite horse in the races, or the reigning actor in the theatre."

At a far later period the court of Louis XIV. of France smiled on preaching and made it a sort of pastime to hear the great pulpit orators of that age. The natural effect of this sort of stimulus in preaching soon proves unhealthy, but at first considerably, and always to some extent, it gives the really earnest preacher a much desired opportunity for addressing people of the highest consideration in society and bringing them to the Saviour, while at the same time it encourages a style of speech adapted to cultured hearers. In both the directions, then, of real eloquence and of artistic oratory the stimulus of social prestige made itself felt in fourth century preaching.

Back of the special stimulus of imperial patronage and social favor, only brought out and emphasized by these, lay the general taste of the age for oratorical display. The great political oratory of free Greece and Rome had long been crushed by despotism, but the love of it had not died out of the hearts of the descendants of those who had heard Demosthenes and Cicero and their lesser fellow-countrymen and orators. The pleadings in law courts offered only a partial off-set to the loss of free political oratory, and the harangues of the Senate had woefully degenerated. Occasions for panegyrical orations there still were, and this style of oratory was still in vogue. The public assemblies for worship of a now favored religion came as a welcome addition, with the charm of some novelty, to these older occasions for popular eloquence. The taste of the times required a certain brilliancy and rhetorical finish, and in order to meet this demand preaching must now seek these aids.

[1] *Hist. of Prea.*, p. 61.

Along with all that has been mentioned, we must remember that in the traditional and accepted educational system rhetorical studies occupied the chief place. If educated at all a man was educated in rhetoric. As lawyer, civilist, teacher, or man of letters, one must needs have had training in oratory. So when the schools were open to Christians, without persecution or social disfavor, there was opportunity for them to receive the customary oratorical training from the best teachers. And not a few who had been trained for other service entered the ministry. The six most notable preachers of the century[1]—four in the East, and two in the West—had all received the best rhetorical culture of the schools; and there were hosts of others. Nor must we lose sight of the fact that in the audiences which heard the preaching of these times there were many who, as well as the preachers themselves, had been educated in the schools of rhetoric. A few cultured and critical hearers make their taste felt more than a multitude of the illiterate. Thus in different ways the education of the times lent its powerful aid to the other influences which combined to produce that pronounced heightening of oratorical power which we see in the preaching of the fourth century.

Besides these external influences, there had been at work in the preaching of the preceding age certain tendencies in the oratorical direction which came to their full development under the favorable circumstances of the new era. These only removed obstacles and encouraged and shaped progress. They could not have produced so great a growth and fruitage unless there had been life and movement within the sphere of preaching itself. The line of progress lay in the direction of the elaborate and structural discourse as distinguished from the informal conversational homily. There was a trend toward the artistic, scientific, oratorical form of address; and this must find its goal. The day for mere expository or hortatory talks as the dominant mode of presenting and urging the great truths of Christianity upon the attention of hearers was passing away. These should always remain as one of the forms of Christian discourse, but a law of internal devel-

[1] Basil, the two Gregories, John Chrysostom, Ambrose, Augustine.

opment was pushing religious oratory on to relatively as high a plane (considering the times) as the secular orations of the best class had occupied. Some of the elements of this tendency claim more specific notice.

Attention was called in our study of the earlier part of the period[1] to the gradual settling of the canon of Scripture. From the books enumerated by Eusebius as received by all, and even from those still disputed by some though received by many, we see that early in the fourth century the entire New Testament as we now have it had practically come into acceptance among the churches as being, along with the Old Testament, the inspired and authoritative Word of God. Under the lead of both the Alexandrian and the rising Antiochian schools the interpretation and application of Scripture had now become the main element of preaching; and especially under Origen's teaching and example had also become more of an orderly discourse. It was perfectly natural that this growth of homiletical exposition should go on into the great sermons which we have in the discourses of Chrysostom and others in the time now under review.

Another important element in the development of preaching was the fixing of doctrine. The great theological controversies and councils of the fourth and fifth centuries were symptomatic of a tendency toward doctrinal definition and uniformity which had been going on for a long time before. Schaff[2] remarks that "in the development of doctrine the Nicene and Post-Nicene age is second in productiveness and importance only to those of the apostles and the Reformation." So great and close is the connection between preaching and doctrine that the discussion and formulation of the latter must of necessity powerfully influence the former. And so in the times which we are now studying the quickened intellectual interest in some of the great fundamental truths of Christianity, the sharp discussions of them, and their final authoritative definition within accepted limits of orthodoxy, all exerted a mighty influence upon both the content and the form of preaching. And the influence was decidedly in the direction of a more elaborate and formal presentation of truth in discourse.

[1] *Supra*, p. 40 f. [2] *Hist. of the Christian Ch.*, Vol. III., p. 6.

Still another factor was the culture of the ministry. We have already observed that in the Apologists and Theologians of the Ante-Nicene age a very intellectual and cultivated class of men had begun to come in increasing numbers to the standard of Christianity. The liberal policy of Constantine naturally increased still further this accession from the educated classes, and the previously mentioned facilities for education now held out to Christian teachers and preachers had also their part to play. Along with this the now well-established custom of having a special class of men for preachers must be remembered. So it is easy to see that the existence of a specially trained and well educated order of men from whom, for the most part, preachers were chosen tended to make preaching more and more artistic and oratorical. The more culture in the preachers, the more rhetorical the preaching, as a rule.

Thus in the providential ordering of events we see that a number of secondary causes combined to produce in the fourth century a remarkable outburst of Christian oratory. We cannot be surprised to find at this period one of the great historic culminations in the character and power of preaching.

2. Characteristics of Fourth Century Preaching

We may now observe in a summary way the leading features of the preaching in this interesting period, though some of them have necessarily been already touched on in discussing the development of the sermon.

Among the outward features which distinguished the preaching of the fourth century we must take note of church buildings and other appliances for worship. In early times the places of worship were few and simple—upper rooms, schools, but sometimes also the synagogues, at least for preaching. In times of persecution the places were retired. The catacombs near Rome were resorted to, and no doubt secret places in other localities, as persecution might require. But in the intervals between these times of violence and distress church buildings had begun to be erected.

Under Diocletian's fearful persecution many of the buildings which had been erected in the calm after the outburst under Decius were destroyed. So one of the noteworthy things in the era of toleration and patronage was the building of houses of worship. In this work the emperor Constantine himself set the example, and several churches were founded by his mother Helena. The form of structure was somewhat that of the *basilica,* or Roman court-room—a long rectangle with level floor provided with rows of seats. But there were modifications of this, which some think were adapted from the arrangements of private houses in which early worship was so often conducted. Besides the auditorium there were platforms or pulpits, and reading desks, called *ambones;* so that the material appliances for preaching were fairly well developed in this age.

Sundays and festival days were the usual times of preaching, but no doubt there were also special occasions of various sorts and frequency. From the earliest times a regular part of the Sunday worship had been the reading of the Scriptures with an exhortation following. But with the gradual fixing of the Christian year—especially the festivals of Christmas, Easter and Pentecost (Whitsuntide),—and with the increasing reverence paid to saints and martyrs on their days, the preaching on these special occasions assumed more and more importance. In later times, as we shall see, many of the series of sermons which were especially prized and preserved were these festival discourses.

The removal of the necessity of privacy, the building of large churches, the social prestige of Christianity, the fashion of attendance on worship, all contributed toward rendering congregations larger and more miscellaneous than in the former times. For a while heathen and heretics were kept in the outer court, but the people, presumably and nominally Christian, occupied the nave, *i.e.,* central part of the building, the men and women separated by partitions. As to posture the practice was perhaps not uniform, and may have varied even at the same place according to times and circumstances, but generally it appears that the people stood during preaching. The congregations were apparently not very orderly, for even the eloquent Chrysostom often rebukes them for inattention. They shifted about, sometimes broke out into applause, and sometimes large numbers rushed from the church at the conclusion of the sermon, not waiting for the orderly closing of the service.

As was to be expected, both from natural development and from the new order of things, the worship in this period became more elaborate and ceremonious. Its contents were enriched, its order assumed greater fixity. The place of preaching was still just after the reading of the Scriptures, with sometimes perhaps a brief prayer between. The selection of the lesson, or portion of Scripture to be read, was not as yet fixed by any general rule for all the churches. The selection seems to have been left to the bishop,[1] but it is not improbable that in some churches there were at least the beginnings of a regular course of selections. The passage read was frequently used as the foundation of the sermon, or was referred to in the discourse; but just what connection there was between the selection of the Scripture and the previous preparation of the sermon—that is, as to which influenced the other—does not appear.

The growing tendency of earlier times, to restrict preaching as a public teaching office of the church to bishops and presbyters, may now be regarded as fixed and final custom. Whatever lay preaching continued was personal, informal and outside the regular work and worship of the churches. It is not improbable that heretics and minor sects retained a greater freedom in this respect; but this is matter of conjecture. The deacons were now regarded as an order of clergy, but their duties in worship were to read the Scriptures when appointed to do so, to assist the bishops in various ways, and to aid in the celebration of the ordinances and in the collection and distribution of the offerings. They were not regularly allowed to preach.[2] This was the special privilege and duty of the bishops, but was shared by the presbyters under episcopal regulation. The presbyters were ordained and appointed to their charges by the bishops, and likewise designated by them as preachers for special occasions. Thus Chrysostom served for several years as deacon at Antioch before he was designated by his bishop as leading preacher in the principal church of the city.

[1] See Schaff, Vol. III., p. 470.

[2] But this rule was not always rigidly enforced.

The contents of the sermon remained substantially what they had been at the close of the preceding age. As the Apostolic tradition had now faded, and the mediæval saints' legends had not yet arrived, the traditional is the least considerable element of fourth century preaching. The great work of Origen and his school, already so often mentioned, shows itself. Preaching is largely exposition of Scripture, often on a short text, sometimes continuous on whole books or parts of books, or on subjects. Doctrine also becomes now increasingly important as homiletical material; but with it, according to the personality of the preacher, is often mingled some speculation and philosophizing. The preacher's knowledge of life, of passing events, of literature, affords abundant illustration; and in some cases, notably with Basil and Gregory, illustration is derived from nature. The application is often close, direct, personal, and not infrequently very telling.

Between the structureless homily or exhortation of the early times, and the closely articulated, minutely analyzed sermon of the Scholastics and the Puritans of later ages, we find the fourth century discourse. Retaining the Scriptural motive and tone, and in large degree the familiarity, of the homily, and avoiding the tedious division and sub-division of the scholastic sermon, the *logos*, or oration, of this age is more assimilated to the classic models of oratory. It has form indeed, but its bony structure is not obtrusive. The delivery was extemporaneous. Some of the extant sermons were written by the preacher before or after delivery—more commonly perhaps the latter,—but many of them were reported by shorthand writers, with or without revision by the author. Thus Gaudentius, bishop of Brescia,[1] a contemporary and friend of Chrysostom, in one of his letters, speaks of certain sermons as not acknowledged by him as his own because they were hastily taken down by reporters and had not been submitted to him for correction; but others he had looked over and put into shape.

Of course the spirit and motive of these fourth century sermons varied with the individual preachers, as is ever the case. But even among the best preachers of the time

[1] See below, p. 97 f.

there is too often apparent the effort to strike and please by rhetorical display and to win applause by popular utterances. The taste of the age called for more oratorical exuberance than is fitting for the themes of sacred discourse, and the preachers did not rise far above their hearers in this respect. But with these drawbacks frankly noted, we cannot fail to see in many of these homilies the mastering desire of the preacher to glorify his Lord and to win the souls of his fellow men. For the Christian hearer there is constant instruction in the doctrines and duties of his religion, together with most earnest appeals and exhortations, rebukes or consolations, as the case might require.

That the life and thought of mankind were mightily and permanently influenced by the preaching of the fourth century there can be no doubt. As always, much of this influence is intangible and cannot be expressed in terms, but it was felt, then as now. The blessing of God was upon the now unknown as then unrecognized labors of many obscure men, as well as upon the known and applauded oratory of the great preachers. Souls were saved and edified, society influenced for good, and the better thoughts of men enriched and stimulated by the spoken Word in this impressive era of Christian history.

3. The Eastern Preachers

It is time to give our attention to some of the more important preachers[1] of this great period; and they naturally fall into an eastern and a western group. Among the eastern preachers, though not especially remarkable for his preaching, was the famous church historian, Eusebius (c. 260-340). He was bishop of Cæsarea, in Palestine, from 315 to his death in 340. He is chiefly known for his exceedingly valuable Church History and his extravagant eulogy on Constantine. He was probably born in Palestine, and was educated at Antioch and Cæsarea. He was a great student and well informed in history and literature. At one time the archbishopric of Antioch was offered him, but he declined the honor.

[1] In the following discussions much help has been derived from the works, already named, of Paniel, Lentz and Rothe.

In the Arian controversy he tried to hold a middle course and was naturally distrusted by the extreme orthodox party. He accepted the Origenistic doctrine of the eternal generation of the Son, and therefore did not deny the proper deity of Christ, but he signed the Nicene Creed with some reluctance. He enjoyed the esteem of Constantine, and more than paid back his imperial patron in a well known and fulsome panegyric. As bishop he was a frequent preacher, but does not hold very high rank in this regard. A number of his homilies remain. They indicate knowledge of Scripture, acquaintance with other literature, a desire to do good, a fair amount of homiletical skill, a rather dry style, though characterized by the excess and over-ornamentation fashionable at the time.

There is another Eusebius, among the many who bore the name, who is worthy of mention as a preacher. This was the good bishop of Emesa, in Syria (d. c. 360), a friend and pupil of Eusebius of Cæsarea. He was a learned and highly esteemed man. Like his teacher he lay under some suspicion of Arian tendency in doctrine, but probably without justice. He also enjoyed the imperial favor. A number of homilies and some fragments ascribed to him remain, but many of these are of doubtful authenticity. From these and the mention of contemporary or later writers it is inferred that he was a preacher of more than ordinary force and eloquence as well as learning. It is much to his credit that in handling the Scriptures he departed from the extreme allegorical interpretation of Origen and his followers and approached nearer to the literal and grammatical exegesis of the Antiochian school.

The famous presbyter of Alexandria, the stout and successful opponent of Arius, the orthodox Athanasius (296-372), later bishop and often exiled, is one of the most interesting figures in church history. He is so celebrated as church leader, theologian, and defender of the Trinity against Arianism that his work as preacher attracts comparatively little attention. There are extant eighteen so-called homilies attributed to him, but their genuineness is seriously questioned, and their homiletical value is inconsiderable, though they show argumentative skill and force. From his standing and reputation, and from his genuine writings, we easily argue that his power as a preacher must have been more than respectable. Broadus[1] says of him, "His style of writing has directness, simplicity, and native force, a vigorous and manly eloquence, such as one seldom meets with in that age of stilted rhetoric."

Something over fifty homilies from this age are ascribed to one Macarius.[2] There were two preachers of this name, an elder and a younger, and it is not certain to which of them the greater part of the homilies belong, nor which to each. The authorities, however, mostly assign them to the elder man, and agree on ascribing them all to one author instead of dividing them between the two. Nor is it apparent whether any relationship existed between the two men. The elder (c. 300-375) was abbot of a convent in Egypt, and the character of the sermons agrees with that fact; for they are mostly sermons to monks inculcating the monastic virtues. Paniel[3] thinks that if the author had led an active life among men he would have been a great preacher, for these homilies show warmth, earnestness, and an oratorical nature. Macarius also has an interest for us in being one of the earliest preachers in whom we find traces of that devout mysticism[4] which was to form so prominent a characteristic of mediæval and later preaching. "His homilies have been appealed to by modern theopathetic mystics as an authority for Quietism. He teaches perfectionist doctrine."[5] Nebe says that Gottfried Arnold translated Macarius' homilies into German, and they were highly esteemed by the Pietists. But he does not agree with Vaughan that Macarius teaches perfection, absolute sinlessness, on earth.

A notable preacher of the age was Cyril of Jerusalem (c. 315-386). Of the two noted fathers who bore the name of Cyril the earlier and better was born probably at or near Jerusalem about the year 315. When about

[1] *Hist. Prea.*, p. 63.

[2] Besides Paniel and others see especially Nebe, *Zur Geschichte der Predigt*, for a good discussion of Macarius. Bd. I., SS. 84 ff.

[3] *Op. cit.*, S. 398 f.

[4] Vaughan, *Hours with the Mystics*, Vol. I., p. 111.

[5] Vaughan, *l. c.;* and Nebe, *op. cit.*, S. 86, *et passim.*

thirty years old he was appointed presbyter at Jerusalem, and was especially charged with the duty of instructing the catechumens in order to prepare them for baptism. An interesting and valuable series of these catechetical lectures remain. They are really homilies, and besides shedding some light on the views and practices of the time and place on the subject of baptism, they afford evidence of the preacher's art and spirit. Besides giving these lectures to candidates for baptism Cyril preached often to the congregation. One of his remaining sermons is on the healing of the impotent man at Bethesda. Paniel criticises it as full of digressions, parentheses, allegorizing—all indicating a youthful author. In 350 Cyril was elected bishop of Jerusalem. Owing to personal and doctrinal controversies he was twice deposed and reinstated. His condemnations were very probably unjust. Toward the close of his life he was greatly honored and loved as one who had suffered for the truth's sake.

Sometime during the fourth century, probably the latter part, there lived and labored at Amasea in Pontus a bishop called Asterius. Little or nothing is certainly known of his life. It is inferred from some allusions in his sermons that he lived in the time of the emperor Julian, but how long before or after that short reign (361-363) does not appear. It seems that he was educated at Antioch, but we cannot say whether he was born there or not. He had a teacher at Antioch, a Scythian, or Goth, who had been a slave but was then a freedman. This man was highly gifted and well read, and under his guidance Asterius studied the Greek classics and cultivated his style. He seems, as so many other good preachers have done, to have begun life as a lawyer, but was chosen bishop because of his piety and eloquence. He had the by-name of Philaretus, "the friend of virtue." We are fortunate in having ten of his sermons [1] which are accepted by critics as undoubtedly genuine, besides some fragments, and a larger number of doubtful authenticity. As to his preaching Paniel [2] remarks that

[1] Five of these have been well translated by Professor E. J. Goodspeed, of Chicago University, and published in a handy little volume, with an introduction by Dr. Galusha Anderson.

[2] *Op. cit.*, S. 567.

Chrysostom himself need not have been ashamed of some of these productions; and Broadus [1] says, "The subjects are moral and historical; he has fine descriptive powers; the style is marked by exquisite richness of expression, and not overwrought. . . . Some of his sermons could be preached in our churches with little alteration, and would be well received."

An exceedingly engaging personality of the Nicene age is that of the Syrian, Ephraim (c. 300-379), or as he is commonly known in ecclesiastical literature, Ephraem Syrus. He has been described as "the most distinguished divine orator and poet of the ancient Syrian church." [2] Owing to his hymns he was sometimes called "the Harp of the Holy Spirit." He was born near the beginning of the fourth century, in Mesopotamia, of heathen parents. His father was priest in a heathen temple, and on the youth's showing inclination to become a Christian, drove him from home. The boy went to the bishop of Nisibis, who took him in gladly and gave him Christian training. In company with this bishop he attended in his young manhood the great council of Nicæa, and became a thoroughgoing and orthodox Christian. Settling in Edessa in Syria about the year 363 he lived as a hermit in a cave, earnestly studying, and preaching to his fellow monks. Though he was not very well acquainted with Greek he managed to have an interview with Basil, the famous bishop and preacher of Cæsarea in Cappadocia, whom he visited and by whom he was ordained a deacon. He later evaded being made a bishop by playing David's rôle at Gath and feigning himself mad. But though he declined ecclesiastical office beyond that of deacon he was a theologian, writer, poet, and also a preacher of great popularity and power. He was faithful in his benevolent ministrations to the sick, and is said to have died as a result of his self-denying labors during the prevalence of the plague.

In his preaching and writings he used his native Syrian tongue. A large number of his homilies remain, but a

[1] *Hist. Prea.*, p. 66.

[2] Schaff, *op. cit.*, III., p. 953, from whom the account in the text is chiefly derived. See also several of Ephraem's homilies in the *Nicene and Post-Nicene Fathers,* Vol. XIII., p. 305 ff.

larger number have of course passed away. Photius says that he composed more than a thousand homilies. Some are expository, some controversial. "They evince a considerable degree of popular eloquence; they are full of pathos, exclamations, apostrophes, antitheses, illustrations, severe rebuke, and sweet comfort, according to the subject; but are also full of exaggerations, bombast, prolixity, and the superstitions of his age." [1]

Far to the North, a famous contemporary of Ephraem's, Ulfilas (313-383), the so-called apostle of the Goths, should not be forgotten.[2] It is said that he came of a Cappadocian family who had been captured by the Goths in one of their raids. But he was born among the barbarians and his name is the familiar Teutonic "Wolf." His parents taught him Greek and Christianity from childhood, and thus was he providentially fitted for his mission among his people. In his thirtieth year he was ordained a bishop, and worked with great zeal for the conversion of the Goths beyond the Danube. But persecution drove him and some of his converts southward, and he obtained permission from the emperor Constantine in 350 to cross over into the imperial dominions. This was twenty-five years ahead of the famous migration permitted by Valens. Here for thirty-three years Ulfilas lived, laboring among the Goths on both sides of the river as far as he could. He was Arian in doctrine, and that accounts for the prevalence of that view among the Goths.

Ulfilas was a faithful, devoted, earnest man, and a diligent bishop. He therefore must have preached much, but we have no sermons from him whereby to judge of his methods and powers as a preacher. Regretting his Arianism, we should yet honor his fidelity and zeal, and never forget his inestimable service of translating the New Testament into Gothic. This is the earliest monument of Teutonic literature, and probably the first translation of the Scriptures made into a barbarous tongue.

More eminent than those of whom we have been thinking was a renowned trio of preachers from the highlands of Cappadocia. On the hardy people of this region the Greeks had imprinted deeply and lastingly their civiliza-

[1] Schaff, *l. c.*

[2] Article in *Herzog-Plitt,* Bd. 16, S. 146.

tion and culture. They are described as a rough and vigorous mountain race, fierce and treacherous; but they have given to history some important characters, among whom were none more famous than the three great preachers and divines who adorned Cappadocia during the fourth century. In the address of the First Epistle of Peter, Cappadocia is mentioned as one of the countries in which lived the Christians to whom that general letter was written. With this early start it is not unlikely that the Christians greatly multiplied in the region, and that by the fourth century (as seems clearly to be the case) there were great numbers of them. The principal city, Mazaca, renamed Cæsarea after the Roman occupation, was at this time the populous and flourishing metropolis of all that region. It was situated on a beautiful stream, with Mt. Argaeus, 13,000 feet, rising sheer and grand near by.

The period covered by the lives of Basil, his younger brother Gregory, and their friend Gregory of Nazianzus, was one of tumult and unrest in church and state. The Christians of Cappadocia, as indeed in all the East, were torn asunder by the Arian controversy; and there was serious trouble during all this time, no matter which party, according to the fluctuations of imperial favor, might be filling the offices. The bishopric of Cæsarea was of metropolitan rank, and on Basil's elevation to it the province contained fifty subordinate bishoprics.

The two families from which these three men sprang were of high social standing, wealth, and lofty Christian character. The parents of Basil, and the younger Gregory were Basil, a rhetorician and lawyer of Neo-Cæsarea in Pontus, and Emmelia, a Christian lady of excellent family from Cæsarea in Cappadocia. The paternal grandmother, Macrina of Pontus, was a noble Christian woman. The family seem to have lived partly at Pontus and partly at Cæsarea in Cappadocia, where Basil (and probably Gregory too) was born. With so pious a grandmother—a devoted admirer of Gregory Thaumaturgus, the bishop and saint of Pontus in the preceding generation—and mother, it is not strange that this admirable family was eminent for piety. Three bishops, Basil, Gregory of Nyssa, and Peter of Sebaste, came from among the sons, and there was also a distinguished lawyer among them. Macrina, the saintly sister, to whom both Basil and Gregory owed so much, never married but led the monastic life, and was highly esteemed as a Christian woman of excellent gifts and lovely character.

Likewise the family of Gregory Nazianzen was of good social and religious standing. The father had an estate at a little village called Arianzus near to the more important town of Nazianzus from which this Gregory has his surname. Gregory's father was a Christian, but in early life belonged to an obscure sect called the Hypsistarians, from which he was brought over to the orthodox faith by the influence and entreaties of his pious and devoted wife, Nonna. This godly woman, like Anthusa and Monica in her own age, and many a good Christian mother since, consecrated her son to God and brought him up from childhood "in the nurture and admonition of the Lord." The father—for that was long before celibacy became a rigid rule—was bishop of Nazianzus for many years, dying at an advanced age in 374. There was also a sister, Gorgonia, and a brother, Cæsarius, who became a noted physician at Constantinople.

Turning now to consider in more detail the individuals of this justly famous group we properly begin with Basil (329-379), afterwards called the Great.[1] Born at Cæsarea in Cappadocia in 329, his early education was attended to by his father, a well-known rhetorician. During his childhood the family seems to have resided in Pontus, for he came thence in his youth back to Cæsarea to go to school. Here he first met Gregory of Nazianzus, who subsequently became his nearest friend through life. After this he went to Constantinople, where he enjoyed the instructions of Libanius, who was later at Antioch the famous teacher of John Chrysostom. About the year 350 or later Basil went to Athens to complete his education. Here he found Gregory of Nazianzus, who had preceded him. While here the two young men formed an intimate and affectionate friendship which with only one temporary interruption, lasted through life. They were congenial spirits in very many ways, and their

[1] Translations of his works in *Nicene and Post-Nicene Fathers*, Vol. VIII.

beautiful and pure attachment is not strange. It is especially worthy of note that amid the temptations and dissipations for which college towns have ever been noted, these two, though not yet committed fully to the Christian life, preserved their purity, and thus honored their Christian nurture.

With longings already stirred for a deeper Christian experience, and with inclinations toward asceticism, Basil left Athens well educated and prepared for the work of life. About this time his father died and he began the practice of law and the teaching of rhetoric at Cæsarea. But though successful and admired, he did not put his whole heart into the work. More and more he was drawn toward the monastic life. He took a journey into Syria, Palestine, and Egypt, studying monastic institutions. On his return he gave up the law, divided his wealth among the poor, and retired to Pontus. His widowed mother and his sister Macrina had already gone thither and were living in a cloister with other women of like mind. Near them Basil found a spot to his liking where he could form with others a monastery. In a letter to Gregory Nazianzen he describes the place and urges his friend to join him in this quiet retreat of piety and study. Gregory came, as we shall see, but did not remain long.

From this quiet cloister Basil was, much against his inclinations, called forth to active service, and was made a presbyter at Cæsarea in Cappadocia in 364. He preached often and with great success. In 370 he was elevated to the metropolitan bishopric of Cæsarea. This made him church ruler over a province containing fifty subordinate bishoprics. He strenuously set himself to the work of his charge, and was especially active against Arianism, endeavoring to fill the places with bishops of the orthodox party. To this end he appointed his brother Gregory bishop of Nyssa, and his friend Gregory bishop of Sasima. These were obscure towns, and Sasima was very displeasing to Gregory, who was hurt with his friend for sending him to such a place. The emperor Valens, being Arian in opinions, was minded to depose Basil, but for some reason did not.

Besides his cares of administration and frequent

preaching Basil was active in benevolence. It was said of him that "only the poor knew how great were the revenues of his bishopric." He founded a hospital—one of the first, if not the very first in Christian history—for the care of the indigent sick, chiefly lepers, and often ministered to them in person. A feeble frame, severe asceticism, and arduous labors tell the story of a life prematurely worn out, and he died in 379 in his fiftieth year. He was greatly beloved in life and deeply lamented in death. His funeral was attended by an immense concourse and was a remarkable demonstration of popular regard.

As a preacher Basil had native oratorical gifts, a very suitable and thorough education, and the inspiring demands of place and age. Besides all this he was a truly noble Christian character, earnestly intent on doing good, and constantly in touch with men in administering his great office. His preaching attracted large crowds and pleased as well as helped both the cultured few and the uncultured many. He sometimes preached short sermons at the hour of noonday rest, and "artisans, laborers, silk-spinners would crowd into the church to listen to the discourse." Of his much praised *Hexaëmeron*—a series of discourses on the six days of creation—it has been said, "The simplest could comprehend them, while the wisest admired them." His clear and often elegant style, though marred now and then with the overdone exuberance of the place and time, showed the traces of his education and taste. His knowledge of human nature and power of illustration were great. Schaff has done well to call attention to his good use of illustration and description from nature. This was something new, for even the great classic orators were deficient in this respect. Basil's use of Scripture was faulty with the strained allegorizing of the Alexandrian school, but it is reverent and telling. Broadus[1] speaks in especial commendation of his treatment of moral subjects and says, "Amid all the admirable temperance literature of our own age, I have seen no more just and vivid exhibition of many of the evils of drunkenness than is given by Basil in his sermon on that subject." Upon the whole

[1] *Hist. Prea.*, p. 69.

we may say that Basil justly won the respect and reputation which he enjoyed in life, and that posterity has accepted and confirmed the verdict of his own age by giving him a secure place among the great preachers of all time.

Among all the famous Gregories of Church History hardly one better deserves his fame than he of Nazianzus in Cappadocia.[1] Enough has already been told of his parents and of his pious childhood. In youth, up to his thirtieth year when he left Athens, he received the best education his time afforded in schools at Cæsarea in Cappadocia, at Cæsarea in Palestine, at Alexandria—where he knew and revered the great Athanasius—and lastly at Athens, where he remained longer than his friend Basil, and where he was urged, on completing his studies, to remain and set up a school. This, however, he declined to do, and returned home by way of Constantinople, where he visited his brother Cæsarius the physician, whom he induced to go on home with him to see their parents. Filial as well as religious interest prompted this action. Cæsarius, however, though a Christian, did not receive baptism at this time, but Gregory was baptized by his father on this visit home and remained there some time assisting his father in various ways—with his theological learning in the church affairs, and with his practical sense in the management of the estate at Arianzus. His heart, however, was deeply moved toward the monastic life, and on the invitation of Basil he joined his friend at the secluded place in Pontus, as already related. He could not have remained here many months, for in 361 on another visit home he was, without his consent, but with the approval and in the presence of the congregation, ordained a presbyter by his father. This sudden and unexpected elevation to ecclesiastical office was not to his liking, and he ran away back to Pontus and Basil. But his sense of duty overcame his irritation and his preferences, and after awhile he returned home once more and was his father's assistant (in fact, though perhaps not by regular official appointment) until the old man's death in 374. Once during this time he was again in retirement for a season; and these fluctuations between

[1] *Nicene and Post-Nicene Fathers,* Vol. VII.

the active and retired life were frequent and characteristic. Duty, with perhaps a trace of ambition, drove him to the one, but taste and temper inclined him to the other. He once in his father's presence explained to the congregation this conflict in his mind between his love of solitude and his deference to the calls of public duty.

Within this period of his life also occurred the straining of his friendship with Basil. One way in which that great prelate undertook to drive out Arianism from his province was to appoint his friends to bishoprics, and to make bishoprics even in small places where there was special need. One of these insignificant places was Sasima, a wretched cross-roads town, very undesirable in every way and territorially in dispute between Basil and his rival Arian neighbor, the metropolitan of Tyana. To this miserable place Gregory was appointed by his friend. Whether some desire to assert his authority and to discipline the ambition of Gregory may have weighed with the main motive of Basil in making this unwise and somewhat ungenerous appointment we may not certainly say. Gregory, while perhaps he did not much care for great place in itself, had enough both of pride and affection to be deeply wounded at the slight thus put upon him by his dearest friend; and while it appears that he allowed himself to be consecrated as bishop it also seems that he never actually took up his official residence at Sasima. He continued to assist his father at Nazianzus, and on the older man's death in 374 it is probable—though the matter is not perfectly clear—that he exercised the office of bishop there. But whether this relation was official or only tolerated it does not appear to have continued long, for soon Gregory was in retirement again, this time at or near Seleucia in Isauria. Here in 379 the news of Basil's death came to him. Long before, no doubt, the temporary breach had been healed and a good understanding resumed between the two. On getting the news Gregory wrote to Gregory of Nyssa a touching and beautiful letter which remains, and sometime later, upon invitation of the church at Cæsarea, he delivered his famous eulogy on Basil.[1] This, though

[1] Translation of portions of it in Fish, *Masterpieces of Pulpit Eloquence,* I., p. 67 ff.

naturally overdone, is an eloquent and feeling tribute, perhaps the best remaining specimen of the orator's genius.

In this same year, 379, Gregory was called to the care of the little depressed and scattered church of orthodox Christians at Constantinople. Under Valens Arianism had been triumphant at the capital, and orthodoxy had suffered. In some way this little flock turned to the eloquent Nazianzen, and he was urged by many of his brethren to undertake the restoration of orthodoxy at the imperial city. He went, and here within two years did the great work of his life. His success in drawing congregations, building up the church, and giving to the Athanasian doctrine once again respectability and power at one of the world's capitals, is one of the most distinct and notable triumphs in the history of preaching. It is true that the reaction from Arianism under the earnestly orthodox emperor Theodosius aided the restoration, but that enlightened monarch recognized the services of the preacher and appointed him to the great Church of the Apostles, afterwards made famous by the eloquence of Chrysostom. This appointment to the archbishopric was not regular, as Gregory was officially still entangled with his wretched bishopric of Sasima, or his assistant-bishopric of Nazianzus, or both; and so the action of a synod was needed to disentangle the affair and give him the promotion in regular official form. The great Council of Constantinople in 381, called by the emperor still further to pass on the doctrine of the Person of Christ, gave the needed opportunity. By this council Gregory was formally declared archbishop of Constantinople, and was inaugurated with great pomp. But there was still dissatisfaction and much murmuring, doubtless emphasized by personal reasons, and Gregory, weary of contention and longing once more for retirement, resigned before the year was out. On leaving he preached a notable farewell sermon in which he freed his mind as to the causes of his withdrawal.

He now returned to his old home at Arianzus, where he busied himself with the care of his estate, his correspondence, his writings, and to some extent, as adviser, with the affairs of the church at Nazianzus. Thus occupied he spent his last years and died probably about 390.

Gregory Nazianzen holds a high and firm place among the world's great preachers. Small of stature and unprepossessing in appearance, he had no majestic presence to help out the flash and force of his oratorical genius. He was sensitive, vain, ambitious, yet struggling with these and other infirmities ever toward the better things in character and usefulness. The imaginative, delicate, poetic turn of his mind united with his deep religious feeling and firmness of doctrinal belief, and with his admirable culture, to produce a Christian orator of the first rank. Many specimens of his eloquence remain. They are marred by the weaknesses of the man, the oriental extravagance of his race, the bad taste and tawdry rhetoric of the age; but in spite of all this their excellences are marked. Bishop W. Boyd Carpenter[1] says of him: " Well acquainted with the sacred Scriptures, he could reason forcibly and expound clearly, and his lively imagination contributed, with his literary culture, to give a charm and beauty to his sermons." And Ullman, quoted by Carpenter, speaks of " the fertility of his imagination, his fire and strength, his rapidity and compactness of thought, his heartiness and truth of feeling, and his occasional loftiness of flight."

Younger by some years than his great brother, Basil, and the third son in the family, was Gregory (c. 335-395) afterwards named from his bishopric at Nyssa.[2] Not much is known of his early life and training. He does not seem to have had (perhaps did not desire) such thorough education as Basil. Yet it is evident from his works that he too was highly cultivated. No doubt his father instructed him, and he himself speaks in affectionate and grateful terms of his debt for learning as well as other things to his brother Basil and his sister Macrina. He had some inclination toward the ministry of the church, and became in early life an *anagnostes,* or reader, in the congregation, probably at Cæsarea. But he quitted this office and became a rhetorician. This was considered a great lapse, and he was warmly recalled to

[1] *Clergyman's Magazine,* Vol. I., p. 235.
[2] Translations in *Nicene and Post-Nicene Fathers,* Vol. V.

duty by some letters (still extant) from Gregory Nazianzen. He gave up his worldly ambitions and though married—when is not known—went into a retired life for a while.

After Basil became metropolitan bishop of Cæsarea he appointed Gregory to the little bishopric of Nyssa, saying that he preferred the place should get fame from his brother rather than his brother from the place. And it was a prophecy, for but for the man the town would long ago have been forgotten. This Gregory did not take his appointment as did the Nazianzen. He was reluctant to take the office—as was the accepted custom—but made no objection to the place, and put himself into his work with zeal. His abilities as a speaker and debater against Arianism were exactly what Basil wanted at that place and time. He was driven, in 376, from his bishopric by the agents of the imperial government, and an Arian was put in his place. But after two years of retirement, on the death of Valens and the revocation by Gratian of decrees of banishment against Athanasians, he came triumphantly back. Soon afflictions came fast upon him in the death of Basil, of Macrina, and others of his family, and later (c. 384) in that of his good wife, appropriately named Theosebia.

In 381 Gregory attended the Council of Constantinople, and is reasonably supposed to have had great influence in framing the creed adopted by that body. He appears to have made several subsequent visits to Constantinople, and to have visited by official appointment several countries in the interests of peace and orthodoxy. He probably lived till the year 395.

As a writer and preacher Gregory Nyssen was philosophic in mind and of strong speculative bent. He reminds us strongly of Origen both in this respect and in the excessive allegorizing of his interpretation of Scripture. He was a frequent preacher, and a number of his homilies remain. Paniel[1] thus describes him: "His eminent oratorical talent, not put in the shade by Basil, Gregory Nazianzen, and Asterius, would yet be far worthier of respect if the Nyssen had held more in check his desire for clever comparisons, his immoderate allegor-

[1] *Op. cit.*, S. 543.

izing, his inclination to glittering rhetorical flourishes, his exaggerations, digressions and prolixity."

These three friends and eminent Christian leaders and thinkers, often called "the Cappadocian Cloverleaf," are an interesting study in the history of the church and of preaching. Basil was the most restrained—or rather the least extravagant—of the three. His was the better taste, the more orderly arrangement. Gregory Nazianzen was the most impulsive and ardent—nervous, petulant, poetic. Gregory Nyssen was the most metaphysical and speculative—keen and profound in thought. Basil was the man of affairs, the prelate, the manager; Gregory Nazianzen was the man of feeling, the poet, the orator; Gregory Nyssen was the man of thought, the philosopher, the logician. All were great preachers, each a striking example of his kind.

John of Antioch (347-407), later named Chrysostom, the Golden Mouth, was the greatest of the old Greek preachers.[1] He was born at Antioch in 345 or 347, more probably the latter date. His father died while he was yet a little child, leaving his mother a widow at twenty years of age. She was a rare woman—young, good looking, cultured, of excellent family and standing, and well-to-do. Suitors were many and pressing, and it is hinted that the emperor wished her to be married to one of his officers. But she refused all offers of marriage and devoted herself to bringing up her boy. She gave him the best educational training that the time and place afforded. At home she taught him the religious life, and for his mental culture she selected the best teachers. At one time he was under the care of the famed Libanius, who had also taught Basil, and that great rhetorician is said to have wished John to be his successor—if the Christians had not taken him! Libanius is also reported to have

[1] The literature on Chrysostom is of course very rich in amount and value. Besides all the works on the history hitherto quoted, and others, the admirable *Life* by W. R. W. Stephens is especially worthy of mention. Of the many editions of his works, original and translations, there is no need here to take account. The *Nicene and Post-Nicene Fathers* series contains the most valuable. Of these the volume of the *Homilies on Philippians* is edited with a very instructive and appreciative introduction by Dr. John A. Broadus. For a good single sermon, see Fish *Masterpieces,* I., p. 83 ff.

remarked, when he heard of Anthusa's devotion to John, "What women these Christians have!"

John was educated for the law, and actually began the practice of it. A great career seemed to open before him, but for the pure and earnest young man the corruptions of that profession and of the worldly life about him were too bad to be endured. He gave up his business and prospects and was on the point of going into a monastery, but his mother's persuasion induced him to postpone this for a while, as it would leave her lonely.[1] He led a very ascetic life at home, and later (presumably after his mother's death) he entered a monastery near Antioch where, under the teaching of Diodorus, he remained for several years and carefully studied the Scriptures.

In the year 381 he was called forth from this retreat by his bishop and ordained a deacon at Antioch. For four or five years he exercised this subordinate office, which gave him much contact with the people—both rich and poor—and acquaintance with practical church affairs. But his great gift of speech deserved recognition and the world needed the exercise of it, so the bishop of Antioch appointed him in 386 to be presbyter and chief preacher in the leading church of his native city. Here he exercised his brilliant ministry for about twelve years. He soon became the most popular preacher of the city and of the age. His fame spread far and wide. During this time there was a serious sedition at Antioch over the taxes, and the mob in a frenzy mutilated the statues of the emperor, the empress, and their sons. Theodosius, though a Christian, had a fierce temper which sometimes broke all bounds; and the people of Antioch on reflection knew that they had much to fear from the emperor's wrath. They sent a deputation headed by the aged bishop Flavian to Constantinople to apologize for the affront and sue for imperial clemency. In this interval of popular suspense Chrysostom delivered the famous series of twenty-one homilies "On the Statues," which have come down to us. The sermons, so opportune and earnest, had a great effect, and remain as admirable specimens of his genius.

[1] Chrysostom himself gives a feeling account of this interview in his treatise *On the Priesthood,* Bk. II., Ch. 2.

Stephens, in his valuable *Life of Chrysostom,* gives the following vivid account of the occasion: "During the absence of Flavian all the powers of Chrysostom as an orator, a pastor, and a citizen were called forth in attempting to calm the fears and revive the deeply dejected spirits of the people. Perseveringly did he discharge this anxious and laborious task; almost every day for twenty-two days that small figure was to be seen either sitting in the *ambo,* from which he sometimes preached on account of his diminutive stature, or standing on the steps of the altar, the preacher's usual place; and day after day the crowds increased which came to listen to the stream of golden eloquence which he poured forth. With all the versatility of a consummate artist he moved from point to point. Sometimes a picture of the city's agony melted his hearers to tears, and then again he struck the note of encouragement, and revived their spirits by bidding them take comfort from the well-known clemency of the emperor, the probable success of the mission of Flavian, and above all from trust in God."

A passage from the second homily illustrates the preacher's manner: "The gay and noisy city, where once the busy people hummed like bees around their hive, was petrified by fear into the most dismal silence and desolation; the wealthier inhabitants had fled into the country, those who remained shut themselves up in their houses, as if the town had been in a state of siege. If any one ventured into the market-place, where once the multitude poured along like the stream of a mighty river, the pitiable sight of two or three cowering dejected creatures in the midst of solitude soon drove them home again. The sun itself seemed to veil its rays as if in mourning. The words of the prophet were fulfilled. 'Their sun shall go down at noon, and their earth shall be darkened in a clear day' (Amos. 8:9). Now they might cry, 'Send to the mourning women, and let them come, and send for cunning women that they may come' (Jer. 9:17). Ye hills and mountains! take up a wailing; let us invite all creation to commiserate our woes, for this great city, this capital of Eastern cities, is in danger of being destroyed out of the midst of the earth, and there is no man to help her, for the emperor, who has no equal among men, has been insulted; therefore let us take refuge with the King who is above, and summon him to our aid."

The homilies, however, were not only eloquent, but most timely and effective, so that thousands were by their means brought to better thoughts. The preacher bore down upon the vices and sins which marred the city; he complained that the people feared the wrath of the emperor more than the wrath of God, and dreaded death more than sin. Altogether these Statue Homilies are one of the most remarkable series of discourses in the literature of the pulpit. With them Chrysostom's fame and power reached their height in the city of his birth. But he was not to spend his life there.

After some years the archbishopric of Constantinople fell vacant, and there was a scramble of eager aspirants for the place. Among these was Theophilus, the unscrupulous and intriguing archbishop of Alexandria. At this time the weak emperor Arcadius, unworthy successor in the East of his great father Theodosius, was under the influence of one of the meanest of his ministers, the infamous Eutropius. This man determined to disappoint all the schemers and bring from Antioch the eloquent John and make him archbishop at the capital. Knowing that both John and the people of Antioch would resist this move, Eutropius resorted to stratagem and force to accomplish his purpose. The preacher was, innocently on his part, persuaded to come outside the city walls for the ostensible purpose of worshipping at some shrine. He was seized by a band of soldiers in waiting and hurried off to Constantinople, where, with the requisite formalities, he was made archbishop and leading preacher at the great Church of the Apostles!—an office which Gregory Nazianzen had peevishly resigned about sixteen years before this time.

Here for a little over six years (397-404) the pure and devoted archbishop administered with rare fidelity and courage his great trust, and the eloquent preacher poured forth the intense and lofty oratory which has filled the world with his fame. He lived the life of an ascetic, using the large revenues of his office in alms and other pious works. He disciplined his venal and corrupt inferior clergy with an unsparing hand, and gave attention without personal ambition to the details of his exacting and responsible office. He concerned himself with benevolences, with missions, with affairs of general interest. In his eloquent preaching he was no time-server, but rebuked without fear or favor all classes and conditions of men. His plainness of speech gave great offence to the beautiful and imperious Eudoxia, the worldly consort of Arcadius. This hatred of the empress and the envy and anger of many of the clergy were the causes of Chrysostom's deposition and banishment.

Under the lead of the infamous Theophilus of Alexandria, and no doubt at Eudoxia's instigation, a synod was hastily called at The Oak, a suburb of Chalcedon across the strait, to consider charges against the archbishop. A formidable list of charges was made out—about forty in number. Many of them were trivial, most of them utterly false, some with just enough show of truth to make them pass—with exaggerations and perversions—for the truth. Under such circumstances Chrysostom's condemnation was a foregone conclusion. He was deposed by a regularly convened and therefore formally legal synod of the church, and was turned over to the government for punishment. The empress saw to that, and an imperial decree of banishment was forthwith served upon the bishop by the military arm of the government. He was escorted across the strait and his enemies seemed successful. But news of his deposition and hasty banishment flew through the city—the people were roused—they gathered in crowds—they shouted, " Give us back our bishop," " We will have our bishop," " Better let the sun cease to shine than stop that golden mouth!" In the midst of the popular uproar an earthquake came. The terrified empress quailed, the emperor gave way, Theophilus took to flight, and orders were given to bring the beloved preacher back. But this could not last. The sentence was not revoked, nor the enmity appeased. Finally, rather than be a source of schism in the church and of tumult in the empire the good and wise man decided to accept voluntarily his condemnation with an appeal to a future general council. (This, it is almost needless to say, was never called.) In order to avoid popular disturbance he left his mule hitched in the usual place near the church, and gave himself up privately through the back way to the guard, who secretly conveyed him across the Bosphorus.

From his place of exile—Cucusus, in the mountains near the border between Cappadocia and Armenia—he kept up correspondence with his friends, continued to care for his flock, his benevolences, his missions; and was much sought in counsel. As he thus continued to be too popular and influential for his enemies, the authorities determined to change the place of his banishment to an inaccessible little town on the Black Sea. On the way thither his feeble frame, worn out with lifelong asceticism and these new hardships, gave way. He died in a little church by the roadside near Comana [1] in Pontus, repeating his favorite phrase, "Glory to God for all things."

Judged by his character, by his sermons as we have them, and by his work and influence, John Chrysostom has been always and with singular agreement among critics esteemed one of the greatest preachers of all time. Even the cold and sneering Gibbon gives a long account of Chrysostom, and though not doing the saint and preacher justice, is compelled by the facts to accord him high praise. Milton in his *Areopagitica*, speaking of the comedies of Aristophanes, says, "Holy Chrysostom, as is reported, nightly studied so much the same author, and had the art to cleanse a scurrilous vehemence into the style of a rousing sermon." Indeed nearly all references in history and literature recognize the easy preeminence of the man. Some indeed give him, all things considered, the very first place after the Apostles. What were some of the principal elements of his success?

To begin with he had excellent advantages. God had endowed him with rich natural gifts of mind and heart—he had a great intellect, and the germs of a noble nature. Then he had the devoted and intelligent care of a pious and lovely mother. His liberal education and early work at the profession of the law developed his mind and gave him knowledge of the world. His retired life of prayer and study strengthened his spiritual

[1] It is an interesting fact that near this very spot many centuries later (1812) died the devoted missionary, Henry Martyn.

life and made him master of the Scriptures. Then he worked as deacon for four years in the great city of Antioch, coming in daily contact with the people and with ecclesiastical details. So, when, a man of nearly forty years, he was called to be chief preacher at Antioch he had behind him a wonderfully varied and complete preparation for his work.

Nor must we lose sight of the things that helped him in the work. He had great places to fill, and inspiring audiences to preach to, both at Antioch and Constantinople. He had at his command one of the greatest languages for oratorical purposes that has ever been spoken by man. Nor must we omit the important fact that the largeness of his mind and breadth of his sympathies in other lines of work helped him in the pulpit. His work with and for the people, his benevolent and missionary enterprises, and his administrative labors, so far from hindering his preaching, made it larger in mould, more popular in effect. He was no bookish recluse, but a man of the people. Their life and souls were his to know and direct.

Chrysostom's faults as a preacher were neither few nor little. As great a man as he will have great faults as well as great excellences. His best work is marred by the oriental intensity and exaggeration, in feeling, in thought, in language. The overmuch was his snare. In theology, while he was true to the Athanasian orthodoxy, he did not escape the errors of his age and race. He overpraises alms, celibacy, monasticism, as meritorious works. His view of sin and its remedy is more moral than evangelical. Strong tendency toward the worship of Mary and the saints appears. Also there is the sacerdotal view of the ordinances. In brief he did not rise above the doctrinal errors current in his day. In his preaching itself there is often loose and forced interpretation of Scripture. Sometimes he doesn't take a text at all, and almost never confines himself to it. While he does not allegorize after the Origenistic fashion, he does not mind twisting a passage to fit his homiletical needs. In the structure of his discourses he is often loose, fond of digressions and sallies, sometimes getting back to his point and sometimes not. In style he is often too familiar, too prolix and repetitious.

But serious as such faults are, they serve in a case like his to set off great virtues, and also to check the undue admiration we may be disposed to indulge. John Chrysostom had from early childhood a deep, sincere, and pure religious character. Piety, earnestness, sincerity, and self-sacrifice were realities with him. Splendid courage, even if it did sometimes approach bravado, was his. He feared not empress, nor people, nor his evil-minded brethren. He spoke the truth no matter whom it might hit. Fidelity to duty as he saw it animated him in all his work. He, too, was one who wore himself out for his Master.

On the basis of such a character as this the more properly oratorical virtues naturally and safely rested. The nameless oratorical instinct—the way to say here and now the thing that ought to be said, the acute readiness to turn the hap of the moment to account—this was his. Command of language, wealth of material, abundance and fitness of illustration, fine imaginative and descriptive powers—these, too, were his. Add to all this a wonderful knowledge of the Bible and of human nature and of the art of applying the teachings of one to the needs of the other, and the splendid equipment of a live and mighty preacher stands confessed. Students of his sermons and of his life unite in a chorus of well deserved praise of his oratory, but none has said a finer thing of him than his pupil and friend, John Cassian:[1] " He kindled his zeal in the bosom of his Redeemer."

4. The Western Preachers

The attractive characters and work of the great Greek preachers of the fourth century have detained us perhaps too long from their lesser but still important Latin contemporaries. But these may be more briefly presented, because they are fewer and less worthy of study than the Eastern preachers whom they imitated. The singular dependence of the Latin mind upon the Greek for ideas and for culture is as well illustrated in the history of preaching as in that of other literature. Not even the great Augustine, any more than the great Cicero before

[1] Quoted by W. Boyd Carpenter, *Clerg. Mag.*, Vol. I., p. 97.

him, was free from this unhealthy dependence; and if not these greater minds, how much less the smaller ones! Hence in passing from the blooming time of Greek Christian preaching in the fourth century to the Latin preaching of the same period we feel a distinct drop. Yet the native vigor and intense practical turn of the Latin genius asserted themselves, and did not fail to give even to the imitative work of the Western preachers some tinge of original power. This was especially true of Augustine, the only really great preacher among them, but shows itself to some extent in the weaker men who preceded him. Augustine therefore represents the culmination of early Latin preaching, and our present survey will appropriately close with him. But we must also give some attention to the great bishop of Milan, Ambrose, and before him to a group of the earlier preachers of less fame.

Among the Latin preachers who come between Cyprian and Ambrose one of the most important was Hilary (d. 368), the highly esteemed bishop of Poitiers.[1] He was born toward the end of the third century at the place which his own work has made somewhat known in church annals, but which the famous victory of the Black Prince a thousand years later (1356) has celebrated in the history of England. Pictavium, in Aquitania, a province of southern Gaul, known in modern times as Poitiers, was the scene of Hilary's birth and labors. He was of good family and apparently well-to-do. His parents may have been Christian, but this is uncertain. He had good educational opportunities, but was a little slow at first in his mental progress. But by hard work he secured good learning. He studied at Rome and in Greece. When he was baptized, or how long before baptism he had been a Christian we do not know; but as delay in baptism was then common, his elevation to the episcopate in his native town shortly after his baptism does not prove a late conversion. His piety and abilities had long been recognized, and somewhere between 350 and 355, because of his learning, his pure life, his zeal, he was called to the bishopric of Poitiers. He had been married, probably in

[1] See Paniel, S. 697 ff., and the biography and works of Hilary in Migne's *Latin Patrology*, tom. 9, 10.

early life, to an excellent woman; but his married state did not hinder his election, as celibacy, though regarded as preferable, was not at this period enforced. He had a daughter Abra, or Apra, to whom he wrote when absent once a curious letter, still preserved, in which he urges her to remain unmarried, advises her on some religious matters, and sends her a morning and an evening hymn. The latter is lost, but the other is the beautiful one beginning *Lucis largitor splendide,* one of the treasures of ancient Christian hymnody.[1] For his zeal against Arianism he suffered banishment (c. 356-361) under the emperor Constantius. During his exile, in Phrygia, he wrote his treatise in twelve books on the Trinity, besides other writings. He was recalled, and then again banished, and seems to have ended his life in retirement about the year 368.

He was sound in the faith, an honest and bold believer in the scriptural doctrine of the Trinity before it had been formulated in the Nicene creed. He gladly accepted that instrument, and was a lifelong opponent of Arianism. As to baptism he held the view then prevalent that it was necessary to salvation, but on condition of repentance and faith. He believed in a strict church discipline and was diligent in seeking to win men to the faith in Christ.

In regard to his preaching not much is to be said. The Benedictine editor[2] of his works says that Hilary expounded the Gospel of Matthew to the people, and that he says of himself, "What he believed he preached, through the ministry of the ordained priesthood, to others; and exercised his calling for the salvation of the people." Jerome speaks favorably of his eloquence, comparing it to the flow of the river Rhone. On this Paniel shrewdly remarks that the Rhone is a rather muddy torrent! No sermons as such remain. But there are a number of treatises, dissertations (*tractatus*), on the Psalms which seem very clearly to have been originally sermons and afterwards written out in commentary style. A glance at these confirms the judgment of Jerome that while Hilary imitated Origen he added some things of his own. Along with some acuteness there is much of idle speculation and allegorizing. There is no eloquence, and the

[1] Migne, *Pat. Lat.*, tom. 10, col. 551. [2] *Op. cit.*, tom. 9, col. 165.

style is not pleasing; but much reverence for Scripture appears and great desire to do good. On the whole Hilary is more important as a churchman and theologian, but deserves respect and consideration as a preacher.

Another Latin preacher and bishop of this age is Zeno (d. 380) of Verona.[1] His bust, along with those of many other distinguished sons or citizens, is found on the porch of the old town hall at Verona to this day; but it is hardly a likeness! It appears that he was born in north Africa early in the fourth century, and was chosen bishop of Verona in Italy in 362, filling that office till his death in 380. He was, like Hilary, a strenuous upholder of the Nicene creed and of church discipline. He enjoyed an excellent reputation for character and works. Some accounts call him a "martyr," but others only a "confessor," i.e., one who suffered but did not die for his faith.

Of his homiletical productions there remain ninety-three *tractates*—some of them very brief. It has been conjectured that these short addresses are either merely notes of what was expanded in delivery, or else were additional remarks or exhortations given by the bishop after the presbyter had preached. He had some merit as an orator—acuteness, fancy, considerable rhetorical culture and skill. He makes frequent—perhaps too frequent—use of illustration and apostrophe. His imitation of the Greek preachers is plain; and allegorizing is abundant and arbitrary.

Our knowledge of Pacianus, bishop of Barcelona (fl. c. 373), is very little.[2] Jerome in his *De Viris Illustribus* makes favorable mention of him as a man of high standing and noted for piety and eloquence. He seems to have been highly esteemed before becoming a Christian and bishop. He was married, and his son Dexter, to whom Jerome's book was dedicated, held high office under the emperor Honorius, after his father's death. Pacianus became bishop of Barcelona in Spain probably about 373, and died in old age in the time of Theodosius, before 392.

Two sermons of his remain. One is an exhortation to penitence. It is practical rather than doctrinal, and

[1] See Lentz, *Gesch. der Christl. Hom.*, Bd. I., S. 147; and Paniel, S. 716 ff. [2] Paniel, S. 731.

contains some passages full of thought and eloquence. The other, on baptism, is not so good. His work shows familiarity with the classics, good knowledge of the Bible, and effective use of illustration. He resembles Cyprian, whom he studied with pleasure. He was evidently a preacher of considerable force, and we can only regret the scantiness of our knowledge of him and his work.

In Gaudentius of Brescia (d. c. 410) [1] we have again an interesting but too little known character. Neither his country nor the date of his birth is certainly known. But it is inferred that he was born at or near Brescia before the middle of the fourth century. In his young manhood he went to the East for travel and culture, and spent several years at Cæsarea in Cappadocia. While there his friend and teacher, the bishop of Brescia, died, and Gaudentius, at the instance of the older bishops, especially of Ambrose of Milan, was chosen bishop and urged by letters to return. The usual reluctance was expressed, but the eastern bishops were requested by their western brethren to deny to Gaudentius the communion until he should consent! This brought him home, and he was duly consecrated. He was required by the older bishops present to preach a sermon on the occasion of his own ordination. This sermon has come down to us and gives the facts just mentioned.

Among Chrysostom's letters while he was in exile is one addressed to Gaudentius thanking him for his interest in trying to secure for the archbishop a revocation of the decree of banishment. The old man says that Gaudentius' effort was a comfort to him in his lonely and neglected state, and speaks of Gaudentius as a friend whom neither time nor distance could estrange. It seems that the Italian did not long survive his distinguished friend, dying probably about the year 410 or later.

Gaudentius was highly honored for his piety and eloquence. A number of sermons of fairly sure authenticity remain. Among his hearers and friends was a citizen of Brescia who through illness missed a series of sermons that the bishop was giving during the fasting season. He asked Gaudentius to send him the sermons to read, as he could not hear them. The bishop agreed and sent

[1] Paniel, S. 771; Migne, *Pat. Lat.*, tom. 20, col. 791.

him not only the ten fast sermons, but four other short addresses on different chapters of the Gospels, and also a panegyric on the Maccabean brothers, who were esteemed as martyrs. Of these last he says that he would not be responsible for them, as they had been taken down hastily and he had not looked over them, but the others (presumably the ten fast sermons) he had revised. Besides these there is the sermon at his ordination, and several others. In one of these he repeats the tradition that Peter was crucified with his head downward, and Paul was beheaded. As a preacher in point of style, thought and oratory he does not hold very high rank, but is worthy of remembrance.

From these less known men we turn to the highly renowned bishop of Milan, Ambrose (340-397).[1] His birth-place was probably Treves in Gaul, where his father was pretorian prefect, i.e., governor with military and civil jurisdiction over several provinces. A pretty story of Ambrose's babyhood is to the effect that bees once alighted on his mouth while he was asleep and the frightened nurse being about to drive them away the father forbade her, saying that it was an omen of future eloquence—honeyed speech. On the early death of his father Ambrose and his brother and sister were left to the care of their mother. The family affection was beautiful and enduring. None of the three ever was wedded; they were devoted to each other. In one of his sermons late in life Ambrose pays noble tribute to his brother, who had recently died, and elsewhere speaks tenderly of his sister.

The family moved to Rome in Ambrose's childhood, and he was educated—like Basil and Chrysostom—for the legal profession. He met with decided success in civil life. His fine talent for government was soon recognized and he was appointed *consular,* i.e., civil governor, of Liguria and Aemilia, with headquarters at Milan. The territory was large, embracing in our times, besides Milan, the cities of Genoa, Parma, Modena, and Bologna. Thus the appointment was one of distinction. It is related

[1] Authorities already noted and works of Ambrose in Migne, *Pat. Lat.*, tt. 14-17; translations in *Nicene and Post-Nicene Fathers.*

that on his leaving Rome to take his office one of the high officers of the imperial court remarked that he would fulfil it "like a bishop." This only referred to the fidelity and conscientiousness which the man would carry to his task, but it was unconscious prophecy.

While Ambrose was governor at Milan, the Arian bishop died, and there was determined effort on the side of the orthodox party to secure the election of a bishop who should represent their views. The Arians were equally determined on their part. On the day of election there was fierce contention, and Ambrose went as governor to the church to quell the disturbance. While he was pleading for peace and order the voice of a child suddenly rang out, "Ambrose for bishop!" The crowd took it up. It was accepted as the voice of God, and both parties united on him, and in spite of his remonstrances elected him on the spot. He was only a catechumen—had not yet been baptized, though long a Christian in heart. He tried to flee, but was overruled, baptized, and in eight days duly consecrated bishop of Milan!

He took office in a humble but devoted spirit, and feeling the deficiency of his theological education, went to work diligently to study the Bible and the Greek theologians and preachers—especially Origen and Basil. He preached regularly on Sundays and often on other occasions. He was much occupied with the cares of his large and exacting diocese, and took great interest in singing and worship. He was very accessible and affable as a pastor and was much beloved by his people. He was a firm disciplinarian and a man of determined courage. The signal instance of this is his refusal to admit the emperor Theodosius to the communion till the choleric monarch had purged himself by penance for the massacre of the populace of Thessalonica.[1] Even the cynical Gibbon[2] is aroused to admiration of this episode in the life of a Christian prelate, and concludes his account of it by saying, "The example of Theodosius may prove the beneficial influence of those principles which could force a

[1] The letter he wrote to the emperor concerning this is a model of fidelity, firmness and courtesy. See Migne, *Pat. Lat.*, tom. 16, col. 1209.

[2] *Decline and Fall,* Vol. III., p. 118 (Am. reprint of Milman's ed.).

monarch, exalted above the apprehension of human punishment, to respect the laws and ministers of an invisible Judge." In other ways also did the high-minded bishop show both his great interest in public affairs and the nobility and elevation of his own character. He was a conscientious and hard worker, and care wore upon him. Likewise the death of his beloved brother Satyrus fell upon him as a serious blow from which he never recovered. He died, not old, in his fifty-seventh year, 397.

Ambrose the man and bishop is greater than Ambrose the preacher. In studying his sermons and orations we cannot help a feeling of disappointment.[1] His principal remains in the way of sermons are his orations on the dead. That (in two parts) on his brother Satyrus is especially good.[2] It is full of love and grief for his brother, but shows the proper feeling of one who is a Christian, a pastor and a teacher, in view of so great an affliction. The oration on Theodosius is also notable. Others of his speeches and sermons were worked out after delivery and lack the fire of actual speech. His expositions of the Psalms are mostly borrowed from Origen, whom, if anything, he outdoes in allegorizing, and his Hexaëmeron is an undisguised copy from Basil. This plagiarism was not then considered so great an evil as it really is, and yet it remains a sad subtraction from the fame of a truly great and good man.

Among the great theologians and preachers of early church history, whether considered in regard to character, abilities, and work, or in regard to enduring influence and fame, no one stands higher than Aurelius Augustinus (354-430).[3] He was born at Tagaste, in Numidia, north Africa, Nov. 13, 354. Augustine's father Patricius was of good family and a man of some influence in his town, but seems to have had a somewhat crabbed disposition and to have been a trial to his godly wife. Her influence

[1] This view is expressed by other critics as well as by Broadus, *Hist. Prea.*, p. 80. [2] Migne, *Pat. Lat.*, tom. 16, col. 1346 ff.

[3] A great literature deals with Augustine, yet rather as man and theologian than as preacher. Various editions of his works are easily accessible; translations in *Nicene and Post-Nicene Fathers.* Paniel hardly does Augustine justice as a preacher. There are more just and appreciative discussions in Rothe, Lentz, Brömel (*Homiletische Charakterbilder*), Nebe, and others.

and prayers had their final reward, and Patricius, long a heathen, became a Christian and was baptized late in life. Among the great Christian mothers of history Monica has a well deserved respect, and her grateful and gifted son has embalmed her memory in beauty and tenderness in the pages of his *Confessions.*

Augustine was sent to the best schools at his home and at Carthage. His pious mother had brought him up in the most tender and earnest Christian influences, but as is sadly too often the case, the temptations of the corrupt world about him proved too strong for the vigorous youth and he became wild and dissolute. He tells us in his immortal *Confessions* the sorrowful story of his downfall and his shames. They need not be repeated here. He ran the hard way of the transgressor and bitterly reaped, in all his after life of remorse and penitence, the fruits of his youthful follies and sins.

He became a teacher of rhetoric at Carthage. A passage in Cicero's *Hortensius* stirred in the young man of nineteen a desire to seek after God and to be a philosopher, and he gave himself with zest to study. From Carthage he went to Rome to teach and study, and from Rome to Milan.

His philosophical studies brought him into contact with the dualism of the Manichaean sect, and for a time he was caught in the meshes of that system. But it proved after long trial unsatisfactory, and he was turning to the Neo-Platonic philosophy in quest of intellectual and moral repose. This was about the time of his removal to Milan, where he began to practise his profession of rhetorical teacher. His patient and faithful mother came to him at Milan—probably after the death of her husband. He also had with him his illegitimate son, whom he had named Adeodatus—strange name for one who, though tenderly loved, was a perpetual reminder of his early manhood's faults. Here at Milan in his thirty-third year, intellectually dissatisfied and conscience-smitten for his evil youth, he came under the influence of the good and noble Ambrose. He went often to hear Ambrose preach, and by the blessing of God upon his mother's faithful labors and the bishop's good life and preaching, he was led to a full and joyful acceptance of the Christian faith.

He was baptized, along with his son Adeodatus, by Ambrose in 387. His pious mother lived to see this fruition of her hopes and prayers, but died shortly afterwards at Ostia, whence they were soon to depart for their old home in north Africa. Likewise the beloved son of Augustine's youth and error died early.

On his conversion Augustine quit his teaching, divided his property among the poor, and gave himself up to study, reflection and writing. Several of his theological and philosophical treatises belong to this period. He returned home and lived in retirement for a few years near Tagaste, when in 391 he was called to Hippo and made a presbyter by the bishop Valerius. On the death of the prelate in 395 Augustine was made bishop in his place. For thirty-five years he exercised that office, writing much, preaching often, administering with exemplary fidelity his charge, and living a life of true Christian nobility.

In 430 Hippo was besieged by the Vandals under Genseric. The aged bishop lay sick and worn in his plain chamber, the only decoration of the walls being passages from the penitential Psalms; thus he passed away August 28, 430, in his seventy-sixth year.

Passing by the greatness of Augustine as a theologian, a controversialist, a writer, we are here concerned with his preaching. He was very diligent in this work, often preaching five days in the week and sometimes twice a day. In his treatise, *On Christian Teaching*,[1] and in his two ordination sermons, he gives us his conception of the preaching office, and it is a high and just one, to which he endeavored to attain himself. He recognizes both the honor and the responsibility of the office, insisting that the preacher must teach by example as well as precept, and that he needs the prayers of his people. Well says Brömel of him: " What he taught that he lived, and what he lived that he taught—that was the power of his preaching."

In his famous and justly admired work, *On Christian*

[1] See Brömel, *Homiletische Charakterbilder*, Bd. I., S. 39 ff., who has a fine analysis and study of the treatise *On Christian Teaching*. This is well translated by J. F. Shaw in Dods' edition of the Fathers.

Teaching, Augustine relates an instance of the effect of his preaching.[1] He was addressing the rough Mauretanians and endeavoring to dissuade them from the feud (*caterva*), which was very common among them. "I strove with all the vehemence of speech I could command to root out and drive from their hearts and lives an evil so cruel and inveterate; it was not, however, when I heard their applause, but when I saw their tears, that I thought I had produced an effect. For the applause showed that they were instructed and pleased, but the tears that they were subdued. And when I saw their tears I was confident, even before the event proved it, that this horrible and barbarous custom was overthrown; and immediately that my sermon was finished I called upon them with heart and voice to give praise and thanks to God. And, lo, with the blessing of Christ it is now eight years or more since anything of the sort was attempted there." Modestly as this is told, it shows what a power Augustine must have sometimes had with his audiences.

In his preaching, as in his *Confessions,* there was the mystical trace—the devotion of a rapt soul, loving communion with God; and in his sermons, as in his theological and controversial writings, there was stern and fearless logic. He cared not so much for graces of style as for depth of matter and power of effect. To convince, persuade, instruct and win his auditors was his supreme concern. For pithy and telling sayings he is justly famous. Though he had been a teacher of rhetoric he was not so careful of order and decoration as would have seemed natural, or would indeed have been proper. He perhaps undervalued these in his intense concern to make his preaching effective. He also undervalued immediate preparation, and often came to his pulpit without having carefully thought out beforehand what he would say. Even so full, acute, logical a mind as his could not wholly overcome the consequences of this error, and his sermons—taken down by shorthand writers—abundantly show the weaknesses of such a method.

In his treatment of Scripture he follows the fashion of his time as to the allegorical interpretation, and perpetrates many a foolish and trivial blunder in exegesis.

[1] *De Doctrina Christiana,* lib. IV., cap. 24.

Sometimes he takes a text, sometimes not; sometimes he sticks to his text, sometimes not. Very many of his sermons are expository lectures on books of the Bible, continuous and fairly complete. Brömel considers those on the Gospel of John and on the Pauline Epistles to be the best, but many on the Psalms are of great devotional and spiritual power. His sermons deal very little with illustration, but the few illustrations he does employ are apt and telling. The deep earnestness of his nature and the power of his thought are the main elements of strength in his preaching. However mistakenly careless of form and beauty, these instinctively, as it were of themselves, appear in his work. Such a powerful soul as his could not but express itself in his preaching, but he might have been more eloquent, more attractive, and far more impressive, then and now, had he been more at pains to adorn his speech. The sermons are of very unequal length, and very unequal merit, as a consequence of his carelessness of preparation.

But take him all in all Augustine was the greatest Latin preacher. While he lived on into the fifth century for three decades, his work and influence belong really to the fourth, and mark the close of that wonderful and fruitful epoch in the history of the Christian pulpit which came to its culmination in Chrysostom and himself. The Greek wave rose first and highest, but soonest ebbed, and never has flowed again. Since Chrysostom there has been no really great Greek preacher. After Augustine also there was a marked decline for two centuries, and a dark period for five more in the West, when again the Latin pulpit, or rather Western preaching under Latin auspices, rose into new power for a time.

PERIOD II

THE EARLY MEDIÆVAL, OR DARK, AGE

A.D. 430–1095

After the times of Chrysostom and Augustine up to the preaching of the First Crusade by Peter the Hermit and Pope Urban II

CHAPTER III

The Decline of Ancient Preaching in the Fifth and Sixth Centuries

We here take up the second general period as outlined for our studies, namely, the long dark age which reaches from the death of Augustine early in the fifth, to the call for the First Crusade at the end of the eleventh century. In the early part of this era the crumbling fragments of decaying ancient civilization were mingling with the crude beginnings of a new and very different stage of progress in human affairs. Vigorous and promising in many ways as these new beginnings really were, the thoughtful men of that gloomy transition could scarcely detect any promise of good in those forces which were accomplishing the overthrow of all that outwardly represented a past of power and glory. Decay was the age-token, and the feeling of hopelessness, the sense of defeat, the consciousness of being near the end of things, were only too common. The letters and other writings of Ambrose already sound the lament over a falling state; and Augustine's great work *De Civitate Dei* found its emphatic thought if not its actual suggestion in the painful yet glorious contrast between dying Rome and the truly eternal City of God. Thus the evening of antiquity closes down in shadows over Europe, and it is a long night of fitful sleep, rude alarms, and barbaric orgies that follows, until the clarion call to the Crusades announces the dawn of the mediæval day.

Preaching, too, after Augustine, entered on a decline from which it did not recover till the twelfth century, and therefore for these studies as well as for general history the terms of the period are correctly placed. In this chapter we are concerned with the preaching of the fifth and sixth centuries, but it will be well to take a short preliminary glance at the history of the times so as to gain the proper orientation for our more specific study of the pulpit.

1. General Sketch of the Times

Upon the death of the great Theodosius in 395 the empire was divided betwen his two weak sons, and there was no more union of the sovereignty in one hand. This division lay deep in the different characters of the people east and west, as well as in governmental convenience and other things; and it had been maturing for ages. It is true that in the sixth century for a short time the victories of Belisarius and Narses brought Italy and north Africa under the sway of Justinian, and that far later, in 1204, the Crusaders captured Constantinople and established a fleeting Latin sovereignty there; but these were episodes, and brief ones. The racial and political division was further emphasized by the schism between the churches, which was fast coming on, but in the sixth century was not yet accomplished. The ancient empire of Rome came to its pitiful end in this time. From without Goths and Vandals, Huns and Lombards, put the finishing touch to the age-long inner decay, and the majestic old structure of the Cæsars toppled and fell. Men were expecting it; and though in itself an impressive event to reflection, the scene which closed the tragedy was paltry enough for a farce. In 476 the last petty Roman emperor, a child in years and absurdly named Romulus Augustulus, surrendered his crown to Odoacer the Ostrogoth, who sent what was left of the imperial regalia to the emperor of the East; and so the great drama ended.

Not till the middle of the fifteenth century did the Turks do for Constantinople what the Teutons had done for

Rome in the fifth. In truth, during the sixth century the remarkable reign of Justinian (527-565) shed some rays of real and lasting glory upon the decadent East. While not himself a man of the first rank in either intellect or character, this emperor was fortunate and wise enough to find and employ men of genius. The military exploits, with the imperfect forces at their command and against powerful odds, of the great generals, Belisarius and Narses, were brilliant, though ineffectual in the end. More lasting was the magnificent work of the great lawyer Tribonian and his associates, who codified the confused and voluminous laws of the empire and thus rendered distinguished and lasting service not only to the science of jurisprudence, but through it to the general good of mankind. Nor must we forget Justinian's services to education, commerce and art, especially architecture. The world-famous church of St. Sophia was rebuilt in his reign, and so pleased was he with his work that on its completion he is said to have exclaimed, "I have outdone thee, O Solomon!"

Out of the chaos of ruin and rapine which marked the barbarian overthrow of Roman sovereignty in Europe something like order slowly emerged in the establishment of powers which eventually became, or contributed toward forming, the leading dukedoms and kingdoms of mediæval times. In Germany there was turmoil and confusion, but the defeat of the Huns at Chalons in 451 at least averted the menace of their conquest of central Europe. In Italy, first the Goths, and later the Lombards, laid foundations of real political power. In Spain the West Goths built up a kingdom which was a basis for future developments. The Burgundian power along the Rhine was important, both at the time, and as a source of coming events of great influence in history. In Gaul the Franks under Clovis, and in Britain the Anglo-Saxons were making the beginnings of France and England.

Meantime, amid the ruins of the old Roman empire and the confused beginnings of mediæval monarchies, the religious and secular power of the papacy was firmly established. Henceforth European history has to deal with a new power emanating from Rome as a centre, and potent still in the affairs of the world. The inner developments of church polity, assisted by outer events and forces, had culminated through various grades of bishops in the institution of five great church rulers, called Patriarchs, and located at the cities of Jerusalem, Antioch, Alexandria, Constantinople, and Rome. The leading position among these naturally lay in dispute between the last two, and this became one of the chief elements of schism between the Greek and Latin churches. In addition to the natural and traditional odds in favor of the Roman bishop two circumstances now powerfully assisted in making him supreme: one was that he was the only Patriarch for all the Latin part of the church and world, the rest being all oriental and Greek; and the other was that the decline and fall of imperial authority and glory in the West enhanced the position of the Patriarch of Rome. All these advantages were opportunely pressed by the talents and force of character of Leo I. (440-461), who not only asserted his claims, but gave them their enduring Scriptural defence by urging in their support the words of Christ to Peter in Matthew 16:18, "Thou art Peter, and on this rock I will build my church," etc. In addition to this Leo exerted great influence at the Council of Chalcedon in 451, and helped by personal pleas to avert or mitigate the horrors of barbarian attacks on Rome under Attila and Genseric. After Leo, Gregory the Great (590-604) did much to confirm and perpetuate the papal authority. In the hands of these two able men, one near the beginning and the other at the end of the epoch we have under review, we may regard the papacy as definitely and finally established. Such were the main influential events in this chaotic but formative era in European history.

2. The Decline of Preaching

In an age like that of the fifth and sixth centuries it would be vain to expect any particular sphere of human endeavor to manifest tokens of vigor which were lacking in the general life of the times. Everything had gone into a decline, and preaching could not be exempt. But we must beware of being caught in the toils of generalization and concluding that there was no preaching at all, or that it was wholly bad. Both East and West there was preaching, and there were some preachers of talent, character, and influence. Yet the general truth holds that it was an age of decay. Let us now take note of some of the general and local causes of this decline, and discuss some of the characteristics of the preaching.

We shall first notice the general causes which contributed to the decline of preaching in the fifth and sixth centuries, and then pay a little more particular attention to those which prevailed respectively in the East and in the West.

The general law of reaction is noticeable in the history of preaching, as it is in other histories. Preaching had reached the highest point of its ancient development in Chrysostom and Augustine. Rothe well remarks that it could go no higher than this without the coming in of a new spiritual life and power, and this is precisely what did not occur. The reaction was to be expected, and it came swiftly and sadly enough. This natural ebb-tide was concurrent with a rough sea of storm and turmoil in the world. The times were evil indeed. Barbarism threatened without and corruption sickened within the church as well as the state. The general corruption in morals affected balefully the lives of the clergy as well as the laity. Ambition, place-hunting, selfishness, greed, and even worse things were not unknown among those whose business it was to live as well as preach the gospel. Of course the faulty living of preachers is a too painful experience of every age of preaching, but when clerical unworthiness gains the upper hand the general effect is disastrous beyond measure. In a flourishing age this sore evil is a drawback, in a declining one it is an acceleration. It was so in these mournful times. While there were many godly and true preachers, it must be owned that not a few were only too willing to be both in the world and of it.

We should not fail also to take account of the growth of liturgy and forms of worship. While these preserved a prominent place for preaching in the services of the church their effect then, as too often since, was to make the spoken word of far less relative value than forms of worship. This tendency, while stronger in later times, was already powerful, and preaching was not vigorous and able enough to overcome the trammels of liturgy. More serious than this was the growth of the hierarchical spirit, the conception of the preacher as priest rather than prophet. An acute student of the history of preaching[1] has remarked: "We find this change, I think, passing over the spirit of preaching after the second or third century. We shall see it reaching its head in the Dark Ages. But perhaps the worst effect of all was that wrought on the preacher himself, changing him from a messenger of God into a petty mediator and dispenser of God's mercies and punishments! This led to the preaching of church discipline rather than Christian morals, of penance rather than repentance. The heart of the gospel was too often wrapped in the rough and insipid husks of externalism, and it was more than the simple sinner could do to get at the kernel." Along with this perversion of gospel preaching went another which also waited for its full development in the mediæval sermons. This was the worship of Mary and the veneration of the saints. These were beginning to be looked upon as intercessors with God, and their votaries sought their mediation to obtain divine grace and mercies. Already in the fourth century traces of this worship are seen, and the development goes on through the fifth and sixth, to the injury of a pure gospel preaching.

Besides these general causes, which were operative in East and West alike, there were some which if not wholly absent from either locality, were yet specially active in one or the other. In the East the reaction was apparently more pronounced than in the West. The fall from Chrysostom was very great. It was not a total collapse indeed, but still the fact remains that no preacher of world-wide fame has appeared in the Greek Church since his day. Account for it as we may, and tone down the statement as much as possible, there is no evading the essential truth of the remark. The reaction was sharp and intense—it has been a long ebb, and history waits for the flow. The Greek mind seemed to have done its best work in preaching when it flowered in John of Antioch, and it fell back exhausted from that achievement. Imitation followed genius. Spontaneity and freshness failed.

[1] Fleming James, *The Message and the Messengers,* p. 101.

The little men of a declining age usually try to live on the brains of the great men who have preceded them. But inexorable history writes it down that the brains of one generation are not sufficient brain-food for the next. Echoes are not living voices—only faint and fainter tributes to greatness, admired but departed. If the bad taste of the age reflected itself in the faults of even fourth century preaching, what shall we say of it as a factor in the decline of which we are treating? The exaggeration, the bombast, the inflated oratory which marred the best preaching of the Patristic Age are hideous faults in the worst. There was nothing yet to correct the taste of either hearer or preacher, and this must have contributed greatly to the decay of preaching. It is true that this is partly conjectural, for we have not so many specimens from which to judge; but what indications there are fortify the natural inference.

The fierce doctrinal controversies which distracted the Eastern Church, and troubled the Western, during the fifth century must come in as one of the prominent causes of the decline of preaching. The rise of great controversies in doctrine has often stimulated preaching. But the protracting of controversy into barren and fine-spun metaphysics, and the degeneration of manly strife for great truths into personal and partisan polemics, have always had a bad effect. Following the Reformation there was an era of dogmatic discussion which reacted unfavorably on preaching, and this was true in the Greek Church of the fifth and sixth centuries. The great Arian controversy of the fourth century stirred the preachers during that epoch to great exertions. Chrysostom, and before him the Cappadocians, had felt the stimulus of endangered truth. But the settlement of the Nicene creed in the Council of Constantinople in 381 had cleared the air after a half century of debate. In the disputes of the following centuries—marked by the Councils of Ephesus in 431, of Chalcedon in 451, and of the second Constantinople in 553—there was a protracted struggle over fine points of doctrine, and the display of much unseemly violence and partisan selfishness. All this had a most unwholesome effect both on Christian character in general and on that of the clergy; and thus in many ways these struggles tended to lower the tone and the effect of preaching. The Greek Church gained the orthodoxy in which she has complacently rested for a millenium and a half at the expense of the very life of her pulpit.

As already remarked the reaction from excellence was hardly so marked in the West as in the East. This was partly because there was not so much to react from. The oratorical excellence of Ambrose and Augustine is not so striking as that of the Cappadocians and Chrysostom. Ambrose is but an echo of Basil, and Augustine as an orator is as much below Chrysostom as Cicero is below Demosthenes—though not in the same ways. Then the followers of the great Latin preachers are not so much behind their models as is the case with the Greeks. Leo and Gregory of Rome are not so distinctly inferior as preachers to Augustine as Cyril of Alexandria and Theodoret are to Chrysostom. Yet notwithstanding this cautionary comparison we still must assign reaction as one cause of decline in the West as well as in the East. Augustine's mighty thinking finds no parallel in his immediate followers. Leo comes nearest, but he is a great way off. It is a long journey from Augustine to Bernard,[1] but that is how far we have to travel before we find another very eminent preacher who uses the Latin tongue, and that is on the eve of its displacement by the new languages of Europe.

The West felt more directly and powerfully than the East the pressure of Barbarian invasion. Alaric sacked Rome in 410, Attila threatened, but was defeated at Chalons in 451, Genseric and his Vandals pillaged the city in 455, and the pitiful remnants of empire were surrendered to Odoacer at Ravenna in 476. The fear of plunder, death and disgrace; the despair of preserving anything from the wreck of the social system; the general sense of helplessness and dread, were not favorable conditions for the cultivation of eloquence, secular or sacred. The weakness and fall of government also were depressing after the patronage of former years. This state of things was somewhat paralleled by that in France after the age of Louis XIV.—an era of splendid pulpit eloquence and court patronage, followed by a long decline.

[1] Died 1153.

Leo I. and Gregory I. are the founders of the papacy. Either one may be considered the first pope, though it rather lies upon Gregory to be so regarded. On the ruins of secular empire came the papacy. The story belongs to general church history, but the thing for us here to notice is that though both Leo and Gregory were preachers of considerable merit, the growth of papal government was not favorable to preaching. Already in Ambrose the governing instinct of the Latin mind had encroached upon pulpit eloquence. And Leo's cares of government, his efforts to aggrandize the Roman see, his bold claim to preeminence based on the primacy of Peter, his successful assertion of doctrinal leadership at Chalcedon, and his services in pleading with Attila and Genseric on behalf of Rome, while they showed him the great leader and prelate, were certainly not distinctive marks of the preacher. So in general the growth of the hierarchy and the strengthening of prelacy were not favorable to the cultivation of preaching. The rise of the mendicant orders of preachers in the thirteenth century, and the great preaching of the reformers in the sixteenth, were not prelatical products.

Along with this we must emphasize what has already been mentioned among the general causes—the larger place given to church discipline, penances, and the like. Ecclesiastical duties and almsgiving as a means of grace were beginning to receive more homiletical attention than grace itself. This was markedly true in the West. Under all these circumstances it is no wonder that preaching declined. The wonder is that it survived, and that amid such untoward influences there were found both East and West some preachers of ability who still held forth the word of life.

A number of the most striking characteristics of preaching in this age have been already indicated in the discussion of the causes which led to its decline. These need not be repeated here, but some additional matters will claim our notice. As with the causes of decline some of these characteristics are general, and some are more notable in the East or in the West.

The sermon retains its character as an expository discourse. It varies still from the more extended address to the briefer homily. In form and content it remains much what the fourth century developed. Only the decline of power is apparent, as has been shown in the preceding discussion. The allegorical interpretation—except in Theodoret and a few others of the Antiochian school—has the field. The enforcing of churchly duties is a large element in the preaching. The growth of liturgical forms, while depressing to preaching, has yet given to it a recognized and permanent place in the services of the church. It has become what a modern German writer on Homiletics defines it even now to be: "Worship in discourse, and discourse in worship."[1]

Besides what has been already pointed out, we should observe that in the East the speculative quality of thought is more prominent, and the rhetorical art and effort more apparent, than in the West. Among the Latins there is less of speculation and more of the practical in doctrinal discussion. Strong emphasis is placed on the church and its life and duties, its liturgy and demands. Less attention is paid to oratorical finery, and the sermons are usually briefer than in the East, some so brief as to suggest that they were only expository remarks, or additional exhortations made by the bishop after the longer discourse of a presbyter.

3. The Greek Preachers

Among the Greeks there were many preachers, and a few who for various reasons were men of note and influence. Of these we shall select for brief mention five less known and two of greater prominence and fame.

A very interesting character is Synesius (d. c. 420),[2] bishop of Ptolemais in Cyrene, north Africa. He was of good family and well educated. At one time he was among the pupils of the famous woman philosopher, Hypatia, at Alexandria. He had read much and traveled extensively, and was an easy-going man of the world, a Neo-Platonist in philosophy. In some way he was brought under Christian influences—of a sort—and seems

[1] "Ein Cultus-Act der Rede, das ist das bestimmende Moment; und ein Rede-Act im Cultus, das ist der abhängige." Th. Harnack, *Geschichte und Theorie der Predigt*, S. 12.

[2] Möller in Herzog; Schaff's *History*, Vol. III., p. 604 f. There is a clever presentment of Synesius in Kingsley's *Hypatia*.

to have had, along with much philosophy, some real Christian views and principles. He owned an estate in the country near Ptolemais, and was fond of country life —gardening, hunting, and the like. He had much influence and was much respected by his neighbors, and the times being troublous he was urged—though married and yet unbaptized—to become bishop of Ptolemais. Synesius felt some honorable scruples, and moreover insisted upon being allowed to retain his wife and his dogs if he should accept the office! Nevertheless he was persuaded by Theophilus of Alexandria and others to accept the bishopric, and was baptized and ordained by the archbishop himself. Though thus conscientiously reluctant to enter the office he made a faithful bishop in kindly care of his flock. Epistles, treatises and hymns of his remain, but only two homilies, and they of small moment. He had the oratorical gift and training, and though we have no fair samples of his preaching to judge by, we may infer that he was a speaker of more than ordinary force.

Among the notable theologians and scholars of this age a high place is held by Theodore (d. 428)[1], bishop of Mopsuestia in Cilicia, the friend of John Chrysostom, the pupil of Diodorus. He was probably born at Antioch, where he was trained in rhetoric by Libanius, and designed for the law. But he was persuaded by his friend John to retire with himself from the world and study the Bible under Diodorus. A bright vision of love crossed his path and he was about to go back to the world, when John's eloquent pleadings again prevailed and Theodore finally devoted himself to the religious life. Soon he was made a presbyter, and in 394 bishop of Mopsuestia. In this same year he preached on some occasion in Constantinople a sermon which received warm commendation from the emperor Theodosius. Yet it is as theologian and commentator that Theodore is best known. Of his voluminous writings not many remain, and some of these chiefly in Latin translations. Among the fragments Paniel notes only a few, and those unimportant, of a homiletical character. His style was not attractive—"neither brilliant nor very clear," according to Photius—and he wearies by too much repetition. Yet he enjoyed

[1] Möller in Herzog-Plitt, Bd. 15, S. 394; Paniel, S. 582.

considerable reputation as a preacher, and it is to his lasting credit that he sought to present the historical and grammatical meaning of Scripture rather than the allegorical.

Homiletic interest, or rather curiosity, is awakened toward Nestorius,[1] the famous heretic who was condemned at Ephesus in 431. The fame of his eloquence had induced the emperor Theodosius II. in 428 to make him archbishop of Constantinople. For a while he enjoyed great popularity as a preacher, but his zeal against heretics made enemies for him; and his opposition to giving the title "Mother of God" to Mary and his error as to the Person of Christ were used against him, and he was deposed and banished. The Council of Ephesus in 431, under the influence of Cyril of Alexandria, made him drink the bitter cup of persecution for heresy which he had himself forced on others. Some fragments and reports of his discourses remain, but as these come from his opponents they cannot be regarded as fair specimens of his work. Rothe, however, conjectures that he must have been a preacher of more than usual abilities.

We have better means of judging concerning Proclus, who was made archbishop of Constantinople in 434. In his young manhood he had served Chrysostom as secretary, and was a careful student of rhetoric. So he had a good chance to learn oratory. He was a presbyter at Constantinople at the time of the Nestorian controversy, and is said to have been the first to attack in a sermon Nestorius' objection to calling Mary the "Mother of God." He enjoyed great popularity as a preacher. Twenty-three of his sermons remain, three on Mary, the rest delivered on feast days and Apostles' days. They are mainly theological and polemical, with little of practical application. He is often declamatory, dealing much in exclamation, antithesis, and other devices for rhetorical effect. The sermons show considerable vigor of expression and liveliness of imagination; they are usually without text, are of unequal length, and commonly have an introduction, and at the conclusion a doxology, after the manner of Chrysostom. Of one of those on Mary Rothe says: "The sixth homily consists almost entirely

[1] Rothe, S. 127 f.

of long dialogues between Mary, Joseph and the angel Gabriel, and Christ himself; and of a very pathetic monologue by Satan!"

There was, in this age, a Basil (d. c. 448), who was bishop of Seleucia in Isauria, from whom there remain forty-three sermons. Little is known of his life. He was a warm, even enthusiastic, partisan of the claims of the Virgin Mary as these were then understood, but he seems to have taken rather a wavering position in the Eutychian controversy. As a preacher he is estimated higher than Proclus. He is hot in polemics against heretics and Jews, given to much empty declamation, and is a far-off imitator of Chrysostom. Yet he has some merits —handles his text historically and fairly well, and makes some practical application.

Two other preachers of this time are of far greater importance than those we have just noticed, both as church leaders and as speakers—one representing the Alexandrian, the other the Antiochian school.

Cyril[1] of Alexandria (d. 444) was nephew of the infamous Theophilus, the enemy of Chrysostom. He succeeded his evil uncle as patriarch of Alexandria about the year 412, and was an apt pupil of his predecessor in selfishness, intrigue, and even violence. Cyril was a member of the synod which condemned Chrysostom, and afterwards when in a later synod the unrighteous sentence against the famous preacher was revoked and tardy justice done his memory long after his death, Cyril voted against the revocation, and compared Chrysostom to Judas! Yet, after all this, it must be said that under pressure of church authority he did admit Chrysostom's name among those of the saints and martyrs on the memorial tablets of the Alexandrian church. As an instance of his violence it is said that soon after taking office as archbishop he closed the churches and seized the church property of the Novatians as being heretics. In 415 the Jews in Alexandria, because of his injustice toward them, raised a riot, and Cyril authorized an armed onslaught on their synagogues. Some were killed, many driven away and their property plundered. This high-

[1] Lentz, I., S. III.; Schaff, Vol. III., p. 942 ff; Rothe, S. 122; Gibbon, Chap. XLVII.; Kingsley's *Hypatia.*

handed assumption of authority brought him into conflict with the imperial governor Orestes. Some writers hold him responsible for the brutal and atrocious murder of Hypatia, the beautiful and accomplished teacher of pagan philosophy in Alexandria. The mob that murdered her was led by Peter the reader, a violent adherent of Cyril, whose sympathies were probably in favor of the proceeding. But there does not seem to be enough evidence to prove that he directly ordered or instigated it. Before, at and after the Council of Ephesus (431) Cyril was the able, unscrupulous and violent opponent of Nestorius and his teachings. He stuck at no measures of bribery and violence to carry his point. Schaff says that "he exhibits to us a man making theology and orthodoxy the instruments of his passions," and quotes Milman as saying, "Who would not meet the judgment of the divine Redeemer loaded with the errors of Nestorius rather than the barbarities of Cyril?" The Catholics find it hard to apologize for canonizing him, and the fine historical romance of Kingsley has given him an evil name in literature.

As a theologian and preacher Cyril is entitled to more consideration than his character would warrant, for he was an able exponent of the Alexandrian school. He posed as the friend of hidden wisdom, and of course pushes very far the allegorical interpretation of Scripture. It was customary for the archbishop of Alexandria to write and send forth at certain seasons an address or circular letter to the churches of his diocese. A number of these appear among the works of Cyril as homilies. Of the twenty-nine remaining, seventeen are said to be concerned with the title of Mary—"Mother of God"—then so hotly disputed. Besides these there remain thirteen other discourses which deal much with that doctrinal strife. The most noted was delivered in the Church of Mary at Ephesus before the famous council of the year 431, after that body had solemnly decreed that the disputed title should be given to the Mother of Jesus. The sermon was deposited among the acts of the council. There is another sermon which treats of the Lord's Supper as a "mystical meal," in which "Christ acts as host." Another treats of the future state of the wicked, and describes with elaborate detail the sufferings of hell. It has many vigorous and striking passages, but it is overdone, and the effect is spoiled by exaggeration. The speaker seemed to take pleasure in picturing the awful fate of the lost. Cyril does not lack fancy and richness of imagery. Some of his sermons show a good deal of logical skill as well as rhetorical effectiveness. But after all Rothe has this to say: "The passionate, violent, angry character of the man impresses itself also on his sermons. His polemic is violent and bitter, and full of passionate personal attacks upon his opponents. Moreover there passes through his addresses a rather consuming than warming glow of feeling and fancy, which, better guided, might have brought forth extraordinary effects." How true it is that the evil traits of a man's character may hinder and even ruin his influence, although he be gifted with unusual talents!

We find a very different sort of man from Cyril in his contemporary and sometimes opponent, Theodoret (d. 457),[1] bishop of Cyrus in Syria. This distinguished historian and exegete was born at Antioch about the year 390. He, like many another eminent divine, was blessed with an especially good Christian mother, who took pains with his education. He was trained in a monastery, and received the impress though not the personal instructions of the eminent teacher Diodorus, who had taught Chrysostom and Theodore of Mopsuestia. This last scholar and prelate had also great, and possibly personal, influence over Theodoret, in whose work is seen the safer historical and grammatical interpretation of Scripture pursued by the Antiochene scholars as compared with those of Alexandria. After 420 Theodoret appears as bishop of Cyrus, a town of no great importance in Syria. He was opposed to Cyril in his violent dealings with Nestorius, though he did not go as far as Nestorius toward teaching the theory of the dual personality in our Lord. He was moderate. Under Cyril's influence he was condemned at Ephesus in 431; and the so-called "Robber Synod" in 449 went so far as actually to depose him from

[1] Schaff, Vol. III., p. 881 f; Rothe, S. 129 ff; Lentz, I., S. 116 ff; Möller in Herzog, Bd. 15, S. 401 ff.

his bishopric. But the Council of Chalcedon in 451 acquitted and restored him on condition of his accepting the condemnation of Nestorius and agreeing to the title "Mother of God" as applied to Mary. These concessions he could make without much compromise, as he was not in full accord with Nestorius in doctrine, though personally opposed to his condemnation, and by no means an admirer of Cyril. As bishop Theodoret led an exemplary life, in fact he had been pious and pure from his childhood, and had served in some of the minor offices of the church with fidelity and success. Even his enemies had to acknowledge the goodness of the man, especially his benevolence and charity. "He owned nothing of value save his books, applying the revenues of his diocese to the public good."

He is especially valuable to posterity as a church historian, continuing the narrative of Eusebius down to the year 429. But as an exegete and preacher he has received high praise from scholars who have studied his works. As a preacher he was active and laborious, visiting other towns than his own and working for the conversion of sinners and heretics. He had no sweeping eloquence, but must have been a clear, keen reasoner. His style is simple and straightforward and not overloaded with ornament. There remain from him an interesting series of ten sermons delivered ten days apart at Antioch before he was made bishop of Cyrus. They treat of Divine Providence. He proves the providence of God from natural religion, from the guidance of nature and of men, from evidences of design (using in an elaborate way the human hand as an illustration), and from the arrangements of society. The last sermon sets forth the incarnation and saving work of Christ as the highest and crowning token of God's providence. Altogether Theodoret was a preacher of considerable ability and importance. Indeed Rothe says of him that "he is the only classical preacher that the Greek church has after Chrysostom." We may therefore close our survey of Eastern preaching in this epoch with him. The Greek preachers of the sixth century are hardly worth study. The age of Justinian, with its great generals and lawyers, produced no great preacher.

In the West as in the East we find in this period a

number of men whose characters and deeds are of considerable interest and importance in Church History, but when we look for any who are exceptionally influential or distinguished as preachers we shall look in vain. Judging from the specimens that have come down to us we can only rate the Latin preaching of the fifth and sixth centuries as mediocre, but it may well be that much of the best work has left no literary remains of itself. Certainly there was no utter dearth of preaching, and we may mention a few of the better known or more important preachers in each century as representatives of their less known brethren. Of the men of the fifth century four only will, for different reasons, and as representatives of different tendencies, receive notice.

Among the great missionary preachers of all time, and adorning this obscure age, was the apostle and saint of Ireland, Patricius, better known to us as St. Patrick.[1] The legends and myths which, however piously meant, have distorted and marred his real image must not blind us to the fact that he was a historic person, and that he did a great and noble work, whose influence and blessing extended far beyond his own age and people. There remain no sermons from him, but his "Confessions" are regarded as genuine, and there are also some letters which may be so accepted. From these we learn the main facts of his life and labors. The story is told with great humility, but it reveals in its very simplicity the noble character of the man, and gives some inkling of the power and success of his preaching. He was born in Scotland, the son of a priest or deacon, at Bonaven, now known as Kilpatrick, probably about the year 372. The barbarous Scots from Ireland (then their main habitation) often made forays into Britain, and in one of these they captured the youth and carried him away into slavery. After a time he managed to escape and return to his native land. But the godless condition of the heathen among whom he had lived as a slave preyed on his mind, and he resolved to go back and preach to them the gospel of

[1] C. Schoell in Herzog, Bd. II., S. 292 ff; F. F. Walrond, *Christian Missions before the Reformation,* p. 7 ff., a brief, popular, but well-considered and interesting account. The sources and literature are well given in the article by Schoell.

Christ. No words can tell the story as well as his own:[1] "Against my wishes I was forced to offend my relations and many of those who wished me well. It was not in my own power, but it was God who conquered in me and withstood them all; so that I went to the people of Ireland to preach the gospel, and suffered many insults from unbelievers, and many persecutions, even unto bonds, giving up my liberty that I might be made a blessing to others. And if I am found worthy I am willing to give up my life with joy for his name's sake." He would sometimes beat a drum to call the people together in the open air, and then would preach to the crowd. He gathered pupils about him, and they would travel over the country reading and expounding the Gospels. His visits were usually brief, but sometimes he would remain longer in one place; and there is an interesting account of his work at the capital, Tara, made famous in literature by Moore's song, "The harp that once through Tara's halls." Here he gained many converts, as well as in other places. Glad indeed should we be if we had any specimens of his sermons to study, but if we had they would probably be very inadequate tokens of his real power in preaching. For we should not have had them (nor probably have been able to understand them if we had!) in the native language in which they were spoken; but only in Latin reports of them made by himself or his scholars. So perhaps we need not much regret the lack. The secret of his power is well expressed in Walrond's words:[2] "In all that he did, and in every moment of every day, he relied upon the constant guidance and support of that God whose word he was engaged in publishing." After years of laborious and successful toil he seems in the evening of his life to have rested somewhat, and to have passed away in peace.

We come into a very different atmosphere when we leave this free, live, devoted missionary of the far West, and drop back among the prelatical and more distinctly Latin preachers of decadent Italy. Of these three may be mentioned as representative, but only one of them is worthy of much consideration.[3]

[1] Quoted from Walrond, *op. cit.*, p. 16. [2] *Op. cit.*, pp. 23, 24.

[3] Information chiefly derived from the works of Schaff, Lentz, Rothe, etc.

Peter (d. 451) was the name of the leading bishop of Ravenna during this falling epoch when the feeble Roman imperial court had removed from the Eternal City to that fastness. His appointment at the seat of government indicates that he was a man of some influence. He filled the office for eighteen years, from 433 till his death. In later times he was surnamed Chrysologus—" golden speech "—probably from the flowing style of his writings rather than from their eloquence. It is a note of declining taste when so tame a writer receives such an appellation. There remain one hundred and seventy-six short sermons attributed to him. They are not strong or sublime, and explain the Scriptures after the allegorical method, but in a simple way and with evident desire to benefit his hearers. He has much to say of alms, fasting, and the other accepted churchly virtues.

From Maximus (d. 465), bishop of Turin, about the middle of the fifth century, there are extant seventy-three brief homilies. He is said to have had a fine faculty for impromptu address, and Rothe keenly remarks that there is sufficient evidence of unpremeditated speech in these sermons! They are full of allegorical interpretation, and they also contain numerous anecdotes of the saints and like material, giving notice of the rise of that style of sermon. They are not of much intrinsic interest or value, but as samples from the times they are instructive. One curious homily discusses an eclipse of the moon, and roundly scolds the people for keeping up the old heathen custom of making a loud outcry, as if that would have any effect in causing the shadow to pass, as if God needed any such help as this in removing the trouble!

The most important Latin preacher of the fifth century after Augustine is Leo (d. 461), the famous bishop of Rome, who is sometimes considered the first pope in the proper sense. He was probably born in Rome, though neither the time nor the place of his birth is certainly known. He had filled some of the minor offices of the church in Rome when in 440, during his absence, he was unanimously and cordially elected bishop. He exercised this office in a faithful and distinguished manner during his twenty-one remaining years of life, and is not without reason called " the Great." He held a very exalted opinion of the supremacy of the Roman see, claiming the right of Rome to pass on all matters of doctrine and practice for the whole church. Leo was a strong theologian and took part with intelligence and success in the doctrinal controversies of his age. In 449 he wrote to Flavian, bishop of Constantinople, a letter against the error of Eutyches as to the fusion of the two natures in our Lord's person. This letter was the basis of the decree of the Council of Chalcedon in 451 which defined the two natures in the one person of Christ. This gave Leo great doctrinal authority through Christendom. He also took an active interest in secular affairs. He is said to have induced Attila the Hun (in 452) to spare Rome, and also to have moderated somewhat the destructive Vandals under Genseric, when they sacked and pillaged the city in 455. Thus Leo was a many-sided and very able man. His life was without reproach, and he gave great and conscientious care to his flock.

As a preacher he has some especial claims to attention. He is the first of the Roman bishops from whom we have sermons remaining. Of these ninety-six are with reasonable probability reckoned genuine.[1] He was a diligent preacher, believing earnestly that this was an indispensable part of his duty as a bishop. The sermons are short—as was then customary in the Latin churches. As we have them it is estimated that even the longest would only have occupied twenty minutes in delivery, many of them only half that time. But the reports may be shorter than the actual sermons were. They are occupied largely with festivals, fasts, saints' days, and other occasions. Only a few are expository at all, nor do they much discuss the great doctrines. They urge the churchly virtues of fasts, alms, and penance, and teach that these are meritorious works. In style they are rather ambitious and brilliant, abounding in antitheses and pregnant sayings. Leo is a warning against making more of style than of matter; for it is a sharp and not wholly unjust criticism of Lentz that if the order of the words be changed, or other words be used to express the thought, the merit would be gone.

While not particularly profound in thought or specially

[1] Migne, *Pat. Lat.*, tom. 54, col. 141; translations in *Nicene and Post-Nicene Fathers,* Vol. XIII.

edifying in tone the sermons contain a good deal that is worthy of note. The sixty-first sermon[1]—eighth on the Passion—discusses the arrest of Jesus, the sinful compliance of Pilate, the greater guilt of the Jews, the meaning of Christ's bearing his own cross and of Simon's sharing it, and how we should see the deeper meaning of the crucifixion as taught by our Lord's own words. Then in a long apostrophe he speaks of the attractive power of the cross, and concludes as follows: "Let us then, dearly beloved, confess what the blessed teacher of the nations, the Apostle Paul, confessed, saying, 'Faithful is the saying, and worthy of all acceptation, that Christ Jesus came into the world to save sinners.' For God's mercy towards us is the more wonderful that Christ died not for the righteous nor for the holy, but for the unrighteous and wicked; and though the nature of the Godhead could not sustain the sting of death, yet at his birth he took from us that which he might offer for us. For of old he threatened our death with the power of his death, saying by the mouth of Hosea, the prophet, 'O death, I will be thy death, and I will be thy destruction, O hell.' For by dying he underwent the laws of hell, but by rising again he broke them, and so destroyed the continuity of death as to make it temporal instead of eternal. . . . And so, dearly beloved, let that come to pass of which St. Paul speaks, 'that they that live should henceforth not live to themselves but to him who died for all and rose again.' And because the old things have passed away and all things are become new, let none remain in his old carnal life, but let us all be renewed by daily progress and growth in piety. For however much a man be justified, yet so long as he remains in this life he can always be more approved and better. And he that is not advancing is going back, and he that is gaining nothing is losing something. Let us run then, with the steps of faith, by the works of mercy, in the love of righteousness, that keeping the day of our redemption spiritually, 'not in the old leaven of malice and wickedness, but in the unleavened bread of sincerity and truth,' we may deserve to be partakers of Christ's resurrection, who with the Father and the Holy Ghost liveth and reigneth forever and ever. Amen."

[1] *Nic. and P.-Nic. Fath.*, Vol. XII., pp. 171 ff.

In the sixth century only three names need detain us, but these are for different reasons well worthy of mention. Fulgentius (d. 533) was bishop of a town called Ruspe in north Africa. He was born about the year 468 of a senatorial family in that region. He had in youth good educational advantages, and he improved them. He was blessed with a good Christian mother. An indication of her influence and of his dispostion is found in the fact that on being appointed to some government position, before entering the ministry, he found the exactions for taxes so harsh and distasteful that he gave up the office. He leaned toward the monastic life, but events called him to activity and to suffering. The Arian king of the Vandals persecuted the orthodox Christians, and Fulgentius was among those who suffered. Against his will he was made bishop of Ruspe, and soon afterwards was banished, along with other orthodox bishops, to the island of Sardinia. Towards the end of his life he was, under some change of sentiment, recalled to his bishopric. He was an able and clear-headed man, well versed in the Scriptures, in the questions of the day, in the older Christian writers, and especially in the works of Augustine, whom he greatly admired and imitated. Ten sermons among those attributed to him are considered to be probably genuine.[1] Some resemble Augustine in style, but the most of them are imitations of Leo. Thus they possess no particular originality or power.

Cæsarius (d. 542), for forty years bishop of Arles, in Gaul, was born near Chalons, about the year 470. He was at an early age a monk in the cloister at Lerins, then deacon, then presbyter, then abbot, and finally in 501 was made bishop of Arles. He was a man of great piety and force of character, and is one of the most important men of his time. He was truly evangelical in spirit and devoted in labors, and was a leader in the Gallican church in his day. He had no easy life. In various ways he was annoyed and even persecuted, on charges of disloyalty and the like, by first one and then another of the barbaric kings—Frank, Burgundian, and Goth. But amid all his trials he was a faithful and diligent bishop, and believed much in preaching. He also gave much and fruitful at-

[1] Migne, *Pat. Lat.*, tom. 65, col. 719.

tention to singing as a part of worship. A number of sermons ascribed to him remain, but not all are certainly genuine.[1] He was earnest in urging faith and a true conception of the work of Christ. In fact he was Augustinian in his theology, and his utterances against the merits of mere churchly works are remarkable in that age. He was accustomed to use many illustrations from life in his preaching, trying to reach the common people and earnestly opposing all sorts of superstitions. His sermons, or those ascribed to him, were much quoted and used throughout the mediæval period. In this respect he almost takes place beside Augustine and Gregory the Great, the three being inexhaustible sources for later plagiarism.

The first stage of this period in the history of preaching fitly closes with Gregory,[2] called the Great, who was bishop of Rome, or, as we may now say, pope, from 590 to 604. He was born at Rome about the year 540 of an ancient and wealthy family of senatorial rank. During the temporary supremacy of the Eastern Empire over Italy in consequence of the decline of the Gothic kingdoms and the victories of Belisarius and Narses, the famous generals of Justinian, Gregory was appointed to a high civil position in Rome. He discharged the duties of his office with fidelity and success; but he had a longing for the monastic life, which found expression for a time in his endowing several monasteries. After his father's death he turned his own house into a cloister, of which he became himself a member, and practiced the strictest asceticism. In 579 he was appointed by Pelagius II., bishop of Rome, a legate or ambassador to the court of Constantinople—a position which he filled with ability, as he was skilled in diplomacy and executive management. After several years he returned and was made abbot of his convent. It was about this time that he is said to have noticed the fair and handsome English prisoners in the slave market, who called forth his admiration and sympathy, and awakened in him a desire for the conversion of that far-off heathen people. In 590 he was elected

[1] Migne, *Pat. Lat.*, tom. 67, col 1041.

[2] Mostly the same authorities as before; works in Migne, and translations in *Nicene and Post-Nicene Fathers*, Vol. XII.

bishop of Rome. While he did not in the matter of the title push the papal claims as far as Leo had done, he held to all the substantial things that his great predecessor had gained, and with much apparent personal humility asserted the supremacy of the Roman see. Schaff well says of him:[1] "He combined great executive ability with untiring industry, and amid all his official cares he never forgot the claims of personal piety. In genius he was surpassed by Leo I., Gregory VII., Innocent III., but as a man and a Christian he ranks with the purest and most useful of the popes." He was very active in all departments of his work, extending his jurisdiction in all the West. He welcomed Spain back from the Arian heresy, the result of Vandal and Gothic influences; he sent the monk Augustine to England to labor for the conversion of the Anglo-Saxons, and performed many other acts of importance as pope. He reformed the liturgy and the music of the Roman church, and gave a start or a fresh impulse to many elements of ecclesiastical life.

Among Gregory's works is a celebrated treatise on the pastoral (episcopal) office called *Liber Regulae Pastoralis*, or, more briefly, "Pastoral Rule." It was written in the first year of his pontificate, and addressed to Leander of Seville. It owes something to the similar work of Gregory Nazianzen, to which he refers in the prologue to part third, but apparently nothing to Chrysostom's treatise on the Priesthood.[2] The work treats of the responsibilities of the pastoral office, of the character of those who should be pastors, of the kind of teaching appropriate to different classes in the flock, and other such matters. It contains much sound advice suitable for all times, together with much that is trivial and weak. There is very little that bears specifically upon preaching, and nothing in the way of homiletical theory or rules; but the general teaching of the book and a few hints here and there show both just ideas and a high regard for the preaching part of the pastor's office. The book enjoyed a great repute in its own and subsequent times, and had the distinction of being translated into Anglo-Saxon by Alfred the Great,

[1] *Ch. Hist.*, Vol. IV., p. 212.

[2] Barmby's *Prolegomena* to the *Pastoral Rule, Nic. and Post-Nic. Fathers*, Vol. XII.

and of being especially recommended by enactments of Charlemagne.

As a preacher Gregory was, like Leo, very diligent. He conscientiously held it to be one of his prime duties to preach and to instruct his people. Sixty-two of his homilies remain, twenty-two on Ezekiel, and forty on the Gospels, based on the passages appointed for the day. Some of the sermons were committed to writing by himself, and others were taken down by reporters and revised by himself. Usually they are brief, but several are of considerable length. As sermons they cannot claim very high rank. The style is often barbarous and inelegant, the arrangement of no special worth, the thought not rich nor deep, and the Scripture interpretation full of the allegorical method and often puerile. The homilies consist usually of short paraphrases of the text, and of moral application of it. Two things deserve especial mention: (1) He puts, as was natural from his monastic bent and training, great emphasis upon the contemplative element of the religious life; and (2) he recognizes and assumes, both by precept and example, the important place of preaching in Christian worship.

The character, the work, the time of Gregory, all unite to make him the Pharos of the transition betwen ancient and mediæval church history. He belongs to both epochs.[1] As Christlieb well says: "There meet in him the decline and the new strengthening (though not the new life) of preaching. On the one side his place is here; on the other he is the beginning point of the Middle Ages."

CHAPTER IV

The Low Estate of Preaching in the Seventh and Eighth Centuries

As the note of the fifth and sixth centuries is decline, so that of the seventh and eighth is chaos. It was a strange, wild time, with everything in confusion. The old East was in its dotage and the new West in its childhood. The great peoples and governments of mediæval and modern Europe were making their crude beginnings.

[1] See Christlieb, in Herzog, Bd. 18, S. 486, 487.

Christianity in all its phases and institutions reflected the character of the times, but even in its corruptions and perversions it was at once the best conservator of the ancient good and the surest guarantee for the future.

1. A Glance at the Times

In order that we may the better place ourselves for studying the preaching and preachers of the period, some of the most important events and movements in both political and religious history should be rapidly recalled.

This epoch witnessed the rise and wonderful early spread of Mohammedanism. The flight of Mohammed occurred in 622, his death ten years later, and in just a century after that, in 732, Charles Martel defeated the Saracens on the plain between Tours and Poitiers. In these hundred years many of the fairest provinces of the Eastern empire had been forever wrung from Greek control, Constantinople itself seriously threatened, Egypt and north Africa overrun and firmly held, Spain subjected, and all western Europe menaced by the Saracen invasion.

In the Byzantine empire some glory was shed on decay by the brilliant but futile victories of the emperor Heraclius, but state and church were torn and weakened by the long and weary strife over the worship of images and by the controversy whether in the Person of Christ there is one will or two.

In the seething, turbulent West new nations, peoples and languages are forming from chaotic elements. Italy witnesses the downfall of the exarchate of Ravenna and with it the final departure of even the most shadowy political connection with the East; likewise the rise of the Lombard kingdom, the nucleus of the Papal States, and the foretokening of a new Empire soon to be established under the Franco-German kings. Germany is as yet missionary ground where a few toilers are sowing seeds of Christian civilization. France, long feeble under her sluggish Merovingian kings, is beginning to assume some semblance of unity and a degree of real power under the vigorous guidance of the mayors of the palace, who at last take the name as well as the substance of royalty and found the illustrious Carolingian dynasty. In England the struggle between Saxon and Kelt progresses, but the consolidation of the Anglo-Saxon kingdom is still in the future. Latin is still the accepted language in all the West for literary, legal and religious purposes, but the Babel of dialects shows some signs of yielding an outcome in later times of vernacular speech and letters. Especially in England is the work of Cædmon and Bede worthy of remembrance in laying foundations for Anglo-Saxon literature.

In the social order, or rather disorder, some forces are to be reckoned with. The kings and lords constitute the ruling class, where military success and personal prowess are the main ideals. There seems to have been as yet no mercantile and burgher class to speak of, and yet these must have existed in some forms, though weak and oppressed. The lower, or governed, class consisted chiefly of two elements: the barbarian followers of the chiefs and kings, rude, illiterate, rapacious; and the downtrodden and despoiled native peoples. In such conditions trade and agriculture could only exist as necessary to life, they could not flourish as elements of civilization. Between the governing and the governed classes there was the clergy, recruiting its ranks from both the others and thus forming a sort of cement—alas! often sadly untempered mortar—for the social fabric. Morals were in a deplorable state, and yet not utterly rotten and hopeless. Roman law lay at the basis of civic life, and yet there was much lawlessness and rapine and some superposition of barbarian usages and laws. The ordeal and torture were common, and the man who could not defend himself had not much chance for "life, liberty and the pursuit of happiness." At the bottom was the old social life with both its good customs and its decay and ruin; then there was the alluvial deposit of fresh barbarian soil with its rank weeds of violence and rapacity, and yet with its choice flowers of courage, honor and respect for woman; and above all was the influence of Christianity which, despite its own corruptions, served to mitigate the ills of the other two elements, and held in germ the hopeful formative forces of the better social order that was to come. The Papacy, now finally independent of the East, establishes its political power in Italy, and by its shrewd alliance with the Frankish kings strengthens itself for its growth and dominance in all the West throughout the Middle Ages.

2. General Survey of Preaching in This Time

Preaching, as usual, shared and to some extent reflected the character of the age. There were materials and qualities of it common to both sections of the church and world, but at the risk of some repetition it will be better to consider the East and West separately. All the old differences—ethnic, geographical, political, linguistic, doctrinal—remained and were emphasized by the new conditions, while still others were added. The preaching of the East has dropped into its conservative old age, and its general character shows little change for centuries; while that of the West, though in a sad decay, has in it latent forces destined to wonderful and varied development in the course of time.

In the Greek Church of this time there was no growth, but there was some ferment. In the seventh century the *monothelete* heresy—the doctrine that the person Christ had only one will though two natures—racked the church as had done the more famous controversies of the earlier times; and in the eighth the zeal of the iconoclastic—image-breaking—emperors and their followers tore church and empire in twain over the question of the reverence to be paid to pictures and relics.

Besides these controversies, which, of course, influenced the clergy and preaching of the times, other conditions affected for evil the sermons addressed to the people. Degeneracy and corruption infected both people and priesthood. Fanaticism was flourishing, superstition abounded. Angels and saints, images and relics received veneration which amounted to worship, while the special emphasis which had long been given to the worship of the Virgin Mother of Jesus becomes excessive. To her are transferred many of the attributes of her divine Son, and some of the events associated with his incarnation and birth are made to do service also in behalf of his mother. Thus her miraculous birth, her presentation in the temple, the doings of her parents are treated as historical and important. Christ is looked upon as the Judge and his glorified mother is appealed to as intercessor and mediator between men and his wrath. Festivals and saints' days abound, many of the sermons that have come down to us are occupied with these, and were doubtless regarded as masterpieces and so preserved. Piety had fallen still further—if that were possible—into formalism, and Christian virtue into regard for churchly observances and requirements. What sort of preaching was to be expected under these conditions?

Theological thinking has almost gone. John of Damascus stands out in solitary eminence among the theologians of the age. He has no equal among his contemporaries or successors, and but few that may be compared to him at all. The exposition of Scripture is wretched. Allegory is gone mad. The clergy are ignorant as well as corrupt, the sermons show little thought and less learning. Harangues on the saints, the images, the festivals, and chiefest of all on the Virgin, take the place of the exposition of the word of God. Few of the sermons have texts, and the quotation and application of Scripture are often forced. Rothe[1] well sums up the situation thus: "The monkish spirit prevails. The dogmatic addresses almost wholly lack the didactic element. All moved about the idea of the miraculous and the incomprehensible, and the whole aim of the preacher seemed to be to awaken astonishment and admiration. To this end they were not ashamed to get material from the New Testament Apocrypha." As was to be expected, the style—bombastic, wordy, overstrained—fully corresponds to the content of these decadent homilies, and we look almost in vain for specimens of real oratorical power.

When we turn to the West we find a different and in some respects more hopeful state of affairs. It is sadly true that preaching is much neglected—perhaps even more than in the East—and the quality and contents of the preaching are no whit better than among the Greeks of the same period. But there are both circumstances and elements of preaching which are suggestive of better days to come, even though as yet the coming is far away. There can be no question that in all its history preaching was at its lowest stage during this period. But though languishing it was not dead, though very inferior in quality it was not wholly bad.

The chaotic state of European society during the sev-

[1] *Gesch. d. Pred.*, S. 158.

enth and eighth centuries was not favorable to preaching. Rude barbarian kings and lords ruled over church as well as state. The people were oppressed, many of them fearfully ignorant and corrupt. The clergy were often grossly ignorant, and sometimes immoral. Yet these very things appealed to devout churchmen and to enlightened statesmen as well, and earnest efforts were made to improve the state of affairs. About the year 762 Chrodegang, Archbishop of Metz, in his *Regula Canonicorum* (c. 44) enjoins that there must be preaching, presumably in all the churches of his diocese, twice a month at least; and better yet on every fast day and Lord's day; and that the preaching must be such as the people can understand. In the *Capitularia*[1] of Charlemagne and his successors numerous regulations are found in regard to the character and duties of the clergy, and preaching comes in for its share of attention. These rules are found as early as the year 769. There is much insistence upon the duty of preaching, and even the material of the sermons is prescribed to some extent; as for example, priests are forbidden "to feign and preach to the people, out of their own understanding and not according to the sacred Scriptures, new or uncanonical things."[2] These efforts in the latter part of the eighth century reveal how greatly preaching had fallen both as to frequency and quality. We shall see later what effect these efforts at reform had upon the preaching of the following times.

Besides these praiseworthy attempts of the authorities to improve preaching there were earnest endeavors on the part of individual priests and monks here and there to gather the people together and preach to them. These missionary movements, though crude and imperfect, were a note of real life in preaching, and had in them the pledge of a fruitful future. We shall see more of this phase of preaching further on.

The clergy and preaching of the age have been very properly classified by historians into parochial, cloistral, and missionary. So far as the clergy is concerned the classification, though proper, cannot be rigid or exclusive. For sometimes, though very rarely, a parish priest or even

[1] Migne, *Pat. Lat.*, tom. 97.
[2] Capit. of the year 789; Migne, *Pat. Lat.*, tom. 97, col. 182.

a bishop, might do some missionary work, or be called on to preach in a monastery. But very frequently the monks preached in the parishes, were sometimes made prelates, and were distinctively the missionaries of the age. When it comes to preaching itself, however, the distinction is apparent enough.

Parochial preaching was that of prelates and priests in churches to the people gathered on Sundays, saints' days, festivals and other occasions. Strange as it may seem there was apparently less of this preaching than of the other kinds, and it was of poorer average quality. Many of the bishops and secular priests concerned themselves very little with preaching. Partly this was due to all the elements of decline which affected the preaching of the age, but more distinctively to the encroachment of liturgical worship and the cares of administration, which we have already seen growing in the preceding period.

Cloistral preaching, as the name indicates, was that done in monasteries, and consisted chiefly of instruction and exhortation to monks and nuns. It may be that persons from the outside were sometimes invited or permitted to attend some of these services, but the aim and character of the preaching was monastic. The preacher might be a visiting prelate or brother, or, very frequently, the abbot, or sometimes a brother appointed for the purpose. In case of the nunneries the preachers were usually the prelates under whose jurisdiction the institutions lay, or monks of the related orders deputed for the purpose. In far later days one of the most famous preachers of the Franciscans [1] began his career as a preacher to the nuns of the associated order. Sometimes these sermons were called "instructions," and sometimes "collations," from the fact that they were not infrequently given while the brethren were at their common meal in the refectory. Naturally the discourses were of a didactic and often of a mystical character.

In addition to the actual cloistral preaching we must take some account of the influence of monasticism upon preaching generally. For it was great and lasting. In the widest view there was the conceded value of the monasteries as refuges and preservers of learning in these evil

[1] Berthold of Regensburg, d. 1272.

times. The monks were taught in the cloistral schools what learning there was. Some of these schools and their teachers, even in this early age and yet more in later times, became and remain deservedly famous. The monastic clergy were commonly far superior both in morals and learning to the parish priests. From the monasteries went forth the best prepared men for the work of the ministry, and many a monk became a distinguished prelate. This was true of the great Spaniards Leander and Isidore of Seville in the preceding times, and of Ildefonso of Toledo in the period now under review.[1] Frequently the monks went forth to preach in the churches and also as missionaries, as we shall presently see more fully. In regard to the work of the monks in England Montalembert [2] gives this interesting account: "It is then to the monks, scattered as missionaries and preachers over the country, or united in the numerous communities of episcopal cities and other great monastic centres, that must in justice be attributed the initiation of the Anglo-Saxons into the truths of religion. . . . . They were expressly commanded to teach and explain to their flocks, in the vernacular tongue, the Decalogue, the Lord's Prayer, the Apostles' Creed, and the sacred words which were used in the celebration of the mass and the administration of baptism; to expound to them every Sunday, in English, the Epistle and Gospel of the day, and to preach, or instead of preaching to read them something useful to their souls. . . . . From this spring those homilies in Anglo-Saxon which are so often to be met with among the manuscripts in our libraries, and which are by several centuries of an earlier date than the earliest religious documents of any other modern language." Since the brilliant Frenchman's time some of these early homilies have been edited and published by English scholars.[3]

Missionary preaching had received its impulse from the work of Patrick and Columba in the preceding period.

[1] See Montalembert, *Monks of the West,* I., pp. 414-427.
[2] *Op. cit.,* Vol. II., p. 608.
[3] See Cutts, *Parish Priests and Their People in the Middle Ages in England,* chaps. II., III,. V., XIV., and especially p. 223 for remarks on the Saxon homilies, which, however, belong to a later date than the eighth century. We shall have occasion later to deal with the *Old English Homilies,* edited by Morris.

In this time it found noble expression in the labors of Columban, Gall, Wilibrord, Winfred (Boniface), and others. It appears that the parochial clergy did little or nothing of this sort of preaching, though the good work of Eligius of Noyon, who was never a monk, is a brilliant exception to this rule. The missionaries were principally monks.

As already intimated the character and quality of Western preaching in the seventh and eighth centuries must be rated lower than at any previous time. After the fall from Ambrose and Augustine to Gregory I. and Cæsarius of Arles, further decay would seem well nigh impossible. But still it is a fact. The bishops preached but little, the common parochial clergy even less; what preaching there was came mostly from monks and missionaries. The sermons are largely imitations, adaptations, compilations, and in not a few cases direct copies of the older discourses. The faults of other days are perpetuated in weak reproductions, no new note is heard, little power is shown; preaching is merely holding on to its traditions with a feeble grasp and waiting for better days.

In form the sermons are still the structureless hortatory homilies of other days. They are usually very short. The style is not uniform; quotations and imitations from older models preserve the manner of the later Latin fathers to some extent; and of course individuals differ in their use of the current church Latin; but the general inference from all this is in accord with the facts—there is no style to speak of at all, no strength, life, beauty, or eloquence.

In contents the Latin sermons are no better than the Greek. The Scriptural exposition is forced and allegorical, often helplessly puerile. Of deep and powerful thinking there are scanty if any specimens. Saints' tales and marvels, extravagant laudation of the Virgin and of relics are largely in evidence. Some gospel is preached, however, and the moral teaching is for the most part correct and earnest. The monastic and churchly virtues receive too great emphasis relatively to other things. We should remember, however, that accounts of the effect of preaching at times upon its auditors give us a better impression of its actual power than we are able to gather from the tame Latin reports of sermons which have come down to us. There was doubtless both better and worse preaching than the preserved discourses exhibit.

Latin was the prevalent language of preaching. All the discourses of this time are preserved only in that tongue; the Anglo-Saxon homilies mentioned before belong to a later date, and there are none as early as those in any other of the nascent languages of modern times. But still, even in this early time—the seventh and eighth centuries—there are traces that at least some of the popular preaching was done in the vernacular dialects. Thus Bede [1] tells how King Oswald of Northumbria interpreted Aidan's preaching to his court, and how "Paulinus preached all day long to the people," presumably either directly or by an interpreter, and how Cuthbert "was wont chiefly to visit the villages . . . . to allure the rustic people by his eloquent preaching to heavenly employments." In France, or Flanders, Eligius of Noyon, who will be noticed later, distinctly says in one of his sermons: "Therefore we address you in rustic speech (*rustico sermone*);" and in another, "Therefore we turn to you using a simple and rustic speech (*eloquio*)."[2] This is not perfectly conclusive, since it may refer to the bad Latin and harsh prounciation of the common people as distinguished from the more cultured, but it is at least an indication of the use of vernacular speech in the Frankish countries in the seventh century. In Switzerland, as we shall see, there is reason to believe that Gall early in the seventh century made some use of the native dialects in his preaching. This interesting and somewhat difficult question of the extent of the use of the rising modern languages in the preaching of the Middle Ages will come up again and again as we proceed to follow the history, but this much concerning the earliest traces of such use it is proper to state here.

From this general account of the preaching of the two centuries under review we must proceed to give brief notices of some of the more important preachers of the age in both the Eastern and Western churches.

[1] See Cutts, *Parish Priests,* etc., pp. 21-24.

[2] Quoted by Cruel, *Geschichte der Deutschen Predigt des Mittelatlers,* S. 9, who says: "The Latin language therefore belongs here, as in all similar cases, only to the written report, and not to the public delivery." This seems an allowable inference, but it should not be pressed too far for reasons mentioned in the text.

3. Preachers of the Greek Church.[1]

There is no occasion for a classification of the Greek preachers of the epoch; but a few of the better known will be mentioned in their chronological order. Very little is known of Sophronius except that he was originally a Sophist, then a monk, and became patriarch of Jerusalem about the year 634. He was early and late a strong opponent of the Monothelete doctrine. Four sermons are ascribed to him, their subjects being as follows: (1) On the Birth of Christ; (2) Panegyric on the Angels; (3) and (4) On the Adoration of the Cross. They are declamatory in style and excessively panegyrical in tone. For example, the cross is apostrophized and called on in a long prayer to show forth its manifold power.

A certain George of Pisidia comes into view about the year 640 as archbishop of Nicomedia, having previously been known as a deacon and librarian at Constantinople. From him we have some poetical and historical writings and nine sermons. They treat of the conception of Mary and of her mother; of the birth of Mary, and her presentation in the Temple; and of her being at the cross and the tomb of the Lord. They show the prevalent tendency to give to Mary not only some of the attributes and offices of her Son, but even to ascribe parallel facts to her birth and infancy. Some of the tales are taken from the Apocryphal writings. Besides these discourses on Mary there is a panegyrical sermon on the saints Cosmas and Damian. Of the whole collection Rothe says: "All these addresses are empty declamations without content and without thought, overloaded with picturings, exclamations, rhetorical figures, and emphasis. They could only tickle spoiled ears, but not teach or edify hearts."

A man of more note is Andrew, who, toward the end of his life, early in the eighth century, was archbishop of Crete. He was born in Damascus, where his early education was received. About the year 635 he became a monk at Jerusalem, and must have lived there a long time, for

[1] For the following discussion the author is chiefly indebted to Rothe's *Geschichte der Predigt,* sections 57-63; though something has been derived from other authorities, and something also from the original sources as given in Migne's *Greek Patrology*.

at the council of 680, which condemned Monotheletism, he was the representative of the patriarch of Jerusalem. After the council he was kept at Constantinople, ordained a deacon, and put in charge of an orphanage, and later was made archbishop of the island of Crete. He was a man of considerable talent, being something of a commentator and also a hymn-writer. One of his hymns has become somewhat familiar to modern singers in Neale's vigorous adaptation rather than translation:

> "Christian, dost thou see them
>   On the holy ground,
> How the powers of evil
>   Rage thy steps around?
> Christian, up and smite them,
>   Counting gain but loss,
> Smite them by the merit
>   Of the holy cross."

As a preacher Andrew has perhaps better claim to notice than any of his contemporaries. Seventeen homilies are ascribed to him, but at least one and possibly others are of doubtful genuineness. They are characteristic of the times, being mostly concerned with Mary and the saints. One of these whom he eulogizes is naturally enough his first predecessor as bishop of Crete—Titus! One of the sermons treats of the Transfiguration, one of the raising of Lazarus, two of the exaltation of the holy cross. His veneration of the Virgin is of the most extreme sort. According to Rothe "he calls her the diadem of beauty, the queen of our race, the holy temple of Christ, the rod of Aaron, the root of Jesse, the sceptre of David, the mediatrix of law and grace, the seal of the Old and the New Testament, the expected salvation of the heathen, the common refuge of all Christians, the restoration from the first fall, the bringing back of the fallen race to freedom from suffering, and much of the same sort." But with all these faults there is a certain elevation of thought and expression, and certainly some oratorical power. He exhibits one peculiarity of the preaching of all this time, that is, putting extensive imaginary speeches into the mouths of Bible characters, the angels, and even God.

There meets us in this time the name of a certain Germanus, who is said to have lived about a hundred years (634-c. 734). He first appears as bishop of Cyzicus, then about 715 as patriarch of Constantinople. From this office he was driven into exile by the iconoclastic emperor Leo about the year 730, and died soon after. He was a zealous partisan of the image-worship, and is highly esteemed by the Greek church as one who suffered for his convictions. There remain from him a few religious poems and some other writings. Among these are a number of sermons, many of which are devoted to extravagant praise of the Virgin. In one of them is a long conversation between the angel Gabriel, the Virgin Mary, and Joseph, in which Joseph makes accusations against Mary and she defends herself. In another he declares that Mary soon after her death was raised again and taken bodily to heaven. The style is much like that of Andrew of Crete, and there is evidence of real oratorical talent.

By far the most important and interesting man of the mediæval Greek church is John of Damascus (d. c. 754, or later),[1] sometimes called by his Arabian name of Mansur, or Momsur. It is rather as a man, a theologian, a writer, than as a preacher that he is justly famous. Judged by his sermons alone he could not be reckoned among the great preachers of history, nor very far above his contemporaries, yet his greatness in the other respects mentioned makes him altogether the most notable Greek preacher after Chrysostom. His admirers have vainly sought to place him alongside the great Antiochene by surnaming him *Chrysorrhoas,* "the golden current."

The story of his life, as accepted after his own times, contains miraculous and fabulous elements which throw some doubt upon that part of the narrative which is not of itself improbable. The accounts say that he was born in Damascus the latter part of the seventh century, the son of a Christian named Sergius, who served the Arab caliph as treasurer and stood high in the ruler's favor. John's education was received from one Cosmas, a pious and learned Italian monk, who had been captured by the

[1] The date lies between 754 and 787. His latest writing is of the earlier date, and his death is noted by the second Nicene Council in 787. Article in Herzog.

Arabs in a foray and sold as a slave at Damascus. Sergius ransomed the saintly man and set him to educate his own son John and also an adopted son called Cosmas, probably after the teacher. Both pupils did well, and John especially distinguished himself, learning grammar, philosophy, mathematics and theology. His father having died, John was appointed by the Caliph to high office. Now comes a highly wrought story from which it is hard to get the kernel of truth which probably lies within it. On account of his defence of the image worship, the emperor of Constantinople falsely, by use of a forged letter, informs the Caliph that John is a traitor; whereupon the Caliph has John arrested and causes his right hand to be cut off. John begs that the hand be left with him in the prison, and in answer to prayer the Virgin joins the hand back to the wrist during the night. The Caliph is overcome by this miracle, pardons John and wants to restore him to his office; but John refuses and leaves Damascus.

Whatever the cause may have been, John did leave his native city and the service of the Caliph and entered as a novice the famous monastery of St. Sabas near Jerusalem. Here it is related that the brethren had so profound an impression of his learning that none would undertake to be his teacher, until at last upon certain conditions an old and austere monk agreed to receive him into his cell as a pupil. We need not follow the details of his severe training in self-abasement. Finally, it is said, the Holy Virgin appeared in a dream to the old monk and bade him remove the restriction he had placed upon John's writing, as she had need of his talents in her service and that of the church. Henceforth his literary labors are great; his numerous writings show diligent activity. He was ordained a presbyter by the patriarch of Jerusalem, and was frequently called upon to teach and preach in the city. It is probable also that he preached upon occasion in other places. Thus with his writings and his preaching he spent the remainder of his days at St. Sabas, where he died about the middle of the eighth century.

His extensive writings embrace works on the image controversy, and on theology, some hymns, and some orations and sermons. His greatest theological work, "The

Fount of Knowledge," is a useful epitome of the Greek theology and is still an authority in the Greek Church. He used the Aristotelian logic, and is thus in some sense the pioneer of the great Latin schoolmen of a later age, who are much indebted to him. He wrote a number of hymns, still prized in the Eastern church; and it is a matter of interest that his adoptive brother and fellow pupil Cosmas was his companion and colaborer in this work.[1] Neale has put us in his debt by admirable reproductions of several of these, "The Day of Resurrection" being the best known.

John's sermons are not free from the errors of his time —forced allegorical interpretation, excessive veneration of the Virgin, highly wrought panegyrics on the saints. There is little of theological or moral teaching in them; they are unnecessarily prolix, but they are clear and forcible in expression and show the logical, scholastic bent of his mind. Such as they are, they served as models for later Greek preachers and found many imitators. An extract from his sermon on the withered fig tree may give a hint of his method. After a stilted introduction dealing with the incarnation he proceeds to say: "Wherefore then as he was partaker and sharer of the [divine] nature (for the nature of the Father and of the Son is one), so, as it were, he serves the will of the household and becomes man and is obedient to the Father even to death, and that the death of the cross, all for the purpose of healing my disobedience! He comes, then, hastening to suffer and hurrying to drink the cup of death, whence is the salvation of all the world. He comes hungering for the salvation of humanity, and finds not fruit in it—for this is what the fig tree, as in a parable, obscurely teaches." Then he goes on to develop this thought, repudiating the literal interpretation.

Theodore Studites (759-826) was born at Constantinople about the middle of the eighth century, and came of a good family. He had an uncle, Plato, who was abbot of a monastery and induced Theodore and other members of the family to take up the monastic life. Theodore became very ascetic and was highly esteemed by his brother monks. Against his wishes he was or-

[1] Schaff, *Ch. Hist.*, Vol. IV., p. 406.

dained a presbyter in 784. He had trouble with the emperors both on moral subjects and in regard to the veneration of the images. He was several times banished, and often cruelly treated. From 797 to 802 he was in favor at court, and at the request of the empress Irene—the zealous champion of the holy *icons*—he became head of the famous monastery of the Studium at Constantinople. He reorganized this and made it the most renowned of all the Greek cloisters of the age. Hence comes his surname.

There remains from him a collection of a hundred and thirty-five short addresses to the monks, which are without text, mostly hortatory, and inculcating the monastic virtues. These discourses were very highly esteemed and were for a long time read in some of the churches in connection with public worship. Besides these homilies there are also sermons of all sorts on the much-used subjects of the day, the Virgin and the saints, the exaltation of the cross, and the like. They are wholly in the taste and manner of the age, full of superstitions, saints' legends, forced figures and empty declamation. However admired in their own times, they bring no good message to ours.

4. Preachers Among the Roman Clergy

Turning our attention now to the West we shall find it both proper and convenient to use the classification of parochial, cloistral, and missionary, although as already stated the distinction in case of the preachers is not so clear as in the preaching. Only a few of each group can be noticed.

Of those who represent the parochial clergy one of the best was the Spaniard Ildefonso (607-667), who was born at Toledo of parents of noble birth and rank. In his youth he was taught by the famous Isidore of Seville. Against his father's will he entered the monastery of Agali, which was the most noted one of that age in Spain, and was the seat of learning and culture. Here Ildefonso was for a long time resident, first as monk and then as abbot. He took prominent part in several synods, and was distinguished for the purity of his own character and for severe discipline of others. In 657 he was, reluctantly on his own part, made archbishop of Toledo.

He was a faithful bishop, but was sorely harassed by many trials and conflicts in that age of turmoil. Arianism and the hostility of the king were not the least of his troubles. He filled his high office for a little more than nine years, and died greatly esteemed by the Spanish Catholics.

His best known work is a treatise against three unbelievers concerning the virginity of Mary.[1] He was a most ardent upholder of all the exaggerated Catholic doctrines concerning the mother of our Lord. The treatise is highly rhetorical, not to say bombastic, in style, and gives us no doubt a better idea of Ildefonso's preaching than the doubtful sermons which are ascribed to him. His reputation as a preacher was considerable, and he must have had a fervid temperament and the oratorical fire; but if the writing on Mary is a fair specimen of his work he did not fall below many of the oriental preachers of the time in the excess of his adulation of the Virgin.

Decidedly one of the most engaging characters of this age was the Frenchman Eligius (588-658)[2], long a courtier of several of the early Merovingian kings, and in his later life bishop of Noyon in Picardy. He was born near Limoges of a pious family, and was well brought up from childhood. Apprenticed to a goldsmith, who had charge of the royal mint at Limoges, Eligius greatly distinguished himself by his fidelity and skill in his calling. Meantime he was constant in his religious duties, and—a truly remarkable thing for a layman in that age—a careful student of the Scriptures. After a while he left Limoges and went to Paris, then the capital of the Neustrian Franks. Because of his skill as a goldsmith, his honesty and excellent character, he became a great favorite with King Clotaire II. Eligius was not corrupted by royal favor nor by the accumulation of wealth. In outward things, such as dress and manners, he conformed for a time to the world about him. But this was for policy rather than liking, for in his heart he was unworldly, even ascetic. As soon as he could do so with prudence he began to show his real feelings in these matters, laying aside his costly clothing and dressing with exceeding plainness. He gave much to the poor; he

[1] Given in Migne's *Latin Patrology.*
[2] *Vita,* in Migne, *Pat. Lat.,* tom. 87, col. 478 ss.

labored for the spread of Christian knowledge, and on his journeys frequently spoke and gave instruction in the Bible as a sort of lay evangelist; he founded cloisters based on the strictest discipline. Thus in various ways he used his influence at court, his personal wealth, and his own time and efforts to advance the cause of religion as he understood it.

When Dagobert succeeded Clotaire as king he retained his father's affection for Eligius and reposed so much confidence in the pious goldsmith as frequently to consult him on affairs of state. This was naturally not agreeable to the more worldly courtiers, and least of all to the ambitious mayors of the palace, who were already rising to the power which later resulted in their usurpation of royal prerogatives and finally of the royal title. The next king, Louis II., was more under the influence of his mayor of the palace, and the removal of the good goldsmith from the court was the next thing in order. To the credit of all concerned let it be said that instead of murder or false accusation the happy expedient was hit upon of making Eligius a bishop and giving him a frontier diocese! So the good man was duly consecrated a bishop and assigned to a region in the northeastern part of France bordering on the Belgic provinces, later known as Picardy, with the town of Noyon as its chief city and the residence of the bishop.

Thus inducted into office the bishop of Noyon proved to be a capable and faithful prelate, discharging the duties of his higher trust with all the fidelity and diligence which had distinguished him in his active business life. Now also his former Bible studies and lay preaching stood him in good stead as a preacher, and his relations to the monasteries he had founded helped him in the administration of affairs in his diocese. He had need of his previous experience, for the difficulties and opposition encountered in his work taxed all his resources and courage. Sixteen sermons of somewhat dubious authenticity are ascribed to him.[1] They exhibit no originality of thought, but have a certain warmth and earnestness. The account of his life indicates that he preached much and believed in it. He sometimes used the "rustic speech," and preached to heathen as well as to his flock.

[1] Migne, *Pat. Lat.*, tom. 87, col. 594 ss., adduced by Rothe.

Among those who preached chiefly to the monks, or whose remaining sermons at least are chiefly cloistral, the preëminent name in this period is that of the saintly Saxon monk Bede (672-735), or Bæda, whom history delights to honor with the title of Venerable. He was born in the north of England at or near Yarrow. In early childhood he was put into the monastery of St. Peter at Wearmouth, and later transferred to that of St. Paul at Yarrow. These monasteries and their neighborhood were the scene of his life and labors. His teacher, Benedict Biscop, was a wealthy nobleman who had turned monk and supplied the monastery with books. Bede was an apt and diligent scholar and became well versed in the Scriptures, in the Latin Fathers, and in other branches of current learning. When he was nineteen years old, though under canonical age, he was made a deacon, and at thirty was ordained priest. He was invited to go to Rome to study and be in line for preferment, he was offered the abbacy of his convent; but he declined both of these flattering offers and devoted himself to learning and to the work of a teacher and preacher. He was a great and much beloved teacher, and a voluminous author. His best known and most valuable work is his *Ecclesiastical History of the Saxons,* which has been for ages one of the most prized sources for the history of the early Saxon period in England.

As a preacher Bede was active and faithful, preaching mostly in the cloister, but also to the people. Of the extant sermons ascribed to him there are a great number,[1] but probably many of them are spurious. Being chiefly reports of sermons to the monks, they cannot be regarded as a fair specimen of his popular power. They are monkish and dry, and full of extracts from the Fathers, especially Gregory the Great. The Scripture exposition is, of course, allegorical, but in other respects fairly good. The style is clear and usually easy, with some warmth but not much power.[2]

[1] Migne, *Pat. Lat.,* tom. 94, col. 9 ss.; and some translations in Neale's *Mediæval Preaching,* p. 2 ff.

[2] Here is a striking saying from his sermon on the Baptism of Jesus, where discussing John's unwillingness to baptize his Lord, he says: "Sed quia vera humilitas ipsa est quam obedientia comes non deserit, quod prius officium expavit humiliter explevit." Migne, *Pat. Lat.,* tom. 94, col. 59.

In Migne's Patrology[1] are given a brief account and some sermons of Ambrosius Autpertus (d. c. 779). The sermons are not certainly genuine, but they have some real homiletic merits, though afflicted with the usual faults of that age. Little is given as to Aubert's life. He was born in Gaul, but became a monk in the monastery of St. Vincent in Volturno, Italy. It is related that he suffered from an impediment in his speech, which was miraculously removed in answer to prayer, and that he became a fluent and eloquent speaker. He was made abbot of St. Vincent, and was evidently held in high esteem both as man and preacher. One of the sermons considered to be his is a rather striking discussion of cupidity. The preacher shows (on the basis of I. Tim. 6:10) that avarice is the root of all evil, hard to eradicate, the source of pride, idolatry, envy, oppression, robbery, and other sins; and yet the effort must be made to tear this evil root out of the life. He makes effective warning in conclusion, and exhorts to almsgiving.

There were a number of monkish missionary preachers in the age we are studying, but only the most famous three will receive notice in our necessarily brief discussion—Columban, Gall, Boniface.[2]

Columban (c. 540-c. 615), so called to distinguish him from the first Columba, who founded the famous monastery at the isle of Iona, on the Scotch coast, is also known as Columba the Younger, or Columba of Luxeuil, from the abbey he founded in France. The name means in Latin "a dove," and was probably given to or adopted by the first Columba as a distinctive surname, and came to the second from the first, most usually in the form Columban. He was born in the Leinster district of Ireland, was a fine, studious lad, and early entered the famous abbey of Bangor, where he studied till he was thirty years old. At that age he felt his call to go forth as a missionary and founder of cloisters to be centers of evangelistic labors among the rude and half-heathen

[1] Tom. 89, col. 1265 ss.

[2] Besides other authorities, and the sources, the author has used with great profit the able and satisfactory work of R. Cruel, *Geschichte der Deutschen Predigt im Mittelalter*, and the brilliant and scholarly but withal somewhat onesided and *tendential* work of F. R. Albert, *Geschichte der Predigt in Deutschland bis Luther*.

people of central Europe. About the year 590 he took with him twelve pupils as companions and went forth to labor in the mountain region of France and in Switzerland. He first established a monastery in the Vosges mountains at Anegratis. It was a wild and desolate country, and there was a struggle to maintain life. But after the first trials the abbey throve and became so full of monks and pupils that Columban decided to move on and establish another at Luxuvium, the modern Luxeuil. Later still another was founded at Fontaines. All these were in the territories of the Burgundian kingdom.

From these cloisters as centers Columban and his pupils went forth to labor among the people for their conversion and spiritual training. After more than twenty years of earnest labors, having incurred the enmity of the famous Burgundian queen Brunhilda, of the king, her grandson, and of certain bishops, he was banished from Burgundy and went into Switzerland. Here he labored for some years under the protection of the Austrasian king Theodebert; but on the latter's overthrow by another branch of the Franks he went to Italy. Here, amid the Apennines, he founded his last monastery, that of Bobbio, the refuge of his last year of life and the scene of his death in 615.

None of Columban's sermons to the people have come down to us, but there have been preserved in Latin fifteen or sixteen addresses, mostly to the monks, called the *Instructions of St. Columban.*[1] Thus while he was a noted and laborious missionary, these sermons, or rather brief reports of sermons, belong to the cloistral class. They deal chiefly with the moral and saintly virtues. The first treats of the Trinity, the second of mortifying vices and attaining virtues, the third of hating the world, and of love for heavenly things, the fourth holds that a man must labor in this life in order to rest in the life to come, the fifth that life is not properly a *life* (*vita*), but only a *way* (*via*), the sixth that this life is like a shadow, and so on. There are in them some great moral truths and Scriptural ideas, many striking expressions, but of course there is much that is forced, allegorical, monkish, and unscriptural. The piety and earnestness of the man are manifest in his work.

[1] Migne, *Pat. Lat.*, tom. 80, col. 229 ss.

The most famous of the twelve pupils who accompanied Columban from Ireland was Gallus (c. 550-640), or Gallun, whom we know best by his abbreviated name, Gall. He was of good Irish family and had been for some time a student of Columban's at Bangor before they together went to Burgundy. He was active with Columban in all his labors, and was most useful to him as an assistant. Gall was gifted in language and had learned while in Burgundy the so-called "Alemanic" tongue, the dialect of an influential branch of the Teutonic folk. It is probable that this language was understood quite generally in Switzerland, much of which was then known as Alemania.[1] When Columban was banished from Burgundy Gall went with him into Alemania, and was very active in labors among the people. The story goes that after the missionaries had settled at Bregenz on Lake Constance Gall one day preached a powerful sermon to the people in their own tongue, and while they were still moved by the discourse he broke in pieces and threw into the lake three idols that had long been objects of worship. It was a bold stroke and produced a lasting impression.

When persecution forced Columban into Italy Gall was prevented by illness from going with him. The elder man regarded the illness as feigned, or at least exaggerated, and was quite angry at leaving his favorite pupil and helper behind, so that he forbade Gall to conduct the services of the mass as long as he himself should live! However, Gall remained behind sick, but managed to reach in a boat Arbon, on Lake Constance, where he had friends who received him and nursed him back to health. On getting well he desired to resume his missionary and monastic life. So pushing on with a guide into the wild country, he established his cell at the place which to this day bears his name—St. Gall. Others gathered about him, and a flourishing monastery was founded. From this station he kept up his mission work till his death in 640.

In the year 615 Gall was invited to accept a bishopric at Constance, but declined, pleading the prohibition of

[1] As is well known the French name for Germany is still *Allemagne,* and for the German language *allemand.*

old Columban, his master, against his saying mass! But he recommended for the place his pupil, John, a native of the country. On the consecration of John as bishop Gall preached a notable sermon in Latin, which John interpreted into the language of the people. It seems clear from the affair at Bregenz that Gall could preach very effectively in the tongue of the people, and his long sojourn in the country and labors among the natives make it incredible that he was not sufficiently acquainted with the vernacular to use it had he so desired. The explanation of the singular circumstance is perhaps rather to be sought in the considerations that as it was a formal occasion and Latin was the ecclesiastical language it was fitting that the churchly tongue should be employed, while to accommodate those who could not understand it, and at the same time to demonstrate his fitness for his high office, John turned the sermon into the vernacular.[1] The sermon is still preserved, its genuineness generally accepted by critics.[2] It is a decidedly interesting performance. Beginning with the fall of the angels and of man the preacher sketches the Bible history from Genesis to Acts, giving emphasis to the work of our Lord and making spiritual application throughout. The special lesson is that men should forsake their sins and heathen follies, and serve the true God. In the conclusion he "calls upon Christians now to live in accordance with their baptismal vow, to avoid sin, to do good, and to care for their own souls in view of the future judgment." [3]

Winfrid (680-755), whom we know best by his Latin name of Boniface, was born in Devonshire, England, of well-to-do parents. He was educated at Exeter and at an abbey called Nhutscelle, which by some has been identified with Netley.[4] It is thought that he adopted his new name of Boniface on becoming a monk. He showed both diligence in study and aptitude for affairs. A longing for missionary life on the Continent seized him. So,

[1] See Albert, *Gesch. der Pred.*, Bd. I., SS. 52, 53. But he seems to me to infer more than is just against the use of the vernacular in Gall's ordinary preaching and in that of others.

[2] Migne, *Pat. Lat.*, tom. 87, col. 13 ss.

[3] Albert, *op. cit.*, Bd. I., S. 57.

[4] F. F. Walrond, *Christian Missions before the Reformation*, p. 81.

with the reluctant consent of his abbot, he went to Friesland to help his countryman Willibrord, who was laboring there as missionary bishop of Trajectum, now known as Utrecht. Winfrid found on arrival that the Frisians were engaged in a fierce war with Charles Martel, the famous Frankish mayor of the palace and "Hammer of the Saracens." As there was little prospect for missionary work for some time to come the enterprising young monk returned home. The abbot of Nhutscelle had just died, and Winfrid was urged to accept the vacant post, but declined, and sought to carry on his missionary work in another way. He went to Rome and obtained a commission from the Pope as general missionary among the Germans. Now his real life work begins, in 719.

After working for a while in southern Germany (principally Thuringia) Boniface came to the conclusion that he could do better if he had the protection of the secular powers. Having previously secured a letter from the Pope to Charles Martel—the real ruler of the Franks in the name of the feeble Merovingian king—he proceeded to court to seek the protection of the powerful Frank. Charles readily granted his request, much to Boniface's joy. While at the Frankish court he had heard of the death of old Radbod, king of the Frisians, and armed with Charles' letter of protection he again went to the aid of his old friend Willibrord among the Frisians. He remained about three years in that country and then returned to resume his labors among the Germans in Thuringia and Hesse. After a fruitful year's work he made another visit to Rome, and was created bishop of Germany without fixed headquarters. Once more he sought and obtained the protection of Charles Martel, and from now on labored for some years among the Thuringians and Hessians, calling helpers from England, founding monasteries, preaching and working for the half-heathen people. It was during this time that he cut down with his own hands at Geismar a huge oak that had long been regarded with awe as sacred to Thor (or Woden, as some have it), one of the heathen divinities. In 732—the very year in which his mighty Frankish protector immortalized himself by defeating the Saracens on the plains of Tours—Boniface was made archbishop and primate of all Germany. His hands were now full with establishing churches and bishoprics, selecting men for offices, and generally settling ecclesiastical affairs in his vast territory. In 745 he was assigned to the archbishopric of Mainz, that his labors and responsibilities might be somewhat lessened in his old age. But after a time the old man turned over his affairs to another, and with the old dreams of his youth he turned once more to the heathen Frisians. In that wild country he received at the hands of a horde of the heathen his martyr's crown, being slain by a party of fierce men to whom he had come with the gospel of peace. Thus Boniface ended his labors in the year 755, though some authorities place it a year earlier.

Historians are not unanimous as to the merits of Boniface's work, nor as to the superior excellence of his character. The Catholic view is expressed in his well-known title of "Apostle of Germany." Extreme Protestants discredit his work, and in some degree his character. They make him bigoted, worldly, bent on subduing the Germans to the papal yoke, preparing the way for Canossa and necessitating the Reformation. As is usually the case in such matters, the truth probably lies between extremes.

There remain fifteen short, probably genuine, sermons from Boniface.[1] They are not missionary discourses, but are addressed to nominal Christians. Thus they seem, as has been well remarked,[2] to belong not to the first half of his life, when he was doing pioneer work, but to his later career of organization and discipline. It is hard to say exactly to what class of hearers they were given, or certainly in what language they were spoken, though of course we have them in Latin. They are without text, but often relate to the Scriptural lesson for the day. They use Scripture freely, but of course in the prevalent allegorical way. They borrow much from the older sources, and deal with baptismal vows, the Creed and Lord's prayer, the churchly virtues, and the like. As sermons and of themselves they are not of much value; but they deserve study as specimens of their

[1] Found in Migne's *Latin Patrology,* and discussed by Cruel, Albert, *et. al.* [2] Cruel, *op. cit.,* S. 23.

kind, and as the remains of a very interesting and important man.[1]

Our survey of the conditions and character of Christian preaching and of the lives and labors of a few of the best preachers during the seventh and eighth centuries justifies the title of this chapter. Preaching was indeed at a low estate. But still it was not gone from the earth, and, though depressed, it was not dead. The sketch we have made does not exhaust the subject. Besides those mentioned, there were many other brave and faithful men who, with imperfect equipment and in trying times, preached the gospel as they understood it to the people of their own days.

CHAPTER V

Voices in the Night; or, Preaching During the Ninth, Tenth and Eleventh Centuries

1. Sketch of the Age

The epoch included in this chapter runs from the death of Charlemagne in 814 to the beginning of the first Crusade in 1095. In the East there were not many events of general historical interest, but the old empire held together still. The accession of the empress Irene in 780 had been a turning point in the image controversy, and the second Nicene Council in 787 had declared in favor of the images. But after Irene some of the emperors had been iconoclasts, and it remained for another empress, Theodora, in 842, finally to settle the long strife in favor of the *icons*. The monks and the women gained the day at last. From 867 to 1057 a line of Macedonian emperors, including, besides others, Phocas, Zimisces, and Basil II., governed with some real ability and suc-

[1] In Serm. I., *De Fide Recta,* speaking of pastors he says: "Quomodo docet quis quod non didicit? vel qualiter pastor esse poterit si pane vitæ gregem sibi commissum pascere ignorat? Non erubescat nesciens discere quod ignorat, nec sciens tardus sit docere quod novit." That last sentence has a suspiciously Augustinian ring, but let us hope it is original! At any rate the passage well expresses a very important principle.

cess. Then the family of the Comneni—Isaac and Alexis—reigned with a show of splendor, but in real weakness, toward the end of the eleventh century. The revival of the Roman empire in the West under Charlemagne was a final stroke to the pretensions of Constantinople in that direction—though any real sovereignty had long ago passed away. On the northeast there were struggles with the rising power of Bulgarians and Russians; and on the southeast the decay of the caliphs was offset by the rise of the Turks, and so the storm that was to bring destruction was already brewing.

In the West events pregnant with influence on subsequent history occur. The death of Charlemagne in 814, the division of his empire among his descendants, and the great settlement of the treaty of Verdun in 843, really founded France and Germany as separate monarchies and left Burgundy as an age-long apple of discord between them. Another step of great importance was the renewal of the empire under strictly German leadership in 962 by the able Otto I. This period also witnesses the incursions of the Northmen in different parts of Europe, especially important being the settlement of the Normans in France and of the Danes in England. The struggles of Alfred, the Danish supremacy, and at last, in 1066, the Norman conquest give to English history a memorable interest. The general expectation in Europe that the world would come to an end with the year 1000 produced both unrest and lethargy in the tenth century. But the relief from that foreboding and the agitation preceding the Crusades awakened the eleventh century, and a new era was about to dawn.

In ecclesiastical affairs the final schism between the Roman and Greek churches is accomplished within this period. The three decisive steps may be mentioned without discussion: (1) The establishment of the Western Empire by the Pope and Charlemagne gave to the papacy prestige and power; (2) The quarrel between Nicholas of Rome and Photius, the ambitious patriarch of Constantinople, resulted in their excommunicating each other about the middle of the ninth century;[1] (3) The final dispute between Leo IX. of Rome and

[1] Schaff, *Ch. Hist.*, IV., p. 275.

Michael Cerularius of Constantinople involved the differing points of doctrine and ritual, and also claims to jurisdiction over recent converts in eastern Europe, and resulted in the mutual excommunication of the churches in 1054.[1] This schism, however, was an affair of ages; the events mentioned only sharply emphasized what was already a fact. The conversion of Russia to the Greek church in the tenth century was an event of world-wide importance.[2]. Count Vladimir, after some hesitation, accepted the Greek faith, married a Byzantine princess, and was baptized along with many of his people in 988. The story of the papacy during this epoch is full of shame and glory. Early in the tenth century began the so-called *pornocracy,* the reign of the harlots, when the see of Rome fell under the blighting influence of corrupt and ambitious women. Much confusion and turmoil went on all through the century till the election of Gerbert as Sylvester II. in 999 brought some little relief; but still riot and confusion disturbed the church, and at one time as many as three popes at once claimed the throne. Finally the emperor deposed them all, and in 1046 Clement II. inaugurates a better day. In 1049 the monk Hildebrand becomes chief adviser to Leo IX., and from then on till his own elevation as Gregory VII. in 1073, and his death in 1085, he brought the papacy to the height of its power and glory. It was a wonderful thing how the institution was brought up from its abyss of shame and made so great a power.

To trace the history of preaching through these dark ages is the task before us, and as the conditions East and West were so different it will be necessary, as before, to treat separately the Greek and Roman churches.

2. The Eastern Church

Only a few general remarks are needed to put before us a view of the Greek preaching of the age, for there was no marked change from that of the preceding time—none for the better certainly, and it hardly could be for the worse.

[1] Schaff, *op. cit.,* p. 318.

[2] Stanley gives an interesting account of it in his *Lectures on the Eastern Church,* p. 284 ff (Scribners' pop. ed.)

In form the sermon is still rather the stately and pretentious oration. It treats of great occasions, and easily retains the exaggeration and bombast of previous ages of decline. It commonly has no text, but the usual themes for laudation. There are a few homilies of less pretentious character, but of no special merit.

In contents there is much sameness. Praises of Mary and the saints on their festivals are the chief material. Little or no doctrine, and only a little good moral exhortation occur. There is a dearth of strong thinking, of grappling with great themes. Grasp of fundamental Christian truth is traditional and feeble, and the application of truth to life is scant and weak. The disciplinary virtues find place, but large and live handling of moral issues is not prominent. The use of Scripture strikes one as more sparing than in former days, and of course the forced and allegorical interpretation is still dominant.

There is much dependence on the past, as the following quotation from Lentz[1] will show: "The free address came more and more into decay; men stuck to what was already at hand and chose especially the homilies of Basil the Great and St. Chrysostom for readings—a custom which lasted long. This was due to watchfulness for purity of doctrine which the church was careful to guard. Accordingly, as early as the Trullan Council, in the year 692, order was made that the bishops should daily, and especially on Sundays, teach religion to the clergy and laity through collections of sound doctrines of Holy Scripture, and that they should not pass the fast-set bounds and doctrinal prescriptions of the godly fathers. When any controversy arose as to the Scripture they must explain according to the 'lights and teachers' of the church, and thus they would win more applause than if they gave their own views."

There was continuous decline in the frequency of preaching.[2] The two chief causes were the ever increasing regard for the mass as being the essential thing in worship, and the growing ignorance of the clergy. More and more these deteriorated, and many were utterly incapable of preaching an original discourse. Such was the fallen condition of preaching among the people who

[1] *Christl. Hom.*, I., S. 132.

[2] Rothe, S. 202.

in this degenerate age still spoke the language and professed to revere the examples of Basil and Chrysostom!

A few of the best among the preachers from whom sermons have come down to us may be mentioned as samples. Of these the first is a certain Gregory (d. c. 817), who was born in the Isaurian Decapolis probably about 731, and served as bishop in that region. There remains under his name a curious and all but worthless address [2] known as "a historical sermon on a certain Saracen who had a vision, was converted, and afterwards suffered martyrdom." The address was a great favorite, and was much used as a declamation in the monasteries. A condensation of it may not be devoid of interest.

It tells how a Saracen officer on a journey with his retinue came to a temple consecrated to St. George and ordered his servants to drive the twelve camels into the temple and feed them. The horror-stricken monks protested in vain. But on entering the sacred precincts the camels all fell dead. The terrified Saracen had the carcasses speedily dragged away and then remained himself to witness the worship. When the mass was celebrated the man saw with astonishment and loathing that the officiating priest took a fair child and cut him into four parts, putting each part into a plate and pouring the blood into a cup. The assembled Christians all partook of this gruesome feast without apparent horror, but as though accustomed to it. At the conclusion, when the priest and others had eaten the consecrated bread that was left over from the distribution, the celebrant took off his robes and, coming to the Saracen, hospitably offered him some beautiful bread. This, the man learned, was the bread from which the consecrated loaf had been selected, whereupon he broke out into fierce words, calling the priest a murderer, a monster, and the like. The pious man was greatly shocked, but when the Saracen explained why he used the opprobrious names the priest's surprise became astonishment, and he said: "You surely must be some great one, for I and my comrades being only poor ordinary sinners see nothing in these elements but bread and wine, as types of the broken body and shed blood of our Lord Jesus Christ. Nor have the holy lights and

[2] Migne, *Pat. Gr.*, tom. 100, col. 1201 ss.

teachers of the church, even such as the saints Basil and Chrysostom and Gregory, seen anything more than this." Whereupon the Saracen was converted on the spot and straightway demanded baptism, but the cautious priest, after telling him what was involved in the Christian faith, referred him to the archbishop, who dwelt far away at Sinai. The Saracen went to the archbishop, was duly instructed and baptized, and began the life of a monk. One day he asked the archbishop how he might see Jesus. The old prelate could not tell him, and the Saracen bethought him of the holy priest in the temple of St. George, and repaired thither. From his old acquaintance he learned that the way to see Jesus was to go back to his kindred, publicly renounce Mahomet, and proclaim Jesus as his Lord and Saviour. The Saracen gladly obeyed these instructions, was promptly put to death for his boldness, and thus obtained the martyr's crown and the beatific vision.

The story is elaborated with considerable prolixity, and while utterly valueless in itself and as a sermon, yet throws a curious light on the taste and customs of the age with regard to some points of interest. It would be pleasing to dwell on these somewhat if space permitted, but the statement that even the "lights and teachers of the church" saw only the bread and wine as types, shows that this man at least had not gone very far in developing the doctrine of the Real Presence.

There was a Christopher (d. c. 836) who was patriarch of Alexandria in the first third of the ninth century. Little is related of his life. He joined with two other prelates in a letter to the reigning iconoclastic emperor in favor of image worship. He was long a sufferer from paralysis, and the active duties of his office were devolved upon an assistant. His interest for us lies in the fact that there remains from him a homily [1] which, in spite of its defects, is really worth preserving, and would be worth translating here entire, excepting its stilted introduction and needless, not to say foolish, digressions. But for these faults its literary excellence is considerable, the language being simple, and the interest sustained to the climax, while the moral lesson it conveys is of peren-

[1] *Pat. Gr.*, tom. 100, col. 1215 ss.

nial importance. Space forbids more than a brief presentation of its course of thought.

The homily is without text, but has this title: "A Soul-Profiting Exhortation Showing to What This Life Is Like, and unto What End It Comes." It is a sort of parable, with applicatory interruptions and other digressions, and runs thus: A man once took up his abode in a fine house, bringing his wife, his only son, his servant, and his other belongings. He was warned that in the house (this life) there dwelt a deadly snake (the demon of avarice), and he was urged at once to hunt out the reptile and kill it, which he was fully resolved to do. But when he came to kill the snake he found that it had left for him a piece of gold of the finest mintage. The man reasoned, "Surely this snake does not wish us any harm, or he would not have left us this piece of gold." So he let the snake alone, and day after day it brought the gold piece. After a while it bit the man's horse, and the animal died. The neighbors urged the man to kill the snake before he should do worse damage. He was about to do so, when the fatal coin again caught his eye and caused him to reason that with the fast accumulating gold he could buy another horse and still have much money left. So it went on as before, until the servant was bitten and died; then the son; then the wife; the man vowing vengeance, cursing the house, bewailing his lot that he ever came into it, in each case; but every time the bright, pure gold piece salved the sore, and plausible reasonings let the snake live on. By and by the man becomes a miser and gloats over his wealth, but suddenly one day the snake bites him and he falls very ill. No physician can cure him, but he prays to God and vows he will mend his life and kill that snake if only he be spared. His prayers are heard and he recovers, but when he goes to kill the snake he finds instead of the usual coin a magnificent pearl. Fatal sight! the fool hesitates, declares he will take better care and not let the snake bite him again. Once more, after many pearls are his, he is bitten; once more prays and vows; once more is spared; till at last God's patience is exhausted, the third bite of the snake is allowed to have its effect, and the wretch dies pleading in vain, condemned by the wise, justly getting the due meed of his folly and sin. The homily concludes with suitable application of the lesson and with earnest exhortation to repentance. It is in refreshing contrast to the stock sermons of the age.

A certain George (d. 880), who was for a while keeper of archives in the great church at Constantinople, and later was bishop of Nicomedia, and a friend of the patriarch Photius, has bequeathed to us nine or ten worthless discourses in the bombastic style of the age. Some of the titles are here quoted from Rothe as illustrating the kind of thing which generally prevailed in his time: The Prophecy concerning the Conception of the Mother of God; Encomium on the Conception of St. Anna, the Mother of the Most Holy Mother of God; Oration on the Conception and Nativity of our Most Holy Lady, Mother of God and Perpetual Virgin, Mary. There are several more sermons on Mary and one on the saints Cosmas and Damian. They are full of exaggeration and padding of all sorts, and are destitute of any merit. Yet no doubt they were highly esteemed in their time.

The learned Photius (d. 886), patriarch of Constantinople near the middle of the ninth century and later, is chiefly celebrated for his quarrel with Nicholas of Rome,[1] which was one of the steps in the great schism. But he was also an author of repute in several fields,[2] and some of his works are of considerable value. He enjoyed a good reputation as a preacher. Of his sermons there are published in Migne's Greek Patrology[3] two entire ones in Greek and two Latin fragments or abridgements. Others besides these are mentioned by scholars as existing in manuscript, but they seem never to have been printed—probably to nobody's loss! Of the two complete sermons one is on the birthday of Mary, in which the preacher remarks: "To-day is the Virgin Mother born of a barren mother, and thus the home for the Lord's sojourning is made ready." This was accepted tradition as to the mother of Mary, whose birth also had to be extraordinary. The other sermon is likewise devoted to the Virgin, having been preached at the dedication of a church built in her honor. They are of the customary sort, loose in con-

[1] Schaff, *Ch. Hist.*, IV., p. 312 ff.
[2] *Id.*, p. 636 ff. [3] Tom. 102.

tents and treatment, full of digressions and padded with fables and the like.

All three of the preceding preachers belonged to the ninth century. Rothe declares that in the tenth century no Greek preacher is worth naming, and we may as well accept his judgment and pass on to the eleventh century, which may be dismissed with brief mention of two only.

Theophanes Cerameus (d. 1052) was archbishop of Taorminia in Sicily, and died about the middle of the eleventh century. From him have come down sixty-two homilies, which are said to be rather above the common run of mediæval Greek sermons. In fact Rothe[1] praises them as being simple in style and free from tawdry declamation, interpreting and applying the text with some skill.

The noted commentator Theophylact (d. c. 1107), who was quite a scholar and a teacher of one of the young emperors, has left us several sermons or addresses, but they follow the fashion of the age and in themselves are said to be unworthy of mention. The sun of Greek pulpit eloquence has long set.

3. The Western Church

In the countries which owed ecclesiastical allegiance to Rome the history of preaching up to the end of the eleventh century went on upon the lines developed in the epoch last studied. Notwithstanding the earnest efforts of Charlemagne and his successors to improve preaching by legal enactments, there was no great improvement. These efforts themselves reveal a bad state of affairs, for laws on morals are usually in advance of attainment. That the laws continued to be made shows that the evils were not remedied, but still that interest in the reform persevered. No doubt all this gave impulse toward a better state of things, but from the nature of the case the evils could hardly be mended by law. There was needed a new spiritual impulse, a reform from within, and this did not come. Then the decay and division of the empire contributed to the failure of these well-meant reforms, and preaching continued to be much neglected

[1] *Gesch. der Pred.* S. 204; and this judgment is endorsed or adopted by Christlieb in Herzog, supplement to Bd. 18.

and of poor quality. On the other hand, however, we must remember that the neglect was not total, any more than in former times. Parochial, cloistral and missionary preaching still went on, and remaining sermons as well as narratives of events still teach us something of the character of the work done.

The missionary work of this age was considerable. In the East, as we have already seen, Russia was attached to the Greek church; and before that, in the ninth century, Cyrill and Methodius, two brothers, had done an excellent work among the Slavs in Moravia. Though Greeks themselves, their converts became connected with the Roman church, but in a somewhat independent way. The missionaries had learned the native language, preached in it, translated some of the Scriptures into it, and secured permission for it instead of Latin to be used in worship. But through political and ecclesiastical rivalries and divisions this good work did not endure, though some fruit came of it. In the West proper much activity went on among the half-Christian population in the lands that had already been brought nominally into the fold, and, in addition, Norway and Sweden, Denmark, the Baltic provinces, Poland, Bohemia, Hungary, all in some measure received the Romish form of Christianity during this period. It was the "dark ages," but the gospel light though burning low was not quenched.

Coming to consider more particularly the preaching itself in these dark centuries we shall find it convenient to discuss in order the clergy, the people, the language used, and the character and contents of the sermons during that age.

The Roman hierarchy was considerably developed. In 1059 the Roman cardinals—a designation which originally included "all the clergy attached to one particular church"[1]—were created a college of electors to choose the pope, and the term "cardinal" is henceforth restricted to these, though after the thirteenth century the Roman cardinals were appointed from other countries as well as from Italy. Archbishops, bishops, priests, deacons, constituted the stated orders of clergy, but there were numerous other officers and titles. Monasticism

[1] Kurtz' *Church History* (Am. ed.), Vol. II., p. 59.

had powerfully influenced the clergy. Some of the abbots had episcopal rank and authority and were called "mitred abbots." Many monks were ordained deacons and priests and were called "regulars," because they lived by monastic rule (*regula*), while the ordinary parochical clergy were called "seculars," as living out in the world (*sæculum*). Other monks were novices, pupils, lay workers. There was much of rivalry and bad blood between the "regulars," who claimed superiority in character and learning, and the "seculars," many of whom no doubt were shamefully ignorant and loose.

Of course there were learned and good men among the clergy of all orders, but the average character was discreditably low. The superior clergy had a good degree of ecclesiastical, social, and even political influence, and many of them fell victims to the vices of avarice and luxury. In fact the whole class was more or less infected with vice; simony, gluttony, avarice, sensuality, flourished among them. While the monks may have been in most cases better than the "seculars" there is painfully abundant evidence that they, too, were often corrupt and vile. Besides moral degradation there was among the clergy much gross and inexcusable ignorance and superstition.

The nobles, the clergy, the common people, were then as long afterwards the three classes of society. The middle class, strictly speaking, had not yet arisen. The clergy, still as in former times, being recruited from both the other classes, for social as well as official reasons made a sort of connecting link between the upper and lower orders of people. Among all classes there was much superstition, immorality, ignorance, violence; and yet the finer virtues of humanity and the noble ideals of the Christian faith were held in honor, and there was much piety of a sort. As to the arts and comforts of life not much can be said; there were feasting and luxury in the upper walks of society, but the exactions of the clergy and the rapacity of the nobles left little more than bare living to the common man. Under such conditions there was evident and sore need of preaching, but it had much to do if it would attain and keep a tolerably decent average of excellence, and even this, alas! it failed to achieve.

Scholars are somewhat divided in opinion as to whether

before the twelfth century there was, properly speaking, any preaching in the vernacular languages of continental Europe.[1] It is generally agreed that although there are evidences of Anglo-Saxon preaching long before this time, the rule certainly in cloistral and prevailingly in parochial preaching, was to use the Latin as the churchly and universal tongue; that no sermons earlier than the twelfth century (except in Anglo-Saxon) are preserved to us in any other language than Latin; and that the use of Latin in worship and preaching was persistently prevalent into even later times.

But in favor of there having been at least some preaching in the vernacular the following considerations are urged: (1) That the fact of preservation in Latin does not prove that many of the sermons were not *delivered* in the language of the people, for Latin was the language of literature, and especially theology, and all *writings* would naturally be in that tongue. (2) Missionary preaching must have been largely if not altogether in the vernacular, either directly or by an interpreter; and there are positive statements and other indications which establish this view.[2] (3) There are laws and regulations from Charlemagne's time and onward which plainly prescribe that at least some preaching must be given to the people in their own tongue. The clearest case is that of a canon passed by the Synod of Tours in 813 which distinctly says: "And that each [preacher] shall strive to translate the same homilies [written in Latin] plainly into

[1] The point, as regards Germany, is ably discussed by Rothe, Cruel, Albert, in the works so often cited, and by scholars to whom they refer. For French preaching the admirable work of M. Lecoy de la Marche, *La Chaire Francaise au Moyen Age,* considers the question more especially in reference to the thirteenth century, but the learned author shows that there are indications of vernacular preaching in French before that time. He notes, however, the variant opinions of French scholars, and confesses the difficulty of the question.

[2] For the cases of Eligius of Noyon and of Gall, see pp. 146, 150, 151 and Lecoy de la Marche, p. 237, who quotes the following epitaph on Notker, d. 998:

Vulgari plebem, clerum sermone Latino
Erudit, et satiat magni dulcedine verbi.

Magni is probably misprint for *magna.* Here we see the contrast distinctly made between the language used for the people and that for the clergy.

the rustic Romance or German tongue, in order that all may the more easily understand the things which are said."[1]

On the other hand some seek to break the force of these weighty considerations by urging, (1) that the non-existence of dialect sermons cannot be overcome; (2) that the indications from "preaching" to the people in the vernacular are inconclusive because the word often meant only reciting the creed, the Lord's Prayer, and the like; (3) that the seeming exceptions only prove the rule; and (4) that the laws and canons show the lack of vernacular preaching and vainly sought to institute it. But this looks too much like special pleading in the interest of a theory. The truth probably lies between extreme positions either way; and there was probably some missionary and popular preaching in the vernacular, though as a rule, always in the cloisters and generally in the churches, the preaching was in Latin.

As to the character and contents of the sermons that have come down to us from that age little needs to be said. The preaching was much as in former times; the best part of it was borrowed from the older preachers, and it was filled with legends, with discussions of the churchly virtues, and the like, to the obscuration of the simple gospel. As a consequence it could not have had much influence on the life of the people. Church services consisted largely of the liturgy, especially that connected with the celebration of the mass, and very little of direct appeal to conscience and thought. After the deep darkness of the tenth century there were some tokens of a better time. The rise of scholasticism about the middle of the eleventh century and the preaching of the first Crusade toward its close were both tokens and causes of a coming revival which was to show itself in the twelfth century, and to reach its height in the truly wonderful preaching of the thirteenth.

As we have seen, the classification of preachers as missionary, parochial and cloistral still holds. The age had no distinguished preachers, though there were not

[1] Et ut easdem homilias quisque aperte transferre studeat in rusticam Romanam linguam aut Theotiscam, quo facilius cuncti possint intelligere quae dicuntur. Quoted by Rothe (S. 184) and others.

wanting in all the classes earnest workers, capable prelates, and learned divines. Some of the best and best known will be selected for brief sketches.

The most distinguished missionary preacher of the age was Ansgar (801-865), who was born of Frankish parents near Amiens and educated at the famous monastery of Corbie. After teaching a while at the twin German cloister of the same name (usually written Corvey) he accepted a call to go to Denmark as missionary. He established a mission in Schleswig in 827. He was especially kind to the poor and needy, and his zeal as teacher and preacher was marked. But the king, who had patronized the good missionary, became unpopular, and was forced to leave the country. Upon this Ansgar also found it best to retire; but a way was opened for him to enter Sweden, where he spent two years in teaching and preaching. In 831 a bishopric was established at Hamburg for all the northern country, and Ansgar was made the first incumbent of the see. The king of Denmark captured Hamburg, plundered the city and burned the church. It seemed as if Ansgar's work was all ruined; but he did not forsake the field, and better times came. Bremen and Hamburg were united, and he was made archbishop of the enlarged diocese. From Bremen as a basis he gradually resumed work both in Denmark and Sweden, and at last met with larger success. He worked on, a saintly and faithful man, to the end of his life in 865. It is known that he preached much and effectively to the people, but no sermons of his have come down to us, and particular estimate of his preaching is therefore impossible.

Among the preaching prelates of the age none stands higher than the celebrated teacher and leader Rabanus, surnamed Maurus (c. 776-856). He, too, was of good French family, was born at Mainz and carefully educated at the renowned abbey of Fulda. For a time he was sent to Tours to be taught by the famous Alcuin, but returned to Fulda and became teacher there. He was ordained deacon in 801, priest 814, elected abbot of Fulda 822, resigned 842, consecrated archbishop of Mainz 847, and retained the office till his death in 856. He was eminent as teacher, scholar, author; was a diligent bishop, and withal an active and popular preacher. He both preached much himself and encouraged others to preach.

While at Fulda he wrote at the request of Aistulph, archbishop of Mainz, a collection of homilies. They were to be used in private reading and also by the priests who should read or reproduce them in preaching. Some extracts from his introduction follow:[1] "In obedience to your commands I have composed a book of sermons to be preached to the people on all subjects which I consider necessary for them. . . . But since I could not, through the variety of my occupations, publish all these at one time, but as opportunity allowed sent them separately to you, I now request you to have them collected into one volume. . . . And this I would principally request as my recompense, that whenever you give this work to pious persons either to read or to preach you would desire them to assist my frailty by their prayers to the most righteous Judge, that I may by His grace for a long time run the course of the present life, and may merit to attain happily to future blessedness." The sermons are not remarkable either in thought or style. They are greatly wanting in originality, being largely borrowed from the fathers and earlier preachers. In one he inveighs against the still surviving superstitious custom of raising a great noise during a lunar eclipse, and inserts in the midst of his own remarks a paragraph, without altering a word, from a sermon by Maximus of Turin[2] on the same subject! This collection contains seventy sermons, and there is a later one which has a hundred and sixty-three discourses. This is thought[3] to have been more especially designed for private reading. The earlier one is the more important. The discourses deal with the fasts and feasts, but also in a striking way with the sins and errors of the times.

A fellow-student of Rabanus both at Fulda and Tours was Haymo (c. 778-853), who also taught awhile at Fulda. Later he was abbot at Hirschfeld, and from 841 to his death bishop of Halberstadt. There goes under his name a collection of a hundred and fifty-four homilies. Most of them consist of extracts and compilations from

[1] Quoted from Neale's *Mediæval Preaching*, p. 30.
[2] See *ante*, p. 123. [3] Cruel, *op. cit.*, SS. 57, 58.

the older church writers. Albert[1] considers them rather as pious extracts designed for private reading than as actually delivered homilies. There is no originality. The collection is a compound of quotations, ridiculous allegorizing of Scripture, exhortations to the churchly virtues, treatises on fasts, saints' days, and so on. They are of no value except as illustrating the taste and habit of the age in preaching.

A like man, of later date, was Fulbert (d. 1029), born probably at Chartres about the middle of the tenth century. Bishop Odo took him up when a boy and trained him for a churchman. He was put to school at Rheims, where he was taught by the celebrated Gerbert, afterwards Pope Sylvester II. Recalled to Chartres Fulbert taught various subjects—grammar, music, dialectic, medicine—and had among his pupils the subsequently famous Berengar of Tours. He was a notable teacher and was sometimes called the "Socrates of the Franks." In his writings he defends already the view of the real presence of Christ in the eucharist, which long afterwards received the name of "transubstantiation," and in the method of his theological treatises there are suggestions of the coming scholasticism. Fulbert was never a monk, and was made bishop of Chartres in 1007. Here he had no bed of roses, but was involved in the troubles of his times. He was a diligent bishop, and enjoyed a good repute as a preacher; but, in the judgment of critics, the sermons that we have from him do not sustain his reputation. They are, as usual, largely compilations filled with allegorizing and excessive veneration of the Virgin in the style of the Greek preachers. For example, he emphasizes the widely spread view that Christ is to be regarded rather as Judge, and therefore the intercession of his human mother is needed by penitents.

The name Ælfric belongs to several Anglo-Saxon churchmen of this period, but especially three are worthy of note: (1) an archbishop of Canterbury (996-1006); (2) an archbishop of York (1023-1051); (3) a certain learned Benedictine monk of contemporary date known as the "Grammarian." Whether the last is a third man or is to be identified with one of the archbishops is a

[1] *Op. cit.*, II., S. 116.

question.[1] Probabilities seem rather to favor his identification with the archbishop of York. He was a very learned teacher and greatly beloved man. In addition to his own work as preacher he translated many Latin homilies into Anglo-Saxon, and thus was not only a leader and founder of English preaching, but was also one of the fathers of English prose. As homilies these discourses hardly rise above the level of their age, but, as Schoell remarks, they are " a pure model of the beautiful Saxon mother tongue, and on that account alone are of the highest significance."

We may fitly close these sketches by the mention of two distinguished monks and prelates of the eleventh century who have left us cloistral sermons.

Peter, called Damiani (1007-1072), was born at Ravenna, the youngest of a large family. His education was provided for by his elder brother, Damian, whose name in grateful recognition of this generosity Peter ever afterwards attached to his own. He early became a monk, and in that very corrupt age was notable for his piety. He boldly denounced the current abuses and in various ways, by precept, regulation and example, sought to reform the morals of the clergy. He was a steadfast friend and ally of Hildebrand in this sorely needed work. He was made a cardinal, then papal legate at Milan, charged to correct disorders in that ever somewhat independent diocese. This post he soon resigned, worn out by conflict and worry. An address which he made to the angry clergy and people when papal legate at Milan is preserved and shows both boldness and eloquence.[2] He lived more quietly after this, writing and working in the monasteries, and died peacefully of a fever at Faenza in 1072, the year before his friend Hildebrand was made pope.

Of his sermons seventy-two remain.[3] They have the faults with which we are already familiar as characteristic of the time—copying, allegory, excessive veneration of Mary—but they show some real oratorical talent and much sweetness of spirit and piety, without much origi-

[1] Schoell, in Herzog, I., S. 185.

[2] There is an English translation in *The World's Greatest Orators,* Vol. III. (G. P. Putnam's Sons); also some discourses in Neale's *Mediæval Preaching.*

[3] Migne, *Pat. Lat.,* discussed by Rothe and others.

nality or profundity of thought. Neale[1] rates them very highly, thinking them the best of the age until we come to Bernard; but Rothe's judgment is not so favorable and is nearer the truth.

The great theologian Anselm (1033-1109) was born in northern Italy, the son of parents of some rank. The father was a harsh man, with little sympathy for the boy's predilections toward piety and the church, but the devout mother, Ermenburga—worthy to be named with Nonna, Anthusa, and Monica—brought up her son with studious care; and though he early lost her, he never lost the impress of her teachings and character. After her death the lad found his home intolerable and left it, making his way over the mountains to the monastery of Bec in Normandy, where his famous countryman, Lanfranc, the scholar, was abbot. Lanfranc was high in the favor and councils of William of Normandy, and was appointed by the Conqueror archbishop of Canterbury. Anselm's life singularly followed that of his master, for in process of time he, too, became abbot of Bec, and later, under William Rufus, archbishop of Canterbury. In this office he so stoutly maintained the church's privileges against the arrogance and greed of the king that he was banished, though afterwards recalled. He lived till 1109.

It was during his banishment that he wrote his immortal treatise on the incarnation and atonement of our Lord, called *Cur Deus Homo*—Why God-Man? His greatest distinction is as a theologian, both on account of this treatise and two others, the *Proslogion* and *Monologion;* and he is rightly regarded as the most potent force in beginning the scholastic theology, though Lanfranc and Fulbert of Chartres had previously given it some impulse. Anselm was a great thinker, and a pure and simple-hearted man. His resistance to William Rufus, though on the wrong side as we now see it, was not prompted by pride or ambition, but was the fruit of conviction; for he held the strengthening views as to the papal prerogatives.

As a preacher Anselm did not rise above his times. It is disappointing to find his sermons so distinctly inferior to his great theological works. Sixteen of his homilies

[1] *Mediæval Preaching,* p. 54.

have come down to us. They seem to be mostly if not entirely addresses to the monks. They are in the nature of running comment—old-fashioned homilies indeed—upon the Scripture for the day. They show no special eloquence, nor much originality or profundity of thought. Allegory, of course, prevails as the mode of Scripture interpretation, and there is a trace of scholastic method here and there. The opening paragraph of his homily on Our Lord Walking on the Sea gives a specimen of his method:[1] "*And straightway Jesus constrained his disciples to get into a ship, and to go before him to the other side, while he sent the multitude away.* In this lection, according to its mystical interpretation, we have a summary description of the state of the Church from the coming of the Saviour to the end of the world. For the Lord *constrained his disciples to get into a ship* when he committed the church to the government of the apostles and their followers; and thus *to go on before him unto the other side,* that is, to bear onward towards the haven of the celestial country, before he himself should entirely depart from this world. For with his elect, and on account of his elect, he ever remains here until the consummation of all things; and he is preceded to the other side of the sea of this world by those who daily pass hence to the land of the living. And when he shall have sent all that are his to that place, then, leaving the multitude of the reprobate, and no longer warning them to be converted, but giving them over to perdition, he will depart hence that he may be with his elect alone in the kingdom. Whence it is added, *while he sent the multitude away;* for in the end of the world he will send away the multitude of his enemies, that they may then be hurried by the devil to everlasting damnation." Thus he proceeds verse by verse, giving special attention to the walking on the sea and the sinking and rescue of Peter.

Our survey of preaching, both in the Eastern and Western churches, during these three dark centuries leaves us with a feeling of depression. It was mostly weak imitation or straightout copying from the past; it had in the West very little and feeble use of the vernacular; in both sections of the world it dealt largely in fables of the

[1] Quoted from Neale's *Mediæval Preaching,* p. 80.

saints, in extravagant and utterly unscriptural laudation of Mary as almost the equal of her divine Son; it laid more stress on the monastic and churchly than on the real Christian virtues; it emphasized the merit of penance and other works, and failed to make prominent the atoning work of the Saviour. Altogether the preaching of the gospel was at its lowest stage during the dark ages that extended from the death of Gregory the Great in 604 to the beginning of the Crusades in 1095. Yet some of the sermons preserved from that time show us that though weak and neglected, preaching still had some power in the world for good, and was able both to preserve and to perpetuate itself, notwithstanding the most serious external hindrances and internal decay. The beginning of the scholastic theology, the sweep of religious feeling aroused through Europe against the infidel desolators of the Holy Land, the yet unexhausted missionary impulse that had been one of the chief redeeming features of the ages of darkness, the reaction from the extreme depression of the tenth century, and the rise of the living languages of Europe as means of literary and religious expression, all are the faint gray streaks of a coming dawn. "The darkest time is just before day."

PERIOD III

THE CENTRAL MEDIÆVAL, OR SCHOLASTIC, AGE

1095–1361

From the times of Peter the Hermit and Pope Urban II. to the close of Tauler's (d. 1361) and the beginning of Wiclif's (ord. 1361) Preaching

CHAPTER VI

Heralds of the Dawn in the Eleventh and Twelfth Centuries

The hints given at the close of the last chapter indicate the beginning of a new era in the history of civilization, of Christianity, of preaching. Towards the end of the eleventh century the forces of this new stage of human progress are gathering strength, they gain in power during the twelfth century, urge the movement to its height in the thirteenth, while in the latter part of that and first half of the fourteenth century the wave recedes to make way for another of different character and results. The period, then, on which we enter in this chapter (1095-1361) may be called the core or center of the Middle Ages; and while its limits are assigned from the point of view of the history of preaching, they yet include events and movements of vast significance in general history. This coincidence is not accidental; it only means that the total life of any great epoch must contain and influence each separate manifestation of that life, and that preaching has shared with other elements of European civilization the quickening impulses and gathered results of this momentous age.

Of the whole period the present chapter takes in only a fraction of the eleventh century and all of the twelfth.

A few observations on the general history of this time will somewhat prepare the way for a study of its preaching and preachers.

1. General Survey of the Twelfth Century

The division of Charlemagne's dominions, and the establishment of the territorial power of the pope in Italy, had shattered the ideal of having one great Western Empire, and left the struggling germs of three great nations to come slowly toward their separate organic lives. These were Italy, Germany, and France. The only one to reach a real national unity in this period was France. In the eleventh century the forces working toward the separate nationality of these different peoples were more or less active. The languages were different. Italian and French were forming themselves on the basis of the Latin, but the rough German preferred its forest ancestry and repudiated the softening touch of the classic speech. The peoples, too, were at bottom different. Frank upon Gaul was a different cross from Lombard upon Italian, and Teuton was not crossed save with itself.

In Britain, which was never under the New Empire, but with the departure of the Roman eagles had pursued her own course, there was even a more distinct development. The Briton had gone down before the conquering Saxon, and now, in the eleventh century (1066), the Saxon must accept the Norman conqueror, and a new turn is given to the language and institutions of England. Such was the national outlook in the end of the eleventh century.

In this time the political aspect of Italy was simply chaotic. In the eleventh century the Normans had established themselves in Sicily, and for ages that island and the southern end of the peninsula constituted dukedoms and kingdoms under various dynasties and nations. In the north the Lombard kingdom gave way to city republics, and these to family governments. Besides these the great cities of Genoa and Venice rose through commerce to wealth and independence, and were fierce rivals in trade In central Italy fair Florence advanced step by step to power and renown. None of these discordant states could offer to the Italian people a strong centre of attraction.

The brilliant attempt of Arnold of Brescia to establish a republic at Rome ended in failure and the death of the premature patriot.

With abundant differences of detail and of national character the political affairs of the German people present a singular parallel to those of Italy, not only in the special period under our present study, but for a longer time. The revival of the empire under Otto the Great in the tenth century gave some hope of national and imperial unity; but while France was now politically separate from the empire, distracted Italy offered constant temptation to conquest, and the shadowy phantom of universal European empire still beguiled the fancy of the German kings. Thus Italy and Germany mingle their own discords into a larger din of utter confusion, and the patient ear of history waited long before hearing the first full notes of harmony. But when we turn our attention to the other two nations we shall find a very different state of affairs.

After the division of Charlemagne's dominions France, as a country, nation, and government, pursued its own line of development. The keynote of its political progress for centuries, including the central mediæval period, was the struggle for royal power. There was a king in name, but he was only the weak, nominal overlord of powerful vassals, several of whom singly were richer and stronger than he, and over whom as a whole his authority amounted to nothing. In the twelfth century Philip Augustus made substantial progress in reducing the power of the great feudal lords and extending his own. After his return from Palestine in 1191 he pressed this policy to the end of his life in 1223, gaining much territory from the English possessions in France and in various ways weakening the nobles. With him the monarchy in France became rich.

Very different from that of her continental neighbors was the political history of England during this great epoch. Like France, she developed a strong national life and government, but her monarchy tended to limitation and not to despotism. The Norman Conquest in 1066 made the king and his nobles the governing class in the country. But the Saxon love of liberty was to be reckoned with always, and the hot Norman blood of the barons was not to be too hastily stirred by royal tyrannies. By these three forces the political development of the English people was mainly guided. The first Norman kings were tyrants in character, but could not always be in fact, and many of the Plantagenets were very able and wise rulers, who knew how far they dared go in the assertion of kingly power.

Among all these peoples, alike in many respects while so unlike in others, there grew during the eleventh century a firmer grasp on life, less dependence on a decayed past and more assertion of conscious strength, reaction from the depression and darkness of the tenth century, more hopefulness and vigor in all the lines of human effort. In the sphere of thought the work of Lanfranc, of his distinguished follower Anselm, and of others of like mind, was laying fast and solid the foundation of that mighty fabric of theological and philosophical dialectics which trained and exercised for three hundred years the best human intellects—scholasticism. In religion the reformatory work of Hildebrand, beginning about the middle of the eleventh century and pursued with ardor all his strenuous life, had awakened the active sympathy of men like Peter Damiani and was bringing forth fruit meet for repentance in the lives of priests and people. Along with this there was among the masses of these nations a nascent sense of power; and at the same time in all classes a consciousness of moral and spiritual lowness and need.

On this gathered fuel fell the spark of eloquence which kindled a wondrous flame of partly religious, partly superstitious, partly political, and wholly adventurous enthusiasm which, in spite of repeated dampers, flared up at intervals during nearly two hundred years, and only flickered out at last from sheer exhaustion. In 1095 at a great council at Piacenza ambassadors appeared from Alexis Comnenus, emperor of the East, calling attention to the menacing and destructive attitude of the Saracens, and begging for help against these violators of the Holy Land. Pope Urban II. heard with sympathy, and the council favored giving the help. But there was not quite enough enthusiasm about it, and Urban, himself a Frenchman, adjourned the council and called another at Clermont, in France, later in the same year. Here his eloquent appeal stirred the audience to a frenzy of enthusiasm. The people, too, were aroused by the preaching of Peter the Hermit and others sent out by Urban, and after a while the first Crusade was started. This is not the the place to follow the long and checkered story of these expeditions. It took two centuries of costly failure to teach the West its lesson.

But during this time Europe was undergoing great changes and getting ready for the beginning of her modern course of development in civilization, which was to come by way of the Renaissance and Reformation several centuries later. The mighty though misdirected efforts of the Crusades had stirred the minds of all classes of the people, from kings and nobles to burghers and peasants. All elements of life were touched with a new breath, and so we shall find that with the Crusades, preaching, too, entered a new phase.

Yet it is, of course, in the realm of church and religion that we find the largest area of contact between the general life of the period and preaching. Some knowledge of general religious conditions as then existing is therefore essential to a good understanding of the preaching of the time; but as the discussion of the pulpit will bring out many of the details of religious life, it will be necessary here only to notice a few of the salient features of the history.

The death of Gregory VII. in 1085 closed a remarkable career and a most important era. The reforms he had carried within the church, and the claims he had asserted for it, left the papacy at the highest point it had yet reached in power and influence. The eloquent championship of the first crusade by Urban II. was another step in realizing and exhibiting the power of the pope in Europe, and also was an addition to papal prestige in that the principal part in the early crusades was borne by the Latin nations, friendly to the papacy, and not by Germany, its rival. Other things that helped on the ascendency of papal power were: the great extension of canon law, that is, of the jurisdiction of the church in causes of various sorts; the rise and extension of orders of monks more directly amenable to the pope than to the bishops; and the great influence of men like Bernard and others who were its devoted adherents.

The Concordat of Worms in 1122 was a compromise between emperor and pope on the long-standing controversy over investiture, that is, whether the prelates in any country should be appointed to office by the pope or the national sovereign. It was against the interest of the civil government that officebearers of so great influence as bishops and higher prelates should hold directly from a foreign power; it was against the interest of the church that its highest functionaries in any land should hold office by appointment of the temporal power. The question was vital; the only real settlement of it could be in the supremacy of one or the other authority. A compromise could only prolong the real feud under seeming peace, or veil the actual power of one of the parties by apparent concessions to the other. The Concordat was such a compromise; it gave to the pope investiture by ring and staff—the symbols of spiritual leadership, to the king appointment by the sceptre, the token of royal authority. The incumbent could not be fully in office without both acts, and thus if (as was usually the case) the royal appointment followed the papal, the king held a veto on the pope's appointments. This and other things left the way open for endless disputes. Yet the Concordat did give something of a breathing spell. But soon the struggle between pope and emperor broke out again, and this time it was the death struggle. The Guelf party, favoring the pope, and the Ghibelline, favoring the emperor, kept Italy and Germany in turmoil for many years. The hard-headed Adrian IV.—the only Englishman ever made pope—offered a firm and successful resistance to the great emperor Frederick Barbarossa. At the turn of the centuries (1198-1216) the greatest of all the popes—Innocent III.—was in the chair. In him the papal power reached its zenith.

In the life and character of the clergy, the moral and religious state of the people, and some other matters vitally affecting preaching, the conditions were so much the same as those which more distinctly and fully characterized the thirteenth century that detailed consideration of these points is deferred to the next chapter. It is quite time for us to come to the preaching of the twelfth century.

2. Preaching in the Twelfth Century

Although the Crusades put the old Eastern Empire and the Greek church more in contact with the West than had been the case for ages, we do not find that this contact (or anything else!) galvanized the corpse of Greek preaching. We may as well here, once for all, dismiss the consideration of it for the time included between the end of the eleventh century and the Reformation. In all this time there was of course preaching; and some sermons and the names of some of the more important preachers have come down to us. But the sermons—many of them yet unprinted and accessible only in manuscript in certain libraries—have nothing remarkable to offer. They are of the conventional type of decayed Greek preaching. Some of the preachers, as John Caleca, Gregory Palamas, George Scholarius, and others are more or less known to historical and theological scholars, but scarcely beyond those limits.

In the West, however, a very different state of things meets us.[1] Here there is at the end of the eleventh century and through the twelfth a distinct improvement in the power and effect of preaching, though as yet not very much in contents. It will be well to pay attention to the signs and causes of this revival.

As France was the leading country in Western Europe during this age it is natural that we should find there

[1] The works which have been principally used in the preparation of the following pages are: *La Chaire Française au XIIme Siècle,* par M. l'Abbé L. Bourgain; *La Chaire Française au Moyen Age,* par M. Lecoy de la Marche; *Geschichte der Predigt in Deutschland bis Luther* (especially Bd. II., *Die Blütezeit der Deutschen Pred. im M.-A.*), von F. R. Albert; *Der Heilige Bernhard und sein Zeitalter,* von A. Neander; *Geschichte der Deutschen Predigt im Mittelalter,* von R .Cruel; *Geschichte der Predigt in Deutschland von Karl dem Grossen bis zum Anfang des 15ten Jahrhunderts,* von A. Linsenmayer (Catholic); *L'Oratoria Sacra Italiana nel Medio Evo,* da Luigi Marenco; *Old English Homilies of the Twelfth Century* (Vol. II. of these in *Publications of the Early English Text Society*), edited, etc., by R. Morris. These will be referred to simply by the name of the author in each case. Many other works, including, as far as was practicable, the sources, have of course been consulted, and general reading has left its impressions in many cases where minute acknowledgment is impossible.

more than elsewhere the evidences of a revived interest in preaching. In other lands, too, there is heightened interest, and indeed throughout the Western European countries there can be no doubt that the darkest ages of preaching are now in the past.

Speaking summarily, we may say that the leading tokens of the revival are two: (1) There is a greater regard for preaching on the part of the clergy themselves. The shameful neglect of the past centuries begins to be redressed, and the mediæval Christian Israel suffers no longer so great a dearth of "teaching priests." Much remains to be done, many faults to be corrected, but there is hope of better things, yea, better things have already begun to be, when the preachers themselves magnify their office. (2) The other token of revival is the converse of this; it is that the people of all classes begin to show more respect for the real preacher and more interest in his message. It is true that scant respect is due, and scant respect is shown, to the still too numerous preaching officials who deserve not the name of preacher. But where a man like Bernard, or Fulco of Neuilly, or, among the so-called heretics, one like Henry of Lausanne, appears, the admiration and love of the people are abundantly in evidence. The very opposition occasionally roused by the preacher showed how great was the power of his word. The bad priests sometimes endeavored to stop the good ones, even using personal violence; and the loose and wicked among the people once in a while raised persecution against the brave men who denounced their sins. Bourgain well says[1] that the popular and worthy preacher was thus exposed to the double peril of persecution by his enemies and overpraise by his friends. Alas! it is one of the perennial perils of a fearless and able ministry. But the fact shows that preaching was no longer to be despised. Moreover the greater crowds which now began to attend popular preaching show this quickening of general interest in the work.

When we attempt to find and state the causes which led to this revival of interest in preaching we are met by the difficulties natural to such inquiries, and yet we may not decline the task. From the point of view of the Chris-

[1] Pp. 8, 9.

tian faith the one great cause lies hidden in the unrevealed designs and movements of Divine Providence, and in the mysterious and gracious workings of that blessed Power of whom the highest authority declares:[1] "The Spirit breathes where he will, and you hear his voice, but know not whence he comes and whither he goes; so is everyone that is born of the Spirit." From the point of view of history and philosophy the deeper cause lies beyond ken in that mighty law of ebb and flow, action and reaction, which directs, yet with no perceived regularity, the course of human affairs. The rhythmic action of this great law is detected in all those larger and nobler activities of man which for lack of a more accurate designation we may call spiritual: the realms of literature [2] and art, of science and philosophy, of statecraft and commerce, of manners and morals, of religion. Even when we admit the mystery of this great law of up and down, of forward and backward, and attempt only to detect and name what we are pleased to call "proximate causes," we cannot always be sure of our ground. For sometimes we call causes what are in fact effects, accompaniments, symptoms.

Yet, bearing in mind these greater and deeper causes, we may go on to present those more evident events and movements which seem to account for the marked revival of interest and power which we observe in the preaching of the twelfth century. In general it may be said that this revival was one element or part of that quickening of life which was felt throughout Europe in this age. And more especially we may distinguish and emphasize the following five things: (1) The reforms instituted by Gregory VII. among the clergy must have had weight. To be sure there was much yet to be done; but a more earnest spirit of devotion, a better life, and a higher regard for preaching as a part of their work seem to characterize the clergy at the beginning of this time. Always when the preachers themselves have a proper conception of their work, and live more nearly up to the standard which their exalted office requires, preaching will be more

[1] John 3: 8—perhaps the most probable meaning.

[2] For an interesting discussion of how this law has worked in German literature see W. Scherer, *Gesch. der Deutschen Literatur,* SS. 19, 20.

earnest and more fruitful. (2) Along with this spiritual quickening among the clergy must be reckoned also the intellectual revival which expressed itself in that form of philosophical thinking in theology to which the name of scholasticism is given. The rise of this mode of thought, especially among the clergy, has already been noticed, and will be more fully discussed later on;[1] but it must here be reckoned, with all its shortcomings, as one of the most potent causes and accompaniments of the revived preaching of the twelfth and thirteenth centuries. When the preachers—even the few, the leaders—think profoundly on religious themes there must be a heightened tone in preaching. (3) Another potent cause, noticed by both Catholic and Protestant writers,[2] was the work of the so-called heretics. Many of these in the twelfth century were thinkers of no mean order, and one of the ways they took to disseminate their views was by preaching among the people. This stirred the Catholics to use similar means to meet what they considered dangerous errors. All through this century and the next, preaching for and against heresy is very common. Scholasticism represented religious thinking in the schools, heresy among the masses. Both stimulated and influenced preaching. (4) We must repeat that the crusades were a powerful factor in stimulating preaching. This they did not only by the general stir they produced, and not only by the partially religious character of the enthusiasm they awakened, but more especially and directly by the use they made of popular preaching. The oral address, whether by an Urban before the princes at Clermont, or by a Peter the Hermit, or a Raoul the Ardent among the people, was the means employed to arouse the masses. After these first preachers came Bernard and others to preach the later crusades. It was not exactly preaching—in the proper sense of the word—but it was the urging of men to immediate self-sacrificing devotion to what was believed to be a religious cause. It appealed to religious motives—at least in part—and thus it revealed and utilized the power of religious eloquence over the masses of men. So, while we well might wish that the object had

[1] See below p. 231 ff.
[2] Linsenmayer, Bourgain, Broadus, and others.

been more truly Christian, the motives purer, and the methods more enlightened, it is yet true that the proclamation of the crusades was a mighty and a permanent step forward in the development of popular preaching. (5) Another notable cause in making the preaching of the age powerful was the increased and more effective use of the language of the people. We have already seen [1] that in the preceding age the national languages were forming, and were coming into competition with the Latin as means of preaching. Now, just when the proclamation of the crusades called for effective popular address, this tendency shows marked advance, so as to make this epoch the transition period to the general use of these languages in the sermons of Europe till in the sixteenth century the triumph of the vernaculars is complete. But this important matter, besides being a cause of revival, requires fuller notice as marking one of the most interesting features of the age.

Whatever differences of opinion may divide scholars as to the use of the popular tongues in the preaching before this time, it is generally admitted that in the twelfth century these languages were widely if not generally employed in the sermons addressed to the people.[2] Lecoy de la Marche has shown that in the thirteenth century the French tongue was chiefly used in preaching to the people in France; and that this usage rests upon a custom growing faster and firmer from preceding times. Other writers have followed the same kinds of investigation for other countries and have reached assured conclusions. The twelfth century therefore witnesses the widespread and firmly fixed, though not yet universal and exclusive, use of the native and living languages of Europe in the pulpit. But granting this, there are several related questions which require to be noticed.

Have we any sermons now remaining in the twelfth century forms of modern European languages? In Italian

[1] See above, p. 165 f.

[2] So for France, Bourgain and Lecoy de la Marche; for Germany Cruel, Linsenmayer, and for the twelfth century, Albert; for Italy Marenco and Zanotto (*Storia della Predicazione nei Secoli della Letteratura Italiana*); and for England *The Old English Homilies.*

there seem to be none.[1] In German there are a great number.[2] In French there seem not to be many published collections, but Lecoy de la Marche and Bourgain have studied and reported a large number in manuscript which they found in libraries and collections. In English the *Publications of the Early English Text Society* contain volumes edited by Dr. Morris of *Old English Homilies,* dating from the twelfth and thirteenth centuries. These sermons in themselves, as we shall see, are of little value, but to the students of language, literature, and theology they are relics of inestimable importance.

Another question—chiefly of literary and philological interest—relates to the state of the languages themselves as compared with their modern descendants. It is only necessary to remark on this point that by the twelfth century the native tongues had already acquired distinctive character and a considerable degree of firmness. There are various literary remains from this age which are highly prized by students and lovers of literature. It is for us a matter of no little interest to find that in that nascent literature of Europe preaching had a place of its own, and has sent on to modern times specimens of its contribution to the general sum. The preacher, as well as the poet and historian, had his place in guiding and fixing the linguistic development of European literature.

The remaining question to be considered is, What was the relation between the Latin and the vernacular languages in the uses of the pulpit? It is rather a complicated question. We must bear in mind several facts. One is that the Latin was actually used in spoken sermons not only in the twelfth century, but much later, along with the growing use of the national tongues. On this point it is of course impossible to determine and express with any precision the exact proportion of use; but it is quite evident that as the employment of the other languages increased that of the Latin declined.

Another fact is that by far the larger proportion of all

[1] Marenco, cap. I., says that there is one Italian sermon which may date from the twelfth century, but as the first one he is sure of belongs to the fourteenth, the point is not settled.

[2] Linsenmayer, S. 245 ff.; Cruel, S. 146 ff.; Albert, I., sec. I; all of whom refer to a number of collections made by other German scholars.

the sermons that have come down to us, not only from the twelfth century, but from the entire Middle Ages, are in Latin. Some of the earlier writers on the history of preaching, as well as some later critics, have been led by this fact to suppose that most of the sermons of the middle centuries were actually delivered in Latin. But the excellent work of Lecoy de la Marche and others has shown that the fact can be easily explained. The explanation is that many of the sermons which were delivered in the common tongues were written in Latin. This was sometimes done by the preachers themselves, either before delivery as sketches or notes, or after preaching as abbreviated reproductions. Sometimes the sermons were reproduced by hearers from notes taken on the spot or from memory. They were written in Latin because that was still the language of writing, of publication, of culture, the common medium of European scholarship. A man would have more hearers when he used the common tongue, but more readers when he used the Latin. The educated disregarded the common tongue as unsuited to writing. It is recalled that Dante, even in the thirteenth century, was minded to write his great epic, as he had written his great treatise on government, in Latin, but for some reason did use the Italian. As for the common people, few if any could read either language.

The next matter of importance for us to consider is the preservation of sermons. And here several items claim attention. First of all we have to make the obvious remark that the most of them have not been preserved at all! This is true of every age, and was no less so of the twelfth century. Many of the preachers of these sermons are now unknown, some have left a reputation for eloquence, but no specimens; while some have left specimens, but, unhappily, no eloquence. Nor is this beyond explanation. For even to-day many of our most effective preachers never get their sermons printed, and the printed sermons of many others are not fair specimens of their power before an audience. Our criticism of any age, as of our own, must on this account be cautious; and it is no wonder that the homiletic remains of the twelfth century hardly convey to us a just idea of the actual and effective preaching of that stirring time.

Another item of interest—already briefly noticed in another connection—is that we have from this age numerous collections of anonymous sermons—some in Latin, some in German, in French, and in English. One of the peculiarities of mediæval preaching—from the time of Charlemagne onward—was the preparation and employment of *homiliaries* or collections of sermons for the use of the clergy. They might use them as models and guides, or might commit and recite them, or, in extreme cases, might read them. This plagiarism was not considered a fault—it found early and authoritative justification in something that the great Augustine had written! Both Rabanus Maurus and Paul the Deacon in the preceding times had made these collections, and the work went on for ages.

The striking thing about the sermons found in these collections is their strong family likeness, their lack of individuality, of originality. When we compare the Latin and English sermons with the criticisms of the scholars who are familiar with those found in the German and French collections we see that these homilies have much the same character in all. The reason lies chiefly in the fact that they are mostly compilations and reproductions of older authors. Among these the prime favorites [1] seem to have been Augustine (or what was reported to be his work), Cæsarius of Arles, Gregory the Great, and Bede—the last-named, as we have seen,[2] being largely a compiler himself.

These collections, then, give us a saddening view of the dependence and tameness of the twelfth century preaching, but we must qualify this judgment by remembering what has just been said about the many unwritten sermons that stirred the age, and also by taking note of what is now to be said about those whose authors are known to us.

For we have also from the twelfth century a large number of authentic sermons. Many of these have the faults of the anonymous ones, but they show, as is natural, more individuality, more original force, more freshness. These sermons exist, for reasons given above, mostly in Latin; but there are some in French, and one

[1] Linsenmayer, SS. 193, 194. [2] See above, p. 147.

of the German collections is ascribed to a certain Conrad the Priest, of whom Albert[1] says, "To the priest Conrad belongs the honor of having left the most important collection of sermons [in German] before Berthold of Regensburg." We shall see more of these later on.

The form and contents of twelfth century sermons offer a curious and not unprofitable subject of study, which has received suitable attention at the hands of the scholars whose excellent leadership we have been following. These sermons did not reach the excellence of ancient times nor that of the following centuries, but they begin to show improvement upon the immediate past. The old form of the simple expository and hortatory homily was retained. There was not so much attention to arrangement and division as we shall find in the sermons of the thirteenth century, but already this tendency to a more logical structure and penetrating analysis begins to show itself. This appears in the sermons of Bernard, who sometimes announces his plan of treatment in advance of discussion. He is considered by some to have introduced, or at least to have improved and popularized, the analytic method, and thus to have set the fashion for all following times. Others, as Broadus,[2] assign a preeminence in this direction to Antony of Padua in the thirteenth century. Both these great popular preachers only used, developed and set going a tendency which was native to the time, which we shall hereafter more fully notice, as it came to its height in the next century—that is, the scholastic method. And it naturally finds a more complete application in the hands of Antony than of Bernard, who was influenced by its beginnings and not its full growth.

Along with this growing fondness in the contemporary mental attitude for logical analysis we must notice the fact that the teaching of homiletics was not neglected in this age. Not only was there probably oral teaching on the subject in the schools for clerical education,[3] but there were numerous homiletical helps provided. These, as we have seen, were partly in the way of sermons or homilies already prepared, and thus were injurious rather than

[1] Bd. I., S. 9. [2] *Hist. Prea.*, p. 103.
[3] Mentioned by both Cruel and Linsenmayer.

helpful. But along with this there were numerous treatises which taught the art of preaching.[1] It is true that these treatises themselves show little originality or power, but the use of them was at least favorable to a better rhetorical practice. And this practice so far shows itself in many of the sermons that Bourgain[2] is led to a too enthusiastic estimate of the rhetorical facility of the preachers of the time, saying that many of them "seem to have known Fénélon[3] in advance."

As to other matters of rhetoric, style did not so much differ with individuals as is common. This is accounted for by the use of homilies, imitation, copying and the like. The style of these homilies is usually tame, but unpretentious and clear. With vigorous men like Raoul the Ardent and Bernard there is of course less of the commonplace and a more pronounced individuality in the style. In some of the sermons there is a turgidity and laboring after effect which reminds us of the later Greek preachers. In others plays upon words, and rhymed prose, or *assonance,* are much sought after. The use of illustration, especially legend and anecdote, was frequent, but not always very clever. Albert[4] calls this whole time the "narrative period" in preaching, from the liberal use of narrative as compared with argument, exposition, and doctrine. Yet he says that it is impossible to declare any one method to have been dominant. As the material was gathered from many sources so were the forms of discourse.

The use of Scripture in the sermons is much as we found it in the preceding ages. How could there be improvement upon the past with such wholesale borrowing from the past? The *pericope,* or reading for the day, often furnishes the basis for the sermon. Sometimes another text is taken and the *pericope* is handled in the discourse; sometimes no text is taken; and sometimes sayings of the Fathers, or even passages from the liturgy, are used as texts. In the sermons there is much quotation of Scripture, but it is often inexact, and oftener still misinterpreted

[1] For full and critical discussions of these see Cruel, S. 244 ff., and Linsenmayer, S. 85 ff.
[2] *Op. cit.,* chap. II.
[3] I. e., his famous *Dialogues on Eloquence,* 17th century.
[4] Bd. II., sec. 1, 2.

and misapplied. The interpretation is of course still allegorical, if possible even more absurd than in former times. Centuries must pass before the pulpit could be delivered—and even yet is not wholly delivered!—from bondage to this ancient and intrenched abuse of Scripture. This was to be expected in the traditional homilies, but even original and powerful men like Bernard are not free from it. Ambrose and Augustine had got it from the Greek Alexandrian school, and the Roman clergy for centuries followed and carried to extremes the methods of these and other revered teachers of the ancient church. For example, Samson, who rose in the night and carried off the gates of Gaza, was a type of our Lord, who rose from the grave and triumphed over death. Gideon's fleece was a prefiguration of the Virgin Mary. Thus: The fleece was wet, and all the earth was dry; before our Lord's birth and during his infancy Mary alone had the treasure and all the earth had him not: then the fleece was dry and all the earth was wet; in his manhood and death Mary was bereft, but all the earth had the Saviour.[1] One of the preachers went so far as to say that "he who does not understand the Holy Scripture and the deep sense of it *otherwise than according to the words which are there written,* to him it tastes no better than if he chews and eats unthreshed and unground corn."[2]

On the whole, with regard to the use of Scripture, the Catholic critics,[3] while admitting faults of interpretation, are far more lenient toward the mediæval use, or rather misuse, of Scripture than are the Protestant writers. For the latter point of view Albert[4] very well sums up the case as follows: Theoretically the Bible was recognized as the source and foundation of preaching. But the following great errors show that in reality it had less influence than in appearance: (1) The use of extra-biblical material as Biblical, that is, the Fathers of the church and legends; (2) Gross and wilful errors of interpretation and application; (3) Extreme use of allegory, even to the point of teaching things contrary to Scripture; (4) Frequent lack of any text at all.

In general the doctrinal and moral teachings of the

[1] Albert, sec. 3.
[2] Id., sec. 4.
[3] As Linsenmayer and Bourgain.
[4] *Op. cit.,* sec. 4.

twelfth century preachers were, from the Catholic standpoint, Christian and sound; and with much of the teaching Protestants find themselves gladly in accord. But, on the other hand, there is, of course, much, both in principle and detail, which from a true Biblical standpoint must be regarded as erroneous and hurtful.

We have just seen that ostensibly the Bible was accepted as the source of teaching, but that in many ways it was departed from or misapplied. Also the great central Christian doctrines were proclaimed and urged, but in many points they were misunderstood, obscured, perverted. Thus the doctrine of the Trinity was accepted, but often there was little if any distinction made between the Persons of the Godhead.[1] Christ is presented as truly divine, and as the only and all-sufficient Saviour; but often his glory is obscured by dwelling on that of Mary and the saints, and his atoning work is overshadowed by wrong teaching as to the merit of works and the intercession of human and glorified mediators. The sinfulness of man and his need of repentance and faith in order to be saved were insisted upon, but repentance too easily became outward penances, and faith a mere acceptance of the church creed. The future life was taught in both its phases of punishment and bliss, but this was mingled with unscriptural teachings as to purgatory, and with other more or less harmful errors. One of the curious teachings, which came indeed probably from a hint of Augustine's, but was much insisted on and used in this time, was that God's purpose in the creation and then in the redemption of man was to fill up the gap which had been made in the heavenly hosts by the fall of the angels. Much attention is paid to the angels, and also to the reality of Satan and his aids. Perhaps the greatest error, which the Catholic writers praise as a glorious truth, emphasized by these sermons, is the adoration of the Virgin. The extravagances of the preceding period [2] had become the settled doctrines of the twelfth century. In one of these homilies Mary is represented as the fishing line and Christ as the hook and the bait. The hook represents the divinity whereby he strangles the devil, the bait represents the humanity whereby he attracts and saves us! Such stuff as this is, alas! only too common.

[1] Albert, ib., sec. 5. [2] See above.

Excepting the errors as to penance and merits and related details, the moral teaching of the sermons is usually satisfactory—Biblical, Christian, strong. Sins and virtues are strongly depicted and vividly portrayed in their contrasted natures, effects and recompenses. Vice is not glozed over nor weakly denounced, wherever found in nobility, clergy, or people. And so, making all necessary allowances and subtractions for errors, perversions and faults of every kind, the sum of our findings as to the doctrinal contents of these sermons would be that, upon the whole, the great essentials of Christian faith and life are presented in them; and that he who would intelligently and sincerely take their teachings to heart would find the Lord Christ as his Saviour, and heaven as his eternal home.

As to the times and subjects of preaching, the latter were often determined by the former, so that sermons on the regular days of the church year—Sundays and feast days—were called *sermones de temporibus;* and those in commemoration of the saints were called *sermones de sanctis.* Besides these there were special occasions, such as dedications, meetings, funerals, and the like. Within these general limits, of course, the particular subjects of the sermons would be determined by the nature of the occasion, the lesson for the day, the choice of the preacher, and so on. The hour by preference was early in the forenoon—apparently sometimes preceding, sometimes following the celebration of the mass. But other hours were also sometimes used, according to circumstances. The place of preaching was of course generally the church or the cloister chapel, but the popular preachers often addressed the crowds in the open air in town and country. The audiences varied both in character and size with circumstances—whether in church or monastery—whether a special or ordinary occasion—whether a popular or dull preacher—as always! Audiences were not always very orderly. Preachers complain of inattention, going out, sleepiness and the like, in well understood fashion. Bourgain tells of one preacher who seems to have had a drowsy audience, and he quietly remarks, "That sleeping man over there in the corner is going to miss the great secret I have to tell, if he doesn't wake up."

It had the desired effect. Men and women usually sat apart. There seems to have been difference of custom in regard to posture. Some of the references in the sermons plainly indicate that the people were standing up, others (as in the case of sleepiness and other indications) quite as plainly show that the people were sitting or reclining. So that there was no uniformity in this matter, it probably varied with time, place and circumstances. The audiences were more free and easy than now, more like a popular assembly. They often expressed approval or disapproval. Even so mighty a man as Bernard alludes in one of his sermons—perhaps more—to this, saying in effect, "I see by the way you shake your heads and whisper that what I am saying does not please you; but it is true," and so on. The preacher was often confidential and conversational with his audience, introducing dialogue, homely illustration, humor, and sometimes even undignified, not to say irreverent drollery. The fresh popular preaching of the twelfth century had not yet got on stilts. Of course there were differences between individuals in this as in other regards. The mode of delivery of sermons was usually that of free speech after more or less of preparation; sometimes the homilies were learned by heart and recited; and there are some indications that sermons were occasionally read from manuscript—possibly not always the preacher's own! [1]

Before concluding our survey of the preaching of the twelfth century it may be well to give a specimen in illustration of some of the points hitherto presented. It is taken from Morris' *Old English Homilies of the Twelfth Century* [2] as translated by him from the Saxon, the subject being the Nativity of Our Lord, and runs thus: "*Natus est nobis hodie Salvator qui est Christus in civitate David.*[3] Good tidings and pleasant to hear the lord St. Luke tells us in the holy gospel, and saith that an holy messenger brought them from heaven to the land of Jerusalem, and told them to the shepherds who were

[1] Lecoy de la Marche, Pars II., chap. V. [2] P. 30.

[3] It was usual in the vernacular sermons to retain the Latin in announcing the text, in quoting Scripture and other sayings, though nearly always the Latin was either translated or paraphrased.

watching over their cattle beside the city of Bethlehem. Listen now and attend how he told the tidings word by word. . . ." The author goes on to explain how great the joy was, and proceeds: "These words the angel said because that man should fill up the angels' seat (which had been forfeited when Lucifer and his company fell out thereof), and not on account of angels' sickness, who have eternal health; but for man's sickness, who are all sick, and have all been so since affliction came upon our first father Adam, as our Lord saith in the holy gospel: *Homo quidam descendebat ab Jerusalem in Jericho et incidit in latrones, etc.* Our Lord Jesus Christ saith that a man went down from Jerusalem to Jericho and came upon thieves, and they spoiled him of all his rich garments and wounded him very sorely, and left him scarcely alive. This is said of Adam, *Qui descendit a beatitudine caeli in defectus hujus mundi.*[1] It was Adam that went out from the perfect bliss of paradise into the wretched state of this world, and led after him then nigh all his offspring." The preacher proceeds to explain that the thieves were the devils who robbed man of the three garments of grace, immortality and innocence, and inflicted on him wounds, that is manifold sins. So God punished him for these sins, and sent many sorrows upon all. Then he goes on: "And in such sickness they longed eagerly for our Saviour; and he came, thanked be he, to heal them of their sin wounds and to clothe them in those honorable garments which the devil had taken from our forefather Adam." He sent messengers to announce his coming—patriarchs, prophets, angels, and now this angel. Not to the great of earth, but to these shepherds.—"Therefore I will tell you (take heed thereto and understand it) what the herdsmen, and what the nightwatches, and what the cattle betoken; and first of all what the wild beast denotes."—Quotes Peter's saying about our adversary the devil, comments on it, and proceeds.—"The flocks which this beast worrieth are sheep, and oxen, and goats, and swine."—Shows how men fall into each of these classes, and goes on.—"Some men lead a pure life and neither do nor say anything unpleasant to their fellowmen, but love God and go each day to church as sheep to the

[1] Probably the words of the Latin homily or of a church writer.

fold, and do gladly their duty to the church and give alms to poor men, and are called sheepish men."—The oxen likewise signify the good "who will do nothing wrong, but labor with the earth and till much for other men's behoof, and these are called oxish [or neatish] men. Of these sheepish and oxish men speaketh the prophet thus, *Subjecisti sub pedibus ejus oves et boves,* that is to say the sheepish and the neatish men are in bondage to Christ."[1] The goatish men, our preacher at some length explains, are the lascivious who live in their evil ways, reek of their sins, and will be punished in hell. The swinish men are those who "pass their lives in eating and drinking as swine, which foul themselves and root up and sniff ever foully and much enjoy foul things, and when they are full they go to the foul mire and therein wallow ———, and therefore they are called swinish men. And in them the devil dwelleth by the leave of our Lord Jesus Christ, as the holy gospel saith."—Quotes the passage in Latin and goes on, "Our Lord drove many devils together out of a man who was out of his wits, and thus healed him, and the devils entreated our Lord Jesus Christ to send them into a flock of swine, and he did so; and the swine ran, as the devils drove them, into the sea and drowned themselves. So giveth our Lord leave to the devil to be in the swinish men of whom I have before spoken, and to dwell in them and to drown them and to bring them out of their wits and to drive them from one wrong to another, from a little vice to a great one, from sin to sin, from evil to evil, and lastly he drowneth them in shameful death and leadeth them with him to hell."

The shepherds, of course, represent "the teachers of holy church which pasture their flocks on sweet pastures which are the good words of Holy Book." The preacher describes and condemns the bad shepherds, and then speaks of the good. These keep watch during the night, that is this life.—"And this life in which we live is compared to night because it is so dark through our horrible sins. In this night there are four night-watches: before evening, which belongeth to children; midnight, which belongeth to youth; cockcrow, which belongeth to grown

[1] Literally, "are in thrallship to Christ."

men; morning-time to old men. These herdsmen that are teachers, as bishops and priests, watch before evening; then are the children well brought up. At midnight he watcheth, when he taketh away the vices of youth and teacheth them the good. At cockcrow he watcheth, when he turneth the full-grown men to God's service. In the morning he watcheth, when he turneth old men to the bliss of our Lord Jesus Christ."—Then with an application to his hearers, and a reference to baptism and the Lord's Supper the homily concludes.

3. Preachers of the Twelfth Century

The number of preachers in the twelfth century seems to have been relatively greater than ever before. Besides all the orders of clergy there were many unauthorized preachers—especially among the so-called heretics. All these men of course differed widely among themselves in character, all the way from the earnest and sincere down to the false and vicious; in talents and culture, from the few of exceptional ability down to the mediocre and the strangely ignorant; in modes of thought and life, from the great prelate busy with worldly affairs to the ascetic hermit who had fled the world; from the absorbed scholar to the rough and ready popular preacher. Classification of so varied a body of men is difficult, no matter what basis we take. The grouping adopted for the last period will still be found serviceable—parochial, cloistral, and missionary or popular. In the thirteenth century we shall find it possible to classify the preachers with some degree of accuracy according to their mode of thinking and working, into scholastic, popular, and mystic; and tokens of this distinction are already at hand in the twelfth century. Thus, for example, Peter Lombard is scholastic, Fulco of Neuilly is popular, and Hugo of St. Victor is mystic; while Bernard of Clairvaux combined in himself the mystic and popular elements, with traces of the scholastic. If we group the preachers simply by nationality our difficulties are not removed; for in many cases it is hard to say to what nation a man properly belongs. Often he was born in one country, was educated in another, worked and died in a third. As for languages all the educated knew and used Latin, and several of them spoke more than one of the dialects. Yet, without being very exact, we may consider them according to countries; and since we find that of the four leading countries of Europe France was very far in advance in the number and quality of her preachers, we shall briefly discuss the others first, reserving the French preachers for more extended notice.

In Italy, as in the other European countries, the number of preachers in this period was large, and many sermons have come down to us in the Latin language.[1] There was also no doubt preaching in Italian, as both Marenco and Zanotto, independently of each other, show.[2] The latter scholar [3] describes the period as one "in which the new art [i.e., new mode of preaching] grew up, rough and without monuments of high value, developing itself under the dominion of the scholastic method and the Latin language." There are few Italian preachers of this age whom it would be profitable to study; but there are three who for different reasons stand apart from the commonplace crowd, and though few, if any, homiletical remains are preserved from them, they yet influenced the course of thought and of preaching in such ways as to claim some notice here.

Near the end of the eleventh century, in a little town of Lombardy, was born, of what parentage is unknown, a boy who was named Peter,[4] and later called from his native region, the "Lombard." His talents gained the notice of a benefactor who provided for his education at Bologna. Thence he went to France, with a letter of recommendation to the great Bernard, who aided him in attending school first at Rheims, and then at Paris in the famous abbey of St. Victor. His progress was great, and he was made bishop of Paris in 1159, but resigned the next year. He was the greatest teacher and representative of the Scholastic philosophy in his time. His famous treatise, "Sentences," exercised a profound influence on his own and subsequent times. Bourgain briefly criticises him as "celebrated theologian, mediocre

[1] See Marenco, *op. cit.*, cap. I.; and F. Zanotto, *Storia della Predicazione nei Secoli della Letteratura Italiana,* cap. I.

[2] Ibb. [3] P. 7.

[4] Works in Migne, *Pat. Lat.*, tt. 191, 192; and notices of his life in various authorities, especially Wetzer und Welte, *Kirchenlexicon,* Bd. 9, S. 1916 ff.

preacher." But his influence on thought and on preaching entitles him at least to this short notice.

Also from northern Italy and contemporary with Peter, was Arnold of Brescia (d. 1155).[1] He, too, as a young man, was attracted to Paris by the fame of its teachers; and there he became an admirer and friend of Abelard, who influenced him profoundly. Returning to Brescia, and being now a priest and preacher, he attacked the corruptions of the church, and maintained that it should free itself from political and other worldly entanglements. Banished from home he spent some years in France, Switzerland and Bohemia. Later he was allowed to be at Rome, but attracting followers, and encouraging a revolt with the idea of establishing a republic, he was taken and executed in 1155. No sermons remain, but his powerful eloquence is admitted by foes and admired by friends; and its monument is in its effects and in the fact that even to this day in Italy his name is dear to lovers of liberty. Apart from his political influence his preaching against Romish evils was moving and powerful.

A very notable man in his day, and still more in his subsequent influence, was Joachim (Gioacchino) (d. 1202), abbot of Floris in Calabria.[2] He was born in Sicily not earlier than 1130. After a pilgrimage to the Holy Land he became head of a monastery of the Cistercian order in Italy, and later was permitted to establish a new abbey at Floris (Fiore), regulated by very strict principles and earnestly devoted to flight from the world and to study. He enjoyed the favor of the emperor Henry VI., and of the empress Constance, and was during his life to all appearance on good terms with the popes, though later some of his writings were condemned. He was a man of great personal influence and probably of eloquence. He does not seem to have preached or taught

[1] The church histories and encyclopedias usually give good accounts of Arnold. The German historian, Giesebrecht, has in modern times given him great fame, and there is a long account of his controversy with Bernard in Neander's *Heilige Bernhard,* S. 222 ff.

[2] Besides the church histories, etc., Sabatier's *Life of St. Francis of Assisi,* p. 46 ff (Am. ed.); and a critical article by E. Schott in Brieger und Bess, *Zeitschrift für Kirchengeschichte,* Jahrgang 1901, S. 343 ff.

much outside of his cloister, but through his monks and his writings he came to have decisive influence upon the course of thought and of preaching. His significance (dimly foreshadowing Savonarola three centuries later) was that of prophet and reformer. Schott[1] thinks that his prophetic scheme was tampered with by his pupils, and we cannot be sure that all which purports to be his is authentic. "The Everlasting Gospel" is the phrase chosen to designate his scheme, which divides history into three great eras corresponding to the Persons of the Trinity and to the three greatest apostles: That of the Father, represented by Peter, the introduction of Christianity; that of the Son, represented by Paul, the early history of Christianity; and that of the Spirit, represented by John, the contemporary age, toward the end of the world. While he believed in the Catholic Church he attacked sharply its corruptions. He mightily stirred the better spirits of his age and place, and the effects of his work were among the influences which shaped the purposes and character of the young Francis of Assisi.[2]

Germany, too, was not without its representatives. We have seen that the collections of homilies among the Germans, whether in Latin or the vernacular, are almost entirely anonymous. Yet in some cases the name of the author, or compiler rather, is given; and of these three—two in Latin and one in German—deserve notice.

One of these goes under the name of Honorius Scholasticus (d. c. 1150), sometimes also called Augustodunensis. It is not perfectly clear that Honorius was a German, as he lived long in France, but the probabilities are that he was.[3] His life is wrapped in obscurity. But he seems to have been born in Germany near the beginning of the twelfth century and to have lived and taught long in an abbey at Autun (Augustodunum) in France, whence he returned to another cloister in his native land, and died near the middle of the century. He was a very prolific writer on a number of theological subjects,[4] and his writings were highly prized especially in south Germany.[5] It is, however, as a preacher and compiler of sermons that he concerns us.

[1] *Op. cit.* [2] Sabatier, *ad loc.*
[3] Linsenmayer, S. 194, and note; Cruel, S. 129 ff.
[4] Migne, *Pat. Lat.*, tom. 172. [5] Linsenmayer, *ad. loc.*

His collection[1] is called *Speculum Ecclesiæ*, "Mirror of the Church;" and the story of its origin and purposes is given in the preface. According to this the brethren of his order addressed to him an urgent request to publish for the benefit of a larger circle the discourses which he had, so greatly to their profit, delivered in the convent. Honorius replies that "the most skillful painters, Ambrose, Augustine, Jerome, Gregory, and very many others, had beautifully decorated the house with a wonderful, heavenly and varied painting;" but as they were perhaps in some measure beyond comprehension, or extracts from them had become through frequent use somewhat trite, he would respond to the request of his brethren and put forth this little "tablet" which he had painted, unworthy indeed to be compared with the great works of the masters, but nevertheless new and likely to be of some help to those who should use it. He calls it the "Mirror of the Church," which "all priests may hang up before the eyes of the church, that the Bride of Christ by it may see what in her still is displeasing to her Bridegroom, and may conform her ways and acts to his image." Then he gives a set of instructions for conducting worship, and says, "Having then by the grace of the Holy Spirit received inwardly the word of God in his name thus humbly begin:" Then follows the first sermon, on the Nativity of our Lord. Near the end, having made a good stopping place, he gives this hint to the preacher: "Here make an end if you wish; but if time permits add the following"—and gives some more. Instructions like this abound throughout the sermons. In one he says that if it is very cold, or very hot, "or any other impediment hinders," the preacher may omit certain parts, otherwise he may add so and so. In another he says, "In all the sermons you ought first to pronounce the verse in the Latin tongue, and then explain in the common tongue (*patria lingua*)." As to the merits of the sermons themselves the general criticism on all similar collections is applicable—except that these have a certain freshness in the compilation and show a trace of originality here and there in handling the materials. There is a good deal of striving after effect, particularly in the use of the

[1] Migne, *op. cit.*, col. 813 ss.

rhymed prose, or assonance, then so popular. It is probable that this was done in some measure to aid the memory of the preacher as well as for rhetorical effect. The *Speculum* was much used, and became a mine from which other compilers and translators liberally helped themselves.

Early in the century, but after Honorius, a certain Werner (d. 1126), of Ellerbach,[1] abbot of St. Blasius in the Black Forest, published a collection of sermons which he called *Deflorationes Patrum*, which, being interpreted, signifies "Flowers Plucked from the Fathers." Not only from many others but very freely from the *Speculum* of Honorius does our worthy Werner gather his flowers without being at all concerned to tell where he had been on his plucking expeditions. Thus in his introduction he states that his purpose was to offer a new collection of discourses for the use of preachers, as the old ones had become somewhat stale, and the people (the poor dear people!) needed a fresh supply. And even this idea was borrowed from Honorius! Of course it goes without saying that the "Gathered Flowers" are somewhat faded and dried up. But, as Cruel remarks, these sermons, as well as those of the "Mirror" were for several reasons above the reach of the less instructed clergy, particularly as they had to be turned into the vernacular when given to the people; and so there was evident need of some collections in the native tongue and of simpler style. This want was met by the production of those numerous collections in German which have already been mentioned. These were partly done directly from the older sources and partly were translations and adaptations from the Latin collections.[2] It is worth while to notice here only that one which bears the name of its author, Conrad the Priest.

In the last decades of the twelfth century a certain priest named Conrad[3] lived and worked in the neighborhood of Lake Constance. He published a collection of sermons in the old German dialect, with a Latin introduction in which he states the purpose of the book. He —like the widow with her mites—offers his little con-

[1] Cruel, S. 144 ff. [2] Linsenmayer, S. 246.
[3] Linsenmayer, SS. 247, 285 ff.; Albert, Bd. II., S. 9, *et passim.*

tribution for the service of the priests of the Lord, "who love Christ, who preach Christ and not themselves, especially the plebeian and popular priests and those to whom perchance abundance of books is wanting, and who more often with blessed Martha have been anxious and occupied with external things, and on this account have the more rarely been able to sit with blessed Mary at the Lord's feet, that is, to give attention to sacred reading." The work contains a full set of sermons for the church year and a number for saints' days, all in the approved style. In all there are a hundred and fifty-four of these sermons, not very different from others in most respects, but easier in style and showing the author's gift of adapting his speech to the common people.

Passing by France for the present and coming over to the England [1] of the twelfth century we find there a state of things in regard to preaching quite like that which prevailed in Germany—a number of collections of homilies in the vernacular, but few preachers of note. We have seen [2] that as far back as the tenth or early eleventh century Aelfric had translated homilies into the Saxon English of the time. There were also other collections [3] earlier than the twelfth century; and when we reach this date the collections become abundant. Unhappily the homilies are both dateless and nameless, but they are shown to belong to the twelfth and thirteenth centuries. Of these Morris says: [4] "None of them seem to be copied—from Aelfric's treatises. Most of them perhaps were originally translated from Latin homilies, though some few have the appearance of original compositions. Omitting a few allusions to the gluttony and drunkenness of the period, and to the profligacy of the clergy, and the rapacity of the rich, there is nothing that throws any light upon the social condition of the twelfth century.[5] The religious instruction given in

[1] See Morris, *Old English Homilies;* and Cutts, *Parish Priests and their People in the Middle Ages in England,* especially chaps. VI. and XIV. [2] Above, p. 170.

[3] Cutts, p. 223; Morris, Vol. I., Preface, p. xi, and Vol. II., Introduction, p. VII.

[4] Vol. II. (Twelfth century), Int. pp. ix, x.

[5] In this respect they are quite different from the French collections, as Bourgain and Lecoy de la Marche have shown.

these homilies is of a very simple character; and all the discourses, while not without interest, possess much quaintness in the mode in which the Scriptures were popularly expounded." In general tone, doctrine, and method the English homilies are very like those in use elsewhere in Europe. As Cutts has pointed out [1] the Norman conquerors did not disturb the parish priests, and yet the Conquest opened the way to a larger influence from the Continent.

Among the English preachers of the century was a certain Ailred (or Ethelred), of Revesby (c. 1109-1166).[2] He was born of good family, near Durham, about 1109, and as a child was most promising in mind and character. He "spent his youth in the court of David, King of Scotland, as one of the attendants of his son Henry, and while there gave a remarkable instance of his sweetness of character by forgiving one of his enemies who had slandered him. David was much attached to him, and would have made him a bishop; but he preferred to become a monk, and entered the Cistercian abbey of Rievaulx in the North Riding of Yorkshire." [3] Later he was abbot of Revesby, and afterwards of Rievaulx. He was highly esteemed by King Henry II., and by his contemporaries generally. He did some successful missionary work among the rude Picts of Scotland, was a historical writer of some importance, and took active interest in the affairs of his time. He suffered from ill health toward the close of his life, but bore his sufferings meekly, and kept at his work to the end. Altogether he appears to have been an amiable, earnest, active man. He died and was buried at Rievaulx in 1166.

He left numerous historical and theological writings, among which are a number of sermons.[4] They are not remarkable, being in the fashion of the age—such as has been sufficiently pointed out. He was so taken with the allegorical method of interpretation and so fertile in finding the spiritual meanings of Scripture that he could spin out a number of them from one word as a text.[5]

[1] *Op. cit.*, p. 84 ff.

[2] Rothe, *Gesch. der Pred.*, S. 218 f; *Dictionary of National Biography*, Vol. XVIII, p. 33 f; Migne, *Pat. Lat.*, tom. 195.

[3] *Dict. Nat. Biog., ad loc.*

[4] Migne, *Pat. Lat.*, tom. 195; Rothe, S. 219. [5] Rothe, *ad. loc.*

A very different man from Ailred was Peter of Blois (d. c. 1200), who was a Frenchman, but claims notice among the English preachers of the time, for reasons that will appear. Born at or near Blois, he was educated at Tours, at Bologna (where he studied law), and at Paris. He lived several years in Sicily, where he was tutor to a royal prince. He did not like Sicily, and though offered ecclesiastical honors there, returned to France, where he taught for a while and held various church appointments. Some time during this period he entered the service of the English king, Henry II., and under his patronage came later to England, where he filled different posts in the church. He was never appointed to high office, and seems to have been a self-seeking, quarrelsome sort of man, with a plenty of self-conceit, but possessed of learning and talents that made him useful. His letters, full of vanity as they are, have some value among historical sources for the period; and his other writings show considerable ability, but not of a very high order. His sermons receive commendation from Bourgain,[1] but Rothe[2] says that the six short sermons remaining from him offer nothing of interest, except that they were delivered in Saxon English and were afterwards written out in Latin by the author himself, who confesses that they were "quite crudely and insipidly written." Thus they hardly represent thè sermons as delivered, and it is worth noting that this Anglicized Frenchman preached in the English of his time. The sermons, as we have them, are lacking in good arrangement, and are full of digressions. Altogether the English pulpit has but a mediocre rank in the twelfth century.

As in other respects, so in preaching, the leading place among the European peoples of the twelfth century was held by France. We are greatly indebted to the labors of Lecoy de la Marche and Bourgain for a vivid portraiture of the preaching of the period. These scholars have not confined themselves to the printed sources, but have given the world the benefit of their studies of many old French manuscripts of that age.

It will be convenient to consider in one group the three

[1] P. 63. [2] S. 219.

most important preachers of the first crusade. Pope Urban II. (d. 1099) was a Frenchman, Odo by name, and was born of knightly family in Chatillon sur Marne, probably early in the eleventh century. While still young he became a monk at Clugny, where he soon adopted the strenuous ideas of Gregory VII. as to the papacy. His worth and talents attracted attention and he was rapidly promoted. In 1078 he was made a cardinal by Gregory VII., and on the death of Gregory's immediate successor Odo was made pope, taking the name of Urban II., in March, 1088. In 1095, it will be remembered, he assembled a council at Clermont, on the soil of his native France, to consider the undertaking of the first crusade. Here a great assembly of prelates and nobles was gathered, and Urban addressed them several times upon the theme that lay upon his heart. One day, in the open air (for no building could accommodate the throng), he poured forth his soul in one of the most effective addresses of history. There is, of course, no exact reproduction of this famous speech. Several reports of it were made [1] and have been preserved. These are quite unlike in form, but much the same in contents. The substance of the report of it by William of Malmesbury [2] is this: Christian people should be ashamed to let unbelievers possess two-thirds of the whole world, including the Holy Land, which they were desolating. He promised full absolution to all who would undertake a holy war to deliver the sacred places from their grasp. If those who went died in the attempt they would be sure of heaven, if they succeeded they would see the sepulchre of the Lord. Why should they fear to die? Let them go forth as soldiers of the cross! The speech awakened wild enthusiasm; men waved their swords and shouted, "God wills it!" Thus the crusades were begun—under the spell of a timely and powerful eloquence. Of Urban's sermons, properly speaking, there are no remains; [3] but he was an active preacher and the tradition of his eloquence is well sustained.

[1] Migne, *Pat. Lat.*, tom. 151. [2] *Op. cit.*, col. 571 ss.

[3] Migne, *op. cit.*, col. 563 ss, gives an address at the dedication of a church, and another at the ordination of Ivo as bishop of Chartres.

Peter the Hermit (d. 1115),[1] according to the more recent opinions, was probably sent out by Urban II. soon after the Council of Clermont to arouse the people in behalf of the crusade. It is now doubted whether he was in Palestine at all before he went with the crusaders. But it appears that he claimed to have been there and to have seen a vision; or this may have been a later invention to embellish the stories of his eloquence. According to the usual accounts Peter was born at or near Amiens early in the eleventh century. The surname, the Hermit, was given him by his contemporaries and indicates that he lived in retirement. But Guibert of Nogent's description of his eloquence [2] leads us to infer that he was a popular and useful preacher—coming from his retirement to preach to the people—before he began the crusade preaching. Guibert says that he never knew a man to be held in such high esteem, that he composed quarrels, made peace, rescued fallen women, was loaded with presents, and regarded as a saint whose word was an oracle. When he took up the crusade preaching his work had a tremendous effect. He stirred the people of all classes, gathered multitudes to his own standard, and without waiting for the princes and military leaders led the hapless crowd. He was unfitted for leadership and could not control his followers. But that part of his story does not belong here. He preached and performed priestly duties for the crusaders, but returned to France (probably after the capture of Jerusalem) and became monk and prior of an abbey at Huy, where he died in 1115.

Along with Urban and Peter should be named Raoul the Ardent (Radulphus Ardens, d. 1101),[3] who was born (date uncertain) near Poitiers, and was known as a parish priest in that region. It appears that he went with one of the expeditions of the first crusade, under William of Poitiers and Aquitaine, and that he died in Palestine about 1101. This is about all that has come down to us concerning his life; but in his case we have a group of more than thirty sermons remaining. They

[1] See Broadus, *Hist. Pre.*, p. 95 f, for a brief notice of Peter's popular eloquence, and for critical accounts see the articles in Herzog and in Wetzer und Welte, *Kirchenlexicon* (Catholic).

[2] Migne, *Pat. Lat.*, tom. 156, col. 704-5.

[3] Bourgain, p. 55; Migne, *Pat. Lat.*, tom. 155.

show that he deserved his surname of Ardent; for they are earnest, with a note of conviction and of concern for the spiritual welfare of his hearers. In denouncing sin he spares none—whether princes, clergy, or people—and yet he mingles with his warnings a tenderness and charity which show forth a true soul. In style he is often rough and in bad taste, but vigor is not wanting; and he exhibits an originality in refreshing contrast to most of the sermons of the age. He espoused the crusade with all his ardor, and like Peter practised what he preached by going himself.

A notable prelate in the early twelfth century was Ivo, bishop of Chartres (d. 1116). He was a man of distinction and influence in his day, and was quite diligent as a preacher. Twenty-four short sermons remain from him.[1] They were highly esteemed, and one of them is preserved even to this day in the Roman Breviary. Bourgain says of him, "Without being eloquent he joined to knowledge a vivid imagination; his method is neat; he does not embarrass with an enumeration of texts, eschews subtle divisions, slowness and lifeless dialect."

Another famous prelate of the early part of the century was Hildebert (d. 1134), at first bishop of Mars, and later archbishop of Tours. He was the contemporary and the equal of great men; but does not seem to have been especially great as a preacher if we judge by his few remaining sermons;[2] but the man enjoyed a better reputation than these sermons indicate; and yet in them are some traces of real worth, as the critic already quoted says that they are "dignified, elevated, paternal, tempered by the sweet authority of the pontiff."

Here we must mention the celebrated theologian, Peter Abelard (d. 1142). For Abelard, too, is among the prophets, though by a slender title. Famous as the unhappy lover of Eloise he has awakened in all times the interest of the romantic; favored with the heresy-hating hostility of Bernard he has claimed the sympathy of the liberal minded; brilliant as a lecturer, he had the admiration of hundreds of students, and his fame endures; acute as a thinker, he has a secure place among the scholastic

[1] Migne, *Pat. Lat.*, tom. 162, and Bourgain, pp. 32, 276, 296.
[2] *Pat. Lat.*, tom. 171; Bourgain, p. 37 et suiv.

theologians of his era; but all in all the man does not rank among the highest, by virtue either of character or work. As a preacher he is remembered by thirty-four sermons,[1] preached probably after he retired to the cloister, and, it seems, written out at the request of Eloise. They are not great as sermons, but only claim mention because of the author's fame in other directions.

By all odds the most prominent figure among the French preachers of the twelfth century is that of the famous Cistercian monk, theologian, mystic, man of affairs, partisan, crusade evangelist, and popular preacher, Bernard (1091-1153), abbot of Clairvaux, and saint not only by canon but by general consent.[2] Bernard was born at Fontaines near Dijon, third son of the brave knight Tecelin and Aleth, a pious lady of excellent family. Though she died while Bernard was yet a boy her influence over him was holy and permanent, and so she takes a worthy place among those noble mothers to whom in all the Christian ages some distinguished preachers have owed the best that was in them. The lad was of weakly frame and unfit for military duty, so he was early destined for the church and educated with that in view. For a short time during his school days he seems to have tasted a bit of the worldly life about him; but the memories of his mother, and the influence of a lonely and thoughtful journey speedily recalled him to higher things, and with characteristic firmness and devotion he turned his back upon the world. It is quite like him that he induced a goodly number of others to join him in this renunciation, his lifelong trait of personal influence thus early exhibiting itself. After leading a retired life for a while he and his companions entered the famous monastery of Citeaux, which had given name to the Cistercian order of monks. The abbey was just then

[1] *Pat. Lat.*, tom. 178, col. 379 ss.

[2] Sources and authorities for Bernard are of course numerous. His works and letters are given in Migne, *Pat. Lat.*, tt. 182-185, with much valuable editorial matter by Mabillon and others. He receives ample treatment at the hands of Bourgain, and notice from all the other historians and critics of the preaching of the period. The great monograph of Neander is still valuable, and the late Dr. R. S. Storrs has done American readers and literature a noble service in his *Bernard of Clairvaux*.

not very flourishing, but the entrance of this fine body of about thirty young men under the lead of such a spirit as Bernard gave it new life. Soon its growth was so rapid as to require division and colonization. One of these colonies was established at Clairvaux (*clara vallis,* vale of light), and Bernard was chosen to be its abbot. This was his heart's home through all his busy life, and with it his name is forever associated. He had later in his career frequent invitations to other places and higher preferment, but he put them all aside and remained simply abbot of Clairvaux.

He practised a rigid asceticism, disciplined his monks with a strict but loving care, taught them and preached to them with all fidelity, received with sweet cordiality the visitors who sought him for help and counsel in the spiritual life, and was in all essentials according to the demands of the age a model monk and abbot.

But a man of his powers could not be hid in a monastery. Soon his wonderful preaching began to attract crowds to Clairvaux, and his capacity for affairs marked him as fitted for severer tasks than the peaceful direction of a cloister. He soon became the most notable man in the church in France, and from thence his influence and activities spread through Italy and Germany. He was especially successful in healing disputes, and was the able defender of Catholic orthodoxy alike against the scholastic subtleties of Abelard and the popular evangelical views of Peter of Bruys and Henry of Lausanne. He favored and helped to shape the foundation of the order of Knights of the Temple. Though refusing to be the head of his own order, he was the most active man in promoting its rapid and wide spread.

On the death of Pope Honorius II. in 1130 the cardinals were divided and chose different men for the papacy. Innocent II., the choice of the minority, had the weaker title, but he was the fitter man. Fearing his rival's stronger party he fled to France and sought protection from King Louis VI. The monarch referred the matter to the bishops of the realm, and they held an assembly to decide which pope they should recognize. Bernard, though not a bishop, was called in and asked to present his views, and he took so decided ground in favor of Innocent and urged his cause with such eloquent persuasiveness that the assembly unanimously decided to recognize Innocent as pope. Bernard visited some of the principal cities of Italy in the interest of his man, and by 1138 his efforts were so successful that he saw Innocent generally recognized and the schism healed. Now he turned back to his beloved Clairvaux to rest and teach his monks. But new labors and burdens were in store for him. Soon came his strife with the acute and philosophic Abelard, whose clever lectures were unsettling the orthodox faith, and none could be found to answer the heretic and force him to retract so well as Bernard. Then came the troubles at Rome about Arnold of Brescia, and Bernard bore an active part on the papal side in this controversy. To Bernard too fell the duty of opposing the work of the evangelical heretics, Peter and Henry, in the south of France. He preached among the people there with great acceptance, but the work of those men was too well done to be overcome even by the eloquence of a Bernard. Finally, in 1146, he was charged by the pope with the duty of preaching the second crusade, and he went through France, Italy and Germany on this mission.

In Germany, though he had to preach by an interpreter, the people were moved to tears and enthusiasm by his voice and manner, while he spoke himself, before the interpreter could translate his words. Thousands were induced to take the cross. He did not accompany the crusaders—perhaps because he was physically unfit to contend with the hardships of the camp, perhaps because the authorities needed him at home—and the failures and disasters which befell the enterprise bore heavily upon his spirits. Yet he went on preaching and teaching all he could at Clairvaux, but being often called upon for those outer tasks from which he shrank, though so well performing them, and ever coming back to refresh his soul among his brother monks in studying and expounding the word of God. At last, worn out with toil, he died and was buried at Clairvaux, August 20, 1153.

It is hard to put into a few words a fair estimate of this great and many-sided man. The faculties of his singularly rich nature were held in admirable poise. The strong and vigorous intellect and the abounding energy of purpose and act were a wholesome offset to the soft and spiritual mellowness of his piety, while this last, like the gentle warmth of an autumn day, suffused the other two, keeping thought from barren and cold speculation, and restraining splendid leadership from ambition and arrogance. The English writer, Vaughan, in his *Hours with the Mystics,*[1] has admirably put the matter thus: "Against the self-indulgence which would sacrifice every active external obligation to a life of contemplative sloth, he protested all his days by word and example. He knew the world and men; he stood with his fellows in the breach, and the shock of conflict spoiled him for a dreamer. The distractions over which he expended so much complaint were his best friends. They made him the worse monk, and by so much the better man." He has been compared by many to Augustine; and Bourgain [2] draws a fine parallel between Bernard and Pascal. He was not equal to either of these in depth of intellect, but the mystical trace was common to all, and the neat and terse way of expressing bright and soulful things.

Bernard was an excellent preacher. He is one of the comparatively few whose published sermons sustain traditional reputation. The stories of his eloquence and its wonderful power over all sorts and conditions of men do not strike us as overstrained when we read, with all just allowances, the discourses which remain from him. Doubtless many other critics would agree with Broadus [3] in saying, "I think that beyond any other mediæval preacher, he will repay the student of the present day." A large number of his discourses are preserved to us.[4] The first given in Migne's edition are seven on the Advent, and these are perhaps most often read. They are characteristic; clear in thought and language, sweet and pious in spirit; full of the current Catholic adoration of the Virgin, but not to the obscuration of the Lord whom he praises and loves. They have many a well-turned and happy phrase, which seems to come with perfect ease and naturalness without the least straining. While not severely analytical the sermons usually have clearly

[1] P. 143.
[2] Pp. 92 et suiv.
[3] *Hist. Prea.*, p. 100.
[4] *Pat. Lat.*, tom. 183.

marked divisions. In the first sermon he thus indicates his plan: "Do you therefore, brethren, to whom as unto babes God reveals things that are hidden from the wise and prudent—consider with sedulous thought, and diligently weigh the reason of this Advent, seeking, namely, who it is that comes, whence, whither, for what purpose, and in what way." He discusses these points in the order indicated, but when he comes to the last, "in what way," he postpones that for next time as being "worthy of a special sermon, especially since to-day's sermon has gone on at length." Following the sermons on the Advent are a number on the holy seasons (*de temporibus*), and then a course of 125 on various subjects (*de diversis*), and the collection concludes with eighty-six on the Song of Solomon. These, according to the editor in Migne's collection, were begun in 1135 and were cut short by the author's lamented death in 1153. He was thus eighteen years (of course at intervals) working at the series, and it reaches only to the first verse of the third chapter. The first sermon treats of the title—why Song of All Songs?—because it is an allegory of the love between Christ and his Bride, the Church. Then come seven different sermons on the first verse, "Let him kiss me with the kisses of his mouth." The minute allegorical treatment of every phase of meaning suggested to the pious mystic by these words is curious, but a trifle tedious. Of course the interpretation is not now generally accepted, and the long drawn series is somewhat wearisome; but as specimens of preaching these discourses have the merits of brevity, clearness, adaptation, and a devout and gracious spirit. To feel their full force we must imagine ourselves among that rapt group of monks at Clairvaux listening while the revered master opens his heart in these loving sermons that breathe out his yearnings for communion with his Lord. We shall then warm toward the preacher and appreciate both his devout feeling and his perfect taste as he says in his opening paragraph: [1]

[1] *Pat. Lat.*, tom. 183, col. 787. The exquisite original defies translation and is as follows: "Revera pauper et inops pulso ad eum qui aperit et nemo claudit super sermonis hujus profundissimo sacramento. Oculi omnium in te sperant, Domine. Parvuli petierunt panem; non est qui frangat eis; speratur id a benignitate tua. O piissime, frange esurientibus panem tuum, meis quidem, si dignaris, manibus, sed tuis viribus."

"Truly poor and needy I knock unto him who openeth and no man shutteth, in regard to the most profound subject of this discourse. The eyes of all look in hope to thee, O Lord. These little ones have asked for bread; there is none to break it to them; that is hoped for from thy dear grace. Break thou thy bread, O kindest One, to those who hunger, by my hands it may be, if so thou deignest, but by thy power."

Resembling Bernard in some respects was Norbert,[1] founder of the Augustinian order of Præmonstrants (d. 1154). Though reckoned with propriety among the French preachers he was born on German soil in Cleves, of good family. After brilliant studies he became a cleric. But he lived easily, sometimes at the court of the archbishop of Cologne, sometimes at that of the emperor Henry. He was loved and flattered by many because of his fortune, his social rank, his fine personal qualities. But from an easy-going and not spotless worldly life he was recalled. Out riding one day he was caught in a storm and stunned by a flash of lightning. On coming to himself he asked, "Lord, what wilt thou have me to do?" and seemed to hear a voice which said, "Forsake evil, do good, seek peace and pursue it." He passed the next days in prayer, and soon begged to be ordained. On being invited by a dean to occupy his pulpit he consented. He enlarged on the vanity of life and lashed the faults of the worldly clergy. The discourse created a commotion. Next day he fell to it again with such effect that one of the priests, whose conscience was smitten, struck him in the face. All this advertised his preaching, and the crowds came. He had found his work. He met much opposition, but also some encouragement from the church authorities, and was very laborious and successful in his work as a travelling preacher. Norbert, like Bernard, was especially gifted and successful as a preacher of peace and reconciler of disputes. He was offered the church of St. Martin, diocese of Rheims, but the canons objected—he was too much of a reformer. Soon afterwards he founded at Prémontré a monastery and order of Augustinian monks, called from the place, Præmonstrants. They were devoted to preaching, and

[1] Bourgain, p. 128 et suiv.

Norbert was thus in some degree a precursor of Dominic and Francis in the next century. He was finally made archbishop of Magdeburg, in which office he died in 1154.

While at Magdeburg he put in order a collection of his sermons to the people, but, unfortunately, only a few fragments survive. But the tradition of his powerful and reformatory popular eloquence remains. He was undoubtedly one of the foremost preachers of the time.

Later, living to almost the end of the century (1196), was Maurice of Sully,[1] the famous bishop of Paris, and founder of the church of Nôtre Dame. He saw a bishopric afar off when yet a poor boy, and refused an alms which was offered to him on the condition that he should give up his ambition to be a bishop. His parents were poor, but somehow the boy managed to get an education, and made the best use of his opportunities. He entered an abbey and was rapidly promoted. He made an excellent parish priest, and was advanced to the office of archdeacon. On the death of Peter Lombard the bishopric of Paris became vacant, and there was some difficulty in finding a successor, though there was no lack of aspirants. There are two stories of how Maurice received the coveted appointment. One is that the electors could not agree—in the embarrassment of their riches—and left it to three of their number to nominate the man, Maurice being a member of the committee. These could not agree, and left it to Maurice; whereupon he named himself, being conscientiously and solemnly of the opinion that he would best perform the duties of the office! The other story is more creditable to him. It is that the electors being at sea asked advice of King Louis VII., and the monarch inquired who was the best pastor and preacher among them all. The answer was that Maurice was the best pastor and preacher, but Peter Comestor[2] was the most learned in the Scriptures. The king gave a wise answer: "Choose Maurice for bishop, and let Peter be a teacher of the monks." So he became bishop of Paris in 1160; and soon afterwards it fell to him to christen the

[1] *Biographie Universelle,* s. v.; Lecoy de la Marche, p. 42 et suiv.; Bourgain, p. 48 et suiv.

[2] The Eater; so called not for his gluttony, but for his greed of learning.

royal infant who was later celebrated as Philip Augustus. He is also famous as having begun the building of the great and historic cathedral of Nôtre Dame, of which the cornerstone was laid by Pope Alexander III. in 1165. The work was of course not finished in Maurice's time, but he carried it well on and got a great deal of money for the building.

There is a pretty story that while he was bishop of Paris his old mother paid him a visit clad in the simple garb of the poor; but that the attendants would not admit her, and the ladies took her away and dressed her up properly to be presented to the great man. But when she was brought to him he said, "I do not know this lady; my mother was never dressed like this, but only in the simple clothing of the poor; I should recognize her in that." Taking the hint the ladies removed the old woman and changed back her clothes, whereupon the bishop received her with all love and reverence as his mother; the rebuke not being meant for her, but for the attendants. Later in life Maurice retired to the abbey of St. Victor, where he died in 1196.

A number of his sermons remain in manuscript, some in Latin and some in the old French of the twelfth century. These last are highly prized by French scholars on linguistic and literary grounds. As they have not been published, we are dependent on the judgment of the critics who have read them for an estimate of their worth. Both Lecoy de la Marche and Bourgain speak highly of them, but Daunou, a literary critic in the *Histoire Littéraire de la France,* takes a less favorable view of their value. Maurice enjoyed, however, great reputation as a preacher, and wrote a book of instructions on the art of preaching.

Toward the end of the twelfth century there appeared in the neighborhood of Paris a priest of the parish of Neuilly, who attracted great attention by the pungency and power of his sermons. His name was Foulques, or, in its Latin form, Fulco.[1] He was of very humble extraction and uneducated. On his first appearance he was laughed at for his ignorance, but he remedied that defect

[1] Lecoy de la Marche, p. 75 et suiv.; and for his life the article in Wetzer und Welte, *Kirchenlexicon.*

by earnest study, and it was not long before he had the great as well as the lowly crowding to hear him preach. He was sometimes almost suffocated by the throngs of people, and men literally tore away pieces of his clothing for souvenirs. He rebuked the great and helped the fallen. He was especially successful in the reclamation of fallen women, for whom he built and maintained a home. The story goes that he once said plainly to Richard the Lion Heart of England that the king had three daughters hanging to his neck from whose embrace he must disentangle himself if he would be saved. Richard said it was a lie, he had no daughters; whereupon the priest named them for him—Superbia, Cupiditas and Luxuria.[1] Instead of punishing the bold preacher Richard replied with bitterness that he would bequeath Superbia to the Templars, Cupiditas to the Cistercians, and Luxuria to the prelates. In 1198 Foulques was selected by Innocent III. as one of the preachers of the fourth crusade. His success was wonderful, reviving the traditions of Peter and of Bernard. Thousands were led to take the cross, and Foulques himself was enrolled among them. But he did not live to see the perversion and failure of the crusade, having died in 1202. No sermons remain from him, but the traditions of his eloquence and success are well founded.

The abbey of St. Victor at Paris was founded by William of Champeaux in 1108, and became famous for a number of distinguished men who studied and taught in its walls. The teaching office, especially as exercised in preaching to the monks, was one of the specialties at St. Victor, and Bourgain [2] tells how the brethren magnified the office by magnifying its difficulty and burden as the turn of each one came to preach. Among the most celebrated of these preachers were Hugo [3] (d. 1141) and Richard [4] (d. 1173). Neither of them was French by birth, Hugo being most probably a Saxon, while Richard was a Scotchman. Both were mystics and Richard was the pupil and successor of Hugo in the priory.

[1] Pride, Greed, and Luxury. [2] *Op. cit.*, pp. 117, 118.

[3] Life and works in Migne, *Pat. Lat.*, tom. 175, with editorial matter by the Abbé Hugonin.

[4] *Pat. Lat.*, tom. 196, ed. Hugonin.

Hugo had been brought up in his Saxon home, very largely under the advice of an uncle, who was an ecclesiastic. He early became a monk, adopting the Augustinian rule. Troubles and civil war drove the uncle and nephew from home, and after passing some time in the Netherlands they sought and found refuge in the abbey of St. Victor in Paris. Here the talents and acquirements of Hugo were highly valued, and in course of time he was made prior. He spent the rest of his life in teaching and preaching in his abbey.

Hugo was one of the most notable of the mediæval mystics.[1] That trait had been in Bernard combined with active popular preaching, in Hugo and Richard it was allied with scholasticism. Hugo taught that in the mental attitude to divine things there are three stages: cogitation, meditation, contemplation. By cogitation he meant thinking, the application of the purely intellectual processes to religious truth; by meditation he understood reflection, or brooding over the truth; by contemplation he intended to set forth the highest effort of the soul, immediate or intuitive insight into truth. In this he distinguished a lower and a higher stage, and this latter was the summit of attainment.[2] In the way of sermons Hugo left, first of all, nineteen homilies on the book of Ecclesiastes, which receive some praise from Bourgain,[3] but are criticised as diffuse and overloaded with digression and allegory. Besides these are other sermons, which have warmth of feeling and ease of expression, but with the faults just mentioned.

Richard of St. Victor, succeeding Hugo as prior, was a Scotchman of hard thinking and energetic character. He was zealous for reform and discipline, but he was at the same time more of a scholastic than Hugo. He was an adept in the hair-splitting subtleties of logical analysis, and also in the most finespun and exaggerated allegorical interpretation of Scripture. This naturally falls in with the spirit of mysticism, and it finds striking exemplification in both the Victorines. Richard subdivides Hugo's

[1] Mysticism and its place in the preaching of the Middle Ages will receive fuller notice further on. See p. 266 ff.

[2] See Vaughan, *Hours with the Mystics*, p. 157.

[3] *Op. cit.*, p. 118.

three stages of the acquisition of truth and life into two each, making thus six steps in the process of finding God. The last and highest is above (and seems to be beyond!) reason, and is reached not so much by thought as by penitence and tears, being a sort of religious ecstasy. Richard left a number of treatises among his works, which had doubtless been given to the monks first as sermons or lectures. They show considerable sprightliness of thought and expression, but with the mystical and scholastic exaggerations already noticed.

The contemporary writings give much attention to the so-called heretics, especially in the south of France. Among them were several leaders and preachers of distinction. Of these especially important were Tanchelm (d. 1123), Peter of Bruys (d. c. 1124), his disciple Henry of Lausanne (d. c. 1148), and Peter Waldo, who about 1170 was sending out his "poor men of Lyons" as colporters and preachers. Sermons from these men are not preserved, but even the testimony of their Catholic enemies and persecutors declares their eloquence, their power over the people, and their enduring success in establishing their opinions in the hearts of their followers. The failure of Bernard to overcome their work we have already noticed, the effort of Dominic to counteract it will be mentioned later. All these things, and many others, indicate that these so-called heretics were men of conviction, of earnestness, of rare persuasive gifts.

CHAPTER VII

The Culmination of Mediæval Preaching in the Thirteenth Century

The thirteenth century is in many respects the focus of the whole period (1095-1361) which we are now studying. In this great century mediæval preaching reached its acme of power. And, as usual, this result was due in large degree to events and characteristics of the times, to which we must give brief notice.

1. Europe in the Thirteenth Century

The four great peoples of England, France, Germany and Italy were they whose political and other national affairs give to the thirteenth century its chief historic significance.

In England the era is noted for constitutional history. In 1215 the barons at Runnymede wrested Magna Charta from the weak hands of John; and though that famous instrument was not a concession to popular rights in our modern sense of that phrase, it yet was a bar to kingly tyranny and to the concentration of power in the royal hands. Later, however, the people found a tribune in Simon de Montfort, by whose efforts there was called in 1265 a representative parliament in which there sat for the first time knights of the shires and burghers from some of the towns. Thirty years later (1295) decisive turn was given to all of England's future political history by the assembling of the "model parliament" of Edward I. This was a really representative body; England's constitution of "king, lords and commons" is fixed for generations to come; the people have at last won a place in directing the affairs of government.

In France affairs took quite a different turn, and the development toward a consolidated and strengthened monarchy went on. The reign of Philip Augustus extended nearly a quarter of a century into the new era, and under him, as we have seen,[1] the monarchical principle made substantial gains. Philip II., who began to reign in 1223, pursued his father's policy, but died young, leaving his son Louis IX. a minor. But the queen-mother, Blanche of Castile, was a woman of character and ability, and as regent she held the reins of government with a firm hand. The preceding kings made the monarchy strong, "Saint Louis" now made it beloved and respected, bequeathing it in 1270 to his son Philip III. (the Hardy), who in turn soon left it to his son Philip IV. (the Fair) in 1285. This acute, unscrupulous, but able monarch holds his own against papal assumptions, and in other ways brings a vigorous and powerful reign over into the fourteenth century. Throughout the thirteenth century, therefore, France is the strongest political power in Europe.

In Germany the tangle continued. The great emperor, Frederick Barbarossa, had died in 1189. His son, Henry

[1] *Ante*, p. 176.

VI., married Constance, the heiress of the Norman kingdom of Naples and Sicily, and from this marriage came the brilliant and unfortunate Frederick II. (1215-1250). His long, eventful and turbulent reign was signalized by the final effort to subjugate Italy, by the death struggle with the papacy, and at last by the fall of his house. The murder of his son Conradin, or Conrad IV., in 1254, ended the long and splendid struggle of the Hohenstaufen against the papacy, and for political supremacy in Italy. After that, for about twenty years, was the Great Interregnum, with its anarchy and confusion, till in 1273 the choice of the electors at last fell upon Rudolf of Hapsburg, the founder of the imperial Austrian line. Rudolf gave up the struggle for Italy, and devoted himself to building up the wasted empire in its proper German character, and with him a new era in German history begins.

In Italy during this fateful century all the discordant elements of her mediæval politics were in seething chaos. In the north the faintly republican constitutions of the Lombard cities were giving way to those family tyrannies which characterized Italian civic history for centuries. In Piedmont the House of Savoy was already laying the basis of its future power. In the northwest Genoa, republican in government, was mistress of the seas and of commerce on that side; while her great rival in the northeast, Venice, was queen of the Adriatic, and under her doges was at the pinnacle of her greatness and wealth. In central Italy fair Florence, with her quasi-democratic government, was a prey to fierce internal discords, and toward the end of this century distinguished herself by sending into exile her illustrious son Dante. Across the peninsula further south stretched the fatal Papal States, the divisive wedge, destined to be the last stronghold of Italy's political dismemberment. In the south Naples and Sicily, the heritage and snare of Frederick II., came after Conrad's death into the hands of Charles of Anjou, but the unpopular French sovereignty fell by the massacre known as the "Sicilian Vespers," in 1282, and the end of the century finds southern Italy under Spanish rule.

Such was the state of European politics during this wonderful century: In Italy and Germany, confusion;

in France, decay of feudalism and tendency to absolute monarchy; in England, growth of parliamentary power and strengthening of constitutional monarchy.

From political events to social affairs in Europe the transition is easy, and we shall here find a more immediate and influential connection with the pulpit.

The mighty impulse of the crusades was felt in every part of the social order of Europe during the twelfth and thirteenth centuries, and with this were united many other forces which contributed to the activity and progress of men during that stirring era.

The crusaders and their followers came in contact with many wares and luxuries hitherto unknown or little known in the West, and they brought home with them a taste for these things. All this stimulated trade, and the merchants became a wealthier and more considerable class of society. Venice and Genoa especially attained to great power and renown, but other Italian cities shared the new prosperity with them. Nor was the new trading impulse confined to Italy. Inland and international trade also was marvellously stimulated, and the cities of Germany, France, the Netherlands, and even England, felt the quickening touch of business. Fairs were held for exchange of wares between the merchants, and these occasions were important not only to the merchants themselves, but to all others. The robber baron, as well as the petty thief, was there; the fine dame, and the shameless courtesan; the gay youth in search of pleasure, and the wondering peasant gazing at the sights; the preacher, too, was on hand, and used his chance to rebuke sin and say a word for Our Lady and the saints. Along with the merchant, the banker and the usurer grew rich. Lending money at interest was esteemed a sin, and the usurer and the Jew, together with the heretic, receive special attention from the preachers. This commercial activity stimulated others, as is ever the case, and thus the whole realm of trade, finance, and labor received in this age an impulse which has endured through all the following centuries of western commerce.

The king and nobles were at the top of the social order and the clergy mingled freely with them, receiving and giving influences both for good and ill. The serving classes—house-servants and tillers of the soil—themselves divided into various orders, which we need not stop to describe, were at the bottom of the social pyramid. But now between these a new order rises, or, more exactly, an old but hitherto little regarded order grows into wealth and power. The decay of feudalism and the growth of the cities by trade give now to the citizen merchant or banker a new importance and power in the social order. In the twelfth and thirteenth centuries we see that great power in its formative stage, in its crude yet vigorous youth; but even thus the young giant gives promise of his coming strength, when he shall be the regnant chief in western civilization. The burghers, or men of the middle class, must be henceforth recognized and dealt with as a power in all social life. Their wealth makes them the envy of the lower class, the spoil of the upper; and their struggle to secure their rights, personal and civic, as against the buttressed power of kings and lords, is in large measure the history of social and political progress for ages to come.

It is needless to say that the intellectual life of the European peoples received a powerful uplift and showed marvellous development in this period. There is a more general diffusion of knowledge. Monks and theologians not only hold their places of leadership, but they go far beyond the heights of former days. As before noticed, their ranks are recruited from all classes, so that culture, like religion, is less affected by caste than the political and social spheres. But now the wealth and leisure of the burgher class afford their sons the means of higher culture, and many of them are found among the earnest students of the time. Nor is even the ruling class untouched by the new zeal for learning. Kings and nobles are not only patrons, but in some cases also the pursuers and possessors of culture. Frederick II., the brilliant and ill-fated emperor, was a man of letters, and is said to have preferred Italy to Germany as a residence, because he could better gratify his scholarly tastes in the southern land.

The universities of Europe arose in this age, they were crowded with students, and they greatly extended the range of studies pursued before. To the seven liberal arts—the *trivium* and *quadrivium*—there were added now the pursuit of law and medicine, and above all of theology. This last was the *scientia scientiarum* of the times. The older schools, perhaps especially those of Charlemagne, had prepared the way for the universities. In this period we find them in Italy, Spain, France, and England. Not till the fourteenth century did they begin their wonderful history in Germany with the foundation of the University of Prague in 1348. About 1250 Robert of Sorbon founded (but upon preceding institutions) the famous school for theology at the University of Paris, which, as the "Sorbonne," has perpetuated the name of his birthplace. That university was already distinguished for the teaching of theology, but this foundation added greatly to its power and fame. Medicine was especially cultivated at Salerno, and law at Bologna. Oxford and Cambridge also attracted students in the various schools. The number of students reached grand proportions. This was especially true at Paris, where, it is said—though it seems an evident exaggeration—that on one occasion the University supplied 20,000 persons to march in the funeral procession of some noted man. The life of the students was marked by many of the characteristics which in all ages have been recognized as the students' own. Many were studious and lived hard for learning's sake, many were idle and spendthrift, coming only for the name of the thing and on pleasure bent; many were disorderly and hard to manage, so that the perennial feud of "town and gown" was a feature of the age, and all were affected with the class spirit, the student way, toward faculty, town, each other and the world in general.

But academic learning was by no means the only intellectual sign of the times. Literature and art likewise had their place of influence. In England the promising and comparatively early development of Saxon literature had received a check and turn by the Norman invasion, but the seed and soil were both ready, and in the fourteenth century Chaucer leads in the founding of English literature properly speaking. In France the troubadours and other poets in the twelfth and thirteenth centuries are founding modern French literature, and in Germany the minnesingers are doing like service, while the great national epic of the Nibelungen probably receives in the thirteenth century the form in which we now have it. In Italy the close of that same century is immortalized by the genius of Dante, and the way is prepared for Petrarch and Boccaccio in the fourteenth. In the sphere of art, sculpture and painting are yet crude, waiting for the kindling of the Renaissance; and music, though one of the seven academic arts, must wait yet longer for its thoroughly artistic development; but architecture achieves great triumphs in the castles, and especially the cathedrals, of that prolific age—monuments alike to the growth of art and to the revival, power and permanence of the religious feeling.

This brings us now to pay some attention to the affairs of the papacy, the clergy, and the general interests of religion in Europe during this age.

At the turn of the century (1198-1216) there sat upon the papal throne the greatest of all the popes—Innocent III. As the vicegerent of Christ and the successor of Peter he claimed sovereignty over all the nations of the earth. He reduced John of England to abject submission, and carried it with a high hand toward Germany, but encountered a serious and tough resistance at the hands of Philip Augustus of France. After him the brilliant emperor Frederick II.—grandson of Barbarossa—conducted the struggle against several popes in succession. He failed. At his death in 1250 the issue lay on the papal side, but both parties were exhausted, and the papacy, weakened from its long struggle, and in the hands of less able and vigorous pontiffs, entered a period of decay. It is true that Boniface VIII. (1294-1303) powerfully reasserted and even extended the claims of Innocent, but Philip the Fair of France was more than a match for the astute Cajetan. After Boniface the papacy was for a long time subservient to France.

In regard to the lower clergy the period offers a number of interesting points. The distinction of secular (those who lived in the world) and regular (those who lived under monastic rule) not only continues, but receives emphasis during this time. The regulars acquire a greater relative importance for three reasons: (1) The reforms in discipline instituted toward the close of the eleventh century were not wholly fruitless; the study of scholasticism and the contemplation of mysticism, together with other influences, combined to make the regular clergy as a rule superior in character and attainments to the seculars. (2) The example, the personal magnetism and eloquence, the indomitable energy, the widespread influence of Bernard of Clairvaux in the twelfth century gave to monasticism a new and long-abiding impulse. Old orders were quickened and new ones created, and monasteries were founded in all lands. (3) The founding of the two great preaching orders of Francis and Dominic in the thirteenth century, their early enthusiasm and comparative purity, gave a fresh turn to monastic life and influence. We shall see later the more particular relation of these orders to preaching. Among the different orders, and between the seculars and regulars as classes, there was great rivalry. The seculars and regulars accused each other of all sorts of evils. Some allowance must be made for partisan dislike, but no doubt there was ground enough for serious charges.

Some of the secular priests and prelates were men of high character and gifts, true to their calling and earnest for all that was good as they saw it. Others were ambitious, selfish, avaricious, luxurious and corrupt. Among the monks there were not wanting men of holy character, of high intellectual worth and culture, of intense and unselfish devotion. Yet among these too the monastic vices found place. There were the lazy, the garrulous, the grasping, and even those who were unfaithful in spirit and letter to the stern vows of their order. On the whole, in this period, the balance of character and influence lies in favor of the regulars. Their decline comes later.

Such a clergy as this, marked by both personal and artificial distinctions, it was to whom were confided the religious interests of Western Europe, so far as those interests were included and represented in the dominant Catholic church. The heretics had teachers and leaders of their own; but the generally accepted religious guides of the people in the centuries under our review were the Catholic clergy. These performed in great city cathedral or little village church the offices of the Christian worship as it was then conducted; they read the Scriptures, preached, prayed, sang, said masses, and heard confessions; they performed funerals and marriages and baptisms; they instructed the ignorant, comforted the sorrowing, visited the sick, cheered the dying, helped the penitent, succored the poor; sometimes they rebuked the sins of the great, and sometimes, alas! they imitated them; they moved among all classes of society, an influence for good, though often tainted with acknowledged evil; and such as they were, frail and faulty at best, they stood as the moral and spiritual teachers of the people, the ofttimes erring, but often also the sincere and humble representatives of the kingdom of God among men.

We come now to consider the state of religion among the people during this period, and only very general terms can be employed in undertaking to describe it; for in so long a time, in so many different places, there was necessarily a great variety of phases and phenomena. Yet the mediæval life was so slow as compared with that of our times, and the unity of the Catholic church was so little broken as compared with sectarian developments since the Reformation, that there was more of sameness in the general type of religious life in all Europe than would on first view seem likely.

The religious life of mankind has ever been characterized by ebbs and flows of feeling; and this was true within the period we have in view. About the time of the first crusade there was a great wave of religious enthusiasm, which found expression in that great movement. This movement was not confined to the clergy—it took hold of king and lord and vassal and serf, and even of the children. In the twelfth century this revival had its ups and downs, but was on the whole fairly well sustained; early in the thirteenth the great preaching orders started another and a different kind of religious enthusiasm—gathering great crowds to hear the preaching of the more popular friars. Toward the end of that century and in the fourteenth and fifteenth there is marked decline.

For the rest the attitude of men to religion and morals was not so strikingly different from that of all the Christian ages as to challenge attention. The works of Bourgain [1] and of Lecoy de la Marche [2] give striking pic-

[1] *La Chaire Française au XIIme Siècle.*

[2] *La Chaire Française au Moyen Age, principalement au XIIIme Siècle.*

tures of society as portrayed in the sermons of the twelfth and thirteenth centuries; and from many other sources also we may be able to construct an outline view of the part played by religion in the life of those far-off times.

There were, first of all, among the people as among the clergy, the sincerely pious and devout, who loved God, made little of worldly things, and tried to live according to the teachings of the church. They had their representatives in all classes, from the saintly Louis IX. of France down to the humble peasant. As among the priests so among the people there was the grand army of the half-way religious—with all grades of half-wayness. Nominally religious, connected with the church, sometimes penitent, often errant, and always worldly, they were the terror and the burden of the truly holy in the earth. In the clergy they might be worldly prelates, living in wealth and luxury, or doubters like Abelard, outwardly conforming to the church, but secretly doubting and expressing as much as they dared without losing their places; among the rulers they might be of the type of Frederick II., ambitious, selfish, bent on glory and power, regarded as a heretic, anathematized by religious authority, and yet with an outward, nominal, occasional sort of regard for religion. There was the jolly burgher, who loved his ducats and his wine, but went to church and communicated perhaps once a year; there was the gay worldling on pleasure bent, and his dame or mistress, with passion for dress and finery, who yet upon occasion could be very pious in talk or passing emotion. And, of course, the utterly irreligious, "who feared not God, neither regarded man," were to be found in all the walks of life. There were the superstitious and the credulous, fearing all things and preyed upon by designers of every sort. And there, too, are the so-called "heretics," refusing the supremacy of the Roman church, some of them no doubt all wild with disorder and rebellion, some half-crazy with fanaticism and follies, but not a few also who yearned for and sought to exemplify and establish a pure New Testament religion over against the pretensions and corruptions of Rome.

After discussing with great clearness and interest the state of society, as presented in the sermons of the thirteenth century, Lecoy de la Marche concludes his admirable book with this striking paragraph: "Our guides have complacently pointed out to us the weaknesses of the prelates and monks, the abuses of power by the princes, the robberies of the lords and their retainers, the ambitions of the burghers, the ruses of the merchants and usurers, the coarseness of the sailors, of the laborers, of the servants, the artifices and coquetry of the women, the peccadilloes of the students. They have given us in a rapid view the state of knowledge, the received ideas in the matter of government, of commerce, of education, the development given to each branch of the human sciences. And by the light of their torch that vast panorama has appeared to us under a darker color than the reality. By an optical illusion common to the moralists of all ages they have judged their contemporaries to be the worst of the generations. 'We are the dregs of the centuries,' says Jacques de Vitry in so many words—*Nos sumus in quos faeces saeculorum devenerunt.* But at the bottom it is the same interests, the same passions, the same struggles which fill all the pages of the great book of history, and at any moment that it is studied the human heart is found to be such as it has been, is, and will be. There is only diversity in the remedies applied to the plagues, and it is when those remedies are furnished by religion that the cure is least distant. The harshness of the criticisms of the pulpit carries indeed its own corrective in itself: so much ardor to combat evil proves that perfection was sought; so much animosity against vice shows what value was attached to virtue."

2. General View of Preaching in the Century

Passing on to take a view of preaching itself at this great epoch in European history, we find that the revival which distinguished the twelfth century went on with great power and with some new features into its successor; and it was not until late in the thirteenth century that the inevitable reaction began to appear. One of the evidences or elements of this continued revival was the enormous crowds which are reported to have gatherd to hear the popular preachers. Even when we make allowances for over-estimates and subsequent exaggerations it still remains probably true that the largest audiences ever gathered to hear preaching were characteristic of this period. It seems that Berthold and Antony had larger crowds than Whitefield in the eighteenth or Moody in the nineteenth century. The effects of preaching on life and conduct were also immediate and profound. Conversion and its fruits are abundantly reported in the contemporary accounts. The martial and adventurous excitement of the crusades had given place to a more spiritual and moral movement, or, to speak more accurately, these gained comparatively on the other.

The most important and significant movement in the first part of the century was the founding and early work of the two great preaching orders of monks, the Franciscans and Dominicans. The primary object of these institutions was to preach. The spur to the establishment of the Dominicans was found in the failure of the pope's emissaries to overcome heresy in the south of France, and Dominic conceived it would be best to meet the sectaries in their own way by sending forth preachers among the people who should live plainly and be diligent in preaching. The Franciscans came into being in response to the example and call of Francis of Assisi, who saw the people in need of the word of God, and went forth in lowly poverty to bring them the message of grace and love. These orders spread very rapidly in the first half of the century, and the friars went everywhere preaching the word. They even went on foreign missions to Africa and Asia. While the primary idea of Dominic was to meet heresy, and so the order was chiefly devoted to teaching, it yet became assimilated to the evangelistic character of the Franciscans, and they in turn, through rivalry, at a later period, paid more attention to learning. In the beginning these orders were comparatively pure, and were fired with the zeal and spirit of their founders. As they grew in numbers, learning and influence they became more worldly, and their power for good decreased. But through this century, or to very near its close, they were in the flourishing period of their character and power.

But though there was much and very effective preaching in this century, and though it attracted great multitudes of hearers, yet in quality and character it did not escape the faults inherited from the long ages of departure from a true Biblical standard. When we compare the preaching of the thirteenth century with that of the two other culminating periods—the fourth and the sixteenth—which preceded and followed it, we shall find that in respect of real Biblical content and sound evangelical character it falls immeasurably below them. It was a sadly distorted gospel which was preached in the thirteenth century. It had suffered from mutilation, perversion, and accretion. The use of Scripture was often only sad misuse—it was either neglected wholly or served merely as a pretext for wholly unscriptural or even antiscriptural teachings. Wild allegorizing, puerile fancies, forced meanings and applications, gross misunderstanding, and sometimes positive irreverence, were only too common in the handling of the word of God. The best preachers were not free from some of these faults, and those of lower grade were of course worse still. The merit of works, the saving value of ordinances, penances, and the like, were presented, to the detriment of gospel truth and sound Christian morals. The glory of the Virgin, the legends of saints and martyrs crowded, and sometimes crowded out, the history and doctrine of Scripture. Scholastic and mystic subtleties often passed beyond the comprehension of the hearers and left the hungry sheep looking up unfed. Yet amid all this failure and perversion the main distinctive truths of Christianity were ably and sincerely presented, and by many earnest voices the saving power of Christ was told, and thousands were brought to his cross. Sin was searchingly analyzed and boldly denounced, and to the ever-present springs of human action appeal was constantly made.

The preachers of the century may be grouped now on a new principle, according to the tendencies of thought and life which actuated them. These tendencies, or modes of thought and life, were the scholastic, the popular, and the mystic. They flowed freely through all the preaching of the age in greater or less volume, and sometimes the same man would combine in his preaching two, or even all three, of these elements. The scholastic magnified the intellectual, the popular the practical, and the mystic the deeper spiritual aspects of the religious life. In this chapter we shall consider the first two.

3. Scholastic Preaching and Preachers

Scholasticism did not begin nor end in the thirteenth century, but it reached its strongest influence and had its greatest representatives in that time; and this is therefore the most appropriate place to note its influence on preaching. Every great movement in philosophy and theology naturally influences the preaching of the age in which it has vogue, and finds defenders and opponents in the pulpit as well as those who are more or less directly moulded by it. Illustrations are numerous, and those of our own time are ready to hand. But our concern here is with scholasticism and its influence upon the preaching of this great thirteenth century.

What is scholasticism? The words scholastic and schoolmen sufficiently indicate the fact that what is called scholasticism was primarily and chiefly an affair of the schools. Anselm in the eleventh century and Abelard in the twelfth are very great names among scholastic preachers of former times, and they were both great teachers, one representing the rigidly orthodox, the other the freer mode of thinking in theology. Scholasticism is the combination of theology and philosophy. It is the application of the Aristotelian logic to the interpretation of Scripture and the deductions of theology. It is the effort and method whereby the speculations of the intellect on the data furnished by church dogmas may be by logical processes harmonized with those dogmas. It was the serious attempt of acute and minute reasoning to give itself the freest possible exercise and largest possible scope within the trammels imposed by ecclesiastical authority and by accepted beliefs regarded as fundamental and final. Scholasticism was a giant in bonds. Perhaps never has the human intellect more strikingly exhibited three of its greatest powers: speculation, analysis, ratiocination. In regard to it the question is not as to the intellectual power involved, but as to data and ends—as to the soundness of the premises, the breadth of the inductions, and the value of the conclusions, rather than as to the ability to perceive, deduce, and classify the material of thought. In penetration and acuteness of insight, in luminous and exhaustive arrangement of matter, and in logical severity and conclusiveness, those old schoolmen were very great thinkers. As a method scholasticism was sure to need and to receive modification; as a philosophy it could no more be final than those held by the old Greeks, or by the more recent German and English thinkers; but as the occupation of the purest and highest intellects of the thirteenth and contiguous centuries it at least deserves respectful consideration at the hands of the philosopher and the historian.

As we shall see, some of the great scholastics were preachers, but the influence of scholasticism upon preaching is not represented in these alone. A vigorous and prevalent method of treating intellectual problems in any age always affects many who cannot be classed with the philosophers, and thus the general mental habits of an age are colored by the dominant philosophy, whether it be accepted or denied, understood or misconceived. The contribution of scholasticism to preaching had regard to both matter and form. In respect to the first the metaphysical subtleties, hairsplitting distinctions, attenuated reasonings, the dogmas, fancies, speculations about things of no particular consequence then or now, all became in some measure the possession of the pulpit. Men of less ability than the great doctors would be sure to pick up the phrases and methods of the leaders of thought without always knowing what they were about.

In the matter of form the contribution of scholasticism to preaching is more important and enduring. The rage for minute analysis was carried too far, but it made the sermon henceforth a more orderly and logical address than it ever had been even in the hands of Chrysostom and Augustine, not to mention the invertebrate homilies of the ages of decline. From now on the sermon must include among the elements of its ideal completeness clear distinction and logical treatment of its material. The tendency will go too far, degenerate, become tedious, ridiculous even—but it will stay. And so at least one of the prime essentials of effective pulpit discourse owes a debt to the scholastic method.

Owing to the rise of the preaching orders of monks

and to other causes, the popular phase of preaching was prominent earlier in the century than the scholastic; and it was not until these orders themselves fell under the influence of the schools and produced great scholars that we find the scholastic method very pronounced and powerful in the pulpit. Still in the early part of the century there are a few notable men, distinguished prelates, who, because of their learning and general position, belong among the scholastic rather than among the popular preachers. Among them are two celebrated English bishops who claim brief notice as preachers.

Stephen Langton (d. 1228) was born in Yorkshire about the middle of the twelfth century, but was educated chiefly at Paris, where he made a warm friendship with the gifted Italian, Lothario, better known as the greatest pope—Innocent III. In 1198 Innocent promptly made his friend a member of the papal household, and in 1206 appointed him a cardinal. The next year, through the influence of the pope, he was chosen by the canons archbishop of Canterbury. But he was not acceptable to King John, and over his investiture there arose the famous controversy between pope and king in which John was at last forced to yield, and in 1213 Langton took charge of his office. He stood firmly for the country's liberty and bore no mean part in framing and securing Magna Charta. He remained in peaceful possession of his diocese till his death in 1228.

There are numbers of unpublished sermons of his cited by Oudin,[1] and Lecoy de la Marche has found and studied thirty-five of these, somewhat jumbled in one collection, and besides a complete and homogeneous series in a manuscript at Ste. Geneviève. They show some real oratorical talent, and as the learned critic observes, "pass completely beyond the coldness and banality only too common in the productions of the time." We are much indebted to the French scholar for having thus shown that this famous English prelate and patriot was also a preacher of no ordinary force.

[1] See Lecoy de la Marche, Pars I., chap. IV., from whom the account in the text is chiefly derived. He discusses Langton among the French preachers because of his education and lecturing at Paris and his long sojourn in France.

The renowned bishop of Lincoln, Robert Greathead (better known in its old French form, Grosseteste; d. 1253), also belongs here. He is called [1] "in some respects the most distinguished of all the English mediæval prelates as regards his personal influence both over the men of his time and its literature." Born of humble parents, he yet obtained education at Oxford and at Paris, and became one of the most learned men of the day. He held several subordinate places in the English church, and was finally made bishop of Lincoln in 1235. He was a diligent bishop, strict in discipline and vigorous in administration of affairs. Though a sincere and duty-loving man, he was hasty in temper and somewhat harsh in manner, and so he made enemies and had many a quarrel on his hands. He did not fail to include among his opponents several of the popes, who desired to put into office men whom the honest and sturdy Englishman deemed unfit. He also stood by Magna Charta, and was a friend of Simon de Montfort. But amid all these official cares he was a diligent preacher, and reports of about forty of his sermons remain. The writer quoted above remarks, "Of those who speak of him, one is especially struck by his courage, another by his universal knowledge, a third by his subtlety in interpreting Scripture, and a fourth by his frequent preaching."

Elinand,[2] or Helinand (d.c. 1225), was born in France, but of Flemish parents who had fled thither. He was as a youth devoted to learning, but before his conversion was much given to the pleasures of the world. After that he became very pious and joined the Cistercian order of monks at Froidmont. His learning was ample and accurate. He had the classic and ecclesiastical writers at his fingers' ends, quoting from them with ease, frequency and effect in his sermons. In one of these [3] he quotes Horace, Virgil, Cicero, Ovid, Statius, Lucan, Terence, Quintilian, Ambrose, Jerome, Augustine, Leo I., and alludes to Bernard, Dunstan, and others. He was himself a writer of repute, his historical work being still one of the important sources of information for his period.

[1] Article in *Ency. Brit.*

[2] *Works* and notice of his life in Migne, *Pat. Lat.*, tom. 112, col. 481 ss.

[3] Sermon XV., on the Ascension; Migne, *l. c.*

As a preacher he was a trifle pedantic, and did not rise above the manner and matter of his age; but he shows warmth of feeling and does not fail to warn his hearers against the sins of the time. In the very sermon in which he displays so much learning he warns the monks, to whom the sermon was addressed, against seeking for itself the learning of this world. He says, "Everywhere knowledge is sought, nowhere life; without which not only is nothing profitable, but even knowledge is nothing. For this reason not even knowledge itself is found, because it is not sought where it is, that is, in the book of life, which also is the book of knowledge, namely, in him who is the Wisdom of God, in whom all the treasures of wisdom and knowledge are hid."

Among the famous prelates and scholars and preachers of the early thirteenth century a good place belongs to Jacques de Vitry (Jacobus de Vitriaco; d. 1240), priest in France, bishop in Palestine, cardinal in Italy.[1] Born probably at Vitry (some say Argenteuil) about 1180, he was early attracted to Oigny by the fame and piety of the noted Beguine, Mary of Oigny, who took a motherly interest in her friend as long as she lived. He studied at Paris and was ordained to the priesthood, and, returning to Oigny, he soon became known for his learning and his oratorical talent. About 1213 he was commissioned by Innocent III. to preach in Belgium the crusade against the Albigenses in the south of France. He had great success and went with the crusaders, preaching both to them and to the heretics, but naturally without much success in case of the latter. Soon after this he was charged by the same pope to preach a new crusade to the Holy Land, and met with much success. Meantime he was chosen by the canons of Acre to be their bishop. On the way to Rome to be set apart to his far-off charge he found at Perugia the lifeless body of the great pope—who had suddenly died there in June, 1216—lying shamefully neglected in the church of St. Laurence. The crowd of attendants had hurried to Rome to the new election! Struck by this evidence of the emptiness of earthly glory, he went on to Rome, where he was

[1] Lecoy de la Marche, p. 53 et suiv.; and the article in Wetzer und Welte.

kindly received by the newly elected pope, Honorius III., one of whose first official acts was to consecrate Jacques as bishop of Acre in Palestine. He discharged the onerous duties of his diocese with faithfulness and ability for some years, and then begged that his resignation be accepted. This was reluctantly granted, and he returned to his beloved Oigny for a short rest. Thence he was called by his friend Pope Gregory IX. and made cardinal bishop of Tusculum (or Frascati), and took up his residence in Rome till his death in 1240.

Jacques de Vitry was in many ways a very remarkable man. Celebrated as a writer, especially of history, his account of affairs in Europe and the East during his lifetime is of great value to historians. As a preacher he was known in many countries, but especially in France. A contemporary, quoted by Lecoy de la Marche, says, "His word moved France as it had not been moved within the memory of man." During his residence at Rome he made a collection of his sermons which remains (partly in manuscript), and is said to be unusual for independence and originality. The first part [1] contains sermons of different lengths, style, etc., suited to different audiences, on the usual subjects of the feasts, the saints, and the like. The second part, yet unpublished, consists of seventy-four sermons addressed to "prelates and priests; canons and regular clergy; scholars; judges and lawyers; theologians and preachers; black and white monks; sisters, gray, white, and Cistercian; regular canons; hermits and recluses; friars Minorites; brothers of the order of the Temple; brothers Hospitallers, and guardians of the sick; lepers and infirm; poor and afflicted, people in sorrow; crusaders; pilgrims; nobles and knights; citizens; merchants and bankers; laborers and vine-dressers; artisans; sailors; servants and domestics; married people; widows and celibates; young girls; children and youth." In the prologue he says: "The greatest prudence and the greatest discernment are necessary in preaching. The same specific does not suit everybody. The physician who would cure all eyes with the same salve is a fool; and that which the eye needs the foot does not." He has great variety in his preaching, and is happy and fruitful in the use of illustration.

[1] Adduced by Lecoy de la Marche, *op. cit.*

At least mention should be made here of the celebrated founder of the theological college—the Sorbonne—of the University of Paris, Robert (d. 1274), who was born at Sorbon near Rheims, was canon at Cambrai, later at Paris, and chaplain to the pious king Louis IX. He was not greatly learned, but a respectable scholar. Some discourses,[1] besides other writings, remain from him. "They contain few passages of an elevated eloquence, but they are rich in moral traits, in examples of all sorts, and in vestiges of the French language, though written in Latin."

Preëminently representative of the dominant scholastic mode of thought were two: Albert, called the Great, and his greater pupil, Thomas Aquinas.

Albert[2] (d. 1280), to whom was given the epithet Magnus, was born in southern Germany, entered the Dominican order at Padua, was highly educated in the learning of the time, became one of the most famous and influential teachers of his age, and prior of the Dominican abbey and school at Cologne. Here he did most of his work as professor and preacher, but also lectured for a time at the University of Paris, whence he returned to Cologne for the remainder of his life, and died there in 1280. He was called "Doctor Universalis."

Several sets of sermons are attributed to him, but many of these are certainly spurious,[3] and perhaps not all the others can be confidently accepted as genuine. But the very fact that so many sermons were put forth under his great name is evidence of his power as a preacher and his influence upon preaching. Those sermons which may be most probably accounted genuine are in the scholastic method, and were very influential in giving vogue and authority to it. There is a set on the festivals and saints' days of which Christlieb[4] says: "By thematic form, through practical use of the text, and simple popularity they are distinguished above many." But his chief fame as preacher rests on another set on the Sacraments. Among them is a series on one text: Prov. 9:5, "Come, eat of my bread, and drink of the wine which I have

[1] Lecoy de la M., *op. cit.*
[2] Most of the authorities previously noted.
[3] Cruel discusses them under the title, "Pseudo-Albert."
[4] Art. in Herzog, Bd. 18, supplement.

mingled." Albert takes these words of the personified wisdom as being those of the Lord Jesus Christ, and a prophecy of the Lord's Supper. On the basis of this interpretation he proceeds through a number of sermons to discuss—in the characteristic way of divisions, subdivisions and distinctions—the institution, the form, the miracle, the participation, and so on, of the Lord's Supper. Almost certainly not his, but called his, and illustrative of his and the scholastic method in general, is a greatly used and prized so-called *Mariale,* that is, a series of sermons or sketches on the Virgin. The text, Luke 1:26, 27—the mission of Gabriel to Mary at Nazareth—was used to suggest a set of two hundred and thirty questions in regard to Mary. Here by the sophistical dialectics of scholasticism there are attributed to the Virgin all sorts of knowledge, as of grammar, rhetoric, law, and other things.

Albert's great fame is merged into and surpassed by that of his renowned pupil, Thomas Aquinas (1227-1274).[1] This greatest representative of the scholastic theology was born of noble parents at Aquino, near Naples, in the year after the death of Francis of Assisi. At five years of age he was sent to be educated at the well-known Benedictine monastery of Monte Cassino, then under the care of an uncle of Thomas. He was a quiet and thoughtful boy, and already, like Origen of old, surprised his teachers by his precocious questions on profound subjects of theology. At this time Italy was rent by the quarrel between the papacy and the emperor Frederick II.—the Guelf and Ghibelline factions. When Thomas was twelve years old the monastery was burned by the soldiers of Frederick, and the boy returned to his home. Soon he was sent to the University of Naples, where after a time he fell under the influence of the Dominicans, and while still a youth joined that order. This step was greatly against the pride and the tastes of his family, who could not abide the thought that their well-born and gifted Thomas should be a mendicant monk, strolling about the country barefoot and preaching. He was fitted for higher things in the church than this. The Domini-

[1] *Works* in the great Paris ed. of Drioux; *Life,* by Vaughan; notices and accounts in many authorities.

cans tried to smuggle him off to France, but he was captured by his brothers, who were officers in the imperial army, and, with his mother's consent, was made a prisoner in his own father's castle. This lasted for two years, during which time it is said that by his father's instigation he was subjected to temptation in order to corrupt him. But this was resisted, and his enforced leisure was devoted to higher things. Three books were the companions of his captivity—the Bible, some works of Aristotle, and the *Sentences* of Peter Lombard, one of the fathers of scholasticism. These he mastered thoroughly, and his subsequent life and labors show also how thoroughly they had mastered him. After two years his family so far relented that he was set at liberty, and later his mother gave up her opposition to his being a Dominican. Thomas was then sent to Cologne to study under Albert the Great. The young man was of heavy build, reserved and shy. His companions nicknamed him *bos mutus*—the "dumb ox." But one day Albert set him to defend a thesis, and he did it with such marked ability that the great teacher said, "You call him the dumb ox, but some day his lowing will fill the world." When in 1245 Albert was sent to the University of Paris to lecture for awhile Thomas accompanied him and enjoyed a first acquaintance with that renowned seat of learning. On Albert's return to Cologne Thomas was for four years his beloved master's assistant teacher, and then was sent back to Paris to study for his degrees. After several years more he was made a doctor the same day with his beloved friend Bonaventura of the Franciscan order. What a long period of studious preparation before he took up in earnest the work of his life!

Ready now for that work the young doctor Thomas Aquinas found his hands full as soon as he took hold. One of his first successes was won in a controversy with the brilliant William of St. Amour, who, in a treatise, had attacked the preaching orders. Thomas was called to Italy by the pope to defend the friars, and he achieved a brilliant success. He became very popular as preacher and lecturer, and was sent by the authorities of his order to many different places to teach and preach. Paris, Bologna, Naples, Rome itself, were the scenes of his triumphs in pulpit and chair. It was thus that the "dumb ox" of former days became changed into the "angel of the schools," the *doctor angelicus* to admiring hearers and readers. But the years of his activity were not to be very many, though prodigiously fruitful. In the early spring of 1274 a council was called at Lyons to consider what might be done to reunite the Greek and Latin churches. Pope Gregory X. sent Thomas, who was then in Rome, to attend the council and advise on points of doctrine. He was taken sick on the way, and died at Fossa Nuova, in north Italy, March, 1274, in the forty-eighth year of his age.

As a theologian, his vast and comprehensive work, the *Summa Theologiæ,* witnesses to his industry, his wonderful acquirements, his logical power, his depth and acuteness of thought, his Catholic orthodoxy. As a teacher and disputant, his title of "angelic doctor" and his numerous treatises reveal something of his popularity and power. As a man and Christian, the story of his life tells of his purity, his gentleness, his patience, his diligence; the respect and admiration of his own and later times testify to the nobility of his character; his love for Albert his master, and Bonaventura his friend, shows the heart of the man; and his humble piety toward his God is illustrated in the tradition of later days, which tells that once while he was praying before a crucifix, the Saviour said to him, "Thomas, thou hast written well of me; what reward wilt thou have for thy labor?" And the saint replied, "Lord, none but thee."[1]

But it is in his quality and work as a preacher that we are here concerned with the great theologian, Aquinas. On his journeys and during his residences at various places as professor and lecturer he was, sometimes to monks and pupils, sometimes on great ecclesiastical occasions, and often too to the common people, a preacher of great acceptance and power. He must have preached without manuscript and in the language of the people, but the brief Latin sketches and outlines of his sermons which remain can give us no just conception of his power before an audience. The current Catholic orthodoxy, as

[1] *Acta Sanctorum,* Mart., die VII., 34: "Thoma, de me bene scripsisti: quam recipies a me pro tuo labore mercedem? Qui respondit, Domine, non nisi te."

he has himself interpreted it in his great books, formed the doctrinal content of his preaching; and there can be little doubt that the scholastic analysis and the argumentative method characterized even his popular sermons; but it is a comfort to know that the people delighted to hear him. Broadus[1] says of him: "Amid the immense and amazing mass of his works are many brief discourses, and treatises which were originally discourses, marked by clearness, simplicity and practical point. He is not highly imaginative, nor flowing in expression; the sentences are short, and everything runs into division and subdivision, usually by threes. But while there is no ornament, and no swelling passion, he uses many homely and lively comparisons, for explanation as well as for argument." It goes without saying that as a child of his time and heir of his past he does not escape the allegorizing and forcing of Scripture which we have come to recognize as inevitable in all mediæval preaching. The following outlines will serve as illustrations of his method.[2]

Outline of a sermon on the *Coming of the King*. Matt. 21:5. First Sunday in Advent.

I. The Dignity of Him Who Comes. (1) A merciful King—in sparing. Isa. 16:5. (2) A just King—in judging. Isa. 34; 16:5. (3) A good King—in rewarding. (4) A wise King—in governing. Ps. 73:1. (5) A terrible King. Jer. 23:5. (6) An omnipotent King. Est. [Apoc.] 13:9. (7) An eternal King. Jer. 10:10; Luke 1:33.

II. The Utility of His Coming. Sevenfold: (1) For the illumination of the world. Jno. 8:12; 1:9. (2) For the spoliation of hell. Hos. 13:14; Zech. 9:11. (3) For the reparation of heaven. Eph. 1:10. (4) For the destruction of sin. Heb. 2:14, 15. (5) For the vanquishment of the devil. Rom. 6:6. (6) For the reconciliation of man with God. Rom. 5:10. (7) For the beatification of man. Jno. 3:16.

[1] *Hist. Prea.*, p. 106 f.

[2] One of the outlines is taken from the Drioux ed. of the Works, the other two from an English translation of some of his sermons: *The Homilies of S. Thomas Aquinas upon the Epistles and Gospels for the Sundays of the Christian Year;* translated by John M. Ashley, Lond., 1873.

III. The Manner of His Coming. In meekness, for four reasons: (1) That he might more easily correct the wicked. Psl. 89:10 [Vulg.]. (2) That he might show to all his lowliness. Ecclus. [Apoc.] 3:19. (3) That he might draw the sheep to himself, and multiply to himself a people. 2 Sam. 22:36. [And a quotation from Bernard]. (4) That he might teach meekness. Matt. 11:29. So four things should commend meekness to us: (a) Delivers from evil; (b) Perfects grace, Prov. 3:34; (c) Preserves the soul, Ecclus. [Apoc.] 12:31; (d) Deserves the land of the living, Matt. 5:5.

The Mystical Ship. Matt. 8:23.

Four things are to be considered in this gospel: (1) The entering of Christ and his disciples into a ship. (2) The great tempest in the sea. (3) The prayer of the disciples. (4) The obedience of the storm to the command of Christ. Morally we are taught four things: (1) To enter into holiness of life. (2) That temptations rage after we have entered. (3) In these temptations to cry unto the Lord. (4) To look for a calm according to his will.

The next sermon continues the same subject and shows how a ship symbolizes holiness:

I. The Material. (1) The wood represents righteousness. (2) The iron, strength. (3) The oakum, by which leaks are stopped, temperance. (4) The pitch, charity.

II. The Form. (1) Smallness at the beginning represents grief for sin. (2) Breadth of the middle, hope of eternal joy. (3) Height of stern, fear of eternal punishment. (4) Narrowness of keel, humility.

III. The Uses. (1) To carry men over seas; in holiness we go to heaven. (2) To carry merchandise; in holiness we carry good works. (3 To make war; in holiness we fight against the demons.

4. Popular Preachers and Preaching

We have already had occasion to observe that the distinctive and emphatic thing in the preaching of the early thirteenth century was the missionary or popular element. Vast crowds, popular enthusiasm, some fanaticism and extremes, but likewise conversion to God and amendment of life were some of its features and fruits.

Under the providence of God a number of coöperating causes may be traced as producing at this time so notable an extension in the power and effect of popular preaching. In a general way greater consideration was now given to the people themselves. Along with the decay of feudalism, the rise of the burgher class, the growth of cities, the acquisition of some political significance by the middle class, the general stir and heightened interest in life, whch have been elsewhere noted, there came greater longing among the people for larger intellectual and spiritual life. This reached and appealed to the minds and hearts of many of the devout. For a century and more Western Christendom had been trying at intervals to wrest by mighty armed hosts the holy places at Jerusalem from the hands of the infidels, but what was doing to deliver the souls of the masses in Europe and elsewhere from the bondage of sin, of unbelief, of moral decay? The people needed, and Christian men must give them, tne gospel of Christ. And the Catholic leaders saw too that many who did not hold the Catholic faith in the traditional and authoritative ways were seeing this need of the people and were spreading heresy among them. So the two motives of a real concern for the people and a jealousy for the Catholic faith were working together to stir up more zeal for preaching in the hearts of some. And these two leading motives became incarnated in two great leaders who now appeared on the scene. Dominic saw that heresy could be more wisely and safely met by preaching the Catholic faith after the manner of the heretics themselves than by persecution or mere churchly teaching; and more devout Francis saw the neglected spiritual condition of the people and heard his call to preach the gospel to the poor. Hence arose the two great orders of preaching monks in whose ranks we find the great popular preachers of the century, and from whom went forth missionaries in many lands at home and abroad. Besides their direct work the example of these preachers had effect on other preachers not of their own companies.

In character and contents the popular preaching was such as has been described as generally prevalent in the age—the current Roman Catholic faith of the Middle

Ages, the traditional allegorical interpretation and other misuses of Scripture, the excessive employment of legends of the saints and other unscriptural material as authoritative, the doctrines of penance, purgatory, and confession, the veneration amounting to worship of the Virgin—all these and other overgrowths upon the gospel we have learned to recognize as characteristics of the mediæval preaching, and they need here be only thus briefly recalled. But we must not forget that along with these things the work of Christ as the Saviour, and the only Saviour, was vividly presented, and the duty of repentance and faith strongly urged together with the practice of the Christian virtues as the fruits and evidences of a real Christian experience. Moreover, the fearful sins of the age—in clergy, nobles, and people—received brave and keen rebuke. These old preachers knew human nature, and they did not hesitate to expose and denounce and try to correct its perennial foibles. Change the language, the allusion to current events, some of the illustrations from prevalent customs and manners, and the main material of their treatment of sin and its remedy would apply to the men and women of to-day as well as to those of the thirteenth century.

In form, the sermons of the popular preachers were largely influenced by the scholastic passion for analysis and minute subdivision. In regard to language they were of course mostly, if not entirely, preached in the vernacular dialects.[1] For illustration and argument there was effective use of every sort of material—legends and tales, fables old and new, the habits (real and imaginary) of animals, the forces of nature (of course oftentimes absurdly misunderstood), the customs of the time, and many other sources, were open books to these prophets of the day. Sometimes queer methods for advertising and effect were resorted to. "Sensational preaching" was by no means unknown. There was many a prototype of the modern Sam Jones variety of "popular" preacher. Tricks and surprises, catchy and coarse illustrations were not infrequent. The humorous was freely employed, and this often degenerated into the burlesque and irreverent.[2]

[1] See Lecoy de la Marche, as above, p. 184.

[2] Friar Cuthbert in Longfellow's *Golden Legend* is not overdrawn.

The marvellous was a mighty help in that age of credulity, and it was worked too hard even by the best of the preachers. But the sermons were also popular in the best sense—they found the people, held them, helped them. Vivid allegory and picturing appealed to the imagination, lively dialogue and sharp home-thrust kept the attention, and warm and tender appeals to the better feelings of men were not without effect. Past masters in the art of popular speech, and of handling great crowds in its use, were Antony and Berthold; but though preëminent, they were not alone.

When we name a few of the more notable men who distinguished the annals of popular preaching in the thirteenth century we must not forget the great army of less known and even of now forgotten preachers who in the spirit of these leaders, and in use of the methods which the leaders exemplify, went among the people preaching the word. Contemporary accounts and the considerable number of sermons—many of them anonymous—which have come down from that age, show us that the prominent and well-known names represent a mighty activity, of which they are only the most notable examples.

The first place in our discussion naturally belongs to the two great men who in the early part of this thirteenth century founded the famous orders of preaching friars—the Dominicans and Franciscans.

Dominic[1] (d. 1221), whose real name has been lost sight of in his assumed and canonized one, was born in 1170, of high family, at Calaruega, in Old Castile, Spain. In early childhood he found his pleasure in going to church, in prayers, in self-denial. He was well educated in youth by an uncle, and at the age of fourteen was sent to the University of Valencia, where he studied hard the required general course, and afterwards made a specialty of theology. During his career as a student he was distinguished above all his comrades for diligence and learning, and still more for his piety. He had a tender

[1] The chief authority is the *Acta Sanctorum*, August, Vol. I., p. 359 ss. Also, *Vie de Saint Dominique,* by the famous modern Dominican, Lacordaire; *Francis and Dominic,* by J. Herkless, a brief popular account; articles in Wetzer und Welte, and Herzog. Dominic did not leave many writings, and of those ascribed to him the larger part are considered spurious.

heart, and was ever ready to sacrifice himself to duty. Thus early, too, he was deeply concerned for the salvation of men and the conversion of heretics. At the age of twenty-four he was called by bishop Diego of Osma to be canon of his cathedral; and in this office he displayed great zeal and preached very often.

Toward the end of 1203 Alfonso VIII., king of Old Castile, sent bishop Diego on an embassy to Denmark to seek a bride for his son. The bishop chose Dominic for his travelling companion. The mission was successful, and the bishop came back to report, but on the return of the messengers the following year to bring the princess to Spain it was found that she had in the meantime died. From this second journey the bishop and Dominic did not directly return, but having communicated their sad intelligence to the king they crossed the Alps and paid a visit to Rome. All these experiences were helpful in the development of the young priest, but now on this return journey from Rome occurred the turning point in his life.

On their way through the south of France the companions stopped a while at Montpelier, where they found three papal legates living in some style and making futile official attempts to bring back the heretical Albigenses to the Catholic faith. Diego and Dominic saw that these methods were useless, and advised the priests to adopt a simple mode of life, go among the people with humble sincerity and use the methods of preaching and personal persuasion which the heretics themselves employed. The counsellors set the example themselves, and thus in 1205 Dominic began to preach among the Albigenses of Languedoc. About the same time he started in a small way a home of refuge for young women to save them from heresy, and this later came to be the female order of Dominicans, as well as being a sort of beginning for the order proper. This soon came into being. For Dominic's zeal and example won others to his side. He took no active part in the crusade against the Albigenses, but at its close, in 1215, he set about the establishing of his order of preachers. One of his friends, Peter Cellani, gave him a house for the gathering company, the bishop of Toulouse favored and helped the enterprise, and so did Simon de Montfort. With this good start Dominic went to Rome to gain the pope's consent. As in case of Francis, Innocent III. was very reluctant. He died, however, before the matter was finally disposed of, and his successor, Honorius III., in December, 1216, gave the requisite authorization, and the order of *Fratres Prædicatores,* or Preaching Friars (Brothers), was fairly established.

Dominic was active in spreading, developing, guiding his order during the rest of his life. He died comparatively young at Bologna in August, 1221. Dominic was himself a preacher of decided ability, and was heard with admiration both by the people and the more cultured audiences of Rome and other places. It is to be regretted that no specimens of his eloquence survive.

Francis (d. 1226), the founder of the order of *Fratres Minores* ("Little Brothers of the Poor"), was born at Assisi in Umbria, central Italy, in 1182.[1] His father, Pietro Bernadone, was a wealthy merchant, worldly, ambitious, and of an evil disposition. He wished his fine and handsome son to figure in society, and was quite willing to supply the requisite means to that end. Francis was of an accommodating spirit in that regard—as most young men would be—and sowed his wild oats pretty freely; dressed well, enjoyed life, and did nothing. But all the while he was secretly dissatisfied at times; the dormant conscience was not dead, the beckoning future forbade rest in an idle and luxurious present. The youth was of a free and generous disposition, kind-hearted, lovable, and popular. With a view to social elevation he enlisted as a soldier in one of the petty Italian wars of the time and was furnished by his father with a fine equipment. He started with his companions on an expedition, but his heart failed him—it is said that he saw a vision—and he returned. Certainly this was not for lack of courage, but because he had no taste for the business.

[1] There is a great literature on Francis. For many reasons he has appealed to sentiment as well as to historic and religious interest. I have found particularly valuable the brilliant work of Sabatier, *Francis of Assisi,* Eng. transl.; a critical study by Walter Goetz in Brieger und Bess *Ztschrft. für Kirchengesch.,* 1901, SS. 362, 525; and for the traditions and atmosphere the *Fioretti di San Francesco.*

Here began his troubles with his father. Filled with strange conflicts, he went to Rome in search of peace. Here he was much impressed by the beggars, and counted it one of the beginnings of his conversion that he was moved to tender sympathy toward the lepers, for whom, in his fastidious days, he had entertained a sickening aversion. It is said that he embraced one of these outcasts and gave him his cloak. The turning point soon came. It was in 1206 while he was praying before a crucifix in the church of St. Damian, near Assisi, that his soul found peace in his Saviour, and his resolution to break with the world and devote himself to the service of his Lord was taken.

A stormy scene with his father followed. Pietro appeared with his son before some ecclesiastical or civil tribunal and made complaint of his disobedience. Francis declared he could no longer walk in the ways his father had planned for him, that all he now had belonging to his father was the clothing he had on. Stripping himself of all, he gave the clothes to Pietro, and ran out; some one kindly threw a cloak about the naked youth as he left, and with this only garment he went to the church of St. Damian to pray and consider his future course. For clothing and food the erstwhile dainty and luxurious Francis was now for the rest of his life dependent upon charity, and this dependence became one of the principles of the Franciscan order. It is a pathetic and beautiful thing that, not knowing what he should now do for his Lord, he noticed that the church of St. Damian, which was his soul's birthplace and his refuge when homeless, was out of repair; and humbly taking hold of the first work that came in view, he set about repairing the edifice with his own hands and with such other help as he could get. This done, he turned to do a similar work at another church nearby, Portiuncula; and there, while attending mass one day, he heard the priest read the tenth chapter of Matthew. It came to him as a message from his Lord, showing him his mission and calling him to it. Now his lifework was found; it was *to be poor and to preach.* "No purse—no scrip—as ye go, preach"—this was the key to his future. His soul had found its burden and its joy.

Francis immediately went to Assisi, up the hill from the church, and preached to the people with power, accepting as before only his necessities from the hands of the charitable. His words and example produced an effect. Soon several other men joined him, and so almost before he knew it, and without previous intention, he was becoming the head of a band of preachers. But they were acting without church authority, only talking from their hearts without clerical ordination, and working together without organization This was in the spring of 1209. So Francis went to Rome to get permission to found a regular order of preachers within the fold of the church. Innocent III., who was then pope, was opposed to the multiplication of orders, and only reluctantly yielded to the persuasion of Francis and the representations of others, and finally gave consent in 1210 to the establishment of the order, on the conditions that it should be wholly subordinated to the church and under a responsible head. Francis joyfully accepted the conditions, and so his "Little Brothers of the Poor" came into being as an organization of preachers who should live by charity and preach the gospel to the people.

It is not surprising that the saintly zeal of Francis should have impressed women as well as men, and that so there should have arisen alongside of the Brothers the auxiliary order of "Little Sisters of the Poor," devoted to charity and to the aid and encouragement of the preaching brothers. This order came into being under the lead of Clara, the pure and tender-hearted friend of Francis, and was in many ways a help to him and his brethren in their work.

Francis was ordained a deacon, and on his return from Rome set up a sort of convent near Assisi. This was at the church of Santa Maria degli Angeli, otherwise known as Portiuncula. In the great modern church which now occupies the site the original little low-vaulted sanctuary is preserved under the dome, as the central object. An inscription tells that this was the cradle of the Franciscan order. Nearby is preserved—also inside the church—the room in which the saint died. Volunteers came in crowds. Their missionary activity was great. Cloisters were established in various places as headquarters with the rapid spread of the order in many lands. Preachers went forth during the lifetime of Francis into Syria, Morocco, Hungary, Germany, Spain, France, England. Francis himself went with a crusade to Egypt and afterwards to the East. But as the order grew it developed tendencies which he could not control and were not wholly in harmony with his ideas. A progressive party, under the lead of Brother Elias, of Crotona, was in favor of making more use of education and learning, and these ideas, as we shall see, at last gained the day. Francis and his more intimate associates were in favor of holding by the simpler principles of the first Rule of the order. These troubles within the ranks and the incessant labors of his active life wore upon the founder's mind and strength. He resigned the headship of the order; suffered much from mental anxiety and bodily weakness, but enjoyed abiding peace of soul and joy in God. He died at Portiuncula, in 1226, only forty-four years old.

Of the extant works attributed to Francis[1] a large proportion are certainly spurious, but a number are reckoned by the critics to be as certainly genuine, while others are in dispute. Among the genuine writings are no sermons, properly speaking, but from several of them we may infer something as to the preacher's thought and style. There is a brief but interesting letter to Antony of Padua,[2] which shows Francis' uneasiness over the coming in of learning as an aid to the preachers, and at the same time illustrates one of his main principles—the insistence upon prayer. Application had been made to admit the brilliant and learned young brother Antony among the authorized preachers of the order, and it is thus that Francis gives his consent:

"To my dearest brother Antony, brother Francis in Christ, greeting. It meets my approval that thou shouldest interpret to the brethren the writings of the Holy Theology; in such way, however, that neither in thee nor in the others (which I vehemently desire) should be ex-

[1] The only edition of the Works of Francis to which I have had access is an old one (1641) by John de la Haye, containing the works of Francis and of Antony of Padua. But the critical studies by Sabatier and by Goetz, referred to in previous note, have of course been regarded in the citations made.

[2] Ed. of de la Haye, p. 4.

tinguished the spirit of holy prayer, according to the Rule which we profess. Farewell." The *Letter to All Christians* is not certainly genuine, and even if so in the main, has probably been retouched by later hands.[2] But as it has much in favor of its genuineness we may quote it in illustration of the doctrine and manner of Francis. The opening address is as follows: "Since I am the servant of all, I am bound to serve all and to administer to all the fragrant words of my Lord. Whence considering in mind that I cannot in person, because of the infirmity and weakness of my body, visit each one, I have proposed in the present letter sent forth to offer to you the words of our Lord Jesus Christ, who is the Word of the Father, and [also] the words of the Holy Spirit, which are spirit and life." After stating the doctrine concerning Christ, and speaking of his birth, his mission, his institution of the Supper, and his prayer in Gethsemane, he goes on: "Nevertheless he placed his will within the will of the Father, saying, 'Father, thy will be done; not as I will, but as thou wilt.' Of that Father the will was such that his blessed and glorious Son whom he gave for us, and who was born for us, should offer himself, through his own blood, a sacrifice and victim on the altar of the cross, not for himself, by whom all things were made, but for our sins, leaving us an example that we should follow his steps. And he wishes that we all should be saved by him, and should receive him with a pure heart and a chaste body. But there are few who wish to receive him and be saved by him, although his yoke is easy and his burden light." Upon this good gospel foundation, however, he proceeds to erect a superstructure partly of the "gold, silver, precious stones" of divine truth and partly of the "wood, hay, stubble" of traditional error. For example, concerning almsgiving, he says, "Let us therefore have charity and humility and do alms, because these wash our souls from the filth of sins; for men lose all the things which they leave in this world, but carry with them the wages of charity and the alms which they did, for which they shall obtain from the Lord a prize and a worthy reward." And so in other places there is noteworthy mingling of truth and error. But is not this ever true?

[1] Goetz, *op. cit.*

And must we not remember the times in which this godly man lived and what he was taught and received for truth?

Francis of Assisi was a truly wonderful man. By natural disposition he was gentle, loving, delicate, and these traits had been mellowed by grace into a rare beauty of character. That he had some fanaticism with his devotion, and was (as many others in his days and since) a strange compound of superstition and piety, may be granted. But he was a loving and lovable man. He loved nature, men, and God. The mystical trace in him was combined, as in Bernard and others, with intense desire and active effort for the good of his fellowmen. His preaching was based on his experience, and enforced by his life. It was simple, winsome, tender, persuasive. He preached in the language of the people and to their hearts. He held up Christ as Saviour and Lord. He spoke against pride and every sin, and in favor of all the virtues, exhorting to penitence, faith, humility, chastity, and love. His style was not ornate and learned, but simple, practical, and effective. Sabatier has well summarized one of the secrets of his wonderful power over men in saying, "He was of the people, and the people recognized themselves in him."

While many popular preachers of this age belonged to no order, or to the Dominican or other orders, it is yet not surprising that the two who are most distinguished for power and success in drawing and dealing with great audiences were both Franciscans—Antony of Padua and Berthold of Regensburg.

The little country of Portugal has given birth to at least two of the greatest preachers of the Catholic church: Antony of Padua (c. 1195-1231), and Antonio Vieyra, who lived in the seventeenth century. While Padua in Italy was the scene of Antony's principal labors and the resting place of his bones, it was at Lisbon that the famous Franciscan preacher first saw the light, and received his education and start in life. Ferdinand,[1] for this was

[1] De la Haye's ed. of the works of Francis and Antony, before mentioned; article by E. Lempp, in Herzog; and a critical article by the same scholar in Brieger und Bess, *Ztschft. für Kirchengesch.*, Bde. 11, 12, 13.

Antony's baptismal name, was born in Lisbon, of noble or knightly family, and most probably in the year 1195. His parents died while he was young, but the boy was well brought up, and received the current higher education, as his writings abundantly show. He early joined the Augustinian monks while a student at the University of Coimbra. But during this period also occurred the event which decided him to join the followers of Francis. The remains of two Franciscan missionaries who had suffered martyrdom in Morocco were brought to Coimbra for interment. Their fate took hold of the fervid imagination of young Ferdinand and fired him with an ambition to win like them the martyr's crown. This was in 1220. He left the Augustinians, and against the wishes of his friends and amid the jeers of his companions, he became a Franciscan missionary and set out to North Africa in search of martyrdom. He assumed the name of Antony in honor of St. Antony, the renowned old Egyptian monk, leaving his name, his former life, and his native place behind him forever.

In Africa, however, instead of martyrdom at the hands of heathen, he found a sick bed and a long and weary illness from fever. Under this providence he wisely concluded that God desired not so much his death as his life, and embarked for Italy to come in closer touch with his new order, and become perhaps one of its preachers. But his faith and humility were destined to further trials. The vessel in which he sailed was wrecked on the coast of Sicily, but he found brethren of his order and with them attended the General Chapter, which met in 1221 at Assisi. Here he seems to have been unnoticed and neglected, but on his humble request was at last received by one of the elder brethren, who took him with himself to a hermitage in the Campagna. Here he remained for a while learning humility and practising asceticism, till at last he with several others came up for ordination to the priesthood. As they were at the town of Forli for this purpose the prior or leader requested one after another of the younger brethren to preach or lecture to the rest; all declined till brother Antony's turn came; he modestly consented, and discharged the duty in such a way as to reveal to his superiors his wonderful oratorical talent. Request was made that he should be appointed one of the travelling preachers, and to this, as we have seen, Francis gave his consent.

Brother Antony was now fully launched on his wonderful though short career as a preacher. From now (probably about 1222) to his early death, some ten years later, his labors in preaching were continuous and heavy. Not very much is certainly known of the first years of his work. He preached in Italy and in many places in France, where he had a marvellous effect on the people. His facility in language must have been remarkable, as he seems to have had no difficulty either in France or Italy in making eloquent sermons to the masses. He took part in leading questions and debates of the day and was especially active and successful in restoring heretics to the faith. At last he was made provincial of his order for northeast Italy, and took up his residence in Padua in 1229. But the labors of office too much hindered his preaching, and he was released from the one that he might give his whole attention to the other. But his time was short.

The Franciscans had a residence given to them in Padua, and another just outside the walls called the Little Ark. In these places Antony lived and worked during the two remaining years of his life. Great crowds thronged to hear him—thirty thousand people, it is said—and of course no building could accommodate them. He preached chiefly in the open air and with wonderful power and success. The region near Padua was at that time given over to many sins. He describes it as a "field thirsting for rain;" and he handles its sins with faithfulness and effect. Great was his success; but he was suffering from dropsy and his labors had exhausted his strength. He kept on as long as he could, but finally gave up and took up his residence not very far from Padua in a great tree, in which a little hut was built for him among the branches. Whether his idea in this was hygienic, or superstitious, or merely whimsical, does not appear. But here in his nest he worked at putting his sermons into shape for publication, until at last he was persuaded, when near the end, to come back to the Little Ark at Padua, where he died June 13, 1231, about thirty-eight years old.

There is, as usual, much difference among critics as to the genuine writings of Antony, but amid the many sketches of sermons in Latin which pass under his name, no doubt some are his, and in form and thought at least represent his method; but they do not and cannot convey to us any suggestion of the language, the expression, and still less the power and moving warmth with which he spoke. From among the so-called *Dominical* (Sunday) *Sermons*[1] a specimen or two may serve as illustration of his manner. Thus: Luke 21:25. *There shall be signs in the sun, and in the moon, and in the stars; and upon the earth distress of nations.* Here four things are noted according to which there are four advents [of Christ], namely, in the flesh, in the mind, at death, and at the final judgment. I say, first, an advent in the flesh—and that is the assumption of human flesh—is noted here: *There shall be signs in the sun.* For the sun is the Son of God. The second is in the mind, spiritually; and this is the purifying of our mind, either a protection against sin, or a conferring of virtues, in this: *In the moon.* The third in death, which is the separation of body and soul, in this: *In the stars.* For the stars will fall from heaven, etc. The fourth in the end of all things (*ultimo fine*), in which there will be apportionment of merits and punishment of wrongs, in this: *And in the earth distress of nations, etc.* On this basis he proceeds to enlarge his points with all sorts of plays upon words, allegorical extravagances and the like.

In another sermon he discusses the message of John the Baptist from the prison, and founds his treatment upon the signification of the persons involved. Thus: Herod represents the world; Herodias the flesh; John in chains the spirit of man in bondage to pleasure; and the two disciples of John stand for hope and fear. But it is really unfair to judge Antony by such imperfect specimens of the mere outlines of his sermons, and those not certainly genuine.

The traditions of his preaching contain much of the marvellous, both as to the astonishing crowds it drew and as to the effects produced by it. But making due allowance for extravagance in these stories, and for later

[1] Ed. of de la Haye.

additions to them, there is sober basis in fact for Antony's great reputation. In his use of Scripture he followed to the most absurd extreme the fanciful allegorical method; but in his division he used sensibly and well, without undue detail, the theological analysis of the scholastics, and did a service to preaching in popularizing a better structure of discourse than that of the homily. In his numerous and telling illustrations he drew freshly and powerfully from the everyday life about him, from nature, from human nature; in earnestness, fervor, and effect his strength is unquestioned; and in drawing power he has never been surpassed, rivalled only by his fellow Franciscan Berthold, later in the century, and by Whitefield, perhaps Moody, and a few others, in modern times.

One of the most remarkable preachers of that age, or indeed of any age, was the Franciscan evangelist Berthold (c. 1220-1272), of Regensburg (Ratisbon), in Bavaria.[1] Not much is known of his life, which, except for his wonderful preaching, was probably uneventful. The man is known almost solely in his work. He was born probably at or near Regensburg in the first quarter of the thirteenth century, most likely not earlier than 1220 nor later than 1225. Nothing is known of his family or family name. He is simply known as "Brother Berthold," in the various forms in which the name is given. At an early age he was taken into the Franciscan abbey at Regensburg, and there educated. Henceforth his name is always associated with this place, which was his home or headquarters during life and his resting-place at death. Here he fell under the tutelage of the pious and devoted mystic, David of Augsburg, who long taught at Regensburg, and was himself a preacher of no mean abilities.[2] The friendship and encouragement of this good man had much to do with Berthold's after success. It is

[1] All the German historians of preaching in the Middle Ages, both Catholic and Protestant, and with pardonable pride, pay much attention to Berthold. There are good discussions in the works of Linsenmayer, Cruel, Albert, Nebe; and an account by Göbel prefixed to his valuable translation of the sermons of Berthold into modern German. Editions in the old dialect have also appeared, and there are copious extracts in some of the writers above named and in the lively sketch of C. W. Stromberger, *Berthold von Regensburg.*

[2] See below, p. 281.

related that during his preaching Brother David would sometimes accompany him, help him with suggestion and cheer, and sometimes sit behind him and encourage him as he preached. Sweet, indeed, is it for the loneliness of genius to be cheered by the intelligent sympathy of a real friend!

Berthold's sermons show acquaintance with the church fathers and other theological literature, but no high degree of learning, nor any marked depth or subtlety of thought. He could not be called either scholastic or mystic, but distinctively a powerful popular preacher in whom the clear arrangement of scholasticism and the warm piety of mysticism showed traces but not ascendency. In his convent sermons he used Latin, and in his other sermons shows familiar and easy acquaintance with that tongue, but his great work was done in the rude old German of his time.

The first mention of Brother Berthold is in 1246, when he was sent to one of the nunneries of his order to lecture and preach. About 1250 he appears as a travelling preacher, creating unwonted enthusiasm, attracting great multitudes which no church could hold, overflowing sometimes even the squares of the towns. He preached on the hillsides from a lofty wooden tower, and it is said even from trees, where a sort of scaffolding would be erected for him. He must have had a very powerful or very penetrating voice, and would take the direction of the wind with a feather and speak "down the wind." During ten years he went through Bavaria, Suabia, Alsace, Switzerland, stopping longer in some places than in others, and sometimes repeating his visits. About 1260 he turned toward eastern Germany and traversed Austria, Bohemia, Hungary, taking in Franconia and Thuringia on the return trip. In some of these lands he could not speak the language and preached by an interpreter. These are the scanty details of a life filled with incessant activity and phenomenal success in preaching the word of God to the people during a trying and fearful time in Germany.

It will be remembered that the years of Berthold's ministry (1250-1272) coincided almost exactly with the period known in German history as the Great Interregnum, when for about twenty years after the fall of the Hohenstaufen emperors there was no king in Germany, and the reins of authority were loosed. Petty sovereigns and lords were without an overlord, and the political, social, and moral disorders of the times were great. In such a time as this the voice of this man came as that of a prophet of old, sent of God to rebuke the wicked and comfort those who waited for better days. In 1272 Berthold died and was buried at Regensburg, where his tomb was long regarded and visited as that of a saint, and his memory held in grateful affection by the people.

There remain some of his Latin sermons, probably only sketches, chiefly of his convent sermons, and perhaps written by himself. These would be valuable if we had nothing else, but fortunately in his case a number—some seventy or eighty—of his German sermons have been preserved in the reports of hearers. Early in the nineteenth century one of the brothers Grimm called the attention of scholars and literary men to these manuscript sermons as choice specimens of early German prose. Since then they have been published in various partial or complete editions, and a Catholic scholar, Göbel, has done good service by turning them into modern German. The sermons are now therefore accessible to those acquainted with the German of to-day, and will repay study.

From these and the traditional accounts we see that Berthold was, above all things, a mighty preacher to the people. He had true piety, conviction, and a sincere desire to save and teach men. He preached not for his own fame or reward, but for the glory of his Lord and the help of his fellowmen. Repentance was his principal theme. Like another John the Baptist he thundered against sin, and called the people to conversion. He powerfully and unflinchingly attacked the sins of all classes. He told the lords plainly that they were like rapacious eagles preying upon the sheep, he rated in no soft tones the judges who rendered unjust decisions for hire, he satirized and denounced the sinful follies of polite society and the baser vices of all orders, he paid special attention to the false and worldly clergy, and before Luther was dreamed of denounced the "penny preachers" who traded in spiritual things; he scored the cheats and fakirs, the dicers and dancers, the lazy, the gluttonous—in fact, sinners of every hue. But his special pet object of attack was the avaricious man, the "geiziger," who stands out with unenviable distinctness in his vivid pictures. Like Antony and other moral preachers of the time he condemned usury with reiterated emphasis. Heresy, too, claimed his attention and he faithfully warned against what he believed to be errors. On the other hand he painted in glowing colors the beauty of the Christian virtues and the present and eternal rewards of the Christian life. Nor was it a mere external morality that he preached; he showed the worthlessness of works without faith, even if he did lay too much merit to the works of faith. He exalted Christ as the only Saviour from an eternal and agonizing hell, the only Guide to the lasting and blessed kingdom of God. Of course, with all this, the characteristic doctrinal and other errors and perversions common to his age fully appear. It was no pure Scriptural gospel that he preached, but mediæval Romanism, yet at its best. He was wonderfully gifted in the art of fresh, vivid, moving popular address. Invective, warning, appeal, exhortation, all were at his command. Imagery and illustration abounded, often homely, sometimes coarse. Vivid dialogues and shrewd hits enlivened discourse; but through all these rhetorical devices shines full and clear the lofty purpose of the speaker to quicken and guide the spiritual life of his hearers. The following outline of one of his most characteristic sermons will give at least a hint of his manner:

On Seven Very Great Sins.

Text (misquoted, and no book and chapter given, probably intended for John 15:11): "I rejoice in thee, and my joy is perfected in thee." Three kinds of people make God glad—each gladder than the other in succession; namely, those who keep from mortal sins, those who are habitually good, and those who die in the practice of goodness. Correspondingly, three kinds of people make the devil glad; namely, those who occasionally fall into sin, those who live in sin, and those who die in sin. But seven kinds of people not only make the devil glad but put a crown on him (see Rev.

12:3). The seven crowns of the dragon are the seven chief sins, and they bring people to the bottom of hell just as the seven princes of Egypt went to the bottom of the Red Sea. Here they are: 1. Those who are damned for the multitude of their sins. 2. Those for the greatness of their sins—such as perjurers, adulterers, excommunicates, etc. 3. The devil's hunters (male and female), such as harlots, procurers, and the penny preachers. 4. Heretics. 5. [Left blank. The editor supposes it was the unpardonable sin, about which Berthold elsewhere manifests unwillingness to speak plainly.] 6. Bad masters and unjust judges. 7. The avaricious. In "enlarging on his points" he does not mince matters at all, but strikes out right and left without fear or favor.

Besides the great men who have been discussed there were a number of less distinguished preachers to the people who worked in the spirit and methods of the leaders. The names of some have come down to us, and there are besides numerous anonymous sermons which have been preserved from that age, and exhibit the popular character.[1]

Among the French preachers may be named Stephen (Étienne) of Bourbon (d. 1261), who preached much, travelled much, and came in contact with many persons of distinction, secular and religious. He wrote a book for preachers containing extracts and examples of sermons, and divided into seven parts representing the seven gifts of the Holy Spirit. There was also William of Auvergne, who was bishop of Paris from 1228 to his death in 1249, and was very influential in church and state. He had popular gifts as a preacher, and excelled, sometimes exceeded, in the use of figures and illustrations.

Of the Germans, besides David of Augsburg, who will be noticed among the mystics, there was a Cæsarius of Heisterbach (d. c. 1240), whose sermons show good skill in construction, variety, and power of oratory. There were also a certain Peregrinus, from whom we have a collection of sketches; and an anonymous preacher in the neighborhood of Black Forest, whose lively and vigor-

[1] For the French and German preachers, the authorities so often cited; and for those of Italy, Zanotto, *Storia della Predicazione.*

ous sermons show alike the influence of Berthold and of Jacob of Voragine. But perhaps the most interesting of these Germans was Conrad of Brundelsheim (d. 1321), who was abbot of the Cistercian monastery at Heilsbronn. A collection of his sermons, or sketches, in Latin, bears the curious title of *Sermones Fratris Socci,* i.e., "The Sermons of Brother Sock." Why he was called "Sock" does not appear. One humorous suggestion, mentioned by Linsenmayer, is to the effect that perhaps he carried his notes in his ample socks; but Cruel offers the more rational guess that it was a nickname given him from some personal habit or occurrence and had nothing to do with his preaching. At any rate, "Brother Sock" gave to his brethren in these rather scholastic Latin sketches a set of sermons to modify and use which show that he was himself no mean preacher to the people; and there is no doubt that his brethren made abundant use of his liberality and often turned them to account.

There was among the Italians a well-known preacher called John of Vicenza (Giovanni da Vicenza, or da Schio), who was renowned as a peacemaker in many parts of Italy, and by whose eloquent persuasions foes and feuds were reconciled. But more important for us than he was Jacob de Voragine (1230-1298), who was a Dominican, and probably had experience in early life as a travelling preacher, but was, when he died, a prelate at Genoa. He thus represents both the parochial and the popular preaching of the time. Not much is known of him, but the traditional accounts represent him as a greatly beloved and admired preacher to the people. His interest for us lies chiefly in the fact that he was the compiler of the stories of the saints in the collection called *Legenda Aurea,* commonly known to us in the singular number as the "Golden Legend." There were, of course, later editions of this book, and it is not possible to determine how much of the work is due to his editorial care and was worked over by him. In the collection are many sermons, mostly on the saints and the Virgin Mary. Christlieb[1] says the book gives us "a deep insight into the etymological fooleries (interpreting allegorically the names of Biblical characters, etc.), the crass superstitions

[1] Art. in Herzog, Bd. 18, supplement.

and the incredibly tasteless love of miracles of that age. Also its numerous sermons show not only the unfruitfulness for real edification of scholastic pedantic trifling and legendary picturing, but they helped much to corrupt taste in preaching." But the sermons are given in a warm, even fiery manner, and are often lively and picturesque in style and imagery, and so very well suited to popular use. Longfellow's *Golden Legend* gives many a hint as to the contents of the book, though by him the best parts were selected, hung on the thread of a pleasing story, and softened and beautified by the spirit of poetry and the gentle sentiment of our poet of the fireside.

CHAPTER VIII

Decline and Mysticism in the Thirteenth and Fourteenth Centuries

In the present chapter we have to do with the latter part of the thirteenth and a little more than the first half of the fourteenth century, that is, as far as the death of John Tauler, the great mystic preacher, in 1361.

Europe was a troubled world in the fourteenth century. The Hundred Years' War between England and France was begun by Edward III. of England early in the century, and was taxing the strength and resources of both nations. Germany was in awful confusion with a disputed imperial succession between Louis of Bavaria and Frederick of Austria; division, civil wars, and other trials desolated the land. Conditions in Italy were no better than formerly—endless squabbles and no hope of unity and strength. After the conflict of Boniface VIII. with Philip the Fair the papacy became a tool of France, and for seventy years (1309-1378) the residence of the popes was at Avignon in southern France, instead of at Rome. Corruption accompanied decay. The papal court by its luxury and turpitude was a stench in the nostrils of mankind, and there seemed no remedy for the desperate case. In such a time preaching fared but ill. We have to note a sad decline in the scholastic and popular types of preaching, but at the same time to describe the growth and power of the mystic type which stamps a somewhat redeeming character of its own upon the age.

1. Decline of Scholastic and Popular Preaching

The great preachers of the Dominican and Franciscan orders had passed away, and the day of the second-rate man had come. Albert and Thomas, Antony and Berthold are memories and models, but no longer living forces. Along with this, popular interest in preaching and popular regard for the preacher sensibly diminished. We do not now hear of so great crowds and so great effects. Furthermore, the quality of sermons which have come down to us from the scholastic and popular preachers after Aquinas and Berthold gives abundant evidence of a falling off in power.

In undertaking to discover and state the causes of this decay we have to fall back upon that mysterious law of reaction which we have so frequent occasion to observe and apply. The two great movements in preaching to which the names scholastic and popular have been given had reached their height and must recede. At high tide there is strength, repose, beauty; but when the waters recede they leave trash and slime behind them to augment the ugly and unclean things which they had covered but not washed away. So the inherent, inevitable, faults and weaknesses which are connected with every great forward movement—whether in the movement itself, as in the wave, or fixed in habit and custom, as on the shore—appear in all their ugliness when the reaction comes. In the scholastic sermons, the over-speculation, the hair-splitting distinctions, the tedious detail of analysis, the frequent sophistries and useless conclusions were at all times ugly faults; but now that the vigor of youth and the freshness of genius were departed this manner of preaching became barren indeed. And still worse was it that the religious spirit which had counteracted and even utilized so much that was weak in scholasticism had itself lost intensity and fervor. In popular preaching, the seeking after effect, the misuse of Scripture, the coarse humor, that could hardly be tolerated even when accompanied by real devotion and spiritual power, became now in their emptiness almost a hideous mockery of preaching. Further, as to both these modes of preaching, we see what is well exemplified in many other spheres, namely, that methods which are rods of power in the hands of masters are rotten reeds in those of feeble imitators. Little Thomases and little Bertholds multiplied, and made odious the things which had done good service in a former generation.

And in addition to these inward causes of decay the standing external hindrances were to be reckoned with. The world, the flesh, and the devil, always and everywhere, are leagued in lively coöperation against good gospel preaching; and these evil allies were as present and as potent in the times which we are discussing as they are in our own. Corruption in society and church, in laity and clergy, was bad enough and getting worse. And, finally, we must notice that growth of power, popularity, and even earthly possessions, had corrupted and weakened the spiritual and fruitful work of the two great preaching orders. Except for the mystics among the Dominicans we have to record a falling off in character, and therefore in the best influence, for both the orders of preachers. Yet we must not think that the decay was total or even more rapid than it really was. History is not best written in antitheses. We may err to distortion by emphasizing contrast. In human affairs evil and good are always present, sometimes one is more evident, sometimes the other.

In order to preserve the continuity of our narrative there is needed a brief mention of some of the more important preachers of the scholastic and popular tendencies during the late thirteenth and early fourteenth centuries. But only a few of the best from the different countries need be named.

In Italy there was a certain Jordan (Giordano) of Pisa, or Rivalto (d. 1311), who is mentioned favorably by Italian writers as a preacher of power in the popular tongue, who was also distinguished both for his piety and his scholarship. He was learned in the languages, and his knowledge of the Scriptures is praised as remarkable.

In Germany there are several preachers worthy of being remembered. One was Nicholas of Landau, who was quite a scholastic, pushing the method of that school to considerable extremes. Another was Henry of

Frimar (d. 1340), who taught in Paris for a while, and then in Prague. From him a number of very scholastic sermons remain. Like him was Jordan of Quedlinburg, who enjoyed a good reputation in his day and left behind him a number of sermons in Latin, which are marked like the others by excess of scholasticism.

In France there were a number of preachers, but none very distinguished in comparison with those of earlier and later times. Famous as a scholar and commentator, though not especially for his preaching, was Nicholas of Lyra (d. 1340), a Franciscan, and teacher at Paris and other places. His commentary on the whole Bible had the name of "postils," or brief homilies, and suggests that a good deal of it was used in preaching. Besides there are some sermons remaining. But Lyra's chief distinction is that in interpreting the Bible he somewhat broke away from the traditional and absurd allegorical method and did something toward bringing in a sounder exegesis of Scripture. Besides, there were two distinguished prelates and canonists (interpreters of canon, i.e., ecclesiastical as distinguished from civil, law) who bore the name of William Durand, the elder the uncle (d. 1296), and the younger (d. 1328), from whom some sermons and a good name remain.

England was not fertile of strong preachers during any part of this period. She was waiting for Wiclif and the Reformation. But of course there were preaching and preachers in England all this while, and two distinguished prelates who belonged to the Dominican order may be named as lights of the period. These were William of Macclesfield, and Walter of Winterbourne (d. 1305). The latter was in the evening of his life a learned canonist and cardinal, and of his earlier days Fuller[1] says, "in his youth he was a good poet and an orator." From this we may perhaps sadly infer that learning and law and office had dried up the springs of his fancy and had left him less effective in speech during his later years. At any rate such and such things have been known to happen to Englishmen—and to others. From this declining scholasticism let us turn to the rising power of mystic preaching.

[1] Quoted in *Dict. Nat. Biog.*, article on Walter of Winterbourne.

2. Rise and Power of Mystic Preaching

Mysticism [1] has appeared in many ages and nations, in philosophy and life, as well as in theology and religion and preaching. It has also more or less affected the preaching of every age; but as some of the most notable preachers of the period we have under notice were mystics, this is perhaps the best place to give to mysticism such brief consideration as our space permits, before discussing its leading representatives in the pulpit of the time.

When we ask what is mysticism? the very associations of the word suggest the extreme difficulty of definition. Like all terms used to describe mental phenomena and tendencies of thought, which have large general import and many shades of particular application, mysticism is hard to define. That is, it is difficult to frame a statement general enough to include all that is meant by the term and brief enough to be put into a sentence and easily remembered. But brief descriptive statements of the essential character of mysticism may be made sufficiently exact to give a good working knowledge of it in lack of accurate scientific definition. Thus Vaughan [2] says: " Philosophers and monks alike employ the word mysticism and its cognate terms as involving the idea not merely of initiation into something hidden,[3] but beyond this of an internal manifestation of the Divine to the intuition, or in the feeling, of the secluded soul." Clarke,[4] greatly influenced by Vaughan, puts the matter rather more simply thus: " The belief that man can come into union with the Infinite Being by means of a wholly passive self surrender to divine influence." And Preger [5] has it: " The characteristic of mysticism is

[1] For Mysticism I have derived most help from the following works: R. Vaughan's *Hours with the Mystics;* Ueberweg's *History of Philosophy;* James Freeman Clarke's *Events and Epochs in Religious History;* Preger's *Geschichte der Deutschen Mystik im Mittelalter.* The authorities on the history of preaching for the period also give much that is helpful.

[2] *Hours with the Mystics,* p. 21.

[3] The etymological meaning of the word.

[4] *Events and Epochs of Rel. Hist.,* p. 276.

[5] *Geschichte der Mystik,* Bd. I., S. 8. " Das Characteristiche der Mystik ist, dass sie ein unmittelbares Erleben und Schauen des Göttlichen anstrebt."

that it strives after an immediate experience and vision of the Divine." In mysticism three forms, more or less allied to each other, are to be distinguished. Vaughan calls them "theopathetic, theosophic, and theurgic;" and Clarke, "religious, philosophic, and thaumaturgic." More simply, these distinctions, which cannot be exact, indicate that the central position of mysticism has three ways of expressing itself: (1) an immediate intuition of truth—philosophic or speculative mysticism; (2) an immediate dealing of the soul with God—religious mysticism; (3) by virtue of these, the ability to perform miraculous or at least extraordinary works—wonder-working mysticism. The philosophic or speculative mystic sees truth not by logical processes but by direct vision, in some ecstasy of high and intense thinking; the religious mystic knows and realizes God not by investigation and reasoning, and not by external means of any sort, but by rapt contemplation, by complete surrender of self to divine influence; the wonder-working mystic claims, by virtue of this supernatural indwelling of truth or of God, the power to exert extraordinary influences upon the minds and even the bodies of others. The last phase has perhaps fewer representatives, and is more commonly regarded as extreme, fanatical, and vulgar; but in its less extreme and objectionable forms is allied sometimes to the philosophic but more naturally and commonly to the religious sort of mysticism. The philosophic and religious types easily pass into each other; what particular form mysticism takes simply depends on whether the mystic is himself rather a philosopher or a religionist. Thus Fichte and Emerson are philosophic mystics; Tauler and George Fox religious ones; while in Eckhart and Behmen the two strains are fused. Let us repeat then, that in religious mysticism the essential thing is the avowed consciousness of an immediate dealing of the soul with God; a surrender of self, a possession by God; a complete union with God, or fullness of God.

What has been said shows how perilous it is either to deny wholly or to accept without qualification the central position of mysticism. That it contains truth is just as clear as that it is not all or solely truth. To deny it wholly is to blind the soul to one of its highest privileges, to accept it solely is to fall into fatal error. For in some phase or degree mysticism may be connected with the holiest piety, or with the grossest sins; with the best and most fruitful religious activities, or with the idlest and most insane speculations; with enduring and beneficent labors and services in the kingdom of God, or with lasting injuries to the cause of true religion; with reverent acceptance of the Bible as authoritative revelation from God, or with a qualified acceptance of it admitting of correction by the inner light, or even at last to utter rejection of it as a divine message, and the substitution of the vagaries of an unbalanced mind.

The errors and exaggerations of the mystical tendency in the religious life may well make us wary of its one-sided and extreme phases, but the element of truth in it keeps it alive. Both those who hail its extremes as new truth and those who dread them as new error need the historic perspective. For in all centuries Christianity in general, and preaching in particular, have profited by the good and suffered by the evil of mysticism.

It may be a question whether mysticism has had its chief seat of power in the cloister, the school, or the pulpit; but it unquestionably powerfully influenced the last through the other two.

The mystical yearning both led to the cloister and was strengthened and encouraged there. The contemplative life, the study of Scripture, the prayers and other influences of convent life were favorable to its development. Hence we are not surprised to find that most of the mystic preaching was given in the monasteries, and that most of the mystical preachers were trained in them. From early times the monastic life had thus laid its moulding hand on the pulpit, and the powerful impulse given to monasticism by Bernard in the twelfth century and by Francis and Dominic in the thirteenth, and the high place held by all three of these men in the pulpit, had great effect in enlarging the influence of monastic mysticism upon the preaching of the thirteenth and fourteenth centuries. Nor must the influence of the other monastic orders be forgotten. Benedictines, Augustinians, Præmonstrants, and others had something to do with the extension of mysticism.

And here we must notice another important and helpful force in developing and spreading mystical views, that is, the nunneries, and the pious women both within and without these institutions. Mysticism has large affinities with the feminine nature, and it is not at all surprising to find that some of its most distinguished representatives and teachers in all its phases and during all its history have been women. It does not fall within the scope of this treatise to discuss this interesting phase of the subject at any length. But Preger [1] has shown that in the twelfth and thirteenth centuries along the Rhine and in the Netherlands—not to speak of other localities—in the cloisters and out of them numbers of mystical women lived and worked. Hildegard of Bingen, Elizabeth of Schönau; the Beguines, Mary of Oigny, Matilda of Magdeburg; the nun Gertrude, and others are mentioned as influential in one way and another in promoting the spread of mysticism. Ecstasies and prophecies, nervous faints, excess of feeling, profuse weeping and various other such phenomena, were frequent characteristics of the feminine religious life of the period. All this prepared the audiences to listen with sympathy and appreciation to the sermons of the mystic preachers. In fact, many of the sermons of this tendency, both Eckhart's and Tauler's, were actually preached in the nunneries, and we owe their preservation to the insight, sympathy, and skill of the pious women who reported and wrote them out.

In the schools as well as the cloisters mysticism had a place of power from which it greatly and permanently influenced the pulpit. Many of these schools were cloister schools, and the most distinguished teachers were members of some one of the orders. It is scarcely a distinction therefore to separate the school from the cloister, except that it gives us occasion to note the specifically scholastic and speculative bent which was given to the mystic trend of thought in the hands of professors. Among these the names of Hugo and Richard come up for mention again, as these distinguished lecturers ex-

[1] *Op. cit.,* SS. 13-141.

pounded their systems at the abbey of St. Victor at Paris in the twelfth century. In the thirteenth the renowned teacher, Albert the Great, at Cologne and Paris, paid much attention to the mystic element in religious thought, and through his widespread influence many preachers of the Dominican order became devoted to this way of thinking. The greatest of the scholastics, Thomas Aquinas, also incidentally gave some teaching in this direction. In life, and probably in preaching, the mystic element was more decided than in his rigorously logical theological system; but even there it was not wholly wanting, though not emphasized or largely developed.

After the mystics of the twelfth century we do not find any distinctly great preacher of this tendency until we come to Bonaventura in the thirteenth; but all along there were those whose preaching kept up the continuity of mystic thought. There was lull but no cessation of mystic preaching between Richard of St. Victor and Bonaventura. With the latter, however, there is a revival of mysticism under the scholastic guidance, and after him the work of Master Eckhart gave the start to the developments which followed and reached their height in those who were taught or influenced by that powerful teacher.

Nor was it only in the preachers of the church and its orders that mysticism was found. There were various heretical sects among whom the teachings flourished, and these were represented by preachers as well as writers whose influence among the people was considerable.[1] Of these, Amalric of Bena, early in the thirteenth century was largely influenced by Joachim of Floris, and had in France a rather large following. Later, a certain David of Dinant is mentioned as a teacher of influence, and a sort of society known as "Brothers of the Free Spirit" became very notable in the late thirteenth and early fourteenth centuries. Thus in many ways and from many sources, mystic teaching impresses itself upon the preaching of the time, and becomes, though not to the exclusion of other tendencies, the characteristic feature of the pulpit of the period.

It is important at this point to consider how widely

[1] See Preger, Buch II., Kap. II., for full discussion.

extended this mystic preaching was, and what was in a general way its character.[1]

In regard to extent it should be observed that the range of the really powerful mystic preaching was comparatively limited. The locality of it was chiefly along the Rhine, on both sides, and in the Netherlands. Of course it was not confined to this region, but here it was more in evidence and reached its greatest influence. As to following, too, it is from the nature of the case clear that mystic preaching can never be so widely and influentially popular as that which is less distinctively marked by the peculiar tenets of mysticism. Partly the lofty religious life which it requires in its better forms, partly the fanatical or at least overwrought phases of it in its less balanced forms, and partly the difficulty of comprehending it in all its forms, make mysticism always the profession of the few, rather than of the many. In comparison then with the mighty scholastic and popular preachers of the age the mystics had smaller audiences, more select, most usually those already Christian, and a far less extensive range of influence.

The particular teachings of the different mystic preachers can be better exhibited in discussing the men themselves, but before that a remark on the general character of mystic preaching is requisite. Its one distinctive common trait was the doctrine of a union of the soul with God. This was the goal of all mystic preaching. The steps by which this fusion of the divine and human were to be attained might be differently described and named, the very nature of the things in question might be differently stated, and the results of the union differently set forth, but this one great idea of immediate intercourse of the Christian soul with God underlies all the mystic preaching. It was this noble aim which gave and still gives to mystic teaching its power; and if this general statement were all, it might well be left unchallenged. But when we come to details we see how in enforcing its greatest thought the mystic preaching became im-

[1] Besides the books on Mysticism in general, those of Linsenmayer, Cruel, and Albert discuss its particular relation to preaching—Linsenmayer of course from the Catholic point of view. The Protestant writers, including Preger, find in this mystic preaching an important preparation for the Reformation.

perilled and fell into grievous errors. For example, the doctrine of the relation between God and man in the hands of Eckhart and his followers came so near to pantheism that the students of his system, then and still, have been divided in opinion as to whether it was or was not really pantheistic teaching. Again, the emphasis upon personal experience and individual dealing directly with God led (and still leads) to undervaluing of the Bible as the one authoritative revelation of the mind and will of God in regard to salvation; and naturally this led to erroneous treatment of many of the most important doctrines of the Scripture, especially those relating to sin and redemption. Again, a peril of the mystic preaching which was not always successfully avoided lay in such insistence upon passivity, as the condition of the mystic union with God as to end in sloth. Not in Bernard, nor in Tauler, nor in those like them, do we find this mistake; but in others there are traces of laying stress upon the contemplative life to the injury of the active.

The differences which prevailed among the mystics themselves in regard to the details of their general system have already been foreshadowed and lead to a clear though not sharply defined classification. Those who adhered to the church theology and the scholastic method, like the Victorines, Albert and Bonaventura, are properly called scholastic mystics. Those who followed the powerful lead of Eckhart in using the church doctrines and the Bible itself only as starting points for profound speculations, growing chiefly out of personal experience, are rightly named speculative mystics. And those who, like Bernard, Francis, and Tauler, combined, both in theory and life, lofty mystical aspirations with active earnest work for the souls of men, are suitably described as practical mystics. But to get a more definite and concrete view of the mystic preaching of the period we must consider it as set forth in the lives and works of its representative men.

3. Leading Preachers of the Mystic School

Following the grouping just indicated we notice first those who were more distinctly influenced by scholastic training and modes of thought.

We have seen that in Hugh and Richard of St. Victor, and later in Albert the Great and Thomas Aquinas, there was a mingling of mysticism and scholasticism, with this difference: that in the first two the mystic element predominated over the scholastic, while in the other two, the scholastic was supreme, the mystic incidental. But there was one great preacher of the age of whom it has been said that he was "the greatest scholastic among the mystics and the greatest mystic among the scholastics." This was none other than John Fidanza, better known by his acquired and canonized name of Bonaventura (1221-1274).[1] The future "doctor seraphicus," scholastic, mystic, cardinal and saint, was born at Bagnorea in Tuscany in the year 1221. His parents were respectable people, though not distinguished. The boy received his father's name of John, but his famous nickname, as he himself relates, came to him in the following fashion: When he was three years old he fell ill, and his pious mother sought in his behalf the prayers of the saintly Francis of Assisi, who was at that time in the neighborhood. After the child's recovery he was shown by the grateful woman to the holy man, who exclaimed: "*O buona ventura,*" which may be familiarly rendered, "O good luck." Henceforth, as in other instances, the nickname has usurped the place of the baptismal one, and history knows the child of St. Francis' answered prayers as Bonaventura.

The boy grew up pure and pious, and, as was natural, early entered the Franciscan order. He loved learning as well as religion, and made excellent progress in his studies. He was sent to Paris and studied under the renowned English scholastic, the "irrefragable doctor," Alexander Hales, who is said to have remarked concerning his pupil, "In Brother Bonaventura Adam seems not to have sinned." Here at the University of Paris he met the promising young Dominican, his fellow countryman, Thomas of Aquino, and the two, though of different orders, formed a lasting and beautiful friendship. Their lives were remarkably parallel. Both became distin-

[1] Besides the authorities already named, *Acta Sanctorum,* July, Vol. III., p. 770 ss; Guillon's *Bibliothêque des Pères de l'Église,* tom. 25; Cardinal Fanna's *Ratio Novæ Collectionis Op. S. Bonaventuræ*—a critical discussion, not an edition of his works.

guished scholars and theologians, they took the doctor's degree the same day, they died the same year, Aquinas in March, Bonaventura in July, 1274; Aquinas on the way to, and Bonaventura at, the Council of Lyons.

Bonaventura was at an early age made general of his order, and filled various church offices with success and distinction. It is said that he was once offered the archbishopric of York, but declined. He was honored as a friend by the pious king Louis IX. of France, hailed by admiring pupils as the "seraphic doctor," and not long before his death was made a cardinal.

Numerous writings of Bonaventura remain, among them very many sketches of sermons. The critics, of course, reject some of these, but enough of them may be accepted as genuine[1] to give such a basis of judgment as we have in other cases. No preacher, as we have often to observe, can be fairly judged by the mere notes and outlines of his sermons, and yet they give some notion of his methods and ideas. From the other works of Bonaventura, however, we may gather his opinions on theology, and infer something as to his manner of preaching. The scholastic method and the mystic spirit are clearly seen. He developed the mystic teachings of Bernard and the Victorines. Like Richard, he held to six stages in the ascent of the soul to the perfection of union with God, but he tried to improve on Richard by further distinctions and different statements. In some of his writings he represents three stages in the Christian life: (1) Fulfilling the requirements of the law; (2) Following the spiritual teachings of the gospel; (3) Attaining to blessedness by the six steps of contemplation. It would take us too far afield to go minutely into these subtleties. His general position is summed up by Vaughan[2] thus: "Bonaventura resolves all science into union with God. The successive attainment of various kinds of knowledge is in his system an approximation, stage by stage, to God—a scaling of the heights of illumination, as we are more closely united with the divine Word, the repertory of ideas." He is thus rather Platonic than Aristotelian.[3] The Christian elements of

[1] See Fanna, *Ratio Novæ Collect.*, etc.
[2] *Hours with the Mystics,* p. 149 f.
[3] Cf. Ueberweg, *Hist. Philos.*, pp. 433, 453 f.; and Preger, Bd. I., S. 251 ff.

his system appear in many ways; for example, the ultimate goal, the sixth stage in contemplation of the divine, is the loving and reverential apprehension of the being of God as revealed in the blessed Trinity. In speaking of the corresponding powers by which man makes the steps necessary to reach the goal of union with God, he says,[1] "But these powers are corrupted by sin; they must be restored by grace, purified by righteousness, exercised by knowledge and perfected by wisdom. Christ both is and works this fourfold help, which may be also described as twofold: grace and truth."

Leaving Bonaventura's mysticism to the theologian and philosopher we come to his preaching. The contemporary accounts of his eloquence are numerous and decisive. He is praised both as *sermocinator ad clerum et prædicator ad populum*—sermonizer to the clergy and preacher to the people. He was fluent, ardent, persuasive. The outlines of his sermons are bare, and they illustrate the scholastic and allegorical methods of his time. One example will be enough to show his manner. The text is Isa. 52:13, "Behold my servant shall deal prudently (Lat. *intelliget,* shall understand); he shall be exalted and extolled, and be very high." He takes the text as a prophecy and commendation, not of Christ, but arbitrarily of John the Evangelist. The outline is as follows: John is here commended: 1. For the holiness of an excellent life, in the words, "My servant." 2. For the clearness of his knowledge—"Shall understand." 3. For the excellency of his doctrine—"Shall be exalted and extolled, and be very high." Now on the basis of his threefold intelligence he was raised to a threefold dignity: 1. Apostolic rank, because he knew useful things; 2. Prophecy, because he knew hidden things; 3. Gospel teaching (evangelist), because he knew high things. Hence he has left us three sets of works: 1. The Epistles, as a preacher; 2. The Apocalypse, as a prophet; 3. The Gospel, as a scribe.

So much for the scholastic; the mystic is revealed in the following quotation[2] from a sermon on the Passion of our Lord: "O death, O passion of my Saviour,

[1] Preger, *op. cit.,* S. 254.
[2] Guillon, *Bibl. des Pères,* tom. 25, p. 83.

source of all good things. Here it is death that gives life, it is wounds that heal; the blood bathes and purifies; the opening of the side unites hearts. O wonderful death which makes all my joy, all my happiness, which crowns all my wishes! No; I will no longer be separated from my Jesus; there is no felicity but in being with him. I will prepare myself three retreats; one in the wounds of his hands, another in that of his feet, the third (Ah! this will be the one where I shall fix my abode) will be in his side. There I will speak to his heart; there I shall obtain the accomplishment of all my desires. So, more and more, will I imitate his most holy mother, whose soul was torn by the sword of the passion of her Son. O wounds of Jesus my Saviour! O dwelling full of charms! With what delights, think you, should be flooded the soul which by these sacred doors enters into the heart of Jesus Christ? which attaches, closely unites itself, unchangeably, to that divine heart? Nay; I cannot express it! Make you trial of it! That is the only means of knowing it!"

The older school of churchly scholastic mysticism, adhering stanchly to the Catholic traditional orthodoxy, and developing its views in the dialectic method of the schools, reached its height and its end in Bonaventura. Toward the end of the thirteenth century we find a powerful mind, a thinker of a new order, who is less careful of dialectic distinction and logical form and minute analysis, and is less concerned to use these in order to harmonize his views either with the established dogmas of the church or with the real meaning of the Scriptures. The experience of the individual soul in its dealing with God comes to the fore as a source and criterion of truth and knowledge, and henceforth we have to deal with a new tendency in the philosophy and theology of Europe. This tendency is represented in those whom we have called speculative mystics.

The leader of these was the celebrated Master Eckhart (c. 1260-c. 1327).[1] What is known and inferred as to his life can be told in few words. There is some uncertainty as to the exact dates of his birth and death,

[1] For studies of Eckhart see Vaughan, Preger and the historians of German preaching before cited.

but it is inferred that he was born about 1260. He was a native of Thuringia in the neighborhood of Strasburg. He early joined the Dominicans and went to the famous school at Cologne for his education. Preger thinks it unlikely that Albert the Great was still living, but the spirit and methods of that great teacher were still dominant there, for if he had died before Eckhart came it was shortly before.

Eckhart also studied and lectured for awhile at Paris, where he got his degree of Master about 1302, it seems by some special influence of Boniface VIII. In 1304 he was made provincial of his order for Saxony, and three years later vicar-general for Bohemia, and was clothed with authority to institute needed reforms in the convents of that region. He lectured and preached with great power in different parts of Germany, and made a second stay in Paris. Later he was prior at Frankfort on the Main, and provincial at Cologne, where he taught in the famous Dominican school and had many pupils.

He was much loved and admired by his pupils, and his moral influence over them was great and salutary. He was very devout, and pure beyond suspicion or blame. He says once that he "baptized himself seven times a day in the blood of Christ," and gives the prayer he was accustomed to repeat. It is full of humility, confession of sin and pleading for cleansing. He mentions as one of the most precious gifts of grace to him that he had been freed from carnal desires. The enemies who resented his discipline, and later attacked his teachings, could bring no charge against the uprightness and purity of his conduct. But many of his teachings were very strange, hard to understand, and often utterly out of harmony with received opinions. Moreover there were mystic teachers of heresy in the neighborhood, and Eckhart seemed to be in sympathy with them both personally and in his teaching. So it came about that charges of heresy were made against him at the instance of his bishop. Nicholas of Strasburg, a brother Dominican and himself a mystic, was appointed by the pope to look into the matter. As was natural, Eckhart was acquitted. But the bishop was not satisfied and renewed the charge, so that a new process was instituted in 1327. Eckhart made an explanation, saying that he had not meant to teach contrary to the doctrines of the church, that he was misunderstood on some points and misrepresented on others, and was open to conviction if he could be proved wrong. The bishop had therefore to refer the case to the pope, and while it was pending before the papal curia Eckhart died, probably in 1327 or 1328.

After his death, in the year 1329, a papal bull was published condemning seventeen propositions from Eckhart's writings and laying eleven more under suspicion of heresy. Eckhart's explanatory and conditional statement was interpreted to be an unconditional retraction of these specified teachings. So the Catholic writers declared that he recanted his errors and died in full orthodoxy; but Preger and other Protestant writers hold that he never did recant the essential teachings of his books, but only professed a willingness to be convinced of his error.

The essence of Eckhart's system was the "mystical union" with God. This he represented in such terms as practically amount to an identification of the soul with God. Thus he says:[1] "He who standeth at all times in a present Now, in him doth God the Father bring forth his Son without ceasing." "In every man who hath utterly abandoned self God must communicate himself according to all his power, so completely that he retains nothing in his life, in his essence, in his nature, in his Godhead." In other words, God is humanized in the mystic, and so the mystic becomes divine. Further: "God and I are one in knowing. God's essence is his knowing, and God's knowing makes me to know him. Therefore is his knowing my knowing. The eye whereby I see God is the same eye whereby he seeth me. My eye and the eye of God are one eye, one vision, one knowledge, and one love." These daring and obscure utterances can be matched with many similar ones. It is true that on the other hand many noble sayings and true thoughts are to be found, for example: "Good works do not make holiness; it is holiness that makes good works." Yet it does not seem possible to acquit him of pantheistic speculations, of extreme and misleading

[1] Quotations are from Vaughan.

statements, and of exalting too much the individual experience as authority. Along with this, his use of Scripture is even more free and sophistical than that of the scholastics. It must mean what he says. And his conception of the fundamental doctrines of grace is essentially defective. Sin, repentance, faith unto salvation, find little place in his system. He preached mostly to monks and nuns urging those who are already converted to attain to fullness of union with God.

One of the most notable pupils of Eckhart was Henry Suso, or Seuse (1295-1366). He was born near Constance toward the end of the thirteenth century. His father was a knight and worldly, his mother a pious woman of the sentimental type. The union was incongruous and unhappy; and the boy was like his mother and much influenced both by her nature and training. He was placed quite young in the Dominican cloister at Constance, after his father had given up all hopes of making a knight of him. Here for years he went through a series of mental sufferings and self-imposed bodily tortures, seeking peace. Meantime his studies went on, some of Eckhart's writings came into his hands, and he was after a while sent to Cologne, where he enjoyed immediate instruction from the celebrated Master. He became thoroughly imbued with Eckhart's teachings, and secretly carried on much of the asceticism that he had practised in his cloister. It was not until his fortieth year that he abandoned this extreme rigidity of asceticism, and then because in an illness he came to see that it was endangering his life. Yet he did not regret having thus broken himself in.

He filled various positions in his order at different places, suffered some persecution for supposed heretical views, and was accused of other things—unjustly—and made to suffer much. The trouble between pope and emperor, and the laying of the land under interdict was a sore trial to the cause of religion. Suso was of those who sympathized with the pope, and owing to the emperor's threats the monastery at Constance, where he was teaching, was virtually broken up, the monks driven away. During his exile he was frequently travelling and preaching in those parts of Germany where he could safely do so. In 1346 some relaxation in the persecution made it possible to reopen the convent at Constance, and Suso returned, only after a while to be hurt in soul and reputation by a false accusation of improper relations with an evil woman. But he lived down the slander, and was, in 1348, sent by his superiors to Ulm, where he spent the rest of his life.

In his teachings he made no advance on Eckhart as to substance of thought. His views and methods were substantially the same as his master's. But he was a more popular preacher than Eckhart. While his soft and sentimental nature made him the idol of the nunneries and of the devout women in all ranks, he was yet an acceptable and moving preacher before the people. Not many of his sermons have come down to us, but they show the same doctrine as his more extended writings and exhibit traces which sustain his traditional reputation for eloquence.

Among the numerous followers of Eckhart's teaching we find the name of a certain John of Sterngassen. This latter designation was taken from a street or quarter of Strasburg, from which it would appear that he was born or lived in that city. He was a preacher of considerable power and was lector, or teacher, in Strasburg about 1318 to 1323. He was a thoroughgoing disciple of Eckhart, and went even further than he [1] in using Scripture merely as a starting point for mystical and experimental speculations. One of his sayings, quoted from Preger,[2] may give a taste of his mystical quality: "What in God is a working [or doing], that must be in me a feeling [i.e., a passive feeling, *Leiden*]; what in God is a speaking, that must be in me a hearing; what in God is a picturing [*Bilden*], that must be in me a beholding. All that God can do, that can the soul feel."

Bernard, Francis, Bonaventura even, have shown us how the mystical type of thought and life could be held along with active and fruitful effort for the salvation of men; and how popular preaching might be when colored by mystic thought. This is no unusual phenomenon in the history of mystic views, and finds excellent illustration

[1] Albert, *op. cit.*, sec. 21. [2] *Op. cit.*, S. 245.

in the lives and works of the preachers we have now to consider, the practical mystics.

We have already met with David of Augsburg as the teacher, friend, and companion of Berthold of Regensburg.[1] But he was also something on his own account. He was a preacher to the people; and as Albert had through his pupils given mysticism a great impulse in Germany, so David by his writings, preaching, and influence did very much to make the German language the instrument of communicating religious instruction. His treatises are regarded as among the best specimens of early German prose. Little is known of his life, but the fact of his being called after Augsburg indicates that that city was his birthplace, or for a time his residence. He lived a longer time at Regensburg in the Franciscan monastery, where he was teacher of the novices, and as such instructed Berthold. After this he was again in Augsburg, where he ended his days. A contemporary writer[2] says, "In addressing sermons to the people he was of an excellent genius." But in his gentler and easier nature he lacked the fire and power of his more famous pupil Berthold. No specimens of his German sermons have yet come to light, but his Latin sketches and German writings indicate in his mystic teachings the influence of Augustine, Bernard, Hugo and Richard of St. Victor. It is not unlikely that he was also influenced by the prevalent mysticism among the devout women of his region, for he explains the nervous and overwrought feelings which were common, as indications that a sense of the presence of God may be too much for the bodily nature to stand. He clearly teaches the "mystic union" with God as the goal of the soul's endeavor. Preger gives the following verse of a poem, not David's but current in his time, as expressive of the mystic feeling toward God:

Flieh ich von dir,	Flee I from thee,
Du kommst zu mir.	Comest thou to me.
Verlass ich mich,	Losing myself,
So find ich dich,	I find thyself,
O überwesentliches Gut!	O superessential Good!

Contemporary with Eckhart was a certain Nicholas

[1] See *ante*, p. 256 f.; and Preger, *op. cit.*, S. 268 ff.
[2] Quoted by Preger, *l. c.*

of Strasburg. He it was who, being charged by the pope with the first trial of Eckhart, acquitted him. He is also called "Brother Nicholas who was lector at Cologne," but when and how long does not appear. Involved with Eckhart, he, too, was under process for heresy at Eckhart's second trial, but must have been leniently dealt with, probably for reasons of policy. Thirteen of his sermons and sketches have been printed, and there are more in manuscript. He is mystical, but by no means so scholastic as Bonaventura nor so deep and speculative as Eckhart. His aim is practical, his audiences popular, his style lively and picturesque. Of course he handles the Bible in the current arbitrary fashion; but, like other popular and practical preachers, he teaches the worthlessness of works as a means of salvation, preaches repentance, and holds up Christ as the only Saviour. The following story, quoted in several of the books from one of his sermons, illustrates not only his individual method, but a style of popular presentation of divine things which was current in his time and later. After having dwelt earnestly on the value of the sufferings of Christ on our behalf, he suddenly takes this turn: "Now we must learn to climb up on the cross of our Lord Jesus Christ. And who are the right sort of tree climbers? It is they who place their love and desires nowhere else, and seek their joy and their comfort nowhere else than in the cross of our Lord Jesus Christ and in his precious worthy passion. I will give you an illustration. Once a cat and a fox were taking a walk together in a field. The fox said, 'Mrs. Cat, what can you do?' The cat said, 'I can climb trees.' 'Oho!' said the fox, 'what a fine art is that.' Then said the cat, 'Mr. Fox, what can you do?' 'To be sure,' said he, 'I can do great things, and have a whole sack full of arts; if once I untie it nobody can equal me.' While they were thus talking there came greyhounds that were about to catch the fox. The cat ran up a tree, and said, 'Now, Mr. Fox, untie your sack! It's time!' 'Ah, Mrs. Cat,' said the fox, 'I lightly esteemed your art, but now it were dearer to me than all the wisdom that ever I learned.'"

The application is made to the worldly wise folks who know all manner of arts and schemes which belong to this world, yet when death comes know not where to run for refuge, but the "good people" run to the tree of Christ's cross and passion.

But the greatest preacher among the mystics of this age was the Strasburg Dominican, John Tauler (c. 1290-1361).[1] In order, however, better to appreciate him and his preaching we must take some knowledge of his times. In 1314 there was a double election of emperor, and the allegiance of the Germans was divided between Frederick of Austria and Louis of Bavaria. The papacy became involved in the quarrel because of the appointments to church offices within the German lands. In the course of the quarrel Louis went so far as to set up a rival pope in his own interest, and John XXII. retorted by declaring the subjects of Louis free of their allegiance, and by laying the imperial lands under the terrible interdict—the suspension of all religious functions. The sympathies of the German people were divided, and the religious orders were also of divergent sentiments. The Dominicans outside of Germany were strongly for the pope, and a general chapter of the order had enjoined the members to respect the interdict. Still there were some who obeyed the emperor rather than the pope, and there were others who felt obliged by the emperor's threats to leave their homes and find refuge in places where his authority did not reach, or where the interdict was not so strictly enforced.

In addition to these political and religious disorders there were great distresses and disasters—earthquakes, floods, destruction of crops by grasshoppers, and worst of all, the plague, which appeared in 1348 and carried off thousands of the population. Along with all this there was frightful moral corruption. Hardened and encouraged by the dreadful disorders, criminals of every sort abounded and vices were unrestrained. Amid these evils the strange fanatical sect of the Flagellants arose. Companies of people made pilgrimages through the country praying and lashing themselves on the bare back till the blood ran down. As among the people so among

[1] Very much the same authorities for Tauler as for Eckhart and the other mystics. There are numerous German and several English and American editions of Tauler's sermons. Cf. Broadus, *H. P.*, p. 110 ff., Ker's *Hist. of Preaching*, p. 125 f., Pattison's *Hist. of Christian Preaching*, p. 112 f.

the clergy there were, on the one hand, the corrupt and hardened, who seemed to be plunged only the deeper into evil by the terrors of the time; and there were also the pious and thoughtful, who found in these things only a louder call to mysticism, the devout and contemplative life, separation from the world, hiding in God.

It was in this time that the saintly and faithful John Tauler lived and worked. He was born of respectable parents at Strasburg, somewhere between 1290 and 1300. Piously inclined from youth, John early entered the Dominican order and pursued at Strasburg and Cologne the regular studies required for advancement. At his home city he no doubt heard both Eckhart and John of Sterngassen preach, and at Cologne he was most probably a pupil of the great master of mysticism. Here he took the regular three years' course of theological study and added an extra one as candidate for the grade of *lector,* or teacher. It was probably in his twenty-fifth year that he was ordained and began to preach and perform other priestly functions at Strasburg. The city of Strasburg took the emperor's side in the controversy with the popes,[1] and lay under interdict from May, 1329, to about 1353, though there were relaxations toward the last of the time; and, in fact, all along the absolute cessation of all religious functions could not be enforced, because many priests disobeyed. In 1328 more rigid commands came to enforce the interdict, and on the other hand the emperor declared that the priests should celebrate the mass or quit the country. Tauler was among those who felt in duty bound to obey the pope and the superiors of his order, though it is not improbable that his sympathies lay the other way. The city of Basel also sympathized with Louis the Bavarian, but did not go so far as Strasburg in forcing the clergy to obey the emperor and carry on the services. Hence many found a refuge at Basel, where teaching in the convents and possibly some other duties were allowed. At any rate we find Tauler at Basel for a part of this time, lecturing and preaching in the Dominican school. Here he met friends of his order—Henry of Nordlingen, Suso, and others—who were mystics like himself, and also came

[1] Though John XXII. died in 1324 the fight was continued by his successors.

in contact with the "Friends of God," a body, hardly an order, of mystics. Among others there was a pious woman, Margaret Ebner, whose influence and sympathy were promotive of the mystical trend in Tauler's life. It was during this time that he established his reputation as a preacher. The sermons of this period are rather of the scholastic sort, with much Latin, and directed chiefly to monks and nuns. But they have earnestness and warmth, and attacked the faults of the monks and clergy in such downright fashion as already to awaken hostility.

Probably in 1348 Tauler returned to Strasburg, whether as teacher in the Dominican school, or convent preacher, or as "general preacher" in the order, is not certain. But there was evidently some relaxation in enforcing the interdict, and at Strasburg the last and most fruitful period of his work was accomplished. His preaching attracted large attendance and was doing much good in the stricken city.

Now comes the curious story of his "conversion"—or "second blessing," as it would now be called. The story has been attacked by Catholic scholars on various grounds, and is now generally discredited by them;[1] but Preger and other Protestants hold that this is interested criticism, and that the story is substantially true. It is to this effect: A certain pious layman from the "Oberland," probably near Basel, who was one of the "Friends of God," and a mystic, came to Strasburg to hear Tauler, being attracted by his great fame as a preacher. After hearing him several times he sought an interview with the preacher, and told him that he was, though preaching to others, not yet himself fully enlightened. He persuaded Tauler that he needed a real experience of things divine, a true losing of himself in God, and the like. Tauler was so unsettled by this that under the advice and help of this "Friend" he gave up preaching, sought retirement, and by fastings, penitence, and prayers tried to find this "higher life." His course was much censured by his friends as fanatical, and derided by his opponents as folly; but he continued it for about two years, when he reached the rest he sought, and found a new or at least a more vivid spiritual life. He now offered to preach

[1] Linsenmayer after Denifle; art. in Wetzer und Welte, etc.

again and was permitted to do so in the cloister chapel. A great crowd assembled. But the long trial had worn his strength and weakened his nerves, so that in standing before the people he broke into weeping, and could not preach. After some days a second opportunity came, and this time his word was with such power that men and women groaned, wept, and fainted away in intense concern and fervor. From now on a new Tauler preached. Sometimes at Cologne—where he was sent by the authorities of his order—but chiefly at Strasburg, in these fearful times of corruption, disorder, disaster, and gloom, the powerful, pleading voice of this faithful witness was heard. He spared nobody's sins, he felt for everybody's distresses, a faithful prophet, a sympathizing priest. He pointed one and all to the Saviour, whom he himself found the only refuge from his own sins and from the awful evils of the times. In such labors and preaching Tauler's last years were spent. When his mortal sickness came he received tender care at the hands of his own sister, who was prioress of a convent at Strasburg, and in a house in the garden of her establishment he entered into rest, June 16, 1361.

A considerable number of sermons attributed to Tauler have been printed in various editions. Some are undoubtedly spurious, and all are reported by other hands than his, largely as in Eckhart's case by the nuns of the convents where he preached. But enough can be counted really his own to enable us to find in these sermons strong support of the unanimous and cordial traditional testimony as to the power and character of Tauler's pulpit work. The sermons are thoroughly pervaded by the mystic ideas and spirit. They are chiefly devoted to awakening the hearers to a truer and purer Christian life, a real union of the soul with God. Incidentally they powerfully attack sin and call to repentance and faith, but their main purpose is to promote the true life in God. In use of Scripture they are allegorical and free, as was only too common, but they are more Scriptural than Eckhart's, and far more practical. They depreciate dependence upon works, and insist upon faith in Christ as the only way of salvation. In arrangement they are not at all careful of the scholastic forms, and are more like the loosely constructed homilies of former times. In style they are lively and popular, full of illustration and imagery, fresh, piquant, sometimes too coarse for the taste of our times, but impressive and acceptable in that age.

In tone and spirit Tauler was evangelical, sincere, lofty, and pure, appealing out of his own experience of grace for a holier life and a more real union with God on the part of his hearers. All the books quote Luther's words in a letter to Spalatin, in which he warmly praises the sermons of Tauler and declares that in no German nor Latin books on theology had he found so great help as in these. Altogether, making allowance for mystical onesidedness, Roman Catholic errors, and traditional misuse of Scripture, and finding him less deeply immersed in any and all of these than most of his predecessors and contemporaries, we must consider Tauler one of the most evangelical, devout, effective preachers of the age; and one of the most worthy to be remembered with affection and respect by all ages.

4. Retrospect and Lessons of the Period

With Tauler we may fitly close our study of this central mediæval period. After him the mystical type of preaching is still found, as we shall see, but the same year in which he died, 1361, a new voice is heard in far away England, and the newly ordained young priest, John Wiclif, sounds the first note of a revolt from papacy which is to shake the world and also make a new era in the history of preaching.

As we look back over this period and endeavor to gather up some of its lessons for our own days we shall find them abundant and instructive. The three great lines of thought and life which we have traced and studied are in some form essential and perpetual. Thinking, acting, feeling; reasoning, doing, brooding; arguing, persuading, meditating; are necessary elements of the work of preaching in all times, and for the age we have been studying we have learned to call them respectively scholastic, popular, and mystic preaching. Scholasticism was the effort to reach ultimate truth by reasoning from divinely revealed doctrines and from ecclesiastically authorized dogmas thence derived. Its data were insufficient, its method dry and monotonous, its processes subtle and often sophistical, and its results unsatisfactory; but its grand aim was to bring, by the highest and most intense effort of the spiritually enlightened reasoning powers, all truth into systematic relation and then declare the beautiful harmony to the world. The failure of scholasticism and the fault of the preaching which it formed, show us the futility of supposing that all truth can be derived from a segment of it, and that life of any sort can be identified with a mode of thought. No philosophy is as large as truth, and no process of thinking is the whole of man's spiritual life.

The great popular preachers of the period likewise bring us a lesson. And it is, though partly both, rather encouragement than warning. The misuse of Scripture, the over use of legendary material, and the grotesque and often coarse methods employed, are the chief faults of this preaching, and they are serious ones. But its power to attract crowds of hearers, and to bring home to them, with an effectiveness rarely equalled and never surpassed, the things which the preacher himself believed, may well excite our admiration and encourage our efforts.

The mystics also teach us that avoiding the extremes of supposing ourselves one with God, and therefore either the infallible media of his mind and will, or the sinless temples of his indwelling, there is yet a higher height of communion with God than we perchance have reached, and a fuller fulness of truth than we have yet experienced. Perhaps, too, by their very errors they may lead us yet to learn that in the true surrender of self to Christ there lie raptures not yet enjoyed, and preaching power not yet attained.

And so as we look back through the thickening haze of centuries upon the colossal figure of this mediæval preaching, we see, in softened outlines and mellowed smoothness, the blending of elements that must be constant in the effort of the human soul to see and to preach the truth as it is in Jesus. The all but perfect preacher shall be he who will combine in consummate synthesis intellectual power, popular eloquence, and personal holiness—he in whom logic controls zeal and tempers piety, zeal respects logic and loves piety, and piety glorifies logic and sanctifies zeal. This message the thirteenth century brings to the twentieth, and alike by its successes and failures bids the preachers of to-day lay it well to heart.

PERIOD IV

THE TRANSITIONAL, OR REFORMATORY, AGE

1361–1572

From the times of Tauler and Wiclif to the death of John Knox. the last of the great reformers

CHAPTER IX

THE RENAISSANCE, AND PREACHING IN THE FOURTEENTH AND FIFTEENTH CENTURIES

The new period on which we enter in this chapter extends from the death of Tauler, the greatest of the mediæval mystic preachers, to the death of John Knox, the last of the great reformers. The characteristics of preaching with which we have grown familiar in our study of the preceding period continued to display themselves, but with a falling off both of acceptability and of power. Already, as we have seen, the scholastic and popular types had begun to fall into decay, and marked evidences of weakness in the mystic type were also apparent. Yet the mystic preaching showed more life than the other two sorts, and gave, especially in the Netherlands and Germany, some help to the rising power of reformatory preaching. So that along with the decline which we have to observe in the general power of the pulpit we shall have to trace the rise of that wave of mighty reformatory preaching which began with Wiclif in the latter part of the fourteenth century, increased in volume with Savonarola near the close of the fifteenth, and reached its crest in Luther and his fellow reformers in the first half of the sixteenth. Meantime the mediæval traditions and methods were continued, but with some correction of more glaring faults, in the Catholic preaching of the age. This period (1361-1572) of about two hundred years may be appropriately styled in the history of preaching the transitional or reformatory age, for it marks the passage from the traditional mediæval method and spirit in the pulpit to those of modern times.

For our studies, however, it will be desirable to divide the period into two great epochs: that of the fourteenth and fifteenth centuries, when the forces of decay and reform struggled side by side in church and pulpit; and that of the sixteenth century, when in the Protestant Reformation preaching reached its third great historic culmination—the first two being in the fourth and in the thirteenth centuries respectively. In the earlier part of the general period, that is, during the fourteenth and fifteenth centuries, the great artistic and literary revival which is called the Renaissance lent its influence to the development of preaching; in the later epoch, the sixteenth century, the Reformation was the guiding force. In this chapter and the next we study the earlier epoch.

1. Europe in the Fourteenth and Fifteenth Centuries

It will be well to recall some of the more important events in the general history of Europe before discussing the social and religious conditions which had a more direct bearing upon the pulpit of the age.

We should remember that in England this was the age of the Edwards and Henrys, of the struggle with Scotland, of the Hundred Years' War with France, of the desolating Wars of the Roses and their close in the reign of Henry VII. In Scotland the romantic age of Wallace and Bruce was followed by the fatal accession of the house of Stuart, of which the fourth James was reigning when the fifteenth century ended. In France the struggle with England absorbed the attention and strength of the nation for a century, but under Charles VII. (1422-1461), the menace of subjection to a foreign power was at last removed, and France entered on a new career of power and influence in European affairs. The monarchy was strengthened by the arts and policy of the cruel and false but sagacious Louis XI., whose two next successors became possessed with the dream of establishing French power in Italy—a fatal inheritance to Francis I. in the next period. In Germany the emperor Charles IV. sought to alleviate the confusion and turmoil by providing for a more orderly and satisfactory election of the emperor. This he did by putting forth in 1356 the famous Golden Bull which vested the choice in seven electors, four temporal and three spiritual lords. This arrangement had great effect on all the subsequent history of Germany. The next important emperor after Charles was Sigismund, who began to reign 1410, and took hold of affairs with vigor and ability. Under him the famous council of Constance was called, which deposed the rival popes and thereby ended the long schism in the papacy, but alas, also condemned to death the noble reformer, John Huss, in 1414. The following emperors were not able to accomplish much in settling the distracted regions over which they held the nominal sovereignty. The interests and jealousies of the various principalities and cities were too great a difficulty for the statesmanship of that age to overcome. Germany must wait generations yet for her political unity. And the political chaos was enhanced by the religious dissensions which were about to bring in the Reformation. In the meantime we must not forget that in the latter part of the fourteenth century the Swiss threw off the imperial yoke and founded their sturdy little republic.

The affairs of Italy and the papacy during this period were sad enough. The political situation of Italy maintained its old confusion. Naples and Sicily constituted for a time an independent kingdom striven for by France and Spain, and eventually falling to the latter. Rome and the Papal States were in a fearful condition during the sojourn of the popes at Avignon (1305-1377). The two noble houses of Colonna (Ghibelline) and Orsini (Guelf) kept up a constant feud. In this time the visionary Rienzi tried to restore the ancient Roman republic (1347-1354), but his attempt failed. The turbulent city of Florence attained high renown in arts and letters, but was a prey to many mutations in government. Likewise the cities of Venice, Genoa, Milan, and other smaller principalities, shared in the political unrest and disunion. Not yet for Italy was there a gleam of national hope.

The papacy, too, was during all this time in a wretched state. It will be remembered that under French influence in 1305 the residence of the popes was transferred from Rome to Avignon in France, where it remained for seventy-two years—the so-called "Babylonian Captivity." Public opinion finally induced the pope to return to Rome in 1377. But at the very next election there was a split. The Italian cardinals were determined, though in the minority, to have an Italian pope, and elected Urban VI. The French cardinals fled to Avignon and elected Clement VII., who resumed residence there. And now for a generation the world is favored with the spectacle of a divided and corrupt papacy. France favored Avignon, and Italy Rome; Spain followed France, and England Italy; Germany was divided. Efforts to heal the schism were in vain until the Council of Constance finally deposed all—there were now three—of the claimants, and declared Martin V. the rightful pope in 1417. But the end of the schism brought no moral reform. The popes that followed were by no means reformers. Pius II. (Æneas Silvius Piccolomini) was a man of letters; Innocent VIII. was given over to vices, and in his time the papal court was a sty of corruption; Alexander VI. (Borgia) was the most infamous of them all, the Nero of the papacy; Julius II. was a statesman and a warrior, by mischance a pope, and he made the states of the church a political power which endured until modern times; Leo X. (John of Medici) was a patron of arts and letters, free and easy, fond of money and luxury, supposed to be a freethinker, and certainly a very unsuitable man for the great crisis that was now at hand.

Long had Spain, with the south under Moorish rule and the north divided against itself, been of little moment in European politics. But in the latter part of the fifteenth century things took a turn. A statesman and patriot appeared in the person of Cardinal Ximenes, and to his farsighted political talents the country owed much, though his religious bigotry inflicted lasting evils upon it. In 1479 the crowns of Castile and Arragon were united by the marriage of the two heirs, Ferdinand and Isabella; in 1492 the Moors were driven out of their stronghold at Granada; and in the same notable year Columbus, under

Spanish patronage, discovered the New World and gave to Spain a prestige and wealth that lasted for generations.

This brief glance at the political situation in Europe during the two centuries we are studying reminds us that it was a time of war, ambition, oppression, cruelty, intrigue, corruption, and yet of far reaching significance in national affairs. Nor was this all, for amid the political and military strife, there was progress in other things.

The arts of peace also flourished and grew. Trade and industry, the art of wealth-production, received important stimulus and development. There was waste and extravagance, but there was also thrift. The merchant and banker became pillars in the state. Commerce grew with the discovery and opening of new lands. As the invention of gunpowder revolutionized warfare and changed the face of the world, so the invention of printing revolutionized literature and set the pace for a new era in the world of letters. The great discoverers and navigators, Vasco de Gama, Columbus, Magellan, and others, filled the world with wonder, and widened the outlook of humanity upon itself and its home. In the fifteenth century new interest was developed in the study of the exact sciences and of the great forces of nature, and this great department of human thought received some of the impulse which has given it so much ascendency in modern times.

In the fine arts, particularly during the latter part of the time, there was great progress. Both instrumental and vocal, both secular and religious music were cultivated, and took on important developments. In architecture the noble movements of the former period went on with power. Churches, towers, castles, palaces, public buildings, bridges, and private residences, all show the great growth of the building art. In sculpture and painting the effort was made, as in music and architecture, to cultivate and impress religious ideas. The decoration of cathedrals and churches was one of the principal aims of later mediæval art; but when in the fifteenth century the revived interest in antiquity made itself felt, a new breath came to art also. The purely artistic—art for art's sake—the beautiful—the sensuous—now goes hand in hand with the religious aims of the preceding age. One need only take a superficial glance at the walls of an art gallery to see how the devoutly religious and the sensuously beautiful struggle side by side for expression in the art of that wonderful age. The earlier Italian work of Giotto and others prepared the way for the wonderful developments of the Renaissance.

We have seen how already in the preceding period the languages of modern Europe were settling into shape, and the national literatures were beginning. That tendency goes on in this period with accelerated power, receives a great impulse from the invention of printing, and in the fifteenth century gets a new life and a new direction by the revival of learning. The strong foundations of Italian literature had already been laid by Dante (d. 1321), Petrarch (d. 1374), and Boccaccio (d. 1375). In other lands also fair beginnings had been made before the new learning came with its breath of power and life. In Germany poetry passed from the knightly and gallant kind of the Minnesingers to the more burgherly and didactic sort of the Meistersingers. German thought found expression also in some prose writings, though these were of no great or world-wide influence. In France, while the poetic strain of the early troubadours was not wholly lost, prose writing found admirable representatives in the naïve and charming Froissart (d. after 1400) and in his followers, especially Philip de Comines (1445-1509), whose narrative of the events of his time is highly valued. In England poetry had its great representative in Chaucer (1328-1400), and prose in the marvellous traveller's tales of Sir John Mandeville (d. 1372).

All these earlier developments prepared the ground for the seed of the new learning which fell richly upon it about the middle of the fifteenth century. All departments of human thought—philosophy and religion as well as art and literature—were powerfully affected by this great movement, which is variously described as the Renaissance, the Revival of Learning, or of Letters, and Humanism—that is, the study of the Greek and Latin classics. Broadly speaking, it was a fresh, intense and naturally one-sided and extreme devotion to the art and literature of ancient Greece and Rome. Like every other literary cult it had its sound and its corrupt elements, its serious aims and its laughable follies, its good and its bad results.

The movement, as was natural, began in Italy, and spread through Europe. Petrarch and Boccaccio were both good Greek and Latin scholars, and their work and example encouraged a taste for classical studies among their admirers and followers.

In 1453 the fall of Constantinople sent many Greek scholars westward, and these found welcome and profit in many of the Italian cities. Notably did the wealthy, cultured, and powerful Medici at Florence encourage this tendency of literature and art; and under the rule of Lorenzo the Magnificent, that fair city became a flourishing center of the new culture. Able and distinguished scholars as well as famed artists added luster to that "city of flowers and flower of cities," as it was proudly called. Here the study of Plato was a reigning fad. Here lived Politian, Marsilius Ficinus and Pico di Mirandola, that wonder of knighthood and culture. And here in their time, as we shall see, preached the stern and eloquent prophet of the age, Savonarola. In other parts of Italy the new learning also had brilliant representatives, such as the Cardinal Bembo and Laurentius Valla, and last but by no means least the popes, Nicholas V., Pius II.—who, as Æneas Silvius Piccolomini, was known to fame as an eminent Humanist before he became pope,—and Leo X., the son of Lorenzo dei Medici, who was on the papal throne and devoted to literature and art when Luther began what the easy-going pontiff was pleased to regard as a "quarrel of monks," but history calls the Reformation.

From Italy the movement spread into other lands. Passing Germany for the present let us recall that in England the new love of learning came with power and laid enduring foundations. John Colet (d. 1519), dean of St. Paul's, and a preacher of force, was an admirable Greek scholar who had studied in Italy and taught with enthusiasm at Oxford. In France the scholarly work of Faber Stapulensis (as the Latinized form has the name) and others belong to this period.

In the Netherlands learning was in touch with piety.

The mystics had not lost influence there. The Brethren of the Common Life, a society founded by the pious and popular preacher Gerhard Groot, gave special attention to the education of the young. Among them in their earlier days studied the gentle Thomas à Kempis; and later, when their greatest leaders were gone and their teaching somewhat deteriorated, came first John Wessel and afterwards Erasmus to get a start in learning in the schools of the Brethren. The names of these two men bring us to the new learning in Germany and its relation to the Reformation.

John Wessel[1] (c. 1420-1489) was born of honest middle-class people at Groningen, and received his early education in the school of the Brethren of the Common Life at Zwoll. It is probable that he at this time came also under the influence of Thomas à Kempis, who lived in the cloister at Agnesberg nearby. The youth was both pious and in love with learning. He pursued his studies at Cologne, Lyons, Paris, Basel, and in Italy. He taught and lectured at many of these places, and was specially influential at Heidelberg in building up the university, on which he left a deep impress. Here after his time some of the leading lights of the Reformation—Melanchthon, Brentz, Butzer—studied, and no doubt felt the influence which Wessel had left behind him. In Italy he came in contact with many of the earlier scholars, and later he was associated with Reuchlin. Along with his learning his pious life and evangelical views prepared the minds of many of his pupils for the coming religious upheaval.

Vast and important as are the interests of nations and of culture during the fourteenth and fifteenth centuries, the affairs of religion are also passing through one of the most tremendous crises of history and approaching the great revolution of the sixteenth century. Catholic writers love to speak of the mediæval centuries—especially the thirteenth—as the "ages of faith." But even at its best the sway of the papacy was not, and could not be, complete. Much less so in the years of darkness and corruption. Even as far as Rome taught Christian truth and correctly represented the Christian spirit, it still

[1] Ullmann's *Reformers before the Reformation,* Vol. II. (Eng. transl.), gives an elaborate account of Wessel.

had to meet the perennial opposition of evil, enmity without and corruption within. Nor was the church ever without the questioning presence inside its fold of those who were more or less discontented with many of its doctrines and practices. And further, there were the so-called heretics who declared from the outside that the Scriptures taught a simpler and purer form of faith and practice than was found in the Roman system. And lastly, there were then, as always, extremists and visionaries of every sort. The awful moral degradation into which the papacy fell during this time made it utterly unfit to contend against the forces of decay on the one hand and of reform on the other, and it is the conflict of these two sets of forces that constitutes the religious history of this great period.

It is well known that the state of religion in this time was very low. Corruption in doctrine and life was general and extreme. The plain annals of the age relate facts that make us blush for our race; the satirists expose and denounce with unsparing hand the vices and follies that prevailed; and the preachers describe, lament and attack sin in many forms and places. The picture of the corrupt age is painted in glaring colors by those who could look directly upon the things of which they tell. Yet, bad as it was, the darkness was relieved by some rays of light. The pure and pious were found even in those evil days; quiet mystics sought God in retirement, and noble spirits, both among clergy and people, were found who lived in this evil world the life of faith and virtue. And not only in the way of satire, but also of heart-breaking sorrow and earnest rebuke, reformers thundered against sins from which they themselves firmly abstained. Nor were there utterly wanting, both among faithful men and excellent women, those who visited the fatherless and widows in their affliction and kept themselves unspotted from the world. In simple justice to the things that make for righteousness we should bear these facts in mind when we come to look more narrowly upon the evil features of the time. One of the worst of these—the corruption of the clergy—we come now to consider.

Adequately to describe the character of the Catholic clergy from the days of Wiclif to those of Luther would tax the picturing powers of a Dante or a Burke. Yet the facts themselves, stated as briefly and as simply as possible, carry their own sad and awful impression without aid from the genius of poet or orator. There was a mediæval proverb [1] to the effect that if a man would enjoy himself for a little while let him kill a chicken, if for a year let him marry a pretty wife, if for life let him become a priest. The easy and envied life of a priest, however, was only the lot of the more favored. Many of them were poor and had to contend with hardships. But there were among the prelates and those who had the better places luxury and easy living that almost baffle belief. Along with these there was a worldliness, a carelessness, a moral obliquity that are only too well attested. Even when we make all necessary deductions for the exaggerated lampoons of the satirists, the idle tales of the people, and the overstatements of aroused and indignant reformers, the real facts at bottom are hideous enough. Ignorance and incompetence were small faults in comparison with the moral unfitness which disgraced the clergy of the age. Avarice and luxury, greed and ambition, simony and extortion, went together. And, worse than these, open concubinage and general looseness of life are well-known sins of the secular clergy. The monks were no better, and even the nunneries did not escape censure. The papacy set the example. Petrarch said that the court of the popes at Avignon was a place where the hope of heaven and the fear of hell were regarded as old fables, where virtue was esteemed an affair for peasants, and sin was regarded as a sign of manly independence. Such moral degradation excited the scorn of the world, aroused the conscience of the upright, drew the tears of the godly, and called on all in tones of thunder for a "reformation of the church in head and members." But little was that call heeded by popes and councils. The answer to it was to come in another way.

In the upper classes of society—the princes and rulers and gentry—there was a moral laxity which shows itself only too plainly in the annals of the age and its other literature. The ties of morality and religion sat very lightly indeed upon the seared consciences of many who esteemed

[1] Quoted by Hase in his Church History somewhere.

themselves the nobility of earth. Cruelty, violence, oppression, fraud, lying and shameless vice stained the powerful and wealthy. The extravagance, luxury, dissoluteness of many fashionable women were only equalled by the corresponding and further-going vices of the men. As for religious belief, it was the exception, and the exception itself was marred by superstition and corruptions of doctrine. But not all of the nobility were bad, there were some illustrious exceptions.

Among the people generally, with such examples of evil as the clergy and upper classes set, the corruption of morals and the degradation of religion were fearful. We may spare ourselves the description of details. Murder, robbery, theft, fraud, unchastity, abounded. No wonder men thought the end of the world must soon come and sweep away a people so sunken in iniquity. In what passed for the Christian religion fearful abuses in practice and wretched corruptions of doctrine went hand in hand with superstitions that well might seem incredible, did not eye-witnesses attest them, and their remnants still prove them to have been sober facts. Magic, miracle, witchcraft and deviltry were all believed in and practised! Relics of the saints were worshipped, and, of course, the saints themselves. Ecstasies and visions, prophecies and miracles were accepted as real divine interpositions by even the pious, while absurd and wicked impostures were freely practised and apparently believed, not only by the innocent people, but even, to some extent, by the cheats themselves! The sale of indulgences, the laxity of discipline, the externalism that corroded the religious life, added to the moral disorders.

Truly it was a time for reform. The better spirits of the age felt this deeply, and there was a deep and growing conviction among all classes that things should and must be changed. In many a quiet home pious parents taught their children virtue and the fear of God; the art of printing spread Bibles and good books among the people; the Brethren of the Common Life in the Netherlands, and similar organizations elsewhere, cultivated and spread piety; in many of the cloisters there were devout mystics who called upon God in prayer; and here and there some brave reformer lifted up his voice and spared not to show this decayed house of Israel its sins.

2. The Preaching of the Times

The state of the Catholic pulpit during the fourteenth and fifteenth centuries may be comprehensively and accurately described as one of decay. The mighty forward movement of the twelfth and thirteenth centuries had reached its limit, and the inevitable reaction followed. Yet, of course, preaching did not suddenly change either its inner character or its external forms and methods, and among these were many elements of permanent value. Besides this conservation of many good features there was the rising protest of the reformatory element, which was more and more making itself felt, till it accomplished a revolution early in the sixteenth century. And so, both the conservative (in a measure) and the reformatory forces of preaching maintained, in the time we are now considering, a struggle against the forces of decline. But these, upon the whole, were in the ascendant.

Let us first pay attention to some of those acquired and preserved characteristics of preaching, which still meet us in the pulpit of the fourteenth and fifteenth centuries. Some of these were good, and some evil, and some mixed. It is not necessary to make this discrimination formally, as it will speak for itself in the discussion, but it should be borne in mind throughout.

The three modes of thought and method which prevailed in the preceding epoch are still found, but all with distinct loss of power—the scholastic, popular and mystic.

Toward the close of the thirteenth century the great masters of the scholastic type of preaching had passed away. Small imitators of the great men now abounded and made the method ridiculous. The wearisome divisions, the tedious refinements, the useless distinctions and vapid subtleties made up only a galvanized corpse, or a dancing skeleton as in some puppet show, instead of a live and vigorous body. The description of the degenerate scholastics of the age given by Erasmus in his *Praise of Folly* has been often cited. He tells how, in the first place, they would begin with an invocation borrowed from the poets; then they would have an exordium of some far-fetched and extravagant nature drawn from the river Nile, or Bel and the Dragon, or the signs of the zodiac, or squaring the circle, or from the elements of grammar, or forced etymologies and the forms of words, all artificial and pedantic to a degree. The third stage would be what in the old rhetoric is called the "narration," or "statement of the case," and here the text of Scripture would be given or slightly alluded to. The fourth part—the main body of the discourse—would introduce almost a new person, for here our scholastic becomes a mighty theologian, and propounds the most wonderful theological subtleties, touching on things found in neither heaven nor earth; and to tickle the ears of the hearers he would adduce the great doctors, the "subtle," the "irrefragable," the "seraphic," and the like; and then would come syllogisms and corollaries, and all sorts of scholastic fooleries. Finally, there would be the "fifth act," in which the preachers show the greatest art by bringing in as application and illustration some fable or legend—the more marvellous and absurd the better—which they proceed to interpret "allegorically, tropologically, and anagogically." Thus these declaimers would produce their "chimeras," more ungainly than the famous one satirized by Horace in the *Ars Poetica,* where the literary painter is said to portray a human head, with a horse's neck, the feathered body of a bird, and the tail of a fish. The pen of the erudite Dutchman was dipped in gall, but there are many witnesses to the essential truth of his caustic description. Truly scholastic preaching was in the sere and yellow leaf!

Yet, as a slight offset to the sad decay, Rothe approvingly mentions the very thing which Erasmus criticises in the application, or fifth part, of the scholastic sermon, namely, the use of fables, legends and other illustrations. This came as a relief from the abstruse and severely doctrinal and analytical character of the strict scholastic method, and was an approach to the freer and more effective popular style.

In the popular preaching of the age traces of all the other types—scholastic, mystic, and reformatory—are found in various degrees. Yet it is proper to retain this class of preachers for separate consideration because it is important to remember that in this age appeal to the multitude was still effectively made by preachers of popular gifts.

As is ever the case in this kind of preaching the preachers fall into three sorts: (1) Those who draw and impress the people by sincere and earnest effort to do good, by good example, by heart-to-heart appeal, by what is meant to be sound evangelical teaching; (2) Those who are chiefly indeed bent on good, but allow themselves large liberty in the use of devices to attract and catch the crowd, such as sensational oddities, humor, and even worse things; (3) Those who see in these devices ends rather than means, and seem to be more intent on making a sensation and raising a laugh than on anything else. Rothe[1] says: "These droll preachers are by no means particular in the choice of their entertaining material; and, along with some real sparks of wit, they heap together the worst platitudes, the most trivial jests, and not seldom downright vulgarities and indecencies. Gabriel Barletta, Olivier Maillard, and Michel Menot—all scholastic preachers—are the leaders of this sort of thing. And precisely in such cases as they do we see that even earnest preachers did not consider this drollery beneath their dignity."

Throughout the whole mediæval period, as we have seen, there are traces of the burlesque and sensational in preaching. But in the fifteenth century, and especially in Italy and France, this always questionable and often thoroughly evil tendency found frequent and exaggerated expression.[2] It is almost incredible to what a degree of irreverence, absurdity, and even indecency this sort of thing was carried. Some of the stories and gibes found in sermons of that age are almost as bad as anything related by Boccaccio. An Italian saying in commendation of any spicy and not too delicate joke was that "it was good enough for a sermon."

Even some of the better preachers, men with really serious aims and personally of excellent character, were not free from this fault, and in the hands of less able and seri-

[1] *Gesch. der Pred.*, S. 261.

[2] Marenco, *L'Oratoria Sacra Italiana*, cap. IV.; A. Méray, *Les Libres Prêcheurs devanciers de Luther et de Rabelais;* Rothe, *Gesch. der Pred.*, SS. 261 ff., 290 ff.

ous men it became a shame and disgrace which no amount of special pleading can justify, and the bad taste of the age can only partially palliate. One of the better sort of the Italian preachers [1]—himself by no means above reproach—writes: "Preachers ought to abstain from levity and not speak idle words and stories to provoke a laugh. Even if sometimes it is necessary to make the people attentive by some modest pleasantry, let it be done moderately and rarely." But of this sage counsellor of moderation to his brethren the following story is told: [2] He had a female admirer who objected to his monk's habit as unbecoming, and said she would like to see him clad in knightly array. He told her to come to hear him preach next day and she should see him and hear him address the people clothed in full panoply. He dressed himself in all the flashy garb of a knight and covered it all with his monastic gown. Thus he began to preach, and took occasion in his sermon to urge the princes and knights to go a-crusading against the Saracens and Turks. He lamented the unwillingness of the rulers to engage once more in this holy warfare, and declared if nobody else would lead he was ready to lay aside his Franciscan gown and put himself at the head of an expedition. Upon this he put off his gown, and stood, a flashing knight with drawn sword; and in this costume he proceeded with his discourse. Even if, in justice to the man, we discredit the alleged motive of vanity that was back of this performance, it was a useless bit of sensationalism and insincerity. Nobody was going on a crusade then, and he was sharp enough to know it.

In an Easter sermon Gabriel Barletta—of whom more will be said later—discoursed thus: [3] "After his resurrection the Lord was looking for a messenger to carry the glad news to his mother. A number offered themselves. Adam said, Let me go, because I was the cause of evil. No, you won't do, because you are too fond of figs and might stop in the road. Abel said, Let me go. No; you

[1] Robert of Lecce, quoted by Marenco, *l. c.*

[2] By Rothe, S. 262, on the authority of Henry Stephens. Marenco also tells the story, only he leaves out the incident of the sweetheart.

[3] Rothe, S. 264. Used by Longfellow in Friar Cuthbert's sermon in *The Golden Legend.*

might meet Cain, and he would kill you. Then Noah would undertake the business. No; you drink too freely. John the Baptist couldn't go, because he wore hairy clothes; and the penitent robber was rejected because his legs were broken. Finally an angel was sent, who raised the song, *Regina coeli, laetare! Alleluia! Resurrexit sicut dixit! Alleluia!*" What trifling and irreverence! and that by a man of real talent, and of generally serious aims! Barletta also, in one of his sermons,[1] tells a story which some readers may recognize as having been related of a much respected minister of recent times in Virginia.[2] A certain priest, in celebrating the mass, observed a woman who seemed much touched, and freely wept as he intoned the service. After it was over he spoke to the woman and asked the cause of her emotion, and she told him it was his voice, which reminded her tenderly of her recently deceased ass!

Marenco[3] says that the excess of this way of preaching became such a scandal that the Lateran Council of 1512 was led to pass its rule forbidding it, and that provincial councils, and later the Council of Trent, acted in the same direction. It is worthy of note that the abuse was so great as to call for this high authoritative repression.

Meantime the mystic type of preaching had also some representatives in this age. Along the Rhine, and especially in the Netherlands, as well as to some extent in France and other countries, we find them. Some of these preachers will claim notice later; here it is sufficient to remark that the mystic preaching of this time was chiefly derived from the masters of the past and did not offer, either in its representatives or its teachings, much of independence.[4]

In regard to the composition and delivery of sermons, there is not much new to tell, as the customs of preceding times were still much in vogue. But several points of homiletic interest require notice.

Besides homiletic helps in the way of collections of

[1] Told by Méray, *op. cit.*

[2] I am glad to run down this foolish story and show that it is as old as it is silly.

[3] *Op. cit.*, beginning of cap. V.

[4] Rothe, S. 267.

material there were put forth in this time a few books which taught the art of discourse. Early in the fifteenth century Nicholas of Clemanges [1] (a pupil of Gerson), in his general work, *De Studio Theologico*, had given some excellent precepts about preaching. Near the same time two Germans published works which, though somewhat crude, made real advance in homiletical theory.[2] Later, probably early in the sixteenth century, two more German works appeared.[3] The first bore the title *Tractatus de Modo Dicendi et Docendi ad Populum Sacra, seu de Modo Prædicandi,* and had for its author one Jerome of Dungersheim. Cruel gives an outline of the work and speaks favorably of it. The other was the *Manuale Curatorum* of Ulrich Surgant, which treats of such subjects, as, What is preaching, Who should preach, How one should preach, Different kinds of preaching, Subjects of preaching, Memorizing, Delivery, and the like. Thus we see that, while the theory of preaching was not wholly neglected, and many practical teachings were given in various ways, there were no really great or important works on Homiletics during this time.[4]

From these books and from the sermons themselves we may gather something as to the contents and form of the discourses of the period. The two matters may be briefly treated together. With differences in detail according to persons, subjects and circumstances, the prevailing method of discourse was about as follows: First, there would be an invocation or brief prayer for divine guidance, then an exordium, or *prothema,* an introduction to awaken interest or pleasure in the hearers. This was not at all or only remotely connected with the subject, and sometimes was far-fetched and bombastic. Then would come the *thema,* that is, the text or passage of Scripture, read in Latin, sometimes translated into the vernacular, and sometimes briefly explained word for word. This, if extended at all, was called *postillating,*[5]

[1] Id., S. 269. [2] Cruel, S. 596 ff. [3] Id., S. 599 ff.

[4] Those of Reuchlin, Erasmus and Melanchthon of course belong to a later date.

[5] The name *postil* for sermon has this origin: In the worship the sermon followed immediately upon the reading of the Scriptures, and the preacher was accustomed to introduce his comment by saying, "After these words of the text," etc. (*Post illa*

and was like the ancient homily. Sometimes, if the *postil* was of much length, it might take the whole time and become the sermon, with only the conclusion added. But more commonly the theme, or announcement and brief explanation of the text, was a subordinate affair, and then came the *dispositio,* or arrangement, the division and statement of the plan of discourse. With the scholastics this was very elaborate; with others it was subordinate and brief. Next came the argument or proof, or discussion and elaboration, with quotations from the teachers of the church. Here, too, was room for scholastic abuses, but the popular sermons would rather here be more polemic in tone and perhaps briefer. Last would come the anecdotes, fables, stories, comparisons, drawn from nature, from habits of animals and all sorts of things, by way of illustration and impression. Finally would be the *admonitio* or *conclusio,* with a brief closing prayer.

Such were the general form and contents of the preaching of these centuries. We see how little place the explanation and real enforcement of the Word of God was likely to have, and in most cases did have, in sermons of this construction. Scholastic subtleties with the more learned and their imitators, examples and tales with the more popular and easy going, were the main contents. As to the doctrine and morals the case continued as in the former times. The prevailing theology of mediæval Romanism was the staple of dogma. The morals of Christianity were usually clearly taught, but with admixture of external churchly regulations and the evils of the teaching concerning penance and indulgences. Among preachers of the reformatory tendency, the attack upon sin and corruption was the main thing in preaching, and many of these men were fearless and able in their polemic, assailing all classes of men and all species of sin without fear or favor.

The Latin still held some place as the language of

verba textus, etc.). So the homily came to be called the *postilla,* from whence a verb *postillare* was made, and a noun *postillatio* to describe the action. The word occurs in Wiclif's writings and other old English literature, but is now obsolete in English, though not entirely so in other languages. Readers of Luther will remember that his Home-Talks are called *Hauspostillen.* See Cruel, S. 123.

spoken sermons. These were mostly, as formerly, those given before universities, church assemblies, in cloisters, and the like; but still some were delivered to the people in Latin, and very many, as in the past, were written out and published in that tongue. But naturally the use of the vernacular gained ground, and, especially among reformers and popular preachers, tended entirely to displace Latin as the language of the pulpit.

As to the delivery of sermons, there is not much to add to what has been said of prevalent customs in the Middle Ages.[1] Places, hours, congregations, length of sermons, occasions, remained as described. The three methods of preparation were employed: some men memorized, some extemporized, some preached from notes. In regard to this Cruel says:[2] "As regards the delivery of the sermon itself, manifold division and subdivision of scholastic sermons, and the multitude of learned citations makes it in many cases scarcely conceivable how such a discourse could be committed and recited from memory. But for that it was customary to use the help of short memory cards, or even the sketch itself, which would be taken into the pulpit. Surgant says on this point: 'He who has naturally a weak memory and cannot remedy it by art must lay before himself a paper with the main and subordinate divisions written on it, or, if he can, the whole sermon, not to read it word for word, but only from time to time to glance at it.'" Bare reading, then, seems not to have been practised, but only memoriter or extemporaneous preaching, frequently with the help of more or less full notes. Doubtless the individual differences of delivery were as marked as among us. Erasmus satirizes the extravagant and ridiculous gestures and inflections of the showy preachers, and the sensational men no doubt resorted to many tricks of delivery for effect. One amusing thing is noticed by Cruel.[3] Sometimes the preachers, when they got to a new division, would say, "Now clear your throats, for this matter is important and must be heard," or, "Clear your throats now, I will soon let you go," or, "This ends the first division, if any one has to cough or clear his throat, this is the place." Sometimes this was done as a device to rouse the congre-

[1] *Ante*, p. 192 f. [2] *Op. cit.*, S. 633 f. [3] S. 634.

gation, and sometimes for this purpose the preacher would put in some lively and not always respectable anecdote. So much for the sermon and its delivery; we must now turn our attention to other matters. (Meantime the weary reader may clear his throat or otherwise refresh himself for a new phase of the subject!)

Enough has already been said to show that, except for the note of reform which is heard in some of the preaching of the time, the sermons of the later fourteenth and all the fifteenth century give evidence of marked degeneration. Yet we must dwell longer on the painful topic and point out more in detail what has thus far been only incidentally discussed.

We have already had occasion to speak of the low character of the clergy during this epoch.[1] Much ignorance, immorality, luxury and ambition, laziness, avarice, and other evil things have to be charged to their account. And this of course was at once both cause and evidence of decay in the pulpit. For in all times the character of the preacher either enforces or enfeebles his preaching. And where the average of character is bad, no matter how noble the exceptions may be, the average of preaching will necessarily be low. Where there is lack of true piety and conviction in the preacher the pulpit work tends to become empty, formal, frigid and without moving effect. And this is the character of much of the preaching of that age.

Always one of the signs of degenerate preaching—as of any literary production—is a slavish dependence upon others, past or present, a want of independence, originality, freshness. Copyists and imitators are found in every age, it is true, but when the masters belong chiefly to a former generation and the small followers mostly abound, the fall is great.

So was it now. We have seen how in all the Middle Ages, from the days of Gregory the Great, and notably in the age of Charlemagne and after, the preachers freely appropriated material from the past and present. In fact the best of them did it without scruple, and the less capable were encouraged to use without stint collections of sermons and other prepared material. This plagiarism

[1] *Ante*, p. 297 f.

and dependence were not regarded as morally wrong, nor does the fatal effect upon preaching seem to have been appreciated. In the decadent age of which we now treat this wretched practice had full swing and was one of the worst symptoms of the prevalent decline.[1]

All sorts of homiletical helps abounded. Some might have been legitimate and useful if wisely handled, but generally they were a temptation to the weak and a snare to the lazy. There were books of outlines, collections of various sorts of material, from so-called "flowers" derived from Scripture and other sources, to fables, tales, illustrations gathered from nature and elsewhere. The invention of printing made it possible to multiply these books, and many of them had great vogue. In addition to these helps, which required at least some effort on the part of the preacher to use in his work, there were collections of ready-made sermons at the disposal of the brethren. One of these actually bore the title of *Parati Sermones,* prepared sermons.[2] The author is unknown, but the book was one of the most popular of the kind, having passed through seventeen editions. The discourses are presented in a simple and clear arrangement and in a style "easily memorized," and were especially popular because they gave so many examples and illustrations. But another collection surpassed even this in popularity, having gone through twenty-five editions. This was the work of a certain John of Werdena and bore the whimsical but significant title of *Sermones Dormi Secure,* that is, "Sleep Well Sermons."[3] The title is explained in a brief introduction, which is couched in these terms: "Here happily begin the Sunday Sermons with expositions of the Gospels through the year, quite well known and useful to all priests, pastors and chaplains, which are also called by the other title of Sleep Well, or, Sleep without Care, for this reason, that without much study they may be appropriated and preached to the people." A few of the sermons are themselves borrowed from other sources, but they are mostly the author's own, who

[1] Noted in all the authorities, but especially well in Cruel, S. 451 ff.
[2] Cruel, S. 474 ff.
[3] *Op. cit.,* S. 478 ff.; and Broadus, *Preparation and Delivery of Sermons,* p. 141 (new ed.).

was spoken of by Trithemius as a "very celebrated declaimer of popular sermons in his time."

One outline may suffice as a specimen of his art. The text is Mark 6:48, "The wind was contrary to them;" and this is the statement of the plan: "There are four spiritual winds which are contrary to us and move the sea of this world: 1. The east wind blows when a man reflects on the sorrowful condition in which he entered this life. 2. The west wind, when he reflects on bitter death. 3. The south wind, when he thinks of the joys of eternity. 4. The north wind, when he thinks of the terrors of the last judgment."

Besides this weak dependence and wholesale plagiarism the preaching of the age showed all the accumulated faults of the past with which our studies have made us familiar. There is no need to repeat them here; but only to remind the reader that doctrine was corrupt, Scripture interpretation allegorical and strained and otherwise faulty, morality often dubious, legends and tales superabundant, and scholastic refinements and excesses unduly prevalent. But degenerate as preaching generally was, we must not forget that there were also indications of the saving presence of a noble life and power. It was not all bad, and to the rise and growth of this better kind of preaching, its nature and effects, we must now give attention.

Beginning with Wiclif, in the second half of the fourteenth century, a new note is heard in preaching. This does not mean that none before him had preached reform by attacking evils and appealing to Scripture as authority against churchly corruptions in doctrine and practice; but it does mean that in lifting up his mighty voice in this way he spoke differently from the most of his contemporaries, and he spoke not wholly in vain. The spirit of the true reformer is not that of the satirist who sees evil and derides it, nor that of the pessimist who sees it only to despair; nor that of the pious mystic, who flees before it to the withdrawn and introspective life; but that of the leader of men, who combines whatever is good in all these ways of regarding evil and adds to them the courage to attack and the hope to overcome, or, at least, to abate the ills of his time.

Was there demand for this new spirit and this new method in preaching? Surely. All those crying abuses which we have reviewed as evils existing in the social and religious life of the times, and as marks of degeneracy in the pulpit, blended into a loud and imperative call for preaching of a sort different from that which prevailed in the two centuries just preceding the Reformation. The wretched and sinful state of society loudly demanded men who should, like John of old, speak in the spirit and power of Elias. And while this is true of every age, from that of Noah to our own, the call came with an emphasis of its own in the fourteenth and fifteenth centuries of European history. If ever the world needed the preaching of a pure gospel it was then; if anything could put a saving leaven into that mass of evil it must be a renewal of real Christianity.

And yet at this very crisis, nay, as a part of the crisis, it was true that the great body or hierarchy claiming to be the representative of God and the authorized interpreter of God's will on earth, was itself marred by unspeakable corruptions in life and doctrine. The religious guides of the people were many of them shamefully and hopelessly corrupt. If men were to be saved by preaching, it must be through preachers different from these. And in doctrine the lapse was equally grave and more widely diffused, for even the good preachers held a very badly mixed theology. It may well be that among some of the so-called heretics of this time there could be found a purer type of doctrine than that which prevailed among the Catholic clergy, but no sermons of theirs have come down to tell us what they preached. The current Roman Catholic doctrine, with all its unscriptural and anti-scriptural accretions, was the staple of the sermons that have survived. Surely it was time for a new note to be heard. What more emphatic call for a true gospel preaching can there be than is found in the co-existence of a depraved ministry and a corrupted theology?

With all these things there was a widespread awakening of conscience in regard to the fearful evils and corruptions of the times. The better spirits of the age looked on these things with grief and shame, and came more and more to feel that upon them rested some responsibility to improve the condition of the world. Among the weak and sinful, too, there was a growing feeling of penitence and desire for better things. Such a feeling as this in a former age preceded and helped to produce the crusades and the great preaching which distinguished the twelfth and thirteenth centuries; in this era it preceded and helped to produce the Reformation and the great Protestant preaching of the sixteenth century. Ullmann well says:[1] "The religious and moral preparation for the Reformation consisted in this, that the Christian spirit found in the members of the Church a new and mighty revival, both in the way that more inward interest of the understanding toward Christian truth was aroused, and that the moral feeling was awakened and sharpened; led back from the outwardness of works to the inwardness of feeling and will."

This awakening of conscience showed itself in many different ways, and was found in many different places. Rulers, statesmen, men of affairs, scholars and literary men, as well as preachers, and pious mystics of both sexes, felt and expressed the need for a renovation of Christian life and teaching, and for a "reformation of the church in head and members." Did all the blended tones of this call go unheeded?

In the preaching of the age there was found with more or less of distinctness and power some response to these earnest demands for reform. In some sense it is generally true that the sermons that have come down to us contain traces of the reformatory tendency, but in many of them it is only a trace. Yet even that is worth something as an indication that the pulpit, decadent as it was in many respects, was not wholly deaf to the call for a better teaching and enforcement of Christian truth.

The most widespread, conspicuous, and, at the same time, easiest part of reform preaching was found in its attack on the corruptions which disgraced the age and compelled the attention of men. This is the necessary commonplace of all reformatory movements, and is greatly in evidence in the sermons of this time. The preacher shared this critical attitude with the philosopher, the historian, the literary man; and these might be mere

[1] *Reformatoren vor der Reformation,* Bd. II., S. 4.

cynics and satirists, showing and denouncing corruption, but not helping much to remove the evils of which they complained. No doubt some of the preaching of the age—as is true of all ages—went no further than this, nor are there wanting indications to support this reasonable inference. The preacher might even thunder in the pulpit against the sins of which he was himself guilty in private. Judas might condemn avarice and treachery, and Simon Magus inveigh with holy horror against the sale and purchase of so-called spiritual dignities, at least of churchly offices. Alas! sometimes the most loud-mouthed assailer of evils is not by any means a reformer.

But a degree better than this cheap and perfunctory attack upon sin was the work of men who, like Barletta, Geiler and Maillard, were good in life and serious in purpose, and yet fell short of being real reformers because they lacked the best spirit and the best method. They scolded and ridiculed, and used plain language, and feared nobody; but they brought no thorough reformation. Nothing is wanting to the completeness of their diagnosis and the painful thoroughness of their probing; but the balm of Gilead is not found in their hands, nor is the health of the daughter of their people recovered. A still further advance is found in the weeping prophet, who sees with grief unto tears, and denounces with a sorrowful despair, the evils for which he perceives no remedy. But the true reformer cannot stop with these. He may combine all these elements—righteous wrath, sharp denunciation, heartbreaking grief, and manifest sympathy for his sinning people—but he must be more and do more than all that is here implied, or he cannot lead and ensure the reformation for which he prays.

That completing element lies in the assumption of leadership and its summons for a following. Some brave, even if hitherto obscure, and modest Gideon must blow his trumpet and summon a following of his brethren. He must say that this task can be done, must be done, and we are the men and this the hour to do it. Here is the confident call of leadership in a righteous cause, a cause believed in, a cause whose ultimate triumph is really hoped for, a cause in which the leaders are willing not only to dare but to do, and not only to do, but, if need be, to die.

Patriotism and philanthropy have furnished many illustrious examples of this spirit, but it is not claiming too much for the Christian ministry to say that in its ranks in all ages reformers of the true and noblest type are to be found. In the age of which we now treat lived Wiclif, Huss and Savonarola. These were no gay satirists of follies which they blithely shared, no blatant censors of sins which they indulged, no sharp antagonists of evils which they fought only with pen and tongue, no gloomy prophets of calamities against which they lifted warning voices merely, not helping hands. Nor were these immortal three alone. Brethren and followers they had, even if comparatively few; and, though the work was too great for them, it was nobly begun and found a larger accomplishment in after times.

In their call to the consciences of men—that residue of moral force which even decay and darkness cannot utterly smother in human society—these reforming preachers had a mighty engine of power and a perpetual incentive to hope. But for the Christian preacher this was not, and never is, enough. He must be more than the moral reformer, while he always must be that. There is for him a higher appeal than to the awakened conscience and the earnest coöperation of men of like mind with himself. The chief element, nay, the real essence, of a religious reformation is its appeal to God. This was the distinctive thing in the work of the great reformers of the sixteenth century, and of those few brave spirits who preceded them in the dark fourteenth and fifteenth.

By what higher warrant than that of human conscience and law may men assail existing evils and call on other men to aid in attacking and overcoming them? Some might say that no higher warrant is needed; but the Christian reformer does not so speak, and history justifies his resort to an authority supreme over these. But what shall be the character of his appeal to God? That leads us to a deeper question. How is the divine authority expressed for men? To what visible and accessible manifestations of the divine will shall resort be made? The question is put in this speculative form only to make clearer the facts with which we are dealing. In its historical form it is simply this: How did the reform preachers of the corrupt age which we are studying make their appeal to God?

The three ways in which God is believed among Christians to indicate his will were all more or less clearly invoked in the reformatory struggles of our period. To some God spoke most distinctly in the consciousness and conscience of the pious and enlightened soul. The dealings of the divine Spirit with devout individuals in their sought and practised communings with God were accepted and utilized as revelations of his mind and will. The real element of truth and strength that is here involved should be frankly recognized. But we see that this mystic strain lapsed only too easily into a belief of direct personal inspiration, and even in so noble a soul as Savonarola went perilously near to fanaticism and ended in comparative failure. This mode of appeal needed, as it ever does, the correction and regulation of something external, stable and definite.

To others God spoke in the church and all its institutions, as the historic and visible manifestation of his presence among men. And while in its human developments there might arise errors in life and doctrine, it is for the church to purify itself in head and members. The appeal must be from the church corrupted to the church aroused to its fallen state. Again, whatever force must be allowed to the idea of common consent in doctrine, as tending to orthodoxy, and to general agreement in morals, as tending to righteousness, shall here also be freely conceded. But varying standards, both theoretically and historically, tend to confusion; and, as a matter of fact, the Catholic Church failed to effect its own reformation. Partly because the real advocates of reform were in a minority and not even then unanimous, and partly because the church and its theology contained many errors that could not be removed without what was tantamount to abdication of some of its strongest claims, thorough reform in this direction was hopeless. Constance and Basel glaringly record this failure, and Trent later emphasized and perpetuated it.

Something more was needed. Accordingly, others sought and found the finally authoritative voice of God in the Holy Scriptures. If the individual Christian experience and the churchly life and doctrine conformed to the Bible they might—always with caution and open to revision and correction—be accepted as subsidiary aids in reaching right conclusions and effecting needed reforms; but evermore and finally the revealed Word of God in Holy Scripture must be supreme authority. Here Wiclif and others laid down the gage of battle; it was on this field they fought and fell, that later reformers might here also fight and triumph.

Historic justice, however, requires that two remarks should here be made as to the use of Scripture by the early reform preachers. One is that they were not absolutely alone in their appeal to the Bible and in their use of it. Others also recognized the Scriptures as authority, but not with the emphasis and finality that make this the distinctive and triumphant thing in reformatory preaching. The other remark is that so deeply seated and universally accepted were false principles of interpretation and application in the pulpit use of Scripture, that even the reformers themselves were by no means clear of them. But it is their glory that here also they made a notable advance and prepared the way for better things.

In the old Teutonic stories the hero, Siegfried, had to take the rusted fragments of his inherited sword and by file and fire and hammer make it over again before it became in his strong hand the ever-victorious weapon of assault upon dragons and all other foes. So the Siegfried of reform must forge anew the sword of the Spirit that out of the rust and breakage of centuries of misuse it might come forth a keen and gleaming blade, ready to hand in every fight for the truth. To some of the heroes thus armed and active, though not, alas! immediately victorious, we shall give our attention in the next chapter.

CHAPTER X

Preachers of the Fourteenth and Fifteenth Centuries

Having discussed in the preceding chapter the times and the preaching that characterized them, we must now consider some of the representative preachers of the various tendencies of thought and methods of work. The older types remained and the preachers of reform—advance heralds of the Reformation—deserve and will receive special study.

1. Preachers of the Older Types

Italy was specially rich in scholastic and popular preachers in the fifteenth century;[1] but only a few of the best can be noticed here. John (Giovanni) of Capistrano (1385-1456) was a Franciscan of the stricter sort. He was a man of some learning and highly regarded in his native land as a preacher. He so distinguished himself by his zeal against heretics that the pope sent him on a mission to Germany, where he had great crowds. Though he preached in Italian and through an interpreter, his lively gesticulation and theatrical manners produced a great effect on his hearers. He likewise preached in Bohemia against the Hussites.[2]

Of far greater importance was Bernardino of Siena (1380-1444), likewise a Franciscan, and soon after his death enrolled among the saints. He came of good family in Etruria and enjoyed good instruction, studying canon law. But soon he divided his wealth among the poor and entered the Franciscan order. He was much grieved over the decay in that famous body, and made efforts at reform among them. As an officer of the order he made a journey to Jerusalem, which he turned to good account in his studies. He developed great talent as a speaker and was very popular. Siena was the principal scene of his labors. He was very diligent in preaching, attracted large crowds, and produced wonderful effects. He was especially successful in attacking gambling, many players being induced to forsake the evil and burn their dice and cups. The story goes that a painter complained to Bernardino that his living was

[1] I have had excellent help in the following pages from the works of Marenco and Zanotto, and from Rothe; also from the old but still valuable work of Ammon, *Geschichte der Homiletik,* which treats especially of the period between Huss and Luther. Rothe borrowed very freely from this work.

[2] See Hering, *Geschichte der Predigt,* S. 80.

taken away because he earned his bread by painting dice, and that the preacher told him to paint instead a disc representing the sun with the name of Jesus in the center. The painter did as he was told, and the demand for these tokens grew so great by Bernardino's influence that the painter got rich. The explanation lies in the fact that in preaching Bernardino would sometimes use one of these pictures to illustrate his sermon and heighten the effect. Thus we see a bit of sensationalism and a tincture of superstition in his work. He carried it so far that the pope put a stop to it as approaching idolatry. The sermons of Bernardino are decidedly of the scholastic type—long, exhaustive, with subtle and numerous divisions and distinctions—and one wonders at their popularity. But he had the oratorical talent—imagination and capacity for kindling emotion—and he powerfully moved the people. He treated moral subjects with good effect, and was far superior to most of his contemporaries.

Even more scholastic than he was Leonardo of Utino (d. 1470), who about the year 1444 was a renowned professor at Bologna and preacher also at the court of Pope Eugenius IV. He was a Dominican and enjoyed great reputation as preacher in many cities of Italy. The sermons which remain from him are remarkable, besides their generally scholastic type, especially for two things: their marvellous learning, and the rigid monotony of their structure. In regard to the first Ammon says,[1] "Every one of these sermons is overloaded with an immense mass of sayings and citations from authors of ancient and more recent times. The very first one, on gluttony, contains whole passages from Gregory the Great, Augustine, Seneca, Cicero, Boëthins, Vegetius, Lucan, Ennodius, Gaufred, Valencio, Maximus, Hugo, Isidore, Jerome and Ambrose." In regard to structure it is curious that every discourse is built on the same plan, as monotonously as the chapters of the *Summa* of Aquinas, by which it was evidently influenced. The introduction describes a soul intent on instruction coming to hear the teaching of the Gospel or Epistle, which is stated in the theme, but has to be proved because the

[1] *Op. cit.*, S. 92.

devil would overthrow it. After the introduction and statement of the theme the plan is to unfold the subject under two general divisions represented respectively by Moses and Thomas Aquinas. Each of these general heads is subdivided into four parts. Under the teaching of Moses the subject is tested by, 1, Natural law; 2, divine law; 3, prophetic law; 4, human law. Under the teaching of Aquinas it is tested by, 1, Natural law; 2, evangelical law; 3, canon law; 4, ecclesiastical law. With ingenious subtlety, native to a scholastic, he makes all of these prove his point, and concludes his sermon with the sentence: "Then the fully instructed soul gave thanks to God for what it heard from its teachers and went home in peace. Amen." In all the more than eighty sermons this same plan appears. The further subdivisions under the topics of the various kinds of law are very numerous—preferably forty!—and this is where scholastic ingenuity and wealth of learned quotation especially appear. Such a method might well seem destructive of all oratorical effect, but the energy, the earnestness, the natural oratorical talent of the preacher overbore his scholastic pedantry and give him power over his hearers, who could but admire his learning and thoroughness while they felt the force of his native eloquence.

The scholastic method did not lack notable representatives in Germany also.[1] Among these we may first mention John Gritsch (d. c. 1430), of whom little is known save that as a preacher of the Franciscan order he was very celebrated at Basel in the time of the famous council there. An interesting collection of his sermons remains. Like those of Leonardo, they are uniform in plan (though of course not Leonardo's plan), and are loaded with citations from the authorities.[2] While the structure is too uniform and artificial, it has the virtues of clearness and neatness. Like many other preachers

[1] Besides Ammon and Rothe, the great work of Cruel, which becomes here in its closing sections extremely valuable. It is a pleasure to make parting acknowledgment to a treatise characterized by so great scholarly research and soundness of judgment.

[2] The following plan, quoted from Ammon, gives a good specimen of Gritsch's manner. The subject is the Transfiguration,

of his time Gritsch makes much use of the classic fables, and is especially fond of Ovid's *Metamorphoses.*

His method of treating these may be illustrated by an example quoted from Cruel: "When Jupiter, the god of heaven, was informed of the corruption of the whole human race he took counsel with all the gods and determined to destroy all men by a flood. Beforehand, however, he decided to go down to earth in another form and learn by personal observation whether the complaints against men were well grounded. In human form he visited the wicked tyrant Lycaon, who prepared him a bed in his house, but secretly sought to slay him. For this he was changed into a wolf, who now ranges howling in the forests. The truth of the matter is really this: that Jupiter was a king of Crete, who, by his magic arts made his subjects believe that he was a god, and as such he received worship. Now, when many had bound themselves to war with him, he disguised himself, in order to spy out the force of the enemy, and so he came to Arcadia to Lycaon, who received him treacherously and in the night tried to kill him. By stratagem he escaped this danger and drove Lycaon as a punishment from his possessions, so that he was compelled to flee to the woods and live by robbery and plundering, so it could be justly said that he was changed into a wolf. In truth, beloved, now do the godless people of the Jews appear as such a wolf Lycaon. For we know that the supreme Jupiter, the Son of God, by his incarnation, came down personally to visit the Jewish people. The Jews, however, sought in wolfish fashion ever treacherously to slay him. But Christ, who knew all things—

Matt. 17:1 ff, and the outline is as follows:

I. Mundi utilitas renuntianda: habet enim,
  1. Infidelitatem in acquirendo;
  2. Instabilitatem in retinendo;
  3. Anxietatem in relinquendo.

II. Humana fragilitas relevanda:
  1. Per secretam inspirationem;
  2. Per uberem largitionem;
  3. Per severam indignationem.

III. Beatitudinis dignitas desideranda:
  1. In subjectione contra mundi praesumtionem;
  2. In dilectione contra mundi dissensionem;
  3. In duratione contra mundi correptionem.

even their corrupt hearts—could not be deceived, that is, he knew that he by the resurrection would escape the death prepared for him, but that the Jews, on the contrary, for punishment would be scattered, and, like hungry wolves, would range over the earth." We see here familiarity with classical literature, a rationalizing way of treating the myths so as to prevent their being any more believed as true, an allegorizing way of making them serviceable in Christian teaching, and clear trace of that mediæval hatred of the Jew which was only too much encouraged by the Church and often broke out in shameful persecutions.

The most renowned of these German scholastics was Gabriel Biel (d. 1495), who for a number of years, under the patronage of duke Eberhard of Wurtemburg, filled with distinction the chair of philosophy and theology at the University of Tübingen. In his last years he retired to a home of the Brethren of the Common Life at Schönau, where he died. Though a busy professor in two departments, Biel was also a diligent preacher. After his death several collections of his sermons were published. They exhibit the extreme of scholastic method, but also deal earnestly and practically with moral and devotional subjects.

Toward the last of the fifteenth century there preached at Leipzig a notable man, George Morgenstern, who attacked in unsparing terms the widespread evils of the age in all classes. He used the dry scholastic method of arrangement, though no doubt with more sap and vigor in actual delivery than appears in the sermons.

After Morgenstern, and early in the sixteenth century, there was one Pelbart, in Hungary, who enjoyed a great reputation among his contemporaries as a preacher of unusual merit. In addition to the scholastic method which characterizes his work there is evidence of some imagination and poetic faculty in his sermons which show therefore traces of real oratorical power.

The popular preachers of the time show a mingling of all the other elements in their discourses. Some join with the scholastic method popular gifts and esteem; some exhibit marked traces of mysticism; and nearly all are given to lamenting or denouncing the current evils and abuses, and are therefore akin to those who, because of their evangelical method and spirit, are more properly called reformers. We need not, however, complicate our discussion by attending to these distinctions, but simply group by their countries the few selected for treatment.

At least one notable preacher of this popular type came originally from Spain, though he labored chiefly in France, where he died and was buried. He was Vincent Ferrar (1357-1419), born of a respectable and pious family at Valencia in Arragon, pious from childhood, a Dominican in 1374, and soon distinguished as teacher and preacher. From a boy he was in love with preaching and had the natural gifts of an orator. At his earliest appearance during the years of his monastic life, his eloquence attracted wide admiration, and crowds gathered to hear him wherever he went.

Later when he went on his journeys, especially at the head of a band of Flagellants, his following was enormous, and he preached daily. His preaching is said to have produced amazing results, and miraculous powers were attributed to him, as in case of Francis and Antony before him. Like them he was canonized soon after his death. He must have had in a large degree the power of moving discourse, but his published sermons do not bear out his extraordinary reputation, being in the dry scholastic style and deeply imbued with the thought and method of Thomas Aquinas.

In the Italian preachers of the fifteenth century the scholastic tendency was especially marked, but along with this not a few of them displayed unusual powers of popular oratory. Among these, three are specially worthy of mention.

Bernardino of Busti (d. c. 1500) was a Franciscan from Milan and was esteemed by his contemporaries as a preacher of extraordinary merit. Ammon relates that whenever on fast days and special occasions the people of the towns in northern Italy desired a preacher of unusual power they petitioned the Franciscan authorities to send them Fra Bernardino. In scholastic character his discourses resemble, without equalling, those of Leonardo of Utino, and many of them are without any oratorical quality. But, as we have so often had to notice, this does not disprove the real oratorical power and fervor of the actually delivered sermons.

Contemporary with Bernardino was his fellow Franciscan, Robert Caracciolo of Lecce, who labored mostly in the vicinity of Naples. He was regarded by his contemporaries as a "second Paul," and had the art of moving to tears. That he was not free from sensational methods we have already seen,[1] but he too was capable of serious work along with his scholastic methods and his popular arts. But by far the most famous Italian preacher of this century, next to Savonarola, was the renowned Gabriel Barletta (fl. c. 1470), of whom it was said by way of proverb, *Qui nescit Barlettare, nescit prædicare*—if one does'nt know how to preach like Barletta he doesn't know how to preach at all. He was born at Barletta near Naples, and took his name from his birthplace. As a preacher of the Dominican order he preached in many different places in Italy, but very little is recorded of his life. A curious collection of sermons, or reports of sermons, has come down from him. He undoubtedly must have preached in Italian, but these sermons are reported in barbarous Latin, with frequent interlarding of Italian words and whole phrases. Discourses of this kind are called "maccaroni sermons." They are not infrequent in the French mediæval collections, as Lecoy de la Marche and others tell us, but Barletta's are the only real specimens in Italian. Marenco[2] thinks that the sermons were certainly delivered in Italian, but that the half-learned reporter gave them in Latin as best he could, but where the Latin was not at hand for phrases or words, he simply gave the Italian. As they stand, therefore, the sermons are curious specimens of reporting and of diction. But beneath their barbarous jargon their method and matter are worthy of note. Scholasticism was in them, to be sure, but the popular note is predominant. The preacher deals in legend and anecdote to a remarkable degree, often descending to the burlesque, the comic, and even the inane and silly. He is a preacher to the crowd, the unenlightened mass that loves entertainment and spice, and is not too particular as to the quality of it either as regards taste

[1] *Ante*, p. 303. [2] Cap. I.

or good sense. The vulgar and coarse, as well as the ridiculous and irreverent, are here, but we should do Barletta injustice to suppose that this was all or the main thing in his work. He was an earnest man and used these trifles rather as means than as ends. He spoke with courage and effect against the evils of the time, and did not descend so low with the light and sensational methods as did many of his contemporaries. He knew how to treat with more than usual delicacy and good sense such themes as conjugal love and the dance.[1] Other moral subjects engaged his attention also, and he had the art of speaking to the point, and at the same time to the hearts of his hearers.

There were in France during this epoch a number of preachers of the popular sort, among whom the most notable were Maillard and Menot. Olivier Maillard (fl. c. 1500) was born in Brittany in the fifteenth century and died early in the sixteenth, exact dates being uncertain. He was a Franciscan, a doctor of the Sorbonne, and celebrated as a preacher, especially at the church of St. Jean en Grave at Paris. He also served as court preacher at times both for Louis XI. of France and for the duke of Burgundy. Pope Innocent VIII., King Charles VIII. of France, and Ferdinand of Castile all honored him with commissions of importance, which he discharged with fidelity and skill. In 1501 he was charged by the pope with the hard and thankless task of reforming the Franciscan order in France. He bravely undertook to do what he was told, but was resisted and even chased from one of the monasteries as a false brother. He paid back this debt, however, very richly in his sermons, where he depicted and excoriated the corruptions of his brethren in no sweet fashion.

His reputation is founded principally on a series of sermons which he preached in Paris probably between 1494 and 1508. They were a holy terror. They spared no class, nor person. King, nobles, priests, ladies, and the people generally were attacked with a boldness that is commendable indeed, but with a bitterness of spirit that could not have been edifying, and a coarseness of language that is without excuse even in that age of license.

[1] Examples given in Ammon, S. 131 ff.

The preacher borrowed the language of the lowest—the slang of the streets and the vulgarities of the dissolute.[1] Once the king, Louis XI., was so plainly attacked that on Maillard's language being reported to him he naturally took offence and sent the preacher word that if he went on in that style he should be put into a sack and drowned. Maillard replied, "Go, tell your master that I shall then reach paradise sooner by water than he can with his post-horses." This was an allusion to the fact that Louis XI. had recently introduced post-horses in France. It does not appear either that Maillard changed his course or that Louis executed his threat. No doubt there was exaggeration and excess of invective in Maillard as well as lack of poise and taste, but he meant well, and his boldness and fidelity should not be forgotten, even though his spirit and style cannot be excused.

Contemporary and like-minded with Maillard was his brother Franciscan, Michel Menot (d. 1518), the place and date of whose birth are unknown. He lived in the reigns of Louis XI., Charles VIII., Louis XII., and Francis I. For a long time he taught theology in the Franciscan school at Paris, and died there in 1518. He enjoyed so great a reputation as preacher that he was called *Langue d'Or,* the Golden Tongue. His sermons were taken down by hearers, reported in the barbarous *maccaroni* style of mingled French and (alleged) Latin, printed in many editions. They must, therefore, be taken with some allowances, but as we have them they exceed those of Barletta and Maillard in coarseness and buffoonery. They portray a terrible state of affairs in French society at that time, and are themselves, in spite of good purposes and a courageous spirit, a mournful comment on the religion and taste of the age.

The greatest German preacher of the popular type in this time was John Geiler of Kaisersberg[2] (1445-1510), who passed most of his active life as preacher in Strasburg. He was born at Schaffhausen, early lost his father and was brought up by his grandparents at

[1] Méray, *op. cit.*, and an art. in the *Nouvelle Biographie Universelle.*

[2] All the German authorities on the period devote considerable attention to him, but the discussion of Cruel, S. 538 ff, is particularly good, and is mainly followed here.

Kaisersberg, whence his surname. He pursued his studies at Freiburg and became a professor of philosophy there; but soon turned his attention to theology and to preaching. He found his work in the pulpit, and in 1478 accepted a call to Strasburg, where, in the Minster, a preaching office had been endowed without the cares of the priesthood. This suited Geiler exactly, and here he did the most of his work, though at the request of the bishop of Augsburg he spent some time there during 1488-89; and in Strasburg and vicinity he often preached in other churches and in the cloisters. At the cathedral during the summer and festival seasons he was accustomed to preach at six o'clock in the morning, at other churches and in the cloister at three in the afternoon.

Geiler's sermons have come down in various German editions, and as they stand are but imperfect reports of his actual utterances. He wrote out and published none himself, but from his Latin sketches and the notes of hearers these sermons have been worked out. But even thus they show the characteristics of the man and reveal a preacher of no ordinary popular gifts and power. Like his Italian and French contemporaries he descended to the coarse and comic to a considerable degree, and far beyond the bounds of good taste even in that age; like them, also, he attacked with sharp invective and reckless daring the sins of all classes—people, clergy, and rulers. His course made him enemies, who resorted to a number of petty persecutions to spite him—such as employing the choir boys to mock during the service, the writing of abusive and indecent letters, following him with derisive calls and mimicries as he went on the streets, and other annoyances of the sort. But he went on his way unmoved, and he won great favor, attracted large crowds, and secured the friendship and confidence of many men of influence, including the emperor Maximilian, who "wrote to him frequently, received visits from him, heard him preach, and received with kindness and interest certain moral counsels which Geiler gave him—to restore peace, to do equal justice to all, and to put an end to the plunderings that had then gained the upper hand." [1]

Though free with his tongue, and not averse to wine

[1] Ammon, S. 219.

and rough jokes, Geiler was otherwise above reproach in his life and earnest and faithful in the discharge of his duties. As a man he was of kindly, frank, accessible disposition; conscious of personal rectitude without pride, and bold in attacking sin without personal grudge or unsympathetic harshness toward the penitent. He was a close observer and had a thorough acquaintance with human nature, and with all the details of life in his time. His illustrations, like those of Beecher and Spurgeon in modern times, are drawn from many sources. Likewise he was a wide reader and well educated, and his sermons show excellent labor put on his preparation. If he lacked the higher degree of originality he at least knew how to make good and individual use of what he learned from others. So there appear in his sermons traces of both scholastic learning and mystic contemplation; but he was above all and chiefly a preacher to the people.

A curious specimen of his work is the series of seven sermons on "The Hare in the Pepper," that is, the seasoned, or spiced, hare. There are two texts for all seven: Lev. 11:6, and (chiefly) Prov. 30:26: "The conies are but a feeble folk, yet make they their houses in the rocks." He compares the Christian to a hare under fourteen points, derived from the habits and fate of that animal, treating one or several of the lessons in each discourse, thus: "1. The hare is timid, so the Christian lives in the fear of God. 2. It is swift in running, so is the spiritual person swift in good things and finds nothing too hard. 3. It runs quicker up than down the mountain, so the Christian up the mountain of God. 4. Dogs are set upon the hare, so the evil spirits upon us. 5. It rests its safety upon flight, so must we flee before evil assaults. 6. It continually moves its lips and mumbles, so should we continually fear God. 7. It has long ears, so also should the Christian have long ears, in order to hear with diligence and eagerness the word of God. 8. It makes its resting place in the rocks, that is, for us, Christ. 9. The skin of the hare must be removed, so must we lay off a threefold skin: temporal good, our own will, outward works. 10. It is roasted in the fire, so we in sufferings and adversities. 11. It is basted, so must we baste ourselves with the sauce of God's grace, with devotion and divine love. 12. It must be tested, whether it is well roasted or not, so must we test ourselves. 13. It must be put in the pepper, that is the cloister[1] and all therein which nips and burns our human nature like pepper. So also must persons out in the world lay on themselves many self-denials and penances. 14. The hare is brought on golden plates to the table, so shall we also some time be set before God as a pleasant savor in the heavenly kingdom and be by him consumed and incorporated with himself."

This last thought is worked out thus: " The hare is put into two golden plates and set on the table before the king, where it is received with pleasure and eaten and incorporated with the king and made one with him. So also the believing Christian, when he has been prepared in the way before described, is borne by the hands of the holy angels on the two golden plates of glory—body and soul—into everlasting bliss before the face of the heavenly King. And as the hare is eaten by the king, so thou, through an unspeakable benevolence, love and joy, art sunken in God and made one with him. Not essentially, as the heretic Amalrich said,[2] but heartily through clear knowledge, love and joy. There is man again in his source, there has he first peace, rest, and bliss, there has the little hare first rightly reached its resting place in the rocks, there its fear has disappeared, its heart flutters no more, it dreads not, for it is safe and knows it is safe. There it experiences what was promised, that God will dry all tears and henceforth there will be neither weeping nor pain. There will come true what the Lord has said, that the humble shall be exalted. The little hare that ran despised here in the vale of tears, was hunted by hellish dogs, flayed and roasted, comes now to great honor."

This gentler strain was not, however, the most characteristic thing in Geiler's work. His " Ship of Fools " and other collections of sermons give forth the sterner, coarser, and less pleasing, but also more vigorous and effective parts of his method. Altogether he is a de-

[1] The sermons were preached in a nunnery.
[2] Amalrich of Bena, a mystic of the extreme Eckhart school.

cidedly important character in his age, and did something to arouse the German mind preparatory to the Reformation.

Coming to the Netherlands we must go back to an earlier date and place ourselves in the second half of the fourteenth century. Here we find among the popular preachers a man remarkable for his personal piety, his excellent success in preaching, and his abiding influence on the best religious life of the age. It is Gerhard Groot[1] (1349-1384), the noble preacher and the founder of the Brethren of the Common Life. Groot was born of wealthy and excellent family at Deventer, the only son of his parents. He was weakly in body but eager in mind, and received a good education at home, at Paris, at Cologne. Returning home well prepared in culture for the work of a priest, he had no difficulty in finding places for beginning his work, and accepted a subordinate position at Utrecht. Well off and cultured, with a taste for luxury and pleasure, it looked as if he must go the way of the worldly clergy. But soon a deeper life was awakened within him by the influence and pleading of a pious friend whom he had won at Paris, and who visited him at Utrecht, and dealt lovingly and faithfully with him. It is a beautiful incident, creditable alike to both the men. Gerhard changed his course, burnt his costly books on magic, gave up his income, put off his fine clothes for a coarse gray garment, and withdrew for ascetic practices, devotion, and further study to a Carthusian monastery at Gueldres. Here he spent three years, when his active nature drove him forth to live and work among his fellowmen. He shrank from the responsibilities of the priesthood, but was ordained a deacon, and this gave him the right of public instruction by preaching.

In this humble spirit Groot began his wonderful career as a travelling popular preacher. He had pronounced success from the start; for back of his admirable preparation, there lay both the natural talent for public speech and the earnestness of a soul bent on serving God and doing good to men. Thomas à Kempis said of Groot that he worked in the spirit of John the Baptist. People of all classes thronged to hear him, wherever he came, and

[1] Ullmann, *Reformatoren vor der Ref.*, Bd. II., S. 54 ff.

he called them to repentance and faith. It was not only his eloquence and earnestness of speech that drew them, but men saw and felt the power of his blameless and consecrated life. He refused pay for his services, and sought no ecclesiastical preferment. It was said of him—precious eulogium upon a preacher—*Fecit quod dixit; sicut docuit, quoque vixit.* He sought to know the experiences of the people and to adapt his preaching to their needs, and he preached in the popular tongue. His zeal was unwearied, the fruits of his labors rich in conversions and real amendment of life.

But his success and his rebukes made him enemies among the worldly clergy, whose vices he knew and denounced, and by their representations he was deprived of his permission to preach. Friends laid the case before the pope, but the appeal was in vain. Groot submitted to the authority of his ecclesiastical superiors and gave up preaching, but turned his attention to teaching unofficially and quietly among the people. Here also his success was great. A visit to the aged mystic, John Ruysbroek, at his abbey near Brussels, impressed Groot not only with the beauty of the mystical life, but also with the orderly and peaceful way in which the monks lived together. He came away with the idea in his mind that pious men without monastic vows might live in common to learn and teach. His views found acceptance with friends, and so arose the Brethren of the Common Life, a sort of pious society for mutual edification, which speedily concerned itself with the education of the poor. The brotherhood grew and extended, and many a poor scholar—Erasmus among them, and John Wessel—afterwards received instruction in early life in the schools of this society. Busied with his order, and his teaching, Groot died in the midst of his years and his usefulness—having caught the plague from visiting a sick friend—when only thirty-four years of age. His sermons do not seem to have been reported and preserved, but the influence of his life and of his brotherhood was great in producing other preachers of evangelical tendency and in preparing the way for the Reformation.

In England as in the Netherlands and generally in Germany, the popular preaching was characterized by a more seriously reformatory spirit than was the case in Italy and France. Wiclif and his preachers, and afterwards the Lollards, did the most of this work; but they come more naturally under the reformatory preachers.

The mystic preachers of the period are naturally fewer in number than those of the other types, but some of them were very notable and influential men. The geographical happens here to be also the chronological order, and we have to do with only three countries—the Netherlands, France, Germany.

The earliest important representative of mysticism in the Netherlands was John of Ruysbroek[1] (1293-1381), who was born at a village from which he took his surname, near Brussels, late in the thirteenth century. He lived to a great age, reaching over to the latter part of the fourteenth century. He was much influenced by Tauler. At eleven years of age he was put to school at Brussels, where he studied four years. Nothing is recorded of any further schooling, and through life he was more devoted to piety than to learning. At twenty-four years of age he was ordained a priest and appointed to a church in Brussels. He was often seen sunk in deep meditation in the streets, not noticing the crowd. But in his teaching he warned against mere ecstatic mysticism and contended for a deep inward piety. Up to his sixtieth year he exercised the priest's office in Brussels with fidelity, but not much is known of the character and effect of his preaching. But the attractiveness of the contemplative life so grew upon him that he retired about 1363 to a newly founded Augustinian cloister near Brussels, where he spent the remainder of his long and peaceful life. Here he gave himself to meditation and writing and to instructing the many who came to learn from the pious old man the life of self-denial and love to God. Among these visitors, as we have seen, was Gerhard Groot. Ruysbroek's writings reveal a mysticism less profound than Eckhart's, less practical than Tauler's, but he had some affinities with both, without being so great as either. In preaching and teaching as well as by personal character, he made his mysticism profoundly and fruitfully influential upon others, and his work was one

[1] Ullmann gives also a good account of Ruysbroek.

of those far-off but important steps which led to the reform preaching and life in later years.

Gerhard Groot has already been noticed among the popular preachers, but he belongs here also, as he had decidedly mystical traits; and he also claims mention here as a necessary connecting link between Ruysbroek and the other great Netherlands mystic who has filled the Christian world with the odor of sanctity in his famous writing—*The Imitation of Christ.*

Thomas à Kempis (1380-1471) was born of humble and hard-working parents at a little Dutch village not very far from Cologne, called Kempen, from which his surname is taken. The family name was Hamerken, but the other is so well established that it has usurped the place of a surname. The boy early showed both intelligence and piety and was glad to avail himself of the free education offered to poor children by the Brethren of the Common Life. After having been aided for a time by their funds he entered their house at Deventer. Here a congenial friend, and the excellent head of the school, Florentius, successor to Groot, both had great influence on the youth, and he was drawn to the life of contemplative piety. After several years he was advised by Florentius that if he desired to lead the contemplative life he should enter a monastery. This delighted Thomas, and he soon entered the Augustinian convent of St. Agnes near Zwoll. For five years he remained a novice, then was made priest, and later superior. Here his life flowed quietly on to its end at the age of more than ninety years. Exercises of devotion, writing and copying, reading, preaching, and exhorting the novices, the brethren and many visitors who came to hear him, occupied his time. Many of his sermons remain, and they exhibit the sweet restfulness, the purity, the love, the quiet devoutness that we would expect from the author of the *Imitation of Christ.*[1] Thomas à Kempis was a thoroughgoing Catholic and monk, and his views are not by any means all

[1] The question of the authorship of this gem of devotional literature cannot be regarded as settled beyond doubt, but the better opinion among critics seems to be that which I heard Prof. Hauck of Leipzig express in a lecture, namely, that the claims of Thomas are the best, and that if not his, the work must be regarded as anonymous.

sound or evangelical, but he was mystical, pious, devoted. His influence was all in favor of purity and reform within the church, and the total effect of his life and work has been sweet and helpful.

In France we find a practical mystic in the famous chancellor of the University of Paris, Jean Charlier (1363 1429), who was born at a little place called Gerson, near Rheims, and, like so many others, is called from his birthplace rather than by his family name. He was educated at the University of Paris, and in 1408 was pastor of one of the leading churches there. His view of preaching is set forth in a passage[1] from one of his sermons: "Many believe that sermons should be delivered only that the people may learn and know something that they did not know before. Hence their scornful saying, 'What is preaching to me? I already know more good than I am willing to do.' But these people are in error; for sermons are not delivered for this reason only, that one may learn something, but also for this reason, to move the heart and inclination so that they shall love, desire, and accomplish that which is good. Therefore the apostle desires not so much that one should learn what is in Christ as that he should be likeminded with him. They, however, who attend sermons only to learn something new are like those of whom the apostle writes that they are ever learning and yet know nothing." In his preaching Gerson boldly and decidedly attacked abuses and degeneracy, especially in the ignorant, worldly, and greedy clergy. He had accurate knowledge of human nature, a keen observation, and much experience of men and things. A Catholic critic[2] says of him that he had "quickness of comprehension, penetration of judgment, rich experience and blooming fancy, extensive reading in ancient classics, solid rhetorical structure, fundamental knowledge of philosophy and theology. Further he had an admirable familiarity with the Holy Scripture." This is high praise, but it has to be discounted by the fact that Gerson did not rise above the scholastic and allegorizing methods current in his day. And the moral quality of his work, high as it undoubtedly is, must also

[1] Quoted by Rothe, S. 300.
[2] Art. in Wezter und Welte's *Kirchenlexicon.*

be painfully discounted by the pettiness and casuistry he displays in treating certain questions.[1]

Gerson was active at the Council of Constance, and boldly sided with the progressive party there in holding that the council was superior to the pope and had the right to depose the three claimants and elect a new pope. Having denounced the murder of the Duke of Orleans, he became unacceptable to the court in France and could not return there. He first found a refuge in Austria, but later went to Lyons and lived there in a convent of which his brother was prior, occupying himself in his later years in teaching little children. He was among the most influential ecclesiastics and preachers of his time, and his own life was above reproach.

It would be strange if in Germany no trace of mysticism should be found among the preachers of this epoch, and doubtless there was more of it than comes to the surface or renders itself conspicuous. For, as a matter of fact, no specially distinguished mystical preacher appears among the Germans of the time. There are two men, however, who though not of the highest rank as either preachers or thinkers claim at least brief notice.

John Veghe[2] (d. 1504) was the son of a citizen of Münster, and is mentioned in 1451 as a member of the Münster house of the Brethren of the Common Life. He was advanced to the position of rector, and in 1481 was made rector of the Sisters' house at Niesink. His "collations," in the low German dialect, have been published and favorably noticed by several German critics. From these notices it is gathered that Veghe did not adhere closely to the scholastic form in preaching, though he was fond of making a series of "points." He made a rather practical use of some of Eckhart's ideas, and in one place there is a clear and bold utterance against the abuse of indulgences. The sermons have the Catholic contents, leaning much on Augustine, but with a practical mysticism, which though below the measure of Thomas a Kempis, is yet rather in his vein. They show also

[1] Quite a list—and a very unedifying one—is given by Ammon, S. 70 ff. Among other things he defends the not uncommon but no less astounding theory that a monk's vow of chastity would be broken by marriage, but not by occasional sensual indulgence.

[2] Hering, *Gesch. der Pred.*, S. 83.

warmth, devotion, elevation, and purity of spirit characteristic of the better type of mystical preaching.

The other representative mystic is the better known and highly esteemed John Staupitz (d. 1524), who, though not very strong as a preacher, yet by his piety, his personal influence, and most of all by his relations to Luther, occupies an important place in the early history of the Reformation. The place and date of his birth are unknown, and nothing definite of his parentage is recorded, except that he was of good family in Meissen. He was educated at Leipzig and Tübingen, where he received his doctor's degree, and was prior of an Augustinian monastery. Later he was made vicar-general of this order, and was appointed by Frederick the Wise professor in the newly founded university at Wittenberg. On a visit to Erfurt he met the young Martin Luther, then much troubled with doubts and fears, and took a warm interest in the young monk. He pointed Luther to Christ alone as the ground of hope, interested himself in his promotion to Wittenberg, and was at first warmly sympathetic with his attack upon the abuses in the church. But Luther went too fast and too far for Staupitz, who never gave up his Catholic views or connection, though he was favorable to reform within the church. Later Staupitz transferred from the Augustinian to the Benedictine order and spent his latter years chiefly in southern Germany, where he died in 1524.

As a preacher Staupitz had no preëminence of talent, but was heard with interest and profit. He held the mystical doctrine of the union with Christ by losing self in him through contemplation. He was not at all an original thinker in any line. But he is chiefly memorable to Protestants because of his helpful friendship to Luther in the early formative stage of the great reformer's career, and is more notable for the purity and piety of his life than for high intellectual achievements of any kind.

In general, these mystics are an important link in the chain of influences connecting the Reformation with the more evangelical types of life which existed and persisted through the dark times of the fourteenth and fifteenth centuries.

2. The Preachers of Reform

The history of preaching has already often shown us that in the times of its highest prosperity the things that make for decline are ever present and active, and that in the times of its lowest depression the forces of reform and purification are never wholly absent. In these two centuries of comparative decline which intervened between the great Catholic revival of preaching in the thirteenth century, and the greater Protestant revival which glorified the first half of the sixteenth, the better elements of preaching were not entirely lacking, and the forces were slowly gathering which out of the corrupted mass of mediæval decay were to produce the great evangelical preaching of the Reformation. So we study some of the reform preachers, beginning with those in the far West.

Up to this time England has played no great part in the history of preaching. She has had preachers among her priests and monks, but none of extraordinary merit or wide reputation. But now she furnishes to the world the "Morning Star of the Reformation," and with the beginning of that tendency enters upon a glorious career in this as in other departments of history. From now on her preachers rank with the first in respect of character, power, and enduring fame.

The great preacher and reform leader, John Wiclif [1] (1320-1384), was born about the year 1320 of good family near Richmond in Yorkshire. The social standing of his people was excellent, and they probably had some means. The boy received good education and was early sent to Oxford, where he distinguished himself successively as student, scholar, teacher, and preacher. Oxford was henceforth the center and principal scene of his life and work. Wiclif's career as a preacher began in 1361, when he was ordained to the priesthood. Immediately his preaching and writings began to attract attention, for his word was with power. He held various places as a preacher while residing, studying, lecturing, and writing at Oxford.

In 1374 the king appointed him to the parish of Lutter-

[1] The surname seems to be local, as was so often the case, and to denote a cliff of the river Wye—Wye-cliff—shortened to Wiclif. Among the variety of spellings the simplest one is adopted in the text.

worth, and he held this place to his death. With it his name is inseparably associated, for here he did the most of his work, as priest and preacher, though living chiefly at Oxford.

Besides his regular parochial work at Lutterworth Wiclif often preached in other places, and his preaching was very acceptable to the people wherever he went. In London he was heard with great admiration by court and people, but naturally not by the clergy, whose worldliness and unfitness he was already attacking with power. Because of political sympathies he enjoyed the favor of the powerful statesman, John of Gaunt, whose protection was worth much to the reformer in his bold attacks on the clergy and the papacy.

Notwithstanding Wiclif's favor with the court and the people, his clerical enemies finally plucked up courage to call the bold preacher to account for his caustic utterances. In 1377 charges of heresy and other things were brought against him before the Bishop of London. But the trial was broken up by a brawl between his protectors and the bishop's following, and nothing came of it. His enemies then got the pope (Gregory XI.) to issue bulls condemning certain teachings of Wiclif as heretical. The bulls also called for the institution of processes against the reformer. But partly because of the sympathy of the University of Oxford, and partly because the bishops themselves were somewhat jealous of having a papal tribunal to deal with accused persons in England, this effort to crush Wiclif was not successful. Once more, in 1378, he appeared before the prelates in London to answer charges, and again through the sympathy of powerful protectors (John of Gaunt and the Princess of Wales among them) the trial came to little, only a mild reproof being administered to the preacher.

In this same year (1378) Wiclif organized his companies of "poor priests," or "simple priests," as they were called, to go about England preaching; and at the same time he set on foot his translation of the Bible into the English tongue. The far-reaching importance of these two measures cannot be overestimated. The "poor priests" were not an ecclesiastical order—Wiclif had a poor enough opinion of the decayed orders—but were simply evangelists and colporters of a more scriptural pattern, who went about among the people preaching in English a simple gospel, teaching, and perhaps distributing copies of the Scriptures done into the native language, together with some of Wiclif's writings. Men of character and education were engaged in this work, and the contrast between their voluntary and devoted labors and the pampered and worldly officialism of the endowed clergy, whether secular or regular, was impressive. No wonder the common people heard them gladly; no wonder the pharisaic priests hated the work and its founder. History repeats itself. Good work was done, and in the hearts of the English folk as in a rich soil, seeds were sown that in after years were to bring a great harvest—but alas, only after the harrow had done its work.

Reform principles made progress in Wiclif's own mind. At first he had attacked the papal claims to authority in secular matters, and in other ways. Then he fell upon the evil clergy and spared not their sins and other unfitnesses for their work. At last he comes to assail some of the Roman doctrines, especially that of transubstantiation. His study of Scripture and his acceptance of it as the supreme authority in matters of faith were coming to make of him a reformer indeed. In 1381 he put forth theses against the doctrine of transubstantiation, embodying much the same ideas as those subsequently held by Luther. A treatise called "Wiclif's Little Wicket," which was a tract, but much in sermon form, and no doubt with many ideas and expressions used in his discourses, is given in Fish's *Masterpieces of Pulpit Eloquence,*[1] and is a good specimen of the spirit and method of the reformer. It is vigorous in style, bold in expression, and acute in reasoning, and makes a sharp assault on the doctrine of transubstantiation.

This latest phase of his development—attacking certain doctrines of the church—mightily stirred up the already angered clergy, and frightened some of Wiclif's friends. John of Gaunt tried to get him to stop. The trouble was emphasized by the rise of a sedition under John Ball, a popular leader and agitator for the rights of the common people, who claimed to have got his ideas

[1] Vol I., p. 118 ff.

of freedom and popular rights from Wiclif. So a council was called in 1382 to take measures against Wiclif and his followers. Some of these were punished, but Wiclif himself was still left at liberty, though articles from his writings were formally condemned. He had the people on his side, and it was hard to bring him to judgment. Yet he and his friends thought it most prudent for him to retire from Oxford to the more quiet retreat of Lutterworth. Here he pursued his parochial duties and busied himself with his writings for his few years more of life. His health, never strong, was now declining, and he died of a paralytic stroke on the last day of December, 1384.

Apart from his vast importance as a reformer, Wiclif would claim attention alone by his eminent merits as a preacher. Sermons from him have come down to us partly in Latin and partly in English.[1] The sermons are based on Scripture, are not wholly free from scholasticism, nor from the current allegorical method of interpretation, nor from some Roman Catholic errors; but they are in the right direction, for they show at least a better interpretation and use of Scripture than was common, and a far more evangelical doctrine. They are vigorous in attack, clever in appeal, and give suggestions of an eloquence which the spoken discourses must have had. For they are but sketches of sermons and were no doubt amplified in delivery. Not only did the author himself amplify them, but the curious directions at the end of many of the short discourses indicate that he intended his "poore preestis" to make free use of the sermons. Thus at the end of the first sermon on the Rich Man and Lazarus, we find the following: "In this Gospel may preestis telle of fals pride of riche men, and of lustful lyf of mighty men of this worlde, and of longe peynes of helle, and joyful blis of hevene, and thus lengthe ther sermoun as the tyme axith." In sermon five we have a good principle of Scripture interpretation thus set forth: "It is noo nede to depe us in this stori more than the gospel tellith, as it is no nede to bisie us what hight Tobies hound. Hold we us apaied on the mesure

[1] The admirable edition by Dr. Thos. Arnold leaves nothing to be desired: *Select English Works of John Wyclif;* edited by Thos. Arnold, Oxford, 1869.

that God hath govun us, and dreeme we not aboute newe pointes that the gospel leveth, for this is a synne of curiouste that harmeth more than profiteth."

A longer extract from the third sermon, founded on Luke 15, will give us an idea of Wiclif's method. The spelling is given in our modern way, though thereby much of the quaint flavor of the original is lost. "In this gospel telleth Christ two parables of comfort, how his people shall be saved allif [although] priests grudge thereagainst, both prelates and religious [i.e., monks], for their pride and covetousness. The story of this gospel telleth how publicans and sinful men were coming to Jesus to hear his lore [teaching]; and he treated them graciously as a good Lord, but scribes and Pharisees grudged against this and blasphemed against Christ, and said he ate with them unlawfully. And this deed may figure things that fall now, sith [since] prelates as scribes and religious [monks] as Pharisees grudge against true priests, members of Christ, that commune with commons, as publicans, and secular lords as sinful men, and say it falleth not to them to know God's law. For they say it so high, so subtle, and so holy that all-only scribes and Pharisees should speak of this law. And these secular prelates may well be cleped [called] scribes, for they, both more or less, write [1] [i.e., keep account of] the money that they pile [pillage] of the people more busily than they print in their souls the knowing of God's law. And these religious [monks] be Pharisees, for they be divided [2] from the common manner of living by their rotten rites, as Pharisees were. Three causes there be why this heavenly leech [physician] received freely these sinful men and ate with them: first, for he would convert them, to the confusion of proud prelates that letted [hindered] the freedom of God's laws to have their course. By this should they meekly know that highness of state maketh not a man evermore better to God. The second cause is that Christ would give his priests in time of grace lore [teaching] and example to do wisely so, and to stand for the freedom of God's law. The third

[1] Play on the word "scribe" from *scribere,* to write.
[2] Play on the original meaning of the word Pharisee, a separatist.

cause is, for Christ would show his general lordship and saving not only of Jews but of heathen men in divers states. These prelates would fain that all God's law were hanging on them for to spoil [rob] the people; for then would they tell this law and put them to false understanding as [that] they might have more winning [gain] of the people."

These were bold words, and they are a fair sample of Wiclif's fearless assault on monks and seculars. The rest of the sermon proceeds on the view that Christ is the shepherd, the angels are the ninety and nine, mankind is the lost sheep. Christ is "the woman"—the wisdom of God—the ten pieces are God's "reasonable creatures," the tenth and lost piece is man. "The lantern that was lighted is the manhood [incarnation] of Christ, the turning up of the house is changing of states that be made in this world by the manhood of Christ."

We know that Wiclif had many sympathizers and followers not only among the common people but also among the influential and the cultivated. Yet among them is no preacher of special renown whose name stands out preeminent like that of the leader himself. To persons of the reform tendency the name of Lollard was applied, probably as a term of reproach, signifying babblers, or praters. It was a custom of these Lollards to expound the Word of God and teach the people the truth of Scripture. That they opposed the papal errors and sought for a better establishment and a greater enlargement of the rights of the people is certainly true, and so far they must have our sympathy and respect; but there is no reason to doubt that with their good there was mingled the ill of extremes, fanaticism, and perhaps sedition. At any rate the Lollards found themselves under the ban of both church and state, and they were persecuted most cruelly. For ten years after Wiclif's death his followers went on preaching among the people, and sowing the seeds of his evangelical doctrine. But the attitude and enactments of the so-called reforming Council of Constance strengthened the enemies of Wiclif, and active measures of persecution were taken against the Lollards. They were repressed, but their opinions were not extirpated. Like those of the "Friends of God" and other parties on the Continent these teachings had root among the people and waited in good soil for sunshiny weather.

Something more than a hundred years after Wiclif, and on the eve of the great Protestant revolution, there appeared at Oxford another remarkable man, a scholar and preacher, who held and advocated reformatory views. This was John Colet[1] (1466-1519), celebrated as lecturer at Oxford and as dean of St. Paul's cathedral in London.

Colet was born in London in 1466, the eldest son of Sir Henry Colet, a man of wealth and influence. John received his early education at London, but was soon sent to Oxford, where he remained seven years and took his degree. The love of learning was deep within him, and he went abroad to catch the new spirit of learning and to study the Latin and Greek classics. He visited Paris and Italy, got acquainted with Erasmus and other Humanists, and returned to England in 1497 saturated with the Revival of Letters, and an enthusiast for classical culture. But Colet was also a Christian and desired the work of a priest. He was ordained soon after his return to England, settled at Oxford, where he gave without fee a course of expository lectures on the Epistles of Paul, using the Greek text and expounding from that. Not only the novelty but the merit and power of these discourses attracted enthusiastic and cultured audiences. Colet's fame as a preacher spread, he held various charges, with Oxford as a center, and in course of time was made dean of St. Paul's and a doctor of divinity. At St. Paul's he instituted a course of expository sermons which attracted great attention. He also established a divinity lectureship there for week days, and was the founder of the famous classical school connected with St. Paul's.

Colet held decidedly reformatory views. He disapproved of confession and other Romish practices. On this account he was not acceptable to the clergy, was accused of heresy and brought to trial before Bishop Warham, but was acquitted. He pleaded for a reform within

[1] There is an excellent article on Colet in the *Dict. of National Biog.*, based on the more elaborate work of Seebohm, *The Oxford Reformers.*

the church on the basis of the New Testament and of the practices of the early Christian centuries, but he was not as thoroughgoing as Luther, nor did he have the dash and vigor of Wiclif. His was the temperament of the scholar rather than that of the general. But his influence and his writings, and especially his work in opening the Word of God, give him a sure place among the early reformers. He was a man of piety and wrote books of devotion, as well as some commentaries and other theological works. His sermons were given, some in Latin and some in English. His ease and effectiveness, clearness and warmth in speech, are attested by those who heard him, but his remaining sermons—as is so often true—do not exhibit the real oratorical power of the man. One of his sermons, delivered before Convocation in February, 1512, is particularly commended as a bold and powerful plea for reform within the church. Colet died just as the Reformation was beginning, in 1519.

In France, as we have seen, the reform movement took the form of satire and invective in such preachers as Maillard and Menot. The position of Gerson was not satisfactory, for though an excellent preacher of mystical opinions and himself a pious man, his reformatory views went no further than in the direction of healing the papal schism. He was the leading man at the Council of Constance which condemned Huss, and he cannot be fairly reckoned among the fore-reformers. Leaving out these three, who have before been noticed, we may mention one man who lived a little before their time. This was Nicole d' Oresme (Nicholas Oresmus, d. 1382), who is celebrated for at least one bold sermon in the direction of reform. He was a man of great learning and probity, who enjoyed the confidence of several kings and held high office in the French church. He was sent on an embassy to the papal court at Avignon in 1363 or 1364, and took occasion, when invited to preach, to deliver a respectful but vigorous message in regard to the evils in the church. He compared the overthrow of Israel to the impending overthrow of the church because of its corruptions. The sermon does not spare the clergy and was a brave and able testimony. But it does not seem to have produced any good result, and Oresme certainly did not start or lead any reform in France.

In Germany we find two distinct groups of reform preachers whose work very decidedly influenced opinion in their country and helped to prepare the way for the great Reformation.

The more notable of these were the Bohemian reformers, among whom were several preachers of power whose names are worthy of grateful remembrance. First among them was one Conrad of Waldhausen [1] (d. 1369), who flourished about the middle of the fourteenth century. He was an Austrian by birth and lived in several different places before he finally settled at Prague. Here he had great influence through his powerful and Scriptural reform preaching. He blazed the path for his followers by asailing fearlessly the moral corruption of the clergy, their empty and formal conduct of worship, and their wordy and fruitless disputes.

A very interesting character is John Milicz, or Militsch (d. 1374), who was a contemporary and follower of Conrad. He was of Moravian birth, but received his education at Prague and settled there. He studied both law and theology and was appointed archdeacon and preacher. He attacked vigorously the want of discipline among the clergy, and also lifted up his voice in opposition to the Roman practice of withholding the cup from the laity at the celebration of the Lord's Supper. This, as is well known, became one of the leading questions with Huss and his followers in Bohemia. When Milicz saw that his views were unacceptable to his superiors he resigned his archdeaconry and accepted a ministerial office about the church. Not officially, but in a simple conversational way, he continued to teach and preach. He used the native Bohemian tongue and talked in simple heartfelt fashion to the people, and his influence grew fast. He lived on the voluntary offerings of the people, preaching three or four times a day—probably on the streets and squares. He learned the German language so as to address himself to that portion of the population. He was skilled in the Scripture and handled it with effect in his discourses.

[1] Rothe, S. 252; Cruel, S. 615.

After a while he ceased preaching for a season of rest, and meantime determined to go to Rome and deliver at headquarters a message against corruption. He put up a notice on St. Peter's church that he would preach. His audacity could not be tolerated, and he was put in jail for his pains, and on being asked what he intended to preach he called for his Bible, which had been taken away from him, and said that was his sermon. He soon got his release, however, and returned to Prague, where he took up his preaching again with great zeal and effect. He taught young preachers, rescued fallen women, and had great influence among the people. On the death of Conrad, Milicz was appointed preacher in his place, and thus resumed his official ministry. But he did not cease to attack the vices of the clergy and the corruptions of the church in his daily preaching. He was accused of heresy, but was acquitted, and kept on preaching till his death, in 1374. Some of his sermons have come down in Latin sketches, but these of course convey no adequate conception of his power as a preacher in the common tongue.

Another of these early Bohemian reformers was Matthias of Janow (d. 1394), who was born at Prague, but educated at Paris, where he took his degree. On returning to his native city and being ordained he began to preach against the current evils, and to urge that the cup should be administered to laymen as well as priests. In fact, he went so far as actually to dispense the wine to the communicants; but he was forced by authority to desist from this. He was rather quiet in his preaching and did more by personal influence and by his writings. Still he was a preacher of no small ability. One of his best contributions to the cause of reform was that he induced a wealthy layman to build at Prague the Bethlehem Church, where the gospel should be preached to the people in their own tongue. We shall see that this church and this wise provision figured largely in the career of the great reformer whom we come now to discuss.

John Huss[1] (1373-1415) was born of humble parentage at Hussinetz, in Bohemia, in the year 1373, shortly before the death of his strongest precursor, Milicz. He

[1] All the German authorities, especially Ammon, S. 51 ff.

received only an imperfect education in youth, and his scholarship always showed the defect of his early training. As a young man, however, he attended the university at Prague and took his degrees of bachelor and master in the regular course. He was a vigorous thinker and early won and ever maintained high rank as a theologian. He also developed power as a preacher and was soon chosen to succeed a very estimable man as chief preacher at that Bethlehem Church which had been built for the very purpose of having the word preached in the Bohemian tongue. As yet he did not espouse the cause of reform, but preached with such acceptance that he drew large crowds, won the favor of all, including that of the queen, and thus firmly established himself in the confidence and affections of the people. Meantime he continued his connection with the university as lecturer on theology. The University of Prague was the first to be established in the German countries, and, though in Bohemia, was largely attended by German students and chiefly officered and governed by Germans. Huss was a patriot and jealous for his native land. He secured a better representation of Bohemians in the government of the university. This blow to their supremacy angered the Germans, and multitudes of them left—professors and students—and founded, upon invitation of the elector of Saxony, the first genuinely German university at Leipzig in 1409.

But there were not only German students at Prague. Other nationalities were also considerably represented, and among the crowd of foreign students were some Englishmen, attracted in part, as others, by the fame and standing of the university, and in part by the fact that intercourse between the two countries was stimulated at this time by a matrimonial alliance between the royal houses.[1]

Some of these English students had come under Wiclif's influence at home, and by their means the views and writings of the great English reformer became known at Prague. Thus some of Wiclif's writings came into the hands of Huss. At first he opposed the English heretic

[1] Richard II. of England had married a Bohemian princess in 1382.

—even with bitterness—but as he read to controvert he was convinced, and soon became a pronounced advocate of Wiclif's opinions.

Huss now began by tongue and pen to attack the papacy and the corruptions of the church. His course astonished his friends and aroused enemies. But once embarked upon it there was no going back, and he became both in courage and ability a worthy follower of his great English master and a worthy predecessor of Luther. His place at least is assured in the ranks of real reformers, for he made the Scriptures the basis of his opposition to the papal perversions and he wavered not, but sealed his testimony at the stake.

The attacks of Huss aroused the church authorities and he was called to account by the archbishop of Prague, who ordered many of his and Wiclif's writings to be burned. Huss justly characterized this as folly, boldly appealed to the pope, and went on his way. But the attention of the pope had already been called to Huss, and he was summoned to appear before the papal court at Rome and answer charges of heresy. This showed him that his appeal was useless and his personal safety would not be secure, so he declined to go. Upon this refusal he was, in 1410, declared a heretic and excommunicated. But he had his following at Prague and kept on his preaching, as both Savonarola and Luther, under similar circumstances, did after him. The new archbishop, however, resorted to stronger measures than his predecessor, and forbade the conduct of all religious services in Prague as long as Huss remained there. This action decided Huss to leave Prague, and he retired to his childhood home at Hussinetz, but still continued to preach, there and at other places as opportunity offered.

In 1414 the emperor Sigismund assembled at Constance the famous council which was to restore peace to the distracted church, rent by schism, disturbed by heresy, defiled by corruption. On the first two points action was taken, the last slightly touched and fatally postponed. In dealing with heresy the council soon proceeded to summon the arch-heretic Huss to appear before it and answer charges as a disturber of the peace of the church. Armed with a letter of protection from the emperor he came.

The sad and disgraceful story is soon told. Huss appeared before the council, explained his views, refused to retract what he held to be the truth, and was condemned to prison and to execution. In open council he exhibited his letter of protection and called on the emperor to acknowledge his signature and seal. Sigismund turned pale and then blushed with shame, but the imperial word was broken on the casuistical plea that it was right to break faith with a heretic.[1] After further imprisonment Huss was led to the stake and bravely died in the flames in the year 1415, just about a century before Luther nailed his famous theses on the palace church at Wittenberg and began the Reformation.

But though dead Huss lived on in his influence and writings. It belongs to general church history to trace the further progress of the Bohemian reformation, its unhappy divisions, its wars and persecutions and defeat. Numerous works of Huss remained, among them some sketches of sermons chiefly in Latin. But these cannot properly convey a satisfactory impression of his manner or power as a preacher before the people. They are poor in all rhetorical respects, bad Latin, dry, too sharply polemic. The probability is that Huss did not have especially oratorical gifts, but in his preaching he carried more weight by the nature of his utterances and by the strength and sincerity of his convictions than by those more pleasing and impressive talents which we call eloquence. But the people loved to hear him, and the history of religion in Bohemia after him is a tribute to his power with men more striking than the imperfect specimens of his sermons that have come down to us.

Mention at least should be made of the noble friend of Huss, Jerome of Prague (d. 1416). He was a knight at the court of the King of Bohemia, a well educated, much travelled, and highly eloquent man. Though not a priest he sometimes informally preached, teaching the views of Wiclif and Huss. Though dissuaded, he accompanied Huss to Constance; but his courage was at

[1] More than a hundred years later, when Luther was arraigned before the diet at Worms, and Charles V. was urged on similar grounds to recall his safe-conduct, that emperor is said to have emphatically refused, saying, "Non erubescam cum Sigismundo antecessore meo."

first not quite equal to the strain put upon it. He tried to get away, but was captured and imprisoned; under stress he renounced the views of the condemned reformers, but ashamed of his weakness he asked for another hearing. In an eloquent address, which has been preserved in a report made by some one who heard it, he renounced his weak renunciation, boldly and ably defended his real sentiments, and met his fate like a man. In 1416 he was burned on the same spot where Huss had died the year before.

Besides Bohemians there were among the Germans themselves some notable preachers of the reformatory order, who helped to prepare the hearts and minds of many of the German people for the great work of Luther and his colaborers. Among these were Jacob of Jüterbogk, John of Goch, Krafft, and others,[1] who not only opposed the general corruptions of the time, but—it is interesting to observe—especially assailed the abuse of indulgences as these had been proclaimed by Capistrano and other papal missionaries in Germany.

Perhaps the most important of these early German opponents of indulgences and the other errors was John Richsrath (d. 1481), commonly called John of Wesel, from his birthplace. He must not be confused with John Wessel, the famous teacher, mystic, and reformer of this time. Of Wesel's parents and early education little or nothing seems to be known, but it is clear that he was an educated man. He came to the University of Erfurt probably about 1440. Later he was made lecturer at Erfurt, and then doctor. He distinguished himself both as professor and preacher, and about 1450 he published a treatise against the reigning theory of indulgences. After this the pope sent Cardinal Cuso to Erfurt to preach and sell indulgences, and still later came the redoubtable Capistrano[2] on a similar mission. Wesel did not hesitate to oppose them in much the same way that Luther afterwards attacked Tetzel.

After some twenty years' service at Erfurt Wesel was for a short time at Mainz, going later to Worms, where for seventeen years he lived and preached. As a

[1] Ullmann gives, in his well-known work, a full account of all these.

[2] Above, p. 317.

preacher he took decided ground against all the more glaring corruptions of the times, and based his opposition on the Scriptures and the Augustinian theology. He is thus in many respects clearly a predecessor of Luther. In his preaching he was more brilliant and fierce than prudent, and as a consequence made enemies and provoked persecution. He was accused of heresy, and proceedings were instituted against him in 1479. The trial went against him and he was put in prison, where, in consequence of hardships too severe for his age, he died in 1481. There can be no question that traces of his work and influence at Erfurt and Worms were helpful in the struggle that was now soon to begin in Germany.

In Italy the voice of reform was not wholly still in the early and middle part of the fifteenth century. Here and there preachers of a more serious turn than the generality of priests lifted up their voices against the manifest and fearful demoralization of the times, and men like Bernardino of Siena and Gabriel Barletta spared not in their denunciations of evil present and ruin to come. But all smaller figures are dwarfed by the eminent greatness of one who, toward the close of the fifteenth century, did a work and made for himself a name as preacher that shall endure through time.

Girolamo (Jerome) Savonarola [1] was born at Ferrara in north Italy, September 21, 1452. His family were respectable and cultivated people. The boy was of a thoughtful, melancholy temperament, and while yet a youth began to think and brood upon the evils of the age. A bright vision of love crossed his path, but the maiden he sought rejected his addresses, and this disappointment increased his melancholy. Like John Chrysostom, he was repelled instead of attracted by the dissolute life of the world in which he lived, and kept himself through life austerely pure.

[1] The standard work on Savonarola is Prof. P. Villari's admirable *Life and Times of Savonarola,* well translated into English by the author's wife. It contains numerous selections from Savonarola's sermons. An edition of these by Baccini has been found useful. There are interesting studies of Savonarola in Mrs. Oliphant's *Makers of Florence,* Mr. W. D. Howells' *Tuscan Cities,* and in George Eliot's *Romola,* which also gives a very vivid sketch of the times.

In his twenty-second year he heard a sermon on the evils of the times and the need of escaping them. This chimed in with his own mood, and he determined to embrace the monastic life. But his entrance into the cloister was not managed in a way wholly to his credit. One day while the rest of the family had gone off to a festival Girolamo left his home, and, going to Bologna, entered the Dominican monastery there. He wrote back to his father an affectionate letter and explained that he had taken that course to avoid the discussion of the matter in the family, as he feared their pleadings might hinder the accomplishment of his resolution.

As a novice and student in the Order of Preachers Savonarola showed great earnestness and diligence both in study and in pious exercises. For seven years the young monk pursued his studies and his self-discipline at Bologna, and then the authorities sent him forth to begin his career as a preacher.

He began at his native Ferrara, but not with much success. He was then sent—in the same year, 1481—to Florence to teach in the famous convent of San Marco and to fill an appointment as preacher in the old church of San Lorenzo.[1] The church was, and even yet remains, an important one in Florence, and the appointment meant recognition of Savonarola's powers. But the series of sermons was a failure. The Florentines did not take kindly at first to the young monk's matter or style, and the audience dwindled to twenty-five perfunctory hearers. A few years were to work a mighty change.

After this Savonarola was sent to other places to preach. During one of his tours in north Italy, preaching much at Brescia, he grew in power before the people. Already he had found the keynote of his future deliverances, the three famous prophecies that henceforth constituted the burden of his message: (1) The church

[1] It is said to be the most ancient church in Florence, having been built in 390, and consecrated by Ambrose of Milan in 393. In Savonarola's time it had been already twice rebuilt, but on the same site and no doubt with some parts of the walls and perhaps other material remaining. Two old pulpits—apparently not now in use—decorated with fine bronze reliefs by Donatello still stand in the church, but whether they were used by Savonarola or not I do not know.

will be scourged; (2) it will be renewed; (3) all will come quickly. His preaching made a great sensation, and the country began to ring with his name and his prophecies. Meantime a chapter of the Dominican order had been held at Reggio, and at this meeting Savonarola had delivered a powerful discourse on his favorite theme. Among the hearers of this speech was that youthful prodigy of learning and piety, John Pico, Count of Mirandola. His admiration for Savonarola became warm friendship. On his return to Florence he had much to tell Lorenzo concerning the eloquence of Savonarola; and the worldly tyrant, who, with all his vices, wished the city to have the best of everything, requested the Dominican authorities to send Fra Girolamo to Florence.

Accordingly, in 1487, Savonarola comes back to the scene of his early failure; but he comes now with a consciousness of power derived from an assured conviction of his mission and from success in other fields, and moreover with such prestige as the admiration of Pico and the patronage of Lorenzo the Magnificent could give. As prior of the convent of San Marco, and preacher in the church attached to the cloister, the austere Dominican finds his work. His attitude toward Lorenzo was uncompromising from the first. He refused to flatter the brilliant and dissolute master of Florence, or in anywise to court or value his patronage. He did not mince his words when speaking of the evils in the city, and he was from first to last the friend of popular government and the foe of the Medicean tyranny. Savonarola's audiences soon overflowed the little church of San Marco, and in the Lent season of 1491 the preacher gave his sermons in the magnificent church of Santa Maria del Fiore (St. Mary of the Flower), otherwise known as the Duomo, or Cathedral, of Florence. In this spacious building thronging multitudes pressed together and stood to hear the powerful eloquence of this Dominican friar. One wonders how he could have made himself heard, but the testimony of witnesses is decisive of the fact.

On the death of Lorenzo the Magnificent, inspired to patriotism by Savonarola's preaching, Florence expelled his son Piero and reëstablished the republic. The new constitution, modelled after that of Venice, was largely formed and adopted by Savonarola's advice and influence. But he was far from being a scheming politician. He bravely and conscientiously sought by his preaching and his personal influence to reform the morals as well as the government of Florence. Personally pure, but inclined to austerity and melancholy, he was too extreme and impracticable in some of his proposed measures. But for a while it looked as if Florence would purge herself from worldly folly and be what the patriot preacher wished—a city where Christ reigned.

As always in republican governments, factions were formed in the city and party spirit ran high. There was, first, the party that favored Savonarola's ideas of government and reform; next, the opposite party, who violently strove against reform; and lastly, a less pronounced party of opposition to the rigorism of Savonarola, who might easily be made to work with the extremists upon occasion. Along with these was a small party of older citizens, friends of the Medici, who desired the return of that family, and bided their time, working with any of the others as suited their views. This political magazine only needed a spark to explode it. The spark fell. Piero di Medici made an attempt to get back into Florence. It failed, but some prominent citizens suspected of favoring his designs were burned to death by the reform party then in power, and this awakened the fierce enmities of the opposition. This was one step toward Savonarola's fall.

We must also take account of the enemies he had in the church. Since the main element of Savonarola's preaching was that which dealt with the existing decay in church and world, it was inevitable that his attack on evil should expose him to the hatred of the corrupt clergy. And two particular circumstances emphasized this general state of affairs. These were the rivalry of the Franciscan order, who were jealous of the preeminence of a Dominican; and the character of the man who from 1492 to 1503 occupied and disgraced the papal chair. This man was the infamous Roderigo Borgia, who reigned as Pope Alexander VI. It was not to be expected that a pope whose own life was an epitome of the worst vices of the age should look with satisfaction upon any effort to reform the clergy, or hear with patience the unflinching exposure and predicted scourging of the evils which afflicted the church. Some of Savonarola's utterances were reported to the pope, perhaps exaggerated and perverted—though they did not require such editing in order to excite the wrath of his unholiness—and he determined to silence the bold preacher. Various means were resorted to without avail. Once the pope invited Savonarola to Rome to confer on these matters, but Fra Girolamo was quite too wise to accept the invitation. Another time, it is said, Alexander offered the monk a cardinal's hat if he would change his course, and Savonarola replied that the only red hat he expected to wear was that of martyrdom. This may or may not be strictly true, but it is at least characteristic. Then the pope resorted to sterner measures. He commanded silence; but the Florentine government, being then in the hands of Savonarola's party, sustained the preacher. The pope then threatened the Florentine merchants in Rome with confiscation of goods. The Seignory felt the force of this argument and counselled the friar to cease preaching for a while. He obeyed; but could not—for many reasons—long remain silent, and in 1496 ascended the pulpit of St. Mark's once more, and in a series of bold sermons went on his way. This introduced the final scene. The pope excommunicated Savonarola and commanded all the clergy and good Catholics to sustain the penalty. At first the government braved the pope and still permitted Savonarola to preach, but it was an unequal fight, and as the friar's enemies in the city constantly gained ground the end was coming into view. This clerical and papal hostility was the second step toward the catastrophe.

The third and fatal cause which coöperated all along and finally precipitated Savonarola's downfall was the indiscretion of himself and his friends. Savonarola was not a man of the same make with Wiclif, Huss or Luther. In both strength of character and soundness of judgment he stands below all of these. And he made the fatal error, which these did not make, of basing his reformatory efforts on the general appeal to conscience and on his own commission as a prophet, rather than upon the Word of God. That, at moments of high ecstasy, and especially when borne along by the torrent of his own oratorical feeling, Savonarola believed he was preëminently inspired of God is no doubt true. That, in moments of depression, he doubted this, is perhaps equally true. As to the people, there were partisans of his who believed in his inspiration more fully perhaps than he did himself, and there were enemies who believed him a cheat. Between them, and of all grades, was the changeable crowd who could be led either way, according to circumstances. And thus came the end.

Among Savonarola's partisans was a certain Fra Domenico, who during the time that Savonarola was not preaching delivered a series of sermons, in which he went to great lengths in attacking the clergy and in asserting his prior's prophetic claims. He declared again and again that he was prepared to test the truth of those claims by the ordeal of fire. That is, he was willing to walk through fire along with one who opposed the claims in the belief that by a miracle he would come safely through while the opponent would perish. This bravado was finally taken up by the Franciscans, and one of their lay brethren was found who said he would accept the challenge and walk through the fire with Fra Domenico. He expected to be burned, but declared he was willing to suffer if he could thereby expose the false pretensions of Savonarola and his party. Alas! for the weaknesses of the great and good; it is the one serious blot on Savonarola that he consented to this wretched business. His compliance can doubtless be psychologically explained, but it cannot be ethically excused. It is to the shame of the city authorities that they permitted the trial to be attempted, and ordered the necessary preparations to be made in the famous square of the Seignory. Here the fuel was laid and the fires even lighted on the appointed day, in the presence of a great mixed and expectant crowd. When the champions and their partisans, including Savonarola himself, appeared, there was discussion first as to whether the men should go through with their clothes on; and, secondly, whether Fra Domenico should be allowed to carry a crucifix in his hand. These arguments occupied nearly the whole day, and in the evening a shower of rain came and put out the fire. At last the Seignory asserted the authority they ought to have used at first and forbade the trial, ordering Savonarola and his monks home. Thus the whole thing ended in a fiasco. The people, disappointed, weary, deceived, turned like hounds upon Savonarola and his friends. The mob raged through the city, and only under protection could Savonarola reach San Marco in safety as he retired from the square.

In the following weeks the tragedy ended. The government was now in the hands of the faction opposed to Savonarola, the pope and clergy were bent on his destruction, and the fatal mistake of the ordeal, and its failure, had discredited his highest claims. In vain did the preacher try to explain and justify the recent events. His last sermon was preached in San Marco in March, 1498, and in it he pathetically expressed his willingness to die for his faults. A mob assailed the convent of San Marco, which was vigorously defended by the monks, and the preacher was held responsible for the riot. Savonarola, Fra Domenico and another of his more zealous partisans were arrested and tried before a tribunal partly civil and partly ecclesiastical. The charges against them were really not worthy of serious consideration—charges of sedition in the city, deceiving the people, and heresy. But their destruction was a foregone conclusion, and what with torture and perversion, and even falsification of testimony, the case was made out, and the three men sentenced to be hanged and burned on the very spot in the Piazza della Seignoria where the fires had been lit for the ordeal. Here, on the 23d of May, 1498, the abominable sentence was executed. The old palace of the Seignory still looks down grimly on the scene, and the spot is now marked by a bronze plate, which represents the well-known features of the reformer in his monk's cowl, with a palm leaf, and an inscription which tells that after four hundred years Florence placed this memorial tablet in honor of the prophet and preacher who had there suffered for his work's sake.

As a man Savonarola was pure and pious from childhood and through life. Not even his bitterest enemies could attack him here. His disposition inclined to melancholy and austerity—a part of the hair shirt he wore next his flesh is still shown in his cell at San Marco. But he was kind and affectionate in nature, made and kept warm friends, and by his personal influence as well as his preaching did much to help and mould the characters of others. His unselfish devotion to his work is beyond all cavil, and his patriotism and love of liberty, without a trace of ambition for personal distinction or other gain for himself, are clearly written in the story of his life. His courage was great, even to death, and yet under torture he flinched and wavered. This, however, was due more to the extreme sensitiveness of his constitution than to lack of moral courage. As some one said, "He had the heart, but not the fibre, of a martyr." The difficult point in his character is that in regard to his prophetic claims. It is impossible to believe that he was a deliberate cheat. It is equally impossible to deny that he went beyond the bounds of sober reason in claiming the gift of prophecy and the immediate inspiration of God, and his consent to have his claims tested by the ordeal of fire and in the person of another is not to be defended. The difficulty is most probably and charitably to be met by the view that Savonarola was sincere in his belief of his prophetic mission, and yet could not feel always sure of it. There was a border land of fanaticism which he did not wholly escape.

As a preacher Savonarola stands among the most eminent in history. His natural gift of oratory was unquestionable. He had that nameless something which throws the spell over hearers and captures them while it lasts. Crowds flocked to hear him, and multitudes were both transiently and permanently moved and moulded by his preaching. His figure was slight but erect and firm, his complexion dark but refined, his nose aquiline, his lips full and mobile, his eye keen and flashing, his hands thin and delicate, his gestures graceful and appropriate; and his voice, at first somewhat harsh, soon was mellowed by use, and became rich, sonorous, full and distinct. In mind he was well endowed with both the reasoning and the imaginative faculty. Scholastic subtlety and acuteness are found in his sermons, as well as cleverness of speculation and sweep of fancy. His training was thorough in the Dominican curriculum, and he was ever a student and thinker. His theology was in accord with the Catholic orthodoxy of his age, having been chiefly formed by Aquinas. But his knowledge of Scripture and his reforming soul encouraged the entrance of many evangelical opinions into his sermons. Yet he was in this regard by no means the peer of the other great reformers. The Catholic elements of thought predominate in his preaching. Besides the scholastic traces, and in spite of the struggle of his better knowledge of Scripture, the allegorical method of interpretation too much prevails and mars the force of his sermons. These would not measure up to the standard set by the later reformers, but they show the resources and power of the man, and as far as reported and printed sermons can they sustain the traditional reputation of the preacher. Their language is clear, simple and pleasing, their thought and feeling elevated and strong.

With Savonarola ends the line of fore-reformers. When he was executed at Florence Luther was a fourteen-year-old lad in school at Eisenach, and helping to earn his scanty living by singing in the streets, and filling one stage of his preparation for his mighty work. Among Luther's predecessors the preëminent names are those of Wiclif, Huss and Savonarola, and the greatest of these in leadership was the first, the greatest in preaching the last. All were persecuted, two suffered martyrdom; but their work was not in vain, and their lives have counted for much among the forces for good in the world. On an old banner, painted by Fra Angelico, carried by Savonarola to call the people to worship, and preserved yet in his cell at San Marco, we read: *Nos prædicamus Christum crucifixum.*

CHAPTER XI

The Reformation, and Preaching in the Sixteenth Century

With the beginning of the great Protestant revolt from the Roman Catholic Church in the sixteenth century a new era dawns upon the world. The gathering forces of new learning, of discovery and scientific progress, and of reformatory movement within the church, which had marked the fifteenth century, all contributed their various kinds of power toward that momentous revolution.

In preaching the new note which had sounded out in the fore-reformers, but had seemed to be stifled by persecution and martyrdom, found a clearer resonance in the work of the great reformers of the sixteenth century. The voice of Savonarola had not long been hushed at Florence before the little university town of Wittenberg, in Saxony, was ringing with the bold challenge of a young monk and professor who was soon to shake the world with a power mightier than that of the eloquent Italian. And the notes were reverberated throughout all Western Europe, even on toward the end of the century, when, in 1572, the last of these strenuous reformers passed away in the sturdy Scotchman, John Knox. The voice of religious reform mingled with all other sounds of movement in this great century, and it is not easy to keep distinct the separate tones. Or, to drop the figure, all other affairs were inextricably mixed with those of religion, and the history of the Reformation is during its progress almost the history of Europe. This makes it desirable that we should give a little attention to general affairs in Western Christendom in this time.

1. Europe in the Sixteenth Century

At the end of the fifteenth century Spain, united, rich, and arrogant, assumes a great rôle in European history. And this leading place is greatly enhanced during the first half of the sixteenth century by the accession of the young king (1519) to the empire as Charles V. After him his narrow and bigoted son, Philip II., in his wars with the Netherlands and England, contrives to lower Spanish prestige in European affairs.

In Italy the old confusion still continues. The papal states, rescued by the military genius of Pope Julius II., were impoverished by the extravagance of Leo X. They played no important part as political forces in this time. Naples was a bone of contention between Spain and France, but it was held by the former. Francis I. of

France tried hard to gain possessions in northern Italy also, but, though victorious at Marignano in 1515, he was defeated at Pavia in 1525, and his attempt was unsuccessful. Still there was no sign of political unity or power for Italy as a whole.

In Germany the opening of the sixteenth century found Maximilian I. on the imperial throne, but he was no great ruler and his grasp of power was feeble. To this shadowy phantom of empire came by choice of the electors in 1519 the young Charles, King of Spain, as grandson of Ferdinand and Isabella, Duke of Burgundy and ruler of the Netherlands by virtue of descent from Charles the Bold, and heir in direct line to the Hapsburg dominions of Austria and its connections in Germany. To this was added the Spanish sovereignty over Naples and Sicily and the newly discovered countries of America. It was a strange combination of circumstances which made this young ruler heir to so great possessions, but the empire added little or nothing to his real authority and much to his burdens. He was a man of courage, wisdom, patience; but the task of regulating so many peoples of different tongues and interests, and just in the throes of the greatest religious revolution of history, was too much even for his talents as a statesman and skill as a warrior. Tired with the struggle he abdicated in 1555, leaving the Austrian possessions with the imperial dignity to his brother Ferdinand, and his other dominions to his son Philip II. of Spain. Ferdinand was not formally elected till 1558, and reigned only a few years, being succeeded by Maximilian II. The political significance of the empire was in nowise enhanced under their reigns.

For the first fifteen years of the new century Louis XII., a man of some ability, was king of France, but bequeathed to his dashing son, Francis I., the fatal policy of aggression in Italy. Francis was by no means the least able of the three brilliant sovereigns—Charles V., the emperor, and Henry VIII. of England being the other two—whose reigns distinguished the age. History has much to tell of his relations with his brother monarchs, of his persecutions of his Protestant subjects, and something of his efforts to promote culture among his people. The brief reign of Henry II. was somewhat promising, but his untimely death left confusion and trouble in France. His three sons—Francis II. (husband of Mary Stuart), Charles IX. and Henry III.—followed in rapid succession, with the shadows and shames that marked their rule. Charles IX. was on the throne when our period closes (1572) and Bartholomew's Night had not long occurred —August 24th.

In England Henry VII., sagacious and economical, built up the weakened royal power and accumulated a considerable treasure, so that his clever, able, unprincipled and tyrannical son, Henry VIII. (1509-1547), found a strong kingdom when he came to the throne. Under him and his children, Edward VI. (1547), Mary (1553), and Elizabeth (1558), with painful fluctuations, and under storm and stress, the modern England as a Protestant nation had its birth.

Turbulent and unhappy Scotland suffered its mournful defeat at Flodden under James IV. in 1513. James V. followed with a disastrous reign, and in turn left the distracted kingdom to his beautiful but ill-fated daughter, Mary Stuart (1542-1587). Long regencies and many conspiracies and tumults marked these unfortunate reigns.

Turning from political to social affairs, we remark that the life and customs of the various European peoples varied, of course, in different lands; but there were matters of general interest in which all were more or less concerned that give to the sixteenth century a place of high importance in the history of civilization. Yet in this sphere the distinctive feature still was the religious, other matters chiefly continued the impulses and conditions brought over from the fifteenth century.

The classes remained as before, but the progress of religion and culture, the upheavals and wars, the final decay of feudalism and chivalry, as understood in the Middle Ages, marked the transition to modern civilization. The great religious and political questions of the age occupied all minds, and there was much debate and change of attitude among the people. Yet the strife did not produce always the sweet flowers of piety; and moral conditions were not so profoundly changed as would seem true on first thought. Catholic writers sneer at the word "reformation" as a misnomer, and adduce sayings of Luther and other reformers in criticism of moral conditions to show that there was no real improvement under Protestant auspices. It is true that fearful evils continued to mar the face of European society, but there can be no doubt that moral reform was upon the whole advanced.

The now established use of gunpowder had revolutionized warfare, and that dreadful curse of humanity was made even more terrible and destructive than ever before. Its waste and demoralization were sad features in the life of the reforming century. Yet, in spite of wars and changes, trade and commerce increased, for the discovery of America and the enlargement of men's knowledge of other lands and contact with them stimulated industry. There were many wild financial schemes and much unrest, and yet the production and power of wealth went on. The general character of the century was one of alertness in all departments of life. The dead past was left to bury its dead, and men were busy in the living present and looking to a grander future.

In science, art and literature the age was full of activity. The discoveries of the fifteenth century had produced a wonderful interest in physical and mathematical science. Copernicus (d. 1543) propounded his theory of the solar system. Tycho Brahe pushed on astronomical science. Paracelsus (d. 1541) made great additions to knowledge in chemistry and medicine, and Francis Bacon, a bright boy of ten years of age at the end of this period, was already beginning to think and giving promise of power to come. The great artists of the Renaissance brought their lives and works over into the new century. Michel Angelo Buonarotti lived and worked on till 1563. Da Vinci (1519) and Raphael (1520) died just as the Reformation began, but Correggio (d. 1553) and Titian (d. 1576) lived through it. In the Netherlands the Van Eycks and Holbein were opening the way for their more brilliant successors, while Albert Dürer (d. 1548) and Lucas Cranach (d. 1555) were laying the foundation of modern German art.

In literature the impulse from the Revival of Letters went on with power. Learning was the delight of the age, and none of the principal lands of Europe were without distinguished representatives in the republic of letters. Spain and Italy furnished in Lope de Vega, Calderon, Cervantes, Ariosto, Tasso, and others, great names to the history of literature, while scholars in more profound fields, like Bembo, Sadolet, Bellarmine, and others, held high place. In England good old Roger Ascham, the teacher of the Princess Elizabeth, must not be forgotten, nor the famous literary men of that well-known circle which adorned her reign. But in the earlier time the leading humanist in England was the brilliant and unfortunate Sir Thomas More, the author of "Utopia," friend of Erasmus, and victim of Henry VIII. In France the scholarly work of Faber Stapulensis (Le Fèvre d'Étaples) belongs to this early period. But the leading literary genius of the time was the satirist François Rabelais (1483-1553). He was a priest upon whom his vows sat lightly, and a monk of two different orders successively without being an ornament to either. But he was a diligent student and a master of several languages, including Hebrew and Greek. His famous satire, *Gargantua and Pantagruel,* scored the evils of the time, sparing neither clergy nor pope.

The greatest of the humanists was the world-famous Desiderius Erasmus (1468-1536), born at Rotterdam, educated in his early years among the Brethren of the Common Life, but owing most of his learning to his own efforts, spurred by an indomitable thirst for knowledge and led by a clear and vigorous intellect. He travelled and studied the classics in France, England, Italy, Germany and Switzerland. Born a Dutchman he was a citizen of the world. One of his greatest services to culture and religion was the editing and publishing of the Greek New Testament. He also wrote a book on the Art of Preaching, and numerous other works, one of the most famous and influential of which was the satire, *Encomium Moriae* (*Laus Stultitiae,* "Praise of Folly"), written in elegant Latin, and dedicated to Sir Thomas More in playful punning upon his name and the Greek title. In the book Folly praises herself as one of the great powers of the world, and thus holds up to ridicule the sins and weaknesses of the age. Prelates and preachers are unsparingly handled, and thus the author served the reform spirit by attacking the grosser evils of the day. But

Luther well said of him that he showed the evil without the remedy.[1]

Along with Erasmus should be named the great German humanist, John Reuchlin (1455-1522), the famous scholar and jurist, the uncle and helper of Philip Melanchthon, the fine Hebrew student and teacher, the friend and maker of scholars, the author of many books. Nor must we forget the knightly friend of Luther, Ulrich von Hutten (1480-1523), scholar, poet, satirist and letter writer, whose trenchant pen and cultured mind were keen blades in the fight against churchly corruption.

2. Course and Effects of the Reformation

The particular events of the Reformation can for our purposes be better considered in connection with the developments in preaching and the lives of preachers. Here it will suffice merely to glance at the general course and effects of the movement.

Those loud calls for reform in doctrine and morals which had sounded out in the two preceding centuries grew in volume, and had to be heard even by the unwilling in the sixteenth century. The storm center was Germany; the occasion well known. In the year 1517 a Dominican friar of considerable talent as a popular preacher, John Tetzel by name, was appointed by superior ecclesiastical authorities to preach and sell indulgences in Saxony. He made a hawking peddler's affair of it, and is said to have declared that as soon as the coin jingled in his box a soul would fly out of purgatory.

Tetzel's conduct aroused the young Martin Luther, Augustinian monk and professor in the Saxon university of Wittenberg, and induced him to attack the practice of dispensing indulgences. This he did by posting a series of ninety-five theses, or propositions, on the door of the castle church at Wittenberg as a public challenge to disputation on the points involved. The theses were read far and wide and created a mighty stir. With this beginning events moved on. Efforts were made by the pope and his partisans to stop Luther from going further,

[1] "Satisfecit quod malum ostendit; at bonum ostendere et in terram promissionis ducere non potuit." Words often quoted.

but to no purpose. Debate only widened and intensified the breach. Luther soon had a following all over Germany. The great events of the Reformation followed fast, and soon involved all Europe. In Switzerland, first at Zürich and later at Geneva, reforming doctrines spread. Even Italy and Spain were somewhat touched by the movement, and in northern and eastern Europe the leaven worked. France was deeply moved, but the persecuting policy of Francis and his successors made the reformers mostly exiles. In England and Scotland, also, the doctrines of the Reformation found acceptance, and wrought out their well-known historic fruits. The effects produced by the Reformation upon the life, the thought and the subsequent history of the world were far-reaching and permanent, especially in the religious sphere.

Looking over the whole field we see that thenceforth the western world has two leading forms of the Christian faith, with many variations on the Protestant side. A new time has come for Christianity. No more is it Rome and heretics, but now it is Rome and Protestantism. In some lands one, in some the other, is in the ascendant; but the history of preaching, as well as of all the other institutions of Christianity, must henceforth be written from two different points of view.

The characteristic of Protestantism was its revolt from a corrupted church on the basis of the supreme authority of the Word of God. This character it has preserved in the main, and from this fundamental principle there have flowed important consequences. One of these has been the great variations among the Protestants themselves. This came from asserting the rights of private judgment in the interpretation of Scripture and of freedom to choose one's belief. Thus what has been lost to unity has been gained to liberty, though only slowly and by degrees has true religious freedom gained a sure and permanent place in even Protestant countries. Another important result has been the parallel march of reverence and criticism in handling the Bible. In some cases reverence has lapsed into literalism, in others criticism has passed into rejection; but the sound mean of an intelligent acceptance of the Bible properly interpreted as the norm of religious belief and practice has held its own and produced splendid results in the spread and maintenance of Christian truth. The far-reaching effect of this principle on preaching we shall see later.

The effect of the Reformation on the Roman Catholic Church has been the seemingly paradoxical one of both weakening and strengthening it. The rivals of Rome's exclusive claim to be the church of God on earth had hitherto been the old and decrepit East and the scattering sects of so-called heretics who had arisen here and there to protest, to suffer, to decline. But now that claim was challenged by representatives of the highest culture and noblest piety in every land of Europe. The movement was too general to be put down as merely a heresy, and too vigorous to be ignored or cajoled.

On the other hand the forces of reform within the church gained power. The corruption of morals which had been one of the prime causes of the Protestant revolt was greatly checked. There has been no Borgia among the popes since the Reformation. Also the pious elements within the old church asserted themselves, and both charitable and missionary enterprises received great stimulus. And finally the great Council of Trent, which was called to deal with all the questions raised by Protestantism, reassured good Catholics everywhere by removing some crying abuses and by putting forth in remarkably clear form the essential doctrines of the Catholic faith. That council, forced by Luther's revolution, is rightly regarded as one of the mightiest bulwarks of the Roman church, giving it a new and stronger lease on life.

3. Relation of the Reformation to Preaching

We come now to consider the more particular relation of the Reformation to preaching. It is at once apparent how close that relation is. The great events and achievements of that mighty revolution were largely the work of preachers and preaching; for it was by the Word of God through the ministry of earnest men who believed, loved and taught it, that the best and most enduring work of the Reformation was done. And, conversely, the events and principles of the movement powerfully reacted on preaching itself, giving it new spirit, new power, new forms. So that the relation between the Reformation and preaching may be succinctly described as one of mutual dependence, aid and guidance.

This applies chiefly, of course, to Protestant preaching, but the Catholic pulpit also was in some degree stimulated and otherwise wholesomely affected by the movement. And thus, in the most general view, a distinctly new epoch in the history of preaching meets us now, and the greatest and most fruitful one since the fourth century. Great as was the Catholic preaching of the twelfth and thirteenth centuries it is not to be compared with that of the sixteenth century reformers either in its character or in its enduring results. Well does Christlieb[1] say: "The age of the Reformation makes the deepest cleft, the sharpest turning-point in the historical development of Christian preaching, as to contents and form, spirit and character." This new character of preaching is commonly recognized by Protestant writers, and its causes and elements assigned with substantial unanimity of judgment. The points are well summarized by Broadus[2] as being: (1) a revival of preaching, (2) a revival of Biblical preaching, (3) a revival of controversial preaching, and (4) a revival of preaching upon the doctrines of grace. Catholic writers also recognize a new era in preaching, but naturally give both the character and causes a different statement from that of Protestants. We shall see more of this when we come to study the Catholic preaching of the age,[3] but here it is proper to take the Protestant point of view.

Discussion of the personality and preaching of individuals among the reformers will be given in the sketches that are to follow; but in viewing the general character of Reformation preaching it will be well to keep clearly before us the following points: (1) The debt of Reformation preaching to the new age; (2) The new emphasis given to preaching as a vital element of Christian worship and life; (3) The influence of their conflict with error upon the preaching of the reformers; (4) The place and use of Scripture in their sermons; (5) The homiletical methods of the time as shown in some of the leading reformers.

[1] Art. in Herzog, Bd. 18, supplement.
[2] *Hist. Prea.*, p. 113 ff.
[3] Below, Chap. XV.

(1.) The Reformation was a part, and a very large part, of that general forward movement in Western Christian civilization which is the glory of the fifteenth and sixteenth centuries. Now the Christian world was emerging from mediævalism, as just a thousand years before it had passed out of antiquity. But how different were the conditions into which these two momentous turning points led! Then it was a fall, now it was a rise; then it was a passage from decay to chaos, now from a lower to a higher civilization; the fifth and sixth centuries trembled with despair, the fifteenth and sixteenth quivered with hope. Preaching felt the throb.

The discoveries of science and navigation enlarged the thoughts of men, the new methods of warfare made great political changes, the art of printing introduced a new age in literature, the revival of classical learning and the new birth of art gave culture a higher tone—and all, as we have seen, quickened the mental energies of mankind. Now, as preaching is in large part and essentially an intellectual exercise and one of the forces of culture, it was inevitable that it should respond to this new breath of life in the world of thought. And it did. There is a new intellectual vigor in preaching, a fresh and strong grasp of mind, which is in notable contrast with the pulpit work of the times immediately preceding. And it is natural that this should be especially true of Protestant preaching, because Protestantism was the party of progress in the religious world.

Also in the sphere of general social and political life the tokens of a new time were not wanting. Feudalism had run its course, the burgher class had come to power, and now, too, though but little as yet and slowly, the great common people must be reckoned with as a force in human affairs. In various ways the right of the common man to be heard and considered is gaining recognition. The Peasants' War, with its mainly just and reasonable demands for popular rights, is one of the many indications in this direction. Popular preaching and the translation of the Bible into the speech of the people show that this recognition of the great masses of humanity was germane to the religious revolution of the time. Luther was himself a peasant's son, and, though he did not approve of the Peasants' War, he never lost his sympathy for the class from which he sprang. In every age the pulpit has had distinguished representatives who stood with and for the people in their aspirations for an enlargement of rights and privileges in social and political life, and this sympathy has not failed to impart vigor and strength to preaching. It was so during the Reformation.

(2.) And now, also, there was laid a new and mighty emphasis on preaching. Not for long centuries had the office been held in such high regard as it won during the Reformation. There were several ways in which this renewed interest found expression.

We have seen how, in the ages of decline, preaching was neglected by the clergy. The preaching orders of monks were long a protest against this neglect, but now they, too, had fallen into decay. Wiclif's "poor priests" were also a rebuke to the negligent clergy, but the Lollards had been put down. The neglect was general, and there were many complaints, but the diligence of the reformers in preaching is something marvellous. Both Luther and Calvin were indefatigable preachers, and their example was contagious.

It is true that the reformers used other means to promote their cause. They invoked and employed the aid of the civil powers in the different ways appropriate to the different countries in which they labored. Thus Luther leaned on the Elector of Saxony, and made his famous appeal to the princes and nobles of Germany; Zwingli, Calvin and the other Swiss reformers sought and secured the coöperation of the councils of the cities; in England, through all the vicissitudes of the reform movement, the prelates and preachers were much mixed up with the court and government; and in Scotland Knox was in constant touch with the Lords of the Congregation and in continual conflict with Mary Stuart. The reformers also made diligent and efficient use of the press and of correspondence, both public and private. Nor did they fail to employ teaching, personal influence, discussion and debate. In fact, every legitimate means of advancing their cause seems to have been used, but none the less it remains true that their chief instrument was the preaching of the Word of God, and that the most of them were exceedingly diligent in the work. A few examples will abundantly illustrate this point.

As is well known,[1] Luther was reluctant to enter on the work of preaching, and only did so at the request of his ecclesiastical superiors while still a monk, in 1515. At once, however, he began to realize the value of preaching, and the orator's instinct within him was awakened, so that he sometimes preached as many as four times a day. After his work as a reformer was fully under way his diligence in preaching was one of his distinguishing marks. During 1529, it is recorded,[2] he preached three or four times a week; in 1541, often four times on a Sunday and two or three times in the week; on holidays commonly twice. His theory grew out of his own practice. In his *Table Talk,*[3] speaking of the urgency of his friends about his preaching, he says: "I am now aged, and have had much labor and pains. Nothing causes Osiander's pride more than his idle life; for he preaches but twice a week, yet has a yearly stipend of four hundred guilders." With such teaching and example before them, it is no wonder to find that Luther's friends and fellow-laborers were likewise zealous preachers and magnified their office by much use.

Calvin's astonishing diligence is also matter of history. Well does Broadus[4] say: "The extent of his preaching looks to us wonderful. While lecturing at Geneva to many hundreds of students (sometimes eight hundred), while practically a ruler of Geneva and constant adviser of the Reformed in all Switzerland, France and the Netherlands, England and Scotland, and while composing his so extensive and elaborate works, he would often preach every day. For example, I notice that the two hundred sermons on Deuteronomy, which are dated, were all delivered on week days in the course of little more than a year, and sometimes on four or five days in succession."

The Zürich reformers were no less busy. Zwingli had set the example of frequent preaching. Leo Jud wore

[1] Nebe, *Zur Geschichte der Predigt,* Bd. II., S. 1.
[2] Nebe, *op. cit.,* S. 5.
[3] Hazlitt's ed., Bohn's Lib., p. 188.
[4] *Hist. Prea.,* p. 121 f.

himself out at it. Bullinger often preached six or seven times a week, till, in his later years, the council, warned by Jud's breakdown, interposed, gave him an assistant, and forbade his preaching more than twice a week.[1]

In England the "unpreaching prelates" were the object of fierce attack by the reformers, who took good care that their own example should enforce their polemic. In his famous *Sermon of the Plough*[2] sturdy old Latimer pays his respects to "unpreaching prelates, lording loiterers, and idle ministers" in these terms: "But this much I dare say, that since lording and loitering hath come up, preaching hath come down, contrary to the Apostles' time; for they preached and lorded not, and now they lord and preach not. For they that are lords will go ill to plough; it is no meet office for them; it is not seeming for their estate. Thus came up lording loiterers; thus crept in unpreaching prelates, and so have they long continued." Further on he continues: "And now I would ask a strange question: Who is the most diligent bishop and prelate in all England, that passes all the rest in doing his office? I can tell, for I know who it is; I know him well. But now I think I see you listening and hearkening that I should name him. There is one that passes all the others, and is the most diligent prelate and preacher in all England. And will ye know who it is? I will tell you—it is the Devil. He is the most diligent preacher of all others; he is never out of his diocese; he is never from his cure; you shall never find him unoccupied; he is ever in his parish; he keeps residence at all times; you shall never find him out of the way; call for him when you will he is ever at home. He is the most diligent preacher in all the realm; he is ever at his plough; no lording or loitering can hinder him; he is ever applying his business; you shall never find him idle, I warrant you." Of Latimer himself, Hooper,[3] Coverdale, Jewel,[4] and many others there are records and statements to the effect of their faithful attention to the preaching part of their work. The same is true also of Knox and his fellow-workers in Scotland.

[1] For further particulars see below, pp. 408, 411, 415.
[2] Fish, *Masterpieces,* I., p. 134.
[3] Below, p. 497. [4] Below, p. 508.

Among the reformers preaching resumes its proper place in worship. The elaborate ritual of the Catholic service had made the sermon but a small affair; the celebration of the mass had become the center of worship, and around that much ceremonial had gathered, so that but little stress was placed upon the reading and exposition of the divine Word. But in the reformed services the mass is abolished, and the exposition of Scripture becomes the main thing. The Lord's Supper is observed periodically, but not at every service. Thus preaching becomes more prominent in worship than it had been perhaps since the fourth century.

Nebe [1] mentions the oft-quoted remark of Luther, that preaching is the most important part of the worship, and illustrates Luther's high regard for preaching by a number of quotations from his sermons, in which he speaks of preaching as "the power and strength of Christendom," and as being the office of teaching all the virtues and duties of Christianity, of converting and edifying souls, and the like. But in all this we must remember that Luther was looking upon preaching as the exposition of the Word of God, and by no means as a man's oratorical performance. Thus in his *Table Talk* he says:[2] "I am sure and certain, when I go up to the pulpit to preach or read, that it is not my word I speak, but that my tongue is the pen of a ready writer, as the Psalmist has it. God speaks in the prophets and men of God, as St. Peter in his epistle says: The holy men of God spake as they were moved by the Holy Ghost. Therefore we must not separate or part God and man, according to our natural reason or understanding. In like manner every hearer must say: I hear not St. Paul, St. Peter, or a man speak, but God himself." So in exalting preaching he was not lifting up the preacher, but the message that he brings from God to the people. This high view of preaching was shared by the other reformers, and became one of the distinctive notes of the Reformation.

There is no doubt that in Protestant worship—especially in the Reformed churches—this tendency went too far, and in course of time the sermon too much encroached upon the other parts of the service. But

[1] *Op. cit.*, S. 6 ff. [2] P. 16.

even in those Protestant churches, as the Lutheran and English, which retained much of the historic liturgy rendered into the language of the people, the sermon acquired a greater place in the order of worship than it had for ages enjoyed. This naturally tended to dignify the preaching office in the minds both of the preacher himself and of his hearers, and with increased respect came increased power.

Along with this higher estimation of preaching it was natural that there should be required a better preparation, both intellectual and spiritual, in the preachers. The mental and moral unfitness of very many of the clergy under the old conditions was one of the main objects of attack and of reform. The reformers were bound by every reason to see that in this respect there should be great and manifest improvement. And they were very careful of it. Certainly some unfit men—ill-educated and ill-regulated—got into the Protestant ministry; but this was the exception. All the reformers insisted on a high standard of religious and educational preparation for the pulpit. It is well known that the leading reformers were themselves men of liberal culture. On Luther's learning—admitted by all—Brömel [1] well remarks that he was a "universally trained" man, all the elements of the culture of his time appear in his sermons: the Latin classics, philosophy, dialectic, natural history—as far as understood in his days—history, the church fathers and other ecclesiastical writers. At twenty-four years of age young John Calvin was one of the most accomplished scholars of the time, and through life a hard-working student. Law, languages, theology, philosophy, history, to say nothing of all Biblical lore, were at his finger's ends. Zwingli was full of the Humanist culture of the age, and his chief impulse as a reformer came from this side. Œcolampadius, Butzer, Capito, Pellican, Jud, Myconius, Bullinger, were all lights of learning as well as of reform. In England Latimer, Cranmer, Ridley, Hooper, Coverdale, Parker, Jewel, and many others were highly educated and learned men. Knox, also, though not so great in this direction as in others, and by no means the peer of Luther or Calvin, was not deficient in such education as

[1] *Homiletische Charakterbilder,* S. 93 ff.

could be had in his time and country, diligently improved his opportunities to study with Calvin while an exile at Geneva, and took up late in life the study of Hebrew and Greek.[1]

Nor were the reformers content to be men of large culture themselves alone, and simply set the example of diligence in study; they were concerned to teach the young men who labored with them and should come after them. Wittenberg and Geneva were seats of Protestant learning, and they were thronged with students from all over Europe. Cranmer was careful to provide for the training of the future leaders of the English church, and brought to Oxford and Cambridge such men as Peter Martyr Vermigli, Martin Butzer, John à Lasco and others. While in the *Table Talk* Luther again and again insists that the preacher should be simple in speech, so that the people could understand him, he by no means undervalues learning, as the following passages show:[2] "A preacher should be a logician and a rhetorician, that is, he must be able to teach and to admonish. When he preaches touching an article he must, first, distinguish it. Secondly, he must define, describe and show what it is. Thirdly, he must produce sentences out of Scriptures, therewith to prove and strengthen it. Fourthly, he must with examples explain and declare it. Fifthly, he must adorn it with similitudes; and, lastly, he must admonish and rouse up the lazy, earnestly reprove all the disobedient, all false doctrine, and the authors thereof." Again, "Young divines ought to study Hebrew, to the end they may be able to compare Greek and Hebrew words together, and discern their properties, natures and strength."

This culture was required not only by the evident proprieties in the case, and by the very nature of the preaching office, but was emphasized by the peculiar circumstances in which the reformers found themselves.

(3.) The stern conflict which the reformers had to wage with error demanded abilities and training of no mean order. The task of Protestantism was not easy. Centuries had hardened into fixed custom the abuses against which the reformers fought; their opponents were often men of keen dialectical skill, and the early

[1] Broadus, *Hist. Prea.*, p. 194 f. [2] Pp. 188, 193.

successes of Protestantism stirred the defenders of the old order to unusual exertions and better training. On the other side, the very character of the errors which they had to oppose served to quicken and render more earnest the preaching of the reformers.

The scandalous corruption among the clergy, and, in fact everywhere, greatly aroused earnest souls who felt that this condition of affairs should and could be amended. Preaching must always amount to something when it has definite evils to attack and specific warnings to give. And the awakening of the general conscience, which has already been adduced as one of the causes of the Reformation, powerfully fortified to the hearers the appeals and warnings and denunciations of the preachers. The consciousness of a high and holy mission to uplift and purify the characters of men by the preaching of the Word of God had a large and fruitful place in the minds and hearts of the reformers.

Necessarily, also, the preaching of these men was much occupied with errors of belief, and was therefore largely polemical and doctrinal. Luther says;[1] "Wickliffe and Huss assailed the immoral conduct of the papists; but I chiefly oppose and resist their doctrine; I affirm roundly and plainly that they preach not the truth. To this I am called; I take the goose by the neck and set the knife to its throat. When I can show that the papists' doctrine is false, as I have shown, then I can easily prove that their manner of life is evil. For when the word remains pure, the manner of life, though something therein be amiss, will be pure also." Externalism had obscured the truth and hidden away the heart of the gospel. The true nature of Christ's work for men and of the means whereby its blessed fruits were available to them must be freshly and more clearly explained. And so the great core of reform preaching is justification by faith—that gracious act of a sovereign but loving God whereby the repentant and believing sinner is for Christ's sake pardoned and acquitted. Penances and purgatory, the almost divine mediation of the Virgin and the saints, the whole theory of merits and indulgences, every form of human satisfaction for sin, must give way before the true doctrine of salvation by grace through faith in an all-sufficient Saviour.

[1] *Table Talk*, p. 186.

"Christ and him Crucified," in a clearer light and a fuller tone, is the burden of the preaching; "justification by faith without the works of the law" is the keystone of the doctrine. "Protestantism was born of the doctrines of grace, and in the proclamation of these the Reformation preaching found its truest and highest power." [1]

(4.) But the glory of Reformation preaching—that great principle in which all others are necessarily involved—was its use of Scripture. In the hands of the reformers the Word of God again comes into its heritage and rules the pulpit.

In the first place the Bible is recognized as the supreme authority in matters of faith and practice—*credenda et agenda.* The great reformers held fast this principle, which has already been dwelt on as the characteristic element of a true reform in Christian doctrine, worship and life.[2] They naturally respected much the feelings, convictions and reasonings of the Christian mind, believing that the Holy Spirit enlightens and leads those who truly trust in God and seek to know and do his will. But these were secondary and subordinate means; if these judgments were in accord with the Word of God they could be accepted, but that Word must be the decisive test, the ultimate appeal. Further, the reformers, though revolutionary, were not disposed to break wholly with the past. Tradition was allowed some place, and many beliefs and practices, more or less modified to suit the new order of things, were retained which might better have been spared. Luther was rather more conservative than Zwingli and Calvin, and the English reformers decidedly more so than Knox. None were ready to go with the extremists of their party, and still less were any disposed to favor the fanatical schemes of those who under cover of reformation would introduce anarchy. This cautious temper is responsible for the retention in some Protestant bodies of some practices—as infant baptism—which had been sanctioned and established by the Catholic Church, but without Scripture authority. But notwithstanding these deficiencies the main contention of the reformers as to the authority of the Bible was clearly and bravely maintained. Tradition and "the Christian consciousness"—

[1] Broadus, *Hist. Prea.*, p. 117. [2] *Ante*, p. 315 f.

to use a modern expression—were firmly held subordinate to Scripture.

This fundamental attitude of the reformers appears constantly in their writings and sermons, and is one of the commonplaces of the history of the Reformation in all lands. A few illustrations, however, may not be superfluous.

Brömel [1] speaks of this use of Scripture by the reformers as "one of the levers by which they removed the rubbish in the old church and brought out to light again the everlasting light of the gospel." Besides Luther he instances Urbanus Regius, Brentz, Cœlius, Corvinus, Dietrich, Mathesius, and others among the pupils and friends of the great leader, who "all not only preached the Word of God, but they so preached it that the Word was quite the main thing, the art of preaching the subsidiary thing." In Luther's *Table Talk,*[2] among many others, are found these characteristic utterances: "A theologian should be thoroughly in possession of the basis and source of faith—that is to say, the Holy Scriptures. Armed with this knowledge it was that I confounded and silenced all my adversaries; for they seek not to fathom and understand the Scriptures; they run over them negligently and drowsily; they speak, they write, they teach, according to the suggestion of their heedless imaginations. My counsel is, that we draw water from the true source and fountain, that is, that we diligently search the Scriptures. He who wholly possesses the text of the Bible is a consummate divine." Again, "Let us not lose the Bible, but with diligence and in fear and invocation of God, read and preach it. While that remains and flourishes, all prospers with the state; it is head and empress of all arts and faculties."

Calvin, of course, repeatedly expresses the same profound conviction, and in a sermon on 2 Tim. 3:16, 17, "All Scripture is given by inspiration of God," etc., he unfolds in detail the supreme authority and sufficiency of the written Word. The first three of the sermons in Bullinger's *Decades* [3] are devoted to the Word of God,

[1] *Op. cit.,* S. 98. [2] P. 3.

[3] *The Decades of Henry Bullinger, that is, Fifty Sermons Divided into Five Decades;* Parker Soc., ed. Thos. Harding. This is a reprint of an English translation published in 1577 and 1587.

and the nature and use of Scripture are at length unfolded. Among many strong sayings the following occurs toward the end of the second sermon as a summary:[1] "Dearly beloved, this hour ye have heard our bountiful Lord and God, 'who would have all men saved and to come to the knowledge of the truth,' how he hath revealed his word to all men throughout the whole world, to the intent that all men in all places, of what kind, age, or degree soever they be, may know the truth and be instructed in the true salvation; and may learn a perfect way to live rightly, well and holily, so that the man of God may be perfect, instructed to all good works. For the Lord in the word of truth hath delivered to his church all that is requisite to true godliness and salvation. Whatsoever things are necesary to be known touching God, the works, judgments, will and commandments of God, touching Christ, our faith in Christ, and the duties of an holy life! all those things, I say, are fully taught in the Word of God. Neither needeth the church to crave of any other, or else with men's supplies to patch up that which seemeth to be wanting in the Word of the Lord."

The English reformers are equally emphatic. In 1534 a set of instructions was drawn up (probably by Cranmer himself) [2] and sent to all the bishops for the guidance of the clergy. One of the items is as follows: "That from henceforth all preachers shall purely, sincerely, and justly preach the Scripture and Word of Christ, and not mix them up with man's institutions, nor make them believe that the force of God's law and man's law is like; nor that any man is able or hath power to dispense with God's law." Latimer, in his third sermon on the Lord's Prayer,[3] thus speaks: "And because the Word of God is the instrument and fountain of all good things, we pray to God for the continuance of his word; that he will send godly and well learned men amongst us, which may be able to declare us his will and pleasure; so that we may glorify him in the hour of our visitation, when God shall visit us, and reward every one according unto his desert."

[1] *Decades,* Vol. I., p. 69.
[2] *Works of Abp. Cranmer,* Parker Society, ed. J. E. Cox, p. 461.
[3] *Sermons of Bp. Latimer,* Parker Soc., p. 354.

It follows from what has been said that the reformers gave to Scripture a better interpretation than that which had prevailed before. The petty and often ridiculous allegorizing which marred even the best mediæval preaching finds little or no place in the sermons of the reformers, save a trace here and there in Luther and some of his followers. It is refreshing indeed to pass from the wild and baseless spiritualizing of the mediæval preachers to the sober, clear, grammatical, and instructive expositions of Luther, Zwingli, Calvin, and others of their schools. Calvin's commentaries on the Bible are still very valuable, and have scarcely ever been surpassed for power to seize surely and express strongly the exact meaning of the sacred Word. In giving this new direction to preaching and basing it thus securely upon a sensible and reasoned interpretation of the Bible the reformers made one of the greatest possible contributions to Christian life and progress.

Again, it naturally follows that among the materials of reformatory preaching the Scriptures held the post of honor and power. Tales of the saints and other stories are banished. The petty fables and impossible adventures which had formed so large an element of mediæval Catholic preaching do not appear in the sermons of the Protestant reformers. Nor do we find in so large a degree the refinements of scholasticism, though this still shows traces of itself and leaves both in the structure and contents of sermons permanent impression. In Luther's earlier sermons there is more of it than in his later, and the dogmatic bent both of his and Calvin's followers is a well known affair of theological history. But all fair allowances and subtractions duly made, it stands out clearly and impressively true that the warp and filling of Reformation preaching was the Word of God.

Nor is it mere citation of texts, more or less apposite as proof of doctrine, that makes the bulk of this Scriptural content. There had been much of this sort of employment of Scripture in the mediæval preachers. But now the pulpit deals more in the exact application of Biblical passages to matters of doctrine; and above all, as we shall presently see, in exposition of the Word as the homiletical form of preaching. All three of the great reformers delighted in expository preaching, and this was one of the most valuable and fruitful and enduring results of their labors. To this day the Lutheran and Presbyterian preachers have had among them many able and distinguished expounders of the Word.

(5.) The homiletical methods of the reformers of course varied with individuals among them. Yet in a general way it may be said that their exposition of Scripture naturally led them back toward the ancient homily as the prevailing sermon form. This tendency was increased by the reaction against scholasticism with its minute distinctions and subdivisions. There is less of logical analysis and of oratorical movement in the sermons of the reformers than in those of many of their predecessors and followers. But still there is no complete recurrence to the old loose homily, no entire renunciation of the more compact homiletical structure which was largely the gift of scholasticism to the pulpit. But this matter of method can best be presented by examples from some of the leading preachers.

Luther cannot be said to have had a rigid and unvarying homiletical method.[1] In his earlier work the traces of his Catholic training appear in the stiffer scholastic form than is to be found in his later sermons. In the *House-Postils,* as reported by Dietrich and others, the other extreme of free and easy conversational comment appears. In the few sermons (some of the *Church-Postils*) which he prepared by writing while at the Wartburg, there is naturally more attention to form and expression than he could bestow in his subsequent strenuous life; and it is said that he himself regarded these as his best sermons. But in the larger number of his discourses, as reported by Cruciger and others, we have his most characteristic method of verse by verse comment on the Gospel or Epistle for the day, or on some extended passage of his own selection. Luther's views of preaching, as being properly an exposition of the Word of God, are unfolded in many places in his sermons and his *Table Talk.* He bent to his work all the faculties of his nature and the

[1] See the excellent discussions in the works of Brömel and Nebe, which, however, have been tested by a measure of independent study.

culture of his mind. His exposition is usually marked by sobriety of judgment, but sometimes drops too easily into allegorizing and into polemics. But both these imperfections are easily understood when his training and nature, his circumstances and incitements are taken into account. All subtractions duly made, it remains that Luther was a mighty expounder of the Scriptures, and he left this method of preaching as a rich legacy to his followers.

Calvin began his career as an expository preacher while yet a young law student at Bruges, when, in an informal way, at the earnest request of the people, he taught the Scriptures to small gatherings. It became the delight and the established method of his life. His preaching differed from Luther's as the men themselves differed.[1] It has less of fancy, less of warmth, less of popular appeal, but more of steadiness, of logical connection, of severely exact interpretation. While he also commonly employed the verse by verse comment, both unity of theme and logical connection of thought are much in evidence. The notable series of sermons on the *Divinity and Glory of Christ*[2] are chiefly expository discourses on passages from the First Epistle to Timothy, with some from other Scriptures. While Calvin preached without notes, his delivery was deliberate enough to permit a reporter to get his exact language, and thus a large number of his sermons have come down.[3] They are prevailingly expository. The structure is no more than what was natural to a very orderly mind which had no need to exert itself to produce connected thinking. The sermon published in Fish's *Masterpieces of Pulpit Eloquence*[4] is on bearing afflictions. The two thoughts that trials are a necessary part of Christian experience, and that under them we have the best of consolations, are the ever-recurring theme, and under a variety of expository comment and illustration, they pervade the entire discourse.

[1] There is a striking parallel in Broadus, *Hist. Prea.*, p. 118 ff. Hering also, *Gesch. der Pred.*, S. 110 ff has some good observations on Calvin as compared with Luther.

[2] I used an old French edition of these while in Geneva, and there is also an old American edition of many of them in a volume of translated discourses of both Luther and Calvin, which has been found serviceable. [3] See Hering, *l. c.* [4] Vol. II., p. 12.

Of the Zürich reformers Zwingli was also prevailingly expository in method, but, strictly speaking, no specimens of his sermons survive. Bullinger[1] left a very large number of discourses, some in the crude old Swiss-German tongue, but many also carefully done into Latin by himself, most likely after preaching. Of these the famous *Decades,* a series of fifty discourses divided into five tens, are a treatise on theology in the form of sermons. They are without text and are topical, but they afford example of the preacher's careful interpretation of Scripture, and suggest the pains and clearness which must have characterized his more strictly expository addresses. In their English dress they were translated during the reign of Edward VI., and became one of the training books for the Anglican clergy. The style is clear, the tone spiritual and devout, the arrangement and division logical and perspicuous. He usually gives at the end a brief and clear summary of the thought. They naturally lack some of the life and vigor of spoken discourse.

The preachers of the English Reformation are not so predominantly expository in method as their brethren on the Continent, inclining more to the topical manner, and even when interpretative comment is followed, the adherence to text is perhaps less marked. Lesson and application are rather to the fore than exegesis. Yet there are instructive examples of pulpit exposition among the remains of the great English divines of the period. Even Latimer[2] has a vigorous and suggestive series on the Lord's Prayer, which were delivered in 1552 before the Duchess of Suffolk, at Grimsthorpe Castle, Lincolnshire. He often strays off, as is his manner, but there is many a shrewd and luminous unfolding of the meaning of the Word. Among the few sermons that have come down from Bishop Hooper[3] is a striking series on the prophet Jonah, delivered before Edward VI. and his council in the year 1550. He thus states[4] his reasons for taking this book as his theme: "This prophet

[1] *Bullinger's Decades,* Parker Soc., four vols.

[2] *Sermons of Latimer,* Parker Soc.

[3] *Early Writings of Bishop Hooper,* Parker Soc., ed. Samuel Carr.

[4] *Op. cit.,* p. 445.

have I taken to interpretate for two causes. The one, to declare unto the king's majesty and his most honorable council, that the doctrine we preach unto his majesty's subjects is one and the same with the prophets' and apostles', and as old as the doctrine of them both, and not as new as these papists, and new learned men of papistry would bear the people in hand. The second cause is to declare which way the sinful world may be reconciled unto God. And for the better understanding of the prophet I will divide him into four parts. The first containeth into what danger Jonas fell by disobeying of God's commandment. The second part containeth how Jonas used himself in the fish's belly. The third part containeth the amendment and conversion of the Ninivites at the preaching of Jonas. The fourth part containeth an objurgation and rebuke of God because Jonas lamented the salvation of the people and city." Besides this general division each discourse is again divided into appropriate parts. While there is much of historical comment and lesson, the application to existing conditions in England is evidently the main thing in the preacher's mind. From Bishop Jewel there remains among other sermons a series on the Epistles to the Thessalonians.[1] These were his last discourses to his flock at Salisbury, and were published from his notes after his death, by his friend John Garbrand. They are replete with Jewel's learning and earnestness, but hardly take very high rank as expository discourses.

CHAPTER XII

Preachers of the Reformation in Germany and German Switzerland

From our sketch of the Reformation and its effects it is fitting that we now come to a more particular study of the leading preachers of the great movement in the lands affected by it; and the natural thing is to begin with Germany and the great leader there.

[1] *Works of Bishop Jewel*, Parker Society's edition.

1. Martin Luther (1483-1546).

Martin Luther,[1] the son of peasant parents, was born at the little village of Eisleben, in Saxony, November 10, 1483. His father and mother were persons of vigorous mould and strong character, and they brought up their children with rigid severity and yet with parental affection, and nourished them in the simple Catholic piety common among the German peasantry at that time.

The Luthers were poor, but by one means and another Martin was sent to school at different places. When about fifteen years old he is at Eisenach, where he adds to his scanty means by singing before the houses of the wealthier folk and attracts the notice of good Frau Ursula Cotta, who gives him his board. In 1501 he is sent to the high school at Erfurt, where he distinguishes himself by hard study and good progress in learning. The father is ambitious that Martin shall be learned and a lawyer. It is at Erfurt, when twenty years of age, that Luther first has in his hands a complete copy of the Bible. He found the Latin Vulgate in the library one day, and was delighted with his discovery. Now he began to give to the sacred Word that loving interest and those lifelong studies which were to work such a revolution in the world. At Erfurt the young man, though full of life and spirits and fond of company, preserved his purity unsullied and was much given to prayer and devout meditation. Scholasticism and theology attracted him, and he neglected his legal studies for these. He also heard some reformatory principles taught and preached at Erfurt during his school days, but they seem not at the time to have made much impression on his mind. He took his degrees in the regular course at the University of Erfurt and was graduated Master of Arts

[1] There is a vast literature on Luther. I have found serviceable for this study, besides works on church history, the great *Life* in German by Julius Köstlin, which is now also available for American readers in the shorter form; Scribners, New York; C. G. Schmidt, *Geschichte der Predigt;* Wm. Beste's *Die bedeutendste Kanzelredner der Lutherischen Kirche des Reformationszeitalters;* and the fine discussion of Luther as preacher by Nebe, *Zur Gesch. der Pred.,* Bd. II., SS. 1-92. An old edition of translations of sermons by Luther and Calvin, the *Hauspostillen,* and some other sermons have also been consulted.

in 1505, second in a class of seventeen. He began his law studies again, to please his parents, but his heart was not in these. Full of internal struggles as to religion, he went to visit a friend, and found him dead—murdered in his bed. Shocked by this scene he went out into the open; a flash of lightning startled him. In the awe and dread of these experiences he vowed he would become a monk. The current of his life entered a new channel.

This decision greatly displeased Luther's parents, and he himself afterwards regretted it, but he adhered to his vow and entered the Augustinian monastery at Erfurt in July, 1505, carrying copies of Virgil and Plautus under his arm. He was fond of study, and was also a rigid and correct monk. He studied the Bible earnestly and prayed much. But all his exercises failed to bring the peace and satisfaction for which his spirit yearned. In this time of conflict and unrest he received help from the pious John Staupitz, vicar-general of the Augustinian order, who in one of his visits to the monastery at Erfurt became deeply interested in the bright and struggling young man. Staupitz told Martin to look to Christ alone, and not to his own works of devotion, as the source of peace. An old monk in the cloister gave him similar advice; and so by his studies of the Bible, by his own struggles, and by the help of those friends, Luther was gradually led on till he found satisfaction and assurance of pardon by trusting Christ alone for salvation.

In 1510 Luther was made professor at the University of Wittenberg, where he was to spend the rest of his life. It was during his early days at Wittenberg that at the earnest request of Staupitz, but with a genuine reluctance and self-distrust on his own part, Luther began to preach; at first in the little cloister chapel, and then, on the sickness of the pastor, in the town church. It is food for reflection that he thus modestly and falteringly took up what was to be the best and principal work of his variously busy life. But as he kept on the reluctance wore away, and he came to love the work of preaching with a devotion that never gave out. About this time, too (1511), occurred Luther's memorable visit to Rome, whither he was sent on business for his order. While in Rome he ascended the "Holy Stairway" on his knees, like many another Catholic devotee; but yet it is true that the worldliness, corruption, and emptiness which he saw among the clergy in Rome, made a lasting impression on his mind, and that the words, "The just shall live by faith," kept ringing in his ears. He came back to his work at Wittenberg, was made a doctor in 1512, lectured on the Psalms, Romans, Galatians, and Hebrews, and became more and more convinced of evangelical views. The theology of Augustine seized his mind, and the mysticism of Bernard and Tauler penetrated his soul. His love for preaching grew, and he began to teach that the preachers should give more diligent attention to their work and should preach less of penance and works, and more of repentance and faith.

In 1517 John Tetzel came preaching his indulgences, and on October 31st of that historic year, Luther put up his theses, and before he knew it the Reformation had begun. The bold deed of the young theologian at Wittenberg came like the notes of Gideon's trumpet to the discouraged in Israel, and called forth a deal of approval and discussion throughout all the land. In two weeks the theses were read all over Germany, and from now on the name of Martin Luther is a household word in German history. The events of his life after this are the events of the Reformation up to his death in 1546.

The story is too long, too full of incident, too important to be fully told here. But it may be well to recall the more important events of that stirring and influential life. Various unsuccessful attempts were made to hold Luther to the Catholic faith, but the pope excommunicated the bold monk, and he retorted by burning the bull of excommunication in 1520. Summoned to the imperial diet at Worms to answer before Charles V. and the assembled magnates, he bravely refused to recant. Then comes his retirement in the Wartburg castle, where he worked at his translation of the New Testament. Called from his retreat by the indiscretion of some of his followers he came back to Wittenberg, where he gave prompt and signal token both of his influence as a leader and of his power as a preacher, when in a series of eight sermons he resumed control of the movement, assuaged the tumult of the extremists and steadied the minds of his friends. Sorely tried in 1525 by the Peasants' War, and by the death of the wise Elector of Saxony (Frederick), he found consolation in his marriage with Katharine von Bora, a former nun. In the family relation he was both good and happy. His home was a comfort to him and a joy to his friends for the rest of his days.

The year 1529 is marked by several memorable events in Luther's life and work: (1) His visitation of the Saxon churches, in which much was done in the settlement of their order and worship, and the unifying of their organization. (2) The issuance of his famous catechisms, which are among the bulwarks of the Lutheran theology. (3) His sad dispute with the Swiss reformer Zwingli over the Lord's Supper. (4) The famous diet of Spires at which the German nobles in sympathy with Luther made, against the unfairness of the papal and imperial side, the Protest which gave an immortal name to the movement. In the next year at Augsburg was presented to the diet the great Confession which defined the Protestant faith. Luther was, for prudential reasons, not permitted to be at Augsburg, but from Coburg, within the Elector's dominions and in easy reach, he kept in touch with the theologians and princes who were at the diet. In this and many other ways he was busy and burdened. Writing, corresponding, teaching, advising, and preaching, he had his heart and hands full of work.

Amid all his labors we must not forget his services to sacred song. He wrote many hymns and tunes, but his immortal paraphrase of the forty-sixth Psalm contains the very essence of his faith and his work: "A mighty fortress is our God."

Luther was far from being satisfied either with himself or his work, and the inevitable drawbacks and disappointments that retarded and damaged the cause of the Reformation were clearly seen and keenly felt. It was natural that he should be weary of life; and his end was fortunate for him, occurring not many months before the disastrous issue of the Smalcald War brought Protestantism to sad straits in Germany.

The story of Luther's end is brief and sweet. In January, 1546, he was invited to Eisleben, his birthplace, to aid in settling a dispute which had arisen between the counts of Mansfeld. He was successful in this mission, and on a Sunday of his stay there, February 14th, he preached his last sermon. His health had not been very robust for some time, though there was no special illness now upon him. He seems to have caught cold, for the next day after preaching he complained of an oppression about his chest, took his bed and in a few days—February 18, 1546—passed to his reward. It is noteworthy that he should have died away from Wittenberg, and at the little place where, sixty-three years before, he had been born. Friends were with him at the closing scene and tenderly ministered to him. One of these, Justus Jonas, asked him of his faith, and the tried veteran expressed his full trust in Christ as his only hope. And so having quoted the Master's own dying words, "Lord, into thy hands I commit my spirit," he passed peacefully into rest. His body was taken to Wittenberg for burial, and there his dust awaits the resurrection, near the chancel of that old castle church, several times damaged and renewed, close to the spot where in his brave youth he had posted his theses and begun the mighty work of his life.

Luther's was by no means a perfect character, but it was a very robust and essentially sound one. The natural man was strong and brave, but somewhat rude and coarse, as his peasant blood and early training would lead us to expect. Yet he was kind-hearted and full of the joy of life. His was that typical German nature in which tender sentiment—love, poetry, music, æsthetic taste—is strangely allied with a coarseness and violence never excusable and sometimes shocking. But this ruder element was not in Luther allied with self-seeking. Overbearing he might be, but he was not selfish. Much that is unpleasant in manner and speech can be forgiven to a man of rugged honesty of purpose and sincerity of conviction. In Luther the regenerate man was not wholly released from the trammels of his clay, but he was truly converted and ever on the way to better things. He was full of the faith he preached; and of love, with a noticeable trace of mysticism; he was mighty in prayer, and even in his busiest and most exacting days did not omit communion with his God. One of his favorite sayings was *Bene orasse est bene studuisse*—to have prayed well is to have studied well. He was regardful of his friends, and honored them, though observant of their faults and not always very considerate in his criticisms. He was devoted to his people and to his God, and unfaltering in his heroic defence of the truth as he saw it. The tried man stood the test of many a tough encounter. He was often lonely, sad, and disappointed. Though in many minor matters he is far from being beyond criticism, he stood the severest tests of character at every essential point, and towers colossal among the heroes of Christian history. Unbiased judgment will not gainsay the dictum of Carlyle: "I will call this Luther a true great man—great in intellect, in courage, affection, and integrity; one of our most lovable and precious men."

As a preacher Luther stands in the first rank of those who by the ministry of God's Word have moulded the characters and destinies of men. Among all his other offices and achievements—as scholar, theologian, author, and leader—we must not forget that, first of all and chiefly, he was a preacher. At first he could hardly be persuaded to preach, but when he once got at it nothing could stop him.

Like many other great preachers he was great not in any one preëminent thing but in a cluster of excellent qualities. Remember the stages of his development as a preacher: first, his monastic and scholastic preparation up to the time of the theses, during which he was diligently studying the Bible and gradually and unconsciously becoming mentally and spiritually saturated with the doctrines of grace; then his break with Rome and the sharp discovery to himself and the world that he had struck out a new path and was burdened with a message that he must deliver; then the enforced months of Bible study and reflection in the Wartburg; and, finally, the mature closing years, beginning with the triumph at Wittenberg when, in a few powerful sermons, he saved the Reformation from wreck by excess. Add to this discipline of events his natural gifts and character; his strong intellect, his fine imagination, his sympathy with the people, his genial disposition, his courage and honesty; add further his learning, his knowledge of the Bible and theology, his keen insight into men and affairs, his facility of speech and power of statement; and add above all his experience of grace and his overwhelming earnestness of conviction that he had and must proclaim the truth of God in matters vital to the souls of his fellowmen—and there is presented a sum of elements which could not fail to make him one of the greatest preachers of all time.

When we read Luther's sermons and note the contents of his preaching, in order to do him justice we must read not from our times back to him, but forward from the times preceding up to him. Thus only can we justly appreciate the immense difference between his work and that of the best mediæval preachers, and estimate aright the value of the service which he rendered to the preaching of the gospel. Compare Luther's sermons with those of Bernard, of Antony, of Berthold, of Tauler, and even of Savonarola, the greatest of his mediæval predecessors, and what a difference strikes us! The earlier sermons, before he finally broke with Rome, naturally have more in common with the past. But even in these the grasp and exposition of Scripture are an important element, and traces of the coming evangelical development are discernible. And so in his maturer sermons we are prepared to find the three distinctive qualities of his discourse: (1) Right interpretation and application of Scripture; (2) Christ alone the Saviour; (3) Union with him by faith the only way of salvation. Everything is built on this foundation. The exposition of the Word is sometimes general and sometimes detailed, but not often allegorical or strained. The context is regarded and the real intent and meaning of the Scripture writers is sought and respected. The saints and the Virgin receive their proper place, and Jesus Christ alone is exalted as Saviour, Intercessor and Lord. Works and penances are rightly judged, and faith in Christ is made the central means in salvation. With these essentials firmly laid as a foundation the structure of argument, illustration, attack and defence, elaboration by story, experience, appeal, proceeds. There is no show of learning, and no effort to strike, but everywhere the evident purpose by all subordinate means of speech to bring God's truth home to the hearts and minds of his hearers.

As to the manner and style of Luther's preaching, not much needs to be said. His outlines show no slavery to the analytical method and are often homiletically faulty; he pays but little attention to introduction and conclusion, the body of discourse is the main thing. He often digresses, but usually has a well-defined theme, though not always clearly stated. Sometimes there is a short text and textual division, sometimes the old homily style of verse by verse comment, and sometimes the more analytical treatment of a longer passage as a whole. In rich and racy vernacular speech Luther was a master. He thought with the learned, but he also thought and talked with the people. Often there is lack of elegance, and sometimes downright coarseness, but on the whole his style of speech was clear to the people, warm with life and sentiment, and vigorous with the robust nature of the man himself. He had a free impressive delivery without affectation or violence. He carefully thought out his sermons; indeed was full of thought all the time, and spoke freely without manuscript as the occasion and the circumstances demanded.

The tone and spirit of Luther's preaching were what his character and views would lead us to expect. He believed and therefore he spoke—out of his experience and convictions—out of his sense of duty—out of love to God and men, and without the fear of man before his eyes.

2. Friends and Followers of Luther

In all parts of Germany there were friends and followers of Luther who deserve honorable mention in a history of preaching.[1] Some of these were preachers of a high order of merit themselves, and though they owed much to their great leader were by no means his slavish imitators.

Though Philip Melanchthon (d. 1560) was not a preacher, yet as the intimate friend of Luther, the theologian of the Reformation and the teacher of many preachers, he claims notice here. He wrote two not very important works on preaching. Even Luther could not prevail on him to preach; and it is said that once after

[1] The works of Beste and Schmidt, mentioned in previous note, have been of special use in studying the friends of Luther.

examining two candidates for the ministry he wept and said, "O poor me! who in writing with the pen am not afraid to express my views before the whole empire, yet dare not do what to these is a little thing, speak before even a small congregation of hearers." Yet he lectured with effect to large classes of students, and even composed lecture sermons (postils) for them, which show good powers of composition. But it was as he said: "If preaching were an art merely, I too could preach." He lacked not the powers, but the call.

Decidedly one of the most notable preachers of the Reformation was the beloved pastor at Wittenberg, John Bugenhagen (1485-1558). He received the customary rudiments of education at his native place, Wollin in Pomerania, and his university training at Greifswald, where he stood high and was graduated young. He became a teacher at Treptow, and in 1512 was made a priest and a lecturer in a school of preachers. His exegetical lectures rivalled his sermons in power and popularity.

By the writings of Erasmus and other things he was kept in deep sadness over the decay in doctrine and morals. A little later Luther's tract on the *Babylonish Captivity* fell into his hands, and though he spoke against it at first, a more careful reading convinced him that Luther was right, and he gave in his adhesion to the reformer. He was attracted to Wittenberg, where he could study the new doctrines at the feet of the leader; but soon after his arrival there Luther went to Worms and the Wartburg. During Luther's absence Bugenhagen stood with Melanchthon in opposing the extremes of Carlstadt and others. He also began to lecture on the Psalms to a few of his fellow Pomeranians in his house, but so great was his success that the house would not hold those who came to hear, and he was induced to give his lectures to a wider public.

In 1522 he married Eva Rorer, who proved a good and true helper to him all his life long. In the same year he was appointed pastor and preacher of the town church at Wittenberg. The interesting old building is still there, and near it the homely house which bears an inscription signifying that there John Bugenhagen lived and labored as pastor for many years. One of his most important works as pastor was to introduce the new order of worship—an event which is recorded on a memorial tablet in the old church near the pulpit where Luther, Bugenhagen, and others of the preachers often stood. Bugenhagen was an excellent pastor and organizer, and in the latter capacity he was frequently called on to visit other places and introduce the new order of worship and church polity. Perhaps no other man—not even Luther, who was not gifted in organization—did as much for the Reformation in this way as Bugenhagen. During these absences Luther preached for him very often and also looked after the pastoral work. He was Luther's confidant, and often cheered and encouraged the reformer in his spells of depression. Being milder and more composed in temper than Luther, and not timid like Melanchthon, he was a very necessary third in that great triumvirate. His views of truth and principles of action were heartily in accord with Luther's, and their cordial mutual esteem and appreciation were never broken.

The organizing genius of Bugenhagen won noteworthy successes in establishing Lutheranism in Brunswick, and in Hamburg and Lübeck. From the last place he was sent back home highly honored, and, as a mark of appreciation, in a coach and accompanied by an escort. On the way a young fellow of the escort, one of those refreshingly stupid and meddlesome persons who serve to break the monotony of life, asked Bugenhagen if he thought the Apostle Peter would have been willing to travel in so much style. The answer is worthy of record: "My son, if the Apostle Peter had visited such kind, good people as your masters in Lübeck he would doubtless have permitted himself to be sent away with respect and comfort; but if he had come upon mean fellows like you he would have gone home afoot."

After these visits Bugenhagen for a considerable time went on with his regular work at Wittenberg, preaching, looking after his flock, and giving lectures at the university. In 1533 he was made a doctor. Later, to his great joy, he was invited by the duke to come to his beloved native Pomerania and confirm the Lutheran order in the churches. After this King Christian III. of Denmark summoned him to Copenhagen to preside over the religious services at his coronation and then organize the churches after the Lutheran order. After these notable labors Bugenhagen returned to Wittenberg and took up his usual work. But soon the shadows began to gather. Luther died; Protestantism was defeated in the field; Wittenberg itself was captured by the imperial forces and passed under the dominion of Maurice of Saxony. Bugenhagen took the position that the new ruler must be accepted and the best possible be made of the untoward change. For this, as well as on some minor theological points, he was sharply criticized by the more extreme Lutherans; ill health and weariness befell him; but in all his trials his brave and patient spirit did not fail. Unterrified by danger, untempted by ambition, he lived his good and active life to the end, and passed away in peace at Wittenberg, in April, 1558.

An able German writer [1] has said: "In the city from which the reformation of the German church was to go forth there were drawn together three men: the first gifted as prophet, the second as teacher, the third as pastor; Luther for Saxony, Melanchthon for Swabia, Bugenhagen for Pomerania." "Dr. Pommer," as Luther sometimes called him, was an excellent scholar, praised by Melanchthon as a *grammaticus,* and was also a sound and popular expounder of the Word of God. As a preacher he was not distinctly great in an oratorical way, falling below Luther, Jonas and others, and even below himself in other respects; yet even here he stood above the common. His preaching was distinguished for its honoring of Christ, its power of exposition, its devout spirit. He loved to preach, and sometimes, in Luther's no doubt just opinion, he kept on too long. Strange that the only remains of his preaching are his funeral discourse at Luther's death, and a sermon in the Pomeranian dialect. Of his other writings there are quite a number. In the printed edition of the funeral sermon for Luther the substance is given, but the personal references are wanting. It is no eulogy, but a strong and sensible discourse of comfort to sorrowing Christians on the noble passage in 1 Thess. 4:13-18, beginning with the

[1] Vogt, quoted by Beste, S. 175.

words, "But I would not have you to be ignorant, brethren, concerning them which are asleep, that ye sorrow not even as others which have no hope." Fitting words from the right man on a momentous occasion, and the discourse is not unworthy of them all.

Next, and very close to the immortal three just mentioned, stood the lovable and eloquent Justus Jonas (d. 1555). He was the son of a burgomaster of Nordhausen, received his early schooling at home, and then studied with distinction at Erfurt and Wittenberg. At first he devoted himself to law, then to theology, and became professor of Holy Scripture and Canon Law at Wittenberg, soon exchanging for the chair of Theology. He was in cordial sympathy with Luther from the first, and stood so close to him in the exciting days at the beginning of the Reformation as to be called "Luther's Jonathan." He accompanied the reformer on his famous journey to Worms, and shared the perils and the triumphs of that great occasion. He was also present at the Marburg colloquy with Zwingli, and in the next year was an influential figure at the Augsburg diet, where the Confession of Faith was put forth. In 1539 Jonas, with Luther and others, at the invitation of Duke Henry, organized the Lutheran church in the duchy of Saxony—at that time, as often before and since, distinct from the electorate. Two years later he was called to Halle to be pastor, not having yet been ordained as preacher, and there, in the old Marienkirche, which still stands in mediæval grandeur, one of the most conspicuous buildings of the town, Jonas preached his first sermon. He was granted leave of absence from his chair at Wittenberg for four years, and these he so successfully filled with labors as pastor and preacher that at the expiration of his leave his flock protested against his departure and he was allowed to remain, being probably released from his professorship. Luther often visited him at Halle, and coming by on that last journey to Eisleben was accompanied by his tried friend to what proved to be his death scene. It was Jonas who stood by the dying hero, asked him if he would die by the principles he had taught, and received his emphatic "Yes." He conducted the first funeral services over Luther at Eisleben, and afterwards delivered a memorial discourse at Halle. The fatal Smalcald War brought great trials to Jonas. Halle was taken by the emperor's army, and a Spanish soldier was instructed to kill the preacher, but the man's heart failed him, and the faithful pastor escaped. He fled and underwent many vicissitudes. In his last years he was Superintendent of the Lutheran churches in the principality of Coburg and died at Eisfeld in 1555.

In comparing him with others Melanchthon said, " Bugenhagen is a grammarian (scholar), I a logician, Jonas an orator, and Luther is all in all." Only a few of his sermons remain in print, but they are worth reading. While not so impressive a speaker as Luther, he was a preacher of excellent merit. His sermons exhibit forcible argumentation, accurate knowledge and interpretation of Scripture, a sound gospel, with a warm nature, good imagination and a lively and vigorous style.

Caspar Aquila (Adler, d. 1560) was one of the younger friends and pupils of Luther. He was of a vehement, though not inconstant nature. He not only filled several pastorates with distinction, but was at Wittenberg one of the scholars who lent valuable service in the translation of the Scriptures. Like others he suffered for his zeal and courage when the issue of the Smalcald War went against the reformers. Charles V. is said to have offered a reward for the bold and fiery man.

As we should expect from his character, Aquila was a warm, soulful preacher. Thoroughly grounded in the Scriptures and filled with Luther's doctrine, he preached with glowing zeal and some indiscretion against the papacy and the Romish errors, but he also knew how to speak words of tenderness to needy souls and set forth the truth of the gospel in clear and forcible expression. In the rhetorical matter of division and order he is more exact and careful than Luther and Jonas, while his style, like theirs, is picturesque and popular.

In South Germany one of the noblest leaders in the Reformation cause was the judicious and faithful John Brentz (1499-1570), who came of respectable and pious parents in a small town of the modern Württemberg, then Swabia. As a student from early years he showed both intellect and diligence. At the University of Heidelberg Œcolampadius was one of his teachers, and among his fellow-students were Martin Butzer and Philip Melanchthon. His sympathies were with Luther from the start, and when he began to teach at Heidelberg, though not a priest or preacher, he could not keep off the theological questions of the time and began to lecture on Matthew. Objection was made, and he was ordained priest, but with undisguised evangelical views. Soon he received a call to be pastor at Hall, an important Swabian town to the northeast of Stuttgart. Here for a long time he worked as a pastor, beloved and strong. He gradually, and with great wisdom and moderation, led his people into reformation views and order, doing away with the mass in 1525. He earnestly opposed the Peasants' War, but was moderate in actions against it. He agreed with Luther as against Zwingli and Œcolampadius as to the Lord's Supper, was at the Marburg Conference, and also at Augsburg when the Confession was published. At the request of the duke of the country Brentz helped to reform the University of Tübingen in a Lutheran sense. The defeat of the Protestant rulers in the Smalcald War brought suffering to Brentz and others. He had to hide, and so near were the imperial troops to finding him once that their lances nearly pierced him as they were thrusting about in the straw or brush which concealed him. It is also told of him—as of some others in similar circumstances—that he was kept from starvation by the good offices of a hen who laid an egg near him every day. He escaped, however, to safer places; and when better times came back he was called to be the leading Lutheran preacher at Stuttgart, where he fulfilled an able and blessed ministry for many years, though not without many trials and sorrows, and died in September, 1570, outliving many of his old companions.

The preaching of Brentz was full of Scripture. He made exposition the principal thing, and in a time of so much theological controversy, in which he bore no little or unworthy part, he yet preached much upon Christian duty and morals. For this he was warmly praised by Luther. As a man he was distinguished for his purity, courage, moderation and fidelity, while his admirable modesty and unselfish desire for the good of his people won for him the confidence and love of men.

Among the younger men who were gathered about Luther a place of honor belongs to Veit (Vitus) Dietrich (1506-1549). He was of humble origin, being the son of a poor shoemaker at Nuremberg. But his promise was observed by friends, and he came to Wittenberg to study, supported by the council of his native town. His attention to study was notable, as well as his amiability and cheerfulness. He was an inmate of Luther's own home, and was brought into admiring intimacy with both Luther and Melanchthon.

While Luther was at Coburg in 1530 watching the proceedings of the famous diet of Augsburg, Dietrich was his tried and helpful companion. In those anxious days the ready cheerfulness and busy and tactful service of his young friend were a great comfort to the heavily burdened reformer. Dietrich's letters to Melanchthon and to Luther's wife present a valuable picture of the great man's fortitude and prayerfulness during the mental and bodily strain of that trying time.

After teaching awhile at Wittenberg Dietrich became pastor of a church at his native town of Nuremberg. The elder Osiander was pastor of the leading church here. He was involved in some controversies, and was, though an able preacher, not a very lovable man. His preaching was rather of the ambitious sort and soared over the heads of the people. Dietrich's more simple nature and his easy, popular style, addressing itself to the children and the poor, were a strong contrast to those of the older man. The consequences are easily surmised—the crowd followed Dietrich, and the jealousy of Osiander was aroused. He made it in various ways unpleasant for Dietrich, but Melanchthon bears emphatic testimony to the admirable patience and humility of his friend under these trials.

Dietrich's sermons are clear, simple, and sweet. The analysis is plain, the language easy, and the spirit devout. Besides his own work he has laid posterity under obligations by his report of Luther's *Hauspostillen,* or "Home Talks," and as these differ considerably from the reports of another auditor it is reasonable to suppose that they reflect a good deal of Dietrich as well as of Luther. Specially worthy of mention is his loving effort to reach the children in his sermons, and well does Beste say of him:[1] "His sermons are the testimonies of a witness who had turned the doctrines of the Reformers into sap and blood, and for that very reason could speak in the most childlike simplicity. They accordingly deserve in the fullest sense the name of children's sermons. Without Luther's fiery spirit they are yet alive with Luther's light and warmth."

There were many other Lutheran preachers of this early period who spread the principles of the Reformation in various parts of Germany. There was the polemic and lofty Andrew Osiander at Nuremberg, the poetic, warm-hearted John Spangenberg, who in several different pastorates gave his clear and popular sermons; Nicholas von Amsdorf, highly esteemed as man and preacher by both Luther and Melanchthon, though somewhat extreme and imprudent; Anton Corvinus, whose short, vigorous sermons won Luther's warm praise, and whose sufferings and toils for the truth were equal to those of any of his brethren; John Mathesius, the modest, retiring teacher and beloved pastor at Joachimsthal, in Bohemia, whose eulogy upon Luther is one of the best sources for the life of the great man; and George Major, who as a boy at Wittenberg enjoyed the love and confidence of the older leaders, heard their discourses, profited by their instructions, and became one of the leading preachers of the Reformation in several different places, notably in that old castle church at Wittenberg, where the theses were posted, and where are the tombs of Luther and Melanchthon.

3. Conditions Preparatory to the Reformation in Switzerland

In the latter part of the fifteenth century there existed in Switzerland conditions which had an important bearing on the course of the Reformation and the character of preaching in that country. The pride and independence of the Swiss had been greatly increased by their recent notable military achievements in Italy and against Austria. But the demoralization of the country was sadly aided by the system of hiring out the brave Swiss soldiers

[1] *Op cit.*, S. 293.

to fight the battles of other lands than their own. The church and clergy in Switzerland were as corrupt as elsewhere, and offered little or no help against this national deterioration. Yet there were some faithful priests and other pious persons who warned against the state of things. Among these was the famous Felix Hemmerlin of Zürich, one of the canons at the Grossmünster, who wrote against many of the existing evils, and his works had considerable circulation. The political independence of the Swiss made them restive if too much pressure was brought to bear on them by church authorities. The failure of the church to institute needed reforms caused the authorities, municipal or aristocratic, as the case might be, to take hold of some of the worst evils and make regulations in the interests of religion and morality. There was a tendency also toward municipal control of church revenues, and in other ways toward giving to the civil authorities a large share in the direction of ecclesiastical affairs. When we add to all this that, through Erasmus and others, the Humanistic movement, with its criticisms of the church, was more or less prevalent in Switzerland, we trace many of the causes which gave encouragement and stimulus to the great work of Zwingli and the rest.

4. Zwingli and His Friends at Zurich

All these preparatory influences were more or less apparent in Zürich, the important and vigorous town which was to become the main center of reformatory activity in Switzerland. Here, in the yet standing Grossmünster, in January, 1519, the great Swiss reformer began his work.

Huldreich [Ulrich] Zwingli[1] was born on New Year's Day, 1484, at Wildhaus, in the mountainous and lofty district of Toggenburg. His parents belonged to an old and respectable family of plain, honest people. Huldreich was the third among ten children. The talents and promise of the boy early attracted notice, and his father

[1] Authorities chiefly used: Rudolf Stähelin, *Huldreich Zwingli, sein Leben und Wirken;* the same author's article in Herzog; article by Prof. Egli of Zürich in *Allgemeine Deutsche Biographie;* Zwingli's *Werke,* Bde. I. & II., by Schuler and Schultess. I have also consulted S. M. Jackson's valuable *Huldreich Zwingli.*

designed him for the church. It was well for the lad that his excellent uncle, Bartholomew Zwingli, was parish priest in a neighboring community. By his advice Huldreich was sent to a good school at Basel, where he remained three years, and thence went to Bern. Like Luther, Zwingli was not only a diligent and brilliant student, but was also a musician, played and sang well, and greatly delighted in the art. Having completed his preparatory studies, the young scholar was advised to go to the University of Vienna, which was then much under the Humanistic influence. Here he studied for awhile, but returned to Basel to take his degrees in regular course, where, along with his university studies, he also taught in a school. Here he formed his enduring friendship with Leo Jud, who shared both his scholarly and his musical tastes.

An event of importance to both these young men was the coming of Thomas Wyttenbach to teach and preach at Basel, in 1505. This man exerted a deep and lasting influence on Zwingli. He was an excellent teacher, and, along with his zeal for culture, he also held religious views which lay in the direction of reform. The main thing was that he emphasized the Word of God as the chief authority in matters of faith. He also exposed the abuse of indulgences, and possibly attacked other errors.

In 1506, having completed his university course, Zwingli was ready for his life-work and was called to be parish priest at Glarus, a town of considerable importance. Before going to his charge he preached his first sermon at Rapperswyl, a place on the shores of Lake Zürich, and read his first mass in his native village. At Glarus Zwingli lived and worked for ten years. He felt from the first the responsibilities of his position, and conscientiously labored to meet them. Though not yet deeply spiritual he gradually made progress, both in the life of piety and in reformatory views of Christian truth. He was no scholastic recluse on the one hand, fond as he was of books and learning; nor, on the other, did he allow the social and administrative functions of his office to divert his attention from his studies. He accumulated books and worked hard upon them. But the crown and core of all his studies was the Bible. In 1513, without a teacher, he began the study of Greek[1] in order to get his knowledge of the New Testament directly from the original. As a natural result of his study of the Scriptures he already began to give them the chief place in his preaching, though not as yet were the scholastic and traditional Catholic elements put aside.

On the social and pastoral side of his life Zwingli was equally active. By nature he was jovial and sociable, made friends easily and kept them. He moved freely among the people, was interested in their life both as pastor and man, and learned their ways of thought and speech. Zwingli loved his country and shared the warlike spirit of his race. But he was, like other thoughtful patriots, opposed both on moral and patriotic grounds to the practice of mercenary warfare. But though opposed to it, yet, as a Catholic and patriot, he accompanied, in the capacity of chaplain, the Swiss troops who fought for the pope against Francis I. of France in 1515. He witnessed the bloody battle of Marignano, where some Swiss fought on both sides, and where the papal army was defeated. More than ever disgusted with mercenary warfare, and having now larger knowledge of life and men, including some insight into papal affairs, the young priest came home to Glarus to resume his pastoral work. But in the summer of 1516 he left Glarus and accepted a call to Einsiedeln.

During his two years' work at Einsiedeln Zwingli made important progress in his development as a reformer. Then, as now, the place was a noted shrine for pilgrimages, because of the possession of an ancient image of the Virgin, which was said to work miracles. Thus the place was a center for Romish superstition and for the Catholic teaching as to merits, indulgences and the like. The hollowness of it all was deeply impressed upon the young preacher's mind. He was prudent enough not to attack these things directly, but he opposed to them the preaching of the gospel of grace and redemption in Christ alone. Not only in his own mind did the evangelical sentiments grow, but he was enabled to impress them upon the many pilgrims who came to Einsiedeln. His

[1] It seems strange that neither at Basel nor Vienna as late as Zwingli's time was Greek a part of the curriculum for the academic degrees.

power in the pulpit was unquestionable, and his name, and to some extent his teachings, were made known in many parts of the country by those who had heard him at Einsiedeln.

In the spiritual life his case was a peculiar one. He had no clearly defined conversion like Augustine's, no such heart struggles as Luther, and never had the spiritual and mystical tone which marked both those great men. Zwingli's was rather a gradual growth in spiritual and moral power, chiefly led by the intellectual apprehension of the evangelical doctrines. Thus we cannot date his actual conversion. Before going to Zürich he had not been wholly free from certain lapses from virtue only too common among the priests of his time. But with shame, even if with a too easy frankness he owned his falls, fought his weakness, and at length, through grace, overcame. He had no sophistical excuses to make, but a manly determination to conquer.

The appearance of Erasmus' edition of the Greek Testament in the spring of 1516 was a great event for Zwingli —as for the world. He got a copy just before leaving Glarus, and at Einsiedeln he made a loving and earnest study of it. Among other methods of study he copied out in Greek the epistles of Paul, in order to impress the language more on his mind. As a preacher he grew in power steadily with his theological and spiritual growth. And so, at the end of two years and a few months at Einsiedeln, he was ready for his life work at Zürich.

In a political sense the city of Zürich was at the time practically free and self-governed. It had control over the canton of the same name, and by having joined in 1351 the four forest cantons—Uri, Schwytz, Underwalden, and Lucerne—it had become an influential member of the Swiss Confederation, in some respects the most important. It was thus fitted to be the center of the Reformation for German Switzerland. In ecclesiastical matters there was also considerable freedom. The two leading churches, the Grossmünster and the Frauenmünster—both dating from the ninth century—were the seats of ecclesiastical foundations that had acquired a great degree of independence in the management of their own affairs.

The city also had gradually gained considerable power in regulating the churches, both in regard to the selection of the canons and the disposal of funds. But, while these conditions were just such as a true leader could make the most of for introducing reformatory principles, the moral and religious state of Zürich was a fearful drawback. Hemmerlin had lifted up his voice against the demoralization of people and clergy, but he had been sorely persecuted for his fidelity and put in jail. The people were outwardly attached to the old faith and to the pope, and there was little real spiritual or moral basis, either in clergy or people, on which to build a true reformation in religion. Yet there was some. The devout and pious were found in Zürich also, and some who felt on humanistic grounds a hearty disgust with the disgraceful corruptions of the time.

On Saturday, January 1, 1519, his birthday, Huldreich Zwingli began his eventful work as "popular priest," or pastor, of the Grossmünster church at Zürich. It was an event for history. He announced to the assembled canons on that day that he would begin his preaching the next day with a course of expository sermons on the Gospel of Matthew, taking the book straight through without regard to the appointed lessons of the church service. This announcement created a stir, but the congregation gathered on Sunday with heightened interest to hear the new preacher and the new method. Success was assured from the start. The people came in unwonted numbers, and the preacher's hold upon the minds and hearts of his hearers was immediate and firm. Distinctly thus the Swiss Reformation began with the preaching of the Word of God. Zwingli afterwards explained the reason for his course in his letter of self-defence, addressed to the bishop of Constance, in 1522. He said he began with Matthew in order to make his people acquainted directly with the work and teaching of Jesus. He then expounded the Acts in a similar way to show how the early church was established on Christ's foundations. Next he took the Epistles to the Galatians and to Timothy to set forth Paul's views of fundamental doctrine and church order; and then those of Peter to show how that apostle agreed with Paul. At the time of writing his defence he was expounding the Epistle to the Hebrews that the congregation "might be led to Christ as the true High Priest and only Mediator between God and men, and might be still clearly taught concerning his saving work and glory."

In the course of this year, 1519, the plague visited Zürich, and its ravages were fearful. Zwingli was away when the epidemic broke out, but promptly returned to his post and faithfully performed his arduous pastoral duties in that struggle with death. The loss of friends, of his younger brother Andrew, who lived with him, and his own serious illness, made a deep impression on the spiritual life of Zwingli, and his brave devotion to his duties in that time of trial made him more than ever dear to the people.

In this same eventful year the work of Luther began to influence Zwingli. Hitherto his development and work as a reformer had been independent of the great Saxon. Luther's Leipzig disputation with Eck in the summer of 1519 gave Zwingli great joy and encouragement. And when, in the next year, the papal bull against Luther was issued Zwingli prevented its publication in Zürich. He unhesitatingly stood with Luther and applauded his course, though he foresaw that this decisive step meant, not only for Luther himself, but for his sympathizers everywhere, separation from Rome. He went on with his preaching, and without much outward opposition attacked yet more clearly and earnestly both the bad moral condition of the church and also many of its doctrines, as purgatory, the intercession of saints, the legends of the saints, the authority of the pope, and especially monasticism.

An event, considered by many as the decisive point in the severance of Zwingli's relations to Rome, befell in the year 1522. Some of his people exercised their Christian liberty by eating meat on a fast day. Zwingli felt that they were somewhat precipitate, but when they were called to account before the authorities for their breach of discipline he defended their course, and this led to his preaching and publishing, in March, 1522, a sermon on Christian liberty in matters of detail. In this he not only questioned the whole matter of fasts as being without

Scriptural foundation, but showed the worthlessness of external works in general.

Zwingli soon determined on a bold stroke. At his suggestion the council of the city issued a call for a great public disputation, to be held at Zürich on the 29th of January, 1523, to consider all the questions in dispute between the reformers and their opponents. The invitation was made very general, but only a few from beyond Zürich and vicinity came. Faber was there, with a small following, representing the bishop of Constance, but the friends of Zwingli were numerously present. He himself appeared with sixty-seven propositions which he had published and proposed to defend. There was really no discussion to speak of. Zwingli had it all his own way. Faber contented himself with denying the right of the city council of Zürich to pass on such questions, asserting the supremacy of the church and the pope, and making other such shifts. The disputation came to an end by noon; and in the afternoon the council passed and recorded a minute to the effect that as Zwingli had not been shown to be in error, he should go on unmolested in his preaching of the Word of God as he had been doing; and, further, that other preachers in the region should preach only what could be proved by Scripture, and that the term heretic should cease to be applied to those who pursued this course.

Reforms in the order of worship took place. One by one the Catholic ceremonies disappeared, making place for the simpler rites of the reformed service. Finally the mass was abolished, and the simpler celebration of the Lord's Supper in the Reformed manner, and according to the New Testament design, was substituted at Easter, 1525. This date and event may be taken as the culmination of Zwingli's work as a reformer, but the strifes and trials of his closing years must be at least briefly recalled that the story of his life may not be incomplete.

Among the followers of Zwingli was a group of men—some of them men of culture—who, though agreeing with him in his opposition to Rome, felt that his reforms did not go far enough, or sufficiently reproduce the doctrines and practices of the apostolic churches. They believed that the State-Church system was wrong, and came to disbelieve in infant baptism. This led to the view that persons who had received that rite in infancy should, on professing faith in their maturer years, receive baptism. Hence they were called Anabaptists, or rebaptizers. In regard to the separation of church and state, Zwingli was unalterably opposed to their views. But on the question of infant baptism he was at first disposed to agree with them, only counselling moderation and patience. But the Anabaptists would not keep still, and being, no doubt, somewhat rash, they were put in the attitude of disturbers of the peace and opponents of the lawful authorities. So at last they were put under the ban, and some of them were condemned and executed. This persecution remains a sad blot on Zwingli's career; but we must remember that these men seemed to him and the Zürich authorities dangerous agitators as well as heretics.

The suppression of the Anabaptists showed Zwingli's power in Zürich and his firm adherence to his principles of a State-Church, but it cost him much trial and sorrow, and neither the extreme measures employed nor the repression of liberty of conscience can be justified. Along with this controversy came the peasant uprising, which affected Switzerland as well as Germany. Zwingli sympathized in part with the peasants, urging the granting of some of their claims, counselled moderation both to them and the civil authorities, and thus secured the ending of the trouble in Switzerland without bloodshed.

Parallel with these troubles was the painful and unfortunate difference between Zwingli and Luther over the Lord's Supper. The controversy began in 1524 and was carried on for some time by writings. Zwingli was firmly persuaded of the soundness of his own views, but was ready to tolerate differences in others if they could hold together in common opposition to Rome. The discussion showed that agreement was impossible; but Zwingli tearfully offered the hand of brotherly love, hoping that they might agree to disagree on this theologically important but practically secondary matter while they were at one in their acceptance of Scripture and rejection of Catholicism. But Luther looked upon such compromise as a betrayal of truth, and declined Zwingli's generous overtures. This was a most unfortunate episode, but in it Zwingli shows to better advantage than Luther.

The third and fatal strife in which Zwingli was involved was of a political as well as religious nature. The five Swiss cantons of Uri, Schwytz, Unterwalden, Lucerne and Zug—the first four being the famous heart of the old Swiss Confederacy—remained firmly Catholic, while Bern, Glarus, and others followed the lead of Zürich and became Reformed. The five Catholic cantons, though weaker than the others in wealth and population, had a preponderating influence in the Swiss diet, and used their advantage against the Reformed views. The matter finally came to blows. The Reformed cantons were somehow unprepared to act in concert, and the delay was promptly utilized by the Catholics. Zürich saw the attacking army almost at her doors and hastily sent an inadequate force into the field. Zwingli foresaw the inevitable defeat, but he bravely accompanied the troops and encouraged them. The fight occurred at Cappel, a town lying between Zürich and Zug, Nov. 11, 1531. The Zürichers were outnumbered and defeated, and Zwingli fell on the field, sword in hand.

The character of Zwingli and the nature of his work of reform were in many respects quite different from those of the other great reformers. His religious life was not so deep or pure as that of either Luther or Calvin, yet it was sincere and strong. His conscientious devotion to duty was marked from the first, and as his knowledge of the gospel grew and strengthened his personal experience of its saving power likewise increased. With him the humanistic, moral, intellectual side of reform was in the lead; and the political bent of his mind was stamped on his measures both by his ardent patriotism and by the character of the place, institutions and people with which he had to deal.

As a preacher Zwingli must occupy a high place in history. Preaching with him, as with Luther, was the main thing, and by it chiefly he gained and kept his hold upon the people and carried out his work of reform. He made it his aim from his first work in Glarus to bring the Word of God home to the people by preaching, and this early resolve only grew with his growth and became the central thing in his life and work.

In form and method of preaching Zwingli was little influenced by scholasticism, and accordingly did not much value analysis. The order of thought was more like that of the classic discourse—showing the influence of his humanistic studies. In language his preaching was popular, clear, and moving. He had less imagination and feeling than Luther, perhaps more than Calvin. But it is not so easy to judge of Zwingli as of the others, because few of his sermons have come down to us. He preached without notes, rarely wrote out for publication, and his sermons were not reported. But the traditional accounts of his methods and power all testify to his wonderful ability in the pulpit. He had a tall, strong figure, a pleasing face and manner, but no great voice. Yet he had that magnetic influence which is ever characteristic of the true orator—people loved to hear him, and were profoundly influenced by what he said. He himself was genuinely surprised by his large congregations, and his friends marvelled at the notable reformation accomplished by his preaching in Zürich. The composite nature of his character and work are fitly set forth in the noble bronze statue back of the old Wasserkirche in Zürich, which represents him standing with upturned face and holding a sword in one hand, a Bible in the other.

Among the assistants and followers of Zwingli at Zürich we notice briefly only the two most important ones —Jud and Bullinger.

Leo Jud,[1] or Judæ (d. 1542), was born at a small town of Alsace in 1482. He was the son of the parish priest, who, like some others, in defiance of the rule of celibacy, lived in an acknowledged relation that was really, though not lawfully, marriage with a woman of respectable family. The name Jud, or Judä, indicates descent (which was remote) from the stock of Israel. The boy Leo was sent to school and enjoyed excellent instruction, not only in the classics, but in morals, from a teacher of character

[1] Good account of Jud in the excellent series, *Leben und ausgewählte Schriften der Väter und Gründer der Reformirten Kirche.* The sketch of Jud is by Carl Pestalozzi, nephew of the great educator.

and talents. Among his school friends was Martin Butzer, who was to be the famous Strasburg reformer of later days. Leo inclined to the study of medicine, and took employment with an apothecary in Basel, at the same time attending lectures at the university. But the humanistic and theological bent of his tastes triumphed over the medical, and he took the regular degrees in course. It was at Basel, as we have seen, that he formed with Zwingli the friendship so important to the lives of both. During the latter part of his course Jud was made a deacon of St. Theodore's church in Basel, and later was ordained parish priest at St. Hippolyte, in his native Alsace. Here he did faithful service for a number of years, preparing both himself and his people for the new life that was so soon to come in the religious world. He and Zwingli kept up correspondence and mutual affection, and so we are not surprised that when Zwingli went, in 1519, to Zürich he should have recommended Leo as his successor at Einsiedeln. Here accordingly Jud next lived, and for four years followed in his friend's footsteps, progressing in learning and grace while preaching much and boldly the new doctrines.

It was a great joy to Zwingli when, a vacancy occurring at St. Peter's Church in Zürich, he could again use his influence and secure his friend's election to the pastorate there. So Jud came to take charge of his new and what proved to be his lifelong office, in February, 1523. At Zürich he stood manfully by Zwingli in all the work and trials incident to introducing the Reformation. Nor was he simply an echo of his friend. He had courage and views of his own, was a faithful pastor, an attractive and instructive preacher, a lovable and pious man, a diligent and laborious scholar. One of his greatest services was his translations, especially of the Bible. He and others labored at this, using, but not exactly reproducing, Luther's work. Indeed before Luther had finished the Old Testament, Jud had translated some of the books, and the first copy of the entire Bible in German was printed at Zürich, ahead of the Wittenberg version.

The death of Zwingli was not only a deep personal affliction to Jud, but he saw in that catastrophe the serious peril of the great work of the Reformation. Fear, reaction, the opposition at Zürich and elsewhere, made a combination of circumstances that well might appall the stoutest heart. Sadly but bravely Leo stood by his post in that mournful crisis; suffered and endured much, and helped no little to rescue and establish on enduring foundations the imperilled work. He was deeply concerned that a suitable successor to Zwingli should be found. He favored the call to Œcolampadius, who declined; with excellent good sense and modesty he refused to be considered for the vacant place himself; and earnestly advised the Zürich council to elect the young and promising Henry Bullinger. This was done, and when Bullinger came Jud gave to the younger leader cordial support and deference, as he had done to Zwingli.

Struggling with opposition, with poverty, with bodily weakness, the heroic little man toiled on to the end, and died, greatly beloved and mourned by his friends, June 19, 1542.

Many writings, but few sermons, survived him. He preached extempore, expounded ably, warned faithfully, but lovingly; attacked boldly, but not violently; spoke with ease and clearness, and, while not a preacher of preeminent gifts, was heard with interest and profit. Zwingli said of him in a letter to Myconius on Jud's election to St. Peter's: "Soon will be there the lion with the mighty voice and the heart thirsting for righteousness; small indeed of person, but full of heroic courage." And his son, gathering some accounts of his life, said of his preaching: "His sermons were buttered and salted. Yet often he complained that when he had with great earnestness attacked great vices and weighty sins, he had not met with success. The cause might well lie in this, that he was by nature so kind, mild and friendly a man. I have also understood from excellent citizens that no sermons succeeded with him better than those on Christian love."

The accomplished, able and highly successful follower of Zwingli in carrying out the work of reformation at Zürich was Henry Bullinger[1] (1504-1575). He was born at Bremgarten, near Zürich, July 18th, 1504, the son of a priest who, like Leo Jud's father and others, lived in otherwise honorable, though ecclesiastically forbidden,

[1] *Väter und Gründer, u. s. w.* His life also by Pestalozzi.

wedlock. In fact many congregations in Switzerland, and perhaps elsewhere, preferred to tolerate this breach of church rules rather than endure worse evils in a celibate priesthood. And so this married priest was beloved by his congregation, and was a good husband and father. Of the other sons there is no need here to speak. Henry showed early promise, both in mind and character, and was carefully taught by his parents and his grandmother and in the local schools. At twelve years of age he was sent to Emmerich, in Germany, to a good school, and later he attended the famous old High School at Cologne. Here, about 1520, Bullinger began the study of theology, just at the time when the strife over Luther's reformatory work at Wittenberg was at its height. What with his reading of the early church fathers, Luther's and Melanchthon's writings, and most of all the Bible, Bullinger soon became satisfied that Luther was right. But he did not pass from the old faith to the new without regret and struggle. Coming home from Cologne, he spent a quiet year at his father's house in Bremgarten, deepening his knowledge and his convictions. Then he was schoolmaster at Cappel for six years. He did not become a priest in the old church, for he could not conscientiously celebrate mass. But he attended church for the prayers and the sermon; and both privately and in his school taught reform doctrines. Bullinger attended the disputations at Zürich in January and in October, 1527. Later he heard Zwingli preach and made his personal acquaintance. Soon Bullinger's work began to tell at Cappel, and before a great while the church and abbey there were reformed. The mass having been done away with and a synod of Reformed ministers established, the way was open for Bullinger to take up the work of preaching, which he did along with his school duties. Meantime he became engaged to a sensible and lovely young lady at Zürich. His letter to her proposing marriage is preserved, and does credit to his sense, candor and tenderness. After a long betrothal they were married, and the union was a happy one for life.

In 1529 the elder Bullinger at Bremgarten declared in favor of the Reformed opinions, and after a sharp struggle the adherents of Rome gained the day and he had to give up his charge. But the Reformed element recovered strength, gained the majority and called the son to be pastor in his father's place. Here he labored for two years; but the war which ended so disastrously for Zürich at Cappel drove Bullinger from home and he received hospitable entertainment at the house of a friend in Zürich. He was there when the defeat of the Zürichers and the death of Zwingli threw the city into consternation and the work of reform into danger.

The great question of a suitable successor to Zwingli was seriously agitating the council and the people. Œcolampadius declined to leave Basel, Leo Jud wisely rejected the overtures made to him, and urged the council to choose Bullinger. He was invited to preach, and his sermons made a deep impression. His election followed, in December, 1531.

In announcing Bullinger's election to the ministers assembled before it, the council took occasion to define their duties, and among items to which no reasonable exception could be taken made some conditions which were a distinct repression of the "freedom of prophesying." They bade the ministers in their rebuke of sin not to use harsh words, and, further, to keep off the ground of civil affairs; in other words, to refrain from criticising the government. Bullinger arose in the painful silence with which the preachers heard this restriction proclaimed, thanked the council in fitting terms for the great honor conferred upon him, agreed cordially with most of what had been laid down as to the duties of the clergy, but said he could not accept the great place offered him without a clearer understanding of exactly what was meant by that fourth article in the council's ordinance as to preaching. He asked for time to consult with his brethren and give his answer at a future meeting. It was granted, the consultation showed the unanimous and proper feeling of the preachers that they could not work under such restriction upon their freedom, and Bullinger, at the proper time, laid the matter before the council in an able speech, in which he showed that the regulation was contrary to Scripture and to sound policy; and distinctly declared he could not accept the place of leader unless the objectionable clauses were modified. Nothing could have shown more clearly Bullinger's fitness for leadership than the promptness, wisdom, firmness and moderation with which he met this first and severe test. The council was seriously divided; the debate was long and anxious, but the majority came to see that to insist on their course would be, not only to lose Bullinger, but Jud and others, and that this meant, at that terrible crisis of reaction and despondency, nothing less than the ruin of the cause of reformation. To their credit they receded, contenting themselves with advice instead of regulation on the points involved. Bullinger then accepted the office of preacher at the Grossmünster and leader of the Reformed churches in Zürich.

He thus began his difficult and enormous labors with a victory for the cause of truth, and all his after conduct was of a piece with this. Wise, patient, courageous, but not fiery and rash, he was the very man to follow the more strong and impetuous Zwingli, and build slowly and surely on the foundations which that splendid leader had laid. Long and arduous were his labors. There was much in Zwingli's work at Zürich that needed completion, and somewhat that needed improvement; and the general interests required great wisdom and exacting labors. But Henry Bullinger was the man for the occasion. His correspondence with Protestant leaders all over Europe, his oversight and counsel more especially toward the Swiss churches, his administration of the difficult affairs in Zürich, his numerous writings and continued studies, his faithfully performed pastoral and pulpit duties, and no less thoughtful and tender concern for his home and his friends, filled and burdened a long and noble life. He suffered great pains in his last and long illness, but bore them with Christian fortitude, till God gave him release on September 17, 1575.

As a preacher Bullinger deserves more than passing notice. Tall of form, with a flowing beard, a benevolent and intellectual expression, a pleasing voice, a dignified yet animated bearing, he had good external qualifications for public speech. His preaching, like that of the other reformers, was chiefly expository. In the first year of his pastorate he preached series of discourses on Hebrews, the Epistle of Peter, and the Gospel of John; and in the first ten years he had gone through nearly all the books of the Bible. His diligence and fruitfulness, especially when his other labors are remembered, were simply amazing. He often preached six, and sometimes seven and eight, times a week. When Leo Jud broke down under similar labors the council became alarmed for Bullinger also, gave him an assistant, and requested him to preach only twice a week. His biographer enumerates as having come down from the eighteen years following 1549 one hundred sermons on the book of Revelation, sixty-six on Daniel, one hundred and seventy on Jeremiah, one hundred and ninety on Isaiah, twenty-four fast sermons, and a great number of single discourses. Besides these and other published sermons there were, of course, a great many more. Many of his sermons were published in Latin for preachers beyond the home land, and others in the queer old Swiss German of the time. Some of them were translated into other tongues. He preached in the simple language of the people, without oratorical effort, but with warmth and earnestness, with sincere effort to bring God's truth home to the understandings and the hearts of his hearers. Thus for many years he held a firm grasp on his congregation and was listened to with interest, respect and reverence to the end of his laborious and faithful ministry. God be praised for the lives and works of such men as Henry Bullinger!

There were other preachers at Zürich and vicinity besides the leaders who have been named, but we must turn to the two other important centers of reform influence in German Switzerland and give brief account of the leading preachers.

5. Reformers at Basel and Bern

Basel (French Bâle) is an important city on the Rhine and near the French border. Noted as a fortress in the time of the Roman empire, it received its name, "The Royal." During the Middle Ages it had a checkered history as an imperial city. It was devastated by plague and earthquake, but survived and grew strong. Here, in the sad fourteenth century, the noisy Flagellants wept and beat themselves, and here, too, pious mystics like Nicholas and other "Friends of God" found home and influence. Here also during the fifteenth century one of the famous so-called Reforming Councils held its long and mostly futile sessions. The revival of learning found welcome in Basel in the circles that gathered first about Reuchlin and later about Erasmus, and some noted printers and publishers fostered this literary distinction. In 1501 Basel took the memorable and decisive step of joining the Swiss Federation; this brought and confirmed larger freedom in both civil and ecclesiastical affairs, making it possible for the city government, as at Zürich, to have large share in shaping the course of events in religious history. In 1513 the great scholar Erasmus made his first visit to Basel to see the publisher Froben (Frobenius) in regard to publishing one of his works, and hither, off and on, he came for the rest of his wandering life, till he died and was buried here in 1536. The great event for Erasmus, Froben, Basel, and the world, was the publication of the first complete printed edition of the Greek Testament in 1516. In Basel, too, in those stirring early years of the sixteenth century, Thomas Wyttenbach taught, and Zwingli, Leo Jud, Pellican, Glarean, Capito, Grynæus, and other scholars noted in Reformation history, spent busy and fruitful school days. Thus at Basel, along with the usual hindrances, were various lines of influence that might be gathered and used for the Reformation if the right man came on the scene as leader. And he did, in the person of John Œcolampadius (1482-1531).

In the little town of Weinsberg, in the present Kingdom of Württemberg, lived a good and respectable citizen and merchant named Hüssgen, some say Hausschein. To him and his pious and sensible wife sons were born, but only one survived. The boy received in baptism the name of John, but in after days, according to the absurd humanistic fashion then so affected, translated or perverted his German family name into the high-sounding Greek Œcolampadius, by which he is known in history.[1]

Born in 1482, he was nearly a year older than Luther, who was about two months older than Zwingli. The delicate but precocious and promising boy owed it to the influence of his pious and intelligent mother that, instead of being brought up to his father's business, he re-

[1] Life by Hagenbach, in *Väter und Gründer, u. s. w.*

ceived a scholar's education. After early instruction at home, John had the advantage of an excellent school at Heilbronn, and later of the University of Heidelberg. The vigorous mind of Œcolampadius ranged beyond his required studies, and he read widely in the church fathers and other writers. Still thirsting for knowledge and further preparation before becoming a priest and preacher, he went for a time to the University of Tübingen, where, among others, he found a congenial friend in the much younger but already remarkable scholar, Philip Melanchthon. Reuchlin was then in Stuttgart, not far away, and Œcolampadius took a course in Hebrew with that famous teacher, and pursued the study further at Tübingen, along with Capito and John Brentz, under a converted Jew.

In accordance with a custom then sometimes permitted there had been founded for Œcolampadius by the liberality of his parents a chapel, or preaching place, in his native village, and before going to Tübingen he seems to have spent a few months there. Now he returns to this his first charge and takes up his work more regularly. He made preaching the first thing, and while his sermons yet retained many of the Catholic habits and methods, they were both more evangelical and more expository than the old sort, and they made a great impression on his people. His first publication was a series of sermons on the seven last sayings of our Lord on the cross.

Between the time of this first work as preacher at Weinsberg and his final settlement at Basel for the work of his life Œcolampadius had a strangely checkered career. Interesting as the details are in themselves and significant in his preparations for becoming the chief reformer at Basel, they cannot here be discussed at any length. We find him for a short time at Basel, then at Augsburg, then, strangely enough, for a few months in a monastery; then a little while chaplain to the reforming knight, Francis of Sickingen. Here he made progress in reforming principles and introduced some changes in worship.

But soon Œcolampadius gave up this place also and accepted an invitation from his friend Kratander, the publisher at Basel, to pay a visit of indefinite duration at his house and wait till a professorship or some place suitable for him should open. It was under these circumstances that he took up what was to be his lifelong residence in Basel, Nov. 17th, 1522.

In a few weeks, the pastor of St. Martin's church being in poor health, a place as vicar was offered Œcolampadius there; and he began his fruitful ministry in that church. At first his duties were not very arduous, and he had time for his much loved studies. About this time, without personal acquaintance, he began a correspondence with Zwingli. He also corresponded with other reformers. Besides his expository and increasingly evangelical sermons at St. Martin's, Œcolampadius began to give—presumably at the university, though by what arrangement does not appear—a course of lectures, expounding, first, the prophecy of Isaiah, and then the Epistle to the Romans. These, as well as his more popular sermons on the first Epistle of John, were afterwards published, and gave great satisfaction to the friends of the Reformation in many quarters. Though Œcolampadius was doubtful of the value of public debates, and deprecated their evils, he yet was led to propose a public discussion of four propositions on the questions of the age. The discussion occurred in August, 1523, in the college chapel, was well attended, and produced good results.

Later came William Farel, the hot-headed, but eloquent, French reformer. He was welcomed by Œcolampadius and encouraged to hold a public discussion, which was attended with interest and did good. But Œcolampadius did not really care much for these public debates. His main work was preaching, and in this he was not only eminently successful in drawing the people, but in greatly instructing and profoundly moving them. He began to preach on week days as well as Sundays, and the people came in eager and large congregations. Thus the seeds of evangelical views of truth were richly sown in the hearts of many of the best and most influential people of the city, and the results were soon seen in many ways. The secular authorities of the city, as at Zürich and Bern, began to take action favoring the Reformation. One of their first acts (in 1525) was to give Œcolampadius the position of leading preacher at St. Martin's, for up to this time he had still been only vicar. This increased his dignity and influence, but it also added to his labors and cares.

From now on for four years the reformation in Basel proceeded in rapid order till, early in 1529, the doing away of the mass and the images in the churches marked its final establishment. During these years of strife and progress Œcolampadius was a busy and laborious man, but he stood his ground and did his work nobly.

The few remaining years of his life were abundantly occupied in preaching, writing, confirming the Reformation at home and lending wise counsel and good influence to the cause elsewhere. The catastrophe at Cappel was a shock from which Œcolampadius never recovered. His own end was near. An illness that proved to be fatal attacked his always feeble and much overwrought frame, and in November, 1531, he joined his fellow-worker and friend where strifes are no more. And so they went—those two great brave souls—one from the battlefield, calm and ready amid strife, carnage and defeat; the other from the Christian's dying bed, hopeful, victorious, and in perfect peace.

Œcolampadius was an active and successful preacher, without the highest oratorical genius. He had no impressive external gifts, being small and feeble of frame, and having a weak though not unpleasant voice. But his vigorous intelligence, sincerity and depth of feeling, ample learning, aptness and power in exposition, clearness and ease of expression, more than made up for lack of the externals. So we do not wonder, when we read his sermons, and remember the traits of his character and the facts of his life, that he should have attracted and held large and eager congregations, and should have accomplished the work he was set to do chiefly by the ministry of the Word.

The successor of Œcolampadius at Basel was Zwingli's warm friend, the eminent teacher Oswald Myconius [1] (1488-1552). Born at Lucerne in 1488, the son of a miller named Geisshussler, he later acquired in some way the Greek name of Myconius—probably a nickname given to him by Erasmus. With others, eager like himself for learning, he studied and then became a teacher at Basel,

[1] Hagenbach again in the series last mentioned.

where, also, he married. While at Basel he was on intimate terms with Erasmus, and there, too, he met Zwingli and Leo Jud. In 1516 he came to Zürich to teach in the school connected with the Grossmünster, and while there deepened his friendship with Zwingli, who was then at Einsiedeln. He was largely instrumental in having Zwingli come to Zürich; but did not himself remain long there, having accepted an invitation to return to his native Lucerne and teach. He espoused warmly the reformatory views, which were unpopular at Lucerne, and was called a "Lutheran heretic." At last the people became so enraged against him that he had to leave, and Leo Jud secured a temporary place for him at Einsiedeln, in 1522. As soon as a vacancy occurred in the school at Frauenmünster, in Zürich, his friends there secured it for him. It was truly a comfort to Zwingli to have the two tried friends—Jud and Myconius—with him in Zürich, one as preacher at St. Peter's, the other as teacher at the Frauenmünster. Here Myconius remained till Zwingli's death. He had in his home an admiring pupil, who relates that when Myconius heard the news of Zwingli's death, he said, "I can no longer stay here!" While not an ordained preacher, he had, at the request of the council, combined oral Scripture exposition, which was really preaching, with his work as teacher, and thus gradually took up the ministry of the Word. His pupil and young friend, Plater, having gone to Basel to teach, and knowing of Myconius' desire to leave Zürich, spoke of his old teacher so warmly to friends that he was authorized to go back to Zürich and conduct Myconius to Basel, where he could visit and preach at the church of St. Albans, where there was a vacancy in the pulpit. His trial sermon was so pronounced a success that he was called to the post in December, 1531. When he began his work at St. Albans, Basel was mourning the recent death of Œcolampadius, and the council was much exercised to find a suitable follower to that remarkable and beloved man and leader. But Myconius' success at St. Albans was so immediate and decided that after a few months the council decided to promote him to the cathedral as the successor to the recently deceased leader.

No one was more surprised at this turn of affairs than

the modest Myconius himself. He thus wrote of it to a friend: "I am named as successor to the sainted Œcolampadius. Great God, what disparity! But God has so ordained. . . . Unexpected and strange is it all to me. Earnestly do I pray God that sooner he would remove me from the earth than that his glory should be lessened by my induction into office." In such a spirit the mild-mannered teacher entered on his new and responsible position, but on the express understanding that he should hold the place only till a more suitable person could be found. None was found. He held the place twenty years, till his death in 1552.

Myconius was a fine teacher and an able expounder of the Word of God. His preaching was simple, clear and eminently Scriptural in matter and tone. He was not fond of display nor endowed with oratorical gifts, but he was heard with great acceptance and profit, for he preached with force and unction. One thing he says of his preaching will doubtless be well understood by many another faithful preacher: "I have been preaching the gospel ten years, and yet I cannot say that in attacking sin I am satisfied with myself. Sometimes I go beyond bounds, sometimes I do too little. I dare not be silent, and yet I cannot strike the right measure, which often not a little disturbs me." Faithful soul! perplexed to find the just combination of the pastor's and the prophet's functions! Yet this modest, amiable, faithful man preached in what was virtually his only charge for twenty years, carried on the work of a greater man than himself, and exerted a wide and lasting influence for the cause he so much loved.

The city of Bern, now the capital of the Swiss Federation, lies in a beautiful situation in the heart of picturesque Switzerland. Founded by the Duke of Zähringen in the end of the twelfth century, it was not so old as some other Swiss cities, but was from the first characterized by the bravery and independence of its people. It joined the Swiss Federation in 1353, having previously won its independence, and at once assumed and ever held a leading place in the affairs of the republic. Like other cities Bern had, through its council, considerable influence and control in ecclesiastical affairs. But here, as elsewhere, the sad demoralization of the people through the practice of mercenary warfare, and of the clergy through the evils so common everywhere, made the religious outlook discouraging in the extreme. There was not so much culture as in other places, and the superstition of many of the people made them easy victims of the indulgence-seller Samson, who rivalled Tetzel in Saxony. Yet there were not wanting among the people and in the council men who were heartily ashamed of the evil state of affairs, and were willing to be led in a better way when the time and the leader appointed of God should arrive. The time was the great reform movement in the sixteenth century, the leader Berthold Haller.[1]

In the memorable year of 1492 the future Bernese reformer was born in the Swabian village of Aldingen. The lad was of delicate constitution, but of quick intelligence and amiable character. He had an excellent teacher at Rottweil, and later studied at Pforzheim under Gerard Simler, afterwards professor at Tübingen. Among his schoolmates was Simon Grynæus, later the noted humanistic teacher at Basel, and the young Philip Melanchthon. Haller then spent two years at Cologne studying the dry bones of the degenerate scholastic theology, which no more satisfied him than it had Œcolampadius before him. He longed for further and more extensive studies, but accepted a place for a while as teacher at Rottweil, and was just about to go to Freiburg for further education when, in 1513, a call came to go to Bern as assistant teacher in a flourishing school. He knew not what was before him when he accepted this place and took up his residence as teacher, with apparently some preaching duties attached to his office, in the city that he was so profoundly to influence for all time.

Haller quickly made friends by his kindly sociable nature, having attracted notice by his eloquence and force of speech. He was elected chaplain of one of the guilds of citizens, and from 1517 held some official position in the church. His duties were varied and exacting from the start, and he never had the leisure for those studies that he so longed to pursue. He never became so great a scholar as many of the other reformers, and regretted

[1] Life by Pestalozzi in *Väter und Gründer, u. s. w.*

often the course of affairs that hindered his development in that direction. He was early attracted by the evangelical views, and his devotion to these was largely stimulated and confirmed by the presence at this time in Bern as canon and preacher at the Münster of that very Thomas Wyttenbach who at Basel had so profoundly influenced Zwingli and Leo Jud. Haller served as deacon under Wyttenbach, and lived with him till his retirement from Bern in 1520. Already in the preceding year a decisive turn had come in Haller's life by his appointment as canon and one of the chief preachers at the Münster. His place had come to him, and he was ready for his work.

Haller began at the great cathedral—a very imposing building still—in a very simple way. He took the appointed lessons as the basis of his sermons and expounded these carefully and with decided evangelical views. Later he added a series of discourses on the Ten Commandments, using Luther's exposition as a guide. His preaching was popular, and his congregations grew large and remained so. In 1521 he visited Zwingli at Zürich and received hearty commendation and help in his work. The friendship was warm and lasting, and there was frequent correspondence between the two till Zwingli's death. About this time the eloquent French Franciscan, Lambert, came to Bern on his way to Germany on a preaching tour. Though yet a monk Lambert was full of reformation ideas. Not knowing German, he preached in Latin to the priests and others, and his attacks on existing evils made a great stir. Some of the clergy were furious and tried to have the council restrain the fiery Frenchman. But that body, on the contrary, upheld him, and took occasion to declare in favor of a larger liberty to the preachers.

Soon Haller began a series of expository sermons on Matthew, influenced no doubt by Zwingli's experiment at Zürich, and his preaching was even more sought after by the people who were thirsting for the gospel truth, and his earnest teaching was having great influence. In 1523 the Bern council passed an ordinance similar to that of Zürich, instructing the preachers to preach the "pure Word of God freely, openly and without restraint." With this good beginning the government became more and more pronounced in favor of the new order of things; and progress, not without friction, setbacks, and various trials, was continually made. The Anabaptist controversy also made its appearance at Bern, and caused much trial to Haller and the rest. In 1527 the Bernese council called for a great conference and debate on all the questions between the Catholic and Reforming parties. It began in January, 1528, and lasted for nineteen days. Zwingli was present, also Œcolampadius, Bullinger, Butzer, Farel, and other leading reformers, besides a fair representation of Catholics. It was a triumph for Reformed opinions and greatly strengthened the cause throughout all Switzerland and beyond. Before the disputants had left the council took action and did away with the mass and the images in the churches. This marked the victory.

It now remained for Haller and his associates to settle and organize the new ecclesiastical constitution and confirm what had been done. The death of Zwingli and the peril that followed the defeat at Cappel were serious wounds to the cause; but the work went on. Haller's long and hard labors had worn him down; he fell an easy prey to disease, and passed to his reward in 1536, only forty-four years old. As a scholar he does not rank as high as the other leaders in the Reformation, but in fidelity and wisdom, in moderation combined with courage and patience, he falls behind none. His preaching bore the character marks of the reform movement in contents and method; in style it was simple and unambitious, but clear, forcible and winning. Its best praise is that it pleased, instructed and moulded the people to whom it was directed.

6. The Strasburg Reformers

This seems the best place to consider the preachers of the Reformation at Strasburg, for though it was a German and not a Swiss city, the leaders there occupied a mediating position between the Lutheran and Zwinglian views, and, on the whole, inclined more to the latter.

Strasburg was one of the ancient free cities of the German empire. It had acquired self-government in

1333, and in 1482 had adopted a new and very liberal popular constitution. Under this the city government had secured a very large control in ecclesiastical as well as civil affairs, and had so limited the authority of the bishop and reduced his importance that he preferred to live elsewhere and be represented at Strasburg by a vicar. The state of the clergy was bad, as usual. But among the best citizens were not a few who detested the existing state of things and were ready for a change. Perhaps the influence of that old mediæval mysticism and the work of Tauler were not wholly gone, and certainly the long and powerful ministry (1478-1510) of John Geiler of Kaisersberg was fresh in the minds of many when the Reformation began. We must also reckon among preparatory tendencies the entrance of Humanism under the auspices of Erasmus, Wimpheling and others. So when Luther began his attack on the papal abuses in 1517 there were many in Strasburg who hailed his bold strokes as the beginning of a real and long-hoped-for reform. Among these was a preacher and priest named Matthew Zell, who was already doing some effective reformatory preaching when, in 1523, the two men came who were to be the leaders in establishing the Reformation in Strasburg; these were Wolfgang Capito and Martin Bucer, or Butzer.[1]

At the then somewhat considerable town of Haguenau, in Alsace, there lived toward the end of the fifteenth century a German family named Köpfel, signifying "little head." Among the sons of the family, born in 1478, was one who received the name of Wolfgang and afterward Latinized his surname into Capito. In after years he remembered to have heard as a lad considerable talk of Huss and Jerome of Prague; of good John of Wessel, who had been imprisoned and died in jail because at Augsburg he had dared to preach that the Bible was above the pope; and of the great "Dr. Kaisersberg," as Geiler was familiarly called, who was preaching with such power at Strasburg. The eager and intelligent boy was educated with a view to medicine as a profes-

[1] An admirable double biography is that of W. Baum in the *Väter und Gründer* series; and a well written article based on this work is found in the (English) *Dict. Nat. Biog.*, on account of Butzer's work in England.

sion, and after preliminary schooling got his degree in medicine at the University of Freiburg. But his heart was not in that branch of study; and his father's death soon after he received his degree made him feel the impotence of his profession, and also left him free to leave it. As he had means to pursue his studies where and as he liked, he turned to law, and then theology, studying at Freiburg, Basel, and Ingolstadt, as suited his pleasure. Thus he was graduated in the three departments of medicine, law, and theology, taking his degree in the last from Ingolstadt. Besides the regular course he read widely, and became one of the most accomplished scholars of his age, being a peer in that brilliant coterie of Humanists that centered in Basel around Erasmus. He was made, in the fall of 1511, dean of the faculty of liberal arts at Freiburg and licentiate—that is, lecturer—in theology. But he desired to preach, and was glad to accept a call to Bruchsal, an inconsiderable pastorate in the diocese of Spires, where he spent several years.

Capito's next appointment was much more to his taste—in 1515 he was made one of the cathedral preachers at Basel. Here for some years he labored with much success, preaching with great acceptance and growing all the time in evangelical convictions. He was one of those men whom insight, breadth and charity prevent from being partisans; who can always see both sides of a quarrel and have sympathy for whatever is good in both. This amiable characteristic often gives rise to suspicions of insincerity, wavering, and doubleness. But Capito was not open to such charges. He agreed with Luther, but disliked his coarseness; he did not hold with Erasmus, but he admired his good points and valued his friendship. Hence he tried in vain to hinder or heal the breach between these men, and to some extent suffered in the estimation of both. He did not believe in rash revolutionary measures, but favored the progress of reformation principles by the slower method of indoctrination and influence. The strifes at Basel became too fierce for his peaceful nature, and he was glad to accept a position—not a very well defined one—as preacher and secretary to that curious jumble of politician and ecclesiastic, petty prince and electoral archbishop, Albert of Brandenburg, at

Mainz. As counsellor of that dignitary he attended the famous Diet at Worms, in 1521, where Luther made his brave stand. More and more Capito was satisfied of the truth of the Reformation doctrines, and his position at Mainz was becoming intolerable. It was a welcome call, therefore, that came to him from the authorities at Strasburg in 1523 to become chief preacher at the church of St. Thomas in that city.

This was a decisive point and the opening of the last stage in Capito's life. On coming to Strasburg he found Matthew Zell at work, and later in the same year (1523) came Martin Butzer. The three worked together in great harmony, according to their different characters; and by their preaching, the intelligent aid of the council, and the providential drift of the age, the Reformation was finally established at Strasburg in 1529. On February 20 of that year the popular assembly by a vote of 184 to 94 ordered the discontinuance of the mass in the churches. Of course there were trials in all this time. Capito had been promoted to the pastorate at St. Peter's Church, and his congregations and influence had increased. He felt the justice of many of the demands of the peasants, but counselled moderation; he saw much that was Scriptural in the Anabaptist contentions, and though deploring their excesses, he judged them much less harshly than did his colleagues; he sympathized with Zwingli's views on the Lord's Supper, but would take no part in the Marburg conference. He had much to do in drawing up the so-called Tetrapolitan Confession—representing the theologians of the four cities of Strasburg, Lindau, Constance and Memmingen—which emphasized the mediating position of the Strasburg leaders. In 1541 the plague visited the city, and among its numerous victims was the venerable and beloved Capito.

Enough has been said of his great learning, his notable moderation and breadth of sympathy. As a preacher he was not preëminent, but Scriptural, clear, winsome. His scholarly expositions, earnestness of feeling, and acceptability of manner, drew always good congregations, who loved to wait on his ministry; and, as in the case of others who stand in the second rank as preachers, the best witness to the power of his preaching is not the tradition of remarkable eloquence, but the enduring good accomplished.

One of the most interesting characters in the history of the Reformation was Capito's colleague at Strasburg, Martin Butzer, or Bucer, as the name is more commonly but less correctly written. His father, a well esteemed man, was a cooper by trade, and lived first at Schlestadt, where Martin was born, in 1491, and later removed to Strasburg, where he became in time a respected member of the council. The story of Martin Butzer's life and work is full of vicissitudes and interest, but as he was more of a theologian and lecturer than preacher, he can claim only summary notice here. For the sake of education he joined the Dominicans, and for a while, in their monastery at Heidelberg, enjoyed university privileges. Released from his vows at last because of growing reformatory principles, he held an assistant's place in a church at Weissenberg. Like a true reformer, he had defied the law of celibacy and married an excellent wife. His reform preaching aroused opposition, and both he and his superior were driven out of Weissenberg.

It was thus that Martin Butzer, in the early spring of 1523, came to his father's house in Strasburg, homeless, without means, with a young wife, soon to be a mother, and accompanied by a friend similarly situated.

Capito and Zell welcomed Butzer as an able recruit in their reforming campaign, but though many in Strasburg sympathized with the new views, and the authorities were leaning that way, it still was not so easy to find a place for a married priest. People had not yet become accustomed to that part of the reform! Still the son of good citizen Butzer was not to be discredited, and the friend of Capito could not be ignored. Soon some place was found for him to teach, expound the Scriptures, and thus really preach; and later, upon the foundation of the university, he was appointed a professor, and with the progress of the reformation there came to him full recognition as preacher and places to preach with authority.

The main significance of Martin Butzer in the history of the Reformation lies in the laborious, earnest, faithful, but ineffectual, efforts he made to harmonize the Lutheran and Zwinglian parties in their unhappy division over the Lord's Supper. It was the problem and the effort of his life, and it brought him much trial and little success. His realization of the beatitude of the peacemakers was reserved for the heavenly life.

When the result of the Smalcald War left Charles V. free to oppress the Protestants, Butzer opposed with all earnestness the emperor's so-called Interim, or effort to enforce a religious truce by compromise. But Strasburg was made to accept the Interim, and Butzer in 1548 left the city and country. At that time, under Edward VI. and Cranmer, Protestantism was in the ascendant in England, and by Cranmer's influence Butzer was offered a professorship of theology at Cambridge. He was glad to accept the place, and so ended his interesting and useful life as professor in one of England's great universities. He was diligent in lecturing and writing while at Cambridge, but his failing health hindered and shortened his activity, and in 1551 he died. It is shameful that under Bloody Mary his body was disinterred and burned; but in the reign of Elizabeth honor was done to his memory.

Butzer had ample scholarship, and held his own with the lights of his time in theological learning. He left numerous writings on many subjects, mostly in Latin. His style was diffuse and obscure, so much so that Calvin once said in speaking of some writing of a like mind, "Butzer himself has nothing so obscure, ambiguous, tortuous." Of his sermons, strictly speaking, there seem to be no important remains. If his spoken discourse was like his writing he must have been hard to follow; but he had a good voice and presence, and his long and successful service in the pulpit shows that, notwithstanding faults of style, and some lack of clearness in thought, he must have been more than an ordinary preacher.

We must not forget that besides these great leaders who have been singled out for notice, there were a great many others, more or less known, who caught the spirit and methods of these and exemplified the peculiar type of Reformation preaching all over German Switzerland. Some would be well worthy of study, both for their characters and methods; but those whom we have had under review are enough to indicate both the general course of the Swiss Reformation and the kind of preaching which characterized it. Nor must we forget the Anabaptists, for whom the gentle Capito had a kindly feeling, the other leaders only opposition and persecution; but it seems best to tell what little is known of them and their preaching in connection with their brethren in other countries.

CHAPTER XIII

Preachers of the Reformation in France and Other European Lands

It was an unhappy thing for France that the character of her monarch and the condition of her affairs in the early sixteenth century forced into exile or obscurity or subserviency the men who would have been her reformers. To those who were too great to be obscure and too true to be subservient exile was the only resource, and hence the center of French reform is not Paris or Lyons, but Geneva. Yet the beginnings were in France.

1. The Partial and Early Reformers

As in other lands, the movement started in France among the churchmen with no thought of separation, but of purification in both doctrine and morals. And though many of those who started the movement remained still in the old church, they are worthy of remembrance for what they began and left to more consistent men to carry on. Several of these deserve notice.

Jacques Le Fèvre d'Étaples, or Jacobus Faber Stapulensis, in the Latin form of his name, was not a preacher, but an eminent humanist scholar, and the beloved and influential teacher of many preachers. He was a man remarkable for sweetness of character, and for all sorts of learning. When he gave his attention to Biblical and theological subjects he touched them with the hand of a master. His views were decidedly in the direction of reform, but, like Erasmus—though very unlike him in many respects—he stopped short when it came to leaving the Catholic church. William Briconnet, bishop of Meaux, and by special permission also abbot of St.

Germain des Prés at Paris, was a pupil of Le Fèvre, and at one time had decided leanings toward reform, though he, too, naturally drew back when separation from the Catholic church became a logical necessity. When Briçonnet became abbot of St. Germain des Prés in 1507 he gave Le Fèvre an appointment as teacher in his abbey, and here for a number of years the pious scholar taught the Scriptures. He published versions of the Bible and a number of long useful commentaries, and he had among his pupils at different times both Farel and Calvin, besides a number of others who in one way or another took part in the religious movements of the age. Le Fèvre's commentaries show that he taught a much purer Christianity than the current Romanism, and it is no wonder that numbers of his pupils became Reformers. Briçonnet, too, after his manner, gave decided impulse to the new movement, for among other things he encouraged in his diocese of Meaux a number of men to preach and expound the Scriptures in the new way. But this work was broken up when the church authorities perceived its drift, and Briçonnet returned to a closer conformity to the old religion.

One who came much nearer at one time to being an active reformer than either Le Fèvre or Briçonnet was Gerard Roussel (1480-1550), who came from near Amiens, and was a pupil of Le Fèvre. He gave sympathy and applause to Luther's first steps in beginning the Reformation. He was one of those who at Briconnet's invitation preached the evangelical doctrines in his diocese, but was required to cease when the authorities withdrew the permission. In 1525 he fled to Strasburg to escape arrest, but was recalled at the instance of Queen Margaret of Navarre, the sister of Francis I., who favored the reformers and helped them all she could. Later Roussel became her confessor, and later still, through her influence, was made a bishop. His reaction toward the old faith and virtual abandonment of the reformed cause afterwards called forth a strong letter from Calvin rebuking him for his course. He was an eloquent and forcible preacher, and though he did not leave the Catholic church he was really one of the pioneer preachers of reform in France.

Coming to those who in the early years followed conscience and logic, and thus came out of the old establishment into new and untried ways, we meet almost first the honored name of François Lambert (d. 1530). He was born at Avignon in 1486. At fifteen years of age he joined the Franciscan order, and soon so distinguished himself by his study of the Scriptures and by his eloquence that he was made a travelling preacher. Like Luther he had great spiritual struggles, and even wished to go into a more strict order of monks for discipline, but this was refused him. About 1520 he read the early writings of Luther and became at once and decidedly convinced that the reformer was right. He was not a man to keep silent, and naturally fell under suspicion of heresy. Notwithstanding this, however, it may be at his own request, he was sent on a preaching tour into Germany in 1522. Going by way of Geneva and Lausanne, he came to Bern, where he met Haller, and was encouraged by him to hold a public disputation on the points involved in the current controversy. Thus he and Haller gave each other help and encouragement, and Lambert went on his way strengthened in his views. At Zürich his remaining doubts were resolved and he decisively committed himself to the Reformation, though this meant severance from his order and exile from his native land. Perhaps he did not regret the first of these results, but the second was always a grief to him. His life henceforth belongs to Germany rather than to France.

He went to Wittenberg in 1523, and there forever renounced Catholicism, married and took a course in theology with Luther, Melanchthon and the rest. It was impossible for him now to return to France, though he tried to get a place at Metz, and then at Strasburg, where he might be near enough to help the cause of his native land. But he failed to become established at either place. At last he came under the notice of Philip of Hesse, who protected him and got him to draw up a plan of organization for the Protestant churches in Hesse. Though his plan had to be modified in many particulars it was the basis of the Hessian church system. In 1527 he was made a professor in the newly constituted university at Marburg, but did not live long to fill this place, being carried off by the plague in 1530. His reformatory views were rather Zwinglian than Lutheran. He was an eloquent and impressive speaker, after the Keltic type, and was often too vehement in action and in word. But he was a true and noble man, and would gladly have given his life to France if he had been permitted.

2. Farel and His Associates

The leading place among the early French and Swiss Reformers belongs to Farel and the two younger men associated with him, Froment and Viret.[1]

The leader of this group, William Farel (d. 1565), was born at Gap in 1489. He was one of a large family, early showed a fondness for study and religion, and, after making good progress in the neighborhood schools, he was sent to the University of Paris for further study. But the quality of instruction had so declined in those days that the ardent mind of Farel was not satisfied by it, and he turned to Le Fèvre for teaching in philosophy. Le Fèvre, it will be remembered, was also teaching the Bible and theology. The study of the Scriptures under that great teacher was an increasing delight to the young man, and it led him to see clearly that there was a woful difference between the Bible and the doctrines and practices of the Catholic church. There was the inevitable struggle between the traditional beliefs and his newfound faith. When he laid his case before Le Fèvre the good teacher said, " My friend, listen well to this: I read the signs of the times and here is my thought—God is going to renew the face of the religious world, and you will be a witness of it." Then and there the young man felt that he must not only witness but take part in the coming change. He gladly availed himself of Briçonnet's plan of campaign, and after remaining awhile longer at Paris, he was found at Meaux in 1521 with that group of ardent young souls preaching and expounding the Scriptures among the people. A stop was soon put to the good bishop's innovation, and the movement was

[1] Besides various encyclopædia articles, accounts in the church histories, and incidental notices in Beza's and Bungener's lives of Calvin, I have found profit and pleasure in reading a bright sketch by Charles Chenévière, *Farel, Froment et Viret,* Geneva, 1855.

suppressed. As Farel had been very zealous and pronounced, he thought it best to go into hiding for awhile, hoping that the storm would cease and he would in time have some opening in France to preach the reform doctrines. But after about a year of inactivity, as the prospects seemed no better, he sadly turned away from France and came, in 1523, to Basel.

Here the excellent Œcolampadius received and encouraged him. It will be recalled that they held a public disputation on the questions between the Catholics and Reformers. Farel put up his theses in Latin and defended them in the same tongue, Œcolampadius interpreting. The result was favorable to reform and encouraging to the Reformers. But it aroused the ire of Erasmus, and he used his influence to have Farel sent away.

After visiting Zürich, and later Strasburg, Farel turned, though not without fear and trembling at first, to French Switzerland. It is pleasant to know that his chief human encouragement in beginning the distinctive work of his life came from the wise and gentle Œcolampadius, who not only urged him to the task, but gave him salutary and needed cautions against the vehemence and excess which were Farel's main fault. He had a successful evangelistic career in the towns of French Switzerland. In some he remained longer than in others, in all he preached the gospel with an eloquence born of conviction, and with all the fire of his race. He did not always keep the good counsel of Œcolampadius—he was a Frenchman—and Farel! Once he snatched the wafer out of the hand of a priest who was going to administer extreme unction to a dying man. This was perhaps the most extreme of his many extravagant actions, and was indefensible on any grounds. It is needless to say that his usefulness in that place was at an end.

Often he was mobbed, insulted, sometimes beaten, but never subdued. When he succeeded in establishing a reformed church in a place he would leave it in the hands of a pastor or pastors. At Orbe, in 1531, he was very roughly treated, but his visit there is memorable for having brought out and started on his way the later associate of himself and Calvin at Geneva, the useful and eloquent Viret.

In 1532 Farel attended the synod at Bern, and then went, at great risk, into Piedmont to a synod of the Waldenses and helped them conform their churches more closely to the divine Word. He saw that they needed leaders and a version of the Bible, and he promised to send them four men who should help them. He was as good as his word, and later sent them the men, among whom was Robert Olivetan, a kinsman and friend of John Calvin, who had helped that young man in his early struggles toward the truth, an admirable teacher who had aided in giving the Reformation a start at Geneva, and a pious scholar whose version of the Scriptures for these Waldensians was one of the earliest translations of the Bible into French.

On his return from Piedmont, accompanied by Saunier, another useful helper and preacher, Farel came to Geneva in September, 1532. Olivetan was then teaching there, and he told Farel that a beginning had been made toward reform, and that some people in Geneva were hungering for the truth. Farel needed no further hint, and decided to remain and preach the reform. He held frequent conversations with those who would come to his lodgings, and as a result fifteen citizens were converted. The news spread, and soon the lodgings would not hold the crowds who came to hear the gospel. This, of course, roused the anger of the Catholics, and there was much excitement. But the city authorities proposed that Farel should meet his opponents in a public discussion of the points in controversy, and that the debate should be held before the council. Nothing suited Farel better, and he and his friends came joyfully before the council on the day appointed. But the priests wanted no fair debate; there was no prospect of victory for them in that. Instead of arguments they resorted to clubs, and made a tumult, breaking up the meeting with violence. Farel and Saunier were beaten almost to death, but finally the authorities succeeded in getting them out of the city. Thus in disorder and violence Protestantism made its beginning in Geneva, but it had come to stay; and this seeming defeat was not the last of Farel. At Granson the two companions, wounded and sore, but not discouraged, recounted their experiences to sympathizers, and among these was Antoine Froment, who was filled with a desire to go to Geneva and find ways to hold together the disciples who had been gathered there, and carry on the work. He went, in this fall of 1532. In the next year, encouraged and in a measure protected by the Bernese authorities, who had strong and growing political influence at Geneva, Farel returned, accompanied this time by Viret. They joined Froment in carrying forward the work. The details of their trials and successes we have to pass over. Suffice it to say that the Reformation constantly gained upon the old faith, both among the people and with their official heads, but there was constant and formidable opposition.

In 1535 the long contest was decided, and by formal vote of the council Protestantism was recognized and established as the religion of Geneva. But much remained to be done both in settling the new order of things and in keeping up the fight with the remaining and vigorous opposition.

In the early summer of 1536 the young John Calvin was passing through Geneva with his brother and sister, seeking in this roundabout way a refuge in Strasburg or Basel. Farel saw in Calvin the qualifications needed just then in a leader for Geneva, and so wrought upon him that Calvin heeded the call as from God and consented to remain and work with the three pioneers in further establishing and strengthening the cause of reform in Geneva.

For a time the four reformers worked on together, but soon Viret went to Lausanne, and in 1538 the party hostile to the disciplinary measures of the reform gained the upper hand, and banished Calvin, Farel and Froment. After awhile Farel became pastor at Neuchatel, which remained his place of residence and the main scene of his labors until his death, in 1565, a few months after Calvin's. The remainder of his long and useful life was full of activity and of successful work. Neuchatel formally adopted the Reformation in 1542, and other signal successes were achieved by the veteran. But his life had reached its culmination in that dramatic and splendid scene when he laid on the heart and mind of John Calvin the cause of reform at Geneva, and resigned into abler hands than his own the direction and consummation of a work that his courage, eloquence and self-sacrifice had so nobly begun.

Farel was not without serious faults of character, chief of which were his rashness and excess. He could not be prudent, and was sometimes vehement to the point of violence and rudeness. But he was sincere, self-sacrificing, devoted and brave. He left some writings, but they are of no great importance. He had studied well in his youth, and was well versed in the Scriptures, but he was a man of action rather than of the pen. He was not a deep but a quick and ready thinker, and a good debater. No sermons remain as specimens of his preaching, and if they did they could not in printed form express the man. But the results of his work and the accounts of his preaching tell us more plainly than written discourses could that he was a man of mighty and moving speech. He had good presence and voice, his words came like a torrent, and his own fiery nature and powerful convictions kindled a glow in those who heard. Sharp and bitter in attack, he could also be tender and persuasive in appeal. Before the multitude, in the popular eloquence that takes hold of the crowd and stirs them profoundly, whether for opposition or consent, there was among the early reformers no superior to William Farel.

Antoine Froment (1509-1581) was born in Dauphiné, and was early converted there under the influence of one of the evangelical preachers of Briçonnet's company at Meaux. He began to preach, but persecution soon drove him to find a refuge in Switzerland, where he met with Farel and took some share in his work. On the expulsion of Farel and Saunier from Geneva in 1532, Froment was working at Granson, and the story of their success and sufferings so worked on him that, with Farel's encouragement, he determined to go to Geneva, and, if possible, find some means to continue the work which they had begun and had been so rudely forced to leave. Arriving in Geneva he opened a school for teaching French, and along with that taught the new doctrines in religion. The pupils told their parents, many of them were interested, others gathered, and Froment's school soon became a place of worship. The opposition was alert and active, and Froment thought he would have to leave. In fact, he did start away, but had not gone far before he began to feel that he was not playing the man, and he determined to retrace his steps and, braving all danger, take up his work again. Later he was joined by Farel and Viret, as we have seen, and the three worked on together till Calvin came, in 1536, and gave a new impetus and direction to the work, till all were forced to retire for awhile in 1538.

The later life of Froment was, unhappily, not creditable. He fell into serious faults. In 1549 he left the ministry, and in various ways made his living. Among other things he was at one time secretary to Bonivard, the famous Genevese patriot and "prisoner of Chillon," at whose request Froment wrote an account of the early days of the Reformation in Geneva. It is believed that Froment sincerely repented of his errors of conduct. The lapse of his later years has been forgotten in appreciation of his earlier services, and his name is inscribed, along with those of Farel, Viret, and Calvin, on the memorial tablet in the temple of St. Pierre at Geneva as one of the honored reformers of the city.

As a preacher Froment had something of the popular eloquence, the rough and ready speech of Farel, but he was not so great a man either in mind or character.

A worthier and abler man than Froment was Pierre Viret (1511-1571), a native of Orbe, in the canton of Vaud, and, therefore, a Swiss by birth. His father was a tailor, who, however, perceived and appreciated the talent and promise of his son, designed him for the church, and in 1527 sent him to Paris to be educated for the priesthood. Here for three years he studied under Le Fèvre, whose teaching planted deeply in his mind the seeds of evangelical truth. But, properly speaking, his conversion to Protestantism and his entrance into the ministry were, under God, the work of Farel. In 1531 that intense reformer was preaching at Orbe, and, as usual, met with opposition and ill-treatment. Viret was roused to sympathy by the indignities put upon the preacher, as well as strengthened in his reformed convictions by the preaching. Farel invited him to share his work and his sufferings, and to begin by preaching then and there, in his own town, the doctrines that he held. Viret consented, and preached his first sermon as a reformer under those circumstances. He was with Farel a good deal in his travels, but also did much independent work. He preached at many places in Switzerland and in southern France, and had his share of interesting and perilous adventures. Once his life was attempted by an angry priest, who wounded him with a sword, and once a fanatical servant girl poisoned his food and he with difficulty recovered. These injuries seriously impaired his health for life. His work at Neuchatel and Lausanne was greatly blessed, and, as we have seen, he worked with Farel and Froment in getting the Reformation established in Geneva in 1535. Two years later, and before the retirement of the reformers from Geneva, Viret accepted a call to Lausanne, where he did excellent and lasting service to the cause of reform, not only as pastor, but also by the establishment of a school, the germ of that noble university which has had so honorable a record in Protestant history.

When Geneva, tired of anarchy in religion and unbridled license in manners, concluded to recall the reformers, Viret was invited to come back from Lausanne, and he returned to Geneva before Calvin. It was greatly to Calvin's delight that he had on his return the help of this true and tried fellow-laborer. But the climate of Geneva proved rather severe for Viret's health, and he sought the south of France. He preached with great success in a number of cities in southern France, and at last, as Chenévière says, " felt himself strong enough to confront the fogs of the Rhone, and respond to a call of the Reformed at Lyons." Here he labored for nearly a year with such wonderful favor that several thousand persons were converted, a strong church was formed, and there was prospect of making Lyons a sort of center for Protestantism in France. But the Catholics were alarmed and procured an edict from Charles IX. that only native-born Frenchmen be allowed to preach in the Protestant churches in France. As Viret was of Swiss birth, he was forced to leave. Geneva tried again to get him, but he preferred a milder climate, and after teaching school for a while at Orange he made his way to Orthez in the little kingdom of Béarn, or Navarre, where the celebrated Jeanne d'Albret, the Protestant princess and mother of the future Henry IV. of France, was holding her court. Protected and honored by the queen, Viret passed his remaining days as preacher and theological teacher at Orthez, and at his death his remains were honored with burial in the royal vault.

In winsomeness, amiability, attractiveness, Viret was superior to Farel and Froment and to Calvin, too; as a preacher he was superior to Froment, and very different from both of the others. While not deficient in learning and culture, he, of course, was far below Calvin, though above Farel. His eloquence had not the thoughtful power of Calvin's, nor the vehement energy of Farel's; it was gentle, persuasive, flowing. His voice was sweet, but weak, and crowds almost held their breath to hear him. There was a charm and persuasiveness that drew and won, while yet, under sense of wrong and against arrogant sin, the delicate lips could quiver with indignation and utter the sharpest sarcasms. In writing Viret was too diffuse, and probably this fault affected his sermons also, though of these no printed specimens remain.

3. Calvin and Beza

Great in many ways and wonderfully useful as were these early promoters of the Reformation in France and French Switzerland, they all come far below the commanding genius and extended influence of one who built upon their foundations indeed, but such a structure as it was not given to them to raise—John Calvin[1] (1509-1564).

In the early years of the sixteenth century there lived in the town of Noyon, in Picardy, a worthy citizen whose name was Gerard Cauvin, or Chauvin. The name was Latinized later into Calvinus, and then abbreviated into Calvin.

His wife, Jeanne Lefranc, was a woman of excellent

[1] For Calvin, besides many general authorities too numerous to mention in detail, I have found specially helpful the following: The brief *résumé* of his life prefixed to Calvin's commentary on the Psalms; *Vie de Calvin*, par Theodore de Béze; *Jean Calvin, sa Vie, son Œuvre, et ses Écrits*, par Félix Bungener, Paris 1862; and some sermons in both the orginal and translations.

gifts and piety, who taught the best Catholic religion of her times to her children. Among these one named for his mother, Jean (John), was born in 1509. A delicate child he was, but marvellously bright, with his keen eyes, clear head, and prodigious memory. His parents early destined him for the church—the mother with the yearnings of piety, the father with those of ambition. Seeing bishoprics or a cardinalate ahead, Gerard worked hard to secure for the gifted youth a suitable education. But as the cost was very great, Cauvin, who had influence with the ecclesiastical authorities, used it to secure for the studious and pure lad an appointment as chaplain in a small church in the neighborhood, that the little salary attached to the place might help defray the expenses of education.

At first the boy John seems not to have been required to discharge any of the duties of his office. Later his father obtained the privilege that he should not even be required to reside near his church, but should be permitted to pursue his studies " when and where he would." And so, in 1523, at the age of fourteen, we find him at Paris, where he studied at various schools and greatly distinguished himself in all departments, but especially in logic and related subjects. His morals were absolutely pure, and his grave rebukes of his companions obtained for him, more in pleasantry than bitterness, the nickname of " The Accusative." Meantime the busy Gerard has secured an additional appointment for the youth, which enables him to go on with his studies. So John Calvin, before he is twenty years old, is chaplain at two places—Noyon and Pont l' Evêque, not very far away. He did not, however, receive ordination as a priest; but had some nominal functions to perform, and seems to have visited his appointments and occasionally to have preached. The arrangement certainly was not a proper one, from any point of view, but it must be remembered that such things were often tolerated, and this was done openly and by regular authority of the bishop of Noyon; that Calvin held these offices with the expectation of fully discharging their duties when he had completed his studies, or of giving himself to the service of the church in other ways; and finally, that when his views changed and he felt compelled to leave the church he voluntarily resigned both offices.

And now Gerard's ambition takes a new turn, and he decides that under the general permission to pursue his studies at his pleasure John may undertake the study of law, and devote himself to that lucrative profession if he should hereafter find it desirable! Under this liberal construction of privilege we find the obedient son—not from his own inclination—next engaged in the mastery of the science of law. He pursued this study with notable success under distinguished teachers at Orleans and Bruges. This training was an important element in his after career.

While at Paris Calvin had been much under the influence of his excellent kinsman, Robert Olivetan, whom he had heard boldly preach the evangelical doctrines. His own earnest study of theology, of the stirring questions raised by the reformers, and, most of all, of the Bible, had been slowly but surely turning his mind toward Protestantism. While studying law at Bruges he forsook neither his Bible studies nor his religious activities. He took up the study of Greek with Alleman (or Walmer, the eminent Swabian humanist, who later also taught Theodore Beza), and in a short time mastered the language and studied the Greek Testament with delight and to good purpose. Meantime the people in the neighborhood, hungering for religious instruction, urged him to lecture and preach. By permission of the authorities he thus informally and often preached and expounded Scripture at the little town of Berri near by. In this way he began his work as a preacher, and thus early was fixed the character of his preaching, as clear and popular exposition of Scripture.

It was during this time, too, that his final hesitations were dismissed, and he found mental and spiritual rest in the full acceptance of the distinctive reformed doctrines and of Christ as the only Saviour. His own account of the great crisis that he then passed is given with characteristic force and terseness in his beautiful Latin in the preface to his commentary on the Psalms, and sets forth the fact that, after he had long been obstinately devoted to the errors of the papacy, God, by his grace, had "reduced his hardened mind to docility by a sudden conversion."[1] He does not go into details, as the more genial Luther did, and we can only conjecture the spiritual struggle which culminated thus. Now, too, the death of Gerard Cauvin left the son free to abandon the law and required his attention to the family affairs at Noyon. Later Calvin is sojourning at Paris and publishing his first book, a commentary on Seneca's *De Clementia.* At twenty-four years of age he is already accomplished in classical, legal and theological training, and walks with firm tread among the scholars of his time. During this sojourn in Paris, not yet having left the Catholic church, possibly hoping still for reformation within it, and waiting for the drift of things, he is not idle, but studying and in various ways teaching the reformed views.

At this time Nicholas Cop was rector of the University of Paris, and being required to deliver a sermon upon some important academic occasion, he asked Calvin to assist him in preparing the discourse. When it was delivered its pronounced Protestantism created a storm. Cop was compelled to flee, and the real author being suspected and hunted, Calvin also was forced to leave Paris. He retired first to Saintonge, where, in various ways, teaching and preaching, he aided the little Protestant flock gathered there; and later went to Nérac to see the aged Le Fèvre, who was living there under protection of Margaret of Navarre. This princess, who in so many ways showed her care for the persecuted Protestants, finally persuaded the king, her brother, to let the Cop affair drop, and Calvin was allowed to return to Paris.

In the year 1534 Calvin went to Noyon and formally resigned the two church offices that he held. He had come to see that reformation within the church was not to be hoped for, and that he must in conscience take his place with the Protestants on the outside. In the fall of that year Francis I., under clerical influences, came out strongly in favor of the old faith, and began a vigorous persecution of the Protestants. This practically

[1] "Deus tamen arcano providentiae suae freno cursum meum alio tandem reflexit. Ac primo quidem, quum superstitionibus papatus magis pertinaciter addictus essem, quam ut facile esset e tam profundo luto me extrahi, animum meum, qui pro aetate nimis obduerat, subita conversione ad docilitatem subegit."

drove the Protestants out of the kingdom. Like others, Calvin sadly left his native land and retired to Switzerland. At Strasburg he was joyfully welcomed by Capito and Butzer, and later went to Basel, where Myconius and others likewise gave him a cordial reception. During this time, with the help of Capito and Simon Grynæus, he learned Hebrew, and was now ready to study all the Bible in the original languages. But the crowning event of his sojourn at Basel was the writing and publishing, in Latin, of his famous *Institutes of Christianity*. This immortal and epoch-making work was one of the principal labors of Calvin's life, and passed through many editions and revisions before it reached its final form in 1559, a few years before the author's death.

The occasion for writing and publishing the work was that, for political reasons, in his quarrel with Charles V., Francis had caused it to be given out that his oppression of the Protestants in France was directed against seditious sectaries like the Anabaptists and others. Calvin determined that a brief and clear statement of what the Reformed commonly believed was called for. The preface, written in French, was a brave and manly appeal to the French king to consider what his Protestant subjects really believed, and not allow himself to be misled by the calumnies of their enemies. The treatise in six chapters was a compendious and lucid statement of the principal points held by the generality of Protestants as against Rome. It was hailed by Reformers everywhere as a clear and powerful expression of the things they held in common; though (if a remark in the preface to the Psalms is correctly understood) it appeared anonymously, the author soon became known, and his name was on every Protestant tongue. From now on John Calvin takes his place with Zwingli and Luther as one of the three greatest reformers of the sixteenth century.

After the publication of his book Calvin made a visit to Italy to consult the Duchess of Ferrara, a princess of France who, under the influence of Margaret of Valois, had embraced Reformed views and favored the Protestants as much as she dared. But her plans were thwarted by the vigilant and determined Catholics, and, both on her own account and that of her guests, it became unsafe for them to remain long at Ferrara. By some force of necessity, or during some lull in the watchfulness of the persecutors, Calvin paid a last visit to his old home at Noyon in the summer of 1536. Here he finally settled his affairs, and, taking with him his brother Antony and a sister, he proposed to find a home in Strasburg or Basel. The direct way through Lorraine was then closed by the war between Francis I. and Charles V., and Calvin came around by way of Geneva, where he arrived in August, 1536.

Farel learned of Calvin's presence in the city and visited him at his lodgings. What first impressions may have been made on the veteran reformer by the pale, thin, feeble-looking student we do not know; but as the interview proceeded Farel began to urge Calvin to stay at Geneva and take hold of the work He eloquently set forth its need of a capable leader, a man qualified by education to carry on the work in a way that he and his associates could not. But Calvin was reluctant; he pleaded his youth, his unfitness, and chiefly his love for study, rather than the untried responsibilities of a life of active leadership in difficult affairs. Finally, under a sudden and irresistible impulse, Farel rose and, extending his hand over Calvin, said:[1] "You have no other pretext for refusing me than the attachment which you declare you have for your studies. But I tell you, in the name of God Almighty, that if you do not share with me the holy work in which I am engaged he will not bless your plans, because you prefer your repose to Jesus Christ!" Calvin himself said that this "terrible adjuration" came to him as the voice of God, and that he yielded, believing that it was the divine will for him to take hold of the work at Geneva. So now, with one brief and sharp interruption, that city becomes his home, and, it may almost be said, his kingdom, for the rest of his life.

Politically Geneva was at this time in a state of transition. Practically it was a republic all to itself, for it had recently become free from the control of both the Catholic bishops and the dukes of Savoy, who had quarrelled over it for generations, and it had not yet joined the Swiss Confederation. There were two popular assem-

[1] Beza's *Life* (old French ed.), p. 22.

blies, the Grand Council and a smaller body; and four Syndics constituted the executive arm of the government.

As we have seen in our sketch of Farel, the council had taken charge of both civil and religious affairs, and had established the Reformed faith as the religion of Geneva in 1535. Just one year later Calvin comes on the scene. But things were really in quite a chaotic state, and the new conditions required greater capacity for organization and direction than any of the earlier reformers possessed. Farel was not mistaken in his man.

At the instance of Farel Calvin was appointed by the council a preacher and teacher of theology. The hand of the born leader soon appeared. Not only did preaching and teaching occupy his time, but he drew up a catechism and a confession of faith, and also laid his strong hand to the reformation of morals by rigid church discipline. Geneva was hardly ready for this, and the measures of the reformers provoked such opposition as to lead at last to a revulsion of feeling that ended in the election to office of men who disliked the reformers, and finally secured, in 1538, their deposition and banishment. Farel settled at Neuchatel, Calvin at Strasburg, where Butzer and Capito arranged that he should be pastor of a small church of French refugees.

During the years at Strasburg (1538-1541) Calvin was busy as preacher and pastor, but also much occupied in theological writing, and in various ways helping on the cause of the Reformation. Here he met and married Idelette de Bure, the widow of a former Anabaptist preacher, and she proved through her life a tender and faithful spouse. But affairs at Geneva deeply concerned him, and his influence was greatly felt. Moral, religious, and political disorder reigned in the city, till, finally, feeling again turned, and first Viret, and then Calvin himself, was called to return and carry on the work of reform.

So in 1541 Calvin is again called as chief preacher and teacher of theology at Geneva. For more than twenty years he filled that post and did a masterly work. We are concerned with him chiefly as a preacher, and it does not fall to this discussion to trace his career as a reformer, as virtual civil guide, if not ruler, of his city, and as theologian and counsellor of the Reformation in many lands. After Luther's death he was the leading figure among the Protestants, and his influence throughout Europe was immense. The one sad blot upon his great career is the persecuting temper which he shared with many others of his time, and which led (though he was not alone to blame) to the execution of the erratic and surely not admirable Servetus at Geneva. While that execution cannot be justified, at least it should be remembered to Calvin's credit that he tried to keep Servetus from coming to Geneva and sought to mitigate the sentence of burning at the stake which was imposed by the city council. To Calvin himself it was a sad and bitter trial.

Sickness and death came to his people and to his family. One after another his three babes died, and after them the true and faithful wife. His own feeble frame, naturally delicate, and worn down by severe study and overwork, was racked with painful disorders. Yet this man of high conscience and inflexible purpose worked on, preaching in each alternate week every day, besides the usual Sunday services, lecturing nearly every day on theology, attending the meetings of the consistory on the days appointed and guiding its deliberations, visiting the sick of his flock, entertaining visitors, conducting a large and taxing correspondence, and, as if these official duties were not enough, writing his commentaries, revising and republishing his *Institutes* and some other works, and refuting heretics! It is simply marvellous how any one man could have done all he did, and the wonder is intensified when we remember that he was a feeble man, always ailing and often ill. His wonderful memory, his power of concentration, his capacity for affairs, his quick and penetrating intellect, his few hours of sleep, and, above all, the driving wheel of his tremendous will help to explain how he could attend to so much, but even this combination of gifts is itself a marvel.

Labors, sorrows, ill-health, overwork and crushing care must have their victory at last over the frail body that contained a mind and soul so great, and Calvin's end was rapidly approaching. Repeated attacks of illness prostrated him, and in February, 1564, he preached his last sermon. His sickness was long and lingering. The venerable Farel came from Neuchatel to see him, and their last interview must have been full of tender feeling for both. One day Calvin assembled the councillors of the city about his bed and gave them a parting address and a solemn leave-taking. In the course of his talk to them he said:[1] " I protest before God that not rashly, and not without being persuaded of the truth, have I taught you the doctrine which you have heard from me; but I have preached to you purely and with sincerity the Word of God according to the charge which he gave me concerning it."

The next day he assembled the "company of pastors," and, after solemnly charging them as to their duties, he likewise bade them farewell. On the twenty-seventh day of May, 1564, he was released from his long and painful struggle and entered into the eternal peace. In accordance with his wishes his funeral services, though largely attended, were without pomp, and no inscription was placed upon his grave. The stone now shown at Geneva marks only the conjectural site, but his name is enduringly written in the works that live after him and in the abiding influences of his life and mind.

Calvin had some serious faults of character along with great and masterful virtues. He was irritable, and his anger was often fierce and lasting. But he was conscious and penitent of this and other faults. Pure and austere in morals himself, he was a rigid disciplinarian and lacking in sympathy for the weak and erring. Grave and serious from childhood, he was deficient in geniality, in humor, in gentleness. He seems to have practised reserve and self-repression, but the tenderer sides of his nature would sometimes, though rarely, appear.

Beza somewhere naively remarks that if Farel's fire and Viret's winsomeness had been added to Calvin's qualities the combination would have made a well-nigh perfect preacher. As it was, the defects of Calvin's character showed themselves in his work as a preacher. There is lack of sympathy and charm, deficiency of imagination, sparing use of illustration, no poetic turn, no moving appeal, no soaring eloquence. But, on the other hand, the virtues of the man and the endowments of the intellect were great and telling. Courage, candor, love of truth,

[1] Quoted in Beza's *Life of Calvin*.

devotion to duty, fidelity to principle and to friends, earnestness of purpose, consecration to God and absorption in his work—these and other splendid traits make us almost forget the defects that have been mentioned. And his marvellous intellect—capacious, penetrating, profound—so wins admiration that we have to remember that in him sympathy and imagination were not equal to reason and insight.

In Calvin's preaching the expository method of the Reformation preachers finds emphasis. His commentaries were the fruits of his preaching and lecturing, and his sermons were commentaries extended and applied. Mostly in the homily form of verse by verse comment, there is yet in them a march of thought, a logical sequence that simply did not choose to express itself in the scholastic analysis. In truth, this lack of analysis and clearly defined connection is remarkable in a man of Calvin's logical power. It shows how the commentator got the better of the preacher. Yet his sermons are not mere commentaries. There is a quickness of perception, a sureness of touch, a power of expression that unite to make the thought of Scripture stand out and produce its own impression without the aid of the orator's art. The style was clear, vigorous and pointed, without ornament, but chastely and severely elegant; without warmth, but intense and vigorous. We do not wonder that Bossuet, Catholic and orator, should find Calvin's style "*triste*" (sad, gloomy); but Beza, who knew the effect of his preaching, said of him that "every word weighed a pound—*tot verba tot pondera.*"[1] Calvin had no striking presence, nor rich and sonorous voice, but he had a commanding will that needed no physical strength to supplement it, and a sustained intensity of conviction that could spare the help of a flowing eloquence.

And so, though the highest qualities of oratory found no place in Calvin's preaching, the power of his thought, the force of his will, the excellence of his style, and, above all, the earnestness with which he made the truth of God shine forth in his words, made him a great preacher and deeply impressed on his hearers the great verities of the Christian faith.

[1] Broadus, *Hist. Prea.*, p. 120.

There were associates and friends of Calvin at Geneva, fellow-laborers in other parts of Switzerland, and, as far as persecution permitted, in France. These noble and useful men preached the Reformed doctrines and cared for the churches of that faith, but none of them attained any marked eminence, except Theodore Beza (d. 1605),[1] the admirer, friend, associate, and successor of Calvin at Geneva, whom Christlieb describes as "the many-sided professor, church leader and tireless preacher." Born of gentle parents at Vezelay, in old Burgundy, Beza was educated at Paris and Orleans. He was designed for the bar, but preferred literature, and was a poet in Latin and French while yet a youth in the gay Parisian world. An illness turned his thoughts to God and the Reformed faith, and upon his conversion he went to Calvin at Geneva. He was gladly welcomed, and soon a place was found for him with Viret at Lausanne, where he taught Greek, expounded the Scriptures, and carried on Marot's translation of the Psalter. He was active in efforts to help the Reformation by writings and conferences, in which his birth and breeding helped the cause. In 1559 he was called to Geneva to teach Greek and help Calvin. He was also installed as one of the pastors, and his preaching was frequent and effective.

His learning and eloquence gave him great influence, and in 1561 he was summoned to take part for the Huguenots in a famous colloquy called by Catherine de Medici, the queen mother, to be held at Poissy, near Paris. Beza achieved notable success in his oration and conduct, but, of course, the Catholics took care that nothing should come of the colloquy in favor of the Protestants. Beza remained in France many months, laboring for his brethren, but at last returned to Geneva, where he was soon called to succeed Calvin as leader. His long and busy life as preacher, theologian, scholar, disputant, continued over into the seventeenth century.

We have little means of judging of his powers as a preacher, for few of his sermons remain, and these are not important. But his labors in the pulpit were great and fruitful. Baird[2] says of his speaking that even his

[1] Article by Heppe in Herzog; Schaff, *Ch. Hist.*, Vol. VII., p. 846 ff; Baird's *Rise of the Huguenots*, passim.

[2] *Rise of the Huguenots*, I., p. 523 ff.

enemies "could not help admitting that he had a fine presence, a ready wit, and keen intellect, and that his excellent choice of language *and ready utterance entitled him to the credit of eloquence.*"

Besides the great leaders of the Reformation and their more immediate associates in those lands where the reform movement had its origin and chief strength, there were in other parts of the Continent of Europe and among the sects in various lands some notable preachers who claim notice at our hands. We begin with those of Spain and Italy.

4. Reformation Preachers in Southern Europe.

Under the pious Catholic Queen Isabella and the learned Cardinal Ximenes there was serious attempt to reform the Catholic church itself in Spain, and this effort naturally included the suppression of heresy as well as the correction of abuses. If the one side of the work satisfied many who wished to see a reformation, so the other discouraged, and by the horrors of the Inquisition persecuted and destroyed those who would have a reformation in any other than a strict Catholic sense. Yet, notwithstanding these fearful odds there were some, even in Spain, who preached the evangelical doctrines.[1]

The pious and devoted Juan de Avila, called the "Apostle of Andalusia," though not a Protestant, preached a much purer gospel than most of his Catholic brethren, and among other things urged upon the people the study of the Bible. But a more pronounced reformatory impulse came from Rodrigo Valer of Seville. He was a wealthy, handsome, popular young man of the world, who suddenly for some reason withdrew from social life and devoted himself to the study of the Scriptures. He became convinced of the evangelical doctrines, and began boldly to teach them both in personal interviews and by addressing the people as he could in public. He also sought personal acquaintance with the clergy, and influenced them toward reformed opinions. His activity, for he was very bold,

[1] In addition to the church histories, encyclopædias, etc., I have found help in Stoughton's *Spanish Reformers,* Lond., 1883; Jules Lassalle's *La Réforme en Espagne,* Paris, 1883; and in an anonymous French work on the same subject published in 1827.

soon attracted the notice of the Catholic authorities, and he was imprisoned, but he was strong and defiant in his views and would not recant nor modify them. He was punished in various ways besides imprisonment. One penalty was that he had to wear a *sanbenito,* or garb of a condemned prisoner, attend mass and hear sermons. But on one occasion he broke in upon the preacher and disputed his doctrine, and after that he was more closely confined. He died in prison when about fifty years old.

Profoundly influenced by Valer was Juan Gil, better known as Dr. Egidio, who was born in Arragon, had greatly distinguished himself as a student at the University of Alcala and had become canon of the cathedral at Seville about 1537. Here he was already attracting notice as a skilled theologian and a speaker of unusual gifts, but was discouraged as to the fruits of his preaching. Valer and he got together somehow, and the intrepid lay evangelist told Gil that his preaching lacked the true gospel element. Egidio began to study the Bible more, and soon his preaching took on a new character. It became warm, evangelical, truly eloquent; and crowds attended his sermons. His eloquence attracted the favorable notice of the emperor Charles V., who proposed to make him bishop of Tortosa. Then the opposition broke out. It was recalled that Egidio had visited his friend Valer in prison and had written an earnest apology and plea for that heretic; it was declared that his so popular sermons were charged with the Lutheran heresy, and that he was misleading the people. He was tried, but though nothing was certainly proved against him he was condemned as a suspect, deposed and imprisoned for a year. Some say he recanted, but he spent his imprisonment in writing some commentaries and other works, and the story of his public recantation is probably a perversion of the facts. He seems to have been set at liberty several years before his death and to have preached a little in retired places; but his public ministry was cut short by his condemnation. He died in 1556.

There were two successors of Egidio at Seville who likewise, with more or less clearness, preached the doctrines of reform. Ponce de la Fuente was learned, eloquent and cautious, avoiding open attack upon the Roman errors but preaching the evangelical doctrines. A writing of his, which he frankly acknowledged, was found; and it contained such plain teaching of Protestant views that he was condemned and imprisoned. After two years of confinement he died. After him came Gregorio Ruiz, who also preached evangelical views; but warned by the fate of his predecessors he was less open and pronounced about it, and managed to escape the Inquisition. Sad was the fate of Carranza, archbishop of Toledo, who had taken a prominent part in the Council of Trent, but was later accused of Lutheranism, and after seventeen years of humiliations, trials and imprisonments died at Rome in 1576. Along with him should be mentioned Augustino Cazalla (1510-1559) who was long a pupil under Carranza, then studied with distinction at Alcala. He was endowed with oratorical gifts and was made court preacher to Charles V. in 1542. He passed nine years with the emperor in Germany and imbibed Protestant views. On his return to Spain he was preacher at Valladolid and undertook to introduce the new views there. But he was not the man for a genuine reformer, and though he gained some converts and preached with zeal for awhile, he was induced under torture to renounce his Protestantism. After death his remains were exhumed and burnt by the Inquisition. With him were associated some others at Valladolid. But in all Spain the officers of the Inquisition were alert, and the persecution of those who dared to teach the Lutheran heresy was vigorous and severe. Reform preaching could not flourish there.

A few words, however, must be said concerning the Spanish exiles who taught and preached in other places the doctrines that were so cruelly suppressed at home. Earliest among these was the celebrated Juan Valdez (c. 1490-1541), whose work at Naples was notably influential in promoting the Reformation in Italy. He and his twin brother Alfonso were of excellent Spanish family at Cuenca, where they were born in the latter part of the fifteenth century. They had good instruction, exhibited great love of learning and were among the most distinguished Spanish humanists. Alfonso held important official positions in the court of Charles V., was often with the emperor in Germany, but had no sympathy for

Luther and his work. Juan, on the other hand, though a very decided humanist and a real friend of Erasmus, advanced very far beyond the Erasmian ideas of reform, and was almost a Protestant. He was not a preacher, but his religious activity, his theological works, and his influence upon preachers and others in Italy were so great that he claims notice here. Some time between 1530 and 1535 he left Spain and took up his residence at Naples, where he does not seem to have had any official or business relations, but to have lived on his income and studied and taught at his pleasure. He was a sort of mystic as well as reformer. He put his Hebrew learning to use by translating the Psalms into Spanish, and his Greek by translating Paul's Epistles and the Gospel of Matthew. He was a man of lovely character, and attracted a large number of friends, especially of pious and learned persons of both sexes. He did not hesitate to teach the evangelical views of Christianity, and his influence on several notable Italian preachers we shall have occasion to recall later.

Juan Diaz was a brilliant and promising young reformer who early came to Germany. He was welcomed and beloved by Butzer at Strasburg, and much was hoped from him in the way of influencing his countrymen, but he was followed by his brother, a fanatical Catholic, who, failing in his effort to bring him back to the old faith, betrayed him and led him to his death at the hands of an assassin. There were also two brothers Enzinas (called also Dryander), who, in Holland and Germany, were distinguished as upholders of reform views. Later was Juan Perez, who had been associated with Egidio and others at Seville, but left Spain in 1551, and came to Geneva, where he was pastor of the Spanish Protestant refugees, afterwards was pastor at Blois, in France, and later still was chaplain of the now widowed Duchess of Ferrara at Montargis. Useful in many ways his most distinguished service was his translation of the Bible into Spanish.

The last to be mentioned is the fruitful and learned author, Cipriano de Valera, who was born at Seville about 1532, early fell under the influence of Egidio, fled to Geneva in 1557, thence went to other parts of Switzerland, to England, and to Holland. He was for three years pastor of the Spanish refugees in London, and tried by writings to spread reformed opinions in Spain.

In Italy the Reformation had a similar course to that in Spain; a humanistic impulse, a reform party within the church, and a persecuted and exiled little band of true reformers.[1] Several of these are worthy of a longer account than can here be given to them. Paolo Vergerio was a lawyer of ability at Capo d' Istria, but, losing his wife, he came to Rome and entered the service of the church. In 1532 he was papal nuncio in Germany and had interviews with Luther, without yet becoming a Protestant. Returning to Italy he preached awhile at Naples and was made bishop of his native town. In 1540 he was in France with Cardinal Este, and was sent by Francis I. to the diet at Worms, where he met Melanchthon and Butzer, and probably Calvin also. He was now much in accord with the reformers, but did not as yet openly avow his opinions. He returned to his diocese and preached them among his people. Called to account, he appealed to the Council of Trent, but was denied a hearing and his case was remanded to the court of the Patriarch of Venice. Vergerio refused to appear before that tribunal, and after awhile, being more and more hunted, he left Italy and went to the south of France, where he preached his views more boldly and became very bitter against Rome. In 1553 he was invited by the Duke of Württemburg to Tübingen. He travelled in other parts of Germany at intervals, and died at Tübingen in 1565. He was rather intemperate in his preaching after he left Italy, and during his earlier career was perhaps not wholly free from dissembling his views for personal safety.

Another reformer was Pietro Carnesecchi, of noble Florentine family, and the friend of Cosimo and Catharine dei Medici. He was honored with various church

[1] Besides numerous general authorities of various sorts, I have had opportunity to consult Tiraboschi's accounts of Vermigli and Ochino in his famous *Storia della Letteratura Italiana,* Vol. X. (Milan ed.). Karl Benrath's satisfactory monograph, *Bernardino Ochino von Siena* (of which there is also an Engl. translation) is the standard work on Ochino. Their sojourn in England gives occasion for fine articles in the *Dict. Nat. Biog.* on both Vermigli and Ochino.

offices, and was prothonotary under Clement VII. But, disgusted with the corruptions of the papal court, he left Rome and travelled in various parts of Italy, teaching and preaching. He was a man of kindly bearing and manners, and was cordially received everywhere. He came to Naples, and was among those who received instruction and help from Juan Valdez, the pious Spanish scholar, but was not yet ready to break with Rome. He was a friend of Cardinal Pole, and perhaps was hopeful of seeing reforms carried out in the church. He paid two visits to France, and from the second, having become more pronounced, he returned to Italy and remained for awhile at Venice. Finally he came once more to Florence, where the Medici tried to shield and save him, but having at last openly avowed Protestant principles, he fell under the sentence of the Inquisition and was executed.

More important than either of these was Pietro Martire Vermigli, who was born of good parents at Florence in 1500. His father was an admirer of Savonarola, and named his son for St. Peter the Martyr, honored among Dominicans. At the age of sixteen Pietro entered the Dominican order and distinguished himself for diligence in study, piety and eloquence. He was early appointed to teach and preach. While preaching with great acceptance at Naples, he came under the influence of Juan Valdez, and adopted decidedly evangelical sentiments. At Lucca he began openly to preach his new views, and with such success that he soon fell under the ban of the Inquisition, and was a marked man. Being at Florence in 1542, he foresaw what would befall him, and decided to escape. He fled with a companion to Switzerland, and was first at Zürich, then at Basel, and was finally at Strasburg with Butzer. Capito's death had left a vacancy there, and Vermigli for several years filled the post of lecturer in theology at Strasburg. In 1547 he was invited by Cranmer, along with Ochino, to become professor of theology at Oxford, a position which he filled with credit till the Catholic reaction under Mary forced him to leave England.

Vermigli then returned to Strasburg, and later went to Zürich, where he died in 1562. Vermigli was a man of pure character, fine learning, and of good gifts as a speaker. His enemies could find fault only with his doctrine. Even Tiraboschi, who writes as a Catholic, admits that he was a pious and learned man, far removed from the "arrogance and fury of Luther," whose chief fault was that he "undertook to defend and sustain the worse cause."

The most powerful preacher among the Italian reformers was the celebrated Bernardino Ochino (c. 1487-1564), who was born at Siena, and named for the famous preaching saint of a former age. Ochino was not his family name, but how he got his surname and its significance are matters of dispute. Not much is known of his childhood and youth. He early joined the Franciscan order in the branch of Observants, and later passed into the more strict ascetic branch of the Capuchins. He was twice elected general of his order, the second time much against his will. Ochino, following his natural bent as well as conviction, interpreted strictly the principle of his order in regard to preaching, and early and continuously devoted himself to that work. He preached with power and acceptance in many of the cities of Italy, and his services were in great demand for the special church seasons. His strict life and fervid zeal also won for him the reputation of sanctity. After he went over to Protestantism the Catholics (even Tiraboschi) have represented his early piety as hypocrisy, but though he was a man of strong impulses and perhaps of some inconstancy, there is no sufficient reason to doubt his sincerity and earnestness. In 1538 he came for the first time to Venice, where he made a deep impression, not only on the crowds of people who came to his sermons, but on the upper and learned classes also. The eminent humanist, Cardinal Bembo, testified in many extant letters to the wonderful ability of Ochino as a preacher, and had him to come back to Venice the next year and after. Among other things Bembo is quoted as saying,[1] "I confess that I have never heard anyone preach more usefully and more savingly than he. . . He reasons very differently and in a much more Christian way than all others who have ascended the pulpit in my days, with more of living

[1] Tiraboschi, Vol. X., p. 539 seg.

grace and love, and with better and more acceptable topics."

Another Catholic contemporary, quoted by Benrath, declares that Ochino "left out the wordy war of the Scholastics, which others brought into the pulpit, and preached with spirit and warmth;" and an enthusiastic hearer said, "He might even move stones to tears." Other such testimonials sustain the judgment of Benrath that Italy had had no such preacher since Savonarola. Nine of these early sermons were published at Venice in 1539, and, judging from the extended extracts given by Benrath, and his good discussion of them, and making the necessary allowances for the difference between printing and delivery, they sustain Ochino's reputation. They are not unlike contemporary sermons in form, have a good deal of Scripture quotation, well handled, and are given in a plain, popular style, with fervor, practical point, and a spiritual aim.

Ochino's conversion to Protestantism was not surprising. Already his preaching sounded out the evangelical note of repentance and faith, as opposed both to the moral decay and the work-righteousness of the time. During his several preaching engagements at Naples, along from 1536 to 1540, he was much associated with Valdez and Vermigli, as with kindred spirits, and doubtless received decided influence from them. His preaching after this began to show more and more of the reformatory element. At Venice, early in 1542, he espoused the cause of a preacher who had been punished for proclaiming evangelical opinions, and in the Lent of that year Ochino himself more distinctly and powerfully set forth the main truths of the Reformation. This led the Catholic authorities to action. He was summoned to Rome "on matters of importance." He hesitated, but decided to go, delaying first at Bologna and then at Florence. It became more and more evident to him and his friends that if he went to Rome he must either renounce his convictions or be put to death. At Florence he met Vermigli, who had already determined to leave Italy. Ochino, after a final struggle, decided to do likewise, and in a few days after Vermigli he too fled.

The rest of his life was full of vicissitude, and its close

pathetic in the extreme, but we can only give here a very brief summary of the remainder of his days. Ochino came to Geneva, where, favored by Calvin and the council, he preached to the Italian refugees, wrote some books, and published some sermons for distribution in Italy. They naturally show now, along with his accustomed fire, more of polemic against Rome and more firmness in the reformed doctrines. After about two years in Geneva Ochino came, after stopping a little at Basel and Strasburg, to Augsburg, where, in 1545, he became pastor of the Italian refugees, and labored as pastor, author and preacher till, in 1547, he and Vermigli, both at Cranmer's invitation, came to Oxford as professors. The reaction under Mary drove them both away, and Ochino came back, first to Basel and then to Zürich. He was now quite old, and in his later writings and teachings had broached opinions on the person of Christ and on the Trinity that were somewhat doubtful, though it is not proved that he held, as accused, decided Socinian views on these subjects. Further, though after his flight from Italy he had married, and there never was any just imputation upon his own life, he had in conversation and in a published dialogue on marriage let fall some expressions that seemed to admit in a speculative way the admissibility of polygamy in certain cases. These views, exaggerated no doubt and largely misunderstood, even by such men as Beza and Bullinger, brought Ochino into suspicion and disfavor with the Protestant leaders. The Zürich council finally denied him a place as preacher and advised him to leave. In his old age, thus discredited, and cumbered with his family, he turned to friends that he had among the Italian fugitives in Poland, and went thither, hoping to find refuge and a place to work on for his few years more of life. His old Catholic enemies in Italy rejoiced over Ochino's dismissal from Zürich as evidence of his thorough apostasy and untrustworthiness, and as corroboration of their many slanders against him. Nor did their enmity stop here, but they procured the enactment of an ordinance by the King of Poland forbidding anti-Catholics of foreign birth to settle and teach in his dominions. And thus once more the poor old man was a fugitive. Some obscurity rests over the fate of his family and over the details of his own closing days, but it appears that he died alone at Schlackau, in Moravia, toward the end of the year 1564. It was a sad ending to what was in many ways a brilliant and noble career. Faults, no doubt, Ochino had, and it would be unsafe to say that the judgment of his critics was utterly without foundation; but there is no doubt as to the devotion of his life to his views of truth, as to the earnestness and sincerity of his labors, and as to his distinguished ability as a preacher.

5. Reformatory Preachers in Eastern Europe.

In the parts of Europe which lay immediately to the east of the centers of the Reformation there were not wanting preachers of character and ability, who set forth the Word of God in the spirit and methods peculiar to the reformers. Few, if any, however, were distinguished by commanding powers in the pulpit, or have as preachers secured a world-wide and lasting fame. We may mention a few of the better known men in connection with their countries.

In Bohemia the followers of Huss became divided, but those who remained nearest to his aims and spirit seem to have been among the Bohemian brethren in the later fifteenth century. Among these Rokytsana and Chelchitsky were leaders and preachers, and after them Matthias of Kunewald. Among their successors the doctrines of Luther received recognition, but no great preachers were developed. We must not forget, however, the excellent German preacher at Jaoachimsthal, John Mathesius (1504-1565), the pupil and friend of Luther, who spent all his working life in this pastorate. He was a much loved pastor and a studious, earnest and instructive preacher. Though a learned scholar, he knew how to speak to the people and give them in lively images, comparisons, proverbs and for the most part, in simple style, sound instruction from his pulpit. His seventeen biographical sermons on Luther are unique in their way, and are among the most valued sources for the life of the great reformer.

Two Austrians, Primus Truber and Hans Steinberger, are mentioned as having preached with some success the doctrines of the Reformation in their own country and in Hungary. But the leading place among Hungarian reformers is held by Matthias Birò Dévày (died c. 1547), who is called the "Hungarian Luther." Dévày was born of good Hungarian family at Siebenburgen toward the end of the fifteenth century. After childhood he studied at Cracow, and was a monk and priest in the Roman church till as late as 1527. Meantime, in spite of severe repression, the reformed views had been making some headway in Hungary. At Ofen, now Buda-Pest, the famous Protestant scholar and teacher, Simon Grynæus, later settled at Basel, had taught for awhile, but had been forced out because of his religious views. Here, also, Paul Speratus, who had been driven from Vienna, had preached. Dévày became much inclined to the Lutheran opinions, and in 1529 went to Wittenberg to study with Luther and Melanchthon. After two years he returned to Ofen, but his activity was so great that the Catholics used their power to have him sent away. He labored in several places, suffered several imprisonments, and, finally, went on another visit to Germany and extended it to Switzerland, where he became more inclined to the Swiss ideas of the Lord's Supper than to Luther's. Returning to Hungary, he labored in various ways and places till his death, about 1547. No sermons of Dévày have come down, but he was diligent in preaching, and doubtless preached with power.

In Poland there were Italian refugees, Vergerio among them, who preached the Reformation; and, besides the orthodox, there were also followers of the Socini. But the best-known native reformer was the famous scholar and theologian, John à Lasco (1499-1560), who came of excellent family at Warsaw, was well educated, and for a time served as priest in his native land. About 1539 he became a Protestant, and, having to leave Poland, he labored for about ten years as pastor at Emden, in Friesland. Thence he came in 1549 to England, where he was pastor of a church of refugee Protestants of various nationalities in London. While in England he was much engaged in literary work for the Reformation, and was associated both with the English Protestants and with Butzer, Vermigli and other foreign reformers, till these were forced to leave by the change of policy on the accession of Queen Mary. A Lasco came to Denmark, then to his old home at Emden, and lastly to Poland, where, as Superintendent of the Reformed churches, he was permitted to labor to the end of his days in his native land. He was more of a writer, scholar, commentator and church organizer than preacher, and no sermons remain to give a fair notion of his pulpit powers. But as pastor and reformer he was active in preaching, and his other work shows that he was a thinker and expounder of excellent ability.

Albert of Brandenberg, who held Prussia for the Teutonic Knights, on becoming Protestant, made the province a dukedom, married and founded a family. Bishop George of Polentz aided Albert in introducing the Reformation. From him several sermons, of no special importance, remain. But Luther sent several preachers to aid in the work, the principal one of whom was John Briessmann (1488-1549), who did much by word and work to establish the Reformation in Prussia. After him came the contentious Osiander, from Nuremburg, but his polemical nature and preaching were not of the highest value to the cause.

More influential and notable as a preacher was Paul Spretter, Latinized into Speratus (1484-1551). He was a native of Swabia, was educated in Italy and at Paris, and early embraced the Protestant doctrines. He preached at various places in southern Germany with good effect, and as early as 1521 was found at Vienna, where in reply to a monk who had defended celibacy Speratus preached a powerful sermon, in which he not only showed that the Catholic practice was contrary to Scripture, but also took occasion to attack the whole system of vows as held in the Roman church. His boldness stirred up the Catholic authorities, and he was summoned to answer charges of heresy, but instead of appearing for trial he left Vienna and was promptly excommunicated. He was called to Ofen (Buda-Pest), but the opposition prevented his settling there, so he turned about and, as he passed through Moravia, going to Germany, he stopped at Iglau, where he was persuaded to remain and preach. This he did so well that he bound the Iglau congregation to him with an enduring affection, but also roused the determined opposition of the Catholic party. This led the authorities after several years to send him away, but he held the love of his flock, and they had a mutual compact that he should serve them again if better times permitted. So, in 1523, Speratus came to Wittenberg, where in various ways he aided Luther and the others till in the next year he was called to Königsberg, in Prussia. Going by Iglau he was released by his old flock there and took up his residence as court preacher in the ancient capital of the duchy of Prussia. For six years he was court preacher there, and then was appointed by Albert bishop (or superintendent) of Pomerania. Altogether he labored for twenty-seven years in Prussia, and did a great work as organizer of the churches, hymn-writer and popular and beloved preacher. The Protestant cause in Prussia owed much to the wise, patient and faithful labors of Paul Speratus.

6. Reformatory Preachers in Northern Europe

In the countries to the north of the centers of Protestantism there was progress in the spread of reformatory opinions, and there were preachers to proclaim and teach them. These preachers labored in the spirit and methods of the German and Swiss reformers, those in the Netherlands, at first Lutheran, becoming at last Calvinistic.

Among the preachers of the Low Countries mere mention[1] may be made of Jan Arends, Peter Gabriel, Nicholas Scheltius, and of Peter Datheen, who is specially noted by Van Oosterzee and Christlieb as a popular preacher of excellent gifts and wide influence. There was also at Oudenarde a man of special merit, Herman Modet (c. 1566), who preached on one occasion in a great assembly near Ghent, where in their hunger for the Word of God the crowded people listened to him for hours at a time. The pastor at Utrecht, Guibert Duishuis, was also a man of influence, and in his doctrinal views was a forerunner of the later Remonstrants.

But in those dreadful days of persecution and trial, which marked the early history of the Reformation in

[1] Christlieb in Herzog, as before; Van Oosterzee in the historical sketch prefixed to his *Practical Theology*.

the Netherlands, there was little opportunity for the development of distinctive pulpit eloquence. The martyrs were the best preachers. The story of one of the earliest of these will serve as a pathetic illustration of the class.[1] Thus runs the account of old Gerard Brandt, the historian of the Dutch Reformation: "John of Backer, who was not yet twenty-seven years old, was tied to a stake, strangled, and reduced to ashes, in the month of August, 1525. He suffered death for having preached in spite of the prohibitions, and because he was married. His examiners had several conferences with him during his imprisonment. They undertook to prove that a man should submit to all the decrees and traditions of the Romish Church, that heretics should be repressed and exterminated by the sword, and that priests should not marry. The preacher answered that he did not recognize any other rule of faith than Holy Scripture, and that it was not necessary to use other language than that of Scripture itself in order to interpret it; that a man should not rashly violate the decrees and canons, but should observe them when they were in accord with the Word of God; that violence should not be employed in religion, but rather gentleness and force of arguments. He complained that there was too much indulgence for the unchastity of priests, while chaste and honorable marriage, such as God approved, would not be tolerated. . . . On the fifteenth of September the prisoner was degraded from his rank [stripped of his priest's garments] on a scaffold and clothed with a yellow garment and hat of the same color, and then led to execution. In passing before the prison where a number of persons were confined for the faith he cried, in a loud voice, 'See, my brethren, I am ready to suffer martyrdom. Have courage as faithful soldiers of Jesus Christ, and, encouraged by my example, defend the truths of the gospel against all injustice.' The prisoners had no sooner heard these words than they clapped their hands and made great shouts of triumph, and to honor the martyrdom of their friend they sang the *Te Deum,* the *Certamen Martyrum,* the hymn *O Beata Martyrum Solemnia,* and their songs did not cease

[1] From the abridged French edition of Gerard Brandt's *History of the Reformation in the Netherlands,* Vol. I., p. 27 ff.

till the martyr had expired. When he was tied to the stake he cried, 'O death, where is thy sting? O grave, where is thy victory? Death is swallowed up in the victory of Jesus Christ.' At last the martyr died, after having pronounced these words, 'Lord Jesus, forgive them, for they know not what they do. O son of God, save me! Have mercy on me!' Such was the end of John of Backer. He was the first who suffered martyrdom in Holland for the doctrine of Luther." We do not know how much or how well this young man may have preached before this, but certainly this was a sermon of supreme eloquence; and the bloody work of persecution in the Netherlands gave only too frequent and sad occasions for many such sermons.

In Denmark the Reformation early gained a footing, and John Bugenhagen was called by King Christian to regulate the Lutheran churches there. Among the native preachers are mentioned Hans Tausen (d. 1561),[1] bishop of Ripen, who was noted for his "fresh, clear and edifying expositions of the Scriptures in forcible speech." His contemporary, Peter Palladius (d. 1560), bishop of Seeland, is also named as a preacher of popular power. Thus the distinctive type of Reformation preaching did not lack in Denmark its able representatives.

In Sweden also this was true, and, besides others, there were the brothers Olaf and Laurent Petri, who have been called "the Luther and Melanchthon of Sweden."[2] Olaf Petri (1497-1552) was born at Erebro, the son of a blacksmith, was educated among the Carmelite friars, but later went with his younger brother, Laurent, to Wittenberg, where they were taught by Luther and the other reformers, and came back to labor for the Reformation in their own country. Olaf became rector of a school at Strengnas in 1523, and combined preaching with his work. Here he gained a helper and able reformer in Laurent Andræ. Later Olaf was appointed preacher at Stockholm, from whence as a center his principal work was done. He was a fiery and sometimes rash and imprudent man, bringing upon himself and his cause the usual opposition and evils resulting from that temper and method.

[1] Christlieb, *op. cit.*

[2] Christlieb, *op. cit.*, and several encyclopædia articles.

But he was brave and true, and a preacher both of learning and popular power. There remain from him both sermons and expository homilies which are said to indicate ability of no mean order in the pulpit.

Of a different stamp was the younger brother, Laurent Petri (1499-1573), who was also educated at Wittenberg, was rather more of a scholar than Olaf, and decidedly of a milder and more moderate nature. Gustavus Vasa appointed him preacher at Upsala, and in 1531 made him archbishop there. He was very useful, both as preacher and prelate, and did especially valuable service by his Bible translations. He was benevolent and conciliatory. From him, as from his brother, there remain both sermons and *postils,* or expository homilies, those on the Gospels being mentioned as of considerable excellence.

7. The Anabaptists and Other Sects in Various Countries

Besides the better known and more widely influential preachers who represent one or other of the three leading phases—Lutheran, Zwinglian, Calvinistic—of the Reformation in Europe, there were numerous others, belonging to smaller sects, or representing only themselves and their following, who should be remembered. Naturally, these were very various in character, doctrines and abilities, and were found in different countries; but they may better be considered in a brief treatment together, and thus our survey of the reformation preaching on the Continent of Europe may be concluded.

Amid many persecutions both before and after the time of the Reformation the ancient Waldensian churches maintained themselves in their Piedmont valleys. We have seen how Farel and Saunier paid their synod a helpful visit in 1532 and encouraged them. Other reformers also took an interest in them, but it appears that not until they were permitted to build churches, about 1555, did preaching among them begin to assume a more dignified form than the simple hortatory homilies of their devotional meetings. In later times they have had several preachers of note.

It was not surprising that the Reformation should have

given encouragement by its revolt from Rome to many fanatics and extremists of various sorts. Among these were some men of decided abilities as preachers and popular leaders, but their faults and excesses hindered their own success, and also, to some extent, compromised and greatly embarrassed the leaders of the Reformation. Among the more extreme may be named, without discussion, the imprudent Carlstadt, whose actions were a great annoyance to Luther and the rest; the so-called Zwickau prophets, who believed in an immediate inspiration; and the ill-fated Thomas Münzer, who, along with many hurtful errors, held also some important truths and led the peasants' uprising to disastrous defeat. Later than these were the so-called "Mad Men of Münster," who disgraced the Anabaptist name and cause by their wild excesses, and who carried with them—reluctantly as it seems in most things—at least one preacher of no little eloquence and influence, Bernard Rothmann. Others who were more or less associated with the Anabaptists and had some talent as popular preachers were Melchior Hoffman, who led a very unsettled life, and was not a man of much culture, but yet knew how to reach and influence people; and the erratic David Joris of Holland, who likewise was a wanderer, but an attractive personality and a sensational and bold speaker.

The name Anabaptist has been applied with little discrimination to a variety of sectaries in the sixteenth century. It was not a name of their own choosing, but was bestowed by their enemies to indicate that they were the rebaptizers, those who insisted that all who had received baptism in infancy should, on conversion, be baptized again. But both the name, and the conception involved in it, does an injustice. These men insisted that infant baptism was unscriptural and therefore no baptism at all, that only repentant and believing persons should be baptized upon profession of faith. But of those who adopted this principle not all held the same views in other respects. Especially is it necessary to distinguish the fanatical and revolutionary element from the more conservative. It is not just to charge all with the errors and excesses of some, and it is only historically fair to recognize that there was no general and well defined body of Anabaptists, but that the name was loosely applied to many different varieties. But partisanry is not discriminating, and so it is true that many deserving men have been called by this name of reproach and accused of crimes which they reprobated.

The Swiss Anabaptists were not of the revolutionary character of Münzer and the men of Münster, but they were stout in their opposition to infant baptism and to the union of church and state, and so they were persecuted and repressed by the civil authorities under the advice of Zwingli and other reformers.

In regard to preaching, there was among them a custom of mission, itinerant preaching—a view that ordination was not vitally necessary, and that lay preaching, even by those who had no learning, was permissible.[1] Hence we find among the Swiss Anabaptists some who were not highly educated, but yet were effective preachers, as Blaurock and others. But, on the other hand, Reublin, Grebel and Mantz were cultivated and able men and strong preachers. In Moravia, Friesland and Holland, also, there were not a few preachers of good learning and popular power among these persecuted people. We may select two of the most eminent for a somewhat more extended notice—Hübmaier and Menno.

Prominently identified with both the Swiss and the Moravian Anabaptists was the scholarly and eloquent Balthasar Hübmaier (d. 1528), who was born at Friedberg, near Augsburg, about 1480. He studied at Freiburg under John Eck, taught school at Schaffhausen for awhile to help pay expenses at the university, and in 1512 followed Eck to Ingolstadt, where he was for a time pastor of the town church and professor in the university. His preaching power was already recognized and he was called in January, 1516, to be cathedral preacher at Regensburg, where he worked for some years. One token of his power over men by speech was the fact that his preaching against the Jews led to their being banished from the town; their synagogue was destroyed, and on the site a chapel was built to the Virgin. But this led to

[1] My colleague, Dr. W. J. McGlothlin, has brought out some interesting facts, including this, in his thesis—on the Bernese Anabaptists—presented with success to the University of Berlin for the Doctorate in 1902.

pilgrimages and other superstitious excesses, and Hübmaier began to oppose these things. Thus he was making a slight beginning toward the reformatory doctrines. Some opposition developed and he was led to accept a preaching appointment at Waldshut in 1521. His study of the Bible and of Luther's writings accelerated his conversion to the principles of the Reformation. He returned to Regensburg for a few months, but his preaching was now so decidedly reformatory that he could not remain there, and came back again to Waldshut. This town was under the Austrian dominion, but was near the Swiss border and not far from important places in Germany. During this second and more extended pastorate at Waldshut Hübmaier's character and convictions as a reformer became settled. His reformatory zeal and his powerful preaching began to tell, and his work resulted in the adoption of the Reformation by the church and people of Waldshut in 1524.

Up to this point Hübmaier was in sympathy with Zwingli, and the Waldshut reform was effected in the Swiss mode. But about now the question of infant baptism began to agitate the Swiss reformers. Zwingli himself entertained for a while serious doubts as to the rightfulness of the practice. Œcolampadius, too, was not wholly convinced. Leo Jud long wavered, and the gentle Capito could always see that there were two sides to the Anabaptist controversy. The question was never decided on its merits, but imprudences on the part of the Anabaptists, and their stubborn opposition to authority, complicated the situation and made it largely a semi-political and partisan strife, wherein men's passions were aroused to punish and resist, and thus disastrous results followed. Hübmaier early became convinced that infant baptism was contrary to Scripture, and began so to teach. In 1525 he received baptism at the hands of William Reublin, and led the majority of the Waldshut church to adopt the Anabaptist view of the Reformation. Meantime he ably held his own with Zwingli, Œcolampadius and others in discussing the question, both orally and in writings. But the issue went against the Anabaptists; they were compromised with the Peasants' War, and its disastrous and bloody ending hurt their cause. Waldshut lacked now the sympathy of Zürich, fell into the hands of the princes, and, being under Austrian control, was forcibly subjected to the Catholic party. Thus ended the Reformation there, and Hübmaier was forced to flee. Now comes a dark place in his career, which it is difficult to comprehend and explain.

Hübmaier came to Zürich, where he was secretly received by friends, but was discovered by the authorities and put on some kind of trial. It is said that he asked the privilege of making a public recantation of his Anabaptist views, and, on being permitted to preach for this purpose at the Grossmünster, he played false, and, instead of renouncing his views, proceeded to defend them with his wonted eloquence and cogency. Afterwards, on being reproached for his breach of promise and of propriety, he is reported to have said that it must have been the suggestion of the devil that made him do so. All the time he was arguing the case with Zwingli and others, and finally it is claimed that he did renounce his Anabaptist views, satisfied the Zürich authorities, and with permission, and perhaps pressure, to depart, received from them money for his journey, and left the city. If the statements of his opponents are to be taken without allowance, Hübmaier certainly does not appear well in this affair. But his side of the controversy has not been written, and from a statement that he boasted at Constance of having come off victor over Zwingli in the arguments, we may infer that his alleged recantation at Zürich was more forced than genuine. At the same time it seems impossible to acquit him of some insincerity and diplomacy in the trying and perilous situation in which he was placed. As to the provision of his travelling expenses from Zürich, it is easy to suppose that the authorities may not have been wholly disinterested in helping the redoubtable champion of Anabaptism to get away.

After brief stops at Constance and other places, Hübmaier came at last, in July, 1526, to Nikolsburg, in Moravia, where the Anabaptists had some strength. Here he received protection from a nobleman, who sympathized with the Anabaptists, and was enabled to employ a printing press and publish his writings. Here, also, he was pastor of the congregation, and speedily, by his rare qualities of speech and persuasion, brought great numbers to accept his views. The Anabaptist cause became very strong throughout all that region. But, unhappily, some rash spirits troubled the prosperity of the movement, and at this juncture Moravia passed from Bavarian to Austrian rule, and persecution began. Hübmaier was promptly called to account. No doubt the Catholic opposition was at the bottom, and it was a religious persecution, but Hübmaier's work at Waldshut gave pretext for accusing him of having occasioned the revolt of that city and of complicity in the peasant uprising of 1525. He was imprisoned, and after various ineffectual efforts to get release, at first wavering but finally refusing to retract his religious convictions, he was condemned. So on a public square in Vienna he was burned, March 10, 1528, his faithful wife encouraging him. He met his end with a martyr's steadfastness; and his noble wife a few days later was drowned in the Danube.

All the accounts agree that Hübmaier was a forcible and eloquent preacher. Œcolampadius, Vadian, even Bullinger, bear emphatic testimony to this effect, and the results of his work at every place where he served as pastor show that he had unusual power of influencing men to action by his preaching. Among his writings it does not appear that any sermons remain, but of one of his works Broadus says,[1] "I find a really beautiful address (A.D. 1525) to the three churches of Regensburg, Ingolstadt and Freiburg, entitled *The Sum of a Truly Christian Life,* to be of the nature of a sermon. The arrangement is good and the divisions distinctly stated. He is decidedly vigorous and acute in argument, making very sharp points. The style is clear and lively; when he has begun you feel drawn along, and want to follow him."

Another man of great popular power and influence, commonly reckoned with the Anabaptists, was Menno Simons (1492-1559), whose work was chiefly in Friesland, Holstein and the adjoining regions, reaching also into Holland. He was the founder of the sect called Mennonites, who have maintained a vigorous life to this

[1] *Hist. Prea.*, p. 131.

day, and have a considerable following in the United States. Menno was born in Friesland, educated, and became a priest and a preacher of considerable force in the Catholic church. In 1531 he became parish priest in his native town of Witmarsum, and his development in evangelical opinions soon afterwards began. About this time the execution of a man for holding Anabaptist views made a profound impression on Menno, and led him to investigate the question of infant baptism. But it was only after several years that he became sufficiently convinced to teach these views publicly. He had no sympathy with the Münster fanatics, nor with all who bore the Anabaptist name. Carefully and earnestly he worked out his own position and devoted his life to teaching and spreading the views which he believed to be taught by the Word of God. As his convictions were nearest to those held by the larger number of Anabaptists, there was no impropriety in his taking charge of an Anabaptist church at Groningen in 1537, where he labored for a number of years, not only in his own congregation, but, by visits and numerous writings, in the adjoining regions, and even beyond them. At one time he had a discussion with the eminent theologian John à Lasco, then working at Emden, in Friesland. The debate was characterized by both ability and charity, a combination not always visible in religious disputes then or since. Later, because of persecution, Menno removed to Wismar, and finally settled in Holstein, where he spent the last twelve years of his active life, dying in 1559.

Menno wrote in the Low-German (*plattdeutsch*) dialect, but his writings were done into Dutch and other languages. He was a prolific author, and many of his writings remain. There do not appear to be sermons, strictly speaking, among them, but doubtless many are the outgrowth of his pulpit work. As a preacher he had the character of a mild but well-convinced and firm defender of his views, a faithful and diligent worker, and a man of eloquence and persuasive power over people.

Upon the whole, the preaching of the sectaries, with all its varieties, was true to the fundamental principle of the Reformation—the sole authority of the Word of God as the basis of preaching and of life in the churches. It also exemplified a noble care for the religious needs of the common people, and displayed a popular power at least not less striking than that of the better known reformers. Altogether those critical years of reform in Europe were strenuous in conflict and in toil, and through their preachers the Word of God came to the people with power.

CHAPTER XIV

Preachers of the Reformation in England and Scotland

Both the causes and character of the Reformation in Great Britain differed in many important respects from those of the movement on the Continent, and yet there was necessarily very close connection and sympathy between these movements. In both cases the relation between the Reformation and preaching was close and vital. Except Wiclif, there was in England no great preacher before the Reformation; since that time there have been no preachers in all the world who, in the essentials of true pulpit eloquence, have surpassed the English Protestant divines. And, whatever may be the explanation of the singular fact, it is true that no English Catholic preacher has ever occupied corresponding rank with his great Protestant contemporaries in his own land or with his more noted Romanist brethren in others. Cardinal Newman is no exception, because his best pulpit work belongs, not to his Catholic, but to his Anglican days. In Scotland the case is exactly parallel; no great preacher before the Reformation, since then, in the Protestant bodies, a multitude. It is idle to conjecture what might have been the influence on preaching if a purified Romanism had been the modern type of British Christianity, but the fact is that the Reformation produced the modern British pulpit.

1. The English Reformation and its Preaching

No doubt the character of Henry VIII. and his suit for divorce from Katharine of Arragon were very influential in bringing on and shaping the English Reformation; no doubt also the patriotic desire for independence of papal authority in England had very much to do with it; no doubt, further, that many churchmen in the country sympathized with both these elements of the situation; but back of all these things there lay in the minds of the great English people a deep discontent with existing religious conditions, and a readiness to be led in mending them. This readiness settled more and more into a fixed and mighty purpose through the troubled reigns of Henry, Edward, and Mary, until it reached its accomplishment under Elizabeth. Not sovereigns, statesmen nor prelates could have wrought out the English Reformation unless there had been among the people themselves an intelligent, vigorous and religiously earnest party of reform, which, though at first not in the majority, yet knew how to make its influence felt. Preaching, as we have seen in our account of Wiclif[1] and his work, had much to do with creating and manifesting this sentiment; and we shall from now on have to consider the great part it played in the powerful movement of the age.[2] Well says Mr. W. H. Beckett,[3] "In an age which was eminently a hearing and not a reading one, the influence of such able and zealous preachers as Latimer, Knox, Ridley, Hooper, Bradford, can scarcely be overestimated. In its preachers rather than its rulers was the strength of the Reformation movement."

The work of Wiclif and the Lollards had by no means spent its force. Beckett shows how the Lollard preaching was most influential in those very regions (mostly in the south and east) where the strength of the Reformation was greatest. He also points out that the lack of records of Lollard persecutions for a long time before the Tudors came to the throne does not, as commonly supposed, indicate that the Lollards had been suppressed; but the cessation of persecution was due to the unsettled state of the country during the Wars of the Roses. As Fuller puts it, "The very storm was their shelter." The revival of persecution under both the Tudor Henrys shows that the Lollards were still in evidence. In their

[1] *Ante*, p. 336 ff.

[2] I have found great pleasure and help in the brief and popular, but at the same time able and scholarly work of the Rev. W. H. Beckett, *The English Reformation of the Sixteenth Century.*

[3] Chap. XX.

preaching they denounced the Romanist doctrines with mighty earnestness and exalted the Scriptures as the sufficient guide to doctrine and duty. This Lollard influence not only disposed the people to desire and hear gladly the evangelical preaching, but also was of force in forming the preachers themselves.

Another highly important sign of the coming change was the reformatory sentiment that found place in both the universities. At Oxford Colet's [1] work was finished on the eve of the Reformation, and his name and influence were by no means forgotten. Cardinal Wolsey had some projects for instituting reforms in the church—disciplinary rather than doctrinal—and it was among his plans to found at Oxford, from the proceeds of certain suppressed monasteries, a new college which should afford a better culture for priests. His career was suddenly cut short, and we do not know what sort of reforms might have come under his guidance. At Oxford Erasmus taught, as well as at Cambridge, during his stay in England. In 1510 his famous satire, *The Praise of Folly,* appeared, with its dedication to Sir Thomas More, and it was much read in England. In 1516, from Basel, his Greek Testament appeared, and had a great influence at both the universities and among the better clergy elsewhere. At Cambridge there was in the early years of the sixteenth century, before the distinctively reformatory events began, a decided tendency in that direction. Several of the most distinguished preachers of the Reformation, as well as others who helped it in other ways, were at this time studying and working at Cambridge. Thus, with Lollard sentiments among the people and the new ideas of learning and theology working at both the educational centers of the nation, there were preparatory influences of the first importance for the preaching of the Reformation. That preaching did not begin in any sudden or particularly impressive way, but gradually grew up and gained power by its own momentum, and by the help of other influences as it went on.

We have already had frequent occasion to observe the natural sympathetic relation of preaching to the age in which it finds its exercise; and both in a general way

[1] *Ante,* p. 342.

and in many important particulars this was manifest in the English reformation preaching. That widespread stimulus of thought which came from the discovery of America, the invention of printing, the revival of learning, all in the fifteenth century, left its traces upon the English mind and the English preaching as it did elsewhere, and it may be dismissed with this brief reminder. More immediate was the effect of the course of events in England itself.

The reigns of the four Tudor sovereigns under whom the Reformation occurred afford convenient as well as historically appropriate waymarks to denote its progress and its influence upon preaching. During the reign of Henry VIII. (1509-1547) the personal character of the monarch counted for something in regard to preaching as well as the general progress of the Reformation, for the king was disposed to manage everything in sight, preaching included. But his partiality for Cranmer and respect for Latimer were strong indirect encouragements of the Reformation, though Henry was in doctrine always far more of a Catholic than a reformer. The great reform parliament (1529-1536) was literally the power behind the throne in his reign, and its reformatory acts, especially those suppressing the monasteries, were of profound importance to preaching. But the Six Articles (1539) were decidedly reactionary in doctrine, and made it very dangerous to preach Protestant views. The reign of the boy king, Edward VI.—really a regency or protectorate (1547-1553)—was most favorable to the preaching of the Reformation. The statesmen who guided the policy of England during this time sympathized with the Reformation, and Cranmer was the leading spirit in ecclesiastical affairs. The Six Articles were repealed, Protestant divines from abroad (Butzer, Peter Martyr Vermigli, Ochino, John à Lasco) were invited to England and put in places of influence, and important acts were passed regarding the supply of preachers for the parishes. But there was no unrestricted liberty to preach; license was required before a preacher was permitted to exercise his ministry, and the requirement seems to have been pretty well enforced. Under Mary (1553-1558) two things virtually put a stop to Protestant preaching in England for a while: (1) the reëstablishment of the Catholic worship; and (2) the martyrdom, imprisonment or banishment of the leading Protestant preachers. But in these dark days the nation was being tested for better times, and the effect of the persecution was to aid rather than hinder the establishment of Protestantism in the next reign.

Under Elizabeth, who began to reign in 1558, the restoration of Protestantism was at first compromisingly cautious and slow. Its final establishment occurred in the latter part of her reign. But yet, in her early days, something was gradually done for the rehabilitation of reformatory preaching. The need was indeed great, for the dearth of preachers during the first years of Elizabeth's reign was fearful. At first, to avoid controversies, preaching was forbidden for a while,[1] the church services being confined to the reading in English of the Gospel and Epistles for the day, the Ten Commandments, the Apostles' Creed, and the Litany. At St. Paul's Cross—the famous scene of so much preaching in better days—there was no sermon from Christmas to Easter. It is true this prohibition of preaching was only temporary, but it aggravated the trouble occasioned by the general disorganization of worship, the unsettled state of the country, and the paucity of Protestant preachers. Thomas Lever[2] wrote to Bullinger at Zürich in the second year of Elizabeth's reign: "Many of our parishes have no clergy; and out of that very small number who administer the sacrament throughout this great country there is hardly one in a hundred who is both able and willing to preach the Word of God." This lack of preachers and preaching continued for a long time. Fourteen years after Elizabeth's accession it is said that as many as thirty-four parishes even in the diocese of Canterbury were vacant. In many churches there was only occasional preaching during the year.

Yet some effort was made to repair the dreadful breach caused in the ranks of the clergy by the persecution under Mary. In December, 1559, Parker was made archbishop of Canterbury. The death of Cardinal Pole, who was appointed to succeed Cranmer, spared Protestantism the necessity of deposing him, and perhaps the shame of re-

[1] Beckett, *op. cit.*, p. 264. [2] Beckett, p. 274.

taliation for Cranmer's wrongs. The appointment of other prelates and clergy followed rapidly. Grindal, who had been much associated with Ridley, and was a fine preacher, was made bishop of London. Sandys, who was also a preacher of some force, was assigned to the see of Worcester; and Jewel, perhaps the ablest preacher of them all, was created bishop of Salisbury. Both Sandys and Jewel had imbibed the German and Swiss ideas of reform, and were thorough-going Protestants. There were many ordinations and appointments of the lower clergy, and to meet the pressing need a temporary order of readers was instituted to read the services and the homilies without administering the sacraments. Thus slowly and with difficulty did Protestant preaching recover strength in England after the sharp check of those five blighting years of Mary's reign.

Recurring now to the earlier days, we must consider another powerful influence upon the history of reform preaching. Most important service was rendered to the progress of the English Reformation and to its preaching by the translation and dissemination of the Bible, and the production of Protestant literature. The English Bible was one of the Reformation's most precious gifts to the world. The work of translation went on from the days of Wiclif to the publication of the King James Version in 1611; and that crowning achievement, as its familiar title page reminds us, was based on the earlier versions—"With former translations diligently compared and revised." Most of these "former translations" appeared within the time we are now studying,[1] and it is impossible to over-emphasize their importance in the development of Protestant preaching, both as regards the quickening of intelligent spiritual interest in the hearers and the more thorough furnishing of the preachers.

Besides the circulation of the Bible, the production and publication of Protestant literature greatly helped the preaching of the reformed doctrines. Erasmus' *Para-*

[1] Tindale's New Testament, 1525-1529; Coverdale's Bible (entire), 1535; "Matthew's" (probably Rogers' publication of translations left by Tindale and supplemented by portions from Coverdale) soon after; then the "Great Bible," and Cranmer's Bible—all before 1550.

phrase of the New Testament was translated into English and appointed to be read in the churches. Frith's sharp *Disputation of Purgatory* appeared in 1531, and called forth a vigorous defence of the doctrine by Sir Thomas More. Tindale's able statement of the doctrine of justification by faith in his exposition of the *Parable of the Wicked Mammon,* and his more important treatise on the *Obedience of a Christian Man,* were powerful contributions to the Protestant cause, and supplied many a preacher with arguments and reinforcements. The two fundamental principles of the English Reformation—the supremacy of the king in the external government of the church, and the sole authority of Scripture in doctrine—were clearly and strongly set forth in the treatise. In 1537 there was drawn up by a committee of bishops and published a work called *The Institution of a Christian Man.* It contained an exposition of the Apostles' Creed, the Lord's Prayer, and the Ten Commandments, very largely with a Protestant coloring; though modifications in a later edition under Gardiner's influence made it more Catholic in tone. The book was intended chiefly to instruct the clergy, and was familiarly known as the "Bishop's Book." In its first form it undoubtedly helped the preachers to set forth the evangelical doctrines. The development of the Prayer Book in successive editions and modifications through the reigns of Henry, Edward and Elizabeth, likewise had a relation to preaching in that its being in English helped to popularize worship, and it also recognized the place of preaching in the service.

More directly connected with preaching, however, was the preparation—long apart—of the two books of *Homilies.* The first of these was published in the time of King Edward "for the staying of such errors as were then sparkled among the people." The idea was much like that which lay back of the old Homilies of Ælfric and the later ones of Wiclif; to aid the less cultured preachers in what they should say, or, in the absence of ability to use the material for fresh sermons, to be read as they were. Three of the twelve are said to have been written by Cranmer; others were contributed by Ridley, Latimer, Butzer, and perhaps others. They set out the principal doctrines of the Reformation very distinctly. The later book was published after the restoration of Protestantism under Elizabeth, being sanctioned by the Convocation of 1562. The work was done by the prelates of that later date, has a larger number of homilies, and is even more distinctly Protestant in tone. In one way these Homilies helped preaching, that is, by affording material to the uninstructed clergy; in another they injured it, by encouraging dependence upon such helps.

Reformatory preaching in England was characterized by the traits common to that movement in all the European countries, but modified by the language and habits of thought of the people, and by the circumstances attending the origin and development of the English Reformation. The first sermon of the *Book of Homilies,*[1] printed in 1548, is entitled " A Fruitful Exhortacion to the Readynge of Holye Scripture," and declares both the sufficiency of the Bible as a rule of faith and the necessity for studying and reading it to the humble as well as to the learned. Thus the cardinal principle of the Reformation is here distinctly laid down, and no doubt was equally emphasized in the sermons by individual preachers. The sermon on Salvation, ascribed to Cranmer, affirms and reiterates the doctrine of justification by faith alone; and the relation of faith and works is thus set forth: " In our justification is not only God's mercye and grace, but also his justice, whiche the Apostle calleth the justice [righteousness] of God; and it consisteth in paiynge our raunsome and fulfillynge of the lawe; and so the grace of God doth not exclude the justice of God in our justification, but onely excludeth the justice [righteousness] of man, that is to saie, the justice of our woorkes as to be merites of deservyng our justification. And, therefore, sainct Paule declareth here nothynge upon the behalf of man concerning his justification, but onely a true and lively faith, which nevertheless is the gift of God and not mannes onely work without God. And yet that faythe

[1] I had the pleasure of using (in the Bibliothêque Nationale, Paris) an ancient edition of the *Book of Homilies* " imprinted at London the XXI daye of Iune in the seconde yere of the reigne of our souvereigne lord kyng Edward the VI; by Rychard Grafton printer to his moste royall maiestie; in the yere of our Lord MDXLVIII."

doeth not exclude repentaunce, hope, love, dread and the feare of God to be joyned with faith in every man that is justified, but it excludeth them from the office of justifyinge. So that, although they be all presente together in him that is justified, yet they justify not altogether." The sermons on faith and good works carry out this idea further, and those on Christian morals are satisfactory.

Of course the *Homilies*, as well as the sermons of Latimer, Bradford and the rest, bring out fully that our sole dependence for salvation is on Christ, and they oppose all externalism. The Romanist doctrines of the mass, transubstantiation, penances, purgatory, papal supremacy, and the like are attacked with the customary Protestant arguments. While the Scriptures are exalted as the rule of faith and are always quoted, and usually, very appositely, there is less of distinctive exposition than in the Lutheran and Reformed sermons. Commentaries could not be constructed from the sermons of the English reformers as they could from those of Luther and Calvin. And the number of preserved sermons is comparatively very small. There are a good many from Latimer, for he had a Swiss friend and secretary who was at pains to write out a large number of them, but from the rest only a very few remain.

Criticisms of individuals will be reserved for the biographical notices, but it may be remarked that from the contemporary accounts, as well as from the remaining specimens of sermons, we see that the English reform preachers held the evangelical doctrine, and they preached it with simplicity and with power. Their courage, constancy, fidelity to truth and duty, and their power to move, win and hold their countrymen, are all apparent in their sermons. To a study of some of these noble men we must now turn.

2. Preachers of the English Reformation

At any time in the history of preaching there are distinguished preachers who are not specially distinguished *as* preachers; their pulpit gifts are not commensurate with their services in other directions. The era of the Reformation in England affords abundant illustration of this fact, and a few of the preachers of this class must be noticed.[1]

We naturally think first of the famous archbishop of Canterbury under Henry VIII. and Edward VI., Thomas Cranmer (1489-1556). The future leader of the English Reformation came of good old family in Nottinghamshire. His mother was left a widow while Thomas was still young, but she cared for his education, sending him to Cambridge at the age of fourteen. Here he remained for eight years, taking the regular degrees in course and being made a fellow of Jesus College. This fellowship he lost through marriage, in accordance with the custom, but was reëlected to it on the early death of his wife. He was thus in residence at Cambridge for a number of years, was made a doctor of divinity and gave lectures on that subject; but when he was ordained a priest and what preaching places he filled in his early career are not mentioned in the accounts of his life.

As is well known, his rapid promotion to high ecclesiastical positions was due to the favor of Henry VIII. because of Cranmer's—no doubt sincere—convictions as to the rightfulness of the king's divorce, and as to the means by which it might be secured. In 1533 Cranmer was made archbishop of Canterbury, and soon thereafter the famous cause was tried before him as Primate of England, and the divorce was granted. Faithful, sometimes indeed subservient, to Henry all his life, Cranmer never lost the favor of his royal patron; and through the reign of the boy king, Edward, he retained and faithfully administered his great office.

Though Cranmer was far from rash or very decided in his reformatory progress, there is no reason to doubt that he was sincere in his growing adhesion to the Protestant views. He was disposed to follow rather than lead in matters of opinion, and he especially deferred much to the wise and learned Ridley. Though not a strong preacher himself, he did occasionally preach. He wrote some of the Homilies; and he gave generous and effective encouragement to such powerful preachers as Latimer, Ridley, Bradford, Grindal and others.

On the accession of Mary, Cranmer was degraded from

[1] In preparing the sketches that follow I have found the articles in the *Dict. Nat. Biog.* of especially good service.

his high offices and imprisoned along with Latimer, Ridley and others. From his prison window he was a mournful witness of the martyrdom of his two faithful companions, and in a few months followed in their way. The timidity and weakness which led him to sign a series of recantations of his Protestant views were only atoned for by the brave and pathetic way in which he came to his true self at the end, renounced his weak and insincere recantations, reasserted his real views, and cheerfully died for them. It is easy to criticise the obvious weaknesses of Cranmer—his over-caution, his vacillation, his subserviency—but his virtues should not be forgotten—his kindness, generosity, forgiving disposition; and his great services to the cause of Protestantism in England in the trying days of his life should be fully recognized.

The chief significance of William Tindale (d. 1536) is as a Bible translator and author, but he was also a preacher of promise, and doubtless would easily have attained eminence in that regard had his life-work not been directed in another and extremely useful channel. He was born in the west of England, near the Welsh border, in the ninth decade of the fifteenth century, and after preliminary training studied with marked diligence and success at both Oxford and Cambridge. After taking his degrees he was ordained priest, and taught for a while in the family of a gentleman in Gloucestershire, and preached at various places nearby, including out-of-door services on the College Green at Bristol. His preaching was effective, and as his views were already verging toward reform, the clergy was aroused and had the bold preacher called to account before the bishop. Tindale defended himself with ability and was released. He is said to have remarked to one of his opponents, " If God spare my life ere many years I will cause a boy that directeth a plow shall know more of the Scripture than thou dost." This shows that already he had formed the purpose of translating the Bible into English.

With this great project in his mind he came to London hoping to receive aid and encouragement from the scholarly bishop Tunstall. This was the very Tunstall who a few years later was to buy up and burn a quantity of Tindale's Testaments. Naturally Tindale got no help in that quarter, but having in some way secured a preaching place in one of the London parishes, his sermons attracted notice and won him the fast and helpful friendship of a certain Humphrey Monmouth, who aided him with sympathy and in practical ways. Coming to the conclusion that he could not safely or successfully accomplish his great design in England, Tindale left the country. The first edition of his translation of the New Testament was published at Worms, in Germany, in 1525 or 1526. Later Tindale moved to Antwerp, where a second edition was published in 1529. Meantime his two great Protestant treatises—the exposition of the *Wicked Mammon,* and the *Obedience of a Christian Man*—had appeared, and gave great help to the cause of reform in England. These writings involved him in a vigorous controversy with the accomplished Thomas More, in which Tindale amply sustained himself against that master of dialectic and style.

While residing at Antwerp and working at his translation of the Old Testament, Tindale met and influenced John Rogers, in whose hands he left his uncompleted work. For, in 1535, Tindale was in some way betrayed into leaving the protection of the so-called "English House" at Antwerp, and was captured by the imperial authorities. It was not to the taste of Charles V. or his agents in the Netherlands to have this arch-heretic busily at work at Antwerp. After a period of imprisonment at Vilvorde, and on the refusal of Henry VIII. to interfere in his behalf, Tindale was executed as a heretic in 1536. At the stake he is said to have prayed, "Lord, open the King of England's eyes." Tindale was a competent scholar, and much of his interpretation and diction has been retained in all subsequent English versions of the Bible.

Next to Tindale should be named his friend John Rogers (d. 1555), who was born near Birmingham about the beginning of the sixteenth century. He was educated at Cambridge and began his ministry as priest in a small London parish, but on going to Antwerp to serve the English congregation there he came under Tindale's influence, and probably was thus led to embrace Protestant views. He married, went to Germany, where at Wittenberg he came in touch with the Reformers and put forth the version of the Bible known as "Matthew's Bible," consisting of Tindale's published and unpublished work, with some parts filled in from Coverdale's version. In 1548, Edward now reigning, Rogers returned to England, and was appointed successively to several different preaching places, the most important being one connected with St. Paul's Cathedral, to which he was assigned by Bishop Ridley.

In his preaching Rogers did not spare the corrupt courtiers about Edward VI., and he thus made some enemies, and was called before the council to answer for some of his utterances. But without cringing or retraction he made so frank and manly a justification of his course that he remained unpunished. In July, 1553, during the brief interval between Edward and Mary, when the unfortunate Lady Jane Grey was acknowledged queen by a small following, Rogers, by order of her council, preached at St. Paul's Cross, but he did not at that time touch upon the political situation. A few weeks later, however, after Mary had been acknowledged queen, he preached again, and this time was not so prudent. According to Foxe,[1] "he made a godly and vehement sermon at St. Paul's Cross, confirming such true doctrine as he and others had taught there in King Edward's days, exhorting the people constantly to remain in the same and to beware of all pestilent popery, idolatry and superstition." It was not wise, perhaps, but it was brave unto daring and faithful unto death—the stake was its earthly, the crown its heavenly, reward. It was Rogers' last sermon. Summoned before the royal council to answer for his conduct, he pleaded that he had only preached the religion established by law; and this was true, for there had not been time to change the reformatory statutes of Edward's reign. But this shrewd plea only embarrassed the persecutors for a time. Rogers was summoned again, confined in his own house, then deprived of his offices as preacher, then imprisoned, several times examined, condemned as a heretic, and after more than a year of trials and imprisonments was finally brought to the stake in February, 1555, the first of that "noble army of martyrs" who suffered under Mary's reign. His wife and

[1] Quoted by Beckett, p. 211.

children spoke to him as he passed to the place of suffering and encouraged him to steadfastness; and De Noailles, the French ambassador, who witnessed the scene, wrote in his report that Rogers " went to his death as though it had been his wedding."

No sermons remain from Rogers to give us an insight into his manner of preaching, but he was held in highest esteem as a preacher by Ridley and other excellent judges; and his courage, fidelity and effectiveness in the pulpit were shown on more than one trying occasion.

A man of very different stamp was Miles Coverdale (1488-1568), also one of the venerated pioneers in English Bible translation, and a preacher of merit and influence. Coverdale was a native of Yorkshire, a graduate of Cambridge, and as early as 1514 an ordained priest. He joined the Augustinian friars and came under the early reformatory influence of Barnes, prior to the abbey of that order at Cambridge. After a time he left the convent and devoted himself to an itinerant evangelizing ministry in different parts of the country. From about 1526 for a year or two there are traces of his activity and success in this work, and then for a long time he disappears from view till the publication of his translation—the first complete one—of the Bible in 1535, just ten years after Tindale's New Testament. During this time Coverdale was probably for the most part abroad and hard at work on his translation. It was published out of England, but the place has been disputed; probably Antwerp has the honor. Coverdale returned to England for a short time about 1538 and got married, but on the fall of Cromwell and the punishment of Barnes, his friends, he prudently left the country and spent a term of years as pastor of a Lutheran church and as schoolmaster at Bergzabern, in the province of Zweibrücken (Deux Ponts), in Germany. Doubtless during his long sojourn abroad, while translating the Bible, he had learned the languages and made the connections which rendered this arrangement possible. The accession of Edward VI., and the now dominant influence of Cranmer and other reformers, gave Coverdale opportunity to come back to England in 1548.

He was received with marked and deserved favor, and

after filling with acceptance several lower places was made bishop of Exeter in 1551. Of his work in that diocese an old chronicler is quoted as saying: "He most worthilie did performe the office committed unto him; he preached continuallie on everi holie day, and did read most commonly twise in the weeke in some church or other in this citie." On the accession of Mary, Coverdale was put out of his bishopric and a Catholic put in, but through various influences he was allowed to leave England instead of being sent to the stake. Stopping for a while with English friends in Denmark and then in Westphalia, he finally made his way back to his old place at Bergzabern, a second time his refuge.

Once more and lastly this good man of long life and many mutations came back to his native land; this was when the death of Mary ended the persecutions and gave distressed and wasted Protestantism a chance to recover itself under Elizabeth. Coverdale had become more Puritan in his views, and now declined reappointment as bishop, though as titular bishop of Exeter he took part in the consecration of Parker as Archbishop of Canterbury. The rest of his life was devoted to preaching in different places, and he was much sought after. Though not so strong a character as some others of the prominent reformers, and though escaping extreme punishment, Coverdale was never recreant to his principles, and through all his long and troubled life was an eminently good and useful man. The general testimony of his contemporaries represents him as a preacher of more than average popularity and influence.

Useful in the pulpit as were all these men, particularly Rogers and Coverdale, there is a group of reformers whose services and fame lay chiefly in their preaching; and the best known and greatest of these was the eminent bishop and martyr, Hugh Latimer [1] (d. 1555).

About the year 1490, or perhaps even earlier, in the county of Leicester, there was born to a well-to-do yeoman farmer the babe who, in course of stressful years, was to become the most powerful and popular preacher

[1] *Sermons and Remains of Bp. Latimer,* with biographical sketches compiled from Foxe and other sources edited for the Parker Society by the Rev. G. E. Corrie, Cambridge, 1844-5.

of the Reformation in England, and to be in his old age a martyr for the cause he loved. This was Hugh Latimer, an only son, but with several sisters. Do these two facts help to account for that naive and refreshingly inoffensive egotism which we find in his sermons? After education in the schools near his home the wide-awake lad was sent very young to Cambridge, where he resided and studied a number of years as undergraduate, resident graduate and preacher. He took his degrees in the regular course; his conduct at college was irreproachable, and he was highly esteemed by his mates.

At first a very decided papist, he fell under the influence of Thomas Bilney and others, and became converted to the reformed doctrines. Many years later (in 1552), when now an old man, in his first sermon on the Lord's Prayer, he thus recalls the memory of that time: "Here I have occasion to tell you a story which happened at Cambridge. Master Bilney, or, rather, Saint Bilney, that suffered death for God's word sake—the same Bilney was the instrument whereby God called me to knowledge; for I may thank him, next to God, for that knowledge that I have in the Word of God. For I was as obstinate a papist as any was in England, insomuch that when I should be made bachelor of divinity my whole oration went against Philip Melanchthon and against his opinions. Bilney heard me at that time and perceived that I was zealous without knowledge, and he came to me afterwards in my study and desired me for God's sake to hear his confession. I did so; and to say the truth, by his confession I learned more than before in many years. So that from that time forward I began to smell the Word of God and forsook the school doctors and such fooleries." This was the start, but there were other influences that helped, and Latimer was fairly entered on the way of the Reformation.

At what time he was ordained a priest we do not know, but his preaching began at Cambridge, and his talent in that direction was not hid. A hearer of his early sermons at Cambridge said, "None except the stiffnecked and uncircumcised in heart went away from his preaching without being affected with high detestation of sin and moved unto all godliness and virtue." His sermons also quickened among his hearers a great desire for reading the Scriptures and for hearing a more evangelical preaching.

This work at the university went on for about two years, but Latimer's zeal and advancing reformatory views awakened opposition. As old Foxe quaintly puts it: "How be it as Satan never sleepeth when he seeth his kingdom begin to decay, so likewise now, seeing that this worthy member of Christ would be a shrewd shaker thereof, he raised up his children to molest and trouble him." So much noise was made that the bishop of Ely, in whose diocese Cambridge lay, determined to hear for himself how Latimer preached, and, without giving notice, came one day, taking pains to arrive after the sermon was begun. Latimer's quick wit, however, was equal to the occasion, and he stopped until the bishop and his retinue were properly seated. Then, remarking that since the bishop had come to hear him, it would be proper to preach what would be appropriate to the occasion, he cleverly changed his text and preached a sermon on the priesthood of Christ as an example to bishops, and unfolded with no less force than tact the high duties of the episcopal office. As his language was respectful and his doctrine scriptural the bishop could take no visible exception to the sermon, but commended it after service as a good exposition of a bishop's duty; but he asked Latimer to agree to preach there soon a sermon in condemnation of the doctrines of Luther. Latimer replied that as Luther's writings had long been prohibited to be read at Cambridge he was not acquainted with his doctrine, but added, "I have preached before you to-day no man's doctrine, but only the doctrine of God out of the Scriptures; and if Luther do none other than I have done there needeth no confutation of his doctrine. Otherwise, when I understand that he doth teach against the Scripture, I will be ready with all my heart to confound his doctrine as much as lieth in me." This answer, rather more shrewd than frank, naturally nettled the bishop, and he replied, "Well, well, Mr. Latimer, I perceive that you somewhat smell of the pan; you will repent this gear one day." The bishop's threat was not idle; for, on further complaint, he forbade Latimer's preaching in any of the churches belonging to the university. On this Robert Barnes, prior of the Augustinian abbey, and himself strongly inclined to reformed views, opened to Latimer the chapel of that institution, it being not under the bishop's control. So Latimer went on with his preaching, and did not lack a congregation.

Soon, however, complaint was made to Wolsey, and Latimer was called to London to explain himself before the great Cardinal. This he did with such characteristic boldness, combined with tact, that Wolsey not only dismissed the charges, but gave the unproved heretic a general license to preach anywhere in England he would! Latimer was not the man either to keep his victory to himself or slight the opportunities of further preaching thus afforded him.

Meantime the attention of Henry VIII. had been called to Latimer, and he had a curiosity to hear the bold preacher. So Latimer was called to preach before the court, acquitted himself well, was liberally paid for his services, and made so good an impression that in 1530 he was appointed one of the royal chaplains. So that now for a while he had at intervals the dangerous and irksome honor of preaching at the court of Henry VIII. In what spirit he discharged that duty we may gather not only from the character of the man and from the reports of contemporaries, but also from several allusions and reminiscences which are found in his later sermons, when, as an old man, he was court preacher again—this time to Edward VI. One of these passages is as follows: "In the king's days that dead is a many of us were called together before him to say our minds in certain matters. In the end one kneeleth me down and accuseth me of sedition, that I had preached seditious doctrine. An heavy salutation, and a hard point of such a man's doing as if I should name him ye would not think it. The king turned to me and said, 'What say you to that, sir?' Then I kneeled down and turned me first to mine accuser and required him, 'Sir, what form of preaching would you appoint me to preach before a king? Would you have me for to preach nothing as concerning a king in the king's sermon? Have you any commission to appoint me what I shall preach?' Besides this, I asked him divers other questions, and he would make me no answer to none of them all; he had nothing to say. Then I turned me to the king and submitted myself to his grace and said, 'I never thought myself worthy nor I never sued to be a preacher before your Grace, but I was called to it, and would be willing, if you mislike me, to give place to my betters; for I grant that there be a great many more worthy of the room than I am, and if it be your Grace's pleasure so to allow them for preachers, I could be content to bear their books after them. But if your Grace allow me for a preacher I would desire your Grace to give me leave to discharge my conscience; give me leave to frame my doctrine according to mine audience; I had been a very dolt to have preached so at the borders of your realm as I preach before your Grace.' And I thank Almighty God, which hath always been my remedy, that my sayings were well accepted of the king, for like a gracious lord he turned into another communication." But, though brave and faithful in his perilous position, Latimer wearied of it, he wished to breathe a freer air and speak his mind without being accused of sedition when he framed his doctrine to suit the needs and sins of his audience.

So in 1531, at the request of friends, Latimer was appointed by the king to a benefice at West Kingston, in Wiltshire. In this parish for several years he exercised a diligent and faithful ministry. He carried out his principle of adapting his discourse to his hearers, and preached the very marrow of the gospel in that racy, homely, clear and vigorous style which renders even his reported and printed sermons so charming. His influence extended far beyond his own parish, and he was accused of meddling; but he had his license to preach anywhere he would, and seems to have used his privilege.

Still the opponents of reform and his enemies would give him no rest from attacks and annoyance. The gospel quality of his preaching was the real trouble, but there were not wanting various pretexts for hindering and trying to silence him. Once he was summoned to London, and detained there for several months from his work, confined, and, it seems, for a time, even excommunicated, because he would not subscribe to certain things required by the bishops in the Catholic interest. But the king finally interfered, and seems to have secured from Latimer some sort of submission or promise to be on his good behavior, and so released him and sent him back to his charge. Latimer still had his share of persecution, and at one time seems to have somewhat compromised his principles, but, if so, it was only a temporary weakness.

Under Cranmer's influence Latimer was once again invited to preach a series of sermons before the king, and in 1535 was made bishop of Worcester. In the following year Cranmer appointed him to preach the sermon before Convocation, and Latimer powerfully attacked in true reformer's style the abuses and corruptions in the church, and more than hinted that the prelates before him had not lived up to their duty in reforming evils. In accordance with custom the sermon was in Latin, but it was translated into English and published, and made a great stir, bringing on the preacher not a little criticism and annoyance; but he went on with his work in his diocese, and was as faithful a bishop as he had been pastor. Latimer's bishopric, however, was not of very long duration; for in 1539, under royal pressure, the famous Six Articles were adopted which reasserted many of the essential Romanist doctrines, including transubstantiation. Latimer could not sign the articles, and resigned his bishopric. For awhile he was placed in custody, but was subsequently released, and for six years was practically lost from view; how he occupied himself being unknown. But his enemies were not satisfied, and in 1547 he was apprehended on some sort of charges and sent to the Tower, where he was confined for the remaining few months of Henry's reign.

On the accession of Edward VI., in 1547, Latimer was promptly released from prison, and in January, 1548, after eight years of silence, he preached again at St. Paul's Cross. On a week day he gave his famous *Sermon on the Plough,*[1] in which he paid his respects to lazy prelates, as well as to some other subjects that needed attention. He was offered again his bishopric at Worcester, but declined, and devoted himself to labors among the people in London and elsewhere, living for the most part with

[1] Fish, *Masterpieces of Pulpit Eloq.*, Vol. I., p. 129.

Archbishop Cranmer at Lambeth. He was by no means idle, but preached much in different places. Among the sermons of this period are the notable ones he delivered before the young king on several occasions. Nearly every Sunday he was preaching somewhere, besides doing much other work for the Protestant cause.

When Mary came to the throne, in 1553, Latimer was from the first a marked man. Opportunity was given him to escape from England, but he declined to leave, and in September, 1553, he was again confined in the Tower. Along with Cranmer and Ridley he was later taken to Oxford for trial, and was imprisoned there for two years, till in September, 1555, a new trial was ordered and he and Ridley were condemned to the stake. The execution took place on the 16th of October, and is thus described by one of the old chroniclers: "When Master Latimer stood at the stake and the tormentors were about to set fire upon him and that most reverend father Doctor Ridley, he lifted up his eyes to heaven with a most amiable and comfortable countenance, saying these words: 'God is faithful who does not suffer us to be tempted above our strength.' And, addressing himself to Master Ridley, he said, 'Be of good comfort, Master Ridley, and play the man; we shall this day light such a candle by God's grace in England as I trust shall never be put out.'"

As a preacher Latimer ranks among the best of his time. The contemporary accounts of his preaching bear most emphatic testimony to its charm, its power, and its practical results. And though he spoke freely, without written preparation, we are fortunate in having excellent reports of a large number of his sermons by the hand of Augustine Bernher, a Swiss, who for some years served Latimer faithfully and affectionately as a secretary and helper. These published sermons confirm the traditions of Latimer's excellence as a preacher. They bear in many traits, both of thought and style, the stamp of a marked individuality. Courage combined with shrewdness and tact, strong convictions and deep feeling joined to a lively wit and quaint humor, clear and firm grasp of truth along with an easy familiarity of manner, indifference to exact analysis and division, yet an orderly presentation and vigorous movement of thought, are some of the things that show themselves to the reader of his sermons. They do not deal so much in exposition as in application of Scripture, but they exalt the authority and reverence the truth of God's Word. "His utterances are as fresh as morning air, or the morning song of the birds. He grasps truth with vigor, handles it with ease, holds it up before you with startling reality." [1] And, it may be added, he fortified his doctrine by his life.

Latimer's companion in martyrdom, Nicholas Ridley (d. 1555) came of an ancient and respected family in Northumberland, where he was born about the beginning of the sixteenth century. He had an uncle, Robert, who was an influential priest and preacher, and never left the Catholic faith. Nicholas was educated at Cambridge and made a fine reputation as a scholar, especially distiguishing himself in Greek. He later pursued his studies at the Sorbonne in Paris, and at the university of Louvain. Not till after the death of his uncle Robert, and then only gradually, did Ridley become a convert to the Protestant faith. He discussed the living questions much with Peter Martyr Vermigli and with Cranmer, the latter of whom leaned much through life on Ridley's learning and judgment. In the latter part of King Henry's reign Ridley was advanced to a good many church honors, was a royal chaplain, a canon of Canterbury, and also of Westminster. During this time he was preaching much, and his reformed opinions were growing and strengthening into vital convictions. During the reign of King Edward his conversion to Protestantism became complete, further honors came to him, and his preaching and writing were a powerful advocacy of the Reformation. He was first made bishop of Rochester and in 1550 promoted to the see of London, instead of Bonner. Ridley showed great consideration to the deposed prelate's mother and sister, whom he permitted still to live in the episcopal residence. He was a staunch friend and patron of Rogers and Bradford, whose preaching gifts he recognized and used by appointing them to places of influence. He was also in close touch with Cranmer and with Hooper, though Hooper's pronounced puritanism and objections to vestments, and other details of remnants from Cath-

[1] Broadus *Hist. Prea.*, p. 192.

olicism, involved the two men in disagreeable controversies. In 1553 Ridley preached before the young king a sermon in behalf of the London poor, and so effective was the plea that Edward sought an interview with the preacher, and the outcome was the establishment of three hospitals in the city. In his court preaching he did not spare the men who, taking advantage of the king's youth and ill-health, were guilty of shameless greed and corruptions.

On the death of Edward VI. Ridley was induced by the Earl of Northumberland to declare in favor of Lady Jane Grey, and in a sermon at Paul's Cross before the Mayor and Corporation of London, on the Sunday after the young king died, the bishop took strong ground against the legitimacy of both Mary and Elizabeth, and denounced in vigorous terms Mary's Romanism as a menace to England. The speedy collapse of Lady Jane Grey's little reign and the proclamation of Mary as queen were, of course, fatal to Ridley. He threw himself on the queen's mercy—a pitiful refuge truly!—but could not renounce his convictions. He was promptly committed to the Tower, then sent with Cranmer and Latimer, as we have seen, to Oxford. During his long imprisonment he wrote letters and some able treatises in defence of the Protestant faith, and toward the last gave out two farewell addresses, full of courage and eloquence, exhorting his brethren to steadfastness and trust. In company with Latimer—the two encouraging each other—and with Cranmer from the prison window sadly looking on, he was burned at the stake October 16, 1555.

Ridley was a profound scholar and an able theologian, perhaps the strongest in this early group of reformers. Parker and Jewel among the latter ones were probably his equals in learning, but his position among the leaders of his own time is indicated in the remark of Bonner or Gardiner:[1] "Latimer leaneth to Cranmer, Cranmer leaneth to Ridley, and Ridley leaneth to his own singular wit." As to his preaching, Foxe[2] says: "Every holiday and Sunday he preached in some place or other, unless hindered by weighty business. The people resorted to his sermons, swarming about him like bees, and coveting the

[1] Beckett, p. 210. [2] Id., p. 211.

sweet flowers and wholesome juice of the fruitful doctrine which he did not only preach, but showed the same by his life." The literary remains from Ridley are disappointingly little, though of excellent quality.[1] He either did not care to publish or did not take time, and there was no one to report and hand down his sermons as Latimer's friend did. The treatise on the Lord's Supper is an able and clear presentation of the Protestant criticism of transubstantiation, and defends the Swiss, rather Calvin's than Zwingli's, view of the ordinance. The *Lamentation for the Change in Religion,* like the former treatise given out from his prison, deplores the bringing in again of Romanism under Mary, and is a weighty defence of the Reformation. The two farewell addresses already mentioned abound in Scripture quotations, breathe a noble courage and trust, glow with love, and are couched in the lofty eloquence of a great soul that was looking death in the face and was not afraid.

After Ridley and Latimer should be named their fellow-laborer and fellow-sufferer, John Hooper (d. 1555), who was martyred in the same year, but some eight months before they were. Hooper came of a well-to-do family in Somerset, where he was born toward the end of the fifteenth century. He was educated at Oxford, and is said to have entered the Cistercian monastery at Gloucester when he was ordained a priest. On the suppression of the monastery he went to London, where he seems to have lived about the court in rather a worldly way for a time. Getting hold of the writings of Zwingli and Bullinger, he became impressed with their views and went back to Oxford with the intention of teaching his new opinions there. But he attracted the notice of the sharp Catholic professor, Richard Smith, who was about to try him for heresy when he left Oxford and became steward for Sir Thomas Arundel. He, as a good Catholic, was much concerned because of Hooper's heresies, and sent him to have a conference with the famous Bishop Gardiner, in hope of curing him. Instead of that the effect of the discussion was but to confirm Hooper in his views. To avoid trial Hooper now left England and spent some time abroad, then came back, then went

[1] *Life and Writings of Bp. Ridley,* Rel. Tract. Soc.

away again, this time to Switzerland. At Strasburg he met with Butzer, and at Zürich with Bullinger.

In 1549, on the establishment of Protestantism, he returned to England, and was at once recognized as a leader among the reformers. He was appointed chaplain to the Protector, the Duke of Somerset, and had frequent opportunities for preaching in London. This he did almost daily, and his sermons attracted crowded congregations. He sympathized with the Swiss theologians, was not much in favor of episcopacy, and decidedly opposed to the use of clerical vestments and other matters of ceremonial retained from the old church. In fact he was of the tendency of thought that under Elizabeth and the Stuarts came to be stigmatized as Puritan. This involved him in controversies with Cranmer and Ridley, who did not agree with these views; but Hooper was very highly esteemed by the young king, who admired his preaching. In a series of sermons before the king on the prophet Jonah he attacked some of the Romish practices that were allowed to remain in the Church of England; but, notwithstanding his Puritan views and his combativeness, Hooper was nominated to the bishopric of Gloucester and urged by the king and others to accept. He had many scruples on matters of detail, such as the form of the oath, the vestments and so on, but finally, some compromises being made on both sides, he yielded and was made bishop of Gloucester in 1550.

As bishop Hooper was devoted and active not only in affairs of administration, but especially in introducing reforms and in preaching. In respect to the last his anxious wife wrote to their good friend Bullinger at Zürich that he should "recommend Master Hooper to be more moderate in his labor, for he preaches four or at least three times every day, and I am afraid lest these over-abundant exertions should cause a premature decay."[1]

Later the diocese of Gloucester was merged into that of Worcester, and Hooper was called by the latter title. He was not so successful in introducing reforms at Worcester as at Gloucester, but worked hard and made earnest friends and stout opponents at both places. He

[1] Beckett, p. 209.

was a man of much gravity, not to say severity, of temper and manner, not so genial as Latimer nor so gentle as Ridley. He once rebuked for his vices a man of high social standing, and so severely that he was assaulted for it; but later, when Hooper was in jail and expecting to be executed, this gentleman came to see him, apologized for the assault, thanked the bishop for helping him mend his life, and urged him to escape martyrdom by recanting.

Though somewhat austere, Hooper was a good and true man, kind and liberal to the poor, upright and devoted in his office, and he made many friends in Gloucester. He was opposed to the claims of Lady Jane Grey and favored on legal grounds the accession of Mary; but this did not save him from arrest and trial for heresy; he had been much too active and successful to escape that. He was imprisoned, examined, condemned, and sent to Gloucester to be burned at the stake that his martyrdom might strike terror to his followers there. In view of his popularity, he was forbidden to speak to the people. His execution was awkwardly managed and his sufferings intense, but he bore them heroically. His martyrdom occurred in February, 1555, a short time after that of Rogers.

Not so famous or so highly placed as the three last mentioned, but scarcely inferior to any of them—unless it was Latimer—in preaching power, was the pious and eloquent John Bradford[1] (d. 1555). He was a native of Manchester, received a good school education and showed decided aptitude for business. This talent got him a position with Sir John Harrington, treasurer and paymaster of the English forces in France. There were some frauds in this office, and Bradford resigned. While probably not deeply involved in the irregularities, he seems to have felt somewhat responsible, and under Latimer's preaching in London he was moved, at great personal sacrifice, to make restitution of a large amount of conscience money to the royal treasury. He engaged in the study of law in London, but soon his mind and heart turned toward preaching, though with hesitation and self-distrust, and he went to Cambridge to study.

[1] *Writings of John Bradford,* Rel. Tract Soc.

This was in King Edward's time, while Martin Butzer was professor of theology there. Bradford's zeal in study, his amiable character and unaffected piety won general esteem. Butzer urged him to begin preaching, but Bradford hesitated and feared, and Butzer said to him, "If thou have not fine manchet bread then give the poor people barley bread." Soon he was ordained a deacon by Ridley at London, and then priest. Ridley saw his value and appointed him a prebendary (salaried preacher) at St. Paul's. Besides the duties of this office there were frequent occasions for his preaching at other places, and he was one of the six preachers appointed under Edward VI. as a sort of itinerant ministry, or general evangelists, in all parts of the kingdom. Thus the three years of Bradford's work as a preacher were abundant in labors. Foxe is quoted as speaking of his work in these terms: "Sharply he opened and reproved sin, sweetly he preached Christ crucified, pithily he impugned heresies and errors, earnestly he persuaded to godly life."

He was a man of deep piety and was often engaged in penitential meditations and in prayer. One of his sayings, sometimes attributed to Bunyan and others, is often quoted. When he saw a criminal on the way to execution he remarked, "But for the grace of God there goes John Bradford." His zeal and success aroused the opposition of the Catholics, and soon after Mary's accession to the throne occasion was sought and found to have him tried and condemned. A certain Catholic preacher—Bradford and Rogers being present—took occasion at St. Paul's Cross to speak disparagingly of the late King Edward and in the highest terms of the bigoted Bishop Bonner. This so enraged the crowd that they were about to mob the preacher, and he appealed to Bradford for protection. Bradford reproved the crowd for their disorder, and he and Rogers, at some risk, protected the man from violence. But the affair was perverted, and it was made to appear that Bradford had really stirred up the people to disorder. So he was arrested and sent to the Tower along with Cranmer, Ridley and Latimer. At one time the four were confined in one room and they employed their time in Bible study and mutual help.

Bradford's imprisonment was long, but honorable to

him. He worked for God among his fellow-prisoners of every sort, endeavoring to lead them to Christ and comfort them in Christ. So trustworthy was he that one of his keepers allowed him sometimes to leave the prison in order to visit the sick and needy outside, and Bradford always returned punctually at the hour appointed, or even before. Nor was this all the good man did, but from his prison he wrote many letters to friends outside, encouraging them to hold on to their Protestant faith amid the trying years, and thus he worked for his convictions by his pen when he could no longer preach. These letters were widely circulated, and had a great influence. Even after his condemnation, in January, 1555, Bradford remained many months in prison, but was at last brought to the stake in June of that year. Fuller, describing his death, says, "He endured the flame as a fresh gale of wind in a hot summer's day, without any reluctancy; confirming by his death the truth of that doctrine which he had so diligently and powerfully preached during his life."

Of Bradford's preaching several valuable specimens remain, and they confirm fully the contemporary accounts of his excellent gifts. His letters and a few treatises set forth in clear thinking, plain style and with warmth the fundamental doctrines and principles of the Reformation; and there are two notable sermons. One of these is rather polemical in tone, being on the Lord's Supper, and attacking the Catholic doctrines, but it, as well as the other, breathes the spirit of the gospel. Bradford is less expository than the Germans, less general and gossipy than Latimer, and at the same time less powerful and fresh. But his grasp of Scripture is accurate and firm, and his manner of presenting the truth, both in arrangement and language, is singularly clear, fervent and winning. During one of his evangelizing tours, early in 1553, Bradford preached a notable sermon on repentance, which he was induced afterwards to write out, and it was published only a short time before the death of the young king. In the preface he tells how he came to publish it. After speaking of the great need of repentance among all classes, he says: "This to the end that for my part I might help, I have now put forth this Sermon on

Repentance, which has lain by me half a year at least as to the most part of it. For the last winter I was abroad preaching in the country, my chance was to make a sermon on repentance, which was earnestly by divers desired of me that I should give it to them written, or else put it forth in print. I, for the satisfying of my promise and profiting of the simple, ignorant and rude, have now caused this sermon to be printed; which I beseech God, for his Christ's sake, to use as a mean whereby of his mercy it may please him to work in me and many others hearty repentance for our sins to the glory of his name. Thus fare thou well in the Lord. This 12th day of July, 1553." It is difficult to speak in too high terms of the sermon itself; for it is the very meat and marrow of the gospel, simply and clearly divided and arranged, put in vigorous, plain yet dignified and noble style, with many felicities of thought and phrase, and charged through and through with the spirit of piety, earnestness and devotion. The text is our Lord's proclamation in Matt. 4:17, "Repent, for the kingdom of heaven is at hand." The introduction is natural and simple, the explanation of the text is correct. He makes repentance to consist of three elements: a genuine sorrow in view of sin, some persuasion or hope of God's willingness to pardon sin for Christ's sake, and a purpose to amend and turn to God, though the actual conversion is rather a fruit of repentance than repentance itself. On this plan his discourse proceeds, with appropriate subdivisions, in which he holds up the motives to sorrow for sin, the tokens of God's willingness to forgive, and the results of a true purpose to amend. In dwelling on God's willingness to forgive, he adduces the death of Christ as the supreme token of the divine mercy in these words: "This death of Christ therefore look on as the very pledge of God's love towards thee, whosoever thou art, how deeply soever thou hast sinned. See, God's hands are nailed, they cannot strike thee; his feet also, he cannot run from thee; his arms are wide open to embrace thee; his head hangs down to kiss thee; his very heart is open, so that therein see, look, spy, behold, and thou shalt see nothing therein but love, love, love to thee. Hide thee, therefore; lay thy head there with the evangelist." The careful reader of this sermon will not wonder at Ridley's emphatic testimony of Bradford: "He was a man by whom God hath and doth work wonders in setting forth his word."

Among the group of England's greatest preachers at this time must be mentioned the famous Scotch reformer, John Knox. His life and work belong principally, of course, to Scotland, and will be treated more fully later; but he spent, during Edward's reign, five fruitful years in England, and left an influence behind him that endured for generations. There is no doubt that the powerful Puritan sentiment in the Church of England was largely due to Knox as well as to Hooper and others.[1] On his release from the French galleys, most likely at King Edward's intervention, Knox came to England in 1549, and was appointed preacher first at Berwick, where he attracted large congregations and introduced reforms. His activity brought him into conflict with Tunstall, bishop of Durham, but Knox had the best of the controversy, and was let alone. Later he was assigned to Newcastle as preacher, was appointed a royal chaplain, and offered the bishopric of Rochester. More resolute than Hooper, he declined the office, for he could not accept episcopacy and other Anglican arrangements as scriptural. When called before the Council to confer on the matter he was told that they were "sorry he was of a contrary mind to the common order," and he replied that he was even more sorry that "the common order" was contrary to the institution of Christ. When it came his turn to preach as royal chaplain before the court, on one occasion he was bold to daring in denouncing the notorious corruptions of some of the high officials about the young king. He is reported to have said,[2] "What wonder is it that a young and innocent king be deceived by crafty, covetous, wicked and ungodly councillors? I am greatly afraid that Ahithopel is councillor, that Judas bears the purse, and that Shebnah is scribe, controller and treasurer." Yet afterwards the preacher reproached himself that he had not been a "true soldier" nor "so fervent in rebuking manifest iniquity" as he ought to have been!

[1] See Prof. Lorimer's book on *Knox in England,* referred to by Broadus, *Hist. Prea.*, p. 194. [2] Beckett, p. 213.

Worthy of mention here was another Scotchman who, after a period of activity in his own country, came to England in 1547. This was John Rough (d. 1557), who had acquired a fair education in Scotland, had also done some effective work as a preacher of reform doctrines, but, escaping to England before the fall of St. Andrews, received appointment as preacher at Carlisle, and later at Berwick, Newcastle and Hull. He did efficient service at all these places till Mary's accession drove him out of England, and he retired to Friesland, where he and his wife supported themselves by knitting garments. He ventured to London on business where he was induced to become pastor of a secret Protestant church. The congregation was betrayed by one of its own members and Rough was captured, tried before Bonner, and sent to the stake in December, 1557. No sermons of his remain, but Knox and others bear emphatic testimony to the power of his preaching.

A very useful man in Edward's days, and still more so in the early years of Elizabeth, was Thomas Lever (1521-1577), who was born in Lancashire, educated at Cambridge and then converted to Protestantism. In February, 1550, he preached with great acceptance at the Shrouds, in St. Paul's churchyard, London, and was invited to preach before the king in the following Lent. In December of that same year he did some notable preaching at St. Paul's Cross, and powerfully denounced existing evils. Some later sermons before the king called forth warm approval from Knox and others. During the days of persecution under Mary he was in Europe in touch with the exiles and other reformers, but returned at Elizabeth's accession and was busily engaged in preaching to the end of his useful life. He was Puritan in his convictions and did not escape controversy and trials in his dealings with the leaders of the Anglican party. It is said of him:[1] "Preaching was his talent. His sermons resembled Latimer's in their bluntness and boldness, and his reputation was made by his sharp rebukes of the courtiers when preaching before Edward VI."

One of the most attractive and interesting figures among the English Reformation preachers is that of

[1] Article in *Dict. Nat. Biog.*

Bernard Gilpin (1517-1583), who was called the "Apostle of the North." He came of excellent family in Westmoreland, was a nephew of the celebrated bishop Tunstall, and had other high connections. He was educated at Oxford, was a fine student, and only very slowly came to Protestant views. When he was ordained a priest in 1549 he scrupled at the oath which recognized the king's supremacy, and only accepted it with a condition; and he disputed ably with Hooper in defence of the Catholic faith. Later he was set to dispute with Peter Martyr Vermigli, then professor at Oxford, but his studies in preparation for this proposed contest upset his mind as to some of the Romanist positions. This was the entering wedge, and gradually he became satisfied of the soundness of the reform views. His uncle Tunstall tried to help him, appointed him to various positions in his diocese of Durham and would not suffer him to be molested, even though Gilpin advanced rapidly in Protestant views and preached them boldly. But even Tunstall's influence could not always shield the outspoken preacher from the relentless Catholics of Mary's time, and in the last year of her reign Gilpin was summoned to London to answer for his heresies. On the way he had a fall and broke his leg, and his prosecution fell through, the queen having died before he got well.

Gilpin was strongly Puritan in his leanings, so that he declined a bishopric and also a professorship at Oxford, because he was not satisfied with the remains of "popery" left in the Anglican settlement under Elizabeth and her prelates. With some trials and controversies growing out of these differences he continued his useful ministry to the end of his life. One only sermon remains from him, but his reputation as a preacher and pastor was very great among his contemporaries, not only for learning, piety and eloquence, but for unusual graces of character.

The last of the Reformation preachers in England to be noticed is that group of distinguished prelates who in the early years of Queen Elizabeth settled the Anglican church system in the forms which have continued to be characteristic of it. None among them had commanding pulpit gifts, but a few at least of the well-known leaders cannot be omitted in a history of preaching.

The scholarly and able archbishop of Canterbury,

Matthew Parker (1504-1575) was noted rather as the wise and conciliatory prelate who successfully guided the Anglican establishment between the Romanist tendencies of the queen and others on the one side, and the extreme Puritanism of the more radical Protestants on the other. Among his numerous writings no sermons are mentioned. The slight merit of the authorship of the homily on Matrimony in the sensible but sapless second *Book of Homilies* is deemed to be his; but concerning his earlier years it is said that "to his acquirements as a theologian he united a popular style of pulpit oratory which induced Cranmer in 1533 to license him to preach throughout the southern province." But the fame of Parker is that of an educator, scholar and prelate rather than preacher.

More of a preacher but less of a prelate than Parker was his successor in the see of Canterbury, Edmund Grindal (d. 1583), who in his earlier years had been recognized as a preacher of no little ability, and had held pulpits of prominence in Edward's time under Ridley, bishop of London. Like so many others an exile in Mary's reign, he returned under Elizabeth to take up the heavy work of restoring wasted Protestantism in England. He was far more Puritan than Parker, nevertheless accepted the bishopric of London and gave Parker and the queen, no less than himself, considerable trouble in his scruples as to many of the proposed Anglican institutions. To get him out of the way he was appointed to the archbishopric of York, and on Parker's death—because for the moment it suited the queen's shifting policy,—he was made archbishop of Canterbury. As he was a peace-loving man and not wholly in accord with the drift of things, his bishoprics were a continual trial to him, and he doubtless would have been happier, and more useful too, had he remained simply a preacher in some place suitable to his learning and talents. A memorial discourse on the death of the emperor Ferdinand, and the fourth homily in the *Second Book,* on Good Works, especially Fasting, seem to be all of his sermons that survive, and these would not make a man famous. The homily, however, presents clearly the Protestant doctrine as to good works and treats the matter of fasting with good sense and clearness.

The successor of Grindal as archbishop of York, Edwin Sandys (d. 1588), was like that prelate in his ecclesiastical principles, but very unlike him in character. He was educated at Cambridge, and was a friend of Martin Butzer while that theologian was professor there. On Edward's death he supported Lady Jane Grey and preached a sermon upholding her cause which is said to have "pulled many tears out of the eyes of the biggest of them," presumably the leading men of the time. Naturally he was arrested by Mary's partisans and put into the Tower, but through somebody's favor he managed to get away to the Continent, where he remained till Elizabeth's accession. He also was more Puritan than Parker, and his views on church polity and some other questions kept him in continual controversies. But his abilities and staunch Protestantism made him too useful to be overlooked in restoring the cause, and he was first made bishop of Worcester, and then, on Grindal's promotion to Canterbury, archbishop of York. During these years something is said of his preaching, and a good deal of his quarrels. Some of his sermons were printed in 1585 and reprinted in several later editions. They are not held to be of very great value.

The best preacher among these Elizabethan prelates was John Jewel (d. 1571), bishop of Salisbury.[1] Born in Devonshire in 1522, he was educated at several preliminary schools and studied in two collges at Oxford. Here one of his fruitful tasks was the making of a critical comparison between the Bible versions of Tindale and Coverdale. Jewel was a laborious student, and worked so hard as permanently to injure his health. On getting his degree he was appointed to lecture for a while on Latin and Rhetoric, and his lectures were well attended. In 1547 Peter Martyr Vermigli came as professor to Oxford, and during his work there he exercised a profound influence upon Jewel. When and where Jewel was ordained is not known, but he appears as a licensed preacher in 1551, became vicar at a small village near

[1] *Works of Bishop Jewel,* with Featley's abridgment of Humphrey's *Life* prefixed, printed at London in 1640; art. in *Dict. Nat. Biog.*, etc. The famous "Challenge Sermon" is reprinted in Fish, *Masterpieces,* etc., Vol. I., p. 146 ff.

Oxford, and got his degree of Bachelor of Divinity in 1552, preaching on the occasion an excellent discourse in Latin, of which we shall see see more later. On the accession of Mary, Jewel was deprived of his places, and, though he sacrificed his convictions and signed certain articles, he was still suspected and found it necessary to leave England. At Frankfort, where were Knox and a number of English exiles, Jewel was coldly received till he made public acknowledgment of his weakness and error in recanting, and reaffirmed his real views. Later he was with his friend Vermigli at Strasburg and Zürich.

In 1559 Jewel gladly returned to England, and became active in helping to restore the Protestant cause. At first strongly inclined to Puritanism, he quickly acquiesced in the Anglican compromises, and became one of the clearest and strongest expounders and defenders of the English church system. Like others, he soon saw that, with the temper of the queen and of a large element of the people, it would be impossible to establish either the Puritan extreme or its opposite. In doctrine, however, he always held with the Reformed confessions and wrote to Vermigli, "As to matters of doctrine, we do not differ from you by a nail's breadth." He displayed much activity in preaching and other work about London. In a sermon at St. Paul's Cross in 1559 he made his famous challenge to the papists, and it was repeated in a sermon delivered before the court in March, 1560, and again at St. Paul's Cross later in the same month. The challenge was to the effect that if any one could prove the essential Romanist doctrines as to the papacy, purgatory, masses, transubstantiation, and so on, by Scripture or by any church teacher for six hundred years after Christ, he, Jewel, would subscribe to it and renounce Protestantism. These sermons were not written before delivery, but the last of them was soon written out and published—"shortly set forth as near as the author could call it to remembrance, without any alteration or addition." The challenge was taken up by two Catholics, and Jewel was led into a controversy which went on for some time.

In 1560, while this debate was on, Jewel was made bishop of Salisbury, and went to his diocese. He found much to do, and was very diligent, not only in visiting and administration, but in preaching, because of the great dearth of preachers. In April, 1561, he filled another preaching engagement at St. Paul's Cross, and in the following year appeared his great and famous *Apology for the Church of England*. This was the first elaborate statement of the Anglican position in a work of first-rate importance, and it was immediately accepted as a clear and powerful exposition of that view. It remains one of the classic treatises of the Anglican ecclesiology. The Apology provoked a fresh attack from the Catholics. What with these writings and controversies, the cares of the diocese, activity in the general work of the church, and assiduous preaching, Jewel's never very strong health gave way. In 1571 he came home from Parliament much exhausted, but immediately undertook a visitation of his diocese. To the remonstrance of a friend he answered, "A bishop had best die preaching," and it was not long before the end came, in September, 1571.

In Daniel Featley's abridgment of Dr. Humphrey's life of Jewel, prefixed to an early edition of his works, occurs a quaint but striking eulogy, a part of which runs thus: "And surely, if ever to any, then unto him his bishoprike was a continuall worke of ruling and governing, not only by the pastorall staffe of his jurisdiction in his consistory, but also in the court of men's consciences by the golden sceptre of God's word preached. The memorie of his assiduitie in preaching, carefulnesse in providing pastours, resolutenesse in reforming abuses, bountie in relieving the poore, wisdome in composing litigious strifes, equitie in judging spirituall causes, faithfulnesse in keeping and sinceritie in bestowing church goods, is as an ointment powred out and blowen abroad thorow the diocesse of Sarum by the breath of everie man's commendation."

Jewel was a sound scholar, with a clear head and a good memory, logical and correct. His writings show the confidence of one who is conscious of accurate learning. His sermons lack warmth, but not conviction; fervor, but not strength; imagination and passion, but not logic and clearness. The Latin sermon delivered at Oxford for his degree in divinity, and done into English by Dr. Humphrey, expresses with force his own views of the preaching office, early formed, but never abandoned. From the text, 1 Peter 4:11, "If any man speak let him talk as the words of God," he deduces the simple theme and division: (1) That the preacher should preach; (2) What he should preach; (3) How he should preach. In urging the importance of preaching, he says: "It is not enough to know I wot not what learning. The devils, perhaps, know more than any of us all. It belongeth unto a pastor not so much to have learned many things as to have taught much." Speaking of people's unwillingness to hear as an incentive rather than a discouragement to diligence, he says, "Let us bring forth the light, and God will open their eyes; let us beat at their ears, and God will give them a heart of flesh; let us give the word, and God will give the Spirit; let us plant and water, and God in due time will give the increase." The famous challenge sermon is naturally rather polemical in tone, and is somewhat overloaded with learned quotation, but it is logical and vigorous and not devoid of occasional passages of feeling and power. In general, Jewel's sermons lack the breeziness of Latimer's and the devout glow of Bradford's, but they are strong, clear and sensible presentations of the doctrines and principles dear to all the reformers.

3. The Scotch Reformation

The religious situation in Scotland before the Reformation was dark and deplorable in the extreme. A turbulent and violent nobility; a wealthy, luxurious, corrupt and rapacious clergy; a people sunken in ignorance and superstition; these are the sombre outlines of a picture whose details may be left to the imagination. Yet some beginnings of better things were made early in the sixteenth century. Some influences of the revival of learning had entered the schools, and the writings of Luther and other reformers, though forbidden, were not wholly unknown. By the time Knox began his early reformatory work, in 1542, the principles of the Reformation had made considerable progress, not only among the common people, but also among the nobility and gentry, and there were not a few who were ready to fight and die, if need be, for the faith.

4. Predecessors of Knox

Besides the influence of teachers, of Reformation literature, of private conference, there were a few preachers [1] before Knox who dared, at great peril from the dominant Romanist clergy, with Beaton at their head, to lift up their voices in favor of reform. Among these three are deserving of special mention.

Patrick Hamilton (c. 1504-1528), the young and noble martyr for the truth, came of a family of rank and distinction, and was born near Glasgow, probably in 1504. He was designed for the priesthood, and after receiving preliminary education in the schools he went to Paris—where he got his master's degree in 1520—and probably to Louvain also. Returning to Scotland, he studied a while at St. Andrews. About 1525 he began to show decided sympathy for the reformed views and to teach them. Falling under suspicion, and being in danger of prosecution, he retired from Scotland and went to Germany, where, at Wittenberg, he studied with Luther and Melanchthon; and at Marburg with the French exile and professor, François Lambert. But the state of his own country bore on his mind and gave him no rest, so that, against the earnest remonstrance of Lambert, he determined to return to Scotland and do what he could to introduce the Reformation. He came back in 1527, married, and began to preach the Protestant doctrines. It is not certain that he had ever been ordained a priest, at any rate, he held no clerical charge, and his preaching was, therefore, irregular, and that fact, as well as his doctrine and his zeal, aroused speedy and fatal opposition. He was summoned before Archbishop Beaton at St. Andrews to answer charges of heresy. He foresaw his fate, but bravely went to meet it. With show of consideration he was granted time to consider and recant, but used his respite instead to proclaim his doctrines as much as he could. He was condemned and executed as a heretic in 1528. His youth, rank, earnestness, and sad death created profound impressions, led many to investigate the

[1] McCrie's *Life of Knox;* Brown's *Life of Knox;* notices by Blaikie in his *Preachers of Scotland,* and by Taylor in his *Scottish Pulpit.*

causes of his condemnation, and thus resulted in furthering rather than suppressing the progress of the new views. His eloquence and zeal gave promise of a noble career as preacher had he been spared to pursue his reforming course.

Another preacher and martyr was George Wishart (d. 1546), who died for his convictions nearly twenty years after Hamilton; having suffered under the second Archbishop Beaton, who was also a cardinal. Wishart came of a family near Montrose, but details as to his early life are wanting. There are traditions and traces of his education and of his good knowledge of Greek—unusual among his countrymen then. About 1538 he, or a person of similar name, appears in certain records in England as under trial for heresy; and about this time it seems that he studied for a while in Germany. Later, in Scotland, he translated the Helvetic Confession and spread it abroad. In 1543 he is found, living in great simplicity and piety, and studying very hard, at Cambridge, in England. The next year he returned to Scotland and took up his reformatory ministry in earnest.

The younger Beaton, the cardinal, was now at the head of the Catholics in Scotland, and was as relentless as his uncle had been in persecution of the reformers. Wishart was to go the way of Hamilton, but he went his course with courage and devotion. A part of McCrie's brief but eloquent account of Wishart in his *Life of Knox*[1] may be better transcribed than condensed: "Seldom do we meet in ecclesiastical history with a character so amiable and interesting as that of George Wishart. Excelling all his countrymen at that period in learning, of the most persuasive eloquence, irreproachable life, courteous and affable in manners, his fervent piety, zeal and courage in the cause of truth were tempered with uncommon meekness, modesty, patience, prudence and charity. In his tour of preaching through Scotland he was usually accompanied by some of the principal gentry; and the people, who flocked to hear him, were ravished with his discourses."

He had a great influence over Knox, who often accompanied him in his preaching journeys. When Wishart

[1] P. 21.

was arrested to be taken before Cardinal Beaton for trial Knox wished to go with him, but Wishart said, " Nay, return to your bairns [his pupils]; ane is sufficient for a sacrifice." Thus he clearly foresaw what was coming. And so, early in 1546, this preacher also suffered at the stake; but left a name and work behind him. His death was speedily and terribly avenged. A strong party, composed of those who had various and sore grievances against the harsh and tyrannous cardinal, captured the castle of St. Andrews and put the cruel prelate to death. Though this murder was occasioned largely by other things than religious animosities, there is probably no doubt that many of the reformers were in sympathy with the conspirators. Even Knox, though he seems not to have been chargeable with any direct share in it, afterwards sought in some degree to justify the act as the deserved execution of one who could not be reached by the processes of law. The conspirators retained possession of the castle of St. Andrews and became the nucleus of the Reformed party in Scotland.

Mention has already been made of the ministry and fate of John Rough (d. 1557) in England, but his earlier work in Scotland claims brief notice here. Far less cultured than Hamilton, Wishart or Knox, Rough had a glowing zeal for the cause of reform and a ready popular eloquence that acquired for him great reputation as a preacher. He had been a monk, but on the Earl of Arran's request had been released from the cloister and made a chaplain to that nobleman. When Arran relinquished the reformed faith and became regent, Rough retired for a while; but after the murder of Cardinal Beaton, and upon invitation of the conspirators, now in possession of St. Andrews, he became a minister to the congregation there. When Knox came to St. Andrews Rough urgently pressed upon him the duty of preaching, as we shall see, but shortly afterwards went to England, where his work has already been described.

5. John Knox and His Work

As is well known, the preëminent name among the preachers of the Reformation in Scotland is that of John

Knox[1] (1505-1572). Not so original or great as Luther, Zwingli or Calvin, he yet occupies toward the establishment of Protestantism in his own country a position similar to theirs relative to the movements associated with their names.

John Knox was born in the county of East Lothian, near Haddington, of respectable parents of the middle class, in the year 1505. His father had means enough to give the boy a good education, and after preparatory schooling he entered Glasgow University, where he studied under John Major, and formed a lasting friendship with the gifted George Buchanan, poet and man of letters.

About 1530 Knox was ordained a priest, but soon afterward began to study the Fathers, with the effect that Jerome led him to the Scriptures and Augustine to a more evangelical theology. Knox lectured at Glasgow and also at St. Andrews, and at the latter place he not only began to teach a better theology, but to denounce corruptions in the church. By the year 1542 he had become fully committed to the reformed faith.

Beaton's attention being directed to Knox, he found it prudent to leave St. Andrews, and soon after found a place of protection as tutor in the family of Hugh Douglas of Langniddrie, a nobleman who sympathized with the reformed views. The son of another gentleman, John Cockburn of Ormiston, was also placed under his care; and Knox's distinctive work as a reformer may now be said in this modest way to have begun. For he not only taught his pupils the rudiments of learning, but the tenets of the gospel; and others besides his scholars were admitted at times to his Bible lectures and catechism. These more public instructions were given in a chapel on his patron's estate. This went on for several years, and Knox attached himself with ardor to Wishart on some of that preacher's expeditions.

After the assassination of Beaton, his successor, Hamilton, pursued the reformers with unremitting vigor, and Knox was seriously thinking of leaving the country. But

[1] The works of McCrie, Brown, Lorimer, and others previously referred to, Knox's *History of the Reformation in Scotland,* and numerous other sources.

his friends and patrons were loath to lose his services as a teacher, and persuaded him to go with his pupils to the congregation of the reformers, who were maintaining themselves still at the castle of St. Andrews. Rough, as we have seen, was already installed there as minister, and he welcomed Knox as an able recruit. Knox continued the kind of instructions he had been giving at Langniddrie, and his expositions of the Scripture and power of speech immediately attracted attention. The result was that, by the unanimous vote of the congregation, and at Rough's solemn and earnest request, Knox was also called as a preacher to the reformers at St. Andrews. It was altogether an interesting, not to say anomalous, situation. Here was an unorganized assembly of reformers, not formally out of the old church, gathered about a nucleus of armed men, who had upon them the guilt of Beaton's assassination, and were maintaining themselves by force against the government; and they had called as their preachers an ex-monk, John Rough, and an ex-priest, John Knox! But irregularities were not of much weight to men who felt sure of the truth they held, and believed they were doing God's will. This first ministry of Knox was powerful, but brief. Rough saw how the matter must end, and retired to England; but Knox held on till the garrison at St. Andrews were defeated by French aid and made captives, in 1547.

The terms of surrender were violated by the victors, and Knox and others were made prisoners in the French galleys. In 1549 he was released and came to England, where, as we have seen, he spent five years. After the accession of Mary he remained in England as long as he could, and longer than was prudent, but finally, in January, 1554, fled to the Continent.

During the five years of his sojourn abroad, interrupted by a long and fruitful visit to Scotland, Knox was variously busy. Part of the time he was at Geneva, where he formed a fast friendship with Calvin. Here he studied with great diligence, and, though nearly fifty years old, took up the study of Hebrew to improve his knowledge of Scripture. The congregation of English exiles called him to Frankfort as their minister, and he accepted and faithfully served them till, in their dissensions over the liturgy, the party favoring the Anglican ritual got the majority and forced Knox out, and he went back to Geneva. Meantime he got news from Scotland that the queen-regent (Mary of Guise, mother of Mary Stuart) was disposed for the moment to be lenient towards the Protestants. This favorable turn of affairs and other circumstances decided Knox to make a visit to Scotland and see what could be done for the cause. Leaving Geneva in August, 1555, Knox came first to Berwick and spent some time with his wife and her good mother, and then secretly proceeded to Edinburgh, intending to return soon to Berwick. But he found much to do in Scotland. At Edinburgh and other places he found the friends of reform eager to learn from him, and in private houses he preached and taught diligently, confirming and building up the Protestants and winning not a few converts.

After nearly a year of this labor he received a call from the English congregation at Geneva to become their pastor, and thought it best, on the whole, to accede to their request. So he returned to that city with his family and had a quiet and helpful pastorate there for several years. But his heart was in Scotland, and he joyfully listened to proposals from some of the leaders there to return and carry out the work of reform. The good results of Knox's visit had been shown, and it was felt that he was the man to carry on the work. He did not need any urging, and so, after some disappointments and delays, he left Geneva to take up his mighty labors, in the evening of his days, in Scotland, and landed at Leith in May, 1559. With this date the last and greatest stage of Knox's career as a reformer begins. On arriving in Scotland he found that circumstances had altered the queen-regent's policy, and instead of tolerating the reformers she was now joining hands with Archbishop Hamilton to suppress them. These measures of persecution awakened sympathy for the reformers, but meantime the Protestant cause was somewhat hurt by the indiscretion of a crowd at Perth, who, after a sermon from Knox, provoked by the attempt of a priest to celebrate mass in the church after the reformed services were concluded, rushed upon the church, destroyed the altar and images, and, proceeding further, when once aroused, sacked the monasteries in the town.

These events led to a state of civil warfare. The government sent troops to Perth, the Protestants gathered forces to defend themselves, and thus the lines were sharply drawn. For Romanism in Scotland it was the beginning of the end; but for Protestantism there was a long and often apparently doubtful conflict before the final victory. Knox's share in that struggle and victory was very great, but, of course, he was not alone. The preachers of less prominence, who had toiled during his absence and helped to maintain the cause, stood by him in his gladly welcomed leadership, and their ranks were continually strengthened by accessions from those who had been less decided, but now came out clearly for the new order. About this time the general body of Protestants had come to be known as "The Congregation," and those nobles who, in accordance with the Scottish feudal habits, took the direction of affairs for the general body, were called "Lords of the Congregation." Thus, in Scotland, as elsewhere, but in consonance with the peculiar institutions of the country, the secular rulers had large share in shaping the course of the Reformation.

Not very long after the affair at Perth the Lords of the Congregation invited Knox to preach on a certain day at St. Andrews, with a view of instituting reforms there. Knox was delighted at the prospect of revisiting the scene of his early ministry and of former defeat and captivity, and of thus fulfilling the prediction he had made while a prisoner in the galleys, that he would one day preach at St. Andrews again. But the archbishop naturally resented the intrusion, and threatened to send a force and have Knox shot if he entered the pulpit. As the Lords had only a few men on the ground, the leaders hesitated, and advised Knox to give up the attempt for the present. But Knox's blood was up, and he insisted on filling the appointment, among other things saying: [1] "As for fear of danger that may come to me, let no man be solicitous, for my life is in the custody of him whose glory I seek. I desire the hand nor weapon of no man to defend me. I only crave audience, which, if it be denied me at this time, I must seek where I may have it." He was allowed to have his way, and on the next day

[1] McCrie, p. 131.

preached without hindrance to a great congregation, the archbishop being afraid to execute his threat. He preached powerfully on our Lord's driving out the traders from the Temple, making the obvious application to the need of reforming Christian worship there and then. Several other sermons followed, and in consequence, not by a mob, but by orderly authority of the rulers of the town, the Catholic worship was abolished, the images and pictures removed from the church, and the monasteries destroyed. This was in June, 1559, and the example set by St. Andrews was followed by a number of other towns.

In July the people of Edinburgh, in a public assembly, called Knox to be their minister, and he accepted, and began his work at St. Giles church. But the regent's forces captured the city from the Lords of the Congregation, and, though Knox desired to remain, he was this time persuaded to prudence, left the congregation (protected by treaty) in the hands of a less obnoxious man, and retired. He now went on an arduous and highly successful preaching tour, visiting in two months many of the most important places in the kingdom. He then settled for a time at St. Andrews, till circumstances should admit of his resuming his position at Edinburgh. During the interval he was of course active in the events which marked the progress of affairs in church and state in Scotland. He preached much, wrote much, and in many ways encouraged and animated the ever-strengthening Protestant cause. The alliance with England and the deposition of the queen-regent by the Lords of the Congregation were followed by the death of the regent. A parliament was called to settle the civil and ecclesiastical affairs of the distracted nation. It met in Edinburgh in the summer of 1560, abolished the Catholic religion, and adopted a reformed confession of faith drawn up by Knox and other ministers.

In April, 1560, Knox had come back to Edinburgh as chief pastor, and for the remaining twelve years of his life that city is the principal scene of his labors. In addition to his preaching and administration of church affairs, and complicated, of course, with both, the main point of interest in his later career is his conflict with Queen Mary Stuart in her effort to reinstate the Catholic religion. The romantic history of that misguided and unhappy lady lies apart from our narrative, but it is necessary to recall that the early death of her father, James V., had left her an infant queen, that her kingdom had been under the regency of Arran, and then of her mother, while she was a minor, absent in France, and married, while yet a girl, to the heir-apparent, afterwards for a very brief reign Francis II. After the death of her mother and then of her husband, the fair but unsuitably trained queen was invited by the Scottish nobles to come and take her kingdom. She arrived in Scotland in August 1561, and it was not long before the troubles of her unfortunate reign began. Though the Protestants were in power and had invited her return, Mary soon showed her fixed purpose to do all that she could to restore the old worship. Her mistake was natural, considering both her faults and her training, but it brought no end of trouble both on herself and her subjects. One of her first acts was to order a solemn mass to be said in Holyrood chapel in honor of her return. The leaders prevented the people from making a riot, and Knox himself counselled patience, but showed his feeling on the subject by saying at the end of his sermon that Sunday:[1] "That one mass was more fearful unto him than if ten thousand armed enemies were landed in any part of the realm of purpose to suppress the whole religion." Extravagant as this language seems, it shows that Knox was alive to the dangers which threatened the Protestant cause from the side of the queen, and events soon showed how just were his fears. But Knox was firm, unyielding, even severe, and in his sermons denounced the papacy and papal practices with no less vigor than formerly. McCrie gives a vivid presentation of the reformer's several famous interviews with the queen during these years. She tried the effect of argument, of flattery, of tears, of imperious anger, all in vain. If the bold preacher was too harsh and unfeeling, he was always faithful to his convictions, and if plain almost to rudeness, he was at least not disrespectful. He ever maintained his right to speak his conscience in his pulpit. Once Knox took occasion in a sermon seriously to object to the queen's marriage to any

[1] McCrie, p. 175

papist. Mary was deeply offended, called the preacher to an interview, and in the course of it burst into passionate tears, and vowed she would be revenged. But Knox said [1] that " her grace and he had at different times been engaged in controversy, and he had never before perceived her offended with him. When it should please God to deliver her from the bondage of error in which she had been trained up, through want of instruction in the truth, he trusted that her majesty would not find the liberty of his tongue offensive. Out of the pulpit, he believed few had occasion to complain of him; but there he was not his own master, but was bound to obey Him who commanded him to speak plainly, and to flatter no flesh on the face of the earth." Strange contrast between these two so brought into contact, with unutterable disharmony of character and of principles—both inflexible in their several ways—the queen lovely even in her faults and weaknesses, the reformer unlovely in his virtues and strength. The crowning effort of Mary was to secure Knox's condemnation on a charge of treason, because of certain expressions in a letter he had written in defence of some of his Protestant brethren, who had perhaps acted imprudently in opposing the Catholic worship at Holyrood during the queen's absence. He was tried before the Lords in her presence, she herself taking the part of accuser in a lively way; but the Lords, to their credit, be it said, were not to be browbeaten nor cajoled, and Knox's firm and candid defence secured his acquittal. This was in 1563.

The queen's marriage with Darnley was in nowise pleasing to Knox, and the royal pair found means to annoy the free-spoken preacher. The murder of Darnley and the queen's flight and indecent marriage to Bothwell excited Knox's horror. He, of course, approved of her deposition, and preached the sermon at Stirling on the occasion of the crowning of her infant son as James VI. Knox greatly rejoiced in the appointment of Murray to the regency, and was filled with satisfaction at the wise administration of that able and incorruptible patriot. The assassination of Murray filled him with grief, and when the queen's party took possession of Edinburgh he was

[1] McCrie, p. 206 f.

forced again to retire for a while to St. Andrews. Soon, however, the civil strife was abated, and he was once more allowed to return, and this time to end his days, among his beloved flock. His health rapidly declined, and in 1572, just as the elevation of Morton to the regency promised better days, the old hero reached the end of his journey. For some time he had been longing to depart, and his last days were filled with peace and serenity in view of his speedy release. He died November 24, 1572. As friends stood about his grave the newly elected regent, the Earl of Morton, expressed the thought of the time and the judgment of posterity in the brief but merited eulogy: "There lies he who never feared the face of man."

The character of Knox was an eminently vigorous one. The strong individuality of the man and his real greatness lie on the surface. He could and did receive influential impressions from others, as from Wishart and Rough, in his early years, and from Calvin during his sojourn in Europe, but he was ever his own man. If, as McCrie concedes,[1] he falls below the three great continental reformers, he is at least to be placed next below them. Inferior to them all as theologian and scholar, he also lacked the geniality and popular power of Luther and Zwingli, and did not approach Calvin in constructive genius nor in fine balance of judgment. In his austerity of morals and censure of evil he was more like Calvin, with whom in views of truth and duty he most nearly agreed. Knox's faults were those of a strong and vehement nature. He was severe in his judgments, fearless and tactless in expressing his opinions, and often unnecessarily sharp and extreme in his language. But he does not seem to have indulged in coarseness such as marred the language of Luther and Zwingli; and, notwithstanding his severity, there seems to have been more exercise, as well as expression of tenderness, than with Calvin. He made and kept warm attachments, and in his personal and domestic relations gave and received affection. His moral fibre was of the toughest sort, and yet once, at least, in the negotiations with the English court, he counselled a crooked policy; and while he did not

[1] P. 290 f.

advise he did in a measure defend the murders of Cardinal Beaton and of David Rizzio. In his personal life he was pure from taint and absolutely free from corruption. Various slanders assailed him by the malice of his foes, but they fell fruitless to the ground. His one absorbing aim in life was to establish the Reformation in Scotland, and to this purpose he brought a disinterestedness, a courage, a hopefulness, a diligence and a faith in God and truth which keep his name safe amid the truly great of history.

Little can be said as to the preaching of Knox beyond what has already been mentioned or suggested in the account of his life and character. The reason is apparent in the following statement of McCrie[1]: "Of the many sermons preached by him during his ministry he published but one, which was extorted from him by peculiar circumstances. It affords a very favorable specimen of his talents, and shows that if he had applied himself to writing he was qualified for excelling in that department. He had a ready command of language, and expressed himself with great perspicuity, animation and force." The occasion referred to by McCrie was this: Soon after his marriage to the queen, Darnley, for appearances' sake, went to hear Knox preach, and took violent exceptions to certain allusions in the sermon. On account of it Knox was inhibited from preaching for a while, and, it seems, at the request of the privy council, or to vindicate himself, wrote out as nearly as he could the sermon that he had preached.[2] One other sermon is mentioned in the list of his writings, and there are some expositions of various Scriptures and devotional or hortatory tracts, which show that the common report of his power in unfolding and applying Scripture is justified. The accounts of his eloquence and the effects of his work in the pulpit are his title to rank among the great preachers. His power over men was wonderful. Small of stature and frail in body, like Calvin, he was far more vehement and excitable than the reserved Frenchman. His eye gleamed and his frame worked with the inward power of his convictions, and his mastery of his audience was that of the born speaker. The first sermon at St. Andrews, when he attacked the

[1] P. 298. [2] Fish, *Masterpieces*, etc., Vol. II., p. 207 ff.

papacy, showed his coming power, and the far later one in the same place, when he defied Archbishop Hamilton's threats and put aside the warnings of his friends to urge the immediate reformation of worship, was a triumph of brave and powerful preaching.

6. Contemporaries of Knox

We must not allow the preëminence of Knox to blind us to the fact that in his time there were a number of other faithful and able preachers of the Reformation in Scotland. One of his own noblest traits of character was the cordial recognition which he gave to the worth and services of his brethren; and in their relations to each other there was nothing arrogant on his part nor subservient on theirs. It will suffice, however, to mention briefly a few of the more prominent of these men, for none of them attained to any distinguished rank as preachers, nor do their sermons remain to exhibit their individual characteristics.[1]

One of the humble and faithful ones who labored amid discouragement and peril in Scotland during Knox's exile was William Harlow. He was not a man of much education, but was well grounded in the Scriptures. He had been a tailor at Edinburgh, but, becoming a Protestant, went to England in the time of Edward VI., and was employed there as a preacher in some humble capacity. He afterwards returned to Scotland and preached "with great fervor and diligence" in different places, to the end of his life.

The man who stood next to Knox in pulpit power and extent of influence was John Willock (d. 1585), a native of Ayrshire. He pursued his studies at Glasgow University, and was for some time a monk at Ayr, but early became reformer and forsook the monastery. He, like Harlow, went to England, but was there in Henry VIII.'s reign, and suffered persecution when the Six Articles were being enforced. Afterwards he was appointed a chaplain to the Duke of Suffolk under Edward, but left England under the next reign and practised medicine

[1] Mention in McCrie's *Life of Knox*, and articles in *Dict. Nat. Biog.*

at Emden, in Friesland. Here he got in favor with the Duchess of Friesland, and was by her sent on an ostensibly commercial and political mission to Scotland in 1555. He used his opportunity to encourage and spread the reform movement. Later we find him settled as preacher at Ayr, where he did good work, and made such strong friends that, though tried for heresy and outlawed, the sentence against him could not be executed. He joined Knox on his arrival at Edinburgh, and he it was who stayed and preached there while the city was in possession of the queen-regent and Knox had to retire for a while. Willock was as firm as Knox, but a great deal more tactful and prudent, and his services at that crisis were particularly valuable. The queen-regent tried to have the Catholic worship restored at St. Giles' church, but Willock's decided, though respectful, resistance triumphed. He gave his opinion, when asked by the nobles, in favor of the queen-regent's deposition, but, nevertheless, visited her in her last illness. He filled various pulpits and other positions of prominence and influence in Scotland, but later, for some reason, went to England, where he died as rector of a church in Leicestershire, in 1585. The friendship between him and Knox was close and cordial, and his services to the Reformation were important and lasting. McCrie says of him, "Willock was not inferior to Knox in learning, and though he did not equal him in eloquence and intrepidity, surpassed him in affability, in moderation, and in address; qualities which enabled him sometimes to maintain his station and to accomplish his purposes when his colleague could not act with safety or with success."

Another of Knox's very close friends was Christopher Goodman (d. 1603), who was born and educated in England, and was one of those Frankfort exiles who objected to the use of the English liturgy there and retired to Geneva. He and Knox were joint ministers to the English church at Geneva, and after Knox came back to Scotland he earnestly urged his beloved and faithful colleague to join and help him in establishing the Reformation. Goodman heeded the request, and, coming to Scotland with Knox's family, he rendered valuable help to the cause. He was for a time pastor at Ayr and also at St. Andrews.

He was highly esteemed as a preacher, but, like his greater friend and colleague, he had a sharp tongue and a vehement spirit that often hurt more than they helped. After a while he left Scotland and returned to England, where he had trouble with Elizabeth's prelates on account of his nonconforming views, and died, a very old man, in 1603.

The youngest of this group, who came into influence chiefly after Knox's death, is James Lawson (d. 1584). He claims mention for two things. One is that he was the first man to teach Hebrew in Scotland; having been appointed to a professorship by the regent Murray at St. Andrews. The other is that from this post he was urgently besought by Knox to come to his help and relief in the pastorship at St. Giles' church, in Edinburgh, when the old reformer felt that his days were few. Knox's last public service was at the installation of Lawson as his colleague and successor in the pastorate.

Besides those who have been mentioned there were others also who preached and toiled for the establishing and confirming of the Reformation in Scotland. The value of their labors and the solidity of their work appear in the subsequent history of Protestant Scotland, and in the power and influence of English-speaking Presbyterianism throughout the world. Many of the greatest divines and noblest preachers whose lives have blessed mankind have traced their religious lineage from Knox and his co-laborers in Scotland.

CHAPTER XV

Roman Catholic Preaching and Preachers in the Sixteenth Century.

Inasmuch as the Reformation introduced and established a new epoch in preaching, it has seemed best to follow that tendency among the reformers themselves, and show how in the lands chiefly affected by Protestantism there flourished numbers of notable preachers. But we must not lose sight of the preaching within the Roman Catholic church during this epoch. For centuries we followed the course of development in preaching within that body, and that development received important modification from forces both within and without the church itself during the sixteenth century. Neither the Catholic church as a whole, nor its preaching in particular, was the same after the Reformation as before it, nor what they would have been without that great movement. It is incumbent upon us, therefore, to consider carefully what was the relation of the Reformation to Catholic preaching; and after that we may profitably give some attention to the leading Catholic preachers of the age.

1. The Reformation and Catholic Preaching

It is fair to say in the outset that Catholic and Protestant writers are not likely to agree, and as a matter of fact do not agree, as to the reality, the extent and the character of the influence which the Reformation had upon Catholic preaching. Thus Zanotto[1] depreciates the effect of the Reformation by emphasizing the fact that there was until the Council of Trent no marked improvement in Catholic preaching, but, rather, a fall after Savonarola, giving as two causes for this decline the polemical spirit engendered by the dispute with Protestantism, and the remnant of merely paganizing influences from the Renaissance. This would imply that all the improvement in the Catholic preaching in the sixteenth century came much later than the Protestant outbreak, and was due to the reformatory measures of the Council of Trent. Now there is truth in all this; but it is not the whole truth. Naturally the Protestant preaching itself showed first the heightened tone of the reformatory impulse, and the Council of Trent did work some reforms. But what made that body pass laws for the improvement of preaching, as well as other measures of reform? It is idle to intimate that the Reformation did not influence it. Another Catholic writer on the history of preaching, the Abbé Boucher,[2] goes even further and says, "The church itself, by its councils, by its most illustrious pontiffs and its most holy doctors, recalled the preachers to hard studies, to the gravity of the priesthood, to the simplicity

[1] *Storia della Predicazione*, p. 147 e seg.
[2] *L'Éloquence de la Chaire, ou Histoire littéraire de la Prédication*, p. 271.

of Christian speech. But this reform could only be accomplished slowly, and took a century to show itself. It was during the sixteenth century that Protestantism came and robbed the church of a large part of Europe. It dried up at the same time the fountain of pulpit eloquence in those unhappy lands. There is talking in the pulpit, but no more preaching." The absurd and extreme one-sidedness and inaccuracy of this representation are apparent, but it is an illustration of how Catholics wish to ignore any possible help which the Reformation may have rendered to preaching, either out of or within the Catholic church. On the other hand, Protestant writers—especially the Germans [1]—may be inclined to depreciate any improvement in Catholic preaching, or, if they see it, to assign the whole of it to the influence of the Reformation; forgetting that the Reformation itself was primarily a Catholic movement, and that not all who desired to promote reforms left the church, so that there was progressive movement within as well as helpful stimulus from without. On one point, however, both sides practically agree, and that is that the improved tone of Catholic preaching—whatever its cause—was not very prompt in displaying itself in the sixteenth century. The immediate and direct influence of Protestantism on Catholic preaching was, for reasons already hinted and more clearly to be shown, not a distinct improvement; for the loss of so many of the best preachers, who went out from the church, and the sharpening of the polemic spirit, were injurious to the Catholic pulpit. Yet there were some elements of improvement at work, and these came to fuller power later in the century, and produced still better fruit in the next.

We must recall here something of the state of Catholic preaching in the early part of the sixteenth century. Romanist writers recognize and concede many of the faults

[1] Thus Christlieb says of the Catholic preaching of the sixteenth century that it "shows itself wholly governed by polemic against the reformatory doctrines. In the everywhere threatened revolt from Rome there is defence of that which exists, and only too often the extirpation of heresy is its ground-theme. The conflict with Protestantism, strong in preaching (most commonly only that!), drives also the Catholic Church to more diligence in the homiletical sphere." *Gesch. der Pred.*, in Herzog.

which Protestants charge against the Catholic preaching of the time. It had suffered from the arid speculation of scholasticism, from the puerile exaggerations of the allegorical method of interpreting Scripture, from the cooling influence of the Renaissance, and from the general deterioration in clerical character and pulpit power. If the reformers magnified these faults and ignored the better elements which remained in Romanist preaching, and if the Catholics only partially realized and confessed the evil and sought to break the force of criticism by charging similar and worse defects upon the Protestant pulpit, why, that is only the way of debate when there are wide differences and strong feelings between parties.

We have seen how the reformers gradually withdrew from the old church; and they carried their preaching with them. But there were left behind in the Catholic church reformers of at least three different varieties: (1) There were scholars both of the cool, satirical sort, like Erasmus, and of the devout and earnest sort, like Le Fèvre. (2) There were the pious and mystical, some who came very near being reformers, like Staupitz, and others, who were unshaken in their allegiance to Rome, like Luiz of Granada. (3) There were the thoroughgoing Romanists, who combined with a real desire for the reform of the church, the equally strong one of putting down or refuting the Protestant heresy. These, too, had their different representatives, such as Caraffa, the prelate, and Peter Canisius, the Jesuit and preacher. Now the forces for reform, represented by such men as these and their followers, were by no means inactive. In Italy especially there was a strong movement for improved conditions in preaching. The order of Theatines, founded by Gaetano, Caraffa and others, had preaching in mind as well as other reforms; and the Capuchin monks of the order of St. Francis were started to revive both the stricter asceticism and the preaching traditions of the earlier history of the order. The eminent prelate and later saint, Carlo Borromeo of Milan, earnestly sought, by precept and example, to bring about a better type of preaching. From Spain the order of Jesuits came forth to labor for the ascendancy of Rome in all departments, and not the least in preaching; and in their ranks earlier and later were found some of the most powerful Catholic preachers. Treatises on preaching and helps for preachers appeared. Valerio, in Italy, and Luiz of Granada, in Spain, put forth works of considerable merit on the art of preaching, and some collections of sermons were made for the benefit of the needy in that direction. Among these was one from the famous John Eck, who disputed with Carlstadt and Luther at Leipzig. Finally, the Council of Trent took the matter in hand, and, among other reformatory measures, passed canons which had the improvement of preaching directly in view. One of these [1] made it the duty of bishops and pastors to see that there should be preaching in the churches at least on Sundays, feast days and fast days; and during Advent and Lent every day.

The facts mentioned show that inside the Catholic church there was during the Reformation epoch a decided movement for the reform of preaching; but there were also stimulative influences from without, which, if they did not produce, at least powerfully coöperated with, these inner tendencies. While the Romanist pulpit did not so much as the Protestant preaching respond to those general external influences which have been pointed out before, it was by no means unmoved by them. These, it will be recalled, were the large, progressive spirit of the new age, the impulse from the revival in arts and letters, the effect of criticism upon abuses, and the like. Traditional and conservative as it was in its mediævalism, the Romanist pulpit could not turn a wholly deaf ear to the world's demand for better things.

More particularly, however, the stimulative influence of the Protestant revolt itself is to be considered. The reformers, as we know, did not content themselves with merely criticising or bewailing the defects and decay of the preaching of the age. Their polemic and their example alike served to emphasize the evil conditions which marred the Catholic pulpit. Men do not like to have their faults pointed out by their opponents, but they sometimes profit by the unfriendly criticism, notwithstanding their resentment and denials. Traces of this influence appear

[1] *Sess. XXIV., de Ref.*, cap. 4; referred to by Rothe, *Gesch. der. Pred.*, S. 385.

in many of the Catholic sermons of the time. John Wild, as we shall see, confessed to having received help from the "innovators;" and in others, where not confessed, the service rendered is at least apparent. Besides this we must consider the effect of rivalry. It was not in human nature for the Catholic preachers to see the Protestants winning such victories by preaching and not be moved to greater and better exertions on their own side. Naturally this effect is more distinctly apparent in Germany, where the conflict was dubious, than in those lands where one or the other party had the advantage. And, finally, the effect of the Catholic polemic against Protestantism must also be considered. Not only in receiving attack and in emulation of their rivals, but in their own sharp and determined attack upon the Protestant position, did the Catholics find stimulus towards the exercise and strengthening, at least in one direction, of their preaching. The injurious effect of controversy on the preaching of both parties must be admitted, so far as the religious spirit is concerned, but both frequency and vigor in the work were promoted thereby.

We may now pertinently ask, Did these forces for improvement really accomplish anything? Do we find as a consequence of these tendencies and influences that Catholic preaching in the sixteenth century was decidedly better than in the fifteenth? The answer cannot be an emphatic affirmative, neither can it be a negative. There was some improvement, but not as much as might have been expected. But forces were set in motion that did alter for the better the general character of Catholic preaching, though, as Catholics themselves show, these improvements were not fully apparent till a later period.

A distinct gain was made in the regard for preaching. Perhaps that regard has never become so high as it was in the thirteenth century, and yet there has been increased respect, as compared with the neglect of the two following centuries. And it is likely that not in any age since the Reformation—unless a part of the eighteenth century be an exception—has the pulpit been as little esteemed among Catholics as it was in the fifteenth century.

A very notable gain has been in the improved character of the Catholic clergy as a whole since the Reformation. This has regard to both morals and culture. The proportion of unfit men in the ministry was appreciably reduced by the reforms of the sixteenth century. This statement does not mean that there were only bad men before or only good men since the Reformation in the Catholic ministry; but it does mean that there has been a great improvement. Ignorance and vice have not been wholly banished from among either Catholics or Protestants, but some things which were tolerated in the fifteenth century have been under the ban ever since that time.

Relatively to the irreverent and often absurd misuse of Scripture, which was only too common in the mediæval times, there has been a notable improvement in Catholic preaching. There is much to be desired in the post-reformation sermons in this regard, but we do not find in modern Catholic preaching anything like as much of that wild allegorizing and unworthy distortion of Scripture as existed before the Reformation. It is worthy of remark that the sermons of John Wild and of Peter Canisius, both of whom labored in Germany in near conflict with the reformers, especially show traces of a better interpretation and application of Scripture, and also of a tendency to emphasize the importance of scripture exposition as compared with other modes of preaching. The only homiletical remains from Canisius are a series of *Notes on the Gospels and Epistles*—that is sketches of homilies on the lessons appointed for the sacred days of the year; and among the far more voluminous works of Wild both expository homilies and commentaries occupy a large place. The quality of the exposition in both leaves much to be desired, but it is by no means so forced and so allegorical as in former times was the fashion.

While the Catholic pulpit has never reached the power over the people that it had in the central Middle Ages—particularly the thirteenth century—it at least recovered much of the ground that it lost in the fifteenth century. This rise in popular power was due to all the foregoing considerations, and was particularly enhanced by the now confirmed use of the vernacular languages as the medium of pulpit address. We saw how this tendency was growing through the Middle Ages; but the Latin sermon has become a thing of the past since the Reformation. On some academic and ecclesiastical occasions, when the audience made it tolerable, the sermon was given in Latin; and for the sake of securing a wider circle of readers many of those spoken in the native tongues were translated and published in Latin, and we have many in that form only, the originals having perished. But the ordinary use of Latin in preaching had ceased before the Reformation, and this happy change received emphatic endorsement and perpetuation at that epoch.

Although some changes and improvements were effected in the general character of Catholic preaching by the purifying forces of the Reformation, yet the characteristics acquired through centuries of development remained essentially unchanged. Among these of course are many features which abide in all preaching and are not distinctively Catholic; but Christian, historic, permanent. These are not here under consideration. But if we speak of some matters distinctively Catholic we enter at once the realm of dispute, for these will seem excellencies to the Romanist and faults to the Protestant.

The place of the sermon in worship remained as it was. The Reformation did not rescue it from its subordination to liturgy. If the Reformed churches went too far in making the sermon supreme, and the Anglican church did not go far enough, the Catholic church allowed it to remain relatively insignificant in comparison with the mass and other ceremonies. The priest in the worship continued to be rather the celebrant of mysteries than the preacher of truth. Ritual to strike the senses and the sentiments, rather than the exposition of divine truth to enlighten the mind and mould the character, remained too much the character of Catholic worship. Under such conditions there was an inevitable depreciation and weakening of preaching.

The Reformation mitigated but did not wholly cure certain faults of method in the Catholic preaching of the times. The scholastic tendency was still too much in evidence, along with the multiplied and pedantic quotation from the Fathers and church Doctors. The best preachers of the age are not wholly free from this—as Musso, Villanova, Canisius—although they do show considerable improvement. But in the hands of those who were not so much affected by the new spirit this defect was still more apparent.

The coarseness and irreverence which found place in many of the mediæval Catholic sermons were not entirely banished from those of the Reformation period. It is not denied that here some reformers were equally guilty with their opponents, but that fact does not excuse either party. Still it must be gladly recognized that in this there was improvement over former times, though not complete amendment. And the same remark, as we have already seen, may be made in regard to the use of the Scripture in the Catholic sermons of the age. Many of them indicate a better practice, but still there is too much of the allegorical interpretation, and of forced application. Besides this the use of extra-biblical material continues. The Council of Trent placed the Apocryphal books on a footing with the genuine Scriptures, and they are quoted and used as such. Tradition and legend still supply sermon material. Tales and eulogies of saints and martyrs exceed the legitimate uses of illustration. The authority of the Fathers and Doctors is too highly esteemed in comparison with that of Scripture.

But the most serious Protestant criticism upon the Catholic preaching of the sixteenth century is that which lies against its doctrinal content. It was this that forced the split; the other matters could have been mended inside the church. But naturally at this point the Catholic refuses to confess judgment, though as to other matters he may be willing to admit the existence of some faults. Those great fundamental Christian verities upon which Catholics and Protestants agree are of course not here in question; and it is not denied that in the Romanist preaching of the sixteenth century, controversial as it was, much essential truth upon both doctrine and morals was proclaimed. At the same time the proclamation and defence of those unscriptural accretions and perversions which characterize the Roman theology are the prominent features of Catholic preaching at the period we have in hand. The mass and transubstantiation; penance with its three elements of contrition, confession and satisfaction; good works and merits, and the nature of faith and justification; the adoration of Mary and the saints;

purgatory and prayers for the dead; all these were preached, not indeed to the total neglect, but yet to the great obscuration of pure gospel truth.

We have already had more than one occasion to observe how large a place controversy had in the preaching of the Reformation period. The reason for this is sufficiently obvious, and its effect in stimulating the preaching of the reformers has been previously noticed. Its place and influence in Catholic preaching are now to be further considered. As a general truth it must be borne in mind that controversy has both good and evil effects in preaching. Its good is seen in the spur to diligence, the clarifying of points at issue, the intellectual quickening, the strengthening of conviction and earnestness, which are its usual accompaniments. Its evil appears in the angry passions, the distortions of truth, the personal animosities, the intemperate expressions, which only too often mar its own legitimate working. Fairness demands the statement that both the good and evil of controversy appear in both the great parties to the religious strife of the sixteenth century, and the preaching of both reformers and Catholics exhibits the corresponding effects. Yet it is also fair to say that in some respects the advantage lay with the Protestants, and their preaching shows on the whole more of the good and less of the evil of polemics than is the case with their Romanist adversaries. This was due to a number of things, a few of which may be instanced: The reformers were the attacking party and many of the things which they attacked were notoriously evil and had to be so admitted, while others which were defended were yet placed in question in the minds of multitudes of thoughtful and devout Christians; they were the ones who made the most sacrifices for conscience' sake, and with whom accordingly the weight of moral power lay; they had a simpler task, for their one great authority was the Scripture, complicated with fewer traditions and dissociated from many historic abuses; they made preaching their main instrument of warfare and more unreservedly and warmly devoted themselves to it. Such considerations as these serve to explain why the evil effects of controversy, though unhappily bad enough, were not so manifest in the Protestant as in the Catholic preaching of the Reformation age. But even if the comparison be not admitted, the fact that polemic against Protestantism was hurtfully prominent in that preaching cannot be denied. Rothe [1] asserts that it was the principal element, and Christlieb [2] has the same opinion. These Protestant judgments are confirmed by Catholic writers also, though they naturally take a very different view of the character of the defence made by the Romanists.[3] Thus Renoux [4] says: "The Reformation met in its way vigorous champions to combat it; the church had its defenders. The preachers took pains to warn the faithful against the perils to their faith, and to refute the new belief which threatened to destroy it; in the pulpit especially the greatest zeal was displayed." The same writer contends that the Catholic preachers were more dignified and less bitter than the Protestants, and far less rude and coarse. Yet he admits [5] that they sometimes descended to ridicule and satire. He instances as an especially keen and effective controversialist the Franciscan archbishop of Brixen, John Nas, and makes several quotations from a sermon of his in reply to a certain Müller—which may be a fictitious name, as there was no prominent Protestant preacher of that name at the time. As Leroux quotes these paragraphs with approval, we may transcribe them as fair specimens of Catholic pulpit polemic against Lutheranism. Thus Bishop Nas: "All the popes opposed the heretics; also the heretics always treated the popes as anti-Christ. That is true, and is so to-day, to the great honor of the pope; for the heretics preach a false Christ, who does not require either obedience to the will of God, nor observance of the divine law,[6] and who does not prescribe either love or penitence, contenting himself simply with faith without works. Now the pope anathematizes and condemns this Christ, he is his enemy, the enemy of all his members and of all his sect. So, then, the pope is rightly called an anti-Christ. He is the enemy of all the false Christs, and condemns them. So this fool Müller does not know what he is say-

[1] S. 385. [2] *Ante*, p. 526, note.
[3] See references to Zanotto and Boucher, ante, p. 526.
[4] *Les Prédicateurs célèbres de l'Allemagne*, pp. 211, 213.
[5] *Op. cit.*, p. 219 et suiv. [6] Calvin, for instance!

ing, he vomits hot and cold without knowing it; there is just as much relation in the analogy which he pretends to establish as there is between the fist and the eye." He speaks of Luther's tract on the *Babylonian Captivity* as "thought and written by the devil." Reverting to his opponent, he says: "This crazy Müller is as consistent in his talk as an empty flour sack. To-day he brags on the Wittenbergers as better than all the rest of the world, he makes them out saints, then all of a sudden, as a conclusion to the discourse, he reproaches their vices and threatens them with coming ruin if they do not like his preaching and put it into practice."

This has a certain vigor and liveliness, to be sure, but what else has it? Doubtless there was better polemical preaching than this represents, doubtless, also, there was worse; but, on the whole, the controversial element of the Catholic preaching of this age cannot be regarded as greatly to its credit, either for depth or dignity.

2. The Leading Catholic Preachers

As compared with the preceding and following times, and as compared with the Protestants of their own times, the number of really great Catholic preachers in the sixteenth century was very small. These were found chiefly in Italy and Spain, with a few in Germany, in the other lands scarcely any that demand serious notice. In England the famous Catholic prelates of the time—Wolsey, Gardiner, Tunstall, Bonner and Pole—were distinguished for other things than preaching. In France a few are mentioned by writers on the history of preaching,[1] as Vigor of Narbonne, Charles de Lorraine, Jean Boucher, Pierre Divolé, Edmond Auger, and others. But it is significant that Boucher, in his so-called "Literary History of Preaching,"[2] himself a Frenchman, should say of this period in France that "the sixteenth century permits us to make the excursion across foreign literatures; we shall return to France for the preachers of the League and of the reign of Henry IV." In other words, even to a French Catholic writer, the preachers of his church and country in the early sixteenth century do not seem

[1] As Zanotto and Christlieb, *op. cit.*

[2] *L'Éloquence de la Chaire*, etc., p. 274.

worth mentioning in comparison with those of other lands. In the countries of northern and eastern Europe a few are mentioned by Zanotto, evidently to fill up, but there were none of distinction. So we may confine our view to the preachers of Germany, Italy and Spain.

In Germany, John Eck, the clever opponent of Luther, was a man of learning and influence, but was not specially significant as a preacher, though he contributed a collection of sketches, or short expository sermons, on the Gospels, in aid of the clergy. A similar service was performed by Martin Eisengrein, also not otherwise significant. There is also a volume of sermons from John Witzel, who was a milder polemic than some and sought a more conciliatory way of meeting Protestantism than was common. More sharp in controversy, as we have had occasion to see, was John Nas, who was an Alsatian by birth, first joined the Franciscans as a lay brother, and was afterwards, because of his readiness in speech, made a preacher, and became one of the cleverest and most noted opponents of the Reformation. But by all odds the most important Romanist preachers in Germany at this period were Wild and Canisius, and they are entitled to more extended notice than the rest.

A man of decided talent and merit was the celebrated Cathedral preacher at Mainz, John Wild (d. 1554), or, in the Latin form, Johannes Ferus.[1] A veil of obscurity covers the birthplace, parentage and early years of John Wild. It appears that he was of German birth, and that about 1520 he joined the Franciscans, no doubt from motives of piety and devotion to the Catholic church. In 1528 he was appointed by the elector of Mainz to the post of afternoon preacher at the Cathedral in that city, and was soon afterwards made guardian of his order for the region about Mainz. Here he was diligent and popular in preaching for many years. His learning, piety and eloquence gave him wide influence; and his amiable spirit and aversion to polemics were remarkable in that tem-

[1] Renoux, *Les Prédicateurs célèbres de l'Allemagne;* various cyclopædia articles; and a Latin *Dissertatio de Johanne Fero, monacho et concionatore Moguntino, teste veritatis evangelicae,* by E. G. Dieterich, presented for his degree at Altdorf in 1723. Also a Latin translation of Wild's sermons, published in 1559.

pestuous age. By 1545 he had become widely known as one of the most important preachers of the times, and he drew large congregations. In 1552 Albert of Brandenburg, also electoral archbishop of Mainz, having become Protestant, found it necessary to reduce the city to his authority by force, and captured it. He greatly respected Wild, and tried to win him to Protestantism by asking him to abandon his Franciscan gown; but Wild answered, "This habit has been with me these many years and has never harmed me; why should I leave it now?" Probably Albert would not have removed him from his place as preacher had he renounced his order; as it was, he was displaced by a Protestant preacher for a while, but on Albert's death he was restored to his pulpit at the Cathedral. He did not, however, live very long after this, but died in 1554.

Wild made and filled his own place among the preachers of his time. In learning he was abreast of the age, being acquainted with Hebrew and Greek, and well read in history and theology, patristic and mediæval. In character he was above all reproach for piety and justly esteemed by Catholics and Protestants alike for his amiability, moderation and earnestness. His theological position was a mediating one.[1] He learned much from the reformers, and approached them in many particulars both of doctrine and method. He said that "from the error of the moderns he had here and there dug out a pearl," but he qualified this by saying further that if he had borrowed from the innovators he believed it was only such things as were in accord with the church doctrines. He proclaimed his independence by saying, "I flatter no one, but purely announce to you the gospel in such a way as I shall answer for it to the Supreme Judge." As a consequence, his writings and sermons were admired and quoted by some Protestants, and Dieterich has shown that it is possible to cull from his works many clear and striking statements dear to the reformers. For example, as to Scripture, in rebuking those who would allege obscurity of the Bible as an excuse for not obeying its precepts, he teaches that the Scripture should be read by all, that it

[1] This point is well discussed and illustrated by quotations in the *Dissertation* of Dieterich.

can be understood by the common man, and that it should be explained by its own light. In one place he roundly says, "*Sola scriptura regula est veritatis.*" And so, while not discarding the Catholic traditions and usages, he puts them below Scripture. One of his utterances is well worth quoting as an example both of his manner and his thought. He says: "In the gospel Christ has touched upon many things which now exist among us Christians, who, after the manner of the Pharisees, are taken up, not only with fasts, but also with all the church regulations; who, as Christ himself said, strain out the gnat and swallow the camel. Yea, there are many things (if, indeed, I must acknowledge the truth and judge of it) in which our Christianity has become nothing else than an empty pharisaism—outward show, in which one finds many ceremonies but little righteousness, much song and little devotion, much appearance and little truth, much word and little spirit, the breaking off from certain kinds of food, but no breaking off from sins. On the former there is insistence, the latter is forgotten. When we hold fast the church regulation it is a great thing, when we despise God's commandment, yea, daily sin against it, no harm is done." This earnest rebuke is only too sadly appropriate to all times and churches, but it is gratifying to find a Catholic of eminence who dared so to express himself in those days.

As a preacher Wild had the talents and spirit that always attract and command attention. During his long service as Cathedral preacher at Mainz his audiences were large and his influence great. His published sermons are numerous. He spoke in German and some of his discourses are preserved in that tongue, but a very large number in Latin translations also. They once had large circulation among both Protestants and Catholics. As he said, they were not intended for the learned alone, but for the common people. In addition to their doctrinal import, already considered, the sermons are marked by their prevailing expository character. They are chiefly homilies on the Scripture books, and easily pass into commentaries, of which he also wrote a number. And so we may sum up by saying that for his emphasis on Scripture, for his grasp of evangelical truth, for his independence and yet moderation, for his earnest piety and amiable character, and for his sustained power in the pulpit, John Wild must be ranked with the very best of the few who attained distinction as preachers among the Catholics of his age.

A very different man, but no less eminent in his diverse way, was the famous Jesuit preacher and polemic Peter Canisius (1521-1597).[1] Born in 1521, of excellent family, at Nimeguen, in the province of Gueldres, he was educated carefully in preparatory schools and at the University of Cologne, where he took the regular degrees in course and was especially devoted to theology. He was the first German of any importance to join the newly founded Society of Jesus, and his accession was hailed with pleasure and proved to be distinguished. In 1543 Faber came to Germany to establish the order there, and Canisius, then twenty-two years old, and already a very promising scholar and preacher, was won. He was sent by his archbishop, at the age of twenty-six, to take part in the deliberations of the Council of Trent, and rendered good service for the short time that he was there. Later he was sent to Rome, where for several years he studied and worked under the immediate supervision of Loyola himself, and also served a year as teacher and preacher at Messina.

After all these preparatory years he was at last sent back to his life work in Germany. At first he taught and preached at Ingolstadt with great applause, and his services were much sought after in many places. At the earnest request of Ferdinand of Austria he was sent to Vienna, where for a number of years he did effective work in the interests of his order and of the Catholic church. During this time he prepared and published a Catechism which has ranked among the works of that character most highly esteemed by Catholics. His preaching also drew great crowds, and did much to give to the Romanist cause its abiding strength in Vienna and throughout Austria. Canisius was offered a bishopric, but steadily refused. Afterwards he labored with great

[1] Authorities before noted, but especially the art. in Wetzer und Welte; Canisius' *Notae Evangelicae,* in an edition published at Freiburg, 1591.

effect in Bavaria, and then in other parts of Germany. He not only put new life and courage into his Catholic brethren everywhere, but is said to have been very successful also in winning back many Protestants to the Romanist faith. So highly were his abilities regarded as a disputant against Protestantism that he was especially deputed by the pope to write a reply to the famous *Magdeburg Centuries,* the church history written from the Protestant point of view. Many engagements and labors hindered the production of Canisius' reply, but when it at last appeared it was considered very satisfactory to his side. Thus variously and strenuously occupied in many places in Germany, Canisius yet lived to old age, not dying till 1597. In his lifetime and since, he has been regarded as the ablest defender of Romanism in Germany during the time in which he lived, his name is held in veneration, not only among Jesuits, but among Catholics generally, and in 1864 Pius IX. pronounced him "blessed"—the degree next below sainthood.

Besides the history and catechism already mentioned, Canisius wrote and published a number of theological and exegetical works. The latter are particularly significant because they show the effect of the Protestant exegesis in forcing this foremost Catholic disputant in Germany also to employ that weapon. The Romanist estimate of Canisius will appear from the following passage from the article in Wetzer and Welte's *Kirchenlexicon:* "Unpublished manuscript expressions of his, still preserved, show how clearly and profoundly he understood the essence of Protestantism. Far more impressive than harnessed defence appeared to him the positive teaching and strengthening of the Catholics; and, therefore, this element dominates in all his writings. Luther's coarse popular wit, passion, agitator's rhetoric, are wholly lacking in him. Instead there appears in his (mostly Latin) works the closest familiarity with Holy Scripture, extensive acquaintance with the Fathers and with the positive and scholastic theology, an earnest humanistic culture, great reading of the works of the Protestant theologians, a dignified polemical readiness to strike, piety, decision, and the mildness of a generally apostolic man." From the prodigious activity of Canisius as a preacher the literary remains are slight—only a volume of expository sketches in Latin, called *Evangelical Notes,* and consisting of comments, in the homily style, on the Scripture lessons appointed for the sacred days of the ecclesiastical year. It is of course not fair to judge his powers by these alone, but, making due allowances for their imperfect form, they hardly sustain the high estimate which Catholics place upon Canisius either as exegete or preacher. Waiving the question of doctrines, the adoration of Mary and the saints, and other distinctively Catholic features, we do not find the depth of thought, accuracy of interpretation, or power of expression which we should expect. Yet the style and spirit are worthy of commendation, and the exegesis marks a notable advance upon the scholastic and allegorical method of former times.

We should naturally expect to find a larger number of great Catholic preachers during this time in Italy rather than elsewhere, and though there is no multitude, the facts justify that expectation.[1] We can, however, from the number of those mentioned by the authorities select only a few of the most important for brief consideration.

Among the preachers of the early part of the century none perhaps had so great a reputation as Egidio da Viterbo (d. 1532). The place of his birth is uncertain, but his surname suggests Viterbo. He seems to have been of humble but respectable origin, but little is known of him until, in 1488, he joined the Augustinian monks. After this he spent some time in studies at various places, including Padua, Florence and Rome. He was fond of Platonic philosophy and gave lectures at Florence. Already, in his young manhood, he preached at Rome with applause, and won the favorable notice of Pope Alexander VI., whose favor, indeed, may not be considered any special compliment, except for his capacity to discern

[1] For the Italian preachers of the period I have chiefly used the following authorities: Zanotto's *Storia della Predicazione;* a bright critical introduction to an *Antologia della Sacra Eloquenza Moderna,* da Ulisse Micocci; notices in the appropriate volumes of Tiraboschi's great *Storia della Letteratura Italiana;* articles in *Encyclopedia Italiana;* Cardinal Fred. Borromeo's *De Sacris nostrórum Temporum Oratoribus;* and to some extent the works of the preachers themselves, as far as available.

talent. He was highly esteemed by the Franciscan Genazzano, the rival of Savonarola, and accompanied him to Naples in 1498, where Genazzano died and Egidio was very ill, but recovered, and his preaching attracted great notice. King Ferdinand of Naples sent him to many places in his dominions to preach, and indeed his fame spread all over Italy. His services were in such demand as preacher during Lent and other seasons that Pope Julius II., it is said, reserved to himself the right of giving Egidio his appointments. This pope also employed him on a confidential mission to Venice. He also served ten years as General of his order. Leo X. greatly admired him, and made him a cardinal in 1517. Such eminent scholars and critics as Bembo and Sadolet speak in the highest terms of his talents and eloquence, and there can be no doubt of his learning and eminence as a preacher. But his sermons seem to have perished in the sack of Rome under Charles V., and no specimens of his pulpit work have survived.

Passing over several men of some note who flourished in the early decades of the century with and after Egidio, we come to a group of three whose work lay from the middle toward the end of the age. First of these is the much-praised Cornelio Musso (d. 1575), who was born in 1511, of good family, at Piacenza. At nine years of age he entered as a novice the Franciscan order, received his early education at their convent at Carpi, showing both diligence in study and promising oratorical talent. While a youth of nineteen he was invited to Venice, and on Annunciation day in the Cathedral of San Marco preached a sermon to the wonder of all hearers. But, like young Bossuet afterwards, he was not unwisely seduced from study by this early recognition of his powers, but the rather devoted himself to his books. In 1530 he went to Padua, where he studied hard under good teachers, making progress in Greek and Hebrew, as well as other branches, and in philosophy and oratory. During all this time he was preaching much, and was heard with admiration.

Soon he was called as preacher to Milan, and also held a lectureship at the University of Padua. Later he lectured on philosophy and theology at Bologna, all the while being much in demand as preacher in various places. In 1541 he is found at Rome, where he is highly regarded by the pope, who frequently takes counsel with him on important questions of theology. As a reward he was made bishop, first of Bertinoro, and then of Bitonto, under which appellation he is best known. It fell to Musso to preach the opening sermon at the famous Council of Trent, and he discharged that duty in a way to win extravagant eulogies from the assembled prelates, showing himself, as Tiraboschi says, "at once a profound theologian and eloquent orator." After the Council of Trent he returned to his bishopric of Bitonto, and was diligent as bishop and preacher there for some years, but was later called to Rome by Gregory XIII., and died there, in 1575.

A selection of ten of his sermons was published as early as 1554, and a number of discourses on various subjects appeared later. Many of them were translated into Latin, Spanish, and French. They had wide circulation, and were much praised by excellent critics among the Catholics. Still, to our thinking, the sermons would be by no means models for imitation, being rather long and minute in some details, not remarkably well arranged, and not always in good taste. Yet, according to Tiraboschi: "If Musso be compared with his predecessors, he is to them like gold to earth."

Not an orator, but a man of high character, a prelate of distinction, a useful preacher and helper of preaching, was St. Charles Borromeo of Milan (1538-1584). He came of a distinguished family in north Italy. He was a faithful student, though at first somewhat slow. The pure and pious lad was early designed for the clerical profession, and his uncle, Julius Cæsar Borromeo, resigned in the boy's favor an abbacy which had considerable revenues. Already the lad showed signs of the coming reformer and saint, for he requested his father to take charge of these revenues and employ them in charity, while he went on with his studies at Milan and Pavia, and preserved his purity amid the snares of college life. Pope Pius IV. was his uncle, and, availing himself of the talents of his young kinsman, appointed him to great offices in the church. Though very young and not yet ordained a priest, he was made cardinal deacon and archbishop of Milan. Borromeo did not approve of such abuses, and reluctantly accepted office in obedience to the pope.

As a cardinal and an official in the pope's household, he lived at Rome as befitted his dignity, but felt all the while that he ought to be ordained and take hold of the work of his diocese at Milan. Though only twenty-three years old, he is said to have been the real ruler of the church in the name of Pius IV., and it is claimed that not for a long time had the affairs of the papacy been so well administered. In these times of much responsibility and public business he gave his nights largely to study, and with him as a centre there was a circle of studious men who used to spend their evenings in scholarly converse at the Vatican.

On the death of Charles' elder brother without heir, he was solicited by his kindred, including even the pope, to resign his church offices and marry. But he said he had wedded another bride; and to be rid of the importunities of his relatives he at once consummated his long-deferred ordination as priest and bishop. Having received requisite authority from the pope, he instituted some much-needed reforms in the discipline of the clergy. He also took hold of the dilatory and much-interrupted Council of Trent, and under his skilful influence that body soon accomplished its labors. To him, with others, was committed the preparation of the Tridentine Catechism, that clear and compact standard of Catholic doctrine.

At last, in 1565, he was free to take up his work, performed in his long absence by deputies, as archbishop of Milan. He found things in great disorder, but he soon proved himself almost another Ambrose; and to this day his name is honored at Milan along with that of his most illustrious predecessor. He set the example of self-denial that he required in his clergy. He was diligent in all the work of a bishop, preaching much and administering affairs with a firm and skilful hand. His determined and vigorous discipline made enemies among the less worthy of the clergy, and one of these attempted his life, shooting at him while he was engaged in prayer in the church. But the bullet somehow did not take effect, and his escape was accounted a miracle. When the plague desolated Italy and visited Milan the archbishop was away, but on its appearance he promptly returned to his post of duty and labored in visitation and charities. He escaped the plague, but not long after fell sick of a fever and died in 1584.

As a preacher, so far as gifts of oratory are concerned, Borromeo cannot be ranked with Musso and Panigarola, but he was as diligent and conscientious in this part of his work as in other things. His sermons were instructive, and spiritually helpful to his people. Of course, one of the leading theologians of Trent was a thorough-going Catholic in doctrine. His voice and utterance were not specially pleasing, but his knowledge of human nature, his earnest spirit, the thoughtfulness of his matter, and the weight and elevation of his character gave to his preaching a power which mere graces of rhetoric could not have brought. His great interest in preaching and the reforms he instituted in that department, apart from his own work in the pulpit, give him a worthy place in the history of preaching.

Toward the close of the sixteenth century the most popular and famous Italian preacher was Francesco Panigarola (1548-1594). Born at Milan, of gentle family, he received careful training in youth, and early gave evidence of a remarkably retentive memory and of oratorical powers of a high order. He studied law for some years at Pavia and Bologna, leading at the same time a somewhat loose life. Recalled to serious thoughts by the death of his father, he determined to preach, and in 1567 he joined the Franciscan order and soon became noted for his preaching talents. In 1571 he went to Paris for further theological education, and while there preached with acceptance before Catherine dei Medici. After spending some time at Lyons and Antwerp, he returned in 1573 to Italy, and during the following years, while preaching much, also taught theology in various convents of his order. He passed two years with Borromeo at Milan, who highly regarded him and used him in preaching. Later Panigarola was appointed to a bishopric, but, through envy, he was falsely accused, and suffered somewhat in reputation for a while. The charges against him not being sustained, he was promoted in 1587 to the bishopric of Asti. Soon afterwards he was called to Paris to help the Catholic cause there as one of the preachers of the League, which his ready acquaintance with French enabled him to do with credit. In 1590 he returned to his diocese, which he administered with diligence till his death, a few years later.

Panigarola had a fine voice and figure and a flowing, pleasing style of speech, but the critics find him somewhat artificial and seeking after effect. His arrangement is usually clear and good, and the expression fluent and agreeable. Tiraboschi considers his fame well founded, but Zanotto is scarcely so sure of it; and if the specimens of his work given by the latter are fair samples of his manner, there is far more evidence of fluency than of depth either of thought or feeling.

Spain was less affected by the Reformation than any other Catholic country, and it is just what we should expect when we find the distinctive Catholic preaching more prominent than in Germany or even in Italy. Of the preachers who were active during the sixteenth century three at least are deserving of special notice: Juan de Avila, Luiz de Granada and Thomas de Villanova.

The most evangelical of the three was the so-called "Apostle of Andalusia," Juan de Avila (d. 1569). He was of humble but respectable birth, received his education at Salamanca and Alcala, and devoted himself with zeal and success to preaching, more especially in Andalusia. He loved to preach to the common people, and his converts were numbered among the thousands. He desired to go as a missionary to the East Indies, but was urgently dissuaded by the archbishop of Seville, who wished to retain his rare preaching talent for the work at home. He began to preach at Seville, but visited many other towns. It is said that he could move his hearers by a single word, by a look even. His wonderful success aroused envy, he did not escape attack, but the Inquisition could not find the charges justified. He refused various high church offices, but was highly regarded in his life and after his death. Many of his sermons were translated into various languages. The abbé Boucher[1] says of him: "We have of him sermons in

[1] *L'Eloquence de la Chaire*, etc.

which there is found much of dash, of warmth, and of passion. But rapidly improvised, they leave much to be desired in respect to form."

Famous both as preacher and as author of devotional books, praised by popes and saints, and admired by literary critics, in his own country, was Luiz de Granada [1] (1504-1588). He was born of poor parents at Granada, in 1504. One day he and another boy had a quarrel, which soon came to blows. A Spanish nobleman witnessed the affair and parted the lads, whereupon Luiz stated his side of the case and pleaded his cause with such good reasoning and eloquence that the count was impressed by the boy's talents, and became so much interested in him that he was allowed to pursue his studies along with the gentleman's sons without charge. At nineteen years of age Luiz entered the Dominican order, of which he became a distinguished ornament. He studied philosophy and theology at the University of Valencia. He worked for his order in various ways, but chiefly as teacher and preacher. He was greatly admired and beloved among all classes. Catherine, the sister of Charles V., offered him a bishopric, and the pope desired to make him a cardinal, but he declined all offers of ecclesiastical preferment, and remained, first of all, a preacher, though he also wrote numbers of books. After a life of industry and devotion he died at Lisbon in December, 1588.

Among his writings the *Guide to Sinners* is considered the best, of which a Catholic author said that it led more sinners to God than it contained letters. One of the leading Spanish literary critics is quoted as saying: "Never has a devotional author spoken with such dignity and sublimity of God. When he pictures our weakness and poverty over against the almightiness and compassion of God, when he represents his infinite love and our ingratitude, he is great, sublime, incomparable. He is among the mystics what Bossuet was among the orators." The same critic praises his style as uniting charm

[1] Short notices in Zanotto and Boucher, *opp. citt.*, various encyclopædia articles, preferably the one in Wetzer und Welte; and best of all some of the works of Luiz himself in Latin, namely, his *Rhetorica Ecclesiastica,* and a beautiful old edition of his sermons, *Conciones de Temporibus,* etc., printed at Antwerp in 1584, now in the Bibliothêque Nationale, Paris.

with ornament, and compares him to Chrysostom in ease, clearness, richness, fulness. On the other hand Rothe,[1] the German Protestant, is not so enthusiastic, for, though admitting the oratorical talent of Luiz, he declares him deficient in training and in taste, and says his sermons lack order and are overloaded with images, comparisons, legends and the like. The truth lies between these extremes of praise and censure.

Beside his books of devotion and his sermons, Luiz published an interesting and, in its time, useful work on the art of preaching, under the title, *Rhetorica Ecclesiastica seu de Ratione Concionandi.* The treatise has not much originality, but shows easy grasp of the principles of rhetoric and a careful reading of the best ancient treatises—Aristotle, Demetrius Phalereus, Cicero, though, apparently, not Quintilian—and also of Augustine's *De Doctrina Christiana.* He treats the usual subjects of Invention, Arrangement, Style and Delivery with good sense and in clear and agreeable Latin. He earnestly insists, both in the beginning and conclusion, on the character of the preacher as the highest essential to good preaching, and urges devotion to Christ and absorption in him in the act of preaching.

The sermons of Luiz were preached and many of them published in Spanish, but there are also Latin sermons. A beautiful old edition of these, published at Antwerp in 1584, contains a large number of discourses. The first sermon on the Advent is based on the text Matt. 21:1,2, our Lord's sending the two disciples to find and bring the ass and her colt for his entry into Jerusalem. The preacher first proposes to expound the Scripture lesson and then discuss the reasons why the church celebrates the Advent; but really there are three divisions, thus: (1) Meaning of finding the ass and colt. They signify the Jews and Gentiles—the latter being as yet unbroken to the yoke of the divine law, and all in bondage to sin—"tied," but Christ gives liberty. (2) Why had the Lord need of these humble animals? First, to show his humility; and, secondly, to show his power to deliver, since as already said the asses represent sin-bound people. [The unfolding of this thought is good, notwithstanding

[1] *Gesch. der Pred.*, S. 385 ff.

the way he gets at it.] (3) Reasons for celebrating Advent. The church, like a good mother, provides these sacred seasons for the spiritual enjoyment and profit of her children; and the Advent has, among other blessings, the reminder of the fulfilling of the promises and prophecies of the Messiah. He enlarges upon our blessedness in receiving fully what the Old Testament believers only dimly foresaw.

The five sermons on penance give the Catholic doctrine, but they contain much that is spiritually and morally sound and profitable. The following passage from the introduction to a sermon on the Epiphany will give a slight taste of his style: "Among all the benefits which the unmeasured kindness of God has conferred on the human race this holds the highest rank; that he has deigned to grant to them the saving knowledge of his divinity, without which light no man could savingly know him. For, as no one is able to see the sun without the light of the sun itself, so no one can piously receive God without the aid of God himself. For it is himself to whom we come, and himself by whom we come; he is the way which leads, and the life to which it leads."

One of the very best of the Spanish Catholic preachers was Thomas Garcias of Villanova [1] (d. 1555). He was born in the diocese of Leon in 1487, but his parents having come from Villanova, he was later called by that surname. His father and mother were poor but pious folk, who in their own narrow circumstances always found means to give to the poor, and their example of self-sacrifice and charity made a profound and lasting impression on their son. Thomas received his education at Alcala, the recently founded university of Cardinal Ximenes, and was so successful a student that soon after his graduation he was appointed professor of philosophy there. Later he was called to the older university of Salamanca to the same chair. But he had long had the intention of becoming a monk, and retired from this high position to enter the Augustinian order in 1520 and devote himself to preaching and the direction of souls. His gifts as a

[1] *Conciones Sacrae illustrissimi et reverendissimi D. D. Thomae a Villanova;* Brixiæ, 1603; with a Life prefixed. In addition some other notices in various authorities.

preacher attracted attention and his fame began to spread. The warm admirer who wrote the life prefixed to Villanova's sermons thus speaks of his powers: "It is a thing most worthy of the greatest admiration that he was able so freely to satisfy by one and the same discourse men of so diverse minds. These are the divine powers of liquid truth and sincere virtue. Of these I was an eye-witness, who took diligent care never to be absent from a sermon of that man."

Villanova attracted the notice of the emperor, Charles V., who made him one of his preachers, and wished to promote him to higher ecclesiastical dignities. Villanova refused the archbishopric of Granada, but was at last constrained by his superiors to accept that of Valencia. But he entered on his episcopal duties in the spirit of his order, came on foot with a single attendant, and clad in his monk's habit. He immediately began a visitation of his diocese and the reform of abuses. This, as usual, provoked opposition and enmity from the corrupt element of the clergy; but he went on his way. He reserved of his revenues only what was needed for his living, and gave the rest in charity and religious works. All the while he was active and frequent in preaching, and gave to his public ministry the effectual backing of a life of purity and piety. The feebleness of his health prevented his attendance upon the Council of Trent. When about to die he gave to the poor what few personal effects he had, and left orders that the bed on which he died should be given to some destitute prisoner.

The published collection of his sermons, done into Latin, contains about a hundred discourses on various subjects dear to Catholics, more especially those on the Church seasons. Some are on the Song of Solomon, a number in praise of the Virgin, and a good many on the saints, all the way from John the Baptist to Augustine and Ildefonso. One of the best of them is a sermon on the Last Judgment, which discusses the subject in a Scriptural way, as well as with good reasoning, and contains some passages of real power. The introduction runs thus: "Being now about to speak of the solemnity and the manner of the final judgment, I beseech thee, benign Spirit, from on high to fall upon our minds and graciously infuse the hearts of thy people, that we may have the sentiments worthy of so great a mystery, and that what we may worthily feel we may pour forth in full speech. Put the right and the well-sounding word into my mouth, and let it sound forth from my mouth as from a trumpet to the people of God—thy own speech—so that both the ears of those who hear may tingle, and they be converted to thee, O Lord, lest thy wrath on that day may swallow them up alive."

Then follows the customary invocation to the Virgin for her intercession, and afterwards the statement of the divisions, which are: (1) The reasons, and (2) the character of the judgment, with appropriate and clear subdivision. In a fine passage—too long to quote entire—he treats of those Scriptures which say that judgment shall be in the hands of Christ, and thus proceeds: "I will not refuse him for a judge whom I have had as a redeemer; the lamb, I say, slain for me, him I request as my judge, him I desire, him I long for with all my strength. I will not accuse him of cruelty, for he is a lamb; I will not hold his friendship under suspicion, for he is my brother and my flesh; nor will I fear for his rectitude, for he is God himself. I will not refuse to appear at the tribunal of him who did not disdain to stand for me at the tribunal of a wicked judge. Whatever he has decreed for me I will willingly receive. Therefore, O most mighty Father, give the King thy judgment! Let him be my judge, who for me was judged." Though he comforts thus, the preacher does not fail to warn against false confidence, saying: "But although I would say these things, let no one, my brethren, let no one deceive himself, let no one sleep, let no one become hardened in sin, in hope of forgiveness; for cursed is he who sins in hope."

In truth, Villanova was a preacher of decided merits. The published sermons, while they do not justify extravagant praise, do exhibit the essential qualities of good preaching—they show a warm and pious heart, a good head for reasoning, good knowledge of the Scriptures, usually a clear analysis, an elevated and at the same time intelligible and impressive style. A Protestant cannot subscribe to his doctrine, and will find other things to demur to in many expressions and turns of thought, but no one who reads his sermons can fail to feel their devout spirit and their oratorical power. And thus with him, as an unusually fit example, we may close our survey of the Catholic preaching and preachers of the sixteenth century.

CHAPTER XVI

Preaching at the Threshold of the Modern World

Our studies have conducted us to the threshold of the modern world. The sixteenth century is the beginning of modernity, as the fifteenth was the end of mediævalism. Renaissance and Reformation mark the death of one, the birth of the other. Mental and spiritual culture are the strong forces in human development, and these received powerful impulse in the ages named. In preaching, as our studies have shown us, no less than in other important departments of this mental and spiritual culture, the forces which wrought great changes came to a head in this time, more especially in the early part of the sixteenth century. So this is a good place to pause in considering the history of preaching and look backwards and forwards. A summary of the progress made may clear our vision of the past from the maze of detail into which we have necessarily been plunged, and prepare us better to take also a general forward look into the three centuries after the sixteenth—a more detailed study of which is deferred to the future.

1. Retrospect

As we look back over the long and varied way by which we have traveled and try to sketch in salient outline the main features of the scenes through which we have just passed, what do we see?

Preaching is distinctively a Christian institution, and yet is founded on certain fundamental things in human character and history. As one of the most widely employed and useful forms of public speech it has held for all the Christian ages an assured place among the institutions of human society. Thus, on rational principles, it establishes a claim for fair and thorough scientific study and treatment. Thus, too, on the historical side, it has availed itself in its forms and technical principles of all the developments in the art of oratory, and has contributed no mean share of example and instruction to that department of literature. But it is, of course, as a vital element of the Christian religion that preaching finds its highest historic value and interest. It derives its warrant from the divine Founder himself. Its historic origins are traceable to the prophets and scribes of the Old Testament, and to the teaching and example of Jesus and his Apostles. Its burden and message are the good news of salvation by Christ. From its origin preaching has a two-fold character—proclamation and teaching. It proclaims the gospel of Christ to men with a view to their acceptance of him as their Saviour and Lord; and it teaches to those who have so accepted him the lofty morality and the inspiring hopes and consolations which that gospel includes. It brings to men's minds the truth of God, to their wills his law, to their hearts his love. In the very beginning, and ever as time goes on, these two elements of proclamation and instruction are variously combined in the Christian sermon, which as a part of the congregational worship is occupied with the explanation and enforcement of the mind and will of God as revealed in Holy Scripture. From this origin the history of preaching proceeds through the centuries.

The accounts and remains of preaching in the times immediately following the Apostles are very meagre, but we know that there was preaching of both the evangelistic and didactic sort. As those who could bear oral witness to the main facts of the gospel history passed away, and the authoritative teachers appointed directly by the Master himself died off, the exposition of the written Word became more and more the essence of preaching as a part of Christian worship. With the spread of the gospel and the rapid acquisition of converts, both by personal exertions and more public discourses, the assemblies for worship and hearing became larger and more varied in character; and thus the combination of proclamation and teaching becomes the fixed character of Christian preaching, the two elements being varied according to circumstances. Naturally, in the assemblies the expository element predominates, and we have for centuries, and, in fact, nevermore wholly abandoned, the homily, or explanatory and hortatory talk, as the prevailing type of sermon. All subsequent modifications grew from this germ. The persecutions, which checked large public assemblies of Christians, naturally had the effect of emphasizing this kind of preaching. But somewhat by the Apologists, and more effectively by Origen, and with the intention to put honor upon the sacred Word, the allegorical method of interpreting Scripture was employed in the homilies, and vitiated preaching for ages to come. With the cessation of the imperial persecutions and the protection of Christianity as the religion of the empire under Constantine, a new era for preaching, as for all Christian interests, begins. All the lines of development receive freer opportunity for extension, and there is especial emphasis upon the oratorical element because of two things: one is the change in the character of the congregations to large public assemblies; the other is the better opportunity offered to preachers for being trained in the culture of the age, a culture chiefly rhetorical. The preacher may now add to his duty of expounding God's Word in Christian assemblies the larger office of being a censor of public morals and the orator before a multitude. These functions—inherent in the ancient prophecy—have never been lost to the pulpit, though sometimes neglected and sometimes abused. This line of development reached its acme in Chrysostom, in the fourth century, whose unrivalled homilies were also often eloquent orations and noble pleas for truth and good morals. The theological and philosophical element of preaching, begun long before in the Apologists, found among the Greeks an able exponent in Gregory of Nyssa, and among the Latins in the incomparable Augustine, whose various and numerous writings contain many homilies full of thought and spiritual power. Toward the close of the patristic period, after the times of these great men, preaching suffered decay. This was partly natural reaction, but was terribly assisted by the tottering and fall of the Western empire, and the serious and incurable enfeeblement of the Eastern.

The upheaval of Europe and the overthrow of the old

Roman civilization under the Teutonic barbarians in the early part of the Dark Ages were serious hindrances, along with inner decline, to the continuance of preaching, much more to its further development. But, in a way, it persisted through all the chaos and confusion of the times; and there were preachers who held it to the previous forms without adding anything of value to them. Monasticism encouraged the mild contemplative life, and here and there a Bede gathered his pupils about him and, after the manner of Origen, gently expounded to them the Word of God. Here and there devoted missionaries like Patrick, Gall, Boniface, went among the heathen or half-heathen, and preached and taught them the gospel as they received it. Here and there a prelate like Eligius of Noyon added to episcopal duties the preaching of the Word, and encouraged by example and teaching the preservation of this vital part of Christian work. Charlemagne, enlightened ruler and far-seeing statesman, was distressed at the decay of preaching and passed rules for improving both its frequency and its quality. But these reforms from the outside had no great effect, and with the failure of Charlemagne's empire after his death, the temporary improvements in the clergy and preaching likewise fell away. The darkness thickens till once more a new period dawns.

In the eleventh century two powerful influences upon the history of preaching come into play. One was the rise of the scholastic theology, with Lanfranc and Anselm, and the other, near the end of the century, was the proclamation of the first crusade by Pope Urban II. and Peter the Hermit. The first came from within and gave to preaching for three or four centuries its characteristic method on the technical side, that is, minute analysis, subtle speculative reasoning on the basis of accepted and authoritative church doctrines. Permanent influence was exerted on preaching in the way of arrangement and form, a method which went to extremes, but has left abiding traces for good in insisting on clear structure and logical reasoning in sermons. The other influence came from without, in the call of the crusades, but was no less effective in a different way. Urban's stirring addresses to the assembled nobles at Clermont, and Peter's vehement appeals to the multitudes, revealed once more the power of human speech to rouse men to action, and gave a much-needed impulse to popular preaching. This, too, produced important results, and left permanent influence both for good and ill. Later the mystical impulse from the monastic and contemplative side brought its less impressive and less extensive influence to these, and added, in the general preaching of the age, that spiritual and thoughtful tone which was needed to complete, if not counteract, the other two. All these elements of preaching were represented in Bernard, the greatest preacher of the twelfth century. Early in the thirteenth century the two missionary preaching orders of St. Dominic and St. Francis were started, and gave a powerful emphasis to popular preaching. Members of these orders went all over Europe, and even into foreign lands, preaching with an enthusiasm and effect unknown for ages, and were heard by gathered thousands of people. Nor did these orders neglect the scholastic and mystical trends of thought, as Aquinas, the Dominican, and Bonaventura, the Franciscan, show. Mediæval preaching reaches in the thirteenth century its highest point of excellence and power, but it is still marred by the allegorical interpretation and by the doctrinal perversions and superstitions of the past ages, by the over-employment of saints' legends and other unscriptural material, and by other faults. Decline is already apparent toward the close of the century, and of the three trends of thought the mystical flourishes longest, finding its best expression in the fourteenth century in the work of that saintly man and admirable preacher, John Tauler. But with him this age closes.

Action and reaction, revival and decline, this is history. The fourteenth and fifteenth centuries were evil indeed for preaching. Every force—scholastic, popular, mystic—that had contributed to the great forward movement of the preceding age fell into degeneracy, extremes, abuses. Pedantry and subtlety without power, popular appeals that sunk to the burlesque, pale and feeble ghosts of former giants, occupied the scene. And along with this mental decline there was a moral laxity in the clergy that is appalling. How could preaching survive this famine and ever flourish again? All was not hopeless. The gathering forces of reform, feeble and few at first, came to be a mighty army, and early in the sixteenth century effected the greatest religious revolution of history, and gave to preaching a significance and power in the world such as it had had in the fourth and in the thirteenth centuries, and in many important respects far better and greater than in those two culminations. The very year that John Tauler died, a young man in England is ordained a priest. John Wiclif begins his work. The preaching of the Bible is the main thing in his work, personally and by others. He comes to see that many things taught by the dominant church for truth have no warrant in Scripture, and his eyes do not mislead him as to the fearful moral corruption in the clergy. He has the courage of his convictions, and powerfully speaks his mind. The seeds of his planting will blossom into flower and fruit at a later day. Meantime, over in the heart of Europe, John Huss of Bohemia gets hold of Wiclif's teachings and they get hold of him, and through him of others. Constance and the stake are his reward; but truth cannot be burnt. Other voices here and there are heard, until after the middle of the century at Florence a Dominican monk makes Italy and Europe listen while, in flaming eloquence, he tells of the corruption and speedy punishment of the church. Savonarola goes the way of Huss, but he, too, is not forgotten. Scarcely twenty years after his martyrdom a young Augustinian monk and professor at Wittenberg, in Saxon Germany, startles the world by a bold attack upon papal indulgences and other abuses. One step leads to another. A chord of slumbering sympathy is touched by a skilful and mighty hand, and it is vibrating still. How quickly they come to the fore, those mighty men and preachers—Luther, Zwingli, Calvin, Latimer, Knox, and their fellow-workers and followers. And preaching that seemed dead is now among the livest forces in the world. Protestantism is born, and a new era for religion and preaching is begun. Age-long faults and abuses in substance and method are corrected. Preaching resumes its rightful place in Christian worship, it eschews the scholastic extremes while retaining the benefits of the scholastic method; it effects for itself a wonderful deliverance from the abuses of a false and overstrained mode of Scripture interpretation; it desires to bring home to the people of every grade the Word of God as being, in its rightly understood teachings, the sole and sufficient guide in religious concerns; and, above all, against all perversions and additions it proclaims anew, and with a power and clearness not heard of since the Apostles themselves, the simple gospel of salvation by grace through faith in the Lord Jesus Christ. With this restored method and message preaching stands at the threshold of the modern world.

2. Prospect

The three and a half centuries from about the middle of the sixteenth to the end of the nineteenth constitute the modern period in the history of preaching. As we know, it has been a rich and powerful epoch in the general history of mankind. Preaching has been no small force in the world during this time, and, as we have just seen, it stood at the beginning of the period revived and newly equipped for the important services which it was to render in this last and greatest epoch in human history. Taking our stand back at the beginning of this modern period, we may look forward to the task of preaching in that coming age, and consider both its developing equipment for its task, and the problems with which it will have to deal.

It will not surprise us to find that, like every other single force in the progress of civilization, preaching will sympathize with the sum of others at each successive stage in its development; that is, it will at every epoch be in touch with the times. But it will unite to the influence of environment the momentum of its past, the established principles of its working methods. In fact, this union of tradition and adaptation assures its readiness for work in every age. Nor should the reflection escape us that a wise balance in these forces is the best equipment. Excess of deference to tradition makes the pulpit stiff, dull, ineffective; excess of deference to environment makes it opportunist, superficial, without lasting fruit. With these general remarks, let us more particularly notice some of the elements of power which Christian preaching will employ in the age which lies before it at the close of the reformatory period.

The two great principles established, or newly emphasized, by the Reformation are the most weighty components of the pulpit's new equipment for service in the modern age; the sole authority of Scripture as a revelation from God, and justification by faith in Christ alone as Saviour from sin. The great body of modern preaching—with due discount for exceptions of all sorts—will be thoroughly pervaded by these two dominant thoughts. Where they are accepted and honored preaching will be strong and fruitful, where they are discredited preaching, however brilliant as oratory, will be meagre of permanent spiritual results. Preaching emerges from the Reformation armed with this double-edged sword, and by this sign it will conquer.

A remarkable feature of modern preaching will be its variety. As a result of the revolt from Rome, and the assertion of the right of private judgment in the interpretation and application of Scripture, there will follow a great variety of churches and preachers. There will now no longer be one only church opposed here and there by more or less feeble sects or audacious leaders; there will now no longer be one authoritatively declared body of doctrine to which all must subscribe, whether they believe it or not, on pain of anathema and the stake. But there will be many bodies of Christians calling themselves churches, and many standards or confessions of faith professing to be derived from the sole authority of the Word of God. The different Protestant bodies in their sum will constitute a formidable denial to Rome's arrogated supremacy, and in their diversities a remarkable contrast to its apparent unity. These "variations of Protestantism" will be one of the stock Catholic arguments against it, but the freedom and variety thus expressed and maintained will prove of more value to true religious life and progress than unreal, because enforced, uniformity and tame monotony could be. In the pulpit this manifold variety is to show itself in methods, aims and effects, as well as in the persons and offices of the preachers. The celibate and the monk will no longer appear the highest type. The man among men—the pious husband and father, the exemplary citizen, the respected member of society, as well as the teacher of divine truth and moral guide of the community—will henceforth be the best kind of preacher. His personality will become relatively more important, and his character will count for more than in former times. This new age is going to be one of infinite variety and many changes, and will need a flexible and widely varied ministry to meet its wants.

The sketches we have had of the leading reformers show us that for the most part they were men of great force of character and intellect. They took hold of the work and the problems of their time with a vigor that commands respect. Their labors, their success, their example, their principles, require strong men to follow them. Though there will naturally be some falling off in the immediate successors of the reformers, the ministry of the gospel in modern times will on the whole be distinguished for vigor of mind, strength of character, and general ability to deal intelligently and firmly with the problems of the modern pulpit.

The requirements of the new age, and the brilliant example of the leading preachers, alike will work to erect a high standard of ministerial character and culture. One of the principal objects of the reformer's attack was the corrupt, lazy and ignorant clergy. And this very thing forced the reformers to raise and maintain a higher standard of clerical conduct and ability. Both morals and culture were to be elevated, and they were elevated. The general standard of spiritual and intellectual culture in the ministry was more improved by the Reformation than by all the capitularies of Charlemagne or canons of reforming councils. This does not say that many bad and ignorant men will not be found, alas! among the preachers of all sects, but it does mean that in this modern period upon the whole the standard of ministerial character and culture will be higher than ever before.

The combination of things which have been spoken of will tend to increase the hold of the ministry upon the people. It is inevitable that the people shall begin to take more interest in preaching when the preachers are men whose character and learning compel respect, and when their message comes more clearly as the voice of God through his authorized spokesman, who deals directly with his Word and unfolds its meaning. The attendance upon preaching will increase again, and its effect in guiding men to the higher things of religion and morality will be more decided and marked. It is then with such an outfit as has been suggested rather than described, that the pulpit of the modern world faces the problems that are to rise before it. What are they?

Along with all other human interests preaching will suffer from the storms of war. Tried and tested in that stern school it will have power to meet other difficulties. Civil war in France, thirty years of desolation in Germany, civil war and revolution in England, the eighteenth century wars in Europe, revolution in America and France, the Napoleonic struggle, and all the nineteenth century wars—all these to live through! How the pulpit will adjust itself to these strifes, and preach the gospel of peace amid the rude alarms of war is one of its heavy problems; but it will find a way. Sometimes the preacher will be with the armies in the field, in camp and hospital holding up the Prince of Peace above the noise and chaos of strife; sometimes at home amid the anxious and bereaved he will be giving the consolations of grace and keeping men's eyes on the heavenly rest while the earth is racked with contention.

Naturally the exigencies of the Reformation quickened the spirit of debate and polemic as to the doctrines of Christianity. Henceforth the pulpit will be largely concerned with this feature of the religious life. Nor will it be a pleasing or edifying part of pulpit work, though often an unavoidable one. Much ability, some remains of scholastic sophistry, and too often a rancorous and unchristian spirit will mark the sermons of this kind. Alas! one of the hardest lessons for the Christian pulpit to learn will be that of "speaking the truth in love."

One of the side results of the Reformation was the liberty of thought which it encouraged in religious affairs. The reformers, however, were not quick to accept the logical consequences of their principles. Many of them, perhaps most, were intolerant of differences from themselves, and Protestant persecutions are an illogical disgrace upon the cause. But the liberty which their principles demanded inevitably had its perils—within the churches it will lead to rationalism—outside it will encourage infidelity. Or rather let us say that among some professing Christians freedom of speculation and criticism will go too far, even to virtual denial of the supernatural origin and exclusive authority of Scripture; and that unbelieving opposition to the Christian revelation will too often pervert liberty into license, and assume a tone of arrogant and often insolent confidence unjustifiable alike by fact or sentiment. All this, preaching will have to meet, and in the nineteenth century the skepticism mentioned will call to its aid the grand achievements in scientific investigation and boldly assail the fundamental verities of Christianity, in the name of the highest thinking and most assured knowledge of mankind. Truly for such a conflict the pulpit will need the best outfit possible and all its best strength of development. Here was lurking a giant whom the reforming fathers could not foresee, but none the less in asserting the principles they did, and holding up the standard they did for the ministry, they were making the best possible preparation for the coming conflict. The preaching, however, of these coming ages is going to show upon the whole an ability to grasp and handle the problem of rationalism and infidelity that its opponents and critics may not willingly admit, but which history will own.

The growth and wonderful developments in the literatures of the modern Christian nations will present a problem of adjustment and mutual service or hindrance to the pulpit. In some respects there will be rivalry, in others stimulus and wholesome interaction. Where doctrine and morals are concerned there will sometimes be sharp conflict, but on the whole preaching and literature will be most friendly. The pulpit will not be overshadowed and displaced, but it will be closely rivalled and often fatigued and discredited by other means of public instruction. Secularism in press and school will by their very rivalry demand the continuance and strengthening of the pulpit. Its relative range will be narrowed, but in that very fact its energies concentrated, and concentrated not in vain, upon its own proper duties. The world has never yet heard such preaching as it will hear in the nineteenth century. For, notwithstanding the newspaper and the book, the pulpit will still remain in modern times the chief instructor of men in morals and religious truth.

Progress of thought and freedom will, in these three modern centuries, bring with them increasing recognition of the common man in civil and social life. The Christian pulpit from our Lord's own days till now has ever been one of the foremost champions of the rights of the individual man, whether high or low. Of course there have been exceptions, and many here and there among the preachers have been found untrue to this high ideal, but upon the whole the history of preaching shows the general truth to be as stated; and as the pulpit of the Reformation faces its future it looks to a coming glorious record in its advocacy of human rights, its rebuke of oppressive wrong, its encouragement of social ameliorations.

Early in the seventeenth century Protestant America will be born—a feeble infant truly, yet bravely grasping its mighty future with two weak baby hands at Jamestown and Plymouth Rock. Here in the dependent colonial days American preaching will mostly follow in form and method the traditions of the old world; but under the strong impetus of the Great Awakening it will begin to strike out its own way and be getting ready for its mighty work in the nineteenth century. Here the firm establishment of the voluntary principle in the choice and maintenance of pastors, combined with complete religious liberty, will give to preaching such opportunities as it never had before to develop adaptability, variety and strength. And right nobly it will take its work.

Better than in the Middle Ages with Francis and Dominic, better than at the Reformation with the reformers absorbed in pressing matters at hand, the modern Christianity will take hold of the problem of world-wide evangelization—and the pulpit will not be found wanting. Pious Francke at Halle will preach missions as well as charity, obscure but devoted Carey at Northampton will tell his hesitating brethren to attempt great things for God and expect great things from God, a few theological students will hold a prayer-meeting at a haystack in

Massachusetts, and the great foreign missionary movement of modern times will be on. Preachers at home will emphasize the Master's "marching orders," and preachers abroad in all lands of the earth will revive the primitive methods of preaching Christ, not on other men's foundations but among the heathen who never heard the gospel of God's grace. Thus, true to its double mission of proclamation and instruction, the modern preaching will delight to recall the Founder's words: "Ye shall be witnesses unto me both in Jerusalem, and in all Judea, and in Samaria, and unto the uttermost parts of the earth;" nor will it faint before its sublime task as outlined by its greatest representative among the Apostles: "And he gave some apostles, and some prophets, and some evangelists, and some pastors and teachers, for the work of the ministry, for the edifying of the body of Christ, till we all come in the unity of the faith and of the knowledge of the Son of God, unto a perfect man, unto the measure of the stature of the fulness of Christ."

BIBLIOGRAPHY

The author does not attempt the impossible task of giving an exhaustive survey of the vast literature which more or less directly bears on the great subject treated in this volume; nor even to mention all the books which have come in various ways under his notice, or have contributed to his knowledge. Only those, and not all of them, which have been actually used or found specially helpful in the preparation of the work are given. Many works of general and church history which have been consulted are necessarily omitted. The enumeration under II. is more nearly complete than under the other heads. It is hoped the classification and enumeration of the following works may be found of some service to any who may wish to pursue the subject further.

I. Works of a General Nature

1. History. (a) *General.* Histories of the various countries involved. Gibbon's Decline and Fall of the Roman Empire; Duruy's History of the Middle Ages; Bryce's Holy Roman Empire; Weber's Weltgeschichte; Lecky's History of European Morals; Seignobos, Histoire de la Civilisation; Langlois and Seignobos, Introduction to the Study of History (translation).

(b) *Ecclesiastical.* Eusebius, Ecclesiastical History; Schaff, History of the Christian Church; Hase, Kirchengeschichte; Fisher, History of the Christian Church; Kurtz, Church History; Newman, Manual of Church History; others of similar character. Of special works a few, such as a number of histories of the Reformation, and more particularly: Baird, Rise of the Huguenots; Cutts, Parish Priests and their People in the Middle Ages in England; Beckett, History of the English Reformation; Montalembert, Monks of the West; Stoughton, Spanish Reformers; and other similar works.

(c) *Literary and Philosophical.* Cruttwell, Literary History of Christianity; Tiraboschi, Storia della Letteratura Italiana; Scherer, Geschichte der Deutschen Litteratur; Histoire Littéraire de la France (Daunou, Hauréau and others); several histories of English literature. Ueberweg, History of Philosophy; Weber, History of Philosophy; Vaughan, Hours with the Mystics; Preger, Geschichte der Deutschen Mystik im Mittelalter. Sears, History of Oratory.

2. Cyclopædias. (a) *General.* The Britannica; the American; Ersch und Gruber, Allgemeine Encyclopädie; Cyclopedia Italiana; and others.

(b) *Biographical.* Dictionary of National Biography; Allgemeine Deutsche Biographie; Biographie Universelle; and several others.

(c) *Ecclesiastical.* Herzog-Plitt-Hauck, Real Encyclopädie für Protestantische Theologie und Kirche; Wetzer und Welte, Kirchenlexikon.

3. COLLECTIONS. Acta Sanctorum; Migne, Patrologia Graeca and Patrologia Latina; the Oxford Library of the Fathers; Dods' (T. and T. Clark) edition of the writings of the Fathers; Works of Chrysostom, Augustine and others in the original in some editions; the Christian Literature Series, *i.e.,* the Apostolic Fathers, the Ante-Nicene Fathers, and the Nicene and Post-Nicene Fathers. Texte und Untersuchungen, Harnack und Gebhardt. Guillon, Bibliothèque des Pères. Brieger und Bess, Zeitschrift der Kirchengeschichte. On the Swiss Reformation the excellent Leben und Ausgewählte Schriften der Väter und Gründer der Reformirten Kirche. Old English Homilies of the Twelfth Century, Publications of the Early English Text Society, edited by Robert Morris, LL.D. The Book of Homilies. Collections of Sermons of the different preachers in their works. Fish, Masterpieces of Pulpit Eloquence; Volume III. of G. P. Putnam's Sons' The World's Great Orators.

II. HISTORY OF PREACHING

1. GENERAL. Works which in a way deal with the whole subject: Broadus, Lectures on the History of Preaching; Ker, Lectures on the History of Preaching; Pattison, The History of Christian Preaching; Fleming James, The Message and the Messengers; R. Rothe, Geschichte der Predigt. Brief biographical notices with specimens of preaching: Lentz, Christliche Homiletik; Fish, Masterpieces of Pulpit Eloquence. Sketches of the history: Christlieb, Geschichte der Predigt (article in Herzog, Bd. 18, supplement, much the most complete treatment yet written); Hering, Geschichte der Predigt (part of a larger work, Die Lehre von der Predigt); the historical sketch in Harnack's Geschichte und Theorie der Predigt; sketch in Van Oosterzee's Practical Theology; also in Hoppin's Homiletics; several others of similar nature. Character sketches: Brömel, Homiletische Charakterbilder; Nebe, Zur Geschichte der Predigt.

2. EPOCHAL. Paniel, Pragmatische Geschichte der Christlichen Beredsamkeit (designed as a complete history, but as it only comes down to Augustine it is placed here; one of the notable books on the subject); Villemain, Tableau de l'Eloquence Chrétienne au Quatriéme Siècle; Moule, Christian Oratory during the First Five Centuries; Neale, Mediæval Preaching; Ammon, Geschichte der Homiletik; Albert, Geschichte der Predigt in Deutschland bis Luther; Cruel, Geschichte der Deutschen Predigt im Mittelalter; Linsenmayer, Geschichte der Predigt in Deutschland von Karl dem Grossen bis zum Anfang des 15ten Jahrhunderts; Beste, Die Bedeutendste Kanzelredner der Lutherischen Kirche der Reformationszeitalters; C. G. Schmidt, Geschichte der Predigt in der Evangelischen Kirche Deutschlands von Luther bis Spener; Bourgain, La Chaire Française au XIIme Siècle; Lecoy de la Marche, La Chaire Française au Moyen Age Spécialement au XIIIme Siècle; Renoux, Les Prédicateurs Célèbres de l'Allemagne; Boucher, L'Eloquence de la Chaire, ou l'Histoire Littéraire dela Prèdication; Méray, Les Libres Prédicateurs devanciers de Luther et de Rabelais; Marenco, L'Oratoria

Sacra Italiana nel Medio Evo; Zanotto, Storia della Predicazione nei Secoli della Letteratura Italiana; F. Borromeo, De Sacris Nostrorum Temporum Oratoribus; Blaikie, The Preachers of Scotland from the Sixth to the Nineteenth Century; W. M. Taylor, The Scottish Pulpit.

III. Lives and Works of Preachers

Much about individual preachers and their preaching has been gathered from the works previously named, and so, to avoid repetition, only additional works are here mentioned.

1. Patristic. Works of the Fathers in various editions, both the originals and translations. Life and Times of Chrysostom, by W. R. W. Stephens. Sketches of some of the more notable preachers by Bishop Carpenter, in the *Clergyman's Magazine,* and afterwards gathered into a volume. Sketches of Patrick and other missionaries in Walrond's Christian Missions before the Reformation.

2. Mediæval. Neander, Der Heilige Bernhard und sein Zeitalter; Storrs, St. Bernard; Herkless, Francis and Dominic; Lacordaire, Vie de Saint Dominique; Sabatier, Life of St. Francis of Assisi (translation); Opera SS. Francisci et Antonii (old edition of De la Haye); Fioretti di San Francesco; Locatelli (editor), A New Life of St. Anthony of Padua (translation), also a new edition of the Sermones Dominicales of Antony of Padua, issuing at Padua; Vaughan, Life of St. Thomas Aquinas; Drioux, Opera S. Thomae; Ashley, Homilies of St. Thomas Aquinas; Card. Fanna, Ratio Novae Collectionis Operum S. Bonaventurae; Göbel, Die Missionspredigten des Franziskaners Berthold von Regensburg; Stromberger, Berthold von Regensburg; Life of Wycliffe, by J. L. Wilson, and other sources; Select English Writings of John Wyclif, edited by Thos. Arnold, Oxford, 1869 (the best); Madden, Life and Martyrdom of Savonarola; Villari, Life and Times of Savonarola; Mrs. Oliphant, Makers of Florence; Baccini, Prediche di F. Girolamo Savonarola.

3. Reformatory. Köstlin, Life of Luther (the original in two large volumes, the translation in abridged form), Luther's Werke, Hauspostillen, Table Talk (Bohn ed.), Luther and Calvin (sermons); Stähelin, Huldreich Zwingli, sein Leben und Wirken; Zwingli's Werke (Schuler und Schultess); Jackson, Huldreich Zwingli; Bullinger's Decades; Chenevière, Farel, Froment et Viret; Calvin, Works (some in Latin and French, and some in English in various editions), Preface to Comm. on Psalms (Latin, a brief account of his life); Beza, Vie de Calvin; Bungener, Jean Calvin, sa Vie son Œuvre et ses Écrits; Benrath, Bernadino Ochino von Siena (translation also); Sermons and Remains of Bishop Latimer, Parker Society's edition by Corrie; Works of Archbishop Cranmer; Sermons of John Bradford; Life and Writings of Ridley, Religious Tract Society; Works of Bishop Hooper; Works of Bishop Jewel; Knox, History of the Reformation in Scotland, and sermon (the only one) in Fish's Masterpieces; McCrie, Life of Knox; Brown, Life of Knox.

INDEX

A History of Preaching

VOL. II.

FROM THE CLOSE OF THE REFORMATION
PERIOD TO THE END OF THE
NINETEENTH CENTURY
1572–1900

TABLE OF CONTENTS

VOL. II.

INTRODUCTION

In a former volume the author has traced the history of preaching from the time of the Apostolic Fathers to the death of John Knox, in 1572.[1] That volume treats four of the six periods into which, for convenience, the History of Preaching was divided. The remaining two periods, namely, the Dogmatic, from the death of Knox to the beginning of the Wesleyan revival, about the middle of the eighteenth century; and the Evangelistic or Missionary period, extending from the work of Wesley to near the end of the nineteenth century, were deferred for later treatment. There might also be added, to complete this scheme, a seventh period, beginning near the end of the nineteenth century and including the age in which we live, which might be called the Humanitarian or Social Period; but its study and characterization alike belong to the future historian.

It was intended to discuss in the present volume the Dogmatic and Evangelistic Periods after the manner of the former study; but the difficulties in the way of retaining that method now appear considerable, and a modification of the original plan is adopted. The great movements of thought beginning about the time of the Reformation, together with the growth and world-wide expansion of Christian peoples, bring in a great variety of modifying circumstances, and make the history of preaching far more complex than in any previous age. Furthermore, the variety of conditions—political, social, literary, and other—in the different countries of Western Christendom has introduced other elements of diversity into the history. A generalization which would fairly describe conditions of preaching in one country might be wholly inapplicable to another at the same epoch. It seems well, therefore, to employ a simpler framework

[1]A History of Preaching; from the Apostolic Fathers to the Great Reformers, A. D. 70-1572. By Edwin C. Dargan. New York, A. C. Armstrong & Son, 1905.

than that originally proposed, and in the present volume the obvious but arbitrary division by centuries is adopted; and the subdivision by countries or languages will serve in place of one more logical perhaps, but less clear. The fragment of the sixteenth century remaining after the death of the great reformers is sketched in the first chapter. The main body of the work is devoted to a consideration of the preaching of the seventeenth, eighteenth, and nineteenth centuries in the various countries of Europe.

These three modern centuries are of the profoundest significance in the history of human progress. Life has been more abundant, knowledge more comprehensive and varied, the processes of civilization more rapid and complex than in any period of human history. The Reformation in the sixteenth century set in motion forces which materially altered the course of things in all time following. That mighty epoch of turmoil and readjustment can not be sharply defined, either at its beginning or at its end, but, like all other revolutions, it is an age of transition in which causes and forces peculiar to itself become visible and emphatic, and powerfully influence subsequent times.

A survey of modern Occidental civilization in its more general aspects of necessity includes some account of political, cultural, and religious affairs. It is not requisite for our purposes to descend to more minute and accurate classifications and inclusions. These three great departments of modern national and social life (with their closely related or included activities) so interlace with each other that no one can be understood or properly studied without giving some attention to all. It follows that any particular subdivision of one of these more general departments must not only feel the influence of all the co-ordinate parts of its own department, but also that of the other two with their respective subordinate elements. So we shall have to consider preaching as a part of the great sphere of religion, and thus as subject to all the molding and modifying influences of religious progress; and we shall likewise have to take some cognizance of national affairs, and even international, in each particular country and time in which our studies may fall; and further, we must have in mind to some extent the progress and fluctuations of culture—especially in art, science, education, and literature—so far as these affect the preaching of the period and country under review.

Applying these principles to the preaching of the three modern centuries, the difficulty of writing a connected history is greatly increased by the largeness of the field and the complexity of its forces. But the task can no more be declined for a history of preaching than for an account of any other subordinate and yet vital part of the general history of mankind within this period. Preaching has been in close contact with all the other forces of civilization. It has played its part in the strenuous give-and-take of the modern life, and takes color from the times just as do other great particular movements. So when we take up the preaching and preachers of any country and age we shall have to keep in mind the general situation in all the other affairs noted, but only so far as may seem necessary to a proper understanding and estimate of the character and effect of preaching itself.

PART FIRST

THE SEVENTEENTH CENTURY

CHAPTER I

Preaching in Europe at the End of the Sixteenth Century

As we look back over the history of preaching from the point at which our present study begins, we can easily discern four great culminations of interest and power. Each was preceded and followed by an age of decline, but in the latter certain preparations and forces slowly gathered strength to produce the height of excellence which ensued. The first of these culminations was the originative period in the first century, when, after the voice of prophecy among the Hebrews had long been silent, the promised Messiah Himself appeared in the person of Jesus of Nazareth. The Founder of Christianity was Himself the first of its preachers; but He was preceded by His forerunner and followed by His apostles, and in the preaching of these the proclamation and teaching of God's Word by public address was made an essential and permanent feature of the Christian religion. After this glorious introduction there came an age of feebleness and obscurity in the Apostolic Fathers and their successors till in the third century, in the hands of the great teacher Origen and some others, public instruction in Christian truth and Biblical interpretation began to assume greater dignity and better form. When, therefore, in the fourth century Christianity was adopted as the religion of the Roman State it is no wonder that preaching rose to its second great culmination in the oratory and influence of John Chrysostom and his contemporaries East and West. After this a still longer period of decline came on, from which the

Greek Church has never recovered; and out of which Western Christianity only slowly emerged till, in the eleventh and twelfth centuries, the reforms of Hildebrand, the rise of Scholasticism, and the proclamation of the Crusades, together with minor causes, co-operated to bring in the third great culmination—the powerful Catholic preaching of the thirteenth century. Again decline, swift and fearful, followed. But in the decay and shames of the fourteenth and fifteenth centuries there were heard occasional voices of mystics and reformers who called to the higher things of the Spirit and the Word, and called not wholly in vain. The Revival of Learning, the increase of power in the middle classes of society, and other external influences lent their aid to the forces of reform; and so in the sixteenth century the fourth great culmination meets us in the preaching of the Reformation. Once more the inevitable decline sets in, but it is neither so general nor so uniform as those of the past, being modified both in character and duration by those vast differences of nation, language, and creed which modern European Christianity presents. Thus, as we shall see, in two of the European countries—France and England—the decline was more quickly redressed than in the others; for in each of these lands a great epoch of preaching appears in the seventeenth century, while elsewhere there is no such power in the pulpit. But in the latter part of the sixteenth century, which, as an introduction to its successor, we are to consider in this chapter, the first falling off of reformatory preaching was manifest throughout Europe.

I. Lutheran Preaching After Luther

We naturally begin with preaching among the Lutheran Churches, both in Germany and the neighboring nations, after the death of Luther and his associates.[1]

[1] P. H. Schuler, *Geschichte der Veränderungen des Geschmacks im Predigen*, 3 Bde., 1792; Lentz, *Geschichte der Homiletik*, Bd. II (1839); Schenk, *Geschichte der deutsch-protestantischen Kanzelberedsamkeit* (1841); C. G. Schmidt, *Geschichte der Predigt in der evangelischen Kirche Deutschlands von Luther bis Spener* (1872); Wilhelm Beste, *Die bedeutendste*

Luther died in 1546. Some of his co-laborers, who were also leaders in the great work of the Reformation, lived on beyond him; but the preaching of the Reformation in German lands reached its culmination in Luther himself and those who were more intimately associated with him. Very notable and very pathetic is the decline in Lutheran preaching in the latter half of the sixteenth century. There was a falling off in freshness. The first edge of the Reformation blade had been dulled. Those who followed the great leaders naturally enough imitated them and tried to hold the Reformation, both in its methods and spirit, to the ideas of the forerunners. There was also a loss in spiritual power. The first deep protest against the evils and abuses which it was the aim of the Reformers to cure naturally lost something of its vitality. Both preachers and hearers lacked the fervor of the first great appealing cause. The sermons are more commonplace and formal; the spiritual response not so clearly reflected as in those of earlier days. As a consequence there was also a falling off in the effects of preaching. It is impossible to assign any one cause for this marked decline; there is a cluster of co-operating causes which may be briefly stated.

(1) The decline must be assigned in part to the great law of reaction. Any great movement naturally has its ebb tide. The great reformatory wave under Luther and his fellow-workers had reached its crest and must retire. Along with this, or as part of it, must be reckoned the loss of leaders. Luther himself died just before the middle of the century. Of his immediate associates many lingered for varying lengths of time after him, but these one by one fell off, and with their departure the fresh vigor of the mighty movement was gone.

(2) We must also remember the troubles of the times. The unsettled state of the Empire and of Europe gen-

Kanzelredner der älteren lutherischen Kirche von Luther bis Spener (3 Bde., 1856-1886); Rothe, *Geschichte der Predigt* (1881); articles on *Homiletik* and *Geschichte der Predigt* in the Herzog-Plitt-Hauck *Real Encyclopädie,* originally written by Christlieb, revised by Schian; John Ker, *Lectures on the History of Preaching* (1888).

erally for so long a period naturally interfered with the power of the pulpit. In some respects these troubles stimulated preaching, but in others the opposite effect was produced. In the very year of Luther's death the Imperial and Catholic side gained upon the Reformers. Wittenberg itself fell into the emperor's hands, and the cause of the Reformation on its military and political side seemed in a bad way. Many Lutherans urged compromise, while others insisted upon standing out even to martyrdom. Thus there was a division of sentiment among the leaders themselves, and all this naturally reacted upon the preaching.

(3) Still another cause of the decline is to be found in the theological disputes which prevailed alike between Catholics and Protestants, and among the Protestants themselves. It has usually been the history of an age of theological disputation that the first part of it stimulates preaching, but the continuance of discussion often degenerates into dogmatic hair-splitting and personal attacks, and so the spiritual power of doctrinal differences and convictions shows decay. This was eminently true of the Lutheran preaching toward the end of the Reformation period.

There was, first of all, the old-time quarrel between Catholics and Protestants. The stout blows which were exchanged among the contestants in the earlier life of Protestantism degenerated into a fist-fight, which brought little glory to either side. A pulpit of continual squabbling can never be one of great power. There was also much controversy between the Lutherans and the Reformed. This, indeed, began with the leaders themselves. On many points, especially that of the Lord's Supper, there was sharp and continued dispute between the Calvinists and Lutherans, and many of the strict Lutherans were exceedingly bitter in their denunciations of their brethren. And finally, to complete this sad story, there was, as already intimated, a good deal of quarreling among the Lutherans themselves. These differences were partly political, but also to some extent doctrinal. The line of orthodoxy was sharply drawn, and those who did not measure up to the strictest Lutheran views were harshly assailed. Later we shall see that among the preachers there were good and faithful men who deplored all these things and proclaimed with better spirit and effect the great principles for which they stood. The dark side is not the only side, but its darkness was very dark.

Something should be said in regard to the homiletical theory and methods which prevailed among the Lutheran preachers of this epoch. Naturally the Reformation gave considerable impulse to the study and teaching of the theory of preaching. Among the Humanists, both Reuchlin and Erasmus[2] had written treatises upon the art of preaching. The latter of these appeared in 1535, and was a very elaborate work, founded upon the commonly accepted rhetoric, but with application to preaching. It could never have been available as a text-book for instruction, though it contains many useful suggestions, and exhibits, both in its amplitude of learning and the excellence of its Latin style, well-known characteristics of the author. Among the Reformers proper, other homiletical books appeared. Luther himself wrote no homiletical treatise, but in his *Table Talk,* sermons, lectures, and other writings, he gave occasional and vigorous attention to many homiletical principles. Hieronymus Weller (d. 1572)[3] published a treatise on preaching which was a sort of compilation of Lutheran preaching and practice. Previous to this Melanchthon[4] had, as early as 1519, published at Wittenberg his *Three Books on Rhetoric,* which was afterwards published in different editions with some changes. This is a very brief outline of the elements of rhetoric condensed from previous teachers and is not of much permanent value, though it may have served the theological students at Wittenberg,

[2]Reuchlin's treatise, *Liber congestorum de arte praedicandi,* published 1504, is of little value. Erasmus published in 1511 a popular and useful rhetoric, *De duplici copia verborum et rerum,* commonly mentioned briefly as the *Copia;* and in his famous Praise of Folly (*Encomium Moriae*) he stings the degenerate preaching of the age. But his great work is the one noticed in the text: *Ecclesiastes, sive Concionator Evangelicus,* Basel, 1535. *Opera,* Leyden, 1704, Peter van der Aa.

[3]See Lentz, Schmidt, and Christlieb, *opp. citt.*

[4]Bretschneider's *Corpus Reformatorum,* Vol. XIII, *Ph. Melanchthonis Elementorum Rhetorices Libri Duo.*

for whom it was principally intended. Nicholas Hemming,[5] a Lutheran preacher at Copenhagen (d. 1604), wrote a book on the art of preaching. A contemporary of his, Aegidius Hunnius[6] (d. 1603), besides other writings, also published a work on Homiletics. None of these works can claim a high degree of value, but they indicate a notable fact in the history of preaching,—that theory usually follows practice. The great work of the Reformers in the pulpit led some of their successors to describe and enjoin homiletical principles which seemed to have made their preaching effective.

As to the methods of preaching, several characteristics require notice. In the post-reformers more attention was given both to analytic and synthetic form. The sermons of Luther and Calvin broke away with a certain joyous freedom from the trammels of the scholastic method. This was especially true of their expository discourses, which were verse-by-verse comments rather than orderly addresses. Yet traces of the rigid analysis of the schools inevitably appeared in the preaching of the Reformers; and the study of homiletics naturally tended to the reinstatement of this method. As is often the case in such matters, a needed improvement went too far. In much of the preaching of the period under review there is too much stiff and formal division of sermons. Another characteristic of the later reformatory preaching is that it becomes more theological and less expository. This was due to two things: (1) A natural advancement in theological thinking; (2) The prevalence of dogmatic controversy. Thus after the free expository methods of the earlier Reformers there arose a more topical and discursive style.

As to the spirit and thought of the Lutheran preaching after Luther, two tendencies must be carefully noted. These, of course, are to be met with at all times and are no more peculiar to the Reformation period than to our own, but the manifestation must necessarily differ with the times and their currents of thought. The two tendencies, however, were sufficiently manifest in this age. They are the scholastic or dogmatic on the one

[5]Lentz, Schmidt, and Christlieb, *opp. citt.*
[6]*Id.*

hand, and the mystical or spiritual on the other. The former is cool and critical, logical and severe. The latter is warm, emotional, sometimes obscure and vague, but usually devout and helpful to piety. It is gratifying to know that not a few preachers were of this kind, but still it must be said that all the Lutheran preaching in the latter part of the sixteenth century was too much under the dogmatic and polemic influence. The more spiritual tendencies had to strive hard for recognition in that stormy time of arid debate and theological intolerance.

Only a few of the more notable preachers require to be mentioned.[7] Of these we note first, Jacob Andreae (1528-1590). He was born of humble parentage in Würtemburg. He had, however, a desire for learning, and pursued his education in the schools, gaining academic training at the University of Tübingen. His pastoral life fell chiefly in the capital, Stuttgart, where he was highly successful as a preacher; but his labors were not confined to the city, for he was much in demand for outside work. He was a very active theologian, sharing in the doctrinal disputes of the times. He was noted as a debater, and was also a wise counselor among his brethren. He was also known and highly esteemed as a strong and eloquent preacher. Next we mention Martin Chemnitz (1522-1586). With Chemnitz we pass from south to north Germany, for he was born in the electorate of Brandenburg. He had the advantage of receiving his education at Wittenberg under Luther, Melanchthon, and others. He was very highly regarded by Lutherans, was a useful pastor in Brunswick, and in his latter life served as superintendent of the churches in that region. He was quite scholarly and learned, but was much loved as a man and popular as a preacher. We next name Lucas Osiander (1534-1604). He was a son of the famous Andrew Osiander of the preceding period, who was noted as a preacher and also as a stout theological debater of a somewhat harsh and contentious spirit. Lucas, however, inheriting his father's abilities, was of a gentler and more tolerant nature. He was educated by his father at Nuremberg, and pursued

[7]Beste, Rothe, Schmidt, *et al.*

further studies at Königsberg. After preaching at several smaller places, he was called to one of the principal churches at Stuttgart, where his life was chiefly spent. He published many sermons which were much read in that time. It is pleasant to recall of him that he adapted himself to the common people and preached with acceptance and power.

The last and most important preacher of this group was John Arndt (1555-1621).[8] There is something very winsome and attractive about this devout and lovable soul. He was the son of a pastor in Anhalt, where he was born. He was left an orphan quite young, but received kind treatment and an education at the hands of friends, at Halberstadt and Magdeburg. He was designed for the profession of medicine, but during an illness he was converted and his mind was led to theology and the pastorate. Upon deciding to enter the ministry he studied theology at Wittenberg, Basel, and other places. Here he took up the regular work of the pastorate. He was well fitted for it in training, character, and piety. He exercised his useful ministry at a number of places—Quedlinberg, Brunswick, Celle, and others. In that disputatious age his quiet spirit and tolerant nature exposed him to much criticism on the part of some extreme and violent men. As is so often the case, he was esteemed weak and compromising where he only meant to be loving and peaceful. He was sensitive enough to feel unkind criticism, but brave enough to bear it with a Christian spirit, and he pursued his own way regardless of clamor and unkindness. As a pastor he was very much loved. His heart went out in tender sympathy to his people, and his own sufferings and trials enabled him to sympathize with others. His preaching was decidedly mystical and pious in tone. The dogmatic and polemic elements are thoroughly subordinate to the devout and spiritual. This was a new tendency in those days, and it had a blessed influence upon a few at that time and upon many of later date. Indeed, in some respects Arndt is the fore-

[8]The same, especially Schmidt (S. 80 ff.), and Ker (p. 172 ff.). Also Schuler, *Gesch. der Veränderangen u. s. w.*, Bd. I, S. 160, who pays a high tribute to Arndt in his efforts to bring in a more spiritual tone in preaching.

runner, if not the founder, of the Pietistic movement which found its culmination in Spener and Francke in the next century.

Arndt published a number of sermons. They have been highly prized as pious literature, and are still read. They are indeed one of the classics of the spiritual life of his own and later times. His career and his writings and his influence all show the value and permanence of a really spiritual note in the preaching of any age, however this may be opposed to the leading tendencies of the time.

II. Reformed Preaching After Calvin and Bullinger.

Among the Reformed preachers[9] toward the close of the sixteenth century there was also a decline of freshness and power as among the Lutherans, and for similar reasons. The state of affairs in all the countries where there were Reformed or Calvinistic Churches interfered with preaching. In Germany, both Catholics and Lutherans opposed the Calvinists. In Switzerland the external conditions were more favorable; but in all the centers, both of German and French Switzerland, the loss of the great leaders was sensibly felt. In France the persecution of the Protestants, which had its beginning under Francis I, found its bloody, fearful consummation in the massacre of St. Bartholomew, in August, 1572. From then on persecution raged along with civil and religious strife till the promulgation of the famous Edict of Nantes, by Henry IV, in 1598. The effects of that famous measure of toleration upon preaching, both Protestant and Catholic, fall to be considered in our study of the seventeenth century. All through the sixteenth century in France, Protestant preaching withered under the blight of intense and ceaseless persecution.

[9]See Rothe, Lentz, Christlieb, *opp. citt.* See also Baird, *The Huguenots and Henry of Navarre;* and the Church Histories. For Holland, J. Hartog, *Geschiedenis van de Predikkunde in de Protestantsche Kerk van Nederland,* 2d ed., Utrecht, 1887; J. J. van Oosterzee, *Practical Theology* (Eng. trans.), an introductory sketch of the history of preaching.

What was done had to be done secretly. The most and best of the preachers did their work in exile.

In the Netherlands external conditions were equally unfavorable. For this was the terrible age of Philip II and the Duke of Alva. The Dutch preaching of this epoch was of a primitive and rather rough character. Yet it had fallen into the slough of the new scholasticism, was tainted by pedantry and ruined by polemics. This tendency was rather encouraged than corrected by the founding of the University of Leyden in 1575, though that event was most important as the beginning of higher training for the preachers of Holland. There were few preachers of distinction, and the literary remains of the period are scanty and of little value. Van Oosterzee says that at the time of the Synod of Wesel (1568), which fixed the liturgy, it was found necessary to warn the preachers against "all hateful and offensive affectation or high-flown style." He complains that the disputes of the University were dragged into the pulpit, and that pedantic and tedious exposition of words and phrases was carried to a hurtful extreme.

It is scarcely necessary to mention by name the Reformed preachers of this epoch. At Geneva, Theodore Beza carried on Calvin's work over into the beginning of the seventeenth century. He was a diligent preacher and his work maintained the influence of preaching, both in the religious and civil affairs of Geneva. His assistants there and in the adjacent towns continued the work of former times, but with no great brilliancy or notable achievement.

At Zurich, after Bullinger came Ludwig Lavater (d. 1586)), Rudolf Walter (d. 1586), and John Wolf (d. 1571), all of whom are mentioned with respect by historians of the period as earnest, faithful, and prominent preachers. But their works have left no permanent impression, nor do they constitute any important factor in the history of preaching.

More important among the Reformed preachers of the period is the name of Andrew Hyperius.[10] He was

[10]Schmidt, *op. cit.,* S. 53 ff.; articles in *RE;* and especially P. Biesterveld, *Andreas Hyperius voornamelik als Homileet.* Inaugural Address, 1895.

born at Ypres, in Flanders—whence his surname—in 1511. His mother was a woman of good social position and high character, and both parents sympathized with the Reformation movement. The father died while Andrew was young, but left careful instructions for the boy's further education, which he had carefully attended to before his death. Andrew was ambitious and eager as a student; he absorbed the best humanistic training of his time. Having attended the preliminary schools, he took his degrees at the University of Paris, but traveled and studied much in other countries, including England, where during a few months' sojourn he taught as well as studied. His sympathy with the Reformed views, and the consumption of his fortune in pursuing his studies, caused him to leave his native land and become a teacher elsewhere. He was thus led to Marburg, where he became professor in the University in 1542. It was here that he spent the rest of his life in preaching and teaching. He was a man of unblemished character, both in domestic and public relations, and his influence, both in the University and in the religious life of Hesse, was extended and wholesome. He produced a number of important theological works, but is especially distinguished for his notable contribution to homiletics. He wrote two books on this subject. The second of these is not of permanent value, being chiefly given to suggestions about the selection of subjects for preaching; but the earlier work, published in 1553, is one of the best and most influential treatises upon homiletics that has ever been produced. In it the evangelical spirit of the preacher goes hand in hand with the learning and thoughtfulness of the trained scholar. In style and arrangement it far surpasses the more voluminous—not to say tedious—work of Erasmus, to which, as well as to others, it doubtless owes something. The treatise consists of two parts. The first book deals with the general principles of rhetoric as applied to preaching, and the second gives a particular application of these principles to some of the special truths and topics with which the preacher must deal.

III. English Preaching After Bishop Jewel.

In England the latter part of the sixteenth century includes the closing years of Queen Elizabeth's reign.[11] There is scarcely a more brilliant epoch in English politics and letters than the close of the Elizabethan period. The adventurous expeditions of Drake, Hawkins, and Frobisher opened up great vistas of enterprise, which seized strongly upon both the imagination and the practical sense of the English people. The vigorous statesmanship of Burghley and Walsingham and their associates gave the English a foremost place in diplomacy and statecraft. The defeat of the Spanish Armada in 1588 gave world-wide and splendid renown to the English fighting qualities and secured for England her position of supremacy on the sea, which has never been vacated. The character and qualities of the queen herself, while open at many points to serious criticism, were such as to awaken the loyalty of her subjects and the respect of foreign powers. In philosophy the great name of Francis Bacon is beginning to be known, and English thought is henceforth a power of the first magnitude in the world's advance. In literature the supreme name of Shakespeare adorns this period, while among the lesser lights those of Spenser, Raleigh, Hooker, and others must be recalled.

Preaching in this wonderful period shows but ill in comparison, both with itself in preceding and succeeding epochs and with the great activity and power of the English mind in other departments of activity. How are we to account for this singular phenomenon? Several causes may be assigned. Preaching was depressed by the effects of the persecution under Queen Mary. Many of the best Protestant preachers had been slain or driven into exile, and in the earlier days of Elizabeth the restoration of Protestantism was exceedingly slow and cautious. Elizabeth herself was at heart more Catholic than Protestant, while for policy she had to

[11]Besides works and biographies of the preachers mentioned, see Brown, *Puritan Preaching in England* (Yale Lectures), Scribners, New York, 1900; Thos. Fuller, *Church History of Britain* (Book IX, 1580-1600); Marsden, *History of the Early Puritans.*

work with the Protestants. She did not approve of preaching, and discouraged it in a good many ways. One of the blots upon her reign is her persecution of the Anabaptists and other evangelical sectaries. In addition to these things, the political and ecclesiastical disputes of the times greatly absorbed the minds of the church leaders. Questions affecting the relations of Church and State were in hot dispute, and some who might have been able preachers, as, for instance, Archbishop Parker himself, were greatly taken up with other affairs. Yet, in spite of these depressing hindrances, preaching still existed and pursued the lines of development which had been begun in former times. In character it was much influenced by the controversial spirit. The rise of Puritanism and the disputes between Puritans and Anglicans were important forces in preaching. In style the extreme Puritanical method had not yet appeared, but the literary expression of the pulpit was not a little damaged by the fancifulness and literary conceits which were notable characteristics of much of the literature of Queen Elizabeth's time.

We may select for special mention a few of the better known preachers in both groups. Among the Anglican divines the most eminent name is that of Richard Hooker (1563-1600), the famous author of the *Ecclesiastical Polity.* His life was beautifully written by the genial old fisherman, Izaak Walton, who loved him very much. Hooker was educated at Oxford, where he made a good record as a scholar and became a fellow and professor. He was ordained in 1581 and preached some acceptable sermons at St. Paul's Cross. He was unwisely and unhappily married, and his domestic life was full of disappointments, which he bore with marked patience and sweetness of temper. In 1585 Hooker was made Master of the Temple in London, and it was while filling this incumbency that he fell into a controversy with his Puritan colleague, Walter Travers, who had the afternoon appointment as preacher at the Temple. The men differed widely in their theological and ecclesiastical views. The controversy inevitably had its unpleasant sides, but it resulted in one of the great contributions to English literature in Hooker's masterly treatise. This was the best defense of the Anglican position which appeared since Bishop Jewel's *Apology*, in the preceding epoch, and remains one of the classics of English literature. Hooker's noble style, clear thinking, and admirable spirit are known to many readers. The book was never quite completed, and some of it was published after his death. He had no doubt elaborated many of its thoughts in his sermons, and we can therefore form some idea of his style of discourse. As for the sermons themselves, not a great many remain, and they do not occupy a very high place in homiletic literature.

One of the most famous churchmen and preachers of this age was Lancelot Andrewes (1555-1626), but as his greatest fame and work belong early in the seventeenth century, under James I, he will more properly be considered among the preachers of that time.

Among the Puritan preachers in the latter part of the sixteenth century there were several men of power, two of whom at least deserve special notice. Henry Smith (1550-1593) was greatly admired by judicious men in his own time, and has left a good name behind him. Quaint and genial old Thomas Fuller praised him very highly and declares that his nickname of the "silver tongued" was "but one notch below Chrysostom himself." He received some education at Cambridge, and then studied with a Puritan preacher named Greenhan. He did not take a pastorate, but was elected in 1587 lecturer at St. Clement Danes, London. Here he achieved great celebrity as a preacher. Anthony Wood speaks of him as the "miracle and wonder of the age, for his prodigious memory and for his fluent, eloquent, and practical way of preaching." His sermons covered a wide range of topics and were marked by many of the literary traits of the times, abounding in quaint conceits and much imagery, but they were sweet and tender upon occasion, and must have produced a profound impression upon their hearers.

The other of these Elizabethan Puritans was William Perkins (d. 1602). He also receives high praise from Thomas Fuller, who says that "his sermons were not so plain but that the piously learned did admire them, nor so learned but that the plain did understand them,"—which is high praise for a preacher in any time. He gave some addresses at Oxford upon the duties of the ministry which afford a good idea of his own aims and purposes in the ministry. Using Isaiah's vision and call, he thus speaks of the burning coal taken from the altar and laid on the prophet's lips: "This signifies that the apt and sufficient teacher must have a tongue of fire, full of power and force, even like fire, to eat up the sins and corruptions of the world. For though it be a worthy gift of God to speak mildly and moderately so that his speech should fall like dew upon the grass, yet it is the tongue of fire; but it must be fire taken from the altar of God; it must be fire from heaven; his zeal must be a godly and heavenly zeal." Besides his sermons, Perkins is noted for having written (in Latin) perhaps the first modern treatise on homiletics by an Englishman. A translation was published in 1613, under the title, *The Art of Prophecying.* Perkins was a very learned and scholarly man, besides being plain in speech. His influence for good was very great, both in his own days and afterwards.

All these men show us that we can not dogmatize concerning the decline of the English pulpit in this age. While comparatively it was less great than in preceding or following times, and did not measure up to the literary splendor of its own age, it was by no means to be despised, either as a force in the national life or in a good measure of excellence and power within its own sphere.

IV. Scotch Preaching After Knox.[12]

Religious affairs in Scotland after the death of Knox were in great turmoil. There was a worldly and political party in the church, the inevitable result of the forces under which the Scottish Church came into being. Knox himself was forced by circumstances to associate the cause of religion with the political party opposed to

[12]See Blaikie, *The Preachers of Scotland from the Sixth to the Nineteenth Century;* Taylor, *The Scottish Pulpit;* McCrie, *Sketches of Scotch Church History;* Calderwood, *History of the Kirk of Scotland,* Vols. III-IV; *Works* and *Life* of Robert Rollock.

Queen Mary. The Protestant nobles, called Lords of the Congregation, had far too much influence within the church for its best spiritual interest. The young king, James VI, very early showed a desire to dominate the church as a part of the body politic, in which he desired to be absolute ruler. The organization of the church had been left incomplete at the death of Knox. Amid these difficulties it was given to one singularly great man to be the guiding genius in the maintenance and development of Scotch Presbyterianism. This man was Andrew Melville (1545-1622). Chiefly known as a reformer and educator, as the steady and unterrified opponent of worldly and royal encroachment, as organizer and leader, he was also a preacher of no little force and power. Preaching, however, was forced into the second place in his strenuous career.

A few of the better known preachers claim at least brief mention. There was James Lawson (d. 1584), the young colleague and successor of Knox at Edinburgh. Of course he did not measure up to the great reformer, but it is a distinction to say of him that he was Knox's own choice for his successor, and that he acquitted himself creditably in an exceedingly difficult position. Along with him should be named another who for a time had been a colleague of Knox at Edinburgh. This was John Craig (d. 1600). Like most of the Scottish preachers of the time, he had caught the fearless and outspoken spirit of their great leader. He had been a Catholic monk of the Dominican order and had studied much abroad. He had shown his courage in the time of Mary and Bothwell. He refused to comply with some desire of the congregation, and showed his independence by resigning. In 1580, James VI, the boy king, chose Craig for his court preacher. His ministry was greatly acceptable, both for its fidelity and its power. He kept his place until his death in 1600. We should also name here the learned teacher and author, Robert Rollock (d. 1598). Chiefly famous in these pursuits, he was also an esteemed and powerful preacher. The following paragraph from Dr. Blaikie's account of him gives some measure of the man: "In a way somewhat strange, Rollock became one of the ministers of Edinburgh. It was the practice for many of the people to assemble early on Sunday mornings in one of the churches called the New Church. How this came about, we are not told; all that we know is that the pious heart of Rollock was concerned to see them idle while they might be listening to the Word of God. With great self-denying zeal he began to preach to them, the hour of service being seven in the morning—a thing that had never been done in Edinburgh before. Rollock seemed to have no other thought than that of occupying usefully a portion of the time liable to be thrown away. All his brethren and fellow citizens were so impressed with his gift and so full of admiration for the man, that they persuaded him to undertake the pastoral office; and at length Rollock gave his consent. His preaching was attended with a remarkable degree of spiritual power and impressions, and the most learned and cultivated classes were as much impressed as the ignorant. Their minds were illuminated as with heavenly light, and their feelings wonderfully stirred up—the result of the clear and practical way in which the preacher presented the truth, and of the deep, sympathetic action of his own heart, moved by the Spirit of God, filled with the truths which he proclaimed." Rollock was a man of amiable and kindly temperament, thus quite a contrast to Knox. Blaikie compares him to Melanchthon in his relations to Luther.

Along with him should also be named a descendant of one of Scotland's most noted and famous families. This was Robert Bruce (1559-1631). He was educated for the law at St. Andrews, but deeply felt his call to preach the gospel, and gave up excellent worldly prospects in his profession. He had a deep spiritual experience, both of conversion and call, and his impassioned and earnest ministry gave every proof of the intensity and fervor of his personal convictions. Before he had quite completed his theological studies at St. Andrews, he was earnestly solicited to become successor of Lawson in Edinburgh. This, however, with good sense, he declined. During his student days he had shown great aptitude in expounding the Scriptures to his fellow-students and during the morning services in church. In 1587 he was called to Edinburgh and reluctantly accepted the place. For awhile he was in high favor with the young king, to whom he rendered services on more than one occasion, but his fidelity in opposing James' desire to restore episcopacy in Scotland cost him the monarch's favor. He was imprisoned for awhile in Edinburgh Castle, and on being released was forbidden ever to return to Edinburgh. He led a somewhat unsettled life as a preacher in his last years. The good men of his own time most highly esteemed him, both as a man and preacher. One of his contemporaries says: "He was a terror to evil-doers, and the authority of God did so appear in him and in his carriage, with such a majesty in his countenance, as to force fear and respect from the greatest in the land, even those who were avowed haters of godliness." And another says: "No man in his time spake with such evidence and power of the Spirit; no man had so many seals of conversion; yea, many of his hearers thought that no man, since the apostles, spoke with such power." He possessed two of the most necessary pulpit gifts, a thorough knowledge of Scripture and a searching application of it to the consciences of his hearers.

V. Catholic Preaching After the Council of Trent[13]

The latter part of the sixteenth century witnessed some improvement in the quality and power of Catholic preaching. This was due to several causes, of which three may be mentioned as the most prominent.

(1) There was in a general way the stimulus of rivalry with the Protestant preaching. This, of course, had its seamy side in the prominence of the polemic spirit, but nevertheless the very existence of Protestantism and the emphasis which it placed upon preaching the pure Word of God, had a decided and helpful effect in improving both the taste and the Scriptural quality of Roman Catholic preaching. This influence was felt all through the sixteenth century, and while not espe-

[13]See the Church Histories; Canons of the Council of Trent as quoted in various authorities on preaching; and Zanotto, *Storia della Predicazione, passim.*

cially prominent toward its close, still has to be reckoned with as one of the forces in the Catholic preaching of the time.

(2) More particularly we must count the effect of the Council of Trent (1545-1563). Among the many Canons passed by that distinguished body, some related to matters of practice and discipline, including preaching. It will be remembered that Cardinal Charles Borromeo, of Milan, was one of the leading theologians in the Council, and that he was especially interested in toning up the quality of Catholic preaching.[14] Doubtless there were others who agreed with him, and so it is easily seen how important the new interest in preaching should appear in the eyes of that body. The Council laid it down as the first duty of a bishop to preach; it regulated also the preaching of the friars; it passed rules for the reformation of certain abuses and for the better education of the preachers. There can be no question that the actions of the Council on these subjects were effective in producing a decided improvement in Catholic preaching. Some Catholic writers have been disposed to assign to this influence alone the marked improvement of the Catholic pulpit in modern times; but, while it is one of the causes, it can not be considered the only one. The influence of Protestantism can not be discounted.

(3) We must also take account of the founding of the famous Society of Jesus.[15] One of the purposes of Loyola in establishing his order was to promote preaching, though its main purpose was to strengthen the papacy and counteract in every possible way the work of the Reformation. Preaching, as one of the principal means of instructing the people and meeting heresy, naturally was much emphasized in the order, and many of its members, from the time of its founding and on through its checkered history, have been among the most distinguished preachers in the Roman communion.

Yet when we come to discuss the principal Catholic preachers toward the end of the sixteenth century, we do not find many who have any particular claim to dis-

[14]See my *History of Preaching,* Vol. I, pp. 525, 528, 545 ff.
[15]The Church Histories; Taylor, *Loyola and Jesuitism.*

tinction. The greater preachers of this century belong rather to its middle period than immediately at its end. There was something of a lull in power among Catholics, as well as among Protestants in the evening of the Reformation epoch. A few Italian preachers are mentioned by Zanotto as having attained some distinction. Among these were Joseph of Lionessa (d. 1612) and Lorenzo of Brindisi (d. 1619). In Germany and France the case was somewhat similar, where Jean Boucher, who preached before both Henry III and Henry IV, is at least worthy of mention as a notable French preacher of his age. For piety and earnestness, both of life and preaching, mention should also be made of the well-known St. Francis of Sales (1567-1622).

A general survey of the Christian pulpit at the turn of the sixteenth century, as has been already pointed out, shows decided symptoms of reaction and decline. Neither among Protestants nor Catholics was there the height of intellectual force, spiritual fervor, and popular success which the earlier and middle periods of the century witnessed in the pulpit. We must turn our faces toward the dawning seventeenth century, when in at least two of the European countries, France and England, a great classic period in the history of preaching arises.

CHAPTER II

Preaching in Southern Europe During the Seventeenth Century

The general historic importance of the seventeenth century in Western civilization is readily conceded; but its points of commanding interest for human progress are shifted from Southern and Central Europe to France and England. In each of these two countries there is also a great age of pulpit eloquence, while elsewhere there is weakness. Decadent Spain and distracted Italy wither under the blight of triumphant bigotry; free thought is suppressed or expelled. Divided Germany suffers for thirty years in the first half of the century the horrors of civil war, and lies prostrate all the century through. In France the monarchy, and in England the people show their strength; and on vast colonial fields in America and India these two great nations are getting ready for their titanic struggle through the next century, with the odds apparently in favor of France. Literature in Italy and Germany has little to show for itself; in Spain the bloom is reached, but is ready to shatter out. In France literature reaches its classic zenith in the reign of Louis XIV; and in England the great Elizabethan age is worthily extended in the masterpieces of the tumultuous revolutionary period. More particular notices of events and conditions, with their influences upon preaching, will better come under each country as we proceed.

I. Portugal

But for one man the little country of Portugal would claim no consideration in a history of seventeenth century preaching. Four hundred years before this time she had given to the world the great Franciscan, Antony of Padua, who was born and educated in Portugal, though his main residence was at Padua in Italy. In this age another Antonio comes on the scene, and the work and influence of Antonio Vieyra add one more celebrity to the pulpit annals of a country singularly destitute of such distinction.

In the latter part of the sixteenth century Portugal lost her political independence, being brought under the dominance of Spain, and it was not till 1665 that the Spanish yoke was thrown off and the house of Braganza established a new dynasty and government. An alliance with England cost the country disastrous concessions that further weakened its political importance throughout the seventeenth century. Portuguese literature was distinguished during the sixteenth century by the splendid work of Camoëns in his *Lusiad* and *Sonnets;* and there were a few other authors of some distinction; but the seventeenth century has little of literary worth. There were besides our preacher, Vieyra, only a few writers on religious subjects who had much influence. In religious affairs Catholicism, with the Inquisition, was dominant, and the Jesuits were strong. In Brazil and other possessions there was opening and stimulus to missionary endeavor, and this gave some life to religious activity; but on the whole neither religious nor other conditions in Portugal were favorable to the development of pulpit eloquence.

Yet a few preachers are mentioned by Catholic writers as entitled to favorable notice. Zanotto[1] names, among the Jesuits, Luiz Cardeyra (d. 1684), who published some sermons; and Emmanuel Reys (d. 1699), who was auxiliary bishop of Lisbon, an eminent preacher, who published four volumes of sermons; also Simon da Grazia (d. 1682), prior at Goa, and author of notable panegyrics on the saints. These are scarcely known beyond their church and country; but, as we have seen, there is at least one Portuguese preacher of the century whose fame is wider than these limits. This was Antonio Vieyra (1608-1697).[2] Like his mediæval namesake, Antony of Padua, he rises far above the average, and has a secure place among the great preachers of all time. And he was more of a Portuguese than the earlier Antony, who did his best work in a country and language not his by birthright. Vieyra spoke and wrote in Portuguese, and his works did much for that language, being even yet esteemed among its classics.

Vieyra was born at Lisbon in the early years of the century, but was taken by his parents to Brazil when seven years old. Henceforth his time was divided between the homeland and her great colony. He was carefully educated in the schools of both the parent land and Brazil. In 1625 he took the vows of the Society of Jesus. The characteristic Jesuit training and traditions were his. He became proficient in learning, in diplomacy, in knowledge of human nature, in facile and elegant speech and writing, in persuasive and moving eloquence. Called to Portugal, he was made preacher at the royal chapel at Lisbon by John IV, who greatly admired and loved him. Entrusted by his sovereign with important political duties, he showed himself an adept in diplomacy. But he loved Brazil and the mission work there, and could not be induced to remain always in the home

[1]*Storia della Predicazione,* p. 317.
[2]Zanotto, *l. c.;* Neale, *Mediæval Preaching,* on Vieyra.

country. Back and forth between Portugal and Brazil his life was spent, with one intermission of importance, when he discharged a preaching appointment of some months in Rome. He lived to a great age, notwithstanding his ceaseless activity and great labors, and died, as he wished, in Brazil.

Besides his published sermons, Vieyra produced a number of other works. His writings are among the classics of the Portuguese language, and his work for education and literature in Brazil is reckoned one of the foremost influences for culture in that land. Selections from his sermons are accessible to English readers in Neale's *Mediæval Preaching*. From these and a slight glance at his sermons in the original a fair idea of the general character of these discourses has been obtained. In contents and theology they are Catholic, of course, and yet with a trace of evangelical teaching not to be expected from a Jesuit of that age. Indeed, it has been stated that in some quarters the sermons are among books forbidden to be read by the clergy, because of their tendency in this direction. The moral tone, for the most part, appears to be unexceptionable. The style is wordy and elaborate, according to prevalent taste, and hardly seems to justify the very high place accorded to it. The knowledge of human nature is keen, the application direct and pungent. There do not seem to be any oratorical flights, such as we find in the French school, nor the quaint and stately dignity which we find in the English classics of the century. But there is a loftiness of thought, a seriousness of purpose, a carefulness and elegance of expression which make the sermons worthy of high consideration in themselves, and, when compared with those of the preacher's Spanish and Portuguese contemporaries, easily of the first rank.

II. Spain

The condition of affairs in Spain during the seventeenth century was not favorable to pulpit eloquence or effectiveness, but a number of preachers are named by Catholic authors as worthy of distinction among their compeers, though none have attained to anything like world-wide fame.

After the defeat of the famous Armada sent against England in 1588, the power of Spain distinctly declines, and the whole of the seventeenth century is witness to that. Philip III (1598-1621) was a weak and fanatical prince, whose favorite, Lerma, mismanaged the revenues, drove out the remnant of the Moors and their descendants, and made other mistakes harmful to the prosperity of the country. Misfortunes continued under Philip IV (1621-1665). The Netherlands were finally abandoned; Portugal successfully revolted; insurrections occurred in the horribly mistreated Italian dependencies, and war with France led to disastrous defeats. Under Charles II (1665-1700) there was no change for the better; another ruinous war with France occurred, troubles in Italy continued, and with this king the proud House of Hapsburg became extinct, making way for the terrible wars of the Spanish Succession and the establishment of the House of Bourbon in the next century.

The religious situation was what might be expected from the triumph of the Inquisition,—the expulsion and persecution of heretics, the dark fanaticism and corrupt lives of the monarchs and their favorites. The Roman hierarchy had had its way, but at fearful cost to the country and to the Roman Church itself as a force for true religion.

But the dark outlook presented by political and religious conditions is somewhat relieved by the glory—even though a fading glory—of Spanish literature during the seventeenth century.[3] When the century opened Cervantes (d. 1616) was famous and still at work. *Don Quixote* is not his only, though his most important, title to fame. Other romances, short or long, lyrics, and some dramas, came from his pen and produced a large following of imitators. Another remarkable literary genius of the century was Lope de Vega (d. 1635), whose especial, but not sole work, was drama. He stirred up many followers. But the chief poet of Spain is Calderon de la Barca (d. 1681), who is held to be one of the greatest of dramatists, especially in tragedy. Besides these great masters, whose fame belongs to all coun-

[3]Ticknor, *History of Spanish Literature,* Harpers, 1849; 3 vols., Period II.

tries and times, there were a number of less known and yet nationally influential writers in all the walks of literature. Among the lesser poets and ballad writers one has, in spite of talent and worth, an unenviable name as having corrupted taste. This was Gongora, who introduced and practiced a bombastic and inflated style, which he and his followers called *cultismo;* but it is also known from him as Gongorism. This affectation was contemporaneous in Italy; and there is dispute between Spanish and Italian critics as to where the chief blame of its introduction belongs. Likewise the same phenomenon appeared in English literature under the name of Euphuism. This wretched folly spread from poetry into prose and vitiated all the literature of the time. Even the masters who satirized it felt in some degree bound to yield to the current of taste. There were a few notable historians in the early part of the century, as Mariana, Sandoval, and Herrera; and later Solis was esteemed the most important. There were collections of proverbs, some treatises on grammar and rhetoric, and on politics. Ticknor mentions with some approval a treatise on *The Idea of a Christian Prince,* by Faxardo, which had some vogue and usefulness. There were also some religious and practical treatises of various degrees of merit, but none of great power or lasting influence. The tyranny of both Church and State was not favorable to the cultivation of eloquence; and the mediæval character of the Catholic Church in Spain, with its elaborate ceremonial sacerdotalism, acted as an additional drawback to pulpit power.

The preaching of the age is thus described by Ticknor:[4] "After the beginning of the seventeenth century the affected style of Gongora and the conceits of the school of Ledesma found their way into the churches generally, and especially into the churches of Madrid. This was natural. No persons depended more on the voice of fashion than the preachers of the court and the capital, and the fashion of both was thoroughly infected by the new doctrines. Paravicino at this period was at the head of the popular preachers, himself a poet devoted to the affectations of Gongora; a man of wit,

[4] *Op. cit.,* vol. III, p. 127 f.

a gentleman and a courtier. From 1616 he was, during twenty years, pulpit orator to Philip III and Philip IV, and enjoyed as such a kind and degree of popularity before unknown. As might have been expected, he had many followers, each of whom sought to have a fashionable audience. Such audiences were soon systematically provided. They were, in fact, collected, arranged, and seated by the friends and admirers of the preacher himself,—generally by those who, from their ecclesiastical relations, had an interest in his success; and then the crowds thus gathered were induced in different ways to express their approbation of the more elaborate passages in his discourse. From this time and in this way religious dignity disappeared from the Spanish pulpit, and whatever there was of value in its eloquence was confined to two forms,—the learned discussions, often in Latin, addressed to bodies of ecclesiastics, and the extemporaneous exhortations addressed to the lower classes; —the latter popular and vehement in tone, and by their coarseness generally unworthy of the solemn subjects they touched." Ticknor adds in a footnote: "Capmany, in his five important volumes devoted to Spanish eloquence, has been able to find nothing in the seventeenth century, either in the way of forensic orations or pulpit eloquence, with which to fill its pages, but is obliged to resort to the eloquent prose of history and philosophy, of ethics and religious asceticism."

On the other hand, the case does not seem quite so desperate when we look over such a list of names, with brief comments, as is given by Zanotto in notes to two of his chapters on the history of preaching in Italy. He mentions briefly contemporaneous preachers of note in other lands, and his list for Spain during the seventeenth century is fairly full. In all he names forty-seven Spanish preachers who published sermons during the century; and these are noted with various degrees of commendation. It is to be supposed that his list is not exhaustive, for it is singular that he does not include Paravicino, who is particularly instanced by Ticknor, as quoted above. Among the more important of those mentioned by Zanotto are the following: Francesco Blamas, of the Philippine Islands, who came to Spain and showed himself quite an orator, afterwards went as missionary to America, and left some sermons in the Spanish language; Francesco Labata (d. 1631), who enjoyed much celebrity, and published, besides many sermons, a sort of homiletical help for preachers; Diego Baeza (d. 1647), who had "great renown" and put forth many sermons on the feasts, on funeral occasions, and for souls in Purgatory; Juan d'Armenta, of Cordova (d. 1651), who was director of several colleges and "passed among the more eloquent orators;" Emanuele Naxera, of Toledo (b. 1624), who had a famous career as preacher for thirty years and left, besides theological works, a number of volumes of sermons, some of which were thought worthy of translation into Italian; Antonio de Lorea (d. 1688), who was much praised for his easy eloquence; the Augustinian, Pedro of St. Joseph, who was called the "painter" from his skill in that art, but was also a preacher of note.

III. Italy

The condition of Italy during the whole of the seventeenth century was deplorable in the extreme. It was an age of darkness and slavery. From the firm establishment of the Spanish power over almost the entire peninsula under Charles V, Italy entered her prison and remained until quite recent times—to use the well-worn phrase—"only a geographical expression." Virtually only Piedmont, under the House of Savoy, and Venice, in the rapid decline of her former greatness, were free from the dominant Spanish misrule. A rapacious line of viceroys wasted the domains which they professed to govern. Futile uprisings in Naples and Sicily only tightened the hateful manacles and increased the sufferings of the people. A feeble line of fourteen popes with difficulty held together the States of the Church. The decayed scions of ducal houses rotted in their sloth and vices in the provinces and cities made famous in former times. Genoa, inwardly corrupt, was the football of contention between Spain, France, and Savoy—by turns a prey to all, and no more strong or great. Venice passed through exhausting wars—which in her declining wealth and power she could ill afford to wage—with her own countrymen, with Austria, and with the Turks. Here alone were there any remains of Italian greatness and independence; and how great was the fall even here! In Savoy, in contrast with the ducal houses of Italy proper, the ruling family showed some strength and held power with a vigorous hand. Piedmont was already becoming, under this famous House, the hope of Italian independence and unity. But that day of realization was far in the future and unsuspected even by the most far-sighted.

Moral corruption accompanied political degradation. Vice of every description flourished among rulers and people. Rapacity, lust, cowardice, instead of being held down, were in the ascendant; cruelty, oppression, and violence were the pastime of the strong; and subserviency, treachery, and hate were the refuge of the weak. Religion had no happier fortune. The Inquisition had snuffed out the spark of reform; the salt had lost its savor, and there was no seasoning for itself. Some of the popes enriched their families—notably the Borghese and Barberini; one, Paul V, tried to revive the high pretensions of mediæval times, only to be successfully resisted by Venice and haughtily humiliated by Louis XIV. Freedom of thought was suppressed, and Galileo was forced to recant. Superstition abounded where vital religion decayed. This was seventeenth century Italy.

As to the literature of the time, Sismondi[5] gives a fearful picture of decay. He mentions and discusses a few writers of more or less prominence, but none of any real greatness. Guarino, Chiabrero, and others wrote some true lyrics. The name of Marini is notorious as corresponding to that of Gongora in Spain, for he it was who introduced in Italy that inflated and bombastic style which marks this era of decadence. Imitators there were in abundance. More worthy of mention is the senator of Florence, Filicaia, who wrote some excellent lyrics with a patriotic flavor and purpose. In this time arose opera—music and the stage using poetry

[5]*Literature of Southern Europe,* Bohn's edition, vol. I, p. 440 f. Cf. also Tiraboschi, *Storia della Letteratura Italiana,* on this period.

only as an inferior aid. The critic's depressing summary is as follows: "Enfeebled Italy produced during a century and a half only a race of cold and contemptible imitators, tamely following in the paths of their predecessors; or of false and affected originals who mistook an inflated style for grandeur of sentiment, antithesis for eloquence, and witty conceits for a proof of brilliant powers. This was the reign of corrupted taste; a taste which strove, by a profusion of ornament, to disguise the want of native talent, and which maintained its authority from the time of the imprisonment of Tasso until the appearance of Metastasio in the zenith of his fame," that is, from 1580 to 1730.

Experience teaches us that under such conditions it would be vain to look for a high degree of pulpit power. Preaching was influenced for the worse by its environment, and fell in only too easily with the faults of the age. It is not a pleasant picture which the faithful and candid pen of Zanotto[6] draws of Catholic preaching in Italy during the seventeenth century, especially its earlier part. From his careful study the following account is chiefly derived.

Although there were some true and good preachers at the opening of the century, such as Joseph of Lionessa and S. Lorenzo of Brindisi, yet it was true that "sacred eloquence in general followed worse than ever the deplorable perversions of literature, which especially showed their follies in the academies." The foreign Spanish rule cramped liberty of utterance in the pulpit. If the preachers attacked too boldly the existing evils they were likely to be denounced as criticising the government under which these evils flourished. Not only the preachers themselves, but their hearers also, felt these restrictions. Some came to hear for their spiritual benefit, but many only formally, and some as eager critics. Connected with this there were allied and derived evils which deplorably affected the preaching of the time. In an apt phrase Zanotto describes it as "heroicomic." Unable to lay its hand upon the real faults and needs of the age,

[6]*Storia della Predicazione,* capp. VII, VIII, so often referred to, and to which I am largely indebted. He naturally gives most attention to Italian preachers.

it sought for capricious novelties and strained effects. While this wretched affectation marred all contemporary literature, it is at its worst in preaching, which depends for its best character on reality and propriety of feeling. Some of this bombast was due to the Spanish influence, with its pride and pompous language; but some also to reaction from the severe classicism of the preceding epoch. The defects of that classic revival were perpetuated; its uses were perverted. Speaking of these bombastic preachers, our critic observes:[7] "That which an ancient orator would have signified with a simple metaphor became in their hands an interminable harangue which served finely to form an exordium. So it happened that the introductions have often only a very subtle connection with the body of the discourse." Some of the more important preachers in the first part of the century, and before the improvements introduced by Segneri led to something of real reform in pulpit methods, must now be noticed.

Of Luigi Giuglaris (1607-1653) the eminent historian of Italian literature, Tiraboschi,[8] says that in him was condensed the quintessence of the seventeenth century style. He had some sparks of real genius, was certainly brilliant, and had a large following; but he exemplified the faults of the age. Honored at the court of Savoy, he was for five years entrusted with the education of the prince Charles Emanuel, for whom he wrote a book of instructions which compares most favorably with the infamous similar work of Machiavelli in the former age. Indeed, Zanotto says it is more solid and important than his sermons. In this Giuglaris shows some oratorical merits: puts his proposition well, holds to his main point, and knows how to make a connected argument. He has much doctrine, exhibits boldness and a dramatic action which attracts attention, and on the whole has a good outline and order of discourse. But his preaching is marred by the current conceits and blemishes, as the following example, given by Zanotto,[9] shows.

It is taken from his Advent Sermons, the one for the third Sunday in Advent; but leaving the gospel for

[7] *Op. cit.*, p. 212.

[8] *Op. cit.*, adduced by Zanotto.

[9] *Op. cit.*, p. 212 ff.

the day, he branches off into a discussion of the instability of earthly goods with a view to teaching a sound humility. The title of the sermon at once suggests the manner of treatment: "The Anatomy of Our Nothingness." For a text he forces to his use the reply of John the Baptist to the deputation from Jerusalem (John 1:19-21), putting his emphasis on the words, "I am not—" *i. e.,* nothing! In the introduction the preacher pictures a learned surgeon with a fresh cadaver upon the table and his dissecting knife in hand. He distinguishes the four greater parts of the body: head, chest, stomach, and members—which include all that remains. Then he subdivides each of these four greater parts into a number of others, mentioning for the head alone twenty-one subdivisions. He then proceeds to give some account of the history of anatomy, mentioning that Averroës distinguished in the human body 529 muscles and 248 bones, of which Galen makes 300. He then compares the humors of the body to the four classical rivers, adding that the numerous veins correspond to the provincial streams. All this rubbish he puts together in order to reach his subject, which he thus sets forth: "As the physicians are accustomed openly to make these anatomical investigations, having for that purpose from the authorities the body of some condemned criminal, in order that the causes of diseases may be ascertained and there be no mistake in the application of remedies; so, while we all are professing to cure our own selves, now from the bruises which envy makes, now from the frenzies caused by choler, now from the paroxysms of wantonness, our nature shows itself with all minuteness, in order that remaining from such an anatomy entirely convinced that we are nothing, we may, with frequency every day taking the cordial of humility, treat medicinally all our diseases at the root." As the surgeon must strip his cadaver, so must we strip away in our self-anatomy all clinging and superfluous garments; the nobleman laying aside his nobility, the merchant his riches, princes and pontiffs the crown and purple, the miter and cloak. He goes on to enumerate and discuss, first in the order of nature and then in the order of grace, the evils, passions, and faults which oppress this poor humanity. Under the order of nature he recurs to his fourfold division of head, chest, stomach, and members, drawing illustration from their various diseases. He gives especial attention to diseases of the brain, beginning with an attack on the literary man, and passing in review poets, rhetoricians, philosophers, lawyers, physicians, and other intellectual workers, showing the vanity of their craft, that he may reprove their pride.

Of the same sort, but even worse, was Emanuele Orchi (d. 1649), a Capuchin monk of Como. In him the exaggeration and bombast, both in thought and language, of the current method have an extreme representative. A volume of his sermons was published after his death, and in the preface the editor remarks, as if expressing the general opinion, that these discourses were not only esteemed worthy of publication, but of world-wide admiration. But this extravagant praise is singularly yet sanely modified in the further remark that they should not serve as models for imitation, for the reason that their "excessive floridity of style is diametrically opposed to that end of the conversion of souls which, after the honor and glory of God, ought to be the sole object" of preaching. Orchi, according to the prevalent custom, bestows great and elaborate attention on his introductions. For example, in a sermon on pride he devotes a long and labored introduction to a minute description of a peacock. Thus:[10] "Behold, sirs, the peacock in love with himself, who, beholding his tail spread in full circle, presents to our sight the remarkable perspective of its full-eyed pomp, and with mute speech addressing those whom he seeks to win, says: 'Hast thou seen that some labored embroidery of the industrious needle, in a finely woven fabric entangling gems amid delicate labyrinths of silk and gold, overcomes by the wealth of art the treasures of nature? Hast thou looked upon some gracious painting of a famous brush on smooth canvas, how, representing to the life a well-proportioned figure in delicate lines, it surpasses with the semblance of a shade the reality of a body? Now, if thou dost compare either of these to the—I know not whether I shall call it embroidered picture or pictured embroidery—

[10] *Id.*, p. 217 f.

of my full-eyed circle, the art of Pallas will seem insipid to thee, and thou wilt esteem as commonplace the school of Apelles; and it needs must be said that with reason I seem to myself a happy bird as I carry on my head, in these delicate plumes of needle and brush, a triumphant crown—the clearest token of the splendid victories of my tail.'" And more of the same sort of foolish dilating follows till the silly bird is described as suddenly catching a look at its ugly legs and dirty feet, when, smitten with shame, it drops its spread tail and slinks away. Thus, he says, there is always some check to human pride. Would that the preacher could have learned his own lesson!

Besides these two leaders there were many other preachers who carried this faulty method to excess. Among them was one, Salvatro Cadana of Turin, theologian and councillor to the Duke of Savoy, who is described as having "a veritable mania" for strained antithesis and paradoxes. In many the folly of the age appears in the titles chosen for sermons, whether singly or in collections. Thus Maria di Simoni, a Capuchin of Venice, called his series of Lenten sermons: "Seraphic Splendors of the Dark Sayings of the More Celebrated Academicians Relucent Among the Shades of Vague Hieroglyphics." Antonio Cagliardi, of Milan (d. 1688), an Augustinian who lived much at Venice and was dear to the rulers and people of that Republic, called a volume of his sermons, "Spiritual Sweetmeats for the Unforeseen Needs of Evangelic Speakers"—apparently a sort of *homiliarium* for lazy plagiarists. Some of the preachers sought whimsical epithets or descriptions for the saints whom they celebrated in panegyrics. Thus one eulogizes St. Catherine of Siena as "The Sacred Earth of the Pharos," possibly meaning the foundation of a heavenly lighthouse; another speaks of St. Augustine as "The Adam of Grace"—which is not so bad; and a panegyric on St. Gaetano bears the title, "The Treasures of Nothing," and much more of the same sort.

Zanotto mentions some more or less eminent Spanish preachers who also preached in Italy, among whom was Didaco Alvarez, a Dominican honored by Pope Clement VIII, and author of a *Manual for Preachers.* Likewise there were Italians who preached in Spain and returned with renown to Italy. Especially notable among these was Nicolo Riccardi, of Genoa (d. 1639), who preached before Philip III and was called by him a "monster" on account of the enthusiasm created at the Spanish court by his style of eloquence; and his discourses were actually published as the "Sermons of a Monster!"

On the other hand, things were not all dark for preaching. Along with these faults of style there was, in the rhetorical structure of sermons, some improvement over former times. Nor was the vicious method of the age accepted without contemporary censure and desire for better things. There were those who criticised, some with satire and some with pain, the absurdities and unrealities of the current manner. There were preachers who knew better and wished for better things, but, as Tiraboschi says, felt obliged to yield somewhat to the taste of the age in order to get a hearing; and doubtless even those who were in earnest and sought to use better methods were unconsciously influenced more than was wholesome by their environments.

Among these men of better purpose and spirit Zanotto praises Girolamo da Narni (d. 1631), scion of a noble family and piously brought up, a Capuchin, who preached in the principal cities of Italy and much at Rome. He was much loved and praised for his good life as well as for the force and fervor of his sermons, some of which were honored by a translation into French. Another preacher of the better sort was Luigi Albrizio (d. 1665), a Jesuit of Piacenza. The example quoted by the historian from the conclusion of one of his discourses does not lack force, real appeal to the conscience without artifice, and a downright and direct moral earnestness. Still another was Tommaso Reina (d. 1653), a Jesuit of Milan, who did not wholly escape the faults of the times, but was highly and justly esteemed for force and earnestness. He had considerable homiletical skill, and knew how to attract and retain attention. In a sermon on Temptation he discusses, with not a little power, the case of Absalom, as thus:[11] "Now comes the impious Absalom, all haughty and full of pride, aspiring to the

[11] *Id.*, p. 234.

kingdom of his father, and therefore with sacrilegious and parricidal arms opening the gap to his uncontrolled passions. Already he imagines himself seated on the paternal throne, covered with purple, crowned with gold; already he appears to himself to be receiving the homage of the people, the tributes of vassals, the presents of princes, the congratulations of his household, the embassies of foreign powers. Already his government is formed, he promulgates the laws, he establishes the sanctions, he rewards, punishes, pardons, condemns, elevates, deposes, ennobles, disgraces, enriches, impoverishes. What doest thou, unhappy one? Whither does thy impiety lead thee? Whither wilt thou be carried by thy mad ambition? Against thy father wilt thou at length lift up sacrilegious and rash arms, and plot death for him who gave thee life? At length to reach the kingdom wilt thou reach the height of all wickedness, putting underneath thy feet the laws of God, of men, of nature? Unfortunate in every way, be it that thou gain the victory, be it that thou lose. If thou win, thou shalt be impious; if thou lose, thou shalt be disgraced."

Toward the middle and end of the century a reaction from the excesses of the earlier school began to appear. The greatest leader in this movement was the elder Segneri, who is regarded as the restorer of Italian pulpit eloquence. But before him Daniel Bartoli (d. 1685)[12] inveighed against the corrupt taste and hurtful abuses of the pulpit, comparing the fantastical preachers to Nero, who during a scarcity of provisions at Rome had a ship to come from Egypt laden with sand to sprinkle on the floors for the games, thus aggravating the sufferings of the eager and hungry populace when they discovered sacks of sand instead of grain. His sharp strictures had some effect, especially among the preachers of his own order, the Jesuits, from whose ranks the leading reformer of Italian preaching arose.

Paolo Segneri (1624-1694),[13] descended from a noble Roman family, was born of pious parents at Nettuno,

[12] *Id.*, p. 254.

[13] *Quaresimale del padre Paolo Segneri della Compagna di Gesù,* due vol. G. Silvestri, Milano, 1827. This work also contains a life of the preacher, and his own introduction, in which

May 21, 1624, the eldest of many sons. His intellectual power was early manifest, and his father gave him good educational advantages. He was sent to a Jesuit school at Rome, where his diligence in study and earnestness and purity of character attracted the favorable regard of his teachers. One of these, afterwards Cardinal Pallavicino, later made of the Latin form of Segneri's name the telling anagram: *Paulus Segnerus—purus angelus es.*

While engaged in his studies, and from an early bent to oratory, Segneri determined to become a preacher, and sought admission to the Society of Jesus. This step was at first opposed by his father, but the earnest youth, by quiet persuasion and patience, at last gained the parental consent, and was received as a novice in 1637. He pursued the studies and other training of his novitiate with great zeal and success; indeed, so severe was his application that he became ill, and his malady resulted in a permanent deafness, a lifelong drawback to his work. Paying special attention to oratorical studies and practice, both in writing and in speech, he became so proficient as to be often deputed to preach even before leaving school. Already he began the preparation of his famous *Quaresimale,* the series of Lenten discourses which remain his most distinctive work.

Upon completing his studies he at once entered upon the work of preaching, being sent by the authorities to various places. In 1661 he gave the Lenten sermons at Piacenza, and in the same year the Advent sermons at Fermo. He wished to go as missionary to India, but his deafness and his special talents for pulpit work at home led his superiors to refuse his request; but they allowed him to alternate his Lenten and other more formal preaching with "missions" or evangelistic meetings in the homeland. In this work he was devoted, laborious, and successful throughout a period of twenty-six years, during which he extended his labors in all parts of Italy, endured many hardships and privations, and finally wore

he gives his views of preaching. Zanotto (p. 256 ff.) has an informing discussion of Segneri, but perhaps is more appreciative than judicial. See also Micocci, *Antologia della sacra Eloquenza Moderna,* who in the beginning of his work has a fine critique of Segneri and several others.

out his strength. He usually began about Easter and continued his missions on into the fall, when he would rest awhile till sent out somewhere to preach the *Quaresimale.* This notable series was first published in 1679. Other volumes of sermons and some highly valued apologetic and devotional writings came from his pen. Age and weariness were already telling upon him when, two years before his death, he was appointed apostolic preacher at the papal court. In a short time, however, he resigned; and died, greatly loved and honored, at Rome, in 1694.

There is but one voice as to the purity of Segneri's character and the earnestness of his convictions; and these shine out in clear light in his sermons and other writings. He has been called by admirers in his own land and church "the restorer of sacred eloquence," and "the father of modern pulpit eloquence" in Italy. It is certain that he introduced among his countrymen a new epoch in pulpit work and set a better example in preaching than had been in vogue for a long time. In the preface to his *Quaresimale* he gives his views of preaching, and they are sound and just. He attacks the current bombastic style, showing how it detracts from the power of the pulpit and is unworthy of the purpose of preaching, which is to save and instruct people, not to astonish and entertain them. So he says, "I have rather made it my duty to imitate Christ, who never cared to draw the people to heaven by any other road than the royal one of veracious reasons." Another point on which he insists is that of careful preparation. Incidentally, he disapproves of light and humorous discourse. His sermons exemplify his principles, for they are serious, thoughtful, carefully prepared, based on thorough study of Scripture—with which he shows great familiarity—loyal to church authority and tradition, and earnestly devoted to the spiritual good of his hearers. They also exhibit knowledge of human nature, the fruit of much observation, without bitterness or cynicism. He attacks with courage and fidelity the current vices and faults, but without coarseness or abuse. His homiletic method is rather that of the classic orators and the ancient fathers than that of the scholastics. Logical analysis is not obtrusive, but there is good arrangement and progress of thought. The introductions are usually quite studied and elaborate, but not far-fetched or strained for effect. Argument abounds and is cogently put. Frequent illustrations, gathered alike from observation and reading, enliven the discourse without being drawn out into wearisome detail. The style is lofty, diffuse, highly wrought, intense; but, while lacking flexibility and ease, it so far surpasses in directness and power the overwrought manner of the time as by contrast to seem simple and severe. It was the unusual merit of Segneri's preaching that drew the crowds to hear it, for he had no special personal endowments to attract or to please. His voice was undistinguished, and his deafness prevented his hearing himself so as to prevent or correct certain faults of utterance; it also led to a monotony of tone in delivery.

The first of the famous Lenten sermons does not take a Scripture text, but the breviary's call to penitence, "Remember, O man, that thou art dust, and unto dust shalt return." The introduction, after a few opening sentences, appeals to those who would dismiss the warning as commonplace, and proceeds: "You know it? How is it possible? Say; are not you those who just yesterday were running about the city keeping festival, some as lovers, some as madmen, some as parasites? Are not you they who were dancing with so much alacrity at the entertainments? Are not you they who were immersing yourselves so deeply in debaucheries? Are not you they who were abandoning yourselves with so much unrestraint backward to the customs of foolish heathendom? Moreover, are you they who were sitting so joyfully at the comedies? Are you also they who were speaking out from the theater-boxes with such warm applause? Answer! And are not you they who, all full of joy in that very night preceding the sacred Ashes, passed it for yourselves in jests, in diversions, in revelings, in laughter, in songs, in serenades, in amours, and please God that it was not even in more unseemly amusements? And you, while you are doing such like things, know certainly that you also have to die? O blindness! O stupidity! O delirium! O perversity!

I was thinking to myself that I had brought with me a most invincible motive to induce you all to penitence and to weeping, in announcing death to you; and perhaps there may be for me even here some divine messenger, conducted through clouds, through fogs, through winds, through bogs, through snows, through torrents, through ice, lightening for me every labor by saying that it can not be that I shall not win some soul by reminding sinners of their mortality. . . .

"Ye angels, who sit as guardians by the side of these, my so honored hearers; ye saints, who lie buried under the altars of this to you so majestic basilica; you from this hour I suppliantly invoke that at every time that I shall ascend this pulpit ye will entreat for my words that weight and that power which they could not have from my tongue. And thou chiefly, O great Virgin Mary, who canst with truth call thyself parent of the Divine Word; thou who, greatly thirsting for it, didst by good fortune conceive it in thy bosom; thou who, fecund with it, didst for the common good bring it forth to light; thou who, from its being hidden and imperceptible as it was, didst render it known and tangible even to the senses; effect thou that I may know how to treat it every day with such reverence that I shall not contaminate it with the profanity of empty formulas, that I shall not adulterate it with the ignominy of facetious jests, that I shall not pervert it with the falsity of forced interpretations, but that I may transfuse it into the hearts of my hearers as pure as it came forth from the hidden recesses of thy bowels! I come unprovided with any other support than a most lively confidence in thy favor. Therefore do thou enlighten the mind, do thou guide the tongue, do thou direct the bearing, do thou weigh all my speaking in such manner as may turn out for the praise and glory of God, may be edifying and useful to my neighbor, and to me may serve for obtaining reward and not be turned into matter of condemnation."

The sermon proceeds to press home the uncertainty of life with great variety of argument and illustration, and with genuine fervor of feeling and of interest in the hearers. Yet, notwithstanding all Segneri's earnestness, there is some artificiality, even in his preaching, which can not but be felt. But on the whole, for solidity of argument, dignity of style, power of imagination, depth of feeling, and loftiness of aim, to Segneri must be accorded a place among the truly great preachers of history.

The reform of preaching was further pushed on by those who admired and followed Segneri. Among them was his successor as apostolic preacher at Rome, Francesco Maria Cacini (1648-1719).[14] Born of good family at Arezzo, he early became pious and studious, and was admitted to the order of Capuchins at fifteen years of age. His talents and zeal brought him quick advancement, and his oratorical gifts were soon recognized and employed by his superiors. He spent some time in France, and was doubtless influenced by the great preaching of the age in that country. Notwithstanding his reluctance, he was appointed Segneri's successor as chief preacher at the papal court, and filled the place with such credit that he was made a cardinal in 1712, retaining in his great office the simplicity of a monk. In his youth he naturally inclined to the faults of the age, but under the influence of Segneri he soon threw off the extremes of bad taste and became an influential leader in the reform of pulpit method. He published a number of sermons, which had considerable reading and influence. Some critics have ranked him even higher than Segneri.

Another notable preacher of this school was Paolo Segneri the younger (d. 1713), a nephew of the more famous man. Though dying at forty years of age, he left a name behind him not unworthy of his illustrious uncle, like whom he was greatly successful in the conduct of missions.

Of course there were those who refused to follow the new path of improvement and kept on the old way of exaggeration, unreality, and bombast. Among these was Carlo Labia, a Venetian by birth, archbishop of Corfu, who published, about 1700, a book on preaching in which he defended the current methods. From the accounts it appears to be itself quite extravagant in style

[14]Zanotto, p. 284 ff.

and tone. There were also others of this school; but it could not last. The better method and spirit established themselves firmly, and so Italian preaching faces the eighteenth century with a more hopeful outlook.

CHAPTER III

Seventeenth Century Preaching in Germany and Northern Europe

While the general conditions of preaching during the seventeenth century were much the same throughout Europe, there was great difference in the particular characteristics of the pulpit in every European country. This difference becomes very noticeable when we pass from the preaching of Spain and Italy to that of Germany and Northern Europe. The change is as great as that of climate and people. The survey of the present chapter will take in the German, Swiss-German, and Scandinavian lands; and in these we shall pass under review the Catholic, the Lutheran, and the Reformed pulpits. But before dealing with these more specific aspects of the subject, it will be helpful to a better understanding if we take a general survey of the conditions and characteristics of preaching in the time and regions named.

I. General Survey of Conditions and Characteristics

During the first half of the century (1618-1648) Germany was desolated by the horrors of the Thirty Years' War, and the neighboring lands were necessarily involved in the troubles. Not only during its terrible continuance, but for ages after its close, that ruinous conflict laid waste all things German. The following extracts, quoted from a competent German historian,[1] will suffice for our purpose. Menzel says: "Germany is reckoned by some to have lost one-half, by others two-thirds, of her entire population during the Thirty Years'

[1]Menzel, *Geschichte der Deutschen,* quoted in *Historians' History of the World,* Vol. XIV, p. 385.

War. . . . The country was completely impoverished. The working class had almost totally disappeared. . . . Immense provinces, once flourishing and populous, lay entirely waste and uninhabited, and were only by slow degrees repeopled by foreign emigrants or by soldiery. The original character and language of the inhabitants were by this means completely altered. . . . Science and art had fled from Germany, and pedantic ignorance had replaced the deep learning of her universities. The mother tongue had become adulterated by an incredible variety of Spanish, Italian, and French words, and the use of foreign words with German terminations was considered the highest mark of elegance. Various foreign modes of dress were also generally adopted. Germany had lost all save her hopes for the future."

Amid such general wreck and ruin it could not be expected that literature would flourish; and German letters during this period show the baleful effects of the time. A critic[2] well says: "The conditions of pure literature were almost wholly wanting. Had a man of high genius arisen, the buds of his fancy must have faded for lack of light and air." The corruption of the language by admixture of foreign elements, the foolish imitation by some German authors of the bombastic Italian school, by others of the flippant French manner, added to the waste and moral deterioration of war, laid a withering blight upon literature. The quantity was small, the quality poor. Some leaders, mostly among the nobles and scholars, strove against the prevalent corruptions, both by forming societies whose patriotic design was to purify and preserve the German language, and by producing a literature which, both by criticism and example, should protest against the extravagances and corruptions which were rife. Among these writers was Martin Opitz (d. 1639), whose poetry—not of a very high order in itself—was yet distinctively German, and

[2]James Sime, article on German Literature, *Encyc. Brit.* For the slight account of German Literature in the text I am indebted chiefly to various articles and compends based on German sources. See especially *A Brief History of German Literature,* by G. M. Priest, New York, 1909, chap. IX; and the studies and examples of German literature in the *Warner Library.*

led the way to better things. Far more worthy of mention is Paul Fleming (d. 1640), who died all too young, but left behind him both love lyrics and sacred hymns which exhibit true poetic genius and depth of feeling. The dramatists and court poets of the period fall very low in servile imitation of foreign styles and in coarseness. Of romances a few appeared, which, though valuable for throwing some light on the times, are commonly marked by poverty of thought, corruption of language, and coarseness of material and expression. The best of them is the *Simplicissimus* of Grimmelshausen (d. 1676), in which the author described much of his own varied experiences during the great war and produced a work of some enduring merits. No important historical work is mentioned by the critics, but it was during this century that Pufendorf (d. 1694) produced and published (in Latin) his great works on jurisprudence, with some historical treatises. Of philosophical writers, Jacob Boehme belongs rather to the preceding age, though he lived till 1624. The great thinker Leibnitz (1646-1706) wrought his powerful work during the seventeenth century, but he wrote chiefly in Latin and French. His famous pupil, Wolf, belongs to the next era.

Deferring for the present any consideration of sermons, we find in this period some other religious writings of more or less importance. Theological controversy raged, and a number of polemic and dogmatic treatises appeared. The study of Hebrew and Greek found expression in many famous and important works, including those of the two Buxtorfs. Nor was practical theology wholly neglected. Several treatises on the art of preaching belong to the period, but they are without value, being given over to a dry and mechanical method. In fact, all theological writing of the period—dogmatic, exegetical, and practical—labors under the weight of pedantry and suffers with the dry-rot of scholasticism. It is mostly written in Latin and therefore can hardly be credited to German religious *literature* at all, however important in the history of German religious thought. In the region of devotional literature a different and far better state of affairs comes to view. This is especially true of hymns.[3] Indeed, some of the classics of German hymnody were produced during this terrible era of suffering and trial. Of didactic and devotional writings there is a fairly good number. The notable preachers, Arndt and Schupp of the earlier time, and Spener and Francke of the later, wrote some treatises of both contemporary and enduring influence and value.

The preaching of the age[4]—to speak here only in a most general way—shared both in the evil and good which characterized the times. The reaction and decline which already set in after the Reformation proceeded on the lines which have been previously indicated. Harsh polemics and narrow dogmatism prevailed among all the warring sects and opinions. The din of dreadful civil strife did not altogether drown the angry controversies of the pulpit. Besides this, the scholastic trend of former times kept on its hurtful course. Dismal dialectics and sapless pedantry often dried up the springs of spiritual refreshment which should have flowed from the pulpit. Surely, if ever the people needed at the hands of a relgious ministry instruction and comfort, it was when war and strife and demoralization were laying everything in ruins. It seems almost incredible that so much of the preaching of that sad time should have been so misdirected. Along with polemics and pedantry we find in some of the sermons of the time that fondness for bombast and fanciful trifling which was a prominent feature of the literary expression of the age. Perhaps this was not wholly an evil—except in its needless exaggerations and extremes—since the pulpit of any time, to be effective, must catch the prevalent manner of expression as far as is consistent with the peculiar aims of preaching; and it is not wholly fair to judge such things as tone and

[3]Besides articles, etc., on literature referred to in preceding note, see Julian's *Dictionary of Hymnology,* the great authority on its subject in English; also other studies, as by Hatfield, Duffield, in this department.

[4]See Christlieb-Schian in *RE,* and works of Schuler, Lentz, Schenk, Schmidt, Beste, Rothe, and Ker, mentioned in note to Chapter I. In addition see Brömel, *Homiletische Charakterbilder* (for Spener and Gerhard); Nebe, *Zur Geschichte der Predigt,* 3 Bde., (for Spener and preceding conditions); Hering, *Geschichte der Predigt;* and others as more particularly noted below.

diction by the standards of taste which prevail in our own times. Much that seems to us unworthy and foolish trifling, yes, even ridiculous conceit and affectation, must have brought some message to hearers and readers accustomed in other modes of oral and literary expression to excesses of artifice and fancy. Some such plea in mitigation may also be urged, though with far less sympathy, on behalf of the occasional coarseness and buffoonery which we find in many sermons of the age. This, we well know, is in nowise a peculiar characteristic of the seventeenth century; it is found in all the ages of preaching—our own not excepted. Yet it is true that in that time some preachers descended, in their satire and ridicule of evil and folly, to depths of vulgarity for which no excuse should be attempted. The better preachers of the time did not fail to note all these symptoms of decay nor to protest against the evils which they saw and deplored. One of the best of them, Christian Scriver,[5] exclaims: "Where to-day are the fiery tongues and the burning hearts of the apostles? Where is Luther's joyous spirit? Where are those who are intoxicated with the love of God, and proclaim the great deeds of God?" Indeed, Elijah is never alone, though to himself he often seems to be so. There is ever a remnant according to the election of grace; and even in this dark era of the German pulpit there were found preachers of a deeply pious and evangelical spirit. The influence of Arndt and others was felt in the earlier part of the century, even during the horrors of war; and the rescuing work of Spener and his Pietist followers in the latter part of the century marks a new epoch in German preaching. From this general view we pass to a more particular account of the Catholic, Lutheran, and Reformed pulpits in Germany and Northern Europe during the seventeenth century.

II. The Catholic Pulpit

Catholic as well as Protestant Germany was hurt by the horrors of the Thirty Years' War; and the preaching in the Catholic pulpits exhibits in its own way the wounds

[5]Quoted by Hering, S. 118.

and weaknesses of the time.[6] Polemics, dogmatism, pedantry, fancifulness, bombast, and coarseness are found; but in some preachers also the better qualities, of which these were the perversions and excesses, together with sincere spiritual purposes and teachings, do not fail to find a place. Abbé Renoux, a French Catholic historian and critic of German preaching, remarks:[6b] "It (preaching) was forcing itself to become classic and to take rank among literary compositions; but, as with us in France, before reaching its goal it made false steps, often missed its way, taking without discrimination emphasis for grandeur, coarseness for simplicity, an undigested erudition for a knowledge of good taste." But these faults were, as among the Protestants, discerned and opposed by the better preachers. The leading influences for improvement came from the preachers of the religious orders, and especially the Jesuits. One of these, Father Scherer, wrote some good instructions for young preachers, directed against the faults of the age, and is quoted as saying:[7] "Preachers, whose business it is by divine grace to win many souls and convert them to Jesus Christ, ought never to forget themselves, for what would it profit them to gain the whole world if they lose their souls? They ought not to be like the carpenters who built the ark in which Noah entered to escape the flood and who found themselves swallowed up in the waters; they ought not to be like the bells, whose sound rings through the church, and which are suspended outside; nor like mile-posts, which show the road to others while they remain immovable." Later than this another noted preacher, Father Staudacher (d. 1672), well says:[8] "The preacher ought to speak of divine things by means of earthly things, and, as need may arise, interest by the charm and beauty of his discourse those hearers who without that would perhaps refuse to listen;

[6] L'Abbé G. Renoux, *Les Prédicateurs célèbres de l'Allemagne,* Tours, 1885; Johann Nepomuk Brischar, *Die Katholischen Kanzelredner Deutschlands seit den drei letzten Jahrhunderten,* 5 Bde., 1867; Joseph Kehrein, *Geschichte der Katholischen Kanzelberedsamkeit der Deutschen von der ältesten bis zur neuesten Zeit,* 2 Bde., 1843.

[6b] *Op. cit.,* p. 227. [7] *Id.,* p. 230. [8] *Ib.*

he must soften and adorn his words as one gilds the edge of a cup which contains a remedy. So, since the preacher speaks of God to men, he must treat divine things humanly, and human things divinely."

Among the published sermons of the age a great number exist in Latin, but they were preached in German—or the substance of them at least. There are volumes[9] (unread by this writer!) of sermons by Matthew Faber (d. 1653), quite a noted Jesuit preacher of the day, a Bavarian; Philip Kisel (d. 1674), of Fulda, who preached with applause at Mainz, Spires, Wurtzburg, etc.; Michael Radau (1675), who, besides sermons, published a treatise on extemporaneous preaching; Philip Hartung (d. 1682), a Bohemian, who preached with great diligence in Moravia and Silesia, and published a volume which bears the title, *Conciones tergeminae, rusticae, civicae, aulicae,* which may be freely rendered, "Sermons of three sorts: for country, town, and college," and illustrates the variety of his labors and the peculiarity of his taste. A number of others, more or less noted among their coreligionists, are mentioned in the books; but two, Scheffer and Staudacher—whose views on preaching have been quoted—deserve somewhat fuller notice.

Michael Staudacher (1613-1672)[10] was a Jesuit father who enjoyed a high reputation for both earnestness and eloquence as a preacher. Born in the Tyrol, he received careful training and practice at the hands of the Jesuits. Several volumes of his sermons were published. He exemplified that mystic and poetic trait which is innate in the German mind and has characterized German preaching in every age. While he did not go to the fanciful lengths of some of his contemporaries, he was sufficiently under the spell of that movement of the age, as the following extract from one of his sermons will show. The sermon has for its subject a comparison of the risen Lord to a flower, and, after noting that the comparison is founded in Scripture, the preacher proceeds: "This celestial flower which was sown in the virginal conception to sprout at the nativity; which flourished in youth, and spread its perfume in the years of

[9]Mentioned by Zanotto, p. 317 f.

[10]Renoux, p. 244 ss.; Brischar, Bd. II, S. 166.

maturity; which faded under sufferings and withered in the tomb; this flower, I say, came forth anew, fresh and living, in the resurrection, it took on a new splendor, and its beauty is more ravishing than ever before. That tomb became a garden-plot where bloomed that most beautiful and precious of flowers, our Lord, our Saviour. . . . The birth of the flowers and their first germination comes to mind. As soon as the earth, on the third day of creation, was separated from the waters of the sea wherein it had been submerged, it began at once to become green and to cover itself with flowers and fruits; thus was it at the saving of the world; scarcely delivered from the yoke of death which had held it in bondage, it appeared with a thousand ornaments. In the same manner the divine tomb on the third day became a magnificent bed of flowers, whence arose the most beautiful, the most holy, the most rare, even Jesus Christ, glittering with immortality! . . . O! could I, O! could my hearers, breathe its perfume! O, that we might carry it in our memories, plant it in our hearts, water it with our pious tears, warm it with the fire of our love! Just as the bees direct their flight toward the roses, so may our souls take their flight toward its fragrant stem, thence to draw the dew of heavenly graces and the honey of veritable joy!"

Contemporary with Staudacher, though living a little longer, was another Jesuit preacher of renown, Victor Scheffer (d. 1717),[11] a Bohemian. He also was of the poetic and mystic type. In a sermon of his on the words of our Lord to the disciples regarding the persecutions which would overtake them, there is much of this strain, but it is too lengthily drawn out to be very effective. But the earnestness and piety of the preacher are in evidence, as a brief extract will show. Quoting Augustine, he has compared the heart of his hearer to a barque vexed by storms here on the sea of earthly experience, and says: "Pious hearers! you to whom this world is a sea of sufferings, I wish to suggest to you a means of consolation. It is included in these words, 'I have told you these things in order that when the hour is come you may remember that I have told you of them.' *Sursum*

[11]*Id.* p. 247 f.

corda! Upward, Christian hearts! Your heart is your barque; it is upward it must tend, or you will never find repose; it is there that are to be found the mountains of Armenia, where rests the true ark of the divine Noah, the cross of Christ; it is from this side that you must direct your flight, O dove of Noah, for in this valley flooded with tears as of a deluge, you will find no refuge; the dove floats in the air like a barque on the waves; the barque must be empty of water if it would land; and the birds have received that instinct of nature that they shake off the dust and the mud when they rise into the air; adieu, earth! they say, as they mount to the skies. O, faithful Christian, lighten your ship: that is, put out of your heart the lusts and the desires of the false earthly goods here below if you would reach port. Adieu, earth, he will say; adieu, vile clay; and he will mount toward the skies."

Another Jesuit preacher of this time was Gerhard Pauli (1648-1715),[12] who was born near Paderborn in Westphalia, and received the Jesuit training at Vienna. Designated as a preacher in 1667, he gave the festival sermons at several prominent places, and attracted notice by his oratorical powers. At first he adopted the artificial and labored style then so common, and sought popularity; but he received a spiritual uplift and took a new line. He burned his fine sermons and began to preach in a simple, more spiritual and earnest way. This drew large crowds and resulted in great good. He had a fine, magnetic nature and gave his best to his preaching. He was called the "German Chrysostom" of his time. He wore out his strength in his work, was several times carried almost fainting from the pulpit, until his superiors finally forbade his preaching. His sermons were published after his death, and reading the extracts given by Brischar we find them clear, simple, appealing, perhaps too full of quotations, but strong in illustration and earnest in tone. A fair sample is as follows: "Historians relate of Phidias, the ancient artist, that he could make the most beautiful statues out of any material that came to hand. It was all one to him—gold or stone, silver or wood, iron or clay: in all he knew how to work the most

[12] Brischar, II, S. 908 ff., and 915 f.

lifelike images. Just such an artist should be our love. If God lays before her the gold of temporal fortune or the hard stone of varied need; if he sets before her the silver of human kindness or the iron of harsh persecution; so must she in all know how to set forth the lifelike image of a pure, divine love. Love and suffering, sickness and health, prison and freedom, poverty and riches, serve her equally well, because she is not working for reward. God alone she seeks, and beyond God nothing."

But leaving these and other men of less influence and fame, we must close our account of German Catholic preaching in the seventeenth century by a short study of the best known, and in most respects, the most important of them all, the Augustinian monk and court preacher at Vienna, Abraham of Santa Clara (1644-1709).[13]

The real name of this famous orator and writer was Ulrich Megerle (or Megerlin), but in accordance with monkish custom, when he entered the Augustinian order he abandoned it and assumed the appellation of Abraham of Santa Clara, by which he remains known. He was born June 2, 1644, in Kreenheinstetten, a little village of Suabia, now district of Moskirch in Bavaria, amid the mountains which shelter and supply the sources of the Danube. The father, Megerle, was a man of respectable standing and an inn-keeper. The little Ulrich among his children early showed the talents which afterwards made him famous, being studious, acute, and fond of speaking. His father cared for his education at the neighboring schools until the lad was twelve years of age. He was then sent to the famous Jesuit school at Ingolstadt, where for three years he studied with diligence and made excellent progress in the branches of learning cultivated there. After this several years more were spent at the celebrated school of the Benedictines at Salzburg, where he completed his academic education in 1662. He now became a novice of the Augustinian order, assuming the name of Abraham of Santa Clara, and

[13]See Kehrein, Bd. I, S. 77 ff. and Bd. II, S. 132 ff.; Renoux, chap. VIII; *Abraham à S. Clara, Judas der Ertz-Schelm;* Bobertag in Bd. 40, *Deutsche National-Litt.*, herausg. von Joseph Kürschner.

passed the years of his novitiate at the convent of Maria-Brunn, near Vienna. After this long training he was made a priest in 1666—twenty-two years old—and began his notable career as a preacher.

The first pulpit work of Father Abraham of Santa Clara was done at a convent of his order at Taxa, near Augsburg, whither he was sent to preach the festival sermons in the year 1666. His unusual gifts as a popular speaker at once attracted attention, especially his humorous and effective hits at common foibles and sins. In a year or two he was sent to be chief preacher at the Augustinian Church in Vienna, and, with the exception of an interval of seven years (1682-1689) spent at Gratz, Vienna was the scene of his labors to the end of his life, in 1709. Thus for about thirty years he was the leading preacher at the Austrian capital. His renown, influence, and opportunity were all enhanced by his appointment as court preacher in 1677 by the Emperor Leopold I—a position which he held to near the end of his course, when he was removed by Joseph I. During this time Bourdaloue was filling a similar position in Paris at the court of Louis XIV, Bossuet having preceded him for ten years previously.

There is inviting parallel and contrast between the two situations—the courts, the monarchs, and the preachers all coming in for comparison. Both courts were worldly and corrupt enough, as that is the way of courts. There was extravagance, show, insincerity, flattery, wickedness, in both. But at Versailles better taste prevailed in art, letters, and manners. There was also greater *prestige* and worldly glory. But none of these were wholly wanting at Vienna. The Hapsburgs have never been deficient in pride and pomp. As to the monarchs, there was much difference and little similarity. The one thing in common was absolutism and its accompaniments at once of tyranny and absurdity. Louis was unquestionably the abler man, Leopold perhaps the better—at least their faults were not the same. In his way, Leopold encouraged religion as well as art, as Louis did in his, with the advantage in sincerity on the side of the Austrian. But when the preachers are put alongside, what a difference! Perhaps it is unfair to

Abraham to compare him with both Bossuet and Bourdaloue; but it is in a measure inevitable. Bossuet was the ideal of oratorical art and taste; yet he sinned against art by excess of art, and against taste by nauseous flattery of royalty and worldly greatness. Abraham was rough, uncouth, even coarse, but he spoke his mind even at court and begged no man's pardon for using great plainness of speech; yet he, too, sinned by the excess of his virtue and descended to depths of vulgarity which no fair criticism can excuse. Bourdaloue, from the preacher's standpoint, was the best of the three. He did not soar with Bossuet, and he did not grovel with Abraham. He did not nauseate by flattery nor amuse by witty satire, yet he also was skilled in human nature and could bravely give reproof where it was demanded. Distinctly, therefore, Abraham falls below both of the famous Frenchmen. If his oratory be compared with that of Bossuet its power must be confessed, but, though given at court, it was oratory for the crowd; if his appeal to conscience be compared with that of Bourdaloue, its basis in thorough knowledge of the human heart must be conceded, but it is the appeal through mockery rather than reason, and awakens laughter rather than tears.

The course of Abraham's career at Vienna was marked by many events both of local and general importance, which he did not fail to turn to account in his work. Specially notable was the visitation of the plague in Vienna in 1679. During the scourge no one was more active, self-sacrificing, and useful than the great preacher. He played the man, and his excellent conduct increased his fame and influence. The change of rulers and the process of years and labors in due time brought about Abraham's retirement and failure in health. He accepted his retirement gracefully and wittily, remarking: "As for me, the court preacher hides himself under the gown of the monk, who scorns all the *prestige* of the world—even though he must sometimes wait his turn for an audience after a Jew! If this misfortune happens to a man of consideration, to an officer, without wounding him—since the Jews have elbow room now in every antechamber—I ought not to distress myself about it." But age and labors were wearing him out, and after a few years he succumbed. He died in great peace of soul December 1, 1709, grasping a favorite crucifix and with the name of Jesus upon his lips. He enjoyed through life the confidence and respect of his fellows, with the dislike only of some whom he reproved; and his fame rests secure amid the great preachers of his time.

Considering Abraham of Santa Clara as a preacher we see, from the brief account of his life, that the three principal conditions of high success were richly met in him: natural talent, suitable training, adequate opportunity. Besides the outfit of the oratorical mind and temper, he had the physical aids of an impressive figure, a fine face, and a good voice. He was, therefore, one of those rare and notable men in whom the main elements which go to make up the ideal orator are found. It is not surprising that he drew very large audiences and made instant and lasting impression upon them. Contemporary and traditional accounts testify with one voice to his power and influence; and were there nothing else to judge him by than these, his place would still be secure among the small group of the most effective preachers of history. That the world has not heard so much of him as of others, his equals or inferiors, is due to his situation in time and place. Had the Austria of the seventeenth century been the Germany of the nineteenth, his fame would have filled the world; or even then had a man of just his gifts and opportunities appeared in France or England he would have been, in his peculiar way, the peer of his mighty contemporaries in those lands; or had he lived in the thirteenth century and pursued the career of a popular traveling preacher, he would have been almost the twin of his famous fellow-countryman, Berthold of Regensburg. For he was a master of living speech; vivacity of action, rapidity of utterance, fluency of language, richness and variety of vocabulary, quick play of humor and imagination, keen insight into human nature, with wide acquaintance with both its general and local traits—all this, together with the native and trained faculty for magnetic extemporaneous discourse, went to the making of him.

But we are not left to accounts and descriptions alone for our knowledge of Abraham of Santa Clara. Though chiefly a powerful, popular preacher, he has, like many others, also left abundant published material by which the contemporary estimate may be critically tested. On the whole he stands the test as well as most. Leaving out all mention of minor works, of which there is some variety, the production on which his fame chiefly rests and by which he must be judged is his *Judas the Arch-Knave.* Originally a course of sermons, it has secured a recognized place in German literature as a religious satire upon human nature in general and its own generation in particular. It professes to be an unfolding of the origin, development, and character, and downfall of Judas Iscariot. But the account of Judas is extended far beyond the Biblical notices, though these are used fairly well, and is derived chiefly from the mediæval legends about the traitor, especially those found in the *Golden Legend* of Jacob à Voragine. It is needless to say how baseless and for the most part silly these are. In each discourse Judas, or that part of his real or supposed career which furnishes the text, is only the starting-point, a deal of other material—often irrelevant and remote—being lugged in. Of course there is the usual homiletical application to the times and audience of the preacher; and this is the main point of value and power. The first sermon in the collection exhibits his method as well as any. Judas was the son of Reuben and Ciboria, of the tribe of Dan, dwellers at Jerusalem. Before the birth of Judas his unhappy mother had a frightful dream to the effect that she should bring into the world a great criminal and scoundrel, who would bring disgrace and woe upon his family and others. This brings up the subject of dreams, which is the topic of the first sermon. Dreams are of three sorts: (1) Those which arise from natural causes; (2) those which are suggested by evil spirits; (3) those which are sent of God. The first are briefly discussed and illustrated. The second class comes in for fuller treatment and gives the preacher occasion to discuss all manner of wickedness as arising from the suggestion of the devil in the dreams of evil men. Some curious and some foolish cases are alleged as instances. It is admitted to be hard sometimes to say positively whether the dream comes from Satan or not. The third class of dreams finds illustration in the cases of Joseph and others mentioned in the Bible, and in many legendary ones. But here again caution must be observed, for it is not easy to tell every time whether the dream has certainly come from God, as, for example, in the case of Pilate's wife; though the preacher would place that under this head. Application is made, by way of digression, of how God uses little, common things such as dreams to draw us to Himself, and more directly, in the conclusion, to urge the duty of disposing the mind aright to receive in sleep any suggestion which God might thus make. If a good dream then comes, be sure to follow its leadings.

Abraham had much varied reading, though not much deep learning. He was no great theologian or thinker; and his use of Scripture is often forced and fanciful. Scherer says that he represents the Romanism of his day, not at its best, but at its commonest, being polemical, proselytising, and unfair, and pushing the peculiar tenets of his Church to their extremes. Catholic critics are naturally less severe in judgment; but they also notice his obvious faults of manner and spirit. As usual with preachers of the impressionistic and popular type, his virtues are often his defects; the exaggeration of strength is weakness. This exaggeration, however, was on the side of seeing with keen vision the evil of his age and hitting it with the club of the giant or piercing it with the rapier of the wit. Abraham, like many others of his sort in all ages and lands, was often irreverent and coarse beyond any need or excuse. He was a satirist and humorist in the pulpit. He did good, no doubt, but would have done more had he been more serious. He may have been less famous, but more lastingly useful had he chastened his scurrility into decency and subdued the wildness of his wit without prejudice to the keenness of his insight or the strength of his wisdom. He was one of the best of his kind; but his kind is not the best.

III. The Lutheran Pulpit

The general characteristics of the preaching of the seventeenth century found sufficient and varied illustration in the Lutheran pulpit, both in Germany itself and in the Scandinavian lands.[14] The close of the Thirty Years' War by the Peace of Westphalia in 1648 gives a convenient division point for all the history of the period, and not less than in other departments for that of preaching also. Yet, as is well known, the Peace only came as the result of exhaustion to all parties, no side gained the ultimate victory, many questions were left unsettled; and while actual warfare ceased, the ravages and desolation and utter demoralization which accompanied and followed the strife left their marks on every element of the religious life, preaching included. Still, the lessons of the war were not wholly lost, and peace gave to the pastors better opportunities for their work; so that it is natural to find on the whole some improvement in all the work, and particularly in the spiritual life of the pulpit toward the end of the century. This improvement is justly regarded by German historians of preaching as epochal in the work of Spener and his followers, Francke and others, under whom arose the great movement known as Pietism. But the germs of this influential spiritual movement were already existent and more or less active in the devouter preachers of the first half of the century, chiefly those who had felt the touch of John Arndt's refined and gentle piety. We may note, therefore, but need not insist upon the middle of the century as a divisional point for our history.

A more appropriate line of cleavage than that of date would seem to be that of spirit and method in the pulpit; and the preachers throughout the century can be grouped according as they signalized in their pulpit work any one or two of those four marked features which are prominent in the age as a whole: polemic dogmatism, scholastic pedantry, fanciful or sensational impressionism, or genuine and earnest spirituality. Now, it is evident to the thoughtful student at a glance that it is far easier to detect and describe these trends or habits of the pulpit of the age than it is accurately to locate any individual preacher in a rigidly defined group distinctively marked by one or another of these features. A man may belong on the whole to one group rather than another and yet give evidence of one or more of the other tendencies in

[14] See literature given in Note 4.

his preaching. Thus John Gerhard certainly falls among the spiritual preachers, but he was at the same time a sharp polemic theologian; and J. B. Carpzov is the very essence of stiff and formal pedantry, and yet his sermons were also given over to strained efforts to strike the fancy; and even such devoutly earnest men as Valerius Herberger and Heinrich Müller yielded too much to the spirit of the age in its demand for the show of erudition and the display of imagery. Nor would it be fair even to those men who were swept away by one or more of the extreme faults of the age to say that they were wholly without regard to the spiritual good of their hearers in their work.

In regard to these features of the age another remark must be made. As stated above—dogmatism, pedantry, impressionism, and spirituality—the account stands three faults to one virtue; and this on a general view is not unjust to the Lutheran pulpit of the seventeenth century. But it is only fair to keep in mind that the three faults noted are but extremes or perversions of pulpit virtues, one-sided or degenerate manifestations of qualities that never can be spared from an effective presentation of truth; that is, courage of conviction, ample knowledge, popular appeal. And on the other hand, it must be sadly remembered that the indispensable virtue of pious devotion may sometimes itself degenerate into a narrow partisanry, which, by ignoring or discrediting the real worth underlying the extremes it attacks, becomes itself a fault.

The Lutheran polemic against Romanism had lost indeed its freshness and power, but none of its asperity. The old strife between Lutherans and Calvinists over the questions which divided them still resounded in the pulpit; and the stricter and more liberal parties of Lutheranism continued to pay each other the compliments of a warlike age.

In respect of the refinements of scholasticism and pedantry we find abundant examples, not only in actual sermons, but also in the homiletical principles that were taught and practiced in this unhappy epoch. There appeared a number of dry and stiff treatises on the art of preaching, published in Latin, and unfortunately read as well as written by preachers. They fall into a particularity of distinction and precept which is tedious in the extreme. Thus the limit was reached in a work of J. B. Carpzov the elder, who specified a hundred different "modes" of preaching.[15] Another treatise kindly reduced the number to twenty-six! But even John Gerhard, one of the best preachers of the time, in advocating a still simpler method, distinguishes and expounds eleven "modes," as follows:[16] (1) The grammatical, (2) the logical, (3) the rhetorical, (4) the histrionic, (5) the historic, (6) the ecclesiastical, (7) the catechetical, (8) the scholastic, (9) the elenctic, (10) the mystical, (11) the heroic. He admits that these are merely technical distinctions which may be variously modified and combined in practice, but he seems to think of them as workable and valuable guides in the composition of sermons, and that under his so much simpler system the more elaborate schemes of other homilists may be reduced. Doubtless all such strained and tedious homiletical theories broke down under their own weight in actual practice, and failed of complete exemplification in preaching; but it is unfortunately true that they did not utterly fail of recognition.

Besides this absurd theory, it must be owned that many sermons of the age are stuffed with undigested erudition. Schmidt remarks:[17] "To what a general dominance this taste attained is evidenced by the circumstance that even the better and the best men of that time were not able wholly to escape it, as, for example, Valerius Herberger fairly overwhelms his hearers with a crowd of stories gathered from all quarters, and in one sermon brings over the souls of his hearers in motley variety the names of kings and emperors, of warriors and scholars, of celebrated men and women." And Nebe[18] satirically exclaims: "Churchly oratory discards Scripture; this logic and polemic can not minister to edification. A man of learning stands in the pulpit before the poor people! And one step down a steep plane leads further still. The whole range of learning and of knowledge presses into preaching and in all the languages of the world demands hospitality!" Besides this ruck of learning there is a

[15]Schmidt, S. 122. [16]*Id.*, S. 123.
[17]*Op. cit.*, S. 125. [18]*Gesch. der Pred.*, II, S. 95.

wild riot of fancy. Illustrations, fables, stories, conceits, images, strained comparisons, overdriven metaphors, seek in vain to redress the grievance of pedantry and popularize in some degree these heavy discourses. This trend did not indeed reach its acme of excess till the next period, but it was well under way.

Some titles of collections and single sermons as well will illustrate both the more restrained and the more extreme practice of this method of preaching.[19] One of the better sort of preachers put out a book with this title, "The Heavenly Lovekiss;" another, "Holy Treasury of Pearls;" another, "Bitter Oranges and Sour Lemons;" another, "Pale Fear and Green Hope in Sleepless Nights." One tried to distinguish himself by the use of paradox in his titles, as for example, "Splendid Poverty," "Salted Sugar," "Heaven in Hell," "The Only-begotten Twin," and the like. Dr. Carpzov at Leipzig gave a course of sermons extending over a whole year, in which he compared our Lord to the various kinds of hand-workmen, a cloakmaker, a lantern maker, a welldigger, and even a brandy burner! Another spoke of the devil as a great ban-dog, and showed: (1) How he bit first Adam and then Christ in the leg; and (2) how Christ drove him back to hell, his kennel. The same, on another occasion, described our Lord as a chimney-sweep, and discussed: (1) The sweeper himself; (2) the flue; (3) the broom. Another discoursed upon sin under the likeness of a hole in one's sock, that begins small but constantly gets bigger. The collection in which these choice specimens find place was called, "The Spiritual Oil-Room," and is said to have passed through thirteen editions.

Finally, on this dark side of the subject, it must be regretfully stated that for the benefit of the less learned and gifted brethren a multitude of helps were provided to cram them with raw information on short notice and supply unlimited illustrations on every possible subject. But we must not think that along with these sad exaggerations and perversions there were no good preaching and preachers. Some of the better men must have at least a brief notice.

Notable among his contemporaries and highly es-

[19] Instances gathered from several of the authors mentioned.

teemed in later times was Valerius Herberger (1562-1627).[20] He was born and brought up at Fraustadt, a quiet town in southeastern Prussia, and here also he spent his life as pastor. His father was a furrier by trade, but withal a man of some talent and a writer of devotional poems. The boy was early left an orphan, but was kindly nurtured by a childless aunt, who sent him to school and intended him for a shoemaker. But the good pastor in Fraustadt—who was also his godfather—told young Valerius that his father had prayed and predicted that he would be a preacher of Jesus to his fellowmen. Thus the youth's heart was trained to his future lifework. He was prepared for his ministry by studies at Frankfort-on-the-Oder and at Leipzig. Called to a position as teacher and then deacon in his native town, he served awhile in these offices, becoming pastor in 1596. Declining various calls to other places, he served the rest of his life as pastor in his home town, where he was much beloved and useful to the end. Herberger's life was consistent with his calling. He lived purely and unselfishly among people who had known him from childhood. During a great conflagration his courage and prayers were a help to the community, and during a visitation of the plague his self-sacrificing and brave ministrations were an inspiration and a solace to his people. His life was inconspicuous, but he had his share of trials and sorrows in those terrible days of strife, and his ministry was a blessing, as his end was peace.

As a preacher Herberger was devout and spiritual. He eschewed angry polemics and sought to win by love and persuasion. He was no deep thinker, nor an erudite scholar; but his thought was sane and Biblical, his spirit earnest, and his method winning. His published sermons lived long after him and were useful in the homiletical and spiritual literature of his own and succeeding times. Their chief fault, as we now see it, was overindulgence in the fancies and conceits which marked the pulpit vogue of his age, leading to forced exegesis, artificial structure, and affectation of style—common faults of this tendency.

A man of a very different sort was John Gerhard (1582-1637), born at Quedlinburg of parents of good

[20]Schmidt, S. 86 ff.; Hering, S. 120.

social standing and carefully educated in common and higher schools. He at first studied medicine to oblige a kinsman, but through sickness was led to a deeper religious life and turned his thought to theology. He studied at Jena and Marburg, and was probably influenced by Arndt. His devotional turn was early shown by the production in his young manhood of perhaps the best known and most valued of his numerous writings, the *Meditationes Sacrae.* Already notable for both learning and piety, he had many and frequent calls during the early years of his life, and indeed was much sought after always. But his work was done as pastor at Heldburg, in the duchy of Saxe-Coburg (1606-1616), and as professor in the University of Jena (1616-1637). His chief distinction is as a theologian and defender of the Lutheran faith. His writings were very numerous, and as a theologian he was ranked even by Bossuet as next after Luther and Chemnitz.[21] Yet he is also entitled to consideration as a preacher, not only because after his pastorate and while professor he continued to perform active and notable service in the pulpit, but because of his homiletical teaching and influence. The defect of his sermons was their heavy erudition—often loaded down with quotations from Latin, Greek, and Hebrew, for which practice he made this naïve excuse:[22] "Next to the sermon I have busied myself to speak in the words of the fathers, and yet these words not always turned into German, because in their own tongue they have a stronger emphasis than in our German." He could not lay aside the professor in the pulpit, yet he was truly concerned for the spiritual welfare of his hearers. As Schmidt well says, "While he was not always sufficiently considerate of the capacity of his congregation, yet he held their needs strongly in view, and correctly recognized that a fruitful application of the gospel to the heart and the life of the congregation must be regarded as the chief requisite of every sermon."

Less able and celebrated than Gerhard, but somewhat like him, was Conrad Dannhauer (1603-1666), professor and pastor at Strassburg.[23] He was a bitter opponent of the Calvinists in the Palatinate, his sermons were

[21] Schmidt, S. 97. [22] *Id.*, S. 99, note. [23] Hering, S. 122.

loaded with learning and strained fancies, but were not devoid of spiritual aims and effects, and his influence was felt by men who learned to avoid his faults. In this connection may also be mentioned Paul Gerhard (1606-1676), a cousin of John, but in every way a different man from his more learned and famous kinsman. His was a sad life, for he was driven from place to place, now by the war, and now because he was not acceptable to the rigid orthodoxy of some leaders who thought more of the letter than of the spirit. Severe personal afflictions also befell him, and he described himself as "a divine tossed in Satan's sieve." But he was a loving and faithful pastor in the several places that he served, a devout and tender preacher, whose influence was pure and sweet against both the rabid polemics and the barren scholasticism of his time. Yet it is not in his sermons, but in his tender and still cherished and widely useful hymns that his chief significance and his enduring influence are to be found.

The most notable of the preachers after Arndt whose work fell within the first half of the century was the beloved John Valentine Andreae (1586-1654).[24] He was a grandson of Jacob Andreae, a stout and famous preacher of the earlier Lutheranism, and was born at Herrenberg in the duchy (now the kingdom) of Würtemberg, where his father was pastor, August 17, 1586. The father soon moved to Königsbrunn, where John Valentine enjoyed the best school advantages, and later completed his academic and theological studies at the University of Tübingen. After graduation he traveled as instructor and companion with some young men of noble family in Germany, Switzerland, France, and Italy. For a time he served as tutor at Tübingen with the purpose, as he says in his interesting autobiography, not only to take care of his now widowed mother, but also "daily through teaching to learn." Next to theology he loved mathematics. Besides the church fathers and Luther, he read much in Erasmus and Hyperius. Altogether he had acquired a manysided and liberal culture when, in 1614, he was ordained and began his ministerial work at the town of Waihingen. He served here for six years,

[24]Schmidt, S. 100 ff.; Hering, S. 121.

meeting with much success and many trials preparatory to the greater ones that were to follow. Würtemberg suffered terribly during the Thirty Years' War, and Andreae was one of the pastors whose work felt keenly the disastrous effects of the conflict. His second pastorate was at Calv (1620-1639), during the height of the struggle. These were years of losses, sufferings, and desolations. Recalling his more peaceful days at Waihingen, where he had some leisure for writing, he says that at Calv he "hung his pen on the willows of Babylon." In 1639 he was made court preacher at Stuttgart, a larger field of influence, but a position whose responsibilities and inherent difficulties were aggravated by the terrible demoralization in church and court following the war. He says his work was like a fight with wild beasts "where victory brings as little honor as defeat brings shame." But toward the end of his life, owing to the good-will of his prince, he was appointed to easier places, first at Bebenhausen, and then at Adelberg, where he died soon after settling, in 1654.

Andreae was a man of lofty and pure character, clear and penetrating intelligence, well rounded culture, and devout spirit. He fell upon evil days, and his righteous soul was vexed almost to despair, but his work was not in vain. He wrote, lived, and spoke with power and effect against both the moral corruptions of the people and the ruinous faults of the pulpit, that is, especially, the harsh polemics and the sapless pedantry which marred and almost nullified the preaching of the age. Of course, he was made to suffer for his convictions, but he did not fail of recognition in his lifetime and later. Spener wrote of him fifty years afterwards as one whom even then for the good of the Church he could wish to call from the dead; and Herder much later still described him as a "rarely beautiful soul" and as one who "blossomed as a rose among thorns."

Contemporary with Andreae, but in far northern Germany, were Joachim Lütkemann (1608-1655), professor and preacher at Rostock, and Balthasar Schupp (1610-1661), pastor at Hamburg. Both of these rose superior to the dogmatizing and pedantic tendencies of the age and preached with spiritual fervor and force. Of Lütkemann, Hering[25] says that he entered on his duties as professor with the motto, "I would rather make one soul blessed than a hundred learned;" and of Schupp, that his effective combination of humor and piety made him like the famous Geiler of Kaisersberg, although more spiritual than he, and "the most popular preacher of morals of the seventeenth century."

Among the men who labored after the peace of 1648, amid the desolation and sorrowful corruption of that age, a few of more than average force and influence deserve mention. Among the preachers of scholastic tendency none had any commanding influence in the pulpit; but the two Carpzovs—John Benedict the elder and younger—professors and preachers at Leipzig, were both men of note. The father (d. 1657) was pastor of the Thomas Church in Leipzig for about fifty years, and also served as professor in the theological faculty of the University. Something has already been said of his homiletical teaching and practice. His two lines of work interfered with each other, and he did not attain to great eminence in either. But he was not all theologian and homilist. One witness at least testifies[26] that "whoever has known the man more closely will acknowledge that he bore in his heart a true piety which also showed itself in many ways." J. B. Carpzov the younger (d. 1699) followed in his father's path, both as professor at Leipzig University and pastor of the Thomas Church. He was like him also in method and spirit. He was involved in controversies with Spener and others regarding Pietism, and the more spiritual method of preaching which that great movement introduced.

Far more important for the history of preaching are the preachers of the rising Pietist tendency, which traces its origin back to Arndt and reaches its height in Spener and Francke. In the latter part of the seventeenth and first quarter of the eighteenth century this more spiritual movement marked almost a revolution in both the theory and practice of German Lutheran preaching. At least some of its leaders must receive consideration.

Heinrich Müller (1631-1675)[27] was born at Lübeck,

[25]*Op. cit.*, SS. 122, 126. [26]*RE*, III, S. 145.
[27]Schuler, Thl. II, SS. 10-14; Schmidt. S. 106 ff.; Hering,

whither his parents had fled for a time from Rostock during the Thirty Years' War. They soon returned to their own city, and in Rostock the delicate youth received his home care and school education. He pursued University studies also at Greifswald, and on returning to Rostock he became a preacher and pastor, though also doing some work as a teacher and lecturer. His work was short, for he died in his forty-fourth year, after a long illness, during which it was said that his sick-bed was "for many members of his congregation a most blessed pulpit."

Notwithstanding his bodily ailments and pressing public duties, Müller was a busy and fruitful writer. Numbers of sermons and other devotional writings flowed from his active pen. His quality as preacher was of a highly spiritual and awakening order. He appealed fruitfully to the feelings and the conscience, and sought not in vain to lead his hearers to a living and working faith in the Saviour. Profoundly pious himself, and keenly observant of the life of the age, he attacked with power and success the formalism of the time and led many to a deeper spiritual life. In his early years he was ambitious of pulpit distinction and yielded to the taste of the time for a pictorial and flowery style of preaching. While he never entirely corrected the exuberance of his fancy, he became more and more chastened in style and sought earnestly by clear, winsome, and at the same time popular method of speech to enforce the truth. His influence, both during life and after, was greatly felt in promoting a truly spiritual pulpit eloquence.

Very much like Müller in type was the equally notable Christian Scriver (1629-1693),[28] whose principal work was done as pastor at Magdeburg, where he served for twenty-three years. His first pastorate was at Stendal, his last (very short), at Quedlinburg. His life was uneventful, his ministry spiritual, devoted, and full of fruit. He was greatly beloved during life, and his sermons had many readers and wholesome influence after his death. Hering says of him: "His utterance is in flow and fullness quite the clearest and most pleasing among the voices of contemporaries, and if not of compelling, yet of charming, force." He was rich and apt in illustration, and while a man of peaceful disposition, he earnestly and ably attacked the ungodly and immoral life of the times. His admirably Biblical and evangelical preaching was fortified and commended by a blameless and lovable character.

The wave of spiritual development in German preaching reached its height in the great Pietist, Philip Jacob Spener (1635-1705).[29] He was born in Rappolsweiler, Upper Alsace, January 13, 1635, of pious parents, who from his birth devoted him to the service of God. To his good birth and early Christian training were added excellent gifts of mind and traits of character. Others besides his parents interested themselves in the training and progress of the promising boy, so that he enjoyed the best opportunities, both of religious and scholastic culture. His studies in the usual branches of learning, as well as in theology, were pursued chiefly at Strassburg, where he enjoyed the instructions of Conrad Dannhauer and Sebastian Schmidt, both eminent theologians. Under a learned Jew, Spener took up the study of Hebrew and pursued it with diligence and success. He had a fancy for recondite subjects, looking into the Talmud, and as a side line devoting some attention to genealogy and heraldry. He traveled and studied in Swizerland (Basel and Geneva) and in France. He had a genuine thirst for knowledge, was always a diligent student, and therefore became a very learned and broadly cultured man.[30] After teaching a short while at Strassburg and Tübingen, he was, without his own seeking and reluctantly,[31] installed as a preacher in Strassburg in 1660. He loved to preach, but partly from natural disinclination and partly because of fondness for study, he greatly shrank from pastoral care. Notwithstanding this

[29]All the authorities on German preaching give much attention to Spener. Particularly valuable are the discussions of Brömel, Bd. I, S. 128 ff.; Nebe, Bd. II, S. 93 ff.; and Schmidt, S. 136 ff. See also Schuler, *Gesch. der Veränderungen des Geschmacks,* Theil II, who devotes much space to Spener's reforms; and Ker, *Lects. on the Hist. of Preaching,* p. 183 ff.

[30]Brömel, Bd. I, S. 128 f.

[31]Schmidt, S. 137, note, says: "Spener never in his whole life applied for a place, but accepted the various calls that came to him almost always with reluctance and only when convinced that it really was a divine call."

he was made pastor at Frankfort-on-the-Main in 1666, where he served for twenty laborious years and was then, at the earnest solicitation of the Elector of Saxony, transferred to Dresden. Here his activity and usefulness both in preaching and writing continued; but attacks and criticisms annoyed him, and finally he broke with the Elector, whose faults he firmly rebuked. His position becoming intolerable, he accepted a post of honor at Berlin in 1691. In this, his last office, he was relieved of pastoral cares, but continued to preach regularly and superintended the affairs of his district. His fourteen years of service here were on the whole peaceful and fruitful. In January, 1705, he celebrated his seventieth birthday with his family, but in less than a month (February 5th) he passed to his reward.

Spener is rightly held to be one of the most remarkable men of the German pulpit. Gifted with a strong and versatile intellect, an eager thirst for knowledge, and trained both by school discipline and the studious habits of years of patient industry, his scholarly outfit was adequate to the extraordinary demands upon it. Pure and pious from childhood, sincere and devoted in service, diligent and laborious in work, of blameless character and lovable disposition, he was eminently qualified for the preacher's task. But in two respects he fell short of the highest pastoral success: he was awkward, shrinking, and reluctant in the personal work of the pastor, though recognizing its importance and trying to discharge it as a duty; and his preaching, with all its excellent qualities, was lacking in rhetorical form and finish and was often heavy and dry. In his reaction from homiletical abuses he was too careless of true homiletical form, and yet he was a great preacher and a great teacher of preachers. It was his lofty spiritual conception of his office that made him a leader of men in spite of his dislike of personal work; it was the spirit, content, and aim of his preaching that made it powerful and effective in spite of its oratorical faultiness.

As early as 1676 Spener published an edition of Arndt's sermons, to which he prefixed an introduction with the title *Pia Desideria*.[32] These "Pious Longings"

[32] Ker, p. 189 f.; Brömel and Nebe, *passim.*

were for the following six things, as summarized by Ker: (1) Wider circulation and study of the Word of God; (2) Co-operation of pastor and people for prayer and edification; (3) The principle that in religion knowledge is not enough, but life as well; (4) Love and wisdom rather than argument in dealing with unbelievers; (5) A theological training which should emphasize heart and life as well as learning; (6) A method of preaching which should aim at conversion and edification—a true spiritual life both in origin and outcome. Spener's earnest opposition to the pulpit faults of his times was characteristic and constant.[33] He deplored and withstood the evil tendency to homiletical over-refinement, the stress on form rather than content; he criticised both the pedantry and the excess of fanciful ornament in preaching; he reacted against the doctrinal polemics and hard intellectuality of the age. In his own preaching, however, he went too far away from good form. He was heavy without being pedantic, he eschewed illustration, and his emphasis on thought and material made his sermons long, wearisome, and hard to hear and read. His style was dull, over full, prolix; his delivery lacked fire. The critics[34] wonder that he was heard with as much interest as is known to have been the case, and their reasonable explanation of his great success and influence lies in two things: (1) That the people were glad to welcome a new manner, even though it taxed their endurance; and (2) that the earnest and practical aim of Spener's preaching offset its lack of pleasing qualities. In doctrine Spener was wholly loyal to the strictest Lutheran standards; but while he correctly taught justification by faith, his main insistence was upon its fruit in sanctification; and while he contended for a pure Biblical teaching, "his polemic," as Brömel phrases it, "concerns chiefly nowhere doctrine, but only life." But it was mainly in his influence with others and not so much in the quality of his own sermons that Spener is to be reckoned as a reformer of German preaching. He sounded a much-needed note at a critical time, and under his lead a body of earnest spiritual preachers arose and left an enduring mark upon the German pulpit.

[33]Nebe gives many examples; *op. cit.*, S. 98 ff.
[34]Both Brömel and Nebe fully discuss the point.

Chief among the immediate followers of Spener must be reckoned the devoted and widely useful August Hermann Francke (1663-1727).[35] Born at Lübeck, he spent his childhood at Gotha, whither his father removed and filled a magistrate's office. But the boy was left an orphan at seven years of age. Like Spener, he had an early bent both toward piety and learning. It is said that at ten years of age he asked his mother for a room of his own so that he could the better study and pray. His studious proclivities were suitably encouraged and his education was received at school and university in Gotha, and further at Erfurt, Kiel, and Leipzig. He early developed a passion for Hebrew and Greek, which he called "the two eyes of theological study." He read the Hebrew Bible through seven times in one year! Yet (like John Wesley long afterwards) his zeal and piety were not crowned until after some years with a genuine and deep religious experience. He caught the spirit of Spener and others of that school and became the leader among those called Pietists. After lecturing and preaching for short intervals at Leipzig and other places, he finally found his lifework as teacher and preacher at Halle. First in a high school and then in the University upon its founding, he taught Greek and theology, and was pastor successively of two different churches. Here also he founded his famous Orphan House, the first of its kind among Protestants, the equally famous Bible House, and preparatory school for missionaries. With power he took hold of home benevolence and foreign missions in addition to his burdensome double work as professor and pastor. Yet among all his labors he put the chief emphasis on preaching. He fully accorded with Spener as to the aim of preaching in beginning and developing the spiritual life of the hearers, and in the principle that a proper interpretation and application of Scripture is fundamental in preaching. Again, like Spener, Francke is said to have been too long and particularizing in his sermons, but he had more of the natural gifts of eloquence, he paid more attention to rhetorical form, and both his style and delivery were

[35]Schmidt, S. 156 ff.; Brömel (only incidentally), S. 141 f.; Hering, 158 f.; Kramer, art. in *RE;* Christlieb, in *RE;* Ker, p. 201 ff.

more pleasing. Notwithstanding his enormous labors in other spheres, he did not neglect his pulpit work, and he drew and retained large and profited audiences throughout his faithful and efficient ministry. He died in 1727, and so his work covers the first quarter of the eighteenth century; but as one of the founders of the Pietist school, he belongs with Spener to the close of the seventeenth.

During this period there were outside of Germany a few preachers of note of the Lutheran faith, some in Holland, but most in Denmark and Sweden.[36] From a number briefly noticed by Christlieb a few of the more prominent may be named. There was Caspar Brochmond (d. 1652), bishop of Zealand, who is described as a strong theologian and exegete, but not much given to personal application of the truth to his hearers. On the other hand, a very practical, experimental, earnest, and widely influential preacher was found in Dinesin Jersin (d. 1634), bishop of Ribe in Jutland. Sweden has to her credit John Rudbeck (d. 1646), bishop of Westeraes, who excelled in learned and able theological exposition. Likewise J. Matthiae (d. 1670), bishop of Strengnaes, who appealed more to the feelings and was esteemed a strong and useful preacher.

IV. The Reformed (Calvinist) Pulpit

We must now pay some attention to the preaching and preachers of the Reformed, or Calvinistic, Churches in Germany, German-Switzerland, and Holland, reserving for separate study the French, English, and Scottish Calvinists.

In Germany the Reformed Churches and people continued to be the objects of fierce doctrinal attacks on the part of the Lutherans. But in spite of this and of the horrors of the Thirty Years' War they managed on the whole to hold their own, and, in fact, gained some ground. Their position was greatly strengthened by the adhesion of the Elector of Brandenburg early in the century. In the capitals of Zurich and Bern and throughout German-speaking Switzerland affairs in Church and

[36] See Christlieb-Schian, *Geschichte der Predigt,* in *RE.*

State were more peaceful and prosperous, being less affected by either the great wars or the sharp controversies of the age. In the Netherlands, as in Germany, France, and England, the turmoil of war and politics was great. This was the century of Dutch greatness and glory. Maurice, Frederick Henry, William II, and after an interval William III of Orange and England, were the famous stadtholders; Olden-Barneveld and the two brothers John and Cornelius De Witt were the statesmen; Van Tromp and De Ruyter were the sea-captains; Rubens and Rembrandt were the painters; Grotius, Arminius, Gomarus, Cocceius were the theologians, who have made this period illustrious in the annals of Holland and the world. Theological controversy raged between the strict Calvinists of the older school and the Arminians and Cocceians who defended the newer opinions.

Reformed preaching, like that of the other communions, felt the touch of the times. It shared and manifested both the faults and the excellencies which have been already fully brought out as characteristic of the age. The polemic spirit, bad taste—sometimes as coarseness, sometimes as excess of fancy—pedantry, cumbersome and tedious homiletics, are found in the Reformed pulpit as in others. But neither are there wanting traces of the more spiritual aims and saner homiletical methods also found among the Lutherans of the time. Very influential among some Reformed preachers was the admirable work of Andrew Hyperius, of which mention has been made.[37] As to the Calvinistic preachers of this century the great names are found among French Protestants and English Puritans, and not in the lands we are now considering. Yet there are a few of note.[38]

In Germany, Abraham Scultetus (d. 1624) was the leading figure in the first quarter of the century. His main work had been done, both as theologian and preacher, in the previous age, but he was still active and useful in the time we are now considering. Born in Silesia in 1566, he received fair educational advantages,

[37]See *ante*, p. 16 f.

[38]Christlieb-Schian, as before; and special art. in *RE* on Scultetus.

though somewhat interrupted by various troubles. He became an excellent teacher of youth, both as private tutor and in schools, and a preacher who was heard with interest in the various places of his residence. Finally, after various trials and changes, in 1590 he settled at Heidelberg, where in several different offices as professor and pastor he ended his course in 1624.[39] Distinguished as a theologian and leader of his church, Scultetus was also a worthy pastor and preacher. Several volumes of his sermons were published, and one, a series of "Church postils," ran through several editions and was translated into other languages. Later in this century Bernhard Meier (d. 1681), pastor at Bremen, is named as one of the most notable preachers of the Reformed faith, of whose sermons on the Gospels and on the Heidelberg Catechism a goodly number was published.

In Switzerland there do not seem to have been in this period any preachers in the German tongue of marked excellence or fame; but Christlieb names two as worthy of mention in maintaining the succession of the Reformed pulpit. These are Felix Wyss (d. 1666), pastor at Zurich, and Samuel Eyen (d. 1700), pastor at Bern.

In Holland[40] the state of affairs existing at the end of the sixteenth century[41] continued, with aggravation, into the seventeenth. Pedantry, bombast, and polemics were the marks of the preaching of the Reformed Dutch pulpit in the early part of the century, but there was some improvement toward the middle and end of the period, introduced by the rival schools of the two famous theologians, Voetius and Cocceius.

Gisbert Voetius (1588-1676)[42] was born at Heusden, and became a distinguished student at the University of Leyden. He served awhile as pastor, but was most eminent as theologian and professor at Utrecht, where

[39]Scultetus wrote, in Latin, his own epitaph which, after stating place and date of birth and death, simply adds: *Caetera dolor et labor fuere*—"the rest was sorrow and labor."

[40]See Hartog, *Geschiedenis van de Predikkunde,* Bl. 73-123; Van Oosterzee, *Prac. Theol.,* p. 146 ff.

[41]See *ante,* p. 16.

[42]Dutch and German encyclopedias for biography, Hartog and Van Oosterzee for influence on preaching.

he worked for forty years or more. He was a stern Calvinist and defender of the Synod of Dort against the Remonstrants and others. Both as systematic theologian and preacher he was more of a controversialist than an exegete, scholastic in type and uncompromising in spirit. But along with his scholasticism and dogmatism he carried a very genuine piety—in fact, he was strongly influenced by the German Pietists. His place in the development of Dutch preaching is defined by his scholastic method, his Pietistic principles, and the controversy which arose between him and Cocceius and long persisted among their respective followers.

The homiletical method and teaching of Voetius are to be found partly in his sermons and partly in his lectures. His ideas were expanded and systematized into several treatises on preaching by pupils of his. Two of these were of some merit and influence: *Tractatus de ratione concionandi,* by Hoornbeek, 1645; and *Manducatio ad sacram oratoriam,* by Knibbe, of which a sixth edition appeared in 1697. Van Oosterzee (following Hartog) describes the Voetian mode of preaching as "wholly analytic; dry and diffuse exposition of Scripture, perhaps alternated or concluded with more or less appropriate exhortation." The text was usually only a suggestion for theological disquisition, and the style was often marked by bombast, when it did not sink to flatness. Yet the pietistic trait of the Voetian method appeared in its earnest insistence upon true piety in the preacher and upon practical application to the hearer as essentials in preaching. Knibbe adopted as the motto for his treatise the Arabian proverb, "Knowledge without practice is like a cloud without rain." Yet it must be admitted that in the sermons of the Voetians—especially the earlier ones—dry scholasticism got the better of useful application, and improvement was greatly needed.

Among the preachers of this school Hartog names and criticises a number whom it would scarcely be edifying here particularly to describe. Not all pursued the same way. In some the application amounts to very little, in some it is distributed through the sermon, in others concentrated at the close with more or less elaboration.

There was a certain Smytegelt who published one hundred and forty-five sermons, in full quarto, on "The Bruised Reed;" there was a Jacob Borstius who stood near to Voetius as a friend, but whose work had the glaring faults of fancifulness and sensationalism. Though he knew how to attract the crowd and spared not to smite sin, he was a victim of inflated bad taste in his preaching.

Over against the Voetians we find arrayed the pupils and admirers of the eminent scholar John Cocceius (1603-1669),[43] who was one of the most noted and learned theologians of his time. Born at Bremen, he was educated at the University of Franeker—then and long afterwards an important school in Holland—where he also served as professor till 1650. In that year he was transferred to one of the chairs of theology at Leyden, where he served with honor and fame to the end of his life in 1669. Distinguished as an interpreter and lecturer on the Bible (especially Hebrew), Cocceius was also a preacher of some power, and he gave public expositions of Scripture and published commentaries. As against the topical scholastic method of Voetius he advocated a return to the expository method, insisting that the main business of the preacher was to interpret and apply the Word of God. The aim was good and the reform was greatly needed, even producing something of a revolution, and precipitating a long and bitter quarrel between adherents and opponents of the method. But unhappily, even among the Cocceians, the taste of the age for pedantry and scholastic refinements often led to a minute and wearisome examination of every phrase and word in the text, together with multiplied and needless definitions and explanations. In theology Cocceius was less rigid in his Calvinism than Voetius; and this, along with the difference of method in preaching, led to the long and mostly profitless quarrel between their adherents. The later Cocceians were divided into two schools: the Leyden group, who pushed this detailed exegesis to extremes, and the Franeker group, also called "earnest Cocceians," who sought to be more practical in application to the spiritual needs of the hearers,

[43]Same authorities as before.

and thus approached the pietistic wing of their Voetian opponents. Early in the eighteenth century, as we shall see, F. A. Lampe was enabled, by appealing to the better spirits of both parties, to effect some reform in the method of preaching.

The most important representative of the Leyden branch of Cocceians was Solomon van Til, who, as professor at Leyden from 1702 to 1707, brings us over into the next century, but as a preacher was chiefly active in the period under review. The other branch was prominently represented in David Flud van Giffen, pastor at Wyckel from 1674 to 1701, who carried his exegetical refinements too far, but yet often preached to the real edification of the people. Hardly so highly rated is D' Outrein, named by several of the authorities, and from whom is mentioned a wonderful sermon on Solomon's bedstead, which is taken as a symbol of the New Testament church!

The Remonstrants (Arminians) had in their eminent professor at Amsterdam, Philip Limborch (1633-1712), not only a learned and able defender of their views, but a preacher of fine skill in exegesis. He held several successful pastorates before he became a professor. To the Remonstrants also belong several strong preachers in the notable Brandt family. The elder Gerhard Brandt (d. 1685), famous as the historian of the Reformation in Holland, gave three distinguished sons to the gospel ministry. The eldest, Caspar (d. 1696), was a learned and much admired preacher; Gerhard the younger (d. 1683) had only a short life, but died highly useful and esteemed; Johan (d. 1708) was noted as a preacher of poetic gifts and vigorous eloquence.

Among the Walloon (French-speaking) preachers a number are mentioned[44] whose influence upon the whole was helpful toward improving the Dutch pulpit methods. They gave large place to moral teaching in their sermons, and more successfully than their Dutch brethren escaped the pedantry and bombast of the age. In the earlier part of the century Louis de Dieu is named with approval, and later Louis Wolzogen, who, besides being a useful preacher, was the author of a sensible treatise

[44]Hartog, Bl. 142 vv.

(in Latin) on homiletics. There was also Alexander Morus at Middelburg; and at Leyden the celebrated Frederic Spanheim the younger, of German descent and Genevan birth and training, a stout Calvinist theologian, and a scholar of high attainments.

A word should also be said concerning the separatist preacher Labadie (1610-1674), who was a Frenchman by birth, a Catholic in bringing up, and served as a priest of the Oratory in his early manhood. Being of reformatory tendencies, he was excommunicated and exiled. He joined the Reformed Church, preached for a time in England, but later in Holland. Protesting against the cold scholastic intellectualism of the orthodox Church, he formed separatist congregations, which finally became lost or merged with others. Labadie was a warm and enthusiastic man and preacher, who—as is ever the case with his type—had both sharp critics and very pronounced friends. He was not without influence upon men of the pietistic tendency in all parties—even Voetius was criticised for having too close relations with Labadie and his movement.

CHAPTER IV

The Classic Age of the French Pulpit

In the ever fascinating and impressive history of the French people the seventeenth century, or more exactly the period which lies between the assassination of Henry IV in 1610 and the death of Louis XIV in 1715, is supremely important. Its great personages and momentous events appeal with power alike to the scientific and the dramatic historian; its forces and achievements attract and burden the philosophic thinker; and its wealth and splendor of literary expression are a lure and a joy to the student, whether he be a thoughtful critic or merely a delighted reader. The first decade of the century witnessed the last years of the knightly Henry of Navarre, who with all his faults had the good of his people at heart, and was in the midst of large designs when the dagger of a fanatical assassin ended his reign before its best fruits could be reaped. His Italian queen, Marie di Medici, proved a weak and incapable regent. During the ministry of her feeble son, Louis XIII, affairs went greatly wrong; but soon after he attained his majority Richelieu came on the scene, and during nearly the remainder of that reign his genius for government made it illustrious in spite of the weakness of the sovereign. Sir James Stephen[1] says, "Richelieu was the heir of the designs of Henry IV, and the ancestor of those of Louis XIV." Louis XIII did not long survive his great minister and real master, and, like his own father, left a boy king and a queen regent to follow him. But Anne of Austria and her remarkable son Louis XIV were of different quality from their predecessors. During and for awhile after the minority of Louis, the crafty policy of Mazarin dominated the queen and government. But the young king soon asserted himself, and on the death of Mazarin in 1661 he actually assumed the reins of government and only relinquished them at his death, fifty-four years later. No finer summary has been penned than that of the distinguished English author already quoted:[2] "The two foundations of the absolute throne of Louis XIV were terror and admiration: The terror of a power which had subjugated the army, the church, the magistracy, the noblesse, and the municipalities; the admiration of a power to which literature and art, arms and fortune rendered their riches and their uninterrupted tribute. King-worship had never before taken so entire a possession of any Christian State. Never had the luxurious pomp of an Oriental court been so intimately and so long associated with the energies, the refined tastes, and the intellectual culture of an European sovereignty. During fifty successive years Louis continued to be the greatest actor on the noblest stage, and in the presence of the most enthusiastic audience of the world."

In a history of preaching we can be only remotely concerned with the military glories, diplomatic achievements, and internal administration of that great reign; yet these influenced all the other elements of the national life, including religion and its institutions. But the lit-

[1]Quoted in *Historians' History of the World,* XI, p. 485 f.
[2]Sir James Stephen, *op. cit.,* p. 525.

erary, social, and religious features and forces of that great age are more directly connected with our subject and can not be left out of view, though requiring only brief notice in a general survey of the causes which made the age of Louis XIV as notable for pulpit oratory as for any other meeting-place of life, thought, and art.

I. General Survey of the Preaching of the Century

The title of this chapter is fully justified by a study of the preaching which we meet with in France and its French-speaking neighbors during the seventeenth century.[3] While in Southern Europe, in Germany, and other lands, preaching, as we have seen, was depressed and comparatively feeble, it came to great power in England and in France. In each of these countries there were special and noteworthy causes which produced a phenomenon so markedly in contrast with the situation in other European lands. We come, therefore, to consider the causes and characteristics of the "classic" French preaching of this age.[4]

First, we must notice the influence of contemporary

[3]Of German authors, Lentz, Christlieb, and Hering, appropriate places in works previously mentioned; of American authors, Broadus, *Lectures on the History of Preaching,* p. 136 ff., New York, 1876; Pattison, *The History of Christian Preaching,* p. 214 ff., Philadelphia, 1903; James, *The Message and the Messengers,* p. 188 f.; Fish, *Masterpieces of Pulpit Eloquence,* II, pp. 3, 4, 21 ff.; Sears, *History of Oratory,* p. 228 ff.; *The World's Great Sermons,* Funk and Wagnalls, Vols. II, III; Wilkinson, *French Classics in English,* p. 137 ff.; of French authors, Bungener (translation), *The Preacher and the King;* Feugère, *Bourdaloue, sa Prédication et son Temps;* Vinet, *Histoire de la Prédication parmi les Réformés de la France au 17me Siècle* (a very valuable work); Berthault, *J. Saurin et la Prédication Protestante;* Card. J. S. Maury, *Principes de l'Éloquence,* ed. Guilleminet, 1805; Abbé Ed. Boucher, *L'Éloquence de la Chaire;* La Bruyère, *Caracteristiques;* Hurel, *Les Orateurs Sacrés à la Cour de Louis XIV,* Paris, 1872; Jacquinet, *Les Prédicateurs du XVIIme Siècle avant Bossuet;* C. A. Sainte-Beuve, *Causeries de Lundi,* tt. IX, X; E. Gandar, *Bossuet Orateur,* Paris, 1867; P. Stapfer, *La Grande Prédication Chrétienne en France* (Bossuet and Monod). Works on French literature, and the lives and sermons of individual preachers in following notes.

[4]See especially Broadus, *op. cit.,* p. 136 ff.

literature in France. This was its Golden Age.[5] The writings of Rabelais, Ronsard, Brantôme, Montaigne, and some others in the sixteenth century had prepared the way for the splendid development which characterized the seventeenth. In the hands of these masters of literary expression the French language had already begun to acquire that clearness, force, and charm which were to make it the splendid vehicle of prose that it came to be in the classic and modern periods. There was much in the French national life of the age, as we have seen, both to stimulate and to form the literary expression of that life; and the task was eagerly accepted and nobly fulfilled. Early in the century Malherbe was court poet, and he set a high standard of excellence in style. Some minor poets and the great dramatists, Corneille, Molière, and Racine, and that consummate artist of the poetic fable, La Fontaine, followed to make the century illustrious. Of philosophers it must suffice to name Gassendi, Descartes, and Pascal—that prodigy in science and in thought, whose beauty of character and felicity of style are pre-eminent. Along with La Fontaine's fables we must not forget the genial child-stories of Perrault, who first put into writing such universal favorites as *Little Red Riding Hood, The Sleeping Beauty, The Tales of Mother Goose,* and other popular tales which have gone into all languages and been retold in many forms. Of essayists, historians, and other writers of thoughtful and descriptive prose there are familiar and brilliant names enough, among whom may be recalled the elder Balzac (apparently no connection of the modern novelist), Rochefoucauld, Madame de Sévigné (the famous letter writer), Madame de la Fayette (the leading novelist of

[5]Of course all the notable French historians and critics give large and able attention to this period, and it is scarcely necessary to adduce them here, though there may be named as specially helpful: Martin, *Histoire de France,* Vol. XV; Petit de Julleville, *Histoire de la Langue et de la Lit. Française; Histoire Littéraire de la France* (Daunou, Hauréau, and others), etc. In English Prof. Saintsbury's *Short History of French Literature,* and his article in the *Britannica* may be named. Wilkinson's *French Classics* in English; the survey in Vol. XI of the *Historians' History;* and that in Vol. XXXI (p. 39 ff, with the literature referred to) of the Warner *Library of the World's Best Literature,* may be consulted by American readers.

her time), Boileau the critic, La Bruyère the satirist, and others of less note. Among these the great masters of religious writing and of pulpit oratory found congenial literary atmosphere and a constant spur to the best expression of thought.

In the political and social spheres of activity we find another great influence in the development of the preaching of this wonderful time.[6] The general intellectual excitement of an age so intensely alert and active in diplomacy, war, development of resources, and other schemes for national aggrandizement, necessarily had its effect upon the pulpit. The great ministers of State and leaders of the national and social life encouraged literature, art, and preaching. But, as Broadus well says:[7] "The most singular of all the circumstances . . . referred to as stimulating the French Catholic preaching of that age was the fact that Louis XIV so greatly delighted in pulpit eloquence. It was a curious idiosyncrasy. He not merely took pleasure in orations marked by imagination, passion, and elegance, as a good many monarchs have done, but he wanted earnest and kindling appeals to the conscience—real preaching. In fact, Louis was, in his own way, a very religious man. He tried hard to serve God and Mammon, and Ashtoreth to boot. His preachers saw that he listened attentively, that his feelings could be touched, his conscience could sometimes be reached. They were constantly hoping to make him a better man, and through him to exert a powerful influence for good upon the court and the nation. Thus they had the highest possible stimulus to zealous exertions. And although they never made Louis a good man, yet his love for preaching, and for preaching that powerfully stirred the soul, brought about this remarkable result, that it became the fashion of that brilliant court to attend church with eager interest, and to admire preachers who were not simply agreeable speakers, but passionately in earnest."

In the religious history of the age there was one great element which powerfully stimulated preaching—

[6]Well sketched by Broadus, *op. cit.*, pp. 138-141; and for the influence of the king and court, pp. 148-150.

[7]Pp. 148, 149.

the religious toleration which prevailed under the operation of the famous Edict of Nantes, which was in effect from 1598 to 1685. That great measure of Henry IV gave relief from persecution to the harried and banished Protestants of France for nearly a hundred years. After the dreadful days of the St. Bartholomew Massacre (1572) to the Edict of Nantes (1598) the preaching among the Reformed (or Huguenots) was necessarily affected by the persecution, but as soon as liberty was given to the pastors to instruct their flocks there was a great revival of Protestant preaching. A noble line of preachers, full of earnestness and power, arose and flourished. Their abilities and success stirred the Catholics to greater diligence, and this was one of the contributory causes toward that marvelous outburst of sacred eloquence which distinguished the age of Louis XIV. It is no less notable that in the eighteenth century, after the death of Saurin (1730) and Massillon (1742), who were only survivals of the preceding age, there were no great French preachers, either Protestant or Catholic. On the pulpit as well as other institutions of France the repeal of the Edict in 1685 laid a killing frost.

Instead of attempting a general characterization of the preaching of this great epoch, it seems best to unfold its leading features as these appear in individuals and groups among the preachers, both Catholic and Protestant.

II. The Catholic Pulpit

Owing to the causes just outlined the French Catholic preaching of the seventeenth century, and particularly toward its close and just beyond it, reached its highest oratorical development. There was an earlier, less gifted succession of preachers who prepared the way for that renowned group who brought French pulpit oratory to its perfection—Bossuet, Mascaron, Bourdaloue, Fléchier, Fénelon, Massillon. Varieties of appeal and of method in the pulpit are well illustrated in the individuals of both the earlier and the later groups, as will appear in the following notices of them; but there are a few general observations which should be made before we discuss the preachers separately.

First of all, it should be remembered that this was Catholic preaching, orthodox and devout. Protestant readers and critics seem sometimes to overlook, or at least to underestimate, this obvious consideration. We can not fully understand or justly weigh any preaching without due regard to its general point of view and to the personal and cherished convictions of the preachers themselves. The universal elements both of the Christian and of the oratorical appeal will inevitably be colored by the creed and aim of the preacher. Romanist doctrines and sentiments pervade these discourses, and a Protestant may be permitted to admire the skill and earnestness with which they are presented without accepting them as his own, or making his very different doctrinal point of view a part of his criticism of the preaching as preaching.

Leaving the doctrinal content and attitude of these wonderful sermons and taking general account of their form and style, we note that their most obvious trait in common is their *art*. And in this statement there is exactly that balance of censure and of praise which careful attention to rhetorical art in preaching demands. Yet it is real art and not mere artifice. The art, especially in Bossuet and Massillon, is consummate. From introduction to conclusion the mastery of oratorical technique is superb. The rules are obeyed, but in the spirit of the master, not of the slave; structure and progress are apparent, but not obtrusive; language is clear, forcible, elegant, and varied as need requires. Bad taste—either in slovenliness and coarseness or in excess of fancy and ornament—is banished. The only serious exception as to taste is that flattery of the great, especially of the king, which sadly mars some of the most notable of these discourses. But even for that—bad as it is—some shadow of excuse may be found in the general habit of the age and especially its remarkable obsession in regard to Louis XIV. Readers of English who recall the absurd tone of the dedication in King James' Version of the Bible do not need to be told to what lengths even truly good men of that age could go in their adulation of royalty. But granting this, and some minor and occasional other defects, it remains true that perhaps never in the history of preaching or of any oratory was the art of eloquent speech brought to such a height of excellence as in this Catholic preaching of the age of Louis XIV.

Yet it would be false criticism to condemn this great pulpit work as mere show oratory. It was far from that. In the quotation from Dr. Broadus already made it is justly stated that these orators were not practicing art for art's sake, but they were really seeking the spiritual and moral good of their hearers. We should, for example, get a wholly one-sided view of Bossuet if we regarded him as a preacher solely from the point of view of his sublime Funeral Orations. In his less stately discourses he knew well how to use his unrivaled powers for the good of his flock. He reminds us very tenderly and simply of this in the closing words of his great oration for Condé, when he says, at the end of a splendid apostrophe, "With you these discourses shall end. . . . I reserve for the flock which I must nourish with the Word of life the remnants of a voice which is failing and of an ardor which shall soon be quenched." Bourdaloue bore down heavily upon the conscience; and Massillon earnestly sought to awaken and guide the purest and noblest sentiments; while Fénelon, least artistic of them all, was a mystic and a saint who longingly endeavored to raise the souls of his auditors to the holy presence of God.

Those earlier and less noted preachers to whom reference has been made included several men of decided gifts, who are only overshadowed by their Protestant rivals and their Catholic successors. The note of improvement over past conditions begins to be heard in Claude Lingendes (d. 1660),[8] Superior of the Order of Jesuits at Paris. He made the mistake, says Zanotto, of writing out his sermons, or rather treatises, in Latin, and thus "they present all the heaviness of the pulpit and of the school." Nevertheless the sermons have merit, and they have the distinction of having been carefully studied both by Fléchier and Bourdaloue. Voltaire[9] asserts that Fléchier

[8]See Maury, p. 101 ss.; Hurel, pp. 5, 28 (who dissents from the view that Lingendes' sermons were written in Latin); Jacquinet, p. 217 ss.; and Zanotto, *op. cit.*, p. 307.

[9]Broadus, *op. cit.*, p. 152.

borrowed considerable passages of his famous funeral oration for Marshal Turenne from Lingendes, and it is stated that even Bourdaloue made what would now be regarded as improper use of his Jesuit brother's material.

In this earlier group should also be named the famous philanthropist and founder of the Sisters of Charity, St. Vincent de Paul (d. 1660). He is said to have been a preacher of great zeal and earnestness; and some sermons remain as from him, but Zanotto thinks they were written out by some hearer who dresses them up in a rhetorical style that the saint would not have approved.

François Bourgoing (d. 1662), born of good family in the Nivernois, educated at the Sorbonne, for a short time parish priest at Clichy, became under Cardinal Berulle one of the founders and finally Superior of the Congregation of the Oratory at Paris. Perhaps without distinguishing merits as a preacher, he has been immortalized by being the subject of one of Bossuet's Funeral Orations.[10] The orator's tribute to Bourgoing's preaching is as follows: "The word of the gospel came from his mouth alive, penetrating, animated, all full of spirit and fire. His sermons were not the fruit of slow and tardy study, but of a heavenly fervor, of a prompt and sudden illumination. . . . Whence came his power? It is, my brethren, that he was full of the heavenly doctrine; it is that he was nourished and filled with the best essence of Christianity; it is that he made to reign in his sermons truth and wisdom; eloquence followed as a servant, not sought out with care, but drawn by the very things he was saying." This judgment is doubtless more generous and oratorical than critical; but it is worth repetition for its own sake.

Two other priests of the Oratory were notable as preachers in this time: Jean Lejeune (d. 1672),[11] famous as a "missioner," or evangelist, who was once smitten with sudden blindness while preaching, but went on with his discourse; and the better known J. F. Sénault (d. 1672),[12] who already gives token of the nobler elo-

[10] *Oraisons Funèbres,* par Bossuet, ed. Garnier Frères, p. 216 ss.; also noticed by Jacquinet with approval.

[11] Jacquinet, p. 140, gives him high praise.

[12] See Jacquinet, p. 182; and Hurel, I, p. 77 ss., who speaks of him as one of the reformers of eloquence.

quence so speedily to follow him, and whose funeral orations on Louis XIII and his mother, Marie de' Medici, have been greatly applauded.

Coming now to that great group of preachers who distinguished the close of the seventeenth and the early years of the eighteenth century, we shall find that of the six selected for notice, three—Bossuet, Bourdaloue, and Massillon—occupy the highest rank as pulpit orators; one—Fénelon—while just below these, is somewhat difficult to place; and two—Mascaron and Fléchier—while justly entitled to respect, certainly fall far below the rest. If method of appeal and the quality of oratory be regarded, we should say that Fléchier, Mascaron, and Bossuet represent the more distinctively rhetorical style and aims, appealing—Bossuet especially—to the imagination and the sense of the sublime; Bourdaloue is master of the ethical method, searching the conscience and convincing the reason; while Fénelon and Massillon more directly appeal to sentiment and stir the religious feelings. If we consider personal character and the value and permanence of spiritual influence, we should perhaps put Mascaron and Fléchier lowest, Bossuet and Massillon midway, Bourdaloue and Fénelon highest. But these groupings, though generally just, are necessarily flexible and incomplete. The true quality and value of each man can only be determined by individual study, for which the order of time will serve as well as any critical classification.

Jacques Bénigne Bossuet (1627-1704)[13] was born at Dijon of good middle-class family, September 27, 1627. His ancestors and his father had rendered honorable service in the legal profession. The boy was well endowed in mind and person, and received high social

[13]The histories of France and of French literature, the histories of preaching and oratory, with numerous critical treatises and special works, all give much attention to Bossuet. See Christlieb-Schian, Hering, Articles in *RE,* Zanotto, Broadus, Pattison, James, Wilkinson, Fish, and the Warner *Library,* previously mentioned; Didot's edition of the *Oeuvres de Bossuet,* and an edition (undated, but recent) published by Garnier Frères, Paris, of the *Oraisons Funèbres et Panégyriques;* E. Gandar, *Bossuet Orateur;* Stapfer, *La Grande Prédication,* etc.; Maury, p. 78, *et passim;* Hurel, I, p. 180 ss.; Ste.-Beuve, *C. de L.,* tom. X, p. 145 ss.

recognition and excellent education. His advantages were great; he used them wisely and well. He was dedicated to the priesthood and received the tonsure in his eighth year. Trained first in the Jesuit college at Dijon, he completed both his academic and theological course at the College of Navarre at Paris. His first academic thesis was submitted in his sixteenth year, and won such applause that his unusual talents and acquirements were subjected to a curious test. The great center of fashionable literary life in Paris had been founded in the time of Louis XIII by the Marchioness de Rambouillet at her splendid home; and its prestige and influence long continued to be a dominant force in the literary and social life of the capital. Says Wilkinson,[14] "At the high court of blended rank and fashion and beauty and polish and virtue and wit, thus established in the exquisitely builded and decorated saloons of the Rambouillet Mansion, the selectest literary genius and fame of France were proud and glad to assemble for the discussion and criticism of literature." It was before one of these assemblies that the gifted young student for the priesthood was by some freak suddenly summoned at a late hour to come and deliver off-hand a sermon on a text assigned. With characteristic self-confidence he undertook the task, and succeeded so brilliantly that he became famous from that moment. On this Broadus[15] wisely says: "All this was very unhealthy, but it shows the kind of artificial relish for pulpit eloquence which already (1641) pervaded the court circle, and what sort of atmosphere was breathed by these great preachers. Some other young men had become popular preachers in Paris before taking orders, and Bossuet was saved from this by the advice of a bishop, who urged him to turn away from such premature popularity and become mature in culture and character before he preached much in the capital. This was doubtless the turning point of Bossuet's career, which decided that he was not to be the meteor of a moment, but an abiding luminary." Bossuet continued his studies to the taking of his degree in 1652, when, at the age of twenty-five, he was appointed to an important charge at Metz. Here, admirably equipped in knowledge of philos-

[14] *Op. cit.*, p. 16. [15] *Op. cit.*, p. 160.

ophy, history, classic literature, theology, the Church Fathers, and the Bible, he labored as priest and preacher for seven studious, growing, and fruitful years. His career as a preacher falls into three periods:[16] (1) These seven years (1652-1659) at Metz, the period of youth and development; (2) the ten years (1659-1669) which he spent as court preacher at Paris, the period of maturity and oratorical fame; (3) the remainder of his life (1669-1704), during the first part of which he remained in Paris as instructor of the Dauphin and preached comparatively little; but after 1682, as bishop of Meaux, he devoted himself to the affairs of his diocese and preached a great deal, no longer as court preacher, but as Christian pastor.

Bossuet entered upon the second of these periods at a fortunate time for his success and fame. Mazarin was nearing his end (1661) and the young king was just entering on his own period of greatest glory. The preacher was already famous in Paris, not only for his youthful triumphs as a student, but also by reason of occasional visits and sermons at the capital during his work at Metz. He preached before the king and court as occasion required, and in various churches of Paris. Of his celebrated Funeral Orations a few of the less valued had already been given at Metz, and some of the more notable were to fall within the last period, but along with some others the two which are commonly considered his masterpieces were delivered in the middle period. These were the orations over Henrietta Maria, the unhappy widow of Charles I of England and sister of Henry IV of France, and her equally unhappy daughter, Henrietta, duchess of Orleans. These magnificent discourses placed the oratorical reputation of Bossuet upon a height secure and enduring, among the very noblest achievements of human eloquence.

The third and last period of Bossuet's work as a preacher began with his appointment in 1669 as bishop of Condom—a diocese remote from Paris and near the Pyrenees. This seems to have been more of an honorary elevation than a real one, as it does not appear that Bossuet ever lived in his diocese, for he resigned it the very

[16]Preface to *Oraisons Funèbres,* p. vi.

next year on his appointment as instructor to the Dauphin, the heir-apparent to the throne. During his incumbency of this office Bossuet wrote for his royal pupil his famous *Universal History*, as well as some other treatises. His writing and teaching occupied most of his time, and he does not appear to have preached very often. But on the conclusion of his term of service—which certainly came to no signal results—his fidelity at least and his other distinguished merits were recognized by the king in his elevation in 1682 to the bishopric of Meaux, a town only some twenty-five miles from Paris. He loved his charge, and was active and earnest in the performance of his episcopal duties. His preaching took on a new phase, or rather reverted to the pastoral method. He preached simply and plainly to the people from mere outlines. Only sketches of these sermons remain, but they are highly prized as specimens of Bossuet's more truly religious and gospel preaching. They show the same admirable outlines, orderly progress, and vivid style that appear in his more elaborate productions, but lack of necessity the grandeur and eloquence of the Orations. Yet it was during this last period that Bossuet, to whom now the nickname "the eagle of Meaux" was given, pronounced three of his great Orations—that for the duchess Anne of Gonzaga (a sufficiently difficult task!), that for Michel Letellier, and that last and in many respects greatest of them all, the one for the prince of Condé. This splendid effort closed that part of his work, and the rest of his life was given to his diocese. He died and lies buried at Meaux, the center of his last labors, resting in the cathedral that he loved.

Bossuet the man appeals less to us than Bossuet the orator. His wonderful gifts and equipment and many admirable traits of character can not be denied, but on the whole he is less winsome than commanding. He was an acute and powerful but not fair controversialist, and though not rude, apt to be overbearing. His early work at Metz, where he came in conflict with various sects of Protestants, with infidels and Jews, sharpened both his wits and his temper in controversy. His *Variations of Protestantism* is certainly one of the ablest and most effective of polemics. His devotion to Romanism and royalty, as well as his patriotism, unfitted him to deal judicially with English affairs. And so his vigorous attacks upon Luther and Cromwell display the splendid powers of the partisan orator and not the balanced analysis of the historical critic. In his famous debate with Claude, the Protestant preacher, his haughty unfairness was open to just exceptions. Also Bossuet's controversies within the pale of his own church brought him more success than esteem. By his stout defense of the "Gallican liberties" and the prerogative of his king as against the Vatican he is supposed to have missed the cardinalate or other high preferment, to which his eminent talents and services would seem to have entitled him. In his controversy with the saintly Fénelon over the latter's Quietism (mysticism) Bossuet gained his point, and his friend was forced to recant some of his expressed opinions; but the temper and method of the two show decidedly to the advantage of Fénelon.

That tendency of the age to flatter the great, and especially Louis XIV, on which comment has already been made, finds only too frequent place in Bossuet's orations. It exceeds the bounds of truth, and even of good taste; and with every allowance made for the manners of the time, it is unnecessary and unbecoming in a minister of God's Word to men and kings. Yet it must be said that Bossuet did not cringe; he could flatter, but he was not base. It is related that in regard to his dispute with Fénelon, the king asked him, "What would you have done had I taken sides with Fénelon against you?" and Bossuet replied, "I should have talked twice as loud." And on another occasion, after Bossuet had in a sermon boldly denounced the theater, Louis tested his candor and courage by asking him in company what he thought of theater-going; and the preacher met the test both bravely and tactfully by answering, "Sire, there are great examples for it, and great reasons against it."

This combination of courage and tact finds some notable illustrations in the funeral discourses. In that for Anne of Gonzaga,[17] for example, princess and duchess and highly connected, it was exceedingly difficult in the presence of royal and noble relatives and other great personages to be even charitably candid without giving

[17] *Oraisons Funèbres,* p. 104 ss.; Warner Lib., Vol. IV, p. 2216.

offense; and yet, on the other hand, to blink and thereby condone the errors of one whose sins had been notorious was impossible for the Christian preacher. Discounting and dismissing the inevitable flattery of rank and blood, we shall find the skill of the preacher admirable and instructive in its handling of his difficult problem. At the outset let Bossuet have credit for believing, as he doubtless did, in the original sincerity and tested reality of the penitence and conversion of the princess. Whether his auditors then agreed with him, or his readers do now, is beside the mark. It seems impossible for him to have undertaken the task unless he was so convinced; and of this his own words leave no doubt,[18] for in describing her conversion he says: "Thus she passed at once from a profound darkness to a manifest light; the clouds of her spirit are dissipated—miracle as astonishing as that where Jesus Christ caused to fall in an instant from the eyes of converted Saul the kind of scales with which they had been covered. Who then would not cry out at such a sudden change, 'The finger of God is here!' The result does not permit a doubt of it, and the work of grace is recognized in its fruits. . . . The princess Palatine changes entirely in a moment: no attire but simplicity, no ornament but modesty; she shows herself to the world at this time, but it was only to declare to it that she had renounced its vanities. . . . Twelve years of perseverance in the midst of the most difficult tests raised her to an eminent degree of sanctity." On this basis the preacher was free to deal candidly, though respectfully and charitably, with the sins of her previous life; but even then he is tactful enough to employ largely her own language in a written confession, language far stronger than he could have used, but which at the same time condemned her faults and emphasized her penitence. With all this in his mind we can see how the orator could thus open his discourse:[19] "I would that all souls far off from God, all those who persuade themselves that

[18] *Op. cit.*, pp. 125, 128, 129.

[19] *Op. cit.*, pp. 104-107. The text announced is Isa. 41:9, 10, which Bossuet renders from the Vulgate thus: "I have taken thee by the hand to bring thee back from the ends of the earth: I have called thee from the furthest places; I have chosen thee, and I have not rejected thee; fear not, for I am with thee."

one can not conquer himself nor maintain his constancy amid combats and sorrows, all those in fine who despair of their conversion or of their perseverance, were present at this assembly. This discourse would make them know that a soul believing in divine grace, in spite of the most invincible obstacles, lifts itself to the most eminent perfection. The princess to whom we render the last duties, in reciting according to her custom the divine office, read the words of Isaiah which I have quoted. How fine it is to meditate upon Holy Scripture; and how well God knows therein to speak, not only to all the church, but also to each believer according to his needs! While she was meditating upon these words (it is she herself who relates it in an admirable letter), God impressed upon her heart that it was she to whom He was addressing them. She believed she heard a sweet and paternal voice which said to her: 'I have recalled thee from the ends of the earth, from the farthest places, from the crooked ways where thou wast losing thyself, left to thine own judgment, so far from the celestial country and from the true way, which is Jesus Christ. While thou wast saying in thy rebellious heart, "I can not subdue myself," I laid My mighty hand on thee and said to thee, "Thou art My servant; I have chosen thee from eternity; and I have not cast away thy proud and disdainful heart."' You see with what words God made her feel the state from whence He drew hear; but hear how He encourages her amid the harsh tests to which He puts her patience: 'Fear not in the midst of the evils by which thou feelest overwhelmed, because I am thy God who strengtheneth thee; turn thee not from the way whither I lead thee, since I am with thee.' . . . Come now, ye sinners, whoever you are, in whatever far-off regions the tempest of your passions has hurled you, were you even in those dark lands of which the Scripture speaks, and in the shadow of death; if there is left to you any pity for your unhappy soul, come see whence the hand of God has drawn the Princess Anne, come see where the hand of God has lifted her. . . . You, then, who gather in this holy place, and chiefly you, O sinners, whose conversion He awaits with such long patience, harden not your hearts, do not believe that it will be permitted to you to bring to this discourse only curious ears. You shall be stripped of all the vain excuses with which you cover your impenitence. Either the princess Palatine will bring the light to your eyes, or she will make fall, as a deluge of fire, the vengeance of God upon your heads. My discourse, of which you perhaps believe yourselves to be the judges, will judge you at the last day; it will be a new burden upon you, as the prophets said, 'the burden of the word of the Lord on Israel;' and if you go not hence more Christian, you will be more guilty. Let us begin, then, with confidence the work of God. Let us learn before all things not to be dazzled by good fortune, which does not satisfy the heart of man, nor by fine qualities which do not make it better, nor by virtues (of which hell is full!) which nourish sin and impenitence, and which prevent the salutary horror which the sinful soul should have of itself." These extracts from the fine exordium, which is too long to be quoted entire, in some degree at least illustrate Bossuet's method of handling with both delicacy and boldness an unusually difficult situation.

In the three greatest of his funeral discourses—those on Henrietta-Maria, Henrietta of Orleans, and the Prince of Condé[20]—the superb oratory of Bossuet appears at its best, "the eagle of Meaux" soars highest. All the deepest feelings, loyalties, convictions of the orator were stirred to their depths; all his felicity of language, height of imagination, splendor of thought were used to their utmost power; pathos, force, sublimity of utterance take the reader captive. What must it have been to hear them! A fine and commanding presence, a piercing eye, faultless action, and a voice resonant, clear, powerful, and yet under perfect control—all these, and the subjects, the occasions, the audiences, combined to make these three deliverances immortal in the history of preaching.

[20]Fish, *Masterpieces,* etc., II, p. 23 ff.; and *The World's Great Sermons,* III, 85 ff., give translations of this great oration. Both translations are very faulty, and the latter—it is to be regretted—omits large portions without even indicating the omissions, thus spoiling the symmetry of the oration. Cardinal Maury, *Principes de l'Éloquence,* p. 80, is in my judgment correct in considering the Oration on Condé the masterpiece of Bossuet's oratory.

Jules Mascaron (1634-1703)[21] is the least known of the group, but he enjoyed a great reputation in his own time, even among the great ones. He was a priest of the Oratory, sometimes court preacher, and so popular as to draw great crowds wherever he preached. He was made bishop of Tulle in 1671, and of Agen in 1679. He also gave funeral orations, some of which were much admired. Feugère says regarding him: "It is to be regretted that the sermons of Mascaron are lost. Mascaron should not be placed in the same line as Bourdaloue or Massillon. . . . Madame de Sévigné has praised him beyond reason, and yet not without reason. . . . He is an orator of the second order, but who sometimes rises to the height of the greater ones." It is related of him (not Bourdaloue,[22] as is sometimes done) that on one occasion in preaching before the king and court he bore down so pointedly upon their sins that the courtiers winced and complained to Louis, who was in one of his better moods, and said, "Gentlemen, the preacher has only done his duty; it is for us to do ours."

Louis Bourdaloue (1632-1704)[23] is undoubtedly one of the greatest preachers of all history. He has not the sublimity nor the beauty of Bossuet, and not the sweetness nor the felicity of Massillon, but for strength and earnestness of thought he is their peer and more than their peer; less the orator and more the prophet than either. The Roman Catholic doctrines of his discourses must be allowed for—he was a priest and a Jesuit, orthodox and strong. The extreme length and fullness of his sermons was a fault he shared with all his great contemporaries—Italian, German, English, as well as his own

[21]Zanotto, p. 308; Hering, SS. 139, 142; Hurel, I, p. 110; Feugère, *Bourdaloue, sa Prédication,* etc., p. 165; some sermons reported to be his are preserved in Migne's *Collection Intégrale,* etc., but they are probably of doubtful authenticity.

[22]Even Broadus fell into this slight error, being misled by Feugère, whose reference is ambiguous.

[23]Feugère, *Bourdaloue, sa Prédication et son Temps;* Bungener, *The Preacher and the King, or Bourdaloue in the Court of Louis XIV; Oeuvres de Bourdaloue;* Fish, *Masterpieces,* II, 46 ff.; *World's Sermons,* II, p. 108 (same editorial fault as in case of Bossuet); Broadus, *op. cit.,* p. 163 ff., and some of the other authorities mentioned before.

countrymen; it was a fashion of the age. On the other hand, the universal elements of the Christian doctrine and morals are firmly held and powerfully presented, and in those long and sometimes heavy and wearisome discourses there are passages of tremendous power. So overwhelming was his assault upon the conscience through the reason that the great general, Condé, as is reported, once said on seeing him enter the pulpit, "*Silence, voici l'ennemi* (Hush, here comes the enemy!)" And a gruffer soldier, an old marshal, forgetful of proprieties and carried by storm by the preacher's appeals, capitulated aloud thus, "Zounds, he 's right!"[24]

Bourdaloue was born in August, 1632, at Bourges, where his father was a highly esteemed lawyer. The legal atmosphere in which the boy grew up no doubt trained and directed his native faculty for close discrimination and reasoning. The moral and religious training of the lad was the care of an intelligent and devoted Christian mother, who lived long enough to enjoy her son's success and renown, dying at a great age only a short time before he did. There was at Bourges a Jesuit college of no little distinction—the very one where Louis de Bourbon, afterwards the great Condé, was educated. Here young Bourdaloue received his college training. His aptitude for mathematics was marked, also for philosophy. He desired to become a Jesuit. Being an only son, it is natural that his father should have opposed his entering the priesthood. Louis ran away to Paris—only sixteen years old—and applied for the novitiate in a Jesuit monastery. His father went after him and brought him home, but the boy was so firm in his choice that his father finally yielded and took him back to Paris to the monastery. Studying and teaching for some years, Bourdaloue disciplined his powers for his future career.

He was nearly thirty years old when the sickness of an appointed preacher occasioned Bourdaloue's first service in the pulpit as a supply. His success was immediate and brilliant. He was sent to different places to conduct "missions." Crowds gathered. Feugère relates this interesting story:[25] "At Rouen the sermons of Bourda-

[24] Feugère, p. 106.

[25] *Op. cit.*, p. 14; well retold by Broadus, p. 165.

loue attracted an immense crowd. 'All the workmen quitted their shops to go and hear him, the merchants their business, the lawyers the court, the physicians their sick.' And Father d' Harrouis, who pays Bourdaloue this distinterested testimony, adds with good humor: 'As for me, when I preached there the year after, I put everything in order again: nobody left his business any more.'"

Thus well prepared for what was to be his life work for the thirty-four years appointed for him (1670-1704), Bourdaloue on the retirement of Bossuet in 1669 was called to be court preacher, and began his work with the Lent of the year following. There were intervals during which he was sent out to other places than Paris and Versailles, but it is wonderful testimony to his character as a man and to his power in the pulpit that for a full third of a century he could have been the most frequent as well as the most respected and best beloved preacher at the court of Louis XIV. Some time before the end he begged permission to retire, but it was refused, and he died in the harness in his seventy-second year. Louis XIV told him once that he would rather have him repeat his sermons every two years than to hear others preach new ones.[26] Nor was it preaching alone that occupied his time; carefully as he prepared his sermons, he yet found much else to do. He was much sought after as confessor, passing sometimes from four to six hours a day in the confessional; he spent much time in visiting the sick and preparing the dying for the end. And so when his last illness came he was ready calmly to say, "Now I must do what I have so often preached and counseled to others."

Bourdaloue was held in high esteem as a man of sincerity and purity of character. The enemies he made—and they were few—were only such as could take offense against a brave and true man who rebuked sin by both word and life. His disposition had that fine combination of gayety and sympathy which awoke affection and confidence. As we have seen, the confessional and the sick-bed were the scenes of his power and influence. But he shone in the social circle also, even in that brilliant court of Louis XIV, and the *salons* of the time.

[26]Feugère, p. 21.

His sympathy and complaisance naturally made him less severe in personal dealing with individuals than he was in rebuking sin in his sermons. One witty lady is credited with the saying, "Father Bourdaloue charges high in the pulpit, but he sells more cheaply in the confessional." But that this was due to sympathy rather than to laxity is both the more probable and the more charitable view. On the other hand, there is good testimony that in dealing with the individual sinner Bourdaloue did not compromise his moral principles. It is believed on good report that he several times refused to absolve the king himself, not seeing in the royal libertine any evident fruits of repentance. Once Louis said to him half jesting, "Father, you should be well pleased with me; Madame de Montespan is at Clagny"—not very far off! But Bourdaloue seriously answered, "Sire, God would be very much better pleased if Clagny were seventy leagues from Versailles." There is no doubt that he sought earnestly and bravely all his life to convert the king and reform the court.

In regard to the preaching of Bourdaloue we are fortunate in having ample resources for forming judgment. These data fall into three groups: (1) The sermons themselves, of which a considerable body remains; (2) the testimony of contemporaries; (3) the opinions of subsequent critics.[27] Taking these in reverse order, we find that criticism, French and foreign, Catholic and Protestant, gives to Bourdaloue an assured place among the great preachers of the world; opinions differ more or less as to some details. The consensus of favorable judgment recognizes the sincerity, earnestness, and spiritual fervor of the man; the high and intense moral quality and aim of the discourses; and the remarkable penetration, force, and skill of the reasoning they display. Differences of opinion and the sum of adverse comment have to do chiefly with details of content, form, and method. The unchristian critic naturally takes issue on many points with the views of the preacher, and the

[27]All these are fully represented in the literature adduced in previous notes, more especially in the comprehensive study of Feugère, to which I am greatly indebted.

Protestant balks at many of the doctrines advanced and modes of expression employed by the Jesuit theologian, while the non-scholastic modern mind is offended and wearied by the minute division of the matter and tedious prolixity of discussion found in these discourses. The inevitable comparison of Bourdaloue as a preacher with his two great contemporaries and rivals divides opinion. The literary critic, admiring the classic splendors and delightful clarity of Bossuet, and charmed by the smoothness, finish, and beauty of Massillon, at once puts Bourdaloue down as inferior in style, and generally in the art of expression. From the point of view of diction and artistic taste—the merely literary canon—the criticism is doubtless just. But this is not the proper canon for comparing and judging preachers of the Christian gospel, to whom form is (or should be) subordinate and only ministrant to the higher things of content and spirit. The critics who look from this watch-tower give Bourdaloue the first place among the three mighty ones.

In this the judgment of their own generation generally agrees. In the famous letters of Madame de Sévigné,[28] as well as other contemporary literature, the pre-eminence of Bourdaloue as distinctively a preacher is displayed and usually conceded. This, however, seems to have been more evident in comparison with Bossuet than with Massillon, who avowedly chose a different method from either of his great predecessors, partly no doubt just to be different, and partly also to avoid their faults. The formal and bony method of the traditional homiletics, which Bourdaloue did not discard nor so skillfully hide as Bossuet, called forth the strictures of Fénelon, and perhaps of others in that time as well as later. Besides this rhetorical infelicity, Bourdaloue fell into a very serious one in delivery. Absorbed in the reproduction from memory of his long and minutely divided and subdivided sermons, he failed to keep his eyes on his hearers, even

[28]These are freely used and quoted by Feugère, *passim*. In one she speaks of his having acquitted himself "divinely well" (p. 13); and in another of "making the courtiers tremble" (id.). A letter from one who hated the Jesuits says (p. 11): "Those good fathers of the Society proclaim him at Paris as an angel come down from heaven."

closing them sometimes for fear of being thrown off the track by anything he might observe in the audience![29] But despite such drawbacks of method and action, crowds came to hear Bourdaloue, listened with admiring attention to his logical and searching sermons, and carried away—even when they failed to practice them—impressive lessons in Christian truth and duty. Even in that worldly and shameful court his faithful ministry was not without fruit, and in more hopeful fields his sowing was not in vain. Many tempted and sinning ones found in him a spiritual father or moral guide, notwithstanding his own errors and their greater sins.

But it is time to give some notion, however slight, of the sermons of Bourdaloue. Confessedly in style they fall below those of his two competitors; confessedly in structure they overdo the minute analytical method; confessedly they are rather too coldly intellectual and argumentative. This was felt by Madame de Sévigné and others at the time, for in one of her letters[30] she says of his eloquence: "I am charmed with it, I am carried away by it, and yet I feel that my heart is not much warmed by it." This is ever the peril of the logical preacher, and Bourdaloue did not wholly escape it. But the style does not want vigor, clearness, and sometimes beauty and charm; the analysis is thorough, complete, logical, helpful to thought and memory; and in not a few passages the feelings are profoundly stirred.

As an example of Bourdaloue's analytical method Feugère[31] cites what he elsewhere refers to as the "terrible sermon" on Impurity. It was provoked by an atrocious crime in high life, and Bourdaloue could not keep silence before the court. It is a good example of twofold division of the subject-matter: Impurity a sign of reprobation, and the principle of reprobation. "Visible sign of reprobation, because nothing in this life can better represent the state of the reprobate after death; principle of reprobation, because nothing exposes us to

[29]Feugère (p. 152 ff.) discusses this matter at length and apologetically, though without admitting that Bourdaloue kept his eyes closed during the whole sermon. He also speaks of his good voice, rapid utterance, and attractive manner.

[30]Feugère, p. 151. [31]P. 91 f.

more certain danger of falling into the state of the reprobate." The first division is thus subdivided: "Four things perfectly express the state of a reprobate soul after death, and are the consequences of impurity: (1) darkness, (2) disorder, (3) slavery, (4) remorse." Again, the elements of darkness are set forth as (a) forgetfulness of self, (b) forgetfulness of his sin, (c) forgetfulness of God. The other points and the other general division are similarly treated. Each point is developed and proved with a thoroughness and comprehensiveness of treatment that leaves no corner of the subject unexplored. Well might it be called a terrible sermon; and it was timely, courageous, and impressive.

In the great sermon on *The Passion of Jesus Christ,*[32] the text is our Lord's saying to the weeping women of Jerusalem, "Weep not for Me, but for yourselves." Starting with the thought that the Passion of Christ was an event for weeping, he draws the lesson that we should rather weep for ourselves than for Him, *i. e.,* for our sins, for these are more sorrowful even than the passion itself. Having derived his theme in this circuitous and rather erroneous way, he proceeds to discuss the relation of sin to the Passion and analyzes thus:

I. Sin caused the Passion. In it we have not only a Divine Sufferer, but a Divine Penitent. Two parts of penitence.

1. Sorrow. In Gethsemane. (1) Not the dread of death; but (2) grief for sin.
2. Satisfaction. On Calvary. (1) How made? He became sin for us. (2) Why made? In Him only a suitable Victim could be found.

II. Sin renews the Passion. God does this in the Eucharist; man by his sins. In the same ways now as originally led to it.

1. Betrayed and forsaken by His disciples.
2. Persecuted by priests and ministers.
3. Mocked by Herod's courtiers.
4. Rejected by the populace, who prefer Barabbas.
5. Insulted by hypocritical worshipers.
6. Crucified by merciless executioners.

[32] Fish, II, 46 ff.

III. Sin defeats the Passion. In two ways:

1. Renders it useless. This broke the Saviour's heart and caused His cry of distress.
2. Renders it even deadly. (1) As to the Jews by their rejection, so to us by ours. (2) Adds to condemnation and justifies eternal punishment. (3) The blood which cleanses the saint befouls the sinner in the sight of God.—Suitable application made all along, and in conclusion.

Passing by errors of intepretation and doctrine, this is a very powerful analysis and presentation of the searching and sad theme. In the sermon are some very striking passages. In making application of his view that Christ in Gethsemane sorrowed chiefly for the sin He was bearing for men, he says:[33] "Behold, Christians, what I call the Passion of Christ, and what formed the first scene of His suffering! Is it thus that we consider sin? And does the sorrow that we feel on account of it produce in us proportionably like effects? Let us now enter into the secrets of our conscience; and, profiting by the model which God proposes to us, let us see if our dispositions, in the exercise of Christian penitence, have at least that just measure which must give it validity. Is it thus, I say, that we consider sin? Do we conceive the same horror of it? Do we lose tranquillity of soul in it? Are we agitated and grieved at it? Is this sin, by the idea which we form of it, a punishment to us as it was to Jesus Christ? Do we, like Jesus Christ, fear it more than all the evils in the world? Does it bring us by remorse for it into a kind of agony? Ah! my brethren, cries St. Chrysostom, touched with this comparison, behold the great disorder with which we have to reproach ourselves, and on account of which we must eternally weep over ourselves. A God-man is troubled at the sight of our sin, and we are tranquil; He is afflicted by it, and we are unmoved; He is humbled for it, and we are bold; He sweats even streams of blood, and we shed not one tear; this is what should terrify us. We sin, and far from being sorrowful even unto death, perhaps after the sin do we still insult

[33]Fish, II, p. 50 f.

the justice and providence of our God, and do we not say within ourselves, like the ungodly, 'I have sinned and what evil has happened to me?' Am I less at my ease on account of it? Am I of less consideration in the world? Does it diminish my credit and authority? Hence that false peace so directly opposed to the agony of the Son of God; that peace which we enjoy in the most frightful condition, which is a state of sin. Although the enemies of God, we do not allow ourselves merely to appear satisfied. Not only do we affect to be so, but we are capable of being so in reality, even so as to be able to dissipate ourselves and run into the frivolous joys of the age. Reprobate peace, which can only proceed from the hardness of our hearts. Peace a thousand times more sad than all the other punishments of sin, and in some respects worse than sin itself!"

In developing the point that Christ was mocked by the courtiers of Herod, and is continually mocked by those in the courts of even Christian princes, Bourdaloue delivers some telling blows, with as much force as courage, to the king and courtiers to whom he was speaking. In another sermon—on a *Perverted Conscience*[34]—he also strikes at the court life, as follows: "I have said more particularly that in the world in which you live—I mean the court—the disease of a perverted conscience is far more common, and far more difficult to be avoided; and I am sure that in this you will agree with me. For it is at the court that the passions bear sway, that desires are more ardent, that self-interest is keener, and that, by infallible consequence, self-blinding is more easy; and consciences, even the most enlightened and the most upright, become gradually perverted. It is at the court that the goddess of the world, I mean fortune, exercises over the minds of men, and in consequence over their consciences, a more absolute dominion. It is at the court that the aim to maintain one's self, the fear of displeasing, the desire of making one's self agreeable, produce consciences which anywhere else would pass for monstrous, but which, finding themselves there authorized by custom, seem to have acquired a right of possession and of prescription. People, from living at court, and

[34]Wilkinson, *French Classics in English*, p. 144.

from no other cause than having lived there, are filled with these errors. Whatever uprightness of conscience they may have brought thither, by breathing its air and by hearing its language they are habituated to iniquity, they come to have less horror of vice, and after having long blamed it, a thousand times condemned it, they at last behold it with a more favorable eye, tolerate it, excuse it; that is to say, without observing what is happening, they make over their consciences, and, by insensible steps, from Christian, which they were, by little and little become quite worldly, and not far from pagan."

Esprit Fléchier (1632-1710) has an assured place among the pulpit orators of the great epoch in which he lived. He was born at Pernes in the south of France, and with the exception of his sojourn in Paris, his life and labors were chiefly spent in that part of the country where also he died, at Montpellier. He was educated at Avignon and completed his academic studies at a very early age. While at school he gave special attention to the study of eloquence, and taught rhetoric for a while at Narbonne. He came to Paris in 1661 and became a catechist in one of the parishes of the city, spending also some time in teaching in various capacities. He gradually attracted attention by his preaching talents, especially excelling in funeral orations, of which he preached quite a number. Louis XIV recognized his worth and gave him various ecclesiastical promotions, till finally, in 1687, he was made bishop of Nimes, and spent the remainder of his life in that diocese. This included Languedoc, which contained many Protestants. The revocation of the Edict of Nantes two years previously made Fléchier's work in this region exceedingly difficult; but he was a man of gentle spirit and kindly disposition. He won the respect and even affection of the people, and died seriously regretted by all.

As an orator he was of the same type as Bossuet, but falls far below him in genius and skill. His orations were too evidently studied, with their carefully balanced periods and set phrases. Feugère[35] says of him that he

[35] *Op. cit.*, p. 164. See also a judicious estimate by Hurel, tom. II, p. 85 ss.

was an "excellent writer, one of those who have best known the resources of language. He conceals under a form too carefully worked out a basis quite poor which smacks neither of simplicity nor naturalness, and he was the Balzac of the pulpit; the cadence of his phrases, the studious balancing of his periods betray the rhetorician. . . . He perpetually commits the fault of confounding sacred eloquence with the academic kind." This criticism, though severe, is not without justice. Fléchier's greatest oration was that on Marshal Turenne, delivered five months after the death of that great general. It produced a profound impression and is really a worthy performance, though exhibiting the faults already pointed out.[36] One of the best paragraphs will give a fair sample of his manner: "Let us then, messieurs, derive from our sorrows motives for penitence, and seek only in the piety of that man, true and substantial consolation. Citizens, strangers, enemies, nations, kings, and emperors mourn and revere him. Yet what can all this contribute to his real happiness? His king even, and such a king, honors him with his regrets and tears—a noble and precious mark of affection and esteem for a subject, but useless to a Christian. He shall live, I acknowledge, in the minds and memories of men, but the Scripture teaches us that the thoughts of man, and man himself, are but vanity. A magnificent tomb may inclose his sad remains; but he shall rise again from that superb monument, not to be praised for his heroic exploits, but to be judged according to his work, whether good or bad. His ashes shall mingle with those of the numerous kings who governed the kingdom which he so generously defended; but, after all, what remains under those precious marbles, either to him or to them, of human applause, the pomp of courts, or the splendor of fortune, but an eternal silence, a frightful solitude, and a terrible expectation of the judgment of God? Let the world, then, honor as it will the glory of man, God only is the recompense of faithful Christians."

One of the best known and worthiest names in the history of French literature and religion is that of the

[36]See Fish, *op. cit.*, p. 70 ff.

pious and beloved François Salignac de la Mothe Fénelon (1651-1715).[87] He came of an old aristocratic family of the region formerly known as Périgord in the southwest of France. His remarkable talents and beautiful character already appeared in his youth. He was carefully educated and trained for the priesthood in the schools at Cahors and Paris, but his private studies and meditations were the main sources of his culture. In his twenty-fourth year he was ordained a priest and gave himself heartily to his work, chiefly in connection with the parish of St. Sulpice in Paris.

Fénelon's preaching was heard with pleasure and profit, but as he did not commonly write and preserve his sermons, only a few[88] remain as specimens of his pulpit work. It is as teacher, writer, and prelate, and above all as a devout and saintly man, that Fénelon is best known. The sermon on *Prayer* is commonplace, indeed almost tame; but it is full of good sense and of deep spirituality. Yet the traditions of Fénelon's preaching represent him as impressive and moving, though neither with Bossuet's soaring eloquence nor Bourdaloue's logical power. His views of preaching are given in his famous *Dialogues on Eloquence.* This book was written in his early manhood, and some of its opinions and expressions would doubtless have been modified had he revised it in later life; but on the whole it must be regarded as containing Fénelon's best thought on eloquence, especially preaching.

There are three interlocutors. A represents the views of the author, and does most of the talking; B is the

[87]Most of the authorities previously referred to, especially Maury, *passim,* and the *Éloge,* p. 379; and Ste.-Beuve, X, 16 ss.; good article by Lechler in *RE;* and a delightful account and apprciation by Wilkinson, *op. cit.,* p. 158 ff. Sermon (rather an essay) on *Prayer* in Fish, II, p. 97, reprinted in *World's Great Sermons,* II, p. 203 ff., apparently entire. Perhaps the best completed edition of Fénelon's *Oeuvres* is that of St. Sulpice, 1843; various separate editions of the *Dialogues sur l'Éloquence,* both in the original and translation, are to be found.

[88]The homiletical remains of Fénelon are found in Vol. II of the *Oeuvres,* p. 520 ss. They consist of ten sermons, including the *Panegyrics,* three "talks" (*entrétiens,* including that on *Prayer*), and eighteen short and simple plans of sermons.

learner with wrong views on many points, but willing to be taught, and finally accepting A's views; C is the interested listener who puts in occasionally with suggestions and side remarks, but in the main agrees with A. There are three dialogues. The first discredits the eloquence of which the aim is display or entertainment, and defends the view that the true aim of eloquence is to instruct the intelligence and improve the morals of the hearers. This is pre-eminently the aim of preaching. This was the better theory and practice even of the ancient rhetoricians and orators. The second dialogue shows that in order to reach this end the orator must prove, picture, and move (*prouver, peindre, toucher*), that is, appeal to the reason, the imagination, the feelings. Now for these purposes the extemporaneous delivery is best, of course after previous study. One should, however, avoid useless and catchy ornaments, and an extravagant and boisterous delivery.[39] The third dialogue discusses the interpretation of Scripture. Here Fénelon shows that the Bible itself gives examples and models for the Christian preacher. In this part he follows Augustine's treatise *On Christian Teaching* pretty closely, except that he discards the allegorical method of interpreting Scripture. Finally, he discusses panegyrics, which should conform to the principles laid down, and concludes with a quotation from Jerome: "Be not a declaimer, but a true teacher of the mysteries of God."

We can not here follow at length the life of Fénelon—his admirable teaching of young girls, and later his wonderful success with the grandson of Louis XIV, his appointment as archbishop of Cambrai, his mistreatment by Bossuet and Louis in the controversy over Quietism, his conciliatory demeanor toward the Protestants, his activity in benevolent deeds, his peaceful death. Well says Professor Wilkinson:[40] "Fénelon was an eloquent preacher as well as an elegant writer. His influence exerted in both the two functions, that of the writer

[39]On this the author remarks with as much grace as wit: "Rien ne me semble si choquant et si absurde que de voir un homme qui se tourmente pour me dire des choses froides; pendant qu' il sue, il me glace le sang."

[40]*Op. cit.*, p. 176 f.

and that of the preacher, was powerfully felt in favor of the freedom of nature in style as against the conventionality of culture and art. . . . Few wiser words have ever been spoken on the subject of oratory than are to be found in his *Dialogues on Eloquence*. . . . Fénelon, as priest, was something more than professional preacher, pastor, theologian. He was a devout soul, the subject of a transcendent Christian experience, even verging on mysticism."

The last of this great group of French Catholic orators was Jean Baptiste Massillon (1663-1742).[41] It is true that his long life extended nearly to the middle of the eighteenth century, but long before its close he had retired from Paris and the court, and he so evidently belongs to the group we have been studying that the discussion could not be complete without including him.

The story of Massillon's comparatively uneventful life is quickly told. He came of humbler origin than his great predecessors, though like Bossuet and Bourdaloue, he had a lawyer for his father. His birthplace was the town of Hières in the sunny south of France, the famed Riviera, east of Marseilles. His engaging disposition and brilliant talents attracted and retained admiration. He was trained in the college of the Oratorians at Hières, and became a priest of that order. Though a born orator, and from his childhood given to declaiming and speaking, he was modest and reluctant at first about preaching. His superiors and friends almost forced him to begin his great career at Paris in 1696, as head of one of the schools of his order. This involved frequent opportunities to preach, both at Paris and elsewhere. His success was assured from the beginning. Crowds flocked to hear him. In 1699 he preached before the king and court at Paris and Versailles. Then from 1701 to 1704 he preached the Lenten

[41]Much the same authorities as before; *Oeuvres Choisies de Massillon* (especially both the *Grand* and the *Petit Carême*); Maury, p. 164 ss.; a study by F. Godefroy, prefixed to Garnier's ed. of the *Oeuvres;* Hurel, II, p. 191 ss.; Ste.-Beuve, IX, p. 1 ss.; Art. by Schmidt in *RE;* sermon on *The Small Number of the Elect* in Fish, II, 138 ff.; reprinted in *World's Great Sermons,* III, p. 3 ff.; a particularly good discussion and several well-chosen and well translated extracts by J. F. Bingham in Warner's *Library,* XVII, p. 9780 ff.

sermons before the king. This series is known as his *Grand Carême* (Great Lent), and includes his most important sermons. In 1715 Massillon preached his world-renowned funeral sermon over Louis XIV. Two years later he was made bishop of Clermont, and in 1718 he was called to preach the Lenten sermons before Louis XV, great-grandson of Louis XIV, and now a boy of eight or nine years. This series of sermons is called the *Petit Carême* (Little Lent), so named from the brevity of the discourses and the fact that they were addressed primarily to a child, though of course in presence of the court and congregation. After this Massillon lived and worked in his diocese at Clermont, as Bossuet had done at Meaux, till he died at the advanced age of eighty years.

Massillon, like Bourdaloue, was great and remains eminent in his sermons chiefly. Bossuet and Fénelon gained distinction in other fields, including literature; but Massillon's sermons *are* literature. It is said that Voltaire kept a volume of them on his table that by frequent reading he might improve his own style. But, exquisite as it is, the style of these sermons is not their chief merit; in fact, it is so faultless as to be almost a demerit, as just such use of them as Voltaire's, the unanimous and unstinted praise of literary critics, and the delight of any reader appreciative of consummate art in diction, combine to show. Nor is their content so out of the ordinary range of contemporary Catholic orthodoxy as to awaken remark. The fundamentals of Christian doctrine and morals with the current and accepted Romanist teaching and tone, are the staple of thought. The peculiar power of Massillon's discourses lies in two things: the spirit which animates and characterizes them, and the method as a whole—not literary style only—in which they present accepted truth. Massillon avowedly chose a different line from the oratorical art of Fléchier and Bossuet and the analytical dialectic of Bourdaloue. On hearing some of these masters soon after coming to Paris, he said to a friend, "I feel their intellectual force, I recognize their great talents, but if I preach, I shall not preach like them."[42] As

[42]Quoted by Bingham in Warner, *Lib.*, XVII, p. 9782.

has been already pointed out, the spirit of Massillon's preaching was that of tender and intelligent appeal to the sentiments, rather than to imagination and reason; and the method was that of skillful adaptation of form to end, the persuasive quality of fitness. In him as much as in any orator is found the exemplification of Matthew Arnold's famous requirement of sweetness and light. But the light keeps the sweetness from cloying upon the taste. Massillon's was clear and trained intelligence; his breadth of culture and sobriety of judgment are apparent in his work, and his knowledge of human nature in general and of his own age in particular is amply in evidence. Some one asked him once how it was that being a priest he knew so much of the sinfulness of mankind, and his answer was at once honest and correct, "From my own heart." To this self-knowledge must be added that which he drew from close and discerning observation, and from the confessional.

The spirit and method which a reader finds in Massillon's discourses came to their hearers heightened and enforced by the personal qualities of the speaker. That nameless power which we vainly strive to express in such futile terms as "magnetism," "unction," "charm," and the like, was his. Aspect, bearing, voice, and gesture, all were pleasing, winsome, and forcible, too, though without any approach to violence. In these respects he was like John Wesley; he did not "tear passion to tatters," but he deeply moved and sometimes electrified his audiences.

Two specially notable instances of this wonderful effect of Massillon's speaking are of record. One was in the exordium of his funeral sermon for Louis XIV. Certainly the occasion and its accompaniments were impressive enough. Could any one rise to them? Massillon did. A great audience filled Notre Dame; the pageantry which had so large a place in the king's life was not wanting at his obsequies; but long before now the vanity of so much pomp had begun to be felt, and the shadows of coming decline and disaster were menacing the realm which the aged and outworn monarch had but just bequeathed to the little grandson of his son. The preacher reverently announced his well-chosen text, Ecclesiastes 1:16, after the Vulgate, "I spoke in my heart, saying, Behold, I have become great, and have advanced in wisdom beyond all who were before me in Jerusalem." Pausing for a moment to let the text make its own solemn impression while he looked with quiet dignity over the scene, and the audience became awed to breathless silence, Massillon said:[43] "God only is great, my brethren; and above all in those last moments when He presides at the death of the kings of the earth. The more their glory and their power have shone forth, the more in vanishing then do they render homage to His supreme greatness; God then appears all that He is, and man is no more at all that which he believed himself to be." The effect was tremendous; not so much, as Professor Wilkinson justly remarks, because the thought was profound or novel, but because it was so eminently true to the feelings of the audience, and so fittingly said.

The other instance is more remarkable still, both in being a double instance and in having no unusual occasion to stimulate and aid the effect. It occurred twice in connection with some sentences near the conclusion of the famous sermon on *The Small Number of the Saved.* The sermon had been delivered with powerful effect elsewhere, and by request was included and repeated in the *Grand Carême* series before the court. It is indeed a masterly effort, as even an imperfect translation shows; but the remarkable thing is that on repeating it, when the preacher came to the passage in question, the second audience though looking for it should, like the first, have been so profoundly moved as to break forth into groans and sobs!

It was on the conclusion of this *Grand Carême* that Louis XIV paid Massillon the striking and oft-quoted compliment: "Father, I have heard in this chapel many great orators, and have been much pleased with them; but whenever I have heard you, I have been displeased with myself."

In the *Petit Carême,* the ten Lenten sermons ad-

[43]*Oeuvres de Massillon, l. c.* The original is: Dieu seul est grand, mes frères, et dans ces derniers moments surtout où il préside à la mort des rois de la terre. Plus leur gloire et leur puissance ont éclaté, plus, en s'evanouissant alors, elles rendent hommage a sa grandeur suprême; Dieu paraît tout ce qu'il est, et l'homme n'est plus rien de tout ce qu'il croyait être.

dressed to the boy-king, Louis XV, all the sweetness and simplicity of style, the engaging manner, and the excellent judgment of Massillon appear. That admirable quality of fitness to audience and occasion never showed to better advantage. Delightful to read, these discourses must have been wonderfully interesting and helpful to those who had the good fortune to hear them. Yet both Maury and Sainte-Beuve after him give to the *Petit Carême* a relatively low place among Massillon's works—Maury hardly considers them oratory at all.

This inadequate discussion of the great French Catholic preachers may fitly conclude with the quotation of a part of the passage above mentioned from the sermon on *The Small Number of the Saved*:[44] "I confine myself to you, my brethren, who are gathered here. I speak no longer to the rest of mankind. I look at you as if you were the only ones on the earth; and here is the thought that seizes me, and that terrifies me. I make the supposition that this is your last hour, and the end of the world; that the heavens are about to open above your heads, that Jesus Christ is to appear in His glory in the midst of this sanctuary, and that you are gathered here only to wait for Him, and as trembling criminals on whom is to be pronounced either a sentence of grace or a decree of eternal death. For, vainly do you flatter yourselves; you will die such in character as you are to-day. All those impulses toward change with which you amuse yourselves, you will amuse yourselves with them down to the bed of death. Such is the experience of all generations. The only thing new you will then find in yourselves will be, perhaps, a reckoning a trifle larger than that which you would to-day have to render; and according to what you would be if you were at this moment to be judged, you may almost determine what will befall you at the termination of your life.

"Now I ask you, and I ask it smitten with terror, not separating in this matter my lot from yours, and putting myself into the same frame of mind into which I desire you to come—I ask you, then, If Jesus Christ were to appear in this sanctuary, in the midst of this assembly, the most illustrious in the world, to pass judg-

[44] Wilkinson, *op. cit.*, p. 151 f.

ment on us, to draw the dread line of distinction between the goats and the sheep, do you believe that the majority of all of us who are here would be set on His right hand? Do you believe that things would even be equal? Nay, do you believe there would be found so many as the ten righteous men whom anciently the Lord could not find in five whole cities? I put the question to you, but you know not; I know not myself. Thou only, O my God, knowest those that belong to Thee! But if we know not those who belong to Him, at least we know that sinners do not belong to Him. Now, of what classes of persons do the professing Christians in this assembly consist? Titles and dignities must be counted for naught; of these you shall be stripped before Jesus Christ. Who make up this assembly? Sinners in great number, who do not wish to be converted; in still greater number, sinners who would like it, but who put off their conversion; many others who would be converted, only to relapse into sin; finally, a multitude who think they have no need of conversion. You have thus made up the company of the reprobate. Cut off these four classes of sinners from this sacred assembly, for they will be cut off from it at the great day! Stand forth now, you righteous! where are you? Remnant of Israel, pass to the right hand! True wheat of Jesus Christ, disengage yourselves from this chaff, doomed to the fire! O God! where are Thine elect? and what remains there for Thy portion?"

III. The Reformed Pulpit

Twenty-six years of persecution and suffering for the Protestants of France lay between the Massacre of St. Bartholomew in 1572 and the decree of toleration of Henry IV in 1598, commonly called, from the place of its promulgation, the Edict of Nantes. Eighty-seven years of comparative peace passed under that beneficent even if incomplete measure of relief, till its fatal revocation under Louis XIV in 1685. Then awoke the horrors of persecution, the *dragonnades,* banishment. Preaching among the Protestants felt the influence of this course of events. The era of toleration under the

Edict, and the first years of exile after the Revocation, mark the highest point to which French Protestant preaching attained, at least until the nineteenth century, and in some particulars without that qualification.

For the study of the Reformed preaching and preachers of this period we are fortunate in having an excellent though posthumous work of that accomplished scholar and critic, Alexandre Vinet, professor at Lausanne early in the nineteenth century.[45] The book contains notices, biographical and critical, of the most important preachers, together with numerous citations from their sermons. This admirable treatment makes superfluous any independent study of the sources, and requires only occasional criticism and supplement.[46]

Vinet declares that in the Reformed Church of the period there were "great theologians, great controversialists, great diplomats, and above all great Christians." While it was true that the men of the highest talent were in the Catholic Church, "at bottom the Protestant Church was richer than its rival. . . . Catholicism outside of the great names had fewer good preachers than Protestantism." The critic candidly admits the literary inferiority of the Reformed preachers, but makes the obvious remark that they had not the advantages of the Catholics for the cultivation of literary taste. "Bossuet said of Calvin, 'His style is sad.' It might have been said of the most of the Reformed preachers. But Calvin is at the same time eloquent, and they are not always that. Their gravity is bare, despoiled of flowers of imagination: nothing in their situation, nothing in their past nor in their future was suited to enliven their style." They also needed to have more theology and polemics

[45]*Histoire de la Prédication parmi les Réformés de France au dix-septième Siècle,* par A. Vinet, Paris, 1860. The work is carefully edited from the mss. of the author, supplemented and filled out from the notes of the students. Broadus (*op. cit.,* p. 152 ff.) praises and follows this work; and I have the pleasure of using the copy which he read and marked for his own brief but vivid account.

[46]The editors in the preface call attention to several omissions, and sagely remark that those who might deem the harvest of original investigation too laborious could find abundant gleanings in the extracts which the volume contains—a remark which I gratefully endorse!

in their sermons than the Catholics. This tended to make their discourses heavy, and to reduce to narrower limits their appeals to feeling and conduct. But if these sermons suffered thus in spirituality and beauty, they gained in solidity and strength. To this must be added their Scriptural character, fruit of the Reformation, in which they far excelled those of the Catholic preachers. The Reformed congregations had in them a large proportion of thoughtful hearers who were versed in both the religious questions and the culture of the times, and these required a cultivated ministry. Vinet mentions that one man was deposed because of his lack of culture. On the whole the Reformed preachers were men of vigorous intellects and trained faculties, and if their style lacked literary art and beauty it did not want the solid qualities of clearness and power.

The preachers fall into an earlier and a later group, and—as was to be expected—those of the later paid more attention to literary finish than those of the earlier group. We shall do well to follow the order as well as the grouping of Vinet in the condensed account which follows.

Pierre du Moulin (1568-1658) is the first to be considered. He was born in Normandy, but received a large part of his education in England. After teaching several years as professor of philosophy at Leyden, he settled as pastor of a church in Paris, at the same time serving for a while as chaplain to the princess Catherine of Bourbon, a Protestant sister of Henry IV. Recognized as a leader among his people, and being familiar with the English language and affairs, he was called by James I to England to advise upon some scheme that monarch had for effecting a union of the Reformed and English Protestants. Later (about 1620) Du Moulin tried to enlist the active efforts of the English king on behalf of the persecuted Protestants of the Palatinate, and his correspondence falling into the hands of the French Government, was regarded as treasonable. Du Moulin saved himself by flight, taking refuge with the Duke de Bouillon at Sedan, which at that time was not French territory. Here he served both as professor of theology and as preacher for the rest of his life, dying at the advanced age of ninety years. His long life was crowned with a noble death. He kept his faculties to the end and, not wishing to die unconscious, he would say to his attendants now and then, "Awaken me, awaken me!" On which Vinet remarks,[47] "An emperor (Vespasian) wishes to die erect, a Christian wishes to die alive."

Du Moulin was a strong theologian and controversialist. The Catholics regarded him as their chief opponent, and long after his death even Fénelon thought it worth while to reply to one of his doctrinal works. But his writings were of a temporary sort, though serviceable in their time. During his long career at Sedan Du Moulin published ten "decades" (series of ten) sermons. One of these sets is dedicated to his three sons, two of whom were preachers, and after saying that he felt it his duty to write them some affectionate counsel so as to keep on speaking to them after his death, he pays this gentle tribute to his wife: "You are children of a mother who was a rare example of piety, of zeal, and of charity toward the poor. She lived as it is proper to die." He gives his sons judicious advice as to preaching and pastoral work, saying among other things:[48] "By serious and careful study endeavor to acquire the knowledge which is necessary to you. . . . The gifts of God ought not to be the cause of negligence. We are in a time in which great knowledge is requisite, and in which the adversaries will not leave us without exercise. God no longer uses the jawbone of an ass to conquer His adversaries." He cautions against the over-use of ornament in speech, urging straightforward simplicity. No doubt warned by his own past experience, he advises them not to meddle with political affairs, but to give themselves wholly to their proper work.

As a preacher Du Moulin was strong, simple, direct. The critic says:[49] "His sermons do not affect the form which had been used formerly. He does not preach, he talks. His plans are not learned, but very simple and little varied. He does not seek the art of multiplying or extending the matter by a subtle analysis; a talk, serious but familiar, of a father with his son would not be other-

[47] *Op. cit.*, p. 49. [48] *Op. cit.*, p. 16 s. [49] *Op. cit.*, p. 21.

wise ordered." The extracts quoted show Du Moulin as a solid thinker, without much of originality or profundity of ideas; as a live and vigorous speaker, vivid and clear, using illustrations and language often inelegant but strong, not an orator of the highest rank, but a virile and effective talker in his own age. Here and there occur passages of real beauty and strength. Here is an example:[50] "It is proper to consider the place where we are, namely, the house of God, where He communicates with us and informs us of His will: a place which the angels surround, which the world hates, which the devils encircle as wolves around the sheepfold of the Lord." Another, where, speaking of the death of Jesus, he says: "In His death He left His money to Judas, His body to the earth, and His soul to His Father, to teach us to have in dying less care for our money and our burial than for the salvation of our souls."

Michel le Faucheur (1585-1658) was a native of Geneva, where no doubt he received his education. His works show a well-trained and well-stored mind. He was pastor first at Annonay and then at Montpellier. Afterwards he was called to Paris, where he served some years before his death at the age of seventy-two.

Faucheur wrote a treatise on oratory, which shows sound knowledge and good sense. But he was known almost wholly by his preaching. He was heard with enthusiasm and made a great reputation. A number of sermons and sketches were published after his death. The analyses and extracts given by Vinet show that Faucheur, while not of the highest grade as an orator, was an admirable preacher. His sermons are, after the Genevan plan, almost wholly textual and expository; and both outline and exposition are clear, usually just and natural, and sometimes very striking. His style is better than Du Moulin's, somewhat more diffuse, but rapid, flowing, nervous. Imagery is infrequent, but illustrations are used happily. Controversy is vigorous, and the main doctrines of the Reformation are presented with force. The thought is eminently Biblical, the application sound and edifying.

Jean Mestrezat (1592-1657) was also born and edu-

[50]Vinet, p. 40.

cated at Geneva, and died as pastor in Paris about the same time as Faucheur. He had a brilliant mind and remarkably early development. At eighteen he taught philosophy at the Reformed college at Saumur, and was called thence very young, on the strength of one hearing, to be pastor at Charenton, that suburb of Paris which had been granted in 1606 as a place of worship for the Protestants, and was destined to have a distinguished line of pastors. The young Mestrezat sustained well the first impressions he made, and through life was noted for his courage and skill as a preacher of the Word.

The passages and analyses quoted from Mestrezat by Vinet sustain his criticisms. These are to the effect that Mestrezat had little of the oratorical faculty, less than either Du Moulin or Faucheur. The style is dry, and the treatment minutely exegetical and analytical. There is little application, less imagination, no pathos. His remarkable popularity and sustained influence are to be explained by the taste of his audiences—brought over from Reformation times and not yet declined—for such minute and forceful exposition of Scripture as Mestrezat knew well how to give. Then one imagines there must have been more of moving and impressive quality in the delivery of the sermons than appears in the printed discourses.

Jean Daillé (1594-1670) was born of good family at Châtelhérault. On completing his education he became tutor to two grandsons of the celebrated Duplessis-Mornay, and accompanied them for two years during a tour of almost all Europe. On his return he became for a while chaplain to his distinguished patron, on whose death he became pastor at Saumur. In 1626 he was called to be one of the pastors at Charenton, where he served for forty-four years, that is, till his death in 1670. He was a man of might in controversy, being regarded as the successor to Du Moulin in this respect. In 1632 he published a famous book, *Treatise on the Use of the Holy Fathers,* which subtly and forcibly attacked the authority of the Church Fathers in controversy. Of this book Vinet says:[51] "The novelty and piquancy of the subject; a plan, simple, pleasing; an excellent method;

[51]*Op. cit.,* p. 184.

a style easy and passably lively without any sharpness, made of this treatise the first truly popular book of controversy."

Daillé was also a preacher of some renown. He published twenty volumes of sermons which, Vinet says, "contain some quite remarkable things." One of these, much praised by a contemporary man of letters, the elder Balzac, discusses the value of the testimony borne by the apostles to the resurrection of Jesus. It is based upon the two arguments: (1) That they did not wish to deceive, and (2) that they were not self-deceived. The arguments are expanded, illustrated, enforced, and applied in a clear, flowing, agreeable style. Daillé was evidently a preacher to compel attention and interest, although not an orator of the highest rank.

Two other preachers of this earlier group are discussed by Vinet: Moise Amyraut (1596-1664), and Raymond Gaches (1615-1668). Amyraut was a theologian and author of a strong book on Christian morals. Skilled as a disputant, he was also a preacher, but carried the methods and spirit of the professor into his pulpit work. He was born at Bourgueil in Touraine, but spent his days as student, professor, and pastor at Saumur. Gaches for a short while served as one of the pastors at Charenton, and while not among the most noted he was distinguished among his brethren for his "fine and joyous imagination which knew how to lay hold of the poetry of Christianity, altogether neglected by his contemporaries. He had also some sensibility, one might almost say unction."[52]

These no doubt are the most important preachers of the earlier school of the Reformed. But there are some, not considered by Vinet, who would have place in a more exhaustive survey, such as Drelincourt—more noted as theologian and disputant than as preacher—and Morus, effective in the pulpit, and pastor at Charenton just before Claude, together with others here and there in France, not so noted, but useful and earnest in their work. But now we must pass on to the later group. Most of these were at the height of their usefulness at the Revocation, and carried—many of them—their gifts and labors into exile.

[52]Vinet, p. 287.

Jean Claude (1619-1687) is one of the great names in French Protestant history. He was born at La Sauvetat, a little town in the south of France, where his father was pastor. The elder Claude was a man of lofty character and solid learning. He paid careful attention to the training of his son, teaching him both literature and theology with great success. Some accounts say that Claude also studied theology at Montauban. Be that as it may, the better part of his education was received at the hands of his father, and by his own diligent lifelong studies. He became pastor of the little church at St. Afrique in the south of France. His pastoral duties there were very light, and this gave him opportunity for study, which he diligently employed. In 1654 he was called to be pastor at Nîmes, where he discharged his duties with fidelity. While there he also taught theology. In 1661 he presided over the provincial Synod of Nîmes, at which a proposal was made for some sort of alliance with the Catholic Church of that region. Of course, this could not have been anything but injurious to the Protestants. Claude declared with firmness that his people could not consent to such an overture without compromising their principles. On account of his stand against the Catholic party, he was forbidden to exercise his ministry further in Languedoc. This was the beginning of Claude's great career of controversy with the Catholics. He went to Paris to see if he could not secure the reversal of this prohibition upon his ministry, but he did not succeed. While in Paris he was engaged in several controversies and published some of his strongest works in defense of the Protestants, including his famous *Defence of the Reformation.* This work brought him great reputation among both Catholics and Protestants. In 1666 Claude became a minister in Paris, and from then on to the Revocation of the Edict of Nantes, in 1685, he was the leading figure among his people. It was in this time that he crossed swords with Bossuet. A lady of high birth, who was about to go over to the Catholics, arranged that these two great men should hold a debate at her house. Vinet well says that this was a spectacular performance, but it remains true that Claude acquitted himself remarkably well in this tilt with the greatest debater on the Catholic side. Bossuet himself admitted that he was afraid for those who heard Claude. On the Revocation of the Edict of Nantes in 1685 Claude was banished and received no indulgence, being required to quit the country in twenty-four hours. He withdrew to The Hague, where he lived only two years longer, preaching among the refugees and working as he could for the benefit of his people. Claude was a great man and a noble character.

Leaving out his controversial works and concerning ourselves with Claude's preaching, there are several matters of interest to be noted before discussing his sermons. Vinet well says[53] that Claude marks the transition between the earlier and later method of preaching. As we have seen, the earlier preachers followed the Reformation method of textual analysis and exposition. They did not produce what are called subject sermons. In Claude we find the beginning of the newer method, which deduces a subject from the text and discusses it on its merits. We see also in Claude the introduction of a far more classic and literary style than among his predecessors. From Claude on to Saurin there is a decided heightening of literary and oratorical power in the Protestant preaching. It is interesting to note here the interplay of influences between the Protestant and the Catholic preaching. The good work of the Reformed preachers in the earlier period certainly stirred up the Catholics to better preaching, and the great success of the Catholic orators of the age of Louis XIV in turn provoked their Protestant rivals to practice a better oratorical method. All this is illustrated in Claude, and not only in his discourses, but in his famous *Essay on the Composition of a Sermon.* This little treatise, notwithstanding its faults, had a great vogue in its own time and for years afterwards; translated by Robert Robinson into the English language, it influenced both English and American preachers, and has been one of the most highly prized of Protestant books on homiletics. It has a number of sound suggestions as to the various homiletical details and is especially valuable in suggesting the proper use of the Scriptures in preaching.

In regard to the sermons of Claude, it is to be re-

[53] *Op. cit.,* p. 303.

gretted that only a few have been preserved. In these our critic finds a marked improvement in style over the past, the evident influence of the taste and manner of the age of Louis XIV.[54] As to analysis, Claude seems to have a great preference for the twofold method of division, as several of his sermons show; he does not descend to subtle and minute subdivisions, but there is good logical order and clearness in his outlines. He has not much imagination nor pathos, but there is a tone of earnest sincerity and modest consciousness of both moral and intellectual rectitude. This gives to his discourses an air of dignity and authority not at all offensive, but compelling respect. His diction is accurate, clear, and strong; now and then it approaches the beautiful, but makes no effort to be fine. It is said that he carefully worked over his writing, being studious to secure accuracy and correctness in speech. The examples given from Claude's sermons indicate a high degree of intelligence and of earnest interest in the lives and characters of his hearers. Perhaps the most important and striking of the discourses quoted is that which he gave at the impressive crisis when the Edict of Nantes was about to be revoked; it was the dramatic moment in the history both of Claude himself and of his people. His text was the promise of God to Abraham in Genesis 17:7, 8. The sermon was put into writing after delivery, and some extracts follow: "My beloved brethren, you have asked for this exhortation; I give it to you with all my best wishes; it was conceived in haste and in the greatest distress of my grief, but as I perceived by the torrent of tears which it brought from you that it was blessed, I scrupled in publishing it to make any change. It is not a regular explanation of the text; grief did not suffer art and method. These are movements of my heart, broken with pain, and counsels of which I conjure you to preserve the memory. . . . When I think of the unhappy posterity which will rise in judgment against us,—alas! unhappy children of more unhappy fathers,—but you will have time hereafter to weep; care now for the single moment which remains to you. God is leaving you; this is the plain proof of it; here is the break: 'I will

[54]*Op. cit.*, p. 308.

not spare them longer; he that dieth, let him die.' And whither should they go, Lord? 'He who is appointed for death, to death; he who is appointed for famine, to famine; he who is appointed to captivity, to captivity.' . . . You will be without pastors, but you have for pastor the Great Shepherd of the sheep, whom you will hear in His Word. . . . You will have no more a temple, but the Sovereign does not dwell in temples made by hands. . . . Holy family of my Father, dear heritage of my God, sacred flock of my Divine Master, if I do not preach to you in this place I shall gather you in my heart; if I do not bless you from this pulpit I shall bless you in my heart, and there you shall be the main subject of my joy or of my grief. . . . Holy Father, keep them in Thy name! Lord Jesus, permit not the gates of hell to prevail against them! And Thou, Holy Spirit, Author of light and of grace, fill them with consolation and holiness! O our God, let not one sheep perish! O! that we may be able at that great and last day to see them all at the right hand of Jesus Christ, and that they may be our joy and our crown in the day of the Lord! Amen." We can see from these extracts the impassioned and sorrowful character of this farewell discourse. We can follow the aging and overwhelmed pastor as he goes into his exile, heartbroken for his scattered and persecuted people. It was a mournful event in the history of France and of the world.

Surely one of the noblest figures in that time of horrors is that of the irreproachable man, faithful pastor, and eloquent orator, Pierre Du Bosc (1623-1692). Du Bosc was born in the famous old town of Bayeux in Normandy, his father being a lawyer of note, who practiced before the courts in Rouen. Pierre was the youngest of thirteen children, and was endowed with excellent gifts of mind and nature, including in marked degree the oratorical temperament. If Claude was the thinker and disputant of his distressed Church at this crisis, Du Bosc was its orator. Vinet[55] quotes the following estimate by the historian Benoit: "He had all the gifts necessary to a Christian orator. He had a mind enlightened by knowledge of literature. He was a good

[55]*Op. cit.*, p. 350.

philosopher, solid theologian, judicious critic. He was very well made in person. He had a voice equally agreeable and strong, a very composed bearing, a robust body, vigorous health."

At the age of twenty-three Du Bosc became pastor at Caen, and could never be induced—though often invited and sometimes urgently pressed—to give up his beloved charge for another. He remained till persecution scattered his flock and drove him into exile. He was made to feel the heaviness and bitterness of the Catholic hostility all his life. Though naturally of a sweet nature, and, as controversialists went in those harsh times, a conciliatory and mild disputant, he was made to suffer for his courage in defending his opinions and the rights of his people. Once he was banished to Chalons for six months, and only allowed to return to his flock on the intercession of friends. A notable incident in his career was his appearance before Louis XIV in 1668 to plead against the proposed abolition of certain courts which had been established under the Edict of Nantes for hearing Protestant causes. This was one of the steps toward the overthrow of the Edict itself. The plea was of course unsuccessful, but it remains a choice and beautiful specimen of an eloquence simple, clear, strong, touching, and manly. Like many another great speech that did not gain a verdict, it did not fail for any fault of itself—the case was hopeless, though the orator was not.[56] At first the king was careless, but the eloquence of Du Bosc soon gained and held to the end his marked attention. He promised to look into the matter, but, like many other royal promises, it came to nothing. After adjourning the audience, Louis said to the queen,[57] "Madam, I have just heard the best speaker in my kingdom," and added, to the attendants, "It is certain that I have never heard such good speaking." As Broadus remarks, this was before he had heard Bourdaloue and Massillon, but he had heard Bossuet, Mascaron, and other orators of the time. Persecutions continued and grew worse. The

[56]Vinet gives it entire, p. 354 ff., and I only regret I can not do likewise, for it is—bating the accustomed flattery of Louis—altogether admirable.

[57]Vinet, p. 363; Broadus, p. 171 f.

great catastrophe was approaching. A year before the Revocation a process was instituted against Du Bosc and his church which resulted, in June, 1685, in a decree for the demolition of the house of worship and the banishment of the pastors twenty leagues from Caen. Churches of refugees in England, Denmark, and Holland at once called Du Bosc, and he accepted the care of that at Rotterdam, and reached there only a few weeks before the Revocation. Here, worn and broken, he spent the last ten years of his life, to the end a faithful pastor, the eloquent preacher of the Word of Life.

He who reads the ample and representative quotations which Vinet gives from the sermons of Du Bosc, and compares the eminent critic's judgments with his own impressions, will find in these discourses the sure token of an earnest eloquence, but yet not of the supreme rank. Du Bosc is indeed less artificial than the great Catholics, but he is far below them in all the particulars that made each one of them great; he does not soar as Bossuet, nor searchingly convince as Bourdaloue, nor sweep the feelings as Massillon. His style is limpid in clearness, his exposition is neat and evident, his arrangement is pleasing and lucid, his imagination is fine without grandeur, his illustrations frequent and varied, but not remarkably striking nor always in good taste. In tone and spirit, Scriptural and ethical content, and sincere desire for the good of their hearers, these discourses of Du Bosc hold a deservedly high place in the pulpit literature and history of their time.

The remaining preachers of this later group of the Reformed are exiles. They also pass over into the eighteenth century, but their works and methods showed the impulse and exemplified the spirit of the great age in which they received their training. They are essentially of the seventeenth century, though living beyond it. Only one of them is great—Saurin—but a few others must at least be briefly mentioned.

Isaac Beausobre (1659-1738),[58] born in Niort, and educated at Saumur, early fled to Switzerland, and then to Berlin, where for forty-six years he was the highly esteemed pastor of the French Protestant Church. He

[58]Not mentioned by Vinet. Art. in *RE,* II, S. 198.

was a strong theologian and disputant, and a faithful pastor. His eloquence was much admired.

Jacques Abbadie (1654-1727)[59] was born near Pau, educated at Saumur and Sedan, and early went to Berlin, where, both as preacher and apologist, he won fame and influence. Later he came to London and was pastor of the French refugees there. He attracted the favorable regard of William III, who appointed him to a deanery of the English Church at Killaloe, in Ireland. Abbadie's *Defence of the Christian Religion* was a great book in its time, and his sermons also were highly valued.

Daniel de Superville (1657-1728)[60] was born and educated at Saumur, but also studied at Geneva, under Turrettin. He was a brilliant student and remarkably mature in youth. Pastor for a time at London, he fled at the Revocation to Rotterdam, where, in two different churches, he lived and worked to the end of his life. Abundance, facility, imagination, benevolence, good sense, sound doctrine distinguished his sermons.

By common consent the greatest of the Reformed preachers of this epoch was Jacques Saurin (1677-1730).[61] The name Saurin appears with credit more than once in the literary and civic affairs of France. The father of the preacher was a leading lawyer of scholarly tastes and pronounced Protestantism at Nîmes, where Jacques was born eight years before the Revocation of the Edict of Nantes. At that memorable crisis the elder Saurin retired with his family to Geneva, where the promising son prosecuted his studies with the ministry in view. But the ardent youth broke off his studies at the age of seventeen and enlisted in an English regiment in the service of the Duke of Savoy, who was opposing

[59] Art. in *RE,* I, S. 18; Notice and sermon in Fish, II, p. 105.

[60] Vinet, p. 480 ss.; Fish, II, p. 121 ff.

[61] Literature previously mentioned, especially Vinet; and add: Berthault, *J. Saurin et la Prédication Protestante;* art. by Bonnet in *RE; Sermons,* translated by R. Robinson, various edd.; sermon in Fish, II, p. 157 ff. See also some notice of Saurin in the accounts of Dutch preaching given in the works of Hartog and Van Oosterzee. Maury, in his *Principes,* p. 167 ss., gives considerable attention to Saurin, comparing him with Bossuet, but finds him pedantic and heavy. Similar judgment is given by Stapfer in comparing Saurin with Bossuet in his *Grande Prédication Chrétienne,* which I recall from memory.

the French invasion of Piedmont. It is said that Saurin conducted religious work among his fellow-soldiers, and also won the regard of his commander, who made him a color-bearer. Louis XIV found it to his interest to conclude peace with the house of Savoy in 1696, and Saurin returned to his thelogical studies at Geneva, enjoying the instructions of Pictet, J. A. Turrettin, and other notable teachers. There is tradition that Saurin was not the most docile and reverent of pupils, giving some trouble with his self-assertion and questions, till one day one of his professors quoted to him the words of Ecclesiastes: "Rejoice, O young man, in thy youth . . . and walk in the ways of thy heart and in the sight of thine eyes; but know thou that for all these things God will bring thee into judgment." The reproof took effect; Saurin became more humble and serious. Before his ordination his speaking gifts were recognized, and "already he was remarked as preacher before he became a minister."

When twenty-three years of age—presumably upon completion of his course of study—Saurin made a journey to England, and was induced to settle in London, as pastor of the Reformed Church, which contained a number of the French refugees. He spent five years as pastor here. Broadus[62] tells us that "here, like a true Protestant, he married a wife.[63] Yet, though a real love affair, this union did not turn out very well. Unexampled as the case may be, the minister's wife was of an unlucky disposition; and being blessed with the company of a mother-in-law, sister-in-law, and two brothers-in-law, she made the house too hot to hold them. A bad manager she was, too, while he, for his part, was negligent and wastefully generous."

In 1705, his health having suffered from the London climate, Saurin made a journey to Holland, and having preached at The Hague with great acceptance, he was urged to settle there. At first he was made, by some special arrangement, a sort of chaplain or pastor to the "nobility," but later became one of the regular pastors of the church of French refugees. It seems to have been

[62]*Op. cit.*, p. 178.

[63]She was English, a Miss Boynton, and this must be taken into account in what follows.

the established custom of the Reformed Churches to have a body or company of pastors, after Calvin's plan at Geneva. Four are mentioned as Saurin's colleagues at The Hague: La Chapelle, Chion, Huet, and Chais, of whom the last became his successor as leading pastor. It is a sad thing that for some reason these men disliked Saurin and often made him the object of unbrotherly criticisms, and even of sharp attacks. It is hardly to be supposed that Saurin was wholly faultless in this painful matter, and the way he was made pastor-in-chief may have caused discontent at the beginning; but there can be no question that envy and spite on the part of these smaller men were the main sources of trouble. Vinet judiciously says:[64] "I can only explain the hatred of which Saurin was the object by his success, the indiscretion of his partisans, and the imprudence with which he let it be seen that he felt his own superiority."

On the other hand, Saurin had a multitude of friends who greatly admired him for his talents and loved him for his qualities. His power and popularity in the pulpit were maintained during a ministry of twenty-five years. It is said that at the height of his powers places were engaged in the church two weeks ahead, the streets were jammed with carriages, and people even climbed up to the windows to see and hear![65] In private life he was genial and generous to a fault. One story, greatly to his credit, should be told. A legacy of large amount was left to him. The will was contested by relatives of the deceased, and Saurin's ever-ready enemies sharply criticised him. To vindicate himself he allowed the case to go to trial; it was conclusively shown that the will was made entirely without his knowledge, and the legacy was awarded him; then, with proper conditions, but without retaining a penny for himself, he divided the estate among the natural heirs. When he came to die he sent for his four colleagues and fraternally interviewed them, asking their pardon if he had ever wronged them, and denying any evil intent in some of the actions they had resented and criticised. For the most part, they seem to have accepted the reconciliation in good feeling; at any

[64]*Op. cit.*, p. 600.
[65]See Broadus, *op. cit.*, p. 179.

rate, Saurin appears in a most amiable and Christian light in the matter. And so at last he closed in peace his varied, much tried, but nobly useful career, at the comparatively early age of fifty-three years.

Saurin had the external qualities for effective speaking—a good person, an agreeable and strong voice, an attractive manner. His intellectual qualities were of a high order, well cultivated and kept in exercise by study and careful preparation. He had a fine imagination, accompanied by penetrating and orderly thinking. He could have excelled as a philosophic theologian had his career taken that direction; but imagination and contact with life saved him from scholasticism, and his strength of thought and feeling sometimes rose to a splendid fervor that swept his hearers with him. His analysis was in the fashion of his time, too minute to suit modern taste; his style, too, was of his epoch, not of ours, in its fullness and detail; but it was usually clear, always forcible, sometimes rising to the sublime, and enriched with beauty. The inevitable comparison of the greatest Protestant preacher with the three famous Catholics of the period leads to the view that he had in lower degree elements of them all. He had not the consummate art of Bossuet, but in power of imagination and occasional flights of eloquence he was not infrequently equal to that orator; his reasoning and analysis were not inferior to Bourdaloue's, but he had not the keen and ample knowledge of human nature which marked the Jesuit father; he was least like Massillon of the three, but in tenderness and fervor he occasionally comes near that type, though without the exquisite finish and sensibility which were Massillon's distinguishing traits. In making such a comparison we must not fail to remember the vast advantages of social position and stimulating environment which aided the Catholic orators to develop just those particulars in which they excelled Saurin. On the other hand, the Scriptural basis and tone of Saurin's thought, and the deep experience of trials, both his own and those of his people, gave to his preaching a deep note of power and pathos which theirs could not have.

Three quotations must suffice us as specimens of Saurin's pulpit work. The clearness of his thinking is illustrated in the following extract from a sermon on *The Price of Truth*:[66] "Before we enter on this inquiry, it is necessary to determine what we mean by truth. If there be an equivocal word in the world, either in regard to human sciences, or in regard to religion, it is this word truth. But, not to enter into a metaphysical dissertation on the different ideas that are affixed to the term, we will content ourselves with indicating the ideas which we affix to it here. Truth ought not to be considered here as susbsisting in a subject, independently of the reflections of an intelligence that considers it. I do not affirm that there is not a truth in every object which subsists, whether we attend to it or not; but I say that, in these phrases, to search truth, to love truth, to buy truth, the term is relative, and expresseth a harmony between the object and the mind that considers it, a conformity between the object and the idea we have of it. To search after truth is to endeavor to obtain adequate ideas of the object of our reflections; and to buy truth is to make all the sacrifices which are necessary for the obtaining of such ideas as are proportional to the objects, of which our notions are the images. By truth, then, we mean an agreement between an object and our idea of it."

A passage from the sermon on *The Nature and Control of the Passions,* based on Peter's exhortation[67] to the "strangers and exiles," shows how strongly and faithfully Saurin could teach and exhort his own exiled flock. Discussing motives to resist the passions, he thus appeals:[68] "Moreover, religious exiles have given up a great deal for conscience, and they must choose either to lose the reward of their former labors, or to persevere. A man who has only taken a few easy steps in religion, if he let loose his passions, may be supposed rational in this; his life is all of a piece. He considers present interests as the supreme good, and he employs himself wholly in advancing his present interest, he lays down a principle, he infers a consequence, and he makes sin produce all possible advantage. An abominable principle certainly, but a uniform train of principle and consequence; a fatal

[66]Saurin's *Sermons,* tr. Robinson, Vol. II, p. 28.

[67]1 Peter 2:11. [68]Fish, *op. cit.,* p. 179.

advantage in a future state, but a real advantage in the present; but such a stranger as we have described, a man banished his country for religion, if he continues to gratify fleshly passions, is a contradictory creature, a sort of idiot, who is at one and the same time a martyr to vice and a martyr to virtue. He has the fatal secret of rendering both time and eternity wretched, and arming against himself heaven and earth, God and Satan, paradise and hell. On the one hand, for the sake of religion he quits everything dear and renounces the pleasure of his native soil, the society of his friends, family connections, and every prospect of preferment and fortune; thus he is a martyr for virtue, by this he renders the present life inconvenient, and arms against himself the world, Satan, and hell. On the other hand, he stabs the practical part of religion, violates all the sacred laws of austerity, retirement, humility, patience, and love, all which religion most earnestly recommends; by so doing he becomes a martyr for sin, renders futurity miserable, and arms against himself God, heaven, and eternity. The same God who forbade superstition and idolatry enjoined all the virtues we have enumerated, and prohibited every opposite vice. If men be determined to be damned, better go the broad than the narrow way. Who but a madman would attempt to go to hell by encountering the difficulties that lie in the way to heaven!"

Finally, to show something of the fine quality, both of Saurin's soul and art, let the following apostrophe to Louis XIV be read from a sermon preached at New Year, 1710, with its good wishes:[69] "And thou, redoubtable prince, whom I once honored as my king, and whom I still respect as the scourge of the Lord, thou also shalt have part in my good wishes. Those provinces which thou art threatening, but which the arm of the Lord upholds; those regions which thou art peopling with fugitives, but with fugitives whom charity animates; those walls which enclose a thousand martyrs whom thou hast made, but whom faith renders triumphant, shall resound still with blessings on thy behalf. May God make to drop the fatal bandage which hides the truth from thy sight! May God forget those rivers of blood with which

[69]Quoted in the original by Hering, *op. cit.*, S. 150 f.

thou hast covered the earth and which thy reign has seen spread abroad! May God blot out of His book the evils which thou hast done to us, and in recompensing those who have suffered them, pardon those who have caused them to be suffered. God grant that after having been for us, for the Church, the minister of His judgments, thou mayest be the dispenser of His graces, and the minister of His mercies!"

CHAPTER V

The Classic Period of the British Pulpit

The tumultuous seventeenth century fills a momentous place in the political, social, literary, and religious life of England and the English-speaking peoples. Amid the crowded and rapidly shifting events of state we need here only recall that this century witnessed the passing of the great era of Elizabeth into that of the Stuart dynasty. The reign of that parody upon royalty, James I (1603-1625), was followed by that of his unhappy son, Charles I (1625-1649), whose tragic execution, by awakening sympathy for the man, has in some measure softened judgment upon his inexcusable errors as a king. Civil war, chaos, and strife came to their fruitage in the military despotism of the Commonwealth under Cromwell (1649-1660), which, by its manifest strength and generally good aims, almost justified its severities and extremes. But these again were darkly balanced by the hideous moral reaction under Charles II (1660-1685), which boldly flaunted its worst excesses in public, but cast over them the glamour of royalty restored, and secured the too easy tolerance of a people weary of war and repression and longing for peace and pleasure. The Revolution under James II (1685-1688) signified once again the exhaustion of the patience of a nation tried beyond endurance by the tyrannies and unworthiness of the House of Stuart; and the transition to a new era and a new century as well was accomplished under the reign of William III (1688-1702).

I. General Survey of the Preaching of the Century

The British pulpit of the seventeenth century was a living factor of the age. It gave and received potent influence in the stirring events and movements of the time; and it can not be understood or rightly valued apart from its intimate connection with the social, literary, and religious facts and forces which helped to make the seventeenth century in England, as in France, an illustrious epoch in the history of preaching.[1]

To one who looks back upon any great historic age, the better and the worse aspects of the moral life of the people, and the finer and coarser features of social manners present striking contrasts as they exist side by side in the enforced companionship of time and place. But to the actors the scene was not a still picture, but a fierce struggle, where the elemental forces for good and evil in the social life of man contended for mastery. This perennial conflict was emphasized by the course of events in seventeenth century England. A turbulent age like that must needs bring to the surface both its best and its worst elements. Vice and crime held high carnival when opportunity offered—as it too often did. The courts of James I and of Charles II were stews of vicious indulgence. Nor was it there alone, but only too generally among the people, that drunkenness, gambling, licentiousness, lying, cheating, frivolity, waste, and all accompanying evils prevailed. On the other hand, we must not forget the abundant and strong protest against these things which we find, not only in the stern prin-

[1]Besides the standard Histories of England and several Church Histories, Histories of Literature and various articles, the following authorities have been consulted: Collier, Fuller, Overton, Blunt, and others on the ecclesiastical history of the period; Tulloch, *Rational Theology and Christian Philosophy in England in the Seventeenth Century; The Classic Preachers of the English Church* (lects. ed. by Kempe), 1877-78; works of Broadus, Pattison, Fish, before mentioned; Brown, *Puritan Preaching in England* (Yale Lectures, 1899); Blaikie, *The Preachers of Scotland;* Taylor, *The Scottish Pulpit; The Evangelical Succession* (a course of lectures on Scottish preachers at St. George's Church, 1882-3); Works and Biographies of the preachers as mentioned below.

ciples and conduct of the Puritans, but in the gentler methods and no less saintly remonstrances of many pious minds. Yet it must be owned that refinement of manners was no token of this age. Even its virtues often became gloomy and severe, while its vices too easily disdained the draperies and disguises of more polished and outwardly decent times. License of manners and coarseness of speech are glaringly reflected in the literature of the times. The splendid genius of Shakespeare conceded too much to this bad fashion of the age, and even the purer mind of Milton has left in his writings occasional allusions and expressions offensive to good taste and true delicacy of soul. The forces of good and evil alike were often aggressive to violence; and cruelties and barbarities were tolerated and practiced, even in the name of law and religion, that now seem incredible. If the scepter of the Stuarts was a rod of tyranny and persecution, the sword of Cromwell was a flaming instrument of vengeance and compulsion.

The sermons of the period show the influence of its morals and manners in many ways. The rebuke of evil is virile and sometimes rude, and the struggles of the time called forth a sharpness of polemic not always consonant with Christian love. The easy morals of some elements of society were also reflected in a few of the clergy of the epoch, though sternly reproved in others.

Not only social conditions, but also habits of thought and expression characteristic of the age, left their impress upon its preaching. There were great thinkers in the seventeenth century whose names are well known, such as Bacon, whose best work was brought over into this era; Hobbes, Newton, and Locke, besides others less prominent and influential. In literature also the period was distinguished. Shakespeare died in 1616, and part of his creative work belongs to the former age, but some of his best plays were written after the century opened, and the first complete edition of his works was the famous folio of 1623. Contemporary and succeeding dramatists never reached his level, of course, and their work was marred by the abominable coarseness which the age tolerated or even demanded, but a few at least produced writings that hold their place in English literature.

Among them were Jonson, Massinger, Ford, and, later, Wycherly, Dryden, and Congreve. Among lyric and minor poets there were Herrick, Herbert, Carew, Waller, Donne, Cowley, and Dryden again; but the pre-eminent name of the period in poetry is that of John Milton, whose great epic is accompanied by some of the most exquisite lyrics ever penned. The century also shows a great variety of prose writers, of whom some of the greatest names are those of the learned Selden, and the quaint Fuller, the lovable Izaak Walton, the stately Clarendon, the gossipy Evelyn and Pepys (though their invaluable diaries were not published till long afterwards); and the religious group, including Chillingworth, Hall, Jeremy Taylor, and the immortal allegorist, Bunyan, who are also among the preachers. A monumental literary as well as religious event was the publication in 1611 of the Authorized or King James Version of the Bible. Under these varied and efficient influences and employments, the English language became in the seventeenth century a strong and splendid vehicle of thought; and its use in the pulpit of the age shows its manifold qualities and powers. It ranges from the quaint homeliness of Bunyan to the involved and stately periods of Barrow, from the poetic beauty of Hall and Taylor to the virile strength of South and the clarity and moderation of Tillotson.

The religious movements of the century are closely intertwined with all its other affairs; but a few of the most important events need to be recalled in order that the preaching of the age may be better understood. In England the compromises under Elizabeth left two leading parties in the Church, and a few vigorous but persecuted sectaries outside its fold. Of these the Brownists (later Independents or Congregationalists) and the Anabaptists (later Baptists) were the most important. The extreme episcopal party in the English Church was composed of two elements: Those who were really Romanists at heart, but conformed for policy, and those who were against Rome, and yet were sacramentarian and ritualist in views and Semi-pelagian in theology. They were pronounced adherents of the doctrine of "divine right" in both bishops and the king. Bancroft and Laud were the leading exponents of the views and designs of this party, with its intellectual and social *prestige,* its narrowness, intolerance, and pride. The other party in the Church was much split up. They are generally called "Puritans," because they advocated that life, doctrine, and church polity should strictly conform to "the pure Word of God," but that designation includes a variety of men and views. Among the Puritans were moderate Episcopalians, willing to accept the episcopacy and the national Church as historically developed, Calvinistic in theology, opposed to ritualism, and strict in life. But along with these was a considerable number who, while not separating from the Church, would reform it from within and bring it back to what they considered the true New Testament model, both in doctrine and government. These were Non-conformists, and might be for a time merely acquiescent Episcopalians, but were chiefly Presbyterians, with a few Independents. Lastly, there were Separatists, who would not remain in the national Church in any form it might take, whether comprehension or compromise, but stood for freedom of worship. These were chiefly Independents and Baptists.

In Scotland, under the masterful leadership of Knox, the Reformed views had triumphed. Romanism was overthrown, and its episcopacy also had gone. Henceforth the Kirk of Scotland was to be Calvinistic in doctrine and ultimately Presbyterian in polity. But meantime, what should be its relation to the church property—buildings, benefices, endowments, and all the rest—formerly held by the Catholics and administered by bishops and priests? And how should the new Kirk be related to the civil government as represented in the sovereign? Fierce debates upon these momentous questions filled the last third of the sixteenth century, after the death of Knox, in 1572. At the opening of the seventeenth century James VI was at the height of his dispute with the Scottish Kirk in his endeavor to force a Protestant episcopacy upon an unwilling majority of the people, and was already madly jealous and tenacious of his royal prerogative.

In this state of mind he became king of England, as James I, in 1603. Thus the Scottish disputes were added to the English and further complicated the religious problems of this stirring century. In each country there was a small group of Catholics at one extreme and of Separatists at the other, but the bulk of the people were for a national Church of some sort, only differing as to what form it should take. James favored episcopacy, and the episcopal clergy in turn favored the royal pretensions. The main body of the people in Scotland were for Presbyterianism and the practical control of the civil government by the Kirk, but a strong minority were for king and bishops. In England there was a more nearly equal division, and now one party gained ascendency, and now the other. At the Hampton Court Conference, in 1604, James promptly and decisively took sides with the High Church party and insulted the Puritans. This policy was inherited by Charles I and pushed to disastrous extremes. The persecuting measures of Archbishop Laud need not here be recounted in detail. They provoked in Scotland the signing of the Covenant of 1638 in determined opposition to episcopacy and ritual; in England, the early protest and revolt of the Long Parliament in 1640, the Solemn League and Covenant of the Parliament with the Presbyterians of Scotland in 1643, and the Westminster Assembly with its Catechisms and Confession in 1642-43. Then came the downfall of Laud in 1645. It looked now as if Presbyterianism would carry the day in both lands. But the Civil War brought the army and Cromwell and the Commonwealth, so that now, instead of a king and bishops, intolerant and trying to enforce episcopacy, and instead of parliaments and assemblies equally intolerant and trying to enforce Presbyterianism, there was the Independent wing of Puritanism, more tolerant of religious opinion, but irresistible for a time in the State. Macaulay thus graphically describes the situation:[2] "The ecclesiastical polity of the realm was in inextricable confusion. Episcopacy was the form of government prescribed by the old law of the land, which was still unrepealed. The form of government prescribed by parliamentary ordinance was Presbyterian. But neither the old law nor the parliamentary ordinance was practically in force. The Church actually

[2]*Hist. of Eng.*, Vol. I, p. 148.

established may be described as an irregular body made up of a few presbyteries and of many independent congregations, which were all held down and held together by the authority of the government." The Restoration in 1660 brought back, along with the king, an intolerant episcopacy and a royalist Parliament to pass the infamous persecuting acts of the reign of Charles II. These were: The Act of Uniformity, requiring all clergymen by a certain date to sign acceptance of everything in the Book of Common Prayer, or lose their places; the Conventicle Act, forbidding any religious meetings to be held except under the Prayer-book Ritual; and the Five Mile Act, forbidding any deprived clergyman to come within five miles of any town where he had formerly held a charge. Meantime the Covenanters of Scotland were harried and hunted. James II secretly wished to restore Romanism, but his Declaration of Indulgence was an illegal measure which alienated the Episcopalians without winning the Dissenters, and did no good. His short reign had an inglorious end, and left the religious confusion worse confounded. At last the dawn of a better day came with the accession of William and Mary, in 1688, and the adoption, in 1689, of the famous Act of Toleration. Episcopacy remained the established Church of England, but other forms of polity and worship were tolerated under certain restrictions. The working out of this great compromise belongs to later times. It brought peace and put an end to violent persecution. But the unwise requirement that the clergy should swear allegiance to the new sovereigns, while many of them were sincerely attached to the old order, again drove from the established Church some of its best and most conscientious ministers.

Preaching necessarily and in various ways felt the influence of all this turmoil in civil and religious affairs, and was itself no small factor in forming opinion and promoting action within and between the various and opposing factions. If there was any Catholic preaching, it was done under cover; and, at the other extreme, the Separatist preachers were often imprisoned and otherwise persecuted. In Scotland only a few Episcopal preachers were of any note—such as Sharp and Leighton; it was the Presbyterians who had the ear of the people and gave tone to the work of the pulpit. In England the two great parties of Anglican and Puritan, alternately in the ascendant and always rivals, stimulated while they opposed each other; and each had a great and powerful body of divines and preachers, whose work has made their age illustrious. Yet the great leaders were comparatively few, as is ever the case, and we must not forget the rank and file of less gifted, less cultivated, and often less worthy men, whose less conspicuous characters and labors did not fail to exemplify both the faults and the virtues of the preaching of their time. The line of cleavage here indicated was found in both the great factions. The learned and eloquent Anglican had his equal among his Puritan brethren; and the narrow and fanatical exhorter among the Puritans had his counterpart in the ill-trained and almost degraded but stubborn parson of many an Anglican parish. And if the pious and faithful obscure were found in both parties, it must also be owned with shame that the canting, hypocritical Puritan was fairly matched by the loose and lazy Anglican. Character and talent, and the want of them, are not things of parties, but of men in all parties.

In the famous third chapter of his *History of England,* Macaulay has given a memorable description of the Anglican clergy at the accession of James II, in 1685.[3] He speaks first of the rural clergy, their poverty and dependence upon the country lords and gentlemen, the poor esteem in which they were held, and yet their important and vigorous influence on the royalist and episcopal side; he grants that "there was at that time no lack in the English Church of ministers distinguished by abilities and learning," but shows that these were to be found at the "few places where the means of acquiring knowledge were abundant, and where the opportunities of vigorous intellectual exercise were frequent." After naming and describing some of the best known of these, the historian summarizes, in part, as follows: "Thus the Anglican priesthood was divided into two sections, which, in acquirements, in manners, and in social position differed widely from each other. One section,

[3]Vol. I, pp. 302-311.

trained for cities and courts, comprised men familiar with all ancient and modern learning; men able to encounter Hobbes or Bossuet at all the weapons of controversy; men who could in their sermons set forth the majesty and beauty of Christianty with such justness of thought and such energy of language, that the indolent Charles roused himself to listen, and the fastidious Buckingham forgot to sneer; men whose address, politeness, and knowledge of the world qualified them to manage the consciences of the wealthy and noble; men with whom Halifax loved to discuss the interests of empires, and from whom Dryden was not ashamed to own that he had learned to write.[4] The other section was destined to ruder and humbler service. It was dispersed over the country, and consisted chiefly of persons not at all wealthier, and not much more refined, than small farmers or upper servants; yet it was in these rustic priests, who derived but a scanty subsistence from their tithe sheaves and tithe pigs, and who had not the smallest chance of ever attaining high professional honors, that the professional spirit was strongest." Allowing for Macaulay's well-known bias against the Tory party, his description on the whole is true to facts; and indeed the distinction of a cultured and uncultured class of preachers is more or less true in all ages, all countries, all sects, all parties.

When, therefore, we seek out and endeavor to describe the features and elements of the preaching of any age and country, we must lay our account with both the fact of this distinction and its effect on our studies. For both the literary remains—chiefly sermons—and the accepted traditions which come down from any period of preaching represent mainly, though not exclusively, the cultured class of preachers. Does our study, then, of these sources lead to an inaccurate and misleading representation of the pulpit of any particular epoch? Not necessarily; for the difficulty is not so great as it seems, and for two main reasons, which may be briefly set forth. The first is that, as indicated already, the published sermons and traditional accounts of the preachers of an age are not exclusively of the more learned

[4]Reference to Tillotson, as explained in footnote.

and influential class. Enough of the other sort are usually preserved to keep a general critical estimate from being altogether one-sided. The second reason is less obvious, but equally good. It lies in the fact that the leaders of any age—in preaching as in other things—are its true representatives. Dr. Broadus has spoken a sage word for every student of the history of preaching in remarking somewhere that "every great preacher is the child of his time." The time-spirit and its fashions are reflected in his work. He is spokesman to posterity for his less gifted and eminent brethren. And then the converse is also true, that these are often learners and imitators of the leading spirits. In their more obscure and practically forgotten labors, the humbler preachers of every generation are wont to exemplify and spread abroad the doctrines and methods of the more highly endowed and placed. With these considerations in mind, we may come to the ample sources for studying the preaching of the seventeenth century in England, confident that such study will reveal without serious error the actual conditions and features of that "classic period of the British pulpit."

Some general characteristics of preaching the British pulpit shared with those of other lands in this epoch, and some were more peculiarly its own. The gains of the Reformation were still visible in the sermons of the seventeenth century. These, in the Protestant preaching, were chiefly the place given to the exposition of Scripture, and the polemic against Rome. Scottish preaching, after Knox, continued to exhibit both of these more than the English. In fact, the English Reformers, though recognizing the authority of Scripture, were not so much given as their Continental and Scotch neighbors to its detailed exposition in the pulpit. If anything, the Puritan preaching of the seventeenth century—influenced so largely by Calvinistic principles—shows more attention to this than that of the preceding age. The Anglican sermons are about the same in this regard, being more inclined to the topical than the expository method. The use of Scripture is generally reverent and sensible, but there is not a little forcing of the Word in the interest of those fanciful and quaint conceits in which the taste of the times delighted, and also in the interest of sectarian interpretations and doctrines.

The controversial element remains very considerable in amount, and often very acrimonious in spirit. Not only was this true of the polemic against Romanism, but it received peculiar emphasis in the fierce sectarian disputes of the age. These had not degenerated into mere logomachy, for the preachers were in the main powerfully convinced of the truth of their principles and were hopeful of making them triumphant in the State. This imparted a tone of moral and spiritual earnestness to the preaching of the age which was not wholly discredited, even by its most extreme and dogmatic controversialism. Yet we can not but feel a twitch of pain in reflecting that even saintly souls like Rutherford and Baxter could, in the language of *Hudibras*,

> "Prove their doctrine orthodox
> With apostolic blows and knocks."

In the matter of division and analysis, the scholastic method of many of the Continental preachers finds abundant employment among their British brethren. Especially do the Puritan divines often descend into a minute and exhaustive subdivision of their matter, which is offensive to modern taste and must have been wearisome and hurtful to spiritual as well as literary effect in any age. Along with this there was an undue amount of pedantry in preaching. Greek and Latin quotations and learned allusions abound. Certainly only a few of the hearers could have followed or appreciated these, and they must be reluctantly set down to a desire to impress people with the learning and authority of the preacher, rather than to impart true spiritual profit to the hearers. It may, indeed, be true that much more of this sort of thing appears in the printed discourses—being intended largely for educated readers—than was actually given in the delivery of the sermons.

Along with this pedantry, we must notice another blemish generally apparent in the preaching of the age, and found in other lands than England. This was the tendency to affectation of style. In the British divines it did not so much tend to bombast and meretricious eloquence as in some of the Italian and French preachers, but, as in case of many of the Germans, it took the shape of conceits of fancy, plays upon words, antitheses, paradoxes, and the like. It was a token of the age, and was not peculiar to the pulpit, but is sadly out of place there. We find it, not only in such poetic preachers as Donne and Taylor, but even in Puritans like Adams, and Separatists like Bunyan. Here again, as with the display of learning, the effort to strike the hearer is too apparent; and to a modern reader the effect is often repellant and wearisome rather than attractive.

One other general criticism on the sermons of the time—in which the British preachers again were not unlike their Continental neighbors—relates to their length and fullness. As in the case of Spener, Bourdaloue, Saurin, and others, we restless moderns can not but wonder at the patience of audiences that could sit through one of these long English discourses. And they were not only long, but many of them, especially of such men as Howe and Barrow, were so filled with thought as to be a severe tax upon attention. There are not wanting traditions that the hearers, though usually respectful, sometimes resented this undue demand upon their patience. Broadus[5] quotes, from Calamy, the following description of a fast-day service conducted by Howe: "It was upon those occasions his common way to begin about nine in the morning, with a prayer for about a quarter of an hour, in which he begged a blessing on the work of the day; and afterwards read and expounded a chapter or psalm, in which he spent about three-quarters of an hour; then prayed for about an hour, preached for another hour, and prayed for about half an hour. After this, he retired and took some little refreshment for about a quarter of an hour (the people singing all the while), and then came again into the pulpit and prayed for another hour, and gave them another sermon of about an hour's length; and so concluded the services of the day, at about four of the clock in the evening, with about half an hour or more in prayer."

If we inquire what it was that, in spite of such faults and blemishes as have been noted, made this preaching

[5] *Hist. of Preaching,* p. 211 f.

great, the answer is not far to seek. Most of the sources and elements of its power have already been indicated or implied in the preceding discussion, but, by way of summary, we may mention as specially noteworthy the following four things:

(1) *Loyalty to the Word of God.* It was one of the Anglican divines of this period—William Chillingworth—who gave utterance to the famous dictum, "The Bible, and the Bible only, is the religion of Protestants." This principle was the very lifeblood of the English preaching of the seventeenth century; its antecedents necessitated and its problems demanded an intelligent, strong, and confident appeal to the authority of God as revealed in His Word. That appeal was made with power and effect.

(2) *Consciousness of strength.* The preachers themselves earnestly believed in the thing they were doing. Never did the legendary Arthur have more confidence in the virtues of his famous brand, Excalibur, than did these great divines in the "sword of the Spirit," as they wielded it in their stout battles against sin and error. They were no perfunctory officials going through the forms of a task prescribed by custom and accepted with weariness, but earnest men who felt that things could and must be brought to pass by preaching the Word.

(3) *Thoughtfulness.* Notwithstanding the learned lumber, the tedious detail, the catchy and strained fancifulness that many of these sermons show, there is also, in many of them, a depth, fullness, comprehensiveness, and power of thought that have been sometimes equaled, but scarcely, if ever, surpassed, in the history of preaching. This is, of course, not true of all—it could not be; but it is so characteristic of many as to be a token of the age.

(4) *Use of language.* It was the tongue of Shakespeare and of Milton, in the days when the work of those masters of speech was new, that these old English divines employed. Its wealth of words, its felicity of phrase, its flexibility of use, its music, its varied adaptation to thought, mood, and need—all these were at the preacher's service, and for the most part he used his instrument well. The strong Saxon soil, the clear and tonic Norman air, and the fresh glow of classic light

united to produce the flowers and fruits of that rich and varied diction which characterizes the sermons of that time.

II. Preachers of the Established Church

In undertaking to sketch the leading preachers of England and Scotland during the seventeenth century, we are confronted with the three usual problems of selection, grouping, and comparative fullness of treatment. Leaving the last to take care of itself as we proceed, we find that the first is greatly simplified by being narrowed to the question of whom to leave out; there can be little doubt as to those whose claim to consideration is established. In the grouping of these for study we might follow the course of events through the century and consider the prominent and influential preachers in each successive epoch—the reigns of the first Stuart kings, the Commonwealth, the Restoration, the Revolution; but, as there would be some overlapping and confusion in this method, it is perhaps better to follow the more clearly marked line of distinction into Anglicans on the one hand, and Puritans and Dissenters on the other, while observing the chronological order in the presentation of individuals. We therefore begin with the great preachers of the Anglican Church.

Launcelot Andrewes (1555-1626)[6] was born in London, in the reign of Bloody Mary. He was carefully educated, and pursued his university studies at Cambridge. He was ordained to the English priesthood and was rapidly advanced in church offices, being early made dean of Westminster, and bishop successively of Chichester, Ely, and Winchester. Of his ample learning, delightful old Thomas Fuller has this to say:[7] "The world wanted learning to know how learned this man was; so skilled in all (especially Oriental) languages that some conceive he might, if then living, almost have

[6]Andrewes' *Works,* in *Lib. of Anglo-Cath. Theology,* Vol. I, containing ninety-six *Sermons,* and including seventeen Christmas sermons given before the court during the years 1605-24, several years omitted.

[7]*Works of Thos. Fuller,* ed. by Nichols, pub. by Tegg, London, 1868, Vol. III, p. 391.

served as interpreter-general at the confusion of tongues." As was eminently fitting, he was one of the company of scholars whose labors produced the Authorized Version of the Bible. Andrewes was a thorough-going high churchman, devoted to episcopacy and King James. He often preached special sermons before the king, and the royal pedant is said to have greatly delighted in them. The sermons of Andrewes are at times artificial and stilted in tone, and often overloaded with learning and Latin quotations,[8] not free from the whimsical fancies of the age, but weighty in thought, exhaustive in treatment, and much occupied with careful exposition of Scripture:[9] but his exposition is sometimes vitiated, both by polemical bias and the play of fancy. In his inner life Andrewes was deeply pious, and though his sermons bristle with sharp controversy, his prayers and meditations breathe the spirit of mystical devotion.[10]

John Donne[11] (1573-1631) was, according to Fuller,[12] "born in London (but extracted from Wales, by his mother's side great-great-grandchild to Sir Thomas More, whom he much resembled in his endowments)." He studied at both Oxford and Cambridge, but having been brought up a Romanist, he could not get a degree. Yet, as he studied law and prepared for civil life, he carefully examined the different doctrines, and became a Protestant. But he was yet a long way from a spiritual conversion, and had no thought of becoming a preacher. He was a man of society, spent his patrimony freely, took his share of the youthful gayeties of the day, and was far from being free of vices. Donne had real poetic

[8]See Pattison, p. 172, for an example; and almost any sermon in the collection. Andrewes was also too much devoted to the minute scholastic analysis of his themes.

[9]Andrewes, with the other great English divines, is often referred to in the scholarly Commentaries of Bishop Ellicott. See also a sketch by J. H. North in *Classic Preachers of the Eng. Ch.*

[10]See an excellent monograph on this side of Andrewes by Dr. Alex. Whyte, which I once read with interest, but have not by me at this writing.

[11]See the excellent *Life* by Izaak Walton; and *Works;* also a fine sketch by Bp. Lightfoot in *Classic Preachers of the English Church;* also a sermon in Fish, I, 153 ff.

[12]*Op. cit.*, p. 362.

talent,[13] and had he devoted himself to poetry, could doubtless have attained high rank. Many of his poems are marred by the grossness of the age—a thing which he later bitterly deplored—but some of them have decided merit. Donne won the love of a young lady of beauty and rank, but her father, with reason, opposed the marriage; but he married her secretly and was afterwards forgiven. He was tenderly attached to his wife, and his best poems are those which her love inspired. As his life amended and he became mature in years, he was persuaded by his friends—including King James I—to become a minister of the Established Church. He was, no doubt, soundly converted, but his past life and those stained writings of his early days—which he could not recall—made him reluctant to become a clergyman. But his scruples were overcome, and so in mature life, and after a season of careful preparatory studies, he was ordained and began to preach. He was a favorite of the king, and his advancement in church offices was rapid. He was appointed a royal chaplain, then vicar of St. Dunstan, dean of St. Paul's, and to some other places of honor and emolument. It was as chaplain to the king and dean of St. Paul's that he did his principal work as a preacher. He lived about fifteen years after his ordination, and died greatly admired and beloved.

Donne ranks deservedly high among the preachers of his time. He studied carefully for his new work, and was well equipped for it in general learning and mental gifts. Not only was he heard with pleasure, and even with what now seems extravagant appreciation of his eloquence, but his published sermons have enjoyed great popularity. They show careful and laborious study of the Bible, though not always a well-balanced exegesis. Donne was strong and convinced in his Anglicanism, though not a bitter extremist; he was devout in spirit, rich in fancy, and vigorous in style, though this is marred by the affectations and pedantry and straining for effect which were common to the age. Yet even now Donne's sermons will repay occasional reading.

Joseph Hall (1574-1656)[14] was one of the best and

[13]See notice and specimens in Warner *Lib.*, Vol. VIII, p. 4771.

[14]*Works of Bishop Hall,* ed. of Peter Hall. Sermon in Fish, I, p. 167.

purest men of his time. He was born of respectable and pious parents, at Ashby-de-la-Zouch in Leicestershire. His father had a large family, and Joseph was a younger son. In a quaint autobiographical sketch he speaks in the most affectionate terms of his mother—esteeming her worthy to be compared with Aleth, the mother of Bernard, and Monica, the mother of Augustine. Notwithstanding their large family, the parents made arrangements for the education of Joseph, whom they early designed for the ministry. By the help of a gentleman who had married his aunt, the boy was kept at Cambridge till he took his degree, and was made a fellow of his college. Afterwards he taught rhetoric at Cambridge for two years, and then entered the minstry, having received an appointment at Halsted in Suffolk. He says:[15] "Being now therefore settled in that sweet and civil country of Suffolk, near to St. Edmond's-Bury, my first work was to build up my house, which was then extremely ruinous. Which done, the uncouth solitariness of my life, and the extreme incommodity of that single housekeeping drew my thoughts after two years to condescend to the necessity of a married estate; which God no less strangely provided for me; for, walking from the church on Monday on the Whitsun-week, with a grave and reverend minister, Mr. Grandidge, I saw a comely and modest gentlewoman standing at the door of that house where we were invited to a wedding dinner; and inquiring of that worthy friend whether he knew her, 'Yes,' quoth he, 'I know her well, and have bespoken her for your wife.'" The friend then told how he had talked with the lady's father about it, and the gentleman was not averse to the match; and then the words of the author go on: "Advising me not to neglect the opportunity, and not concealing the just praises of the modesty, piety, good disposition, and other virtues that were lodged in that seemly presence, I listened to the motion, as sent from God; and at last, upon due prosecution, happily prevailed; enjoying the comfortable society of that meet help for the space of forty-nine years."

After several years' service in his first charge, Hall accompanied a friend—Sir Edmund Bacon, a descendant

[15]See the brief autobiography prefixed to *Works,* Vol. I, p. XIX.

of the famous philosopher—on a trip to the Continent, and improved his opportunities of observation and learning. About a year and a half after his return he was transferred to Waltham, where he spent twenty-two years as rector, filling, in connection with that, offices at Prince Henry's court and as a prebendary at Worcester. He filled several missions abroad by royal appointment, the most important being at the famous Synod of Dort, in 1618, where he rendered distinguished services. Later he was made bishop, first at Exeter, and then at Norwich. He was envied and annoyed, first by one party and then by another—as is the fate of moderate men. He was accused before Laud as being too favorable to the Puritans; and later, on the assembling of the Long Parliament, as being a bishop, he was deprived of his see, put in the Tower for awhile, robbed of his property, and badly treated generally, dying in poverty, but in peace, in 1656.

As a preacher Bishop Hall ranked with the first of his age in character, learning, and eloquence. His sermons do not rise above the faults of the time in respect of forced interpretation of Scripture, conceits of style, pedantry, and the like. But they abound in noble thought and spirit, and notwithstanding the faults mentioned, their style is elevated, strong, and eloquent. His most famous work is his *Contemplations Upon the Principal Passages in the Holy Story*. Doubtless much of this was originally sermons. Devout, noble, and helpful, it deserves its fame as one of the original and enduring literary monuments of the Anglican Church. In regard to his preaching, he says himself,[16] in speaking of his work at Waltham and Halstead, that he preached three times a week, "Yet never durst I climb into the pulpit to preach any sermon whereof I had not before, in my poor and plain fashion, penned every word in the same order wherein I hoped to deliver it; although in the expression I listed not to be a slave to syllables."

William Chillingworth[17] (1602-1644) was born at

[16]*Op. cit.*, p. XXVI.

[17]*Works of Chillingworth,* with life by Birch, three vols., Oxford, 1838, containing the nine sermons which remain. Sermon in Fish, I, p. 193 ff. See also a judicious appreciation of Chillingworth and his influence on liberalism in English religious

Oxford, his father being a reputable citizen who afterwards served the city as mayor. William Laud, afterwards noted as archbishop, stood as godfather to the child. He was educated at Oxford, taking the degrees in regular course. The points in controversy between the Catholics and Protestants being much discussed, Chillingworth fell under the influence of a Jesuit, Fisher, and was induced to become a Catholic, and then to go to the Catholic College at Douay in France for further study. But it was only a temporary aberration. Laud took the matter up and corresponded with Chillingworth, who soon saw the error of his course and returned to his first faith. This led to much criticism among the Catholics, and to Chillingworth's writing his famous treatise, *The Religion of Protestants a Safe Way to Salvation.* He was offered places in the Church, but had scruples on some points in the Articles and would not subscribe. Finally, however, he overcame these, and received several appointments as preacher; but his ministry was of short duration, only about six years. He was a stanch royalist and churchman. He has deservedly high rank as a preacher. His use of Scripture is reverent and sensible, and his exposition strong and clear. His style is vigorous and not so loaded with affectation and pedantry as is common with others of that age. The argument is able, but the analysis is not always clear; and the unity and structure of a well-articulated sermon are not always in evidence.

William Laud (1573-1645)[18] has gained an unenviable name in English history as the extreme champion of High Church views and the active abettor of the tyrannous measures of Charles I in church and state. But he is entitled to at least a brief notice among the preachers of this troubled epoch. He was born at Reading, Berkshire, the son of a wealthy clothier, who gave him the best advantages for education, both at the schools of his native town and at Oxford, where he took a degree with distinction and was made a fellow of St. John's College.

[18] *Works of Archbishop Laud* in the *Anglo-Catholic Theology,* Vol. I, containing the seven sermons—all that remain. They were all preached before the kings—two for James I and five for Charles I—and by their command, on special occasions, some of great historic interest.

Ordained in 1601, he began his notable career as a churchman in several minor places, till in 1611 he became president of St. John's College and a royal chaplain. Promotions rapidly followed. He became dean of Gloucester, bishop of St. David's, of Bath and Wells, of London, and finally archbishop of Canterbury. His persecutions and tyrannies led to his fearful account with the Long Parliament, by which he was tried for high treason, and after a long process, in which he defended himself with ability, he was condemned and executed in 1645.

Laud's remarkable career and mistakes as a churchman and the apparent tool of Charles I in his efforts to impose Anglican uniformity must not blind us to his merits as a man and preacher. That he sincerely believed in the doctrines and principles which he advocated and for which he suffered can not be doubted. His writings and the testimony of his friends show that with all his unrelenting severity toward Puritans, he was a man of piety. We find this strange paradox too often to question its reality in his case. As a preacher Laud is to be judged by seven published sermons, preached mostly on state occasions—king's birthdays, anniversaries, and the like. They are not so much occupied with gospel doctrine as with the discussion of the high theory of royal and ecclesiastical supremacy which Laud held. They are heavy and pedantic, like Andrewes' sermons, though scarcely so able. Yet in their clear analysis and vigorous presentation, they show that Laud must have had considerable powers as a preacher had they been more fully given to the work of the pulpit.

The later group of Anglican preachers come within the troubled era of the second half of the century—the times of the Commonwealth, Restoration, and Revolution. It was a time of many vicissitudes and trials, but among Anglicans (as well as others) there were men of mark in the pulpit, of whom a few must be named.

One of the most famous of the Anglicans was Jeremy Taylor (1613-1667),[19] son of a barber at Cambridge,

[19]Works of Taylor in various editions, Heber's the best. *Life* by Bishop Reg. Heber; volume on Taylor in the *English Men of Letters* series, by Edmund Gosse. Sermon in Fish, I, 567; another in *World's Great Sermons,* II, 29. See also Tulloch, *op. cit.*, I, p. 344 ff.

where he was born and educated. The gifted child entered the grammar school at six, studied diligently, and was a wonder to his friends and teachers. He entered Caius College, Cambridge, at thirteen, and took the degrees in course and was made a fellow at twenty! Though under age, he was ordained while in college, and at the request of an older college-mate, who was sick, took his place as a supply at St. Paul's Cathedral, London. The remarkable preaching of the rarely gifted youth attracted large crowds; for no such eloquence had been heard in that famous pulpit since the death of Dr. Donne, a few years before this time. He was regarded as "an angel come down from heaven," and was recommended to Archbishop Laud for an appointment. At an interview, Laud remarked upon Taylor's extreme youth, and the young divine responded with as much sweetness as wit that "it was a fault for which he begged his grace's pardon, but if he lived he would mend it." But though the archbishop recognized Taylor's unusual talents and learning, as well as beauty of character, he felt that a few more years of study would be better for him, and therefore had him elected a fellow of All Souls' College, Oxford. Thus the future preacher and bishop had the distinction of enjoying the high honors and privileges of both the universities. In a few years Laud caused Taylor to be appointed to the charge of Uppingham, Rutlandshire.

Here for four years he faithfully discharged the duties of a pastor, married a good and sensible wife, and produced his first published writings. Taylor was a pronounced royalist and churchman, and was driven from his rectory at Uppingham. He was for a time a chaplain to the king, but later, during the Civil War, found a place of refuge as chaplain to the Earl of Carbery, at Golden Grove in Caermarthenshire, Wales. Two clergymen of the Church of England, friends of Taylor, had established a school near the home of Lord Carbery, and they employed Taylor as one of the teachers. Thus, during the Commonwealth, by preaching to the little congregation at Golden Grove and teaching, he managed to take care of his family in congenial employment. His pen also was busy, and during his ten years of retirement at

Golden Grove he gave to the world some of the most famous of his writings. These included the treatise on *Liberty of Prophesying, The Great Exemplar,* the companion works on *Holy Living* and *Holy Dying,* and two series of sermons, the first, *Twenty-eight Sermons* (1651), and the second, *Twenty-five Sermons Preached at Golden Grove* (1653), the two being afterwards published under one title, *Eniautos* (*A Year*), as embracing sermons for the Christian year.

But the shadows of trial and suffering soon began to gather. The deaths, near together, of both the devout Lady Carbery and of Taylor's amiable wife gave meaning and beauty to his immortal treatise on *Holy Dying.* Other sorrows fell, and trials came thick and fast. Criticisms and attacks assailed Taylor; he in some way lost his position at Golden Grove, fell into poverty, was imprisoned for a short time in Chepstow Castle—for what cause is not very clearly made out—and seems to have alienated some of his best friends. Meantime he had married his second wife, Joanna Bridges, who had a little home some twelve miles from Golden Grove, and here during his trials his children were cared for. Soon after his release from prison one of his little sons died, and not long afterwards two more took smallpox and died. This left him one son only of his first marriage. Soon his friends made some arrangement for him to be supported by private contributions, while he acted as a sort of chaplain and priest among his now persecuted fellow-royalists. Later, with Cromwell's consent, he was appointed to an English Church parish at Portmore, near Dublin, Ireland, where he found for several years a refuge for himself and his little family. He had come to London to see about the publication of one of his works when the joyful news of the impending Restoration of Charles II was announced, and Taylor was one of those who signed the call for his return.

It seems strange that a man of Taylor's loyalty and rare ability should not have been appointed to a high place in the restored English Church; but either because of some lingering prejudices, or because his services were deemed more important in Ireland, he was made vice-chancellor of the University of Dublin and elevated to the bishopric of Down and Connor in Ulster. He rendered distinguished services in the reorganization of the University; and was zealous and active as a bishop in his difficult diocese. But Ulster was the stronghold of the Presbyterians, and they provoked the mild author of the *Liberty of Prophesying* to become an intolerant and even a persecuting prelate! The place and the task were alike uncongenial to Taylor; his disappointments were great; his burdens and sorrows heavy, and he soon broke down under the load. Death came as a welcome messenger in his fifty-fourth year, after a life of many trials and incessant labors.

Jeremy Taylor is one of the small but distinguished group of preachers whose sermons alone, leaving out his other writings, give him a place in the first rank of English men of letters. Coleridge[20] regarded him as one of the four great masters of English during the first half of the seventeenth century, the others being, of course, Shakespeare, Bacon, and Milton. Gosse apparently endorses this view, and then seeks to explain the comparative neglect of Taylor in regard to the other three. The critic is perhaps not far wrong in saying "that the fame of Jeremy Taylor has been injured among general readers by the fact that he is a divine, and among divines by the fact that he is an artist." The second part of this criticism is indicative of the distinguishing quality of Taylor's sermons. In thought they are not strikingly original or profound; in general structure and form they do not depart from the accepted rules of homiletical composition. Their title to pre-eminence lies in their exquisite literary quality. The two chief faults of the age are in them—pedantry and fancy. These are heightened by excess of imagery and ornament. Beauty of style is too much sought after. The sermons lack virile directness and popular force. They suited the small audience at Golden Grove, and the quiet of an island of flowers in a stormy sea; they are redolent of beauty and charm; their exquisite fancy, richness of imagination, purity and elevation of feeling, elaborate and musical diction, are generally recognized by readers and critics. Their spiritual aim and ethical effect are

[20]See Gosse, *Jeremy Taylor,* p. 211.

worthy, but after all it must be owned that they belong rather to literature than to life. The following paragraph gives, as nearly perhaps as any such brief quotation could, a fair sample of Taylor's manner:[21] "Since we stay not here, being people but of a day's abode, and our age is like that of a fly and contemporary with a gourd, we must look somewhere else for an abiding city, a place in another country to fix our house in, whose walls and foundation is God, where we must find rest, or else be restless forever. For whatever ease we can have or fancy here is shortly to be changed into sadness or tediousness. It goes away too soon, like the periods of our life; or stays too long, like the sorrows of a sinner. Its own weariness, or a contrary disturbance, is its load, or it is eased by its revolution into vanity and forgetfulness. And where either there is sorrow or an end of joy, there can be no true felicity, which must be had by some instrument and in some period of our duration. We must carry up our affections to the mansions prepared for us above, where eternity is the measure, felicity is the state, angels are the company, the Lamb is the light, and God is the portion and inheritance."

Robert Leighton (1611, or 13-1684),[22] born at Edinburgh or London, and educated at Edinburgh, was the son of an earnest Presbyterian minister, who suffered persecution. Robert also was Presbyterian in his early life, but in hope of reconciling parties he became, after the Restoration under Charles II, an Anglican, and reluctantly accepted a Scottish bishopric. Several years later he was made archbishop of Glasgow, but was not contented, and finally resigned and ended his days in retirement. Bishop Burnet[23] says of him: "He had the greatest elevation of soul, the largest compass of knowledge, the most mortified and heavenly disposition I ever yet saw in mortal; he had the greatest parts as well as virtue, with the most perfect humility, that I ever saw

[21]*Holy Living and Dying,* Bohn's ed., p. 312; quoted also by Gosse, p. 94.

[22]*The Whole Works of Robert Leighton, D. D.,* with a *Life,* by John M. Pearson; Blaikie, p. 142 ff.; and *Evang. Succession,* 173 ff.

[23]*History of His Own Times,* quoted by Pattison, p. 187.

in man; and had a sublime strain in preaching, with so grave a gesture, and such a majesty, both of thought, of language, and of pronunciation, that I never once saw a wandering eye when he preached, and have seen whole assemblies often melt into tears before him." Leighton was undoubtedly a man of deep piety and amiable character, but his sermons, though sweet and spiritual, were like the man himself, lacking in force.[24] Yet they are full of pious feeling, devout in tone, clear and simple in style for that age, not overloaded with pedantry or flowers, and sincerely devoted to the edification of the hearer.

Isaac Barrow (1630-1677)[25] was the son of a London merchant, who, both by interest and feeling, was attached to Charles I. The mother died when Isaac was only four years old, and the boy grew up with such propensities to untidiness and fighting that his father is said to have remarked that if it pleased the Lord to take any one of his children he hoped it would be Isaac. The boy was sent to the famous Charterhouse school, but his faults hindered his progress until he was, by a happy thought, sent away to a school in Essex, where he waked up and began to apply himself to study. He received his university training at Cambridge, where he not only distinguished himself as a scholar, but was noted for his good morals and excellent conduct. Taking the degrees in course, he was elected a fellow of Trinity College, and applied for the Greek professorship, but was not elected. His attainments were simply marvelous. He had mastered Latin and Greek as a matter of course, besides he had learned what there was to know in his time of astronomy, botany, and anatomy, and for a time had studied medicine; but his conscience impelled him to theology, in which he became deeply learned, leaning to the Arminian system. But his favorite intellectual pursuit was mathematics, where he not only became expert as a master and teacher, but made original and valuable contributions toward later developments. But perhaps

[24]Cf. Broadus, p. 203.

[25]*Works of Barrow,* edited by Tillotson, with two accounts (by Hill and Hamilton) of his life prefixed. Sermon in Fish, I, p. 264. Wace, in *Classic Preachers.*

his chief distinction in this field was that he was the friend and the teacher of Isaac Newton.

Missing the Greek professorship on account of his Arminian views—which were unacceptable to the Cromwell government—Barrow raised a little money by the sale of his books, and traveled, spending some time at Paris, Florence, and Constantinople, where he remained a year, chiefly occupied in reading the entire works of Chrysostom in the original. Returning in 1660, he was ordained, and now received the Greek professorship at Cambridge, together with some smaller posts as preacher. Then he became professor of geometry, and later by special appointment he held the Lucas chair of mathematics, which he voluntarily resigned in 1669 into the hands of his great pupil, Newton. This was in order to give himself more to preaching, as he might be called on. In 1672 he was appointed Master of Trinity College by Charles II, who remarked that he was giving the post to the best scholar in England. Barrow discharged his duties with fidelity and success, preaching as occasion offered. He also wrote out many sermons which were never actually used. He was now at the height and near the end of his brilliant career. One of his biographers[26] gives this suggestive hint of his character: "He had possessed but a scanty estate, which yet was made easy to him by a contented mind, and not made a trouble by envy at more plentiful fortunes; he could in patience possess his soul when he had little else; and with the same decency and moderation he maintained his character under the temptation of prosperity." Ever careless of himself, he contracted a fever through over-exertion and died during a visit to London, in May, 1677, in his forty-seventh year. He was surely worthy of the memorial to his memory in Westminster Abbey.

As a preacher, Barrow needed the corrective of the active and practical life of a pastor.[27] He never had a pastoral charge, nor filled any position in the Church at all worthy of his unrivaled powers. He was not popular as a preacher. Audiences grew weary of his too lengthy discourses and the fearful tax upon attention caused, both

[26]Hill, in preface to *Works,* Vol. I, p. XIX.
[27]Cf. Broadus, p. 215.

by their depth of thought and fullness of style. Once—the story goes—he was actually silenced by the exasperated sexton, who rang the bells after an hour or two of preaching. Once again, it is said, some one timidly and suggestively asked Barrow if he did not himself become fatigued in preaching, and he replied that he did sometimes become weary of standing so long! Charles II wittily called him a very unfair preacher because when he treated a subject he did not leave anything for any one else to say. Readers of Barrow's wonderful sermons can easily account for these stories, and see how severe a strain this sort of preaching must have put upon the attention of even the cultivated and thoughtful few. It never could have appealed to the multitude. But the unhurried reader may find even now in these great sermons a rich treasury, both of thought and expression. Thorough in thinking, analytical and exhaustive in treatment, logical in reasoning; full, yet not redundant, in language; majestic and lengthy, yet not involved or obscure in sentence structure, the discourses of this great and luminous intellect still compel admiration and stimulate thought. Broadus[28] judiciously counsels: "Read Jeremy Taylor to enrich the fancy, but Barrow to enrich the intellect and to show how the greatest copiousness may unite with great compactness and great energy of movement." One paragraph must suffice as illustrating what has been said of Barrow's manner. It is from the great sermon on *The Crucifixion of Christ,*[29] where the preacher is elaborating the point "that this way of suffering had in it some particular advantages conducing to the accomplishment of our Lord's principal design," and after instancing its publicity, says: "Another advantage of this kind of suffering was, that by it the nature of that kingdom which He had intended to erect was evidently signified, that it was not such as the carnal people did expect,—an external, earthly, temporal kingdom, consisting in domination over the bodies and estates of men, dignified by outward wealth and splendor, managed by worldly power and policy, promoted by force and terror of arms, affording to men the advantages of outward safety, peace, and prosperity; but a kingdom purely spiritual, heavenly,

[28] *Op. cit.*, p. 216. [29] Fish, I, p. 270.

eternal, consisting in the government of men's hearts and spirits, adorned with endowments of piety and virtue, and administered by the grace and guidance of God's Holy Spirit, maintained and propagated by meek instruction, by virtuous example, by hearty devotion and humble patience, rewarding its loyal subjects with spiritual joys and consolations here, with endless rest and bliss hereafter; no other kingdom could He be presumed to design who submitted to this dolorous and disgraceful way of suffering; no other exploits could He pretend to achieve by expiring on a cross; no other way could He govern who gave Himself up to be managed by the will of His enemies; no other benefits would that forlorn case allow Him to dispense; so that well might He then assert, 'My kingdom is not of this world,' when he was going in this signal manner to demonstrate that great truth. It was a touchstone to prove men's disposition, and to discriminate the ingenuous, well-disposed, humble, and sober persons, who would entertain our Lord's heavenly doctrine with acceptance, notwithstanding these disadvantages, 'not being offended in Him,' from those perverse, vain, proud, profane people, who, being scandalized at His adversity, would reject Him."

Toward the end of the century a group of divines marks the transition from the quaint beauties of Adams, Donne, Hall, and Taylor, and the elaborate and ponderous stateliness of Owen, Howe, and Barrow, to a simpler and more direct and popular method of preaching. Of these, Tillotson and South are the most notable and will receive fuller notice directly, but with them two others should at least be named. Edward Stillingfleet (1635-1699)[30] was more distinguished as bishop, theologian, and controversialist than as preacher, but he was famous in the pulpit also. The garrulous Pepys[31] speaks of hearing "the famous young Stillingfleet," whom some of the bishops and others believed to be "the ablest young man to preach the gospel of any since the apostles," and declares that "he did make a most plain, honest, good,

[30]Among the great mass of Stillingfleet's sermons and other writings, listed in the accounts of his life and in the catalogue of the British Museum, reference is here made to four volumes of *Sermons Preached on Several Occasions*, pub. 1696-1701.

[31]Quoted by Pattison, p. 207.

grave sermon, in the most unconcerned and easy yet substantial manner that ever I heard in my life." Among Stillingfleet's published sermons (the second in Vol. I) there is a strong and manly discourse on the text, "Fools make a mock at sin," preached before Charles II and his court in 1666. For boldness combined with good taste, it is wholly admirable. There is no bravado, no "braving the lion in his den," no covert allusions or dark hints, no pointed or sensational attack on persons or conditions, nor yet any subservient flattery or glozing over well-known evils. It is an unflinching, respectful, serious, intelligent, and well-reasoned exposition of a theme which surely made its own application at that place and time. In general, Stillingfleet's sermons are marked by a high and clear intelligence, judicious weighing of things, and a fairly clear style for that age. There is no soaring, no ornament, little or no play of imagination or pathos. These discourses do not kindle now, and they hardly did so when delivered; but they are forceful, able, and of a high tone. Yet it is an ethical and philosophical tone. Even on such texts as Luke 15:18 (the Prodigal's resolve), and 1 Timothy 1:15 (the "faithful saying"), the evangelical note is hardly struck at all; it is ethical reasoning throughout. Tulloch,[32] not without reason, reckons Stillingfleet among those whose influence favored Latitudinarian and Broad Church tendencies.

William Beveridge (1638-1708),[33] bishop of St. Asaph, was an exceedingly learned man and withal a devoted and beloved pastor and bishop. Among the "classic preachers"[34] he is described as the "Scriptural" one, and his sermons are often quoted in exposition by Ellicott and other commentators. Beveridge's sermons—of which a great number have been published—cover a wide range of doctrinal and textual exposition. While not so labored as those of Andrewes, they, too, are rather overloaded with learning—Latin, Greek, and Hebrew quotations. There is rarely any beauty of language or happy conceits of thought or phrase, but a plain and forcible exposition of Scripture. Imagination

[32]*Op. cit.,* I, p. 411 ff.

[33]See *Sermons* (Vol. I-VI) in the *Anglo-Catholic Theology.*

[34]*Op. cit.,* study by W. R. Clark.

is wanting, and while there is an undercurrent of deep and genuine feeling, there is no warmth, no glow of passion, nor intensity of appeal.

John Tillotson (1630-1694)[35] was born at Halifax, in Yorkshire. He did good work at the preparatory schools, especially in the languages, and entered Cambridge University in 1647. He took the degrees in regular course. He served two years as a curate in Hertfordshire, and made good promise by his amiability and eloquence. His promotion was steady and deserved. He married a niece of Cromwell, and doubtless this led him to take a more liberal view of dissenters than did many of his fellow-Anglicans. He filled various rectorships and other church offices in London and Canterbury. He was opposed to the measures of James II, and favored the cause of William and Mary. On their accession he was made, in 1689, dean of St. Paul's. Sancroft, being a Non-juror, was removed from the archbishopric of Canterbury, and Tillotson was appointed in his place in 1691. He was also made a member of the privy council, but he did not long survive his highest honor, dying in November, 1694.

As a man, Tillotson was able, learned, faithful, amiable, and charitable. His acceptance of William and Mary and his elevation to the see of Canterbury made him enemies among the stronger Anglicans, but he bore their attacks with marked patience and restraint. After his death a bundle of harsh letters was found among his papers, on which he had written, "May God forgive them. I do."

As a preacher, Tillotson occupied in his own day a much higher rank than his published sermons would seem to justify. Bishop Burnet[36] says, "He was not only the best preacher of the age, but seemed to have brought preaching to perfection; his sermons were so well liked that all the nation proposed him as a pattern and studied to copy after him." All his life he was heard with pleasure and profit by large audiences, and his published sermons were much read long after his death. While he was not so strong, either in thought or style, as some of his

[35] *Works,* with *Life* by Birch; sermon in Fish, I, p. 252.
[36] Quoted by Broadus, p. 218.

great predecessors and contemporaries, his sermons are much simpler in plan and language, and so they appealed more to the people. In fact, he introduced a new mode of sermon composition, which not only affected the subsequent development of the English pulpit, but was strongly influential in Holland and elsewhere in Europe. Broadus is doubtless correct in assigning the comparative neglect of Tillotson to-day to the fact that his arguments against infidelity and Romanism no longer appeal to the modern mind, and his style, which was new in his own time, has no longer the freshness which it then had. Tillotson's sermons are marked by great clearness of thought, and express sound sense and vigorous argument; they do not abound in beauty or warmth.

Robert South (1633-1716)[37] was, like Barrow, the son of a London merchant, who was also an intense loyalist. The boy was well educated from the start, being trained at Westminster School, under the famous Dr. Busby. The tombs of Busby and South are still seen near together in Westminster Abbey. South got his university training at Oxford, taking his M. A. degree in 1657. He got into some trouble on account of his Royalist opinions and his courage in expressing them. On the Restoration he was, of course, in favor, and received rapid promotions. He became canon of Christ Church, Oxford, in 1670. Various changes and promotions followed. He refused an archbishopric in Ireland under James II, whose Declaration of Indulgence he conscientiously opposed. He refused to sign the invitation to William and Mary, but after the Revolution he accepted the fact of their sovereignty, though not approving of it. He refused to take a bishopric which had been vacated by a Non-juror, and did not favor the Act of Toleration. He was not very active under Queen Anne, but in his last years was engaged in preaching and publishing his sermons.

As a preacher South ranks, for many reasons, among the greatest of his age and country. He had adequate intellectual outfit, being naturally gifted and carefully

[37]*Sermons,* in various editions; *Life,* prefixed; study by W. C. Lake in *Classic Preachers;* sermon in Fish, I, p. 285, reprinted in *World's Great Sermons,* II, p. 221.

trained; his learning was ample; his mind clear, strong, and intense. He disdained the elaborate fancifulness and labored conceits of the preceding age. He sharply criticised the overwrought style of Jeremy Taylor. In his own preaching he was clear and forcible, with occasional beauties, though these were unsought and unstudied. The fatal defect in South's preaching was its lack of spirituality and tenderness; he was more mind than heart. His invective is sharp, cutting, and by no means always just; but his good sense and steady courage command respect, while the freshness, vigor, and splendid movement of his style give him an assured place among the great masters of English prose. So able a critic as Henry Rogers says:[38] "Of all the English preachers, South seems to furnish, in point of style, the truest specimens of pulpit eloquence. His robust intellect, his shrewd common sense, his vehement feelings, and a fancy always more distinguished by force than by elegance, admirably qualified him for a powerful public speaker. His style is everywhere direct, condensed, pungent. His sermons are well worthy of frequent and diligent perusal by every young preacher." One of his most notable sermons is that on the *Image of God in Man,* from which the following extract is taken. He is discussing the unfallen man, the ideal Adam, in whom the image of God had not yet been marred. In laying out the thought that this image was impressed upon the understanding, the will, and the affections, he begins with the understanding, as follows: "It was then sublime, clear, and aspiring—and, as it were, the soul's upper region, lofty and serene, free from the vapors and disturbances of the inferior affections. It was the leading, controlling faculty; all the passions wore the colors of reason; it was not consul, but dictator. Discourse was then almost as quick as intuition; it was nimble in proposing, firm in concluding; it could sooner determine than now it can dispute. Like the man, it had both light and agility; it knew no rest but in motion, no quiet but in activity. It did not so properly apprehend, as irradiate the object; not so much find, as make things intelligible. It did arbitrate upon the several reports of sense,

[38]Quoted by Pattison, p. 210.

and all the varieties of imagination, not like a drowsy judge, only hearing, but also directing their verdict. In sum, it was vegete, quick, and lively, open as the day, untainted as the morning, full of the innocence and sprightliness of youth, it gave the soul a bright and a full view into all things, and was not only a window, but itself the prospect. Briefly, there is as much difference between the clear representations of the understanding then and the obscure discoveries that it makes now as there is between the prospect of a casement and of a keyhole."

III. Puritan and Non-Conformist Preachers

We must now retrace our steps from the beginning of the century, taking up in similar manner the notable series of dissenting preachers, who were the contemporaries, the rivals, and in many cases the equals of their brethren of the Established Church. Of these we may distinguish the Puritans proper, that is, the Low Church Episcopalians inclining to Presbyterianism or Independency, and then the Presbyterians—Scotch and English—the Independents, and the Baptists. All of these groups furnished distinguished preachers whose names and methods we must now briefly present.

Thomas Adams (d. after 1630),[39] known as "Puritan Adams" and also as the "Shakespeare of the Puritans," has left a good name and some striking sermons behind him; but very little is known of his life. From allusions in his sermons it is gathered that he was pastor for a time at the village of Willington in Bedfordshire, during the early part of the reign of James I, and later in London. He appears as a preacher at Paul's Cross in 1612, but evidently lived long after that date, as his sermons were published in 1630, during his lifetime. Besides a considerable number of sermons, Adams published an exposition of the Second Epistle of Peter, which probably represents a series of expository discourses. All this indicates a long ministry and much preaching.

The *Sermons* and *Exposition* have been highly regarded by many competent critics. Southey is quoted by

[39] *Works;* Brown, *Puritan Preaching,* p. 89 ff.; sermon in Fish, I, p. 180.

Brown[40] as naming Adams the "prose Shakespeare of Puritan theologians, scarcely inferior to Fuller in wit or to Taylor in fancy." His keen portrayal of human nature, his weight of thought, clearness and vigor of expression, and wealth of fancy are all evidenced in his work. The following from a discourse on *The Three Divine Sisters—Faith, Hope, and Charity,* gives some inkling of his quality:[41]

"Hope is the sweetest friend that ever kept a distressed soul company; it beguiles the tediousness of the way, all the miseries of our pilgrimage. Therefore, *dum spiro spero,* said the heathen; but *dum expiro spero,* says the Christian. The one, while I live, I hope; the other also, when I die, I hope: so Job, I will hope in Thee though Thou killest me. It tells the soul such sweet stories of the succeeding joys; what comforts there are in heaven; what peace, what joy, what triumphs, marriage songs, and hallelujahs there are in that country whither she is traveling, that she goes merrily away with her present burden! It holds the head while it aches, and gives invisible drink to the thirsty conscience. It is a liberty to them that are in prison, and the sweetest physic to the sick. Saint Paul calls it an anchor. Let the winds blow, and the storms beat, and the waves swell, yet the anchor stays the ship. It breaks through all difficulties, and makes way for the soul to follow it. It teacheth Abraham to expect fruit from a withered stock; and Joseph, in a dungeon, to look for the sun and stars' obeisance. . . . Though misery be present, comfort absent, though through the dim and waterish humor of thy heart thou canst spy no deliverance; yet such is the nature of Hope, that *futura facta dicit.* It speaks of future things as if they were present. 'We are saved by hope.' We have our inheritance in hope; which gives us the right of the substance, though not the substance of the right: assurance of the possession, though not possession of the thing assured. This tells us that no man should grieve much and long; God making our misery either sufferable or short."

Thomas Goodwin (1600-1679)[42] was born in Suffolk. He received his university education at Cambridge, where

[40] *Op. cit.,* p. 89. [41] Fish, I, p. 183. [42] Brown, p. 98 ff.

he became fellow of Catherine Hall, and, after ordination, a licensed preacher to the University. Later he was pastor in London, and a member of the famous Westminster Assembly of divines. This indicates the change in his church views and relations. Under Cromwell he was president of Magdalen College, Oxford. In 1647 he received an urgent invitation from John Cotton, of Boston in New England, to come to that colony and work with him in the New World. Goodwin had made his preparations to go, even his books had been sent aboard the ship, but he yielded to the earnest remonstrances of his people and remained their pastor. Goodwin was a man of excellent character and abilities. He had a decided evangelical religious experience, both at his conversion and in the subsequent growth of his Christian life. It is this spiritual note which characterizes the sermons of Goodwin, though they do not lack strength of thought and adequacy of learning. In comparing him with others, Brown says:[43] "Comparing him with eminent contemporaries like John Owen and Richard Baxter, it has been said that Owen preached earnestly to the understanding, reasoning from his critical and devout knowledge of Scripture; Baxter preached forcibly to the conscience, reasoning from the fitness of things, while Goodwin appealed to the spiritual affections, reasoning from his own religious experience, and interpreting Scripture by the insight of a renewed heart."

While Goodwin's sermons have something of the well-known faults of the times, his own declaration shows that he avoided the extremes of fancy and pedantry, for in contrasting his own methods with those of others, he thus at the end of his long life opens his heart about his own preaching:[44] "But my heart, upon this, my turning to God and setting His glory as my resolved end of all my actions and ways, did soon discover to me the unprofitableness of such a design [*i. e.,* imitating a certain flowery preacher]; and I came to this resolved principle, that I would preach wholly and altogether solid and wholesome words, without affectation of wit and vanity of eloquence. And in the end, this project of wit and vainglory was wholly sunk in my heart, and I

[43]P. 100. [44]Id., p. 105 f.

left all, and have continued in that purpose and practice these threescore years, and I never was so much as tempted to put in any of my own withered flowers that I had gathered and valued more than diamonds, nor have they offered themselves to my memory to the bringing them into a sermon to this day; but I have preached what I thought was truly edifying, either for conversion or bringing them up to eternal life."

Richard Baxter (1615-1691)[45] is perhaps the greatest single name in the history of English Puritanism, and this is so rather by virtue of character than by eminence of intellect or of learning. The life of Baxter falls into three well-defined periods: (1) The early years, 1615-1646; (2) The pastorate at Kidderminster, 1646-1660; (3) The later years, 1660-1691. It was a long battle with bodily feebleness and a great variety of opposing circumstances, but it was rich in wholesome Christian influence and fruitful of good works.

Richard Baxter was born at Rowton in Shropshire, of respectable but humble parents. Being of a delicate constitution, he was unfitted for hard physical labor, but his acuteness and eagerness of intellect qualified him for scholarly pursuits and culture. But having no means to secure an academic education, he was left to secure his intellectual culture by such irregular schooling and private reading as he could find. At one time he read diligently in the library of the Rev. Mr. Wickstead, a chaplain at Ludlow, being especially interested in devotional works. He learned much and was able to pass a satisfactory examination for orders at the age of twenty-three, when he was ordained by the bishop of Worcester, and began preaching at Dudley and Bridgenorth. Though in ill-health he was very studious, and in 1640 became curate and lecturer at Kidderminster, which was later to be the scene of his remarkable pastoral labors. This first term of service lasted only two years, but left an impression which led to his recall a few years later. During the Civil War Baxter twice served for a short time as chaplain in the Parliamentary army, and also preached as occasion called for at Coventry and other

[45] *Works,* with *Life* by Orme in Vol. I; Brown, *Puritan Preaching,* Lect. VI; sermon in Fish, I, p. 210.

places. Besides his customary bad health, he suffered a long and dangerous illness which brought him near the grave. It is significant that during this period of disquiet and sickness he produced the best known and best loved of all his works, *The Saints' Everlasting Rest.* Both by temperament and conviction Baxter was essentially a moderate, conservative, mediating man. He abhorred tyranny and extremes on either side of the civil conflict; he sympathized with the Parliament, but he protested against the execution of Charles I, and had the courage to tell Cromwell at the height of his power that the Commonwealth was an usurpation, its measures were objectionable, and that the old form of monarchy was more acceptable to the people. While in the army he labored to moderate extremes of all sorts. In church matters also he occupied a middle position, rejecting High Church pretensions, and yet being neither a fully convinced Presbyterian nor Independent. So also in theology he took up a mediating position between Arminians and Calvinists. He formulated and urged various schemes of toleration and comprehension for all parties and opinions which divided the leaders of his age. His theories were impracticable, but his spirit and character commanded the respect of the good and thoughtful, though he was made to suffer at the hands of the intolerant and partisan.

In 1646 the people at Kidderminster, remembering his earnest work of a few years before, urged that he be made their minister, but the place was still held by the unworthy old incumbent with whom Baxter had formerly worked, and he was unwilling to displace the old man and set him adrift. Baxter therefore accepted the post of "lecturer," and really did the work of the parish from the beginning, though for a time the old vicar was officially its incumbent. In this unpromising parish, composed mostly of weavers, with only a few people of culture and ideals, with the additional difficulty of having had very unworthy ministers for a long season, afflicted with ill-health and other trials, Richard Baxter labored for fourteen years. It is one of the most notable instances of pastoral work and success in all history. A transformation was wrought. It was a case where intense and laborious personal and pastoral work was supplemented by devoted and earnest preaching. In his *Reformed Pastor,* his autobiographical sketch, and his sermons, Baxter gives good insight into his methods of visitation, catechising, and teaching. It is amazing and almost incredible how a feeble man could have done all this work besides producing some of his best known writings and constantly preaching.

Baxter welcomed the Restoration in 1660. Like many other moderate royalists, he hoped the restoration of the old form of government would settle the country, and that the new king would have learned something from the mistakes of his predecessor. He welcomed the king, took part in the Savoy Conference, declined an offered bishopric, and desired to be reinstated at Kidderminster under the new government and continue his labors there. But for some reason this was declined, and for the rest of his life he was without a settled charge, though frequently preaching as opportunities were offered, mostly in London, where he married and chiefly resided. In 1685 he was arraigned before the infamous Judge Jeffreys on a charge of preaching sedition. His trial was a horrible travesty, and he was condemned to imprisonment in the Tower, where he spent eighteen months, occupying himself with his writings. At last released on the plea of ill-health, he gradually declined, and died in 1691.

In preaching, the bodily weakness and want of comeliness in Baxter were offset by a bright and speaking eye and a mellow and persuasive voice. His actual preaching produced a profound effect, but we can not judge his sermons fairly by the standards of modern taste and methods. Like those of all the Puritans, they seem to us intolerably prolix, minute, tedious in detail. But when compared with others that have come down from that time laden with the same faults, they show to advantage, at least in two particulars: the style, though quaint and prolix, is clear and strong; and the sermons are remarkably free from the affectations and pedantry and straining after effect which we find in so many. The one distinctive trait, or rather pre-eminent virtue, in Baxter's preaching, as reported by tradition and evident now in the printed sermons, is what Broadus aptly calls its "tremendous, earth-shaking earnestness." All his writings have this note, and his own oft-quoted lines infallibly describe it:

> "I preached as never sure to preach again,
> And as a dying man to dying men."

Brown also well states the matter thus:[46] "This man's power, then, and the secret of his success lay in the natural human way he spoke to men, and the divine earnestness which possessed his soul. He spoke directly from Christ to the people. Christianity was to him no mere set of doctrines to be received or a code of ethics to be followed; it was the power of an endless life."

Some indication of this note of profound personal conviction may be seen in the brief extract which follows from a sermon on *Making Light of Christ and His Salvation*:[47] "Dearly beloved in the Lord, I have now done that work which I came upon; what effect it hath, or will have, upon your hearts, I know not, nor is it any further in my power to accomplish that which my soul desireth for you. Were it the Lord's will that I might have my wish herein, the words that you have this day heard should so stick by you that the secure should be awakened by them, and none of you should perish by the slighting of your salvation. I can not now follow you to your several habitations to apply this word to your particular necessities; but O that I could make every man's conscience a preacher to himself that it might do it, which is ever with you! . . . I will say no more but this at this time: It is a thousand pities that when God hath provided a Saviour for the world, and when Christ hath suffered so much for their sins, and made so full a satisfaction to justice, and purchased so glorious a kingdom for His saints, and all this is offered so freely to sinners, to lost, unworthy sinners, even for nothing, that yet so many millions should everlastingly perish because they make light of their Saviour and salvation, and prefer the vain world and their lusts before them. I have delivered my mes-

[46] *Op. cit.*, p. 178. [47] Fish, I, p. 222.

sage; the Lord open your hearts to receive it. I have persuaded you with the words of truth and soberness; the Lord persuade you more effectually, or else all this is lost. Amen."

The Presbyterian group of preachers contains a number of strong and learned men, mostly Scotchmen, but some Englishmen also. Only a few of the leaders can be selected for brief notice.

Alexander Henderson (1583-1646)[48] was, after Knox and Melville, the most important and influential of the founders of the Kirk of Scotland. In early life an Episcopalian, he was converted under a sermon by Robert Bruce, and soon became convinced that Presbyterianism was right, adopting that belief with characteristic earnestness. He was one of the leaders in framing the famous Covenant of 1638 to resist "prelacy" in Scotland; he was largely instrumental in securing the adoption of the Solemn League and Covenant with England in 1643; and it was he more than any other one man who gave to the Westminster Confession and the two Catechisms their final form. Henderson was born in Fifeshire, and got his academic training at St. Andrews. He served as pastor at Leuchars, near St. Andrews, and, after 1638, at Edinburgh, where he also was rector of the University. As a preacher he was both popular and powerful, balanced in thought, strong in argument, effective in manner. The published sermons of Henderson were all preached in that critical time in 1638 between the signing of the Covenant at Edinburgh and the meeting of the Assembly at Glasgow. They show a masculine intellect, a firm faith, a quiet but determined courage. The tone is noble and modest, the grasp of the subject is clear and firm; there is power of appeal and a secure sense of being right without pride or bitterness.

David Dickson (1583-1663),[49] affectionately known as "Dickson of Irvine" from having served for twenty-

[48]See *Sermons, Prayers, and Pulpit Addresses,* by Alex. Henderson, ed. by R. Thomson Martin, 1888; printed from an old ms. but well attested; with *Life* by Wodrow prefixed; Blaikie, p. 98 ff.; *Evangelical Succession,* 2d Series, p. 89 ff.

[49]See *Select Practical Writings of David Dickson,* ed. by T. Thompson, including a number of sermons; also Blaikie, p. 102 ff.

three years as pastor at that town, was a greatly beloved and useful preacher. He was born at Glasgow and educated at the University of Edinburgh. He began his notable ministry at Irvine in 1618. Here he was a faithful and beloved pastor, a steady student, a popular and forceful preacher and writer. His expositions of Scripture were sound and scholarly, and were long useful. He is remembered in hymnology, too, for his translation or paraphrase of the hymn, *O Mother Dear, Jerusalem,* of which he has been often erroneously supposed to be the author. Reluctantly leaving his small parish, he yielded to a sense of duty and became professor of divinity, first at Glasgow, and then at Edinburgh. After the Restoration he was ejected, and did not long survive. He was a noble man and preacher, pious, evangelical, moving, and successful. Crowds attended his preaching, and many were converted and built up under it. The sermons show strong grasp of the theme, fine spiritual insight, and a beautiful blending of severity and tenderness in rebuking sin, with a quaint and refreshing style that charms both by its simplicity and pungency.

Samuel Rutherford (1600-1661)[50] presents us with the striking contrast of a holy, mystical, devout soul joined to a sharp, narrow, partisan, dogmatic, and intolerant mind. His famous *Letters* to his flock and friends are one of the classics of devotional literature; but the other side of him is remembered by the famous rebuke he received at the mouth of Cromwell, who once sternly suggested to him to consider the possibility of his being mistaken. He was born in the parish of Nisbet, in Roxburgshire, and was educated at Edinburgh. On his ordination he became pastor at the little village of Anworth, where his faithful and much-blessed ministry was distinguished by personal piety and devotion, by earnest and fruitful preaching, and by wisdom and tenderness in counsel, as his admirable *Letters* show. He later became professor at St. Andrews, was a leading

[50]See *Communion Sermons* of Rutherford, ed. by A. A. Bonar, 1876 (with biographical notice), and *Quaint Sermons* by Rutherford (same editor), 1885; notice by Blaikie, p. 112 ff., and lecture by A. T. Innes, Esq., in *Evangelical Succession,* p. 127 ff.

delegate at the Westminster Assembly, and otherwise much concerned in the great disputes of the age. Rutherford appears to least advantage in his controversial works, which, though strong and sometimes profound in thought, are marred by bitterness and intolerance; but his devotional works and sermons exhibit a poetic and mystic temperament which, after the fashion of the age, often found expression in quaint and fanciful ways. He loved to preach, and preached with effect. There is a quaint, delightful flavor in Rutherford's sermons. They show all the varied qualities of his mind—devout mysticism, philosophical thinking, and sharp controversy. But he glorifies his Saviour in all. There is a particularly interesting and striking series of discourses on "The Forlorn Son," as he calls the Prodigal.

Of the English Presbyterian preachers, the most important name is that of Edmund Calamy (1600-1666),[51] who was born and brought up in London. He took his university degree at Pembroke Hall, Cambridge, and being ordained in the English Church, served for a time as chaplain to the bishop of Ely, then as lecturer at Bury St. Edmunds, and later as rector at Rochford. But becoming more and more dissatisfied with episcopacy, he announced himself a Presbyterian about 1639. He then became "lecturer," or preaching pastor, at the strong Presbyterian Church of St. Mary's, Aldermanbury, London. Here a ministry of twenty years was greatly honored and blessed. He was heard by large audiences of cultured and thoughtful people. Like Baxter, he was moderate and conciliatory, desiring to find a middle way in which all could unite. He opposed the execution of Charles I, and favored the recall of Charles II, who offered him a bishopric if he would come back to the Established Church. Under the Act of Uniformity he was forced to resign his place, but did not try to gather an independent congregation, living quietly in London a few years more. The sermons of Calamy show that his reputation as one of the most popular and effective preachers of his time was well deserved. They are

[51]*Dict. of Nat. Biog.*, for his life; and for sermons, *The Art of Divine Meditation* (a series), 1680; and *The Godly Man's Ark* (often reprinted, most recent ed., 1865).

fearless and yet devout in spirit, strong in thought, effective in expression.

There were many good and learned divines and preachers among the Independents, though these were naturally neither so numerous nor so influential as the Episcopalians and Presbyterians. Chief among them were Owen and Howe.

John Owen (1616-1683)[52] was born at Stadham, near Oxford, the son of a clergyman, and descended from an old Welsh family. John was put to a tutor at Oxford, and quickly prepared for college, which he entered at the age of twelve! Though an ambitious and diligent student, he took part in the games and activities of the University and did not lose his health. There is no definite account of his religious experiences, but they came early, and he escaped the vices of college life. During the ascendency of Archbishop Laud at Oxford, Owen, against the wishes of his kindred, left the University. He had, however, already secured his degree of M. A. at the age of nineteen, and had also been ordained to the Episcopal ministry. He became private chaplain and tutor in two families, who were royalists, and on the breaking out of civil strife, Owen promptly sided with the Parliament. This cost him his place and decided his future. His royalist Welsh uncle who had long cared for him now cast him off, and he was left, without means and in great depression of spirits. to shift for himself as best he could. In some way he received help from friends, and later secured a church at Fordham, where he led a quietly studious pastoral life, married, and enjoyed peace. Later he received appointment as preacher at Coggeshall. It was here that he finally became an Independent in his views of church polity. He several times preached by invitation before Parliament, and reluctantly accompanied Cromwell on his campaigns in Ireland and Scotland. During the Commonwealth Owen filled with admirable ability and courage the exceedingly difficult position of Vice-chancellor of the University of Oxford, preaching also at Christ Church. He was not a subservient man, and

[52]Owen's *Works*, complete, ed. by Goold, with *Life* by Thomson prefixed.

in some way offended Cromwell, and gave up his hard post in 1658. He retired to his native village of Stadham, where he had acquired a little home. He spent his time largely in writing, though occasionally preaching till silenced by the Acts of Charles II. Even then he preached sometimes in secret, and more openly as the rigidity of the persecuting laws became somewhat relaxed. He was still regarded as the leader of the Independents, and his active pen ceased only with his life.

Owen was a man of exalted character, esteemed by friends and opponents for his inflexible adherence to principle. Twice married, his domestic life was happy. As a pastor he was faithful and beloved; as a theologian he ranks among the greatest of his age, and his numerous works—some of them still valuable—were called forth by the needs of his time. His *Exposition of the Epistle to the Hebrews* is a monumental work. As a preacher Owen was heard with interest and respect; but making every allowance for the taste of the age, it is difficult to see how his sermons could have been other than tedious and heavy, even to a Puritan audience. The thought has, indeed, the weight and fullness of other great minds of the time, but the logical coherence and clearness of Barrow and Howe, for example, are wanting; the popular tone of Baxter, and even of South, is not in sight, and as for style, nothing comparable to the beauties of Taylor or the simplicity and directness of Tillotson is to be thought of. In sum, Owen was far greater as a man, a leader and thinker, than he was as a preacher; but the greatness of his character and the power and value of his thinking gave interest and influence to his preaching in spite of its want of the distinctively oratorical qualities.

John Howe (1630-1705)[53] was a clearer thinker and a more effective preacher than Owen, but was in other respects not unlike him. He, too, was the son of an Anglican clergyman, and born at Loughborough, in Leicestershire, but his father was ejected for non-conformity, and retired, first to Ireland, and later to a place

[53] *Works* and *Life* of Howe, by Dr. Edmund Calamy, is the edition here referred to. But numerous other editions, partial and complete are accessible. Sermon in Fish, I, p. 238.

in Lancashire. John received good teaching at the hands of his father, and was sent to Cambridge, where he took his B. A. degree in regular course. Then he went also to Oxford, and again received the degree there, and later that of M. A. also, with a fellowship at Magdalen College. He was ordained by non-conformist divines, and began preaching first in connection with his university work, but later settled as pastor at Great Torrington in Devon. Then he served both Oliver and Richard Cromwell as one of the chaplains at Whitehall, returning at Richard's fall to Great Torrington, where he served again till the Act of Uniformity silenced him in 1662. He preached secretly as he could until 1671, when he retired to Ireland, where a lenient bishop permitted him greater liberty in preaching while he served as chaplain to Lord Massarene. In 1675 the relaxation of the persecution permitted his return to London, where his preaching to a congregation of Dissenters was connived at for a time, but in 1685 he went to Utrecht for a sojourn, preaching "in his own hired house" and in the English church for a year or so, till the Declaration of Indulgence, in 1687, permitted his return as pastor to his London flock. The Revolution and Act of Toleration now left him unmolested as an Independent preacher to this London church to the end of his life, in 1705.

In person Howe was tall and dignified; in mind great and learned; in character singularly unselfish, devoted, and pure. His extensive and exhaustive sermons taxed the patience even of his select hearers. It is said that one of his women parishioners once remarked that Mr. Howe was indeed a great divine, "but, dear good man, he spends so much time in laying the cloth that I lost my appetite for the dinner." One of his best sermons, *The Redeemer's Tears Over Lost Souls,* as given by extracts in Fish's *Masterpieces,* exhibits this wearisome prolixity and other defects of Howe's preaching, but it also shows the sweep and depth of his thought, the elevation of his thinking and feeling, and the occasional flowing eloquence of his style. The oft-quoted opinion of Robert Hall[54] is well worth giving here entire: "I

[54]*Works* of Robert Hall, Vol. III, p. 78; an appendix giving reported conversations.

have learned far more from John Howe than from any other author I ever read. There is an astonishing magnificence in his conceptions. He had not the same perception of the beautiful as of the sublime; and hence his endless subdivisions. . . . There was, I think, an innate inaptitude in Howe's mind for discerning minute graces and [also] improprieties, and hence his sentences are often long and cumbersome. Still he was unquestionably the greatest of the Puritan divines."

The Baptists, though comparatively few in number and opposed by some of the strongest social and political influences, had among them some preachers of power and distinction and not unworthy to be mentioned along with the celebrated men of other faiths who have been named.

John Bunyan (1628-1688),[55] the world-famous author of the *Pilgrim's Progress,* also of the *Holy War, Grace Abounding,* and other devotional works, is better known as writer than preacher. But a preacher of wonderful force and power he certainly was. One would expect to find in the sermons of the author of *Pilgrim's Progress* that admirable combination of spiritual insight and fervor, of picturesque and vivid imagination, and of racy, homely, vigorous, and appealing English diction which characterize that immortal production. This expectation is not fully met in the published sermons. In fact, one feels a distinct disappointment—the sermons are those of the Puritan pattern of the day, prolix, tedious, minutely divided, with labored effects and conceits, and the style is often too homely and dry. But put the *Pilgrim's Progress,* and its praises by the critics, out of your mind; recall and allow for the customary Puritan faults; then read a few of the sermons, and perhaps the spiritual warmth, the force of imagination, the clearness and power of style will appeal to you still and stand on their own footing as elemental characteristics of Bunyan the preacher. Then you will not wonder that back of these few published Puritan sermons there lay a well-defined

[55]*Life* by John Brown; his own narrative in his *Grace Abounding,* often prefixed to various editions of *Pilgrim's Progress;* several editions of his *Works;* Lec. V in Brown's *Puritan Preaching;* sermon in Fish, I, p. 225. For literary appreciation see Macaulay's *Essay* on Southey's *Life of Bunyan,* and his estimate in *History of England,* chap. VII.

popular tradition of Bunyan's attractiveness and power as a preacher of the gospel, and that this was well sustained by the crowds that attended and the fruits that followed his preaching.

John Bunyan was born at Elstow, a village of Bedfordshire, of poor and untaught parents, his father being a tinker, that is, a mender of metal vessels, a trade which John himself followed at times, as well as lace-making by hand. His mother died when the boy was quite young, and the father's marriage a few months afterwards was deeply resented. John joined the army (probably, but not certainly, the Parliamentary side) when sixteen or seventeen years old, and became very godless, profane, and wicked. On leaving the army (1646) he settled to his trade as tinker at Elstow, and though utterly without means, he married a girl as poor as himself. He says,[56] "This woman and I came together as poor as poor might be, not having so much household stuff as a dish or spoon betwixt us both." But she brought piety and two books that had been her father's: *The Plain Man's Pathway to Heaven,* and *The Practice of Piety.* These the young couple read and studied together, and the godly wife's prayers and influence were at length rewarded with the conversion of her husband. She died early and unknown, but her work remains. Bunyan was baptized into the fellowship of the Baptist Church at Bedford, by the pastor, John Gifford, in 1655. Soon he was asked to preach, his gift being recognized, and consented, making from the start a profound impression. He also began to write, his first published work being a controversy with a Quaker. Working with his hands and preaching as occasion called for, he was useful and busy. About 1658 he married his second wife, Elizabeth, much younger than himself, whose sufferings during his long imprisonment and piteous appeals before the judges have won for her a place of pathetic interest in the religious annals of the age. On the Restoration, in 1660, Bunyan was forbidden to preach, arrested for disobeying, and thrown into Bedford jail, where he spent twelve years. Friends helped his wife and children; he made lace in the prison, received visits from his wife and children, especially his

[56]Brown's *Life*, p. 54.

blind daughter, and other friends. But the chief interest of this time of trial is that it gave to the world *The Pilgrim's Progress,* which was written in Bedford jail. Toward the last the rigors of prison life were much relaxed and Bunyan was allowed occasionally to go out and even to preach. At last, in 1672, the act of pardon let him out of prison and gave him liberty to preach. He soon became pastor of the Baptist Church at Bedford, and served to the end of his life. His preaching attracted and profited large congregations, and he often visited London, where he was gladly welcomed and heard. It was on one of these visits at the home of a friend that he became ill and died, in August, 1688. He was buried in Bunhill Fields, City Road, London, where his tomb is visited by many who have learned to love him through his wonderful allegory of the Christian life.

Recurring to Bunyan's preaching, let it be remembered that its chief excellence lay in the vividness and reality of its spiritual power. He himself is quoted by Dr. Brown[57] as saying, "I preached what I felt, what I smartingly did feel, even that under which my poor soul did groan and tremble to astonishment." And one of his pastors, in a preface to one of his earlier works, wrote:[58] "He hath through grace taken these three heavenly degrees, to-wit, union with Christ, the anointing of the Spirit, and experience of the temptations of Satan, which do more fit a man for that mighty work of preaching the gospel than all the university learning and degrees that can be had." The closing sentences from a long and earnest sermon on the *Barren Fig-Tree*[59] will give a slight taste of Bunyan's quality as a preacher: "And now, could the soul be annihilated, or brought to nothing, how happy would it count itself! But it sees that may not be. Wherefore it is put to a wonderful strait. Stay in the body it may not; go out of the body it dares not! Life is going; the blood settles in the flesh, and the lungs being no more able to draw breath through the nostrils, at last out goes the weary, trembling soul, and is immediately seized by devils, who lie lurking in every hole in the chamber for that very purpose. His

[57]*Puritan Preaching,* p. 146. [58]Brown's *Life,* p. 113.
[59]Fish, I, p. 236.

friends take care of the body, and wrap it up in the sheet or coffin; but the soul is out of their thought and reach, going down to the chambers of death! I had thought to have enlarged, but I forbear. God, who teaches man to profit, bless this brief and plain discourse to thy soul, who yet standest a professor in the land of the living, among the trees of His garden! Amen."

Vavasor Powell (1617-1671),[60] sometimes called the "Whitefield of Wales," was born of good family in Radnorshire. He was well educated in youth, and took a course at Oxford. Ordained as a minister of the Established Church, he began his work without a deep spiritual life, but on reading Puritan books and talking with leaders, he was converted and became a Non-conformist, and later a Baptist. A great ministry in Wales followed, and multitudes of converts were won. In 1642 he returned to London and did great preaching in the city, making many converts, and forming a church. In 1646 he again went on a mission to Wales, armed this time with a letter of commendation from members of the Westminster Assembly. This tour also was greatly successful, and interesting stories are related in illustration of his power over audiences. Being republican in sentiment, he fell under Cromwell's displeasure. First by one side, and then the other, he suffered imprisonment at various times, spending in sum eight years in thirteen different prisons. He was in the Fleet prison in London when he died. His death was peaceful and triumphant. He published some sermons and other works, including a concordance. He evidently had that fervid eloquence for which so many of his countrymen have been noted. The effects of his preaching were immediate and powerful. It is said that he established as many as twenty churches in Wales, and that he gathered some twenty thousand followers.

Benjamin Keach (1640-1704)[61] was the most famous and able Baptist preacher and divine of his time. He

[60]Article in Cathcart's *Baptist Encyclopaedia; Life,* by David Davies, Lond., 1896; a list of his writings is given in the Appendix, but no sermons seem to be available in English.

[61]Article in *Baptist Encyclopaedia,* Benedict's *History of the Baptists,* Vol. I; Keach's *Golden Mine, Exposition of the Parables;* sermon in Fish, I, p. 299.

was born in Buckinghamshire, and converted at the age of fifteen. By a study of the Bible he became convinced of Baptist doctrines and lived to be one of their clearest and ablest defenders. At first Arminian in sentiment, he soon embraced the Calvinistic theology. He was ordained as pastor of a Baptist church in Southwark, and held it the rest of his life. He was a stout disputant, and crossed swords to good purpose with Baxter and other strong controversialists. His services were in frequent demand, both by pen and disputation, among his Baptist and other dissenting brethren. He suffered, not only the usual persecutions during the period after the Restoration, but was shamefully treated besides. In 1664 he published his *Child's Instructor,* in which he argued against infant baptism. For this he was arraigned before Hyde (afterwards Lord Clarendon) and condemned to the pillory, where he was subjected to ignominy and insult, but bore his sufferings in the spirit of a martyr. He was a voluminous author, and wrote many controversial and devotional works, besides his published sermons. These show a fine insight into Scripture, a clear and convincing argumentation, a devout and earnest spirit, and a style usually simple and clear and not without graces of expression and occasional eloquence. His exposition of the Parables is a series of sermon notes. The interpretation is for the most part sensible and judicious, but sometimes falls into the forced allegorizing and fancifulness too common in that and other ages. *A Golden Mine Opened* is a volume of forty sermons published in 1694. They present a varied character, a good deal of strength, and not a few quaintnesses in the way of both title and treatment. The first one, for example, bears the title, *A Trumpet Blown in Zion, or an Alarm in God's Holy Mountain.* The sermon in Fish's *Masterpieces* scarcely gives Keach at his best, but presents his clearness, force of reasoning, and view of Scripture in a characteristic way. Keach's success is the best commentary on his character and work. The odds against him were great, but he won the fear and respect of his foes, and the esteem and confidence of his friends, dying in peace and honor at sixty-four years of age.

PART SECOND

THE EIGHTEENTH CENTURY

CHAPTER VI

General View of the Eighteenth Century. Catholic Preaching in Southern Europe

For preaching, as for other departments of human activity, the history of Europe in the eighteenth century is neither so interesting nor so important as in the seventeenth and the nineteenth. In general history this relatively lower value of the eighteenth century has often been noted, and sometimes exaggerated. For altogether apart from the place of the eighteenth century as a link in the chain of events and causes, it has to its credit many great movements in the progress of European civilization. The rise of Russia and of Prussia to vital influence in Europe, the development of the British colonial enterprises in India and America, the century-long conflict between England and France on many fields, the independence and federation of the United States, and the great upheaval of the French Revolution make it forever impossible to underrate the historic significance of the century in which these momentous events took place. And in the less dazzling but no less important affairs of commerce, science, thought, literature, and the arts, both industrial and æsthetic, there were affairs not only of great intrinsic importance, but of still greater value as preparations for the more extensive and wonderful achievements of the nineteenth century.

This line of remark applies also to the history of religion in general and of preaching in particular in Europe during the eighteenth century. As compared with both the immediately preceding and following centuries there is noticeable depression of both inner power and of appealing interest. It was not a distinctively great epoch, yet not wanting in strong men nor in important and fruitful movements.

The striking features of the century, in the larger affairs of Christianity and in its pulpits as well, are in contrast—rationalism and evangelism. This is especially true of Protestantism; Romanism was not so greatly affected either in one direction or the other, but suffered from a general decline in which there are only a few traces of power. The Catholic countries in Southern Europe lay depressed and cold, while France suffered from the decay following the exhausting glories of the great age of Louis XIV, till the great explosion of the Revolution shook the foundations of religion as well as of the state.

In the leading Protestant countries—Germany and England—and from them elsewhere, there was a cold wave of skeptical recoil from the religious enthusiasm of earlier times. Deism and latitudinarianism in England, philosophic skepticism (partly due to English Deism and partly to French infidelity) and rationalistic criticism in Germany, combined to make the eighteenth century the "dark age of Protestantism"—as it has not inappropriately been called. In Germany the feeble remnants of Pietism offered some resistance to the prevalent Rationalism. In England the reaction was far more effective and of far greater after results. This was the great Whitefield-Wesley revival, for which there was in America also a corresponding movement in the Great Awakening. The English revival did not at first greatly affect the Continent of Europe, but its influence and fruits were felt there early in the nineteenth century. But in Great Britain itself, and thence in after generations throughout the world, that great evangelical reaction was one of the most mighty and significant movements in all the history of Christian preaching. The features of preaching thus generally indicated will be more particularly dealt with as we discuss pulpit conditions in the separate countries and their groups of preachers, giving our first attention to the Catholic preaching in Southern Europe.

I. Spanish and Portuguese Preaching

The political and religious history of Spain during the eighteenth century need not detain us long, for general affairs had no more than the usual connections with our particular subject of preaching; and preaching was only an accepted and established custom of ecclesiastical life which had no special or vital influence upon the progress of events. The century is notable in Spanish history as that of the Bourbon dynasty. This famous House came to the throne of Spain in the person of Philip V, duke of Anjou and grandson of Louis XIV. His accession led to the famous War of the Spanish Succession, which involved all Europe, established the fame of the English Duke of Marlborough, and ended with establishing the Bourbons in Spain, though at fearful cost to the country. On the whole, the Bourbons—Philip V, Ferdinand VI, Charles III, Charles IV—proved rather good monarchs as monarchs go. They sought the good of the people they ruled and were above the average in personal character, but they confronted difficulties in internal government and in foreign complications to which their abilities were not equal, and the history of Spain during the century is that of continued decline and loss. In religious affairs Catholicism remained supreme, but two important checks to the absolute domination of the papacy were administered during the century; one was the curbing of the power of the Inquisition, and the other was the overthrow of the Jesuits, whose expulsion from Spain (1767) was followed by the suppression (1773) of the Order by the Pope, an action forced by the Spanish Government.

The Bourbons encouraged literature,[1] but the decay which had set in toward the close of the preceding period was incurable, and their efforts were not crowned with distinguished success. Philip V founded a Spanish Academy, modeled after that of France, which did some good work in purifying the language, but failed to stimulate the production of a great literature. Ticknor says:[2] "All elegant culture had so nearly disappeared before the accession of the Bourbons, and there was such an insensibility to its value in those classes of society where it should have been most cherished, that it was plain the

[1]See Ticknor, *History of Spanish Literature,* Vol. III, p. 213 ff., for the literary history of the Bourbon period.
[2]*Op. cit.,* p. 224.

resuscitation must be the work of time, and that the land must long lie fallow before another harvest could be gathered in. During the entire reign of Philip V . . . we shall find undeniable traces of this unhappy state of things; few authors appearing who deserve to be named at all, and still fewer who demand a careful notice." From the middle of the century there was some improvement, and the historian names and discusses a few writers in the various departments of literature, but there were none of commanding genius in any sphere, only a few who attracted much notice, even at home, and fewer still whose names became known in the world.

In such a state of national decline and literary eclipse we should look in vain for preaching to be marked by either intellectual force or spiritual power. The triumph of the Inquisition in the complete suppression of Protestantism and of any freedom of thought in the dominant Church left the Roman doctrines outwardly established as the staple of preaching, but shorn of vital power and wanting the stimulus of a healthy opposition. The inflated style of Gongora still held place among many of the leading preachers;[3] and along with this there was a coarse and irreverent style of open-air and mission preaching which made up in vulgarity what it lacked in real popular force. A sharp satirical attack was made on this style of preaching by Father Isla (1703-1781),[4] a Jesuit, educated at Salamanca, and himself a preacher of no mean powers. He is one of the few writers of his time whom Ticknor mentions with warmth, and that historian's account of him is, in part, as follows: "From the age of twenty-four he had been a successful preacher, and continued such until he was cruelly expelled from his own country. But he perceived how little worthy of its great subjects was the prevalent style of Spanish pulpit oratory—how much it was degraded by bad taste, by tricks of composition, by conceits and puns, and even by a low buffoonery in which the vulgar monks, sent to preach in the churches or in the public streets and

[3]Ticknor, *op. cit.*, p. 237 and note.

[4]See Ticknor, *op. cit.*, p. 259 f.; and an excellent monograph by Bernard Gandeau (Paris, 1891), *Les Prêcheurs Burlesques en Espagne au dix-huitième Siècle, Étude sur le Père Isla.*

squares, indulged themselves merely to win applause from equally vulgar audiences and increase the contributions they solicited by arts so discreditable. It is said that at first Father Isla was swept away by the current of his times, which ran with extraordinary force, and that he wrote in some degree as others did. But he soon recognized his mistake, and his numerous published sermons, written between 1729 and 1754, are marked with a purity and directness of style which had long been unknown, and which, though wanting the richness and fervor of the exhortations of Luis de Leon and Luis de Granada, would not have dishonored the Spanish pulpit even in their days." Besides condemning the bad preaching of the age by his own later example, Isla published a clever satire called *Father Gerund,* in which he lashed with wit and force the popular preachers of this sort. He described the character and methods of his man and put into his mouth specimens of preaching, taken from actual sermons, which amply sustained his strictures. The book set all Spain laughing—after the manner of *Don Quixote*—and, along with the French influence from Bossuet and others, effectually drove from Spanish preaching the excesses which it attacked.

Only a few other Spanish preachers are noted by the authorities[5] as of more than the average worth. Of these Pasquale Ranzon (d. 1711) is named as having enjoyed a considerable reputation at the opening of the century. Along with him should be mentioned his contemporary, Benito Viñales de la Torre, who was professor of theology at Barcelona, and later a court preacher, in the early period and had some fame for eloquence. Others are mentioned by Zanotto as having published sermons—including a few who preached in the Spanish settlements in America—but as the historian gives neither extracts nor comments, they could scarcely have been men of great importance.

In Portugal political, ecclesiastical, and literary conditions present only a few matters of unusual interest. The first half of the century was a period of poverty, misgovernment, and decline, redressed in the latter half

[5]See works of Zanotto and Lentz, previously mentioned, and articles in Wetzer und Welte, *Kirchenlexikon.*

by the strong ministry of Pombal. The Lisbon earthquake, in 1755, awakened the sympathy of the world. As in Spain, the Inquisition was curbed and the Jesuits expelled. Literature feebly imitated French models, lacked originality and power, and has no names of eminence. Letters flourished more in Brazil than in the mother country. Preaching shared the decline of the times and presents no characteristics of power. The authorities referred to name at least one man, Emanuele de Gouven, as rising above the average. He was an Augustinian monk who had unusual gifts of voice and oratory, drew great crowds, and published some sermons. There was also John of St. Margaret, who taught philosophy and theology, was regarded as quite an orator, and published a number of political, moral, and panegyrical discourses. A few others also are mentioned, but without special notice or commendation.

II. Italian Preaching

The general condition of affairs in Italy during the eighteenth century showed no improvement over that of the seventeenth. The country was still the football of foreign rulers. Only decadent and intriguing small States like Genoa, Venice, Tuscany, Parma, and the Papal States, maintained some semblance of Italian native governments, and these were weak, disunited, and corrupt. The failure of the Hapsburg line of Spanish sovereigns and the accession of the Bourbons left the Italian interests of the rival houses a constant source of dispute between Austria and Spain. In these quarrels and the terrible wars they caused France was involved, in the early part of the century through the Bourbons, and later, toward its close, by the Revolution. Meantime the House of Savoy secured the kingdom of Sardinia and was preparing for its future mission as the maker of united Italy. But this was far away. The Italians were throughout the eighteenth century divided, decayed, despoiled, almost hopeless. Even the intervals of "languid peace" in this century of strife brought no true prosperity or power to the Italian people. Capable patriots were too few; mere insurrections were futile; the day for Italian independence and unity was indeed far distant, not yet even in sight.

Italian literature in the eighteenth century,[6] though not great in range or power, nor comparable to that of the sixteenth or of the nineteenth century, shows improvement over that of the seventeenth. Its distinctive achievements are in the field of the drama, but with some lyrics and satires of note; there is not much of notable prose. The lyrical dramas and other poems of Metastasio gave him an European and permanent renown among the writers of his country. Goldoni's comedies and his autobiography are also among the treasures of Italian literature; while the fine and earnest satires of Parini directed attention to the follies and weaknesses of the age. Less worthy than these were Gozzi, who wrote striking comedies; Cerretti, who was a minor poet and a rhetorician distinguished for the excellence of his teachings and of his own style, and Meli, "the greatest of Sicilian poets," who was also professor in the University of Palermo. But the greatest name in Italian literature in this century is that of Vittorio Alfieri (1749-1803), whose powerful tragedies, with all their defects, bear the unmistakable stamp of genius. The degenerate and oppressed condition of his country appealed powerfully to Alfieri, and his pleas against tyranny in his dramas and other writings did much to awaken and encourage the spirit of liberty among his countrymen.

Ecclesiastical affairs in Italy were much complicated with the political and religious disputes of the time throughout Europe. The popes who ruled during the eighteenth century were for the most part highly regarded as men of good personal character, and they attempted various reforms in ecclesiastical discipline. But they were in the toils of the papal system, and much tossed about among the warring interests of their age. The disputes over Jansenism and Jesuitism, the aggressions of Bourbons and Hapsburgs, and finally of republican France; the vain efforts at reform of the clergy and correction of abuses, together with the natural desire to

[6]See Sismondi's *Literature of Southern Europe.* Bohn's ed., Vol. I, p. 475 ff.; and the *Warner Library* for notices of the various authors mentioned.

preserve their States and their dignity, gave the popes of the eighteenth century many an anxious hour and brought more than one to a premature grave. Doctrinal, churchly, and moral conditions were much as they had been in the preceding century. The people were outwardly connected with the church and observed its feasts and fasts and other customs, but the demoralization of all classes was fearful; and the influence of French skepticism, especially toward the end of the century, was plainly to be seen.

Preaching suffered under these untoward conditions.[7] After the improvement brought in by Segneri and his followers there was another decline, and the whole eighteenth century was more or less affected by it, though its earlier decades showed still the wholesome influences of Segneri and the great French preachers of the preceding period.

Naturally the doctrinal and moral content of preaching changed little, if at all. Protestantism and free thought had been suppressed. The only material for a critical judgment of Italian preaching during this epoch is a consideration of its style, spirit, and fruits, and our discussion needs not to keep these sharply distinguished as it proceeds. A general description, derived chiefly from Zanotto and Micocci, and the examples quoted by these critics, will suffice to set before us the main features of eighteenth century preaching in Italy.

Perhaps the most conspicuous fault of the preaching of the age as a whole was its artificiality. There was a straining after oratorical effect, a perpetual effort to strike the fancy and stir the feelings of the auditors. Naturally, as Zanotto says, this induced sentimentality rather than true sentiment. There continued to be much imitation of foreign—especially French—models. Bombast and bad taste disfigured style, and there was a deplorable lack of true spiritual fervor and power.

Though there was a good attendance on the part of the people, it was largely conventional and habitual rather than serious and devout. The preacher was regarded rather as a performer who should strike and please by

[7]See Zanotto, *op. cit.*, cap. IX, X; and Micocci, *Antologia della Sacra Eloquenza Moderna*, p. 21 ss.

his oratory than as a religious guide and helper who should lead and lift his hearers to God. Naturally this conception of preaching led to the treatment of striking topics rather than to exposition of Scripture or of doctrine with a view to spiritual edification. Some of the topics chosen for discourse show how far from the proper office of the pulpit some of the preachers strayed in their efforts to find striking themes. Some discoursed on philosophic subtleties instead of the doctrines of the Church, others took such subjects as *Egotism* and *Antipathy;* even such trivial topics as *Curiosity, Laughter, Tranquillity,* and the like. We see in all this the Catholic and Italian aspect of that cool, rationalistic wave of eighteenth century thought which desolated the contemporary Protestant preaching of Germany and England.

As to the causes of this decline of pulpit power in Italy, so far as it was local and Catholic instead of general—even world-wide—it is interesting to see how a Romanist critic, after admitting the facts, summarily states the reasons for them. Micocci[8] lays down the general principle that "corrupt times and men also corrupted eloquence;" and this remark is preceded by the five following considerations as causes or elements of the decay: (1) The fight against the Jesuits and their suppression in 1773 removed many able preachers from the Italian pulpits. (2) Jansenism, which, after the suppression of the Jesuits, spread much in Italy, joined itself with the "raving rationalistic philosophy" in criticising the enthusiasm of sacred eloquence as fanatic exaggeration, and thus had a freezing effect on preaching. (3) The spread of extracts, translations, anthologies, from the French orators of the classic age injured originality and the following of native models. (4) Foreign domination corrupted both morals and literature and created a style of eloquence no longer properly Italian. (5) There arose a tendency to conciliation and compromise with the errors of the age, and thus to a weakening of religious feeling. With the third and fourth of these assigned reasons no exception is here taken. The others also are doubtless partly true causes,

[8] *Op. cit.*, p. 27.

and satisfactory from the Catholic point of view. But one who is accustomed to Protestant modes of thinking feels rather disposed to wonder why the measure of liberty of thought indicated by these movements did not improve instead of injuring preaching. It would seem that the suppression of Jesuitism—after the actual removal of some strong preachers of that order—was in the line of enlightenment; and the spread of Jansenism (a more Scriptural view of Roman doctrine) should have also been an advance. But the explanation of this failure probably lies in the hint that Jansenism rather tended to rationalism, and this is what the critic probably had in view in his fifth reason; so that the slight advance toward a larger liberty of thought and expression in the pulpit was counteracted by the drift toward a cool and deadening skepticism.

On the whole, it appears that the Catholic preaching of Italy in the eighteenth century—like the rationalist Protestant pulpit in other lands—lacked the vital element of conviction, of enthusiasm, and therefore of a spiritual and compelling earnestness. But there were also better elements in this preaching, and as the century went on these asserted themselves rather more. There came to be less of bombast and straining, less display of classic learning, a better proportion in the treatment of materials, more of Scriptural comment and quotation, and a clearer moral and spiritual aim in preaching.[9]

A few of the more notable preachers of the earlier half of the century are noted and characterized, and some examples of their work given, by the critics whose works are here followed. One of the best of these earlier preachers was Bernardo Maria Giaco (1672-1744), a Neapolitan by birth, gifted in mind, trained by Jesuits, but taking the cowl of a Capuchin. He was of feeble constitution, and therefore did not produce much, though diligent in teaching and preaching as his health permitted. Some of his panegyrics and other discourses were published after his death. The specimens quoted show that Giaco had the oratorical gift, but he had not escaped from the swelling and overdone style of his time. He shows fine imagination and facility in language, but lack

[9]Zanotto, p. 328.

of restraint and of power. More polished and likewise imaginative and oratorical was Saverio Vanalesti (1678-1741), a Jesuit from Naples, whose florid and picturesque style was greatly admired by many.

More important than either of these was Sebastiano Paoli (1684-1751), of Lucca, whom Zanotto describes as "a man of superior genius who obtained great renown, not only as orator, but also as a literary man furnished with varied erudition." Giving himself to preaching as well as to letters, he was heard with applause in various Italian cities and also at Vienna, where he preached the Advent sermons in 1721 at the court of the emperor, Charles VI, and the Lent sermons the next year. In these, after the manner of the French court preachers, he managed to speak with conscientious boldness and yet retain the respect and appreciation of the sovereign. A few sentences from one of these discourses show something of his spirit and style.[10] Addressing himself directly to the emperor, he says: "Yes, most august one, there will come a day of confusion and disorder, when, to make place for the new reign of God, the foundations of your own shall be turned upside down. I hope that you shall see again, written then indelibly in that vast and interminable eternity, your victories and your triumphs. I hope that you shall rejoice to read, there above, the series of those glorious undertakings which you have made in the world for the advantage of your realm and for the support of our Catholic religion. But this can not prevent that you also shall be subject to inquiry—inquiry accompanied, for you and for all those who are like you, by two terrible circumstances; which, as I hope, they shall render you more glorious because innocent, so you must believe they would render you more wretched if you should be guilty. Princes know much: it is their fault if, knowing, they do not govern their realms with due attention. Princes have much power: it is their fault if, having power, they do not purge their realms of vices. These are the two circumstances which will aggravate in that day the faults of princes; and these shall be the two points on which I shall give myself now, for the first time, the most happy honor of discoursing to you."

[10]Zanotto, p. 339.

Girolamo Tornielli (1693-1752) is justly esteemed the greatest of the Italian preachers of the first half of the century. He was born at Cameri, near Novara, and entered the Jesuit Order at seventeen years of age. He pursued the prescribed studies with earnestness and success, and then taught for some years, thus developing his powers of exposition. Having given evidence of oratorical ability, he was in great demand as a preacher in the principal cities of Italy, where he attracted great audiences of cultivated people and won considerable renown. While preaching at Bologna he ruptured a blood vessel, and died at his work. He had a poetic turn and wrote some songs to the Virgin, but his fine imagination showed to better effect in his sermons than in his poems. He published a series of Lenten discourses and another of panegyrics, which were reprinted several times after his death. He was not a deep or logical thinker, but his strong fancy and skill in elaboration of language suited the taste of the age and captured his hearers. Extracts from his sermons[11] show a lively imagination and some oratorical skill, but also the common faults of excess and over-anxiety to strike and captivate. The following estimate by Micocci[12] is overdrawn, but may be quoted as the judgment of a modern Catholic and Italian critic: "In his sermons are admired all the gifts of a great orator. His style is spontaneous, insinuating; the sentence is harmonious, orderly; there is not a word which is not appropriate and fitting; and he was adorned with a wise and opportune erudition, joined with a judicious use of the writings of the Fathers. Lively are his images, his thoughts select and sublime, his reasoning clear, just, effective. Moreover, he had learned to study nature and to know men; hence he depicts with fidelity and vividness the manners of the age, and succeeds admirably in moving the feelings. That which in others would have been pomposity in him is nature; and to these fine gifts he joined an admirable delivery and gesture."

A simpler, more direct and spiritual manner of preaching is found in two men of this time who have each been honored with a place in the Roman calendar of saints. The earlier of these, belonging to the first half

[11] Zanotto, p. 342 ss.

[12] *Op. cit.*, p. 22.

of the century, was St. Leonardo of Port Maurice (1676-1751), who adopted a popular and simple style of speech, discarding the highflown manner of the pulpit orators, and sought to awaken in his hearers a real longing for spiritual things. Later in the century came the famous St. Alfonso dei Liguori (1696-1787), founder of the Redemptorist Order, a preacher of some note and power, but better known as the writer of devotional and moral treatises.

Recurring to the line of pulpit orators, the authorities we have been following give the names and brief descriptions of quite a number who fall within the second half of the eighteenth century, when the stilted and fanciful method was yielding to a clearer and more direct appeal, and the rationalism and skepticism of the age called for a stronger note of controversy in preaching. Among these were named with respect and some measure of praise Emmanuele Lucchese (1720-1766), a Sicilian, who preached with acceptance at the courts of Savoy and Naples, and before the Venetian senate; Giovanni Granelli (1703-1770), a Jesuit, who filled from time to time the most eminent pulpits in Italy, and was heard with applause by the empress, Maria Theresa, at Vienna; Ignazio Venini (1711-1778), also a Jesuit, who was compared by admiring contemporaries with both Segneri and Massillon, because of his searching addresses to the conscience and his knowledge of human nature; Girolamo Trento (1713-1784), likewise of the Order of Jesus, distinguished for vivid imagination and a certain dignity of manner; Piero da Pedarobba (1703-1785), a Minorite, noted for moving eloquence and a lofty character which won his hearers; and Giuseppe Luigi Pellegrini (1718-1799), of Verona, highly esteemed by his contemporaries and heard with edification in many places, especially at Venice and Vienna, who distinctly discarded the lofty, artificial style of the French orators and sought to touch by simpler methods the hearts and consciences of his hearers.

The line of eighteenth century preachers in Italy is closed by Adeodato Turchi (1724-1803), who is perhaps the greatest of them all. The glowing words of Micocci[13] are no doubt too strong when he speaks of

[13] *Op. cit.*, p. 29 s.

Turchi as "an orator among the most illustrious whom sacred eloquence boasts," but his characterization is not beyond bounds, when he adds: "His style, sufficiently eloquent, runs along always as limpid and free as his thought; but sometimes there is a little redundancy and he has foreign modes and phrases not conformed to Italian taste. Altogether, he holds an eminent place in the history of sacred oratory, since he knew how to maintain the dignity of gospel preaching amid the aberrations of the philosophic innovations of his time, which tried, with partial success, to overthrow true Christian eloquence." The more sober estimate of Zanotto emphasizes Turchi's defects, but yet accords him a sure place among the greater Italian preachers.

Turchi was born at Parma, and was named Carlo at his baptism, but on becoming a Capuchin monk in after years he assumed the name of Adeodato. He was trained by the Jesuits, though he did not join their order. On his graduation he taught theology for a time in several schools, but his gift of eloquence marked him for the career of a preacher, which he discharged with success, giving the customary season's sermons in a number of the cities—Arezzo, Pisa, Florence, Genoa, Bologna, Rome, and others. He gave the Advent sermons with great applause at Parma, and then at Naples. At last he was settled as preacher at the ducal court of Parma, and was later consecrated to the bishopric of that diocese, an office which he filled with distinction for fifteen years before he died. Turchi was of an amiable and jovial disposition, and greatly beloved by his friends. He was earnest in his preaching and set himself firmly and intelligently against the skepticism of the age. The somewhat extended extracts given by Zanotto from his sermons indicate a clear intelligence, acute observation, a vivid style, and earnest moral purpose in his preaching. The following paragraph from the introduction to a sermon on the future life will give at least a slight suggestion of Turchi's manner:[14]

"We have them also in our days—those who call themselves fine spirits,[15] unprejudiced, philosophic, who say

[14]Zanotto, p. 405 s.

[15]"Begli spiriti," an evident adaptation of the French *beaux esprits.*

they do not believe in a life to come, and are inwardly persuaded that man ends all at death. They seem to be enamored of nullity and to hold as the supreme good their total annihilation. But how did there ever arise so great a love of nullity along with a desire so accepted and so innate as we have in us of living forever and never making an end? I confess, my hearers, that this idea of destruction and of annihilation causes me shuddering and horror. This 'I' at least which I feel so vividly in myself, and to which I am for very necessity so strongly attached, shall it so soon melt away and be dissipated into nullity and be confounded in the chaos of senseless matter to be reproduced in its time into a tree, a rock, a ferocious beast? In order to adopt an opinion so desolating it is necessary to be perfectly stupified; I add more, it is necessary to be impious. An honest man groans only to think of it! Libertines alone can agree to it, and that not because they do not *feel,* but because they do not *wish* a life after death. That is their rock [of offense], that is the terrible phantom which terrifies them. They fear a punishment for their brutal life. They would have no difficulty in believing the other doctrines of religion; but when there is discussion of a future life, of a terrible judgment which threatens them, of an endless punishment for their misdeeds, ah! there they rage, they writhe, and that they may not believe this sole article they refuse to believe all the rest. And ah! if they could only annihilate along with their own spirit the law-makers, the magistrates, and the laws that pursue the delinquents in human society! What a fine world this would be for them where it would be possible to commit with impunity every strange crime, without fear of punishment either in the present life or in the life to come; what a fine world it would be for them! As for me, I would gladly leave it while they were dividing it and rejoicing together, and would not hesitate to depart from it at the earliest possible moment." After this exordium, he invites the doubters to reason with him calmly and charitably, and exhorts the great intellects to address their powers to this question, earnestly insisting that those very powers themselves are proof that man is not merely material, but spiritual also; and that his moral sense fortifies this argument. On the whole, the pulpit oratory of Italy in the eighteenth century finds no unhappy nor unfit culmination in Adeodato Turchi.

CHAPTER VII

German Preaching in the Eighteenth Century

The history of the German people during the eighteenth century is that of a great period of transition and preparation.[1] The desolation and decay of the seventeenth century were beginning to be redressed, but there was no political unity in Germany during the eighteenth century. The Holy Roman Empire, so-called, was merely a shadow, hastening to its final departure under the strong hand of Napoleon in 1806. The German people regarded the Empire with some reverence as a name and a symbol, but it had no real authority and no appreciable weight in European affairs. The Hapsburg dynasty were intrenched in Austria and some of the other German States, and also ruled over Bohemia and Hungary, but the union of Austria and Hungary in an empire was a far distant event not yet imagined. Austria was the strongest power in Germany, which was divided into a number of petty states and principalities, as it always had been. One among these, however, pushed its way to the front and grew, during the eighteenth century, into a position of first-rate importance in European affairs. This was the kingdom of Prussia. During the seventeenth century the Electors of Brandenburg had developed that duchy into a strong German power. Frederick I, son of the Great Elector, determined to become a king; but as only one king at that time was allowed among the Electors, he could not make the duchy of Brandenburg into a kingdom, so he took his title from his eastern province of Prussia and had himself proclaimed and crowned king of Prussia in 1701. His son

[1]See Bayard Taylor's *History of Germany;* Bryce's *Holy Roman Empire;* and the appropriate volumes and chapters in the *Historians' History of the World;* appropriate discussions in the *Church Histories* of Kurtz, Newman, and others.

and successor, Frederick William I, strengthened the kingdom, disciplined the army, and laid up a considerable treasure. This enabled his distinguished successor, Frederick II, called the Great, to prosecute those remarkable wars which finally left Prussia, at the end of the century, among the first powers of Europe. The death of the Emperor Charles VI, without male heirs, left his daughter, Maria Theresa, the heir to his ancestral estates; but there was question whether a woman could hold the empire. By an act called the Pragmatic Sanction, Charles VI fixed the succession upon his daughter. Her claims were accepted by some of the powers, resisted by others. She was a woman of remarkable strength, energy, and character, and succeeded in holding the affections of both her Austrian and Hungarian subjects. The century was marked by her conflicts with Frederick II, who robbed her of the province of Silesia, and established Prussia as the German rival of Austria. We know how this duel terminated in 1866 and 1871, but these events were yet far distant. The great rivalry between these two powers did not wholly obscure the importance of the lesser German States. Saxony, Bavaria, Hanover, Hesse, and others made some contributions to the progress and the history of the German people. Joseph II of Austria, the son of Maria Theresa, undertook to introduce reforms tending toward greater political and religious liberty, but he was ahead of the age in his ideas and unable to carry out his plans.

In the sphere of thought Germany was not idle during the eighteenth century. Philosophic skepticism made its appearance with the work of Wolf as Professor at Halle, in 1705. English deism gave rationalism its start, and French infidelity under Voltaire and others greatly stimulated skepticism and irreligion among the German people. The religious complexion of the people remained outwardly as it had been settled after the Thirty Years' War. Austria and Bavaria, with some minor States, remained Catholic. Prussia, Saxony, and others remained essentially Protestant. The Lutherans were naturally in the ascendant, but there were also Reformed churches and teachers of some standing. The overthrow of the Jesuits and the reforms of Joseph II somewhat weakened the Catholic power in Germany. In the Lutheran churches the controversy between the Pietists on the one hand and the Rationalists on the other was considerable. The rulers of Prussia endeavored to effect a union between the Lutherans and the Reformed, but with only a moderate degree of success. Controversies raged over these efforts, as well as over theology. One of the notable religious events of the century was the founding and development of the Moravian Brethren, whose persecutions in Bohemia and Moravia led them to seek a refuge in Saxony, where they found welcome upon the estates of the pious Count Zinzendorf, who became their leader and virtually their founder. This sect has been distinguished throughout its history for a kind of mystic piety and the earnest prosecution of missionary labors in all parts of the world.

German literature during the eighteenth century[2] slowly grew into the greatness and glory which characterize its modern development. Early in the century it began with imitations of English and French masterpieces, but soon Gottsched undertook to purify the language and reform somewhat the literature of his people. He was attacked by Bodmer and others, but his teachings and example as to purity of style had some effect. Some minor poets, such as Haller and the earnest Christian, Gellert, prepared the way for a better time, so that about the middle of the century Germany was ready for the birth of her great classic period in literature. This was led by the pious and gifted Klopstock, who opposed the current rationalism, and wrote his notable religious poems. He was followed by the great Lessing, whose criticisms and dramas abide among the classics of German literature. Following these, or contemporary with their latter years, came Herder, not a creative genius of the first rank, but a critic and lover of literature, whose influence and inspiration were a strong force in the development of German letters. The closing decades of the eighteenth century and the early part of the nineteenth were rendered illustrious by the work of Schiller

[2]Priest's *Short History of German Literature;* and the notices and examples of the different authors as given in the *Warner Library.*

and Goethe, whose varied and abundant labors in prose and poetry, but especially the latter, lifted German literature to its modern eminence.

In religion the eighteenth century in Germany witnesses a conflict between three forces. First of all, there was the age-long and the world-wide moral struggle. The deterioration of morals caused by the wars was very great. Pure religion had a hard time to maintain itself where the bonds of society and of political loyalty were so constantly interrupted. Then there was the conflict already alluded to against infidelity and rationalism. While German thought did not wholly reject the Bible and the Church, as did the more revolutionary tendencies in France, nevertheless it undermined the authority of both. Rationalism accepted the Bible as literature open to criticism, and regarded the Church as a convenient institution for the teaching of morals and the outward maintenance of worship and religion. Against both these forces—moral deterioration and religious rationalism—the devout believers in Christianity maintained a brave and glorious struggle. While the eighteenth century was a dark age, it is nobly illustrated for Germany as well as for England by the earnest work of those who still accepted the Christian religion as divine and gave their lives and talents to its defence and propagation. All the influences which have been thus briefly sketched naturally had their effect upon the preaching of the century, of which we shall now make some survey, and then discuss some of the greater and more important preachers.

I. General Survey[3]

The Catholic preaching of Germany during the eighteenth century was neither so strong nor so varied and distinctive as that among the Protestants. It was slower to feel the better manner, which in Italy had come in

[3]The works of Schenk, Lentz, Rothe, Hering, Broemel, Nebe, Christlieb-Schian, Ker, Fish, Zanotto, Renoux, previously mentioned. Articles in *RE,* in Wetzer und Welte's *Kirchenlexikon,* and in the *Allegemeine deutsche Biographie,* where needed. Additional works: Doering, *Die deutschen Kanzelredner des 18ten u. 19ten Jahrhunderts;* Sack, *Geschichte der Predigt in der deutsch-evangelischen Kirche von Mosheim,* u. s. w.; Schuler,

with Segneri, and in France with the classic preachers, than was the Lutheran and Reformed preaching. And later on in the century it was likewise slower to feel the chilling influence of the philosophic rationalism which characterized many of the Protestant preachers in Germany and many of the Catholic preachers in France. Yet it was to some extent affected by both these forces. It showed in process of time more tendency to break away from the old, crude scholastic structure, but found it hard to shake off the stilted, forced, pedantic style so common in those days. There was still too much straining after effect, and employment of devices and conceits to strike and dazzle the hearer. Along with the philosophic rationalism, and the so-called Illuminism which followed it, near the turn of the century there arose a more spiritual and evangelical tendency in German Catholic preaching which came to fuller expression and power early in the nineteenth century.

It is scarcely necessary to say that the content of Catholic preaching continued to be the accepted Romanist doctrines, with the usual polemic against Protestantism. But, as in France, the presentation of morals—particularly as the century advanced—gained upon that of doctrine and became characteristic. The polemic against Protestantism found among some a new sting in the current rationalism which desolated many Lutheran pulpits, but in others was modified toward the latter part of the century by the rise of a more spiritual movement under Sailer and his school.

Protestant critics, like Lentz[4] and Rothe,[5] in showing the faults of Catholic preaching, are apt to be a little one-sided and sweeping in their judgments. On the other hand, Kehrein,[6] from the Romanist point of view, assumes a more judicial attitude, and shows that both the

Geschichte der Veränderungen des Geschmacks im Predigen; Kehrein, *Geschichte der Katholischen Kanzelberedsamkeit der Deutschen,* u. s. w.; Brischar, *Die Katholischen Kanzelredner Deutschlands seit den drei letzten Jahrhunderten.* Sermons and biographies of individual preachers as far as available.

[4]*Geschichte der Christlichen Homiletik,* Bd. II, S. 364.

[5]*Geschichte der Predigt,* S. 474.

[6]*Geschichte der Katholischen Kanzelberedsamkeit,* Bd. I, SS. 59 ff., 107 ff., 153 ff.

faults and virtues of the age were found in both the Catholic and the Protestant pulpit, though he seems to grant that improvements were rather slower in maturing among the Catholics. The old faults of pedantry, bad mixture of style, cram of quotations, catchy expedients to amuse and strike, with wearisome and minute divisions of the subject-matter, lingered on too long. Kehrein pays a just tribute to Spener[7] in leading a reform among Protestants, and to some extent among Catholics, too. The Wolfian philosophy is also credited with some influence[8] on the prose style of Germany, and therefore, in a second degree upon preaching, in the direction of clearness and purity and the effort to say the thing for the benefit of the hearer. But this trend went to the extreme of the over-use of definition and logical demonstration, landing often in dry rationalism.

In the period from about 1770 on into the nineteenth century Kehrein[9] notices the influence of the new literary spirit in Germany—the great classic period of modern German literature—the special leading of Mosheim and his following in improving pulpit methods among Protestants; and the somewhat helpful but also somewhat injurious effects of the philosophy of Kant and Fichte—helpful in stimulating practical moral appeal, injurious in leading some preachers into an unintelligible philosophic style and a moralizing rationalistic tone. But these, together with the other and earlier influences noted, naturally had more distinct as well as more ample illustration in the Protestant preaching of the period, which must now be briefly described.

In discussing the Protestant preaching in Germany during the eighteenth century it is not necessary to consider the Lutheran and Reformed Churches separately, though well to bear in mind this confessional distinction occasionally in regard to doctrine, localities, and individual preachers. We may also lose sight of the stricter and broader Lutherans, as new issues and alignments arose, and the older polemics gave place to newer and perhaps less rancorous disputes. The polemic spirit, characteristic of the German theological mind, was by no means dead or absent from German preaching in the

[7] *Op. cit.*, S. 65 f. [8] *Op. cit.*, S. 66. [9] *Op. cit.*, S. 148 ff.

eighteenth century; but the field of battle and the weapons of warfare were somewhat changed.

The preachers and preaching of German Protestantism during this epoch fall into three distinct and clearly marked groups or schools,[10] making, of course, the necessary allowances for some mingling of tendencies and methods, and remembering always that these distinctions can never be anything more than approximations to scientific exactitude. The three tendencies or schools are the Pietistic, the Rationalistic, and the Supernaturalistic or Mediating. In a way, these forces or modes of thought operated side by side, and often in conflict; but Pietism historically preceded the other two, which more nearly paralleled each other.

The Pietist principle was exaggerated and weakened by the followers of Spener and Francke, and lost its hold upon the leaders of the German pulpit; the Rationalist movement was the natural recoil from the one-sidedness and the faults of Pietism, aided by the rise of philosophic skepticism and of the new critical method of Bible study and exposition; the Supernaturalist, or Mediating, school of preachers arose in obedience to an instinct which recognized the failure of both the other methods of preaching, yet sought in mending their faults to keep whatever was good and permanent in each. The influence of Pietism distinctly declined after the first third of the century; the other two schools were at close grips through the remainder of the period and on into the early decades of the nineteenth century. Neither could be with entire correctness called dominant at any time; but along about the middle of the century the mediating principles of Mosheim and others were largely exemplified in the German pulpit; yet the parallel force of rationalism was strong and aggressive, and reached its height toward the end of the century; but this supremacy was held in check and in part counteracted by the evangelical work of such men as Reinhard, Lavater, and others about the turn of the century.

[10]Nearly all the authorities mentioned above, but especially Ker, *Lects. on Hist. of Preaching*, Lects. XII-XV, and the art. in *RE*. Here, however, it is well to refer also to Christlieb's original article in the older edition, as Schian has considerably modified the point of view in regard to Rationalism.

Now, as to the characteristics of these modes of preaching something must be said. The earlier Pietism, as we have seen,[11] laid great and needed stress upon Christian feeling, upon the experience of grace, upon the union of the soul with Christ and its edification in Christ; it discarded the scholastic analysis of themes and sought to interpret and apply the Word of God directly to the conscience and life of the hearers; it struck anew and with telling effect the evangelical keynote of sin and grace, and the worthlessness of work-righteousness. But in its critique of over-refinement in analysis and effort to strike, it neglected form too much; and in its insistence on feeling and experience it did not give due heed to intellect and the moral life. In its later forms it fell into cant, its faults became more and more manifest, and its inadequacy to represent either in chair or pulpit the whole of Christian teaching grew more and more apparent.

But over against this decay we must take note of the continuance of Pietism in two vigorous offshoots. One of these was in South Germany, particularly about Stuttgart, where the pious and scholarly Bengel exerted a blessed and long-continued influence in favor of a deep spiritual and evangelical method of interpreting and applying Scripture. The other was chiefly in Saxony, but spread through the world. This was the great Moravian movement, reinforced and then led by Zinzendorf, combining an often extreme type of mysticism with beautiful piety of life and admirable missionary zeal.

The older form of opposition to Pietism, proceeding from the stiff scholastic orthodoxy of Lutheranism, now virtually disappeared. The newer check took two directions, both with much of good in them, but the latter with evil tendencies that came to a sad outcome in Rationalism. The earlier form of recoil from the one-sidedness, narrowness, and cant of Pietism at its worst was led by such men as Rambach, Reinbeck, Sack, Cramer, and more especially Mosheim. This school maintained a no less real, but a broader, evangelical teaching and life, presenting the full scope of doctrine and duty on the basis of sound Christian experience and faith. It rejected the pietistic contempt of form and style, and in-

[11] *Ante*, pp. 51, 70, 73.

sisted that the accepted principles of oratory should be employed in the preaching of Christian truth. This wholesome reform was both needed and welcome, and students of German preaching are practically unanimous in putting Mosheim along with Spener as one of the great leaders in the modern development of pulpit eloquence in Germany.

The rationalistic development of preaching was in part, but in part only, a reaction from Pietism. The philosophic teaching of Wolf at Halle, early in the century, affected both in matter and form the preaching of those who fell under its influence. Its severe critical, not to say skeptical, reasoning was opposed to the simple faith of the better Pietism, and to the vaguer raptures of the more extreme type; its exactness of definition and clear statement of argument had a salutary influence upon style in the matters of directness and simplicity. But when, later in the century, the Wolfian skepticism was reinforced by the influence of the English deism and of the French infidelity, Rationalism reached its height; and its influence on preaching was disastrous. In some cases, too, the formal side of this preaching showed evil traces in the over-use of argument and the tedious multiplication of definitions. Along with this the new critical attitude toward the Bible must not be forgotten; the rationalistic method was beginning its modern course of development. In some preachers it helped to a far better understanding and application of Scripture; in others it came to a virtual denial of any proper divine or supernatural element in the Bible, and thus to a weakening of its authority as the certain voice of God on doctrine and morals.

In regard to doctrine, the rationalistic preaching was very unsatisfactory. It had no well-defined conviction, but a critical attitude. The distinction—now beginning to be made—between religion and theology was employed to evade or depreciate doctrine, as of little utility to the common man, and therefore not required in pulpit discussion. But even such scanty treatment as is given, directly or indirectly, to the great distinctive truths of Christianity is disappointing. This is true, even of the best representatives—such as Spalding and Zollikofer—

and, of course, of the more extreme types. The nature of God, the incarnation, the atonement, the resurrection, justification by faith, and the other great teachings are little heard of; and when they are presented, it is with no certainty of grasp or loyalty of personal acceptance.

At first, and in the hands of such men as have been named, the treatment of morals was far more satisfactory than that of doctrine. In fact, in the earlier stages of the rationalistic movement this was its strong point. It was here that its critique of the later Pietism was effective, and its own work was vigorous and clear. But alas! even here degeneracy soon appeared, and devout Germans to this day mention with shame the wretched travesty upon Christian preaching which was found in some of the rationalistic pulpits of the latter part of the eighteenth century.

A few illustrations, gathered from authentic sources, will make plainer this woeful fall.[12] One of these later preachers, in discussing the life of our Lord, took as his theme, "Recollections of Jesus Christ," and, among other things, considered why Jesus did not set up a home! Another, at Easter, discussed the "Danger of Being Buried Alive;" another, "The Fear of Ghosts." In pushing the theory of practical utility in preaching, some of these pulpiteers descended to such themes as "The Advantages of Travel," "The Preference of Stall-feeding for Cattle Over Grazing," "The Unspeakable Blessing of Potato Culture." The value of coffee as a beverage was urged; while the importance of vaccination for the smallpox was a frequent topic of pulpit discourse.

But the evangelical note was not wholly wanting; the work of Spener and Bengel and Mosheim was not in vain. The extreme of rationalism was its own severest critic to sensible men, and the futility of even the boasted Illuminism as a substitute for religion was apparent to many. To some extent even Herder—child of culture that he was—saw this and strove for a deeper Christian teaching and life, but the later supernaturalism found clearer expression and more effective and lasting influence in Lavater and Reinhard.

[12]All the authorities which have been named mention these things; but see especially Schuler, *Gesch. der Veränderungen des Geschmacks,* etc., III, S. 202 ff.

II. The Catholic Preachers

The excellent works of Brischar[13] and Kehrein[14] name and discuss a number of German Catholic preachers for this period; they also, sometimes by full sermons and sometimes by illustrative extracts, put before us the means of judging the work of the most important men. It is a pleasure to acknowledge the fullest indebtedness to works which have rendered unnecessary independent research in a difficult and unaccustomed field.[15]

At the beginning of the century a number of Jesuit preachers are named by Brischar, and described with approval; such as Reittmair (d. 1711), spoken of as "the sacred Tully;" Scheffer (d. 1717), and Tam (d. 1719). Of these and a few others, the author says:[16] "They held themselves far from the tastelessness, the false pathos, and the mixed diction of the degenerate style then in vogue." He further praises their good German style, and the examples given seem to justify his approval. Later came a number of others who did good work, but especially Franz Hoger (1664-1720), who with large experience of the world combined a trace of mysticism, and was a master of his material, with a fine gift for antithesis and the use of figures, which naturally sometimes leads him too far. Along with him is named Matthäus Pecher (1663-1729), who had great learning, showed some originality in the choice and statement of his themes, was something of an artist and poet, and acquired great reputation as a preacher.

But the most notable of German Catholic preachers in the first half of the eighteenth century was Franz Hunolt (d. about 1740 or 1746—dates seem uncertain).[17]

[13] *Die Katholischen Kanzelredner Deutschlands seit den drei letzten Jahrhunderten;* von Johann Nepomuk Brischar, 5 Bde., 1867.

[14] *Geschichte der Katholischen Kanzelberedsamkeit der Deutschen von der ältesten bis zur neuesten Zeit;* von Joseph Kehrein, 2 Bde., 1843.

[15] Other authorities on German preaching, though themselves largely indebted to Brischar and Kehrein (except Lentz, who preceded them), have also been consulted; and, where needed, articles in Wetzer und Welte, and the *Allgemeine Deutsche Biographie.*

[16] *Op. cit.,* Vorrede, XII.

[17] Wetzer u. Welte, VI, col. 430; *Allg. deut. Biog.,* Bd. 13, S. 421; Brischar, Bd. 5, S. 1 ff.; Kehrein, Bd. I, S. 121.

He is described in the encyclopaedias as the most famous Catholic German preacher of his century. The article in the *Allgemeine deutsche Biographie* says that in a time when German preaching had fallen very low Hunolt's sermons show great excellence in the way of simplicity, directness, naturalness, and earnestness of aim. Other critics agree in general with this judgment, and the examples given by Brischar seem to bear it out. Hunolt was born in Siegen, Nassau, but the date is uncertain. He presumably enjoyed the Jesuit course of instruction, as he belonged to that order, and his sermons exhibit the traces of culture. He was made cathedral preacher at Treves sixteen years before his death, and filled the place with distinction. His sermons were published in 1740 under the title *Christliche Sittenlehre der evangelischen Wahrheiten,* as though seeking to combine the ethical with the evangelical doctrines of Christianity. The collection was several times republished, and seems to have had considerable reading and influence. From the specimens of Hunolt's preaching given by Brischar, one would rate him highly on his merits, and still more highly by comparison. He shows keen penetration and knowledge of human nature—doubtless helped by the confessional—with a plainly seen and earnest desire for the salvation and improvement of his hearers. The division is simple, usually twofold, the language plain and straightforward. We find no swelling words and catchy phrases, but strong appeal, candid dealing, and notable power in the use of telling illustration from life. He was a strong preacher, and doubtless deserved his fame.

The second half of the century, as we have seen, witnessed both in the Catholic and Protestant pulpits of Germany a deterioration in the tone and content of preaching, along with much improvement in form and style. The philosophizing and rationalizing spirit invaded the pulpit and chilled preaching to the quick. It is not worth while to adduce names and instances of this perversion among the Catholics—some of the Protestants will be considered later—but only to mention several of the better sort, who strove against the spirit of the age in its worse, and sought to exemplify it in its better tendencies and aims.

Ignaz Wurz (1731-1784)[18] was born at Vienna, entered the Jesuit Order at sixteen, pursued the usual thorough course of training, including a few years of service as teacher, and then was designated as preacher. His gifts at once attracted attention, and his character respect. In 1764 he preached a notable sermon at the coronation of the Emperor Joseph II. He was made professor of pulpit eloquence at Vienna, and wrote a treatise upon it, quite useful in its time.[19] He held this office when his order was suppressed, in 1773, but lectured on for awhile till opposition forced him to desist, in 1776, when he retired to a pastoral charge which had long before been assigned to him by the foresight and kindness of the Empress Maria Theresa. It was here—at Pierawart, in South Austria—that he ended his days in peace.

As a preacher Wurz was much admired and beloved, and occupies a distinguished place in the history of German Catholic preaching. He preached and published many sermons. In the preface to his sermons he declares, with equal candor and good sense, that he has not sought the strange and out-of-the-way things, but the old and yet ever-new commonplaces, while endeavoring to conceive and express these in his own way. He has taken from theology and philosophy what seemed necessary or useful to his purpose, but has studiously avoided "school-theology, school-method, school-quarrels, adherence to any one system, and the like." In a manly sermon on the true cause of religious unbelief—based on Caiaphas' demand to Jesus to declare himself (Matt. 26:63)—Wurz shows that much of the current demand for positive proofs of religion was mere dogmatic prepossession, and proceeded from a corrupt heart and a will anxious to throw off restraint. One of his most notable discourses was the funeral sermon for Maria Theresa.[20] The text is taken from 2 Maccabees 7:20, 21—the account of a brave Jewish woman who had suffered the loss of her sons under the tyrant, and of whom it is said: "But above all was the mother marvelous and worthy of mention . . . filled with a noble temper

[18] *Allg. deut. Biog.*, Bd. 44, S. 354; Kehrein, I, 130 ff.; and II, 241 ff. [19] *Anleitung zur geistlichen Beredsamkeit.*
[20] Kehrein, II, 241 ff.

and arousing her womanly thought with manly passion." This last expression gives him his theme, and he extols the beloved and admired empress from the two points of view that "she exalted the virtues of the female sex by her manly courage," and "adorned her manly undertakings with the virtues of the female sex." On these two pillars he builds the stately edifice of his panegyric. It does not reach the height of Bossuet, nor the exquisite phrasing and unction of Massillon, but it does strike a manly and loyal note of true appreciation of a great and worthy character, and in this point of view at least has some advantages over the courtlier funeral orations of the French preachers. The style of Wurz is marked by purity, clearness (wonderful for that time), vigor, loftiness, and harmony.

At the turn of the century the noblest figure among German Catholic preachers is that of the eloquent and spiritual John Michael Sailer (1751-1823), professor in various institutions, and finally bishop of Regensburg.[21] Sailer was born of humble and poor parents at a little village in Upper Bavaria, and was pure in character and promising in mind from a boy. In one way and another he managed, by the encouragement and assistance of his parents and the village priest, to pick up the rudiments of learning and finally to go to Munich, in 1761—ten years old!—for study in the schools there. A kind schoolteacher gave him bed and breakfast, he got his mid-day meal for looking after the child of a gentleman in the city during some hours, and his supper with other charity students in one of the schools. He pursued this program, and similar ones, as long as necessary; studied hard, and managed to get on till, in 1770, he entered the Jesuit Order, and began the studies required, at Ingolstadt. But the downfall of the Jesuits, in 1773, interrupted his carrer under their auspices. In some way, however, he managed to keep on his studies at Ingolstadt for several years more, meantime having been ordained to the priesthood in 1775. He had, as most thoughtful young men, his mental and moral conflicts during this

[21] *Allg. deut. Biog.*, Bd. 30, S. 17 ff. (a very careful and excellent article); Wetzer und Welte, X, col. 1536; Kehrein, I, 159 ff., and II, 285 ff.; Renoux, p. 332 ss.

period, but came through them into peace. He began his long and fruitful career as an author with a Latin treatise on Christian evidences—the result of his own mental struggles. He was made tutor and then (1780) full professor at Ingolstadt; but soon the school was reorganized on a different basis, and Sailer with others was retired on a small pension. About this time he produced an excellent and long-famous book of devotion which fed many pious souls, but provoked others—less pious, perhaps—to bitter controversy. The over-orthodox saw in its fresh phraseology and turns of thought heretical departures from the faith, while to many others these things and the warm spiritual tone of the book seemed a deep Jesuit trick to catch the unwary and make converts to Romanism! Sailer's friendship with Lavater and with other of the so-called *Illuminati* of the age exposed him to sharp attacks from the extreme Catholics and cost him a professorship which he held for awhile at Dillingen. At last the royal family of Bavaria recognized in Sailer one of the best men, best Catholics, and best scholars of the age, and gave him a professorship in the once more reorganized University of Ingolstadt in 1799. But owing to the Napoleonic wars and troubles of the time, the institution was moved, in 1805, to Landshut, where Sailer became rector. Here, as preacher and lecturer, his learning, eloquence, and piety drew crowds to hear him, both in pulpit and chair, and his spiritual influence was profoundly felt. His critics continued to pelt him from both sides, and additional offense was given to his Catholic opponents by his spiritual sympathy with the evangelical movement which arose in South Germany with Boos, Gossner, Lindl, and others, who were ultimately driven out of the Catholic Church, and some went off into fanticism. It was, however, only their mystical, pious, evangelical views which appealed to Sailer; he remained true to his church. In the reorganization of affairs after the downfall of Napoleon, Ludwig I of Bavaria tried to have Sailer made a bishop, and finally succeeded in having him made assistant and then full bishop at Regensburg. But the honor came to him only in his old age; and after a few years of labor at his post he died.

Sailer was justly esteemed—in spite of his critics—a great Catholic teacher and preacher of the more pious and evangelical sort. His devotional books and sermons, his liberal and evangelical spirit put him on a different plane from that of the average Romanist priest in his own or any age. Kehrein[22] says that Sailer's writings all give evidence of "genuine Christian spirit, of true Christian love of humanity, and of great skill in language description. He sought above all to represent religion as the highest and most important thing for men." Sailer himself is quoted as saying, "A Christian discourse must never enjoin a mere morality, never the law without the Lawgiver, never virtue without religion, never love without the Spirit who pours love into the heart, never holiness without the Redeemer Christ." The sermon given[23] from Sailer is one of a pair on *The Gospel of the Divine Vocation of Men on Earth,* suggested by the war of the Archangel Michael with Satan (Rev. 12:7, 8), and preached on St. Michael's day. The example of the great archangel is for us all. To fight *for* God, and to conquer *with* God is the sum of a Christian's calling here below. Not that God needs our championship, but it takes a fight against evil if by us the Light, Love, and Life that God is can come victoriously into the hearts of men. The theme is unfolded with clearness and simplicity, enforced by frequent statement, and discussed—barring a few errors of detail here and there—with admirable skill and power. It is a strong, earnest, spiritual discourse, and worthy of the preacher's fame.

Contemporaries of Sailer, whose work, like his, passed over into the nineteenth century, but chiefly belongs to the eighteenth, are three men who, above many others, deserve a brief mention. J. A. Sambuga (1752-1815)[24] is described as "the cherished shepherd of his spiritual flock, whose temporal and eternal welfare lay much upon his heart," and as a preacher of no mean gifts. J. A. Schneider (1752-1818)[25] ranks high among the best Catholic preachers of Germany, having filled important pulpits at Leipzig, Dresden, Cracow, and other places. His sermons show clearness, force, fire, and culture.

[22] *Op. cit.,* I, S. 159 ff.
[23] *Op. cit.,* II, S. 285.
[24] *Op. cit.,* I, S. 167.
[25] *Id.,* S. 180.

He was very acceptable to cultivated and fashionable audiences, but without flatteries and worldly compromises. J. L. Colmar (1760-1818)[26] was born and educated and began his work in Strassburg. He was made bishop of Mainz in 1802, at the instance of Napoleon, and did a great work for the rehabilitation of the Catholic Church there after the ravages of the Revolution. His mild and loving disposition won many friends of all classes and churches; but he was a man of great firmness and courage, who often in those trying days risked liberty and even life in the performance of duty. His preaching—as both the statements of Kehrein and the sample given show—was clear and simple, breathing a spirit of true loyalty to his faith and of concern for the spiritual good of his hearers. It is far removed from the tawdry and stilted style affected by so many in those days.

III. Protestant Preachers

After all, it is the Protestant preachers who have given all that is really distinctive, both in matter and form, to modern German preaching. In the eighteenth century, as we have seen, these preachers may be generally and correctly classified into the three groups of Pietist, Rationalist, and Supernaturalist (if contrasted with the Rationalists) or Mediating (if compared with both the others). Taking up first the Pietist group, we find among the leaders three representatives of very different types—Bengel, Oetinger, and Zinzendorf.

John Albert Bengel (d. 1752)[27] was born near Stuttgart, educated there and at Halle, held several pastorates before finding his lifework as pastor and professor at Stuttgart, where he lived and labored for many years. It is not distinctively as a preacher that Bengel is important in the history of preaching, for while he was a beloved man and pastor, a warm, gentle, balanced, thoughtful, and instructive preacher, his greatness did not lie in his pulpit work. As a lecturer and commentator on the Scriptures he won and retains an exalted place

[26]Kehrein, I, S. 180, and II, S, 331; Renoux, p. 324 ss.

[27]Ker, 225 ff.; Christlieb-Schian in *RE* 15, S. 686; and Hartmann (revised by Hauck), *RE* 2, S. 597 ff.

among those scholars whose learning and piety have unfolded and enforced the Word of God. His famous *Gnomon* (*i. e.,* index-finger), a brief and wonderfully suggestive Latin commentary on the New Testament, is the best known, but not the only fruit of his exegetical studies. His teachings and character strongly and permanently influenced for good many preachers, both in his own and subsequent days, and did much to preserve in South Germany an evangelical type of preaching which escaped both the decay and the extremes of the later Pietism.

F. C. Oetinger (1702-1782),[28] likewise of South Germany, was an admirer and in some ways a follower of Bengel. But he lacked the balance and poise of his master, was a mystic to the verge of theosophy. He was born in Würtemberg, studied at Halle, and held various pastorates, the last and longest being at Murrhard, where he died at an advanced age. In spite of his philosophical and theosophical speculations, he held fast to the Scriptures as the Word of God, opposed Rationalism, and often preached to the edification of his people. This is the more remarkable seeing that he was no orator, and often was obscure in style. Yet he was evangelical, and spoke with a warm heart.

Count Nicholas Zinzendorf (1700-1760)[29] was one of the most notable men of his age, and his interesting life-story deserves a fuller notice than is possible here. He was derived from a noble Austrian family who became Protestants, and, because of the rigid dealings against them, sold their possessions on Austrian soil and came to Saxony. Nicholas was born in Dresden, of a second marriage, and, on his mother's marrying again after his father's death, was left to the care of his grandmother and uncles. He thus received a kind, but peculiar, bringing up. Sent to Halle to school, he was teased by his comrades and tyrannized over by his teachers, but his sound conscience and fine intelligence compelled respect and won success. Here, too, he fell under the

[28]Sack, S. 161 ff.; *RE* 14, S. 332 ff. (Joh. Herzog), and 15, S. 686 f.

[29]Ker, p. 229 ff.; Rothe, S. 444; *RE* 21, S. 679 (Becker, revised by Müller).

pastoral care of the pious Francke, and the pietistic strain in his character was encouraged and established. From Halle he went to Wittenberg to study law, at the wish of his guardian, but was more interested in theology, and remained under the influence of Pietism, developing thus early his own type of religion—that of a complete surrender to Christ and abiding personal union with Him. Still acting on the persuasion of his relatives, he took an official position in Dresden, but his heart was far more engaged in religious affairs. He acquired an estate, with his patrimony and a legacy from his uncle, and with the aid of a like-minded pastor, who was a Pietist, he endeavored to establish a religious community controlled by his ideas. At this juncture he learned that the remnants of the Unity of Brothers (Bohemian and Moravian, especially the latter) were seeking to emigrate from Austrian to some Protestant territory, where they might enjoy immunity from persecution. He offered these pious people an asylum on his estate at Bertelsdorf, which henceforth became known as Herrnhut (the Watch of the Lord) and the center of the Moravian brotherhood. Thus Zinzendorf became the rescuer and virtually the second founder of that pious and active Christian community. He was their protector, teacher, poet, bishop, preacher. He visited other parts of Germany, also England and America, in the interests of his community. His travels and labors of administration were extensive and laborious, and his writings were not inconsiderable in amount. Worn with toil, but happy in its large fruits, he died in his sixtieth year, full of peace.

As a preacher Zinzendorf had great natural gifts, and added to these a religious experience of sincerity and depth. He had a clear intellect, a warm heart, and oratorical fire; with these a rich fancy and a passionate love for Christ and the souls of men; wealth of ideas and of language was not lacking; and thus his outfit as a preacher was adequate. But he was careless of form and style, spoke often without sufficient preparation and with a jargon of mixed French, German, and other words which was hostile to any elegance of speech. His sermons would not be tolerable reading now, though many of his hymns remain in use. Rothe well says of him:

"Had Zinzendorf grasped Christianity all around, and developed his talent under the control of the understanding and of a sound taste, he would have been one of the most extraordinary of preachers."

In the early part of the century there were several preachers of note in the Reformed Church in Germany,[30] who were more or less under Pietist influence. H. J. Ulrich (1683-1731) was *antistes* at Zurich, an active pastor and highly esteemed preacher, who declined more than one important call to Germany, and whose sermons were translated into Dutch. But he was of the older scholastic type, with its rigid analytical form and abundant pedantry. D. E. Jablonsky (1660-1741), long time one of the court preachers at Berlin, was not so original as Ulrich, but was "especially distinguished with the beautiful gift of bringing religious truths home to the heart by naïve, touching pictures." He had had a varied history and training—at Dantzig, Frankfort on the Oder, and at Oxford, for his learning; and as pastor at Magdeburg, Lissa, and old Königsberg—before his long and useful ministry at Berlin. He was interested and active in the evangelical union efforts, and was much beloved and very useful as a preacher, though of the old-fashioned scholastic sort and not highly endowed with oratorical qualities.

Passing now to the preachers of the Rationalist group, we shall omit the extreme types and only name a few of the best representatives. Of these one of the earlier and more moderate was J. F. W. Jerusalem (1709-1789),[31] who was born at Osnabrück, studied under the famous professor Gottsched at Leipzig, traveled in Holland and in England, where he came in contact with the liberal Baptist preacher, James Foster. He was much inclined to philosophy and liberalism; tried to extract the kernel of Christianity from all sectarian shells, and was one of the first by voice and influence to insist upon that marked and almost one-sided ethical preaching so characteristic of the eighteenth century everywhere. He became court preacher, and tutor to the heir-apparent of the ducal

[30]See Lentz, II, S. 325; Rothe, S. 420 ff.; articles in *Allg. deut. Biog.*

[31]Lentz, II, S. 221; Rothe, S. 427 ff.

house of Brunswick, at Wolfenbüttel. He was a strong preacher, full of fire and style; and he had many admirers and imitators. Rothe compares Jerusalem to Mosheim in his appeal to the cultured classes, and in his oratorical feeling; but rates him far below the great historian in evangelical conviction and power. His idea of preaching—given largely in his own words[32]—was that as a recognized institution of society it must give "instruction in religion as the great means of enlightenment, the strongest guide to righteousness, and the surest source of all true peace;" that it must "lead men to enlightenment and morality," must study social conditions, warn against dangers to public and private virtue, and by teaching and example advance the cause of good morals.

John Jacob Spalding (1714-1804)[33] was of Scotch descent and was born the son of a Lutheran pastor in Pomerania, who gave him the foundations of his education. Later he attended school at Stralsund, and the University of Rostock. He was not greatly helped at Rostock, but going as tutor to Greifswald, he continued his studies. Later he assisted his father for a time, then went as pastor to Lassahn for eight years, and thence to Barth, where he served fourteen years. In 1764 he was called to one of the greater churches in Berlin and held it till 1788, when, on account of old age and dislike of certain state-church policies, he retired from active work, though he lived on in peaceful and gradual decline till 1804.

Spalding was happy in family and social life. He was three times married, and fortunately each time. His last wife tenderly cared for his old age; he was wont to call her his guardian angel. His sons and daughters were a comfort to him, especially one daughter who was married to S. G. Sack, one of the several notable

[32]Quoted in footnote by Rothe, S. 428.

[33]Schuler, *Gesch. der Veränderungen,* etc., III, S. 57 ff.; Doering, S. 463 ff.; Lentz, II, S. 227; Rothe, S. 431; Ker, p. 248 ff. Of Spalding's own works, *Gedanken über den Werth der Gefühle im Christenthum,* of which there is an Eng. transl. by A. B. Evans; and *Ueber die Nutzbarkeit des Predigtamts und deren Beförderung,* of which the same translator has given an abridged paraphrase and arrangement.

preachers of that name. Spalding's intercourse with the leading clergymen and other influential men of the age was constant and mutually helpful. Among his friends were Jerusalem, the Sacks—father and son—and Lavater, who when a young man paid Spalding a long visit at Barth, and learned much from him, though they differed so widely in their views of Christian truth and policy.

Spalding's personal attitude toward the fundamental Christian doctrines was not so heterodox as is commonly assumed. But, as is often the case, he advocated tendencies and views which others took up and pushed to their logical results in opinions and practices far out of harmony with evangelical Christianity. While he personally seems to have accepted the supernatural element in Christianity, the general authority of Scripture as a divine revelation, and the deity and atoning work of Jesus Christ, he depreciated all these in his teaching and example and laid emphasis on morality and utility as the chief ends in preaching. He taught that the difficult doctrines, such as the Trinity, the Person and Atonement of Christ, and the like, should have no place in sermons to the people. As a preacher Spalding was winsome in bearing, with a good though not strong voice, an earnest though quiet manner, appealing to intellect and conscience rather than to feeling. His principal activity was as pastor and preacher, but he was also from the first a writer on various subjects, and he published a number of sermons.

The best known and most influential of his books[34] were those on *The Value of the Feelings in Christianity,* and *The Utility of the Preaching Office,* from which both the dominant theory of his ministry and the qualities of his mind and style may be easily gathered. He discusses the feelings in a cool, sensible, intellectual way; but in opposing the pietistic, one-sided valuation of them he goes too far the other way and does not value them enough. In eloquently and cogently defending the usefulness of preaching as a social force he lays the weight of his argument on its ethical rather than evangelical aspect, and thus really discounts its true function. It is the oft-repeated story of attacking one extreme by going

[34]See preceding note.

to the other, criticising one-sidedness by being one-sided in the opposite quarter. In reading these books now one must have the feeling that both of them were overrated alike by admirers and critics; but they were voices of the time on one side of a great divide in the theory and practice of preaching.

George Joachim Zollikofer (1730-1788)[35] was not a Lutheran, but pastor for many years of the Reformed Church at Leipzig. He was born at St. Gall, Switzerland, the son of an accomplished and eloquent lawyer who was fond of theology also, and to whom the boy owed much in the direction of his bent and his early culture. He, of course, attended the schools of his native place, then pursued academic learning at Frankfort-on-the-Main, at Bremen, and then at Utrecht. After traveling in Holland and studying quietly at home for a year, he began his work as pastor in several small places. But he acquired fame as an eloquent preacher so quickly that he was called, in 1758 (when twenty-eight years old), to the Reformed Church at Leipzig, where he found his life-work. Naturally he was not at his maturity at first, but steadily grew in power and influence, and was esteemed one of the best pulpit orators of the age as well as a man of pure and lofty character. He was orderly and neat in preaching, as in home and habits, careful of details, and courteous in manner; broad in culture, without being a great scholar; well endowed with the externals of oratory—a good voice, excellent accent, pleasing delivery; with a clear and persuasive style, a good flow of thought, and a serious and impressive demeanor in the pulpit. He was very eloquent and classic according to the then accepted standards, but was cool, moralistic, and vague in theology, with no firm grasp of evangelical realities either in thought or, apparently, in experience. He was no great theologian, and his philosophy was mildly but intelligently Wolfian. His religious opinions tended to Pelagian views of man and Socinian views of the person and work of Christ. He is quoted as saying:[36] "If the apostles had written to Christians of our times, in our language, and with reference to the

[35]Schuler, III, S. 194 ff.; Lentz, II, 327 ff.; *RE* Bd. 21, S. 711; Sack, S. 185 ff.; Ker, p. 250 f.; sermon in Fish, I, p. 485.

[36]By Sack, *op. cit.,* S. 189.

character and grade of our knowledge, they would certainly have expressed themselves very differently; they would have left out of their mode of expression all that relates to sacrifice, priests, means of cleansing, ransom, holiness." The closing words of a sermon on the *Ennobling Nature of Christianity* will give a fair sample of Zollikofer's preaching:[37] "Wouldst thou then feel and assert thy dignity, O man! Wouldst thou display it in all its luster? Then be a Christian, be wholly a Christian; be wholly animated by the sense and spirit of Christianity. Believe its doctrines with thy whole heart; follow its precepts with fidelity and fortitude; firmly repose on its promises; frame thyself entirely on its Founder, Jesus! The spirit of Christianity will free thy soul from every base sentiment, every unworthy desire. It will elevate thy mind, enlarge thy heart, make thee feel thy powers, and ever transmit thee new. It will raise thee above all that is visible and earthly; will constantly give thee a greater resemblance to Jesus, the pattern of all human perfection; and constantly unite thee more intimately with God. Animated by the spirit of Christianity, thou wilt justly esteem every faculty, every talent, every power that God hath given thee; carefully incite and exert them, constantly produce as much good by them as thou canst. Informed by the spirit of Christianity, thou wilt never act like a slave; never allow thyself to be governed by any sensual appetite, or any unruly passion; thou wilt not cringe with servility before any mortal; thou wilt constantly think and act with generosity and freedom. Animated by the spirit of Christianity, thou wilt ever be more active, more indefatigable in goodness; wilt never be weary in striving upward, and contending for the prize that awaits the conqueror. Animated by the spirit of Christianity, thou wilt already in this mortality think and act like an immortal; and wilt perform a thousand acts of goodness, and enjoy a thousand comforts, which he can neither perform nor enjoy who is unmindful of his immortality, or can not rejoice therein. O how exalted and divine is the spirit of Christianity! the spirit of wisdom and power, of love and felicity! May its animating influ-

[37]Fish, I, p. 494.

ence quicken, warm, and enliven us all! May it rouse us to the noblest sentiments of ourselves, inspire us with godlike energy, with the most active zeal in goodness, and penetrate and warm us with love toward God and man! How great, how illustrious will then our dignity be, and how much greater and more illustrious will it become, from one period of our lives to another, and from eternity to eternity!"

The epitaph on Zollikofer's tomb[38] at Leipzig was certainly meant to be highly eulogistic, but it is indeed pathetic: "He lives on here in his influence, and there in the sphere of souls where Socrates and Jesus live."

Other preachers of the Reformed Church in this period were more evangelical than Zollikofer. Especially worthy of mention are the elder and younger Sack,[39] A. F. W. Sack (1703-1786), and his son, Samuel G. Sack (1738-1817), who was also son-in-law to Spalding.

Coming now to the Supernaturalist or Mediating school, we find that the way was ably led by John Jacob Rambach (1692-1735),[40] who, both in his sermons and in his lectures at Halle, insisted on a sound interpretation and application of Scripture as against the wrong methods of both the philosophic and the extreme pietistic schools. He urged that a sermon should have good order, clearness, simplicity, solidity. Along with him should be named J. G. Reinbeck (1683-1741),[41] who was nearer to the philosophical school than Rambach, studied under Wolf at Halle, and admired without blindly following him. He began his ministry as assistant at Halle, but was later called to Berlin and preached there till his death.

But the greatest name among his brethren of this school is that of the eminent scholar and church historian, Johann Lorenz Mosheim (1693 or 4-1755).[42] Of him Rothe says: "Through him preaching in Germany first came under the jurisdiction of taste. Furnished by nature with decided oratorical talent, and standing midway in the stream of the contemporary spiritual life upon

[38]Cited by Ker, *l. c.*

[39]Lentz, II, 325; Rothe, S. 421.

[40]Schuler, II, S. 127; Lentz, II, 170; Rothe, S. 409 ff.

[41]Lentz, II, S. 176.

[42]Lentz, II, S. 187 f.; Schuler, II, S. 159 ff.; Rothe, S. 424; Nebe, II, 137 ff.; Ker, p. 241 ff.

the summit of his time, familiar with polite literature in the same degree as with theology and philosophic learning, master as few in his time of the German language, cultivated moreover by study of the French and English pulpit orators—especially Tillotson; moved and fructified inwardly by the newly germinating consciousness on the natural side of the spiritual life, he was just the man to grasp and lead to actual realization the idea of a distinctively spiritual eloquence."

Mosheim was born at Lübeck, the son of an army officer, who was a Catholic, but his mother, to whom his early training was chiefly due, was a pious Lutheran. The boy had good educational advantages, and improved them; was tutor in a gymnasium and student at the University of Kiel, where he was ordained and served as assistant pastor. He was professor and preacher at Helmstädt, and later at Göttingen. He was never a pastor, but often pastor's assistant, and sometimes court preacher at Wolfenbüttel and at Brunswick, in connection with his duties as professor and lecturer on church history. His grasp of evangelical truth was firm, his own religious experience deep and genuine. His manner of preaching was much influenced by the English Tillotson and the French Saurin. Naturally from his position and culture his appeal was chiefly to the educated classes, with whom he was deservedly popular as a preacher and highly esteemed as a man. We have already seen that his influence on preaching in Germany has been wholesome, profound, and permanent.

After Mosheim, whose activity closed about the middle of the period, we pass on to a distinguished group whose work fell toward the close and at the turn of the century. Among these must be reckoned the famous literary man and writer, Johann Gottfried Herder (1744-1803),[43] who was born in East Prussia of poor but pious parents, in whose humble home the Bible and hymn-book were the first books to awaken the interest of the future great writer. His remarkable talents attracted attention, and in one way and another his early education was provided for. Among his pastors and helpers was an army surgeon,

[43] Rothe, S. 441; Doering, S. 103 ff.; Sack, S. 138 ff., and others. Excellent sermon on the Bible in Fish, I, p. 497 ff.

who led Herder to study medicine; but his preference was for theology and literature, in which he soon became proficient. After teaching for a time, he became pastor among the Germans at Riga, where he remained several years, then traveled, then was pastor at Brückeburg, and finally was made court preacher at Weimar in the famous days of Goethe and others. His literary tastes and talent for writing made him at once one of the brilliant coterie which adorned German letters at that celebrated epoch, and both his religious views and his preaching were inevitably modified, and not in the direction of sound evangelical thinking, by that worldly and philosophic atmosphere. But it is rather remarkable that he did not drift further away from a firm supernaturalism than he seems actually to have done. Herder was of a deeply poetic and spiritual nature, and his religious side had been warmed and nourished by the influence of Hamann and Jung-Stilling. In character he was devout, pure, and lovable—a true friend, an affectionate husband and father, a kind and sympathetic pastor. His preaching naturally exhibited the qualities of his thought and style as a writer and cultured student. His sermons[44] are described as "poetic rhapsodies," often somewhat vague in thought and obscure in style, too frequently lacking in definite theological view, but warmly spiritual in feeling. But the sermon given by Fish does not merit Rothe's strictures, being a clear, strong, devout, and sincere defense of the divine origin and right use of the Scriptures.

More distinctively a preacher, though far less of a thinker and literary man, than Herder was the famous court preacher at Dresden, Franz Volkmar Reinhard (1752-1812).[45] He was, take him all in all, the leading

[44]Rothe, *l. c.*

[45]Reinhard's life is best understood from his own *Geständnisse* ("Confessions"), giving account of his preparation for his lifework, his ideas and methods of preaching, etc. They are in the form of letters to a friend, were published in 1810, and have been well translated into English by O. A. Taylor, Boston, 1832. Reinhard's sermons were published at various times, and the collected edition is in thirty-nine volumes. The two volumes, published 1709, of sermons preached during the previous year were used for the study given in the text. See also Lentz, II, S. 242; Rothe, S. 454 ff.; Nebe, II, S. 181 ff.; Ker, p. 252 ff.; Fish, I, p. 515 ff.

preacher in Germany at the end of the eighteenth century, and therefore claims a somewhat extended notice.

Reinhard's father was an old-fashioned Lutheran pastor at the little village of Vohenstrauss, in the duchy of Sulzbach, where Franz was born, in 1752. The elder Reinhard was a highly respected man and a preacher of considerable powers and local reputation. The boy owed much to his father's careful training and worthy example. He was taught Latin and trained to Bible study. His future homiletical skill was foreshadowed in his reproducing at ten years of age the outlines of his father's sermons after hearing them. Thus his fondness for clear division and logical order was fixed for life. In 1768 he was sent to school at Regensburg, and soon afterwards his father died, having made such provision as he could for the son's further education. Reinhard's means were very limited, but he invested some of them in books—having already developed a passionate fondness for German literature, especially Haller and Klopstock, whose poems he read with delight. He found helpful teachers at Regensburg, and studied hard, being especially influenced by Demosthenes, whose virile and chaste eloquence appealed more to his taste than the ambitious and affected stuff which often passed in that age for real oratory.

By the kind help of friends and his own strict frugality Reinhard was enabled further to pursue his studies at Wittenberg. Here he began to preach, testing first his powers, as a novice, and later taking up the work more seriously. He prepared himself for a teacher, taught as tutor and with success, then was made professor at Wittenberg, and taught with great applause. He was also made preacher to the University, and took up this office with great and conscientious devotion. Such was his preparation for his work as a preacher, and this was the beginning of his great career in the pulpit. Recognized as one of the ablest preachers of his time, he was called, in 1792, to be court preacher at Dresden, and he filled the post with distinction for the twenty remaining years of his life, to 1812. Reinhard was twice married, both times happily, and in private life as well as in official station bore a character above reproach and adorned with the Christian virtues. While conscientious in the acceptance and discharge of his pastoral duties, Reinhard was pre-eminently a preacher, and it is in this light that we must now view him.

In the sixth letter of his *Confessions*[46] he speaks of the wholesome influence of Demosthenes upon his ideas of eloquence, and insists that a discourse should be well ordered, its matter devoted to the best interests of the hearers, clothed in fit and impressive language, without bombast, but easily flowing. "Then," he says, "my discourse will be clear for the intellect, easy to be remembered, exciting to the feelings, and captivating to the heart. Then I shall speak of religion with that perfect simplicity, exalted dignity, and benevolent warmth with which we ought always to speak of it." This was a clearly defined and high ideal, and Reinhard faithfully endeavored to live up to it, with as much success as the common and the individual human imperfections admitted.

In the ninth letter,[47] with accustomed clearness and evident sincerity, Reinhard explains his theological position. In his growing youth there was the inevitable spiritual crisis and struggle, but he came to peace by trust in God through Christ. Of his manhood he says: "In my struggles after the truth I could not fail to perceive that strict and systematic connection, unity of principle, and consistency of thought in religion could be acquired only by adhering either entirely to reason or entirely to the Scriptures; and hence in reality only by the Rationalist or the Supernaturalist." He was led to make his choice between the two and adopt the supernaturalist position chiefly by two potent considerations: (1) His early acquired and persistent reverence for the Bible as the true Word of God; and (2) the need and yearning of his heart for release from sin and the assurance of things divine—which he could find only in Christ and in the Bible. But this did not lead him to throw away reason nor shut him up to narrow views. He shows that those who try to take a middle course between these two principles are vacillating and uncertain, with no sure guide and no definite system of thought. He mildly complains that he had been misjudged by some critics who accused

[46]Taylor's trans., p. 40 ff. [47]*Op. cit.*, p. 62 ff.

him of insincerity, and by some friends who felt moved to apologize for him. But for himself, both mind and heart found rest in his position, and what he had found he must preach to others.

In his preaching he candidly admits many imperfections. His homiletical training had been scanty and faulty, and he could not propose himself as a model. His sermons were written out—two each week—and committed to memory. They were thus often produced with haste and lacked polish. His method of division was often too formal, but he needed this logical arrangement for himself, and found it helpful to his hearers. His thought and style are confessedly often out of the reach of uneducated people, but he had first the University audience at Wittenberg, and then the cultivated congregation at Dresden.

A perusal—partly cursory and partly more careful—of a number of Reinhard's sermons preached during the year 1808 leaves these impressions: His faults were those of too great sameness here and there, and occasional forcing of his topic from his text—due in large part to his being hampered by the prescribed gospel or epistle for the day. The excellencies of Reinhard, however, outweighed these drawbacks. The reader even now will find in his sermons clarity of thought and usually of style, elevation of mind and character, serenity and firmness of faith in the eternal verities of Christianity, reverence toward God, and a sincere desire to benefit man; no self-seeking nor ambition for oratorical or philosophical display, no sensationalism or novelty, but the instinct of instruction and helpfulness.

The last of this remarkable group to be noticed here is the famous and gifted Swiss, Johann Caspar Lavater (1741-1801).[48] He was the youngest of twelve children of a physician of standing at Zurich. A highly nervous, imaginative, and sensitive child, he seems not to have been understood or properly managed in his home. But instead of becoming embittered and ruined, his isolation drove him to God in prayer and childlike trust. Thus

[48]Doering, S. 189 ff.; Sack, S. 120 ff.; *RE,* Bd. 11, S. 314; an old volume (1778) of Lavater's *Kasual-predigten,* containing also some *Gedichte.*

as early as his eleventh year he found in need the divine consolation and help, and through life the reality and the love of God in Christ were an anchor to his soul. Already he began to exhort his school-fellows and to develop that remarkable faculty for natural and tactful religious conversation which distinguished him through life. He was ever gifted with that sort of individual appeal which the nomenclature of modern religious effort calls "personal work." His quickness in reading character from faces led him early into the study of physiognomy, of which he made a sort of fad—chiefly by way of recreation from graver pursuits—and tried to raise to the dignity of a science.

Lavater was well educated in the schools and at the University of Zurich, and studied theology under Breitinger and Bodmer. An episode in his early career gives an illustration of generosity and courage characteristic of the man. A councilor and prominent citizen of Zurich wronged a poor man whose cause Lavater espoused, both publicly and by writing a scathing letter to the offender. As Lavater had impulsively acted without the forms of law, the enraged and discredited citizen threatened a lawsuit, and it was deemed best that the young man should leave Zurich till the storm blew over. This was the occasion of that long visit which he paid to J. J. Spalding at Barth, and improved so well by intercourse with that distinguished preacher.

On his return to Zurich, Lavater took up the work of the ministry in earnest, serving several years in various churches and subordinate positions till finally he was invested as chief pastor and preacher at the St. Peter's Church, and so continued till his death, in 1801. He was happily married and was exemplary and affectionate in his domestic life. As a pastor he was much beloved in personal contact with his flock. His genial and clever ways endeared him to his friends without damage to the spiritual influence of his sincerely pious character. He had his critics and foes. These made merry or serious attack upon his studies and writings on physiognomy, and accused him of undue self-esteem amounting to vanity. There was some justice in these criticisms; but he lived to realize that he could not make a great science out of his fad, and he grew in the grace of humility. In the trying times of the French Revolution and the beginning of Napoleon's dictatorship in Europe, Lavater was the brave and loyal Swiss patriot, as well as the faithful Christian pastor. During the occupation of Zurich by the French under Massena, in 1799-1800, Lavater was true and faithful to his country and his charge. While ministering to the wounded in the streets after some affray, he was shot in front of his own house by an enraged French soldier to whom he had declined to give a glass of wine. He lingered for a year, but at last died from the effects of this brutal wound. Let it be remembered that he refused to reveal the identity of his assailant, but the rather prayed for his conversion.

Lavater was a great gospel preacher. He firmly held the evangelical doctrines, sincerely accepting and teaching the divine revelation and authority of Scripture, the deity and atonement of Christ, the need of regeneration, and the work of the Holy Spirit, with those involved and accompanying truths which go to make up the evangelical system. But he escaped the narrowness and cant which have too often been justly criticised in many who held these views. Lavater's preaching was characterized by warmth of heart, earnestness of soul, richness of fancy, clearness and vigor of thought, and force yet variety of style. Naturally his manner would differ with occasion and degree of preparation. He did not write his sermons, and the carelessness of the popular speaker sometimes appeared in his style. Comparatively few of his sermons were written out after delivery and published.

Looking through an old volume of these one may find several discourses to attract his notice and reward his reading. There is a strong and tender one on 1 John 4:19, "We love Him because He first loved us;" and from Peter's answer to our Lord in John 6:68, "Lord, to whom shall we go? Thou hast the words of eternal life," there is a rhapsody of trust in Jesus amid temporal, moral, intellectual, and spiritual difficulties. But perhaps the most characteristic and striking sermon of the collection is a fast-day sermon, preached in Zurich in 1771, and published by request, but reluctantly, and with an apology and statement that the author had tried to reproduce it exactly as it had been delivered. The text is 2 Kings 22:11, the account of King Josiah's rending his garments on finding the book of the law and realizing how far he and his people fell short of its observance. There is, first, a good exposition of the Scripture narrative, then an earnest prayer, and then the application to occasion and audience. Why should we here in Zurich act in the spirit of Josiah, and rend, not our garments, but our hearts? Three reasons are urged: (1) Because we do not love God as we ought; nor (2) our neighbor, (3) nor practice self-denial. This simple, even commonplace, division gives basis for a discussion which brings out many of the best qualities of the preacher—his soulful love and trust toward God, his deep and affectionate concern for his flock, and the elements of his oratory already mentioned. Of course, the faults of his temperament and style also appear in some degree. An extract will give a fair sample of Lavater's manner. It is taken from an impassioned appeal at the end of the first division of the sermon—that a sense of the love of God and our failure suitably to respond to it should lead us to penitence: "Yes, rend now, O ye blinded ones, rend not your garments, but your hearts, that ye love not a God of whose love heaven and earth are full; that ye love not a God who, out of the light that no man can approach unto, came down into the night of our human woe and took upon Himself the sin and death of a whole world and gave up the last drop of His sin-abolishing blood for our eternal salvation, willingly and amid unspeakable sufferings; that ye love not a God who, with all His love-worthiness, with all the riches of His eternal glory, would give Himself to you, quicken you with His life, animate you with His Spirit, enlighten you with His own wisdom, flood you with the joy of His divine love, make you partakers of His divine nature; that ye love not a God without whose love no intelligent creature either in heaven or on earth could be blest, without whose love heaven itself would be a hell! Yes, only rend your hearts,—or rather, rend thou them, O omnipotence of my God! Rend thou them, adorable holiness of Him before whom the seraphim veil their faces! Rend thou them, O Spirit of my crucified Redeemer, who didst cleave the rocks and graves and rend yon veil of the Temple! Rend ye them with your dazzling light, ye ever-shining wounds of Him who founded the earth and whose works the heavens are! Rend thou them, O blood that flowed on Golgotha—most holy blood, whose emblem we have this day drunk in the cup of thanksgiving and love—that they may awake these sleeping souls—that their eyes may be opened to love that which alone is worthy to be loved, which alone and eternally can satisfy them and make them blest!"

In the same sermon, further on, after making an earnest appeal to Zurich lest trouble should befall the state, Lavater gives us this warm outburst of self-revelation: "Yet why do I thus speak? I, who am myself a sinner in this town, like others? I who so often myself forget my God and break my holiest resolutions and vows? How dare I, weak, unstable, who feel myself so far removed from being able to say after the apostle, 'Be ye followers of me, as I am of Christ,' how dare I thus speak of other sinners? Ah! forgive it me, thou most gracious (*allerbeste*) God, Thou who knowest my sincere longing for the salvation of these souls as well as Thou knowest my own frequent and great weaknesses. Be it so, Thou knowest that it comes not out of a proud or harsh, but out of a sympathetic heart, which often must wish that to itself also some one might even thus frankly and shamingly speak."

In closing thus our study of eighteenth century German preaching with a view of a soul like Lavater's, it will surely not be out of place to give one more quotation from him, this time from one of his poems—a sentiment for him as well as for ourselves:[49]

> "Fürchte dich nie! Du bist geliebt von der Lieb' und bist ewig!
> Lass der Sterblichkeit eilenden Traum nicht sehr dich bekümmern,
> Sorge nur, dass du erwachst zum Anschaun unsterblicher Liebe!"

[49]Lavater's *Worte des Herzens,* S. 2.
Fear thou never! thou art beloved by Love and art eternal!
Let not mortality's hastening dream trouble thee overmuch;
Care only that thou awakest to the vision of immortal Love!

CHAPTER VIII

French Preaching in the Eighteenth Century

French history during the eighteenth century is full of suffering and horrors culminating in the Revolution.[1] The Revocation of the Edict of Nantes, in 1685, may be taken as a turning point and the beginning of a great decline in France. The expulsion of nearly a half million inhabitants, including many persons of high standing, as well as thousands of honest and capable artisans, and the persecution of those who remained behind were serious blows to the prosperity of France. The king was now growing old; his wars had drained the treasury; the magnificence of his court had set the pace for very expensive living among the higher classes; and taxes and oppression ground the faces of the poor. Sorrows multiplied in the palace, and early in the eighteenth century the famous monarch found himself a lonely old man with a great-grandchild of five years to be his successor on the throne of France. Of the reign of Louis XV it can only be said that it was dark, corrupt, and injurious. The king himself was utterly devoid of the best traits of humanity, mean-spirited, sensual, cruel, and cowardly. He was the most unkingly king of his time, utterly unworthy and unfit to meet the terrible responsibilities of his position. His court was a sty of iniquity and a disgrace to decency. The finances of the kingdom were in terrible disorder. The upper classes were proud, rapacious, and extravagant; the middle classes groaned, and the poor starved. To such an inheritance came, in 1774, the good and promising young king, Louis XVI, with his beautiful young queen, Marie Antoinette. The young monarch was amiable and well disposed, but neither his natural capacities nor his goodness of heart were sufficient to meet the awful difficulties with which he was confronted. There can be only sympathy and pity for the royal pair. Expedient after expedient was tried to check the drift of things toward the awful catastrophe, but it was too late. After more than a century

[1]White, *History of France;* and Vol. XII of the *Historians' History.*

of royal tyranny and oppression, of exhaustion of the nation's strength in the interest of crowned selfishness, no king, however well disposed, could stem the tide of popular discontent and national decay. After everything else had been tried in vain, the king and his advisers at last determined, in 1789, to convoke the representatives of the people to consider the state of affairs. The memorable meeting of the States-General wherein the Third Estate, the common people, asserted at last their rights, resulted in the overthrow of the monarchy, the aristocracy, and the Church, with all the horrors of the French Revolution. And just as the close of the century was coming another terror was arising in the military despotism of Napoleon Bonaparte. Such was the history of France in the eighteenth century.

In literature[2] the case of France is not unlike that of England. As compared with the seventeenth century there was a decline in the number and quality of great authors, but still there were a few famous names to adorn the epoch. At the opening of the century Le Sage published his famous *Gil Blas* and set all the nation a-laughing. Although the scene was Spanish, the tone was entirely French. The *Memoirs* of St. Simon contributed an unusually interesting chapter to French history. One of the greatest historical and philosophic writers of the world, Montesquieu, gave his great writings to the world about the middle of the century. His *Spirit of the Laws* remains one of the great treatises in historical jurisprudence; while Quesnay contributed stimulating discourses to political economy. The Abbé Prévost produced a number of works, among them his classic novel, *Manon Lescaut,* but the greatest and most versatile writer of the century was undoubtedly the cynical and brilliant Voltaire, who gave himself that name as a matter of fancy, his real name being François Arouet. Voltaire exercised a profound influence on his own time and subsequent times. More brilliant than profound, he yet touched as with an electric wand the intellects of his

[2]The standard histories of French literature; specimens and discussions in the *Warner Library* for the period; Sainte-Beuve, *Eighteenth Century Portraits* (translations published by Geo. P. Putnam's Sons).

day. He was one of the most prolific writers of any time in nearly all departments of literature. His skepticism in religion and his lack of moral earnestness have made his influence baleful rather than helpful. Along with him should be mentioned J. J. Rousseau, whose readable and widely spread writings were revolutionary, both in politics and morals. Nor must we forget the Encyclopedists, especially Diderot and D'Alembert, whose works prepared for and furthered the Revolution. Some names of less note than these also occur, among whom must be mentioned the famous scientist, Buffon, and, of women writers, Madme Du Deffand and Madame d' Epinay. Besides Barthélemy, Beaumarchais, and Saint-Pierre, whose exquisite little story of *Paul and Virginia* has been a universal favorite. Authors like these remind us that even declining ages in national history may often produce writers of the first rank.

The most important features in the religious history of France during this century have already been alluded to. The persecution of the Huguenots went on during the early part of the century. The moral corruption and insincerity of religious life, both in clergy and people, was subversive of religious power. The suppression of the Jesuits in 1773, as in other countries, came too late to accomplish any real reform. The terrible explosion of the Revolution, from 1789 and on, upset the foundations of religious faith in France for a while. Atheism and immorality seemed to be triumphant, and unhappy France came to the beginning of the nineteenth century with only remnants of religious faith and feeling left among her people. It was amid such conditions as these that the French preaching of the eighteenth century ran its course.

I. Brief General Survey

For French preaching, as for that of other European peoples, the eighteenth century was a time of reaction and decadence.[3] There is no aspect in which it does not

[3]The Church Histories, general and particular; for the Protestants, Baird, *The Huguenot Emigration;* Smiles, *The Huguenots in France After the Revocation.* For general surveys: the works of Rothe, Lentz, Christlieb, Hering, previously mentioned.

appear inferior, and in many lamentably inferior, to the preaching of both the seventeenth and the nineteenth centuries. The Protestants had been forbidden to hold worship, and many thousands of them had fled to other countries rather than either conform to the Catholic Church or give up their religious services altogether. One other recourse was left: to worship by stealth as they might be able. In some parts of the country this was possible, and, as we shall see, a few pastors remained, tended with care, and taught as they could, the scattered and persecuted flocks of the Reformed. But, of course, these unhappy conditions were unfavorable alike to the actual exercise of preaching and to its literary expression and preservation. In foreign lands there were a number of French Protestant churches with their pastors and preachers, but here again it is easy to see that the conditions were adverse to a high development of preaching. We shall notice later how the general characteristics of the age were shared by the preachers of the Reformed Churches.

The Catholic Church, though outwardly triumphant over her rival, was far from flourishing in any spiritual sense. She was torn asunder with the Jansenist-Jesuit quarrel, and the laxity of morals in high society—encouraged by the corruption of the court—made a mockery of true religious life. The general decay in all branches of the national life was necessarily felt in the church and its pulpits. The reaction from the brilliant but overstrained and costly age of Louis XIV was as manifest in preaching as elsewhere. And it must be acknowledged that no genius comparable to those which had adorned that brilliant epoch appeared in the French Catholic pul-

For Catholic preaching: Zanotto gives some mention, and there are some notices in Maury's *Principes de l'Éloquence;* but three notable works of recent date deal directly with the subject, viz., those of Bernard, Candel, and de Coulanges, mentioned below; for the sermons and brief notices of the preachers, the great work of Migne, *Collection Intégrale et Universelle des Orateurs Sacrés;* Lives and works of the preachers, as far as available. For Protestant preaching; Couriard, *Essai, sur l' Histoire de la Prédication chez les Réformés de France et de Hollande;* Charles Coquerel, *Histoire des Églises du Desert;* Daniel Benoit, *Trois Prédicateurs sous la Croix au 18me Siècle;* and *Les Frères Gibert.*

pit during the whole eighteenth century. The decline is so manifest that criticism has gone to an extreme in speaking of it as a decadence almost complete; in fact, an utter collapse. A little reflection on the French history of the age, and any study of the sermons that remain from the preachers of the century, will show that in this case, as in many similar ones, decline is not total collapse, that inferiority does not mean utter worthlessness, that comparative weakness does not imply total lack of power. Two considerations—to say nothing of others—should serve to balance and correct so faulty a judgment. The first is that many of the faults and weaknesses which appear in eighteenth century preaching were characteristic also of the seventeenth, with which on the whole it is unfairly compared. And the other is that a careful study of the French Catholic sermons which have come down from the eighteenth century will show that though as a rule and on the average inferior to those of the seventeenth century, they were not wholly destitute of excellence or of power.

II. Catholic Preaching and Preachers

For all the purposes of historical and critical treatment, French Catholic preaching during the eighteenth century lies chiefly between the years 1718 and 1789. The latter date brings us to the outbreak of the great Revolution which threw everything into confusion in France, and was markedly disastrous to all the interests of the Catholic Church, including preaching. During the last decade of the century there was comparatively little preaching, and among the faithful few who labored on amid the turmoil and uncertainties of that time of trial there were few if any preachers of distinction; and those who are worthy of notice went over into the nineteenth century. The earlier date (1718) is the year of Massillon's retirement from the court and pulpits of Paris to take up for the remainder of his life his duties as bishop of Clermont. The retirement of Massillon ended the brilliant era of which he had been one of the three most eminent representatives.

The preaching of the century has been carefully

studied and described by three modern French scholars, to whose thoughtful labors the following discussion owes much, though other authorities and, as far as possible, the sources, have also been consulted. Candel[4] treats only the first half of the century, but with detailed and patient study of many preachers of the various orders. De Coulanges[5] (said to be the pen-name of the *abbé* Rosne) studies and presents the time as an age of acknowledged decadence, carefully considering the evidences and tokens of decline. Bernard[6] discusses only the years from 1718 to 1789, with critical studies of a large number of its representative preachers and sermons. He subdivides the period into five shorter ones in the following suggestive way: (1) 1718-1729, transition from the classic age to the new one; (2) 1729-1750, rise of the so-called "academic" pulpit eloquence; (3) 1750-1763, flourishing of academic and rise of apologetic preaching; (4) 1763-1778, a critical period in which semi-philosophic essays were common in the pulpit; (5) 1778-1789, period of reaction and effort to revive the better spirit and method of former times. This scheme, though somewhat artificial, has its merits; but it is better for our purposes simply to divide the century midway. The earlier period (1700-1750) extends from the close of the classic age to the rise of apologetic preaching forced by the skeptical philosophy of the Encyclopedists and Voltaire; and the second (1750-1800) from the rise of this philosophic preaching to the end of the century.

Taking up first the earlier period, we find that owing to the influence of Massillon, who was an Oratorian, and of Archbishop Noailles, who favored the Jansenists, the leading preachers in Paris were at first those of the Oratorian order who were inclined to Jansenist views. In Paris the Jesuits had been discredited by Pascal and the Port-Royalists, and during Noailles' administration they were forbidden to occupy the pulpits there, notwithstanding the fact that Bourdaloue had been a Jesuit. The quarrel was hot and stubborn, involving not only

[4] *Les Prédicateurs Français dans la première Moitié du Dix-huitième Siècle,* par J. Candel.

[5] *La Chaire Française au XVIIIme Siècle,* par A. de Coulanges. [6] *Le Sermon au XVIIIme Siècle,* par A. Bernard.

the preachers and prelates, but both the devout and the worldly among the laity. This fierce controversy within the church had an injurious effect upon preaching, both in lowering its tone and spirit and in discrediting it in the eyes of mankind. The Oratorians in the days of their ascendency put forth some books on preaching,[7] and from them came the leading preachers at the capital for some years. But the day of Oratorian ascendency declined and that of the Jesuits returned when, in 1729, Noailles was succeeded in the archbishopric of Paris by Cardinal Vintimille. This prelate was opposed to Jansenism, with its more pronounced evangelical and mystical tendencies, and favored the Jesuits and their party. Henceforth, till their downfall later in the century, the Jesuits led in the pulpit. They were ready for their recall, for during the time they were forbidden to preach in Paris they had not been inactive in the provinces nor in training their best men for the more important charges.

At this point it may be well to say a word as to the supply of preachers, and the relation between the capital and the provinces in this matter. Recalling the old distinction between the secular and the regular clergy—the former being priests (*curés, abbés*) of parishes, and the latter monks of one or another of the numerous orders—we note that the seculars were not enough to do all the preaching required. Of course, not all of these were actually parish priests, or prelates; some were without settled charges, "preachers by career," who preached as opportunity offered. Candel[8] remarks: "The French pulpit, illustrated chiefly by the Oratorians as long as the episcopate of Noailles lasted, owed nevertheless a part of its glory to the seculars, who, remaining almost always aside from the theological quarrels, deserved by their prudence to be then called or tolerated in the pulpits of Paris." There were always some good preachers among the seculars in France, notwithstanding the greater

[7]Candel (p. 11) mentions several, and especially one entitled *Maximes sur l'Éloquence de la Chaire*, first published anonymously in 1710 and sometimes wrongly attributed to Massillon. It was the work of Father Gaichiés, commonplace and without depth, but it presents the accepted principles of sacred oratory with some force, and had a considerable vogue and influence.

[8]*Op. cit.*, p. 245.

vogue of the monks, and that not only among the parish priests, whose duties included preaching, but also among these "orators of career," or preachers by profession, to whom Paris gave their fame and the court their living! Certainly there was only now and then a Bossuet or a Fléchier among them, but others of less genius were worthy of note. These *abbés* and bishops, as was to be expected, were as a rule more worldly, ambitious, self-seeking, fond of popularity, than the monks; and they the more readily fell into the easygoing compromises with the current philosophy and lowered moral standards of the age.

It was natural that preachers of distinction should sooner or later appear at Paris. The capital attracts the ambitious and challenges the earnest. Louis XIV drew everything of value and show to his court. Thus preachers of the orders who showed unusual gifts would be sent by their superiors to the capital, and among the secular clergy interest, ambition, influence, as well as better reasons, combined to bring leading preachers to Paris. Nearly all the famous preachers began their work outside of Paris, and proved their powers before they were summoned to appear at the royal chapels or in the leading pulpits of the capital. And many of them came at intervals to preach series of sermons at the annual festivals—Advent and Lent—and return to the provinces. Some, as Bossuet, Mascaron, Massillon, Surian, and others, were made bishops and ended their careers in the work of their dioceses. Thus many of the most notable preachers began and ended their ministry outside of Paris.

Besides, there were many worthy and useful preachers who were never called to the Parisian pulpits at all, but gave their time and labors to their work in all parts of France. To these M. de Coulanges,[9] in discussing the ambition and other faults of the clergy, pays a striking tribute which deserves to be quoted. He writes: "It has not been sufficiently remembered that at that epoch there were also apostles full of the Spirit of God, who preached with ardor and success the true gospel. Besides the humble pastors of the towns and villages, who

[9]*Op. cit.*, p. 24.

had a horror of sophisticating the Word of God, numerous missionaries[10] traversed France, moved the multitudes and led them as penitents to the feet of the altars. . . . Though they never thought of posterity, and showed themselves solely anxious to do good to the people, whose joys and sorrows were their own, the names and works of a number of them have reached even to our times. If one would find anywhere, in the age of Voltaire, the true character of sacred eloquence he must seek it in the simple instructions of the *curés* and missioners who preached 'plainly but familiarly.' They exercised on the people a power which sometimes approached the marvelous—they had the knowledge of divine things, and it is to them far more than to the pretentious orators that the words of Holy Scripture may be applied: *The lips of a priest keep wisdom, and the people seek the law at his mouth.*" These just and sensible words could be said—with only the necessary changes for time and place—of every age in the history of preaching.

In regard to contents the French Catholic sermons in the earlier period of the century show no marked changes as to doctrine. They are based upon the accepted Romanist dogmas and ceremonials throughout. The language and tone are thoroughly Catholic. But exposition of doctrine as such finds little place; it is assumed, taken for granted, built upon, but neither argued nor enforced. Scripture is often quoted, sometimes misquoted, and often misapplied, rarely explained or expounded. Quotation from the Fathers and other authorities continues, but is not carried to the ridiculous extremes of former times. Controversy occupies a less prominent place. There is only occasional conflict with Protestants and heretics, and the tone is milder. Traces of the Jansenist and Quietist (mystical) disputes are found; but these affected preaching more indirectly as to its spirit than directly as to its thought-material. Apologetic in regard to the fundamentals of Christianity, as opposed to unbelief in general and the rising tide of skepticism in particular, becomes more pronounced about the middle of the century; only a few of the earlier

[10]Evangelists of various sorts, of whom Bridaine was the most celebrated.

preachers deal with it in their sermons, and then not very thoroughly. Bernard[11] finds only in Molinier and Pacaud of the very earliest group—both of them admirers of Bossuet—any clear apologetic preaching. They both appeal rather to the psychological than to the historical evidences of Christianity, and they draw freely from the great orators of the preceding age. Just later, as the influence of the new school of skeptical thinkers begins to be felt, allusions are found in some of the sermons, but there is as yet no serious realization of the great significance of this movement nor any attempt to meet it with intelligence or firmness. One of the best of the preachers[12]—Ségaud—declared that disdain seemed to him a sufficient defense against infidelity, and Pérussault said that religion did not need controversial defense. Yet to confirm the faith of believers, he did sometimes dwell on the internal proofs of religion, its blessings and comforts.

The main staple of the preaching of the age was morals. By far the largest number of sermons deal with conduct; and it must be said that for the most part they do this in a satisfactory and earnest manner. The terrible moral conditions of the time awakened the deepest concern in the hearts of the serious-minded among both clergy and people. Of course, there were some who treated these conditions lightly, or with satire, but for the most part the preachers assailed vice and crime both in good taste and an earnest spirit. The treatment is usually well grounded in the teachings of the Bible, and exhortation is based upon the duty of obedience to God and the faithful observance of the baptismal vow. But the fault—which all the preachers did not escape—of making sermons mere moral essays and appeals for the conventional virtues was not to be denied. The courage and decency with which the preachers attacked evil are worthy of praise. It was a happy combination which they inherited from Bossuet and the other great preachers of the classic age, who, in banishing coarseness from the pulpit, had not bated a jot of boldness or power in their denunciation of sin. Father de Neuville[13] once finely said: "Ye sacred altars! I have no other support to offer you than

[11] *Op. cit.*, Period I, Chap. II. [12] Bernard, p. 122.
[13] Quoted by Bernard, p. 146.

my voice; and you shall not reproach me with a timid silence." Such expressions are not infrequent, and they are evidently genuine. There were then, as always, preachers whose own lives were not free from the taint of corruption, and some who dealt with the evils of the time in a timid or compromising way; but most of them were faithful to warn, rebuke, exhort the people of all classes in one of the most degenerate and corrupt societies known to history—the age of Louis XV.

In regard to the theory of preaching and the structure of sermons, the accepted principles and commonplaces of homiletics were set forth, without much freshness or force, in a number of treatises. The most important and influential of these were those of Gaichiés, *Maximes sur l'Éloquence de la Chaire* (1710 and on), and of the Jesuit father, Gisbert, *L'Éloquence Chrétienne dans l'Idée et dans la Pratique* (1715 and on). Both these works passed through various editions, were widely read, and taught many preachers the technical side of their work. Besides the treatises, there were also the usual collections of model sermons, outlines, excerpts, and the like, to aid the lazy and help by suggestion the more independent preachers. In his famous *Dialogues sur l'Eloquence,* Fénelon had criticised the abuse of divisions, the refinement of analysis, in sermons; but he had not, either in theory or his own practice, rejected them altogether. The sermons of the age show differences in different men, but, on the whole, the structure tends both to stiffness and to too much elaboration. There was vast improvement, but there was room for more. The fashion was to state and reiterate in various ways the divisions and general course of thought at the end of the introduction, make a short invocation to the Virgin Mary, and then state the first head again and proceed with the discourse. The sermons are prevailingly topical, and there is little of exposition either of Scripture or doctrine.

The general character and style of the sermons of the period follow the lines of development which were established in the preceding age. There was a deterioration—decided and age-long—in power, but forms and fashions change little, and slowly. These characters had been fixed by the masters of the classic age. Admirers and imitators of the loftiness and splendor of Bossuet easily fell into the snare of bombast and turgidity. Those who preferred the argumentative and exhaustive method of Bourdaloue made analysis and completeness tiresome, and degenerated into a cold philosophic aloofness that took the heart out of preaching. Massillon's unction, art, sweetness, effect, easily lent themselves in imitation to assumed feeling and artifice, both in expression and delivery. But the better side, the real elements of beauty and power, which all these methods exemplified were not altogether wanting. Of course there was variety, both in groups and in individuals; there was combination of methods, and mixture of manners and of aims, as must ever be the case, no matter what the time and its ruling ideas. But in general, as Candel[14] points out, there were two lines of development in French preaching after Massillon: (1) the "simple" or "natural" style adopted by the followers of Bourdaloue; and (2) the "academic," "classic," or pompous and affected manner employed by those who thought they were reproducing the tone of Fléchier, Bossuet, and others. With either of these the feeling and delicacy of Massillon might be followed, as well as his art of impression. That is, it is not worth while to make a separate group or school of those who tried to profit by his methods; they naturally fell in rather with the "affected," "academic," or bombastic and flowery sort. In making descriptions and distinctions of this kind it is always necessary to remind ourselves that they are more or less vague and variable, with representative preachers of both extreme and moderate types; and that along with the faults which such critical designations imply there were qualities of power which did not fail to appeal to the thought as well as the taste and feeling of the age. The men who learned the art of preaching from the orators of the French classic age could not be a mere crowd of degenerate imitators.

In the second period of the century the course of development in French Catholic preaching does not require so full an account; for the characters and qualities it exhibited were only a continuation of those already described. There is only one important modification to

[14]*Op. cit.*, Introd.

be dealt with: the attitude of the pulpit toward the hostile critical philosophy and skepticism which dominated French thought in the second half of the eighteenth century. Bayle, Diderot, D'Alembert, and, above all, Voltaire, with others of less fame, in numerous and popular writings, and with wonderful dialectic and literary skill, assailed in various ways the teachings and institutions of traditional religion in France. The attack was fresh, vigorous, alive with new thought, and conducted by writers of real genius; the defense was traditional, timid, destitute of leaders of the highest sort; the result was disastrous. In general, we may note four phases in the attitude of the pulpit toward the dominant philosophy, and they follow in a general way the order of time. (1) Among the preachers there were some who were ignorant of the true force of this new foe; they failed to grasp its meaning or power, and treated it slightly and slightingly. (2) There were those who saw more plainly the threatening evil, their fears were aroused, and they tried to meet the attack, but weakly, timidly, without adequate and fundamental knowledge, either of their own ground and forces, or of those on the other side. (3) There was also a group of preachers who fell into the evil themselves. They either went wholly over to the enemy, though retaining their places; or they took a tone of compromise and concession that resulted in no good either to themselves or their cause. (4) Lastly, when it was too late, there came a reaction in favor of a more positive defense of the fundamental Christian truths and institutions.

When we pass the whole eighteenth century under review, it is evident enough that there was, as already noted, in the French Catholic preaching a marked and deplorable falling off in every quality which makes the pulpit powerful and effective. But before we further study this decline we should bear in mind—besides those already mentioned—a fact which students and critics of successive ages have too often neglected or overlooked in their studies, whether of art, literature, government, society, or religion. It is simply the obvious truth that in all departments of human effort and progress the good and bad, strong and weak, pure and corrupt, fruitful and fruitless, always coexist; but sometimes one set of forces gains upon the other and we have successive eras of flourishing or declining power. This has ever been true of the history of preaching, and it was amply illustrated in the French Catholic preaching of the eighteenth century.

Already friendly critics from the inside, like Fénelon, and unsympathetic critics from the outside, like La Bruyère, had sharply called attention to the defects and faults of preaching in the age of Louis XIV. It was of that splendid era that La Bruyère wrote:[15] "Christian preaching has become a show: that evangelical sadness which is the soul of it is no more seen; it is supplied by the advantages of mien, inflections of the voice, regularity of gesture, choice of words, and long enumerations. People no longer hear seriously the Holy Word—it is one sort of amusement among a thousand others." And it is related that Louis XIV once asked Boileau why it was that a certain rather obscure but earnest preacher was drawing such crowds, and the wit replied: "Sire, people always run after novelty; and this is a preacher who preaches the gospel." Allowing for the element of truth in both of these witty sayings, they may be fairly set over against each other; and they could be spoken of almost any age of preaching. Certainly it is true that many of the elements of decay which critics note in the eighteenth century were brought over from the much lauded age which preceded and conditioned the new one. De Coulanges justly says,[16] "At the moment even of the splendor of eloquence the makers of decay were already at work; the worm is hidden in the fine fruit."

Besides this continuation of evils already at work, we must recall once more that general law of reaction which is so often apparent in the course of events. A great strain is followed by relaxation; and the unhealthy stimulus to "pulpit eloquence" in the classic age was naturally followed by a season of comparative feebleness. That this decline did not so seriously affect French

[15]Quoted by A. de Coulanges, *op. cit.*, (p. 322) from La Bruyère's *Caractères et Moeurs de ce Siècle* (Oeuvres, tome 2, p. 220 ss.). [16]*Op. cit.*, p. 9.

thought and literature in other departments as it did in preaching is chiefly due to the rise of a new school of reflection and production in such writers as the Encyclopedists, Montesquieu, and most notably Voltaire. And this is precisely what did not occur in the sphere of the pulpit. Sore as the need was for a new breath and for new and different methods in preaching, these did not appear. No great and commanding genius arose to found a new school. In England the dull and cold formality of eighteenth century preaching was broken in upon by Whitefield and Wesley, and the general low state of the pulpit was thus greatly redressed. But in France, even if Whitefield had something of a counterpart in Bridaine, there was no Wesley to found a school and perpetuate it in an organization. Indeed, what place was there for a Wesley in the religious situation of France—where Protestantism was banished or forlorn, and triumphant Catholicism was going to decay? The Establishment in England disowned Wesley, but it could neither suppress nor banish him; in France it would have been otherwise for any similar leader.

The superficial opinion (if sincere) of Voltaire, that the reason for the decline of pulpit eloquence in his time was that the masters of the preceding age had exhausted both the subjects and methods of preaching and condemned their successors to poverty of materials, is too absurd to require serious refutation; but it does suggest one of the main causes of the decline. This was that the preachers of the eighteenth century in France—especially the first half of it—were such admirers of their predecessors that they were content to imitate them rather than to improve on them. This attempt to perpetuate a past glory by imitation is disastrous in every sphere of intellectual effort; it is simply ruinous in preaching, which so much requires individuality, independence of mind, and constant adaptation to changing conditions. In noting imitation as one of the principal causes of decay in the sermons of the age, De Coulanges[17] finely says, "Talent is by nature slave to genius." And servile imitation is one of the worst sorts of intellectual and moral weakness. How it leads to the imitation of faults rather

[17]*Op. cit.*, p. 18.

than excellencies, to the exaltation of mere method over spirit, of form over substance, are matters of common critical observation; and they are signally illustrated in the French Catholic sermons of the eighteenth century.

It is now time to notice a few representative preachers of the age. For this selective study the works already quoted have proved admirable guides, and the great collection of the sermons of these preachers (and many others) made by the industry and editorial skill of the Abbé Migne[18] has been of inestimable service. Among the thousands of preachers who worked in this age, and the hundreds whose printed sermons remain, it is, of course, only necessary to select a few of the better known and to bear in mind that there was an earlier and a later group, falling respectively in the first and second half of the century, and distinguished broadly, though not very sharply, by the different tone given to preaching on the rise of the skeptical philosophy of Bayle, Voltaire, and others.

In the earlier group the leading name is still that of Massillon, who lived till 1742, but he left Paris early in the Regency during the minority of Louis XV, and gave the remainder of his days to the work of his diocese of Clermont.

A contemporary and *confrère* of Massillon was Jean Baptiste Surian (1670-1754).[19] In many respects he was not unlike his greater brother, whom he admired and imitated. Like Massillon, he was of the South, an Oratorian, and in his preaching laid stress on feeling and effect. He was born at Arles, educated at Aix and at Caen, made a reputation as a preacher in various places, and was finally called to Paris in 1708. Here he preached along with Massillon for several years, preaching in the most important pulpits, and giving the Advent sermons at the court in 1717 and 1724, and the Lenten series of 1719 and 1724. As a reward for his zeal and eloquence he was made bishop of Vence in 1728. He was also made

[18]*Collection Intégrale et Universelle des Orateurs Sacrés,* etc., par J. P. Migne; 86 vols.; referred to briefly hereafter as Migne, vol. and column given—the columns being numbered, two to each page. Other authorities, biographical or critical, will be given as required.

[19]Bernard, p. 46 s.; Candel, p. 59.

a member of the Academy in 1733. He was a loving and faithful bishop, and died much esteemed in 1754. Candel[20] quotes a contemporary critic of Surian as saying that "nature had not refused him any gift which goes to make the great orator." He had a good voice, fire, feeling, and zeal; he was well read in the Fathers and the classics, and kept in touch with the literature of his time. He owed much of his success as an orator to his personality and delivery; for his printed sermons are not of the highest order of merit. He is rhetorical and classic, but his style is marred by labored and affected phrases; and his thought is not profound or varied.

Two other Oratorians of this early period are the brothers Terrasson,[21] André (1673-1723), and Gaspard (1680-1752). They were of a notable family at Lyons that gave able men to both the bar and the pulpit. Still another brother was an *abbé,* but does not appear to have been distinguished as a preacher. Both brothers were trained in the schools of the Oratory, both filled preaching stations at various places with great acceptance and success, and both were finally called to Paris, where they preached at various churches, as appointed by the authorities, and won their distinction as pulpit orators.

André Terrasson preached the Lenten sermons of 1715 at St. Honoré in Paris, and drew large and cultured audiences. On being appointed preacher at Notre Dame, he continued to attract, and more than the usual part of that vast floor-space had to be supplied with chairs. André was handsome in person, with good action and a fine voice. He was fervent and vigorous in delivery and wore himself out. After over-exertion in the pulpit at Notre Dame he took cold and died. He was simple in life and manner, and somewhat austere in presenting the moral code of Christianity, which he did, however, with courage and power.

Gaspard Terrasson was in Paris filling an appointment at one of the smaller churches when André died, and he was called upon to take his brother's place and

[20]*Op. cit.,* p. 60.

[21]Notices and sermons in Migne, tome 29; mention in Bernard and Candel, *passim.*

complete the series of Lent sermons at Notre Dame. He did so with success, and for about six years more, at intervals, he was heard in the chief pulpits of the capital. But his somewhat indiscreet utterances on the controversy over the bull of condemnation of the Jansenists brought on him the disfavor of the new archbishop of Paris—Vintimille—and he was forced to retire. He went at first to Savoy, then took charge of the small parish Church at Treigny for a time, but finally, in old age and feebleness, he was forgiven and allowed to return to Paris, where he died in 1752.

Gaspard Terrasson was rather more polished as an orator than André, his sermons show more care and labor in their general style. They are stiff and formal in analysis and statement, and are at times overloaded with phrases. He is said[22] to have been the first to use in the pulpit those affected and stilted and vague phrases which the writings of the philosophers were beginning to make the fashion, such as, "The Supreme Being," "The Sovereign Governor of the world," and the like. But he has a good share of imagination and feeling, and was brave and outspoken in his dealing with the sins of the age.

Several other Oratorians—Molinier, Dutreuil, Pacaud—are named and criticised by the authorities, but none of them are rated very high as preachers. Pacaud (1685-1760) was the best of these, and is described by Candel[23] as "a man very sweet and very good; one can not imagine a writer more polished and more amiable." But he was too labored in style, and affected in phraseology.

After the forced withdrawal of the Oratorians from Paris the Jesuits came back, and until the suppression of the order (1773) they furnished the leading preachers for the more important places. Only two of these in this earlier period rose to much fame—Pérussault and Ségaud—of whom the latter is the more worthy of notice.

Guillaume Ségaud (1675-1748)[24] was born at Paris,

[22]Both Candel and Bernard make the statement.
[23]*Op. cit.*, p. 161.
[24]Sermons in Migne, *tome* 47; notices in the other authorities.

and there also died. After the usual course of study prescribed among the Jesuits he was sent out to preach in the Provinces, and made quite a success, especially at Rouen. On being called to Paris he is found preaching at the main stations there during a period of about twenty years. He was a man of agreeable manners, kind heart, true piety, and pure life. In the short sketch of him in Migne's collection a letter is given from the superior of his order, after his death, greatly praising his virtues as a man. He made and kept many friends; and Louis XV granted him a pension. Notwithstanding some negligence in thought and style, his sermons show considerable ability, fluency, unction, penetration, without profundity or originality of thought, but with analytic skill, an erudition that tends to pedantry, and a varied style, sometimes clear, simple, and direct, sometimes labored and prolix. Among the best of his sermons are those on "The Last Judgment," "The Forgiveness of Injuries," "The Temptations of the World," "Practical Faith," and "The Love of One's Neighbor." A few sentences from the introduction to the sermon on "The Last Judgment" will give some idea of Ségaud's manner.[25]

After regretting that the familiar ideas of death, judgment, and hell do not affect us as solemnly as they ought, he shows how they should make us feel, but yet it is not in the ordinarily accepted terrors of these things that the greatest impressiveness lies: "It is not enough for a criminal soul to be separated from its body, the instrument of its fall; the body must be reunited with it to be the companion of its sufferings after having been the accomplice of its disorders; it is not enough that it shall endure in a secret judgment the rigorous examination of all its crimes, it must drink the shame of them in the eyes of the universe; it is not enough that it shall feel itself crushed under the weight of the arm of an avenging God, it must highly recognize His justice and make amends to Him in the sight of heaven and earth. . . . That which will make the Last Judgment so terrible to sinners will not be its accompaniments, it will be its end. . . . Jesus Christ will there report all

[25]Migne, t. 47, col. 61, 62.

the particular judgments which He will have passed in secret, in order to submit them to the censure of the universe, to oblige all creatures to assent to their justice, to force the convicted themselves to sign their arrest and to subscribe to their condemnation—exhaustless source to them of confusion and despair! For that end He will examine three things which alone concur to form a legitimate judgment: the law, the crime, and the punishment—the law by which they shall be judged, the crime of which they shall be convicted, the punishment to which they shall be condemned; the law, to judge if it be not unjust; the crime, to see if it be not supposititious; the punishment, to know if it be not excessive. He will demonstrate to them the equity of the law, the verity of the crime, the fitness of the punishment." These are the main topics of the discourse, and they are developed with clearness of thought, knowledge of human nature and of the age, logical acumen, reasonable simplicity of style, and proper feeling.

Decidedly the most original and powerful preacher of this period was the great missioner (evangelist), Jacques Bridaine (1701-1767).[26] He was born near d'Uzés, in the south of France, at a little village called Chusclan, where, in 1882, a monument was erected to his memory. His parents were poor but pious Catholics, who early impressed their faith upon the boy's soul. His talents and character attracted attention, and he was educated by the Jesuits at Avignon. The authorities soon discovered Bridaine's gift for speaking, and before he had completed his course of study he was sent to take the place of some one in an emergency, and acquitted himself so well that his work and reputation alike were fixed. On one of these early appointments—at the town of Aiguesmortes—seeing that the people were slow to

[26]Candel and Bernard both give fairly good accounts of Bridaine. See also Maury, *Principes de l'Éloquence,* p. 86 ss.; and Azais, *Bridaine et ses Missions,* including an *Oraison Funèbre de Bridaine,* by Bishop Besson. For some reason Migne did not include any sermons from Bridaine in his great collection, but the lack is well supplied by an excellent edition in several volumes, *Sermons de Père Brydayne,* 4me ed., Lecoffre Fils, Paris, 1867.

assemble, he seized a bell, and robed in his preaching garb, rang it through the streets. The people were surprised, their curiosity awakened, they came in crowds, and were rewarded for coming, for Bridaine was not the ordinary village priest or traveling monk of the day. Soon he was ordained (1725), and the great and toilsome work of his life began. It can not here be traced in detail. Though little known as such, Bridaine was in his own day and among his own people one of the greatest of evangelistic preachers—he will bear comparison with Berthold of Regensberg, and, in modern times, with Whitefield and Moody. He held, in all, two hundred and fifty-six "missions," many of them in the larger cities, as well as in smaller places; thousands were moved and led to faith by his work, and thousands more were strengthened and helped in the moral and spiritual struggle. In the intervals of his preaching—often late into the night, as well as during the day—he was diligent in the confessional and in other personal touch with individuals. He was also skillful in securing the co-operation of others. At Marseilles a band of forty young men, converted in his mission, became his willing helpers. He used various "methods" and devices for attracting and impressing the people—processions, choruses, banners, and the like. He sought and obtained the approval and co-operation of the parish priests in his work. He also had public avowals of renewed faith or of first confessions of Christ. In fact, many of the "methods" of modern evangelists seem to have been anticipated by this Jesuit priest of the early eighteenth century.

Bridaine conducted notable missions at Montpellier and at Lyons, and in 1744 he first came to Paris and held a successful mission at Chaillot. It was nine years later (1753) that he came to the church of St. Sulpice and conducted the famous mission there, which, through Cardinal Maury's account in his *Principes de l'Éloquence,* has given Bridaine a name among the great orators of France. The splendid "exordium" attributed by many to Bridaine, and often quoted and referred to as a model of manly eloquence, has been proved to be the wily cardinal's own work, in its literary form, though resting upon a basis of fact.[27] Bridaine did make a bold and eloquent address in his opening sermon at St. Sulpice and deeply impressed his hearers. Thereafter he conducted other missions in Paris and many other places. Finally, worn out with his enormous labors, he died at Roquemaire in 1767.

Bridaine's published sermons, reported by others and some of them probably revised by himself, imperfect as they are, exhibit the usual qualities of the popular preacher. Evidently they do not represent him at his best, any more than Whitefield's do that great orator. In both cases the man was infinitely more than the pale report of a printed page can put before us. But in these sermons appear both the good and bad of the type of preaching which Bridaine so eminently represented, a type made familiar by noted examples in all times. The essential quality is that real though elusive one which in its sum of effect, we call "capturing the crowd." Now the defects of this quality are well known—the exaggerations, the negligence, the easy familiarity, the occasional want of dignity even to coarseness, the overuse of humor and pathos, the anecdote. But its elements of power are equally well known: sympathy with people of all kinds, knowledge of their real wants, simplicity and directness of language and argument, imagination and power of portraiture, dramatic effect, occasional "flights" of eloquence, fervor and earnestness of appeal. All these are more or less observable in Bridaine's sermons, and are sustained by the traditional accounts of

[27]The facts about the matter are, briefly, these: Maury gives the famous piece as having been heard by himself at St. Sulpice. This was impossible, for he was then a child of five years at his home in the South. Later when a youth of seventeen in school at Avignon he heard Bridaine and was, with others, profoundly moved by him. There was present an old man who had heard Bridaine's powerful opening address at St. Sulpice years before and gave young Maury an account of it. From this hint and his own impressions of the man Card. Maury later (as a sort of banter with a friend) himself composed the exordium, and then gave it place in his book as a sample of Bridaine's eloquence. In a letter to a friend he subsequently acknowledged the fraud. I am indebted to Bernard (p. 199) and to Boucher (*Hist. de l'Éloq. de la Chaire,* p. 409) for the facts contained in this explanation. They now do Bridaine no harm, and Maury no good.

his remarkable power over his audiences. It is said[28] that, on one occasion, after having powerfully described in a sermon on death the horrors of dissolution, he paused and said to the people, "Now follow me, and I will lead you to your home," and then, to the solemn chanting of the *Miserere,* he conducted them to the adjoining cemetery and made the closing appeal of his sermon from a tomb. In sum, he preached, as Azais says, quoting a phrase of La Bruyère, *"simplement, fortement, chrétiennement"*—simply, powerfully, *christianly;* and this was Bridaine.

Among the preachers not of any monkish order—the so-called seculars—the most noted of this period was the *abbé* Poulle[29] (1703-1784). Born and educated at Avignon, he held several posts and won fame as a preacher before he came to Paris, where he preached at the court in 1750. From this time on he was one of the best known preachers in Paris, and had a large following. He did not write his sermons, but after retiring from active work he dictated eleven—presumably his best—to his nephew, and it is by these that he is judged. They have little to commend them, except the commonplaces of pulpit teaching. They are wordy, pretentious, and affected.

Of the preachers whose activity lay in the second half of the century—ending with the confusion and trials of the Revolution—only a few require special notice. A number are named and characterized at greater or less length by the authorities we have followed, such as: Father Elisha, a Carmelite friar, whose sensational sermons were heard by considerable crowds; of the Jesuits (before their suppression in 1773), Perrin, Griffet, Chapelain, who are of the third grade of orators; Clément, among the seculars, who really had considerable talent and learning; and, later in the period, Lenfant, Beauregard, and Boulogne, who spoke with boldness against both the skeptical philosophy and the moral corruption of the times, but too late and with too little real power to do more than raise a voice of earnest

[28]Azais, *Bridaine et ses Missions,* p. 91 ss.

[29]Migne, t. 55; Boucher, *op. cit.,* p. 391; Candel and Bernard, *passim.*

protest against the forces of evil that had gained the upper hand and were sweeping all old things away. Three only of the notable preachers of the age are selected for more particular notice: De Neuville, De Beauvais, and the *abbé,* afterwards cardinal, Maury.

There were two brothers De Neuville[30]—or Frey de Neuville, as the name is more fully written—who were active preachers in this time, but the elder (Pierre) was rather more of an administrator than orator, and our study is of the younger, usually known as Charles de Neuville (1693-1774).[31] He was born of good family at Coutanes, but in his childhood his parents moved to Vitré, in Normandy, where he was brought up. He was a gifted child, bright in intellect and pure in character. His religious bent was so decided that he sought and obtained the consent of his parents to his becoming a Jesuit. He accordingly entered that order in his eighteenth year, and enjoyed the thorough training customary among the Jesuits, including the several years of teaching after the completion of the academic studies. De Neuville was a very successful teacher, but his manifest gift in speech betokened the preacher, and the authorities of his order designated him for that work. He was first heard at Paris, in 1735, and at once attracted notice. Henceforth, till the suppression of the Jesuits, in 1773, he often preached in the important pulpits and at the customary Advent and Lent seasons in Paris. His life was uneventful, except for the struggle in his last years against the impending overthrow of his order, which he endeavored in vain to avert, but accepted with pained submission. He was of affable and courteous nature, and was much occupied as spiritual father and confessor. In social life he was affectionate and gay without compromising his dignity, and so made many friends. He toiled laboriously upon his sermons. Long meditation, hard reading, and careful polishing went into

[30]Sermons and brief accounts of both are given in Migne's *Collection* (t. 57), the elder being called Pierre Claude Frey de Neuville, and the younger Anne Joseph *Claude* Frey de Neuville; but he is usually known as *Charles* de Neuville. Perhaps his third name was Charles, and the editor in Migne is in error.

[31]Migne, t. 57; Candel and Bernard, *passim;* Maury, *Principes de l'Eloquence,* some criticisms.

the most of them. His position was firmly taken upon the Catholic theology, and he was well versed in the Scriptures and the Fathers; but his preaching is distinctly and predominantly moral, and in his later years—owing to the growth of skepticism—apologetic. He endeavored to meet the hostile assaults of unbelief, but his spirit and methods were those of an earlier age, and his defense was inadequate, though earnest and brave. He sympathized with those who were shaken in faith, and encouraged them; he knew the heart of his time in the moral sphere, and while he denounced its sins and follies, he pleaded for the higher things and sought to restore and comfort the penitent. The fall of the Jesuits saddened and weakened his closing years, and he died at Paris, an old man, in 1774.

De Neuville's preaching has been very variously judged, both in his own times and since. By friends and admirers he was extolled as a marvel of learned and polished eloquence. Even Lord Chesterfield chimed in with the chorus of local praise and declared that De Neuville was the greatest French preacher of his time. Others, on the contrary, looked upon him as self-seeking, eager for applause, and condemned his sermons as pedantic, pompous, wordy, and brilliant, without depth of thought or height of aim. Naturally, the truth lies between. De Neuville did not wholly escape the faults with which he has been charged, but his sermons are not mere glittering verbiage and pretentious display. They contain, as the character of the man ensured, much of sincere and thoughtful appeal to the remnants of better spiritual life in a distressing and decadent age. But alas! he saw not how to grasp the good that struggled amid the seething evils of the new era and use it as a weapon both of defense and attack. He had a fine imagination, but it was not duly controlled; a gift of language, but it was diffuse, redundant, and sometimes bombastic; an oratorical nature, but it led him away into forced antithesis, over-emphasis, and other exaggerations. Take him all in all—both for weakness and strength—he is typical of his time.

Jean Baptiste de Beauvais (1731-1790)[32] shared with

[32]Migne, tom. 71; Bernard, *passim.*

De Neuville the reputation of being the best preacher of this later period. He was much younger than De Neuville, whose work was nearly done when De Beauvais began to preach in Paris. We accordingly find in De Beauvais a more modern and timely note, and a more vigorous and intelligent grasp of the terrible problems of the age—immorality and skepticism. His attack upon the first was brave, outspoken, and uncompromising. He spared not king nor courtier. Louis XV once spoke of him as "the lost child of the gospel"—so out of place was he amid his surroundings. But the weak and vicious monarch respected the man whose warnings and teachings he would not heed, and made him a bishop. Toward infidelity and its attack on the Catholic faith the attitude of De Beauvais was not so clear and strong as toward moral corruption. At first he took a line of concession and almost of compromise, hoping to win and hold the wavering in that way; but toward the last he saw and pathetically acknowledged his mistake, when many of the worldly-minded clergy had themselves gone over to the enemy, and the foundations seemed to be destroyed.

De Beauvais was born and brought up at Cherbourg, the son of a lawyer, who died in the boy's childhood, but made provision for his education. He was eager for study, and would have become a Jesuit but for the overthrow of the society, which was impending during his youth and soon accomplished. Still, in one way or another the ambitious young man found ways to qualify himself for his chosen work. His career does not present many striking points of interest. He had notable success as preacher in Paris during the closing years of Louis XV, and was appointed bishop of Senez—a faraway diocese in the south of France. But after a few years of faithful though uncongenial service, he gave up his bishopric and returned to Paris, preaching as occasion offered. He was appointed a clerical member of the States-General in 1789, but found himself out of place in that famous assembly, which soon came under control of the revolutionary forces and passed into its successors. The Terror was not far away when De Beauvais died, in 1790.

In his preaching De Beauvais was freer from the current faults than most of his contemporaries—caring less for show and effect, and being more simple and straightforward in style than many of the others. As a sample of his dealing with unbelievers—those who were honestly shaken in soul and were seeking light—take this striking prayer, which, in one of his sermons, he puts into the mouth of such a supposed doubter: "Let the unbeliever say to the Supreme Being: O God, Thou who seest the depth of the heart, Thou knowest how I desire to render to Thee the worship most agreeable to Thee. I am an unbeliever, but am not impious. God of my ancestors! to whom I was dedicated in my chilhood; pious parents engraved the Christian faith upon my feeble heart, but the new opinions of my time, the specious reasonings of the new philosophy, my own passions, have effaced its characters. O God, since so many proofs attest that this religion is Thy work, make it live again in my soul! I can not yet make my indocile reason submit to it. . . . Christianity tells me that Thou owest nothing to Thy creatures; but it also tells me that Thou desirest all men to come to the knowledge of the truth. O Supreme Intelligence, deign to enlighten my darkness! . . . What must I do to be saved? I believe in Thee; help Thou my unbelief."

An illustration of the firm and fearless manner in which De Beauvais dealt with moral questions before the king and court is afforded by a brief extract from a sermon on Truth.[34] He makes the simple division that it is our duty (1) to speak the truth, and (2) to hear the truth, and after discussing the first head and making an honest avowal of his own purpose to speak the truth at all hazards, he comes, under the second head, to say: "Among the prejudices particularly attached to high conditions, none is more common and dangerous than the love of flattery and the fear of truth. As much as one loves a false man who knows how to keep silence or to disguise that which gives offense or to speak only that which pleases, even so much does the inflexible virtue of a true man offend delicacy. Such is the twofold error which I am endeavoring to correct. O, that we could

[34]Migne, tom. 71, col. 45, and 53.

make men feel how much that adulation, which seems so sweet, is really fatal to them; how much that truth, which seems so harsh, would be salutary to them!"

We come to a very different type of man—as much above De Beauvais in talent and power as he was below him in sincerity and principle—in the famous *abbé* and, later, cardinal, Jean Siffrein Maury (1746-1817.[35] The future orator and prelate was born of humble parentage at Valreas, in the south of France, and received his education at the Seminary of St. Charles, at Avignon. At twenty years of age he came to Paris to seek his fortune as a tutor, with a view to entering orders later. He began soon to write and publish, and his *Éloge de Fénelon* won him fame and notice from the Academy. He was ordained at Sens, and his talents and capacity were so evident at his examination that Cardinal de Luynes at once gave him a post of some sort, and his career as orator, writer, man of the world, and preacher by profession, was fairly begun. In 1772 his *Panegyric on St. Louis* brought him renown and honors, and in 1785 his famous *Panegyric on St. Vincent de Paul* won him the coveted prize of a membership in the Academy, besides great applause, both at home and abroad. Meantime he had been made an *abbé,* and his services as preacher were in great demand. He filled various stations before the court, as well as other important appointments, during the years, and in 1786 he became prior of a rich benefice near Paris. As a writer and critic his reputation was established by his able and still read *Principes de l'Éloquence de la Chaire et du Barreau,* in which he unfolded with force of thought and excellence of style the accepted principles of sacred and forensic eloquence, accompanied with keen and competent, though not always just, criticisms of many orators ancient and modern.

Maury's life and character were by no means above reproach. He was worldly, insincere, self-seeking, and did not escape suspicion of graver moral delinquency; but of his talents, learning, and extraordinary oratorical ability there can be no question. Had his moral and spiritual

[35] *Nouvelle Biog. Universelle;* Bernard, p. 489, and *passim;* Boucher, *Éloq. de la Chaire,* p. 398 ss.; Maury, *Principes de l'Éloquence,* ed. of 1810, containing the *Éloges* and Panegyrics.

power corresponded with his splendid mental gifts and skill in using them, he could easily have been the greatest preacher of his time and place. He was brilliant, ready, vigorous in conversation as in speech, but withal haughty to the verge of insolence—a man to command admiration without respect, and influence without love.

Maury was elected a member of the famous States-General of 1789, and became at once the leader of the clerical party. Upon the fall of the Bastille he fled, believing that the revolutionary forces would at once put an end to the old *régime;* but he was arrested and brought back, and on resuming his duties as a member of the body he is said to have remarked, "I shall either perish in the Revolution or by fighting it I shall gain a cardinal's hat." And so it turned out. On the floor of that famous assembly he was the redoubtable champion of the old order of things in church and state. His courage, his readiness, his indomitable bodily vigor, his quickness and power of retort, his resourcefulness, his unceasing vigilance and activity in debate, made him a worthy antagonist of Mirabeau, who recognized him as his ablest opponent. He more than once turned the laugh on Mirabeau with his sallies, as once, when the great popular orator, seeing a supposed flaw in Maury's argument, said, "Now I will close M. the *Abbé* in a vicious circle," and Maury retorted, "Then you must embrace me." But with all his eloquence and unrivaled powers, he could not keep back the catastrophe. On the dissolution of the Constituent Assembly, and the full inauguration of the Revolution, Maury fled to the emigrant nobles at Coblentz, where he was received with acclaim as the hero of a fallen cause. Later, at Rome, his eminent services, though not successful, were recognized at their worth and he received first an Italian bishopric, and later his cardinal's hat. He was of the conclave that elected Pius VII to the papacy, and later, on advice of that pontiff, accepted Napoleon and returned to Paris. It is said that Napoleon once jocularly asked him what he thought of the Bourbons now, and he answered, "Sire, towards them I have no longer faith nor hope, but am left alone with charity." Maury deeply offended the pope by accepting at the emperor's hands, without the pontiff's authority, and without being discharged from his Italian bishopric, the post of archbishop of Paris. When the Bourbons returned to power Maury was, of course, disgraced as a renegade, though he tried hard to make his peace with Louis XVIII, as he had done with the pope. He was mortified by his fall and died soon afterwards, in 1817.

Such was the checkered and interesting career of this remarkably gifted man, of whom as a preacher we can, alas! only say, "What he might have been!" Before his return from Italy, Maury destroyed his sermons[36] (of which there must have been a considerable number), and his quality as a preacher has to be determined by the traditions of his eloquence, and the few orations and panegyrics which remain. Judged by these, he appears to no great advantage. They are pretentious, bombastic, and high-flown. One does not wonder at Bernard's describing even the famous oration on St. Vincent de Paul as a "bizarre" performance, notwithstanding that it won him a place in the Academy; and the impression of his preaching before the court of Louis XVI, even at the height of his career as preacher, is perhaps not unjustly preserved in a saying attributed to that unfortunate young king, who, after hearing him once, remarked, "If Monsieur the *Abbé* had but spoken of religion he would have touched upon everything."

It is fitting, but depressing, that our survey of French Catholic preachers during the eighteenth century should close with one who was a distinguished example, among many less striking ones, of that unhappy epoch—brilliant talent for speaking perverted to rhetorical display, and imperative opportunities and possibilities misused or missed altogether by compromise with the world.

III. Protestant Preaching and Preachers

There is unhappily not much to say, though much that is far better to say, concerning the Protestant preaching in the French tongue during the eighteenth century.[37]

[36]Boucher, p. 398.

[37]See Lentz, Rothe, Christlieb, previously quoted; Berthault, *J. Saurin et la Prédication Protestante;* Hartog, *Geschiedenis van de Predikkunde* (where he treats of the Walloon preachers

We must first of all remember that this preaching, among its many features of contrast with that of the French Catholics, presents the aspect of a dispersion. Three different fields divide our attention: (1) France itself, with its churches and pastors "of the Wilderness," persecuted and worshiping by stealth; (2) Switzerland, with its eminent theologians and pastors; (3) the scattered churches of the exiled in various lands, but chiefly the so-called Walloon (*i. e.,* French-speaking) congregations in Holland. But in this diversity there was, besides the two evident unities of the French tongue and the Reformed faith, another, that of the spirit. As compared with the faults of the French Catholic and the German Lutheran preaching, the pulpit work of the French Reformed preachers shows to good advantage. It would be too much to claim that it wholly escaped the pronounced evils of the age—the pretentiousness of manner and the cool and philosophic moralizing—which we find to a greater or less extent everywhere in the pulpit of this century; but it is only fair to say that, upon the whole, the preaching of the French Protestants of the period shows rather more of true Scriptural content and of direct spiritual appeal than we meet with among their Catholic and Lutheran or their Dutch Reformed contemporaries. It is scarcely necessary to attempt here anything more in the way of a general characterization. Something more definite will necessarily appear as we briefly trace the outlines of the French Reformed preaching in the various lands, and bring under review the work of individual preachers.

We begin with the churches and preachers of the Wilderness, that is, the oppressed and banned remnant of the Protestants remaining in France after the Revocation of the Edict of Nantes, in 1685, and the persecutions of Louis XIV. The stronghold of the Huguenots was the southeastern part of France, amid the Vosges

in Holland); Couriard, *Essai sur la Prédication chez les Réformés de France et de Hollande;* Charles Coquerel, *Histoire des Églises du Désert;* Baird, *The Huguenot Emigration;* Smiles, *The Huguenots in France After the Revocation;* Benoit, *Trois Prédicateurs sous la Croix au XVIIIme Siècle,* and *Les Frères Gibert;* Cyclopedia articles, and Lives and Works of the preachers so far as available.

and Cevennes Mountains. The hardy mountaineers had risen in revolt to defend their faith by arms, and one of the shadows of the latter years of the Grand Monarch had been the war of the Cevennes, or of the Camisards, as it is sometimes called. The Regency in the early years of Louis XV had continued the policy of repression; but there was still a body of unsubdued and loyal believers throughout the region named. To organize anew the congregations, to minister to them as pastors, and to maintain in the caves and defiles of the mountains such secret meetings for worship as were possible, was the difficult and dangerous task of the Protestant preachers in France throughout the eighteenth century till the Revolution. These faithful "pastors of the Wilderness" were under the ban, they were hunted, watched, pursued, some were banished, and some were even hanged; but they put their duty to God before obedience to tyrannical human oppression, and discharged their perilous offices with such courage, consecration, patience, wisdom, and fidelity as have won them imperishable glory. Of course, the literary remains of the preaching of these men of God is practically nothing. They preached and taught as they could in those assemblies guarded by watchful outposts, but likely to be betrayed by spies and surprised by soldiers at any moment. But how could those tender and often eloquent appeals be put into writing and print? We have only the traditions of the actual spoken word, but these bring to us the story of its power to save, to comfort, to animate, yes, and to restrain and guide a faithful people through a century of oppression, but not of despair.

Chief among these heroic pastors was Antoine Court (1696-1760). He was born at Villeneuve, and from early youth formed the purpose to devote himself to the work of reviving and putting on some permanent basis the organization and worship of the Reformed congregations. He disapproved of armed resistance from the first, and throughout his career, and set himself by peaceful means to maintain the cause. He was hardy, brave, yet prudent and tactful, with fine sense and a native gift of eloquence. He had no schooling to speak of, but by hard study he endeavored to repair the defects of his education. His plan, formed at the early age of eighteen, and adhered to through forty years and more of exacting and perilous service, embraced four main purposes: (1) To convoke and instruct the people in secret assemblies; (2) to combat the fanaticism to which many had been led by the Camisards, and to avoid armed resistance; (3) to re-establish the discipline and worship of the Reformed faith; (4) to provide for the raising, training, and continuance of a ministry for the churches. This last thought found expression in the founding of that famous school at Lausanne where so many of the French Reformed pastors have been educated. Court received help from various sources—some coming even from England—and the school was established about 1730. Court became pastor at Lausanne, and kept his eye on the school as well as on the whole work, making frequent and hazardous journeys among the congregations and attending the meetings of the synods. There are no sermons remaining from Court, but Coquerel, the historian of the Churches of the Wilderness, has found among the records a sort of apostrophe or prayer which he thinks was written by Court. He gives it in full,[38] and comments as follows: "From the point of view of the form of the language, it is right to add that such appeals, in a style at once so energetic and so pure, pronounced by a young man of twenty-four years, deprived of every advantage of education beyond that which he had given himself, makes us see that all the disorders of the persecutions and the ruin of the academies had not been able to interrupt that tradition of good eloquence of which the Reformed Church and the school of Saurin had furnished so many models."

Among the earliest students at Lausanne was Paul Rabaut (1718-1794), who became with Court the other most important leader and preacher among the Reformed. His life-story is full of the romance of heroism, in which his fair and faithful wife had her full share. His tours among the churches, his zeal, his labors, his perils and escapes, his indefatigable diligence, his unshaken constancy and courage, his wise and intelligent leadership, made him the worthy younger follower and helper of

[38] *Hist. des Églises du Désert,* I, pp. 106-109.

Court. There was great affection and congeniality between the two, and they labored together in loving accord. Rabaut was pastor mainly at Nîmes, but he traveled much among the churches. A few sermons remain from him, and of them Coquerel says:[39] "Much of simplicity and unction, more of sweetness than vehemence; little of dogmatic discussion; more of charity than of depth; doctrinal exposition invariably sustained by moral counsels. . . . As to form, they are all very methodical; they glitter with the logic of their divisions."

Besides these two great leaders, the Churches of the Desert had other pastors and preachers of less ability and prominence, but of great courage, usefulness, and zeal. Some of these were captured and hanged, some were banished, all suffered. Accounts of the lives of some of them remain, and their labors were not unfruitful; but their preaching has lived only in its effects.

In Switzerland the preaching in the French tongue continued, not only at Geneva, Lausanne, and other centers of the Reformed faith, but at many other places. Upon the foundations laid by Calvin and Beza, and through the controversies of the seventeenth century, this preaching had acquired a strong Biblical character, and at the same time a decided theological cast which still mark its contents and quality when the eighteenth century begins. Great theologians like the two Turrettins, Werenfels, Pictet, and Osterwald left the imprint of their character and methods upon the French-Swiss sermons of the age. But, whatever may be said of other preachers and localities, we shall see that these sermons for the most part happily succeed in departing from the scholastic manner, the affected and pedantic style, and the rationalistic coolness so common in that time. They have a certain flavor of Pietism and an evangelical warmth in spite of their dogmatic cast.

Only a few of the more eminent names among these theological preachers need here be recalled. Samuel Werenfels (1657-1740), one of the most notable theologians and Biblical scholars of his church and time, succeeded his father as leader of the church and professor of theology in the University at Basel. This

[39] *Op. cit.,* II, p. 503.

was the scene of his lifelong and useful labors. He was the friend of the young Turrettin and Osterwald, and they were of like spirit. Of his labors and numerous writings in the theological and controversial sphere there is no need here to write. Though a German-Swiss in name and speech, and using the Latin mostly for his theological works, he was asked, in 1710, to become associate pastor and preacher for the French Church at Basel, a duty which he discharged for several years to the great gratification of his associates and edification of the congregation. At their suggestion these French sermons were published, and they remain still an interesting example of how a great theologian of that age could preach to the hearts of cultured people.[40] They discuss the great fundamental truths of the Christian faith, in a style simple and clear. In the introduction to the first one of the series, second in the volume, the preacher apologizes for using his manuscript, as the French language was not his mother-tongue; but he had no need to excuse the straightforward, simple diction in which he expounded with admirable force and feeling some of those great doctrines which had been his lifelong study. The sermons are devoid of all pedantry and seeking after effect. Werenfels was something of a Pietist, of Bengel's type, and he spoke for the good of his hearers, not his own applause.

Benedict Pictet (1655-1724), the nephew and successor of Francis Turrettin in the chair of theology at Geneva, and also a pastor of the church there, was born in that famous seat of the Reformed worship, received excellent training, traveled, studied, and held intercourse with distinguished scholars and preachers in France, Holland, and England. In addition to his great labors and numerous writings as professor of theology, he was recognized as an able and eloquent preacher of the Word, and a volume of sermons is found among his numerous remains.[41] It would be both interesting and profitable to translate and transcribe here, did space per-

[40] *Sermons sur des Vérités Importantes de la Réligion,* par Samuel Werenfels. Basle, 1715.

[41] *Dix Sermons sur divers Sujets,* par Benedict Pictet, pasteur et professeur. Geneva, 1718.

mit, the admirable introduction in which the author kindly but firmly criticises the bad taste and wrong motives of much of the preaching of the age, and avows his own purpose to adhere to the simplicity that is in Christ, and to preach for the spiritual good of his hearers rather than their pleasurable gratification. And it must be said that for the most part he lives up to his aim. The sermons are rather scholastic and stiff in form, and a little theological learning must perforce sometimes appear; but they discuss practical subjects in a practical way, and do not fail to make earnest and skillful appeal to the souls as well as the intellects of their hearers.

Jean Alphonse Turrettin (d. 1737) was the son of the famous Calvinistic theologian and disputant, Francis Turrettin, was born at Geneva, and received (like his cousin, Pictet) excellent training, improved by travel and association with other learned divines. He departed widely from the stern and uncompromising attitude of which his father had been so notable a representative. He was a mild and lovable man, who sought by concession and charity to mollify and unite Christian thinkers of various schools. He was greatly loved, both as professor and preacher, at Geneva, and published some sermons which reflect both the fine intellect and the amiable qualities of the man.

Jean Frederic Osterwald (1663-1747), the third of that "triumvirate of Swiss theologians," of which Werenfels and Turrettin were the other two, was, like his two friends, the son of a notable man, the honored pastor at Neuchatel. He, too, had admirable training in youth, perhaps a little too varied and a little too forced, but his remarkable talents and continued application extended and solidified his attainments. He succeeded his father as pastor at Neuchatel in 1699, and held the office with great honor and esteem till his death, in his eighty-fourth year. Besides his work as pastor and preacher, Osterwald wrote much on various theological subjects, particularly in Bible translation, lectured with great success and appreciation to students for the ministry, and left behind him many long useful and widely translated and read religious works. There is a volume of his sermons, published at Geneva in 1722, which exemplify his character as a preacher.[42] In the dedicatory epistle addressed to his fellow-pastors, and in the body of the first sermon (on the Seriousness of Religion), Osterwald makes significant allusion to the distressing evils of the times and the inadequacy and unfitness to deal with them aright of any preaching but a simple and sincere presentation of the great truths of Christianity. The sermons unfold those truths, they deal with vital and practical themes, they are direct and pointed, but not ambitious in style, and they show deep concern for the hearers and over the evils of the age; but they are strong in faith and hopeful in tone. They exhibit the fashion of Saurin and others for formal division and minute subdivision, but not to the wearisome degree of some of the German discourses of the time.

Among the French Protestant exiles in foreign lands, and particularly the Walloon (French-speaking) churches in Holland were a number of noble and justly famous preachers. In the early years of the eighteenth century most of these brought over into the new era the spirit and manner of the heroes of the Revocation, such as DuBosc, Claude, and especially Saurin, whose brilliant ministry at The Hague extended to nearly a third of the new period. Along with him should at least be named the celebrated Jacques Basnage (1653-1725), pastor at Rotterdam, and later at The Hague, but better known as a man of learning and an accomplished diplomat and counselor, though of earnest life and piety, than as preacher. There were also the eloquent Christian apologist and preacher, Jacques Abbadie, and the famous pastor of the French Reformed Church in Berlin, Isaac de Beausobre, both of whom have been noticed in our account of the seventeenth century.

Passing thus hastily over these, and omitting others who might well claim notice here, we must, in concluding this survey, pay some attention to two distinguished pastors of French churches in Holland—Chatelain and Chais.

Henri Chatelain (1684-1743) was born at Paris the year before the Revocation, and carried, an infant, by his Protestant parents to Leyden. Here he received his

[42]*Douze Sermons sur divers Textes de l'Écriture Sainte,* par J. F. Ostervald. Geneva, 1722.

school education, then studied awhile with a famous teacher at Amsterdam, then took his university course at Leyden, and after that visited England and pursued some studies at both Oxford and Cambridge. He was called as pastor to the St. Martin's French Church in London in 1710, thence to The Hague in 1721, and finally to Amsterdam in 1728, where he labored till his death, in 1743. He has been described[43] as a pleasing and sensible preacher, clear in his interpretation of Scripture and in unfolding his views, and largely influenced in his method of preaching by the English, especially Tillotson and Doddridge. A number of his sermons[44] were published by his widow soon after his death, and they confirm the judgment just noted; but they also exhibit a cool moralizing tone which is far from the evangelical warmth of the Swiss preachers; they are not marked by any height of imagination or depth of feeling, and can make no claim to true eloquence.

Charles Pierre Chais (1701-1785) was born and educated at Geneva, and on his graduation traveled in Switzerland, Alsace, Holland, and France, observing and studying. He came to Paris in 1727, and in the next year was installed as one of the pastors at The Hague, along with Saurin and the rest. Like the others, he seems to have disliked Saurin, but on the death of the great preacher was regarded as the "least unworthy" to succeed him in the chief place. Though urged to return to Geneva, besides receiving other important calls, he gave to The Hague the services of his long life. He wrote a number of books on various theological subjects; but his greatest work perhaps was the founding of an institution for the sick and poor. As a preacher[45] he was not great nor eloquent, but cultured in style, clear in thought, traditional in method, and not untainted with that rationalistic morality which too often in this century was allowed to take the place in the pulpit of a warm and sure exposition and application of gospel truth.

[43]By Hartog in his *Geschiedenis van der Predikkunde,* etc., bl. 150 vv.

[44]*Sermons sur divers Textes de l'Écriture Sainte,* par Henri Chatelain. Amsterdam, 1744.

[45]His sermons were published in two volumes after his death. *Sermons sur divers Textes,* etc., par Charles Chais. Tt. 2, La Haye, 1787, 1790.

CHAPTER IX

DUTCH AND SCANDINAVIAN PREACHING IN THE EIGHTEENTH CENTURY

In Holland and the northern countries of Europe the general conditions of life, literature, religion, and preaching were not unlike those which we have learned to recognize as characteristic of Europe in that epoch. What needs to be said by way of introductory statement in regard to the history and literature of the respective countries will be better presented separately, as we notice the preaching in each land.

I. DUTCH PREACHING IN THE EIGHTEENTH CENTURY

Little is required to remind us of historical and literary affairs in Holland at this time.[1] The great glories of the Dutch struggle for independence during the sixteenth and seventeenth centuries were followed by a decline in the eighteenth century. The death of William III of Orange, in 1702, without issue left vacant the office of Stadtholder, which had been filled for so long by his illustrious house. Later in the century the office was revived in his cousin, William of Friso, and was made hereditary; in reality becoming a monarchy, though not formally so until the nineteenth century. The States of Holland took some part in the great European movements of the century, but their internal affairs were of no world-wide interest. Wars with France and England depleted the wealth and lowered the prestige of the country, causing her the loss of some colonies beyond the seas, and of some influence in the world. The French Revolutionists conquered the country and made it into the Batavian Republic, soon to become a dependent kingdom under Louis Bonaparte, and on his abdication to pass under Napoleon as a part of the French Empire in the early years of the nineteenth century.

Dutch literature of the eighteenth century has only one name of the first importance, that of William Bilder-

[1]See the authorities previously mentioned—*Historians' History*, Vol. XIV, and *Warner Library* for the literature.

dijk, patriot and poet, who lived on into the first third of the nineteenth century, and whose writings are still highly prized by his countrymen. Other writers of less influence are the brothers Van Haren, poets and statesmen; the learned essayist and clever satirist, Fokke, with Bellamy, Loosjes, Van Helmers, and the eminent historian, Van Kampen.

The Dutch preaching of the eighteenth century had its national characteristics.[2] Though there were some Catholic preachers in Holland, they were not of sufficient importance or influence to claim notice here. The Protestants were mainly of the Reformed Church, and among these the triumph of Calvinism at the Synod of Dort (1618) had left that type of theology the dominant one and the standard of orthodoxy. But the Arminian party had made their *Remonstrance,* and hence were called Remonstrants; and though in the minority, they had in their ranks not a few able and influential men. The French-speaking, or Walloon, Reformed churches had been strengthened, both in their membership and their ministry, by the refugees whom the revocation of the Edict of Nantes (1685) had driven out of France. Besides these three branches of the Reformed Church, there were some Lutheran congregations with their pastors, and a considerable body of Baptists (Mennonites), who numbered among them some preachers of power and influence.

The Rationalist type of preaching does not appear to have had so much power or so general prevalence in Holland as in Germany and England during the eight-

[2]Works of Rothe and Lentz, previously mentioned, though there is not much of value on Dutch preaching in these. The Christlieb-Schian article in *RE* is for Dutch preaching largely derived from Van Oosterzee; but some of the articles on individuals are of especial value. The sketch in Van Oosterzee's *Practical Theology* (Eng. trans. by Evans of his *Praktische Theologie*) owes rather more than is distinctly acknowledged to the thorough though labored and difficult work of J. Hartog, *Geschiedenis van de Predikkunde in de Protestantsche Kerk van Nederland.* This scholarly work is a mine of information, and to it is due nearly all that is given in the text, though it has been found necessary to supplement it sometimes from articles in Van der Aa's *Biographisch Woordenboek der Nederlanden,* and from other authorities mentioned.

eenth century, but traces of it are discernible, chiefly in the moralistic preaching of certain Remonstrants and Walloons. Pietism also had its representatives, especially among the followers of Voetius, who had received influence from the teachings of Spener and Francke. The fierce disputes of the seventeenth century had deeply impressed upon Dutch preaching the dogmatic and polemic character common to so much of the sermonic and other religious literature of the times.

Along with this, it seemed as if the scholastic homiletical method of the seventeenth century had become a necessary feature of orthodox Dutch preaching. Its dryness, length, pedantry, and wearisome detail of definition, analysis, and quotation, do not appear to have been as much relieved as in Germany and England by those conceits of fancy and phrase which we find in the seventeenth century divines of those two countries. It was perhaps this which led Mosheim to say that the Dutch had no pulpit oratory—a dictum caught up by other German writers and naturally contested by the Dutch, at least in its extreme form. But it is conceded by all that at the opening of the eighteenth century preaching in Holland was sadly in need of reform; but, as we have seen, influences were already at work in that direction.

The quarrel between the Cocceians, with their minute exposition of the text, and Voetians, with their neglect of form and comparative depreciation of Scripture in insistence upon experience and practical fruits, was at its height when the century opened. In 1702 there came from Detmold, in Germany, to the University of Franeker a young student who was to work a reform in Dutch homiletics. This was F. A. Lampe (d. 1729),[3] who, after going back to Germany and serving as pastor for some years, was called as professor and university preacher to Utrecht in 1720. He held the double office till 1727, preaching once in two weeks in German. But many of his sermons were translated into Dutch and published, so that both his teaching and example were influential in introducing the better method with which his name is associated. His lectures on homiletics in the Uni-

[3]See art. in *RE,* Rothe, and especially Hartog, Bl. 128, *et passim.*

versity of Utrecht were published in Latin[4] from notes of his pupils, and they had wide circulation and wholesome influence.

Lampe perceived the faults of both the Voetians and Cocceians, as well as the harmfulness of their prolonged and often acrimonious dispute as to method. He therefore sought, by combining the good points of both schools and by appealing to the better spirits of both parties, to bring in a sounder and more edifying style of preaching. With the Cocceians he agreed that the correct interpretation of Scripture was essential, but he insisted that prolonged and minute discussion of each word and possible meaning of the text had no place in the pulpit. With the Voetians he agreed that feeling and spiritual results must be aimed at, but these must be properly related, both to Scripture doctrine and the moral life, and that a clear division and style of speech were necessary for the conveyance of truth to the hearer. Lampe's method was, as Hartog well says, psychological; that is, it took the point of view of the auditor and urged that, as preaching was for his benefit, it should be adapted to his condition and seek to make on him the right impression. Lampe's views appealed to many of all parties and his reform was in a large degree successful, but so inveterate was the habit of analysis and definition that some of his pupils fell into the fault of classifying the hearers and making appeal to each class in turn! Sometimes the confused listener could not find himself in the maze. So, too, in spite of many good and successful efforts, many of the old faults persisted, and the middle of the century finds Dutch preaching sadly in need of further improvement, especially in the direction of simplicity and the real edification of the audience.

Many were beginning to see and feel this need and to seek a better way when, in 1768, Ewald Hollebeek published his epoch-making book, *On the Best Kind of Sermons,*[5] wherein he vigorously condemned the pedantic expository method and the other abuses in vogue, and urged the adoption of the better manner of the English divines, especially Tillotson and Doddridge; that is, of

[4]*Institutionis homileticae Breviarium.*

[5]*De optimo concionum genere,* etc.

deriving a topic from the text and presenting that with such clearness and fitness as to reach the mind and heart of the hearer, with special reference to his spiritual and moral needs. The book raised a strife, as was to be expected, but found many friends and pupils who undertook to carry out its teachings. Many of the older set opposed the innovation and condemned it as the practice of Socinians, Anabaptists, and the like, thus trying to put upon it the taint of heresy as well as novelty. But men like Hinlopen, Chevallier, Bonnet, and others defended and practiced the new views and methods, and they gradually won acceptance. Further in the direction of improvement were the example and influence of Jodocus Heringa, who, however, belongs more appropriately to the early part of the nineteenth century.

Of individual preachers the authorities we have been following mention and discuss quite a number, of whom, however, only a few require notice here; for even of these it was only a still smaller number who reached more than local or national fame.

We may briefly condense what Hartog gives concerning the preachers outside of the dominant Reformed Church. The Lutherans[6] had no very distinguished men, though Van Velten of Amsterdam, and Müller of Leeuwarden, and some others are named as leaders. The Lutheran preaching was naturally much influenced by the tones and tendencies which gave character to the contemporary German pulpit. Reflections of the Pietistic, Mediating, and Rationalistic schools, and of the various homiletical methods taught and practiced in Germany are found also among the Lutheran preachers of Holland.

Among a number of less noted but capable and worthy Baptist (Mennonite) preachers, Hartog[7] gives particular attention to Johan Stinstra (1709-1790), not because he deems him the best, but because he is the best known. He gave two sorts of sermons—some learned and some popular—and in both his good qualities as a preacher appeared. His discourses on *Ancient Prophecies* belong to the more scholarly sort; but in a clear and forcible sermon on Matt. 22:21 ("Render unto Cæsar," etc.), he turns

[6] Hartog, bl. 218 vv. [7] *Op. cit.*, bl. 193 vv.

the general principle of that great text into a very appropriate and timely application to the sin of smuggling; and in other of his discourses he shows how he could make good use of moral subjects. That he was not wholly free from the Rationalism of the day perhaps appears in the statement that he was at one time accused of Socinianism; but Hartog does not discuss the matter. As a preacher, Hartog rates higher than Stinstra, Johan Denknatel (d. 1759), in whose sermons the Pietistic side of the Voetian school of preachers finds frequent and characteristic expression. He also had the faults of his time and school, but he was well acquainted with human nature, and spoke with feeling and effect to the heart of man.

The Remonstrants (followers of Limborch and the Brandts of the seventeenth century) were ably represented in this period by Adrian van Cattenburgh, for a time pastor at Rotterdam, and then for twenty-six years (1712-1738) professor in the Remonstrant College. A volume of his sermons was published at Leyden, and Hartog finds them of some worth as to clarity of exposition, though marred by some pedantry. Like others of this school, he laid large emphasis on moral preaching. Others of the Remonstrants are briefly mentioned and characterized; but we may pass them by.

Of the French Reformed (Walloon) preachers of the age Hartog[8] names and discusses a number, but as these preached to French congregations, and, of course, in the French tongue, only a brief account of them is needed in an account of preaching in Holland. We have already considered the most important of these in the account of French preaching, and need here only recall a few names. Before Saurin, the most important of the Walloon preachers seems to have been Henri Chatelain (1684-1743), preacher in London, then at The Hague and at Amsterdam. We recall the great exiles, Du Bosc, Superville, and others, and, greatest of all, Saurin. Later in the century are named as leaders Chaufpié, Royer, Courtonne, and Chais, the successor of Saurin at The Hague. These French preachers exerted some influence in the promotion of greater clearness and better taste

[8] *Op. cit.*, bl. 150 vv.

in the preaching of Holland; but some of them were more or less infected with the moralistic and rationalistic spirit of the age. But, leaving all these less numerous and less important parties and men, it is, of course, to the preachers of the national Reformed Church that we must look for what is most distinctive in the Dutch pulpit of the century.

Of those whose work lay chiefly or wholly in the first half of the century, before the reforms introduced by Hollebeek became effective, only a few need be named. Leaders among them were Til, Braun, D'Outrein, and Groenewegen,[9] who to a greater or less degree exemplified the old and waning scholastic analysis, pedantry, and bombast. One of the worst of them was Albert Voget, professor at Groningen and later at Utrecht (from 1735), who, though a pupil of Lampe, did not much resemble his master, but practiced many of the faults condemned by him. Hartog justly criticises for its bombast and bad taste a panegyric pronounced by him upon the Prince of Orange.

But there were also representatives in this earlier group of the better tendencies in pulpit method, though Hartog has to regret[10] that they have not left more material for correctly appreciating their work and influence. Here account should be taken of the famous scholar and theologian, Herman Venema (1697-1787),[11] pupil and successor of the learned Vitringa at the University of Franeker, where he served for fifty years. Part of the time he was university preacher, but his sermons were dry and scholarly rather than popular, and it was chiefly in his lectures and his influence on his pupils that his help toward the better manner of preaching was found. Of these pupils Conradi is named[12] with approval, and with regret that little or nothing of his work was published, since during his long service as professor and preacher at Franeker (1740-1781) he was regarded by many as the best preacher of his time.

After the middle of the century there are found in

[9]See Lentz, II, S. 303; Rothe, S. 418 ff.; Hartog, *passim.*
[10]*Op. cit.,* bl. 135.
[11]Hartog, *l. c., RE,* Bd. 20, S. 491.
[12]Hartog, bl. 135.

Holland a number of excellent preachers, from whom a few are selected for brief notice.

Ewald Hollebeek (1719-1796),[13] the leader of the wholesome reform in preaching, was born at Havensted, where his father was pastor. He received his university training at Leyden, was ordained, and served as pastor at several smaller places before going to Middelburg in 1747. Thence he was called to be professor at Groningen, where he served ten years, and was then made professor at Leyden, and so continued to the end of his life. It was in 1768 that he published his famous book and led the way to modernizing the preaching of Holland. All the authorities pay due respect to his teaching and influence as being of capital moment in the development of a higher type of pulpit work.

Among those who welcomed, practiced, and furthered the new so-called "English" method of preaching advocated by Hollebeek was Paul Chevallier (1722-1796),[14] long pastor and professor at Groningen. Born at Amsterdam, the son of a sea-captain, whose early death left him fatherless, he was carefully brought up and educated by his mother. He was an eager student and improved his advantages at the preparatory schools, at the gymnasium at Lingen, and at the University of Leyden. Ordained to the ministry in 1744, he held various pastorates, and was then called to Groningen, as teacher in the Academy and as pastor of the church, in 1751. Here he found his life-work, and in the exacting duties of his double office proved eminently useful to the end. He was a man of extensive learning, a fine teacher—especially of Church History, a faithful pastor, and a popular and successful preacher.

Gisbert Bonnet (1723-1805),[15] descended from an old French family, and younger brother of another noted preacher, was born at Naarden, and early showed remarkable talents. His early schooling was crowned by a diligent and successful course at the University of Utrecht. His first pastoral charge was at Amersfort,

[13]Van der Aa, Dl. 8 (2) bl. 993; Hartog, bl. 233; and the German authorities, *ll. cc.*

[14]Van der Aa, Dl. 3, bl. 346 vv.; Hartog, bl. 241.

[15]Van der Aa, Dl. II, bl. 853 v.; Hartog, bl. 244; Van Oosterzee (Eng. tr.), p. 150.

then at Rotterdam, later at The Hague, when (1761) he was soon called as professor and preacher at the University of Utrecht, where he spent the rest of his life. He published many lectures, books, and sermons. Bonnet's biographer sums up his estimate by saying: "He won renown as having been one of the most eloquent and famous pulpit orators of his time, and one of the most skillful and able teachers at the University of Utrecht. He was a man of eminent piety, broad learning, extraordinary clearness of judgment, and rare eloquence." And Van Oosterzee says that "from him dates the practice of devoting the first part of the discourse, of not too great extent, to the explanation of the text [thus preserving something of the older expository method]; the second, to the formal treatment of the subject to which the text refers [thus adopting the new topical method]; and closing the whole with a part apportioned to the application constantly modified in accordance with the nature of the subject and the wants of the hearers. The best illustration of his method is to be found in his own published sermons, which, whatever their faults in point of detail, may be regarded as models for the period to which they belong."

The last of this notable and influential eighteenth century group was the great Utrecht pastor, Jacob Groot Hinlopen (1723-1803),[16] of whom Van Oosterzee writes that "during more than half a century he was a living protest in his congregation against all scholasticism, a daily sermon on the practical nature of Christianity." Hinlopen was born at Hoorn, and attended school there and at Hardwyck. Later he took courses both at Franeker—where he was greatly helped by Venema—and at Utrecht. Ordained in 1745, he held several short pastorates until he was called to Utrecht, in 1751, and labored to the end of his long and useful life. He had ample knowledge of the Bible, and was a keen and original interpreter. His intercourse with his congregation was full of frankness and love; and his sturdy patriotism and devotion to the House of Orange, as well as his personal influence in his city, were shown by the fact that during the ascendency of the French Revolution

[16]Van der Aa, Dl. 8 (1); bl. 825 v.; Hartog, bl. 229; Van Oosterzee, p. 150.

in Holland General Pichegru found it desirable to banish him from Utrecht for a time.

Hinlopen's sermons have been described as "simple, pleasing, popular." Hartog quotes a fine tribute to him from Jodocus Heringa, himself one of the great Dutch preachers of the next period and one who owed much to Hinlopen's preaching for his own success. Heringa's estimate is as follows: "Among all teachers whom I personally have heard teach, I do not remember ever to have met one who in my opinion combined more wisdom with knowledge, more foresight with zeal, more charm with reverence, more humility with the consciousness of what he was and had, than the God-fearing and man-loving servant of Jesus Christ in the congregation at Utrecht—Jacob Hinlopen." So with this noble figure our imperfect survey of eighteenth century Dutch preaching may fitly close.

II. Danish and Norwegian Preaching

In the Scandinavian countries[17] there was close political union between Denmark and Norway throughout the eighteenth century, and their history and literature require no separate consideration. The line of kings during this century was not particularly distinguished. The middle of the period was marked by the influence of Struensee, a German favorite of the queen, who introduced some measures of reform in political and social conditions, but soon met and deserved his downfall. Later in the century, under the wise leadership of Count Bernstoff, Danish commerce assumed importance in the world and led to war with England, during which befell, in 1801, the famous battle of Copenhagen by the British fleet under Parker and Nelson, which reflects more credit on the brave and patriotic Danes than on the stronger and victorious English.

In Danish-Norwegian literature the greatest name of the early eighteenth century is that of Ludvig Holberg (d. 1754), whose numerous writings are highly prized by his people. In fact, in his comedies Holberg struck out a new path, and in his other works—historical and

[17] See the appropriate volumes of the *Historians' History* and the *Warner Library* for the history and literature.

critical—he raised a high standard of excellence. Indeed, he is regarded as the father of modern Danish literature. After Holberg came Johannes Ewald (d. 1781), who did some notable work, chiefly in tragedy, but his comparatively early death cut off a career of some promise. These two, with others of less power and distinction, prepared the way for the masterly work of Oehlenschlager, with whom begins the great Danish literature of the nineteenth century.

The established and dominant religion in Denmark, Sweden, and Norway since the Reformation has been Lutheran. It is, therefore, just what we should expect when we find that the institutions of Christianity, including, of course, preaching, exhibit in the modern centuries the characters and features of German Lutheranism, with the natural modifications of country and language. Accordingly, we find in the three northern lands those phases of eighteenth century preaching which have already been described as existing in Germany during the corresponding period. There was a group of the strongly orthodox and dogmatic Lutherans who followed the scholastic method of Carpzov and others, and were as polemic and positive as could be desired by their brethren in German lands. There was another group who received and furthered the teachings and influences of Spener and Francke, and thus represented, though in a feeble and second-hand way, the improvements introduced by the Pietistic school in Germany, not failing also to follow the weaknesses and faults of that movement. Yet again the Rationalistic party—with its clear but lifeless and philosophic morality and utility in preaching—was not without its representatives. And finally the off-set to all the others in the principles of Mosheim and Reinhard had likewise some following among the preachers in the northern lands. It is, therefore, not necessary to discuss these features of preaching again in detail, but only to mention briefly some of the leading preachers in Denmark and Norway during the eighteenth century.[18]

[18]As I do not read the Scandinavian languages and have had no access to the original sources I follow in the brief sketch in the text the few hints of Van Oosterzee (*Prac. Theol.*, p. 142 f.), the Christlieb-Schian article in *RE*, and such articles as are found in *RE* on several of the preachers named.

In Denmark there appears to have been no great preacher of the evangelical, or Pietistic, school, though the principles and methods of that party had been introduced by a German, Lütkens, who became court preacher at Copenhagen in 1704. He found co-laborers and followers, but none rose to high rank as preachers. Bishop Hersleb (d. 1757), of Seeland, and also one of the court preachers at Copenhagen, is mentioned as in some sort an opponent of Pietism and as being a preacher "whose powerful eloquence his contemporaries could not sufficiently praise."

Christian Bastholm (1740-1819) was the leading representative of the Rationalists. He was an extreme example of his kind. He, on the suggestion of his father, took up the ministry as a means of livelihood suited to his tastes for study and as a useful institution of the State for the moral and intellectual instruction of the people. He proclaimed, practiced, and defended these principles with learning, acuteness, and a vigorous eloquence which brought him worldly applause and honors in his lifetime, but no enduring fame or influence beyond it.

In Norway the orthodox churchly party was ably represented by Johan Nordal Brun (d. 1816), bishop of Bergen, who is said to have possessed "fiery eloquence and poetic gift," and to have shown in the pulpit "a fullness of fancy and rhetorical brilliancy." He espoused warmly, even if not very profoundly, the side of the Supernaturalists—such as Mosheim and Reinhard in Germany—as against the Rationalists. Like Mosheim, he published a volume of "Sacred Discourses" which were once highly valued. Of the Rationalistic school were N. S. Schultz (d. 1832), pastor in Drontheim, and, more decidedly, Claus Pavels (d. 1822), preacher at Christiania, and later bishop of Bergen. The evangelical and Pietistic school was powerfully represented by the notable evangelist and popular lay preacher, H. N. Hauge (1771-1824), of whom a fuller notice is desirable.[19]

Hans Nielsen Hauge was of peasant parentage, and born in the parish of Thun in 1771. He had only limited school advantages, and at home his spiritual

[19] See the art. by Odland in *RE,* VII, 478 ff.

as well as intellectual life was fed by earnest study of the Bible and a few devotional books such as his pious parents had. With his natural mental acuteness and his strong spiritual bent, the youth had also a fine talent for business and a strong inclination to excel therein. But he was turned from this career and led to devote himself to earnest labors for the salvation of his fellowmen partly by grief and pity and repulsion in view of the moral and spiritual lowness he saw around him, and chiefly by a deep inward conviction that he was called of God to do what he could for the spiritual uplift of his people. He began by personal conversations and the forming of little groups for prayer, conference, and exhortation. His organizing genius and business ability led to the forming of these into societies, somewhat akin to Wesley's in England; but they never separated from the State Church, and Hauge was ever only a lay preacher. He did preach, however, with deep and persuasive conviction, traveling mostly on foot over miles and miles of territory, and reaching hundreds of the people with his personal as well as public ministries. Many were led to Christ and to a truer life in Christ by his own efforts and those of his followers, and his work did much to counteract the ruinous effects of Rationalism and prepare the way for the more spiritual movement in Norway in the early years of the next period. Hauge's sermons naturally lacked the culture of the schools, and had the faults of his type, but they were earnest and sincere and had a powerful influence upon the people. It is mournful to say that he was persecuted by the church and state authorities, tried on many false charges, imprisoned, fined; but he bore himself well in his trials, and left an honored name and an enduring influence behind him as of one devoted to the service of God and the good of men.

III. Swedish Preaching

As to Sweden, Europe had not forgotten Gustavus Adolphus; and the meteoric military career of the youthful Charles XII in the first decade of the eighteenth century seemed likely to revive Sweden's influence in European affairs. But the sudden termination of the young king's life, after his return from his defeat at Pultowa and following exile, removed Sweden again from any leading place in modern history. Charles left a debt-loaded country, no great achievements except a few brilliant but fruitless battles, and no direct heirs. To his sister and her husband devolved the crown of Sweden, but under such conditions as made it a mere title without real power. The history of Sweden for the rest of the century is a record of political dissensions and of royal incapacities, slightly relieved by some good work on the part of Gustave III toward the end of the century.

Three important names in widely different spheres adorned the literature of Sweden during this time. Olof van Dalin (d. 1763), poet and historian, though not a profound or original writer, is rightly regarded as the initiator of the modern era in Swedish letters. Emanuel Swedenborg (d. 1772) was a genius in the domain of religious and philosophical thought, and a man of pure life, broad learning, and profound mystical and speculative thinking. As a thinker and writer he remains one of the most esteemed men of his age, but his literary and philosophical value outside of his own country has been somewhat underestimated on account of the mystical and unaccepted element in his religious speculations. Under the literature of science the Sweden of the eighteenth century bears the great name of Carl von Linné, better known under the Latinized form of Linnaeus, the father of modern botany and one of the greatest of scientists. Though he wrote in Latin and for the learned, the works of Linnaeus in the original and translations hold an immortal place in literature because of the author's clearness and kindling interest, both in thought and in expression. Besides these three great leaders, there were three poets, Bellman, Kellgren, and Leopold, who greatly pleased their contemporaries and did much in preparing the way for the nobler development of Swedish literature in the next epoch.

In Sweden the orthodox and rationalistic parties seem, though not inactive, to have had no particularly able or noted preachers. But the evangelicals were nobly represented by the court preacher, Andrew Nohrborg (d. 1767), who was somewhat like Bengel in spirit;

and Erik Tollstadius (d. 1759), pastor in Stockholm, who attracted great throngs to hear his warm and spiritual discourses. In Sweden there seems to have been, according to Christlieb,[20] "a certain fusion of the old orthodoxy with deeper pietistic inclination of the heart, but of a peculiar Swedish coloring, inasmuch as for the practical Swedish character a comparative undervaluing of 'mere doctrine' was much further removed than for the later German Pietism."

CHAPTER X

British Preaching in the Eighteenth Century

The eighteenth century marks a great epoch in the development of the British Empire. England was, of course, the center, but there was wonderful expansion into many parts of the world. The internal affairs are easily recalled. The succession of sovereigns was begun by the reign of Queen Anne, after the death of William III, in 1702. William was unpopular but great, while Anne was popular but weak, being much under the sway of Marlborough and his wife. On her death, in 1714, the House of Hanover, in the person of George I, began its rule in England. George II reigned during the middle of the century, and the end of it found the good but incapable and obstinate George III on the throne. During these reigns the great parties which have alternately governed modern England were more or less clearly defined and formed. A few favored the Stuarts, under whom two futile attempts (1715 and 1745) were made to recover the crown for that misguided house. These circumstances led to the strengthening of ministerial responsibility and the real government of the country by the House of Commons. The century is distinguished by a number of great ministers and statesmen, such as Marlborough, Bolingbroke, Walpole, the two Pitts, Fox, and Burke. Important events were the Act of Settlement, 1701; the Act of Union with Scotland, 1707. Later in the century, under the lead of an obscure and not very worthy man named Wilkes, three great measures

[20] *RE*, XV, S. 699.

were agitated, viz., Parliamentary reform, the publicity of Parliamentary proceedings, and the freedom of the press. The external affairs of the kingdom were surpassingly important. Off and on during the century, and for fifteen years beyond it, there was the terrible struggle with France. There was also England's part in the Seven Years' War, which resulted in the aggrandizement of Prussia as against Austria in Europe, and of England as against France in India and America. The British conquest of India was decided in 1757. The American Revolution wrested from England her colonies, but established the great Republic of the United States in 1775-1783. The close of the century, 1799, witnessed the beginning of England's final conflict with France, against Napoleon, to be ended at Waterloo in 1815.

In literature the eighteenth century for England means less than the seventeenth or the nineteenth, but still there were many writers and movements that could not be spared from the development of English thought and letters. This century, in literature as in politics, was a robust, transitional, and preparatory age. Not so original as the Elizabethan, nor so copious and polished as the Victorian, the period of Queen Anne is marked by a certain stiffness and artificiality, as instanced in the work of Pope and others. The beginning of English fiction is found in the still popular romance of Defoe, while the writings of Steele, Addison, and Swift fill an important place in the development of English prose. The early Georgian period has to its credit the minor poetry of Thomson, Young, and Gray, while fiction is represented in the tedious tales of Richardson and the coarse stories of Fielding. Bolingbroke and Johnson contributed much to prose, and David Hume begins a long line of distinguished historians. In theology Butler and Law are notable names. The later Georgian epoch, toward the end of the century, is lit up by the genius of Goldsmith, Burns, and Cowper in poetry, while fiction grows both more human and pleasing in the work of Goldsmith and Jane Austen. Dr. Johnson continues to write his ponderous prose, Adam Smith puts forth his famous study in political economy, Gibbon writès his masterpiece on the *Decline and Fall of the Roman Em-*

pire, and the splendid political genius of Burke illuminates statesmanship. These were the masters. There were others who labored with them and made the eighteenth century literature in England, though not comparable to that of the following age, both respectable and strong.

Religious and moral affairs in England during the eighteenth century were for the most part in a deplorable condition.[1] Political corruption was rife, vice was unblushing and hideous, coarseness, profanity, drunkenness, gambling, and debauchery desolated the land. The growth of deism and skepticism in all classes was marked. Philosophical writers, such as Bolingbroke, Hume, and Gibbon, brought churchly religion into contempt with thinking people. In the preface to his famous *Analogy,* published in 1736, Bishop Butler wrote: "It has come to be taken for granted that Christianity is no longer a subject of inquiry; but that it is now at length discovered to be fictitious. And accordingly, it is treated as if, in the present age, this were an agreed point among all persons of discernment, and nothing remained but to set it up as a principal subject for mirth and ridicule." Again later, in his *Charge to the Clergy of Durham,* in 1751, Butler emphasizes his complaint in the following terms: "It is impossible for me, my brethren, upon our first meeting of this kind, to forbear lamenting with you the general decay of religion in this nation; which is now observed by every one, and has been for some time the complaint of all serious persons."[2] Even among professed Christians there was great laxity of life and want of devotion to truth. Many of the clergy were utterly unworthy.[3] There was dense ignorance and much practical heathenism among the lower classes of the people.

Yet there was a brighter side. There were not a few noble Christian characters and earnest representatives

[1]See the historians generally on the period; particularly Lecky's *History of England in the Eighteenth Century, passim;* Green's *History of the English People,* Bk. VIII, ch. 4, near the end; and cf. Ryle's *Christian Leaders of the Last Century,* Chap. I.

[2]Butler's *Works,* Gladstone's ed., the *Author's Preface* to the *Analogy,* Vol. I; and Vol. II, p. 397.

[3]See Green, *l. c.;* and Lecky, Vol. I, p. 84.

of true Christianity. In defense of the Christian faith, Joseph Butler contributed his immortal *Analogy,* and argued the Deists off their own ground; while on the side of feeling and pious mysticism, the devotional work of William Law, Thomas Boston, and others fed true piety among the devoutly inclined. But the great redeeming feature of eighteenth century England was the rise and progress of the revival under the popular preachers, George Whitefield and John Wesley.[4] This great movement reclaimed thousands of the lower and middle classes of the people, and to some extent reached also the upper classes. It changed the current of English thought and life towards a higher morality and a more spiritual religion. Consequent upon the revival came, toward the end of the century, the evangelical movement, corresponding to the Pietism of Germany some decades before. This movement doubtless had its narrowness and one-sidedness, and was open to criticism on those accounts, but it emphasized some neglected aspects of Christian doctrine and life and left a wholesome influence upon modern English religion. Along with this we gratefully trace the dawn of modern philanthropic and missionary enterprise. It is only necessary to say that the latter part of the eighteenth century witnessed the self-denying labors of John Howard, William Wilberforce, and William Carey, and the birth and early training of that ornament of her sex and time, Elizabeth Fry. All these political, literary, and religious movements had their more or less intimate relations to the development of preaching, which shared both the strength and the weakness of the times.

I. General View of Preaching

As in politics and in literature, so in preaching the eighteenth century in England has a marked individuality and an important place of its own. The pulpit of the period can with no more justice be neglected or underrated than can the philosophic thought or the literary product of the age. The state of morals and religion, and the general literary taste and tone of the times,

[4]Green, Bk. IX, ch. III; Ryle, chap. II.

made their impress upon the character and quality of preaching, as these are revealed to us in the traditions and notices and likewise in the abundant published sermons which have come down to us. There is ample material for studying and judging the epoch.[5]

The low moral and spiritual tone of a large, but certainly not respectable, group among the clergy disastrously affected both the character and influence of their preaching. The pulpit work of these men was naturally perfunctory and cold. Nor could their sermons claim originality or freshness, even where they were not bought or shamelessly appropriated from others. And in other preachers, who escaped the taint and condemnation of moral looseness, there was often found a cool, rationalistic tone, such as we have noted already in certain groups of French and German preachers of this age. This type of preaching found for the most part dignified yet pronounced expression in the Latitudinarians of England and the Moderates of Scotland. Even among many who would not be properly placed among the rationalizing preachers, but among the orthodox and theoretically evangelical, there was preaching which it would require more charity than judgment to pronounce other than lifeless and tame.

Yet the situation was not entirely hopeless; there were redeeming features among the drawbacks, and not a few positive virtues of a commanding order. The hidden life of piety among the people, small leaven though it was, demanded and responded to a presentation of the gospel which should nourish the heart as well as the reason. Nor was such a preaching wholly lacking through the century, even apart from the special movement under Whitefield and Wesley and their associates. Still the significant and outstanding evangelical preaching of England during the eighteenth century is forever as-

[5]The histories—both religious and general—of England, Scotland, and Ireland for the period; sketches and notices in works previously mentioned, such as Christlieb, Broadus, Pattison, Blaikie, Fish, and others; best single work is *The Christian Leaders of the Last Century* (eighteenth, of course), by Bishop J. C. Ryle; Works and Biographies of individual preachers; articles in the *Dictionary of National Biography,* and other cyclopedias.

sociated with the names and labors of these two illustrious leaders and their fellow-workers in the great revival. Their preaching was eminently popular and Biblical. Ryle well says:[6] "They preached fervently and directly. They cast aside that dull, cold, heavy, lifeless mode of delivery which had long made sermons a very proverb for dullness. They proclaimed the words of faith with faith, and the story of life with life." The fruits of this preaching were to be found, not only in the religious and moral reformation already noticed, but also in the great improvement in preaching itself, particularly as regards directness of aim, simplicity of speech, and a more pronounced evangelical content.

The character of preaching, of course, differed both with groups and individuals; but there are certain general features to be observed before we study the several schools and their leading representatives. One striking thing (as in Germany and France) in the British preaching of the century is the relatively large and prominent place given to morals. This was characteristic of all schools. The Latitudinarians had little else; and while they did not go so far afield in minor morals as did some of their German contemporaries, their sermons often are little more than essays on conventional morality, based as much on reason and philosophy as on the law of God. "The celebrated lawyer, Blackstone, had the curiosity, early in the reign of George III, to go from church to church and hear every clergyman of note in London. He says that he did not hear a single discourse which had more Christianity in it than the writings of Cicero, and that it would have been impossible for him to discover, from what he heard, whether the preacher were a follower of Confucius, of Mahomet, or of Christ."[7] Among the churchly orthodox, against whom such a grievous charge as has just been quoted can not be laid, Christian morals, distinctly derived from the Bible as the authoritative Word of God, found frequent expression. The most profound and reasoned exposition of the ethics of the gospel in that age occurs in a famous series of sermons preached by Joseph Butler while yet a young man. We shall see more of these later on. Nor was moral

[6] *Christian Leaders*, p. 25. [7] Ryle, *op. cit.*, p. 15.

preaching by any means neglected by the evangelical revivalists. Wesley and his associates and sympathizers strenuously insisted upon a holy life as the necessary fruitage and token of a sound conversion; and to this preaching, as we have seen, was largely due that visible improvement of manners and heightened moral tone of modern English life, both public and private, which contrasts favorably with the situation in the later decades of the seventeenth century and throughout the eighteenth.

As to theology, there was in the preaching of the century a variety of types. The Latitudinarians and Moderates—whether churchly or Unitarian—had no theology to speak of; doctrine was the least considerable element of their work. Arminianism was found in many churchmen, as during the previous century in Barrow and others; and it received powerful stimulus and permanent standing at the hands of Wesley and Fletcher among the Methodists. In truth, that type of theology ought to be called Wesleyan, for Arminius is almost a forgotten personality, while Wesley's name and teaching have become worldwide. Calvinism remained the dominant type of doctrine among the Dissenters—except the Wesleyan Methodists—and the evangelical (low-church) divines of the Church of England. This system received great impulse in the preaching of Whitefield and the Calvinistic Methodists, chiefly in Wales. It is to be regretted that angry polemics marred the writings and to some extent the preaching, both of the great leaders and of the rank and file, in this great and never settled controversy over the so-called doctrines of grace.

The more strictly homiletical or technical aspects of eighteenth century English preaching are scarcely of so striking and varied interest as we have found them in other European lands. The English preachers had never been as much given to the expository homily as either their Reformed or Lutheran brethren on the Continent. So the topical method of composing sermons, with a good deal of the scholastic analysis, had been prevalent in the preceding period and remained the dominant method in the eighteenth century, though with less elaborate refinement of division and subdivision. The style of expression necessarily varied with individuals, but was in general solemn, stately, and elevated, inclining to stiffness, not wanting in power, but sometimes too elaborate and polished. What it lacked in spontaneity, freedom, and freshness it sometimes made up in carefulness, dignity, and impressiveness. There was less of fancifulness, of straining after effect in phrase, of pedantic or pompous or ornamental affectation, than in the former times. Solidity and strength rather than showy display were sought. The wholesome influence of Tillotson was still felt; even though preachers of the flowery type of Hervey—he of the once-famous *Meditations*—were sometimes to be found.

II. Some of the Leading Preachers

It will be convenient to study the British preachers of the century according to nationality, and classify them under this larger division into such groups as we may find appropriate. It is evident that the English, Scotch, Welsh, and Irish characters in their divergences would show distinctive traces in the pulpit; while along with and across these the different schools of doctrinal and ecclesiastical thought could not fail also to leave their impress. The large and obvious general distinction of Anglicans and Dissenters covers also the minor distinctions of groups or schools within the Established Church, and the various denominations of Non-Conformists.

In the Anglican body it is proper to distinguish four groups or schools of preachers, as follows: (1) The churchly orthodox; (2) the latitudinarian and worldly; (3) the evangelical; and (4) the revivalists, meaning Whitefield and Wesley, with their sympathizers and fellow-workers among the clergy of the Church of England. Properly speaking, these would belong under the third group, the evangelical clergy, but both their methods and their importance make it desirable to consider them separately.

Beginning with the churchly orthodox among the Anglican clergy we find one of the most distinguished preachers at the opening of the century to be Francis Atterbury (1662-1732).[8] He was the son of a rector in

[8] *Works* in four vols., with biographical account; cyclopedia articles; sermon in Fish, I, p. 306 ff.

Buckinghamshire, educated at Westminster School, and at Christ Church College, Oxford. As student and writer he was bold and showy, rather than accurate or profound in scholarship. His controversial qualities were early displayed in his much applauded defense of the Church of England against a Catholic critic, and in the literary field by his sharp dispute with the great Cambridge scholar, Richard Bentley, over the spurious *Letters of Phalaris*. Though applauded by partisans of Oxford as against Cambridge, and showing acuteness and power in debate, neither the scholarship nor the temper of Atterbury appear to advantage in this performance. Under Queen Anne, Atterbury was made Master of Christ Church College, one of the royal chaplains, and later bishop of Rochester, to which see at that time the deanery of Westminster was attached. On the death of Queen Anne he favored the return of the Stuart dynasty, and plotted with the Jacobites against the House of Hanover. Being convicted—though on circumstantial evidence—of treason, he was banished and forbidden to receive or correspond with his friends, excepting his immediate family. He died in Paris, but his remains were permitted to be interred—without ceremony—in Westminster Abbey.

Though not accused of gross wrong, Atterbury was not an admirable man. His contentious and arrogant spirit marred his undoubted talents as a disputant, whether in speech or writing. As a literary man he was a friend of Pope, Swift, and other men of letters. His own style was marked by clearness, strength, and a certain elegance, without much of grace or charm. He was of the school of Tillotson, and the influence of his sermons was decidedly in the interest of directness, simplicity, and force. The opinion of even so judicious a thinker as Doddridge, that in Atterbury's writings "we see language in its strictest purity and beauty," and that he was a "model for courtly preachers" and "the glory of our English orators," seems now extravagant; but it shows how highly the pulpit abilities of Atterbury were esteemed in and near his own time. His sermons still read well, but in spite of acknowledged literary worth, they are wanting in evangelical power and in the strength and spirit of the great preachers who preceded him. A short extract from his noted sermon on *The Terrors of Conscience*[9] will afford a worthy example of his best style: "The disorders and reprehensions of conscience are not a continued, but an intermitting disease, returning upon the mind by fits and at particular seasons only; in the intervals of which the patient shall have seeming health and real ease. The eruptions of burning mountains are not perpetual, nor doth even the smoke itself ascend always from the tops of them; but though the seeds of fire lodged in their caverns may be stifled and suppressed for a time, yet anon they gather strength, and break out again with a rage great in proportion to its discontinuance. It is by accidents and occasions chiefly that the power of this principle is called forth into act; by a sudden ill turn of fortune, or a fit of sickness, or our observation of some remarkable instance of divine vengeance, which hath overtaken other men in like cases. Even Herod was not always under the paroxysm described in the text, but surprised into it unawares, by his 'hearing of the fame of Jesus,' and then his heart smote him at the remembrance of the inhuman treatment he had given to such another just and good person, and filled his mind anew with forgotten horrors."

A man of very different type from Atterbury was the famous bishop of Durham and author of *The Analogy of Religion,* Joseph Butler (1692-1752).[10] Butler's father was a merchant at Wantage, and a Presbyterian in religion, who wished to educate his gifted son for the ministry of his own denomination. But Joseph leaned to the Church of England, and accepted an offer of university education at Oxford, where he received his final training as a brilliant student of Oriel College. He already showed in his young manhood those wonderful powers of close and profound thinking which remain his chief distinction. He had a correspondence with Dr. Adam Clarke on the *Being and Attributes of God,* and upon

[9]Fish, I, p. 215.

[10]Various editions of the *Works,* and of the *Analogy;* especially the beautiful ed. by W. E. Gladstone (1896) in three vols., with subsidiary notes; several biographical sketches in *Works* and the cyclopedias. The *Sermons* (twenty-one in all) are in Vol. II of Gladstone's ed.

receiving orders, even before his graduation, he was appointed preacher at the Rolls Chapel, Oxford, in 1718. This was a signal honor for a young man of twenty-six years, but Butler proved in every way worthy of it. It was here that he preached that notable series of fifteen sermons on Christian morals, which not only established Butler's reputation as a great thinker for his own age, but remain one of the standard and classic contributions to ethical philosophy and Christian thought. We shall recur to these sermons later. They were published in 1726, and in that same year Butler left the Rolls Chapel and became rector of Stanhope, a small country parish to which he had been appointed. For seven years he labored with conscientious diligence in this secluded place. But this retirement no doubt helped to maturity some of the great thoughts of his famous *Analogy,* which was published in 1736, after he had received some minor promotions. After this his advancement was more rapid. In 1738 he was made bishop of Bristol, in 1740 dean of St. Paul's, and in 1750, near the close of his life, bishop of Durham.

Butler was a man of great purity and simplicity of character, very benevolent and hospitable, and though he never married or enjoyed domestic life, he was highly valued by a large circle of friends. In speaking of the great qualities of his mind, Gladstone[11] has also paid noble tribute to Butler's character, in these words: "From beginning to end the *Analogy* and the *Sermons,* to some extent, are avowedly controversial; and the prosecution of such work powerfully tends to cast the mind into a controversial mold. But in Butler this tendency is effectually neutralized by his native ingenuousness, by the sense that his pen moves under the very eye of God, and by the knowledge that the sacred interests of truth must be eventually compromised by overstatement. . . . The student of Butler will, unless it be his own fault, learn candor in all its breadth, and not to tamper with the truth; will neither grudge admissions, nor fret under even cumbrous reserves."

The *Sermons*[12] of Butler include the fifteen on morals, published in 1726; six more preached on public occasions, and the *Charge to the Clergy of Durham,* which, though

[11] *Op. cit.,* III, pp. 2, 5. [12] Vol. II, of the Gladstone edition.

not a sermon, contains valuable suggestions on preaching, and, though brief, is a weighty and thoughtful document. The fifteen Rolls Chapel sermons, however, are those by which Butler is to be judged as a preacher. The arrangement and titles are as follows: (1, 2, 3) Upon Human Nature, or Man Considered as a Moral Agent; (4) The Government of the Tongue; (5, 6) Compassion; (7) The Character of Balaam; (8, 9) Resentment and Forgiveness of Injuries; (10) Self-deceit; (11, 12) Love of Our Neighbor; (13, 14) Piety, or The Love of God; (15) The Ignorance of Man. These sermons are very profound in thought, very judicious and fair on disputed points, unequivocally Christian in principle and tone, but very hard reading, alike for the closeness of their reasoning and for the inexcusable heaviness and involution of their style. The most interesting to read is, perhaps, that masterly and discriminating analysis of the *Character of Balaam;* and the most famous and influential the two (11 and 12) on the *Love of Our Neighbor.* Of course, such discourses, either in actual delivery or in after study, are as far as possible removed from being "popular;" but the thoughtful reader will be richly repaid for hours spent over these great deliverances of a master mind.

That Butler himself was aware of the difficulties of his writing, and, in part at least, of the justice of the criticism passed upon it, appears from the candid, though even then reserved, manner in which he speaks on this point. The passage is quoted in the preface to Gladstone's edition of Butler's *Works,*[13] and is reproduced as a curious example of Butler's style even when he almost apologizes for its faults: "It must be acknowledged that some of the following discourses are very abstruse and difficult; or, if you please, obscure; but I must take leave to add that those alone are judges whether or no and how far this is a fault, who are judges whether or no and how far it might have been avoided. . . . . Thus much, however, will be allowed: that general criticisms concerning the obscurity, considered as a distinct thing from confusion and perplexity of thought, as in some cases there may be ground for them, so in others they may be

[13]Vol. II, pp. 4, 5.

nothing more at the bottom than complaints that everything is not to be understood with the same ease that some things are. . . . However, upon the whole, as the title of sermons gives some right to expect what is plain and of easy comprehension, and as the best auditories are mixed, I shall not set about to justify the propriety of preaching, or under that title publishing, discourses so abstruse as some of these are; neither is it worth while to trouble the reader with the account of my doing either."

Samuel Horsley (1733-1806),[14] famous bishop and disputant, was the son of a clergyman who held various livings—among them St. Martin-in-the-Fields, London, and Newington Butts, Surrey (now part of London), both of which Samuel also later held for a time. He was born in London, educated at Cambridge, ordained young, and received a number of appointments, with rather frequent changes. His promotions were rapid: Bishop of St. David's, then of Rochester (at the same time dean of Westminster), and lastly of St. Asaph's. He was a remarkably able and versatile man, being a strong mathematician and at the same time a notable Hebrew scholar, while he was also an assiduous and vigorous administrator of affairs in each of his three dioceses. In the House of Lords he took an active interest in public affairs and was a frequent and respected debater. It is related that he once invited the famous Lord Thurlow to hear him preach, and the graceless politician replied, with certain profane garnishments: "No, I hear you talk nonsense enough in the House, where I can answer you; and I will not go where I can't talk back." Horsley's most important and famous controversy was with the eminent scientist and Unitarian theologian, Dr. Joseph Priestley (d. 1804), who undertook to prove that the doctrine of the divinity of Christ, and so that of the Trinity, was of later historic origin than the early centuries. It is generally admitted that Horsley completely refuted his able opponent, exhibiting both great learning and acuteness as a reasoner. Hors-

[14]See *Sermons of Bishop Horsley,* 2 vols., 1810; and *A Great Bishop of a Hundred Years Ago,* by H. H. Jebb (his great-grandson), 1909.

ley's sermons produced a profound impression on his hearers—Coleridge and DeQuincey, with others, being witnesses. His preaching was remarkably simple and clear for that age, showing usually a simple division, a good deal of ingenuity (indeed, sometimes too much) in interpretation, and the use without the parade of learning. The sermons are solid, sensible, argumentative, without much imagination or appeal to feeling, yet not without occasional traces of such appeal.

It is scarcely necessary to say that among the latitudinarian and worldly clergymen—of whom, unhappily, there was a considerable number—few became distinguished, and these few for other things than their sermons. Naturally the first name that occurs is that of Dean Swift, of Dublin, but he more properly will claim attention along with the Irish preachers.[15]

Along with him comes Laurence Sterne (1713-1768)[16] rector of Sutton, author of *Tristram Shandy, The Sentimental Journey,* and *The Sermons of Mr. York.* These last are cool, satirical, conventionally moral, pleasingly written, indeed, but utterly wanting in gospel content or spiritual power. The man was selfish, pleasure-loving, intoxicated with his literary and social success, worldly, stained, discredited. Alas! he was one of many merely professional clergymen in that age, most of whom had not even a literary or other incidental claim to preserve them from a well-merited obscurity. Of these Bishop Ryle[17] bitterly says: "All over England country livings were often filled by hunting, shooting, gambling, card-playing, swearing, ignorant clergymen, who cared neither for law nor gospel, and utterly neglected their parishes." But over against these there was a strong group of evangelical and earnest men who preached a pure gospel and lived as they preached; to whom it is a pleasure now to turn.

George Horne (1730-1792),[18] devout commentator on

[15]See below, p. 347 f.

[16]See various edd. of the works mentioned in the text, several literary and cyclopaedia accounts, and particularly the discussion and extracts in *Warner Library,* Vol. XXIV, p. 13,899.

[17]*Christian Leaders,* p. 128.

[18]*Works* and *Life* (six volumes, 1799), by his friend and chaplain, Wm. Jones.

the Psalms, and exemplary bishop of Norwich, was born at Otham, in Kent, where his good father, Samuel Horne, was the excellent and beloved rector. A notable remark of the elder Horne reveals his hatred of insincerity when he said, "I had rather be toad-eater to a mountebank than flatter any great man against my conscience." He was a man of great gentleness and consideration of others, and this trait was beautifully shown in his own household. It is said that instead of resorting to shaking or loud calling, he used to awaken George by playing the flute near him. No wonder he became fond of music! The lad received careful elementary instruction at home, then attended school at Maidstone, in Kent, and then became a student of University College, Oxford. He was an excellent student in all branches, especially theology; and his gifts and character were honorably recognized in his election, without solicitation, as a fellow of Magdalen—not his own college. Taking orders in 1753, he preached often at Oxford and other places, while steadily working at his literary pursuits, as became an Oxford fellow. It was during this time that he began his notable *Commentary on the Psalms,* which occupied him twenty years, and remains one of the great works in English on that subject, though devotional rather than exegetical in method.

In 1771 Horne was made a royal chaplain, ten years later dean of Canterbury, and in 1790 bishop of Norwich. He was a man of learning and piety, a skillful and good-tempered disputant, a valued and useful churchman in the various positions he filled.

As a preacher Horne attracted attention from the first. In opinion he was what would later have been called evangelical or low-church. He sympathized with evangelistic and popular religious movements more than was usual with the clergy of the Established Church. As read to-day, his sermons reveal no very remarkable powers; they are sound and pleasing, of that good and useful sort which are ever needed. There is in them more of imagination and ornament than was common to the Anglican preaching of that time, but there was no excess in these. The style is somewhat stilted and *Blairesque,* but without ostentation of elegance or learning.

One of the most earnest and useful, though comparatively little known, preachers of the evangelical group was William Grimshaw (1708-1763),[19] rector of Haworth. Grimshaw never preached in London, never published any sermons, and only a few pieces of other kinds, and is only remembered by several accounts of his life and the traditions of his earnest preaching and self-denying labors in his difficult parish, and by his frequent evangelistic work beyond its borders. Haworth has become famous in literary history as the home of the Brontë sisters, whose father was rector there in the first half of the nineteenth century, from about 1820 and on. But it was Grimshaw that gave to the harsh and somewhat uncouth parish whatever of religious character it won and held. His preaching made no pretension to elegance or greatness, but was in form adapted to the plain people, to whom he chiefly appealed. Yet it glowed with evangelical conviction and fervor, and was the means of leading hundreds of souls to Christ. Though a man of some eccentricities of character and conduct, Grimshaw was held in well-deserved esteem by those who know how to value so noble and fruitful a man as he was, and he died greatly beloved and honored by thousands throughout the region where he lived and labored.

A better known representative of the evangelical school was William Romaine (1714-1795).[20] The son of a French Protestant refugee, Romaine was born and brought up at Hartlepool, county of Durham, where he attended school, and was later sent to Oxford. Here he studied hard for six years, and received his M. A. degree in due course. His scholarly attainments were recognized by all, and found fruitage in a concordance to the Bible and the translation and editing of a Hebrew lexicon. His skill and ability as a controversialist were shown in his effective critique upon Bishop Warburton's *Divine Legation of Moses*—a long discredited rationalistic performance. But along with these labors in the literary field of theology, Romaine was active also as a preacher, having been ordained in 1736-37. Some uncertainty as to place and dates is found in the record of the first ten

[19]Ryle, *op. cit.*, p. 106 ff.

[20]*Works,* with *Life* by W. B. Cadogan, ed. of 1837; Ryle, p. 149 ff.

or eleven years of his ministerial life, but among his different appointments he seems to have held pretty steadily to one as curate of Banstead, near Epsom. His work as author and preacher having attracted attention, he was called upon to fill various occasional appointments in London—one as chaplain to the Lord Mayor, about 1741. But these occasional services did not for some time lead to a settled appointment, and Romaine was on the point of leaving London for final settlement in a country charge when, on the way to the ship, he met a man who recognized him by his resemblance to his father and asked if his name was not Romaine. This naturally led to friendly conversation, and it turned out that the gentleman had some influence which led to Romaine's being chosen, in 1748, as "lecturer" at St. Botolph's Church—a post calling for preaching at regular intervals, but with a salary of only eighteen pounds a year! Of course, the duties admitted of other posts and labors. Thus Romaine began his checkered career as a London clergyman. He had some infirmities of temper and manner, and a leaning to controversy; but far more than these incidental matters, it seems to have been his popularity as a preacher and the pronounced and unequivocal way in which he held and preached his evangelical views that led him into such frequent collisions with the rectors and vicars in London. Again and again on being recommended and even appointed to places, he was opposed and hindered in his work. More than once he was forced into lawsuits to defend his right to preach! Once when a suit was decided in his favor, the vicar or rector of the parish refused to have the church lit up, and kept the congregation waiting in the street till the exact hour of seven o'clock, when the doors were opened. The bishop of London finally interfered and ordered the church to be opened and lighted before the hour of service. During this time Romaine preached two sermons at Oxford, in which he plainly proclaimed the doctrine of the atonement and imputed righteousness as held by evangelicals, and on this account he was forbidden to preach at Oxford any more. He published the sermons, with a brief explanation, and it is strange evidence of the religious decline of the times that preaching like that should have been put under the ban of the Church of

England. Finally—by the influence of Lady Huntington and other prominent persons, yet not without a lawsuit—Romaine was duly appointed, in 1766, as rector of St. Anne's Church, Blackfriars. Here he served with great fidelity and success to the end of his life.

Romaine's sermons are not specially profound in thought, but are thoroughly evangelical in doctrine, simple in plan, and clear in style. They do not rise very high in feeling or imagination, but present gospel truth in a manly, straightforward, sincere, and earnest manner. His preaching attracted large audiences; and he deserved his popularity.

A quaint and eccentric, but deeply spiritual and successful, preacher was the evangelical and evangelistic vicar of Everton, John Berridge (1716-1785).[21] His father was a farmer who, disgusted with John's lack of knowledge of cattle and distaste for farm life, once threatened to send him to college and so make him "a light to the Gentiles." The threat was fulfilled, and the undesigned and irreverent prophecy also. John was sent to Clare Hall, Cambridge, where he proved a diligent and successful scholar, taking the academic degree in course and being elected a fellow of his college. In his early youth he had had very serious religious impressions, but these suffered unhappy decline during his college days. He was ordained and began his work as a preacher without the deep piety or earnestness of his later life. He was brilliant, witty, popular, and sociable, and therefore much sought after; but his spiritual life was low, and, his fellowship affording him the means of living pleasantly at his college and reading as he liked, he was in no haste to take up any steady work as a minister. But, in 1749—he being now thirty-three years old and finely educated, as well as naturally endowed—a change came over his feelings, and he determined to take up his lifework with seriousness. With this design, he accepted a post as curate of Stapleford, a parish near Cambridge, and began to preach regularly. Ryle says:[22] "Berridge entered on his duties as curate of Stapleford with great zeal and a sincere desire to do

[21] *Works* with *Memoir,* by Richard Whittingham, 2d ed., 1864; Ryle, p. 216 ff. [22] *Op. cit.,* p. 222.

good, and served his church regularly from college for no less than six years. He took great pains with his parishioners, and pressed upon them very earnestly the importance of sanctification, but without producing the slightest effect upon their lives. His preaching, even at this time, was striking, plain, and attractive. His life was moral, upright, and correct. His diligence as a pastor was undeniable. Yet his ministry throughout these six years was entirely without fruit, to his own great annoyance and mortification." He had not yet learned by personal experience the deep spiritual realities of the truths which he preached; but a better day, for him and his hearers, was at hand.

The vicarage of Everton, in Bedfordshire, was in the gift of Clare Hall College, and to this place Berridge was appointed in 1754, and held it the rest of his life. For the first two years of his ministry at Everton, Berridge pursued the same course as at Stapleford, and with the same barrenness of results; but then, by one means and another, he was led to a deeper personal experience of grace, and his preaching at once took on a new tone and power, and became henceforth rich in spiritual fruits.

Very earnest and faithful in his own parish, Berridge extended his labors far beyond its limits, preaching much in the neighboring counties, and even farther. Strange to say, he was not molested by the worldly incumbents into whose fields he pushed his itinerant labors. Nor did he content himself with what he could do alone, for he provided lay preachers to instruct those who had been gathered by his own work, paying their expenses out of his own income. He co-operated with Whitefield and the Wesleys, though he held a post in the Established Church—which was unjustly denied to them. After some thirty years of faithful and arduous toil, this queer but devout old preacher passed to his reward, having long before selected his grave and written his own quaint and humble epitaph, which required only the date of his death to fill it out.

Only outlines of some of his sermons and a farewell sermon remain. These hardly reveal the man, only his good and earnest thinking, for in actual delivery he was striking, peculiar, often odd and undignified, but deeply in earnest, popular in style, and abundantly fruitful in winning souls. Doubtless there was much in his manner and methods that was offensive to good taste, but his aim was high, his character sincere, his piety unquestioned.

One of the best known and most remarkable preachers of the evangelical school was John Newton (1722-1807),[23] curate of Olney, in Bucks, and rector of St. Mary Woolnoth, in London. Son of a sea-captain, born in London, early losing his mother, receiving little or no education, he grew up a wild, disobedient youth. His early life was filled with adventure and wickedness of every sort, alternated with periods of religious profession and partial reformation, and kept true to one constant attachment—his love for his cousin, Miss Catlett—from early boyhood. He went on voyages, was impressed into the royal navy, deserted, was left to die on the coast of Africa, suffered extreme hardships, and finally was brought to repentance and faith. Yet even after this he engaged for a time in the slave trade. During his voyages he read much, learned Latin and Greek, and studied very hard. Finally quitting the sea, he obtained a post as inspector of vessels at Liverpool. Here he devoted himself to religious work, and was urged by friends to become a candidate for orders. He felt that he had some gifts for the work of the ministry, and that his remarkable experience could be made serviceable to others; but he shrank from the work, and was not offended when his first application for ordination was refused. Later, however, he was accepted and ordained, and became curate for an absentee rector at Olney, in Buckinghamshire. Here he spent about fifteen happy and useful years in earnest labors. Most interesting during this time was his helpful friendship and protection to the unhappy poet, Cowper. The *Olney Hymns,* their joint production, appeared during this time, and, along with much now intolerable verse, contained some of the choicest treasures of English hymnody from the pens of both the friends. At the instance of an influential friend, Newton became, in December, 1779, rector of the parish of St. Mary Woolnoth, in London, where he spent

[23] *Works,* 2 vols., 1834, with a *Memoir* by Rev. John Cecil, and Newton's own *Authentic Account* of his life, as far as it goes.

the rest of his useful life, having reached his eighty-fifth year.

Newton's remarkable experience, his sound and unquestionable conversion, his native strength of mind (self-cultured though it was), his earnest devotion to his duties, rather than shining gifts in the pulpit, gave him his strength and influence as a preacher. He published sermons, both while at Olney and in London. Among the latter is a series of fifty on the passages of Scripture used in Handel's Oratorio of *The Messiah,* but more interesting from that fact than from any unusual merits of their own. Yet Newton's sermons are in general worthy of regard for their soundness and earnestness, and for their excellence of composition, considering he was a self-taught man. They are in the usual homiletical form of the age, and make no pretension to oratory or display.

Other members of the evangelical group must be passed over with only hasty mention. There was the excellent Henry Venn (1724-1797),[24] the faithful and fruitful rector of Huddersfield, whose *Complete Duty of Man* was once a much-read book; also James Hervey (1713-1758),[25] of Weston Favell, whose highly ornate *Meditations* and dialogues of *Theron and Aspasio* enjoyed a popularity now hard to comprehend, but his sermons were more restrained and practical; and the eminent hymn-writer, A. M. Toplady (1740-1778),[26] whose brief life and ministry, though marred by controversial faults, were not fruitless of good. Despite the defect of temper indicated, it is pleasing to remember that the young author of *Rock of Ages* was also a preacher of real talent, and died highly esteemed by his flock.

From the evangelicals we easily pass to the great revivalists, George Whitefield and John Wesley, some of whose fellow-workers and associates also should claim at least brief mention.

The history of preaching since the apostles does not contain a greater or worthier name than that of George Whitefield (1714-1770).[27] His life was busy, eventful,

[24]Ryle, p. 254 ff. [25]*Id.*, p. 328 ff. [26]*Id.*, p. 358 ff.

[27]The literature on Whitefield is too large to be discussed here. His own *Journal* (published during his lifetime) forms the basis of the biographies of him. Of these the standard among the older ones is *Memoirs of the Life of the Rev. George White-*

and crowded with striking details; his character had enough of human weakness to check extravagant eulogy, but stands out lofty, pure, magnificent, beyond injuring by malice or depreciating by criticism; his abundant labors were, and in their fruits remain, a benediction to mankind; his preaching, for earnestness, eloquence, and immediate effect, was the admiration of his own age, and is one of the most sacred traditions of the Christian pulpit for all time.

Whitefield was born in Gloucester, the son of an innkeeper, who died leaving several children, of whom George was the youngest, only two years old. The widow married again, and she for a time, and one of her older sons afterwards, kept up the tavern. It was scarcely to be expected that a lad so brought up should escape serious faults of conduct, and George became a typical "bad boy." His mother, however, was a good woman, and her influence was not wholly lost. The evil and good strove together in the youth, and for a time it looked as if the bad would win. George was full of mischief and pranks at home and school, fell into profanity, sometimes drank more than was good for him, now and then stole some money from his mother, afterwards quarreled with his brother's wife and left home. Meantime he enjoyed some school advantages, and was quick and ambitious to learn. He hated the tavern business, especially being a bar-tender, and all the while his conscience was struggling within. On leaving Gloucester he went to another brother at Bristol for a visit, and while there his mind was turned with penitence to more serious thoughts of religion; but this was only a transient reformation. While spending some time with his mother, and longing for an education, he made successful application for a servitor's place at Pembroke College, Oxford, and accordingly entered there at the age of eighteen. His ex-

field, by John Gillies, London, 1772; of later accounts, the best are the *Life,* by L. Tyerman, 2 vols.; and J. P. Gledstone, *George Whitefield, M. A., Field Preacher,* New York, 1901; see also the admirable account in Ryle, *Christian Leaders,* p. 30 ff. Of the *Sermons* an old edition in one volume has been used, and later a small volume of *Selected Sermons of George Whitefield,* with introd. and notes by A. R. Buckland, London, 1904. See also sermon in Fish, I, p. 333, and another in *World's Great Sermons,* III, p. 93.

perience at the tavern both gave him skill and saved his pride in waiting upon his fellow-students. He was a cheerful companion and a faithful student during his Oxford days. Best of all, this period witnessed his genuine conversion to God and his consecration of himself to the work of the ministry.

At Oxford, Whitefield observed with growing admiration the conduct of the "Methodist Club," in which the Wesley brothers were leaders, and becoming acquainted with Charles Wesley, he was led by him to join the group in their pious exercises and works of charity. Yet he perceived, earlier than did the Wesleys, that, however sincere and well-meant these practices were, they were not the gospel way of salvation, and his soul could not find peace in his own efforts and deeds. Dissatisfied, and earnestly seeking the true way, he was at last led to a whole and hearty personal trust in Christ alone for salvation. He thus describes his experience:[28] "About the end of the seventh week, after having undergone innumerable buffetings of Satan and many months' inexpressible trials by night and day under the spirit of bondage, God was pleased at length to remove the heavy load, to enable me to lay hold on His dear Son by a living faith, and by giving me the spirit of adoption, to seal me, as I humbly hope, even to the day of everlasting redemption." He goes on to describe in glowing terms the joy that filled his soul, and the abiding and unwavering conviction of this as the way of salvation which possessed and held his mind through life.

Soon afterwards he was ordained a deacon (1736) and began his flaming and powerful work as a preacher. Regarding his ordination, he says:[29] "I endeavored to behave with unaffected devotion, but not suitable enough to the greatness of the office I was to undertake. At the same time, I trust I answered every question from the bottom of my heart, and prayed heartily that God might say, Amen. I hope the good of souls will be my only principle of action. Let come what will, life or death, depth or height, I shall henceforward live like one who this day, in the presence of men and angels, took the holy sacrament, upon the profession of being inwardly moved by the Holy Ghost to take upon me that minis-

[28]Quoted by Gledstone, p. 22. [29]*Id.*, p. 29.

tration in the Church." The spirit in which he thus took up his ministry pervaded it through all its brilliant yet burdensome course to the end. Years after (September, 1764), on some criticism of being a rambler, he wrote to Wesley, "Fain would I end my life in rambling after those who have rambled away from Jesus Christ." And a few years later (January, 1767), in a letter to Cornelius Winter, he said, "The greatest preferment under heaven is to be an able, painful, faithful, successful, suffering, cast-out minister of the New Testament."[30] And this was Whitefield himself.

On the Sunday following his ordination, June 27, 1736, Whitefield preached his first sermon.[31] It had been prepared for a "small society," which accounts for its subject, *The Necessity and Benefit of Religious Society;* but it was delivered, by request, in St. Mary's Church, at Gloucester, where he had been brought up. Let his own account describe the event:[32] "Last Sunday, in the afternoon, I preached my first sermon in the church of St. Mary-le-Crypt, where I was baptized, and also first received the sacrament of the Lord's Supper. Curiosity, as you may easily guess, drew a large congregation together upon this occasion. The sight at first a little awed me. But I was comforted with a heartfelt sense of the divine presence, and soon found the unspeakable advantage of having been accustomed to public speaking when a boy at school, and of exhorting the prisoners and poor people at their private houses while at the university. By these means I was kept from being daunted overmuch. As I proceeded I perceived the fire kindle, till at last, though so young and amidst a crowd of those who knew me in my childish days, I trust I was enabled to speak with some degree of gospel authority. Some few mocked, but most seemed for the present struck; and I have since heard that a complaint was made to the bishop that I drove fifteen mad the first sermon! The worthy prelate wished that the madness might not be forgotten before next Sunday."

We can not here follow the course of that great and busy career thus so earnestly begun; a mere outline must

[30]Quoted (both) in Tyerman's *Life, vol.* II, p. 478.
[31]*Sermons of Whitefield,* No. V, p. 93.
[32]Quoted by Ryle, p. 35.

suffice. While studying still at Oxford, after taking his degree, Whitefield was asked to preach at different places and churches. In London he filled a number of important pulpits, attracting great crowds and producing wonderful effects. In various country places and among uncultured people it was the same way. Being urged by the Wesleys and invited by General Oglethorpe to go to Georgia, he accepted, but preached in many places, especially Bristol, while waiting. Finally he got off in the latter part of 1737, and began his American ministry. Returning to England in about a year, he was ordained priest, but the clergy looked upon him with distrust as an enthusiast, and he was not invited to preach in the churches. This led him to take up (February, 1739) his wondrous open-air preaching. His first sermon of this sort was preached to the colliers at Kingswood, near Bristol. Henceforth field-preaching was his principal work. Later in that year he went back to America, where he preached from Georgia to New England in a wonderful revival. So several times more (thirteen in all) he crossed the seas, having visited America seven times, dying there at last. But during the times he spent in England he continued his work of preaching to thousands in city and country, including a great and fruitful work in Scotland. In 1741 occurred the sad breach over doctrine between him and Wesley. Whitefield was Calvinist, Wesley Arminian; Whitefield impetuous, Wesley cool and logical; each thoroughly persuaded he was right; both to blame for some details in the controversy. Pass it by; they did. Happily and lovingly they were reconciled before death, and Wesley preached a noble memorial sermon for his friend, and has left in his *Journal* many tributes to his worth.

In September, 1769, Whitefield sailed on his last voyage to America. Occupied during the spring of 1770 with his orphanage at Bethesda and work in Georgia, he began in the summer his traveling work. He preached in many places, and with the usual effects, and pushed slowly his way to New England. Here, at Newburyport, Massachusetts, worn out with labors and grievously suffering with asthma, he came to his journey's end. On Saturday, September 28th, preceding his appointment at

Newburyport for Sunday, he was persuaded to stop and preach in the open air at Exeter. He had ridden some miles already and was so fatigued that one of his friends said to him, "Sir, you are more fit to go to bed than to preach." He assented, but lifting his hands and his face, he gave that ever memorable saying:[33] "Lord Jesus, I am weary in Thy work, but not of Thy work. If I have not yet finished my course, let me go and speak for Thee once more in the fields, seal Thy truth, and come home and die." His prayer was granted. He preached to a great crowd on 2 Cor. 13:5, "Examine yourselves, whether ye be in the faith," and with great fervor and effect. After dinner he went on to Newburyport, to the home of his friend, Mr. Parsons, and there, worn down as he was, while ascending the stair to go to bed, he stopped, with the candle in his hand, and spoke to the gathered company till the candle burned out. In the night his asthma came on more violently than usual, and early that Sunday morning he passed to his coronation.

The inner spirit and outward effects of Whitefield's preaching have already been somewhat indicated. His entire consecration and consuming earnestness, his humility and self-sacrifice, his extraordinary diligence and wearing toil, his joy in his work and conviction of its value to men—all these are known. The remarkable effect of his speaking on his audiences is testified to in a great many ways. That his first sermon was said to have driven fifteen persons wild with excitement is but an introductory instance of powers sustained to the end. He moved great audiences as only a few here and there have been able to do. Thousands, tens of thousands, according to Wesley's statement in his funeral sermon, were converted under his preaching. John Newton said it seemed that he never preached without fruit. Shrewd and thrifty Benjamin Franklin, determined beforehand not to be moved by his appeal for his orphanage, emptied his pockets when it came. Garrick the actor, Hume the skeptic, Chesterfield the worldling, agreed that Whitefield was the most wonderful orator of his age. In a letter to Lady Huntington, Bolingbroke wrote:[34] "Mr. Whitefield is the most extraordinary man in our

[33]Tyerman, II, p. 596, *et al.* [34]Gledstone, p. 246 f.

times. He has the most commanding eloquence I ever heard in any person."

The assemblage of oratorical gifts in Whitefield was truly remarkable. There was evident sincerity and sympathy and good-will which won the hearer at once; there was the high and subtle quality of soul which we call magnetism; there was intensity, sometimes passionate fervor, of earnestness which was often a veritable storm; there was a charm and grace of aspect and action, natural, winsome, irresistible; and with all this a voice of marvelous volume, penetration, and harmony. His splendid imagination and dramatic power were controlled, and therefore really heightened in effect, by the loftiness of his aim and the evident unselfishness of his appeals.

In the light of the well authenticated traditions of Whitefield's eloquence, his printed sermons undoubtedly produce some disappointment in the reader. But two things must be borne in mind: first, that the sermons as we have them were mostly reported, and often very ill reported, by others; few if any were carefully prepared beforehand or accurately reproduced afterwards by Whitefield himself; second, even in case of those which come nearest to being what he actually said, we must remember that no printed sermon could express a preacher of Whitefield's type. Broadus has put the matter felicitously, even if a little too strongly, thus:[35] "The sermons we have were mere preparations, which in free delivery were so filled out with the thoughts suggested in the course of living speech, and so transfigured and glorified by enkindled imagination, as to be utterly different from the dull, cold thing that here lies before us—more different than the blazing meteor from this dark, metallic stone that lies half buried in the earth."

But, making proper allowances, and judging the best of these discourses on their merits, one can not help feeling that critics have gone too far in emphasizing the admitted contrast between the spoken and the printed discourses of the great preacher. On a careful reading they do not seem to be as unworthy of their author as they are often reported to be. Though not profound nor wide in range of thought, they are marked by firm-

[35]*Hist. Preaching*, p. 222.

ness, clarity, and sanity in thinking; by force, clearness, fitness, and often beauty of style; by insight, imagination, pathos, breadth of sympathy, and sincere and fervent feeling. When to these excellent qualities of discourse—as discourse—you add the *plus* of such oratorical qualities as have been described, and the still greater increment of the whole-souled Christian convictions and earnestness of the mighty preacher, some not wholly inadequate notion of his preaching may be gained.

As an example of his simplicity and earnestness in appeal, take some sentences from the close of his sermon on *The Kingdom of God:*[36] "My dear friends, I would preach with all my heart till midnight, to do you good; till I could preach no more. O that this body might hold out to speak more for my dear Redeemer! Had I a thousand lives, had I a thousand tongues, they should be employed in inviting sinners to come to Jesus Christ! Come, then, let me prevail with some of you to come along with me. Come, poor, lost, undone sinner, come just as you are to Christ, and say, If I be damned, I will perish at the feet of Jesus Christ, where never one perished yet. He will receive you with open arms; the dear Redeemer is willing to receive you all. Fly, then, for your lives. The devil is in you while unconverted; and will you go with the devil in your heart to bed this night? God Almighty knows if ever you and I shall see one another again. In one or two days more I must go, and, perhaps, I may never see you again till I meet you at the judgment day. O my dear friends, think of that solemn meeting; think of that important hour, when the heavens shall pass away with a great noise, when the elements shall melt with fervent heat, when the sea and the grave shall be giving up their dead, and all shall be summoned to appear before the great God. . . . I know that many of you come here out of curiosity: though you come only to see the congregation, yet if you come to Jesus Christ, Christ will accept of you. Are there any cursing, swearing soldiers here? Will you come to Jesus Christ, and list yourselves under the banner of the dear Redeemer? You are all welcome to Christ. Are there any little boys or little girls here? Come to

[36]Fish, I, p. 347.

Christ, and He will erect His kingdom in you. . . . All of you, old and young, you that are old and gray-headed, come to Jesus Christ, and you shall be kings and priests to your God. The Lord will abundantly pardon you at the eleventh hour. 'Ho, every one of you that thirsteth!' If there be any of you ambitious of honor, do you want a crown, a scepter? Come to Christ, and the Lord Jesus Christ will give you a kingdom that no man shall take from you."

John Wesley (1703-1791),[37] the founder of Methodism, came of preaching stock. His father, grandfather, and great-grandfather were clergymen of the Church of England, and his mother's father, Dr. Samuel Annesley, was a notable Nonconformist divine of London. Samuel Wesley, the father, had been educated at Oxford, and was rector of Epworth, in Lincolnshire, serving also the parish of Wroote, not far away. Susannah Wesley was one of the great mothers of history. Her training of her children was strict and peculiar. Years after John's childhood she wrote out, at his request, a description of her methods, which he has preserved in his *Journal*,[38] and which makes interesting reading, but is too long to quote here. There were nineteen children, a number of whom died in infancy or early childhood. The eldest,

[37]There is a vast literature on John Wesley and the beginnings of Methodism. Only a few of the best or most necessary books need to be mentioned here. Of biographies those of Whitehead and Moore have an established reputation, but belong to the older method of writing biography; Southey's *Life* has more literary than historic value, and is scarcely fair to Wesley and his work; the monumental work of L. Tyerman, *Life and Times of John Wesley*, 3 vols., New York, 1876, is now the standard authority; more recent is the brief, readable, and discriminating *Life of John Wesley*, by C. T. Winchester, New York, 1906. Wesley's careful and elaborate *Journal* was published in parts during his lifetime, and afterwards collected and published entire in four volumes; recently Mr. P. L. Parker has laid the Christian world under obligations by publishing an abridgment in one volume under the title, *The Heart of Wesley's Journal*, New York (undated). This is referred to henceforth as "Journal." See also Ryle, *op. cit.*, p. 64 ff. Of Wesley's *Sermons* various editions are accessible. The one most used for this study is that edited by T. O. Summers and published by the Southern Methodist Concern at Nashville, Tenn. See also sermon in Fish, I, p. 319, and another in *World's Great Sermons*, III, p. 73.

[38]P. 93 ff.

Samuel, became a teacher of distinction, and was a help in many ways to his younger brothers. The sisters were intelligent and interesting, but in one way or another were unhappy in their married lives and a care to the family. Charles, five years younger than John, was his beloved associate in after years, and the author of well-known hymns. But the most famous of the remarkable family was John, who was born the 28th (O. S. 17th) of June, 1703, at the Epworth rectory. He owed much to his remarkable mother, both for his native gifts of mind and character, and for the direction and development of these in childhood and early manhood. His correspondence with his mother during the time he was preparing for the ministry did much to decide the principles on which he took up the work and the type of his theological thinking. Mrs. Wesley had thought through the theological systems of the day and had adopted decidedly the Arminian views.

After his careful home training, John was sent to the famous Charterhouse School in London, where he remained five years, and was a successful student. In 1720 he entered Christ Church College, Oxford, and took the regular course, finishing in 1725. The following year, much to the delight of his fond old father, he was elected a Fellow of Lincoln College, which enabled him for some years after to continue his residence and studies at Oxford, with some intermissions. How diligently he improved his privileges is well known. He became a good scholar in Hebrew, Latin, and Greek, in theology, and in other branches of learning. French and German he mastered later. This good foundation, together with the studious habit acquired, enabled him during the busy years of his later life to keep up his reading to an extent that would have been impossible to an untrained man.

John Wesley had received careful Christian nurture in his home, but during his boyhood manifested no special religious or irreligious tendencies. But when on the eve of graduating at Oxford, in 1725, he began to take more earnest views of religion and to consider if it were his duty to enter the ministry. He read books of devotion, prayed much, corresponded seriously with his parents and his brother Samuel, and finally decided to consecrate himself to God and to the work of preaching. Was this his conversion? So far as conversion is a surrender of self to Christ for His service, it was; but it was not till thirteen years later that Wesley came to that full sense of personal trust in Christ and of joy in the pardon of sin which are necessary to a full Christian experience. But there is no doubt of the entire sincerity of his devotion of himself to his Lord at the earlier date, and of his serious pursuit, even if with mistaken views, of personal holiness. So, in 1725, John Wesley was ordained a deacon in the Anglican Church, and entered on the life of a preacher of the Christian faith. At first his preaching, like his own life and experience, lacked the element of true gospel grace and power. It was outwardly conformable to the doctrines of his church, sought to promote piety in the hearers, and was clear and correct in style, as became an Oxford scholar; but the note of spiritual power and the effect of spiritual fruitage were wanting. It was about the time of his election to the Lincoln fellowship that he wrote to his brother Samuel the words that have become historic: "Leisure and I have taken leave of one another. I propose to be busy as long as I live." Passing words—significant prophecy—tremendous fulfillment! While continuing his studies at Oxford, he obtained permission to spend some time as his father's assistant at Epworth and Wroote, being ordained to the priesthood in the meantime. After two years or more he was recalled to the duties of his fellowship at Oxford, and entered the "Methodist Club," which had been formed by his younger brother Charles and some other earnest-minded young men as a society for mutual help in piety and the practice of charity. John at once became the leader of the group, and the nickname of this association of students has been strangely perpetuated in the history of Methodism. This first stage of Wesley's ministry continued ten years, when a great change occurred in his life.

In 1735, after the death of their father, John and Charles Wesley accepted an urgent invitation of General Oglethorpe to go with him as chaplains and teachers to his colony of Georgia. Charles soon returned, but John remained over two years. He was at this time a rigid ascetic, both for himself and others, his spiritual life was not yet ripened, and he had much to learn in practical judgment. His mission was regarded by himself as a failure; perhaps it was not so much so as he thought, and it is certain that, along with some serious trials and disappointments, it was an important stage in his own development. Coming home to England in 1738, he just missed seeing Whitefield, who was outward bound on his first voyage to America. Wesley was depressed, but seeking for light, when he fell in with Peter Böhler, a German, who had come to London to establish a Moravian society. It was under this influence that, one night at the meeting of the little society, he "felt his heart strangely warmed;" the cloud that had so long enveloped him lifted, and he entered into assured peace and joy in Christ as his Saviour. From henceforth his life and preaching were different. After some months, including a visit to the Continent, he became settled in his views and desirous of engaging in the work of preaching. But the London clergy were suspicious and prejudiced, and it was only occasionally that he and Charles were allowed to preach in the churches. No settled places were offered them. They worked with the Moravian society in prayer-meetings and in study of the Bible. Near the end of 1738 Whitefield came back from Georgia to receive ordination as priest in the English Church, and to solicit funds for his orphanage near Savannah. He was overjoyed to find his friends in the possession of their new experience of grace, and they took counsel together as to what their future should be. Whitefield was denied access to most churches, but on occasion of his being invited and attempting to preach at St. Margaret's, Westminster, a quarrel occurred. It was then that Whitefield determined to preach in the open air, at Kingswood, near Bristol. He urgently invited John Wesley to come and join him in the work; but Wesley was extremely reluctant to preach outside of a church. Finally, however, he came to it, and on Monday, April 2, 1739, he preached his first open-air sermon to a crowd of about three thousand people at Kingswood. This was the beginning of a campaign of fifty-two years.

A word must now be said about the nature of Wesley's life-work. For a long time there had existed within the Church of England numbers of societies for the study of the Bible and mutual edification of the members. The Moravian Society in Fetter Lane, London, was of more recent date. Wesley continued some months to worship and work with them; but differences inevitably arose. Moreover, some twenty or more persons came to Wesley and asked him to form them into a society for study and prayer, under his direction. Thus he withdrew gradually from the Moravians and started societies, or took hold of those already existing, in various parts of the kingdom as he traveled and preached. The work grew, and in process of time these societies were thoroughly organized and the Methodist system was in full working order; but it was not till after Wesley's death that the societies separated from the parent Church.

Coming back to the beginnings of Wesley's itinerant ministry and the first movements toward organizing his societies, we find him, under date of June 11, 1739, recording in his *Journal* an extract from a letter he wrote to a friend who had criticised his course. Let some quotations be noted:[39] "As to your advice that I should settle in college,[40] I have no business there, having now no office and no pupils. And whether the other branch of your proposal be expedient for me, viz., to accept of a cure of souls, it will be time enough to consider when one is offered to me. But in the meantime you think I ought to sit still, because otherwise I should invade another's office. . . . God in Scripture commands me, according to my power to instruct the ignorant, reform the wicked, confirm the virtuous. Man forbids me to do this in another's parish; that is, in effect to do it at all, seeing I have now no parish of my own, nor probably ever shall. Whom then shall I hear, God or man? . . . I look upon all the world as my parish; thus far I mean that, in whatever part of it I am, I judge it meet, right, and my bounden duty to declare unto all that are willing to hear the glad tidings of salvation. This is the work which I know God has called me to; and sure I am that His blessing attends it."

[39]*Journal*, p. 55.

[40]He probably means Lincoln College, Oxford, where he still held his fellowship.

We can not follow here the details of the busy and fruitful years of Wesley's life from these beginnings to about 1783, when the *Journal* gives some indications of declining strength, which increase till, in the record of June 28, 1788 (his eighty-fifth birthday), he gracefully accepts the situation and admits that at last he begins to feel the infirmities of old age! How crowded were the years of his long service with astonishing labors and successes, his own wonderful *Journal* is the best witness. Written with straightforward simplicity, without boasting or seeking for effect, it is a record of toils and a revelation of character suited to awaken wonder, affection, and gratitude. He preached in all parts of the kingdom—England, Scotland, Wales, and Ireland—in cities, towns, villages; sometimes in churches, but most commonly out-of-doors; sometimes to thousands, and sometimes to a few gathered in private homes or in the societies. His favorite hour of preaching was five o'clock in the morning, so that the working people could come before the day's work began. On Sundays he usually preached three times, and often added other services of prayer and exposition. His health and endurance were surprising, improved with age, and lasted, as we have seen, to his eighty-fifth year. Under date of April 21, 1770, he records that up to that time he had ridden horseback above a hundred thousand miles. A life so filled with action necessarily abounded in incidents—some wonderful, many commonplace, some filled with adventure and danger, many marked only by the daily grind of duty done, some joyous and inspiring, some comfortless and dull, some pathetic, and some amusing. Augustine Birrell has described the *Journal* as "a book full of plots and plays and novels, which quivers with life, and is crammed full of character."[41] In addition to the story of his evangelistic labors and successes, we must remember the vast work of organization, superintendence, and attention to details of every sort that Wesley performed in connection with his societies; the great number of tracts, treatises, letters, pamphlets, books, sermons, that he wrote, besides the *Journal;* his frequent and sometimes vexatious and painful controversies, alike with

[41]Quoted in introd. to *Journal,* p. XVI.

friends and foes; and the unceasing demands upon his time and patience for personal interviews.

Nor in candor should we omit some reference to Wesley's uniformly unfortunate love affairs, and his unhappy marriage. There was an early affair while he was at college which seems not to have amounted to anything; but the episode of his courtship and rejection at Savannah does no credit to his judgment or proper feeling, even granting that the girl and her friends were chiefly to blame. Later the unfortunate affair with Grace Murray, a young widow, inferior to Wesley in every way, who jilted him for one of his friends, John Bennett, partly (it is said) by Charles Wesley's advice, left a sore which did not quickly heal. But most painful of all was his marriage, when approaching fifty years of age, to a widow with two children and some property; a woman in every way unworthy of him, who made his life miserable with nagging and foolish jealousy, and even—it must be feared—with positive abuse and cruelties, until she finally, after twenty years of married life, left him, never to return. Of course it would not be fair to acquit any man of blame in such a series of mistakes, but it appears on the whole that in these regrettable affairs Wesley was more sinned against than sinning.

Toward the end, and notwithstanding increasing infirmities, the record of labors continues. The old man is still traveling, writing, teaching, preaching, making plans and appointments for the future. On his last birthday (June 28, 1790) he makes note of his decline, but with no tone of complaint. In the last entry of his *Journal,* Sunday, October 24, 1790, he says: "I explained to a numerous congregation in Spitalfields Church 'The whole armor of God.' St. Paul's, Shadwell, was still more crowded in the afternoon, while I enforced that important truth, 'One thing is needful;' and I hope many, even then, resolved to choose the better part." His last sermon was preached February 23, 1791; his last letter was written the next day—to Wilberforce, encouraging him in his crusade against slavery. Two days later he took his bed, and gradually and peacefully sank to his rest on March 2, 1791, being nearly eighty-eight years old. Among his last sayings, caught and treasured by his attendants, the two best remembered are his singing, "I 'll praise my Maker while I 've breath," and the good words of cheer, "The best of all is, God is with us."

The character of John Wesley, like that of all great men, was a growth and not the achievement of a day. There was excellent material, admirable training, severe testing, great opportunity, tireless diligence, indomitable will—how could he help becoming great? Flawless he was not; there was enough of the common and inevitable human frailty to put a check on undue hero-worship. A tendency to self-esteem occasionally crops out in his *Journal* and other writings, but it was firmly held down by a real humility before God and "saving common sense" in his dealings with men. More in evidence was that phase of this fault which shows itself in pride of opinion, love of rule even to being overbearing at times. Had he not been a man of admirable temper and self-control, this disposition would have led him into graver faults and severer trials than it really did. The singular bad judgment he displayed in his love affairs and some other dealings with women must be assigned to weakness and not to fault. He was unfortunate and lacking in tact, but not evil-minded. A more serious weakness was his tendency to superstition and fanaticism, as shown (among other things) in his more than half-belief in ghosts and witches, and in his use of the lot on several important occasions. But grave as these and other faults were, they seem little and venial when set beside the undeniable and excellent traits of Wesley's character. His purity of soul, his deep experience of divine grace, his utter consecration to God, his quiet but determined courage, constancy, and endurance, his spotless integrity, his splendid self-mastery, his courtesy, gentleness, refinement of manner and of mind, his punctuality, diligence, and decision in his work, his cheerfulness, hopefulness, and sweetness of temper, his winsome personality, along with his masterful genius and dominating will, all make up an assemblage of qualities which placed and keep him high among the great characters of history.

Wesley's equipment for his task was adequate. He had a fine and well preserved constitution and abounding health. Though small in stature, he had an unusually handsome face and a dignified figure and carriage. His Oxford training counted all through life—Hebrew, Greek, Latin, German, French were at his command; his knowledge of history and literature was ample; and his reading in philosophy and all branches of theology was wide. He read on horseback and at odd times more than the average man with the best facilities! His organization of his societies was clear, well-defined, compact, and his enlistment and direction of workers remarkable. The massive power of Methodism as a religious force is the best tribute to his splendid administrative capacity.

Wesley's preaching was eminently characteristic of the man. As to contents it was Arminian in theology, evangelical in doctrine, and full of Scripture; in thought it was rich, logical, clear, and strong; in imagination not deficient, yet not especially marked; in feeling intense but not vehement; in style clear and sweet, without notable eloquence or passion; not so stilted as was the usual manner of his age, and yet to our taste lacking in ease and simplicity. In delivery he was calm, but there was a subdued intensity and glow that powerfully moved his hearers.

One of the best and best-known of Wesley's sermons is that on *The Great Assize*.[42] It was preached at the time of the assizes, or, as we should say, court, held before Sir Edward Clive, in Bedford, March 10, 1758, and published by request. It is a good specimen of his manner, exhibiting his logical order, careful thinking, ample knowledge, good style, chastened imagination, and deep feeling. The text is Romans 14:10, "We shall all stand before the judgment seat of Christ." The introduction and division are as follows: "How many circumstances concur to raise the awfulness of the present solemnity! The general concourse of people of every age, sex, rank, and condition of life, willingly or unwillingly gathered together, not only from the neighboring, but from distant parts; criminals, speedily to be brought forth, and having no way to escape; officers, waiting in their various posts, to execute the orders which shall be

[42]Fish, I, 319 ff.

given; and the representatives of our gracious sovereign, whom we so highly reverence and honor. The occasion, likewise, of this assembly adds not a little to the solemnity of it: to hear and determine causes of every kind, some of which are of the most important nature; on which depends no less than life or death; death that uncovers the face of eternity! It was, doubtless, in order to increase the serious sense of these things, and not in the minds of the vulgar only, that the wisdom of our forefathers did not disdain to appoint even several minute circumstances of this solemnity. For these also, by means of the eye or ear, may more deeply affect the heart: and when viewed in this light, trumpets, staves, apparel, are no longer trifling or insignificant; but subservient, in their kind and degree, to the most valuable ends of society. But, awful as this solemnity is, one far more awful is at hand. For yet a little while, and 'we shall all stand before the judgment seat of Christ.' 'For, as I live, saith the Lord, every knee shall bow to Me, and every tongue shall confess to God.' And in that day 'every one of us shall give account of himself to God.' Had all men a deep sense of this, how effectually would it secure the interests of society! For what more forcible motive can be conceived to the practice of genuine morality, to a steady pursuit of solid virtue, and a uniform walking in justice, mercy, and truth? What could strengthen our hands in all that is good, and deter us from all that is evil, like a strong conviction of this, 'The Judge standeth at the door;' and we are shortly to stand before Him? It may not, therefore, be improper or unsuitable to the design of the present assembly to consider:

I. The chief circumstances which will precede our standing before the judgment seat of Christ.

II. The judgment itself; and

III. A few of the circumstances which will follow it." After clearing and fully discussing each of these heads, the preacher applies his subject powerfully to the various classes before him, and concludes as follows: "O, who can stand before the face of the great God, even our Saviour Jesus Christ? See! see! He cometh! He maketh the clouds His chariot! He rideth upon the wings of the wind! A devouring fire goeth before Him, and after Him a flame burneth! See! He sitteth upon His throne, clothed with light as with a garment, arrayed with majesty and honor! Behold! His eyes are as a flame of fire, His voice as the sound of many waters! How will ye escape? Will ye call to the mountains to fall on you, the rocks to cover you? Alas, the mountains themselves, the rocks, the earth, the heavens, are just ready to flee away! Can ye prevent the sentence? Wherewith? With all the substance of thy house, with thousands of gold and silver? Blind wretch! Thou camest naked from thy mother's womb, and more naked into eternity. Hear the Lord, the Judge! 'Come, ye blessed of My Father! inherit the kingdom prepared for you from the foundation of the world.' Joyful sound! How widely different from that voice which echoes through the expanse of heaven, 'Depart, ye cursed, into everlasting fire, prepared for the devil and his angels!' And who is he that can prevent or retard the full execution of either sentence? Vain hope! Lo, hell is moved from beneath to receive those who are ripe for destruction! And the everlasting doors lift up their heads, that the heirs of glory may come in!

" 'What manner of persons, then, ought we to be, in all holy conversation and godliness?' We know it can not be long before the Lord will descend with the voice of the archangel, and the trumpet of God; when every one of us shall appear before Him, and give an account of his own works. 'Wherefore, behold; seeing ye look for these things,' seeing you know He will come, and will not tarry, 'be diligent, that ye may be found of Him in peace, without spot and blemish.' Why should ye not? Why should one of you be found on the left hand at His appearing? He willeth not that any should perish, but that all should come to repentance; by repentance, to faith in a bleeding Lord; by faith, to spotless love; to the full image of God renewed in the heart, and producing all holiness of conversation. Can you doubt of this, when you remember the Judge of all is likewise the Saviour of all? Hath He not bought you with His own blood, that ye might not perish, but have everlasting life? O, make proof of His mercy, rather than His justice; of His love, rather than the thunder of His power! He is not far from every one of us; and He is now come, not to condemn, but to save the world. He standeth in the midst! Sinner, doth He not now, even now, knock at the door of thy heart? O, that thou mayest know, at least in this thy day, the things that belong unto thy peace! O, that you may now give yourselves to Him who gave Himself for you, in humble faith, in holy, active, patient love! So shall ye rejoice with exceeding joy in His day, when He cometh in the clouds of heaven!"

Of the associates and fellow-workers of Wesley there are a number whose character and works justly entitle them to more extended notice than is feasible in this account. Charles Wesley (1708-1788), younger by five years than John, and, like him, educated at Oxford, was for a short time associated with his brother in the work in Georgia, became also the subject of a "conversion" or at least a deeper realization of spiritual things, engaged in the itinerant ministry with John, but married and gradually left off that mode of work. He was the "sweet singer" of Methodism, and left many well-known and precious hymns to enrich Christian hymnody. The Perronet family, of whom Edward, the author of *All hail the power of Jesus' name,* was the most important, also furnished several preachers to the movement. Besides these there were several lay preachers of notable gifts, of whom the most remarkable were John Cennick (also a hymn writer), Thomas Maxfield, and John Bennett. Thomas Coke and Francis Asbury belong rather to the history of missions and of American preaching. After the Wesleys themselves, the most important man among the early Methodists was John William Fletcher (1729-1785),[43] vicar of Madeley. He was a French-Swiss by birth, the family name being De la Fléchière. He was educated chiefly at Geneva, but came to England as a tutor. He learned the English language very thoroughly, and—what was more signal—fell in with the Methodists, and was led to a deep experience of grace. Being ordained in 1757, he preached as opportunity of-

[43] *Life,* by Joseph Benson, 1817; good account in Ryle, p. 385 ff.; *Works* in 7 vols., 12mo, 1826.

fered, and became, in 1760, vicar of Madeley, a rough mining town in Shropshire, where he did the work of his life. But, about this same time, Lady Huntington established her seminary for training preachers at Trevecca, in Wales, and engaged Fletcher to have the oversight of the work there, as far as his duties at Madeley permitted. His visits to the institution were frequent, and his influence on the students was great and wholesome. He also worked with the Wesleys and Berridge in evangelistic labors and journeys as much as he could. Fletcher was a man of pure and lofty character, a devoted pastor, as well as ceaseless toiler in other spheres of duty. He was an ardent Arminian in theology, and was drawn into many controversies. His famous *Checks to Antinomianism* was long the standard of Wesleyan theology in opposition to Calvinism, and still remains one of the classics of Methodist theological and polemical literature. But notwithstanding his doctrinal battles, Fletcher was a man of deep devotional nature and spirit, lovable and beloved. In the seventh volume of his *Works* there are nine sermons in full and thirty outlines. Their doctrine is evangelical to the core on sin and atonement, Arminian in the interpretation of the divine sovereignty and the danger of falling from grace, firm and unequivocal in moral and spiritual teaching, without going to the extreme of perfectionism. In form the sermons have usually a simple outline, though a little more elaborate than is now the taste. The style is clear, sweet, and winsome, remarkable English for a foreigner to have written. There is no exuberance of imagination or marked fertility of illustration, though these are not wholly wanting. The tone is deeply spiritual, and the method chiefly hortatory, with some argument and exposition.

There was a relatively small but important group of Nonconformist preachers throughout the eighteenth century, who have left a broad mark on the religious thought and life of English-speaking people. Here we must place the gifted, pious, and eccentric Rowland Hill (1745-1833),[44] who, though ordained as a deacon in the Established Church, could never induce any bishop to put

[44] *Life of the Rev. Rowland Hill, A. M.*, by the Rev. Edwin Sidney, A. M., 2d Amer. ed., New York, 1835.

him into the priesthood; so that he occupies a somewhat anomalous position, but is rather to be reckoned with the Dissenters. He was born of an old and honorable family in Shropshire who have furnished several distinguished men to English history. As a child Rowland was bright and humorous, but also deeply inclined to religion. He was converted under the leading of his pious elder brother, Richard. Educated at Eton and Cambridge, he enjoyed and wisely used the best advantages. During his career at Cambridge he was active in religious work, dealing personally with his fellow-students, and working among the poor, somewhat like the Methodists at Oxford. He was invited by good old Berridge to visit him at Everton, which he did frequently and to his great profit spiritually. The college authorities were opposed to Hill's methods, particularly his lay preaching. But he received encouragement from Whitefield, Berridge, and others, and pursued his way, being fully persuaded that he was doing the will of God. Harder yet to bear was the opposition of his father and other members of the family. On his graduation at Cambridge he applied for ordination, but was refused by six bishops successively to whom he made application. So Hill determined to pursue his course of itinerant evangelization. His father reduced his allowance almost to the starving point, but still the heroic young man persevered. He preached all over the kingdom, wherever he could find hearers—and he usually attracted crowds wherever he went. Of course, he found friends and helpers among those who valued his work, as was the case with Wesley and Whitefield and their fellow-workers. But his position was trying and precarious. He found an admirable helper and sympathizer in his wife, who encouraged him in his work, but recommended prudence and tact. When Hill was about to proceed to his degree of M. A. at Cambridge, he again made application for ordination, and was so far successful as to be inducted into the diaconate of the English Church. He obtained the curacy of Kingston, a small parish in Somersetshire, which he held for many years. Meantime he pursued his itinerant ministry wherever he could, and his preaching was very acceptable and fruitful.

Finally his converts, admirers, and friends erected for him the famous Surrey Chapel in London, and this remained the scene of his labors to the end of his life, which extended over into the first third of the nineteenth century.

Rowland Hill was greatly loved as a man and pastor, and his work was blessed to the conversion of thousands. He was a man of marked eccentricities of speech and sometimes of conduct, but these were no blemish on his character or reputation—only occasional infractions of good taste. His humor was spontaneous and natural, sometimes irrepressible; but it often enlightened and helped his discourse, rather than marred it. The depth of his piety, the strength of his mind, and the unselfishness of his devotion to the cause of Christ and humanity could not be questioned. His preaching was marked by the character of the man—earnest and evangelical, but original and often quaint. He preached without manuscript, and often from the suggestion of the moment, but his well-stored mind, rich experience of religion and life, and responsiveness to environment more than made up for lack of careful writing. Sheridan is said to have remarked, "I go to hear Rowland Hill because what he says comes hot from the heart." His few printed sermons naturally conveyed little notion of the actual man. His vivid imagination, quick and tender sympathy, and earnest feeling, relieved by occasional flashes of wit and humor, made him effective and often eloquent as an extempore preacher.

Among the Independents we have the name of the great and famous hymn writer, Isaac Watts (1674-1748).[45] Besides writing hymns and being the author of useful text-books on logic and other subjects, Dr. Watts was a preacher of well-established reputation and influence, though not of the highest rank. Southampton was the place of his birth. Here his excellent father taught school, and suffered persecution, even to imprisonment, for his nonconformity. A pathetic story relates how the wife sat at the prison gate with the puny infant Isaac

[45]*Complete Works,* 6 vols., quarto, London, 1810 (ed. of Doddridge and Jennings), and separately; *Discourses on the Love of God,* London, 1770; *Life* by E. Paxton Hood.

in her arms, waiting to see her conscientious and faithful husband. The child was feeble in body, but great in brain. He was carefully taught by his father, then at school in Southampton, then at Stoke-Newington, in London. After school, Watts became tutor in the family of Sir John Hartopp, a distinguished Nonconformist, who attended a dissenting Church in Mark Lane under the care of Dr. Chauncy. Watts joined this Church, became a teacher in it, then (1702) its pastor. The church was removed to a better location, and an assistant was employed to do most of the work; but Dr. Watts remained pastor all his life, preaching as often as his feeble health permitted. Owing to his weak health, he was invited by Mr. Thomas Abney, a wealthy member of his flock, to visit him indefinitely at his home at Theobalds, near London. The visit lasted almost a lifetime; for the lovable poet-preacher became an inmate of the home, for whose children at first he wrote those "Divine and Moral Songs" that for several generations made his name a household word in thousands of Christian homes the world over.

The sermons of Dr. Watts are not marked by the poetic quality and fervor that his hymns would lead us to expect. But they are clear, readable, and instructive. They would not awaken much interest now except as coming from him, for the particular modes of thought and expression which they exemplify belong to their own times rather than to ours, and the style and analysis alike are somewhat labored and heavy. The sermons usually end with a devout meditation or prayer.

High among the Independents stood the learned and evangelical Philip Doddridge (1702-1751),[46] pastor and teacher at Northampton. Doddridge was born at London, the twentieth child of his parents. But of all the children only an older sister and himself survived infancy. He was of feeble constitution, but was tenderly nurtured, both in body and mind, by his pious mother. Left an orphan when about thirteen years old, he was kindly cared for by friends, and properly educated. The Duchess of Bedford became so interested in the promis-

[46]Various edd. of the *Works* in whole, and of the *Expositor,* and *Rise and Progress,* separately. *Life* by Job Orton.

ing youth that she offered to educate him at either University, but it was on condition that he should enter the ministry in the Anglican Church, and Doddridge conscientiously declined. Friends provided for his entering the Academy for Dissenters at Kibworth, near Leicester. Here he was taught, and later himself became teacher as well as pastor. He served awhile also at Harborough; but, in 1729, was called to Northampton. He took his students with him there, and labored for about twenty years as teacher, pastor, and writer. Many young men, especially of the Independents, were trained by him for the ministry. But his health gave way in the too severe strain he put upon his strength. Hoping for help from the climate, he went to Lisbon, but died there a short time after his arrival.

Among Doddridge's writings are a number of excellent and still highly valued hymns, his famous *Family Expositor*—a paraphrase and commentary on the New Testament—and his long useful, devotional treatise, *The Rise and Progress of Religion in the Soul.* Along with these he published at intervals several volumes of sermons, among them a thoughtful series of discourses to the young. Doddridge was exemplary in pastoral work and in preaching, and was greatly and justly beloved by his flock. His sermons are judicious rather than weighty in thought, evangelical in theology, clear in order and style, but with no special unction or eloquence.

The Baptists have three men of especial distinction in this epoch, first of whom in the order of time is the somewhat erratic but gifted Robert Robinson (1735-1790).[47] He was of rather humble origin, his father being an excise man. His mother was well connected, but unhappily married. The boy was brought up in hardships, but was bright and ambitious, and acquired some learning. Apprenticed to a hairdresser in London, he improved his spare time in reading. Hearing Whitefield preach, he was greatly moved and interested in Methodism. He began as a lay preacher among the Methodists, but set up an independent congregation at Norwich, soon became convinced of the correctness of

[47] *Miscellaneous Works,* with *Memoir* (by B. F.), London, 1807.

Baptist views, and became a member of that body. He had married without much prospect of a living, but was called to a small congregation of Baptists in Cambridge. The salary was so small that he was forced to do other things for a support, and in the meantime his love of writing asserted itself and he wrote some productions. He had mastered French by some means, and published translations of Saurin's sermons and of Claude's *Essay on a Sermon.* These literary labors brought him some reputation as scholar, but not much money, and he became a farmer and trader. Besides, he sometimes preached at other places than Cambridge. His hymn, *Come, Thou Fount of every blessing,* gives him more fame than all his writings, though these were important in their day. He preached without notes, and was heard with pleasure and profit. A few of his sermons were written out and printed, and though they show talent and varied learning, they are nearly all on moral subjects and have now little of interest or value. Robinson did not escape some criticism, both as to doctrine (thought to entertain some Arian opinions) and conduct; but perhaps without entire justice. He was a remarkably gifted man, and had also many admirable traits of character.

Andrew Fuller (1754-1815),[48] the eminent theologian and missionary leader, was also a pastor of excellent gifts and a preacher of strong though not shining qualities. He was born, the son of a farmer, near Ely, in Cambridgeshire, at the little village of Wicken. His parents were Dissenters and attended the Baptist Church presided over by Mr. Eve, a high Calvinistic preacher. Andrew became in early youth subject to decided religious impressions, and also became dissatisfied with the extreme type of theology to which he had to listen in the preaching of Mr. Eve. Thus early he showed his aptitude for theological thinking. By little and little young Fuller was led to take up the work of public exposition of Scripture, and his pastor having resigned, he often led the public worship, until finally the little church invited him to be ordained and take the pastorate. He had been converted and baptized in 1769, and though

[48]*Complete Works* with *Memoir,* by Andrew G. Fuller (his son), Am. ed., 2 vols., Boston, 1833.

without college instruction, he had been a diligent and thoughtful student, and was not ill-equipped for the humble beginning which he now was led to make. His self-improvement was rapid and thorough. His salary was distressingly small, and he was forced to do other things to take care of his family. Under such seemingly untoward circumstances this really great man was formed for the work he had to do. In 1782, reluctantly and after much urging, he accepted the call of the Baptist Church at Kettering, where he discharged the duties of pastor till his death. Here he studied, wrote, attended to his flock, and took great part in the religious movements of the day, especially in organizing and helping on the Baptist Foreign Missionary Society. His writings had great influence, being widely read, not only in his own denomination, but more generally. Both Princeton and Yale Colleges conferred on him the degree of D. D., but with characteristic modesty he declined to use the title. He was a careful and judicious thinker, and a strong expounder of the Scriptures.

In Fuller's *Works* there are many discourses, outlines of sermons, and a few sermons written out in full. Characteristically he was an expository preacher as to method, and a solid preacher as to thought. There is little warmth—no heat; imagination is scarcely in evidence at all; and "flights of eloquence" nowhere appear. The sermons on themes are orderly, discriminating, logical; the expositions (on Genesis, the Apocalypse, the Sermon on the Mount, etc.) are careful and plain, in homily form; the style is clear and even, but lacks grace, fervor, and movement. Excellent good sense and timeliness for their day characterize the writings of Fuller, and they did good and enduring service; but they have not enough literary quality to make them standards, and their adaptation to contemporary thought has, of course, passed away with their own times.

William Carey (1761-1834)[49] is a name most highly honored in the annals of the foreign missionary enter-

[49]See *Carey, Marshman, and Ward,* by J. C. Marshman, London, 1864; there is also an older *Life* by his son; *Biographical and Literary Notices of William Carey* (with a bibliography of his writings), by John Taylor, London, 1886.

prise, and he claims mention in the history of preaching because of one famous sermon which is forever associated with his name and cause. Carey was of humble parentage and born in Northamptonshire. Both his father and grandfather had served the parish as clerks, and Carey himself in early life was an Anglican; but with his conversion to God came also his conversion to Baptist views, and he was baptized by Dr. John Ryland in 1773. Four years later he became pastor of a little Church at Moulton, but supported himself and family by mending shoes. Later he became pastor at Leicester. His remarkable aptitude for acquiring languages went on with his other work, and he became a great self-taught scholar. After the organization of the Baptist Missionary Society, in 1792, he went as its first missionary to India, and never returned to England. His great work as a missionary pioneer and scholar in the Indian languages does not properly belong here. As a preacher he probably would not have attained great distinction, but it fell to him to preach the annual sermon before the Nottinghamshire Baptist Association, which met at Nottingham in May, 1792. He had long been thinking and praying over the religious needs of the heathen and of the duty of Christians to give the gospel to all the world. He had published his tract on *The Obligation of Christians to Use Means for the Conversion of the Heathen.*[50] His soul was aflame with the subject. He took as his text the words in Isa. 54:2, 3, and deduced from them the famous discourse on the theme: "Expect great things from God; attempt great things for God." The sermon produced a profound impression, and under the lead of himself and Andrew Fuller, who nobly seconded his efforts, the great modern missionary movement was inaugurated. This famous historic sermon was not published; it is doubtful if it ever was written out. It is not found in any list of Carey's writings that has been examined for this work. Its thought is no doubt elaborated in the pamphlet already mentioned, which has been often republished. It is a notable instance of the effect of one sermon,

[50]Many times republished, recently in *Highway of Mission Thought,* ed. T. B. Ray, Nashville, 1907—a collection of missionary sermons.

and yet the sermon itself is preserved only in its abundant fruits.

Passing from the English pulpit to that of Scotland,[51] we have to notice that the Revolution of 1688, the settlement of William and Mary as king and queen, and the Act of Toleration were events of great moment in the religious history of Scotland, as well as England. The Act of Settlement distinctly allowed Presbyterianism as the established religion of the country, and thus the long and fatal efforts of the Stuarts to establish episcopacy in Scotland fell down. But the conditions were mixed; the Scottish Parliament, before its discontinuance in 1707, had passed some rules not altogether acceptable to the rigid Presbyterians. This was true, also, of the first meeting of the General Assembly. The easy entrance of Episcopal clergymen—many of them unfit—into the Presbyterian ministry created much discontent. Then the establishment of patronage, that is, the appointment of ministers over parishes, not by election or consent of the congregation, but either by lay or church authority, was a great sore. This tension and division of feeling was emphasized by a theological controversy between the stricter and more liberal groups, especially over a theological treatise called the *Marrow of Modern Divinity*—hence called the "Marrow Controversy." The evangelical party defended the book, the worldly party attacked it. All these causes, combined with some others, led to a secession from the Church, led by the Erskine brothers. This secession left the evangelical party within the Established Church weakened in their conflict with the liberalistic wing, which came to be known as Moderatism. The popular or evangelical party stood for the old truth, the old ways, and an intenser religious life and discipline; while the Moderates were more cold, worldly, literary; preaching morals rather than the gospel. They were the counterpart of the German Rationalists and the English Latitudinarians. The preaching and preachers, accordingly,

[51]See W. G. Blaikie, *The Preachers of Scotland,* pp. 184-267; The St. Giles Lectures (First Series) on *The Scottish Church,* Lec. IX, *The Church of the Eighteenth Century,* by John Tulloch; also McKerrow's *History of the Secession Church;* works and biographies of the preachers named.

fall into two groups: Evangelicals (including Secessionists), and Moderates.

Among the early Evangelicals the leading figure is that of Thomas Boston (1676-1732).[52] He was born at Dunse, where his father was an intense Presbyterian and suffered for his principles. Thomas when a boy spent some of his time in prison with his father. He was converted at the age of twelve under a sermon from Henry Erskine, father of the two famous brothers. Boston grew in Christian experience. By hard endeavors and his father's help he managed to get to Edinburgh for his collegiate and theological education. He then taught awhile as tutor, was licensed, and began preaching; finally was ordained, and settled as pastor over a small country parish in 1699. Boston's autobiography reveals much of that introspection and study of frames and states which we find in many of the journals of Christians of that age. He was diligent and successful in his pastoral work, and preached to the edification of his people. He married a fine and lovely girl, concerning whom, after thirty years of married life, he speaks with a tenderness and enthusiasm beautiful to read. In 1700 Boston found in the cottage of one of his flock that famous book, *The Marrow of Modern Divinity.* He was pleased with its teaching, and induced a friend to publish a new edition of it. The book, as we have seen, was unacceptable to the liberal party and occasioned a great dispute, in which Boston took conspicuous part. In May, 1707, he was called to Ettrick, where he remained the rest of his life. Here he was full of earnest, spiritual, and fruitful labors. In 1712, by the advice of a brother minister who had seen and approved his notes, Boston was advised to prepare for publication his series of sermons on *The Fourfold State of Man.* He completed writing them out in a year, but the book was not published till about 1719. It became and long remained a famous and much-read classic of evangelical teaching. In the opening paragraph of the first sermon, Boston thus clearly states his theme: "There are four things very necessary to be known by all that would see heaven. First, what man was in the

[52]*Select Works* (with *Life* based on his autobiography) of Thos. Boston, ed. by A. S. Patterson, 1847.

state of innocence as God made him. Secondly, what he is in the state of corrupt nature as he had unmade himself. Thirdly, what he must be in the state of grace as 'created in Christ Jesus unto good works,' if ever he be made a partaker of the 'inheritance of the saints in life.' And, lastly, what he should be in his eternal state as made by the Judge of all, either perfectly happy or completely miserable, and that forever. These are weighty points that touch the vitals of practical godliness; from which most men and even many professors, in these dregs of time, are quite estranged. I design, therefore, under the divine conduct to open up these things and apply them." The sermons exhibit a firm and uncompromising grasp and exposition of the evangelical type of theology. In form they are scholastic to the limit, with a number of heads, divisions, points, doctrines, applications, uses, improvements, etc., in the most approved style. But with all this excess of analysis there is clear unity of theme, with completeness and mastery of treatment. There is want of imagination, illustration, and glow, but not of feeling, which is deep and intense. Other sermons, as those on *The Crook in the Lot,* that is, the adversities which God permits or appoints in our earthly lot; on *Prayer,* and a number of other subjects, show the same qualities. Boston was a man of might in his own small parish, and extended his influence far beyond. After a faithful service as pastor and preacher, and through many trials, he passed to his reward, a much loved and much opposed, but true and faithful man.

The name of Erskine is notable in the Evangelical ministry of Scotland. Henry Erskine, under whose ministry Thomas Boston was converted, was a brave, faithful, and godly Presbyterian minister, who suffered many vicissitudes in his career of many removals. He was the father of the two notable Secessionists, Ebenezer Erskine (1680-1756) and Ralph Erskine (1685-1752).[53] Both the brothers were educated at Edinburgh, Ralph (being the younger) in a better time and to better advantage.

[53]See A. R. MacEwen, in *Famous Scots* series (No. 34), 1900, *The Erskines* (Ebenezer and Ralph); also *A Collection of Sermons on Several Subjects, by Ebenezer and Ralph Erskine,* ed. by T. Bradbury, 1738.

Both became ministers of the Established Church, Ebenezer first at Portmoak, near Loch Leven, and later at Sterling; and Ralph at Dunfermline, where he spent his life. Both took the Evangelical side and led out the Seceders, forming the first Associate Reformed Presbytery. In this movement Ebenezer was the leader. The Secession was accomplished about 1733, though it was not till seven years later that Ebenezer was formally expelled from the Assembly. Ralph joined the Secession in 1737, seeing no way to effect reforms within the Establishment. Their congregations were led with them, and many other churches and ministers joined in the movement. It is sad to relate that within their own ranks came further dissensions and trials, but the Erskines were following conscience, and through all their troubles they lived and taught and preached with great power. The doctrines of grace were recommended by them with great unction and force. They were not so strong in thinking as Boston, but they excelled him in tenderness and in the joy of salvation. They attracted great crowds, —especially Ralph,—people coming from long distances, particularly on communion occasions. Their published sermons are of the extreme analytical type, with elaborate introduction, formal statement of heads, divisions, doctrines, points, etc. They abound in Scripture quotations, but are sparing in the use of illustration. Definition, distinction, argument, and appeal are the main things; but there is a spiritual glow through all the bony structure and wearisome refinement of analysis. There is a warmth of conviction and pastoral concern in the quaint modes of expression that still make appeal, even to the reader whose taste is offended by the faults mentioned—which were largely the faults of the age in which the preachers lived.

After the Secession the Established Church enjoyed comparative peace, and though an Evangelical party remained in it, the trend of things was decidedly toward Moderatism. The Moderates frowned upon what they called "enthusiasm," "fanaticism," etc. They were for a cool and moral Christianity, a gospel of good taste and literary excellence. A warm and glowing Christian life or a deep conviction and proclamation of the doctrines of grace was far from their thoughts.

Perhaps the most extreme representative of this school was Alexander Carlyle (1722-1805).[54] He was the son of a Presbyterian minister, born at Prestonpans, where his father was, as he describes him, "An orthodox and popular orator, entirely beloved and much caressed by the whole parish." Carlyle was educated at both Edinburgh and Glasgow. His choice of the ministry was entirely professional, without any conviction either of divine leading or of personal devotion. He was led to it chiefly by the persuasion of his family and friends. Of his views and sentiments in entering the ministry he has written his own condemnation in these words:[55] "I had only one sermon to deliver before the Presbytery of Haddington to become a preacher. . . . The genteel people of Prestonpans parish were all there; and one young lady, to whom I had long been attached, not having been able to conceal her admiration of my oratory, I inwardly applauded my own resolution of adhering to the promise I had made my family to persevere in the clerical profession." In such a worldly spirit he became minister at Inveresk, where he served for fifty-seven years—until his death. In his *Autobiography,* written when he was eighty years old, but not published until 1860, he reveals himself as a man utterly worldly, though respectable, without warmth or devotion, but with good taste, fondness for society, literature, and company. His few remaining sermons (no need of any more!) are wholly destitute of gospel truth or fervor, though written in good taste and agreeable style. No wonder even Hume airily rebuked him once for giving to a congregation where he heard him preach one of "Cicero's Academics," and that Sir Walter Scott, in speaking of his alleged poetry, should have described him as "a shrewd, clever old carle, no doubt, but no more a poet than his precentor," on which Blaikie[56] justly remarks that Sir Walter might have said with equal truth, "no more a minister of the gospel."

A younger contemporary of Carlyle was John Logan

[54]See Sermon on the *Usefulness and Necessity of a Liberal Education,* Edinburgh, 1793; and in Vol. 2 of *The Scotch Preacher* (1775) a sermon on *The Tendency of the Church of Scotland,* etc.; *Autobiography of Alex. Carlyle, D. D.,* ed. by J. H. Burton, 1860. [55]*Autobiog.,* p. 201. [56]*Op. cit.,* p. 225.

(1748-1788),[57] who claims for his talents, his errors, and his misfortunes at least a brief notice. He was born in Midlothian, his father a farmer, and both parents pious Seceders. He was carefully brought up. His parents earnestly desired that he should be a minister, and sent him to Edinburgh for education. Here Dr. Robertson befriended and helped him. He was distinguished as a student, became tutor for awhile, and then minister at Leith. He tried faithfully to discharge his duties, and was very eloquent and popular as a speaker, but personally he was not deeply pious nor in love with his work. Ambitious of literary distinction, he essayed writing in several departments. He wrote a drama called *Runnymede,* which was acted in Edinburgh. This raised a storm. Logan became depressed, drank too much, retired from his work, went to London, and died there in distress. Undeveloped as historian and poet, he might have done well in either line of writing. Some of his hymns and paraphrases of the Psalms are among the treasures of the Scottish Church. His sermons, published by his executors after his death, show far more of religious feeling than those of Carlyle; and more of heart power, native eloquence, and fire of imagination than those of Blair, but their warmth is scarcely evangelical. We miss the tone of one who had experienced the divine life in the soul, though there is something to win sympathy and even respect.

The most famous representative of the Moderates was the celebrated Dr. Hugh Blair (1718-1800).[58] He was born of a good family, his father being a highly respectable merchant of Edinburgh. Blair took his degree at the University of Edinburgh with great applause in 1739. His first charge as pastor was at Collessie, in Fifeshire, but he was soon transferred to the Canongate Church in Edinburgh, and, after faithful service and some promotions, to the High Church, where he served forty years. Blair paid great attention to rhetoric and literature, and was made professor of these subjects in the

[57]*Sermons of John Logan, LL. D.,* with an account of his life, 1810.

[58]*Sermons of Hugh Blair, D. D.* (with account of his life), ed. by J. Finlayson, 5 vols., beginning 1777.

University. His *Lectures on Rhetoric* were published, passed through many editions, and continued for a generation one of the favorite text-books on that subject. As preacher and pastor Blair was circumspect, irreproachable, dignified, and amiable. His eloquence was admired, his hearers were numerous, his influence was widespread, and his character respected to the end of his regular and orderly life. His sermons began to be published in 1777. They had wide acceptance, translation, and circulation, and were long considered models of style and taste. Their failure to interest modern readers lies just here. Their strong point was their appeal to taste, not to thought nor to depth of religious feeling, and so when taste changed they fell into disregard. Macaulay is too severe in speaking of Dr. Blair as a "poor creature," but still he could not be ranked as one of the great preachers of his age and country. His sermons are cold presentations of the accepted Christian doctrines and ethics, without the warmth of evangelic earnestness or the driving power of great conviction. There is want of vitality, and the elegance which characterizes them has passed away along with the starched frills, powdered wigs, and buckled knee-breeches of that age.

Neither the withdrawal of the Secessionists nor the rationalistic coolness of the Moderates left the Established Kirk destitute of evangelical preachers. Some were still found who cherished the doctrines of grace and proclaimed them with earnestness and fruit. One of the best-known of these was John Maclaurin (1693-1754).[59] He was born in Argyllshire (where his father was a preacher), the eldest of three sons, who were early left orphans and cared for by an uncle. One died young, the other became a distinguished mathematician. John received the usual training at Glasgow, and was a hard student. He settled as pastor, first at Luss on Loch Lomond, and read much during this country pastorate. He was soon called to Glasgow, where he served to the end of his life. He was very active as pastor, counselor, and leader. He corresponded with Jonathan Edwards and others interested in evangelistic movements, but in that

[59] *Sermons and Essays of John Maclaurin,* with *Life,* by John Gillies, D. D., 1802.

work he was prudent and sensible. Only three of his sermons were published, one of which became famous and was long regarded as a notable masterpiece, on *Glorying in the Cross.* These sermons are sound and Scriptural in doctrine, not tediously analytical, and have far more of feeling than those of the Moderates, but they lack something of simplicity, showing no particular gift of style, and somehow they do not melt or stir as one would expect. Even the great sermon on *Glorying in the Cross* gives one a certain disappointment on reading it now. Blaikie[60] is not far wrong in saying that it is rather a treatise than a sermon.

Other Evangelicals are named and discussed by the historians, but the most important remaining one is John Erskine (1721-1803),[61] who was a cousin of Ebenezer and Ralph, and the son of a very distinguished lawyer. He had the advantages of wealth, social position, education, and general culture. Though his father naturally wished him to become a lawyer, his heart was given to God for the ministry. Ordained in 1744, he first served a small country church, and then a larger church at Culross. In his early life he published a vigorous treatise on *The Natural Light of Reason and the Consequent Accountability of All Mankind.* He invited Whitefield to Scotland, and defended that great evangelist when he was sharply criticised for his methods. In 1758 he became pastor at the New Grayfriars Church, and some years later at the Old Grayfriars Church, where he was associated with the famous Dr. Robertson, the historian and professor. Erskine was not so favorable to Wesley (on account of his theology) as to Whitefield, though he held some correspondence with Wesley. He was opposed to the war with the American Colonies, and both preached and published on the subject, arguing against the policy. He was active in many ways, by pen and voice, and most earnest in his pastoral work. Sir Walter Scott, whose parents were members of Erskine's congregation, has given a fine and famous description of

[60]*Op. cit.*, p. 256.

[61]*Discourses Preached on Several Occasions,* by John Erskine, D. D., 2 vols., 1804-1818; second vol, with *Life,* by H. M. Wellwood.

the preacher in his novel of *Guy Mannering*.[62] After speaking of his ungainly person, his fair complexion, and scanty gesture, the novelist says: "Something there was of an antiquated tone of argument and metaphor, but it only served to give zest and peculiarity to the style of the elocution. The sermon was not read; a scrap of paper containing the heads of the discourse was occasionally referred to, and the enunciation, which had first seemed imperfect and embarrassed, became, as the preacher warmed in his progress, animated and distinct; and although the discourse could not be quoted as a correct specimen of pulpit eloquence, yet Mannering had seldom heard so much learning, metaphysical acuteness, and energy of argument brought into the service of Christianity." Considering that Scott himself was more in sympathy with Moderatism than with Erskine's views, this testimony acquires additional value. Erskine's sermons were published in two volumes, the second appearing after his death. In several of them he touches on the duties of the pastoral office. In one of them he says:[63] "Christ crucified and salvation through Him; the law as a schoolmaster to bring men to Christ; and exhorting the disciples of Jesus to adorn His doctrine by the conscientious performance of every duty, ought to be chief subjects of our sermons." Again he says: "Little pains may serve to display criticism and literature on subjects which do not need them, or without occasion to plunge so deep in abstract philosophical speculation that the bulk of an audience shall lose sight of us. But it is incomparably more difficult to compose a popular discourse in a style plain, elegant, nervous, grave, and animated; neither bombast nor groveling; neither scrupulously exact nor sordidly negligent." This very well describes the quality of Erskine's own sermons as they impress the reader. They are weighty in thought, but not abstruse; orderly in arrangement, without tediousness; clear and forcible in style, without pretense or undue polishing. They are animated by a true purpose to present the gospel of the crucified Redeemer in a way to win a personal acceptance of Him from the hearers.

[62]Quoted by Blaikie, p. 263.
[63]*Discourses,* Vol. I, pp. 114, 116.

We turn now to preaching in Wales,[64] and we must not forget that the Anglican Church was strong in that principality. The sees of St. David's and St. Asaph's have been filled by some of the most illustrious of the English clergy, but the distinctive preaching of Wales has been largely in the Welsh tongue and by Dissenters—chiefly Methodists and Baptists. Welsh pulpit eloquence has been specially characterized by imagination and fire. The native language is said to possess peculiar charm and fitness for this kind of speech. Not a great many sermons of Welsh preachers have been preserved from the eighteenth century in the English language; but there was great preaching and very effective work by many Welsh preachers during that epoch. The work of Vavasor Powell and others in the seventeenth century prepared the way for the great revival in the eighteenth. In the early part of the century there was great coldness, both in the Established Church and among Dissenters, but the revival began about 1735.

The most notable of the preachers was Daniel Rowlands (1713-1790). He was the son of the rector at Llangeitho, Cardiganshire. He was educated at home, and designed for the ministry, was ordained in London in 1733, and became his father's curate. He preached without a spiritual conversion, and was a gay and lively young parson, but under a sermon of Griffith Jones, in 1735, he was soundly converted, and immediately changed the spirit and method of his preaching. At first his preaching was denunciatory, but grew in grace and gospel power. Crowds came to his services, and he was invited to preach in a neighboring parish. He went, and a great revival ensued. The bishop reproved and silenced him for insubordination, but the people built for him a chapel at Llangeitho, and thus he withdrew from the Established Church. He had great success in his ministry, and also itinerated, preaching in many parts of the country with great power. He was a man of deep piety

[64]See E. Paxton Hood, *Vocation of the Preacher* (1886), chapter on "The Preachers of Wild Wales;" Owen Jones, *Some of the Great Preachers of Wales,* 1885; Daniel Davies, *Echoes from the Welsh Hills* (1883), with an essay by J. R. Kilsby Jones on *Characteristics of Welsh Eloquence;* account of Daniel Rowlands in Ryle's *Christian Leaders,* p. 180 ff.

and consecration, and highly gifted with the oratorical imagination and feeling.

Along with him should be mentioned Howell Harris (1714-1773), who was born at Trevecca, Brecknockshire. In 1735 he went to Oxford to study for orders, but became dissatisfied and returned to Wales. He began to exhort and form societies independently of Whitefield and Wesley in England, and of Rowlands. He applied for ordination, but was refused on account of his methods, and remained a lay preacher to the end. He worked much and cordially with Rowlands. He also met Whitefield in 1739, and Wesley later.

Another of the noble evangelistic preachers of this time was William Williams (1717-1791), who was converted under Harris's preaching, and turned from his medical studies to the work of preaching. He, too, after being ordained, was virtually driven out of the Established Church because of his evangelistic methods. Besides his preaching, which was full of power and success, Williams has given to Christianity two immortal hymns, which are well-known in their English dress, viz., *Guide me, O Thou Great Jehovah,* and *O'er the gloomy hills of darkness.* Still another of these revival preachers was Robert Roberts (1763-1802), who came from humble circumstances, without much education, but was a man of remarkable native gifts and greatly blessed in his preaching. At the end of the century we find the famous Christmas Evans (1766-1838), but his life in its height of power and influence belongs to the next century.

Passing by political and social conditions in Ireland during the eighteenth century (they were surely bad enough!), a word must be said of the religious situation.[65] There were three elements: Catholic, Anglican, Presbyterian. The Catholic was native and the preference of the majority. Not the peasantry only were Catholics, yet that religion was held mainly by this class with great tenacity, much ignorance, and fanaticism, but also with devotion and courage. The people were oppressed, de-

[65]W. E. H. Lecky, *History of Ireland in the Eighteenth Century,* 5 vols.; W. D. Killen, *Ecclesiastical History of Ireland,* 2 vols.; *Ireland and Her People* (a collection of brief accounts of Irish celebrities); articles in *Dict. Nat. Biog.,* and in the *Catholic Encyclopaedia;* lives and sermons of preachers named.

prived of their just rights, and kept in subjection by force. Protestantism (Church of England) was an alien institution forced on a reluctant people; the whole body of Anglican churches and bishops was sustained by taxation and bayonets, yet there were a few natives who accepted the Episcopal Church. What a picture does that Church present with its absentee prelates, its incompetent curates, its persecuting bishops! In the north there was an influx of Scotch Presbyterians, and these were hostile alike to Catholicism and to English prelacy, with not a few quarrels among themselves.

Among the Catholics there were no preachers of special distinction. The natives preached mostly in the Gaelic, and cared little if at all for literary distinction. Lecky describes two sorts of Catholic priests in this epoch.[66] One sort were those who had been educated at various Catholic schools in Europe and brought to Ireland the culture of those schools. They did not produce any writings of lasting value, but they were cultured, and preached in good taste. Priests of this kind were chiefly active in the latter part of the century. Before that there were many of the uncultivated and ignorant sort, who were themselves often fanatical, superstitious, violent, and sometimes coarse. The only preacher of much note in the latter part of the century was Bishop Doyle, who, however, was more of an administrator than a preacher. He is said to have been the first Irish Catholic preacher of note who preached in the English tongue. Of the Protestant preachers only a few are worthy of note.

John Abernethy (1680-1740)[67] was the son of a Presbyterian minister at Coleraine, in Ulster. During the Revolutionary troubles, which occurred in his childhood, he was taken by a relative to Scotland. Later he returned, but was sent back again to the University of Glasgow, and afterwards to Edinburgh, for his education. He settled as preacher at Antrim in 1703, and continued there for twenty-seven years, when he was called to Dublin. After some difficulties, he finally settled there in 1730, and remained to his death.

[66] *Op. cit.*, III, p. 354 ff.

[67] *Sermons on Various Subjects, by John Abernethy, M. A., with a Preface containing the Life of the Author*, 3d ed., 2 vols., London, 1762, ed. Duchal.

Abernethy's sermons show that his drift was decidedly in the direction of Moderatism—they lack depth and warmth of evangelical religion. They are ethically sound, and in style quite pleasing, but would awaken little if any interest in a reader of to-day.

Far more famous, though not as a preacher, was the celebrated Jonathan Swift (1667-1745),[68] dean of St. Patrick's, Dublin. Though born in Dublin, Swift was of English family. His father was rather a thriftless man, and the family suffered hardships, though helped by the liberality of an uncle. Swift's mother returned to England, and Jonathan was sent to Oxford, where he finally got his Master of Arts. His uncle's death left him penniless, and his early years were a struggle. By the help of Sir William Temple, he was ordained and assigned to the parish at Kilroot, near Belfast. His literary activity had already begun, he having written *The Battle of the Books* and *The Tale of a Tub*. As is well known, he also wrote many political pamphlets. He went back and forth between England and Ireland, was most anxious to obtain preferment in England, but never did. Finally, in 1713, he became dean of St. Patrick's Cathedral in Dublin, holding the position to the end of his life.

Swift's political and literary career lie apart from our topic. His unamiable character and his strange conduct toward two women who loved him, his unacknowledged marriage to one of them (Esther Johnson, known as Stella), the gloom and darkness of much of his personal life, finally ending in insanity and death, are sad shadows upon his life. As a churchman, according to the low standard of his times, he had some ideas of conscience and duty. He sought to promote the interests of the Established Church. He professed a formal and doubtless sincere attachment to the accepted doctrines of Christianity, but without depth of conviction or feeling. The defects of his character and the faults of his conduct, though serious, were not scandalous. He espoused the cause of Ireland in a number of ways, and his memory is respected by those who love that unhappy country.

[68]Various edd. of *Works* of Swift (collected and separate); account and extracts in *Warner Lib.*, XXIV, p. 14259; *Life*, by Sir Henry Craik, London, 1882; *Sermons* (with *Life* prefixed), 2 vols., 1790 (?).

Swift's sermons are without evangelical content and without the warmth of personal and deep conviction. They are cool moral essays, often with a vein of satire native to the author. Their style is as clear as a sunbeam, their outlines natural and simple, and their diction luminous and refreshing. The sermon on *The Trinity* is a remarkable discourse as coming from such a man. There is an entire absence of rancor and metaphysics. It is a plain, common-sense treatment of the doctrine as a mystery beyond but not contrary to reason and to be accepted because revealed of God in the Bible. The other sermons are wholly of a moral nature—one on *The Condition of Ireland,* one on *Mutual Subjection,* one on *Conscience.* There is also a sermon on *Sleeping in Church,* based on the episode of Eutychus, in which the preacher finds occasion, not only to berate that fault, but generally to reprehend both the neglect and the undue criticism of preaching. The topic is scarcely suited to the dignity of the pulpit, but no reader of Swift needs to be told that from the points of view of literature and wit, the treatment is delightful.

Undoubtedly the greatest Irish preacher of the century was Walter Blake Kirwan (1754-1805).[69] He was born in Galway, of Catholic parents, and was educated for the Catholic priesthood in various European schools, especially St. Omer's and Louvain, where he was ordained and became professor of philosophy. He then became chaplain to the Neapolitan ambassador at the British court. In 1787 he became a Protestant, believing that he could do more good as a preacher in the Established Church. He had great success, was a genuine orator, especially noted for his pathetic appeals on behalf of charitable institutions. He held various charges, finally was made dean of Killala, which he held to his death. Kirwan's published sermons naturally lack the glow and warmth which characterized their free delivery, but still they are flowing and oratorical in style, though somewhat careless in arrangement. They want the evangelical element which was partly due no doubt

[69]*Sermons of W. B. Kirwan,* with a sketch of his life (supposedly by his daughter, Wilhelmina), 1816; Lecky, Vol. II, p. 506 ff., and V, p. 86; sermon in Fish, I, p. 583.

to the fact that they were charity sermons, but even granting that, there is surely more room than is found for the gospel. Of Kirwan's splendid oratory, one of the strongest witnesses was his friend, the great orator, Henry Grattan, who is quoted as saying: "He called forth the latent virtue of the human heart and taught men to discover in themselves a mine of charity of which the proprietors had become unconscious. In feeding the lamp of charity he almost exhausted the lamp of life. He came to interrupt the reposé of the pulpit, and shake one world with the thunder of the other. The preacher's desk becomes a throne of light."

PART THIRD

THE NINETEENTH CENTURY

CHAPTER XI

PREACHING IN THE NINETEENTH CENTURY. THE PULPIT OF SOUTHERN EUROPE

In the history of human progress there is no greater era than the nineteenth century. Besides the wonderful advance in the material elements and forces of civilization, there were great movements in political, social, and intellectual life. The great problems of human thought were profoundly considered from many new points of view and with new data. In every department it was a century of investigation. No period of human history has been marked by so eager a quest for truth, or was so crowded with contributions to the sum of knowledge. The bewildering mass of material gathered in every sphere of research is beyond estimate. This search for facts and reality has been in the main characterized by intense desire to know the truth and to use the facts obtained in the interest of intellectual and moral advancement. There was necessarily much unrest and stir in all departments of thought. Religion and preaching powerfully felt the movement of the age. In fact, many of the best movements were led by these forces.

In the nineteenth century preaching maintained its place amid the forces of human culture. The pulpit of the period ranks high in comparison with the past. In fact, this era marks one of the four great culminating points in the history of the Christian pulpit after the apostles. The three preceding culminations were those of the fourth, the thirteenth, and the sixteenth centuries. While the preaching of the nineteenth century was not marked by any one or two outstanding characteristics, but rather exemplifies the heightening of power in all directions, it is perhaps on that very account to be regarded as the greatest of the four epochs mentioned. This general character applies to the preaching of the century as a whole. The pulpit of the United States came to its power in the nineteenth century, and that in other countries and in missionary lands has also features of great interest. Our attention, however, in this volume is confined to the preaching of Europe, of which a brief survey must now be made.

I. General Survey of the European Pulpit

The preaching of Europe in the nineteenth century was, of course, the product of all the past. As we have traced its history since the Reformation we have seen a long, involved, and mighty process of evolution. In all European lands the varied elemental forces which combine to make pulpit oratory have been in evidence.

The first thing we naturally think of is to compare the European preaching of the nineteenth century with that of the preceding ages. In such a comparison its superiority must at once be admitted. Taken all in all, the preaching of Europe has never been so good, so successful, so powerful as in the nineteenth century. Yet, in making this statement, and making it with confidence, due allowances must be made. In the first place, we must remember the differences of time and taste. If old Schuler could have continued his remarkable *History of the Alterations of Taste in Preaching* through the nineteenth century, he would have had to write a much stouter volume and to have employed much wider research. Perhaps the main thing he would have had to recognize would be the many different standards of taste which prevailed. As in all other matters, so in preaching the nineteenth century differed widely from the past, and it was so pleased with itself that its own standards of judgment and taste were not always fair to those of previous ages. The style of preaching, whether referring to language or method, which characterized the seventeenth and eighteenth centuries was no longer acceptable in the nineteenth. We must always remember that contemporary taste decides the form of literary or oral expression, and the different standard or standards of the nineteenth century are no more in force for preaching than for other methods of intellectual expression. The taste in music and other arts, as well as in all forms of literature, shows this. When, therefore, we speak of the superior excellence of nineteenth century preaching over that of the past, we must always remember that this is said from the point of view of reigning taste. The preaching which captivated and moved the nineteenth century audiences would not have had so great effect in the eighteenth and seventeenth centuries, could it have been anticipated and practiced then; and in the same direction the preaching which moved and pleased the audiences of those centuries does not strike the same level when read in the light of nineteenth century criticism. But when we make, as we must, this allowance, it still remains true that the nineteenth century pulpit of Europe as a rule is far in advance of preceding times in all the essentials of pulpit eloquence; and this brings us to another consideration which must be borne in mind in making a comparative judgment. We must remember that the preachers of the nineteenth century could profit by the faults and failures of the past. Historical and critical studies brought the leaders of thought and mode into judicial contact with past errors. If the nineteenth century pulpit had shown no improvement on that of the past, it would have written itself down a failure. In addition to this, it could avail itself of the wonderful progress already alluded to in all departments of intellectual life.

When we compare the preaching of the nineteenth century with that of the three culminating points before noted, we should be able the better to appreciate its excellence. As to intellectual power and grasp of Christian truth, the European pulpit of the age in question shows well in comparison. The points under discussion were somewhat different, but the sermons of the nineteenth century show at least as much of mentality as those of the sixteenth century; and when brought into comparison with the thirteenth and with the fourth century, the balance would lie in favor of the nineteenth. If we press the comparison on the point of spiritual fervor or moral power, the nineteenth century will not suffer. Again, it appears to be not far from an average with that of the sixteenth, and superior to the thirteenth and to the fourth. Another point of comparison, where a just opinion is more difficult to reach, is that in regard to adaptation and influence. On this point it is exceedingly difficult for one age fairly to judge any other, for no doubt the preaching of the fourth century, of the thirteenth, and of the sixteenth was better adapted to each one of those epochs than that of the nineteenth (had it been possible to anticipate it) could have been; so that the fairest thing we can say on this point is that the preaching of the nineteenth century was certainly no less fitted to impress its own age than that of each of the preceding historic culminations. Thus, on a hasty, but it is hoped not unfair, comparison of the last great culmination of pulpit power with those of preceding times we should not go astray in assigning the supreme place to the nineteenth century.

When we compare the preaching of the nineteenth with that of the seventeenth and eighteenth centuries, which we have just been studying, the comparison is both easier and more difficult: easier because the contrast is closer; more difficult because the points are more numerous and complicated. Here we can only speak in general terms, leaving for minute considertation as we go along many of the particular points. On the whole, we shall find in the sermons of the nineteenth century less of dogmatism, less of coldness and formality than in the immediately preceding times. We shall find more of ease, flexibility, and adaptation, perhaps also we shall find more effect in reaching the mind and life of the people. So far we have spoken of the comparative excellence of the nineteenth century preaching. Leaving now the comparative method of judging it, we must notice a few of the salient features of the nineteenth century preaching as a whole.

One of the most remarkable of these features is variety. It may safely be said that never before in the history of the Christian pulpit was there so much variety as in the nineteenth century. The point is easily illustrated. Take, for instance, the differences of creed and sect. The Reformation, with its various groups and parties, introduced the modern era of almost infinite sectarian divisions. In the acceptance and the expression of Christianity, both among individuals and groups, naturally every creed and sect found their advocates in the pulpit; and with increasing freedom of utterance there was added variety in doctrine and traditions. This variety appears also in the matter of method and style. Individual preachers here and there felt more liberty to depart from traditional and academic methods of presenting the Word of God; and while something of formality and sameness always remains in the literature, whether homiletical or other, still great differences also appear. In Europe we must remember also the different languages; the vernacular tongues had now long been in use for pulpit work, and the literary development of these various languages was especially marked in the nineteenth century. The preaching of each country and tongue and dialect adds its interest and charm, together with the qualities of each particular language, to the appearance of the nineteenth century preaching as a whole.

The contents of preaching remained substantially the same—the great doctrines and morals of the Christian faith as presented in the Scriptures. But the interpretation of the Bible was much improved. Exegetical scholarship was never so accurate in the Christian pulpit as in the nineteenth century. There was a more general and manifest desire among the preachers to get and apply the exact meaning of the Word of God. As a consequence there was far less than in former times of allegorizing, or strained and fanciful use of texts. There also appeared, particularly as the century advanced, less readiness to adopt the traditional pulpit interpretation and application of texts. Individual preachers made more effort to find for themselves the meaning of Scripture for their immediate purposes. Yet along with this we have to remember that faults in the use of the Bible still persisted in many of the sermons. And far more to be regretted than this per-sistence of old faults was the loosening in many preachers of profound respect for the Bible as an authoritative revelation of the mind and will of God. If a greater and more sympathetic appreciation of the human and historic elements of Scripture appears, so also does there come in less positive and personal acceptance of it as the direct Word of God.

But it would not be true to say that the traditions of homiletical method were entirely banished from the pulpit of the nineteenth century. This is manifestly impossible, and as undesirable as impossible. Improvement there was,—leaving off of some incumbrances, the development of some excellencies; but no sudden cutting away from the principles and methods of the past. The great improvement of homiletical teaching, both academic and literary, is noticeable. And this teaching is not revolutionary, but evolutionary. Besides the generally accepted doctrinal content of preaching, the use of experience remains a most important element of the sermons of the century. Perhaps, on the whole—though it is not wise to dogmatize upon the point—there was increasing use of this sort of material. Making allowance for differences in individual preachers, the personal experiences of both speaker and hearers finds effective use in most nineteenth century sermons. There is also a large infusion of humanitarian, social, and ethical elements in the contents. This also varies with persons, times, and places, and grows toward the end of the period, but is prominent enough in the whole course of nineteenth century preaching to call for special remark.

The literary quality of nineteenth century preaching in Europe reaches and maintains a high level throughout the period. While there is no slavery to form and method, much attention is paid to the best canons of rhetorical art and taste. In all the European countries and the leading Churches and sects this is true. The ministry as a class presents a very high degree of scholarly and literary culture. One can not read widely and attentively in the sermonic literature of the period without being impressed with this fact. There is less of pedantry and display than in some former periods, but for thoughtful and studied yet popular and skillful expression, the European preaching of the nineteenth century will bear searching comparison with any other method of speaking or writing in that great period of literary activity and excellence. It may be true—though not demonstrable—that sermons, in comparison with other literature, were less read than in former times; but they were never more worthy to be read for their literary excellence alone than in this period. Among the preachers of modern Europe there are not a few masters of literary expression, some of whom have become famous and found extensive reading, while many equally worthy have not obtained wide popular recognition.

No less impressive is the practical aim of preaching in this great century. The two primary purposes of preaching—the didactic and the proclamatory—have not been lost sight of. The first has comparatively more prominence, especially in the printed sermons; but the evangelistic note is also heard.

The forces opposed to the Christian pulpit were much the same in the nineteenth as in the earlier centuries. Only some assumed different forms and received greater or less attention as occasion demanded. The same old sin and unbelief had to be attacked. Human nature changes not with the progress of events and the evolution of material and social forces. The selfishness, immorality, vice, and crime of humanity are much the same in all time. The rejection of the spiritual appeal of religion was as characteristic of Europe in the nineteenth century as of any region and people in any age. The prophet's function was as hard and thankless then as ever, his call and task no less weighty and imperative. Also the preachers of this as of earlier ages found themselves confronted with a constant and unresponsive class of nominal believers. The worldliness and indifference of professing Christians were ever in evidence and gave to the modern pulpit, as to the ancient, one of its chief difficulties and most frequent themes.

In addition to these perennial foes, we must not fail to notice two others, which, though not entirely absent in some form or other from all periods, came to a prominence, character, and strength in the nineteenth century different from what we have found in any preceding age. These were the rationalistic criticism of the Bible, and the scientific hostility to traditional Christanity. The former, indeed, came over from the eighteenth century—as we have seen,—but in the hands of several influential groups of German scholars assumed more formidable shapes and became more aggressive and confident in its attacks upon the traditions of Christianity than ever before. The pulpit had to take its solemn account with this tremendous force. Then, too, the wonderful development of physical science and the rise of the British school of scientific speculation about the middle of the nineteenth century made an epoch for preaching as for other departments of human thinking. Materialistic evolution as a theory of all causes and phenomena, not only attacked the foundations of the Christian faith, but threatened to become the substitute of all spiritual thinking, until, toward the end of the century, the inadequacy of so one-sided a view of life began to produce the inevitable reaction. This scientific opposition to historical and spiritual religion was a fearful opponent of preaching and at the same time a powerful stimulus to it. Both phases of this effect are traceable in the sermons of the period. The pulpit did not decline its serious task, but grappled it with both ability and courage of a high order.

The attitude of preaching toward both the scholarly and the scientific criticism of current Christianity in this era naturally varied much in character and quality according to conditions of time, place, and persons; but in a general way the preachers fall, with other thinkers, into the three well-known groups of advanced, mediating, and conservative. The advanced group contained those preachers who more or less fully accepted the theories of the hostile critics and scientists, and in their effort to interpret and adjust Christian doctrine into some harmony with the new theories departed very widely from the creeds and methods of former times. This school delighted to call themselves "liberal," and often were not sparing in arrogant criticism of their "traditionalist" brethren. The conservative group, at the other end, were equally convinced that most scientists and critics were out-and-out infidels intent on destroying the very foundations of the Christian faith and of true religious life. Between these an ill-defined group of mediating thinkers were found, inclining now to one or the other side, or trying to find the real elements of truth and right held by the opposed groups and combine them in some sort of just and enduring harmony. We shall see that all these schools had their representatives in the pulpit, with varying degrees of ability and influence, there being both large and little men in all groups. We shall be able to see this more distinctly when we come to closer range with the preaching of the various countries, epochs, groups, and individuals in our ensuing study.

II. The Pulpit of Spain and Portugal

It is not necessary to make more than passing reference to the political and social conditions in Spain and Portugal during the nineteenth century in order to introduce what little there is to say concerning the preaching on the Peninsula during that period. Spain was shorn of her American Colonies in the early years of the century, and of Cuba and the Philippine Islands during its closing days. Internal revolutions and trials marked her history. From the French occupation under Napoleon's rule down to the end of the century the struggle of dynasties, of parties, of people, and Church were sharp and ceaseless. Turmoil and decline, financial difficulties and popular distress were the rule. For Portugal also a similar state of affairs has been characteristic of modern times. The independence of Brazil and other losses occurred, along with internal disputes and struggles.

In literature there were distinguished names in both countries.[1] They felt the breath of the nineteenth century in this sphere perhaps more than any other. Of Spanish poets there were Zarate, Espronceda, Zorrilla, and others; of historians, Lafuente, Canovas del

[1]See accounts in *Warner Lib.*, Vol. 31, p. 24 ff., and the references to other places. Also cyclopaedia articles.

Castillo, and others; of novelists, Balagua, Alarcon, Pereda, Galdos, and Valdes were in the lead; of statesmen and orators, the most distinguished was Emilio Castelar. In Portugal some of the more eminent names in literature in this period are those of Almeida-Garrett, Herculano, Ribeiro, Diniz, and Braga.

In religious affairs[2] the Catholic Church continued to be dominant and to use its power to the utmost. But its supremacy felt the check of some Protestant work in the Peninsula, chiefly by colporteurs and evangelists; and also that of political opposition to the clerical power, and some movements toward religious freedom and the separation of church and state.

In preaching no great names appear of men known and influential beyond their own countries. The improved literary taste of the century doubtless had its effect upon the style of sermons, and the lesson given by Isla in rebuke of the burlesque method was fruitful in banishing that wretched travesty from the Spanish pulpit. Portugal seems not to have furnished any preachers of distinction; and Spain only a few.[3]

Among the most renowned were Jose Macedo, Benedetto, Francolin, bishop of Charcas, Emmanuel Gonzales y Sanchez, canon of the Cathedral of Seville, and Ildefonso Infante, who published *Conferences* on the Church and its doctrines. Riesco le Grand published a series of Lenten discourses in 1851 which attracted notice. He was a Franciscan monk of Santiago. Atiliano Melnigzo, Cistercian and vicar-apostolic, published "mission" sermons; and from Juan Gonzales, of Valladolid, there appeared eight volumes of sermons embracing the widest range of subjects and enjoying a second edition. From this slight notice we perceive that the Catholic pulpit was not silent in Spain during the nineteenth century, but it can not be called distinguished.

As for Protestant preaching,[4] while there was some, it was depressed and discouraged. There was sometimes

[2]See Kurtz, *Church History,* Am. ed., Vol. III, p. 394 ff., and the art. on Spain in C. Werckshagen, *Der Protestantismus am Ende des XIXten Jahrhunderts,* 2 Bde., 4to., Berlin, 1902, Bd. II, S. 1090 ff.

[3]See Zanotto, *Storia della Pred.*, p. 542.

[4]See Kurtz and Werckshagen, as in note 2.

nominal toleration, but little real freedom in religion. The names of Ruet and Matamoras are given as those of faithful laborers who preached as they dared and could, through persecutions and trials. Strong Protestant congregations were gathered at Madrid, Seville, and other places, but they had a checkered history.

III. The Italian Pulpit

To understand properly the preaching of modern Italy, we must briefly recall the chief political, literary, and religious events in the remarkable history of that famous land during the nineteenth century.[5] The century opened for Italy under the shadow of French dominion. The supremacy of Napoleon and the various changes under his government lasted until 1815, when, by the Treaty of Vienna, the old political status was restored. Austria was supreme in the north, except for the growing rivalry and power of the kingdom of Sardinia. The States of the Church still controlled the central part of the peninsula, while in the south Naples and Sicily were restored to King Ferdinand under the title of the Two Sicilies. Among the people there was great discontent with this divided state. Patriots and statesmen, especially Mazzini, wrote much and encouraged the hope for better things. The Revolution of 1848 gave an opportunity to the patriots for a short time, and a Republic was erected in Rome and the pope put to flight; but the Revolution did not accomplish all that was desired, yet from 1850 on there was growth toward unity under the advance of the House of Savoy. Victor Emmanuel II, the wise king; Count Cavour, the patient and sagacious statesman, and Garibaldi, the agitator, patriot, and general, were leading Italy to her unity and strength. The French alliance, in 1859, resulted in the victories of Solferino and Magenta which broke the Austrian rule and established the kingdom of Italy with its capital at Florence, in 1861. Garibaldi captured Sicily, overthrew the Bour-

[5] *Historians' History,* Vol. IX, p. 566 ff., and the authorities there quoted. Also a good brief sketch in McKenzie's *Nineteenth Century,* and for the time since 1850 in *The Reconstruction of Europe,* by Harold Murdock, New York, 1889.

bons, and thus the south of Italy was united to the kingdom under the victorious House of Savoy. In 1866 the Prussian victory over Austria was improved by the Italians to drive the Austrians from Venice and attach that region to the new kingdom. Only one step remained to the accomplishment of Italian unity. That was the annexation of the States of the Church and the establishment of the capital at Rome. This was accomplished in September, 1870, when the French troops supporting the pope were withdrawn to defend France from her German invaders. So at last Victor Emmanuel entered Rome and established his throne over a united Italy. Since that great event Italy has made great progress, though amid many trials of various kinds. The kingdom, however, is well established upon constitutional principles, and the three kings who have reigned since 1870 have been men of courage, wisdom, and popularity.

The literary history of nineteenth century Italy presents great strength and growth in all departments.[6] There were great writers during this growing period of Italy's political power. Of historical writers eminent names are those of Botta (d. 1837) and Cantu (d. 1895) and F. De Sanctis (d. 1883). With these should be reckoned Silvio Pellico, whose account of his imprisonment became famous, and Joseph Mazzini, the great political writer (d. 1872), and P. Villari, writer of lives of Savonarola and Machiavelli. Of poets there was the passionate patriot Aleardi (d. 1878), and Carducci, who was greatly beloved among his people. Of novelists and story writers the eminent name of Manzoni first occurs to mind, though he was also a poet of distinction. Later came Verga, Farina, and Edmond De Amicis, whose beautiful stories are written in the choicest modern Italian. The latest writers of this group are the well-known D'Annunzio and Foggazzaro. In the hands of these masters the traditions of Italian literature have been ably sustained, and the literary distinction of Italy in this period is as brilliant as her triumph in the political sphere.

[6]See *Warner Lib.*, Vol. 31, p. 18 ff., with the references to other volumes of the *Library* for accounts and specimens. Also other recognized authorities on Italian literature.

Religious movements[7] in Italy during the nineteenth century were closely interwoven with its political history. The gradual unification of the kingdom under the House of Savoy, a constitutional monarchy, carried with it an ever greater degree of religious toleration, to the final establishment of freedom of worship throughout Italy. Against the progress of Italian political unity and the liberal policy toward other forms of Christianity the popes continually protested. In 1814 Pius VII restored the order of Jesuits, and they came back to power determined on the further strengthening of the papacy. Pius IX became pope in 1846. At first he showed liberal tendencies, but the Revolution of 1848 caused him to react and he became one of the most thoroughly reactionary of the popes. In 1854, without a council, he proclaimed the doctrine of the Immaculate Conception of the Virgin Mary, thus placing her almost on a level with her Divine Son. Ten years later, in 1864, he published his famous Encyclical and Syllabus. In these documents he advocated very high Catholic principles and condemned Protestantism and modern progress in no uncertain terms. In 1870 the decree of Papal Infallibility was passed by the Vatican Council, but soon afterwards the triumph of Victor Emmanuel took away the temporal power of the pope. The later popes have maintained the policy of their able and distinguished predecessor. Roman Catholicism has been uncompromising, and still fights Protestantism and progress as much as possible.

Parallel with the maintenance of the highest Catholic pretensions have gone the Protestant movements for evangelizing Italy. Early in the century the emigrant Protestants formed congregations in some of the Italian cities, and chapels for the use of the embassies of the various Protestant powers were permitted. The liberal constitution promulgated by the House of Savoy in 1848 was strictly adhered to, and with the growth of the kingdom religious freedom went hand in hand. The Waldensians of Piedmont pushed into Italy. Under these

[7]See Kurtz, *op. cit.*, p. 389 ff.; Newman, *Church History*, II, p. 444 ff.; G. B. Taylor, *Italy and the Italians, passim,* and especially p. 377 ff.; Werckshagen, *op. cit.*, art. on Italy (Bd. II, S. 1062 ff.) by Prof. E. Comba.

varied influences a Free Church of Italy was formed, but through internal divisions it was somewhat weakened, though many strides have been made towards the establishment of a native Protestantism in Italy. German, English, and American Protestants have established missions in Italy, and through the co-operation of all these forces considerable advances have been made in the direction of strengthening the Protestant cause. Necessarily, the various movements and events thus briefly recalled were intimately and influentially connected with the history of preaching.

Taking up, now, the study of the preaching and preachers of Italy during the nineteenth century, we naturally begin with those of the Catholic Church.[8] Here we find two phases or characteristics which are distinguished in time as well as method. From the French Revolution and the disturbance in Italy during that period to about the middle of the nineteenth century, when the modern revolutionary movements occurred, we find a style of preaching different from that which characterizes the latter half of the century. Of course there was no sharp line of cleavage, but there is a notable change of general tone and manner which will be more clearly indicated as we proceed.

Regarding the first of these periods as a basis, we shall say that, after the turmoil in the latter part of the eighteenth century and the greater quiet which came following the overthrow of Napoleon, in 1815, the Catholic preaching of Italy assumed a more scholarly and academic style. The Revolution had helpfully affected preaching by drawing away the preachers from the commonplace topics and methods of the past. The pulpit had to grapple with a great crisis in human thought and with a time filled with new political and social theories. But following that came a lull which gave time for more studious reflection, and we have a period of expository and hortatory preaching giving more attention to instruction in doctrine and morals and to spiritual edification; but the style of preaching became more studied and more academic again, and there was

[8]Zanotto, *Storia della Pred.*, p. 423 ff. (capp. XI, XII); Micocci, *Antologia della Sacra Eloquenza Moderna*, p. 30 ff.

a tinge of classic romanticism which tended too much to ornament and display. So there is in many preachers of this earlier period some recurrence to the bombastic and flowing style which had too often in the past marred the oratory of the pulpit.

In the latter part of this century, however, there is quite a change again. The stirring events since 1848, and especially of 1870, had a profound influence upon the Catholic pulpit. Two phases of this influence are especially to be noted; one good, the other mixed. The good influence was in the direction of making the preaching more simple and popular. The Catholic pulpit had to meet what it esteemed the gravest errors in doctrine and the most dangerous forces against its own supremacy. It found, also, that the aristocracy was becoming less and less amenable to religious influences, and accordingly there must be increasing appeal to the common people. These two things called for and occasioned a more direct, vigorous, and popular mode of address, and this was certainly an improvement. On the other hand, the demands of the hour induced too much of the polemical and argumentative method in the pulpit. Zanotto complains that there was too much dependence upon mere human reason and philosophic arguments. In part, he traces here the influence of Lacordaire and other French preachers of the apologetic school. There arose a tendency to make sermons mere defenses of the traditional faith or sharp and often indiscriminate attacks against all modern ideas. This led in a measure also to the neglect of moral and spiritual teaching.

So far as doctrine was concerned there was no great change. The Roman system as developed through the ages remained the substance of Catholic preaching, though, as we have seen, there was constant effort to bring it to bear on modern opposition and attack. In the effort to popularize religious teaching and meet errors among the people, missions, or evangelistic meetings, became much in vogue. These were subject to some abuses, and rules for their regulation were devised. Following the French models, there also arose a style of preaching called "conferences." These were free talks on popular themes rather than carefully studied sermons based on Scripture or doctrine. These also became subject to abuse and were regulated by authoritative rule. In both the early and latter periods thus indicated there were strong preachers who exemplified in their work the various phases of preaching which have been sketched. To some of the more important of these men we must now give attention.

Among a large number of preachers in the early years of the century, named and criticised by the authorities followed here, only a few need be mentioned. Pier Luigi Grossi (d. 1812), a Carmelite friar, had some reputation for eloquence, a clear intelligence, and a vivid imagination; but he employed a somewhat pompous style. Pacifico Deani (d. 1824), a Minorite, also attained fame as a preacher of both learning and popular gifts, who left after him a large number of published discourses on the usual themes. A more pronounced follower of the exaggerated and pompous manner of the day was Nani di Loiano (d. 1828), who attracted many enthusiastic hearers and whose sermons were often reprinted. Antonio Cesare (d. 1828), Francesco Villardi (d. 1833), and Francesco Finetti (d. 1842) ranked among the preachers of the first class in their times; but the most noted of this earlier group was Giuseppe Barbieri (1771-1852).[9] Born at Bassano, in the Venetian territory, and carefully educated, he early manifested great aptitude for study and eloquence. He was professor of sacred rhetoric at Padua, but after some years of service, entered the active ministry and became a much admired preacher. Although his style too much followed the strained and over-polished manner, and he sometimes fell into a pompous and wordy vein of speech, he had a strong native intellect and an ample culture that made him worthy of respect in spite of his faults. He was himself not unaware of the exaggerations of the time, and commented upon them in a treatise on the state of contemporary eloquence. He published many sermons. An extract, quoted by Zanotto from Barbieri's eulogy on St. Vincent de Paul, shows considerable brilliancy of conception, a fine flow of language, but

[9] Zanotto, p. 464 ff.; Lentz, *Gesch. der Hom.*, Bd. II, p. 359.

the usual exaggerations of expression and straining after effect. Lentz says that Barbieri avoided the worst defects of his age (it must have been bad, indeed, if he was moderate!) and exhibited a "true fullness of oratorical splendor and a harmonious rhythm."

Of the preachers who illustrated the second half of the century, one of the most famous was Gioacchino Ventura (1792-1861).[10] He was a native of Sicily, and in his young manhood joined the order of Theatines, of whom his lofty intellect and his earnest piety caused him to be made general. He spent some time in Rome, where he preached often, especially at the Church of St. Andrew and at St. Peter's. He preached the funeral of Pope Pius VII, and delivered a striking eulogy on the famous Irish orator and patriot, Daniel O'Connell. At first he sympathized with the movements for independence and freedom in 1848, but, grieving for their failure, he left Italy and sojourned in France, first at Montpellier, and then at Paris. Notwithstanding his foreign accent he created a profound impression in Paris by his eloquent sermons, many of them delivered at Notre Dame. After awhile he became reconciled to the pope, and returned to Italy, where he continued preaching to his death. Judging from pretty liberal extracts quoted from Ventura's sermons by Micocci, we should not fail to class him among the better preachers of his time and church. His style is popular, clear, and full of vigor. The two Italian critics are quite right in praising him for introducing a vastly improved method of preaching. He had genuine oratorical gifts, both of imagination and feeling. His doctrine is intensely Catholic, and his attacks upon Protestantism and philosophy are narrow and often unfair. Micocci over-praises him in calling him the "prince of modern sacred eloquence" and a "universal genius," but he made a great impression upon his hearers, both in Italy and France.

Next to him comes Vincenzo Stocchi (1820-1881),[11] a Jesuit, born of an honorable family in Senalunga. He pursued his literary education at the Seminary of Pienza, and through life continued an earnest student.

[10]Zanotto, p. 491 ff.; Micocci, p. 33 ff.; *Encycl. Italiana,* s. v.
[11]Zanotto, p. 501 ff.; Micocci, *passim.*

He joined the Jesuits in 1840, and in 1853 became professor of eloquence in one of their colleges. He sometimes conducted missions, and preached with great success at Venice, at Florence, at Rome (where he remained twelve years), and lastly at Bologna for the last ten years of his life. The matter of Stocchi's preaching is thoroughly Catholic, and his opposition to modern ideas is pronounced. He had a smooth and flowing style, carefully wrought out, but not overwrought. The extracts given by the critics impress us with his earnestness and with his logical power. A few sentences from a sermon on *The Cross* will give some idea of his manner. Speaking of the Saviour, he says: "Being made flesh, this Word of the Father, as He had in His incarnation no other end than that He should save us, so all His works in the flesh are works of a Saviour. While He tarried in the maternal bosom He was a Saviour. If He was born in Bethlehem and cries a Babe in the cradle, He is still the Saviour. He is Saviour in fleeing to Egypt, and in returning thence. If in youth He labors in the carpenter's shop; if poor and on foot He passes from place to place, sowing the seed of His doctrine; if He eats, if He drinks, if He prays, if He works, if He suffers, if He sleeps, He is still the Saviour. Every breath of His bosom, every beat of His heart, every drop of His sweat, every tear of His eye, are the sighs, throbs, tears, and sweat of the Saviour. This is the one and only name which belongs to this prodigy of two substances—omnipotent and weak, infinite and a babe, wounded and incapable of suffering, eternal and temporal, mortal and immortal, glorious and abased—in one word, God and man." In general, Stocchi's work, while clear and popular, is sometimes too rhetorical, though earnest in tone and feeling.

Another worthy preacher of this period was Giulio Arrigoni (1806-1875),[12] born at Bergamo. He preached much in Lombardy, Piedmont, and Tuscany, and received great applause as a preacher of unusual gifts. For a while he taught theology in the University of Pisa, and tried to popularize his subject. He was a great admirer of Segneri, whose preaching profoundly

[12]Zanotto, p. 501; Micocci, p. 80.

influenced his own. He died archbishop of Lucca, and left a good repute behind him. In a striking sermon on *The Love of Pleasure,* the following sentences occur: "Human life in this condition is usually accompanied by an empty heart ill adapted to raise itself to anything noble and dignified, because where the senses are all the time active and alert, the soul is deadened and, in fact, apart from every virtuous exercise. . . . This eternal need of dissipation and diversion is nothing else than a prolongation of infancy and an impoverishment of the spirit. . . . What greater degradation than this continual busying one's self to do nothing, passing only from gay company to the shows of the stage, from noisy banquets to the sad quarrels of gambling. Alas! I here touch a bleeding sore among us, and one which covers us with shame. Yes, of gambling, that passion of unfeeling souls which makes of rational man the sport of chance; which is an insensate amalgam of prodigality and avarice." In this whole sermon there is power of language as well as soundness of thought, and when the preacher comes to balance the real pleasures of a pious life over against those of sin, he shows both poise and penetration. There is another sermon, on *The Christian Mother,* which is admirable, not overdrawn with sentimentality and effort to say pretty things, but expressing what good men feel in pleasing and acceptable speech.

The last of this group whom it is worth while to notice is Carlo M. Curci (1809-1891).[13] He was born at Naples, the son of a noted lawyer. In early youth he became a Jesuit and was an earnest member of that order, but in later life he accepted and defended liberal views, opposing the temporal power of the pope, and believing in a united Italy. He also held some evangelical views. He insisted that the church should devote itself to spiritual work and leave politics alone. These sentiments brought on him the criticism of the extreme Catholics, but Curci was a man of real vigor. His thought is not very profound, but is strong and well reasoned. The style is somewhat heavier and less popular than that of the other preachers mentioned. In a sermon on *The Problem of Death,* he takes hold

[13]Zanotto, p. 503 ff.; Micocci, *passim.*

of the materialism of the day quite strongly from the Catholic standpoint and has some solid things on death and immortality.

On the whole, the specimens read of Italian Catholic preaching in the nineteenth century leave these impressions: It is not very profound, though thoughtful; too bitter at times in its polemic against Protestantism and modern thought; thoroughly convinced of Catholicism as to doctrine; earnest and persuasive in spirit; for the most part simple and pleasing in style, often eloquent, but some times inclined to rhetorical exaggeration.

Protestant preaching in Italy during the nineteenth century presents an interesting story.[14] In the earlier part of the period the Waldensians were active in Piedmont, and to some extent pushed their labors into other parts of the country. But there was much opposition and persecution, and it was not till the middle of the century and afterwards that the Protestant Italian pulpit amounted to much. Since the establishment of the kingdom in all Italy with freedom of worship guaranteed by the government, there has been a great development of evangelical preaching. Three groups of preachers distinguish the modern times. First, there are the foreigners—German, English, and American, who came to establish missions and churches. Many of these learned the language well, and preached to the edification of their congregations. A second group is made up of the evangelists and pastors attached to these missions. Some of these have done excellent work as preachers, scholars, and pastors; a few have been reckoned eloquent and influential. But the third group—which is the first in time and significance—is that of the native preachers, who have presented the evangelical opposition to the Church of Rome. Not a few of these have attained distinction as leaders and preachers. Three remarkable men claim special mention.

The Waldensian Church had a noble representative in Giovanni Pietro Meille (1817-1887),[15] long pastor

[14]See Taylor, and Comba, as mentioned in note 7.

[15]See *Sermoni di G. P. Meille* (with a brief account of his life), ed. by "A. M."—probably a member of his family, Florence, 1890; Taylor, *passim.*

in Turin, and a preacher of excellent gifts and usefulness. He came of an old Piedmontese family in the parish of Bobbio, where his father cultivated a little farm and also taught school. Later the family moved to another parish, to a more important school. Here the future pastor was trained in the rudiments of learning, and later went to Lausanne, where he spent about ten years in studies. Young Meille enjoyed the esteem of Professors Monnard and Vinet, the latter of whom is said to have remarked that the young man was "born for the pulpit." After his graduation, Meille taught in the Waldensian college for a time, but also preached as opportunity came. During 1848-9, Meille and several other young men spent some time at Florence perfecting themselves in the Italian language (French being their native tongue), and doing some evangelistic work. The Sardinian government had favored the little Waldensian church at Turin, and religious liberty was making some progress. The Waldensian Board determined, in 1850, to strengthen that work, and their choice naturally fell upon Meille as well fitted to take the pastorate. Here, accordingly, he came in that year, and found the work of his life.

After several years of hard foundation work, a large and suitable house of worship was built and dedicated, the pastor preaching on the occasion a noble sermon, setting forth the history and labors of the Waldensians. The church grew and prospered, attracting many of evangelical opinions. Among these were the evangelical preachers, Mazzarella and De Sanctis, who labored with Meille for awhile. But the variant Protestant elements—not all Waldensians—fell into some dispute, and De Sanctis led out a disaffected body, who were not satisfied with the older and slower methods of the Waldensians. This split hurt the cause for a period, but Meille labored to build it up again, and with success. He retired from the pastorate a few years before his death, after having done a valuable and enduring work. As a preacher Meille had decided gifts—a good delivery, a clear and pleasing style, and unction. He labored on his sermons, and they are full of thought and Scripture, with a deeply earnest spirit and thoroughly evangelical views.

The following is a description of a morning service held on one occasion at the Waldensian Church at Turin:[16] "It was not now the mellifluous and rather Frenchified word of Signor Meille. . . . It was instead a robust voice, a speech purely Roman, which thundered against the innovations of the papacy and enchained the attention and the sympathy of the congregation. It was a noble and sympathetic figure, that of the preacher. Tall and imposing in person, the spacious forehead was plowed in the midst with a deep furrow. His look was at the same time sweet and severe, truly fascinating. His gestures were few and dignified. Although he was but a little over forty, yet his hair, which he wore long, and the beard framing his manly face were already sprinkled with gray. It was Luigi De Sanctis." This eloquent and able leader of Italian Protestantism was born at Rome in 1808, and died shortly after 1885. In his youth he became a Carmelite monk and devoted himself earnestly to the service of the Catholic Church, but both the doctrine and life of the Church gradually drove him away. "Intellect and heart were at one in his decision to separate himself from the Church of Rome" (Taylor). This he did in 1849, fleeing to Malta, and writing letters explaining and justifying his course. Here he married an English lady, who became a great help in his subsequent work. De Sanctis was invited to reside at Geneva, which he did for three years, then going to Turin as associate with Meille, as already related. Here the unhappy division occurred in the Waldensian Church, with its dissonant elements. This led De Sanctis and Mazzarella to found the "Free Italian Church." The movement spread with the progress of affairs, but unwise views later crippled these Churches, and before his lamented death De Sanctis returned to the Waldensians, and served for several years as professor in their school at Florence. De Sanctis was a clear thinker, a strong and impressive speaker, and a man of deeply earnest life. His preaching and writings were of the first importance in the early developments of the native Protestantism of Italy.

[16]Taylor, *op. cit.*, p. 386 ff.; and compare notice in Comba's article in Werckshagen, *op. cit.*

Another of this noble group of patriots and preachers was one whom Dr. Taylor[17] describes as "the most splendid figure in Italian evangelization"—Alessandro Gavazzi (1809-1891). Born at Bologna, he was carefully educated and early became a priest of the Barnabite order. For a time professor of rhetoric at Naples, he soon entered the active ministry, and preached with applause in many places. But his liberal drift became soon apparent to himself and others, and he was regarded with suspicion. In the troubles of 1847-9 he took the patriotic side, and delivered at Rome a great eulogistic address on the soldiers who had fallen in the struggle. He opposed the French occupation and the restoration of the pope, and acted as chaplain in Garibaldi's army. By some means he was more fortunate than his friend, Ugo Bassi, who was captured and shot, and escaped into England, where he supported himself for awhile teaching Latin and Italian. But his personality and his splendid gifts as orator could not be hid. He addressed immense and enthusiastic audiences in England and America, but was almost mobbed by the French-Canadians on one occasion. In 1858 he was truly converted and became a Protestant under the helping guidance of Luigi de Sanctis. They were fast friends and co-laborers henceforth. He was connected with the Free Italian Church after the unification of Italy, and labored earnestly for the evangelization of his native land. He was much beloved and honored by all evangelical denominations and worked with all as he could. Some of his sermons were translated into French, but he did not leave a large literary fruitage of his varied powers and learning. He was chiefly a man of action and a soulful orator, who mightily moved his hearers and set in motion strong influences for the work he had so much at heart.

Of later preachers mention should be made of Ravi, who founded the first evangelical church in Sicily, and later devoted himself much to missions among the Jews; and of Rostagno, for some time the eloquent and attractive pastor of the Waldensian Church at Rome, where he preached to large and attentive crowds.

[17] *Id.*, p. 430 ff.; also Comba, as in note 16.

CHAPTER XII

The German Pulpit of the Nineteenth Century

The history of the German people during the nineteenth century is full of thrilling interest.[1] In the early years of the period Germany lay prostrate and humiliated under Napoleon. The famous victories of Austerlitz and Jena brought both Austria and Prussia under his iron hand. In 1806 the phantom of German empire was dismissed from history. But it was impossible for even such a military genius as Bonaparte to maintain a condition of affairs so abhorrent to natural justice and so galling to a brave, aspiring people as was the French ascendency over Germany. The German folk rose in their strength from disaster and defeat and finally drove the conqueror out in 1813. But the rulers rather than the people arranged the state of things at the Congress of Vienna, in 1815, and the dream of German unity was not yet near to reality. The various political units which divided the German folk could not yet find a sound and enduring basis of union. The two leading powers were Prussia and Austria, with the balance of weight with Austria, though her rival was pushing and constantly increasing in strength. There was a disappointed element of the people to whom the arbirtrary power of Hapsburg or Hohenzollern was not the ideal of German political destiny. The longing for freedom and unity could not be suppressed, however much it might be silenced and discouraged. During the revolutionary movements of 1848 Germany was in turmoil, and it seemed as if a large measure of popular liberty would be obtained, but the thrones were as yet too strongly entrenched to be upset. The monarchical principle conquered, though some reluctant concessions in the way of constitutional government were won in most of the German States. Prussia and Austria, in 1864, forced Denmark to surrender her claims to the Schleswig-Holstein lands, and then fell out over the division of the spoil. Prussia won in the memorable six weeks' war

[1]Bayard Taylor's *History of Germany; Historians' History*, Vol. XV; and other authorities.

of 1866, and thus established her supremacy as leader among the German powers. The terrible but short war with France in 1870-71 put the finishing touch to Prussia's acknowledged hegemony, and her king was acclaimed emperor of a new federal German empire, Austria alone of the more important States being left out.

These great military and political events were matched by progress in the arts of peace. In no age has Germany developed her natural resources and grown in wealth and strength as in this era. Her commerce and manufactures, her inventions, her growth in population, her leadership among the forces of civilization have all been pronounced and acknowledged. The development of patriotism, of national feeling, has been very strong, along with great political differences amongst the parties and powers which have divided her national life. In all departments German thinkers have had a great influence in the world. Whether in politics, music, art, business, philosophy, science, criticism, or literature, the power and suggestiveness of German thinking have been frankly recognized by the world. The lack of clearness, the passion for individual freedom of utterance, the constant conflict of theorists, with the rise and fall of schools and opinions, have been marked phenomena of the German mind in modern times.

German literature[2] in the nineteenth century did not maintain, much less surpass, the strength and glory of its classic period, which matured toward the end of the eighteenth, and lingered with Richter and Goethe into the first decades of the nineteenth century. Lyric poetry, however, distinguished itself in the beautiful work of Uhland and Heine. The modern German drama had only a few names of importance during the nineteenth century, such as Grillparzer, Hebbel, Ludwig, and latterly Sudermann. Musical drama, however, had in Richard Wagner its most illustrious representative. Fiction, as in other countries, had in Germany during the nineteenth century a great development. The brothers Grimm in the earlier part of the period gave great vogue to German popular tales. Short stories also flourished

[2]Priest's *Short History of German Literature;* Wilkinson's *German Classics for English Readers;* sketches and specimens in *Warner Library, passim.*

from Kleist, in the earlier years, to Paul Heyse, Storm, and Keller, toward the middle and end of the century. Longer novels were written by Auerbach, Ebers, Freytag, Spielhagen, Rosegger, Sudermann, and others. It is, however, in the literature of philosophy and criticism that the Germans have excelled. Here belong the philosophers Hegel, Schelling, Schopenhauer, and later Hartmann, Wundt, and Nietzsche, together with the critics, the Grimms, the Schlegels, Scherer, Fischer, and others. Nor should their great historians, such as Niebuhr, Ranke, Treitschke, Mommsen, and others, be omitted. In brief, we may say that German literature in the nineteenth century was strong, varied, often profound, touched with romance, but steeped in philosophy.

Religious affairs during this period are also of great and varied interest.[3] King Frederick William III of Prussia endeavored, in 1817, to effect a union of the Lutheran and Reformed Churches. The new body was called the Evangelical Union. The effort was in large measure successful, but not wholly so. The stricter Lutherans refused to come into the body, partly because of their long-standing dispute with the Calvinists, and partly because the ritual was more elaborate than they desired. The union movement, however, secured a large following, both in Prussia and some of the other German States, though the old Lutherans still remained a very considerable party.

Among the Catholics in the early part of the century there arose an evangelical movement led by Gossner, Boos, and others. It was largely a reaction against extreme Catholicism, but was opposed and cast out. The movement fell into fanaticism and was not permanent, though not without some good fruits. The restoration of the Jesuits in 1814 strengthened the papal party in Germany, as elsewhere. The Jesuit and generally High Church type of thought, known as Ultramontanism, had its strong adherents in Germany, but was not without opponents. In 1870 the dogma of Papal Infallibility, passed by the Vatican Council, was strenuously opposed by some of the leading German Catholics, as Hefele, Döllinger, and other distinguished scholars. Some of

[3]Kurtz's *Church History* (Am. ed.), Vol. III, appropriate sections; Newman's *Manual of Church History,* Vol. II, *passim.*

these yielded and accepted the doctrine, but others formed an Old Catholic party, which commanded some influence for a short time, but has not proved a permanency. The Ultramontane efforts were vigorously opposed also by Bismarck and other political leaders in Germany. They dreaded the influence of the Jesuits, against whom the Imperial Diet passed strong repressive laws, known as the Falk Laws. Latterly, however, the political exigencies of the empire have led to a more cordial relation with the Catholics. In recent times, especially in Austria, an Anti-Catholic movement has originated under the cry, "Away from Rome." Thus within the Catholic body there were some stirring movements in Germany during the century.

Among the sects there was some advance, with the larger measure of toleration which the country has enjoyed since 1848. Minor parties and groups had more freedom. Among these the Baptists gained strength and did some worthy work in various parts of Germany.

German theology and criticism have had great influence upon the modern pulpit, both in the Fatherland and throughout the world. We can here only briefly outline the principal elements of modern German religious thinking. The overthrow of Napoleon and the freeing of Germany from the French yoke were regarded by the people as a direct interposition of Providence. Amid the general rejoicings gratitude to God was not forgotten, and this attitude caused a considerable reaction from the cold Rationalism of the eighteenth century. There was a wave of genuine evangelical feeling throughout Germany. Along with this the influence of the great theologian and preacher Schleiermacher must be reckoned. Recoiling from the bald Rationalism which had desolated German religion in the preceding epoch, he insisted upon a return to religious feeling, making the center of his thought to be faith in God, or, as he called it, the feeling of dependence upon God. Schleiermacher did great service in recalling the heart of Germany to a deeper religious experience, but on the intellectual and critical side he was too sympathetic with Rationalism. The older form of Rationalism was indeed dead, but under the lead of Strauss and Baur a new rationalistic criticism of the

New Testament arose about 1835, and this went on in various forms but increasing power throughout the century. Through the influence of Wellhausen and his school, this criticism was largely directed to the Old Testament, and, under the name of Higher Criticism, or destructive criticism, has been a potent force in Biblical studies and theological thought for a generation. Along with this newer criticism came a sort of continuation of Schleiermacher's influence in the theology of Ritschl and his school. Religious experience was magnified and the accepted forms of religious expression retained, but large deference was paid to the advanced type, both of critical and philosophic thought. Together with these forces must be reckoned the rise and power of scientific Materialism. The theories of the English school were accepted and pushed to a great extreme in Germany, especially under the teachings of Haeckel. More recently the radical philosophy of Nietzsche has been hostile to true religious sentiment, as well as to traditional Christianity. Still another influence in Germany must be dealt with as affecting the religious life in all its bearings, that is, Socialism. The teachings of Marx and other socialistic thinkers have involved large elements of materalism, and thus far have been hostile to religion. This attitude has been emphasized because the government has been identified with the State Church, and so the political has blended with the religious situation.

On the other hand, along with all these hostile forces and problems there has been a steady evangelical and earnest maintenance of the true Christian faith. Many of the preachers have held firmly to the traditional Christian doctrines, and among the people a true spiritual life on the basis of the New Testament Christianity has maintained itself. Toward the end of the century there were not wanting signs of a strong and wholesome reaction in favor of a real Biblical and spiritual thought and life.

I. General View of Preaching

All the conditions and forces which have been described powerfully influenced German preaching during the nineteenth century. The national feeling had its effect upon preaching in giving a heightened tone of strength and independence to the German pulpit. Both the classic and the romantic influence in literature strongly reacted upon pulpit work, more especially as to form and style, but somewhat as to thought. It is easy to see how the philosophic and religious movements affected the preaching, and this will be more apparent as we proceed. It is necessary to discuss separately the Catholic and Protestant preaching.

Though the distinctive preaching of Germany since the Reformation has been Protestant, there has also been strong and worthy pulpit work among the Catholics.[4] This was true, not only in Southern Germany and Austria, where the older Church has remained strongest, but in other parts of the land as well. Upon the whole, and as was to be expected, the Catholic pulpit was not as much influenced by the progress of modern thought and activity as was the Protestant. There were, however, progressive elements in the Catholic Church, both in the evangelical direction and in the line of independence of thought and criticism. These tendencies were not without fruits, for they were ably represented; but the strenuously traditional and orthodox element in the Catholic Church proved to be the strongest. The restoration of the Jesuits in 1814 was a reactionary measure and gave strong help to the Ultramontane party. During the first two decades of the century there is not much to note in the Catholic preaching. It was the terrible time of Napoleon's supremacy, at the end of which Germany was still divided. It is true that the evangelical impulse given by Sailer continued over into this earlier period, yet parallel with this the chilling influence of the Illumination with its Rationalism was still felt. But about 1820 the spiritual reaction which followed the overthrow of Napoleon influenced Catholics as well as Protestants to return more warmly and devoutly to the old faith. Kehrein thinks that it was easier for the Catholics than for the Prot-

[4]Kehrein, *Geschichte der katholischen Kanzelberedsamkeit unter der Deutschen,* 2 Bde., Regensburg, 1843; l'Abbé Renoux, *Les Prédicateurs célèbres de l'Allemagne,* Tours, 1885; Zanotto, *Storia della Predicazione;* of Protestant writers, artt. in *RE,* especially Christlieb-Schian, with some others previously noted.

estants to return to a more spiritual preaching because they did not have so far to come and were greatly helped by the restoration of the Jesuits, among whom were a number of strong preachers. The progress in knowledge and literary art, together with the intensifying of patriotic feeling, had a salutary influence on eloquence in general, and naturally upon that of the pulpit. It is true that some of the sermons were of the order of cold discussions and orations decked with rhetorical brilliancy and ornament. Some preachers paid too much attention to secular events with a polemical purpose and effect. Along with the more spiritual and orthodox preachers there also remained some of a more worldly and partisan kind. Kehrein describes "a cold indifferentism in which many preachers seem to be ashamed both of themselves and of their Church, and sought to hide their identity so as to move on a smooth generality; and to this was opposed not seldom a somewhat bitterer zealotism which could not omit in any sermon casting a polemical side-glance on the Non-Catholics." We shall see later how some of these tendencies were represented in individual Catholic preachers.

On the Protestant side of preaching a vigorous and abundant life showed itself amid great variety of parties and schools of thought.[5] The old Rationalism which had flourished in the latter part of the eighteenth century and lingered over into the nineteenth was no more a strong impulse in preaching, but its sway had been very widespread. So much so that Rothe remarks,[6] "About the year 1800 we find in evangelical Germany all other schools of preaching as good as died out, only that of the Illuminism, the so-called philosophico-moral is left." This statement is too sweeping, for Reinhard and Müslin, both representative men, were opposed to this extreme, and they were certainly evangelical, as Rothe himself elsewhere shows. But there is a large

[5]Works of Rothe, Christlieb-Schian, Sack, Nebe, Brömel, Hering, Werckshagen, Ker, previously mentioned; Fish, both the *Masterpieces of Pulpit Eloquence,* and the *Pulpit Eloquence of the XIXth Century;* Stiebritz, *Zur Geschichte der Predigt in der evangelischen Kirche,* Gotha, 1875; L. O. Brastow, *The Modern Pulpit,* New York, 1906; and *Representative Modern Preachers,* 1904.

[6]*Op. cit.,* S. 452.

measure of truth in the statement. Hence, the first thing we have to note in the German Protestant pulpit of the nineteenth century is the decided reaction against the older forms of Rationalism. This reaction may be characterized as twofold, proceeding in part from the side of feeling as represented in Schleiermacher and his school, and in part from a more decided evangelical recurrence to Biblical and evangelical orthodoxy. We may mention as a third force that worked somewhat with this, the founding of the University of Berlin, in 1810, an event which, coming at the time it did, represented both the patriotic and religious movement of German life. Against the coldness and deadness of the old rationalistic method all these forces operated, and not in vain, to bring in a warmer, more genuine, more highly Christian life and power in the pulpit of Germany. Schleiermacher's *Discourses on Religion* appeared in 1799, and they produced a profound impression throughout Germany. Men began to see that too much stress had been laid on the purely intellectual and logical in religion, and too little scope had been permitted to faith and feeling. Henceforth a new breath is felt in the German pulpit. There were many who took up the new movement with earnestness and with power. Deeply spiritual men like Klaus Harms in the north and Ludwig Hofacker in the south appealed not in vain to the deeper piety of the German people. With this good start the evangelical trend of German preaching came to great power along about the middle of the century in such men as Nitzsch, Tholuck, Krummacher, Koegel, and others. This side of preaching was represented chiefly, though not wholly, by active preachers, men who were in contact with human life. Its representative preachers were strong and popular. Christlieb, writing about the year 1886,[7] says that during the preceding forty years there had been more unity in witnessing for Biblical evangelical truth than had prevailed in a hundred years, and "the great majority of German preachers is to-day positively evangelical."

On the other hand, we must take account of the per-

[7] *RE* (2d ed.), Bd. XVIII, S. 621.

sistence of Rationalism. A few preachers like Rohr and Wegscheider still leaned to the old philosophic school of Rationalists, and they had some influence, both through their writings and in the pulpit. This group receives little respect at the hands of German historians of preaching, who called them "stragglers;" but, as remarked above, the rise of New Testament criticism under Strauss and Baur, about 1835, and the powerful reinforcement which came from the materialistic philosophy after the middle of the century, brought in a new and strong type of Rationalism into German thought, and this laid its damaging hand upon the pulpit. Preachers of this type, however, were found chiefly among the university professors, or those who were rather academic than popular. Of course there was all along a group of those who may be called mediating preachers, who made concessions to the new Rationalism without going all the way with it. In the latter part of the century the Ritschlian school of theology produced its characteristic effect. Men talked of repentance, faith, atonement, inspiration, in the old terms, but with a meaning borrowed largely from the time-spirit. Feeling and morals were exalted, but a definite grasp of Scriptural authority and thought was wanting. The familiar language did not bring the old message.

When we undertake to classify in groups the German preachers of the nineteenth century we encounter the usual difficulties. Distinctions can not be sharply made, and there is much combination and overlapping. German critics are apt to be a little subtle and arbitrary in making these groupings. Two obvious methods may be adopted. The more evident is that by church relation: whether Lutheran, Reformed, Union, and the various sects; but there is little use in maintaining any grouping of this sort. The second method, which is quite a favorite with the critics, is that of grouping according to theological position; in general, whether rationalistic, evangelical, or mediating; but under these a number of smaller groups which it would be more confusing than edifying to follow out. Still, such a classification, even though not perfect, is proper and suggestive.

The character of German preaching in this period appears in both its content and form. As to material or contents, the theology would be determined by that of the preacher himself, but as a matter of fact there is not a great amount of formal theology in modern German preaching. Here the classification pointed out above prevails. The somewhat vague theology of Schleiermacher and Ritschl and their followers is contrasted with the more definite and Scriptural views of men like Tholuck, Luthardt, and others like them. In all of the more popular and earnest preachers there is much appeal to feeling. Both of the groups just mentioned make much of this, and popular preachers like Hofacker and Krummacher make feeling the main element of their work. There is a good deal of apologetic and critical material. Sometimes this assumes the polemic form, but the attack on current unbelief is not so sharp as in previous centuries. The attitude of the pulpit toward attack is brave and firm, and for the most part competent, but is more respectful and does not descend to personalities as was too much the case in former times. Scriptural material is much in use, and the exposition of the Bible gains much from the great progress made in Biblical scholarship. For the most part, there is a much saner and a more practical use of Scripture than in former times.

As regards the form of preaching, there is vast improvement over the seventeenth and eighteenth century methods. While something of the older homiletical division and stiffness is retained, the plans and subdivisions of sermons are much simpler and in better taste. The double introduction remains, and the outline is usually plainly laid down and strictly adhered to. The style in many of the preachers, unhappily not in all, tends to more ease and clearness. In a few it is vivid and sweet, but in too many it is still involved and heavy. There is evidence of a high standard, both of homiletical and cultural ideals. The sermons show careful training, large knowledge, virile intelligence, and strength of purpose.

A few words must be said regarding the homiletical teaching in Germany during the nineteenth century. In this department there was excellent progress. Here again we must recall the widespread and powerful influence of Schleiermacher. In his lectures at the University of Berlin on *Practical Theology* he gave a strong and needed impulse to improved pastoral training, both in homiletics and the cure of souls. In the early part of the century also Theremin, in his little book, *Eloquence a Virtue* (published in 1814 and 1837), had maintained a high standard of moral character as necessary in preaching, and Rudolf Stier, in his *Keryktik* (1830 and 1844), had endeavored to emphasize the evangelistic or proclamatory side of preaching. Excellent treatises were later published by Palmer, Hagenbach, Nitzsche, and Otto. All these insisted on a Scriptural type of preaching, with good taste and an earnest effort to benefit the hearer. Later in the century Th. Harnack, von Zezschwitz, Hering, and others published learned, practical, and earnest treatises on homiletics. In this case, as in others, improved practice has brought in improved theory (as Christlieb justly remarks), and then improved theory helps a better practice. On the whole, the nineteenth century marks, both for the theory and practice of preaching, the highest point that has ever been attained by the German pulpit. This is said in no way to disparage the glorious work of the Reformation, which restored to Germany a Biblical preaching and made possible the developments of modern times. But after the Reformation, as our previous studies have shown us, there was a falling off in the power of German preaching, both in the seventeenth and eighteenth centuries. It has come to its own only in the nineteenth.

II. German Catholic Preachers of the Nineteenth Century

Early in the century there was a considerable movement in the German Catholic Church toward a more spiritual and evangelical life and preaching than that which had prevailed in the preceding period. This was largely due, as we have seen,[8] to the character and work of Sailer (d. 1832), who was still active in the first three decades of the new century. Along with

[8] *Ante*, p. 214 ff.

him, though scarcely so able or influential, must be reckoned Martin Boos (1762-1825),[9] a Bavarian, born of humble parentage, early left an orphan, but cared for and educated by friends, mainly an uncle in Augsburg. During his student days he experienced a genuine conversion and found peace in the Saviour. His doctrine and preaching were too much like those of the Lutherans to suit the Catholic authorities, and though no formal heresy nor the least unworthy conduct could be made out against Boos, he suffered much persecution in one way and another. But he won friends and followers in the various places where he wrought his faithful and spiritual work, and his preaching was blessed to the saving of many. Of this group also was Ignatius Lindl (d. after 1829),[10] a powerful orator, who attracted great crowds to hear his evangelical preaching in several places, but became obnoxious to the authorities and was finally cast out of the Catholic Church. He went off into some fanaticism, and became lost in a sect, but in his early work he was a strong preacher of gospel truth and did much good. The most important of this group was John Gossner (1773-1858).[11] Influenced by Sailer and Boos, and long associated with Lindl, he, too, was finally forced out of the Catholic Church, and became, in 1829, pastor of the Bohemian (Protestant) Church in Berlin, where he served for seventeen years as pastor. In his last days he still preached in Berlin in connection with a charity establishment which he had founded. Active in home and foreign missionary endeavor, diligent in writing, in care for souls, in preaching, Gossner led a busy and fruitful life. Had he and his fellow-workers been permitted to remain in the Catholic Church, they would have been among its chief ornaments.

Though these gospel preachers left their Church, others remained in its fold, and some of them preached with power. There was Francis Xavier von Schwäbl (1778-1841),[12] born in Reissbach, Lower Bavaria,

[9]Christlieb-Schian, *op. cit.;* art. by Ahlfeld in *RE;* Kurtz, *op. cit.*, III, p. 237. [10]Christlieb-Schian, and Kurtz, *ll. cc.*

[11]*Id.*, and art. by Hollenberg in *RE.*

[12]Kehrein, I, S. 258 ff.; II, S. 406 ff.; Renoux, p. 426.

student at Salzburg, Munich, Ingoldstadt, professor at Landshut, parish priest in various charges, and finally bishop of Regensburg from 1833 to his death. Though not so great as Sailer, he is worthy to be placed along with him in both character and services. He was a mild and lovable man whose character enforced his word in the pulpit. His preaching was marked by sincerity, earnestness, a good flowing style, and pleasing delivery. Schwäbl paid attention to passing events, but not in a sensational manner. Kehrein gives an address from him at the opening of a seminary for priests at Regensburg, in 1836, while Sailer was bishop there. It is unpretentious, but earnest in feeling, clear and winsome in style, devout in tone, judicious in thought. It teaches the essentials of preaching for all ages and churches. The four necessary things for a priest—which he should learn in his seminary life and ever afterwards practice—are: the spirit of separation from the world (in the right sense, not leaving it to its sins), the spirit of prayer, the spirit of knowledge, the spirit of consecration. The opening paragraph of his discussion of prayer is well worth quoting, and is as follows:[13] "Prayer is the ornament, the essential duty of the priesthood, is the soul of all priestly official actions. Without it the priest is no longer fit for any holy service and is useless to the Christian people. He sows, and God gives no increase; he teaches, and his word is sounding brass; he sings the praise of the Lord, but his heart is far from Him, and he praises Him only with the lips of his mouth. Prayer is like oil in the lamp of the priestly life; if the oil gives out, the wick can burn no more. In the troubles and labors of his calling prayer instills into the priest every comfort; without prayer, however, he is a being without life and light, a thing of shadows, whose most sacred actions are nothing more than the recurring motions of a soulless machine; his official duties are then for him the yoke of a slave, only dry, hard, oppressive labors, unless prayer sweetens the care of them or lightens their pains, or for their slight results comforts him by its confiding look to Him who blesses the sowing at the due time appointed in heaven."

[13]*Op. cit.*, S. 408.

Of similar devout spirit was the gifted and soulful Melchior Diepenbrock (1798-1850),[14] bishop of Breslau, and cardinal. He had a most interesting history. Born of noble family in Bochold, Westphalia, he grew up a wild and indocile youth, became enamored of military glory, and sought a soldier's education and life under and then against Napoleon, but was disciplined for insubordination and dismissed from the army. Yet he was an ambitious student, and made good progress in study and general culture, in spite of his irregularities of conduct. His conversion was notable. Sailer was invited to visit the Diepenbrock home, and young Melchior angrily declared he would absent himself during the good man's visit. But in some way the guest arrived the day before he was expected. At dinner the stubborn youth sat as far out of range as he could, and Sailer, perhaps thinking him shy or possibly divining the true state of the case, at the end of the meal went up to the boy and pleasantly asked him to take a walk with him about the grounds. Refusal was impossible. The interview lasted for only half an hour, and neither one ever told just what passed. But the wild boy was led to Christ; the change was immediate and thorough. He attached himself at once to his spiritual father, studying under him at Landshut, then becoming his private secretary and helper until his death. It was a beautiful friendship. After Sailer's death Diepenbrock's promotion was rapid. He was made cathedral preacher at Regensburg, in 1835, later bishop of Breslau, and then cardinal shortly before he died. Among his sermons are two panegyrics upon bishops of Regensburg—Wittmann, who immediately followed Sailer, but lived only a short time, and Schwäbl. These are both admirable in their way, and Renoux quotes also from other sermons which show the poetic turn, depth of feeling, beauty of language, and earnestness of purpose which characterized the preaching of Diepenbrock. Kehrein[15] gives the following extract as illustrative of his views of preaching as well as his style: "The sermon is to me a living word which has its value, its significance, and its effect through

[14]Kehrein, I, S. 490; II, S. 593; Renoux, pp. 368 ss. and 414 ss.
[15]Bd. II, S. 593 ff.

the vital and vitalizing relation in which the Christian preacher has to put himself toward the eternal truth and toward his hearers, as mediator between the two. The pervasive electric spark of the inner spiritual movement, not self-made, but coming from above, that is the enlightening ray and the fructifying germ of a Christian sermon. A printed one is a living breath hardened to a dead ice-flower on a cold window-pane."

One of the most remarkable preachers of the age was John Emanuel Veith (c. 1788-1876).[16] He was a Bohemian, of Jewish family, educated for a physician, but was converted in this thirtieth year, and became a preacher of unusual powers. At first he entered the Redemptorist order of monks, but later left them in order to have better opportunities of preaching. He received important appointments, and drew and held large congregations at Vienna and other places. But his ministry was mostly at the Austrian capital. He had a fine combination of qualities for the popular preacher: imagination, humor, brilliancy of epigram, sarcasm, poetic quality, keenness of argument, richness of illustration. Specimens of his work, given by both Kehrein and Renoux, show a master of popular discourse and bear out the judgment of Kehrein, who says of him:[17] "Veith's productions commend themselves by liveliness and wealth in images and comparisons, but great knowledge of nature as of the history of the world and of families. Depth of feeling and genuine Christian spirit, as well as great familiarity with the Fathers and Holy Scripture, allow us to forget that sometimes the argumentative intellect is too prominent, and sometimes the dignity of the pulpit is not guarded."

The last of this group to claim notice here is Henry Foerster (d. 1881),[18] successor of Diepenbrock as bishop of Breslau, and one of the notable German prelates who came into conflict with the imperial government in the so-called *Kulturkampf*, i. e., the enforcement of the Falk laws against the inroads of Catholicism after 1871. He was living when Kehrein and Renoux wrote, and they

[16]Kehrein, I. S, 364 f.; II, S. 504 ff.; Renoux, p. 508 ss.
[17]Bd. I, *l. c.*
[18]Kehrein, I, S. 390; II, S. 549; Renoux, p. 488 ss.

give only slight notices of his life, but good specimens of his sermons. These show a very cultivated mind, a noble and clear style, and a good deal of attention to rhetorical art. But the spirit is devout and pleasing, the thought worthy of attention. Foerster is said to have influenced Draeseke and other important Protestant preachers. He was given to the expository homily as a method, and his exposition and application show traces of the modern scholarship and taste. One of the discourses quoted treats of Christ as the Light of the World (John 8:46, 12:12), with this neat outline: He is the Light because He brings (1) The Truth of Heaven to Our Faith; (2) The Offering (Sacrifice) of Heaven to Our Love; (3) The Bliss of Heaven to Our Hope. The original is more striking because of the alliteration in the leading words: *Wahrheit, Weihe, Wonne.*

III. Protestant Preachers

It would probably be agreed among German students of their own preaching that the three men who have most profoundly influenced the modern German pulpit were Luther, Spener, and Schleiermacher. Widely different in character and environment as these men were, there was one thing in which they were very much alike, and out of that one thing came chiefly, though not exclusively, their great influence upon preaching. This one thing was their view of the personal relation of the soul of man through faith to Jesus Christ as the Saviour. This ground-thought found different expression in each of these great men. In Luther it was justification by faith; in Spener and Schleiermacher it was the life of piety as growing out of the mystical union between Christ and the believer. In Luther and Spener the Biblical element was more pronounced and authoritative than in Schleiermacher. The men and the times were very different, and each man in a sense was the child of his age. Each has left a broad mark upon the religious life and thought of Germany, but each in his own way. It is said that when Neander heard of Schleiermacher's death he remarked that he was a man from whom a new epoch in theological thinking would date, and it was even so. Schleiermacher's thought (and his thought found living expression in his preaching) represents a recoil from the cold and irreverent Rationalism and the morally fruitless speculations of Illuminism, which had their hurtful influence upon German preaching in the latter part of the eighteenth century and early years of the nineteenth. Luther recoiled from scholastic and corrupt Romanism, Spener from scholastic and narrow Lutheranism, and Schleiermacher from scholastic and cold Rationalism. They all recognized the value of religious feeling and the indispensable necessity of union with Christ, thus emphasizing the mystical element in Christian experience and the need of enforcing this in the pulpit.

As already noted, the German Protestant preachers may be grouped according to their theological and ecclesiastical positions, or simply in the order of time. The latter method is followed here, and we note an earlier, middle, and later group of preachers, whose theological views and relations will be indicated in each case. We naturally take first in the earlier group, during the first third of the century, the great and influential thinker whose name introduces the new epoch.

Friedrich Daniel Ernst Schleiermacher (1768-1834)[19] was the son of a strongly orthodox preacher of the Reformed faith, who was serving as an army chaplain in Breslau when his remarkable son was born. As a child Schleiermacher was marvelously bright, studious, and thoughtful. Both parents watched tenderly over his mental and moral training. He likewise owed much to the intelligent and sympathetic care of an older sister, Charlotte, to whom he was tenderly attached through life. After careful home training, Schleiermacher was

[19]*Life* (autobiography) and Letters of Schleiermacher, tr. by F. Rowan, 2 vols., London, 1860. Sack, Brömel, and Nebe (*opp. citt.*) all have excellent discussions of Schleiermacher as a preacher; see also art. in *RE* and other authorities. In German there are various edd. of the *Werke, Predigten,* and the *Reden über die Religion; Predigten* von Fr. Schleiermacher, 4 Bde., Berlin, 1843. In English see Ker (*op. cit.*), Brastow, *Representative Modern Preachers,* p. 1 ff.; *Selected Sermons of Schleiermacher* (with an account of his life), tr. by Mary F. Wilson, F. & W., N. Y., not dated; sermon in Fish, *Masterpieces,* I, p. 525; reprinted in *World's Great Sermons,* III, p. 201.

sent, in his fifteenth year, to the Moravian school at Niesky, and later at Barby. In these two schools he remained four years. The aim of the father was to protect the intellectual development of the son against the current Rationalism, as well as to implant in him the seeds of an earnest piety. In part only was the plan successful; for free thinking was in the air, and the boy was a thinker. He loved reading, and was of an inquiring mind. The strenuous and, it must be acknowledged, somewhat harsh and one-sided orthodoxy in which he had been reared itself raised some doubts in his mind. He felt keenly that the traditional modes of thought and expression failed to answer his questions. His father was greatly distressed at the boy's state of mind, and was rather harsh with him. The Moravians also could not retain the young man among them, as he was no longer clear in his Christian belief. It was a very painful crisis in his life, but one through which thousands of young men have had to pass. The affectionate sympathy and help of his sister Charlotte at this time was a great comfort to him, and the pious training in which he had been brought up kept his heart strongly attached to Christ while his intellect was disturbed with many speculations.

He was fortunate in finding at Halle, whither he was now sent, a very helpful guide in his mother's brother, Stubenrauch, who was a professor there. Here for two years he remained, reading very widely and thinking through the problems which disturbed his mind. He loved the Moravian type of piety, loved Christ, and he had deep feeling; but his mind was beset with many doubts, and the philosophy of the age, as well as its literary trend, encouraged his revolt from the traditional orthodoxy. His whole subsequent career shows this struggle and division in his soul. Though personally he came to greater peace of mind, his theological position was never a very clearly defined one. Many of his sayings show intellectual sympathy with Rationalism, but he was no Rationalist in the proper sense. A characteristic remark of his is often quoted: "For his intellect alone I love no man; Schelling and Goethe are two mighty intellects, but I shall never be tempted to love them." On leaving Halle, in 1790, he became a tutor in the family of a Prussian nobleman, and later taught in an orphan house in Berlin. In 1794 he was ordained, and accepted a country charge. Two years later he became chaplain of the famous hospital in Berlin, called The Charité, where he remained till 1802. It was during this time that he was greatly occupied in varied literary labors—for one thing, translating from the English the sermons of Blair and Fawcett. It was at this time also that he published the first edition of his famous *Discourses on Religion* (1799). For three years he held a pastorate in Stolpe, and in 1805 was called, as professor of theology and university preacher, back to Halle. On the breaking up of this university by Napoleon, in 1807, Schleiermacher returned to Berlin, where he served a small church for two years, and finally, in 1809, became pastor of Trinity Church (Dreifaltigkeitskirche). Here he found his life-work and remained pastor of this great church to the end of his days. In addition to his pastoral labors, he was made professor of theology in the University of Berlin, where his lectures were heard with applause and profit by many students. Schleiermacher was not only preacher and professor, but an active, sympathetic, and wise pastor. How one man managed to fill these three important positions with such eminent success in all remains a marvel. It is explained in part, of course, by his wonderful natural endowment. He was a highly gifted man; but the other part of the explanation must not be left out: he was a very conscientious and laborious man. In a sermon on laziness, he declared that to be one of the chief vices, the parent of many others. It was certainly one which had no place in his make-up.

In domestic and social life Schleiermacher was genial and affectionate. His great learning and wide culture, his intellectual and personal sympathies, his deep feeling and intense patriotism caused him to be greatly loved and honored in a wide circle of friends. Though of small stature and somewhat deformed about the shoulders, he had a pleasing and intellectual face. There was almost a feminine, though by no means effeminate, trace in his nature. It is said that he once expressed the wish that he had been a woman! The romance of his married life is characteristic of the man. After an early disappointment he remained single for many years, but during the wars a young pupil and friend of his left his wife and children to the care of Schleiermacher. The young man was killed in battle; Schleiermacher continued to take care of the widow and children; and the expected happened. Though his wife was much younger than himself, it was a very happy union. One of the most beautiful things in his career was the tender sermon which he preached after the death of his only son. He was a man of large heart as well as brain, pure in life, and of high and noble purpose. He died in great peace and Christian hope, in the sixty-sixth year of his age.

Schleiermacher's preaching can not be understood without some reference to his general theological position. As already suggested, this is hard to define. It was, perhaps, not clear to himself, certainly not in his younger years. In feeling and sympathy he was closely allied with the evangelical spiritual element of Christianity. But on the intellectual and speculative side he was a philosophic Rationalist. Consequently, he does not belong entirely either to the orthodox or to the rationalistic party. The warmth of his feeling, his personal trust in Christ, and the energy of his thinking made him a strong foe of the older type of Rationalism. Its extreme development, at least in the pulpit, received its deathblow at his hands. He spoke of it as consisting of "ill-connected fragments of metaphysics and ethics which is called rational religion."[20] Yet in his relation to Scripture he was a Rationalist. The Old Testament made little appeal to him, and he used it not much in his preaching. In later times he would doubtless have sympathized with the higher critics. He was free also in his dealing with the New Testament writings, valuing them chiefly as the revelation of Christ. His famous principle that religion consists in the feeling of absolute dependence upon God is interpreted by his teaching and experience of the mystical union with Christ. His Moravian piety kept in his soul the great

[20]Quoted by Sack, *op. cit.*, S. 276.

principle of Zinzendorf: "I have one passion only: It is He! It is He!" And yet this absolute trust in Christ and love for Him did not make Schleiermacher accept in the full Scriptural sense the doctrine of our Lord's atonement. He believed in and constantly spoke of Jesus as the Saviour and the only Saviour, but his conception of the person and work of Christ was rather that He saves us by dwelling within us, purifying us, keeping us in touch with Himself and God. His view of the Trinity was not clear; he teaches little concerning the Holy Spirit. Though he spoke the language of the church, he was no ardent upholder of church doctrines as such. His gentleness of nature kept him from being polemical, but he does occasionally criticise with severity those who hold to the letter of Scripture and doctrine. Thus, while believing in the deity and saviourhood of Jesus, he was not in full sympathy at all points with traditional orthodoxy. So, to repeat, he was not in accord with either the out-and-out Rationalists or with the evangelical group of thinkers. In moral teaching he was far more satisfactory. Here his teachings ring true to the essence of the Christian system. His ethical teaching is founded both in the teachings of Christ and in the personal experience of Christ's indwelling in the soul.

As to Schleiermacher's preaching, it was for substance one with his theological thinking. It had the defect and the value of his central theological position. It grew out of his own religious feeling, and it appealed to the religious feeling of his hearers. It was inadequate through what it lacked rather than erroneous in what it emphasized. He seemed to address himself almost exclusively to those whom he believed to be already Christians, and his effort was to arouse and encourage and strengthen within them the love of Christ and the practice of Christian virtues. His preaching was not distinct enough in its presentation of the essential principle of the gospel, but it was profoundly spiritual and uplifting within its somewhat restricted range. His method of preaching was admirable. He carefully and thoroughly thought out his subject, making prolonged and patient study of it in all its bearings, and then he preached without notes, or with only a brief outline. His published sermons were either from shorthand reports reported by others, sometimes revised by himself, or written out by himself after delivery. They are usually well-analyzed and logical. He had his division and subdivisions carefully in mind, and made them clear to the hearer as he proceeded. The practical aim of his sermons is evident throughout. It was to awaken feeling, not, however, for feeling's sake, but that it might become fruitful in conduct and life. The style of his discourse is characteristically German. It was reasonably clear, always pure and lofty. He avoided ornamentation. There is no straining after effect. We do not find much of illustration, but his imagination appears in occasional flashes of description. There is little or nothing of formal argument, but the logical power of his thought exhibits itself. There is no appeal to surface feeling, no effort to bring tears or produce a sensation; but there is depth of feeling and more definite appeal to the higher reaches of Christian sentiment in the conclusion of his sermons. The style is flowing, and the movement of thought and appeal is winning and elevated. He could not be called a popular preacher, and yet as early as seven o'clock in the mornings his church was filled with the thoughtful and cultivated people of Berlin to hear his elevated and powerful presentation of the truth as he held it. The greatness of his mind, the sincerity of his aims, the sympathy and breadth of his touch with men are greatly apparent in his work.

A very characteristic sermon is that given in Fish's *Masterpieces* on the resurrection of our Lord as a model for the new life of a Christian. Taking the words of Paul in Romans 6:1-4 as his text, he develops the points of similarity between the resurrection life of the Saviour and the regenerate life of the saved. The three main points of comparison are: First, the origin of both lies in the same power of God to raise the dead; second, the nature and character of the two are similar in many points; and third (which seems a little strange), the risen life of Jesus appeared to be incomplete, showing itself only occasionally, and this corresponds to the imperfect life of the Christian. In developing the second point, that the new life of the Christian resembles the risen life of Jesus in its character and manner, he says:[21] "Although a new life, it is still the life of the same man, and most intimately connected with that which preceded it. So with our Redeemer. He was the same, and was recognized by His disciples as the same, to their great joy. It was the identical form; the marks of His wounds He bore, as a memento of His pains and a sign of His death, even in the glory of His resurrection, and He retained the profoundest and most exact recollection of His former state. Even so, my good friends, is the new life of the soul. If the old man of sin is dead, and we live now in Christ, and with Him in God, we are still the same persons which we were before. As the resurrection of the Lord was not a new creation, but the same man Jesus came forth out of the grave who had sunk down into it, so there must have lain already in the soul, before it died the death which leads to the life from God, a capacity for receiving in itself, after the body of sin should have deceased, the life from God; and this life now unfolds itself in the same human soul, under the previous outward relations, and with the same quality of its other powers and faculties. We are wholly the same, except that the fire of the higher life is kindled in us; and we all bear the signs of death also, and the recollection of our former state abides with us. Yea, truly, in various ways and often are we reminded of what we were and did before the new life-summons sounded in our hearts; and not easily do the scars heal over of our wounds, and the manifold traces of these pains amid which the old, sinful man must needs die, that the new man might live. But the glad faith of the disciples rested in the fact that they recognized the Lord, in the glory of His resurrection, as the same which He had been; and so our confidence in this new life as a permanent, and to us now, a natural condition rests solely in this, that we find ourselves in it to be the same persons that we were; that there are the same inferior and higher powers of the soul which before served sin, but are now converted into instruments of

[21]Fish, *Masterpieces,* I, p. 528.

righteousness; yes, and in all the vestiges of that death as well as of the former life, we are touched with a lively sense of the momentous change which the quickening call of God has wrought in us, and are incited to the warmest thankfulness therefor."

Of the same age as Schleiermacher, and almost exactly contemporary with him, was the famous Reformed pastor at Bremen, Gottfried Menken (1768-1831).[22] The son of a merchant at Bremen and of a pious and wise mother, he had a careful nurture and a happy childhood. Educated in the schools of his native city, and at Jena and Duisburg, he yet did not owe much to the schools, but most to his own application and reading, for the ripeness and fullness of his culture. Already while a schoolboy his talent for speaking and his piety of life were recognized, and he was sometimes appointed to preach. On leaving the university he became assistant pastor to a blind preacher at Uedem, where he remained several years, and read much in philosophy and literature. Then he served for a time at Frankfort-on-the-Main, and then at Wetzlar. Finally, in 1802, he was called to Bremen, first at St. Paul's Reformed Church, where he worked for nine years, and then at St. Martin's, where he continued to his resignation in 1825. Menken had a real and deep experience of inner union with Christ after conflicts. His life, though happy in his Lord and in his work, had its shadows. He aroused some antagonism, his marriage was uncongenial and unhappy, and he was often sick and in pain; but his work was fruitful and his influence wide and beneficent.

Menken's theological position was his own. He opposed with all his earnestness the older Rationalism, taking a firm stand upon the Bible as the inspired Word of God and the real revelation of the divine thought and purpose; he accepted Christ as the only Saviour and true Revealer of God; but his view of the atoning work of Christ was defective, being somewhat like that of Schleiermacher. He minimized sin and the need of satisfaction, though exalting Christ as Lord and the Giver of eternal life through faith. Though a Reformed pastor, he was out of harmony with the Calvinistic theology

[22]Sack, *op. cit.*, S. 297 ff.; Brömel, II, S. 85 ff.; art. by Ph. Haenchen, in *RE*.

on many points. Thus he stood somewhat alone in his thinking, but he gave stout blows against the older philosophic and moral Rationalism, and, with Schleiermacher, wrought nobly for a better acceptance and comprehension of the revelation of God in the Bible. But he was far more Scriptural and evangelical than his greater contemporary. His method of preaching was that of the homily. He avoided themes and their logical analysis, making his sermons consist almost exclusively of expository comment on some passage of the Bible, preferring the historical treatment. He estimated the Old Testament much more highly than Schleiermacher and others of that day. He was very careful in the preparation of his discourses, and many of them were published and preserved in various editions. Though not especially fond of pastoral work, he gave much attention to the training of children. He was chiefly active and chiefly great in the pulpit, and drew many to hear his spiritual and instructive teachings of the things of God.

Along with Schleiermacher and Menken, who opposed the old Rationalism so strongly, we may mention one of its late but vigorous defenders in J. F. Röhr (1777-1848),[23] who was educated at Leipzig, and began his ministry there, but was chiefly active as leading preacher at Weimar. He held to a "rational" view of religion in the older sense—the Bible was a human record of the things it contained, Christ was the human Representative and Teacher sent from God, we must believe in Providence, in human virtue, and immortality on grounds of the human reason—and all the rest of the old rationalistic talk. Röhr was a strong man, and sharply opposed Schleiermacher as well as the more evangelical preachers. His many published sermons, and his "Letters on Rationalism" had much influence with those of his way of thinking, and are an echo of past days.

The newer type of rationalism, which the German critics distinguish as "speculative," found an able though not extreme representative in the first half of the century in J. H. B. Dräseke (1774-1849).[24] Of him Tholuck

[23]Sack, S. 368 ff.; art. by Franck in *RE.*

[24]Sack, S. 347 ff.; Nebe, II, S. 286 ff.; art. by Tholuck in *RE;* Stiebritz, SS. 52 and 512.

speaks as one of the most brilliant preachers of the modern German pulpit, comparing him to a meteor more brilliant than warming, and passing away as a meteor with his time, but the latter part of his judgment is scarcely deserved, for Dräseke had considerable influence during his life, and his sermons were read long after, though perhaps not much in more recent times. He published during his lifetime a great many sermons, and the volumes were eagerly accepted and read. Very notable among them was a series addressed to *Christian Believers* in Germany, and another on *Germany's New Birth,* and still another on the *Kingdom of God.* From extracts and outlines, as well as from the judgments of the critics to whom reference is made, we may gather a fair notion of Dräseke's standpoint and manner of preaching. But first a word or two as to his life.

Dräseke was born in Brunswick, of a very busy civil officer and a very pious mother, who lived until after he was grown and had begun his notable career as a preacher. He studied at the University of Helmstädt, becoming, in 1795, pastor in a small town, and, in 1804, at Ratzeburg, where he served for ten years. Although he was a Lutheran, he was called, in 1814, to the Reformed Church of St. Ansgar, in Bremen, as pastor for the Lutherans in that city. This was a customary arrangement. It was here that Dräseke did the best work of his life for about eighteen years. He was highly esteemed, indeed almost worshiped in Bremen, and his great popularity somewhat turned his head. His best friends could not acquit him of vanity. In 1832 King Frederick William III of Prussia, who greatly admired him, appointed him chief preacher in the cathedral at Magdeburg, to the office of General Superintendent of the province of Saxony, and with the title of Evangelical Bishop. Here for some years he did admirable work, and was heard in various parts of the province with great applause, but his last days were embittered. Personally he was a believer in the divinity of our Lord, but some of the strong Rationalists having made objection to the worship of Christ, Dräseke felt compelled to condemn them. He desired to dismiss the chief offender from his office, but the case was appealed to a higher church court and compromised, the bishop being instructed to warn and rebuke the offender. This event greatly disturbed Dräseke, and led to his resignation. At first the king would not accept it, but finally consented. In 1843 Dräseke retired from his active work and took up his residence at Potsdam, where he died in December, 1849.

Dräseke's theological position was mediating between Rationalism and evangelical orthodoxy. He rejected the older Rationalism and, with Schleiermacher and Menken, accepted and preached the personal union of the soul with Christ as the Saviour, but he came to this position more gradually than either of his contemporaries. In his earlier years he was not so clear as he later became. The human side of the Bible and of Christ were more emphatic in his teaching; but with years and experience he came to stronger faith, and we have seen how he finally broke with the old rationalistic party. His views of the inspiration of Scripture and of the atonement of Jesus were not satisfactory. He preached a moral gospel rather than that of free grace. His theology was Pelagian in regard to sin and salvation. On the homiletical side his preaching deserves high praise. It was brilliant, popular, powerful. He had strong individuality, departing from stiff rules and traditional methods. He used antithesis, strong statements, sweeping appeals. Of course there was some exaggeration and aiming at effect, but his thought and style alike were fresh, strong, and impressive. He had in marked degree the genuine oratorical gift.

There was in this earlier group a number of earnest, efficient, and highly respected preachers who held and preached evangelical opinions. Notable among them was the devoted Moravian bishop, Johann Baptist von Albertini (1769-1831).[25] His parents were of good family and position, his mother a highly gifted and devotedly pious woman. The parents moved from their first home to Neuwied on the Rhine, where was a congregation of Moravians to which they desired to attach themselves. It was here that Albertini was born, and his childhood years were spent under the guidance of these consecrated parents. His youth was passed at the Moravian

[25] Stiebritz, S. 45, S. 504; Nebe, II, S. 345; Sack, S. 316; art. in Plitt in *RE*.

schools of Niesky and Barby, where he received his education, and where he had all through the course the companionship and friendship of Schleiermacher. The two, though unlike in many points, were bound in a close and congenial intimacy of soul, based on intellectual, moral, and spiritual affinities and on somewhat similar experiences in religion during their schooldays. Both were distressed with doubts, both loved the Moravian principles and piety, both clung in personal faith to Jesus Christ. Though they parted at the end of their schooldays and pursued very different careers, their friendship was unbroken through life.

At the close of his brilliant course as a student, Albertini was appointed a teacher in the school at Niesky, and after several years, in the more advanced one at Barby, where he had received his own training. Personally he was a beloved and successful teacher. Philosophy, mathematics, natural science—all engaged his attention. Botany was a favorite subject, and the fruit of his studies was published in a treatise of recognized value on mushrooms. He was also expert in the classics and history, as well as literature. He was fond of poetry, and his own poetic gift was not inconsiderable, finding expression in many hymns and other religious lyrics.

In his study and teaching of the Bible Albertini became more and more settled in his theological opinions and in his personal acceptance of Jesus as Saviour and Lord. After struggle he came into light and peace. His position was much clearer and firmer than that of Schleiermacher. He occasionally preached while still teaching at Barby, but the sermons of these early days are rather cold and rationalistic. But the fervor of his heightened religious experience soon appeared in his more spiritual and earnest discourses. He was appointed to the full office of a preacher at Niesky in 1804, and in 1810 was ordained an elder. He filled this office with acceptance and distinction in various places, till he was made a bishop, in 1814, and resided at various places—Gnadenfrei, Herrnhut, and Berthelsdorf, where he died, greatly beloved and lamented, in his sixty-third year.

As a preacher Albertini perhaps ranks highest in his

own Church. He was distinctively Moravian in his type of thought and feeling. The mystical union with Christ was the essence and core of his preaching, and all else radiated from this center. This led to some one-sidedness and disproportion in his treatment of themes, but Albertini was true to all the main contentions of the evangelical system and presented them with conviction, earnestness, force, and charm. His classical culture, purity of style, soundness of taste, sincerity of soul, and devout piety appeared in his winsome sermons. These were widely read among the pious, and remained long as classics of German evangelical literature. Albertini was more generally read than any other Moravian preacher; his style was far more acceptable and polished than that of Zinzendorf, and he accordingly had a wider reading and, on the whole,—so far as preaching goes,—a more wholesome influence among the German people.

Another useful preacher of the early evangelical group was Franz Theremin (1780-1846),[26] long the honored cathedral and court preacher at Berlin. Theremin's father was a French refugee pastor at Gramzow, a small Prussian town, where Franz was born and received his early training. As a youth he studied at the French gymnasium at Berlin, and took his university course at Halle. Here he studied philology under F. A. Wolf, and theology under Knapp, and had as fellow-students and friends among others the poet Chamisso and the future church historian Neander. He completed his theological studies at Geneva, where he was ordained in 1805. The accounts give nothing as to his life and work till his call, in 1810, to the pastorate of a French Reformed Church in Berlin, where he labored four years. He desired, however, to preach in German rather than French, and the opportunity came when, in 1814, he was appointed cathedral (*Dom*) preacher in Berlin, a position which he filled with distinction and success for thirty-two years—the rest of his life. In theology Theremin held with conviction and fervor to the evangelical essentials; in church relation

[26]Sack, S. 356; Stiebritz, SS. 46 and 505; Nebe, II, S. 235; Brömel, II, S. 116; Palmer in *RE;* sermon in Fish, *Masterpieces,* I, p. 547.

he passed easily from the Reformed to the Lutheran confession, accepting unionist views; in homiletical skill he was a master of style, having formed his oratorical principles upon Demosthenes and Massillon, upon whom he wrote a treatise; his views of preaching are set forth in his famous little book, *Eloquence a Virtue,* in which he insists on character as the first essential of oratory; his sermons are rather thematic than expository, sound in doctrine, devout in spirit, clear and flowing in style, eloquent and moving in substance and manner, without much depth or originality of thought.

In this group also belongs Ludwig Hofacker (1798-1828),[27] who was born in Wildbad, a town of Würtemberg, where his father was pastor. His father was a preacher of some force, and was called to a church in Stuttgart in 1812. The mother was a woman of strong character and devout piety, and her two sons, Ludwig and William, proved to be excellent witnesses to her maternal fidelity and Christian training. Ludwig, in 1816, became a student at the University of Tübingen. For the first two years of his course he was rather a rollicking student, being of a jovial disposition and much liked by his comrades. While he fell into no serious vices, he was given over to worldliness and pleasure, and did not profit much in learning. But in the beginning of his third year, when he began to take up the study of theology, he became more serious. Soon he was smitten with a sense of his sins and distance from God. He began to pray much, and to read books of a mystical tendency. About this time he suffered a sunstroke, which undermined his health and left him a sufferer through life; but on recovering he devoted himself wholly to the service of his Lord, and the remainder of his short life was filled with earnest service in the pulpit. He was only thirty years old when he died, and because of ill-health, had only four years of active service in the pulpit. Two years he served in St. Leonard's Church at Stuttgart—the first as assistant to his father, the second as full pastor after his father's death—but his health broke down, and for more than a year he was

[27]*Predigten,* 22te Ausg., Stuttgart, 1898 (with account of life); Sack, 338; Nebe, III, 124; Brömel, II, 138; Ker, 328 ff.

disabled. In July, 1826, having somewhat improved in health, he accepted the pastorate at Rielingshausen, a village near Marbach, and not very far from Stuttgart. Here he preached and served as pastor till his lamented death, in November, 1828. A short life, but a great work. Hofacker is one of those few and noteworthy men like Spencer, Summerfield, Nott, and others, who died greatly lamented in early manhood, but have left behind them a good work and an undying fame.

Hofacker's sermons were first printed in part during his lifetime. Soon after his death his brother William, also a beloved preacher, gathered all his sermons together—about eighty in number—and published them. They had an immense circulation, the twenty-second edition was put forth in 1839, and up to that time about 80,000 copies had been sold. The edition here referred to was printed in Stuttgart in 1898, showing that these wonderful sermons are still read. When we ask the reason of this great influence from so young a man, it is not far to seek. Two things especially strike us in the sermons. One is their thorough and deep Scriptural evangelical tone, the other their sweet and genuine simplicity. Back of them lies the deep heart experience of the young man; through doubt and pain he had found his Lord and loved Him, and brought his message out of personal contact with his Saviour to the heart of his hearers. Such a voice was needed in those rationalistic days, and the people thronged to hear a man who brought with no uncertain sound the gospel of grace and salvation through Christ. Hofacker must have had, like the young Spurgeon of later days, a winsome manner as well as a strong and sweet message. He was not driven to vanity by the great popularity which he enjoyed, but humbled by it; in fact, he could not understand it. All the German writers and critics pay emphatic tribute to the worth of the man and the timeliness and beauty of his message. He was no deep thinker, and there are evident faults of manner and style, some of the crudeness of youth; indeed, it would have been wholly unnatural had this not appeared. His sermons are one-sided in that they are chiefly addressed to sinners and pay little attention to the training of Christians, but that was the message needed then and there. Hofacker was a true evangelist. In the first sermon of the collection, on the Triumphal Entry of Our Lord into Jerusalem, he deals especially with the words, "Say to the daughter of Zion, behold thy King cometh to thee in meekness." He pleads for the entrance of the Lord into the heart, and thus tenderly expresses himself: "O, whoever would have an open heart for Him and let Him in, how happy would such a man be! how many reasons for joy would such a heart have! not only on the feast days, not only in the church, but at home in his chamber, in his business, in his daily circumstances. For everywhere He meets his own. He is always coming; He has been coming for 1,800 years to the daughter of Zion. He comes in His Word, He comes in His Spirit, He comes in His Supper, He comes at the most different times and under the most different circumstances. He comes in good and bad days, through suffering and through joy. His gracious voice is everywhere audible, on the street, in the field, when thou in the sweat of thy face dost eat thy daily bread as well as when thou restest on thy bed. He meets us often in the meanest circumstances. He is always coming, but He can not always come in. The doors are often shut to Him, because His enemy dwells in the heart. His knocking, the footstep of the coming One passes unheard, the noise inside is too great, the cry is too great, the traffic, the sin-traffic, the traffic that thinks of this world is too great in the heart, the sleep of sin is too heavy, we can not hear Him; the heart is too earthly, too proud. It will not recognize the lowly Son of man who would enter in humility as the King of Peace. Jerusalem had a noble temple and beautiful services therein, and distinguished priests and high priests and a great pride, therefore she despised Jesus of Nazareth, who came not with conqueror's might and glory, but in lowliness. Such a King, such a Messianic Kingdom they would not have. And so it goes yet with the poor hearts of men. But be only still, let thyself be little, and bow thy heart in the dust, abhor only in thyself all that will be puffed up and is contrary to the mind of Jesus, then wilt thou understand the call of the Spirit, 'Thy King cometh to thee,' and open with joy thy heart to Him, and thy King will come to thee and rule in thy heart."

Hofacker had no arts of eloquence nor sensational novelties, but with his soul he preached Christ and Him crucified. This was the open secret of his power and success. He died comparatively a youth, but being dead he yet speaketh. He passed away in pain, but yet in peace, and his last words were: "Heiland! Heiland!—[Saviour! Saviour!]"

Another great evangelical and evangelistic preacher of this time appeared in North Germany. This was Klaus Harms (1778-1855).[28] Harms was a man of the people and gloried in his origin. He was born in Holstein, the much disputed province, of German population, but at that time under Danish rule. His father was a well-to-do miller, and he himself served at that trade. His parents were religious and early desired that Klaus should become a preacher. It is said that when a boy he repeated to the servants one of Schmolck's hymns with so much earnestness and effect that people said he was a born preacher. His parents were not able to afford him the best education, but he studied and worked at intervals. On his father's death he inherited a small sum, and in this way he was enabled to study at the University of Kiel, where he made good use of his opportunities and mended the lacks of his culture. Though morally earnest, he was of rationalistic tendencies, and the university at that time was under the sway of rationalistic views; but Harms could find no spiritual satisfaction in Rationalism. The study of the Bible was bringing him to a sense of deep spiritual need when, at that crisis, a friend of his said to him one day: "Klaus, I have just got a book that I think you will like. I can not make much of it, but I think you can. Come by my room and I will lend it to you." The book was Schleiermacher's *Discourses on Religion*. Harms joyfully took it to his room, shut himself up with it, having told the servant to deny all visitors, began to read it, and read it through by midnight. The next

[28]Sack, 330; Nebe, III, 401; Brömel, I, 178; Stiebritz, 45, 505; Carstens in *RE;* Fish, I, 535; Ker, 338 ff.; Petersen in Werckshagen, II, S. 602.

morning he arose early, it being Sunday, and read the book through again by evening. It was in a sense the means of his conversion; at any rate, it brought him to see the utter spiritual worthlessness of the old Rationalism, and he would have no more of it. Turning now with renewed interest to the study of the Bible and of the Lutheran theology, he found in this the resting place for his mind. He accepted decidedly and finally the evangelical doctrines. He saw man to be a lost sinner, and Jesus to be a perfect and sufficient Saviour. He had found his soul and his message at the foot of the cross, and henceforth through life he was a strong and powerful preacher of the gospel of salvation by grace. He began to preach at Kiel while still a student, then served for a little while as tutor for a neighboring pastor, preaching occasionally to the people, where a little congregation heard him gladly. He was called as pastor to a church at Lunden, in Ditmarsch. While here he published his first collection of sermons, and they were well received. In 1816 he was chosen archdeacon in St. Nicholas' Church, in Kiel. This post he held till 1835, when he was advanced to a higher position in the same church. The year preceding he had declined the king of Prussia's invitation to become Schleiermacher's successor at the Trinity Church, in Berlin. In his latter years he received various honors, his talents and services being widely recognized. In 1849 a partial blindness and advancing age caused him to lay down his work. He died, greatly beloved and honored, in 1855.

Harms as a preacher was, like Hofacker, decidedly evangelistic. He attacked with all his might the current Rationalism, and turned the hearts of many to a better faith. In 1817, the anniversary of the Reformation, he put forth, after the manner of Luther, ninety-five theses in defense of the evangelical faith. This provoked a great controversy, but Harms maintained his cause with vigor, if not always with good taste. As to the form of his preaching, this was more studied than that of Hofacker. He did not go deeply into exposition, though this was not wholly lacking in his work. His divisions were usually clear and striking, his spirit was elevated and sincere. He knew how to adapt himself to the popular needs, both in thought and style, and yet he attracted a large hearing from among the more cultured. During his whole career he was the most popular and powerful preacher in North Germany. His published sermons, though scarcely so widely read or so long useful as those of Hofacker, had great circulation and influence in their day. The man and his work gave a great and blessed impulse to evangelical preaching over against the dull Rationalism of the early part of the century.

We pass now to a group of evangelical preachers whose work lay mainly in the second third of the century. First to be named among them is Karl Immanuel Nitzsch (1787-1868).[29] He was born near Leipzig, the son of a pastor who later became professor of theology at Wittenberg, where Karl received his education. He taught for a while after his graduation at Wittenberg. In 1811 Nitzsch was ordained as deacon and preached at the Castle Church. In 1817 he received the degree of Doctor of Theology from the University of Berlin, and after serving as pastor at Kemberg, he was made professor of theology and university preacher at Bonn. He performed his double office with great distinction and success, besides writing a number of theological treatises. Finally, in 1847, he was appointed to a high church office and professorship of theology in the University of Berlin, where he also served at various times as preacher in important churches. He lived to a great age, and was actively at work nearly to the end. His eyesight and hearing both failed him towards the last, but the gentleness and patience of his disposition never left him. It is beautifully said of him somewhere that he remarked, "I can't see, nor hear, nor write, I can only love." Nitzsch early and firmly assumed a definite evangelical position in theology; as Sack well says: "His richness of thought was united with a decidedly grounded direction of the feelings upon the revelation of God in Christ. There resulted a progress from the revealed

[29]Sack, S. 371; Nebe, III, S. 205; Stiebritz, SS. 47, 506; Hering, S. 230; F. Nitzsch and Christlieb-Schian in *RE;* Fish, XIX cent., p. 63.

mysteries and truths in which the conception of God was biblico-theistic. The revelation appears as fact, miracle and self-witnessing of God; the person of Jesus Christ as of the eternal Son and Mediator who yet appeared in time; and the work of salvation as a fact of experience; faith as practice." Certainly there was nothing original in this, but it shows the clear and definite standpoint of Nitzsch over against the uncertainties of Schleiermacher and the rhetorical expressions of Theremin. Nitzsch was a man of the highest dignity and holiness of character. His influence over pupils and hearers was full of blessing. He had some vividness of imagination and a great sincerity and depth of feeling, but his style is involved, hard, and unattractive. He must have been difficult to follow, and his readers have not been very many, but those who have learned his method have not failed to profit by the power of his thought and the devoutness of his sentiments.

Along with Nitzsch should be named the beloved and distinguished professor and preacher, Dr. August Tholuck (1799-1877).[30] He was born at Breslau, son of a goldsmith, who designed him for his own business, but the young man preferred learning to jewelry. Already in his childhood he displayed remarkable gifts for learning. His early studies at Breslau were continued at the University of Berlin. He was especially fond of the Oriental languages, but studied widely also in other directions. He says, in his own account of his life, that in his twentieth year he read for the first time the Epistles of Paul, and under the great blessing of God a short time afterwards he was led to believe in the crucified One as Paul preached Him. He soon decided to devote himself to the study of theology, and took up the work under Marheineke and others. So remarkable were his talents and learning that he was made professor of theology at Halle when only twenty-five

[30]Sack, S. 377; Brömel, II, S. 158; Nebe, III, 280; Stiebritz, SS. 197, 580; Hering, S. 231; Kähler and Christlieb-Schian in *RE; Fish,* XIX cent., p. 33; *Sketch of the Life and Character of Prof. Tholuck* (with some sermons and other writings), by E. A. Park, Edinburgh, 1840; also some sermons translated in Fish and Poor's *Select Discourses from the French and German,* New York, 1858.

years old, and two years afterwards succeeded the venerable Dr. Knapp. He was a prolific writer also on various theological subjects all through his long life. His commentary on the Psalms enjoyed great distinction and was translated into different languages. His appointment to Halle was much disliked and opposed by the Rationalists there, but he did excellent service in overcoming their influence. As a teacher he won the love and confidence of his pupils. He often walked with them and cultivated their intimacy and friendship. His health was not strong, but he lived a long life and performed great services. He also filled various preaching offices in the province of Saxony, being university preacher at Halle most of the time, and once serving a term in Rome as pastor to the German Embassy there. He published many sermons, and exercised a blessed ministry during his whole life. As a preacher he was Scriptural, earnest, and powerful. He spoke to the heart rather than to the intellect, and in a style adapted to the comprehension of the people.

Tholuck's preaching was eminently the fruit of his own experience. A highly gifted, widely learned man, he had come through difficulties to a personal experience of Christ as his Saviour. He therefore sympathized with the difficulties of the cultivated classes, and his appeal was especially to these. Like Mosheim, in the preceding century, he believed that learning and culture should be used in sermons so as to make their impression upon the thoughtful and cultivated. There is little of the doctrinal in Tholuck's sermons. He was not much of a churchman, nor does he emphasize in a theological way the main doctrines of the Bible. He says little or nothing about the Trinity, nor does he offer any theory of the atonement, but with deep feeling he presents Christ as the Revealer of God and the Saviour of sinners. Tholuck's learning never degenerates into mere pedantry. His historical allusions and illustrations are natural and apt. The style is more conversational and personal than is usual with German professors. He had a vivid imagination, but it was duly controlled. The main element of his preaching was feeling, deep, genuine, contagious, pure, and strong. His sermons were heard by large audiences, and by many generations of students at Halle. In printed form they had wide circulation in Germany and other lands. Thus both in spoken and written discourses, this gifted and devoted professor was one of the mighty forces in the German pulpit of the nineteenth century. His great gifts and learning were consecrated to his Lord. He ended his days in great peace. His last words were, "I fear not for myself; the death of Christ avails for me."

Another but quite different preacher of the evangelical type was Ludwig Harms (1808-1865),[31] the celebrated pastor at Hermannsburg. He was not related to Klaus Harms. His father was pastor before him at Hermannsburg, and he became assistant to his father in 1844, and afterwards his successor. His father was a man of strong character; his mother a pious woman, an excellent housekeeper, and loving mother. Her children were well brought up. It was in 1817 that the elder Harms became pastor at Hermannsburg, where he and his son ministered all their lives. Ludwig received his education at the gymnasium in Celle and the University of Göttingen. Here he studied under some of the most notable professors of the age, and was well trained. Harms was thoroughly evangelical alike in experience and in doctrine, but he was withal a very stout Lutheran of the pietistic sort. His preaching was with power, but was often sharp and rude. He preached with effect to the common people. Besides his preaching and pastoral work, he is noted in missionary history as the founder of the Hermannsburg Missionary Society, which was established in 1849, was supported largely by the common people of Harms's church, but grew very much and has become one of the leading missionary societies of modern times. It has worked chiefly in Africa, though in other lands also.

Among the evangelical preachers of the German Reformed Church the name of Krummacher stands very high. Several of the family have become distinguished. Friedrich Adolph was not only a teacher and pastor of note, but has obtained a permanent place in German literature through his famous *Parables*. Daniel Gottfried

[31]Nebe, III, S. 401; Stiebritz, SS. 85, 529; Hering, S. 237; Uhlhorn and Christlieb-Schian in *RE*.

was a younger brother of his, and was also noted as a strong and earnest preacher. Emil W. was a younger brother of Friedrich Wilhelm, and very much like the better known preacher. There have been others also of the younger generation who are more or less known as able preachers, but the greatest name of the family is that of the famous court preacher at Potsdam, Friedrich Wilhelm Krummacher (1796-1868).[32] He was born at Mörs, a small town, where his celebrated father was teaching school and preaching. The parents were both cultivated and pious. The family moved to Duisburg, in Westphalia, where the father taught and preached for six years, then moved again to Bernburg, where Friedrich and his brothers attended the gymnasium. Later he pursued his university course, first at Halle, and then at Jena. Both institutions were at that time strongly under Rationalist influence. Krummacher found no satisfaction in this. His home training and his father's earnest sermons had kindled deeper longings in his soul. Revolting from Rationalism, studying the Bible and books of piety, he found rest and peace in a personal trust in Christ. In this, like Tholuck and others, he was never shaken. He had a varied early ministry, becoming pastor successively in several Westphalian towns, especially Elberfeld, where he settled in 1834, and did a great work. His preaching attracted large crowds and was productive of much spiritual fruit. In 1847 the king of Prussia invited him to succeed Marheineke at the Trinity Church in Berlin, so long the scene of Schleiermacher's ministry. At first the change was very trying, for the spiritual conditions in his new parish were different from those which Krummacher left behind, but he soon won his way and attracted large audiences. About 1853 he was appointed court preacher at Potsdam, a position which he held till his death, in December, 1868. He was a great favorite with the king of Prussia, and was faithful in his ministry to all.

As a man, Krummacher was jovial, hearty, and af-

[32]Nebe, III, S. 242; Stiebritz, 83, 528; Hering, S. 235; Kögel and Christlieb-Schian in *RE;* Sermon in Fish, XIX Cent., p. 83; *Elijah the Tishbite,* and *The Suffering Saviour* (Am. ed.); in the original, *Neue Predigten,* Bd. II, *Der Leidende Christus,* Leipzig, 1868, containing 58 sermons on the Passion of our Lord.

fectionate, fond of his friends, and frankly egotistical. As a preacher he held with all his might to the Reformed doctrines. He was an ardent student of the Bible, and thoroughly believed in its divine inspiration. While not distinctively a theologian, his grasp of doctrine was not hazy or indefinite. He accepted the sinfulness of man and the vicarious atonement of Christ. He was Calvinistic in his theology, and earnest and warm in the presentation of his views. His homiletical method was free and independent. While not a slave to rule, he usually followed a good outline and arrangement of his matter. His style is popular and clear, full of feeling and warmth. He had a rich and soaring imagination, which he used freely. His exposition of Scripture is occasionally somewhat fanciful, but usually able and sound. His illustrations are abundant and apposite. His series of discourses on *Elijah the Tishbite* made a great impression, because they went back to the Old Testament and used a method of character study and historical exposition which were at that time somewhat new. The sermon found in Fish's *Pulpit Eloquence of the Nineteenth Century,* despite some defects, is a model of modern expository preaching. In the great series of sermons on our Lord's passion, *Der Leidende Christus* (The Suffering Saviour), Krummacher is at his best. The firmness of his faith in the atonement of Christ, the depth of his feeling, the richness of his imagination, the power of his appeal, the clearness and popularity of his style, and chiefly the warmth and force of his eloquence are all in full evidence.

Among the evangelicals of South Germany no name stands higher than that of Johann Tobias Beck (1804-1878).[33] Born of humble parents, at Balingen, in Würtemberg, he received his preparatory schooling there, then completed his university course at Tübingen, where he was in close friendship with William Hofacker and other earnest Christians. In 1827 he became pastor of a small village church, and was an earnest preacher and disciplinarian, not always wise, but serious and earnest, and his work did much good in a rather rough and wild parish. Soon a more congenial place was found

[33]Brömel, II, S. 187; Nebe, III, S. 370; Stiebritz, SS. 141, 553; Hering, S. 242; Kübel and Christlieb-Schian in *RE.*

for him at Mergentheim, where he labored for seven years, and then became professor and preacher at Basel, where he served till 1843. While at Basel, besides his lectures and sermons, he was busy with other writings, and took deep and active interest in foreign missions. At the instance of Baur and others, he became professor and preacher at Tübingen, where he remained to the end of his life, though not preaching much in his last years on account of various ailments.

Beck had marked peculiarities as a preacher; his theological and ecclesiastical position was somewhat free. He inclined to the mysticism of Bengel, even verging upon the theosophy of Oetinger. He was not a systematic theologian nor a decided churchman, yet he accepted in the main and in his own way the church doctrines. His view of the person and work of Christ was similar to that of Tholuck and others of that time. He firmly accepted the divinity and mediatorship of Jesus, but without clear definitions of His atonement. Deep and warm personal attachment to Christ was the essence of his creed. In regard to the Bible, he firmly held it to be the Word of God, and did not go with the Tübingen school in their critical theories, but he held a free view of inspiration. Above all things, he was an expounder of the Scripture. This was his strong point. As to method, he discarded homiletical rules and struck out in his own way. He reverted to the homily form of explaining a passage, making application as he proceeded. He was often obscure in thought and style, but his great services in the unfolding and applying of the Bible to the thought and life of his own age gave him great influence and a name as one of the most remarkable of German preachers. A clever summary of his method has been given in the saying that "he preached in the chair and lectured in the pulpit."

Here also we must notice Friedrich Ahlfeld (1810-1884),[34] who was born at Mehringen, Anhalt, of honest and pious parents of the working class, and came to be one of the most noted preachers and pastors of his time. He had a hard struggle to get an education, but his fond and faithful mother and his own pluck made

[34]Nebe, III, S. 422; Stiebritz, SS. 232, 597; Hering, S. 238; Lechler and Christlieb-Schian in *RE*.

success possible. He was prepared at various schools, and finally entered the University of Halle, where he enjoyed great advantages, and improved them. He began to preach in his student days, being ordained in 1833. His faithful and pious mother was a tender and delighted hearer of his first sermon. Escaping the rationalistic tendency, Ahlfeld became more deeply pious and devoted. After teaching and preaching in various small places, he became pastor, in 1838, at Alsleben, where he served for nine busy and fruitful years. Then, through Tholuck's influence, he was called to the Laurentius Church, at Halle. The church had recently suffered by a schism and the difficulties were great, but Ahlfeld's noble preaching and wise and earnest work were greatly blessed. His fame grew and he received many calls to other places, but declined them till, in 1851, he was called to the Nicolai Church, in Leipzig. This he accepted and held for more than thirty years, up to his death. He had a very rapid delivery, and on the occasion of his first sermon in Leipzig a citizen remarked, "It is very fine, but he makes no commas nor periods."

As a preacher Ahlfeld was remarkably gifted with intuition and liveliness. He had a rich fancy, keen insight into life and character, dramatic power, a fine gift of narrative and description, together with warm feeling and a clear and popular style. These qualities, together with his devout earnestness, made him a powerful and influential preacher for the masses. His personal life was deeply pious, and in this he had the congenial and loving help of a good wife. His theology was stanchly Lutheran, but his sympathy and breadth made him loving toward all Christians. All in all, Ahlfeld was one of the most acceptable, beloved, and useful of modern German preachers.

There was a later group of strong and gifted evangelical preachers who lived and worked toward the end of the century. Among these was the consistory-councillor and court preacher at Leipzig and at Berlin, B. B. Brückner (1824-).[35] The authorities at hand give no accounts of his life and training, but the specimens

[35]Nebe, III, S. 429; Stiebritz, SS. 175, 569; Christlieb-Schian in *RE.*

and criticisms of his work show him to have been a preacher of noble powers and of the modern spirit. He had a keen intellect, a broad culture, a strong and striking style. His insight into his age was penetrating yet balanced, his grasp of the Christian verities was firm and hopeful, his homiletical method sufficiently but not stiffly formal. He delighted in antithesis, in strong though not extreme statements. His diction was vivid and vigorous, not involved or wearisome. His plans were often striking and excellent. In a sermon on the woman at Jacob's well, he thus states his points: (1) No soul is so erring that the Lord can not find it; (2) No occasion is so insignificant that the Lord can not use it; (3) No force is so weak that the Lord can not help it up; (4) No beginning is so little that the Lord can not lead it on to a blessed end.

Along with Brückner came Julius Müllensiefen (1811-1893),[36] who was long time pastor of the Marienkirche at Berlin, and a preacher of winsome manner and wide influence. He had been profoundly influenced by Schleiermacher and Gossner, and was specially gifted in leading seekers and doubters to a peaceful trust in Christ, such as his own rich experience had won. His easy and flowing style corresponded to his irenic and gentle spirit; as Hering describes it: "Perspicuous and clear, without the employment of strong rhetorical means; never stormy, but ever heartfelt and earnest, it recalls the saying about the waters of Siloah, which go softly."

In South Germany, along with and after Beck, were a number of important preachers, such as Adolf von Harless (d. 1878); Wilhelm Löhe (d. 1872), who was a powerful orator; Sixt Karl Kapff (d. 1879), especially distinguished for piety and a sweet and mystical tone of discourse; and Wilhelm Hoffman (d. 1873), who, though a South German by birth and training, worked chiefly as missionary secretary at Basel, and later in Prussia. Chief among these, however, was the Suabian poet and preacher, Karl von Gerok (1815-1890).[37] His religious

[36]Nebe, III, S. 425; Stiebritz, SS. 179, 572; Hering, S. 249.

[37]Nebe, III, S. 427; Braun in Werckshagen, II, S. 637 ff.; Stiebritz, SS. 277, 616; Hering, S. 243; art. by Mosapp in *RE*. *Predigten auf alle Fest-Sonn-und Feiertage,* Bd. I, Stuttgart (undated).

and patriotic poems have given him a place of his own in German literature, and his earnest, spiritual, gospel sermons in his high office as leading preacher at Stuttgart have secured his position among the most important and useful of modern German pulpit orators. The high esteem in which Gerok was held by his contemporaries is well expressed in this appreciation by Nebe: "Gerok has deep feeling, a very mobile, easily kindled soul; his spirit is of fine make, stands upon the height of modern culture, and makes use of the aid which the culture of every time has brought to him. He is well versed in the Scripture, and to Him of whom the Scripture bears witness belongs his whole heart; at His feet he lays devotedly down all his native gifts. He has a large heart, no trace of narrow confessionalism; his harp has only melodies which kindly attract, thankfully praise, joyfully worship. The style is in every aspect excellent, exemplary, classic; pure and clean, brilliant and clear, fresh and lively, full of perpetual youth, of lovely charm, of genuine popularity, of life-warm clarity." A perusal of Gerok's sermons will go far in justifying this generous praise. They reveal a genuine, poetic, sentimental nature, a fine and liberal culture, a loving heart, a loyal soul; and they are couched in an eminently readable and engaging style.

Among professors of theology who also did noble work as preachers in the latter half of the century occur the honored names of C. E. Luthardt and K. F. A. Kahnis, at Leipzig; of Julius Müller, at Halle, and—in more recent times—of Julius Kaftan, at Berlin.

The high office of cathedral and court preacher at Berlin was adorned in the latter part of the century by the incumbency of Rudolf Kögel (1829-1896),[38] who stands at the head of recent pulpit orators in Germany. He was of poetic and oratorical temperament, gifted and highly cultivated in mind, at home in modern thought and literature, master of a clear, noble, and powerful style. His thought was clear, but deep and thorough; he knew men, and the times in which he lived. Its difficulties and problems, its strong and weak places, had been

[38]Art. by Rietschel in *RE;* Dibelius in Werckshagen, II, S. 642 ff.; Nebe, III, S. 432; Stiebritz, SS. 178, 571; Hering, S. 250.

thought through; and his preaching was a word of power as well as a joy to the true believers of his time.

After Kögel, and at the turn of the century, came another great preacher to the cathedral and imperial court at Berlin. This is the strong and yet tender Ernst Dryander.[39] Twice did the author have the privilege of hearing him in the summer of 1902. A man of noble, intellectual face, of clear utterance, easy style, winsome manner, appealing voice. There is a deep earnestness arising from an evident but not obtrusive experience of religion, and a simple, hearty persuasion of the divine verities of the Christian faith. A small volume of sixteen *Evangelical Sermons,* published first in 1882, on the occasion of Dryander's leaving Bonn for a charge in Berlin, gives the reader some idea of the preacher's position and merits. The sermons are remarkably simple and heartfelt, showing (but not obtrusively) the preacher's culture and grasp of modern ideas and problems, and placing the emphasis on the saving gospel of Christ as still the emphatic need of the human soul.

CHAPTER XIII

The Dutch and Scandinavian Pulpits of the Nineteenth Century

It is natural and proper to pass from the preaching of Germany to that of the Netherlands and the Scandinavian countries. For, except the French part of Belgium, these arc closely related in language, religion, and habits of thought to their Teutonic neighbors. As in the two preceding centuries, so in the nineteenth much of German thought and method was reflected in the Dutch and Scandinavian pulpits.

I. Preaching and Preachers in the Netherlands

Hitherto in this history nothing has appeared as to preaching in Belgium;[1] nor indeed now is there any-

[39]Christlieb-Schian in *RE; Evangelische Predigten,* 7te Ausg., Halle, 1902.

[1]See *Historians' History; The Warner Lib.,* and other authorities for history and literature; Kurtz, *Church History,* Vol. III, p. 356 ff., for religious matters; Werckshagen, *op. cit.,* II, S. 1037 ff.

thing definite to say. For, so far as appears, no great personality nor any distinctive movement has arisen in the pulpit of that country. Politically its history has been closely woven with that of France and Holland, with both of which it has at different times been connected as a dependency. Its separate political existence since 1830 has not as yet brought to light anything of special interest in the pulpit. Nearly half the people speak French, nearly half Flemish, and a few both languages. The country has begun to develop a national literature in the work of Henri Conscience and latterly of Maurice Maeterlinck. Its religion has been predominantly Catholic, and the affairs of the Church have been inextricably mixed with politics; in fact, the Catholics are the leading political party. Some tendencies to modern ideas have struggled against the ruling ultramontane forces, but not with success. Some Belgian prelates joined the Old Catholics after 1870, but the movement did not come to much. There have been some Protestants in Belgium, and though they have enjoyed toleration with a growing measure of religious liberty, they have not developed any appreciable strength as a force in the political or literary concerns of Belgium; and naturally, not a pulpit of power.

In Holland the case has been quite different.[2] The pulpit of the nineteenth century was strong, both in its *personnel* and in its national and distinctive tone. The forces which were gathering strength during the eighteenth century came to their fruitage in the nineteenth with a comparatively rich Dutch theological and homiletical literature.

Political affairs need not detain us long. The century opened with Holland under the heel of Napoleon—first, a Republic dominated by France, then a kingdom under Louis Bonaparte for a brief period. On the fall of Napoleon the House of Orange was recalled and the kingdom of the Netherlands established (1815), including Belgium, which separated, in 1830, into an independent monarchy. In the troubles of 1848 important concessions were made by the crown, and the Dutch people escaped serious disasters, and gained still larger

[2]Same authorities; Kurtz, *op. cit.*, p. 351 ff.

popular freedom. Since then, under the form of a constitutional monarchy Holland has really been a democracy. The increase in population and wealth has been marked. The modern spirit has been active in all departments of the national life.

Dutch literature in the nineteenth century has shown the qualities and spirit of the modern era. Van Kampen, the historian, and Bilderdijk, the poet and historian, were still at work in the early part of the century. Isaac da Costa, a Jew of Portuguese descent, converted to Christianity under the influence of Bilderdijk, contributed valuable works, both to poetical and theological literature. Poetry and fiction found able representatives in Bogaers, Dekker, Haverschmidt, and Maartens—especially the last, who, however, has chosen to write in English. Historical and literary criticism found strong upholders in Hofdyk, Ten Kate, Huet, and others. Theological learning and religious literature were ably represented in Da Costa, Van Heusden, Loman, Kuenen, Van Oosterzee, Kuyper, and others of the various schools of thought.

Religious history in Holland during the nineteenth century presented many points of interest. The French conquest, with all its ruinous effects, left at least one benefit in the introduction of general religious freedom. Both in Belgium and Holland this enlargement of toleration produced great conflicts, but of a quite different nature. Belgium was Catholic, Holland Protestant. What the Catholics opposed in Belgium they were glad to take advantage of in Holland. So, when the Reformed Church was restored, on the creation of the monarchy in 1815, it was done along with the toleration of all other forms of worship, which likewise drew their sustenance from the State. This was a bad arrangement and led to great controversies. Later the great statesman Thorbecke, in furthering the cause of perfect religious liberty, made even greater concessions to the Catholics, so that they were encouraged to attempt the restoration of their ancient hierarchy in Holland. Naturally this produced a storm of indignant protest throughout the land. Meantime in the Protestant ranks there were serious divergencies and controversies. The situation about 1830 is thus presented by Kurtz: "In the prevailingly Reformed National Church rationalism and latitudinarian supernaturalism had to such an extent blotted out the ecclesiastical distinctions between Reformed, Remonstrants, Mennonites, Lutherans, that the clergy of one party would unhesitatingly preach in the churches of the others. Then rose the poet Bilderdijk, driven from political into religious patriotism, to denounce with glowing fury the general declension from the orthodoxy of Dort. Two Jewish converts of his, the poet and apologist, Isaac da Costa, and the physician, Cappadose, gave him powerful support."

The writing and influence of Da Costa and others produced a powerful movement in favor of a more orthodox and spiritual teaching and practice, but this led to a serious schism, and the forming of a separate Church in 1839, called The Christian Reformed Church. In the older Reformed Church there arose the three usual parties: (1) the radical rationalists, who were very strong, and found their leaders in such men as Loman, Scholten, and Kuenen, who virtually denied any supernatural element in Christianity; (2) then the mediating school had such able leaders as Van Oosterzee, De Groot, and others, who remained in the Established Reformed Church and tried to bring it to a more evangelical position; finally (3), there were the strictly orthodox Calvinists, who, under the lead of the thinker and statesman, Dr. Abraham Kuyper, long maintained a vigorous struggle within the establishment, but finally withdrew and united with the older separates who had gone out with Da Costa. Thus the religious life of Holland in the nineteenth century was one of great turmoil and constant struggle between the semi-skeptical school of modern criticism and the traditional Calvinistic orthodoxy.

In regard to preaching, the good influence of Hinlopen, Bonnet, and others in the preceding century led to a vast improvement in homiletical theory and practice.[3] We have seen how in the seventeenth and eighteenth centuries a dry scholastic method had prevailed

[3]See, as before, the article by Christlieb and Schian in *RE;* Werckshagen, *op. cit.*, art. by Cramer, Bd. II, S. 917 ff.; Van Oosterzee, introduction to *Practical Theology;* Hartog, *Geschiedenis van de Predikkunde;* Van der Aa, *Biographisch Woordenboek.*

in the Dutch pulpit, but earnest and in large degree effectual struggles had been made, and not in vain, to introduce better methods. Accordingly, we find in the nineteenth century that Dutch preaching feels the forward movement of the modern spirit. As already noted, the evangelical and rationalistic parties opposed each other and acted as spurs to each other. On the whole, the evangelical revival in the early part of the century was the main cause of the heightened tone of Dutch preaching throughout the period. The preachers who professed and taught evangelical doctrines were most popular and most effective in developing the Christian life of the people. A few of the most notable of these preachers may be passed in review.

Chief among them in the early part of the century was the gifted and beloved Jodocus Eliasson Heringa (1765-1840).[4] He was born at a small town in Friesland. At ten years of age he was sent to the Latin School at Groningen, and after that preparatory course, went through the university there with great distinction and honors. He was ordained, and began his ministry as assistant pastor to an old and weak man. In this difficult office he acquitted himself so well that he naturally became the successor to his aged colleague. In 1802 he was called to the double office of professor and preacher at the University of Utrecht; and though, on account of modesty and a preference for the pastoral service, he was reluctant to undertake the double burden, he yielded to duty and found therein his life-work. Leyden and other places tried to get him, but he held to his post at Utrecht until his death. Like other Dutch and German preachers, he was distinguished both in the chair and the pulpit. He saw much trouble during the French Revolution and supremacy, but behaved with great prudence and firmness. His course was of great service to his university and the cause of religion. He lived to an honored old age, much respected and beloved by his countymen generally, and by large numbers of devoted pupils. Like Bonnet and others, and like Francke, at Halle, he combined his two offices with great distinction. He was very learned, and very popu-

[4]Art. in Van der Aa; Van Oosterzee, p. 151; Hartog, bl. 279.

lar with the students. As a pastor he was faithful and beloved. As a preacher, the cyclopædia notice of him says: "Great was his renown as preacher and instructor in homiletics. Very early a competent critic gave him high praise as pulpit orator. His preaching was popular, simple, and cordial. He knew how to enlighten the understanding with Bible truths and to move the heart in a most Christian way." His Bible expositions were very highly prized, and his influence upon many rising preachers was great and enduring.

E. A. Borger (d. 1820)[5] is mentioned by Van Oosterzee with high praise as a preacher of remarkable genius. The critic says that he could "animate and enchain an audience, and soared like a royal eagle far above the crowd of powerless imitators and envious detractors. Whatever weak sides may have been justly found in his two volumes of *Leerredenen,* there is not one of his discourses which does not present traces of a master's hand, or which does not, upon reading again after so many years, still powerfully affect and touch." Borger seems to have been original in method and powerful in expression, an able apologete and an eloquent speaker. Sometimes he was too much given to ornament and display, but was on the whole a preacher of great power and lasting influence.

P. van der Willigen (1778-1847)[6] was a pupil of Heringa, clever, bold, and clear-headed. He was pastor at Hillegom, and died at Tiel, on retiring from active work. He held liberal opinions inclining to Rationalism. He was strong intellectually, but lacked evangelical warmth and force.

Later in the century and about its middle comes another group, of whom J. I. Dermout (d. 1867)[7] was in many respects the most powerful and brilliant. He was educated at Utrecht, began his ministry at Zeist, and, after several years in various places, he came, in 1805, to The Hague, where he worked for forty-two years. Four volumes of sermons were published at various dates between 1819 and 1846. He was a master in the analysis of his text. He also possessed great ease and power

[5]Van O., p. 152; Htg., bl. 317.
[6]Chr.-Schian in *RE;* art. in Van der Aa.
[7]Van O., p. 153; Htg., bl. 286, 331.

in applying Scripture truth to human life. He was nicknamed "the Napoleon of the pulpit" because of his sweeping and forcible manner of speech. Along with him comes J. H. van der Palm (1763-1840),[8] famous professor and preacher at Leyden. He also was particularly strong in exposition of Scripture, and published many sermons which were widely circulated and had much influence upon the younger ministry. Hartog says that none had greater influence than he in bringing into use in a many-sided and tactful way the principle of Scripture exposition and application. Van der Palm was a native of Rotterdam, where he pursued his academic studies. During the French troubles he was silenced for a time, but after the wars he settled as professor and preacher at Leyden. In 1806 he delivered a discourse on the Christian ministry, in which he set forth and emphasized with great power the principle that the preacher above all things must adhere to and teach the Word of God. He published many sermons in illustration of his principle, and thus he became a model for many of his brethren. Another distinguished member of this group was A. A. van der Hoven (d. 1855),[9] a learned and useful professor among the Remonstrants. He had a noble son, who was also distinguished as a preacher and teacher of that period. Van der Hoven was a remarkable orator, full of unction and eloquence. In 1825 he published a striking monograph on Chrysostom, in which he held up that great preacher as a model, insisting especially on naturalness and simplicity. This he practiced himself, for his manner was impressive and appealing without being overstrained. Van Oosterzee says that it was impossible to form a due judgment of him from merely reading his sermons; "One must have personally listened to his unequaled delivery in order to explain the magic power of a preaching which to the last could with undiminished force hold spellbound a numerous audience." He preached without notes, but with great ease. He had a good voice, attitude, and gesture, and is acknowledged to have been one of the most successful of modern Dutch preachers.

After the middle of the century we come upon a group

[8]Van O., p. 153; Htg., bl. 301.
[9]Van O., p. 154; Htg., bl 348 vv.

of modern Dutch preachers, among whom should be mentioned C. E. van Koetsveld,[10] pastor at The Hague. He published, in 1864, a strong volume of sermons on the *Apostolic Gospel,* in which he stoutly opposed rationalistic critical views. He also was successful as a preacher to children, and altogether was a man of influence and widely respected. Over against him should be named C. P. Tiele (1830-1902),[11] who as a preacher and writer represented quite ably the liberalistic trend of opinion. The mediating school of professors and preachers was admirably represented in the distinguished theologian, writer, and preacher, J. J. van Oosterzee (1817-1882).[12] He was long pastor and professor at Utrecht, belonged to the Established Church, but held orthodox views. He was learned in modern thought and literature, had mastered the German critical theories without accepting them. His great work on *Practical Theology* is one of the classics on that subject. As a preacher Van Oosterzee was both strong and popular. During eighteen years of service his preaching attracted thousands. He was especially gifted, and in great demand as a preacher on particular occasions. He was a master of the modern expository method, seeking and unfolding the exact meaning of Scripture, but applying it with unction, force, and success to the modern conditions and the modern mind.

The best known and probably the ablest representative of modern Calvinistic orthodoxy is the celebrated theologian, preacher, and statesman, Dr. Abraham Kuyper. He was long pastor at Amsterdam, and after striving in vain to hold the Established Church to the faith of its fathers, he took the lead in establishing a Free Reformed University at Amsterdam, in 1880. The object of this school was to teach the true evangelical faith as opposed to the critical theories of Scholten, Kuenen, and their followers. Dr. Kuyper has written notable books, one of them on *The Work of the Holy Spirit,* which is the leading modern treatise on that subject. Carrying his religious principles into politics, he led a

[10]Chr.-Schian in *RE.* [11]*Id.;* art. by Cramer in *RE.*

[12]*Id.;* Hartog, bl. 390 vv; art. by Doedes, revised by Van Been, in *RE.*

successful party in the State and for a time was Prime Minister. Dr. Kuyper is better known as a writer and leader, but the vigor of his mind and character were no doubt felt in the pulpit during his service as pastor at Amsterdam.

II. Preaching and Preachers in the Scandinavian Lands

The three Scandinavian countries had a varied and somewhat tumultuous history during the nineteenth century.[13] All were more or less disastrously involved in the troubles of the Napoleonic *régime* in the early years of the century. Denmark part of the time sided with Napoleon, part of the time played neutral, and thus in both ways incurred the enmity and felt the power of England. Sweden fell under the influence of France, and Bernadotte was elected king; but though he was one of Napoleon's marshals, he was not subservient to the tyrant, but opposed and finally turned against him. Norway was forcibly separated from Denmark in 1814, and though erected into an independent kingdom, was compelled to form a political union with Sweden. Though the two countries were under the same sovereign all through the century, they were never really united, much less fused, and early in the twentieth century (1905) the union was dissolved, Norway becoming a separate kingdom. Sweden lost Finland to Russia in 1809, and gained no real or lasting advantage by the union with Norway. Denmark attached to itself the German provinces of Schleswig and Holstein, but so unwisely used her power over them that they revolted in 1848, though unsuccessfully. Their condition appealed to the German people, but these were not united, and nothing but trouble and complications ensued until finally, in 1864, Prussia and Austria forced Denmark, in a brief and brave war, to surrender the two duchies. After 1866 they were absorbed by Prussia. Besides these relations to the other European powers, the internal affairs of the three lands were marked by political disturbances and changes. Den-

[13]For history, literature, and religion, authorities previously referred to; especially Werckshagen (Nielsen), *op. cit.*, S. 981 ff.

mark and Norway have been more favorable to modern ideas of liberty than Sweden.

Scandinavian literature had in all three countries a notable development in the nineteenth century. Some of the most distinguished writers of modern times adorn the literary annals of Denmark and Sweden. The greatest of Danish poets was Oehlenschlager (d. 1850), who enjoyed a well-deserved reputation among his countrymen. After him came Ingemann, who also was most highly esteemed as a poet and novelist. Most widely known of all Danish writers beyond his own country is the delightful writer of child-stories, Hans Christian Andersen; but he did other work also which entitles him to distinction. Of later date came Brandes, noted as literary critic; Drachmann, the poet; Allen, the historian; and among religious writers, to be named later, Grundtvig and Kierkegaard. Among Norwegians the great names of Ibsen, Björnson, Lie, and Boyesen (who also belongs to America) are well known as leaders in various fields of literary workmanship. The Swedes have in their constellation such stars as Tegnér, Atterbom, Almquist, Fredrica Bremer, and the delightful Finnish writer, Runeberg, besides a number of others. The literary ideals and spirit, as well as the favorite forms of literary expression, which characterized European letters in the great century we have under review, had strong hold upon the Scandinavian peoples and produced a rich fruitage.

In religious history we must recall that the three countries were prevailingly Lutheran. In Denmark and Norway, especially after 1848, modern ideas of religious liberty gained foothold and led to the entrance and spread of other forms of doctrinal and ecclesiastical life. In Denmark the Baptists got a start from their brethren in Germany and had considerable spread. In Sweden, though subjected at first to many persecutions—before the harsh laws against other than the Established Church were repealed—the Baptists had, after 1855, a wonderful growth and strength. The Catholics also took advantage of the freedom of religious worship and sought to establish themselves, but without great success. In religious life and thought the same general conditions which we have had to remark elsewhere in Europe were more or less prevalent in the three Scandinavian countries. The Established Church was divided into the radical rationalistic and the more conservative groups, and among the people many pious and sometimes extreme mystics sought in various ways to protest against the evils and declension of the age.

Preaching in these countries as elsewhere naturally felt the influence of the modern spirit in science, literature, and criticism. Improvement in method and in popular application was apparent in Northern European preaching as in that of the other countries. As the author is not at home in the Scandinavian tongues, he is greatly indebted for the brief study that follows to a collection of Scandinavian sermons translated into German and published (1882) by O. Gleiss, pastor in Westerland.[14]

In Denmark, J. P. Mynster (d. 1854)[15] led the way in opposing Rationalism and bringing his people back to evangelical views. In 1801 he was pastor at Spjellerup, Zealand; in 1810, at the Frauenkirche, in Copenhagen, where he also gave lectures on psychology in one of the colleges. He was made court preacher there in 1825, and then bishop of Zealand in 1834, holding the office for twenty years, to the end of his life. He has been described as a man of "comprehensive learning, deep knowledge of human nature, and lofty spirit." His successor and friend, H. L. Martensen, bears this testimony to the good Bishop Mynster: "He belongs, in our fatherland, to those who can not be forgotten, for he was to many the best that one man can be to another—a way to the Way." Our authority gives two sermons from him, the first being on *The Law Our Schoolmaster to Christ.* It contains nothing very new, is somewhat lacking in unity, and covers too much ground, but it shows a clear conception of the truth, a fine spirit, and an easy, unpretentious presentation of the matter in a loving and sympathetic way. The other is a sermon on

[14] *Aus dem evangelischen Norden; Zeugnisse von Christo in Predigten aus der skandinavischen Kirche unsrer Zeit,* von O. Gleiss; Gütersloh, 1882; Chr.-Schian, and Werckshagen as before.

[15] Chr.-Schian in *RE,* Gleiss, Einl., S. IV, and SS. 17, 171.

Christian Hope, for the Easter festival. It is admirable in conception, spirit, and manner, and contains some fine sayings. Evidently the preacher was soundly evangelical and gifted with a moving manner of discourse.

A very remarkable personality was Sören A. Kierkegaard (1813-1855).[16] He was born in Copenhagen, and after the customary education, he stood, in 1840, the required examination for entrance into the ministry, but he never was a recognized pastor nor filled any church office. But he was very active with his pen, and has a secure place among the religious writers of his time and country. In preaching he was a free lance; wherever he was offered or could make an opportunity, he preached earnestly to all who would hear him. He was intensely individualistic, having little regard for the church as an institution or for church life as such. His writings and personal influence were profoundly felt in the religious life of the North and extended beyond his own country. Gleiss gives one sermon from him on Matt. 6:24-34—*Lessons from the Lilies and Birds.* It is really a sort of running exposition on the whole passage strung on the idea of the carefree example of the birds and lilies. It is full of keen and searching though original terms of expression and essential Christian teaching. It is rather a somewhat dry though beautiful essay than a sermon.

One of the great religious leaders of Denmark was the eloquent and pious N. F. S. Grundtvig (1783-1872),[17] born in Zealand, where his father was pastor, he took the examination for orders in 1803, becoming a tutor in a private family, and a fellow at the University of Copenhagen. He was a busy student, devoting especial attention to mythology. In 1812 he became assistant to his father for a while, then came back to Copenhagen, where he worked as teacher and writer on historical, poetical, and theological subjects. His religious interest now became deepened, and an intense spiritual life developed within him. In 1821 he was pastor at Praesto. He had an unfortunate theological controversy with Professor H. N. Clausen, of Copenhagen, which grew bitter and personal, and ended in a lawsuit. The case went against

[16]Chr.-Schian, and Michelsen in *RE;* Gleiss, IV, and 288.
[17]Same; Gleiss, pp. V, and 201, 240.

Grundtvig, and he was forced out of his position. Once more he came back to Copenhagen, and with two friends began to publish a monthly theological journal. Finally, through the king's favor he was again put into a pastor's place at a famous hospital in Copenhagen, in 1839, and here he ministered with great faith and earnestness to his death, in 1872. It has been said, "As Mynster for the church, and Kierkegaard for the individual, so Grundtvig labored for the people." His whole effort was to promote a national Christian life and culture, and though his methods and spirit were those of a born fighter, he was in reality a deeply spiritual man. Even his opponents recognized that to him the Danes owed more than to any one man the revival of their religious life in the early part of the century. In Gleiss' collection there are two sermons, one on *The Flock and Shepherd,* and the other on *The New Birth.* They contain nothing very remarkable, but indicate both the spiritual earnestness and popular power of the preacher.

From the celebrated professor, preacher, and bishop, H. L. Martensen (1808-1884),[18] Gleiss gives four sermons. These show a happy combination of the three indispensable qualities of a modern gospel preacher: (1) Power of thought—whether in the grasp of Scripture truth or the general problems of religion and philosophy; (2) a warm and genuine spiritual feeling, both of piety toward God and of loving interest in the people; (3) a simple, straightforward style and general manner of address, unambitious but not unadorned, intent on the transfer of his own thought and feeling to the hearer. In a word, we have in Martensen sound, able gospel preaching without great oratorical or philosophical effort. The sermons do not exhibit a very sharply defined structure. Sometimes they seem to pass a little beyond the exact teachings of the text, but on the whole they are eminently Scriptural and practical. The life of Martensen was without striking incident. He was born at Flensburg, educated at Copenhagen, ordained in 1832, traveled and studied in Germany (at Berlin and Heidelberg), became professor at Copenhagen, and court

[18]Chr.-Schian and Madsen in *RE;* Gleiss, pp. VI, and 1, 91, 163, 378.

preacher there. On the death of Mynster, in 1854, he was made bishop of Zealand and filled the office to his death. As a thinker and theologian Martensen became known far beyond his own land through his strong works on *Dogmatics* and *Ethics*.

Besides those mentioned, Gleiss gives sermons of various degrees of power, but all of an evangelical character, from Bladel, Fog, Kok, Monard, Leth, Birkedal, Helweg, Frimodt, and some others. Of these, D. G. Monard, bishop of Lolland and Falster, is the most important. He was highly regarded as a preacher, both at home and abroad. Five sermons of his are given.[19] They show a deep evangelical spirit, a clear and personal grasp of the truth, an earnest zeal for God and men, and a manly yet winsome presentation.

In Norway, particularly in the latter half of the century, a number of evangelical preachers appear. There was W. A. Wexels (d. 1866),[20] who was pastor in Christiania. He was evangelical in doctrine, and earnestly opposed to Rationalism. Besides his sermons, he published a *Book of Devotion for Common People,* which sold, up to 1872, one hundred and twenty thousand copies. Contemporary with him was O. A. Berg (d. 1861),[21] who published a volume of short, taking, popular sermons. In Gleiss' collection there is only a brief mention of the names of those Norwegian preachers from whom he gives sermons. There is Christian Knudsen, of Drammen, from whom is given a strong and striking sermon on *The Missionary Service of the Church of Christ, Its Glory and Its Hope.* From J. C. Heuch, pastor and professor in Christiania, there is a sermon on *The Trial, Conflict, and Victory of Faith,* a vigorous and interesting study of the case of the Syrophenician woman. J. G. Blom, secretary of the Lutheran Institution at Christiania, is represented by a comforting and helpful discourse on John 16: 16-20, *The Shortness of the Time of Tribulation.* There is also a good discourse from J. Munch, of the Inner Mission of Norway, and an earnest evangelical, but not especially striking, sermon from O. Berggsen, chaplain in Christianssand.

[19]SS. 9, 221, 256, 330, 360. [20]Chr.-Schian in *RE.* [21]*Id.*

In Sweden Van Oosterzee[22] informs us there was a great improvement in methods of preaching about the beginning of the nineteenth century; and the revival of evangelical life and teaching in the churches, though slower in appearing than in Denmark and Norway, yet had some notable representatives in the pulpit. Among the preachers mentioned as worthy of special notice are Wallin, of Stockholm, who was also a hymn-writer, and was affectionately called the David of the North. L. S. Odmann, at Upsala, and P. C. Hagberg, at Lund, are named as important men in the early part of the century. G. Rogberg (d. 1842) was a professor at Upsala. He began as a rationalist, but became evangelical and preached the old doctrine with great power and success. His was a helpful and widely influential ministry. Esaias Tegnér (d. 1846) was a beloved pastor at Lund. Besides his effective work in the pulpit and the pastoral office, he was a lovable and popular poet and also a theologian of considerable ability. Perhaps the most important preacher in the middle of the century was J. H. Thomander, bishop of Lund. He was of Scotch descent, and had the "fervid genius" of his ancestry. He was hailed by his friends as a new Luther. He earnestly opposed Rationalism, and had a great following. His contemporary, Bishop Reuterdahl, was more of a mediating theologian and preacher, whose method and spirit were somewhat like those of Schleiermacher in Germany. Among later preachers mention is made of Lindblad, Emanuelson, Tören, and Rudin as preachers of excellent repute in Sweden. Besides these of the Established Church, a number of dissenters arose; among them the Baptists, who have had great success among the people. They have exemplified a popular method of preaching and have laid strong emphasis upon evangelical views. Among the leaders and preachers, F. O. Nilsson and Andreas Wiberg are worthy of special mention.

[22]*Op. cit.*, p. 143 ff., and *RE* as before.

CHAPTER XIV

The French Pulpit of the Nineteenth Century

French history during the nineteenth century is full of change and of surpassing interest and importance to mankind.[1] The despotism of Napoleon signalized the first fifteen years of the century. It was a brilliant and bloody time. Then came the restoration of the Bourbons, after the defeat at Waterloo; but this dynasty was not popular. Another Revolution in 1830 brought in the Citizen King, Louis-Philippe. This compromise between monarchy and republicanism did not succeed, for it did not enjoy the respect of either party. It fell ingloriously, in 1848, and was succeeded by another short-lived Republic, till, in 1852, Louis Napoleon, a nephew of the great emperor, first assumed dictatorial and then imperial powers and established the Second Empire. In many respects this period marks great advances in France in all the elements of civilized progress in modern times. The Empire, however, was not strong nor popular. The fatal war with Prussia, in 1870, resulted in its overthrow, and the Third Republic, after fearful internal convulsions, was finally established.

In the arts, sciences, and literature France had a brilliant history during the nineteenth century. In regard to literature it is only necessary to recall the great names of the elder and younger Dumas, of Victor Hugo, Alfred de Musset, George Sand, Balzac, Maupassant, Zola, and a host of lesser writers of poetry and fiction. In history there were a number of distinguished names: Guizot, Thierry, Michelet, Thiers, Duruy, Langlois, and Seignobos, and others. Criticism and essays found distinguished representatives in Souvestre, Taine, Sainte-Beuve, Brunetière, Bentzon, and many others. Philosophy claims the great names of Jouffroy, Comte, Cousin, Janet, and a number of others. Many other writers in all the departments besides these well-known and distinguished ones gave to French literature during the nine-

[1]See appropriate places in the *Historians' History;* the *Warner Library;* or other standard works on French history and literature.

teenth century a power and renown comparable only to its classic period in strength and beauty, and far excelling that in extent and influence. The French genius was extremely brilliant and fertile during this great period of the national history.

The religious history of France in this epoch was as varied and interesting as that in other spheres of the national life.[2] Napoleon restored Catholicism after the horrors of the French Revolution, but he did it with two decided checks upon its power. One of these was the political reservation to the state of a larger measure of control over the church than had been the case before. This agreement with the pope is known as the Concordat, and under it the struggles between the papacy and the French government had their ups and downs throughout the whole century. The other check to Catholic power was the granting of toleration to the Protestants. Napoleon permitted the establishment of a Protestant training seminary for the Reformed Church at Montauban, and another for the Lutherans at Strassburg. Of course, the restoration of the Bourbons was hailed by the papacy as a boon to their cause, but both the independence of the French Catholic Church and the toleration of Protestants had become too well settled to be overthrown. Still, the majority of the people being Catholic, it was not easy for Protestantism to flourish greatly against the many forms of persecution and opposition which were still found. Napoleon III stood firmly for the Gallican liberties and tolerated Protestantism, yet, on the whole, his protection of the pope and the influence of the Empress Eugénie were strong bulwarks to Catholicism. Under the Third Republic freedom of worship was assured to all churches and parties. Very strong anti-clerical feelings were aroused in the latter part of the century which led to the final separation of church and state early in the twentieth century.

There has been a vast deal of skepticism and irreligion in modern France. In the Catholic Church Modernism has been usually quickly and severely repressed; occasionally strong men have either been forced to submit to ultramontane views or have been forced out of

[2]See Kurtz, III, p. 378, and other church historians.

the Church. Nor have Protestants been free from the divisions and controversies of modern religious thinking. In the first half of the century there was a wave of evangelical revival, but rationalism and radical criticism have also had large place and strong influence within the Protestant party. Of course, all these influences, secular and religious, have had their influence upon the development and the exercise of preaching. The French pulpit of the nineteenth century, among both Catholics and Protestants, was brilliant, intellectual, and strong, though not so widely admired nor perchance so influential as in the seventeenth century.

I. General Survey of Preaching

The opening years of the century were unfavorable both for Catholic and Protestant preaching. In its triumph over Protestantism the Catholic pulpit had decayed, as we have seen. Through the eighteenth century it had never been strong or great. It suffered terribly from the Revolution, and so had to meet the nineteenth century with greatly weakened power. Among Protestants, while the freedom of worship accorded by Napoleon gave new opportunity for pulpit eloquence and influence, the blight of Rationalism was sorely felt. These drawbacks made themselves apparent certainly during the first two decades of the century; but in order to trace the development of French preaching it will be necessary to treat separately the Catholic and Protestant pulpits.

On the whole, the Catholic preaching of France during the nineteenth century scarcely measures up to the high standard of its classic development of the seventeenth, but as the century wore on there was a decided improvement over the preaching of its immediate predecessor. Hence, while the nineteenth century preaching shows marked intellectual power and great advance in simplicity and popularity of style, and while a number of able and distinguished orators adorned the pulpit of the epoch, we must still look to the classic period in the age of Louis XIV for the highest point which French pulpit oratory has reached. The early decades of the nineteenth century show the traces of the weakness and decay which characterized French preaching toward the close of the eighteenth century. It is true that a few notable men like Boulogne, Frayssinous, MacCarthy (of Irish descent, but born a Frenchman), and some others were conspicuous and influential in the pulpit, yet they did not redeem this early period from the charge of weakness and decline. A Catholic writer (Scannell, in the *Catholic Encyclopedia*), writing of Lacordaire, says: "The clergy in the first part of the nineteenth century went on preaching as before, speaking on the same subjects, bringing forward the same arguments, using the same methods, forgetting all the while that they had to appeal, not only to believers, but also to infidels. It was Lacordaire's merit that he discerned the necessity of a complete reform; new subjects, new objects, new methods must be adopted." This new movement began about 1830; some ten years later, as we shall see, than the revival of the Protestant pulpit. From this time on the improvement in the French Catholic pulpit is distinct and great.

The causes of this heightened character and power in French Catholic preaching are not far to seek. First of all, it was due in large measure to the general progress of the age. This was a note of civilization the world over. The nineteenth century was alive in France as elsewhere, and no department of the intellectual and moral life of the people could or did escape the impulse of that alert and progressive epoch in human culture. More particularly, there was in France itself a vivid and varied intellectual life. It is well known to observers that while the French Revolution desolated and destroyed, it also stimulated and constructed. In science and literature, as well as in political, social, and industrial affairs, France was among the leading peoples of the age. The constant change and debate in her political life, the oratory of the bar and of the tribune, the critical and argumentative essay writing, the psychological and keen literature of fiction, all had their influence indirectly but powerfully upon the pulpit. As already hinted, it is fair also to think that, as in the early part of the seventeenth century, so likewise in the early part of the nineteenth, the revival of evangelical Protestant preaching acted as a wholesome suggestion and as a spur by way of rivalry to the Catholic pulpit.

Within the Catholic body itself there were at least three special forces which promoted a quickening of power in the pulpit. One of these was the old and never dead assertion of the so-called Gallican liberties. Both the Napoleons favored the assertion of French rights as against the encroachments of the papacy, and there was always in France a party who responded to this call. A second force was the rise of the great movement headed by Lamennais, Lacordaire, and Montalembert, which sought to reconcile high Catholic doctrine with political and social liberties and progress.[3] Lamennais founded his paper, *L'Avenir* (The Future), and the other two were associated with him. Their motto was, "God and the future." They were really republicans in politics, and put themselves unhesitatingly and powerfully on the side of social improvement while trying to remain loyal and orthodox Catholics. The positions were incompatible, and failure was inevitable. The paper was condemned. Appeal was made to the pope, and he decided against the policy of the reformers. Lacordaire and Montalembert submitted and remained Catholic. Lamennais revolted, and finally died without the pale of the Church. The third force was Ultramontanism, over against the Gallican liberties, and over against the struggle of the liberal Catholics. The highest papal pretensions were asserted and maintained. The powerful help of the Jesuits was felt in this struggle. We have seen how Gregory XVI condemned the liberal Catholic movement of Lamennais, but it remained for Pius IX to push the Catholic pretensions to their extreme expression, proclaiming, in 1854, the dogma of the Immaculate Conception of the Virgin; issuing, in 1864, the famous Encyclical and Syllabus, and obtaining through the Vatican Council, in 1870, the decree of papal infallibility. The high Catholic party in France favored these ultramon-

[3]Besides accounts of the leaders in cyclopaedias and other authorities, see an illuminating discussion by Leroy-Beaulieu in the *Revue des Deux Mondes* for Aug. 15 and Dec. 15, 1884—*Les Catholiques libéraux et l'Église de France de 1830 à nos jours.*

tane principles, but all along there was a strong and vigorous opposition. Men like Dupanloup opposed the decree of infallibility, but submitted when it was passed. Men like Loyson (Father Hyacinthe) protested within the Church as long as they could, and finally left it. Even up to the close of the nineteenth century and into the twentieth the turmoil of these conflicts has continued. The assertion of the rights of government as against the claims of the Church, and the ultramontane denunciation of Modernism are well-known movements of recent date.

Along with this movement, which imparted great vigor to French preaching in this epoch, we should observe the effect upon the spirit and style of preaching. There is more adaptation to popular thought and feeling. This is shown alike in the championship of moral reforms and in the flexibility, clearness, popularity of style. The discourses become less formal. Frayssinous and Lacordaire introduced and popularized the kind of pulpit address known in France as *conferences.* These were topical addresses, informal and direct, usually without a text or with one only as a motto. They dealt with religious and moral subjects generally, but with these as associated with social problems, and sometimes with political questions.

The Protestant preaching of France for two-thirds of the century has been presented in a thoughtful and well-written, though not very profound study, by M. Alfred Vincent.[4] It is not possible to agree with this author at all points, but the following discussion owes much to his suggestive treatise. Both in matter and form the discourses of French Protestant preachers up to 1820 show the lingering influence of eighteenth century Rationalism. Their view of preaching is that of the moralist rather than the evangelist, and the style, while usually clear, is labored and cold. Great stress is laid upon natural religion and the moral virtues. Sin, for example, is treated in its outbreaks in particular vices rather than in its nature as a corruption of the human

[4] *Histoire de la prédication protestante de langue française au dix-neuvirème siècle,* par Alfred Vincent, Geneva and Paris, 1871.

soul. Immortality on the basis of philosophy is constantly affirmed, but the Christian doctrine as such does not receive due attention. Little or nothing is said of the Holy Spirit and of regeneration, and naturally the person and work of Jesus are presented rather from the philosophic and moralistic point of view than from the Scriptural and evangelical.

What M. Vincent notes as the second phase of Protestant preaching appears during the period from 1820-1850, and he calls it significantly The Awakening. Through the influence of the earnest Scotchman, Robert Haldane, who resided in Geneva about the year 1816, a wave of revival was felt in French Switzerland. This movement was led by the pious and eloquent Cæsar Malan, who began to preach the evangelical doctrines. He met much opposition, and lost his place in the Established Church of Geneva, but some earnest followers were turned to him, and he established an independent evangelical Church. This movement gained the sympathy and adherence of such men as Gaussen, Vinet, Merle d'Aubigné, and others. Spreading into France itself, it found its greatest representative in Adolphe Monod, with whom were associated his brothers, Frederick, William, and Horace, as well as some others, such as Grandpierre, Secrétan, Martin, and others. These constituted the distinctively evangelical school. They insisted upon the usual tenets of that school, such as the inspiration and authority of Scripture, depth and degradation of sin, the need of salvation by grace, the divinity and atonement of Christ, and the need and reality of regeneration by the Holy Spirit. The usual faults of this school are not lacking. There is some one-sidedness and exaggeration, with occasional intolerance of those who do not accept the doctrinal statements of this party.

The third phase pointed out by M. Vincent is that of Liberalism, from 1850-1866. As a matter of fact, however, this tendency was contemporary with the other, but came to a larger scope and influence during the period; so much so that it may not incorrectly be taken as the dominant and descriptive note of the time. There was in this trend a recurrence to the moral and human view of Christianity prevalent during the first period, but with a difference. Historical and exegetical study of the Bible, and the great progress of scientific study and thought, put the revived Liberalism on a much higher plane than had been occupied by its rationalistic predecessor. Also this newer liberal preaching dealt more with the individual experience, as well as with social questions, and so came much nearer to the hearts of men than the preaching of the older school. The great progress of opinions in the direction of freedom of worship and in other ways made for the wider extension of this mode of preaching. Its doctrinal basis was deficient, both in its accord with Scripture and tradition. It felt too much the strength of its own freedom to be a safe guide. On many vital points of the Christian faith it was too indefinite, vague, even evasive, but it seized with power the problems—intellectual, moral, and social—of its time. It is well to distinguish, as Vincent does, two groups of preachers who were under the influence of this modern spirit. There were the extreme Liberals, like Colani and the two Coquerels; and there were the orthodox Liberals, such as Vinet, Monod, and, more recently, Bersier.

In regard to the contents of preaching in relation to the age, the Protestant pulpit of France throughout the nineteenth century exhibits a lively interest in public questions, and for the most part an intelligent and vigorous dealing with them. The great social and political changes which mark the history of France throughout the century come in for their share of attention. The preachers, as a rule, spoke boldly and clearly on these matters. They exhibited a fine balance of sympathy with forward movements, and yet all respect for the authority of custom and law. The aggressive tone of Romanism, both at the restoration of the Bourbons, and more emphatically upon the revived influence of extreme Catholicism after 1848, provoked a vigorous and intelligent restatement of the Protestant positions. The rise and growth of critical and scientific opposition to traditional Christianity produced a certain measure of apologetic preaching. While this was somewhat weak and traditional in the earlier stages of its activity, it grew in power, intelligence, and ability in the latter half of the century.

In regard to form the French Protestant preaching

of modern times deserves high praise. While some little stiffness and coldness marked the early decades, there was a constant adaptation of preaching, both in style and tone, to the modern mind. The fondness for display characteristic of a former time was largely gone. Simplicity, naturalness, directness are notable qualities of the modern French pulpit. Homiletical principles are understood and employed, but there is no excess of analysis nor forcing of genius by rule. Freedom and spontaneity use method without constraint. The style is prevailingly admirable. It is clear, flexible, lofty, correct, and elegant. In the hands of the masters it rises occasionally to noble eloquence and powerful movement. In such men as Vinet, Coquerel, Monod, and Bersier the best French of the nineteenth century is not borrowed, but natural.

II. Leading Catholic Preachers

Among the notable preachers at the turn of the century we find the Abbé de Boulogne (1747-1825).[5] He had gained renown in the reign of Louis XVI, refused the oath of allegiance to the Revolutionary Government in 1793, was arrested, but released on the fall of Robespierre. Under Napoleon he was restored to his office, and made bishop of Troyes in 1808. He offended the emperor by his independence, in 1811, and was imprisoned. On the restoration of the Bourbons he was released, and retired to his diocese, being later made archbishop of Vienne. As a preacher Boulogne had in full measure the pomposity and swelling style of the eighteenth century, but along with these defects his discourses are marked by force and by occasional passages of eloquence and power.

Less pompous and more eloquent was the remarkable Jesuit of Irish ancestry, Father MacCarthy, whose fervid oratory and strong devotion to Catholic interests gave him great reputation in this early period.

More important than either of these was the famous bishop of Hermopolis, Frayssinous (1765-1841).[6] He

[5]See the Abbé Boucher, *L'Éloquence de la Chaire*, p. 415 ss.; sermons in *Orateurs Sacrés*, tom. 47.

[6]Boucher, p. 449; *Or. Sac.*, tom. 77.

was born in the diocese of Rodez, educated at Paris, refused the oath of allegiance to the Revolution, and retired to his home. In 1801 he came back to Paris to teach theology, and began a course of theological catechisms at the Church of the Carmes. The congregations overflowed, and he continued his work at St. Sulpice. The imperial police kept strict watch upon his utterances, and he was at one time silenced, but was later permitted to resume his preaching. These informal and timely addresses paved the way for the more distinctive work of Lacordaire. Frayssinous was highly praised by Lamennais and his contemporaries, but some of this praise was due to his striking personality and oratorical action. His sermons now seem rather cold and commonplace, but they deal with apologetics, and touch social and political questions. The style has something of the pomp and straining after effect, which was a heritage from the preceding period. On the whole, Frayssinous was not great, but important as a connecting link between two epochs.

The leading figure in the new movement, as has already been pointed out, was the eloquent and distinguished J. B. H. Lacordaire (1802-1861).[7] He was born near Dijon, where he was educated in his boyhood, completing his studies at Paris. Here he began the practice of law, and became a pronounced liberal in politics and theology. Through the influence of a friend he was won to a more definite acceptance of Catholic views, and decided to study theology. He was ordained a priest in 1827, and was appointed a chaplain in some family. This sort of work did not suit him, and he was on the point of going to America when, in 1830, the Revolution of July broke out and offered a new time and opportunity for liberal political principles. It was then that Lamennais, who was still a devout Catholic, invited Lacordaire to co-operate with him on his famous journal, *L'Avenir*. The principles and purposes of these men are thus briefly described by a writer in the *Catholic Encyclopedia:*

[7]Boucher, p. 437 ss., who quotes Ste.-Beuve, Guizot, and others, and refers to a *Life by Frisset,* and to *Sermons;* Art. by T. B. Scannell in *Cath. Encycl.; Conferences,* Trans., by Henry Langdon, New York, 1870. *God and Man, Conferences,* tr., London, 1872 (original 1851).

"Their program was to renounce all State protection and assistance, and to demand religious freedom, not as a favor, but as a right. They advocated free speech and a free press, and exhorted the Catholics to avail themselves of these weapons in defense of their rights. Their religious teaching was strongly ultramontane." As we have seen, they were denounced, appealed to the pope in 1832, and their paper condemned. Lacordaire submitted, and this occasioned, along with some other things, a breach between him and Lamennais, who finally attacked the Church. Lacordaire, after his submission, began to give conferences at Stanislas College. These were criticised and referred to the archbishop of Paris, who, on reading them, was so pleased with their loyalty to Catholic views, while yet appealing to the modern spirit, that he appointed Lacordaire to give the Lenten sermons at Notre Dame in 1835, and again the next year. This was the beginning of his fame and power as a preacher. This new method and the personal magnetism of the preacher attracted great crowds and produced deep and abiding impressions. Lacordaire retired for rest and further study. He determined to become a monk, and was greatly interested in the long-decayed Dominican order of preachers. He joined this order in 1839, at Rome, and endeavored to revive its power in France. On returning to the pulpit of Notre Dame he created quite a surprise, appearing with the tonsure and in the habit of a Dominican friar. He preached off and on at Notre Dame and in other prominent pulpits. During the course of his conferences in 1852 he spoke out boldly against Louis Napoleon's assumption of imperial authority. He was, of course, silenced by the government. He spent his last days in educational work. An oft-quoted saying of his was, "I hope to die a religious penitent, but a liberal impenitent."

The *Conferences* of Lacordaire are still worthy of study as examples of a new and striking method of pulpit address. They show fine argumentative power, clear though sometimes subtle thought, some degree of imagination, and a noble flow of feeling and language. There is no text and no formal division into parts, though the arrangement is not loose. The introductions are short, merely pointing out the topics to be dealt with.

These are then freely and flowingly treated. Lacordaire had a striking personality and delivery. His voice was weak at first, but grew in power as he proceeded, and sometimes rang out with striking force. His method was to speak freely after careful preparation and arrangement of his material. As with all speakers of his sort, many of his most brilliant and effective passages came during the actual delivery. He was often eloquent and impressive.

Another famous preacher of conferences at Notre Dame was the eloquent Jesuit, Francis Xavier de Ravignan (1795-1858).[8] He was born at Bayonne, early joined the Jesuit order, and was educated in their system of learning and theology. He, however, was not a deeply learned man, but was a thoroughly devoted one. His language was not always polished, but strong, and his feeling was intense. He filled the stated appointments at Notre Dame quite often, alternating with Lacordaire and others. He naturally favored the ultramontane views and royalty. He was struck and wounded by a missile in the Revolution of July, 1830. He was very highly esteemed in his own order, one of whom described him as "virtue preaching truth." He gave a series of conferences on *The Spiritual Life,* addressed to Christian women in the convent of The Sacred Heart at Paris. A few men by special privilege were admitted to the galleries. They were published from notes taken down by a hearer, and have been translated into English. They are simple and unpretentious in style, but devotional, practical, and full of feeling. They were very appropriate to the audience. While, of course, presenting the Catholic doctrines and practices with all earnestness, they contain many passages of earnest exhortation appropriate to the general Christian life. The conferences at Notre Dame addressed to great popular audiences were naturally of a different tone and method of approach, though founded on the same principles.

L. E. M. Bautain (1796-1867)[9] was a native of Paris and educated there. He became professor at Strassburg,

[8]Boucher, p. 443 (refers to *Sermons,* and a *Life* by Pontlevoy); *Conferences on the Spiritual Life,* trans., London, 1877.

[9]Boucher, p. 455 (refers to *Conférences sur la Religion,* etc.); *Extempore Speaking* (tr.), New York, 1859.

and later *abbé* at Paris. He gave some conferences on *Religion and Liberty* which indicate philosophic thought. He published the useful treatise, which has been translated into English, on *Extempore Preaching*. He was recognized as a preacher of brilliant gifts.

Charles Joseph Félix (1810-1891)[10] was a very distinguished Jesuit preacher of the middle and latter part of the century. He often filled the pulpit at Notre Dame after Lacordaire and Ravignan, and in large measure sustained the traditions of that pulpit. Born at Neuville, department Du Nord, he was educated at preparatory schools and then at Cambrai. In 1833 he was made professor of rhetoric, and became a Jesuit in 1837. He began his ministry in Belgium, at various places, taking at one time some studies at Louvain. In 1850 we find him teaching and preaching at Amiens. He drew great crowds and was much applauded. From that time he was often called to preach at Paris, giving conferences and sermons at some of the principal churches, and was finally appointed chief preacher at Notre Dame (1853-1870). He lived later at Nancy and Lille, and preached much in the cathedrals of France and Belgium. Lalande, in the *Catholic Encyclopedia,* says of him: "The eloquence of Father Félix was characterized by clearness, vigorous logic, unction, and pathos, even in his reasoning. He lacked imagination and the enthusiasm of Lacordaire, but he was more skilled in dialectic and surer in doctrine. His diction was richer than that of De Ravignan, and while he was less didactic than Monsabré, he was more original." He published a series of Easter sermons called *Retreats*. There are six volumes of these. They discuss the Catholic doctrines with special bearing upon the spiritual and moral life. They are thoroughly Romanist in teaching, and of decided ultramontane principles. The style is flowing and correct. The discourse is well reasoned and often eloquent.

Another prelate and preacher of distinction in this

[10]Boucher, p. 452; Art. by Louis Lalande in *Cath. Encyc.;* three vols. of the *Retraites,* those on *La Prévarication, La Confession, Le Châtiment,* Paris, about 1888. See also a brief but brilliant sketch by Prof. W. C. Wilkinson, *Modern Masters of Pulpit Discourse,* p. 301 ff.

period was Charles Émile Freppel (1827-1891),[11] bishop of Angers. He was a native of Alsace, where he attended preparatory schools. He received his university training at Strassburg, and later, after a brilliant examination, obtained the degree of Doctor at the Sorbonne. He was ordained a priest in 1847, and appointed a chaplain at St. Genévièvе, at Paris. His sermons on *The Divinity of Christ* attracted notice and were published. He frequently preached in the great churches in Paris and elsewhere. In 1869 two volumes of his sermons were published and had considerable circulation. He was made professor of sacred eloquence at the Sorbonne, and his lectures were well attended. He published a notable reply to Rénan's *Life of Jesus.* Freppel was highly esteemed by the pope, and was made bishop of Angers in 1870. He could have received higher honors, even a cardinalate, but declined. He upheld the ultramontane principles, but was in touch with modern movements. As a member of the Chamber of Deputies after 1870, he was highly esteemed. A collection of his works in seventeen volumes was published at intervals in Paris from 1869-1888. In these are many panegyrics, orations, discourses, and pastoral letters. They deal with questions of the day from the Catholic standpoint. The style is clear and modern, but not of particular charm or power. Freppel does not appear to have had the sweeping eloquence of Dupanloup and others, but was a faithful, scholarly, and widely intelligent preacher.

One of the most important leaders, prelates, and preachers of the Catholic Church in France was the celebrated bishop of Orleans, F. A. P. Dupanloup (1802-1878).[12] The future bishop and scholar was born in humble circumstances in Savoy, but in his early childhood he was brought by his mother to Paris, where, through her hard work and sacrifices and his own diligence, he managed to secure an education. His talents were speedily recognized and, on his ordination, places and promotions quickly came to hand. In 1834 he gave

[11]Lalande in *Cath. Encycl.; Oeuvres Pastorales et Oratoires,* Paris, 1869, and after.

[12]Art. by J. F. Sallier in *Cath. Encyc.;* Boucher, p. 449; some sermons in *Or. Sac.,* t. 83; *Ministry of Preaching,* tr., New York, 1890.

a notable series of conferences in the cathedral at Orleans. A few years later he held appointments as Superior of the Seminary and also as Vicar General of Paris. In 1849 he was made bishop of Orleans, holding that office to the end of his life. He was a very active bishop, administering his diocese with great intelligence and diligence. He was also a very prolific writer on the topics of the day. He was much interested in social and benevolent measures, and in educational and literary pursuits. He was a liberal Catholic, though a convinced one. He opposed the dogma of infallibility, voting and speaking against it in the Vatican Council to the very last. He was perhaps the ablest opponent of that measure. It was not that he did not accept it personally, but he believed it was very inexpedient to define and proclaim it. When it was passed, however, like a loyal Catholic he accepted it, and did not go off with the so-called Old Catholics. Dupanloup was an ardent patriot and took a deep interest in all that concerned his country's welfare. In politics he was a monarchist, though advocating a constitutional government under the house of Bourbon. He was made a member of the Chamber of Deputies, and later a senator under the Third Republic. Besides his regular sermons, of which many were published, he put forth a number of panegyrics and funeral orations. He also wrote a very good treatise on *Sacred Rhetoric,* and a number of volumes on *Education.* He had a fine presence. His delivery was graceful, easy, and commanding. He had a clear voice and a very expressive countenance. His discourses, even in print, show a warm and fiery eloquence, which, of course, must have been more apparent in the actual delivery. Boucher, speaking of his preaching, says, "Very solid at bottom, very brilliant in form, very pure and correct in his diction, he was remarkable for brilliancy, vigor, dash; he put all his soul into his speech."

Perhaps the greatest, most popular, and widely known French Catholic preacher of his time was the famous Father Hyacinthe, whose real name was Charles Loyson (1827-?).[13] This remarkable man was born in the south

[13]Cyclopaedia articles, and various other sources; *Discourses on Various Occasions,* trans. by L. W. Bacon, New York, 1869.

of France, the home of so many gifted orators, and was brought up at Pau. His father was a teacher, and carefully directed the early education of his son. Later Loyson pursued his education at St. Sulpice in Paris, and was for some years a teacher. He joined the Carmelite order of monks about 1860, and after his novitiate began to preach at Lyons. His remarkable powers in the pulpit at once attracted attention, and he received various appointments of greater and greater dignity till, in 1864, he preached at the Madeleine, in Paris, and was then appointed preacher at Notre Dame; a place which he filled with great power and popularity till he was silenced for his liberal views and expressions, in 1869. He made a visit to America and was very warmly received by the Protestants, but he still avowed himself a Catholic, though a liberal one. He was released from his monastic vows in 1870, though still recognized as a preacher in the Catholic Church. He protested against the dogma of infallibility, and in consequence went with the Old Catholics, in 1871-72. He opposed the celibacy of the clergy and defended their right to marry. He put these principles into practice by marrying an American lady in 1873. After that he preached for a while to an independent Catholic congregation in Geneva, but later led a somewhat wandering life. He is said to have visited Algiers, and then Greece, where it was reported he had joined the Greek Church, and was welcomed by the Patriarch while at Athens. In recent times a public notice states, that along with a number of Protestants of various denominations, he was present, March 7, 1904, at a celebration, under the auspices of the American Methodist Church in Rome, Italy, of the centenary of the British and Foreign Bible Society. Since his excommunication he could not fairly be reckoned among Catholic preachers, but previous to his separation, and in the palmy days of his work at Paris, he stands at the head of those who by distinguished pulpit gifts and wonderful influence over assemblies have adorned the Catholic pulpit of modern France. Great crowds attended his preaching, attracted not only by his splendid oratory, but also by his liberalism and the undercurrent of protest against extreme ultramontane sentiments.

In regard to later Catholic preaching, we may quote an interesting paragraph from a letter of Bersier, the famous Protestant preacher, to Dr. Broadus, written in 1876. The statement is as follows:[14] "The Catholic pulpit is singularly sterile at our epoch in France. We may say that since Lacordaire, Ravignan, and Father Hyacinthe, no orator has appeared of real excellence. Father Félix, of the order of the Jesuits, has preached with a certain success for several Lent seasons at Notre Dame, and just now they are trying to bring into vogue the name of Father Monsabré. But neither of them rises to the height of his task. Their fundamental characteristic is the ultramontane logic, developing inflexibly the principles of the Syllabus, hurling them as a defiance against contemporary society, and saying to it: Submit to Rome, or thou art lost. No profound study of the Scriptures, no psychology, nothing truly interior or persuasive. It is the method of outward authority brought into the pulpit, with the arid procedures of the scholastic demonstration—a thing at once empty and pretentious."

Monsabré, to whom Bersier refers, was a Jesuit of considerable ability, and is regarded as a preacher of the first rank in his time; but by far the ablest Catholic preacher in the last part of the century was Henri Didon (1840-1900.)[15] He was born at Touret, in Dauphiné, amid the beautiful mountains. He received his early education at Grenoble. At eighteen years of age he entered the Dominican order as a novice. His four years of study were completed at his ordination. He then went to Rome and pursued further studies. Returning to France, he received appointments to preach at various places, including Marseilles and Paris, where he was heard in some of the more important churches. Like the liberal Catholics of the earlier time, he was republican in politics and in great sympathy with the modern spirit, both in science and in social problems. In 1879 he made some notable sermons and writings on the subject of

[14]Broadus, *Lectures on the History of Preaching,* p. 185, note.

[15]Cyclopaedia articles, and a good account by Th. Bentzon in *Century Magazine* for Sept., 1900; *Science Without God,* discourses transl. by Rosa Corder, London, 1882.

divorce. The next year he went still further and spoke in criticism of the attitude of his Church toward modern science. He was accused of preaching contrary to the principles of the Syllabus and was silenced for awhile. He spent, then, a long retreat at a monastery of his order in the island of Corsica. During this time of retirement he traveled and studied some years in Germany. In 1892 he was permitted to return to Paris and preach at the Madeleine. He had not been forgotten, and his return created great interest in the city. Crowds thronged the famous building from all classes of society. Programs of the services were sold on the outside, and tickets for places had to be secured in advance. He did not now put himself in opposition to his Church, but spoke upon the great religious questions. One series of sermons was on *The Divinity of Christ.* His great effort was to reconcile the belief of his Church with the modern spirit, but he was not so great as Lacordaire and his associates. Like them, he was doomed to failure. The career of Didon bears remarkable similarity to that of his great predecessor, Lacordaire. Both were Dominicans, both tried to reconcile Romanism with modern thought and social activity. Both were reproved, both submitted, and both ended their days in educational work after retiring from the pulpit.

In personal character Didon was frank, straightforward, and sympathetic. He was a little intoxicated by his own fame, but that perhaps was to be expected. The critics who have heard his preaching and read his books assure us that his published works do not possess the merit of his sermons. His personal magnetism, earnest delivery, and commanding presence gave to his spoken words greater force than his writings show. Bentzon, who both heard and read Didon, has given a fine picture of the preacher in the article here referred to; and among other things, thus speaks of him: "Père Didon did not display a settled opinion against any person, but was moved by a perfect sincerity and limitless desire to transmit to his hearers the ardent faith which held possession of him. The vast torrent of his eloquence sprang from his innermost heart. At times, though, there are to be found in it traces of declamation and slight offenses against good taste. In his predilection for what was modern he freely introduced into the noble and dignified language of the pulpit familiar and discordant words sometimes borrowed from the current slang." The course of sermons on the relation of science to religion shows good qualities of mind and speech. They evince careful preparation, modern sympathies, and a clear and forcible address.

III. Protestant Preachers

The Protestant preachers in the French tongue are found not only in France itself, but in French Switzerland, and to some extent in Holland and Belgium. It will not be necessary, however, to consider these last apart from their French brethren, but it is desirable to distinguish between the Swiss and French groups, though they naturally were closely related to each other in movements of thought and in actual contact. We begin with the Swiss group.

At Geneva and throughout French Switzerland the rationalistic influences of the late eighteenth and early nineteenth centuries were in full swing. There was in Geneva a cold and critical spirit under which evangelical opinions and movements had greatly declined. The revived preaching in Switzerland and France was due to a reaction against the rationalistic influence. In this reaction there was a number of able and devoted preachers and leaders, such as Malan, Gaussen, Vinet, and Merle D'Aubigné, of whom brief notices follow.

Cæsar Malan (1787-1864)[16] was born of a French family at Geneva, which traced its origin to Dauphiné. The father of Cæsar was somewhat a free thinker, being a reader of Voltaire and Rousseau, but was outwardly devoted to the cause for which his ancestors had suffered. His wife was a woman of devoted piety, and her influence over her son was blessed and helpful. The boy showed aptitude and thirst for learning, and received the best education of the time in his native city. Here also he began to teach, and was recognized as a capable and

[16]Art. by E. Barde in *RE;* sermon and sketch in Fish, *Pulp. Eloq. of the XIX Cent.*, p. 149 ff.

inspiring instructor of youth. He was happily married, in 1811, to a Swiss-German lady, whose sympathy and piety were strong influences in Malan's subsequent career. Like many others under the State-Church system, Malan entered the ministry and was ordained without having experienced a real conversion. He preached in the various churches of Geneva as occasion or duty required, but he was not satisfied in mind or heart with the cold moralistic conception and presentation of Christian truth which then prevailed in Geneva as elsewhere. Association with some students of more evangelical sentiments, and with other friends, especially a sort of society which remained from a Moravian group of former times in Geneva, together with his own searching for light, led Malan to a true conversion and a clearer acceptance of evangelical truth. At this juncture, about 1816, Robert Haldane, the eminent evangelical layman of Scotland, made a long visit to Geneva. The influence of Haldane confirmed Malan in his tendency toward evangelical sentiments and greatly strengthened and comforted him in his efforts to lead a movement in that direction. On the 5th and 6th of May, 1817, Malan preached in Geneva two notable sermons, in which he proclaimed with earnestness and fervor the need of repentance and the doctrine of justification by faith alone. The sermons gave great offense to the authorities and the rationalistic preachers of Geneva. On retiring from the pulpit he was made to feel their coldness and opposition, and as yet even his wife did not fully share his sentiments. Depressed and grieved, he returned to his home, but there was Haldane to greet him with encouragement. The pious Scotchman grasped his hand and said, "Thank God the gospel has been once more preached in Geneva." The breach between him and the State Church began here, and soon became final. Malan was forbidden to preach in any of the churches of the city. He built, however, a little chapel on his own land, and numbers gathered to hear him. Through all trials and some internal dissensions the movement grew until an independent evangelical church was established. Meantime Malan had been deprived of his office as preacher and was now dependent in large measure for his support upon the voluntary contributions of sympathizers and friends. He traveled extensively in Germany, France, and Switzerland, and even as far as England, preaching to gathered companies of evangelical worshipers. It is an interesting fact connected with his visit to England that he was in close friendship with Henry Elliott, the father of Charlotte Elliott. This gifted and pious lady was a lifelong invalid, and at the time of Malan's visit she was suffering great depression of spirits and unable to see clearly the way of salvation in Christ. In conversation, Malan said to her, "Come just as you are, Charlotte." It was this that led her into peace, and out of that experience she wrote that widely influential hymn, *"Just as I am, without one plea,"* a hymn which has been blessed to the spiritual life of many thousands. Malan's preaching work as a pastor of his congregation in Geneva was greatly blessed. He was a singularly attractive and winsome man, and his speech was warm, persuasive, and moving. After many years of earnest and fruitful labors, he passed to his reward an aged man, in 1864. His preaching was marked by intense devotion to the evangelical theology, earnest exposition of the Scriptures, and simplicity and pointedness. The sermon given by Fish on *The Piety of Young Daniel* is marked by great simplicity of thought, a clear outline, and warm exhortation. There is no soaring eloquence, but impressive and well-reasoned appeal.

Along with Malan should be mentioned S. R. L. Gaussen (1790-1864),[17] who was also a native of Geneva, where his father held public offices. Young Gaussen received his education at Geneva, and was ordained pastor at Satigny, a suburb. He sympathized with the movement toward evangelical sentiments led by Haldane and Malan and, like the latter, incurred the hostility of the civil and church authorities in Geneva. It was against him and Malan that these authorities issued, in 1817, their notorious decree which forbade the preachers to discuss the union of the two natures in the person of Christ, original sin, predestination, and the way in which grace works. But Gaussen and others believed in their cause and persisted in preaching the truth. Sharp controversies

[17]Art. by Riggenbach in *RE;* sermon and sketch in Fish, *op. cit.,* p. 139 ff.; Vincent, *op. cit.,* pp. 24, 31, 48.

continued until finally Gaussen was ejected from his pastorate at Satigny, and was forbidden to preach in any of the churches of the Canton. D'Aubigné had also suffered similar deprivation, and these two, with others, founded the Evangelical Society of Geneva, which established a school for teaching young ministers of their views, and for those preaching the gospel in the country. It was in connection with this school that Gaussen did the principal work of his life, teaching and defending the evangelical faith. As a preacher he has been described as combining in a high degree manly energy with delicacy and fervor of feeling. His style was marked by richness and vivacity. It was sometimes diffuse, but was flowing and often kindled into eloquence. Fish gives from him a striking discourse occasioned by the fall of Charles X, that is, the Revolution of 1830. It affords a fine example of the use of a great event, yet from a Scriptural standpoint, without sensation, but with earnest appeal to the higher motives, as these words will show: "But let us end as Christians should do, by raising our hearts and our prayers to God. Although the catastrophe which has shaken a neighboring empire has been placed before us, it has only been that the subject might fill us with spiritual reflection; but as this event, in whatever manner it may be viewed, has caused much misery, and may be the occasion of much more, let us raise our hands toward the mercy seat with praise and supplications and thanksgiving as ordained by St. Paul."

The ablest and most scholarly and accomplished member of this group was the eminent professor and literary critic, Alexandre Vinet (1797-1847).[18] He was born in the canton of Vaud, near Lausanne, of a family descended from Huguenot exiles. His father was a man of high character, but somewhat stern. His discipline was very strict. The mother, however, was full of gentleness and piety, and her influence was strong in develop-

[18]*The Life and Writings of Alex. Vinet,* by Laura M. Lane, Edinburgh, 1890; *Le Vinet de la légende et celui de l'histoire,* par. J. F. Astie, Paris, 1882. Art. by A. Rüegg in *RE;* sermon and sketch in Fish, *Masterpieces,* II, p. 183; Vincent, pp. 81, and *passim; Christian Philosophy—Select Discourses,* tr. from the French, Lond., (Rel. Tr. Soc., undated); *Gospel Studies,* tr., with Introd. by Robert Baird, D. D., New York, 1849.

ing the character and genius of her gifted son. In early youth his breadth of mind and versatile genius appeared. Literature, philosophy, questions of the day, as well as theology, attracted his keen and thoughtful interest, and in all these subjects he became both a deep student and a wise and kindling preacher. He was educated principally at Lausanne, but already in his twentieth year he was appointed professor in the gymnasium at Basel. Here he lived and taught for twenty years. He was ordained and preached frequently in the French churches at Basel and elsewhere, though he never was a pastor. He experienced a deep spiritual change about the year 1823, partly owing to a serious illness. Henceforth he taught and preached clear evangelical doctrines. In manner he was winsome and attractive. His literary output during his stay in Basel was very large and varied. Essays on public questions, brilliant literary criticisms and studies, as well as sermons and other religious writings bear witness alike to his diligence and to his learning and thoughtfulness. In 1837 he was called to the chair of Practical Theology at Lausanne, where he labored for the ten remaining years of his life. Naturally the change was at first a trial to him and he felt as if he were not successful, but his friends and pupils speak far otherwise. He took part with Malan, D'Aubigne, and other leaders, in opposing the rationalism of the Established Church, but his learning and culture, as well as the breadth of his sympathies, saved him from the narrowness which was characteristic of too many evangelicals. He was an ardent defender of freedom of thought and conscience, and while sincerely believing and defending evangelical orthodoxy, he was tolerant of other views. As a teacher of homiletics he was a great master. Unfortunately his two important works on that subject appeared after his death and without his final revision. The *Treatise on Homiletics* was made up from the notes of his pupils and his own imperfect manuscripts. Notwithstanding these defects, it had great influence in molding the views of many preachers in France and elsewhere. It was translated into English and widely used in America. The other work was his admirable *History of Preaching Among the Reformed During the Seventeenth Century.* Some of

Vinet's sermons were published at various times. They indicate all the qualities which have been mentioned and more. Clear conception and warm exposition of Biblical truth are their fundamental notes. Excellent homiletics without the parade of analysis or art, a fine and beautiful style, a mellow and appealing unction were characteristic of Vinet's preaching. Altogether, both as a teacher of preachers and himself a preacher of high rank, though never an active pastor, Vinet is worthy of the highest respect and of careful study. Besides the qualities indicated, he had and used a vigorous imagination, which never ran away with him. His illustrations are apt and forcible, his reasoning acute and candid. The total impression of his manner is that of a rarely gifted, highly cultured mind deeply intent on communicating the truth of God as it was given to him to see it.

J. H. Merle D'Aubigné (1794-1872)[19] was associated with Malan, Vinet, and others in the awakening movement at Geneva. His family name of Merle received the addition of D'Aubigné from his grandmother, who was of high lineage. The father was a citizen of Geneva, but carried on a mercantile business in Marseilles. The youth felt himself drawn toward the work of preaching and became a student at Geneva about the time the religious awakening began. At first he sympathized with the rationalistic side, but was led, under the influence of Malan and Haldane, to both a spiritual and an intellectual acceptance of the evangelical views. Soon after his conversion he went to Germany, and at Berlin attended the lectures of Schleiermacher, Neander, and others. In 1818 he was ordained by the company of pastors in Geneva, and took charge of the Reformed Church at Hamburg. Here he had a successful and earnest ministry of about five years. At that time Holland and Belgium constituted one kingdom. Though Belgium was Catholic, the king was a Hollander and Protestant. He resided part of the time at Brussels, and appointed young Merle D'Aubigné as court preacher there. Here his min-

[19]Art. by Duchemin in *RE;* sermon and sketch in Fish, *XIX Cent.*, p. 123 ff.; Vincent, *passim; Discourses and Essays,* tr. by C. W. Baird, with introductory sketch by Dr. Robert Baird, New York, 1846.

istry continued for about seven years. About 1830 he resigned his position at Brussels and returned to Geneva, where he became associated with the evangelical pastors in founding the theological school for the training of young men in those views. Here, with much preaching, both in Geneva and elsewhere, he found his busy and fruitful life-work, varying his double and arduous duties with occasional travel. Besides his activity as preacher and professor, he was a very prolific writer on many theological and other subjects. The great work of his life was his long-popular and interesting *History of the Reformation,* which was translated into other languages and had a wide circulation, both in England and America. As a preacher D'Aubigné held with firmness and intelligence the theology of his school. His learning was felt, but not made obtrusive in his pulpit work. His sermons were pious, earnest, and effective. He had sufficient imagination and feeling to make them popular and impressive. His style was clear, flowing, and attractive.

Other French-Swiss preachers of this period,[20] less important than those mentioned, were Jacques Martin, pastor in Geneva about 1840, who was characterized by great vigor and vehemence of feeling and style. J. E. Couriard, also pastor in Geneva, and historian and critic, without great distinction as a preacher; B. Bouvier, Viguié, and Trottet, who had a style of animation and a flowing eloquence. It does not appear that any of the preachers of the rationalistic group had any special excellence as preachers.

Passing now to the more distinctively French group of preachers, we shall not find it necessary to distinguish between those of France proper and those who preached in nearby regions, as there was frequent interchange. A very famous and beloved family was that of the Monods. The father, Jean Monod, served as pastor in Copenhagen and also in Paris. Four of his sons became active and highly esteemed preachers in the French Reformed Church. These were Frederick, Adolphe, William, and Horace. The best known and greatest of them was the eloquent, spiritual, and beloved Adolphe Monod

[20]See Vincent, *passim.*

(1802-1856).[21] Adolphe was the fourth of twelve children. The parents of this interesting and striking family were unusually gifted and cultivated, both in mind and character. The mother was a Dane of Copenhagen, where Jean Monod served as pastor of the French Reformed Church for some years, and where Adolphe was born and spent his early childhood. Besides his admirable home training, both in intellect and in character, he attended schools in Paris, and obtained his philosophic and theological education at the University of Geneva. The cold moralistic influences then prevalent in the Faculty there were not favorable to the development of piety or of a genuine Christian faith. Adolphe, always more or less inclined to depression, was chilled by the religious atmosphere, but the evangelical influences which were beginning to be strong under Malan and D'Aubigné, were not without their effect upon the spiritual development of the gifted young man. Thus, about the year 1825, he became truly converted to Christ, and from then on to the end of his life occupied unfalteringly and with great peace of mind a firm position of evangelical belief and of personal union with his Lord. He had had, of course, the inevitable intellectual struggle with skepticism, but here likewise had come forth conqueror and reached a secure vantage ground of well-reasoned theological opinion. Traveling in Italy, he was persuaded to remain at Naples for awhile as pastor of the French Reformed Church in that city. This, however, was only temporary, and in a year or two he was called to the French Reformed Church at Lyons. This was really the beginning of his life-work, which falls into three periods: the pastorate at Lyons, 1827-1836; the professorship at Montauban, 1836-1849; and the pastorate in Paris, 1849 to his death, in 1856.

[21]Fish, *XIX Cent.*, p. 164 ff.; Vincent, *passim;* art. by Bonnet in *RE;* Paul Stapfer, *La grande prédication chrétienne en France—Bossuet, Adolphe Monod; Saint Paul, cinq discours,* par Adolphe Monod, Paris, 1859 (also Eng. trans.); *Les Adieux d'Adolphe Monod,* Paris, 1857; *The Parting Words of Adolphe Monod* (Eng. trans.), New York, 1875; also some sermons trans. in *Select Discourses from the French and German,* by Fish and Poor, New York, 1858.

At Lyons Monod was associated with other pastors, as was the custom in the French Reformed Churches. These pastors, as well as the majority of the congregation, were rationalistic and worldly. The discipline of the church had grown lax, the preaching was fruitless, and consequently spiritual life at a very low ebb. Monod's preaching struck a new note. He proclaimed Christ as the Saviour from sin. He emphasized the sinful side of man as lost without the grace of God. He urged repentance and consecration with all his heart. Of course such preaching created a great stir. Monod's worldly-minded colleagues would have none of it. They even went so far as to complain to the city authorities with a view to removing Monod from his office. Only one thing was left for the pious and brilliant preacher to do. He could not surrender his views, nor could he forsake the few who had been called to a higher Christian life through his ministry. Forbidden to preach in the Established Church, he set up a separate congregation. The little flock of the faithful ones met first in an upper room. Soon the quarters became too narrow, and a little chapel was erected, where a great work was done for the cause of Christ. The evangelical life of Lyons and of France received from that little pulpit a blessed and gracious impulse, as well as a large and fruitful work whose influence abides even till now.

For some reasons not quite clear Monod accepted an earnest call to a vacant professorship of theology in the Protestant Seminary at Montauban in 1836. It will be remembered that this seminary was permitted to be founded by Napoleon in the early part of the century as a concession to the Protestants. It remained a long time the chief if not the only theological institution of the French Reformed Church. So earnest a worker and eloquent a preacher as Monod could not confine his labors to a theological chair. He often filled the pulpits of Montauban and the surrounding region, and during his vacations traveled and preached to the Reformed congregations, especially in the south of France. He was everywhere greeted by great congregations, and his ministry was blessed with many fruits. It was during this time that his unusual powers as a preacher became manifest and celebrated throughout France.

It is not surprising, therefore, that he should have been called to be one of the pastors at the principal Reformed Church in Paris, whither he went in 1849. He preached at the large Church of the Oratory in the mornings, and his hearers were very numerous. In a small chapel connected with his church it was his custom to give on Sunday evenings talks on the Bible of a simple and practical nature. These more familiar expositions were very highly regarded by those who attended them, many of his friends esteeming them more highly than his more elaborate morning sermons. In this great work Monod labored for seven or eight years. The last several months of his life were full of suffering and pain. He fell ill of a lingering and hopeless disease, under which he gradually faded away. During several months of his decline it was his custom on Sunday afternoons to allow a few friends to gather in his sick room, and from his dying bed he spoke short messages of wonderful beauty and spiritual power. After his death many of these, which had been taken down by friends, were published in a little volume under the title, *The Farewell of Adolphe Monod.* The little book was translated into German and English and was very widely read. These discourses formed a fitting close to a life of singular piety, beauty, and devotion.

It is difficult to speak without exaggeration of the beautiful, almost perfect, character of Adolphe Monod. There was that sweet combination in him of natural gayety and of Christian seriousness which supplemented each other and made him a man of winning, gracious, appealing personality. Stapfer, speaking of his college days, says that "the prime characteristic of Adolphe Monod was a gay humor and great ardor for all sports, and less of natural facility for study than a serious purpose to succeed, animated by a lively self-respect." This tendency to light-heartedness was not only controlled and developed by the serious purposes of his later life, but was offset in his sensitive nature by a corresponding tendency to depression of spirits from which he often suffered. From his conversion on through life Monod was characterized by a simple, unswerving, and beautiful piety. He was never spoiled by his success nor by the almost extravagant appreciation of his friends. Conscious of his own weaknesses and fully depending on the grace of God, he exhibited a constant and beautiful humility. He never repelled even the humblest who sought his sympathy and his aid. Rich and poor alike found him a tender and wise counselor and helper. He loved children and they loved him. He published two volumes of sermons that he had preached to children. The enemies and rivals who distressed him were those who disliked his doctrine and were shamed by his life. He was indeed a saintly, lovable, almost perfect man.

Of his native intellectual gifts it is possible to speak with almost equal enthusiasm. He had that fine combination of intellectual acuteness, power of imagination, and depth of sympathy which goes to make the great orator. His thought may not be very profound or original, but it is very clear, strong, and logical. His imagination was chastened by his piety and subdued by native good taste and admirable culture. He had studied profoundly the theological and philosophical thought of his time and was master of the professional learning of his day, though he made no claim to being a critical scholar. General culture also was at his command. He read appreciatively and widely in the best literature of the world. His sermons show no pedantry or display, but they breathe the very spirit of a cultivated man. In form and style Monod's preaching presents the very highest point of homiletical achievement according to the standards of his time. He was formed in the period midway between the classic stiffness of the eighteenth century and the more familiar manner of the later nineteenth. His style is rather too classic for present taste, but is far more flexible and popular than that which prevailed in the epoch preceding Monod's day. His diction is beautiful French, limpid yet vigorous, combining long and short sentences in good proportion, never involved, never tedious, fresh, sparkling, often sublime. Through all there is a tenderness and sweetness, a beauty and a charm which carries no note of weakness with it, but pleases and moves at the same time. It is no wonder that many critics consider Monod the best of all modern French preachers. Even Lacordaire generously said, on hearing Monod, "We are all children beside him." Professor Paul

Stapfer, in a brilliant treatise on *The Great French Preaching*,[22] takes, as illustrating his theme at its highest point, Bossuet and Monod. Among other things, he says, "Great artist by temperament, Monod was so also by conscience; for he considered it a duty to take all the literary care of which he was capable to convince and persuade men of the truth which saves." Such tributes from men who, occupying very different angles of vision, could not accept Monod's doctrines, pay unconstrained and genuine respect to his great powers as a Christian orator. The only criticism of any real importance is that Monod's sermons are too elaborate and polished; but the simplicity and sincerity of his appeal forbid us, even in the presence of such perfect art, to call it art for art's sake.

The published sermons of Monod appeared at various intervals. As early as 1830 he published discourses which dealt with the essence of evangelical doctrine and were widely read. Again, in 1844, a volume of sermons appeared which discussed *The Arguments for the Christian Faith.* Later there appeared two sermons on *The Calling of a Christian Woman.* In 1852 the little volume containing the *Five Sermons on the Apostle Paul* appeared. This was his masterpiece. These sermons were translated into every language, and have been widely read. After his death the dying messages referred to above were published, and also his collected sermons in three volumes containing, respectively, discourses delivered at Lyons, Montauban, and Paris.

From the sermons to women Vincent quotes several striking paragraphs, one of which is as follows:[23] "Woman of the world, who hast consumed thy fairest years in cares, innocent, I hope, but frivolous and unworthy of thee; intoxicating and intoxicated, or turning aside to the profit of thy pride the empire which God has entrusted to thee for His glory and for the good of His people; behold, instead of that existence, brilliant indeed, but brilliant like a falling star; resounding, but which resounds like an empty vessel; see here a life glorious and full, where thou shalt find at length, in

[22]*La grande prédication,* etc., p. 178.
[23]*Op. cit.,* p. 255 ss.

finding thyself, that contentment which thou hast (is it not true?) demanded in vain of the world. Detach thy heart from vanity and give it to charity! Trust me! Forsake that artificial life which supplants and shortens the true one! Keep for thy home the toil of thy days and the repose of thy nights. Count as lost the days wherein thou hast not done some good. Enjoy in fine the happiness of being woman, and thou shalt know that when one has been made to be for man a 'helpmeet for him,' it is worth more to be useful to him than flattered by him, and to serve him rather than to fascinate him."

One of the most notable of modern sermons is that given from Monod by Fish in his *Pulpit Eloquence of the Nineteenth Century* on the text, "God is love." The graceful and impressive introduction begins as follows:[24] "In a small town of Italy, which, eighteen hundred years since, an eruption of Mount Vesuvius buried beneath a flood of lava, some ancient manuscripts, so scorched as to resemble cinders more nearly than books, have been discovered, and, by an ingenious process, slowly and with difficulty unrolled. Let us imagine that one of these scrolls of Herculaneum contains a copy, and the only one in the world, of the epistle from which the text is taken; and that, having come to the fourth chapter and eighth verse, they have just deciphered these two words, 'God is,' and were as yet ignorant of what should follow." A paragraph follows in which the answer is held in suspense, and then he goes on: "At length the momentous word love appears! Who could desire a better? What could be conceived comparable to it by the boldest and loftiest imagination? This hidden God, this powerful God, this holy God—He is love! What need we more? God loves us. Do I say He loves us? All in God is love. Love is His very essence. He who speaks of God speaks of love. God is love! O answer, surpassing all our hopes! O blessed revelation, putting an end to all our apprehensions! O glorious pledge of our happiness, present, future, eternal!" The conception of the sermon is striking and original. It is built around the two thoughts: First, what impression would this statement make upon one who had never heard it before;

[24] *Op. cit.*, p. 167 f.

and second, what impression it ought to make on Christians who have heard it often. In developing the first thought he uses an actual incident reported by the Moravian missionaries in Greenland of a heathen who had listened without emotion to proofs of the existence of God, but was melted and moved by the proclamation of His love. Monod very cleverly and touchingly develops the thought of how this appeal might have affected the heart of this heathen, considering the end that God had in view in the gospel—that is, the salvation of man; and the means whereby that end would be reached—through the sending of His only begotten Son; and the way in which the Son discharged the commission—by the sacrifice of Himself; and lastly, the cause of God's love thus expressing itself, which lies deep in His nature. In making the transition to his application, the preacher thus speaks:[25] "Yes, 'God is love.' This alone would explain the fact that He has so loved—whom? angels? saints? No; but us, His enemies—us individually—me, and you who hear me. 'God is love!' Love is His essence, His substance, His life. 'God is love!' Love sums up all His works and explains all His ways. Love inspired Him to the creation of a holy, and to the redemption of a fallen race. Love prevailed over nothingness to give us existence, and triumphed over sin to give us glory. Love is the object of the admiration of angels, and will be ours in eternity. The thoughts of God are love; His will is love; His dispensations are love! His judgments are love;—all in Him is love. 'God is love!' But the heart of Kajarnak expressed this more fully than all our discourse has done. At the sound of this good news, we see this heathen—if we may still so call him—we see him hanging on the lips of the missionary, his heart is affected, his conscience troubled. He exclaims: 'What did you say? Repeat that again—I, too, would be saved!' And wherefore he rather than you? Why should not this same doctrine which has made a Christian of this heathen upon the shores of Greenland—why should it not make this day in France, in this assembly of more than one nominal Christian, a Christian in spirit and in life? I have asked you, in order to disturb your habitual

[25] *Id.*, p. 179.

apathy, to put yourself in the place of this Greenlander who heard the gospel for the first time in his life; but be on your guard against the supposition that this condition is indispensable in order to be affected by it; as that the gospel has lost its virtue by having been so often announced to you; and that the coldness that we lately deplored in you, is a necessary consequence of your position. It is a necessity of sin, of negligence, of ingratitude, of unbelief, and of nothing else. Your position is a privilege, did you but know how to improve it; and you would have the power as soon as you had the will." From then on to the end he appeals with earnest eloquence to his hearers to make a suitable response to the greatness of God's love to them.

The little volume containing Monod's *Five Discourses on St. Paul* gives us the cream of his thinking and preaching. He was then at the height of his power and influence in Paris. His object in giving the series of five discourses, as he states in the preface, was not to present a study of the life and writings of the apostle, but to present the example of Paul as the type of Christian life most desirable, then as always, to be cultivated. In thus presenting the example of the apostle Monod takes five points of commanding importance in Paul's life, viz.: (1) His work; (2) his Christianity, or his tears; (3) his conversion; (4) his personality, or his weakness; (5) his example. The first discourse is on the text, 1 Cor. 15:10, "I have labored more abundantly than they all." A striking and rapid account of the apostle's great labors enables the preacher to press upon his hearers the need of such diligence on the part of Christians in modern times. The second discourse is based on Paul's address at Miletus, to the Ephesian elders, as reported in the twentieth chapter of Acts. This enables Monod to explain what he calls the Christianity of Paul, or his tears. Three times tears are mentioned in the passage, and it is around these notices that the thought of the sermon revolves. He introduces it thus:[26] "The doctrine of Paul, his faith, his charity, his zeal, his activity, his devotion, his patience, his watchfulness, all is in this discourse, so short, yet so substantial, which may be

[26]*Cinq discours,* etc., p. 47.

regarded as a sort of funeral oration anticipatory of all his apostolic work. Amid so many different traits from which is formed the Christianity of St. Paul as painted by himself, I seek one salient trait which dominates the rest and which makes the unity of the portrait. I find it in the tears of the apostle. The more that the indomitable energy of the greatest of the apostles seems to contrast with this moving symptom of human infirmity, tears, the more am I struck with the place which they occupied in the scene at Miletus." He then notes the three places where tears are mentioned in the passage, viz., where Paul says that he served the Lord with tears, and a little further on reminds his hearers that he had warned them during three years with tears, and at last that he mingles his tears with those of his hearers when at parting they "all wept sore." He goes on to show how these tears revealed and expressed the Christian character of the apostle; how they are compatible both with his courage and with his Christian joy; how towards God they were tears of grief because of men's sins and neglect of God and His grace; how toward men they were tears of deep concern, of interest, of charity; and finally, how they were tears of tenderness and sympathy, revealing the character of the apostle in its love for his brethren. The conclusion of the discourse is as follows:[27] "The tears of the holy apostle have explained him to us. The power of his apostolate was in his personal Christianity, and his Christianity was a weeping Christianity. Weeping from grief, he has conquered by respect. Weeping from charity, he has won by love. Weeping from tenderness, he has attracted by the human simplicity of his gospel. This concerns us, O Christians! Paul, is it necessary to repeat? is for me in this discourse only a means, the end is yourselves; let us rather say, it is Jesus Christ in you. Far from my thought be it to glorify a man. Let the Lord alone be glorified; and Paul would not be Paul unless he said, with John the Baptist, 'He must increase while I must decrease.' No, I do not come to glorify Paul, but I come to humble you and altogether to stir you by that which has made a man, to whom the infinite distance which separates him

[27]*Id.*, p. 81 s.

from his Divine Master has nevertheless permitted so great advance over us. It is needed that a true people of God should be formed who may be at once the generous people of the cross, the devoted people of love, and the simple people of nature, but of nature restored to itself through grace. Let those remain far from our holy enterprise who prefer prosperity to the cross, selfishness to love, appearance to reality. But thou, already a people of tears, awake! sow with tears in order to harvest with a song of triumph. Paul who wept so much, does he now regret his tears? . . . To-day like him! to-morrow with him!"

The third sermon, on Paul's conversion, presents that subject as an example of a true Christian conversion, and enforces it with clearness and eloquence, but without great originality. The fourth discourse presents, from the remarkable passage in 2 Cor. 12th chapter, the personality or weakness of the apostle. This also is a beautiful discourse presenting the apostle's weakness of bringing up, including his intellectual and moral fallibility; his bodily weakness, which interfered with his ministry; and his weakness of speech, to which the apostle himself several times refers. The last of the five discourses sets forth the example of the apostle, as outlined in the third chapter of Philippians, especially the words, "Be ye therefore followers of me." This great theme is likewise unfolded and presented with beauty of language and power of spiritual appeal. Certainly the careful and sympathetic student of Monod can not fail to recognize his easy eminence in the pulpit of his time. He was one of those gracious and winsome men who combined tenderness of heart with strength and splendor of intellect, and consecrated, with beautiful humility and devotion, all his talents and his time to the service of man, and of God.

The immediate successor of Monod in the Church of the Oratory at Paris was J. H. Grandpierre,[28] who was a man of eloquence and thorough evangelical piety. The sermon found in Fish's collection indicates these characters. He, of course, was not so great as his predecessor, but was not unworthy to follow him. There were

[28]Fish, *XIX Cent.*, p. 186 ff.; Vincent, *passim.*

also others of this group who were well worthy of mention, such as Bastie, A. Bouvier, and others.

The liberal group, with a tendency to the critical rationalism of the nineteenth century, had a number of strong and vigorous men. The earliest of them was Colani,[29] pastor for a short time of the French Church of St. Nicholas at Strassburg, and later professor in the university there. He published a number of sermons, both during his pastorate and while professor. According to Vincent he was distinguished by "suppleness and facility, a lively sentiment of actuality, novelty of ideas." He had great influence in the liberal wing of French Protestantism. Along with him should be mentioned A. Viguié, pastor at Nismes, who had the southern vivacity of feeling and liveliness of imagination. Unquestionably the greatest of this group was Athanase Coquerel, Sr. (1795-1868).[30] He was born in Paris, and studied theology at Montauban. In 1818 he became pastor of the French Church in Amsterdam, where he labored for twelve years. He was an acceptable pastor and a preacher of decided merit. He early began to publish sermons, and continued it at intervals through life. In 1830 he removed to Paris as pastor of one of the Reformed Churches there, and remained to the end of his life the leading preacher of the liberal wing of his church. His eloquence presented a fine combination of penetration of thought, clearness of style, and rapidity of movement. He had not the tenderness and spirituality of Monod, but in clearness of thought and felicity of style he ranks well along with the great evangelical preacher. Besides his sermons and other writings, Coquerel published a very clever, sensible, and suggestive treatise on homiletics under the title, *Practical Observations on Preaching.*

Athanase Coquerel, Jr., also pastor of the Reformed Church in Paris, had much of the ability and characteristics of his father, with perhaps a greater degree of force and persuasiveness in delivery. Of this group also were Fontanés, Réville, Pelissier, and others. These liberal preachers presented rather the moral and practical

[29]Vincent, p. 71, etc.

[30]Fish, p. 194 ff.; Vincent, p. 66, *et passim; Observations pratiques sur la prédication,* par Athanase Coquerel, Paris, 1860.

aspects of the Christian life, being sparing of doctrines and more or less in sympathy with the radical criticism of their age; but they were men in touch with the times and spoke, as Vincent says, to the man of the nineteenth century in the language of the nineteenth century. In the cities of Holland[31] there were French pastors of more or less distinction who leaned rather to the liberal school. Among them are mentioned Secrétan (d. 1875) at The Hague, a preacher of depth, and D. T. Huet (d. 1874), for thirty years preacher at Rotterdam, and held in high esteem.

It is fitting to conclude this brief study of nineteenth century Protestant preachers in France with a sketch of one of the noblest representatives of the modern liberal evangelical school of thought, Eugène Bersier (1831-1892).[32] Though most of his life was spent in Paris, he was a native of Switzerland, where he was born in 1831. His father died while he was quite young. He was blessed with an intelligent and pious mother. His boyhood education was received at Geneva, but for some reason his mother brought him to Paris at the age of sixteen, where he pursued further studies. About 1850 he made a long visit to the United States, and while in this country fell under the wholesome influence of a well-known American divine, who took a deep interest in the spiritual development of the attractive and promising French youth. It was under this influence that he felt his call and made up his mind to preach the gospel of Christ. On reaching this decision he went back to Geneva for further study, and was a pupil of D'Aubigné and others. Later he carried on his theological studies in Germany under such great teachers as Tholuck, Julius Müller, and Dorner. Bersier was thus both spiritually and technically well equipped for his work when, in 1855, he took charge of a church in the famous Faubourg St. Antoine, in Paris. Later he became assistant to Edmond de Pressensé in the Free Reformed Church. He immediately took high rank, both as an enlightened, public-

[31]See Van Oosterzee, *Prac. Theol.*, p. 154; Vincent, *passim.*

[32]See the *Gospel in Paris* (sermons and sketch), London (Nisbet), about 1875; *St. Paul's Vision and Other Sermons*, tr., and biographical sketch by Marie Stewart, New York, 1881; Wilkinson's *Modern Masters of Pulpit Discourse*, p. 253 ff.

spirited pastor and as a pulpit orator of the first rank. He used his influence in every way against the war with Prussia in 1870. During the siege of Paris and the fearful days of the Commune, in 1871, Bersier was active, philanthropic, and helpful, speaking words of comfort, leading his people to trust and hope. He shared the sufferings of his fellow-citizens during that time of horror. He once said to Dr. W. C. Wilkinson: "During the siege of Paris our straits were extreme, both from danger and from lack of food. It was a red letter day at my house, during the time of the worst with the city, when we could get a rat for our table. Bombs from the enemy's guns fell everywhere about us. One fell into my own study. But all this terror and famine were as nothing compared with the shame and horror of the Commune." After the war Bersier led his congregation in the building of a noble edifice near the Arc de Triomphe, called from its situation, Église de l'Étoile. Here for the remaining years of his life he preached with great power and effect, and built up an intelligent and highly cultivated congregation. Besides his own people, strangers frequented the church, and his preaching was widely blessed. A simple but elegant mural tablet near the pulpit briefly tells the story of his eminent service as pastor and preacher.

Bersier published some seven or more volumes of sermons. A number of these have been translated into English and published in New York and London. One with the title, *The Gospel in Paris,* gives a number of the sermons and a slight account of the preacher. An admirable critical account is that of Dr. W. C. Wilkinson, in his *Modern Masters of Pulpit Discourse.* In the introductory note to his discussion, Professor Wilkinson says: "During that whole winter (1861-62) I often, indeed almost regularly, heard M. Bersier preach. I also saw and heard him again and again in the weekly prayer-meetings of his church. He was a noble looking young man, with a sweet, rich voice, that added full weight to the impression of his personal presence. There was a dignity mingled with a simplicity in his bearing, a fervor in kindling, a sobriety in his thought, a force always admirable within measure in his utterance, that gave promise of the eminence as preacher in due time to be his." On hearing him some years later, when he was in middle life, Dr. Wilkinson found the impressions of those early days amply confirmed, and in speaking of a volume of his published sermons, says: "I am testifying without reserve that purer gold of thought better beaten into perfect expression I should not know where to look for in any volume of sermons. It has been in my way to make some study of Bossuet, of Massillon, of Bourdaloue, and of Saurin, and I can truly say that in summary of merit the average sermon of Bersier need not fear a comparison with the average sermon of any one of those masters of pulpit eloquence." Professor Wilkinson proceeds to justify this high, perhaps somewhat extravagant, opinion by a keen criticism, accompanied by citations from some of the sermons. We may not be able to go so far as Professor Wilkinson, but certainly Bersier in his published discourses occupies a very high rank among the best preachers of France. He had an admirable presence and delivery; as we have seen, his preparation, both in technical learning and of general culture, was adequate. He had penetration of mind, great logical skill, simplicity yet suggestiveness of analysis, and a free and swinging style, depth of conviction, and a touch with his times both large-minded and large-hearted. Decidedly evangelical in his earlier sermons, he became later in his life more tolerant of departures from traditional orthodoxy. Yet on the whole his grasp of the gospel of Christ was personal, well-reasoned, and fervent. His presentation of truth had the ring of conviction and the persuasiveness of true eloquence.

CHAPTER XV

The British Pulpit of the Nineteenth Century

In no nation of the world did the nineteenth century stand for more than in England and the connected lands. Notwithstanding all her former glories, it is true that in the nineteenth century England came to her highest point of greatness. Military and naval prowess, commercial and industrial progress, social and political achievement, literary, scientific, and artistic work all constitute a crown of glory for this great and widely spread people in this age that no detraction can tarnish, nor even real and confessed fault can spoil.

The wonderful vigor of the English national life in this age appears with full power in the religious sphere as well as in others. Great men, great ideas, great movements, with the stress and clash of progress and debate, were fully manifest. And all parts of the religious life of a live and mighty people were concerned. Questions of ecclesiastical polity and practice, affairs of ritual and forms of worship, profound problems of theology, and practical questions of immense importance concerning works of benevolence and missions stirred the minds of the English people. It goes without saying that all these interests were closely connected with preaching. The British intellect and character in both their strength and weaknesses appear in the pulpit of the century; but it is simple truth to say that at no time and among no people does the Christian pulpit appear to greater advantage on the whole than in Great Britain during the nineteenth century. And this is true from every point of view. Judged by intellectual power and depth of thought, compared with other modes of spiritual activity, tested by practical fruits, and studied in the pure light of literary criticism, the nineteenth century English pulpit occupies an exalted rank in the annals of Christian preaching.

For the purposes of this study of British preaching and its relation to the events and movements of the age, it will be convenient and appropriate to divide the century into three periods of nearly equal length, as follows: (1) From the opening of the century to the rise of the Oxford movement, 1801-1833; (2) Thence to the disestablishment of the Irish Church, 1833-1868; (3) Thence to the end of the century, 1868-1900.

I. The First Third of the Century, 1801-1833

This early period was filled with events of great importance in the after history of England and the world.[1]

[1]See Knight's and other Histories of England; the *Historians' History;* McKenzie's *Nineteenth Century* (brief survey), etc.

The century found Great Britain engaged in her colossal duel with Napoleon, which was terminated on the field of Waterloo, in 1815. The short and to both contestants rather inglorious war with the United States ended with Jackson's victory at New Orleans, in January, 1815, though as a matter of fact peace had been concluded at Ghent several weeks before the battle was fought. Before taking up his famous Peninsular campaign and winning his victory at Waterloo, Wellington had gained important victories in India and secured the British supremacy there. Australia also had been more fully brought under direct home influences and contributed to the commerce and widespread power of the great British empire. In domestic affairs the period was one of immense importance, and rich in results for later times. The sovereigns did not count for much. Poor George III was often ill, and finally lost his reason in 1810. The Prince of Wales was made prince-regent and exercised the royal power till he actually succeeded, in 1820, and reigned ten years more as George IV. Among the incapable and morally worthless kings who have burdened the English throne, the fourth George has a chief place. He lived without respect and died without lament. His brother succeeded as William IV in 1830, and reigned seven years. It is not at all to her sovereigns, but rather in spite of them, that England owes her glory in this period. It was her people that made her truly great.

In 1801 the Act of Union with Ireland led to the discontinuance of the Irish Parliament and to the tremendous agitations which have characterized the political relations of the two islands ever since. In 1832, after long and bitter agitation, the famous Reform Bill was passed which extended the franchise and corrected some of the more glaring abuses of representation in Parliament. Some of the most oppressive laws against Catholics were repealed, and O'Connell was seated in the British Parliament in 1829. The slave trade had already been put down, and the abolition of slavery throughout the British empire was accomplished in 1833. In many other paths of civilized progress great advances were made. Old laws of a cruel nature were repealed, prisons were reformed, child labor repressed, philanthropy and education were pushed forward. In sciences and arts great progress was made. Industrial improvements were inaugurated, but not without great suffering among hand-workers, whose means of support were taken away by the introduction of machinery. The first railway was successfully put into operation by George Stephenson in 1830. Perhaps the most astonishing progress was apparent in manufacturing and commerce. Though the long struggle with Napoleon laid an enormous debt upon the country, the commercial interests of England were vastly extended by the results of the war.

In the sphere of literature England's greatness is no less apparent.[2] This was an age of wonderful intellectual activity and literary achievement. We have only to recall some of the leading names in English literature to remind ourselves how large a place is filled in that sphere by the first three decades of the nineteenth century. In poetry Burns and Cowper came over from the last period and illuminated the opening of the new century. It was the active period of Crabbe, Campbell, Southey, Scott, and Moore among the lesser poets; and of Byron, Coleridge, Keats, Shelley, and Wordsworth among the greater ones. In fiction the near approaching era of its classic power was heralded by the admirable works of Jane Austen and the unparalleled romances of Walter Scott. In essay writing some of the masters were brilliantly exemplifying that style of literary expression, such as Jeffrey, Sydney Smith, Wilson (Christopher North), Talfourd, Lamb, DeQuincey, and the young Macaulay. In the field of oratory, though Burke was no more, and Pitt and Fox had passed away early in the century, they had stimulated a set of younger men whose fame is secure in the history of political and forensic eloquence. Erskine and Grattan were still active after the century opened. Brougham made his greatest effort at the trial of Queen Caroline, in 1820. The accomplished George Canning was at the height of his power and popularity, and the Irish patriot and orator, Daniel O'Connell, was in the full tide of his influence and renown.

[2]See the *Warner Library,* and any of the numerous Histories of English literature, for the period.

Great activity and movement also characterized the religious life of the English nation during this time.[3] The evangelical and missionary impulses and forces of the last century came over with force into the new. Missionary organization went on, and the young societies founded during the last decade of the eighteenth century were gathering experience and strength for the larger developments that awaited them. One of the most important organizations was that of the British and Foreign Bible Society, in 1804. Humane and charitable work accompanied this missionary movement, and the thought and activity of Christian workers were directed with telling effect against abuses and evils at home. Theological opinion and the rise and growth of parties and schools of thought were sufficiently in evidence. The evangelical party was in the ascendant, but its day of greatest influence was ready to decline just toward the close of this era. It had wrought a great work, and was destined to remain one of the greatest forces of English Christian life through the whole century. But its critics were also strong, and seizing on some of its more vulnerable points, were not slow in making their attacks felt. Cant and one-sidedness were undoubtedly apparent in much of the current evangelicalism. But its eminent piety and admirable services to religion and humanity can not be gainsaid when we recall the names and work of such men as Wilberforce, Carey, Simeon, and others. In the Established Church the three parties—Low, High, and Broad—came now to be clearly contrasted and to follow their divergent lines of work and influence. Evangelicalism was identified with the Low Church party. The Broad Church party began to gain power under the lead of men like Coleridge, Whately, and Thomas Arnold. The High Church group had never been wholly without influence, but this tendency was just on the eve of taking on its most significant phase of the century in the rise of the Oxford movement under Keble, Pusey,

[3]See the general and Church histories, and more especially J. Stoughton, *History of Religion in England* from 1800 to 1850, with Supplement to 1880; J. H. Overton, *The English Church of the XIXth Century*, 1800-1833; Tulloch, *Movements of Religious Thought in Britain During the XIXth Century* (Harper's ed., N. Y., 1886).

and Newman, in 1833. Its full development belongs to the next period. Among Dissenters the evangelical wing was strongest, but the liberalistic trend was not wholly wanting, especially with the Unitarian element in the English Presbyterian Church. On the whole, while the other parties were not wholly inactive, the dominant force in the religious life and thought of England in this period was Christianity of the evangelical type.

It would have been passing strange and contrary to all historic precedent if an age such as this had produced no great results in the pulpit.[4] As we have seen, immense energy characterized the English people. War, commerce, and manufactures stimulated the mind; literature glowed and throbbed with intense and productive life; liberty and reform shook the state with power; religion found expression in far-reaching activities at home and abroad, in wide and growing intellectual research, and in a sincerity and reality of Christian living not confined to sects and parties, but more or less pervading them all. These varied influences were felt already in this earlier period, but not in full force till later. It was hard in this opening era of the new century to shake off the coolness and blight of the Latitudinarian and Moderate schools of the eighteenth century. The evangelical pulpit was strongest, but only a comparatively few preachers were of unusual merit. Overton says:[5] "Regarded purely as a spiritual force, the Evangelicals were undoubtedly the strongest party in the Church during the first thirty years of the nineteenth century. So much was this the case that spiritual earnestness was in itself a presumption that a man was an evangelical." But, as he[6] further points out, evangelical preaching made its appeal chiefly to the feelings, and was most com-

[4]There is, unhappily, no general history of British preaching for this or any other period. Notices are to be found in the works previously mentioned; sketch in Pattison's *Hist. of Christian Preaching,* chap. XII; Hoppin's *Hom.,* p. 212 ff.; remarks in *Our Bishops and Deans,* F. Arnold, 2 vols., London, 1875 (referred to as *OBD*); and there is a thoughtful study in *The Modern Pulpit,* by L. O. Brastow, New York, 1906, pp. 174-316; but our chief sources must be collections of sermons and biographical sketches, cyclopaedia articles, and the lives and works of individual preachers, as referred to in subsequent notes.

[5]*Op. cit.,* p. 51.

[6]*Op. cit.,* p. 137 ff.

monly delivered without manuscript, so that the printed sermons as we have them hardly give the measure of the effect of even the best preaching of the time. Men like Southey, Sydney Smith, and others sharply criticised the preaching of the age; and even Heber,[7] writing to a young clergyman, cautions him to "avoid singularities," and instances "the High Churchman who shuffles in a pompous tone through his nose, and the Evangelical minister who preaches extempore." It is a noteworthy fact that the three greatest preachers of this time were outside the Anglican body: Robert Hall, Edward Irving, Thomas Chalmers.

The contents and style of the early nineteenth century sermons claim brief notice. The doctrine was not as yet greatly varied from the accepted evangelical standards. Of course, the High Churchmen gave great emphasis to the sacraments and decried the "excitement" of their Evangelical brethren. But the oratorical triumphs of Irving, before he fell into his later vagaries, the splendid pulpit work of Hall, and, toward the last of the period, of Chalmers, showed that evangelical sentiments could be preached in the very best way. Some one said of Robert Hall that "he redeemed Dissent from vulgarity." The praise was little and grudging, but it was a straw which showed the course of the wind. The Broad Churchmen adopted a critical attitude toward all others (as their manner ever is) which strongly implied their exclusive possession of wisdom and moderation, but their polemic was not often bitter (excepting always the redoubtable Sydney Smith!), and their views, while somewhat vague and shifting, would not now be regarded as very seriously departing from orthodox opinion. Both High and Broad Churchmen opposed the Calvinism of the Evangelicals. As to style, it is hard to put down any general characteristic as widely prevalent amid so great variety of individual method. But, broadly speaking, it may be said that the eighteenth century vogue was still too common—there was too much stateliness, precision, carefully worked out elegance, or the attempt at it. There was want of flexibility, familiarity, humanness. The discourse was too aloof from life, however high it might soar in

[7]Quoted by Overton, *l. c.*

thought and feeling. The method was English; topical rather than expository. The interpretation of Scripture was not yet scientific and painstaking, being rather traditional and superficial. Analysis tended to minuteness and formality in many of the sermons, though the stronger men of the time were no slaves to scholastic division of their matter. On the whole, the sermons of the leading preachers of this age show strong thinking, high intellectual worth, profound earnestness, with a certain consciousness of power. But so much allowance has to be made in these general statements for the differing qualities of groups and individuals that it will be better to try to bring out the features of the preaching by a study of the leading preachers themselves, rather than to attempt further broad characterization.

Taking up first the evangelical group,[8] a word should be said concerning the so-called "Clapham Sect." John Venn, William Dealtry, Henry Blunt, and some others, along with several pious laymen and Miss Hannah More, were leaders in this group, who resided principally at or near Clapham, where Venn and others preached. They exercised great influence throughout the country. Along with them should be named Isaac Milner, Thomas Gisborne, Claudius Buchanan, Edward Bickersteth, and a few more. John Newton, in his old age, was still preaching at St. Mary Woolnoth. The eminent bishop of Calcutta, Daniel Wilson (1778-1858),[9] received his appointment to India in 1832, but was at this time active in the ministry chiefly in London, where he held several pastorates. His long useful series of sermons, or lectures, on *The Evidences of Christianity* were given in the Church of St. Mary, Islington. The line of argument in these discourses has long been out of date, but they were thorough and able for their time. They deal with their subjects in a topical manner with some formality of outline, but in a clear and easy style and with thinking adapted to the average intelligence.

The most important member of the evangelical group

[8]Overton, chap. III; Stoughton, Vol. I, Chap. IV.

[9]Art. in *DNB*, etc.; notices in Overton and Stoughton; *The Evidences of Christianity*, by Daniel Wilson, 2 vols. (*Lib. of Christian Knowledge*), Boston, 1833.

was the pious and beloved Charles Simeon (1759-1836),[10] for fifty years pastor in Cambridge. While a student at King's College, Cambridge, in 1779, he was required as an undergraduate to attend the Lord's Supper. This led him seriously to inquire into his fitness. He read Venn's *Whole Duty of Man,* joined the Society for the Promotion of Christian Knowledge, and in other ways sought to develop his spiritual life. In reading a sermon or treatise of Bishop Wilson on *The Lord's Supper* he was led to put his whole trust in Christ, and grew clearer in his evangelical convictions. He was ordained in 1782, and not very long after was appointed to Trinity Church, Cambridge, at a merely nominal salary. At first he met with opposition on account of his views, but by patience and self-sacrifice lived to overcome it. The opening of the nineteenth century found him strongly entrenched at Cambridge, drawing large congregations and exercising a very helpful influence upon the student body, as well as in the parish. He had his faults, being somewhat proud and irritable, but he mellowed with age, and was at all times a sincere and deeply pious man. Pure in life and unselfish in purpose, he was greatly beloved by all who knew him. It is said that a casual company of fifty or more students being assembled, the question was raised as to whom they would seek for counsel in trouble, and on a ballot nearly all were found to have named Simeon. He was an indefatigable student of the Bible. Besides his sermons, he published many volumes of homiletical outlines covering the whole Scripture. These sketches and skeletons of sermons were very widely circulated, and while they doubtless did some good, they might easily have been a snare to preachers who were not very diligent. Sometimes the analysis is forced and fanciful, and nearly always too formal. The thought is not profound, though spiritual, and the aim is always practical and edifying.

The High Church party were at this time called the "Orthodox" in the English Church.[11] Those who became leaders in the Oxford movement will receive notice later. In this earlier period Bishop Lloyd of Oxford, the cele-

[10]Art. in *DNB,* and account in Overton, Chap. III; *Works* (esp. *Horae Homileticae,* and Appendix), 21 vols., ed. T. H. Horne, Lond., 1833.

[11]Overton, *op. cit.,* Chap. II.

brated Christopher Wordsworth—Master of Trinity College, Cambridge—Bishop Middleton, and a few others, were leaders. But the best representative of this school in the pulpit was Hugh James Rose (1795-1838).[12] His father was a clergyman of Scottish lineage. Hugh was born at Little Horsted, Sussex, and was educated at Wickfield School and Trinity College, Cambridge, where he was graduated in 1817. Ordained the next year, he soon became vicar of Horsham, where he worked with success for two years, published some writings which attracted notice, and then spent a year studying in Germany. He preached and published a good deal and held various places, especially at Hadleigh, in Suffolk. Then he became "perpetual curate" at Southwark to the end of his life. The promoters of the Oxford movement received some encouragement, but also a good deal of cautioning, from Rose, but he could not restrain them. He was highly esteemed by his party, both for the matter and manner of his discourses. He was cautious, clear, and thoroughly devout in the presentation of his views. He was considered by those who heard him often a very impressive preacher.

The liberalistic party, later called Broad Church,[13] were rather in this period the beginners of a tendency than the leaders of a well-defined movement. They were largely influenced by the thinking of Coleridge, Whately, and others. Richard Whately (1787-1863) was not specially distinguished as a preacher, but was made archbishop of Dublin in 1831. As a logician and apologetic writer and philosophic thinker he filled a large place in his time, and influenced both contemporaneous and subsequent thought. F. D. Maurice was beginning his work in this time, but he more properly belongs in the next period. The most important name among the preachers of the Broad Church tendency is that of the eminent teacher and man, Thomas Arnold (1796-1842).[14] Ar-

[12]Art. in *DNB,* and Overton, *l. c.*

[13]Overton, Ch. III; Stoughton, Vol. I, Ch. IV; Tulloch, *op. cit., Lects.,* I, II.

[14]*Life and Correspondence,* by A. P. Stanley, New York, 1846; art. in *DNB,* and notices in Overton, Stoughton, and Tulloch; sermon in *World's Great Sermons,* Vol. IV, p. 133 ff.; *The Christian Life, Sermons Preached Mostly in Rugby Chapel,* London, 1841.

nold's fame rests chiefly upon his great work as the Master of Rugby High School. His powerful personality, his honesty and high-mindedness made him one of the greatest of English educators. Born in the Isle of Wight, he received his preliminary education in various places, but got his university training at Oxford, where he became a fellow of Oriel College about 1815. His life has been beautifully written by one of his famous pupils, A. P. Stanley, and his influence among his students is delightfully described in Thomas Hughes' *Tom Brown's Schooldays at Rugby.* Arnold wrote various essays and treatises, and left a valuable fragment in his *History of Rome.* A volume of his sermons, preached to the boys at Rugby, revealed his qualities as a preacher. He discarded homiletical analysis, used a plain and straightforward style, and spoke with large-hearted feeling and earnest moral purpose to his youthful auditory. While the sermons show a great moral enthusiasm and admiration of Christ, they are not distinguished by evangelical sentiments or warmth of personal conviction.

Among the dissenters of the period there were a good many of very high rank and a few who are to be reckoned among the most important preachers of history. Already we have noticed the work of the eccentric but highly eloquent and useful Rowland Hill,[15] whose work lay chiefly in the end of the eighteenth century, but he was still preaching at the Surrey chapel, and lived until 1833. Among the Baptists Andrew Fuller[16] was in the evening of his days, but still active at Kettering for the first fifteen years of the new century. In Wales John Elias followed Rowlands and others as an evangelistic preacher of great eloquence and success.

But, leaving these preachers of the transition, we come to William Jay (1769-1853).[17] He was born at Tisbury, of humble parentage. He received only a slight rudi-

[15] *Ante*, p. 327 ff. [16] *Ante*, p. 332 f.

[17] *Autobiography and Reminiscences*, New York, 1856; *Works*, 3 vols., New York, 1849; and the *Evening and Morning Exercises* in many edd.; also sketch and sermon in the valuable *Pulpit Memorials*, by Evans and Hurndall (being sketches and sermons of twenty Congregational Ministers), London, 1878, with an introd. by Dr. John Stoughton. Very helpful; hereafter referred to as E. & H. See also a sketch and sermon of Jay in Fish, *Mast.*, I, p. 397.

mentary education, and up to the age of sixteen had only a few religious books. He was apprenticed to a brick mason. On returning from his work one Saturday evening, in 1783, he stopped at a cottage where religious services were being conducted, and was awakened and soon accepted Christ. In 1785 he was received by Cornelius Winter into his house at Marlborough to be trained for the ministry in the Congregational body. He made good progress with his studies, preaching his first sermon at the age of sixteen. At the end of his study period, in the spring of 1788, he was sent by Mr. Winter to supply Rowland Hill's place at the Surrey Chapel. The people were surprised at first, but heard the youth with interest and satisfaction. Soon he accepted the care of a small church near Chippenham, but was discouraged and did not remain long. In January, 1791, he was called to Argyle Chapel, at Bath. He held this charge for nearly sixty-two years, resigning about a year before his death on account of age and infirmities. Jay was a much beloved and respected man, and useful to the end of his ministry.

Some of Jay's characteristics as a preacher may be noted. Something was due to his natural gifts. He was not fluent nor eloquent in the usual sense. He was very simple and straightforward in style and address, eschewing the stilted manner then too much in vogue. Sheridan said he had a "manly oratory." His preaching was simple, evangelical, and eminently Biblical, both in thought and style. The specimen sermon given in *Pulpit Memorials* illustrates these characteristics. It is an ordination sermon for the Rev. H. F. Burder, and is based on the apostle's request for the prayers of his brethren in 1 Thessalonians 5:25. The outline is simple and suggestive, urging the ground of necessity and of equity as a reason for the request. It discusses in a wise, though not particularly original or striking, way the work and responsibilities of the ministry. Besides his many sermons, Jay published a series of prayers and meditations called *Evening and Morning Exercises,* which held a high place among the devotional books of former generations, and fed the piety of many believers throughout the English-speaking world.

Another Independent preacher of the period was the Scotchman, Ralph Wardlaw (1779-1853).[18] He was born at Dalkeith, but his father moved to Glasgow, where Ralph was educated, both at the grammar schools and at the university. At first attached to the Secession Church, he became Congregationalist in opinion by studying the Scriptures. A congregation was gathered about him and a church built for him in Glasgow, where he performed his life-work. He labored diligently as pastor, student, and author. He was involved in a number of controversies, which he conducted in good spirit and with great ability. As a preacher he was not distinguished by any marked single characteristic, but exhibited in his preaching a combination of mental power with spiritual strength and a good carrying style. Judging from the specimen given, his preaching was rather discursive and theological, but was analytical, orderly, and neat. He was a moderate Calvinist in theology. His best known work was long a classic on its subject—*Independency*.

Among the Methodists Jabez Bunting was coming into influence and fame, but his principal activity belongs to the next period. The most important Methodist preacher of this epoch was the eminent theologian and missionary secretary, Richard Watson (1781-1833).[19] He was born of humble parents, but had some early schooling, and was apprenticed to a carpenter; but on his conversion he joined the Methodists and was released from his engagement so as to enter the ministry. Ordained in 1800, he for a time left the regular Methodists, but later returned to them. His chief work was his *Theological Institutes,* which long remained the leading authority on theology among the Methodists. But he was also an eloquent preacher, naturally a strong theologian; and being much interested in missionary work, he presented that great cause with fervor and power.

Among the Presbyterians in England Unitarianism had come in and the strongest preacher of this school was the famous Thomas Belsham (d. 1829),[20] who did very

[18]Sketch and sermon in E. & H.

[19]Sermon in Fish, *Mast.,* I. p. 423 ff.; *Sermons and Sketches,* 2 vols., New York, 1848; *Institutes,* various edd.

[20]See Stoughton, I, ch. VIII, and art. in *DNB.*

much to advance the Unitarian views. While he was chiefly noted as a writer, he was also recognized as a preacher of considerable force.

In Scotland the Moderate party had a few preachers of note, but there were also some men of strong evangelical views. Among these high place belongs to Andrew Thomson (1779-1831),[21] whose work lay chiefly in Edinburgh. He was of strong evangelical sentiments, but believed in using literary art. He was considered a great preacher in his time, as well as a powerful platform orator. He was highly influential among the leaders of the Scottish Church in his party, but by far the two most notable Scotch preachers of the age were Irving and Chalmers.

Edward Irving (1792-1834)[22] was born at Annan, Scotland, on the same day as the poet Shelley. He was a native of the same country as Thomas Carlyle. Irving's father was a tanner, his mother the daughter of a small farmer, but though in humble life, they were respectable people of sturdy character and vigorous intelligence. The boy gained prizes at school, and was fond of attending church services. He heard the Seceders preach at Ecclefechan, the little village made famous in *The Memoirs of Carlyle.* At the age of thirteen Irving went to Edinburgh University, where he graduated in 1809. He was schoolmaster for a while, and among his pupils was the bright and attractive Jane Baillie Welch, to whom Irving became sincerely attached, but who later became the wife of Carlyle. It has been supposed that there was some regret on both Irving's and Miss Welch's part that their early attachment did not result in marriage; but at the same time Irving won the affection of another of his pulpils, Isabella Martin, the daughter of a neighboring preacher, whom, after an engagement of eleven years, he married, and who was the faithful companion of his years

[21]See Blaikie, *Preachers of Scotland,* p. 272 ff.; Taylor, *The Scottish Pulpit,* p. 180 ff.

[22]See Stoughton, I, chap. XVI (p. 374 ff.); art. in *DNB* (rather depreciatory); W. Wilks, *Edward Irving, an Ecclesiastical and Literary Biography,* London, 1854; Mrs. Oliphant, *Life of Edward Irving,* London, about 1865; *Sermons, Lectures, and Occasional Discourses,* by Edward Irving, London, about 1835; Blaikie, p. 290; sermon in Fish, *Mast.,* II, p. 336 ff.; and in *World's Great Sermons,* Vol. IV, p. 103 ff.

of eminence and also of suffering and disappointment. Certainly the friendship of Irving and the Carlyles was strong, and seems never to have been disturbed, though Carlyle has been criticised for alleged ingratitude towards his older and gifted friend. During his life as a schoolmaster Irving occasionally preached as assistant to Mr. Martin, but left his school in 1818 and went to Edinburgh to study for some profession. The yearning to preach, however, was strong within him. It is said that he burned his old sermons and made a fresh start. Chalmers was now at the height of his success at St. John's Church, Glasgow. He heard Irving preach, and invited him to become his assistant. This arrangement continued for awhile, but Irving naturally felt overshadowed by his great associate, and was too ambitious and conscious of his own powers to be long contented in a subordinate position; so he welcomed an invitation to preach for a weak and declining Presbyterian Church at Hatton Garden, London. He accepted the care of this Church, and was ordained at Annan, Scotland, and belonged to that Presbytery, though preaching in London. He entered on his London work in July, 1822, having preached a farewell sermon on leaving Glasgow—a sermon marked by great cordiality and humility of feeling. His success in London the first several years was simply wonderful. One of his biographers says, "In the first quarter, it is recorded, the seat holders at the Caledonian Asylum Chapel had an increase from 50 to 1500." He at first preached in Gaelic, at least at one service, to the Scotch members of his flock, and his support was very small, but the Duke of York, afterwards King William IV, heard him preach, befriended him, got the condition of his preaching in Gaelic removed; and some friends pledged his salary. Of his beginning in London Dr. Stoughton remarks:[23] "A singular phenomenon appeared within the religious world when the first quarter of this century ran near its close; a Presbyterian minister, then unknown to fame, came to an obscure place of worship in the metropolis, and took all ranks of society by storm. . . . He produced an excitement which, from the extent to which it prevailed, the class of persons it affected,

[23] *Op. cit.*, p. 374.

and the prophetic fervor which it displayed, rose to the importance of a national event. . . . He spoke to men at large, to people of fashion in particular. Never since George Whitefield had any one so arrested attention; and Irving went far beyond Whitefield in attracting the respectful, even the admiring, notice of lords, ladies, and commons. His name was on every lip. Newspapers, magazines, and reviews discussed his merits, a caricature in shop windows hit off his eccentricities." Other accounts are to the same effect. The carriages of the great and rich thronged the street in front of his chapel. Men and women of the highest social rank, and great leaders in politics as well as business crowded his chapel. Lord Brougham took Mackintosh to hear Irving, and Mackintosh repeated at the dinner-table a beautiful sentence which he had heard from Irving in prayer. This drew the great orator, George Canning, to go to hear Irving. Afterwards, in a speech in the House of Commons, Canning alluded to Irving and said that he had heard a Scotch clergyman preach the most eloquent sermon he had ever listened to. Though pleased and surprised at his wonderful popularity, Irving remained humble in his mind, certainly at first. His marriage to Isabella Martin proved to be very happy, though she was scarcely a strong enough character to counterbalance his tendency to extremes. The best side of his work was of short duration. He soon began to take up opinions on prophecy and other things which tended to fanaticism. His church disapproved of his extreme views, so he led off a large number, and a new church was built for him in Regent Square. Here for a short time the crowds continued, but soon they began to fall off. His long and violent sermons repelled. He also came to adopt sacramentarian views of the ordinances and was somewhat unsound as to the sinlessness of our Lord's humanity. He was deposed by his Presbytery of Annan for his alleged heresies in 1832. He now instituted the so-called Catholic Apostolic Church, aiming to conform it to the Scriptural model with angels, apostles, evangelists, and with the gifts of healing and speaking with tongues. Several churches were formed on this model, some of which still exist, the sect being known as Irvingites. In 1834 Irving went to Scotland to draw members to his views, but he had fallen ill and his health gave way. He died in that year and lies buried in the crypt of the cathedral at Glasgow.

The estimates of Irving varied widely during his life and also after his death. But even his critics acknowledge his purity of character and opinion, and his devoted and conscientious service. He was led away by his enthusiasm and was perhaps not well balanced in mind. One of the best estimates of him is that of William Arnot, in his *Life of James Hamilton,*[24] who says: "Impelled by the fire of his own spirit within and drawn by the plaudits of an admiring multitude without, Mr. Irving's momentum became too great; he could not stop—he could not even slow. From expounding prophecy he allowed himself to be drawn on almost to the bound of prophesying on his own account." And Dr. Hamilton himself is quoted as thus describing him:[25] "The dupe of his own imagination, still more the victim of his misplaced affection—for all along much of his creed had been absorbed into the system through the fancy and through his cordial admiring tendencies—the idealist had become the simple visionary." Irving's preaching was very unequal. At times he was wonderfully eloquent and persuasive. Dr. Stoughton does not hesitate to say that occasionally Irving's work was worthy of Chrysostom. His biographer, Wilks, also praises highly his sermons and the earnestness and fire with which they were delivered. He quotes from one of Irving's earlier discourses the following beautiful words on prayer:[26] "Prayer is the spirit's discourse with the Father of spirits, whereby she taketh high privilege to unburden her obligations, to unbosom her affections, to express her loyal fealty to her God and King; whereby she conveyeth up to heaven the finer senses of the soul which hath no entertainment on the brute earth, but seeketh its home in the purified sphere of heaven on high. Prayer is the heart's offering towards God, the soul's sacrifice, the only effectual death of pride and selfishness, the source of humility, the breath of piety, and the life of religion."

Among Irving's sermons is a series on *The Parable*

[24]Pp. 177 ff. [25]Wilks, p. 183. [26]*Id.*, p. 49.

of the Sower.[27] A reading of these leads to the following judgment. In Scriptural content they are not closely expository nor filled very much with Biblical thought or quotations. In thought, while the range is large and ample, there is tendency to discursiveness, even occasional rambling. The discourse is not closely argued, nor is the thinking profound. It is striking without being original or deep, yet often it soars in speculation and becomes vigorous in argument. While there is sweep and majesty in the presentation, there is much of fervid declamation which shows that the preacher had not thought all around his subject or fully mastered and co-ordinated his ideas. Yet there is knowledge of human nature, insight and sympathy, along with occasional invective. The attack is now fiery, now solemn. The pleading is often tender, sometimes nobly eloquent. The style is diffuse, elaborate, with long sentences and masses of words, considerable repetition, and elaboration of thought in varying language. The arrangement is not made prominent, yet is usually clear, though lost sight of in the elaboration. The spirit of these sermons is solemn, faithful, sincere, sympathetic, and humble; yet with the personal humility there is firmness of conviction and consciousness of power which both wins and surprises. Some of the critics express surprise that Irving's theological and long discussions should have been listened to with so much interest, but there was evident power in the man as well as in the message, his own earnestness and enthusiasm swept his hearers along. Irving's is one of those pathetic cases where marvelous gifts and powers have been marred and almost wasted by lack of balance, of sobriety, of consistent purpose. No finer tribute to the man has been paid than that of his lifelong friend and supposed rival, Thomas Carlye:[28] "His was the freest, brotherliest, bravest human soul mine ever came in contact with; I call him, on the whole, the best man I have ever found in this world, or hope to find."

The greatest Presbyterian preacher of the age was the famed and eloquent Thomas Chalmers (1780-1847).[29]

[27]*Sermons,* etc., Vol. II. [28]Quoted by Stoughton, *l. c.*

[29]*Works* of Dr. Chalmers, 25 vols., Edinburgh, various dates; an old ed. of the "Astronomical Discourses," with this title: *A series of Discourses on the Christian Revelation Viewed in*

Though his life and some of his most important work extended into the next period, he was at the height of his powers and fame as a preacher at this time, so that he may properly be studied at this point of our survey. Scotland has had a distinguished and mighty line of preachers. Next to Knox stands Chalmers, and, like Knox, he was especially great in the pulpit; but his easy pre-eminence there was upheld by abilities which would have commanded success in other fields, and by actual achievements in various associated lines of effort. For he was also a great teacher, first of mathematics, then of moral philosophy, and lastly of theology. And besides these, he was one of the most eminent practical pastors of his age or of any age. His work among the poor during his pastorate in Glasgow, his admirable organization of charity work in his parish, was not only highly successful then, but is well worthy of study in these days of institutional and social work. And still further, as a church leader and founder he was equally distinguished; for it fell to him to lead in the great Disruption of 1843, and to give a successful start to the grand work of the Free Church of Scotland. These things are mentioned here so that after a brief survey of his life we may leave them aside and study Chalmers distinctively as a preacher. But it must be remembered that, like John Chrysostom, like Bernard, like Knox, like Wesley, like Spurgeon, he made his great abilities of leadership subservient to his pulpit work.

Thomas Chalmers was born at E. Anstruther, a village on the coast of Fifeshire, northeast from Edinburgh. He was the sixth of fourteen children. His parents

Connexion With the Modern Astronomy, by Thos. Chalmers, D. D., Minister of the Tron Church, Glasgow. N. Y., 1817; *Sermons and Discourses,* 3d complete Am. ed., 2 vols., New York, 1848; sermon and sketch in Fish, *Mast.,* II, 320 ff.; *Memoirs of the Life and Writings of Dr. Chalmers,* by his son-in-law, Rev. Wm. Hanna, LL. D., 4 vols., Edinb. and N. Y., 1849-52; also *Correspondence,* ed. by Dr. Hanna; and abridgment of Hanna's *Memoir* by Dr. Moffat; brief *Life,* by D. Fraser (*Heroes of Christian History*); notices by Blaikie, in *Preachers of Scotland,* p. 276, etc., and by Taylor, in *The Scottish Pulpit,* p. 194 ff. Pattison, *Hist. Christian Preaching,* ch. XI; Hoppin, *Hom.,* 216 ff. All follow Hanna for facts, but give useful and interesting accounts.

were commonplace, honest, hard-headed, shrewd, God-fearing Scottish people. His mother, very busy with the care of her large family, left him much to his nurse, who was an incompetent and cruel person. He afterwards said her unkindness and deceitfulness haunted his memory through life. He was sent early to school, and was not brilliant. At St. Andrews' University, while still quite young, too young for a college career, he was not diligent at first; but in the third year of his course his dormant faculties awoke and he began to apply himself with earnestness. Mathematics was his favorite study, but philosophy also attracted him. He read Edwards *On the Will* at the age of fourteen, and said the reading of it put him into "an elysium of delight." He began to study for the ministry at about fifteen years of age, and took a four years' course. This was in accordance with the wishes of his family and friends. He was not yet converted, though piously brought up. Already his gift of expression began to appear. It is said that when it became his turn to lead the chapel exercises, people from the outside came in to listen to his eloquent prayers. At nineteen he was licensed to preach, one of the members of the Presbytery remarking that he was "a lad o' pregnant pairts." He preached a little here and there, but was chiefly intent on studying mathematics. He also pursued some studies at Edinburgh. He was then called to the little parish of Kilmany, and at the same time was assistant professor of mathematics at St. Andrews. He served as pastor at Kilmany for twelve years, from 1803-1815. His early ministry was not marked by deep piety or devotion, though he was conscientious in the outward discharge of duty. For some reason he did not retain his place at St. Andrews, but set up a private school, where he taught for awhile. Now came the great spiritual crisis in his life which resulted in his true conversion to God. There were several lines of influence which were used by the Holy Spirit to produce this great change. He was invited to write an article on Christianity for an encyclopedia, and in studying for his subject he became detached from his mathematical ambitions and seriously engaged on the foundations of Christian truth. About the same time he had a serious illness, which sobered his thoughts, and then there came a sad affliction in the death of one of his sisters. He earnestly read Wilberforce's *Practical View of Christianity.* Under these varied lines of influence he was thoroughly converted in 1811. His new spiritual life led to new views of his work. His ministry had hitherto been without much fruit, but now his parishioners noted the wonderful change in their brilliant young pastor, and many conversions among them were the results of his change. He was happily married in 1812.

A new period of Chalmers' life and ministry begins with his removal to Glasgow, in 1815, where he served as pastor, first of the Tron Church, and then of St. John's, to 1823. This was the period of his great work as a pastor and preacher. His famous series of *Astronomical Discourses* was given in the Tron Church, and his equally remarkable parish work was done at St. John's. It will be remembered that for a part of the time he had associated with him the brilliant and unhappy Edward Irving. From such successful work as preacher and pastor he was called, in 1823, to be professor of moral philosophy at the University of St. Andrews. His accepting this position was rather surprising, and so remains. He occupied this professorship for five years, preaching occasionally, but not as pastor. He had great personal influence over his students, both in an intellectual and spiritual way. His lectures on *Moral Philosophy* were published in book form, but, while sound and able, they were not distinctively great. From 1828-1843 Chalmers was professor of theology in the University of Edinburgh. This suited him much better than either mathematics or ethics. His masterly powers in thought and expression not only charmed his students, but drew crowds of eager listeners to his lecture room. He paid visits to England in 1830 and again in 1837, where, notwithstanding his ungainly appearance and his broad Scotch brogue, he was heard with admiration.

This is not the place to write the history of the famous Disruption in the Scottish Church, in 1843. Many of the most pious and evangelical of the ministers in the Established Church were dissatisfied both as to questions of discipline and moral tone in the Establishment, and also as to the methods by which ministers were put into office. The movement was not unlike the Secession under the Erskines in the eighteenth century. Chalmers was head and front to the movement, and in the famous Assembly of 1843 it was he who led the procession of ministers who departed from the Established Church and set up the Free Kirk of Scotland. As was natural and fitting, Chalmers became professor in the Free Church College in Edinburgh, and held the place to the end of his life, in 1847. He still had great success as a lecturer, but also was much interested in the general work of the church, and preached to a congregation of Free Church people in Westport. In the last year of his life he paid another visit to England, where he preached with great success and effect. Soon after his return from this visit he fell quietly asleep, literally passing away in his sleep, on Sunday night, after preaching, May 30, 1847.

In character Dr. Chalmers possessed and nobly illustrated the virtues of his race: balance of judgment, caution combined with vehemence when aroused, sturdy honesty, strength of will and high moral aims. He had some consciousness of his powers and inclined to imperiousness, but there was also a genuine humility of soul before God. One of his biographers quotes from his journal this characteristic prayer: "Extinguish my love of praise, O God; and now that my name is afloat on the public, let me cultivate an indifference to human applause." In the family circle, among friends, and in society Chalmers was a genial and lovable man, notwithstanding his strength and decisiveness. His force of character eminently fitted him for a public man and leader. Few of the weaknesses which have marred the work of great men attach to him. He was terribly in earnest but not self-seeking, impetuous but thoughtful, strong, wise, trustworthy, and pure.

The work of Chalmers has already been briefly outlined as a professor, moral reformer, and religious leader. We are here concerned with him as preacher. In method he was remarkable; for he read his sermons and yet contrived to put into his delivery all the fire and fervor which usually go with extemporaneous speaking. His style, with its long sentences, hardly lent itself to free delivery, but if he had accustomed himself to this method it probably would have better suited his temperament. There is a story to the effect that some one criticised Chalmers for reading his sermons in the pulpit, when an ardent female admirer promptly answered, "But it was fell reading, though!" And this was the truth. There was wonderful power and mastery in the man, in the thought, in the style itself, that a manuscript could not chain, nor reading reduce to tameness. Besides this defect, if it can be so called, Chalmers did not have a prepossessing appearance, and his voice and manner lacked smoothness and grace.

Another peculiarity, and perhaps the most marked one in Chalmers' preaching, was his method of repeating the same idea with great variety of expression. He would take some one great thought and hold it up from every point of view, exhibiting all its sides, changing the phraseology and the illustration, but keeping that one thought ever before the hearer. The famous criticism of Robert Hall upon Chalmers perhaps exaggerated this characteristic. In a conversation with a friend, Hall said:[30] "Did you ever know any man who had that singular faculty of repetition possessed by Dr. Chalmers? Why, sir, he often reiterates the same thing ten or twelve times in the course of a few pages. Even Burke himself had not so much of that peculiarity. His mind resembles . . . a kaleidoscope. Every turn presents the object in a new and beautiful form, but the object presented is still the same. . . . His mind seems to move on hinges, not on wheels. There is incessant motion, but no progress." This interesting description presents the truth with singular force, but perhaps overstates the point. There is more progress in thought than Hall would seem to have allowed, but he had probably heard only one and read only a few of Chalmers' sermons. The series of expository lectures or sermons on Romans shows the great power of Chalmers' thought, his lucidity of exposition, and thoroughness of thinking. The famous series of *Astronomical Discourses* preached at the Tron Church, Glasgow, during his ministry there exhibit many of the best excellencies of Chalmers' preaching. The ser-

[30] *Works* of Robert Hall, Vol. III, p. 79 f.

mons, as explained in the preface, were called forth by the use which some opponents of Christianity were making of recent discoveries in astronomy. The main point of the infidel objection was that the science of astronomy, by revealing the greatness of the universe, had discredited the Biblical conception of man's importance as the crown of God's creation and the object of His providential care and redeeming love. The objection was amply met for the time at which these discourses were given. Great progress in science since then and the shifting of emphasis in theological thought also make the point of view now somewhat out of date, but at the time when they were spoken these great sermons were both timely and profound. They showed a mastery of the science at its then stage of development, honesty and sobriety of judgment, along with unshaken conviction of Christian truth. The style of the discourses is also now left behind. It partakes of the grandiose manner of the eighteenth century, but it is sweepingly eloquent, in many places truly magnificent. This set of discourses ranks high among the best specimens of British oratory.

In the second discourse,[31] on *The Modesty of True Science,* Chalmers takes the text, 1 Cor. 8:2, "If any man think that he knoweth anything, he knoweth nothing yet as he ought to know." In the course of the sermon he pays a beautiful tribute to the mind of Isaac Newton, to his method of research, and to the modesty of his spirit. He then proceeds to state and refute the infidel objection, which he does in this way: "In the astronomical objection which infidelity has proposed against the truth of the Christian revelation, there is first an assertion, and then an argument. The assertion is, that Christianity is set up for the exclusive benefit of our minute and solitary world. The argument is, that God would not lavish such a quantity of attention on so insignificant a field. Even though the assertion were admitted, I should have to quarrel with the argument. But the futility of this objection is not laid open in all its extent, unless we expose the utter want of all essential evidence even for the truth of the assertion." He then goes on to show that the objection is not well founded, but based

[31] *Astronomical Discourses,* p. 76 ff.

on speculation, and in the unfolding of this thought occurs this splendid passage: "The man who could embark in an enterprise so foolish and so fanciful, as to theorize it on the details of the botany of another world, or to theorize it on the natural and moral history of its people, is just making as outrageous a departure from all sense, and all science, and all sobriety, when he presumes to speculate or to assert on the details or the methods of God's administration among its rational and accountable inhabitants. He wings his fancy to as hazardous a region, and vainly strives a penetrating vision through the mantle of as deep an obscurity. All the elements of such a speculation are hidden from him. For anything he can tell, sin has found its way into these other worlds. For anything he can tell, their people have banished themselves from communion with God. For anything he can tell, many a visit has been made to each of them, on the subject of our common Christianity, by commissioned messengers from the throne of the Eternal. For anything he can tell, the redemption proclaimed to us is not one solitary instance, or not the whole of that redemption which is by the Son of God—but only our part in the plan of mercy, equal in magnificence to all that astronomy has brought within the range of human contemplation. . . . For anything he can tell, the Eternal Son, of whom it is said, that by Him the worlds were created, may have had the government of many sinful worlds laid upon His shoulders; and by the power of His mysterious word, have awoke them all from that spiritual death to which they had sunk in lethargy as profound as the slumbers of non-existence. For anything he can tell, the one Spirit who moved on the face of the waters, and whose presiding influence it was that hushed the wild war of nature's elements, and made a beauteous system emerge out of its disjointed materials, may now be working with the fragments of another chaos; and educing order and obedience and harmony out of the wrecks of a moral rebellion, which reaches through all these spheres and spreads disorder to the uttermost limits of our astronomy."

Perhaps the best known of Chalmers' sermons is that on *The Expulsive Power of a New Affection.*[32] Dr. W.

[32] Fish, *Mast.*, II, p. 320 ff.

G. Blaikie says that this sermon was suggested by Dr. Chalmers seeing a stage-coach driver whip one of his horses without apparent reason, and on inquiry the man said the horse had a habit of bolting at that place and he desired to give the animal something else to occupy his mind. In meditating on this incident, Chalmers began to think how the love of God taking possession of the heart of man would drive out the evil, and that this was the true method of spiritual and moral advancement. The only thought of the sermon which, after Chalmers' peculiar manner, is restated and variously illustrated, is thus presented in the opening paragraph of the discourse: "There are two ways in which a practical moralist may attempt to displace from the human heart its love of the world—either by a demonstration of the world's vanity, so as that the heart shall be prevailed upon simply to withdraw its regards from an object that is not worthy of it; or, by setting forth another object, even God, as more worthy of its attachment; so as that the heart shall be prevailed upon, not to resign an old affection which shall have nothing to succeed it, but to exchange an old affection for a new one. My purpose is to show, that from the constitution of our nature, the former method is altogether incompetent and ineffectual—and that the latter method will alone suffice for the rescue and recovery of the heart from the wrong affection that domineers over it. After having accomplished this purpose, I shall attempt a few practical observations."

But quotations even more extended than these can not present at all adequately a great preacher like Chalmers. The strength and penetration of his mind, the splendor of his imagination, the depth and enthusiasm of his convictions, the magnificence of his language can only be fully appreciated by one who reads more at length in these great sermons. Such a reader will bring away with him not only impressions like those just given, but the large and more telling one of a great soul striving to interpret and impress great thoughts through the medium of adequate speech.

The Baptists of the period were well represented in its early years by Andrew Fuller, who died at the height of his powers, in 1815, and whose work has already been presented. Here also belongs the noted essayist, John

Foster (1770-1843).[33] He was born of intelligent and pious parents in Yorkshire, was converted in boyhood, and baptized by Dr. Fawcett. Feeling called to preach, he was prepared by Dr. Fawcett, and in the Bristol Baptist School. He held several pastorates, but a throat trouble prevented his success as a public speaker, though his sermons were admirably thought out and well written in the style which made his essays deservedly famous. These are not so much read now, but for two or three generations held a high place among the classics of English essay writing. Perhaps the two most famous of these essays were those on *A Man's Writing Memoirs of Himself* and on *Decision of Character.*

In Wales there flourished at this time that wonderful preacher, Christmas Evans (1766-1838).[34] A rude and rather wild youth, he had the misfortune to lose one eye in a fight; but on his conversion, giving himself wholly to the service of Christ, he became a preacher possessed with all the imagination and fiery eloquence of his race. Robert Hall said of him that he was "the tallest, the stoutest, and the greatest man he ever saw; that he had but one eye, if it could be called an eye; it was more properly a brilliant star, it shone like Venus." Though he had but little education, he used well what he had acquired. His imagination was his strong point, and with it that magnetic quality which thrills and moves an audience. In these two elements of oratory he reached a consummate success. His sermons were preached in his native Welsh, but translations of them and extracts are accessible in English. They exhibit that marvelous faculty of description which appeals to warm-hearted people with peculiar power. It is true that the fancy runs riot and was not disciplined by sufficient education or sobriety of judgment; but for successful popular elo-

[33]*Life and Correspondence of John Foster,* by J. E. Ryland, 2 vols., 1846; *Essays* in various edd.; sketch and sermon in Fish, *Mast.,* I, p. 411 ff.

[34]*Memoirs of the Rev. Christmas Evans,* by J. Davis, 1840; *Life of Christmas Evans,* by E. P. Hood; also a sketch by Hood in *Vocation of the Preacher;* and by Owen Jones in *Some Great Preachers of Wales,* p. 159 ff.; *Sermons on Various Subjects,* by the Rev. Christmas Evans, translated (from the Welsh) by J. Davis, 1837; sketch and sermon in Fish, *Mast.,* II, p. 595 ff.

quence among his own people, Christmas Evans ranks among the most remarkable preachers of his age.

Easily the leading figure in the Baptist pulpit of this period, and indeed one of the best of all English preachers, was the eminent pastor, essayist, and preacher, Robert Hall (1764-1831).[35] His life story is a simple one so far as outward events are concerned, yet it was in some respects a remarkable life and worthy of careful study. Hall was born at Arnsby, a little village in Leicestershire, where his father, Robert Hall, Sr., was pastor of the little Baptist Church, and himself a preacher of high character and excellent talent. The younger Robert was the fourteenth child, very feeble in constitution from his birth. In fact, he was an invalid and sufferer from birth to death. He was more fortunate than Chalmers in having an excellent nurse, whose loving care of him throughout his feeble childhood was almost like that of a mother. His own mother was so occupied with the cares of a numerous family that it was impossible for her to give all the attention which so feeble a child required. Robert early displayed a most remarkable intellect. The stories of his precocity are well founded and are sufficiently wonderful. His education began by his nurse teaching him to read by learning the letters and inscriptions on the tombstones of the churchyard, where she often took her little charge for the air. It does not appear that this unusual schoolroom left any gloomy or funereal traits in the mind of the boy. The child was a reader and thinker almost from his cradle. At nine years of age he had read Edwards *On the Will* and Butler's *Analogy,* with appreciation of their arguments. There was a tailor in the village, a member of the elder Hall's Church, who was much given to metaphysical thinking and talk, and in his shop the little Robert was often found discussing profound questions of philosophy. At eleven years of age he was so far advanced in his studies that the teacher, a Mr. Simmons, told his father that

[35]*Works of Robert Hall,* ed. Dr. Olinthus Gregory, 3 vols., N. Y., 1833; Vol. III contains a *Memoir* by Dr. Gregory, a fine critique upon Hall as a preacher by John Foster, and other valuable material; *Life* by E. P. Hood in *Heroes of Christian History,* London and New York; sermon and sketch in Fish, *Mast.,* I. p. 363 ff.; Pattison, ch. XI; Hoppin, p. 212 ff.

he could take the boy no further. Robert was then sent to school to the Rev. John Ryland, at Northampton—a strong but rather peculiar man. Robert remained only some eighteen months under his instruction, but made excellent progress, especially in Latin and Greek. After an interval occasioned by ill-health, he was sent to the Bristol Academy, where he remained three or four years.

Hall was serious from his childhood. His good old nurse declared that he was converted at seven years of age, and throughout his life his character was free from spot and his pious devotion to his Lord was unbroken. When fourteen years of age he was baptized by his father, and received distinct impressions of duty in regard to the ministry. But before this he had written several religious essays, and preached to his brothers and sisters while yet a little boy. He completed his studies at Bristol. The English universities not being at that time open to Dissenters, Robert Hall went to the University of Aberdeen, in Scotland, for his collegiate education. Here he became greatly distinguished as a student. He formed strong friendships, among them one with the afterwards notable Sir James Mackintosh. After several years Hall was graduated Master of Arts and with distinction, having pronounced a Greek oration, which was received with great applause.

During his schooldays at Bristol, having been licensed by his father's church, he made a beginning at preaching. But his first efforts were not successful. He was overcome with diffidence. But during his course at Aberdeen, in 1783, he became assistant pastor to the Rev. Caleb Evans, at Broadmead, Bristol, at first during the vacations; but on completing his course, in August, 1785, he was appointed classical tutor in the Bristol Academy, along with his work as associate pastor of the Church. A very interesting entry in the journal of Andrew Fuller, under date of May 7, 1784, reads as follows: "Heard Mr. Robert Hall, Jr., from 'He that increaseth knowledge increaseth sorrow.' Felt very solemn in hearing some parts. The Lord keep that young man." A similar passage is also found in the journal of Dr. Ryland. These two notices, as well as other things, show that Hall's character and intellect made a profound impression upon his older brethren, but they seem to have had a not unnatural fear that his intellect might lead him into unchristian speculations and that his success might lead him to pride. Their prayers were answered; Mr. Hall grew in grace and knowledge, as in experience. During his five years' association with Mr. Evans at Bristol the younger man was much the superior of the two, and under such circumstances some friction was inevitable. It must be said to the credit of Mr. Hall that his behavior under these trying circumstances was admirable.

In 1791 he was called to succeed the famous Robert Robinson as pastor of the Baptist Church at Cambridge. He met some peculiar difficulties there, and was not much pleased with Cambridge; but his preaching drew large and intelligent audiences, both from the town and the university. His ill-health and acute sufferings, together with the burdens of his pastorate, broke him down. His mind became unbalanced for a time, but he recovered. A second and later attack was more serious. He was placed under the care of Dr. Cox, near Bristol. On being taken to this sanitarium, as we should now call it, one of the inmates, who was an acquaintance of Hall's, expressed great surprise and asked with sympathy, "Whatever brought you here, Mr. Hall, whatever?" Mr. Hall, tapping his head, replied, "What never brought you here, sir; too much up here." On his recovery, Dr. Cox gave him three prescriptions; (1) leave Cambridge, (2) smoke, (3) get married. He did all three, and never lost his mind any more. Much to his regret and that of the congregation, he resigned at Cambridge; and the smoking was probably somewhat soothing to his nerves; he married a woman of excellent sense and character, though by no means his equal in intellect or culture. To her loving care and constant devotion he owed much of that mitigation of suffering and relief from care which enabled him to do the great work of his remainder of life.

Hall removed from Cambridge to Leicester in 1806, where he served as pastor of a Baptist church to the year 1825. This was the principal scene of his labors. Notwithstanding his continued sufferings and the severe attacks of that distressing pain in his back which pursued him all his life and finally ended it, he was a very successful pastor and a preacher of marvelous gifts and power. His congregations, while not so cultivated as those at Cambridge had been, yet contained a number of thoughtful people who could appreciate Hall's style of work; but he was also active and beloved among the middle and lower classes of hearers. A noble statue in the principal park at Leicester still commemorates his life and labors in that city. After nineteen years of successful labors in Leicester, Mr. Hall felt the need of a less exacting work, and accepted the invitation of his old church at Bristol to return to them. This he did, and served there from 1826 to his death, in 1831. He thus returned to the scenes of his boyhood and of his early ministry, being now about sixty-two years old, to end his days where he had begun his work. His pastorate here has been well described as "brief and bright." He was much beloved, and the work of the pulpit was not so burdensome as it had been. But his lifelong malady gained upon him, his bodily sufferings were frequent and intense. He bore his pain with exemplary fortitude and beautiful resignation. The closing struggle was itself a triumph of spirit over clay, of the soul through sufferings. On one occasion, after a paroxysm of pain, he said to his physician: "Did I complain, sir? I did not mean to." And so he passed away in great bodily distress, but in perfect peace of soul.

The character of Robert Hall was suitable to his genius. He was honest, sincere, outspoken, with a tendency to severity. He had a keen wit, and could be very sarcastic when he chose. Speaking of a certain bishop who had been spoiled by office, he said: "Poor man, I pity him. He married public virtue in his early days, but seemed forever afterwards to be quarreling with his wife." He was no great admirer of Dr. Gill. In a talk with Christmas Evans, who did admire that author and expressed his wish that Dr. Gill's works had been written in Welsh, Mr. Hall said: "I wish they had, sir; I wish they had with all my heart, for then I should never have read them. They are a continent of mud." We have already noticed his opinion of Chalmers. Of Wesley he said: "The most extraordinary thing about him was, that while he set all in motion, he was himself perfectly calm and phlegmatic. He was the quiescence of turbulence." Of Whitefield he spoke as presenting the contrast of mediocrity in writing with wonderful power in speaking, which could not be expressed in writing, for "it is impossible to paint eloquence." In his pastoral work and relations with others Mr. Hall was kind, affectionate, and sincere.

A study of Robert Hall as a preacher can not fail to be of deep interest and profit. The themes of his discourse were varied, usually along the lines of gospel truth, but with occasional excursions into topics for the times. His purpose always was to glorify his Master and to preach, as it was given to him to see it, the truth of God. Most of his published sermons are topical, but while at Cambridge it was his custom at one of the services to give an expository lecture. The matter of his sermons presents a fine combination of philosophic thought with Biblical truth. He held firmly the essential doctrines of Christianity as understood by evangelicals. But the philosophic bent of his mind led him often to treat these topics from that point of view rather than that of feeling and exhortation. Along with his deep thinking there is wealth of learning and of reflection and observation. All the elements of successful speech are found in his work: thought, accuracy of information, logical analysis, imagination purified and controlled by culture, depth of feeling with no excess of vehemence, and a splendid style. The best criticism upon Hall's style is its "too uniform stateliness." It lacks variety, flexibility, ease; and this is all the more remarkable because it is pre-eminently a style of speech rather than of writing. Hall did not write out his sermons before delivery. He carefully prepared them by thought and prayer, and spoke from an outline. Afterwards he reproduced them by dictation, sometimes while lying upon his back on the floor of his study to gain some ease of his pain. Hall's delivery and voice lacked something of grace and power. His action was not studied or lively. His voice was rather feeble, and on that account he adopted and used with excellent effect great rapidity of utterance. He said of himself that "slowness of speech in his case would have been fatal to effect, that he must make up in rapidity what he lacked in strength and fullness of tone." His theory and practice were doubtless correct. This method of delivery required both for himself and the audience occasional pauses which were all the more effective because they were natural.

Two of the most famous of Hall's sermons dealt with topics of the day. The great discourse on *Modern Infidelity*[36] had its suggestion in the horrors of the French Revolution, then fresh in the minds of men. It was preached first at Bristol, in October, and then at Cambridge, in November, 1800, and was published by request, being reproduced in the manner already mentioned. This great discourse is well worthy of careful and frequent reading. Its admirable thinking, ample culture, easy mastery of theme, and splendid style give it a place indeed among the "masterpieces of pulpit eloquence." No outline or extracts could convey an adequate notion of its power, but the following paragraph has been so much and justly admired that it may well find a place here. Speaking of the results of the teachings of infidels, he goes on to say:[37] "More than all, their infatuated eagerness, their parricidal zeal to extinguish a sense of Deity must excite astonishment and horror. Is the idea of an Almighty and perfect Ruler unfriendly to any passion which is consistent with innocence, or an obstruction of any design which it is not shameful to avow? Eternal God, on what are thine enemies intent! What are those enterprises of guilt and horror, that, for the safety of their performers, require to be enveloped in a darkness which the eye of Heaven must not pierce! Miserable men! Proud of being the offspring of chance; in love with universal disorder; whose happiness is involved in the belief of there being no witness to their designs, and who are at ease only because they suppose themselves inhabitants of a forsaken and fatherless world!" More appealing in its pathos and almost perfect beauty is the famous sermon on *The Death of Princess Charlotte*[38] from the words of Jeremiah 15:9, "She hath given up the ghost; her sun has gone down while it is yet day." This

[36]*Works,* I, p. 23; Fish, *l. c.*
[37]*Id.,* p. 48; Fish, *op. cit.,* p. 392.
[38]*Works,* I, p. 177.

tender and beautiful discourse takes place alongside of the memorable funeral orations of Bossuet. Some of its passages and descriptions have been quoted by English historians, and it remains one of the choice examples of its kind.

II. The Middle Period of the Century, 1833-1868

The second division of the nineteenth century presents a wonderfully great and fruitful period in the life and thought of the British people.[39] The death of the old and inefficient King William IV, in 1837, introduced the long and brilliant reign of Queen Victoria—a reign that will be ever memorable alike for the character and influence of the sovereign and for the great events and movements which marked its course. The first half of that reign will occupy us in this section.

There were no very important wars during this time; the progress was chiefly that of inner development through Parliamentary struggle and the debates of opinion. Yet the inglorious war with China, in 1842, opened the treaty ports of that great empire to Western commerce and Christian missions; the short and yet too long war with Russia in the Crimea, in 1854-55, was marked by great sufferings in the camps of the allies before Sebastopol, and illuminated by the beautiful service of Florence Nightingale and her corps of nurses; the terrible Sepoy mutiny in India, in 1857, brought forth deeds of suffering, endurance, and valor that live in English history.

Political affairs were characterized by great struggles of parties and statesmen. The passage of the Reform Bill of 1832 was followed by a large extension of the suffrage and the introduction of new men and measures into the constitutional progress of the nation. Further extensions followed in 1857, and again in 1868, so that practically universal manhood suffrage came at last to prevail. Debates on the removal of the import duty on grain (the Corn Laws), on various measures in the interest of freedom and social ameliorations, on the enlarge-

[39]Much the same general authorities as before on national, social, literary, and religious affairs; McCarthy's *History of Our Own Times;* Stedman's *Victorian Poets,* etc.

ment of religious liberty and the general progress of education, and other improvements occupied the minds of the nation and exercised the powers of thought and oratory of some of the greatest statesmen of modern times. It was the age which heard and echoed the thoughts of such men as Macaulay, Canning, Peel, Cobden, Bright, Palmerston, Russell, Derby, and toward its turn and at the height of their earlier struggles, of Disraeli and Gladstone.

Some of the greatest of English writers adorned this epoch. Powerful thought in all the spheres of intellectual effort found noble expression in a literature distinguished for variety, amplitude, beauty, strength, and fruitfulness. Some of the leading orators have already been named. Of poets there were Landor, Hood, the Procters, Clough, Fitzgerald, Mrs. Browning, and the greater names of Tennyson, Robert Browning, Matthew Arnold, and Swinburne, whose labors went on into the last period of the century, but who were doing some of their most distinctive work during this time. Fiction was represented by the masterly work of Dickens and Thackeray at their best, and of George Eliot at her beginnings. Besides these of the first rank, there were Charlotte Brontë and her sisters, with Dinah Maria Mulock, among the women, and among the men Kingsley, Bulwer, Reade, Collins, and others of less fame. The field of history is splendidly represented in the work of such men in various lines of research as Macaulay, Hallam, Grote, Thirlwall, Milman, Knight, Buckle, the Rawlinsons, and others whose principal contributions came in the next period, but who were at work already in this time. Essayists and biographers of various talents and subjects were found in Macaulay, Carlyle, Harriet Martineau, Lockhart, Helps, and Ruskin. Science and philosophy found illuminating, even revolutionary, expression in the writings of men like Sir William Hamilton, Faraday, Brewster, Hugh Miller, Sir Charles Lyell, Herschel, the Mills, Whewell, Darwin, and Spencer, who, with Tyndall, Huxley, and others, passed over into the later period. Religion and theology, in all their different forms and schools, were illustrated by the productions of Whately, Maurice, Newman, Neale, Keble, the Hares, Alford,

William Smith, Stanley, Bickersteth, Martineau, and a host of others, some of whom were also among the leading preachers of the time.

Religious events and movements within this epoch were of general interest and profound importance. Enlargement of the political privileges extended to Catholics and Dissenters began with the Catholic Emancipation Bill of 1829, but went on in various directions, so that throughout this whole period and on into the next there was growth of toleration and of the dissenting bodies of Christians. Sentiment in favor of the disestablishment of the Anglican Church in Ireland was growing, and came, as we shall see, to its fruition at the turn into the next period. Within the Anglican body the three tendencies which have ever to some extent divided opinion became more distinct, and fell into groups or parties to which the names of Low, High, and Broad Church were now more clearly and appropriately applied. The Low Church party carried on with ability and maintained with power the evangelical principles, which more and more escaped the reproach of cant and narrowness. The High Church party had a remarkable development in the Oxford or Tractarian movement, which will receive more detailed notice later. The Broad Church party also received great impetus, partly as reaction from Evangelicalism, partly as renewal of strength in a force which had never died out though held in check by the evangelical revival, and partly as result of that general growth of liberalism in religious thought which has been characteristic of modern times. Criticism—historical and philosophical—of traditional Christianity became rife, and there emerged a decided and painful hostility on the part of many scientific investigators and thinkers toward the long-accepted facts and doctrines of the Christian faith. The effort on the part of many churchmen to follow the trend of scientific thought and yet retain what was regarded as essential in the Christian tradition was the informing principle of the Broad Church group.

Along with this must also be reckoned the growth of humanitarian and social improvement, in which, however, all three parties shared in their different ways. There was on the part of Christians generally a more intelligent and active participation in movements and efforts for social good; particularly in the improvement of the condition of the poor and the laboring classes. The introduction of machinery had reduced many hand-workers to want and to a savage hostility toward the capitalistic classes. The abolition of slavery and the beginning of missionary effort in foreign lands were credited chiefly to Evangelicalism. But members of the Broad Church group, especially Kingsley, Maurice, Robertson, and others, championed the cause of the poor. In this novelists and poets joined, and statesmen and leaders of public opinion were not silent. The revolutionary movements on the Continent of Europe, about 1848, had their English counterpart in the Chartist agitation. Thousands of people signed a petition or demand of rights which was intended to be a new Charter of popular liberties. Many of the demands of the Chartists were one by one granted and enacted into legislation. Many individual Christians of all parties sympathized more or less with the movement, but it was not identified with any particular party.

Among Dissenters there was naturally no High Church party; but in the various denominations the line of cleavage between groups which corresponded to the Anglican Low and Broad Church groups was to be found. The Presbyterians in England had become infected to such a degree with Unitarianism as virtually to have lost their distinctive character as a denomination; though men like Irving and his successor, Hamilton, served the more orthodox Scottish Churches. Among Baptists and Independents men here and there leaned to Arian or Socinian views, but, on the whole, Evangelical principles maintained their hold upon the Nonconformist churches and preachers.

In Scotland the Secession and later the Relief Presbytery movement had withdrawn some of the Evangelicals from the Established Church, but a considerable number remained, and the revival of Evangelicalism in the early years of the century had increased the numbers of that party and given them a strong opposition to Moderatism. In 1847 the Seceders and Relief Presbyterians came together to form the United Presbyterian Church, a body of decidedly evangelical sentiments and earnest missionary work. The remnants of Moderatism and the evils of lay patronage gave to the evangelical part of the Established Church considerable trouble as the century advanced. Finally, in 1843, under the courageous leadership of Chalmers and others, more than four hundred ministers withdrew from the Established Church and organized the Free Church of Scotland. This was known as the Disruption, and, though apparently evil, resulted in much good. The lay members of the Church rallied to the support of the withdrawing ministers, churches and manses were built, salaries provided, colleges founded, missions established, and other good works undertaken and successfully carried out. This splendid self-sacrifice and generosity on behalf of the principle of freedom for the churches to choose their own pastors, as well as in the interest of a more evangelical type of doctrine, were not without fruit both in the withdrawing church itself and in the older Establishment. This also stimulated men to larger efforts for the common cause, and so a greater amount of work was done for the whole church than would have been done if the two parties had remained in the same body, disputing with one another.

Recurring now to the High Church movement within the Anglican Church, it will be necessary to go somewhat into detail in order to estimate aright the influence of this movement upon ecclesiastical thought and more directly upon preaching.[40] The passage of the Reform Bill, in 1832, alarmed some of the most devoted adherents of the English Church. They feared the church would fall too much under political influences and control. Voicing this alarm, John Keble, the famous author of *The Christian Year,* preached, in 1833, a notable sermon on "National Apostasy," in which he sounded the note of warning. Keble was a High Churchman and an Oxford man. His views were shared by a group of others at Oxford. John Henry Newman was absent from England at the time, but on returning joined in with Keble and the

[40]See *The Oxford Movement,* by R. W. Church; *Five Great Oxford Leaders,* by A. B. Donaldson; Newman's *Apologia;* Stoughton, Vol. II, Chap. II, especially p. 45; Tulloch, *Lect.,* III, p. 58 ff.; histories and articles.

others. Soon the group received the efficient sympathy and active help of E. B. Pusey, a great scholar and a man of high social standing and wide influence. The group began to issue *Tracts for the Times* in defense of the historic Anglican Church and presenting decided High Church views of the ordinances and related matters. These writings created a great discussion. Low and Broad Church people both attacked them, and the controversy waxed warmer and warmer till, the Roman Catholic drift becoming more and more apparent, there grew up a genuine alarm lest the movement were a deep-seated scheme to deliver the English Church back into the fold of Rome. The appearance of the famous *Tract XC,* in which the Romanizing tendency became quite apparent, led the bishop of Oxford to exert his authority and suppress further publications of the sort. But this neither ended the controversy nor the movement. Some of the Tractarians, including Newman, went over at last to the Roman Catholic Church, but others, like Pusey, remained within the Anglican body. Following soon after Newman's defection came the famous Gorham case, in 1847. Mr. Gorham was a Low Churchman, who at his ordination failed to give his High Church bishop satisfaction as to the matter of baptismal regeneration, and was refused induction into his charge. The case was carried before various courts, and finally decided by the Privy Council in Mr. Gorham's favor. But the High Church party, notwithstanding this check, were still strong and aggressive. The whole movement lent great interest to theological thought at the time and had a profound influence, beyond the immediate occasion, both upon the progress of religious thinking in England and upon the pulpit; for some of the notable preachers of the age were of this party.

In all the sects and parties we find a vigorous ministry throughout this period. There is a goodly number of men of exceptional weight and power in the pulpit, and generally a high average of culture and efficiency. The breath of progress, the stir of alert industry, the excitement of conscious advance, which characterize the national life of the age are all felt and manifest in its pulpit. It responds to the demand for practical results.

It is less formal and traditional, less elaborate and stilted than in the past, without being less thoughtful or effective. But the many varieties of opinion and practice in religious and ecclesiastical affairs, the controversies of every kind and range—sectarian, critical, scientific, apologetic, social, political—all bearing upon the attitude of the pulpit upon vital current issues, caused a bewildering variety of pulpit expression.

The Roman Catholic Church has naturally not had many exceptionally notable preachers in the British Islands; for the church has had little opportunity to develop a great ministry in the strongly Protestant England, Scotland, and Wales; and in Ireland, though numerically in the ascendant, the Catholics have not had the best conditions for training that native eloquence for which the Irish are justly celebrated. Of course, the Romanist theology has been the main basis of Catholic preaching in English as in other tongues, and the modern statements and ultramontane views have found expression in sermons. The polemic presentation of Romanism has been necessarily somewhat cautious, but has shown vigor and power. Besides these customary elements, British Catholic preaching has paid great attention to moral and social questions, and its style has not wanted the strength and elegance of nineteenth century English.

A few of the more notable men among the Catholics of the period deserve more than mere mention. The famous and widely useful temperance orator, Theobald Mathew (1790-1856),[41] was born in county Tipperary, Ireland, and educated at Kilkenny and Maynooth. After his ordination he had charge of a chapel at Cork, where his earnest eloquence and kind manners, joined with his active work in behalf of the poor, gained him many friends and an ever-widening influence. About 1830 (it is said, at the suggestion of a pious Quaker) he began his extraordinary work in behalf of the temperance cause. Beginning at Cork, he pleaded for abstinence from intoxicating liquors, induced hundreds to sign the pledge, and formed total abstinence societies. The work grew on his hands, and his services were called for in all parts of Ireland. Thousands were rescued from drunkenness by

[41] Cyclop. articles.

his persuasions. His labors extended to England and the United States, and great enthusiasm and success followed his moving addresses. He was well called "the apostle of temperance" in his time. Another leading Irish Catholic preacher of the age was Father Thomas N. Burke (1830-1883),[42] who was born in Galway, and educated in Italy, but, returning to his native country, was active chiefly in Dublin as a priest and preacher of the Dominican order. He came on a visit to the United States in 1871, where he preached and lectured to large and enthusiastic audiences. His *Lectures and Sermons* were collected and published in this country in 1873. During this tour Burke became involved in a controversy with the English historian, J. A. Froude, who was traveling and lecturing in the United States at the same time. Burke had the eloquence of his race, the courage of his convictions, and the ardor of a sincere Catholic. He was most highly esteemed among his fellow Catholics as a preacher of rare powers. Mention at least should be made of Father Thomas J. Potter, of Dublin, whose two books on preaching—*The Spoken Word,* and *Sacred Eloquence*—give him a place among modern teachers of homiletics, and whose own work in the pulpit was recognized by his contemporaries. Archbishop Walsh, better known later as a prelate interested in political and ecclesiastical affairs in Ireland, was also in this period acknowledged to be a preacher of power and influence.

The best known English Catholic prelate and preacher of the period was Nicholas Wiseman (1802-1865),[43] the celebrated cardinal of Westminster, who was born of English parentage, at Seville, in Spain, but was educated in England and at the English College at Rome, where he served as professor for a short time. Coming to England in 1835, he soon became known as a preacher and writer of decided gifts. In 1850 he was made a cardinal and archbishop of Westminster. His appointment gave great umbrage to English Protestants, who looked upon this movement to restore the Roman hierarchy in England as a first step toward the deliver-

[42]Art. by Hogan in *Cath. Encycl.*
[43]*Lectures on Science and Religion,* 3 vols., Baltimore, 1852. Stoughton, II, Chap. XIII.

ing of England back into the Roman Catholic fold. But the storm subsided after awhile. Among the numerous writings of Cardinal Wiseman (chiefly theological and polemical) there are several volumes of sermons. These discuss with force the usual Catholic topics of discourse, but also include a volume of *Sermons on Moral Subjects.*

The Tractarian Movement in the Anglican Church resulted in the accession to the Catholics of several prominent preachers from the High Church party, of whom the two best known are Manning and Newman. The latter will more appropriately be noticed under the preachers of the English Church—in which his best pulpit work was done—but a word should here be said of Henry Edward Manning (1808-1892).[44] Born in Hertfordshire, Manning received his excellent education, first at Harrow, and then at Balliol College, Oxford, whence he was graduated in 1830. After filling some unimportant places as a preacher, he was made archdeacon of Chichester in 1840. Being a strong High Churchman and Tractarian, he was naturally dissatisfied with the action taken against the movement by the authorities, and finally, after the Gorham decision, left the English Church and became a Catholic, in 1851, some years later than Newman. On the death of Cardinal Wiseman, in 1865, Manning was made archbishop of Westminster, and later a cardinal. Like his predecessor, he also was a prolific writer on ecclesiastical and polemical subjects. His numerous published works contain a variety of sermons on devotional and social topics, as well as on the accepted Catholic doctrines and practices. The style is that of an educated Englishman of the time, but does not show unusual excellence. The reasoning is clear and vigorous, but always proceeding first from High Church, and later from Romanist premises. The tone is lofty, sympathetic, and spiritual where not too polemic; the appeal positive and hortatory.

In the Church of England during this period there

[44]*Cardinal Manning,* by A. W. Hutton, Boston, 1892; *Sermons,* London, 1847; a sermon on *The Triumph of the Church* in *World's Great Sermons,* V, p. 61.

were in all three of its groups a number of noted and useful preachers. Of the Low Church party the leading name is that of Henry Melvill (1798-1871).[45] He was the son of an army officer, and born in Cornwall. He was thoroughly educated, taking his university course at Cambridge. Both by conviction and experience he was well grounded in evangelical sentiments. After ordination he preached for a time at Camden Chapel in London, then became chaplain to the queen, and finally canon of St. Paul's. Melvill was a very sound and popular preacher. Large crowds attended his ministry, and he was heard with great pleasure. He was thorough in preparing his discourses. He paid little attention to social or political matters or to general learning. He wrote out his discourses very carefully, but with a view to their popular delivery. They were written for the pulpit, not for the fireside. As read now the sermons appear too polished, artificial, rhetorical; but they breathe a deep piety and high moral aim, and are clothed in a lofty and impressive style. The sermon given in Fish's collection is a very fair specimen of Melvill's best work. It is full of thought, well argued, and carefully elaborated.

Hugh MacNeile (1795-1879)[46] was another Low Church preacher of great renown and widespread influence. He was born in County Antrim, Ireland, and educated at Trinity College, Dublin. He intended being a lawyer, but during an illness, while traveling in Switzerland, his mind was turned to serious things, he was converted and entered the ministry. He began his work in Ireland, but later came to England, where he filled several minor places, and in 1834 was appointed to a position in St. John's Church, at Liverpool. Later he was transferred to another church in the same city, and it was here that his principal work was done, though he held some other offices, including the deanery of Ripon. MacNeile published a number of sermons and

[45] *Sermons,* 2 vols., ed. by Bp. McIlvaine, N. Y., 1853; Stoughton, II, p. 76; Fish, *XIX Cent.*, p. 503, a fine sermon on Gal. 6:7.

[46] Art. in *DNB;* Stoughton, II, Ch. IV; Fish, *XIX Cent.*, p. 568 ff.; *Miscellaneous Sermons* (selected from *The Pulpit*), 2 vols., London, undated.

addresses which are well worth reading, though they do not reveal the peculiar qualities of his ardent and appealing nature. He had the Irish temperament and was at his best in moving personal appeal and flights of extemporized eloquence. He was personal, magnetic, and lovable, won many friends, and turned the hearts of hundreds to the service of his Lord.

The High Church party during this time produced some of its most distinguished representatives. One of the most engaging personalities among them was that of Walter Farquhar Hook (1798-1875),[47] whose life has been most interestingly written by his son-in-law, W. R. W. Stephens. He was born in London, the son of a clergyman, and nephew of the famous literary wit, Theodore Hook. He had a fine mother, and good early training. He was bright, impulsive, irritable, humorsome, but with good feeling and principles, and was early inclined to religion. He was fond of literature, though an irregular reader. He once knocked a boy down for calling Shakespeare a fool. Hook studied at Christ Church College, Oxford, and got his degree, though he studied by spurts. In 1821 he determined to enter the ministry, was ordained, and took up his work as a curate at Whippingham. He took much interest in his parish work and also in his studies. His promotion naturally followed. His great work was done at Coventry, where he was rector from 1829-1837. On settling there he made a fortunate marriage. His wife was a great help to him. In 1837 he moved to Leeds, where he also did excellent work, serving till 1859, when he became dean of Chichester. Hook was a very remarkable man. As a preacher his personal qualities and earnest pastoral labors helped to draw and hold his congregations. Though not pleasing in personal appearance, there was a certain magnetism in his manner, and he had a rich tenor voice which he used with good effect. The matter of his sermons was not specially remarkable. On his favorite theme of the Church he was logical, learned, able. In general, his sermons are plain, earnest, simple in style, warm in appeal, and strong in thought, with no

[47]Art. *DNB; Life and Letters of Dean Hook,* by W. R. W. Stephens; *Sermons on Various Subjects,* London, 1841.

special excellence of arrangement or style. Though a pronounced High Churchman in his view of the church and its ordinances, Hook did not join the Tractarian movement, though he often advised with and sometimes criticised its leaders.

Of these, three of the most important fall within the period we are now studying, viz., Keble, Pusey, and Newman. As preachers the first two require only brief notice. John Keble (1792-1866)[48] was well born and educated, a man of many graces of character and of thought. He was long rector of Hursley, and best known as the author of a famous series of religious short poems, *The Christian Year.* Associated with Hurrell Froude and Newman at Oriel College, Oxford, he took an active part in the Tractarian movement. After the passage of the Reform Bill, in 1832, much fear was felt concerning the attitude of the government toward the Established Church—its control by secular and unfriendly influences. This led Keble to preach, in 1833, his famous sermon on *National Apostasy,* in which he dealt with the question of the Church and State. This is justly regarded as the beginning of the Oxford Movement. Edward B. Pusey (1800-1882)[49] was a typical Englishman of the highly cultivated, highly born, and wealthy class. Thoroughly trained at Eton and Oxford, he became a great scholar, especially in Biblical learning. He was a weighty preacher and a man of very high tone. His adherence to the Oxford Movement gave great weight to it; after him, it was often called by his opponents Puseyism. Pusey's sermons present very sacramental views of the church and ordinances, but he never went over to the Catholics.

The most important person and preacher in the High Church movement was John Henry Newman (1801-1890),[50] who was one of the most remarkable men of

[48]See art. in *DNB,* and references at note 40.

[49]Same as for Keble.

[50]Authorities previously quoted; also *Cardinal Newman,* by R. H. Hutton, London and New York, 1890; *Apologia Pro Vita Sua,* London, 1865 (new ed. 1873); *Parochial and Plain Sermons,* 8 vols., complete ed., London, 1868; *Oxford University Sermons,* Lond., 1871. Wilkinson, *Modern Masters,* p. 145; Brastow, *Representative Modern Preachers,* Chap. VI.

the century. The son of a London banker and of a mother of Huguenot descent, Newman was carefully trained and educated in his childhood. He was early sent to Oxford, but on account of his father's reverses in business he rather hurriedly took his degree at the age of nineteen. In 1823, however, he was elected a Fellow of Oriel College, and soon afterwards was ordained, and began to preach at a small place near Oxford. His residence in Oriel College brought him into contact with the other leaders of the High Church movement, especially under the influence of R. H. Froude and of Keble. In 1828 he was appointed vicar of St. Mary's Church in Oxford, and held the place till his resignation, in 1843. It was in this famous pulpit that he did the most and the best of his preaching. During the years 1826-1831 he was a tutor at Oxford, but his personal influence was so strong in disseminating High Church views among the students that the authorities remonstrated, and he resigned. Unconsciously to himself, and as yet unnoticeably to others, his drift toward Rome was already developing, though it was twenty years before he finally became a Catholic. At this time he had no thought of leaving the English Church. He went abroad in 1833 in great distress of mind. It was after an illness, and on board ship in the Mediterranean, in 1833, that he wrote his world-famous hymn, *Lead, Kindly Light.* Returning to England, he found that Keble's sermon on *National Apostasy* had made a great commotion. The High Church party, led by himself and Keble, and in the next year by Pusey, began to issue the famous series of *Tracts for the Times,* in which extreme High Church views were advocated. A number of these tracts were written by Newman, until finally, in 1841, his famous *Tract XC* appeared and created a storm. It was now plain to others, and must have been plain to Newman himself, that his true place was in the Roman and not the Anglican Church, for *Tract XC* interpreted the Thirty-nine Articles in a thoroughly Romish sense and subtly argued that one might with a good conscience hold Catholic doctrines and still remain in the Anglican communion. At this point the bishop of Oxford interfered and forbade the issuance of any further tracts. The

Tractarians submitted to authority and the publication ceased. The work, however, had been done, and henceforth there remains in the English Church an extreme ritualistic and sacramentarian group. For Newman himself there were but two more steps. In 1843 he resigned the incumbency of St. Mary's and went into retirement. After two years of further reflection, he formally entered the Roman Catholic Church, in 1845. He was now settled and happy, and put himself with vigor into his new work, being ordained a Catholic priest in 1846.

As a Catholic, Newman continued his work and exerted a wide influence, but it was long before he came to occupy his former commanding position among his countrymen, who were keenly disappointed and grieved at his transfer of church allegiance. He established a community of priests at Edgbaston, near Birmingham, and this was long his home and the scene of his work. He was sent to reorganize the University of Dublin in 1854, and spent several years there. In 1864 he had a painful controversy with Charles Kingsley, who accused him of falsehood. This led to the publication of his *Apologia Pro Vita Sua,* in which he explained how he had step by step been led to become a Catholic, and affirmed the sincerity and earnestness of his convictions. The book produced a very favorable reaction toward Newman personally, restoring him in large measure to the affection and confidence of his countrymen. Of course, some looked upon it as a shrewd and insincere piece of work, but the general judgment accepts it as the final statement of Newman's own view of himself. The book is beautifully written and in excellent spirit. In 1879 Newman was made a cardinal, and in his old age, after a brief illness, he passed peacefully away, August 11, 1890.

As a man Newman was a great personality and influential character. On the moral side, he was without reproach, from youth up a warm friend, refined and gentle, genial, magnetic, spiritual. He had not the qualities of a great leader, but was thoroughly courageous and firm in maintaining his own opinions and infusing them into others. On the intellectual side, he was thoughtful and studious, especially fond of history and theology, presenting a fine combination of the logical and yet speculative, of the firm yet progressive quality of mind. His logical theories of "certitude" and "assent" contain an element of fallacy which easily led to self-deception and enabled him to persuade himself of what he wanted to believe without violence to his conscience. His learning was ample, and his thought deep and intense, colored largely by sentiment. His imagination was strong and rich, chastened by culture and spiritualized by religion. On the religious side, Newman was serious from a child. One who reads his *Apologia* can not fail to believe that he experienced a genuine conversion about the age of fifteen, and in his earlier years he held evangelical views. How his associates at Oriel led him into High Church opinions, and these finally carried him to Rome, is brought out in the story of his life; but through all these changes he was intense, high-minded, and devout.

Newman was a voluminous author. His works include historical and theological works and essays, a logical treatise ill-named *The Grammar of Assent,* several stories, and a very striking poem, *The Dream of Gerontius,* and his immortal hymn already mentioned. We are more concerned, however, with his numerous sermons, of which several series have been published, including *Parochial and Plain Sermons,* given chiefly at St. Mary's, and *Sermons to Mixed Congregations,* which were delivered after he became a Catholic. Newman's personality had much to do with his impressiveness as a preacher. His strong intellect, ample culture; deep-toned, earnest, vivid imagination; winsome manner; soft, persuasive voice, and subdued intensity of delivery are all testified to by those who heard him preach. In his printed sermons the characteristics of the man inevitably appear, and the main qualities of his work are easily traced. As for matter, there is a good deal of Scripture, though not profound exegesis. There is sufficient, but not elaborate, illustration. Argument predominates, and yet it is not formal or obtrusive. Doctrine all along is prominent, showing intense thought, deep experience, and conviction, and some speculation. As to method in preaching, Newman is informal and easy, with no clearly marked divisions or care for symmetry of that kind. He usually gets his thought from the text, and keeps that one thought prominent to the end. There is unity and progress, but he seems to follow the logical process natural to his awakened mind without careful planning beforehand or rigid adherence to arrangement. As to style, Newman's is admirable nineteenth century English. It is clear, vigorous, often beautiful, sweet without sentimentality, and strong without coarseness. It is serenely and simply what it is, without trying to be remarkable; and so it is without artificiality or labored effort. The critics are almost unanimous in their praise. Dr. W. C. Wilkinson is one of the few competent judges who has taken the pains to point out many defects and faults in a manner of expression which has perhaps too easily been taken as a model of all the good qualities. His brilliant critique certainly goes to show that what is universally conceded to be excellent is not necessarily perfect.

The Broad Church party also presents in this period a number of men distinguished by their opposition both to Evangelicalism in its narrower forms and to High Churchism. They were influenced chiefly by Coleridge in England, and by Schleiermacher and others of the liberal school in Germany. Among the earlier preachers of this group chief place belongs to the brothers Augustus William Hare (1793-1834) and Julius Charles Hare (1796-1855), whose lives have been beautifully set forth in the *Memorials of a Quiet Life*.[51] They were sons of an English clergyman of high character and culture. They were both well trained and educated, and Julius, the younger, became especially learned in German theology and literature. They were the joint authors of *Guesses at Truth*, a book of detached thoughts which had a wide reading in its day. The pulpit work of Augustus Hare is represented in a volume of *Sermons to a Country Congregation* which show no very remarkable powers, but are plain, earnest, pastoral discourses. Julius Hare's pulpit work has found permanent expression in a once widely read and very useful series of discourses on the *Mission of the Comforter*, being expository lectures on the doctrine of the Holy Spirit as

[51]Besides works mentioned in the text see artt. in *DNB;* Stoughton, II, p. 218; Tulloch, p. 27 ff.; Brastow, *Modern Pulpit*, p. 216.

taught in John 14-17. Hare's spirit was elevated and earnest, his learning ample, his mind broad and tolerant, but his style is too diffuse and prolix. He was a good, but never a great, preacher.

One of the three greatest names in the Broad Church group is that of Frederick Denison Maurice (1805-1872).[52] The son of a Unitarian minister and brought up in that way of thinking, Maurice, however, left the Unitarians and joined the English Church. He was educated at Cambridge, but, settling in London, he fell under the influence of Coleridge and others, who led him to become a clergyman. In 1836 he was appointed to a chaplaincy at Guy's Hospital. He became professor of English literature, and later of theology, at King's College, London, but in 1853 retired on account of his liberalistic views. He taught moral philosophy at Cambridge from 1866 until his death. Maurice's lectures on *The Kingdom of God* and numerous volumes of sermons, besides other writings, were the output of his literary activity. Maurice was largely influenced by Coleridge and by Schleiermacher, between whom and himself there was considerable similarity. His vague theology and indefiniteness of thought hindered his usefulness as a preacher, but won him the sympathy of many men of like minds with himself. His high character and noble purposes were generally recognized. He took great interest in social questions, and along with Kingsley and Robertson, did much to help the poor and the laboring classes. His personal influence as well as his preaching was widely felt in a large circle of those who sympathized with his opinions and aims, but he can not rank among the greatest preachers, either in theological literature or in the pulpit.

Charles Kingsley (1819-1875),[53] also of this group, was one whose name bulks largely in English literature

[52]Art. in *DNB,* based on biography by his son; *Prophets and Kings of the Old Testament,* a series of sermons, London and Boston, 1853; Stoughton, II, p. 220; Tulloch, *Lect.* VII; striking sermon in *World's Great Sermons,* V, p. 25.

[53]Art. in *DNB,* etc.; *The Good News of God,* sermons, New York, 1859; *Sermons for the Times,* New York, 1856; *The Gospel of the Pentateuch,* and *David* (Vol. XXX of the *Works*), London, 1885. Tulloch, *Lect.* VII, *WGS,* VI, p. 149.

and thought. The son of a clergyman of Devonshire, he received his education at Cambridge, and became rector at Eversley, in Hampshire. This was the principal scene of his labors. He at once took a deep interest in the poor and in the working classes. His sermons to the villagers were short and striking, and won the confidence of his people. He sympathized with Maurice and others in their efforts to do something for workmen and the poor of London. His famous novel, *Alton Locke* (1850), was one of the first to deal with the social and industrial questions of the day, and put the author distinctly in the group of so-called "Christian Socialists." He published other novels, including the famous *Hypatia* (1853), and some poems. There are also a number of volumes of sermons preached at various dates. Kingsley's sermons were brief and pointed, careless of homiletical arrangement, and not rigorously logical. The style of his sermons is better than that of his novels, where it is rather prolix. Kingsley was a strong personality, and in preaching spoke with vehemence and force.

One of the most pathetic and yet powerful figures in all the history of English preaching is that of Frederick William Robertson (1816-1853).[54] The man was more than his life, which can be briefly sketched. He was born in London, of a family remarkable for military talents and prepossession. Frederick himself was strongly inclined that way, but his rather delicate constitution, his intellectual bent, and his serious religious inclinations led his father and other friends to wish him to become a clergyman. The boy was fond of reading, and carefully trained by his parents in childhood. He got his principal academic education at Edinburgh, both in high school and university, because his father was stationed there for a considerable length of time. Frederick was so anxious to be a soldier that his father permitted him to apply for a commission, but he failed to secure the appointment, and then yielded his own wishes and decided to take clerical

[54] *Life and Letters of Fred. W. Robertson,* by Stopford A. Brooke, Harper's ed., 1 vol., N. Y., undated; *Sermons of Fred. W. Robertson* (do.); E. P. Hood, *Vocation of the Preacher,* p. 133 ff.; Tulloch, *Lect.* VIII; notices in Pattison, and Hoppin, *opp. citt.;* fine study by Brastow, *Rep. Mod. Pr.,* Chap. II; various other studies and notices.

orders. Five days after this decision he was offered a commission in the army. He was sorely disappointed, but kept his word to his father, and so at twenty-one years of age he entered Oxford University to prepare for the ministry. Here he devoted himself with ardor and great success to his studies, laying deep and broad the foundations of that general and technical culture and learning which his sermons and other writings so amply display. While at Oxford he earnestly opposed the Tractarian movement, though in regard to the ordinances he was already more in sympathy with High Church views than with those of the Low Church party. On the other hand, he had been brought up in evangelical sentiments, but became greatly dissatisfied with what he conceived to be their narrow views. Thus he entered his ministerial life a strange compound of opinions, vigorously opposed both to the High and Low Church parties as such, and yet having some affinities with both. Ordained in 1840, Robertson took up his work with a tone of regret and sadness, as if he had missed his calling, and with a mind unsettled as to his exact theological affiliations; but he was sincerely devoted to Christ and conscientious in the performance of his clerical duties. He began as curate at Winchester, but felt that he was a failure, was dissatisfied with himself and his work, soon gave up the place, and traveled abroad. At Geneva, while despondent and unsatisfied, he met an English family, and, as it seems, rather hurriedly married one of the daughters. Little is said in his biography about his married life, but such hints as have come down at least suggest that it was not altogether a suitable and happy one. Returning to England, Robertson accepted a curacy at Cheltenham, where he spent five arduous and faithful years. His ministry here was despondent though earnest. Always dissatisfied with himself, he was much loved and respected by the people. He began to show the high traits which later distinguished him, and there was marked growth both in Christian character and in mental power. His subordinate position galled him much, and this, with his morbid sensitiveness, led to his resignation. He again traveled in Europe, and on return took work for a little while at Oxford. Finally, in 1847, he was appointed incumbent of Trinity Chapel, at Brighton, and with this pulpit his brilliant but sad ministry is memorably connected. He was very diligent in parish work, took active part in the social and intellectual life of the town, gave lectures to the workingmen, sympathized with the poor, and put his very heart's blood into his preaching. But his health was feeble, his life sad, his disposition somewhat embittered, and in various ways he was made to feel the brunt of opposition and discouragement. His vicar disliked him and desired his place for a favorite of his own. Robertson's liberal views led him into conflict with the evangelical wing of his church, and he was out of harmony also with the High Church group. He was one of the loneliest of men; proud, sensitive, disappointed; defiant, and yet sad. He closed his strangely pathetic life in August, 1853, at the early age of thirty-seven years.

The annals of English preaching do not contain a more interesting story than that of Frederick Robertson. In character, as we have seen, he was high-minded, pure, courageous, yet sensitive to morbidness, tender-hearted and yet proud, lonely and reserved, yet widely tolerant and tenderly sympathetic with those who were in trouble. In his pride he seemed to court opposition, and yet when it came it wounded and crushed his almost feminine nature. His very face, as shown in his portraits and in that beautiful bust in the Bodleian at Oxford, shows the character of the man. Feminine delicacy and masculine intellect combine with a winning expression of spiritual force. In theology, as we have seen, Robertson occupied a position of his own. While not in sympathy with either High or Low Church, he was not so rationalistic as many of the Broad Church school.

Robertson's preaching also presents a remarkable story. It appears that only one of his sermons, that on *The Israelite's Grave in a Foreign Land,* was published before his death. This was preached on the first day of public mourning for the queen dowager (widow of William IV) in December, 1849. It is based upon Joseph's request that his bones should be carried up by the Israelites when they went up from Egypt. The publication of this sermon sheds an interesting light upon those that were published after Robertson's death. In the preface to it he says:

"The sermon is published as nearly as possible as it was spoken. It was written out concisely for a friend on the day of its delivery, with no intention of publication. Afterwards it seemed better to leave it in that state, with only a few corrections and the addition of a few sentences, than to attempt to rewrite it after an interval too great to recall what had been said. This will account for the abruptness and want of finish which pervades the composition." He goes on to disown certain publications purporting to be sermons of his, so that this remains the only authorized publication during Robertson's life. After his death his sermons were collected and published. They are in the same form as that of the sermon just mentioned. It thus appears that Robertson wrote out after delivery in condensed form the sermons by which he is known. In the delivery they were undoubtedly much elaborated. As we have them, they are compact and brief. Robertson's method of preaching was this: He made a careful expository study of the Scripture, usually taking full notes. The division is nearly always twofold. He was fond of thinking in pairs and antithesis. He thought carefully over his notes, but it is not certain whether he used them in delivery or not. There was not much action. He was self-restrained, though intense, in feeling. His voice was good and well controlled. There was nothing artificial in his manner. He had a very expressive mouth and a flashing blue eye which well interpreted his feelings and thoughts. The published sermons had extraordinary success. They have appealed, not only to preachers the world over, but have had wide reading in many circles, religious and literary. They show great intellectual power and resource, quick perception, retentive memory, and usually a discriminating insight where intense feeling did not hinder. Imagination and illustration with sufficient culture are everywhere manifest. In spite of their condensed and imperfect form, the sermons have great literary charm. The style is pure, glowing, clear, attractive. The homiletical excellence of these sermons is beyond dispute. Careful interpretation of Scripture, simple twofold division, and clearly marked subdivisions give a unity of structure and a completeness of treatment notwithstanding the condensed form. Along with these qualities, the higher elements of great preaching are here. There is keenness and depth of spiritual insight, quickness of sympathy with those who are in doubt and trouble, courage and sincerity with occasional note of defiance, and yet withal a deep and tender earnestness and evident piety and devotion to the person of the Saviour, and a longing to help the hearer. These make up a sum of qualities which give to these discourses their unique and commanding place in the literature of the pulpit. Altogether, Robertson comes as nearly as any one to fulfilling those striking words of Sidney Lanier, a kindred spirit:

> " . . . . . The catholic man who has mightily won
> God out of knowledge, and good out of infinite pain,
> And sight out of blindness, and purity out of a stain."

In the various bodies of Dissenters during this period there were many strong and well-known preachers. Selection is difficult, and condensed treatment is necessary. While a few important men stand out above the rest and must be noticed, it would be possible to construct a fair sketch of Nonconformist preaching from among names that are not even mentioned here. Among the Independents the first name which occurs is that of John Angel James (1785-1859),[55] who was born in Dorsetshire, the son of a merchant, and was apprenticed at the age of thirteen to a linen draper. He was converted in youth, and began to teach in the Sunday school. His talent for speaking and teaching, his earnestness of religious life, attracted notice, and he was urged to enter the ministry. He read much, and finally, by the assistance of friends, took a two years' course of study under the celebrated Dr. Bogue, at Gosport. He was then called to be pastor at Carr's Lane Church, Birmingham. This was his only pastorate, which he held for more than fifty years, and it was here that his life's work was done. He was happily and helpfully married, active and useful as a pastor, and a prolific writer on practical religious subjects. Many of his devotional books were widely read and very useful in their day. Two are especially noteworthy, *The Church*

[55]Sketch (by R. W. Dale) and sermon in Evans and Hurndall, *op. cit.;* also in Fish, *XIX Cent.,* p. 518 ff.

in Earnest, and *An Earnest Ministry,* in which his aims and experiences as a preacher found expression. No doubt most of the chapters of his many devotional treatises served first as sermons, and from them a good idea of his preaching may be had. James was not profound in thought, nor technically learned, though widely read. His sermons are characterized by thorough evangelical piety and thought, a clear and pleasing though somewhat flowing style, and a high spiritual aim.

Another highly esteemed preacher of the time was James Parsons (1799-1877),[56] who was the son of a Congregationalist preacher at Leeds, and educated for a lawyer. He was fond of the political orators. On his conversion he entered the ministry and took a theological course. He took charge of a dissenting chapel at York, where he spent his life, hence his nickname, "Parsons of York." Besides his effective local work, he was often called on for public services in other places, and was very popular in London. Despite a weak and peculiar voice, and some other drawbacks, he was a man of rare powers in the pulpit, who had the art of compelling attention by the clearness of his thought and the intensity of his convictions. A specimen sermon shows good grasp of his theme, logical arrangement, and earnest application, with good illustrations and a moving style.

Unquestionably the greatest Congregational preacher of the period was Thomas Binney (1798-1874).[57] Born at Newcastle, he enjoyed only moderate advantages in his childhood. At seven years of age he was apprenticed to a bookseller and was kept busy, but he found time to read in the bookshop, and especially from his fourteenth to his twentieth year he read widely and studied hard, taking Latin and Greek at evenings with a Presbyterian minister. His father was a Presbyterian elder, and the

[56]Sketch and sermon in E. & H.

[57]Art. (by G. B. S.) in *DNB;* sketch in *Great Modern Preachers* (anon., Lond., 1875—slight but clever sketches of a dozen preachers, some of them eminent—hereafter referred to as *GMP*); study (with sermon) by Edw. White in E and H; *Thos. Binney, His Life, Mind, and Opinions,* by E. P. Hood, London, 1874; *Sermons Preached in the King's Weigh House Chapel,* 2d series, 1829, with an introductory sketch by Dr. Henry Allon; sketch and sermon in Fish, *XIX Cent.,* p. 580 ff.

boy early took an interest in church and religious affairs. Why he became a Congregationalist is not clear. He attended a Congregational theological school in Hertfordshire, where he remained three years. On graduation he was pastor for a short time in Bedford, then in the Isle of Wight, and finally (1829) at the King's Weigh House Chapel, London, which was the principal scene of his labors to the end of his life. Binney was a pronounced Nonconformist, and attacked the Established Church with vehemence and power. In many other ways he took part in ecclesiastical and political controversies. In 1857 he visited Australia, where he preached with great power and acceptance. He became the leading figure in his denomination, and received many honors. In 1869, after forty years of service, he resigned his pastorate, though he continued to write and preach occasionally to the end of his life.

Binney was a strong though an unequal preacher. Perhaps his own view and practice are indicated in a saying of his. A young preacher asked him the best way to preach, and he answered, "Gather your materials and set fire to them in the pulpit." He had good personal advantages, a large frame, noble brow, splendid eyes, a manly and yet unaffected deportment. His manner in the pulpit was devout, impressive, sincere. His thinking showed a fine combination of caution and boldness. His style was vigorous and strong. He was odd and yet free fiom sensation and studied effects. His sermons are marked by careful mastery of the text and of other Scriptures bearing on it, by judicious and balanced thought, by excellent feeling, reverence, sympathy, by manly strength both of style and manner, and by tenderness in appeal. In the second series of *Sermons Preached in King's Weigh House Chapel* occurs a fine biographical and critical sketch, from the pen of Dr. Henry Allon, which well presents Binney in the following terms: "Mr. Binney's eminence as a minister of Christ rested upon bases which could scarcely be demonstrated. His name is not connected with any monumental achievement, either in philanthropy, oratory, or literature. For reasons which may appear in the course of these remarks, he has left behind him no work which can be regarded as an adequate expression of his indisputable power. His reputation, like that of many great men, was won by the impression made by great faculties and noble character in their normal exercise, in his case in the common fellowship and counsel of ministers, and in such preachings and writings as the ordinary course of a minister's work gives occasion for. Able as are some of his sermons and pamphlets, to those otherwise unacquainted with him or his work they will not seem to justify the reputation and reverence which were accorded to him. These were evoked by the stable qualities of the man—a great intellectual, social, and religious presence—rather than by any specific achievement." This judicious statement is in general true of so many great preachers, as well as of its immediate subject, as to justify its quotation at length.

The Methodists had a number of strong and influential preachers during this epoch, of whom two are of special prominence. Jabez Bunting (1779-1858),[58] was born and brought up in Manchester. His parents were poor, but his mother a woman of decided character and an ardent Methodist. By various means the boy managed to get some education, and began to preach when nineteen years of age. He studied and grew in the actual work of an itinerant Wesleyan preacher. He occupied many pastorates, both important and unimportant, and filled various church offices with distinction. He had a reverential and impressive manner in the pulpit, and was heard with great attention. His sermons show profound and well convinced spiritual experience, intense practical aim, without speculation and with little of formal argument, taking fundamental Christian truth for granted. There is large acquaintance with Scripture, but apparently not much with literature, or even theology in a scholarly way; but there is marked ability in handling the truths in the preacher's range with good, robust language without affectation or straining. The treatment is mostly textual, the analysis clear, even if at times too formal and elaborate. Above all, the sermons exhibit great spir-

[58]*Life,* by his son, T. P. Bunting, continued by G. S. Rowe, in 2 vols., London (?); *Sermons,* 2 vols., ed. by W. L. Thornton, Lond., 1861; sketch and sermon in Fish, *XIX Cent.,* p. 580 ff.

itual power with occasional flashes of a true eloquence born of noble qualities.

The other leading Methodist preacher of the time was William Morley Punshon (1824-1881).[59] He, too, was born of poor but pious Methodist parents, at Doncaster, and was early left an orphan. He received some education, but entered the counting house of his grandfather to prepare for a business career. He was a great reader, and began preaching at the age of seventeen. Pursuing his studies, he formally joined the Conference in 1845. His gifts and fidelity won him esteem, and he filled various charges with success and respect. He sprang at one bound into fame as a religious orator by a great lecture on *The Prophet Elijah,* delivered at Exeter Hall, London, in 1854. After this he was much in demand for occasional sermons and lectures. In 1867 he was sent to Canada, where he did much for Methodism, both by his preaching and his administrative work. On returning to England, in 1873, he served various Churches, was president of the Conference, and finally Missionary Secretary. He led an active and useful life up to the end. His health declined and he passed away in 1881. Among his last utterances were the words, "Christ is to me a bright reality." And this was significant also of his preaching. He was sound in the faith, unshaken by the rising tide of critical skepticism, anchored on the eternal verities. He had distinguished and notable oratorical powers in voice, manner, and language. His addresses and sermons were somewhat artificial in style, like those of Melvill and others, and would be out of date in the present age. But to their hearers they were impressive, highly wrought, and sometimes sweeping deliverances of a strong mind and an impassioned spirit.

The Presbyterians had to their credit in this epoch two distinguished preachers in London, one in Ireland, and a large number in Scotland. In London, at the National Scottish Church in Covent Garden there ministered the popular and somewhat sensational John Cum-

[59]Sketch in *GMP;* art. in *DNB; Life* by F. W. Macdonald, Lond., 1887; critique by Wilkinson, *Mod. Mast.,* p. 415 ff.; *Sermons* (Introd. by W. H. Milburn), New York, 1860; *Lectures and Sermons,* Boston, 1873.

ming (1807-1881).[60] He was born near Aberdeen, and educated at the University there. He received his license at the end of his course, and acted for awhile as private tutor. In 1832 he was called to the church in London which he occupied to the end of his life. His preaching soon attracted great congregations, and his church was rebuilt and enlarged. The income from pew rents reached 1,500 pounds, but Cumming refused more than 900, devoting the rest to religious and charitable purposes. He was active in philanthropy, was something of a controversialist, and very popular as a preacher. His lectures and sermons on prophecy were tinged with sensation, but the body of his preaching was evangelical, effective, and strong.

James Hamilton (1810-1867)[61] was born at Strathaven, Scotland, the son of a clergyman, and educated at the University of Glasgow. In 1841 he was called to the National Scotch Church, Regent Square, London, of which the famous Edward Irving had been pastor some years previously. The church, which had suffered by the withdrawal of Irving, was built up again under the ministry of Hamilton, who was a preacher of decided merits. He and his church went out with Chalmers at the Disruption, in 1843. Hamilton was an excellent preacher, pastor, and friend, a steady, all-round worker. Besides his sermons, he wrote a good many books which had quite a circulation in their day. His work both in the pulpit and with the pen was fortified by his devoted Christian life. In his preaching he showed a fine imagination, almost a poetic instinct, richness of illustration, with some exuberance of style. His thought was founded in the evangelical theology.

In Ireland there was the celebrated Henry Cooke (d. 1881),[62] pastor and professor at Belfast, a strong theologian, vigorous polemic, capable church leader, and a preacher of popular and effective power. The sermon

[60]Art. *DNB;* sketch and sermon in Fish, *XIX Cent.,* p. 691 ff.; *Twelve Urgent Questions* (essays on texts), Phila., 1855; *Voices of the Dead* (do. on Heb. 11), Boston, 1854.

[61]*Life of James Hamilton,* by Wm. Arnot; sketch and sermon in Fish, *op. cit.,* p. 725 ff.; *The Royal Preacher* (Lectures on *Ecclesiastes*), New York, 1851.

[62]Sketch and sermon in Fish, *XIX Cent.,* p. 739 ff.

given in Fish shows sufficient learning and strong, active intellect, firm belief in the gospel, and an animated though not particularly engaging or highly rhetorical style.

It is, of course, to Scotland that we must look for the great Presbyterian preachers, and here there was such a number that only a few of the best known may be noted. Prominent among them was the delightful Dr. Thomas Guthrie (1803-1873),[63] who was born at Brechin, Forfarshire, received his education at Edinburgh, was pastor at Arbroath, and later at the Old Grey Friars Church in Edinburgh. Dr. Guthrie, like Chalmers, was not only a great preacher, but an active pastor and social philanthropist. He went out with the Free Church in 1843, and was one of the most effective preachers in that body, being for a long time pastor of St. John's Free Church, Edinburgh. There was a vast humanness in Guthrie. He had no great learning, but an intense practical aim for results. His personal touch was sympathetic, kindly, moving. In the pulpit he was one of the greatest masters of illustration in his time or in any time. He knew how to use a good story, and move the feelings of his hearers. He is a strong type of the successful evangelistic pastor. One of his most effective series of sermons has the title, *The Gospel in Ezekiel,* containing twenty discourses based on texts taken from that prophet. One of these, *The New Heart,* on Ezekiel 36:26, is an excellent specimen of Guthrie's manner. The analysis is somewhat loose, and the thought is by no means profound, but the warm glow of feeling is lit up by imagination, and the evangelical earnestness is unquestioned.

Robert Smith Candlish (1807-1873)[64] was born at Edinburgh, and educated at Glasgow. He was one of the younger followers of Chalmers in establishing the Free Church. He was for a long time pastor of the famous

[63] *Autobiography and Memoir* (by his Sons), New York, 1877. *Man and the Gospel* (sermons), London, 1867; *The Gospel in Ezekiel* (series of sermons, New York, undated); study by Brastow, *Rep. Mod. Pr.,* p. 350 ff.; sermon and sketch in Fish, *op. cit.,* p. 623 ff.; and in *WGS,* V. p. 1; Taylor, *Scot. Pul.,* p. 268 ff.

[64] *Scripture Characters* (sermons), Edinburgh, 1872; *The Book of Genesis Expounded in a Series of Discourses,* 2 vols., Edinburgh, 1868; Blaikie, p. 293; Taylor, p. 265 ff.; sermon and sketch in Fish, *op. cit.,* p. 714 ff.

Free St. George's, in Edinburgh. He then followed Chalmers as professor in the Free Church College at Edinburgh. He was a powerful expository preacher without the graces of oratory. He moved by the power of his thought and the vigor of his style. He read his sermons, but, like Chalmers, he delivered them with such vehemence as to make them strongly impressive. He was felicitous in the selection of his texts, which were correctly interpreted and well handled. His thought showed sound doctrine, vivid imagination, frequent and usually good illustration, often experimental. There is no striking originality or depth, little of formal argument, but earnest application. The arrangement is generally simple, natural, and forcible. The style is clear and strong, with no special eloquence, and yet not too commonplace. It is vivid and fresh, but a trifle exuberant, profuse in adjectives, and inclined to verbiage.

In the Established Church of Scotland two specially notable preachers, besides others, adorn this epoch. Norman McLeod (1813-1872)[65] was one of the most eminent of modern Scotch preachers. He was born in Argyllshire, where his father was a clergyman. He was of good Gaelic stock, and loved the Highlands with all his big heart. He was brought up in his native country, but studied at both Edinburgh and Glasgow. He also pursued some theological studies in Germany. On completing his preparation he was pastor at Dalkeith, then at Edinburgh, and lastly at the Barony Church, in Glasgow. It was here that he performed his principal labors. It is hard in brief compass to put a worthy estimate upon this lovable, large-hearted, and many-sided man. His genial nature bubbled over in fun and pleasantry, but his loyal heart beat true to the profounder things in human nature and life; and while he was a liberal in theological thought, his soul was centered upon the person of his Lord and Saviour. It is a beautiful tribute to the man that he was both a favorite and an adviser of Queen Victoria during her sojourns in Scotland, and that he was equally loved and trusted among the poor

[65] *Life of Norman McLeod,* by his brother, Donald McLeod, 2 vols. in one, New York, 1877; *Simple Truths for Working Men,* by Norman McLeod; sketch and sermon in *WGS,* V, p. 177 ff.

of his flock in Glasgow. The late Dr. John Watson is authority for the story that, on one occasion, a peasant woman in Glasgow being ill with a malignant fever, sent not for McLeod but another pastor. On his asking why she had not sent for her own pastor, the old woman said, "Na, did ye think I wad send for Norman in a case of typhus?" "Norman," as he was affectionately called, was too valuable to subject to such a risk. There is a noble statue of him near the Barony Church which the visitor to Glasgow still looks upon with interest. Norman McLeod has a good place in Scottish literature by reason of his genial and admirable stories of Highland life. Among his poems, one excellent hymn survives and is often sung:

"Courage, brother! do not stumble,
  Tho' thy path be dark as night;
There's a star to guide the humble,
  Trust in God, and do the right.
Tho' the road be long and dreary,
  And the end be out of sight,
Tread it bravely, strong or weary,
  Trust in God, and do the right."

Of his published sermons there is a little volume with the title, *Simple Truths Addressed to Workingmen.* These are only what they profess to be, plain Scriptural talks for plain people, full of gospel and good sense, easy to read, yet mingling good, fresh thinking with the beloved old commonplaces, and charged with the big-hearted feeling characteristic of the man.

The other great Scotch preacher of the time was John Caird (1820-1898),[66] born at Greenock, and educated at Glasgow. He was pastor successively at Edinburgh, Errol, and Glasgow. In later years he was professor, and then principal, at Glasgow University. He was a powerful thinker, perhaps too much influenced by Hegel's philosophy, especially in his later years, but in his earlier ministry he was a powerful gospel preacher. A volume of these earlier sermons shows him at his best.

[66] The lectures by Caird on *Fundamental Ideas of Christianity,* Ednb., 1899, contain *Memoir* by Edward Caird; *Sermons* by Rev. John Caird, D. D., Ednb., 1866; sermon and sketch in Fish, *op. cit.*, p. 654 ff, (reprinted in *WGS,* VI, p. 167); Blaikie, p. 317.

They are strong and clear, both in thought and language, full of apt illustration and powerful yet tactful application to life. The most famous of Caird's sermons, and one of the most famous of modern times, was that on *Religion in the Common Life,* which has been frequently republished. Read in the light of present thinking, it does not strike with the novelty of view which it had when first published. It owed its extraordinary circulation and influence largely to the circumstances under which it was preached and published, yet also, it must in justice be said, to its admirable treatment of a great and practical theme. It was preached before Queen Victoria and the Prince Consort, on her invitation, at Balmoral Castle, in 1855. After hearing it, both the queen and her husband asked for the manuscript and read it with great pleasure. By the queen's "command," it was published and sent forth with this royal endorsement. It attained a remarkable circulation and established the fame of its author. The text is Romans 12:11, "Not slothful in business; fervent in spirit; serving the Lord." It is based on a current but natural error in interpretation, as the "business" referred to in the text is not our ordinary daily occupation, but properly diligence in religious work. But the theme, *Religion in Common Life,* is in itself one of great importance. In argument and illustration the discourse is forcible; in thought, clear and Scriptural; in arrangement, simple and progressive; in style, admirable, almost faultless, yet without artifice; in tone and spirit, earnest and faithful. The tact with which the preacher appeals to the queen to discharge her high office in a Christian spirit is perfect. There is neither flattery nor unseemly assumption. The tone is dignified, manly, respectful, but firm.

Coming back to England, we find among the Baptists of the period several preachers of influence and distinction. Among them was Dr. F. A. Cox (1785-1853),[67] who was born at Leighton, and possessed of some wealth. He received his education at Edinburgh, and after filling some smaller pastorates, served for forty-two years at Hackney, in London. He was prominent in denominational and Nonconformist affairs, and respected by the

[67]Art. in *DNB;* vol. on *Scripture Female Biography.*

great men of the time. While a sound scholar and a judicious leader, he was also useful and highly esteemed as pastor and preacher. Among his writings, and probably based on sermons, is a volume with the title, *Scripture Female Biography,* which is well written, but not of any commanding importance.

Baptist W. Noel (1798-1873)[68] came of noble Scottish lineage, and was educated at Cambridge. Becoming a clergyman in the English Church, he was pastor at St. John's Chapel, in London. In theological opinion he was decidedly Low Church and evangelical. With these tendencies, earnest study of the Bible led him to become a Baptist in 1847, at the sacrifice of his place and under the censure and disappointment of his family and friends. True to his convictions, he was baptized and ordained, and became pastor of John Street Chapel, near his former parish. Here he worked as pastor till 1868, when he resigned on account of old age. He was a man of pleasing appearance, fine cultured face, with a clear voice and good delivery, and a fine command of language. His preaching was marked by evangelical sentiments, and showed in its style and general manner the mind of a cultivated, refined man.

William Brock (1807-1875)[69] was a native of Devonshire, and had a very interesting early life and training, which it would be pleasant to dwell upon did space permit. With difficulties he obtained some education and entered the Baptist ministry, serving for awhile as pastor in Norwich, and afterwards, from 1848 onward, of the famous Bloomsbury Chapel, in London. Brock was an admirable pastor and a strong though not brilliant preacher. He published a number of sermons, especially a volume called *Midsummer Morning Sermons,* an excellent series to young people. He also wrote a life of General Havelock, which had a wide circulation in its day.

The greatest Baptist preacher of the age was the already famous though still young Charles Haddon Spur-

[68]Art. in *DNB; Sermons,* 3 vols. (from the *Pulpit*), about 1833; sketch and sermon in Fish, *XIX Cent.,* p. 541 ff.

[69]*Life,* by C. M. Birrell (father of the famous essayist); *Midsummer Morning Sermons.*

geon (1834-1892).[70] The Spurgeon family is of Huguenot name and origin. Its ancestors left France under the persecutions, and one branch settled in the county of Essex, near London. The grandfather of Charles, the Rev. James Spurgeon, was pastor of the Independent Church at Stambourne, Essex, for fifty-four years. The father, John, likewise became a Congregational preacher, but was also engaged in business at Kelvedon, where Charles Haddon was born, June 19, 1834. His mother, *née* Jarvis, was an excellent and pious woman, and gave her children good training. But for some reason Charles became his "grandfather's boy," and spent most of his early childhood in the parsonage at Stambourne, under the care of his grandparents and his maiden aunt, Miss Ann Spurgeon. A bright and thoughtful child, he was carefully brought up, and early showed a great fondness for reading his grandfather's books. He was also sent to school, but was not remarkable. Later he returned to his parents, now removed to Colchester, where, through their sacrifices, he enjoyed good schooling for several years. His moral and religious training had been excellent, but he had his boyish doubts and struggles, and did not have his personal experience of grace till December 15, 1850, when he was converted under a sermon on Isaiah 45:22, preached by an unknown preacher in a humble Primitive Methodist chapel in Colchester. Becoming convinced of Baptist views of the act and subjects of baptism, he joined the Baptist church at Isleham, and was baptized by its pastor, Rev. Mr. Cantlow, May 3, 1851. Soon afterwards he transferred his membership to Cambridge, joining the church there of which Robert Hall had been pastor, and a "lay preachers' association" connected with it. Thus he began preaching,

[70]Various accounts and *Lives,* as those of Needham, Cook, Conwell, Pike, Shindler, and others; but the great source is the *Autobiography* in four large volumes, London and New York, 1898, compiled from Spurgeon's writings and papers under the supervision of his widow. Studies by Wilkinson, *Modern Masters,* p. 181 ff., and by Brastow, *Rep. Mod. Preachers,* p. 383 ff., are valuable among the newer appreciations. Among Spurgeon's numerous writings his *Lectures to My Students,* and *Art of Illustrating* have special homiletic interest. The various series of the *Sermons* have appeared in many editions; latterly the *Spurgeon Memorial Library,* New York, Funk & Wagnalls Co.

and soon was called to be pastor of a little Baptist church at Waterbeach, not very far from Cambridge. Meantime he had been teaching as usher, or assistant, in various schools, and pursuing his studies. It was thus he was employed at Cambridge. By a singular mistake he missed an appointment to confer with Dr. Angus in regard to being educated at Stepney College, in London. His early preaching at Waterbeach was crude, but wonderful in one so young.

The famous old Baptist church in London of Keach, Gill, Rippon, and Angus had run down. Somehow they heard of this promising and wonderful youth, and gave him an invitation to visit them. It resulted—much to the surprise of all—in his call to the pastorate. He felt as led of God and accepted, beginning work in April, 1854. He was a success from the first. Congregations soon overflowed the old house, and removal became necessary. Many were added to the membership, and the church was greatly strengthened and encouraged. The usual difficulties as to enlargement or moving were encountered; it was decided to enlarge, and meantime worship in Exeter Hall; on return, with the great crowds the chapel was found disappointingly small still. So it was finally decided to move and build a great tabernacle. Meantime the church worshiped in Music Hall, Surrey Gardens, where a panic and disaster occurred, and only emphasized the necessity of a better building. Finally the Metropolitan Tabernacle, on the Surrey side, was built and finished, with a seating capacity of about 6,000. Work began in it May, 1861. Here crowds gathered twice every Sunday to hear the great preacher, hundreds were added to the church, great benevolent and religious enterprises were undertaken—as the Pastors' College and the Stockwell Orphanage—and great work done. Spurgeon was happily and suitably married in January, 1856, to Miss Susannah Thompson; and she proved a true helper, though she became an invalid. He likewise owed much to the efficient help of his brother James, who became co-pastor in January, 1868, and worked with him to the end. In 1884 Spurgeon celebrated his fiftieth birthday, in the full tide of his wonderful career as preacher, builder, author, and leader.

But his health had been undermined by his long and arduous labors, and though the work went on he gradually declined, and he often went to Mentone, France, for rest, where he died January 31, 1892.

The preaching of Spurgeon was wonderful in power and popularity, which continued undiminished to the end of his life. Professor L. O. Brastow, in his *Representative Modern Preachers,* gives a fairly good critical estimate of Spurgeon, but his study is, on the whole, somewhat reluctant and depreciatory. All the more emphatic, therefore, is the statement, "He was doubtless the most impressive and permanently successful evangelistic preacher of his age." In a much more just, even if partial, study, Dr. W. C. Wilkinson thus describes this aspect of Spurgeon's wonderful evangelistic ministry: "The spiritual fruitfulness was, from the first, no less remarkable than the intellectual triumph of Mr. Spurgeon's ministry. Within ten years from the commencement of his London pastorate, 3,569 persons had been baptized into the fellowship of the church. I have before me, as I write, an authorized statistical table of figures for the years 1861-1877. This exhibits a steady annual increase of numbers, an increase not once interrupted, in the membership of the church, up to 5,152 in 1877." The statement is not perfectly clear, but means apparently the total addition was that for the period included—an average of over 300 a year, by steady growth. Besides these baptisms into his own church, there were hundreds of others led to Christ by his preaching, and many more were converted by the ministry of his printed sermons, of which nearly 2,500 have been published, with an average sale of 25,000 copies of each. In the study of so marvelous an activity and fruitfulness, we must consider his characteristics.

In speaking of Spurgeon's limitations, it is only just to remind ourselves that no one man ever has had or can have all the excellencies actually exhibited in one and another of the great preachers of history, nor all that are conceivable in the imaginary perfect preacher. So even Spurgeon had his deficiencies, and some of them are instructive. His thought was not particularly original or profound, moving chiefly amid the accepted commonplaces of religion and the evangelical theology. Indeed, this was one element of his power with the common people. His culture showed the lack of a full academic education; and though he read much, there were large sections of modern thought and literature which he never entered. The structure of his sermons was often homiletically faulty and careless. More serious was his frequently inaccurate exegesis; and sometimes he did not seem greatly to care. Like Beecher, he was sometimes hasty in preparation. He too often allowed other things to crowd his sermon. And so there was not much variety; but it is a wonder there was not more sameness.

What, then, were the elements of his power? The natural man was well endowed. While he had a homely face and a stocky figure, he had a fine expression, and was gifted with a voice of great sweetness, smoothness, compass, and sympathy. In intellect he was alert, clever, sound, and strong, with fine imagination, large and shrewd observation, and wide reading, with retentive memory. In temperament he was genial, winsome, sympathetic, hearty. Candor and sincerity were evident traits, with simplicity and strength of character. The Christian showed in all his work. To his pious upbringing was added the deep experience of a definite and decisive conversion, and the joy of his salvation by grace resounded in no uncertain tones throughout his whole ministry. He was a mighty man in prayer, and his devoted loyalty and consecration to Christ were manifest in all that he did. Faithfulness and courage were not wanting in the rounding out of his manhood in Christ. The pastor's heart was his, and though he could not visit much, he kept in personal touch with his great flock in many telling ways; and his leadership was wise, loving, progressive, masterful. The preacher, however, was ever pre-eminent. In doctrine he was an old-fashioned evangelical Calvinist from beginning to end. In use of Scripture he was rich, devout, effective, though sometimes at fault in interpretation. His style was rich, racy, homely, powerful Saxon—sometimes undignified, but ever clear and strong, and often sweet and eloquent. His delivery was free, easy, and natural; and he spoke without notes, his sermons being reported and revised, not written beforehand. In spirit—faith, hope, and love breathed in his preaching. The glory of God in saving men was his ruling motive. Great was his work and great his reward.

Wilkinson well says: "Mr. Spurgeon is a great preacher, rather than a preacher of great sermons. If this is not praise, it certainly is not dispraise. To preach great sermons is, no doubt, the prouder intellectual triumph; but the more useful service, and the rarer moral attainment, is to be a great preacher." Hence it is peculiarly difficult to judge Spurgeon by any one sermon, and still more by brief quotations. But, as specimens of his manner, the two following extracts are given. The first is from one of his youthful discourses (1856), on *Songs in the Night:*[71]

"Man, too, like the great world in which he lives, must have his night. For it is true that man is like the world around him; he is a little world; he resembles the world in almost everything; and if the world hath its night, so hath man. And many a night do we have—nights of sorrow, nights of persecution, nights of doubt, nights of bewilderment, nights of anxiety, nights of oppression, nights of ignorance—nights of all kinds, which press upon our spirits and terrify our souls. But, blessed be God, the Christian man can say, 'My God giveth me songs in the night.'

"It is not necessary, I take it, to prove to you that Christian men have nights; for if you are Christians, you will find that you have them, and you will not want any proof, for nights will come quite often enough. I will, therefore, proceed at once to the subject; and I will speak this evening upon songs in the night, their source—God giveth them; songs in the night, their matter—what do we sing about in the night? songs in the night, their excellence—they are hearty songs, and they are sweet ones; songs in the night, their uses—their benefits to ourselves and others. . . .

"Any fool can sing in the day. When the cup is full, man draws inspiration from it; when wealth rolls in abundance around him, any man can sing to the praise of a God who gives a plenteous harvest, or sends home

[71] *Sermons,* 2d Series, p. 167 ff.; Fish, *XIX Cent.,* p. 606 ff.

a loaded argosy. It is easy enough for an Æolian harp to whisper music when the winds blow; the difficulty is for music to come when no wind bloweth. It is easy to sing when we can read the notes by daylight; but the skillful singer is he who can sing them when there is not a ray of light to read by—who sings from his heart, and not from a book that he can see, because he has no means of reading save from that inward book of his own living spirit, whence notes of gratitude pour out in songs of praise."

The other extract is from a much later sermon (1888), on *The Blood of the Lamb, the Conquering Weapon:*[72] "Brethren, if we are to win great victories we must have greater courage. Some of you hardly dare speak about the blood of Christ in any but the most godly company; and scarcely there. You are very retiring. You love yourselves too much to get into trouble through your religion. Surely you can not be of that noble band that love not their own lives unto the death! Many dare not hold the old doctrine nowadays because they would be thought narrow and bigoted, and this would be too galling. They call us old fools. It is very likely we are; but we are not ashamed to be fools for Christ's sake, and the truth's sake. We believe in the blood of the Lamb, despite the discoveries of science. We shall never give up the doctrine of atoning sacrifice to please modern culture. What little reputation we have is as dear to us as another man's character is to him; but we will cheerfully let it go in this struggle for the central truth of revelation. It will be sweet to be forgotten and lost sight of, or to be vilified and abused, if the old faith in the substitutionary sacrifice can be kept alive. This much we are resolved on, we will be true to our convictions concerning the sacrifice of our Lord Jesus; for if we give up this, what is there left? God will not do anything by us if we are false to the cross. He uses the men who spare not their reputations when these are called for in the defense of truth. O to be at a white heat! O to flame with zeal for Jesus! O my brethren, hold you to the old faith, and say, 'As for the respect of men, I can readily forfeit it; but as for the truth of

[72] *Memorial Lib.*, Vol. XIX, p. 320.

God, that I can never give up.' This is the day for men to be men; for, alas! the most are soft, molluscous creatures. Now we need backbones as well as heads. To believe the truth concerning the Lamb of God, and truly to believe it, this is the essential of an overcoming life. O for courage, constancy, fixedness, self-denial, willingness to be made nothing for Christ! God give us to be faithful witnesses to the blood of the Lamb in the midst of this ungodly world!"

III. The Closing Years of the Century: 1868-1900

The last third of the nineteenth century, including the second half of Queen Victoria's reign, was crowded with affairs of the deepest interest and significance, affecting not only the widely extended empire over which she reigned, but the larger world. Every sort of intense and active life was felt, both at home and abroad. Only a slight touch upon the most important events is needed to recall rapidly the history of the era, recent as it is in the memory of most readers.[73] This was the age of Gladstone and Disraeli, Earl of Beaconsfield, whose leadership of their respective parties, the Liberal and Conservative, and their alternations in office, as the tide of popular approval of their measures ebbed and flowed, make up a brilliant political history. Reforms in the suffrage, the disestablishment of the Irish Church, educational policies, Home Rule for Ireland, colonial and foreign interests, especially in the East and in Africa, kept political and party interest on keen edge most of the time. After the aged and beloved queen had, with great pomp and glory, celebrated her jubilee, the painful Boer War in South Africa cast a gloom over her closing years. Internal affairs showed continued progress in humane and liberal movements. More and more the claims of the poor and laboring classes were recognized, and many abuses were redressed. Education made advances, the universities were (1871) thrown open to Dissenters, and the problems of general education were engaging much attention when the century closed. Commerce and manu-

[73]Much the same authorities as before, as far as they bear on this period.

factures continued to flourish, and the industrial arts were furthered in many ways.

Literature increased, both in volume and variety, and, on the whole, maintained its power. Every phase of literary expression could show a group of able and brilliant representatives. Both in the severer and in the lighter forms of thought and writing there was enormous production. Scientific and philosophic thought was especially great and influential. Darwin's *Origin of Species* had appeared in 1859, but his *Descent of Man* (1871) belongs to this period. Spencer, Huxley, Tyndall, and others of that influential school were as active in literary expression as in research and thought, and a host of other thinkers were as eager as the leaders to find reading for their opinions. In historical, biographical, and critical writing the age is highly distinguished. What an array of talent, both for inquiry and for expression, is found in such writers as Lecky, Froude, Freeman, Green, Stubbs, Fyffe, Gardiner, and other historians; in Trevelyan, Masson, Forster, Stanley, Mrs. Oliphant, Morley, and other biographers; in Carlyle, Ruskin, Matthew Arnold, Symonds, Hutton, Stephen, Gosse, Pater, Birrell, and still other essayists and critics well known to fame. In poetry, Tennyson and Browning were still at work, while Morris, Swinburne, Matthew Arnold, the Rossettis, Lang, Henley, Watson, and others were heard in their different ways. In the rich and wide field of fiction the growth was luxuriant, tangled, infinitely various in aim, style, appeal, effect. Enumeration is impossible, judgment almost as varied as the product itself. But it can not be forgotten that this was the age of George Eliot, Wilkie Collins, Charles Reade, Trollope, Black, Blackmore, Hardy, Mrs. Ward, Meredith, Kipling, Stevenson, Doyle, and hundreds of lesser writers of novels and stories which have taken hold of their generation with a vigor and charm both astonishing and mighty. The literature of religion and theology likewise found in every branch abundant and able expression. In Biblical scholarship—exegesis, criticism, archaeology; in historical research, ancient, mediæval, modern; in apologetics and theology; in devotional and poetical writings, and in sermons, the output of books has been in keeping with that in other departments, both in respect of quantity and quality. A few of the leading names readily occur to mind, when we recall such men as Lightfoot, Westcott, Hort, Sayce, Driver, Cheyne, Liddon, Mozley, Dale, Fairbairn, Orr, Rainy, Ramsay, Neale, Keble, Bickersteth, Ryle, Whyte, Matheson, Nicoll, Meyer, Moule, MacGregor, Morgan, and a host of others in the various branches of Christian literature. Sermons will, of course, receive fuller notice later.

Humanitarian effort and social questions occupied much attention on all sides. Novel writers and poets, statesmen and clergymen, in their several ways, took hold of the many-sided social problem at all its angles. Slum work in the cities, improvement in the habitations of the poor, both on the farms and in the cities; various measures of poor relief, attention to moral problems and rescue work, social settlements for the suggestion of higher ideals and for some forms of benevolent effort on behalf of the lower classes—all were pushed on in various ways. The churches took up the work, and many preachers and other workers did great service in this way. The Salvation Army carried on its benevolent work from many centers of its vast organization. Along with some radicalism and some impracticable schemes, much real service was done for the improvement of social conditions. In general, this effort to comprehend and solve the accumulated problems of modern life was one of the most impressive features of the last three decades of the nineteenth century in England.

In the more distinctively religious and ecclesiastical sphere conditions noted in the immediately preceding time remained substantially the same, but the note of progress was distinctly heard. Parties in the churches, both the Establishment and the Nonconformist bodies, were much the same, and yet with such variations as the new era naturally brought on. There was some shifting of emphasis, some change of view on old questions, some progress on lines of tendency already set up. In the Anglican body the groups of High, Low, and Broad Church could not be so easily separated as formerly. Two or three causes contributed to this confusion. One was the great common work of social amelioration, which appealed to all parties and found able advocates in all. Another was the fight against materialism, and the reaction toward mysticism in all or most of the denominations. And still another lay in the progress of tolerance and mutual respect between all sects and parties. Yet for convenience of study and grouping, and because the fundamental distinctions still were operative, it is best to retain the old nomenclature. The Low Church party was more conservative of the evangelical traditions and type of doctrine; the High Churchmen mingled with a strong bent to extreme ritualism and their traditional sacramentarianism a large interest in social betterment and a good degree of mystical piety; while the Broad Church element, sharing these later tendencies of the religious life, were more sympathetic as well with liberalism in thought on the scientific side as with the theories of the modern German critical school of Biblical interpretation.

Among Dissenters also the distinction of conservative or evangelical, and liberal or rationalistic, remains. The Free Churches in England of all the sects were more or less divided on this line of cleavage; and in Scotland, both in the Established and Free Churches, the same phenomenon appears. It was characteristic of the age, and appears in all lands and in all parties to a greater or less extent. Modern Christianity shows everywhere the struggle to adjust itself to scientific and critical attack upon traditional beliefs and practices, to participate without loss of distinctive Christian aims and motives in social progress, and to find refuge, both from the weakening of faith in confessional statements of Christian truth and from the terrible encroachments of worldliness on the life of piety, in new emphasis on personal communion with God, which finds expression in many ways. In England the Keswick school of religious leaders and writers is the protagonist of the newer mysticism, and in its ranks many able and forceful preachers and authors are found. Along with these forces, mention must be made of the progress of evangelistic measures and efforts at home and of missionary labors abroad. All the great societies were greatly strengthened; contributions were never so large, and administration was wise and businesslike, while extensive work on the foreign fields was pushed with great vigor and success. At home the great evangelistic campaign of the American evangelists, Moody and Sankey, in the seventies, followed by others, encouraged and promoted revival efforts of great variety in character and results. Outdoor preaching was much practiced, and the personal hand-to-hand method of appeal was also much used. Altogether, in the English countries at the close of the nineteenth century there is in the sphere of religious life and thought a variety, activity, and power which are the outcome of previously working forces now come to their highest stage.

Again we have to remark how powerfully the forces and influences which have been thus hastily sketched acted upon the pulpit of the age. It was part and parcel of those mighty influences—intellectual, moral, spiritual—which at once expressed and molded the religious life and thought of this great epoch in English history. It was neither silent nor inactive on the most important questions and measures of the time. Never more alive and vigorous, never more enlightened and cultured, never more thoughtful and trained for service, never more courageous and resolute, never more intensely devoted to its task, the British pulpit showed itself strong, earnest, capable, practical. Its almost infinite variety still impresses the student of its literature, as it must have done the observers and participants of its manifold activity. This great variety, shown in every aspect of preaching—content, form, quality, effect—makes general characterization both difficult and to some extent misleading, but a few salient general features may be remarked.

The apologetic and polemic element of preaching is well to the fore in the English sermons of the end of the nineteenth century. Yet there is a difference of tone and temper. So far as attack and defense toward hostile forces are concerned, there is a fine combination of caution and strength in most of the sermons of this character. Some denunciation and exuberant rhetoric may occasionally be found, and some unfitness of preparation and spirit for suitable encounter with the foe may show itself here and there, but, on the whole, there is marked candor and ability in dealing with the opponents of Christianity. Inside the Christian circle, too, there is less of sectarianism and bitterness in the warfare of parties and denominations. Preachers of the various divisions of Christianity came to deplore those divisions and to moderate the sharp tone in which they expressed their sentiments toward their brethren of different creeds from their own. As regards the Biblical content of sermons the modern English discourse is more exegetical and expository, less topical and discursive, than in former times. Yet this remark is subject to some qualification for individual preachers, though true on the whole. As has already been noticed, the sermons are very practical in aim and more popular in style than in the earlier and even the middle periods of the century. Robert Hall and Henry Melvill would not have appealed to audiences in the last third of the century as they did to the people of their own times. While the address of the pulpit is thus more familiar, direct, short, simple, and practical, its diction is not on the whole undignified or slovenly. There is a strain of fine culture in it which appeals to literary taste as well as to modern habits of thought and expression. Yet by no means may these general words of approval be taken as denying faults of spirit, content style and taste, or weaknesses such as must be allowed for as corresponding to many of the virtues noted.

But it is time to pass on to the study of the various groups and individual representatives of the British preaching of the epoch under review. And in such study we have again to remark that, leaving out a few commanding figures who appear in any survey of the leading preachers of the age, the bewildering number of men of the second and lower ranks makes it possible to select only a few representatives. Others equally worthy must be left out; and the fair-minded reader will not need to be asked to make still further allowances for the opportunities and likings of the student who can only describe and pass judgment on those who have in various ways come under his notice, without pretense of exhaustive research in a field practically boundless.

Among Roman Catholics, Walsh, Manning, and Newman, mentioned in the last section, were still at work as preachers; and to these we may add Father Harper, who preached a series of rather philosophical discourses endeavoring to adjust Catholic theology to modern conditions of thought; and Father Bernard Vaughan (a kinsman of the archbishop), who, a little after our period (1906-07), preached in London a series of rather scathing and sensational sermons on current social sins,[74] which attracted great crowds and were the talk of the town for a season. The sermons are not deep in thought, and are rather wordy and rhetorical in style, but they show considerable knowledge of the subject (one wonders how obtained), good imaginative and invective powers, with wholesome warnings and appeals.

In the Church of England, as we have seen, the former distinctions remain, but it is not always easy to classify individual preachers; but in a general way, some more clearly, some less, they may be grouped as before. Beginning with the Low Church group, we find one of the chief among them to be John Charles Ryle (1816-1900).[75] He was the son of a banker in Macclesfield, where he was born, educated, and for a time engaged in business. He took his course at Oxford, and was ordained in 1841. He filled several unimportant churches, and then was made honorary dean of Norwich, in 1871. In 1880 he was appointed bishop of Liverpool, a newly formed diocese, and filled with marked industry and fidelity his responsible office to the end of his useful life. Bishop Ryle wrote a good many tracts, pamphlets, and short books on a number of different questions. One of his most useful books, to which frequent reference has been made in this volume, is his *Christian Leaders of the Last Century.* Besides that, he published a number of sermons and other devotional works. He was one of the leaders of the Low Church party, thoroughly evangelical in doctrine, and greatly influential. As a preacher Bishop Ryle was not distinguished for remarkable powers in any direction. He was a safe, sensible, earnest, and cultivated man, but with no special gift of genius or

[74]*The Sins of Society,* sermons by Father Bernard Vaughan, S. J., London, 1908.

[75]*Expository Thoughts on the Gospel,* New York, 1866; *Boys and Girls Playing,* and other sermons to children, N. Y., 1881; Sketch and sermon in *Anglican Pulpit of To-day* (anon), London, 1885—a good and useful collection, hereafter referred to as *APT.*

oratory. His thought moved in customary evangelical grooves, but with ease and force. His style is simple and sweet, not marked by high eloquence, but a purity and loftiness of tone which comports well with his mental and spiritual qualities.

Far more eloquent than Ryle was the distinguished bishop and archbishop, William Connor Magee (1821-1891).[76] He was the son of an Irish clergyman of the Anglican Establishment, and grandson of Dr. William Magee, archbishop of Dublin, and author of a once notable work on the Atonement. Magee was educated at Trinity College, Dublin, and after ordination filled several posts in Ireland, but was called to England and rapidly rose in popularity and power. He was for a time rector at Bath, and in 1856 went to London as incumbent of Quebec Chapel. From 1860-1868 he returned to Ireland, where he filled several important appointments, and whence he was called, in 1868, to be bishop of Peterborough. He had a seat in the House of Lords just in time to make a great and famous speech against the disestablishment of the Irish Church. This great deliverance established his fame as an orator of the first rank. Though he did not carry his point, his speech was commonly conceded to be the ablest on that side of the question. He was an extemporaneous speaker, gifted with the fire and eloquence of his race. His published sermons and addresses naturally do not indicate the height of his powers, but they suggest what he was. A few months before his death, in 1891, Bishop Magee was raised to the archbishopric of York, but did not long survive the receiving of this high honor. Magee was noted for his genial wit, which sometimes passed into sarcasm. His thinking was clear and forcible, though not great. His style is flowing and easy, oftentimes rising into eloquence. He was evangelical in sentiment, and very highly regarded among his countrymen. Liddon has spoken of Magee as the greatest orator of his time. By many he was considered as second only to Gladstone or John Bright. Besides his sermons, he published some ad-

[76]See *Our Bishops and Deans,* Vol. II, p. 139 ff.; *Christ the Light of All Scripture and Other Sermons,* Lond., 1892; sketch and sermon in *APT;* Brastow, *MP,* p. 210; *WGS,* VII, p. 1.

dresses and two lectures on preaching, in which he defended the extemporaneous method of delivery, but insisted on earnest preparation, both general and special. This theory unfolds his own practice. Like many preachers of this kind, the impression of his actual work is far greater than that of his published sermons, though these are marked by sound thinking, earnest purpose, a clear order and a pleasing style.

William Boyd Carpenter (1841-),[77] one of the liberal evangelicals in the latter part of the century, was graduated from Cambridge with honor in 1864. He held several places in London, and attained rapid success and reputation as a preacher. In 1882 he was made canon of Windsor, and in 1885 bishop of Ripon. He discharged his duties with great acceptance, and besides his popular sermons, he wrote some valuable articles on distinguished preachers of past ages and a judicious treatise on preaching. He gave the Hulsean Lectures at Cambridge in 1878, and the Bampton Lectures at Oxford in 1887. His sermons were usually delivered without notes and in a very effective manner. His published discourses are largely expository in treatment and lay emphasis upon the evangelical doctrines, especially upon the presence and power of the Holy Spirit. Besides his more notable sermons and lectures, Dr. Carpenter published a very pleasing set of addresses to children.

Among the High Churchmen of this period we may first mention Edward Meyrick Goulbourn (1818-1897).[78] He was a native of London, educated at Eton and Oxford, where he became a Fellow of Merton College in 1841. In 1850 he followed Tait as Head Master at Rugby, holding the place for eight years. He then became vicar of St. John's Church, Paddington, London, where his preaching became very acceptable. In addition to his scholarship and highly trained mind, he had a pleasing delivery and a very winsome style. In 1866 he was made dean of Norwich, but retired in 1889, spend-

[77]*Permanent Elements of Religion* (Bamp. Lec.), London, 1889; *Truth in Tale* (to children), London, 1885; Brastow, p. 212; *APT*, ser. XV.

[78]See *OBD*, II, p. 295 ff.; sketch and sermon in *APT*; *Thoughts on Personal Religion*, Am. ed., N. Y., 1864.

ing the evening of his days at Tunbridge Wells. Among his numerous sermons and other devotional writings, his best known volume is *Thoughts on Personal Religion,* published in 1862, really a series of sermons. These admirable devotional discourses are distinguished by delicacy and elevation of thought, deep piety, and an easy, delightful style. This well-known classic of devotional literature has fed the spiritual life of thousands of readers.

The most celebrated High Church divine of this period was Henry Parry Liddon (1829-1890).[79] The English mind, language, and culture at their best in various epochs have made notable contributions to the literature of every department of human thought. The pulpit of the Anglican Church has richly shared this wealth of intellectual power. Our own age has shown no exception in this regard, and among the foremost of modern naturally gifted and highly cultivated English divines easily stands H. P. Liddon. He was a son of Captain Liddon, of the Royal Navy, and was named Henry Parry in honor of the great Arctic explorer. He was born at North Stoneham, Hampshire, the eldest of ten children. His parents moved to Devonshire, where he received his early schooling, and was a playful but high-minded boy. He attended the famous King's College school in London for two years, and entered Christ Church College, Oxford, in 1847, where he took his degree with distinction in three years. He had already been inclined to High Church principles, and after Newman's defection he was identified with the High Church party and was a stanch supporter of Pusey. He obtained a theological scholarship in 1851, and soon after that was ordained. For several years (1854-59) he was vice-principal of Cuddesdon College. Here he taught young preachers, and had great influence upon his pupils, but his pronounced High Church opinions were not altogether acceptable to the authorities and led to his retirement. Returning to Oxford, he became vice-principal of St. Edmund's Hall,

[79] *University Sermons* (first issued under title, *Some Words for God*) ed., London, 1869; 4 vols. of sermons on the Church festivals; *Sermons on Old Testament Subjects,* London, 1891; etc.; *WGS,* VII, p. 123; art. by Scott-Holland in *DNB;* account in Donaldson's *Five Great Oxford Leaders;* OBD, II, p. 153 ff.; Wilkinson, p. 217; Brastow, *MP,* p. 202.

where he was greatly active with Pusey and others in promoting High Church sentiments. He held various preaching appointments during these years, and was already recognized as a great power in the pulpit. In 1866 Liddon was chosen to take the place of another man without the usual time for preparation as Bampton Lecturer. The subject of his lectures was *The Divinity of Christ.* This work has been recognized as one of the completest and most satisfactory discussions of that subject in modern times. Its thorough conviction, ample learning, acute and profound reasoning, and eloquent style have given it a high and permanent place among the great theological treatises in the English tongue. Certainly one sees and feels various defects, both in the thinking and the expression, but, allowing for these, the treatise remains an acknowledged masterpiece. In 1870 Liddon was made Ireland Professor of Exegesis at Oxford, and also a canon of St. Paul's Cathedral, where he took his turn as preacher twice a year and drew great crowds. This double service suited Liddon exactly. He was a competent theological scholar, a brilliant and kindling teacher, and a preacher of renowned ability. He retained his canonship at St. Paul's for twenty years, declining higher honors, but resigned his professorship in 1882, on the death of his friend Pusey, whose life he desired to write. His health began to fail in his later years, and he took a tour abroad in 1885. Several bishoprics were offered him, but he declined. He died suddenly, September 9, 1890. Most appropriately, he lies buried in the crypt chapel at St. Paul's. On his tomb there is a recumbent figure of him well presenting his refined and noble face.

Liddon was one of the recognized leaders in the High Church party, the lifelong friend and admirer of Pusey. In the troubles over ritualism in the case of Mr. Mackonochie, Liddon sympathized with his friend, but counseled moderation. On the other hand, he became involved in a controversy with Capel, a Catholic priest, who very cleverly maintained that the ritualistic party in the English Church was so near to Rome that they had as well follow Newman and come in. Liddon strongly defended himself and, in general, the Puseyite position.

He had no sympathy with Broad Church views, and several times refused to preach at Westminster Abbey on Stanley's invitation, because that eminent Broad Churchman insisted on inviting to preach there such men as Maurice and even Colenso, the heretical bishop of Natal. The correspondence between Liddon and Stanley is interesting, as showing how mutual respect and even admiration may exist between men of such divergent views and also how frank and yet polite each could be. It is needless to say that Liddon was squarely opposed to the rationalistic teachings of the modern German criticism. Some one has said "that his typical abhorrence was a misty Teutonism." Canon Scott-Holland, in his delightful article in the *Dictionary of National Biography,* says: "In private life Liddon's companionship was an uncomparable and unfailing delight. . . . Intensely domestic and lovable and unaffected by any worldly ambition, he was totally free from the peculiar moral weakness to which a great popular preacher is proverbially liable. His most striking characteristics were a passionate chivalry, a burning courage, and a delicious humor." And Archdeacon Farrar, in his chatty book on *Men Whom I Have Known,* tells that he once heard an intelligent woman ask Liddon how he could keep from being self-conceited over his preaching; it was so good, and he was so much praised for it. His answer was to the effect that the awful responsibilities involved in the work were surely enough to counteract such feelings and keep a man humble. It was a frank and manly answer. He knew he had great gifts; he felt his responsibility for them. Though so well fitted for domestic life, Liddon was never married, but was much beloved in the families of his kindred, where he was a genial companion and a liberal giver.

The qualities and worth of Liddon's preaching are foreshown in his noble abilities, admirable culture, and great earnestness of conviction. It is needless to say that his sermons defend and expound pronounced High views of the church and its ordinances. His sermons show great elevation—mental, moral, spiritual. This loftiness is exemplified even in the details. The reader feels on every page that he is dealing with a great soul. Naturally, the sermons are marked by a clear and broad candor. There is no evasion of difficulties, but every disposition to treat objectors and their objections fairly. Liddon might be mistaken, but he could not be insincere. In stating objections to his own views, he endeavored to put them as plainly as he could, and then meet them with all his strength. And he was a man of might, capable, clear-headed, well-informed, logical, intense. To these splendid qualities were added the charm of a handsome face, a graceful action, and ringing voice, although he read his sermons. Magnetic power went forth from him and mastered his audiences. His sermons were usually very long, but the delighted listener cared not to note the time. Thousands gathered at St. Paul's Cathedral when he was announced to preach, and though from many points in that vast building hearing was difficult, in some places almost impossible, the listeners strained their attention to catch his eloquent words. As to the permanence of Liddon's influence there are doubtless some drawbacks. Both the length and loftiness of his discourses, their lack of popularity and ease, their extreme High Church opinions, with opposition to modern criticism, all count against the permanence of Liddon's influence as a preacher. But on the other hand, the splendid qualities of his style, the sincerity of his conviction, and the masterful grasp and power of his mind will cause him to be read as one among the models of nineteenth century Anglican preaching.

The High Church group, along with and after Liddon, who is its highest pulpit representative, contains an unusually large number of cultivated, thoughtful, spiritual, and effective preachers. What is remarkable about this group is that, including so many eminent scholars and men of books, it should also exhibit so remarkable a degree of success in the pulpit. All the men now to be named, and some others with them, are worthy of careful study and should receive, if it were possible, more extended biographical and critical notice than our present limits permit. Perhaps the most thoughtful and profound of the group was James Bowling Mozley (1813-1878),[80] a Lincolnshire man, and educated at Oxford.

[80]Art. in *DNB; Sermons Preached Before the University of Oxford,* etc., New York, 1876; Brastow, *Rep. Mod. Pr.,* p. 309 ff. —a good study; *WGS,* Vol. V, p. 207 ff.

He was a thoughtful student and received many honors. He was a student of Oriel, and a Fellow of Magdalen College. He remained with the Pusey group when Newman went over to Rome. He filled some places as a preacher, being made canon of Christ Church and University preacher. In 1865 he delivered the Bampton Lectures on miracles, one of the most masterly discussions of that difficult subject. Canon Mozley published a number of sermons, particularly a volume called *University Sermons.* They are marked by profound thought, great candor, and, considering their depth, an unusually clear style. One of these on *The Reversal of Human Judgment* has been pronounced by some critics as the most thoughtful of modern sermons; and Mozley has well been called "the Butler of the nineteenth century." The comparison is apt, but Mozley is far superior to Butler in literary art.

Richard W. Church,[81] born at Lisbon, spent much of his early life in Italy, but was educated at Oxford, and a brilliant student. He is notable as the historian of the Oxford movement, was preacher at St. Mary's, and later dean of St. Paul's. Dean Church was a very thoughtful and useful preacher and writer on a variety of subjects.

Joseph Barber Lightfoot (1828-1879)[82] is usually reckoned among the High Churchmen notwithstanding his liberal views of the Episcopate. He was born at Liverpool, and educated at Cambridge. He was the most eminent modern English scholar in the department of patristic literature. Owing to his liberal views, preferment came rather slowly, but he was finally made bishop of Durham. He was active and earnest as a bishop, taking part in moral reforms, an earnest advocate of total abstinence, and sympathetic with the work of the Salvation Army. His sermons are not overburdened with scholarship, but are practical and clear. The sermon

[81]Sketch and sermon in *APT;* Brastow, *Mod. Pul.,* p. 199; *The Gifts of Civilization and Other Lectures and Sermons,* London, 1880.

[82]Brastow, *op. cit.,* p. 198; *The Contemporary Pulpit Library, Bishop Lightfoot* (anon.), with preface by Westcott, London, 1894; *Sermons by Bishop Lightfoot,* London and New York, 1890 (reported).

delivered on his consecration as bishop of Durham is on *The Vision of God* (Rev. 22:4). After a neat allusion to Butler as the greatest of the bishops of Durham, he proceeds to discuss his theme, considering the threefold vision of Righteousness, Grace, and Glory. The sermon is admirable in spirit, excellent in style, and effective in presentation. Here also should be named another great Cambridge scholar and the successor to Lightfoot in the bishopric of Durham, the distinguished Cambridge graduate and New Testament scholar, Brooke Foss Westcott (1825-1901).[83] Westcott served, after his graduation, as Assistant Master at Harrow, as canon of Peterborough, Professor of Theology at Cambridge, and canon of Westminster. In addition to his eminent service as a scholar and teacher, he was a preacher of considerable merit, taking active part in practical affairs. He published a volume of very judicious and strong sermons on the *Social Aspects of Christianity,* as well as sermons of a more directly spiritual kind. Another famous Cambridge scholar and prelate was Edward White Benson (1829-1901),[84] who was a schoolfellow of Lightfoot and Westcott, was Assistant Master at Rugby, and filled various offices till his appointment as archbishop of Canterbury, in 1884. He scarcely ranks so high in the pulpit as others of this group, but is worthy of note among them.

Recurring to the Oxford group,[85] we find among these the distinguished historical scholar, canon, and later bishop, William Stubbs (1825-1901), long professor at Oxford, and sometime canon of St. Paul's. He was made bishop of Chester in 1884. His qualities as a preacher appear well in a sermon on humility, which is a simple, manly, spiritual plea for this virtue, well illustrated by various examples. Later distinguished members of this group are Henry Scott-Holland (1847-), educated

[83]*Life and Letters,* by his son, 2 vols., London, 1903; *APT,* sketch and sermon; *Social Aspects of Christianity,* London, 1887; *The Incarnation and the Common Life* (various discourses), Lond., 1893; *The Victory of the Cross* (sermons), London, 1888.

[84]Sketch and sermon in *APT,* and a vol. of sermons in *Preachers of the Age,* London and New York, 1892.

[85]Sketches and sermons in *APT,* and notices in Brastow, *op. cit.;* brief notices in Camden-Pratt's *People of the Period,* etc.

at Eton and Oxford. He filled various offices, and became canon of St. Paul's in 1884. He took great interest in social questions, published some volumes of sermons, and contributed some of the essays to *Lux Mundi.* With him and still living should be named Charles Gore, who was also an eminent scholar at Balliol College, Oxford, Fellow of Trinity, President of Cuddesdon College, select preacher at Oxford, Bampton Lecturer, canon of Westminster, and bishop of Birmingham. Bishop Gore's numerous sermons and writings ally him distinctly with the High Church party, but clearly under the movement of the modern spirit. In intellect and culture he ranks among the leaders of his Church. Here also should be placed Canon W. J. Knox-Little,[86] who was born in Ireland, and educated at Cambridge, was rector at St. Albans, and later canon of Worcester, and preacher at St. Paul's, where, even during the week-days, great crowds were drawn to hear his earnest preaching. Among his sermons is a notable one on *Thirst Satisfied* (Ps. 42:3), which shows the inadequacy of human and earthly things to satisfy the soul. It should find its true fullness in God through Christ. This familiar thought is presented to a modern audience in an eminently modern and effective way.

Passing now to the Broad Church group of modern English preachers, the first name which occurs among them is that of the admired and distinguished Arthur Penrhyn Stanley (1815-1881).[87] This elegant scholar, accomplished gentleman, liberal-minded prelate was born in Cheshire, the second son of Edward Stanley, bishop of Norwich. His father's mother was an Owen of Penrhyn, Wales, whence his middle name and his prized Welsh blood. His family was highly connected, and he married the daughter of an earl. All that English culture in school and society offered was absorbed by him. A brilliant student at Rugby under Arnold, and afterwards at Oxford, he laid broad the foundations of his

[86]*The Journey of Life,* vol. of sermons in *Great Preachers of the Age* series, London and New York, 1892.

[87]*Life and Letters of A. P. Stanley,* by R. E. Prothero, 2 vols., London and New York, 1894; *Sermons in the East* (preached before the then Prince of Wales, Edward VII, during his tour in the East), New York, 1864; sermon in *WGS,* VI, p. 53.

culture. Honors and promotions in the Church rapidly followed his ordination. He was honorary chaplain to the queen, often preached at Oxford, but took most pride in that post which he filled with such distinction, and by which he is best known, dean of Westminster Abbey. It was here that he did the principal work of his life. Besides his *Life of Arnold* (a masterpiece of biography), his *Lectures on the Jewish Church* (influenced chiefly by Ewald), his charming descriptive work on *Sinai and Palestine,* and other notable writings, he published a number of volumes of sermons. These are not distinguished by oratorical gifts, but generally by the three excellent qualities of clearness of thought, breadth of mind and sympathy, and a very agreeable and forcible style. Some of his memorial sermons especially show all these traits. Notable among them, one on Thomas Carlyle.

Another famous dean of Westminster was the versatile, brilliant, intense, and popular Frederic William Farrar (1831-1903).[88] He was born in India, where his pious father was chaplain at Bombay. He was educated at King William's College, Isle of Man, and at King's College, in London, where he studied under Maurice and Plumptre. Later he studied at Trinity College, Cambridge, where he lived hard and supported himself. After graduation, he served as teacher, first at Marlborough, and then at Harrow; later at Marlborough again. All the while he was preaching to his boys, as well as at other places, and engaged in some of those numerous theological writings by which he has become distinguished. In 1876 he was appointed by Mr. Disraeli canon of Westminster and rector of St. Margaret's adjoining. His preaching and other public and parochial services attracted great throngs to St. Margaret's. In 1883 he was made archdeacon of Westminster, an office which he filled with distinction for a number of years. At last, in 1895, he was appointed by Lord Rosebery dean of Canterbury, where his labors were less exacting. He

[88]*Life,* by his son, R. A. Farrar, London and New York, 1904; numerous writings and sermons, particularly the vols. on *The Silence and Voices of God,* N. Y., 1877, *Eternal Hope; The Fall of Man,* Lond., 1893, and *Sermons on the Lord's Prayer,* New York, 1893. *WGS,* VII, p. 229.

took great interest in this great old cathedral, and here peacefully ended his busy days. As a preacher Dr. Farrar was very remarkable. He did not carefully polish his sermons; they often showed hasty preparation and a too exuberant rhetorical style. He was inclined to vehemence and extreme statements, but he had a well-stored mind, an ardent temperament, and retentive memory, was apt in quotation and illustration, and powerful in appeal. These qualities, notwithstanding his faults, give him a secure place among the most important and influential preachers of his day.

Later representatives of the Broad Church group included many notable men, among whom was Frederick Temple (1821-1902).[89] He was a distinguished graduate of Oxford, and became Head Master at Rugby, then bishop of Exeter in 1869, bishop of London in 1885, and finally archbishop of Canterbury after Dr. Tait. His liberalism provoked some opposition to these various promotions. Dr. Temple was a man of high character and a strong, pleasing preacher, as several of his sermons which have been read show; yet he would not rank among the greater preachers of the age. Mention should also be made of J. M. Wilson, who also was first distinguished at college and as a teacher at Rugby, and then at Clifton College. He published a number of sermons and other discourses, and gave lectures on pastoral theology at Cambridge. The sermons indicate great breadth of view, with simplicity and clearness of expression.

Toward the close of the century there were a number of able and distinguished Anglican preachers, some of whom are still living, and whom it is not worth while to classify according to their church affinities. These are all animated by the modern spirit to a greater or less extent in its three elements of criticism, socialism, and mysticism. A solid scholar and thoughtful preacher is J. E. C. Welldon, educated at Cambridge, long time Master of Harrow, translator of Aristotle's *Rhetoric.* Appointed bishop of Calcutta, he resided for awhile in India, but ill-health enforced his return. He has preached

[89]For Temple and most of the following such notices and sermons as are to be found in *APT,* Pratt's *People of the Period,* Brastow, etc.; Temple's *Rugby Sermons,* 3 vols., London, 1870-76.

in recent years as a canon of Westminster Abbey and dean of Manchester. A manly and excellent series of discourses to boys, delivered at Harrow and later published, are noted for simplicity, directness, and strength. It is one of the writer's most pleasant recollections to have heard two sermons from Bishop Welldon at Westminster Abbey in the summer of 1903. A large man, with no grace of delivery or charm of voice, he yet impressed the hearers by the quiet earnestness of his manner, the strength and candor of his thought, the straightforward directness of his style, and the evident spirituality of his mind.

Quite different from Welldon is Canon Hensley Henson, preacher at St. Margaret's. Somewhat radical, gifted with a brilliant style, with an eager and intense spirit, he has attracted large audiences, and has taken some delight in saying unexpected things. Canon Henson was born in 1863 in Kent, received his university education at Oxford, where he also was Fellow of All Souls, and lectured on English Church history in 1886. He filled various appointments in the Church, and was select preacher at Oxford on several occasions. Small in stature, and apparently of feeble constitution, with a thin voice, he has not much of a presence to aid the effect of his brilliant and eloquent discourse, but there is a flashing eye and a magnetism of manner which holds the attention, though he reads closely. There was also Alfred Ainger, Master of the Temple, who was born in London in 1837, and trained at King's College and at Cambridge. His afternoon services as preacher at the Temple attracted large audiences, and besides he has greatly distinguished himself as a literary critic. Distinguished leaders in the newer mysticism are Bishop H. C. G. Moule, of Durham, and Prebendary Webb-Peploe, of London, who, besides their official work, have preached with great acceptance, and published books bearing upon the development of the spiritual life. Altogether, the Anglican pulpit at the turn of the century maintained its high plane of cultivated intellectual power, of profound interest in the moral welfare of society, and in thoughtful appeal to the higher spiritual life.

This closing period of the century also shows among

the various Dissenting bodies a large number of important preachers, and though there are a few only who stand out as do Parker and Maclaren above all the rest, those who come next to the masters are neither few nor weak. The Congregationalists are well represented by a considerable array of worthy names, among whom we may take first that of the honored and admired pastor of the Surrey Chapel in London, Christopher Newman Hall (1816-1902).[90] He was born at Maidstone, Kent, his father being proprietor of a newspaper there. Hall was educated at various preparatory schools, and took some honors later at the University of London. He early entered the Congregational ministry, and filled one important place—at Hull—before coming to the chapel made famous by Rowland Hill in a previous generation. For some years he ministered at this historic place, but it began to prove unsuitable for the congregation, and the new Christ Church Chapel, on Westminster Bridge Road, still on the Surrey side of the Thames, was erected. Here Hall preached to the end of his life. He published many sermons and several notable tracts, of which one, *Come to Jesus,* attained a remarkable circulation in many different languages. Hall's sermons are conservatively evangelical, Scriptural, edifying. They breathe an earnest piety and concern for the spiritual good of the hearer, are well analyzed, and couched in a smooth and easy style, with good illustration and warm appeal.

Greater than Newman Hall in intellectual force, though less than he in emotional power, was the strong man and thinker, Robert William Dale (1829-1895),[91] the colleague and then successor of J. A. James at Carr's Lane Chapel, in Birmingham. Dale was born in London, the son of a small tradesman, not especially successful in business, and of a vigorous but anxious mother. The parents were members of the Tabernacle Church at Moorfields. The boy got some primary education in various London schools, and assisted awhile at one of

[90] See Camden-Pratt's *People of the Period;* Fish, *XIX Cent.,* p. 830; *WGS,* VI, p. 85; *Sermons* (with a sketch of Surrey Chapel, etc.), London and New York, 1868.

[91] *Life,* by his son, A. W. W. Dale, London, 1898; numerous writings; *Sermons on the Ten Commandments,* London, 1895; *WGS,* VII, p. 103.

them as teacher. More teaching and reading went on with the years, some youthful writing, some special preparation at a Congregational college for ministers, then the association, first as assistant, and then as colleague, and then as successor to James at Carr's Lane; and the work of a long and busy and useful life. Pastor, publicist, writer, theologian, lecturer, preacher—all in one active, strong, intellectual, conscientious, faithful man. Who can estimate the value of a life like this? And Dale's was a profoundly worthy life. As preacher he was patient and thorough in thought, careful in interpretation, clear and strong in style. He felt himself, and others also perceived, that he emphasized the intellectual aspects of truth rather to the hurt of the emotional and applicatory; but he was deeply in earnest to convince and so persuade men of the essential verities of the Christian faith, and to make these fruitful in life.

The greatest figure, however, among the Congregationalists of the period is confessedly that of the rugged, powerful, world-famous Joseph Parker (1830-1902).[92] In Parker, as in a number of other preachers who have mightily moved the men of their times, we have a conspicuous instance of what is currently but very inaccurately called the self-made man. He owed little to his origin and little to his opportunities for technical education, but by the sheer force of a mighty will and a powerful native intellect, he rose from humble surroundings and through many difficulties to a commanding position among the great preachers of the world. Joseph Parker was born at Hexham, in Northumberland. His father was a stonemason and a rugged, hardworking man; his mother a tender, loving woman, whose gentle nature and influence were not lost upon her somewhat rough but affectionate son. Both parents were earnest Christians and Congregationalists. The boy grew up full of force and self-assertion, a leader in play, somewhat overbearing, but courageous and resolute. He got

[92]*Life,* by Wm. Adamson, D. D., London and New York, 1903; numerous writings; sermons in many volumes and editions, as, *The City Temple Pulpit,* New York, 1882; *Sermons and Notes,* 2 vols., New York, 1882; *These Sayings of Mine,* New York, 1881; *The People's Bible* (notes of sermons on the whole Scripture), 27 vols., New York, 1886 and on; *WGS,* VII, p. 199.

common school education in his youth, but never had any college or university training. From his boyhood he was inclined to religion, largely under the influence of his pious mother. In later life he writes: "I remember the Sunday night when, walking with my father and a most intelligent Sunday school teacher, I declared my love to Christ and asked Him to take my child-heart into His own gracious keeping. The whole scene is ever before me. The two men, father and teacher, explained to me what they knew of the power and grace of Christ, and by many loving words they tempted my tongue into the first audible expression of thought and feeling. It was a summer evening, according to the reckoning of the calendar, but according to a higher calendar, it was in very deed a Sunday morning through whose white light and emblematic dew and stir of awakening life I saw the gates of the Kingdom and the face of the King." Soon after Joseph joined the church a difference arose in the congregation, and he with his parents separated for a time from their old church and attended a Methodist congregation. Later, however, they returned, and even during their temporary separation Joseph taught a Sunday school class in the Congregational church. This Sunday school teaching and some speaking showed his dawning talent and led him into the ministry. He was recognized as a youthful local preacher and preached his first sermon when a boy of eighteen, standing on the cross beams of a saw-pit in the open air. The sermon was naturally a crude affair, but it was delivered with characteristic conviction and energy. Writing of it years later, he says, "Some persons are kind enough to think that even now I am not wholly destitute of energy, but I can assure them that at eighteen volcanoes, tornadoes, whirlwinds, and other energetics cut a very secondary figure when I was on the saw-pit."

He could not be satisfied to carry on his father's work, and determined definitely to enter the ministry. Returning to the Congregational body, he married a fine, good girl, and took his first pastorate at Banbury, on a salary of about $600 a year. The church was greatly run down, but under his vigorous, even if inexperienced, ministry it prospered greatly and was built up into a comparatively strong congregation. The chapel proved too small, and a larger one was built at considerable expense. This, too, soon overflowed. Meanwhile the young preacher was studying, writing, thinking, and growing, both in pulpit power and the administration of affairs. Many calls to other places came, but he refused them, until at last after some hesitation he felt constrained to accept charge of the Cavendish Street Church (Congregational) in Manchester. Here he wrought with growing power for eleven years (1858-1869). The promise of his earlier ministry was amply redeemed. In the great manufacturing town congregations grew, the church was developed in all activities, and the powerful influence of Parker's strong and vigorous ministry was felt throughout the city. His fondness for the pen continued, and a number of writings flowed from his busy brain. Here, however, his first great sorrow came upon him in the loss of his first wife. This was in 1863. In 1869 came an urgent call to take charge of an old but now declining church in London. It was in that street called The Poultry in the City.

After much consideration Parker decided to accept the call, on the condition that a new site and new building should as soon as possible take the place of the old. The old location was sold, and finally the renowned City Temple was built near Holborn Viaduct. This remained the scene of his great ministry to the end of his life. The City Temple was opened in 1874. Parker was not, strictly speaking, a great pastor, not giving his time much to visiting, but, like Spurgeon, he was a masterful leader. His fondness for writing never forsook him. A great many books have come from his prolific pen which it is not necessary here to describe. One of the most interesting of these was a series of lectures which he gave early in his London life to students for the ministry. It bears the title *Ad Clerum,* and is a striking and sensible treatise, derived largely from his own experience, upon the art of preaching. How he found time to write so much along with his administrative cares and the preparation of his remarkable sermons is to be explained by his boundless energy and the native gifts of his mind. In all his work the pulpit was preeminent. He was a master of assemblies, and his preaching was abundantly fruitful in the lives and thoughts of his hearers. His second marriage, shortly before coming to London, with Miss Emma Common, proved a very happy and helpful one. She was a winsome and active woman, and identified in many ways with his work. Though fond of children among his kindred and congregation, he was never blessed with them in his own home. His long and active ministry in London was crowded with the varying details of a busy city pastor's life. He lived at Hampstead a number of years, coming into the city for his church work. He paid a visit to America, where he was warmly received, and preached in Plymouth Church. He was spoken of as successor to Henry Ward Beecher, whom he greatly admired, but naturally preferred to remain in London. His services were in much request in England and Scotland, and during the week he would often accept appointments for services in other places. His Thursday noon addresses attracted large congregations to the Temple, and were attended by numbers of visitors from other countries. Through pen and pulpit and personal influence, Joseph Parker rounded out a life of eminent service, passing away in November, 1902.

In character Parker combined the elements of his origin and up-bringing. The sturdy and somewhat rough and overbearing nature of his Northern ancestry never forsook him, but the winsome gentleness derived from his mother found place alongside of his outward harshness. He was a true friend, a loving husband, and always fond of children, with whom he could be as sportive and gentle as he was often stern and brusque with men. Perhaps his greatest fault was his undisguised self-conceit, which often appears in men who are trained in the rough school of experience as he was. As a preacher Parker was gifted with many of the greatest qualities. Depth of conviction, intensity of feeling, energy of utterance were his. His thought showed a fine combination of conservatism with independence. In the main, he held, but not slavishly, the essential evangelical doctrines. His strong common sense kept him from vagaries, while his sturdy independence allowed no man to do his thinking for him. As a student and expositor of the Bible he was great. He loved to set forth the truth in continuous exposition. His *Peoples' Bible* is the fruit, both of his textual studies and his homiletic habits. Many volumes of expository sermons came from his study, but he was successful also in topical preaching, and some of his addresses were sublime and powerful. He could be terrible in refutation and invective. While not a deep philosopher, he had an essentially masculine mind, and he thought thoroughly into his subjects. His imagination was rich, soaring, but for the most part kept in control and not betrayed into false excess. His diction was varied, ranging from the familiar and conversational to the impressive and elaborate. Illustration, argument, appeal, all glowed in the manner of his treatment. He knew men and his times, their needs, and the power of the gospel. It was his task and his delight to apply the divine remedy in thought, feeling, and purpose to the perennial needs of men as realized in his own generation.

A suggestion, at least, of Parker's manner in his early prime may be found in the following extracts from a striking and original sermon on *The Future Considered as Known and as Unknown.*[93] Selecting two texts which present this double aspect of his theme, he states the first thought as follows: "Let me suggest in the first place that we owe a great deal, both in the way of stimulus and in the way of education, to the very mysteriousness of the future. What poetry is there in a straight line? What enjoyment is there in a road that is never bent into curves or broken into undulations? It is expectancy, call it hope or fear, that gives life a rare interest; hope itself sometimes brings with it a sting of pain, a fear now and again brings with it even something of weird pleasure. Hope turns the future into a banqueting house. Ambition forecasts the future with great plans of attack and defense. Fear anticipates the future so as to get from the outlook restraint and discipline. Life that has no future would be but a flat surface, a stiff and cold monotony, a world without a

[93]Fish, *XIX Cent.*, p. 830.

firmament—a mere death's ground occupied by people not yet quite fit for burying! But with a future it is a hope, an inspiration, a sweet and gracious promise; it is, too, a terror, for we know not what is behind the cloud, nor can we say what foe or friend will face us at the very next corner! We live a good deal in our to-morrows, and thus we spend money which does not fairly belong to us; yet how poor we would be if we could not turn our imagination to some account, and mint our fancies into some little gold just to clink in our hands that we may scare our immediate poverty away! . . . The Past is a worn road; the Future is a world in which all the ways have yet to be made. I would bind you, then, to a general estimate of the future, as being, by the very fact of its being future, a high educational influence—an influence that holds you back like a bit in your foaming lips, and an influence that sends you forward with the hunger of a great hope, relieved by satisfactions which do but whet the desire they can not appease. Thank God that there is a future; that there are days afar off; that there are clouds floating in the distance, beautiful enough to be the vesture of angels, solemn enough to be the sheaths of lightning!" After discussing his theme, he closes with the thought of how the future, both as known and unknown, should lead us to trust in God, and concludes with this paragraph: "I will hide myself in the everlasting, and then the future will come upon me without fear or burdensomeness; even to-day I shall be master of to-morrow, and even death will be but a shadow on the sunny road that leads up to heavenly places. I would live as one who is called to immortality in Christ Jesus, and for whom all the future has been graciously arranged. I am no longer at the mercy of accident, casualty, misfortune; my King, my Redeemer, He whom my soul trusteth, has gone on before to prepare a place and time for me. So I will arise, and speed after Him with burning and thankful love, knowing that how devious soever the way, and how bleak and cross-cutting soever the wind, there is sweet home at the end, the gladness of which shall throw into oblivion all hardship and weariness. I do not ask to know the mere detail of the future. I know enough of time unborn to say unto the righteous, it shall be well with him; to say to the penitent at the cross that he shall share the Lord's paradise; to say to them who mourn, the days of your tears shall be ended, and the time of your joy shall be as a sea whose shore no man can find! Is it dark with thee, my friend? It has been quite as dark with myself, and yet I have seen light descending on the rugged hills, and making those hills as steps up to heaven. Art thou afraid of the coming days, lest they bring with them edged weapons, pain, grief, loss, friendlessness, and desolation? Put thy hand into the palm wounded for thee, the palm of the one Infinite Saviour. He knows all—He is the Treasurer of the future—the great dragon is tamed by the fire of his eye—and they who trust Him with all their love shall be set amidst the safety, the peace, and the glory of His eternal Zion."

Coming after these three mighty ones in the end of the nineteenth and passing over into the twentieth century we have a number of able and distinguished Congregational preachers who must regretfully be passed by with only brief mention. Robert F. Horton, pastor at Lyndhurst Road Chapel, Hampstead, ministers with fine mental and spiritual force to a large congregation, has written some notable books, published several volumes of sermons; and while somewhat "broad" in some of his views, presents the essence of the gospel in Christ and is a mystic of the modern school. Reginald J. Campbell, successor of the great Parker at the City Temple, London, began by exciting curiosity and hope; but has shown, both in his spoken and published utterances, a vagueness of thought and unreliableness of theology which have disappointed the judicious, though he has attracted a congregation of those to whom his breadth of sympathy, indefinite thought, and pleasing manner make appeal. C. Silvester Horne, pastor at the Tottenham Court Road Chapel, the historian and leader of his people, is also a preacher of acknowledged gifts and influence. G. Campbell Morgan, widely known on both sides of the Atlantic as a leader of the modern mystical school, a writer of delightful devotional works, and a vivid and judicious expounder of the Word, is also a preacher of wonderful gifts, holding and instructing large congregations with a magnetism and eloquence that need no other aids to make them impressive. P. T. Forsyth is the incisive professor and writer on subjects of the keenest modern interest in theology and preaching, and carries his fine gift of striking utterance and fresh thinking into his sermons. J. H. Jowett, sometime pastor at Carr's Lane Chapel, Birmingham, as the notable and worthy successor of James and Dale is now (1911) pastor of the Fifth Avenue Presbyterian Church, New York. His well-poised evangelical theology, modern culture, and fresh and virile thinking are aptly mated with a style of admirable finish, perfect transparency, and terse vigor. Jowett was regarded by not a few as being, after the death of Maclaren, the leading preacher of England.

The Methodists had a number of men of power in their pulpits in England at the close of the nineteenth century. Three stand out as specially distinguished. Hugh Price Hughes (1847-1902)[94] was born at Carmarthen, Wales, where his father, himself the son of a Methodist preacher, was a surgeon of excellent standing and character. Hugh received good early training and was the subject of conversion in his youth. Soon he began to exhort, and while away at college wrote to his father that he had decided to preach. The father was delighted, and Hugh received the necessary further training required for entrance into the Conference. He passed a very creditable examination for ordination, and was soon on the road to honors and usefulness in the great body of English Methodists with whom he had cast his lot instead of remaining in Wales. He followed the rounds of an itinerant minister in his church, serving with great success at some of the more important charges. He had a specially successful work at Oxford, where a great revival was due to his labors. Hughes took a deep interest from his early life in all the modern movements for social and industrial improvement. He was never a partisan in politics, but used his influence not in vain on moral questions when these arose. He was

[94]See Camden-Pratt, *People of the Period;* a sketch by "H. K.," London, 1903; and a volume of sermons mentioned in the text in the *Great Modern Preachers* series.

a fluent and brilliant speaker, not widely learned nor profoundly thoughtful, but strong, brave, intelligent, and earnest in advocacy of evangelical sentiments and high moral living. A volume of sermons from him on *The Ethical Teachings of Christianity* contains a series of short discourses which are clear and vigorous in thinking and expression. He does not escape some one-sidedness and dogmatism—does not always appear to have thought all around a subject before giving his positive opinion upon it. Yet he is popular and impressive, driving home the practical and ethical side of religion with force and spirit.

Mark Guy Pearse (b. 1842)[95] was born at Camborne, destined for the medical profession, but instead felt his call to be a Methodist preacher. He has filled positions of importance as preacher, leader, and occasional speaker in his own country, and has on several occasions visited the United States. On one of these visits the writer had an opportunity to hear a strong and spiritual sermon from him. His manner was somewhat dictatorial, but the substance and style of the discourse were both of high order. He also was much concerned in current moral reforms, and spoke on them with pungency and effect.

More classic and cultured than the two preceding is the keen and brilliant William L. Watkinson (b. 1838).[96] He is a native of Hull, where he received his early training. His sermons show an admirable culture, broad and deep, which is probably quite as much the fruit of years of eager reading as of academic foundations and impulses. Dr. Watkinson has filled many of the most important charges in his denomination, doing exceptionally fine work in a pastorate at Liverpool. He has also been editor of the leading Methodist journal, besides filling other posts out of the pulpit. On a visit (several years before this was written) to the United States, Dr. Watkinson came to several of the theological seminaries, including that of the Southern Baptists at Louisville, and

[95]Brief notice in Camden-Pratt; *Sermons for Children,* London, 1876, clear and sprightly talks.

[96]See *WGS,* VIII, p. 180; and the volumes of sermons mentioned in the text.

delivered courses of lectures to the students. These were marked by his well-known incisiveness of thought, aptness of illustration, wisdom of counsel, and beauty of style. Besides the lectures, he was heard with delight in the pulpit. Dr. Watkinson has no particular grace or impressiveness of manner or voice, but there is a charm about his look and easy utterance which goes well with the excellent qualities of his expression already indicated. Among his several volumes of sermons two have come under the writer's notice. The earlier of these, *The Blind Spot and Other Sermons,* contains discourses marked by those fine qualities of insight, style, and illustration which have already been pointed out; and the other, *The Supreme Conquest,* contains the title sermon and other discourses preached during the visit to America mentioned above. If anything, these enhance the impression of the venerable preacher's noble gifts. A deep spirituality, as well as the fine intellectual qualities of the true preacher of Christ, appears in all Dr. Watkinson's work.

The Presbyterians in England claim several preachers of merit during this period, among whom perhaps the best known was John Watson, of Liverpool (d. 1907), better known in literature by his pen-name of Ian Maclaren. Besides his stories and some theological writings, his sermons also have been widely read. He was a preacher of decidedly broad views, but was effective, and heard with interest. The distinguished editor of the *British Weekly,* Sir W. Robertson Nicoll, eminent as literary critic, man of learning, brilliant theological writer and apologist, is also a preacher of recognized ability and power. He was born in Scotland, and served various churches there before coming to England. A volume of his published sermons, *The Lamp of Sacrifice,* shows clear and strong thinking, evangelical views, yet responsive to the modern spirit, and a fine, strong, appealing style.

In Scotland the number of well trained and effective preachers was very great. Modern thought, both in philosophy and Biblical criticism, made great inroads upon evangelical traditions in the Scottish pulpit. A volume of *Scotch Sermons,* to which a number of leading preachers contributed, showed wide departures from the traditional faith; and the controversy over Professor W. Robertson Smith made a sharp issue between the orthodox and progressive element. Preaching was also affected by the union of the United Presbyterians and Free Churches with the unhappy divisions and litigations which followed.

Among the preachers brief mention should be made of John Ker (d. 1886), an eminent professor and preacher of the United Presbyterian Church. Other distinguished professors of the modern period who have also been noted as preachers are Doctors Stalker, Iverach, Rainy, Orr, and Denney. The blind philosopher, poet, and mystic, George Matheson, was heard as a preacher with great attention, and his books of brief devotional thoughts have been an inspiration and comfort to thousands. At Free St. George's Church, Edinburgh, Alexander Whyte has ministered for many years to the edification and delight of a large congregation. His books on *Bible Characters,* originally consisting of sermons, have been read with great interest and profit by many readers. His sometime associate, Hugh Black, now living in New York, is a soulful preacher and the author of pleasing books. The distinguished professor of Old Testament literature, George Adam Smith, a teacher and author of broad critical views, published also some sermons characterized by great spiritual force, poetic quality, and a vivid and popular style of address.

Returning to England, our view of British preaching in this period will close with a brief survey of some of the leading Baptist preachers of the age. William Landels (1823-1899)[97] was born near Berwick, on the Scotch side. His father was a small farmer, and the boy was brought up to economy and hard work. He did not receive much schooling, but by dint of hard study overcame the deficiencies of his education. Converted in a Methodist revival, he soon after began to preach, and became a Baptist in 1846. He was pastor in Birmingham, later at Regent's Park Church, in London,

[97]*Life,* by his son, T. D. Landels, London, 1900; sermons on *The Young Man in the Battle of Life,* London and New York, (undated).

and finally at Dublin St. Church, Edinburgh. Dr. Landels was rather broad in his theology, and had a painful controversy with Spurgeon over doctrine. He was a strong and successful preacher who left his impress upon the thought and life of his people.

Among those who have lived and worked over into the twentieth century, we should name the prolific writer, modern mystic, active pastor in various places, F. B. Meyer, whose spiritual sermons and other writings have been a benediction to many. The venerable Archibald G. Brown, long pastor in the East End of London, and most recently at the Metropolitan Tabernacle, was through long and strenuous years a powerful and successful preacher. John Clifford, born 1836,[98] the distinguished Nonconformist leader, and pastor of Westbourne Park Chapel, has been for a long time one of the most forceful personalities and impressive pulpit orators of his time. He was born in Derbyshire, baptized at fourteen, received some academic training, and came to London as pastor of Praed St. Chapel in 1858. This has been his only pastoral charge, though the name was changed on removal. Dr. Clifford is noted for the vigor and incisiveness of his manner, the thoroughness of his thought, the devoutness and courage of his ministry. Though somewhat broad in his views, he has presented in speech and writing the great essentials of the Christian faith, and has been in later years a recognized leader of the Nonconformist forces. Among the younger men at the close of the century, J. T. Forbes, of Glasgow, the magnetic and thoughtful preacher; W. Y. Fullerton, of Leicester, an energetic and successful pastor; Thomas Phillips, who is doing a great work at the famous Bloomsbury Chapel, in London; and John Wilson, of Woolwich, for thirty-three years pastor and preacher, honored and beloved, are worthy of larger mention than could here be made.

Chief among the mighty of his own denomination, and towering above all sectarian distinctions, stands the great figure of Alexander Maclaren (1826-1910).[99] It

[98] *WGS*, VIII, p. 123; account in Camden-Pratt, etc.

[99] *Alexander Maclaren, the Man and His Message*, by John C. Carlile, London and New York, 1901; accounts in magazines, etc.; Wilkinson, p. 115; notably an article by Rev. Jas. Stuart in

would be interesting, if space permitted, to dwell in a comparative way upon the three great representatives of the English Baptist pulpit during the nineteenth century: Robert Hall, Charles H. Spurgeon, Alexander Maclaren. Alike as they were in so many essential things, they were strikingly unlike in personal characteristics, mental quality, and pulpit powers. Hall was a great metaphysical thinker, Spurgeon a moving, popular preacher, Maclaren a profound and instructive Bible scholar—each in his own way great, strong, and famous.

Alexander Maclaren was born in Glasgow, the son of a merchant who was also a Baptist preacher. David Maclaren was highly esteemed in his little congregation as an expounder of the Word of God, and a man of high character. In 1836 he went to Australia to take charge of an important business enterprise, leaving his family in Edinburgh. During his father's absence Alexander was converted and baptized into the fellowship of the Hope St. Baptist Church, Glasgow, when about eleven years old. On the return of David Maclaren from Australia he took charge of the business of his company in London, where the family thenceforth resided. In 1842 Alexander entered the Baptist College at Stepney, in London. Here he was much influenced by Dr. David Davies, the eminent Hebrew scholar, and became from the first a close and enthusiastic student of Hebrew and Greek, as well as of other subjects. He was a shy and modest, but very painstaking and accurate, student. It is interesting to note that outside of his college he perhaps owed most for his development to the preaching of Henry Melvill and Dr. Thomas Binney. He used to say that Dr. Binney taught him how to preach. Maclaren stood examinations at the London University for his arts degree, and won prizes in Hebrew and Greek. Besides his collegiate studies, he read widely in literature, being especially fond of the English poets.

In his last year at college Maclaren was invited to supply the Portland Baptist Chapel at Southampton, a small and run-down church. The people were pleased

Review and Expositor (Louisville), for Jan., 1911; many separate volumes and editions of his sermons and complete ed. of *Sermons*, Funk & Wagnalls Co., New York. Single sermons in Fish, *XIX Cent.*, p. 888; *WGS*, VII, p. 65.

with the young preacher and determined to wait for him to finish his course. He was then regularly called and ordained, and began on a salary of sixty pounds a year. He was a faithful preacher and student from the first, not especially devoted to pastoral and social work, though not wholly neglecting it. Through life his first emphasis was on the pulpit and on the study as a means to its enrichment and power. Regarding this work at Southampton, in a bright address to young students, he long afterwards said: "I thank God that I was stuck down in a quiet, little, obscure place to begin my ministry; for that is what spoils half of you young fellows. You get pitchforked into prominent positions at once, and then fritter yourselves away in all manner of little engagements that you call duties, going to this tea-meeting, and that anniversary, and the other breakfast celebration, instead of stopping at home and reading your Bibles, and getting near to God. I thank God for the early days of struggle and obscurity." We have here an interesting light on the studious and spiritual growth of the young preacher. It was also during this brief ministry, in March, 1856, that the young pastor married his cousin, Marion Maclaren, of Edinburgh. Twenty years after her death, in his old age, Maclaren wrote of her to a friend: "She was my guide, my inspiration, my corrector, my reward. Of all human formative influences on my character and life, hers is the strongest and best. To write of me and not to name her is to present a fragment."

The little church prospered and grew, but a man of Maclaren's gifts and powers could not be kept in so small a field. In 1858, after urgent solicitation, he accepted the pastorate of the Union Chapel at Manchester, and this remained the scene of his labors till old age and infirmities led to his retirement, in 1903. Though it was a Union Chapel, the membership was predominantly Baptist, and Maclaren himself firmly held the distinctive principles of that denomination. His career in Manchester shows the wide influence which one who is chiefly and almost solely a preacher can exert. True to the principles of his earliest ministry, Maclaren continued through life to be pre-eminently a student and preacher. He paid, of course, some attention to the care of his flock as a pastor; he took part in the municipal and intellectual life of his city; he engaged in the larger movements of denominational and religious life; but his first and highest distinction is that he was a mighty expounder of the Word of God, primarily in the pulpit, then through his published sermons, and incidentally through helpful and scholarly commentaries and other expositions. All sorts of honors came to Dr. Maclaren. He was the recipient of notable kindnesses and appreciation in Manchester on several occasions. He was twice president of the Baptist Union, and president of the Baptist World Congress, in London, in 1905. He received the degree of D. D. from both Edinburgh and Glasgow Universities. In 1896 the citizens of Manchester had his portrait painted for their art gallery, and on the presentation of the portrait the Anglican bishop of Manchester made the address and said, "In an age which has been charmed and inspired by the sermons of Newman and Robertson, of Brighton, there were no published discourses which, for profundity of thought, logical arrangement, eloquence of appeal, and power over the human heart, exceeded in merit those of Dr. Maclaren." Many attempts were made to draw Dr. Maclaren from Manchester, and though he disliked the climate and sometimes complained of that and of the heavy work, he kept on and was not allowed to resign, though often feeling like it, until, in 1903, he was made pastor emeritus and retired from the active ministry. On the fifth of May, 1910, he passed peacefully away, full of years and honors, confessedly one of the strongest and most helpful preachers of his time.

No critical or descriptive account can do justice to the excellence and power of Maclaren's preaching. He has been widely recognized in his own and other lands for those outstanding qualities which have given him his eminent place among the great preachers of the world. First of all, he had the physical outfit of an impressive speaker—an erect figure, good action, a flashing eye, an expressive countenance, a carrying voice. The character lying back of the utterance was one of singular purity, depth, simplicity, and humility. Of course, he had his faults, but these were not such as to damage the effect of his public work. His beautiful home life, his delightful friendship, his fidelity in his charge, all supported his public ministry. His training for his task was, as we have seen, admirably adapted to accomplish just the work that he did. A keen, trained, disciplined intellect, accurate knowledge of the original languages, easy acquaintance with the best Biblical scholarship, and, above all, an ardent love for the Bible, made him an incomparable explorer into its storehouse of truth and a wonderful expounder of that truth to others. But though primarily a student of the Bible, he was not a man of one book, but of many. The traces of his wide and much enjoyed reading, especially in the poets, abound throughout his sermons. He kept in touch with the progress of thought, and rejoiced in all the uplifting social and humane movements of his age. But he was no one-sided optimist; he saw and felt sadly and keenly the sinful needs of his generation, and endeavored with all earnestness to apply to those wants the saving and sanctifying power of the gospel of Jesus Christ. Dr. Maclaren's theological position was candidly and thoughtfully evangelical. His sermons show how his heart and mind were anchored on essential Christian truth. In contents and form these sermons are models of modern preaching. The exegesis of Scripture, as has been indicated, is thorough and accurate. The analysis, while not obtrusive, is always complete, satisfying, clear. Robertson Nicoll somewhere has remarked that a man who reads one of Maclaren's sermons must either take his outline or take another text! Maclaren's style has all the rhetorical qualities of force, clearness, and beauty. It is not obtrusive or strained, is eminently natural, smooth, dignified, and at times eloquent. The tone and spirit are all that could be desired. Piety towards God, reverence, good taste, and a deep yearning for the spiritual good of his hearers animate his discourse. Maclaren's sermons have, next perhaps to Spurgeon's, been the most widely read of all in their time; nor are they likely soon to lose readers. They are so complete as expositions of the Bible, so lofty in tone, so free from that which is merely temporary and catchy, both in thought and style, that they can not but appeal to the minds of men long after the living voice has ceased to impress them upon living hearts.

It is fitting that with one in every way so worthy of a lingering regard this survey of modern European preaching should conclude. Our long journey has reached its goal. We have followed through a little more than three centuries the history of the Christian pulpit in all the countries of Europe except the East and Russia. From the days just after Zwingli, Luther, and Calvin, on the Continent, and Latimer and Knox in Britain, on through the changing epochs of the modern age to the verge of our own century we have pursued our studies. If the reader's task has been considerable, the author's has been large and weighty. Oftentimes he has been tempted in sheer discouragement to lay the burden down; and now that his undertaking is done, the sense of relief and the joy of achievement are mingled with regret at leaving a fascinating study, and with disappointment over the inadequacy and imperfection of the work. Yet both the labor and its result have deepened the conviction that the task should have been attempted, and that it is worthy of more research and a far better setting forth than it has here received.

We have seen how preaching in modern Europe has been intimately related with all those elements and forces which have produced and maintained the intellectual, moral, and religious progress of the most enlightened peoples. Sovereigns, statesmen, warriors, merchants, laborers, artists, writers, philanthropists, philosophers, thinkers, and leaders in every walk of human society have contributed in their several ways to that progress, or sometimes through fault and failure hindered or retarded its course. So also the Christian preacher. He has contributed his part to the general sum of good, or he has by fault or failure hindered where he ought to have helped. We have found him in every land, speaking in every tongue, now at the courts of kings, now in the homes of peasants, sometimes in the open air to thronging crowds, but most often in his own peculiar place in cathedral, church, or chapel, where in the midst of Christian worship he has lifted his voice to speak of the things of God and the soul.

Our survey shows what variety has existed in the preaching of modern Europe. Different periods, countries, languages, customs, creeds, tastes, methods, personalities, have had their necessary and most interesting influences in preserving the history of preaching from the dullness of a dead monotony. Nor has the law of action and reaction been wanting. Times of flourishing and of power have been followed by seasons of loss and decay, and these in turn have given place to happier days.

The many men and sermons that have been studied can not fail to impress us with the dignity and importance of preaching as a force in the development of modern Europe. Making no extravagant claims, and conceding every just allowance that candid criticism may require, our study has brought before us an inspiring history. It presents, when seen whole and large, a spectacle of high endeavor and noble achievement in the loftiest sphere of human effort—the region of the spirit. Here we have seen strong intellect, ample culture, strenuous toil, lofty character, self-sacrificing life again and again consecrated to the high and holy purpose of so presenting the truth of God to men as to win them out of sin and loss to righteousness and eternal life. Men of the highest sort in natural gifts and trained powers have in these later centuries, as well as in the middle and earlier and back to the first, heard the voice of One who said, "As ye go, preach, saying, The kingdom of heaven is at hand."

BIBLIOGRAPHY

No mention is here made of the numerous works of general reference of which constant or occasional use has been made in the preparation of this book. Such works include histories of the lands, peoples and epochs treated; histories of the Church, of Doctrine, and similar topics; histories of philosophy and of literature; encyclopaedias, general, ecclesiastical and biographical; and many works and helps of a miscellaneous character. To save space the lives and sermons of individual preachers are also omitted. Both these and many of the general works mentioned are referred to in footnotes and can be found by reference to the index. The bibliography includes only those works which treat of the history of preaching in Europe from the close of the sixteenth to that of the nineteenth century. A few literary or critical studies, where they bear on preaching, are also included.

AMERICAN AUTHORS

L. O. Brastow, "Representative Modern Preachers," New York, 1904; "The Modern Pulpit," New York, 1906. J. A. Broadus, "Lectures on the History of Preaching," New York, 1876. E. C. Dargan, "A History of Preaching" (Volume I, closing chapters), New York, 1905, and part of article on "History of Preaching" in the "Schaff-Herzog Encyclopaedia," New York, 1910. H. C. Fish, "History and Repository of Pulpit Eloquence," 2 volumes, New York, 1856 (later 2 volumes in one as "Masterpieces of Pulpit Eloquence"), "Pulpit Eloquence of the Nineteenth Century," New York, 1857, and on. J. M. Hoppin, "Homiletics" (with sketch of the History of Preaching), New York, 1883. F. James, "The Message and the Messengers," New York, 1897. T. H. Pattison, "The History of Christian Preaching," Philadelphia, 1903. W. M. Taylor, "The Scottish Pulpit from the Reformation," New York, 1887. W. C. Wilkinson, "Modern Masters of Pulpit Discourse," New York, 1905. "World's Great Sermons," 10 volumes, ed. G. Kleiser, New York, 1908.

BRITISH AUTHORS

"The Anglican Pulpit of To-day," (anon.) London, 1885. F. Arnold, "Our Bishops and Deans," 2 volumes, London, 1875. W. G. Blaikie, "The Preachers of Scotland from the Sixth to the Nineteenth Century," Edinburgh, 1888. J. Brown, "Puritan Preaching in England," London and New York, 1900. "The Classic Preachers of the English Church," (2 series of critical essays by various authors), ed. J. Kempe, London, 1877–1878. G. J. Davies, "Successful Preachers," New York, 1884. D. Davies, "Echoes from the Welsh Hills," with an introduction by J. R. K. Jones on "Characteristics of Welsh Eloquence," London (?), 1883. A. B. Donaldson, "Five Great Oxford Leaders," London, 1902.

Evans (E. J.), and Hurndall (W. F.), "Pulpit Memorials," (sketches and sermons of 20 Cong'l preachers), London, 1878. "The Evangelical Succession" (addresses at St. Giles on Scotch preachers), Edinburgh, 1883. "Great Modern Preachers," (sketches and sermons, anon.), London, 1875. E. P. Hood, "The Throne of Eloquence," London, 1885. "The Vocation of the Preacher," London, 1886. O. Jones, "Some of the Great Preachers of Wales," London (?), 1885. J. Ker, "Lectures on the History of Preaching," Edinburgh, 1888. J. C. Ryle, "The Christian Leaders of the Last Century," London, 1868.

DUTCH AUTHORS

P. Biesterveld, "Andreas Hyperius voornamelik als Homileet," Leyden (?), 1895. J. Hartog, "Geschiedenis van de Predikkunde in de Protestansche Kerk van Nederland," 2d ed., Utrecht, 1887. J. J. van Oosterzee, "Praktische Theologie," 2d ed., Utrecht, 1877–1878 (English trans. by Evans, New York, 1874).

FRENCH AUTHORS

A. Bernard, "Le Sermon au XVIIIme siècle," Paris, 1901. E. Berthault, "J. Saurin et la Prédication protestante jusq' à la fin de règne de Louis XIV, Paris, 1875. E. Boucher (abbé), "L' Éloquence de la Chaire," Lille, 1894. F. Bungener, "The Preacher and the King," or "Bourdaloue at the Court of Louis XIV," (several edd. both original and translation). J. Candel, "Les Prédicateurs français dans la première moitié du dix-huitième siècle," Paris (?). A. de Coulanges, "La chaire française au dix-huitième siècle," Paris, 1901. J. E. Couriard, "Essai sur la Prédication chez les Réformés de France et de Hollande," Geneva (?). A. Feugère, "Bourdaloue sa prédication et son temps," 2d ed., Paris, 1874. E. Gandar, "Bossuet Orateur," Paris, 1867. B. Gaudeau, "Les précheurs burlesques in Espagne: étude sur le père Isla," Paris, 1891. A. Hurel, "Les Orateurs sacrès à la cour de Louis XIV," Paris, 1872. P. Jacquinet, "Les Prédicateurs de XVIIme siècle avant Bossuet," Paris, 1885. La Bruyère, "Caracteristtiques et moeurs de ce siècle" (Oeuvres, tom. 2). J. S. Maury (card.), "Principes de l'éloquence," ed. Guilleminet, Paris, 1805. J. P. Migne, "Collection intégrale et universelle des orateurs sacrés," etc., tt. 86, Paris (?) G. Renoux (abbé), "Les Prédicateurs célèbres de l'Allemagne," Tours, 1885. C. A. Sainte-Beuve, "Causeries de lundi," (various edd.) tt. IX X. P. Stapfer, "La grande prédication chrétienne en France—Bossuet et Monod," Paris, 1898. A. Vincent, "Histoire de la prédication protestante de langue française au dix-neuvième siècle," Geneva and Paris, 1871. A. Vinet, "Histoire de la prédication parmi les Réformés de France au dixseptième siècle," Paris 1860.

GERMAN AUTHORS

Wilhelm Beste, "Die bedeutendsten Kanzelredner der älteren lutherischen Kirche von Luther bis Spener," 3 Bde., Dresden, 1856–1886. J. N. Brischar, "Die katholischen Kanzelredner Deutschlands seit den drei letzten Jahrhunderten," 5 Bde., Schaffhausen, 1868–1871. A. Brömel, "Homiletische Charakterbilder," Bd. 1, Berlin, 1869, Bd. 2, Leipzig, 1874. Th. Christlieb, "Geschichte der Christlichen Predigt," (supplement to Vol. 18 of the Herzog-Plitt "Real-Encyclopädie," Leipzig, 1888; revised with some additions by Schian for last ed.; J. M. H. Doering, "Die deutschen Kanzelredner des 18ten und 19ten Jahrhunderts," Neustadt, 1830. O. Gleiss, "Aus dem evangelischen Norden," Gütersloh, 1882. H. Hering, "Geschichte der Predigt," (first half of a treatise "Die Lehre von der Predigt"), Berlin, 1897. Jos. Kehrein, "Geschichte der katholischen Kanzelberedsamkeit der Deutschen von der ältesten bis zur neuesten Zeit," 2 Bde., (?), 1839. A. Nebe, "Zur Geschichte der Predigt," 3 Bde., Wiesbaden, 1879. R. Rothe, "Geschichte der Predigt von Anfängen bis auf Schleiermacher," (ed. Trümpelmann), Bremen, 1881. K. H. Sack, "Geschichte der Predigt in der deutschen evangelischen Kirche von Mosheim bis auf die letzten Jahre von Schleiermacher and Menken," Heidelberg, 1866. C. G. F. Schenk, "Geschichte der deutsch-protestantischen Kanzelberedsamkeit," Berlin, 1841. C. G. Schmidt, "Geschichte der Predigt in der evangelischen Kirche Deutschlands von Luther bis Spener," Gotha, 1872. P. H. Schuler, "Geschichte der Veränderungen des Geschmacks im Predigen," 3 Thln., Halle, 1792–1794. J. J. Spalding, "Uber die Nutzbarkeit des Predigtamts," 1772. L. Stiebritz, "Zur Geschichte der Predigt in der evangelischen Kirche von Mosheim bis auf die Gegenwart," Gotha, 1875. C. Werckshagen (assisted by various authors), "Der Protestantismus am ende des XIXten Jahrhunderts," 2 Bde., Berlin, 1902.

ITALIAN AUTHORS

U. Micocci, "Antologia della sacra Eloquenza moderna," Turin, 1897. F. Zanotto, "Storia della Predicazione nei secoli della letteratura italiana," Modena, 1899.

INDEX